Programming
Microsoft® Office

Don Schuy

SAMS
PUBLISHING

201 West 103rd Street
Indianapolis, IN 46290

Publisher
Richard K. Swadley

Acquisitions Manager
Greg Wiegand

Managing Editor
Cindy Morrow

Acquisitions Editor
Christopher Denny

Development Editor
Fran Hatton

Software Development Specialist
Kim Spilker

Production Editor
Deborah Frisby

Copy Editors
Kezia Endsley
Christine Prakel
Tonya Simpson
Angie Trzepacz
Johnna VanHoose

Editorial Coordinator
Bill Whitmer

Editorial Assistants
Carol Ackerman
Sharon Cox
Lynette Quinn

Technical Reviewer
Ricardo Birmele

Marketing Manager
Gregg Bushyeager

Assistant Marketing Manager
Michelle Milner

Cover Designer
Tim Amrhein

Book Designer
Alyssa Yesh

Vice President of Manufacturing and Production
Jeff Valler

Manufacturing Coordinator
Paul Gilchrist

Imprint Manager
Kelly Dobbs

Team Supervisor
Katy Bodenmiller

Support Services Manager
Juli Cook

Support Services Supervisor
Mary Beth Wakefield

Production Analysts
Angela Bannan
Dennis Clay Hager
Bobbi Satterfield

Graphics Image Specialists
Becky Beheler
Steve Carlin
Brad Dixon
Teresa Forrester
Jason Hand
Clint Lahnen
Cheri Laughner
Mike Reynolds
Laura Robbins
Dennis Sheehan
Craig Small
Jeff Yesh

Production
Carol Bowers
Georgiana Briggs
Mona Brown
Michael Brumitt
Jama Carter
Charlotte Clapp
Mary Ann Cosby
Terri Edwards
Judy Everly
Donna Haigerty
George Hanlin
Michael Henry
Aleata Howard
Louisa Klucznik
Ayanna Lacey
Kevin Laseau
Shawn MacDonald
Donna Martin
Steph Mineart
Kim Mitchell
Casey Price
Brian-Kent Proffitt
Erich J. Richter
SA Springer
Jill Tompkins
Tina Trettin
Susan Van Ness
Mark Walchle
Dennis Wesner
Michelle Worthington

Indexer
Chris Cleveland

In memory of
Michael James Schuy
1968 - 1994
"little brother"

Overview

Contents

Foreword

In twelve years of creating software-based business solutions, my company has never had a toolset quite like Microsoft Office. Where we once printed to disk files and then created tedious import routines, we now effortlessly move data between Access and Excel. Where we once copied and pasted individual addresses, we now automate large mail merges from Access into Word. Boring DOS screen prompts have been replaced with complex data entry forms with suggested values and validation. And we do all this with relative ease because the Basic language makes Microsoft Office highly programmable.

When I first started PC programming in the early 1980s, I was using Basic—first Commodore Basic and later Microsoft Basic. As the 1980s went by, Basic lost ground to other productivity languages, and we put it aside in favor of xbase, R:BASE, Revelation, and similar tools. By 1990, however, Basic had caught up with us again and was back in our toolbox, thanks to the revolutionary design of Visual Basic. Over time, Visual Basic began to appear in a variety of Microsoft products, and today it provides the programming engine for all of Microsoft Office.

Although programmability is its greatest strength, programmability is not the only virtue of Microsoft Office. Here are some other reasons why you should probably be using—and mastering—Microsoft Office now:

- It is well-rounded. The combination of spreadsheet, word processing, database, and presentation capabilities means that there is "something for everyone." Almost any business problem can be solved with one or more of these applications.

- It is extensible. You really can't grow out of these applications. When you have mastered each one individually, you can learn to make them work as a team. When you have climbed that peak, you can extend them with calls to the Windows API or to other OLE-enabled applications.

- It is deep. You can be productive at any level, whether you are recording simple macros or writing complex SQL statements for data retrieval (you can learn both of these techniques in this book).

- It has a future. Each individual Office application is the best-selling product in its class, and Office is the best-selling application suite. Thus, the investment you make in learning Office will not go away, because Office will not go away. Microsoft is committed to Office for the long haul as both a concept and a product.

So why would you want to learn to program with Microsoft Office Basic? Where is the value for you? The answer depends on what you do each workday. If you are young and looking for a career path, there are good positions in consulting and Information Systems (I.S.) groups for bright people with Basic coding skills. If you are in an I.S. group now, sooner or later you'll have to add Basic coding to your Cobol or RPG skills, so why not get started? If you are a business manager, business owner, accountant, or other professional, your filing cabinets and desktop are probably piled high with important data—with Microsoft Office you can put the data to work for you in new ways.

Here are some examples of the kinds of solutions we create every day in Microsoft Office:

- A customer information system that tracks contacts and financial information in Access, and exports the information to customized Word reports and to Excel for mathematical analysis.

- A Visual Basic application against an Access database that catalogs Word documents, Excel spreadsheets, and PowerPoint slides and uses the power of OLE to display them on demand.

- An inventory control system in Access that manages contracts, receipts, and usage, and both sends information to, and receives it from, the corporate mainframes.

- A customized Excel query tool that pulls summary data from a huge Access database and drops it into pivot tables for analysis.

At the core of each of these solutions is the kind of Basic coding that you will learn in this book. The book is filled with practical examples and lots of code, and it provides a great step down the road toward your mastery of Microsoft Office.

Stan Leszynski
Leszynski Company, Inc.
Bellevue, Washington

Prologue

My First Program

Like many people, my first exposure to programming computers was in using the BASIC programming language.

On Saturday afternoons somewhere in the mid to late '70s, I would ride my bicycle down to the neighborhood Radio Shack store where a salesman was kind enough to let me sit and tinker with one of their TRS 80s.

The first program that many folks would write in those days was something like this:

```
10 PRINT "HELLO THERE"
20 GOTO 10
```

You would then type RUN and watch the computer do this:

```
HELLO THERE
HELLO THERE
HELLO THERE
HELLO THERE
HELLO THERE
HELLO THERE
HELLO THERE
HELLO THERE
HELLO THERE
HELLO THERE
HELLO THERE
HELLO THERE
HELLO THERE
HELLO THERE
HELLO THERE
...
```

You would get a funny and almost guilty feeling in knowing that you just threw the computer into an endless loop from which it could not stop on its own. More significantly, the thrill you got in doing this simple program would spark a life-long addictive habit.

You told a *machine*, a lifeless being, to do something, and it immediately sprung to life at your beckoning. Wow! This was going to be "way cool."

A Computer Bought on Bubble Gum Profits

My first real programming exercise came a few years later. It was on a Commodore VIC 20.

My little brother Mike and his buddy Jason were in junior high school, and they developed an enterprise that netted them quite a sum of money. They would sneak to the store at night and buy a handful of Bubble Yum brand bubble gum at a quarter for each 5-piece package. In school the next day, they would use the concept of supply and demand and sell the gum for up to 25 cents a piece.

After a while Mike got busted and was told to quit because the activity would hurt the student store's profits. Michael had managed to save a hundred dollars from his efforts, and with mild coercion on my part, together we went downtown and bought the computer for *him* from K-Mart.

The VIC 20 came with a single spaceship shoot'em-up game on a cartridge that was quite good and we played it a lot. It sure beat the Atari Pong game which had long since been abandoned. Our real interest, however, was in playing with BASIC.

I typed in a lengthy program that would randomly draw a cavern that scrolled up the screen. A star character (*) represented a spaceship, and the player would have to steer the ship down the cavern and pick up letters along the way. You received points for collecting letters, and you died on hitting a cavern wall.

We didn't have any storage medium for saving the program. We would leave the computer on for days at time so as not to lose the work, but eventually it would be turned off and my program would vanish into oblivion.

Later, I would turn on my brother's computer and type in a new version of the program. In doing this repeatedly, I discovered better ways to write the program, ways that made the program shorter and less of a chore to type.

The Glory Days of *Compute!* Magazine

The first time I bought my own computer was when I was earning my own paycheck as an Airman in the U.S. Air Force stationed at Ramstein Air Base in Germany around 1983.

I was supposed to be saving my money for college, but the draw of computers was too compelling. I rationalized spending the money on an Atari 800 XL because I could buy the word processing cartridge and do all of my night school papers on it. I actually did write a few papers and short stories on the machine, but to be honest, I played a lot of games on it, too.

Some of my most enjoyable computing days were on this little machine. *Compute!* magazine was in its heyday. Every month you would get a fat issue with a game written in five or so different versions of BASIC for all the popular home computers of the day—Apple II, Commodore 64, Atari 800, Texas Instruments TI-99, and the IBM PC junior.

I remember the IBM PC being incredibly expensive and utterly boring in the way of graphics support (it had no sprites!), and I believed it had no future at all. Sprites were little hardware-supported bitmaps that your program could use as game pieces moving across the screen.

The *Compute!* magazine articles and all the spiral-bound *Compute!* books of those days were great. You could actually type in the programs, run them, and then modify them.

The listings were cryptic and so hard to key in without introducing mistakes that the magazine developed a checksum scheme in order to help you locate your typing errors. A resident program was loaded so that as you typed the program in, a number/letter code (the checksum) would be displayed which you would compare against the checksum listed in the article. If the codes didn't match, you knew you had a typo somewhere in the line.

By doing all of the work to type the programs in and correct your typing errors, you eventually saw enough of the programs that you started to understand how they worked.

I wrote my own game on the Atari 800 XL, borrowing a neat assembly routine that I found in a *Compute!* magazine article for some scrolling animation. This game was an improvement on the VIC 20 game I wrote earlier and was called Nightmare Descent. To get it all to fit in the available memory of Atari BASIC and make it run efficiently, I had to use one- and two-letter variable names and place multiple statements on a single program line.

The following code is a truncated listing of that Atari BASIC program, which looks a lot like many of the BASIC programs that were eventually written on those early computers. I must confess now to understanding only about five percent of what it is doing.

```
0 DIM T$(17):GOTO 470
1 YR=YR-0.2:GOTO 10
2 YR=YR-0.2:XR=XR+0.2:GOTO 10
3 XR=XR+0.2:GOTO 10
4 XR=XR+0.2:YR=YR-0.2:GOTO 10
5 YR=YR+0.2:GOTO 10
6 YR=YR+0.2:XR=XR-0.2:GOTO 10
7 XR=XR-0.2:GOTO 10
8 XR=XR-0.2:YR=YR-0.2
10 IF XR>2 OR XR<-2 THEN XR=SGN(XR)*2
20 IF YR>2 OR YR<-2 THEN YR=SGN(YR)*2
30 XR=XR+SGN(XR)*-0.02:YR=YR+0.03:Y0=Y0+YR:X0=X0+XR:LA=PEEK(207):IF LA=193 THEN
40 IF LA>LB THEN SOUND 2,1,6,8:FOR A=1 TO 4:NEXT A:SOUND 2,0,0,0:LB=LB+10
50 POKE 756,SC+CH*4:CH=CH+1:IF CH=4 THEN CH=0
```

```
60 IF PEEK(53252)>1 THEN 300
70 IF PEEK(53263)>0 THEN 490
80 S=STICK(0):IF S=11 THEN DR=DR-1
90 IF S=7 THEN DR=DR+1
100 IF DR<1 THEN DR=8
110 IF DR>8 THEN DR=1
120 IF Y0<12 OR Y0>98 THEN YR=YR*-1.4
130 XX=INT(X0):POKE HP(0),XX:POKE HP(1),XX:POKE HP(2),XX:YY=INT(Y0):SH=DR*11-10
140 P0$(YY)=S0$(SH,AP):P1$(YY)=S1$(SH,AP):P2$(YY)=FR$(SH,AP)
150 IF PEEK(D)=0 THEN 170
160 IF STRIG(0)=0 THEN POKE 706,255:SOUND 0,27,8,3:F=F+1:G=INT(F/20):POKE D,ASC
170 POKE 706,0:SOUND 0,0,0,0:GOTO 10
180 REM   Nightmare Descent (c) 1986 Don Schuy
190 GRAPHICS 1:POKE 710,0:POKE 708,136:POKE 752,1:T$="nightmare descent":DR=1
200 FOR A=1 TO 17:FOR Y=0 TO 8:POSITION A+1,Y:? #6;T$(A,A):NEXT Y:FOR Y=0 TO 7:
210 NEXT A:T$="C 1986  DON SCHUY":FOR A=17 TO 1 STEP -1:POSITION 2,13:? #6;T$(A
220 FOR A=1 TO 202:POKE 709,A:NEXT A:FOR A=1 TO 200:NEXT A:GRAPHICS 18 :LB=0:IF
230 POKE 1555,CL(4):POKE 559,0:POKE 704,68:POKE 705,169:POKE 707,38
240 X0=120:Y0=50:XR=0:YR=0:P0$(Y0)=S0$(1,14):P1$(Y0)=S1$(1,14):P2$(Y0)=FR$(1,14
250 FOR H=0 TO 3:POKE 53252+H,90-H*9:NEXT H:D=ADR(M$)+85:POKE D,255
260 FOR H=0 TO 2:POKE HP(H),X0:NEXT H:POKE HP(3),0:FOR A=0 TO 3:POKE 708+A,CL(A
270 DL=PEEK(560)+256*PEEK(561):POKE DL+3,103:FOR X=DL+6 TO DL+15:POKE X,39:NEXT
280 POKE 203,0:POKE 204,0:POKE 207,0:POKE 205,PEEK(560):POKE 206,PEEK(561):POKE
290 POKE 54279,ADR(B$)/256:POKE 53277,3:SOUND 1,1,16,1:A=USR(1536):RETURN
300 IF PEEK(53252)=2 THEN F=20:POKE D,255:PPOKE 53278,255:GOTO 80
310 Z=LA*5+Z:POKE 207,193:P1$=B$:P2$=B$:POKE 704,74
320 FOR B=15 TO 0 STEP -2:FOR A=1 TO 8:SOUND 0,55,16,B:P0$(INT(Y0)+2)=CR$(A*11-
330 P0$=B$:SOUND 0,0,0,0:SOUND 1,0,0,0:POKE 53277,0:GRAPHICS 18:POSITION 4,3:?
340 FOR U=0 TO 9:IF Z<=HI(U) THEN NEXT U:GOTO 440
350 FOR B=9 TO U+1 STEP -1:HI(B)=HI(B-1):H$(B*12+1,B*12+12)=H$(B*12-11,B*12):NE
360 POSITION 3,6:? #6;"enter your name":POSITION 4,9:? #6;"------------":POKE 7
370 FOR A=1 TO 12:GET #1,K:IF K=126 AND A>1 THEN POSITION 2+A,8:? #6;" ":T$(A-1
380 IF K=155 THEN A=13:NEXT A:GOTO 410
390 IF K<65 AND K<>32 OR K>90 THEN POKE 694,0:POKE 702,64:A=A-1:NEXT A
400 POSITION A+3,8:PRINT #6;CHR$(K):T$(A,A)=CHR$(K):NEXT A
410 HI(U)=Z:H$(U*12+1,U*12+12)=T$:U=11:NEXT U
420 TRAP 440:CLOSE #1:OPEN #1,8,0,"D:SCORE.DAT":PRINT #1;H$:FOR A=0 TO 9:PUT #1
440 CLOSE #1:TRAP 40000:FOR A=1 TO 600:NEXT A:GRAPHICS 17:POKE 710,0:? #6;"
450 FOR A=0 TO 9:? #6;? #6;" ";H$(A*12+1,A*12+12);
460 FOR B=1 TO 6-LEN(STR$(HI(A))):? #6;" ";:NEXT B:? #6;HI(A):NEXT A:FOR A=1 TO
470 EX=EX+1:GOSUB 190:POKE 53278,64:POKE 77,0:F=20:Z=0:GOTO 10
480 REM    Safe Landing
490 Z=Z+1000:GRAPHICS 0:? "OK LANDING":FOR A=1 TO 500:NEXT A:GOTO 330
500 DIM F1$(1),F2$((INT(ADR(F1$)/1024)+1)*1024-ADR(F1$)-1),B$(384),M$(128),P0$(
510 DIM S0$(91),S1$(91),FR$(91),CR$(91),LA$(1),A$(71),HP(3),CL(4),D$(9),H$(120)
520 FOR H=0 TO 3:HP(H)=53248+H:NEXT H:POKE 53259,1:POKE 53260,255:SC=PEEK(129)-
530 B$=" ":B$(384)=" ":B$(2)=B$:M$=B$:P0$=B$:P1$=B$:P2$=B$:P3$=B$:LA$=CHR$(255)
540 S0$=""
550 S1$=""
560 FR$=""
570 CR$=""
580 D$=""
590 L=0:F$="D:NIGHT.FNT":GOSUB 640:GOSUB 630
600 OPEN #1,4,0,"D:SCORE.DAT":INPUT #1;H$:FOR A=0 TO 9:GET #1,B:HI(A)=B:NEXT A:
610 A$=""
620 FOR A=1 TO 71:POKE 1535+A,ASC(A$(A,A)):NEXT A:FOR A=0 TO 4:CL(A)=PEEK((SC+1
630 L=16:F$="D:SCREEN0"
640 OPEN #1,4,0,F$:POKE 853,SC+L:POKE 852,,0:POKE 857,16:POKE 856,0:POKE 850,7:
650 CLOSE #1:RETURN
```

Whatever you do, please don't dig your Atari 800 XL out from its box in the back of the closet underneath the stairs and try that listing out. Besides being an exercise in self-torture, the program is missing a few pieces and data files that are required for it to run.

Casual Programming

What happened in those early days of computing is that regular people, like you and me, would find the time to sit down and write programs without any intention whatsoever of being a "programmer."

I've used the term, "casual programming," to represent this kind of activity, which I believe has diminished in some ways and might be considered a lost art. The casual programmer was a student, teacher, business professional, or anyone who might write a program on their own without really thinking of themselves as some kind of computer technical wizard.

The casual programmer often wrote programs that looked and functioned the same as software developed professionally. Some people even turned their programming projects into marketable programs. The main motivations for programming were, however, to explore the new world of computers, see how they could be used, and (to be quite honest) to have some fun.

How GUI Killed the Casual Programmer

Not long after this, computers got bigger and began to sprout graphical user interfaces (GUIs) and newer, complex operating environments. Apple turned into Mac, Commodore turned into Amiga, Atari turned into Atari ST, the PC turned into Windows, and the Texas Instruments, well...their calculators are doing just fine, thank you.

Although these new computers were friendlier for "end users" to use, they became a problem for the casual programmer. Games were being written in assembly language by masters of that craft; at college you were being taught Pascal; and if you programmed anything at all in these new graphical environments, then C became the language of choice.

To learn and use C, not only did you have to master the use of memory allocation and pointers to pointers to pointers, but your bookshelf quickly became burdened to the point of falling off the wall by all of the heavy volumes of Application Programming Interface (API) calls that you were required to know. Windows had as many as 1,500 callable functions!

Unfortunately, home computing also turned into something different—something called Nintendo and Sega. I always thought of computers as the ultimate game machine, but it never occurred to me that someone would sell millions of computers without keyboards. This was a major setback for the home-computing revolution, but admittedly, games did get much better because they were being paid for. Games on computers were too easily pirated. Still, it saddens me to think that you will never again be able to buy a popular computer from your paper route money or from bubble gum selling profits.

BASIC wasn't considered a cool language to use anymore. Like many other programmers, I spent a few years programming everything in C. I sacrificed the motorcycle I had ridden all over Germany to have enough money to buy a 286 clone. The computer contained a 5 1/4-inch floppy drive, an amber monitor, 1MB of memory, and a 30MB hard drive. It was pretty hot stuff in those days. Also, like many other programmers who started out programming for recreation, I started making a living by writing programs. Many of us believed that we would never program in BASIC again.

Interestingly enough, a popular side project for C programmers was to write their own interpreted language supported with a set of high-level routines similar to the commands in Basic. It seems that however much we enjoyed the elegance and speed of C, we wanted to make programming accessible to regular people again, not just to us techno-geeks.

Basic is Back!

Suddenly Visual Basic came into the scene. The folks at Microsoft found a way to wrap up many of the components of their popular Windows environment into a high-level, object-based programming environment with a newer and more mature version of Basic to drive it. Building a Windows application was now within reach of regular people, and Visual Basic quickly became the best-selling language product of all time.

Building on the success of Visual Basic and the recognition that it was a genuine language for the masses, Microsoft set out on a strategy to make all of its Office applications programmable using a common programming engine. Microsoft dubbed it Visual Basic for Applications (VBA). VBA is the language component of Visual Basic, moved into the environment of each of the Office applications. You now have Basic in a spreadsheet, Basic in a word processor, and Basic in a database.

Today, the Basic programmer has within his or her grasp the power of Access, Excel, Word, and Visual Basic; VBX and OCX custom controls; OLE automation; and Jet and ODBC database technology. The Basic programmer is once again the master of his or her own machine, just as in those early days—and what a powerful machine it has become!

With the return of Basic, something else returned from the good old days of computing. In a magazine article or a programming book such as this one, you should be able to find program listings that you can type in, run, and modify, just as I did in the early days.

There is no better way to learn programming or to learn about a particular programming environment than to actually read and run good coding examples. Any experienced programmer will tell you that to learn programming you must read programs.

A Little Secret about Basic

"If Basic is so great and powerful now," you might be wondering, "why are so many people still programming applications in C and C++?"

You would be surprised to see how many large software projects are now written unashamedly in Basic. A good software developer chooses the right tool for the job and saves a lot of time by doing so. A C++ compiler would certainly be a better tool for some projects, but as Basic becomes more powerful, many more jobs are now falling within its realm.

In general, folks are using Basic to accomplish higher-level application building where quick development and fast response to changing needs are critical.

If you are an experienced "crack" developer who hasn't taken a look at Basic in a while, then it's time to look again. Much of what you think about Basic has changed. Read Chapter 1, "Today's Basic," and Chapter 3, "How Basic Interacts with the Outside World," for a quick overview of where Basic is today. Then look at what I've built using it in the remaining chapters.

If you still aren't convinced, go to your local Access or Visual Basic user group and talk to some fellow developers and see what they are doing. You will find that the applications they are building are downright incredible, and they've saved a bundle of money by choosing Basic.

Contacting the Author

If you have any comments, corrections, bug reports—or heck, just want to shoot the breeze—please e-mail me at my CompuServe ID: 75450,3064.

You can also write to me at my residential address:

> 18315 N.E. Woodinville-Duvall Place
> Woodinville, WA 98072

My best wishes to you in all of your Basic programming adventures!

Don Schuy

May 1, 1995

Acknowledgments

This book would not have been in your hands right now without the support and encouragement from all of the following people:

Many thanks to Petra Berleb, editor of the prestigious *Office & Database* magazine in Germany, for making me a published writer and getting all of this started.

Thanks to all of the folks at Sams Publishing who let me take this thing on and for making it happen. Please take a good long look at the publisher's credits page. This book looks good and reads well only because of the fine work that all these people do on a daily basis. In particular, I really enjoyed working with the book's development editor, Fran Hatton, and the book's editor, Deborah Frisby, who both had undying enthusiasm for the project and helped a first-time author get it right. Thank you Ricardo Birmele (a.k.a. "_Birm") for a complete and thorough technical review.

Thanks to Stan Leszynski, Sid Stusinski, Jill Wagner, and Patti Leszynski of Leszynski Company, Inc., for allowing for this massive distraction and for fully supporting it. Jill also reviewed some of the early chapters, and the chapters are certainly better because of it.

Thanks to Dave Yarnall, who contributed a flood of ideas and whose helpful critiques got the book on the right track at the beginning. The Learning Computer game in Chapter 9 and the Excel Time Killer games in Chapters 11 and 12 all originated from Dave's wonderfully creative brain.

Tom Philbrick also played a role in getting my writing to a start with his "PNWAUG" newsletter. Thank you, Tom, for contributing the original ideas for Pretty Printer in Chapter 4, Calendar Wizard in Chapter 5, and the Address Book project in Chapter 13.

Thanks to Alan Corwin and Roger Lengel, who reviewed several chapters each. I asked you not to pull any punches, and you didn't.

Thanks to Bryan Minugh and Tim Schuy (the hardware guys) for keeping my computer up-to-date and tuned on a family man's budget.

I'd also like to thank Mark Curtis at CCG for keeping the work load light enough for me the first few weeks at my new job so that I could complete the book.

The largest contribution of course comes from my lovely wife Ying. She kept the family running smoothly and kept me going. And thanks to the rest of the gang…Elizabeth, Stephanie, Mimi, and Charlie, for your inspiration and for putting up with Dad.

About the Author

Don Schuy is a contributing writer to the *Access/Visual Basic Advisor* magazine in the United States and the *Office & Database* magazine in Germany. He is co-inventor with Dave Yarnall of patent #5,359,729, a special method for storing equations in a multi-dimensional spreadsheet. Don started his programming career in 1989 with Timeline Inc. of Bellevue, Washington. He then moved on to work with Leszynski Company, Inc., for a year before recently joining the Curtis Consulting Group (CCG) in Redmond, Washington. Don lives with his charming wife Ying and their four children: Elizabeth, Stephanie, Mimi, and Charlie.

Introduction

Basic and the Casual Programmer

Programming Microsoft Office is about programming in the Microsoft Office environment, and it demonstrates today's Basics *in action*.

The book uses a workshop approach that gives the reader the kind of experience one normally can get only from working alongside other experienced programmers. Rather than show you just some technical details about a particular set of development tools, this book can show you something about the art of programming itself and can help you gain insight about how programs are designed and constructed.

The tools used in this book are undoubtedly the most popularly used products of their kind. This is important to the reader who is intent on gaining skills that will help make him or her employable as a professional programmer.

Programming Microsoft Office is also written for the many potential *casual programmers* out there, people who, at least for the time being, have no intent whatsoever to make a profession out of their programming efforts. If you want to explore programming for the fun of it, reading this book is a good place to start.

Part I of this book investigates how Basic has changed since the early days. We look at the steps needed to write and run the "Hello There" example in each of the programming environments used in this book.

We move on to creating some useful and fun utilities in Word Basic, including a Study Mate program that will help you score big on the next exam. Then we take a quick look at some of the newer language constructs that will be used in Basic in the following chapters.

Part II contains a collection of short projects designed to be quick in turn-around and to be useful as much as they are fun. A few may be more entertaining than practical, but you will pick up some tricks and techniques along the way.

Among the programs you will create in Part II are

- A **Calendar Wizard** to generate calendar pages in Excel
- **Sticky Notes** for a functionality similar to Post-It Notes in your Access databases
- **Screen Writer** utilities in Word for budding young filmmakers

- **A Learning Computer** game in Access to show off how smart your computer can be
- **Secret Diary** in Visual Basic to keep your best secrets in a safe place
- **Excel Time Killers**, a set of simple games in Excel
- A sophisticated **Address Book** application in Access with Query-By-Form search capabilities
- The **Picture Builder+** Access property builder that can classify and catalog your icon collection

Part III contains two advanced projects that span several chapters each. The projects in this section demonstrate the full potential building applications using Basic and the Microsoft Office applications. The projects in this section are

- **Survey Wizard**, a complete online survey taking and analysis system developed in Access
- **S.W.A.T.**, a bug/issue tracking system for one or more developers to manage projects

Your Part

To make *Programming Microsoft Office* work best for you, you should simply focus your attention to the program examples.

The chapters of this book are written with the assumption that the reader follows along step-by-step to re-create the applications. This, of course, is entirely optional; the completed programs are on the book's companion CD-ROM.

Try the programs out, read the code, and modify them to your heart's desire. You might consider reconstructing one or two of the example programs from scratch to get the real feeling of what it was like to create them.

As you read this book, don't feel intimidated if you don't know everything about Basic programming as you start. What you don't know, you will pick up as you go, and it's okay if some of the programming details seem fuzzy when you first look at them.

If you are already a Visual Basic programming maestro, you will still find this book a valuable resource. The clever and useful sample programs throughout the book are inspiring and might lead you to more than a few tricks that you haven't thought of.

Advanced readers will also find in this book some hard-to-find and detailed coverage of creating third-party add-in products for the Office applications, including how to build your own Wizards.

I promise that *Programming Microsoft Office* is not a book *"for dummies"* as other books proudly proclaim in their titles. Instead, this book is for you, the reader who might not know everything (or anything) about programming yet, but wants to dig right into the depths of it. From time to time, the book introduces some concepts that are advanced for even experienced programmers.

This book definitely is *not* is a simple replacement for your software manuals. Many books are written about software products with the intent to do better than the manuals included with the product. You are encouraged to use your manuals, online help, and other books for reference while you read, use, and enjoy *Programming Microsoft Office.*

Software Requirements

To work with the code in the example programs, you need the software listed below. Nearly half of the book's programs are written in Access Basic, so you really should get yourself a copy of it if you don't have it already. Access comes with Microsoft Office Professional, but if you bought the plain Microsoft Office, you will have to purchase Access separately.

If you have a later version of the software listed below, you should still be in good shape; the programs should still be executable as-is or with some modification. The documentation included with the product will indicate what needs to be done, if anything, to load and run programs created by a prior version.

Microsoft products used in this book

Program	Coverage
Excel 5.0	20 percent
Word 6.0	20 percent
Access 2.0	50 percent
Visual Basic 3.0	10 percent

Companion CD-ROM

All of the software developed in this book is included in the companion CD-ROM and is ready for use. The run-time libraries for Visual Basic are included so that you may run the Visual Basic example programs even if you don't have Visual Basic.

See Appendix A for instructions on how to install and use the programs on the companion CD-ROM.

Conventions Used in This Book

The following typographic conventions are used in this book:

- Code lines, commands, statements, variables, and other special computer terms usually appear in a special `computer` typeface.
- Placeholders in syntax descriptions appear in *italic* typeface. Replace the placeholder with the actual filename, parameter, or whatever element it represents.
- *Italics* highlight technical terms when they first appear in the text and are sometimes used to emphasize important points.

Sometimes lines of code can be very long, too long to represent as a single line within the margins of the book. In those cases you will see a special icon ➥. When you see the ➥ icon before a particular line, you should consider that "line" part of the preceding line. If you are typing the code, be sure to type in the ➥ line as a continuation of the preceding line.

In parts of the book I describe how a form or other object is created. Usually I list only the actual property settings that should be changed from their default values. In some cases, I list the defaults also when they are significant to making the form or control work as expected.

Icons

Within each chapter, you will encounter several icons that help you pinpoint the current topic. The following icons are used:

The road map icon indicates that I am presenting an overview of what is going to happen in the chapter.

The chalkboard icon is used when you step back to do a little design work before jumping into the coding.

The rocket science icon is used in a few places where the material gets technical or esoteric.

This icon indicates that the book is directing you to act, that is, to type or use the mouse. It's not really expected that you would re-create all of the projects on your own (completed versions of the programs are on the book's CD-ROM), but the chapters are written so that you may do so if you choose.

The examine icon identifies a section where the book directs you to look at some code. (There is a lot of code in this book!)

 The Try This! Question icon identifies short programming exercises, some easy, some hard. (These occur most often in the earlier chapters.)

 The Try This! Answers icon appears at the end of the chapter, where the answers to Try This! questions are presented.

 The checklist icon appears at the chapter summary, identifying a list of items you learned in the course of building the chapter's project.

Getting Started

CHAPTER 1

Today's Basic

In this book, you will create programs in Basic. Why Basic? Quite simply, programming in Microsoft Office is programming in Basic.

Today's Basic has changed considerably from the BASICs programmers used in the early days of computing. Basic is still the easiest way to write short and quick programs; *that* part hasn't changed. Today, however, it's also frequently used as a platform for serious and extensive software-development efforts.

In this chapter, you will take Basic for a test spin in each of the four different programming environments that you'll use in this book: Visual Basic, Word, Excel, and Access. You will learn some essentials about the language Basic, and you will learn the fail-safe way to handle errors in your programs.

Note that much of the following chapter is introductory material. If you are an advanced or moderately skilled Visual Basic programmer already, you'll want to skim this chapter and the following two chapters quickly—or skip them altogether.

If, on the other hand, you feel you need more of a refresher on Basic than the first three chapters provide, see Appendix D, "Basic in a Day," and Appendix B, "Using Objects in Basic." Appendixes D and B are on the accompanying CD-ROM and provide a more complete introduction to the Basic language starting from the ground up.

Where Are the Line Numbers?

Forget the line numbers. Don't admit that you ever programmed using line numbers. It's a test nowadays. If you admit to have ever having programmed with line numbers, everybody will know that you are old. The neighbor kids will start calling you "sir" or "madam," and you won't get invited to parties anymore.

> **NOTE**
>
> Compared to today's Basic, the earlier versions of the Basic programming language had fewer ways to control which statement executed after another one. Each program line began with a line number. The GoTo statement along with a line number was used to jump from one place to another in the program listing. This lack of structure in the language and in the programs written in it gave the earlier Basics a bad reputation among proponents of structured programming.

Today the way we youthful kids organize a program in Basic is through the use of procedures. The shift from line numbers to procedures for organizing a program preceded Visual Basic, but many people's conception of Basic stems from before this significant change. In fact, some people would go so far as to say that the Basics we use today aren't really BASIC and are entirely different languages altogether.

I like to use the word BASIC, with all-uppercase letters, to refer to the older versions, those that used line numbers. The all-uppercase form reminds me so much of what those old programs looked like—you know, before the Shift key was invented. When I am referring to today's Basic language, I use the mixed-case form, Basic; this form represents the look of the lines in my programs today.

"Hello There" in Visual Basic

Without line numbers, where does your program begin execution?

In Visual Basic, you have two options. The starting point for your program is either a subroutine called Main or a form that you can select to be loaded. In the second case, your code begins executing as a result of events that occur in the program environment. You'll see how events work in the next chapter.

In the preface of this book, I told you of my very first BASIC program:

```
10 PRINT "HELLO THERE"
20 GOTO 10
```

Let's try this same little prank in Visual Basic.

1. Double-click the Visual Basic icon in Program Manager.

   This creates a new default project called Project1. A *project* is a collection of forms, modules, and VBX controls that make up a program. The Project1 project displays a Form1 form, as shown in Figure 1.1.

2. Close the Form1 form.

3. With Form1 selected in the project window, select the **File|Remove File** command to delete Form1. (You don't need it.)

4. Select the **File|New Module** command. This opens a new module with the default name of Module1.

5. In the Module1 window, type the text shown in Listing 1.1.

FIGURE 1.1.

Visual Basic's default project.

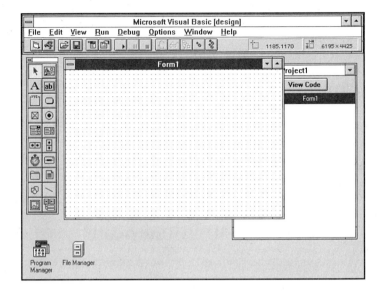

Listing 1.1. "Hello There" in Visual Basic.

```
Sub Main ()
  Do
    Debug.Print "Hello there"
  Loop
End Sub
```

Your screen should now have the Module1 window shown in Figure 1.2.

FIGURE 1.2.

"Hello There" in Visual Basic.

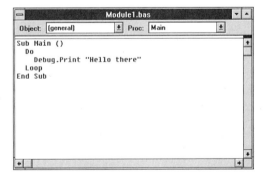

"Hello There" is ready to run now. Select the **Window**|**D**ebug command to open Visual Basic's Debug Window. Press F5 to begin execution, or select **Run**|**S**tart from the menu. In the Debug Window, you'll see Hello there printing repeatedly, as shown in Figure 1.3.

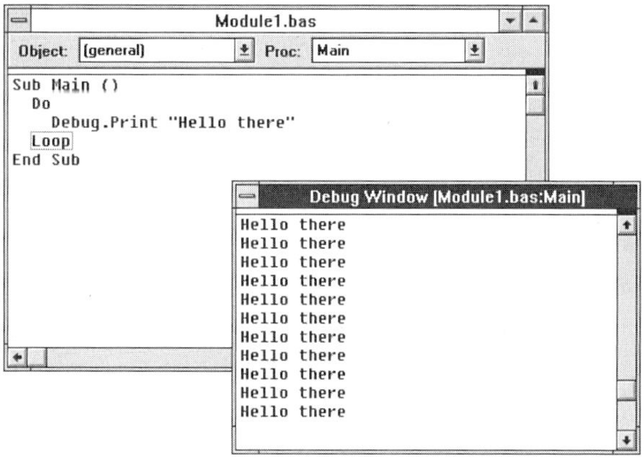

FIGURE 1.3.

Running "Hello There" in Visual Basic.

To stop the program, press Ctrl-Break. This temporarily pauses execution. To really stop the program, select the **Run|End** command from the Visual Basic menu.

As you can see from this little example, it doesn't take much effort to get something quick and dirty up and running in Visual Basic. Next I'll discuss the other Basic programming environments on your computer.

The Basics You Already Own

I'll bet millions of people have Basic on their computers and don't even know about it. It's sitting there snuggled away in some remote sector of the hard drive, just dying to be awakened and put to good use.

I'm not talking about the Quick Basic that comes free with DOS. Remember DOS? Your great-grandfather typed all of his computer commands in DOS before there was Windows. No, what I'm talking about is Word Basic!

Maybe you are "in the know" about this one. Many people, however, bought Word strictly for word processing and don't have any idea that, built smack-dab in its middle, Word has a great little programming language.

Basic is a living resident inside your spreadsheet and your database, also. Quite frankly, your favorite Microsoft Office applications are possessed. With a little programming, they can come alive in ways that the average application user never thought was possible.

"Hello There" in Word 6.0

In Word 6.0, you must use a document window as the place to see the results of your program. After all, the primary reason behind having Basic in Word is so that you can use Basic to help you in the creation of documents.

To find out how a program writes to a document window, you can turn on the macro recorder and type something in. Then you can turn off the macro recorder and take a look at the program that was *generated*.

Did that last part ring a bell there? The macro recorder in Word (and in Excel) actually creates working Basic code. You'll be taking advantage of that fact often as you work on writing programs with this book.

Here are the steps to create the "Hello There" program in Word Basic.

1. Double-click the Word icon in Program Manager to start Word.

2. Select the **Tools|Macro** command to open the Macro dialog box.

3. Enter `HelloThere` for the name of the macro to record, as shown in Figure 1.4.

FIGURE 1.4.

Getting ready to record a Basic program in Word.

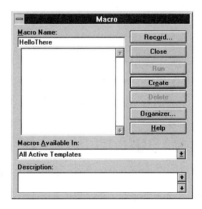

4. Press the Rec**o**rd button.

5. A Record Macro dialog box is displayed; this dialog box enables you to assign the recorded macro to a toolbar button, menu command, or key assignment. Click OK.

You are now ready to record. As shown in Figure 1.5, a small window with Stop and Pause buttons is displayed so that you can stop recording when you are done.

If the Stop button window is blocking your view of where you want to type, you can click the title bar and drag that window out of the way without affecting your recording. In fact, you can browse all of the Word drop-down menu commands (as you try to figure out what to do) without affecting the recording. A command is recorded only when you actually perform an action that affects the document or affects your current editing status on the document.

FIGURE 1.5.

*Word displays a small
Macro Recorder
window with Stop
and Pause buttons.*

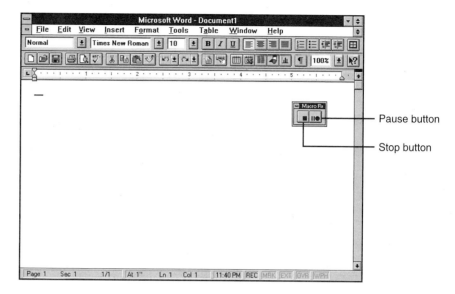

Pause button

Stop button

6. Type `Hello there` in the document window and press the Enter key. Your screen should resemble what is shown in Figure 1.6.

FIGURE 1.6.

*The macro recorder
records whatever you do
to the document.*

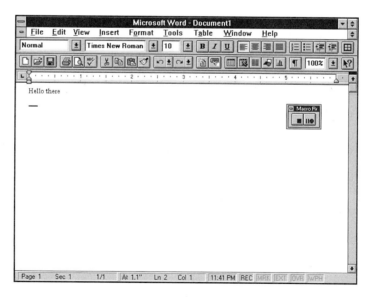

7. Press the Stop button.
8. Select the **T**ools|**M**acro command again.

   Now in the Macro dialog box, you see the `HelloThere` macro listed as an available macro, as shown in Figure 1.7.

FIGURE 1.7.

The recorded macro shows up, ready to use or modify.

9. Click HelloThere in the list of macros so that it is selected.
10. Click the **E**dit button.

Clicking the **E**dit button brings up a macro editing window that displays the following recorded program:

```
Sub MAIN
Insert "Hello there"
InsertPara
End Sub
```

The program's appearance on the screen is shown in Figure 1.8.

FIGURE 1.8.

Word's macro recorder creates code that you can read and modify.

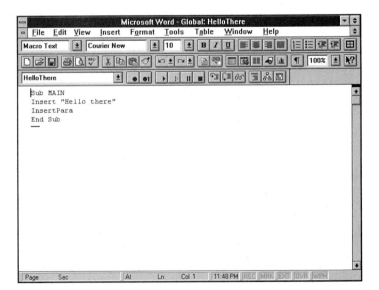

Word's Insert statement is used to send text to the current document window. InsertPara is used to insert a paragraph (the result of pressing the Enter key).

Now that you know something about the Insert and InsertPara commands, you don't have to use the macro recorder to take advantage of them next time. Just type them into your program, and they work the same.

You can add a loop to "Hello There" to make it run continuously.

How you do this in Word is a little different than how you would accomplish the same thing in Excel, Access, or Visual Basic. The flavor of Basic in Word 6.0—known as "Word Basic"—isn't quite as modern as the other Basics. In Word Basic, there are no Do...Loop loops, so you must use a While...Wend loop instead.

1. Add a While...Wend loop to the program. See Listing 1.2 and Figure 1.9.

Listing 1.2. "Hello There" in Word Basic.

```
Sub MAIN
  While -1
    Insert "Hello there"
    InsertPara
  Wend
End Sub
```

FIGURE 1.9.

Adding a loop to repeat the macro recording indefinitely.

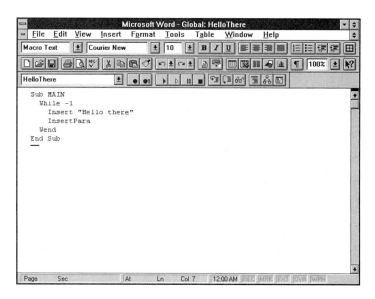

2. From Word's **W**indow menu, you can switch between viewing the document window and the macro edit window. Go back to the document window to test the program.

3. Select the **T**ools|**M**acro command.

4. From the Macros window, click HelloThere from the list of available macros and then click **R**un.

The document window begins filling up with Hello there lines. You can press the Esc key to stop the program. Figure 1.10 shows what you see when you stop the program.

FIGURE 1.10.

The Word "Hello There" program fills a document with Hello there lines until you halt the program.

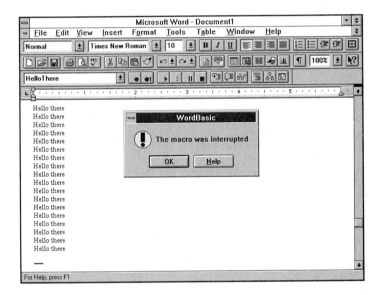

On closing Word, answer "no" to the dialog boxes that ask you if you want to save your work. You won't be needing the HelloThere macro for anything.

"Hello There" in Excel 5.0

In Excel you can use Basic to modify a workbook just as you used Word Basic to modify a document. Excel, however, has a debug window. For this example, you can use the debug window for output just as you did in Visual Basic.

1. Double-click the Excel icon in Program Manager.

2. Select the **I**nsert|**M**acro command. From the cascading menu, select **M**odule, as shown in Figure 1.11.

FIGURE 1.11.

Adding a module sheet to an Excel workbook.

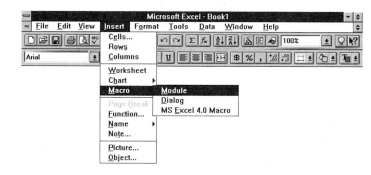

3. Enter the `HelloThere` subroutine into the module sheet, as indicated by Listing 1.3 and shown in Figure 1.12.

Listing 1.3. "Hello There" in Excel VBA.

```
Sub HelloThere()
  Do
    Debug.Print "Hello there"
  Loop
End Sub
```

FIGURE 1.12.

"Hello There" in an Excel module.

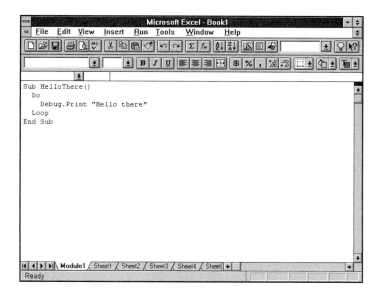

4. Select the **View|D**ebug Window command or press Ctrl-G to display the Debug window.

5. With the Immediate tab selected, type `HelloThere` into the Immediate pane, as shown in Figure 1.13.

FIGURE 1.13.
Preparing to run "Hello There" in Excel.

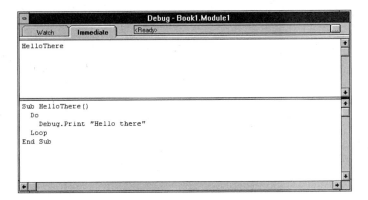

```
HelloThere




Sub HelloThere()
   Do
      Debug.Print "Hello there"
   Loop
End Sub
```

6. Press the Enter key after you type HelloThere. The subroutine begins executing.

The Immediate pane repeats the Hello there text until you press the Esc key to stop execution.

TRY THIS! QUESTION 1.1.

Use Excel's macro recorder to record entering Hello there in a worksheet cell. Then try to modify the program so that Hello there fills a column of cells.

See the solution to this problem at the end of this chapter.

"Hello There" in Access 2.0

You've got just one more application to go.

1. Double-click the Access icon in Program Manager.

   To do any programming in Access, you first need to open an existing database or create a new one. Let's create a new one. (After you are finished, you can delete this new database by using File Manager.)

2. Select **File|New** from the menu.

3. At the New Database dialog box, select the directory and filename for the newly created database. Alternatively, you can press OK to accept the default.

   Access displays a new, empty database with a database container window that has tabs to list the current tables, queries, forms, reports, macros, and modules in the database, as shown in Figure 1.14.

FIGURE 1.14.

*Starting a new
database in Access.*

4. In the database container window, click the Module tab and press the **N**ew button.

5. In the Module window, type in the HelloThere subroutine exactly as you did in Excel. See Listing 1.4 and Figure 1.15.

Listing 1.4. "Hello There" in Access Basic.

```
Sub HelloThere ()
  Do
    Debug.Print "Hello there"
  Loop
End Sub
```

FIGURE 1.15.

*"Hello There" in an
Access module.*

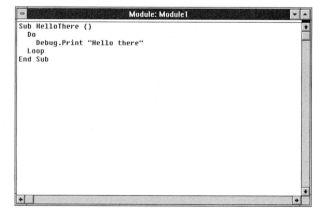

6. With the module window still open, select the **V**iew|**I**mmediate Window command.

7. Enter HelloThere into the Immediate Window, as shown in Figure 1.16.

FIGURE 1.16.

Preparing to run "Hello There" in Access.

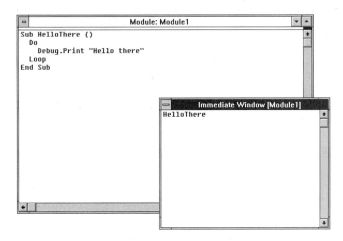

8. Press Enter to execute the program, just as you did in Excel.

The Immediate Window repeats Hello there over and over as expected. Access is like Visual Basic in that you must press the Ctrl-Break keystroke combination in order to stop execution.

Organizing Your Program with Subroutines and Functions

Now that you know the minimum required to enter a program and get it running in each of the Basic environments used in this book, let's knuckle down and cover some essentials of Basic. To add some complexity to your programs, you need to understand how a larger program is divided up in manageable pieces.

The components of a Basic program's code are the two different types of procedures: *subroutines* and *functions*. I use the word *procedure* in this book when I'm referring to both types.

The first part of a procedure is its *declaration*. If it's written well, a procedure's declaration often tells you everything you need to know about how to use the procedure in other parts of the program. The declaration is the first line of a procedure. It indicates the name of the procedure and what values are passed to the procedure when you are using it.

Declaring a subroutine looks something like this:

```
Sub SubName(ArgumentList)
```

SubName is any valid identifier name. (That is, *SubName* must begin with a letter character. Following the first letter, *SubName* can have more letters, numbers, and underscores, too. *SubName* can't have spaces in it or other nasty keyboard characters.)

The name of your subroutine should help remind you about the subroutine's purpose. Some people apply naming schemes to help them create a meaningful name and to keep all of their subroutines and functions organized. For example, you might use an object-verb approach to keep sorted together those subroutines and functions that work with a particular object, like these:

```
FileClose
FileOpen
FileRead
FileWrite

PasswordAssign
PasswordValidate
```

The *ArgumentList* part of a subroutine declaration defines the list of values that must be passed into the subroutine. The name of each variable passed is followed by a definition of its data type.

As an example, consider a `PasswordAssign` subroutine that would associate a password with a particular user. (You'll use this subroutine in creating a diary application later in this book.)

The subroutine declaration could look like this:

```
Sub PasswordAssign(Username As String, Password As String)
```

To the person who uses the subroutine, this declaration indicates that it must be passed two strings to be properly used. The names of the subroutine and arguments can make the code self-documenting. Consider that the subroutine could have been declared like this:

```
Sub Assign(X As Integer, Z As String)
```

This second example contains significantly less information about what the subroutine does. I advise you to avoid writing declarations like this one.

Calling the `PasswordAssign` subroutine within a program would be done this way:

```
PasswordAssign "Elizabeth", "KeepOut"
```

This looks just like using any keyword provided in the Basic environment, doesn't it?

A *function* is the same thing as a subroutine, except that a function additionally returns a value as a result of the call. A function is a procedure that returns a value.

Here's a pseudo-representation of what function calls are supposed to look like:

```
Function FunctionName(ArgumentList) As ReturnType
```

ReturnType indicates the data type of the value that the function returns.

Along with the `PasswordAssign` subroutine, you are going to need a `PasswordValidate` function to verify that a correct password is entered. You could have the `PasswordValidate` function return True (-1) to indicate that a good password was entered, and False (0) to indicate that a snoopy person's bad guess was entered instead.

The function declaration could look like this:

```
Function PasswordValidate(Username As String, Password As String) As Integer
```

Unlike a call to a subroutine, when you make a call to a function in your program, you must use parentheses around the arguments being passed to the function. Here is what a call to the `PasswordValidate` function would look like:

```
PasswordOK = PasswordValidate("Elizabeth", "KeepOut")
```

Good Morning, Mr. Schwartz!

The "Hello There" program isn't much in the way of sophistication, is it? Let's create a slightly larger program, one that "sings" a song. You can do this one in Excel, Access, or Visual Basic. In the following instructions and figures, I'll be using Excel.

The name of the program and the song is "Good Morning." The output of your program can be sung to the tune of "Happy Birthday."

1. Create a new module, as you did in the earlier instructions for "Hello There" for whichever Basic you are using.

2. Enter the `Main` subroutine into the module window, as shown in Listing 1.5.

Listing 1.5. `Main` **subroutine.**

```
Sub Main()

  SingTo "Mr. Schwartz"
  SingTo "Mrs. Washington"

End Sub
```

The `Main` subroutine calls the `SingTo` subroutine twice. Each time, the program passes an *argument* that indicates to whom to sing.

3. Enter the `SingTo` subroutine, as shown in Listing 1.6.

Listing 1.6. `SingTo` **subroutine.**

```
Sub SingTo(strName As String)

  Dim intStanza As Integer

  For intStanza = 1 To 3
    SingStanza intStanza, strName
  Next intStanza

End Sub
```

The complete "Good Morning" song has three stanzas. The `SingTo` subroutine uses a `For...Next` loop to call `SingStanza` three times.

4. Enter the `SingStanza` subroutine, as shown in Listing 1.7.

Listing 1.7. `SingStanza` **subroutine.**

```
Sub SingStanza(intStanza As Integer, strName As String)

  Dim intLine As Integer

  intLine = intStanza * 2 - 1

  SingLine intLine, ""
  SingLine intLine, ""
  SingLine intLine + 1, strName
  SingLine intLine, ""
  SkipLine

End Sub
```

The `SingStanza` subroutine determines which lines of the song to sing. In the first stanza, lines 1 and 2 are used. In the second stanza, lines 3 and 4 are used.

`SingLine` is called to sing each line. When lines 2, 4, or 6 are indicated, the name of the sung-to person is passed also. Otherwise, an empty string is passed.

5. Enter the `SingLine` subroutine, as shown in Listing 1.8 and Figure 1.17

Listing 1.8. `SingLine` **subroutine.**

```
Sub SingLine(intLine As Integer, strName As String)

  Select Case intLine
  Case 1
    Sing "Good Morning to you!"
  Case 2
    Sing "Good Morning dear " & strName & "!"
  Case 3
    Sing "Good Afternoon to you!"
  Case 4
    Sing "Good Afternoon dear " & strName & "!"
  Case 5
    Sing "Good Evening to you!"
  Case 6
    Sing "Good Evening dear " & strName & "!"
  End Select

End Sub
```

FIGURE 1.17.

Entering the SingLine subroutine in an Excel module sheet.

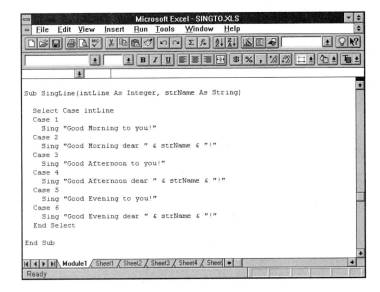

The `SingLine` subroutine uses the `Select Case` construct to sing the desired line as indicated by a number from 1 to 6. The `strName` argument is assumed to hold a value when lines 2, 4, and 6 are sung.

NOTE

The ampersand operator (`&`) is used in the `SingLine` subroutine to concatenate (join) two strings.

6. Enter the `SkipLine` subroutine, as shown in Listing 1.9.

Listing 1.9. `SkipLine` **subroutine.**

```
Sub SkipLine()

  Sing ""
  Sing ""

End Sub
```

The `SkipLine` subroutine puts two lines of space between stanzas to make the output easier to read.

7. Enter the `Sing` subroutine, as shown in Listing 1.10.

Listing 1.10. `Sing` **subroutine.**

```
Sub Sing(strLine As String)

  Debug.Print strLine

End Sub
```

The `Sing` subroutine does the "singing" by printing the line in the Immediate window.

You are now ready to run the program.

8. Type `Main` in the Immediate Window and press the Enter key. Figure 1.18 shows what happens.

FIGURE 1.18.

Excel singing to Mrs. Washington.

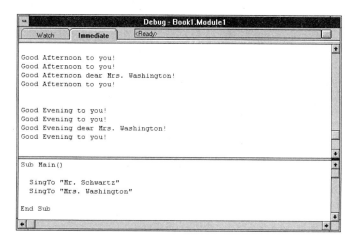

TRY THIS! QUESTION 1.2.
Can you create the "Good Morning" program in Word Basic?

Controlling the Flow of a Basic Program

I know, lectures are boring, but you need to know a few more concepts. Every good programmer must have a handle on these "rules of the game."

Within a program, there are three classic ways that the flow of execution moves from line to line. These can be classified as sequential execution, branching execution, and looping execution. In the "Good Morning" program, you used all three. Can you spot where each was used?

Sequential execution means that a language supports the execution of one line after the other. You expect that to happen, so let's move on.

Branching execution occurs when your program "makes a decision" to go down one path of execution or another. The different constructs for branching in Basic are `If...Then...Else` and `Select...Case`.

The `If...Then...Else` construct works like this:

```
If Expression Then
    Statements
End If
```
or:
```
If Expression Then
    Statements
Else
    Statements
End If
```
or:
```
If Expression Then
    Statements
ElseIf Expression Then
    Statements
End If
```

The *Expression* is usually a comparison of two values but may be a function call or other combinations of things. If the evaluation of the expression returns a non-zero value, the expression is considered True. A zero value indicates False.

In the simplest form of an `If...Then...Else` construct (where `Else` isn't used), if the expression is True, the *Statements* are executed. Where `Else` is used, an alternative set of statements are executed for the False condition.

Even though there may be many `ElseIf` statement blocks, an `If..Then...Else` construct is always considered a two-way switch. Based on the expression evaluated, either one path of execution or another is followed. (The other path may happen to lead to the evaluation of further `If` expressions that are also two-way switches.)

The `Select...Case` construct is branching that occurs with a multiway switch. Based on one expression, one of many paths may be executed. This construct takes the following form:

```
Select Case Expression
Case ValueList1
    Statements
Case ValueList2
    Statements
Case ValueList3
    Statements
Case Else
    Statements
End Select
```

The `ValueList` following each `Case` keyword is one or more values separated by commas. If the expression value matches any of the values in the `ValueList`, then this set of statements will be executed. If no matches are found, the statements after the optional `Case Else` keywords are executed.

The third form of program execution flow is *looping*. Different forms of looping constructs exist, but all basically repeat one or more statements until some criteria to break the loop is met.

The most well-known and beloved form of looping comes from BASIC in the old days—the `For...Next` loop.

The `For...Next` loop is readable and convenient. In one line, it indicates where a counter starts, where the counter ends, and how the counter is incremented.

```
For Counter = Start To Finish
    Statements
Next Counter
```

For example, the following program fragment could be used to print the numbers 1 to 100:

```
For n = 1 To 100
  Debug.Print n
Next n
```

The `For...Next` loop defaults to incrementing its counter variable by 1. You can change that with the `Step` keyword:

```
For Counter = Start To Finish Step StepValue
    Statements
Next Counter
```

The following code would count even numbers going backward from 50 to 2:

```
For n = 50 To 1 Step -2
  Debug.Print n
Next n
```

Some later forms of Basic looping are `While...Wend` and the various forms of `Do...Loop`.

The `While...Wend` loop executes the statements in it, as long as a test expression returns True.

```
While Expression
    Statements
Wend
```

If the expression returns False right from the start, the statements within the `While...Wend` loop never get executed.

The `Do...Loop` loop has more flexibility than the `While...Wend` loop in that you can control when the test is performed. There are several different flavors of the `Do...Loop` loop.

When the test is at the top of the loop, the expression is evaluated before executing the nested statements for the first time. Like the `While...Wend` loop, this type of loop may never execute the statements at all, because the test may fail on the first pass.

`Do While` loops continue the loop while the test expression remains True. `Do Until` loops continue the loop while the test expression is False:

```
Do While Expression
    Statements
Loop
Do Until Expression
    Statements
Loop
```

When the test expression is at the bottom of the loop, the statements within the loop are always executed at least one time. Then, depending on the expression, the loop is continued or terminated:

```
Do
    Statements
Loop While Expression
Do
    Statements
Loop Until Expression
```

You don't have to allow that a loop has some way to exit. In the "Hello There" example, you used the following construct, which is an *endless loop:*

```
Do
    Statements
Loop
```

The user can intervene while a loop is executing by pressing Esc or Ctrl-Break. A loop can also terminate early through code, for example when the `Exit For` statement is used as an early exit from a `For...Next` loop.

```
For Counter = Start To Finish
    If Expression2 Then
        Exit For
    End If
    Statements
Next Counter
```

Similarly, the `Exit Do` statement can be used to jump out of a `Do` loop prematurely.

```
Do Until Expression
    If Expression2 Then
        Exit Do
    End If
    Statements
Loop
```

Does there seem to be some redundancy here? In Basic, you'll often see more than one way to accomplish the same thing. When you have a choice, use whatever method you find easiest to read.

GoTo

A Basic program can change its flow of execution in yet another way. A `GoTo` allows the execution to jump from one line to any other line in the same procedure.

In the past, many programmers argued about whether it was appropriate to use `GoTo`s in a program. Probably more than anything else, `GoTo` contributed to BASIC's old reputation for allowing the creation of unreadable programs. I refer you to the Nightmare Descent listing in the Preface if you are curious about why.

Throwing out `GoTo` completely, however, was and is an overreaction. Today there are some commonly accepted uses for the `GoTo` form of flow control over program execution.

The usage of `GoTo` in this book's programs deals with error handling or any other early exit from the normal execution of a procedure. I'll explain why.

Within a procedure your code may open files or database tables. These files and tables must be closed properly on leaving the routine, and there may be additional things to do—for example, releasing allocated memory, closing forms, setting the mouse cursor back to normal, and who knows what else.

It's called cleaning up after yourself. It's just like wiping your feet before coming in, hanging up the towel after drying your hands, and closing the refrigerator door after taking something from it.

To facilitate the cleaning-up business, most procedures I write have two labels: a Done label and an Error label. Labels are the things that GoTo jumps to now that we don't use line numbers. Following the Done label is a section that does cleanup. It releases any allocated resources that may have been opened or used in the procedure.

In the next section, you will see how error handling in Basic is all set up.

GoTos for Error Handling

Listing 1.11 shows a template that could be used to begin any subroutine or function.

Listing 1.11. A procedure template.

```
On Error GoTo xxError

xxDone:
  Exit Sub

xxError:
  MsgBox Error$, 48, PROGRAM
  Resume xxDone
```

I use this template so regularly that I have a Windows Notepad icon in the Startup directory set up to load a file that includes it.

To create this template, do the following:

1. Enter into Notepad the template text shown in Listing 1.11.
2. Save the file. For the purposes of this discussion, I'll assume that it was saved under C:\NOTES\TMPLATE.TXT.
3. Open the Startup group window in Program Manager.
4. While you hold down the Ctrl key, click and drag the Notepad icon into the Startup window. This creates a new copy of the Notepad icon.
5. Select the new Notepad icon and press Alt-Enter to edit its properties.
6. Enter the following:

   Description: Template

   Command Line: NOTEPAD.EXE C:\NOTES\TMPLATE.TXT
7. Check the **R**un Minimized check box ON. See Figure 1.19.
8. Click OK to save the changes.

FIGURE 1.19.

Automatic loading of a procedure template in Notepad.

The next time you start up Windows, the Notepad icon will be displayed at the bottom of the screen with the Template file loaded and ready for use.

To start a new procedure, I go through the following routine. For the purpose of this example, let's assume you are writing the `PasswordAssign` subroutine in Access 2.0.

1. Open a module window and enter the declaration for the routine:

```
Sub PasswordAssign (Username As String, Password As String)

End Sub
```

2. Press Alt-Tab as many times as necessary to switch to the Notepad session.

3. Select all of the text. The keystrokes for this are Ctrl-Home to move to the beginning of the text and Ctrl-Shift-End to select and move to the end of the text. See Figure 1.20.

FIGURE 1.20.

Selecting the text in the procedure template.

4. Copy the template text into the clipboard buffer by pressing Ctrl-C.

5. Press Alt-Tab again to switch back to your program.

6. Place the text cursor on the `End Sub` line. Paste the template into the new subroutine or function by pressing Ctrl-V. See Figure 1.21.

FIGURE 1.21.

Pasting in the procedure template.

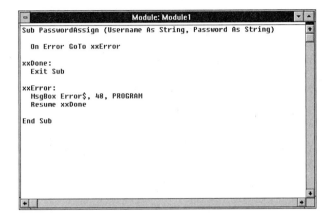

7. Next, double-click the procedure name and press Ctrl-C to put it in the clipboard.

8. Select the **Edit|Replace** command to bring up the Replace dialog box.

9. Enter xx into the **F**ind What text box.

10. Tab to the **R**eplace With text box and press Ctrl-V to enter the procedure name.

11. Make sure the change affects only the current procedure. Press Alt-P to set the Search option to Current **P**rocedure. See Figure 1.22.

FIGURE 1.22.

Modifying the procedure template for the current procedure.

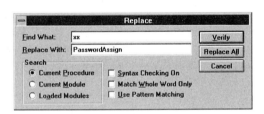

12. Select the Replace A**l**l button to make the change.

The final result should appear as shown in Figure 1.23.

This long series of steps is certainly a target for automation. You may want to create a program that adds the error handling to a procedure after the declaration is entered.

FIGURE 1.23.

Error handling setup in the PasswordAssign *subroutine.*

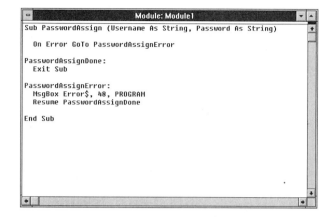

```
Sub PasswordAssign (Username As String, Password As String)

   On Error GoTo PasswordAssignError

PasswordAssignDone:
   Exit Sub

PasswordAssignError:
   MsgBox Error$, 48, PROGRAM
   Resume PasswordAssignDone

End Sub
```

Error Handling in Detail

Let's take a look at the stub for your `PasswordAssign` function, line-by-line.

The first line after the declaration uses the `On Error` and `GoTo` keywords to set up Basic's error trapping. If Basic finds a problem it can't deal with, it jumps to the code after the `PasswordAssignError` label:

```
On Error GoTo PasswordAssignError
```

Without some kind of error trapping, your program will stop execution dead in its tracks. Assigning your own error trapping enables you to catch the error, display a more polite error message if you prefer, do your cleanup, and then get out of the function gracefully.

The `Done` label is where any cleanup occurs. This should be the single exit point for the procedure, so that the code following the `Done` label is always executed before leaving:

```
PasswordAssignDone:
   Exit Sub
```

Because of the `On Error` line at the beginning of the procedure, the code following the `Error` label is jumped to when any error raised by Basic occurs. Using the code in your template, a message box is opened to display the error message.

After the error message box is cleared by the user, the program resumes execution at the `Done` label in order to perform an orderly exit:

```
PasswordAssignError:
   MsgBox Error$, 48, PROGRAM
   Resume PasswordAssignDone
```

In the preceding program lines, PROGRAM is a global constant string set to the name of the program. As the third argument to the MsgBox statement, it is displayed in the error message box title bar. The constant could be declared in a module's declaration section like this:

```
Global Const PROGRAM = "Secret Diary"
```

A typical error message looks like the one shown in Figure 1.24.

FIGURE 1.24

An error occurs because of a missing Passwords table.

In the error handling section, you can check for different error codes and display better messages than Basic provides on its own. For example, it would be helpful if the message in Figure 1.24 indicated what type of object Passwords was, a table. The Basic statement, Err, returns the error code value. Your program can check this value and act accordingly.

Using *GoTo* to Get Out

The second place I commonly use GoTos is just after a function call. Frequently my functions return a status code indicating whether they ran successfully or not. I like to return 0 for success and -1 for failure. In this way, I can code function calls as I do in Listing 1.12.

Listing 1.12. You can use GoTo as a way to bail out when things have gone astray.

```
If ReadFile( strFilename1 ) Then GoTo DataConversionDone
If ReadFile( strFilename2 ) Then GoTo DataConversionDone
If ReadFile( strFilename3 ) Then GoTo DataConversionDone
z = WriteFile( strFilename4 )
```

In Listing 1.12, suppose that the WriteFile call works only if all three ReadFile calls finish successfully. If any error occurs in a ReadFile call, then in the ReadFile function an error message would be displayed and a value of -1 would be returned. The test after the call would jump over any remaining function calls so that the entire process could be aborted.

You could do this without `GoTos`, but your code would look like Listing 1.13.

Listing 1.13. An alternative that avoids the use of `GoTo`.

```
If Not ReadFile( strFilename1 ) Then
    If Not ReadFile( strFilename2 ) Then
        If Not ReadFile( strFilename3 ) Then
            z = WriteFile( strFilename4 )
        End If
    End If
End If
```

I find the first version easier to read. How about you?

Remnants of the Past

With the introduction of procedures in Basic, you would think that `GOSUB` and `RETURN` statements are a thing of the past. I haven't seen them used in a long time and I would have guessed that they didn't exist anymore, but when I looked at online help in Access, I found they still are there. This is probably in consideration of people who are moving code from older BASICs into the new Basics.

Even line numbers still exist! Quite to my surprise, the following version of "Hello There" runs in Access 2.0:

```
Sub HelloThere ()
10   Debug.Print "Hello there"
20   GoTo 10
End Sub
```

Summary

In this chapter you accomplished the following:

- Took Basic for a test spin, using Visual Basic, Word, Excel, and Access
- Learned about using subroutines and functions
- Created a larger program by using subroutines
- Learned about sequential execution, branching, and looping
- Used `GoTo` as a means of handling exceptions in your procedures

In the next chapter, you will break any ties with the past and cover some new features in Basic that never existed in old BASIC.

TRY THIS! ANSWERS

1.1. The program in Listing 1.14 fills a column of cells in Excel with `Hello there`. How did you do it?

Listing 1.14. "Hello There," writing to a column of cells in a workbook.

```
Sub HelloThere()
  Dim intRow As Integer

  intRow = 1
  Do
    Range("A" & intRow).Select
    ActiveCell.FormulaR1C1 = "Hello there"
    intRow = intRow + 1
  Loop
End Sub
```

1.2. Listing 1.15 shows my version of "Good Morning" in Word Basic.

Listing 1.15. "Good Morning" in Word Basic.

```
Sub MAIN

  SingTo "Mr. Schwartz"
  SingTo "Mrs. Washington"

End Sub

Sub SingTo(strName$)

  For intStanza = 1 To 3
    SingStanza intStanza, strName$
  Next intStanza

End Sub

Sub SingStanza(intStanza, strName$)

  intLine = intStanza * 2 - 1

  SingLine intLine, ""
  SingLine intLine, ""
  SingLine intLine + 1, strName$
  SingLine intLine, ""
  SkipLine
```

```
End Sub

Sub SingLine(intLine, strName$)

  Select Case intLine
  Case 1
    Sing "Good Morning to you!"
  Case 2
    Sing "Good Morning dear " + strName$ + "!"
  Case 3
    Sing "Good Afternoon to you!"
  Case 4
    Sing "Good Afternoon dear " + strName$ + "!"
  Case 5
    Sing "Good Evening to you!"
  Case 6
    Sing "Good Evening dear " + strName$ + "!"
  End Select

End Sub

Sub SkipLine

  Sing ""
  Sing ""

End Sub

Sub Sing(strLine$)

  Insert strLine$
  InsertPara

End Sub
```

CHAPTER 2

Word: Study Mate

If you have been using Microsoft Word to create all of your personal or business corre-
spondence, you are probably already a skilled user of Word. To become a real expert,
however, you must become familiar with one of its most powerful features, Word
Basic.

In the last chapter, you dug into just enough theory to start writing some Basic programs. In this chapter, you will find out what it's like to create a program in Word Basic
and why you would want to do so in the first place. Then you will apply what you've
learned and produce a fun and useful flash card program called "Study Mate."

I encourage you to perform the steps outlined in this chapter and reproduce each program as you read along. However, you will find the complete program on the companion CD-ROM included with the book if you don't have time to rebuild the project on
your own.

Why Does My Word Processor Need a Programming Language?

It isn't exactly novel that Word has its own built-in programming language. Word pro-
cessors and text editors have had built-in programming languages for years. Some programming languages, AWK for example, were designed specifically for text processing.

The primary use for a programming language in a word processor is to handle repetitive
tasks.

I'm sure you know what I mean by *repetitive tasks.* These are tasks for which you sit at
the keyboard, typing the same keystrokes over and over until your hands ache and your
fingers feel as if they are going to fall off. You need not do that.

Using a combination of macro recording and programming, you can make Word perform those repetitive tasks for you. You can also write programs to calculate and display
statistics about your writing. You can even create a document-based application using
Word as a software-engineering tool.

If you have a need for any application that involves creating documents, think Word
Basic first.

Using the Macro Recorder

The simplest form of Word Basic programming is to use the Word macro recorder. As
was described in Chapter 1, "Today's Basic," the Word macro recorder creates Word

Basic code. For many tasks, however, you don't have to be concerned about what the program looks like; you just play the macro when you need it.

Any time you find yourself doing the same set of keystrokes and mouse clicks repeatedly, you should recognize this as an opportunity to create and use a Word macro. Recording macros is so easy that it is often done for one-time use in making corrections to a single document; then it's thrown away.

Text Markers

Here's a useful example of the value of macros. If you are like me, you don't create any document in a single pass. You write what you can quickly on the first pass, and you leave markers to indicate what you have left undone.

Later, as you are finishing up the document, you search for the markers to find the unfinished sections.

Some markers I use are *xx* and ***. Sometimes I use two markers, << before the note and >> after it.

When I use the *** marker, my document might look like what is shown in Figure 2.1.

FIGURE 2.1.

A document with markers to indicate unfinished sections.

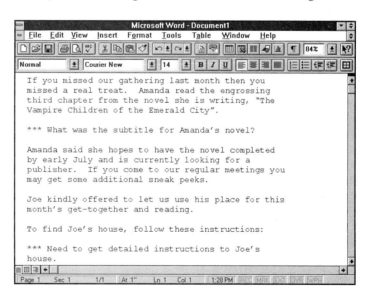

When you choose which characters to use as your markers, be sure they aren't something that might appear in regular text.

Finding Markers

Without the benefit of macros to find each of the markers in your document, you could use the **Edit|Find** command. You could then use Shift-F4 repeatedly to find each occurrence of the marker.

If, during scanning through markers you use **Edit|Find** to search for something other than the marker, pressing Shift-F4 causes Word to search for the last text located with a Find, rather than your marker text. To find the next marker, you'll need to use **Edit|Find** again and reenter the marker as the text to be found.

This may not seem tedious, but in heavy word-processing chores, it's helpful to shave off any keystrokes you can, especially for things you do frequently.

With the Word macro recorder, you can record a macro that finds the marker. You can then assign the macro to a special key combination, Alt-M for example.

Then each time you press Alt-M, the next marker in your document will be found, even if you used **Edit|Find** to find something else during your search for markers. By pressing Alt-M repeatedly, you can quickly look for all of the unfinished sections in your document.

Creating the *FindStarMarker* Macro

Here's how you record the macro:

1. Select the **Tools|Macro** command.
2. Enter `FindStarMarker` as the name for the macro, as shown in Figure 2.2.
3. At the bottom of the dialog box, you can enter a description of what the macro does.

    The description isn't a required entry. You put it there to remind yourself about what the recorded macro does.

FIGURE 2.2.

Creating the
`FindStarMarker`
macro.

4. Press the Record button.

   Before you start the recording, you have the option to assign your macro to a toolbar button, custom menu command, or key combination. You can make the assignment now or do it any time after recording the macro.

5. In the Record Macro dialog box (shown in Figure 2.3), press the button with the keyboard picture.

FIGURE 2.3.

You can assign a macro before recording it.

Next, the Customize dialog box is displayed. It enables you to assign a recorded macro to a toolbar button, menu command, or key-press combination. Select the different tabs in the dialog box to make each of the assignments.

6. With the text cursor at the Press **N**ew Shortcut Key text box, press Alt-M.

   Entering the Alt-M key assignment into the Customize dialog box is shown in Figure 2.4.

FIGURE 2.4.

Assigning the Alt-M key combination to the FindStartMarker *macro.*

7. Press the **A**ssign button to accept the key assignment.

8. Press the **C**lose button to begin recording.

The macro recorder displays its toolbar with the Stop and Pause buttons. The following are the steps to perform in the recording session:

1. Select **Edit|Find** to bring up the Find dialog box.

2. Enter *** (or other marker) as the text to find.

   Select Down as the Search option in the Find dialog box if you don't want the search to start again at the top of the document when it reaches the end of the document. Selecting Down is especially helpful with large documents, because with those it's sometimes difficult to determine whether or not you've passed the end.

   Figure 2.5 shows the Find dialog box being used while a macro is being recorded. In the upper-right corner of the document window you can see the Macro recorder toolbar with its Stop and Pause buttons.

FIGURE 2.5.

Recording the FindStartMarker macro.

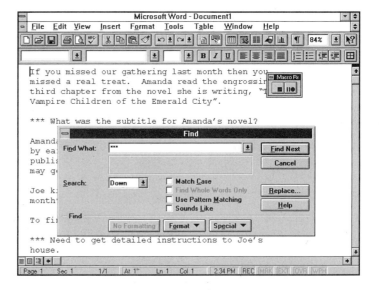

3. Press the **F**ind Next button.

   If your current document has your marker text in it, you will see it selected in the document window.

4. Press the Cancel button to close the Find dialog box.

5. Press the Stop button on the macro recorder toolbar window.

You are finished. Press Alt-M repeatedly to find the remaining markers scattered throughout your document.

Global Macros

On closing Word, your new macro is stored in the NORMAL.DOT template that is loaded each time Word starts. This means your macro will be available for use in any document; the macro will not be confined to the document in which you recorded it.

TRY THIS! QUESTION 2.1.

After the macro is already recorded, try changing the key assignment to something other than Alt-M.

Try adding a menu command, **Edit|Find Star Marker**, that runs your recorded macro. How did it go?

Creating a Custom Toolbar

Rather than have all your macro programs hidden behind secret key-press combinations, you can create your own Custom toolbar and place buttons on it to run your macros.

1. Select the **View|Toolbars** command to open the Toolbars dialog box, as shown in Figure 2.6.

FIGURE 2.6.

The Toolbars dialog box lets you turn on and off the displayed toolbars and create new ones.

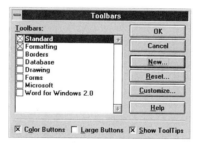

2. Press the **N**ew button.
3. In the New Toolbar dialog box, enter a name for your toolbar, as shown in Figure 2.7.

   The name you enter is what will be displayed in the Toolbars dialog box when you select which toolbars are displayed.

FIGURE 2.7.

Entering a name for a new Custom toolbar.

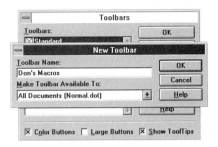

Next, the Customize dialog box appears to allow you to place buttons on your new toolbar, which is shown in the upper-left corner of the document window in Figure 2.8. While you are here, you can add a button for the FindStarMarker macro that you created earlier.

4. In the Categories list box, select Macro.

5. In the Macros list box, you will see the FindStarMarker macro listed.

FIGURE 2.8.

Adding a button to the Custom toolbar.

Toolbar button is added to the Custom toolbar.

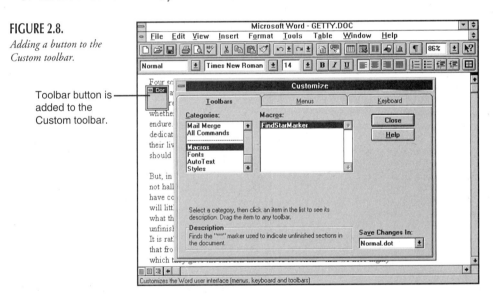

6. Click FindStarMarker in the Macros list box and hold the mouse down. A square outline of a button appears at the mouse pointer.

7. Drag the button outline across the screen to the Custom toolbar and drop it in the toolbar.

   The Custom Button dialog box is then displayed to enable you to choose a picture for the button (as shown in Figure 2.9). You can choose the button marked "Text Button" to enter text, instead of a picture, to appear on the button.

FIGURE 2.9.

*Choose text or a picture
for your toolbar button.*

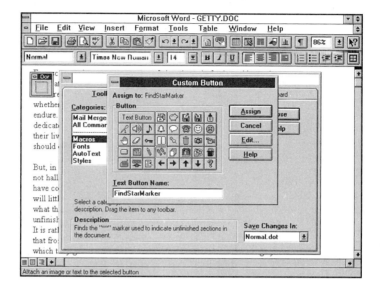

8. Click any picture (I chose the footsteps picture), and press the Edit button.

    The Button Editor dialog box (shown in Figure 2.10) enables you to modify the button picture or create a completely new one.

FIGURE 2.10.

*The Button Editor
enables you to change
the picture for your
button.*

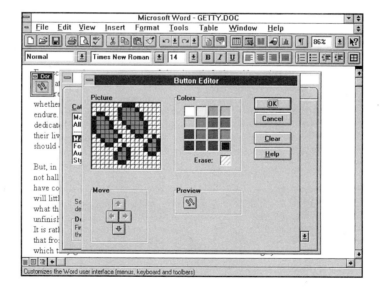

9. Click the **C**lear button to erase the picture. Figure 2.11 shows the button after the footsteps picture has been erased.

FIGURE 2.11.

Use the Clear button to start a new button picture from scratch.

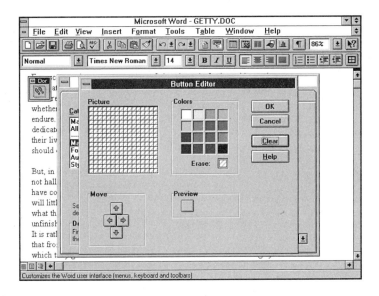

10. Draw the picture for your toolbar button. I drew a picture of three asterisks to remind me of my marker text. The drawing in the Button Editor dialog box is shown in Figure 2.12.

FIGURE 2.12.

The FindStarMarker Custom toolbar picture.

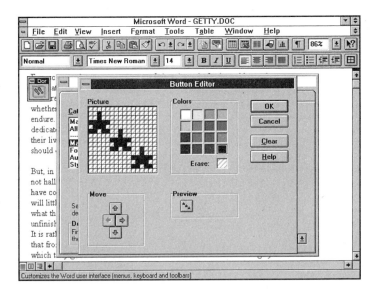

11. Press the OK button to close the Button Editor.
12. Press the Close button to close the Customize dialog box.

To modify an existing toolbar, you can go directly to the Customize dialog box by selecting the **Tools|Customize** command.

Word Count

Were you ever curious about how many times you used a particular word in a document? You can write a Basic program to find out.

Creating Word Count

To create a word count program, you can start by using the macro recorder and finish by coding manually. For this program, you'll add a button to the Custom toolbar created in the preceding section.

1. Select the **Tools|Macro** command.
2. In the Macro dialog box, enter WordCount as the name of the macro to create.
3. Press the Record button.
4. In the Record Macro dialog box, press the Toolbars button.
5. In the Customize dialog box, click WordCount and drag it to your Custom toolbar. Drop it next to the FindStarMarker button that you created earlier.
6. Select a picture for the button, then press the **E**dit button if you want to draw your own picture. See Figure 2.13 for the picture I drew.

FIGURE 2.13.

Drawing a toolbar button for the WordCount macro.

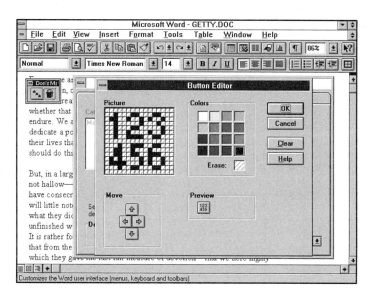

7. Close the Button Editor if you modified the picture.

8. Close the Customize dialog box.

The macro recorder starts now. Following are the steps to perform in the recording session.

1. Select **Edit**|**Find** to open the Find dialog box.

2. Enter some text to find in the current document, as shown in Figure 2.14.

FIGURE 2.14.

Using the Find dialog box while recording the WordCount macro.

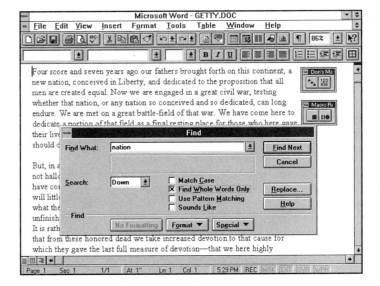

In my document, I have President Lincoln's "Gettysburg Address" from Microsoft's Encarta CD. I entered nation as the word to search for.

3. Press the **Find** Next button.

4. Press the Cancel button.

5. Press the Stop button on the Macro Recorder toolbar window.

Editing Word Count

If that last set of steps seemed similar to the macro you recorded earlier, in fact it was. Now, however, you will add some handwritten code and make this macro much more useful.

1. Select **Tools**|**Macro** from the menu.

2. Select the WordCount macro and press the Edit button.

Word will display the WordCount macro in a document window ready for editing, as shown in Figure 2.15.

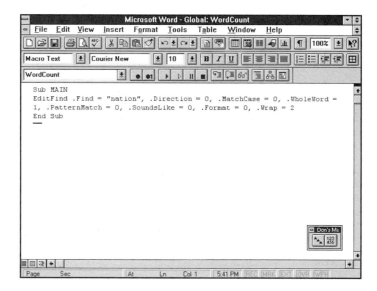

Named Arguments

Each Word macro begins with a MAIN subroutine. Inside of WordCount's MAIN subroutine is a single statement, EditFind. Like other statements in Word, EditFind uses *named arguments*.

Named argument values are indicated by entering a period and the name of the argument, followed by an equals sign, and the value for the argument.

Unlike arguments in regular Basic subroutines and functions, named arguments can appear in any order. Also, many of the arguments are optional and can be excluded altogether.

Word needs named arguments because some of its statements have a horrendous number of arguments. A typical example is the FormatFont statement; it takes 18 arguments.

A Word Basic Online Reference

You can get some help to learn about the EditFind statement.

1. Place your cursor on the EditFind statement and press the F1 key.

The help window displays a topic on the EditFind statement, as shown in Figure 2.16. This topic describes what the statement does, what its arguments are used for, and what values are appropriate for the arguments.

FIGURE 2.16.

The Word Basic help file is a reference for all the statements and functions used in Word Basic.

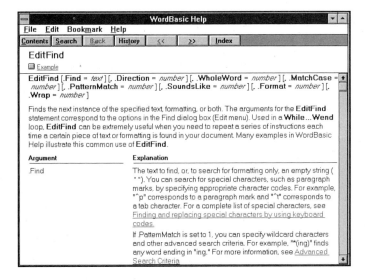

If you get an error stating that the help file is not found, you may have elected not to install the Word Basic help file when you installed Word. You will need to run Setup again, and this time you should make sure that the Word Basic help file is installed.

The Word Basic help file is WRDBASIC.HLP in your Word directory.

The best part of the Word Basic help file is the example programs. You can copy code examples out of the help file and paste them into Word as a starting point for your own routines. I used the second example in the help topic shown in Figure 2.17 as a basis for the Word Count program.

FIGURE 2.17.

The Word Basic help file has many useful examples.

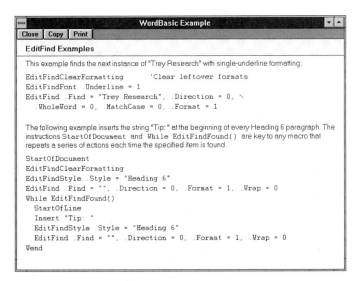

Rewriting Word Count

Now you can modify the Word Count program using the information we gathered by observing the code that the Macro Recorder produced and our investigation through the Word Basic help file.

Trust me on this one. I'll explain the details of the changes in a little bit.

1. Modify the MAIN subroutine so it reads as shown in Listing 2.1.

Listing 2.1. Word Count.

```
Sub MAIN

'   Count how many times a word is found in a document.

    Dim Count
    Dim Word$

    Count = 0
    Word$ = InputBox$("Enter the word to search for:", "Word Count")

    StartOfDocument

    EditFind .Find = Word$, .Direction = 0, .WholeWord = 1
    While EditFindFound()
        Count = Count + 1
        EditFind .Find = Word$, .Direction = 0, .WholeWord = 1
    Wend

    StartOfDocument

    MsgBox Word$ + " was found " + Str$(Count) + " times.", "Word Count"

End Sub
```

Figure 2.18 shows the Word Count program being entered in Word.

FIGURE 2.18.
Entering the Word Count program.

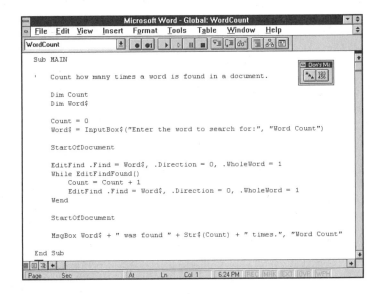

```
Sub MAIN

'    Count how many times a word is found in a document.

    Dim Count
    Dim Word$

    Count = 0
    Word$ = InputBox$("Enter the word to search for:", "Word Count")

    StartOfDocument

    EditFind .Find = Word$, .Direction = 0, .WholeWord = 1
    While EditFindFound()
        Count = Count + 1
        EditFind .Find = Word$, .Direction = 0, .WholeWord = 1
    Wend

    StartOfDocument

    MsgBox Word$ + " was found " + Str$(Count) + " times.", "Word Count"

End Sub
```

Testing Word Count

Let's give Word Count a whirl and see if it works.

1. Switch to the document window by selecting it from the **W**indow menu.

   If you don't have any text in the current document window, enter some or load an existing document.

2. Press the Word Count button on the Custom toolbar.

   If all goes well, the macro will run after you enter it. Don't feel bad, though, if you get an error message like the one shown in Figure 2.19. It's not uncommon to make several typos when keying in a programming listing from a book.

FIGURE 2.19.
Oops! Time to fix the typos.

If you do have errors, switch to the macro window and correct them. Word highlights the error, giving you a quick indication of which line the error is on.

TRY THIS! QUESTION 2.2.
Can you find the error in the code listed in Figure 2.20?

FIGURE 2.20.

Word highlights the offending line.

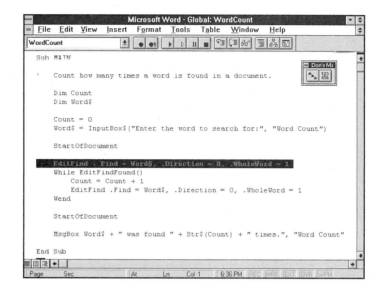

After your program is running successfully, an input box is displayed, prompting you for the word to count.

3. Enter the word for the search and count. As illustrated in Figure 2.21, I'll count how many times *nation* is used in the "Gettysburg Address."

FIGURE 2.21.

Counting occurrences of nation in the "Gettysburg Address."

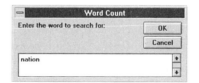

4. Press the OK button.

In Figure 2.22, Word Count displays a text box showing how many occurrences of the word it found.

FIGURE 2.22.

Results from the Word Count program.

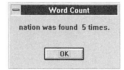

Word Count Under a Microscope

The first line in the MAIN subroutine is a comment. As with each of the other Basics used in this book, a comment in Word Basic begins with a single quote character. Any text after the single quote is ignored by Basic.

```
Sub MAIN

'   Count how many times a word is found in a document.
```

After the comment we "dim" a couple of variables.

```
    Dim Count
    Dim Word$
```

Dim is short for "dimension." With Dim you are telling Basic that you will use a variable of a given name and data type.

Data types are easy in Word Basic. You have two:

■ Number

■ String

A *number* variable can store both integer values and floating point values. A *string* variable stores text. A string variable is always followed by a dollar sign in Word Basic.

In the next two lines of the MAIN subroutine, the Count variable is initially set to zero, and the Word$ variable is set to a string entered by the user through the InputBox$ function in Word Basic.

```
    Count = 0
    Word$ = InputBox$("Enter the word to search for:", "Word Count")
```

The StartOfDocument statement moves the text cursor to the top of the Word document.

```
    StartOfDocument
```

The EditFind statement is called to find the text stored within the Word$ variable.

```
    EditFind .Find = Word$, .Direction = 0, .WholeWord = 1
```

The EditFindFound function returns True (-1) if the EditFind statement successfully found the text being searched for.

A While...Wend loop uses the result of the EditFindFound call to determine whether the loop should be entered each time or terminated. On a successful call to EditFind, the loop is entered and the Count variable is incremented by 1.

Within the loop, the EditFind statement is used again to find the next occurrence of the text being searched for.

```
While EditFindFound()
    Count = Count + 1
    EditFind .Find = Word$, .Direction = 0, .WholeWord = 1
Wend
```

After the counting is done, `StartOfDocument` is called again to move the text cursor back to the top of the document window.

```
StartOfDocument
```

The `MsgBox` statement is used to display the resulting count. The message displayed is constructed by concatenating several strings.

```
MsgBox Word$ + " was found " + Str$(Count) + " times.", "Word Count"
```

```
End Sub
```

That's it!

You've learned the essentials of Word Basic and even put together a couple of useful utilities. Now it's time to put your knowledge to work.

Introducing Study Mate

Study Mate is a flash card program that you can use to quiz yourself in preparation for an exam. A few short sessions with Study Mate will surely improve your test scores.

Creating a set of flash cards in Study Mate is as simple as typing in the questions and the answers. Study Mate uses its own custom toolbar buttons to flip randomly from card to card or to view them in sequential order. Click the button with the question mark picture, and a question is randomly selected and displayed as shown in Figure 2.23.

FIGURE 2.23.

Displaying a Question Card in Study Mate.

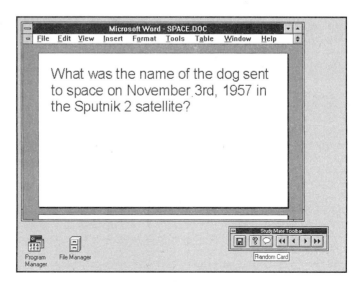

Click the button with the cartoon balloon, and Study Mate displays the answer card for the current question, as shown in Figure 2.24.

FIGURE 2.24.

Displaying an Answer Card in Study Mate.

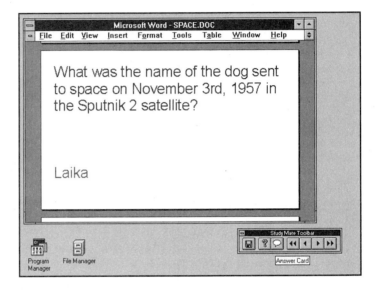

Using a Template

The key to building any application successfully in Word is to know Word's features and to use them well. In other words, don't write code for something that Word can handle alone.

Rather than create a program that prompts for questions and answers to place in the flash cards, you will create instead a Word template that can handle creating the cards with no code at all.

You will use code to create a button to save the cards after they are entered and other buttons to actually use the cards.

A *template* is a Word document used as the basis for creating another document. When you select **File|New** to create a new document, the New dialog box enables you to select from a list of many provided templates and Wizards on which to base your new document.

Within the Study Mate template, you will store page size settings and Word styles that allow for easy creation of the flash cards. Your program will also be stored in the template, making the buttons available to any document based on the Study Mate template.

You don't want to store any components of Study Mate in the default NORMAL.DOT template, as you did with your other macros. Using a separate template enables you to make copies of the template for others, so they too can use the application.

Creating the STDYMATE.DOT Template

To create the STDYMATE.DOT template, do the following:

1. Select the File|New command.
2. In the New dialog box, click Template in the New option group to create a template instead of a document, as shown in Figure 2.25.

FIGURE 2.25.

Creating a Word Template.

3. Click OK.

Getting Word to look like a deck of flash cards took a little experimentation on my part. Here are the steps I came up with.

1. Select View|Page Layout to display the open document in pages.
2. Select File|Page Setup.
3. In the **M**argins tab of the Page Setup dialog box, enter the following settings as shown in Figure 2.26:

    Top: 0.25"
    Bottom: 0.5"
    Le**f**t: 0.25"
    Right: 0.25"
    He**a**der: 0.2"
    Foote**r**:   0.2"

FIGURE 2.26.

Setting the flash card margins.

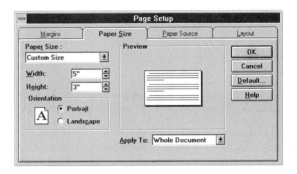

4. In the Paper **S**ize tab, enter the following settings, as shown in Figure 2.27:

   Width: 5"
   Height: 3"

FIGURE 2.27.

Setting the flash card page size.

The page will change to a 3"×5" card, as shown in Figure 2.28.

Next, create a Word style for entering question text in a flash card.

1. Select the Format|**S**tyle command to bring up the Style dialog box, as shown in Figure 2.29.

2. In the Style dialog box, press the **N**ew button.

3. In the New Style dialog box, enter `Question` as the name of the new style.
   The Style for Following Paragraph entry will default to Question.

4. Clicking the F**o**rmat button displays a drop-down menu, as shown in Figure 2.30.

5. Click **F**ont from the drop-down menu.

FIGURE 2.28.
A single flash card page.

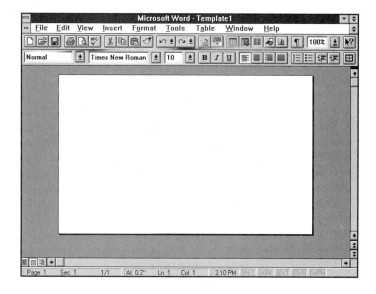

FIGURE 2.29.
Use the Style dialog box to create new styles or modify existing ones.

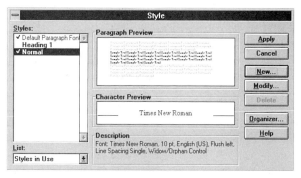

FIGURE 2.30.
The Format button drop-down menu.

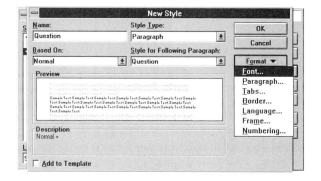

6. Select the font options for how you want the question text in your flash cards displayed. I chose the Arial with a regular font style, size 20, and the color blue, as shown in Figure 2.31. Press OK.

FIGURE 2.31.

Setting font options for the Question style.

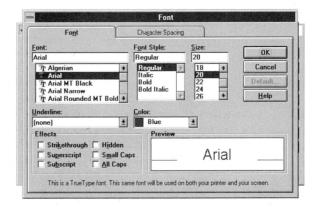

Back at the New Style dialog box, the preview window displays a paragraph of text with the font you selected, as shown in Figure 2.32.

FIGURE 2.32.

The New Style dialog box's preview window displays the style as it will appear in the document.

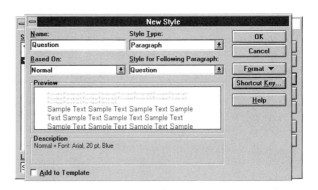

Next, you can add a key assignment to allow for quick selection of the new style.

1. Press the Shortcut Key button.

   The Customize dialog box that you used to create toolbar buttons appears.

2. With the cursor in the Press **N**ew Shortcut Key text box, press Alt-Q. Press the **A**ssign button to enter the key assignment, as shown in Figure 2.33.

3. Close the Customize dialog box.

4. Press OK in the New Style dialog box.

FIGURE 2.33.

Assigning Alt-Q to the Question style.

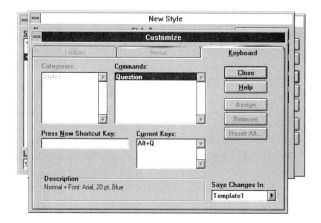

Add a second style to display Answer text in a flash card.

1. In the Style dialog box, press the **N**ew button again to add a second style.

2. In the New Style dialog box, enter Answer as the name of the new style.

3. Select the Question style at the **B**ased On prompt.

   The **B**ased On selection is a shortcut. It means start with all the settings of the selected style when you create the new style.

4. Select the Question style for the **S**tyle for Following Paragraph as shown in Figure 2.34.

   The style set as **S**tyle for Following Paragraph will automatically be used after you enter a paragraph in the current style.

   This means that after you enter an Answer to a flash card and press the Enter key, the current style switches back to the Question style, ready for you to enter the next question.

FIGURE 2.34.

Creating the Answer style based on the Question style.

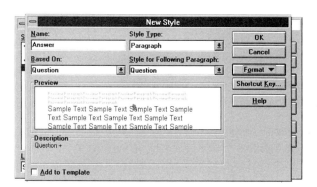

5. Click the **Fo**rmat button, and select **F**ont again from the drop-down menu.

6. Select how you want the font displayed in an answer on a flash card. I changed the color to red and left everything else the same (as shown in Figure 2.35).

FIGURE 2.35.

Selecting the font options for the Answer style.

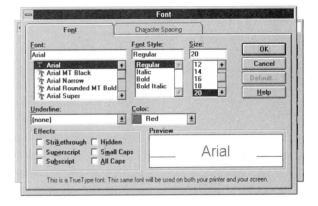

7. Press OK to close the Font dialog box.

8. Press the Shortcut **K**ey on the New Style dialog box to assign a key-press combination to the Answer style.

9. With the text cursor on the Press **N**ew Shortcut Key text box, press Alt-A. Word enters the text `Alt+A` into the text box, as shown in Figure 2.36.

FIGURE 2.36.

Assigning Alt-A to the Answer style.

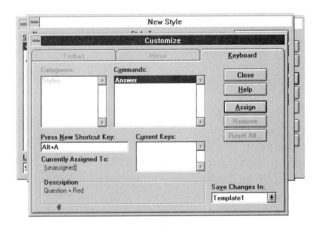

10. Press **A**ssign to enter the key assignment.

11. Close the Customize dialog box.

12. Press OK to the New Style dialog box.

The Style dialog box now displays the two added styles. Clicking either of them displays each style in the preview window, as shown in Figure 2.37.

FIGURE 2.37.
The Style dialog box displays the new styles.

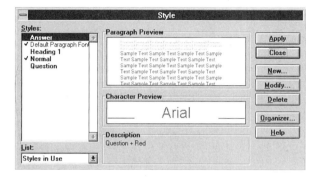

Now you're ready to start using the template. First, save your work so far.

1. Close the Style dialog box.

2. Select **F**ile|**S**ave.

Because you are creating a template, Word doesn't allow you to just save it anywhere. It *must* be saved in the TEMPLATE subdirectory of the directory where you installed Word.

The Save As dialog box allows you to enter a filename, but it won't allow you to change directories.

3. Enter STDYMATE.DOT as the filename for the template, as shown in Figure 2.38, and press OK.

FIGURE 2.38.
Saving the Study Mate template.

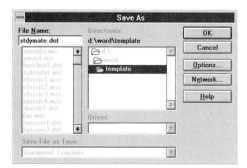

Entering Questions and Answers

The template is ready for entering questions. The intention is not actually to enter the questions in STDYMATE.DOT, but you can temporarily fill a few pages with questions and answers to assist in developing the rest of the application. Before you save the final version of the template, you will clear out the pages so that a document based on the template will begin empty.

You can select the Question style from the leftmost combo box on the Formatting toolbar, or use the key assignment we made for it and press Alt-Q.

1. Press Alt-Q and enter the first question as shown in Figure 2.39.

   Enter any question you like. You could even enter Question 1, because you need this only for testing.

FIGURE 2.39.

Filling in a Question Card.

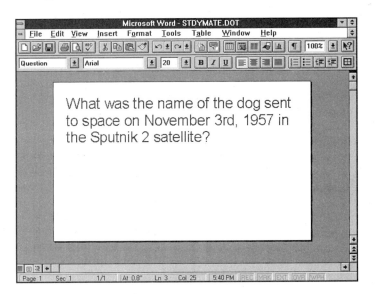

2. Press Enter enough times to get to the top of the next card.
3. Enter the question again, exactly as typed in the first card. Use copy and paste to avoid retyping it.

   You don't have to recopy the question on the second card, but I think doing so produces a nice effect. When the question card is displayed, it looks as if the answer popped up on the same card.

4. Press Enter enough times to get to the last line on the second card. If you go too far, press Backspace to go back.
5. Press Alt-A, or select the Answer style from the Format toolbar.
6. Enter the answer to the question as shown in Figure 2.40.

FIGURE 2.40.

Filling in an Answer Card.

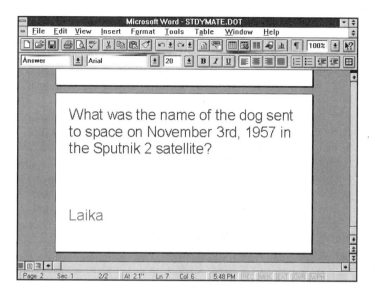

7. Press Enter to move to the next card.

The current style switches back to the Question style so you can immediately enter the next question. Repeat the steps above and enter as many questions as you like. Remember that this is for testing purposes and is going to be erased eventually, so don't work too hard at it.

Here are the questions I entered, all produced from browsing facts listed in the Space Exploration topic on Microsoft's Encarta CD:

Question: What was the name of the dog sent to space on November 3, 1957, in the Sputnik 2 satellite?

Answer: Laika

Question: What was the name of the first U.S. satellite successfully launched on January 31, 1958?

Answer: Explorer 1

Question: What was the name of the USSR spacecraft, launched on January 31, 1966, that was the first to land on the moon without being destroyed?

Answer: Luna 9

Question: Which USSR spacecraft, launched September 12, 1970, brought back a 4 oz. sample of lunar soil?

Answer: Luna 16

Question: What was the name of the first lunar roving vehicle?

Answer: Lunokhod 1

Question: On which planet did the U.S. spacecraft, Viking 1, land?

Answer: Mars

Creating the Study Mate Toolbar

The next thing you need to do is to create Study Mate's toolbar. The toolbar will have the following buttons:

- Save Cards   Update doc page count and save cards
- Random Card   Randomly jump to a question card
- Answer Card   Show the answer for the current question
- First Card   Jump to the first question card
- Previous Card   Move to the previous question card
- Next Card   Move to the next question card
- Last Card   Move to the last question card

1. Select the **View**|**T**oolbars command.

2. In the Toolbars dialog box, turn off any displayed toolbars by clearing each check box in the Toolbars list.

3. Close the Toolbars dialog box.

4. Select **T**ools|**O**ptions.

5. On the View tab, look for the Window group. Clear each check box in the list so that the status bar and scroll bars are not displayed, as shown in Figure 2.41.

FIGURE 2.41.

Clearing the Word status bars and scroll bars.

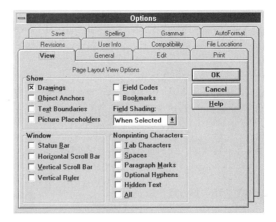

6. Click the Restore button on the top-right corner of the Word window so that the application is not maximized.

7. Resize the Word window so it displays a single flash card, as shown in Figure 2.42.

FIGURE 2.42.

Resizing Word so it shows one flash card at a time.

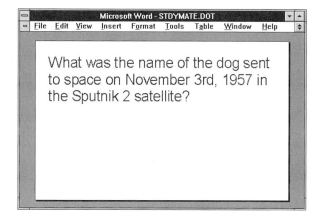

Next, enter the `SaveCards` macro. Figure 2.43 shows an example.

1. Select **Tools|M**acro.

2. In the Macro dialog box, enter `SaveCards` as the macro name and click the Create button.

3. Enter the `SaveCards` macro as shown in Listing 2.2.

Listing 2.2. The `SaveCards` macro.

```
Sub MAIN

' Recalculate document statistics
  ToolsWordCount

' Save the document
  FileSave

End Sub
```

The `ToolsWordCount` statement tells Word to recalculate the document statistics. That's the same thing as selecting the **Tools|W**ord Count command.

You need to call `ToolsWordCount` because a function that you will create later to return the total page count relies on the document statistics information stored within the document. After adding flash cards to the document, the user is expected to press the Save Cards button to see them immediately when displaying the cards.

Incidentally, it's no magic that I know how to use this or any other Word Basic statement used in the Study Mate program. Whenever I needed a desired result, I recorded it with the macro recorder as detailed in the earlier examples.

I also did lots of toying around with Word to find what needed to be recorded in the first place. This is the nature of creating programs in Word.

FIGURE 2.43.

*Entering the
SaveCards macro.*

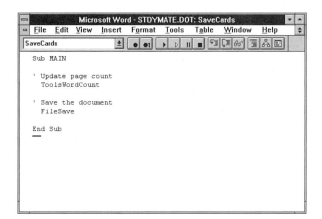

With the following steps, create the Study Mate toolbar.

1. From the **W**indows menu, switch back to the document window.
2. Select the **V**iew|**T**oolbars command.
3. In the Toolbars window, press the **N**ew button, as shown in Figure 2.44.

FIGURE 2.44.

*Adding a new toolbar
for Study Mate.*

4. In the New Toolbar window, enter `Study Mate` as the name of the toolbar, as shown in Figure 2.45.

FIGURE 2.45.

Naming Study Mate's toolbar.

Note that under the label **M**ake Toolbar Available To, the text box contains `Documents Based On Stdymate.dot`. This means that as you create new documents with flash cards based upon the Study Mate template, the toolbar will automatically be available to each one as you open it.

5. Press OK to close the New Toolbar window.

Add a button to the Study Mate toolbar to run the `SaveCards` macro.

1. In the Customize dialog box, select the word Macros in the **C**ategories list. Click the `SaveCards` macro from the Macro**s** list and drag-and-drop it in the Study Mate toolbar window, as shown in Figure 2.46.

FIGURE 2.46.

Creating the Save Cards button.

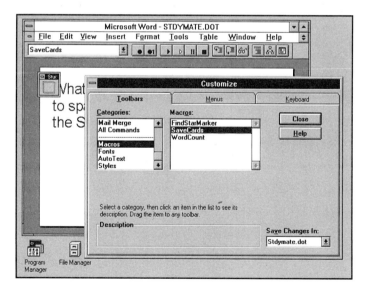

2. In the Custom Button dialog box, select a picture for the Save Cards button and modify it, if you like, by pressing the **E**dit button. The Button Editor dialog box will appear, as shown in Figure 2.47.

FIGURE 2.47.

Drawing the Save Cards button.

3. Close the Button Editor dialog box (if you used it) and close the Customize dialog box.

4. Test the Save Cards button to make sure it works. It should save the current document.

You can drag the Study Mate toolbar to any location on the screen. When the mouse cursor is over the Save Cards button, a yellow tool tip is displayed, showing the name of the macro as shown in Figure 2.48. A nice touch is that a space is added where appropriate in the macro name.

FIGURE 2.48.

Testing the Save Cards button.

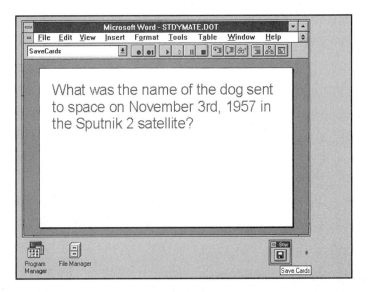

If you get an error, edit the macro and make sure it matches Listing 2.2.

Auto Execution Macros

The next macro I will discuss is automatically executed on opening a Word document that uses the Study Mate template. Word has five *auto macros* that run at different events:

AutoExec   When Word is started
AutoExit   When Word is exited
AutoNew   When a new document is created
AutoOpen   When an existing document is opened
AutoClose   When a document is closed

To create a macro that executes on any of these events, give your macro the appropriate name.

1. Select **T**ools|**M**acro.
2. Enter AutoOpen as the macro name, and press the C**r**eate button.
3. Enter the AutoOpen macro so that it matches Listing 2.3.

Listing 2.3. AutoOpen **macro.**

```
Sub MAIN

' AutoOpen

' Display a random card to start with
  RandomCard

End Sub
```

The AutoOpen macro calls the RandomCard macro that you will create later. When the flash card document is opened, it will begin with a randomly chosen question.

Before you can get much farther, you will need to create a few routines that you can use in several places. That's the topic of the next section.

Creating a Word Basic Procedure Library

As you've already seen, each Word macro starts with a MAIN subroutine. When you call a Word macro, you actually invoke its MAIN subroutine, not a subroutine by the name of the macro.

The MAIN subroutine can have supporting subroutines and functions. You can also call these subroutines and functions from another macro. To do this, when you make the call, you include the name of the macro that the subroutine or function came from.

A subroutine from another macro is called like this:

```
MacroName.Subroutine ArgumentList
```

A function from another macro is called as follows:

```
MacroLibrary.Function(ArgumentList)
```

When you call a function in a macro library, you don't need to include the parentheses if no arguments are being passed.

The Library Macro

Now create your own macro library. We'll appropriately give it the name Library.

1. Create a new macro with the name Library.
2. Enter the subroutines and functions in Listing 2.4 into the Library macro.

Listing 2.4. Library **macro.**

```
Sub MAIN

' By design, this macro does nothing on its own. It is a library
' of routines used by the other macros.

End Sub

Function GetPage

' Read the current page as stored in STDYMATE.INI

  GetPage = Val(GetPrivateProfileString$("Run", "Page", "STDYMATE.INI"))

End Function

Sub SetPage(Page)

' Write the current page to STDYMATE.INI

  Dim z
  z = SetPrivateProfileString("Run", "Page", Str$(Page), "STDYMATE.INI")

End Sub

Function CountPages

' This is a dialog box record variable. It stores all of the
' information found in the Word Count dialog box. It is only
' accurate for the last time that the ToolsWordCount statement
```

```
' was called.
  Dim dlg As ToolsWordCount

' Get Word Count values, which includes the Page count
  GetCurValues dlg

' Return the number of pages
  CountPages = Val(dlg.Pages)

End Function

Sub GotoPage(Page)

' Jump to the desired page and save the current page setting

' Hide updates because this is going to be ugly
  ScreenUpdating 0

' Jump to the top
  While PrevPage()
  Wend

' Jump down to the desired page
  For Count = 1 To Page - 1
    NextPage
  Next Count

' Save the current page
  SetPage Page

  ScreenUpdating 1

End Sub
```

The *Library* Macro Under a Microscope

Each procedure in the library has a specific job, each except for MAIN. In this macro MAIN is a real slacker. The procedures and their jobs are as follows:

- ■ MAIN   Does nothing
- ■ GetPage   Returns the current page
- ■ SetPage   Sets the current page
- ■ CountPages   Returns the total number of pages
- ■ GotoPage   Jumps to a specified page

MAIN

The MAIN subroutine is in the Library macro because every Word macro must have a MAIN subroutine. If you execute the macro from the Macro dialog box, it will do nothing because MAIN is empty.

GetPage and *SetPage*

The `GetPage` and `SetPage` procedures use a Windows-style .INI file as a storage place to simulate global variables. Keep reading. I'll eventually get to the details!

CountPages

The `CountPages` function returns the value Word stores in a document to indicate how many pages the document has.

The `CountPages` function uses a *dialog box record.* This is a special type of variable that holds all the values stored in a Word dialog box. If you execute the **Tools**|**W**ord Count command, you will see all the values available to the `ToolWordCount` dialog box record.

The `GetCurValues` statement is executed to populate the dialog box record variable. You can then reference the different values like this:

- ■ `dlg.Pages`   Number of pages
- ■ `dlg.Words`   Number of words
- ■ `dlg.Characters`   Number of characters
- ■ `dlg.Paragraphs`   Number of paragraphs
- ■ `dlg.Lines`   Number of lines

I used this method to determine how many pages are in a document because it was preferable to trying something like checking how many times the `NextPage` statement would execute before the end of the document was reached. However, using this method requires us to have the Save Cards button on the Study Mate toolbar to ensure that the document statistics are kept up-to-date.

You can get additional information from other dialog box records. Look up `DocumentStatistics` and `FileSummaryInfo` in Word Basic's online help if you are curious. Remember—use Word's features before you use your code.

GotoPage

The `GotoPage` subroutine does exactly what its name implies. The subroutine uses the `ScreenUpdating` statement to turn off screen repainting while it is busy flipping from one page to the next. At the end of the subroutine, `ScreenUpdating` is turned back on, giving the effect that you jumped directly from one page to the next.

I made several attempts at this one before I got it right. I tried using the `PageUp` and `PageDown` statements, but they scroll the page only enough to make the cursor visible.

One minor disappointment for me is that the `ScreenUpdating` statement has no effect on the mouse cursor. While `GotoPage` is running, there is an excessive amount of flickering as the mouse jumps back and forth between pointer and hour-glass mode a few hundred thousand times.

The following section describes why `GetPage` and `SetPage` use an INI file to store a global value.

A Word Basic Oddity

There are no global variables in Word Basic!

You can create a *shared* variable that is accessible to the subroutines and functions within a single macro. Unfortunately, this has limited usefulness because the shared variables are empty each time the `MAIN` subroutine begins executing. You cannot store values in shared variables and expect them to be around on the next program run.

With all of these barriers in place, how do Word macros communicate with each other? Or even with themselves between runs? For the most part, they don't.

To get around this fact, one trick is to copy data to the clipboard and have the next macro read from the clipboard. This is impractical in many cases, because the clipboard may be used for other things between calls.

Another way to pass data back and forth is to write a value into the document, then later find it and read it back out. This modifies the document, however, so the user will be prompted to save changes when they close the document, even if no changes were made.

Another solution is to use the `GetPrivateProfileString` and `SetPrivateProfileString` functions. These write values to an application's INI file. This solution is good because it is easy and doesn't have the drawbacks of the other work-arounds.

Finally, a fourth solution would be to use Basic's file I/O statements. You could create a file in which to store temporary values, then read them back when you need them. Given that `GetPrivateProfileString` and `SetPrivateProfileString` do this already with hardly any work on your part, it's best to use them instead.

GetPrivateProfileString and *SetPrivateProfileString*

The `SetPage` and `GetPage` procedures in the `Library` macro use `SetPrivateProfileString` and `GetPrivateProfileString` as a way to store and retrieve the current page number.

These two statements are neat. I never would have thought this, but creating your own personal .INI file really is easy.

To write a value to an INI file, call `SetPrivateProfileString` with the following arguments:

```
SetPrivateProfileString INISection$, KeyName$, Value$, INIFilename$
```

If the INI file doesn't exist, it will be created in the user's Windows directory. You can specify another directory if you wish.

The INI file STDYMATE.INI, created by Study Mate, has a single section, `Run`, with a single keyname, `Page`. The file looks like this:

```
[Run]
Page= 5
```

The `GetPrivateProfileString` function is used to read a INI file setting. It is called with the following arguments:

```
GetPrivateProfileString(INISection$, KeyName$, INIFilename$)
```

`GetPrivateProfileString` returns a string so the `GetPage` function uses the `Val` function to convert it into a number.

The *RandomCard* Macro

Now that you have a set of library routines, let's put them to use.

The `RandomCard` macro is the code that gets executed upon pressing the Question mark button. The job of the `RandomCard` macro is to choose randomly a question other than the current one, and then display it.

1. Create a new macro, `RandomCard`, and enter the code in Listing 2.5.
2. Select **View|Toolbars**.
3. In the Toolbars dialog box, select the Study Mate toolbar and press the **Cus**tomize button.
4. From the **Categories** list, select Macros.
5. Click the `RandomCard` macro and drag it to the Study Mate toolbar, as shown in Figure 2.49.
6. Select from the available pictures in the Customize Button dialog box, or edit your own.

Listing 2.5. `RandomCard` **macro.**

```
Sub MAIN

' RandomCard
' Randomly jump to a Question page

  Dim Pages
  Dim Page
  Dim RandomPage

' Get the number of pages
  Pages = Library.CountPages
```

```
' Bail out if we have less than 3 pages to avoid an endless loop
  If Pages < 3 Then Goto RandomCardDone

' Get the current page
  Page = Library.GetPage

' Jump back up to here in case we choose the current page again
TryAgain:

' Randomly select a page to jump to

' Pick a number between 1 and the number of questions
  RandomPage = Int(Rnd() * (Pages / 2)) + 1

' Change the question number to a page number
  RandomPage = RandomPage * 2 - 1

' Try again if we selected the current page
  If RandomPage = Page Then Goto TryAgain

' Jump to the selected page
  Library.GotoPage RandomPage

RandomCardDone:
End Sub
```

FIGURE 2.49.

Adding the Random Card button.

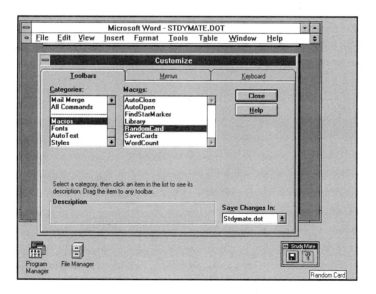

The RandomCard macro uses library routines to get the current page and total number of pages.

If the total number of pages is less than three, there could be only one actual question card in the document. In such a case, the subroutine exits early by jumping to a

RandomCardDone label; otherwise, it would get into an endless loop in the code that tries to find another card to jump to.

The following line uses the Rnd function to calculate a number from 1 to the total number of questions.

```
' Pick a number between 1 and the number of questions
  RandomPage = Int(Rnd() * (Pages / 2)) + 1
```

This number is then converted to a page number:

```
' Change the question number to a page number
  RandomPage = RandomPage * 2 - 1
```

The RandomPage subroutine uses a GoTo to make another attempt at finding the page number when the generated one ends up being the same as is currently displayed.

After a page is selected, the library subroutine GotoPage is called to jump to the appropriate question page.

AnswerCard

The AnswerCard macro displays the answer card for the currently selected question card.

1. Create an AnswerCard macro using the code in Listing 2.6.
2. Add another button to the Study Mate toolbar to run this macro.

I chose the cartoon balloon picture for the answer button. Use any picture you like from the pictures available, or draw your own.

Listing 2.6. AnswerCard **macro.**

```
Sub MAIN

' AnswerCard
' Display the answer to a question by jumping to the next page

  Dim Page

' Get the current page
  Page = Library.GetPage

' Are we on a question?
  If Page Mod 2 = 1 Then

    ' Move to the answer page
    NextPage

    ' Save the current page
    Library.SetPage Page + 1
```

```
      End If

End Sub
```

The `AnswerCard` macro calls the `GetPage` subroutine to determine which page is currently displayed.

The `Mod` operator is used to see whether a question or answer page is currently displayed. The `Mod` operator returns the remainder of a division operation. Because question pages are always on an odd page number, dividing the question page number by 2 will always produce a remainder of 1.

If it is determined that the current page is a question page, the next card is displayed by calling the `NextPage` statement.

The last statement of the `AnswerCard` macro calls the `SetPage` subroutine to save the current page.

FirstCard

The `FirstCard` macro jumps to the top of the set of flash cards.

1. Enter the `FirstCard` macro, as shown in Listing 2.7.
2. Add a button to the Study Mate toolbar to execute the `FirstCard` macro.

For the graphics on this and the remaining three buttons, I drew my own arrows to resemble the record navigation buttons on Access forms. Figure 2.50 shows the picture being drawn for the First Card button.

FIGURE 2.50.

Drawing a First Card button for the Study Mate toolbar.

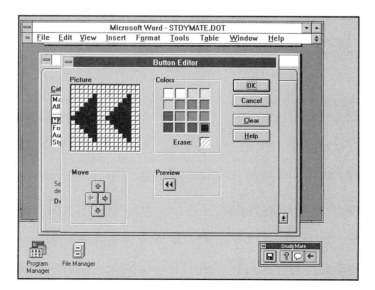

Listing 2.7. `FirstCard` **macro.**

```
Sub MAIN

' FirstCard
' Move to the first card

  Library.GotoPage 1

End Sub
```

PreviousCard

The `PreviousCard` macro moves back to the previous question card. If the current page is on an answer card, you must press the Previous Card button twice to go back to the previous question.

1. Create the `PreviousCard` macro, as shown in Listing 2.8.

2. Add a button to execute the `PreviousCard` macro.

Listing 2.8. `PreviousCard` **macro.**

```
Sub MAIN

' PreviousCard
' Move to the previous question

  Dim Page
  Dim PagesMoved

' Get the current page
  Page = Library.GetPage

' Don't move if on the first page already
  If Page > 1 Then

    ScreenUpdating 0

    PagesMoved = 1

  ' Are we on a question?
    If Page Mod 2 = 1 Then
      PrevPage
      PagesMoved = 2
    End If

    PrevPage

    ScreenUpdating 1
```

```
' Save which page was moved to
  Library.SetPage Page - PagesMoved

End If

End Sub
```

Before moving to the previous page, the `PreviousPage` macro checks to make sure the current page isn't already page 1.

NextCard

The `NextCard` macro moves to the next question card.

1. Add the `NextCard` macro, as shown in Listing 2.9.
2. Add a button to execute the `NextCard` macro.

Listing 2.9. `NextCard` **macro.**

```
Sub MAIN

' NextCard
' Jump to the next card

  Dim Pages
  Dim Page
  Dim PagesMoved

' Get the number of pages
  Pages = Library.CountPages

' Get the current page
  Page = Library.GetPage

' If there are more questions
  If Page < Pages - 1 Then

    ScreenUpdating 0

    PagesMoved = 1

' Are we on a question?
    If Page Mod 2 = 1 Then
      NextPage
      PagesMoved = 2
    End If

    NextPage

    ScreenUpdating 1
```

continues

Listing 2.9. continued

```
' Save which page was moved to
  Library.SetPage Page + PagesMoved

End If

End Sub
```

The NextCard macro checks to make sure there is actually a next card to jump to. It then moves ahead one or two pages to get to the next question.

LastCard

The final macro, LastCard, jumps directly to the last page.

1. Create the LastCard macro, as shown in Listing 2.10.
2. Add the final button to the Study Mate toolbar and set it to execute the LastCard macro.

Listing 2.10. LastCard macro.

```
Sub MAIN

' LastCard
' Jump to the last question card

  Dim Pages

' Get the page number for the last question
  Pages = Library.CountPages

' Jump to one before the last page
  Library.GotoPage Pages - 1

End Sub
```

The LastCard macro calls the CountPages function from the Library macro, then jumps to the page before that, which should be the last question page.

Figure 2.51 shows the complete Study Mate toolbar after all of the buttons have been added.

FIGURE 2.51.

The complete Study Mate toolbar.

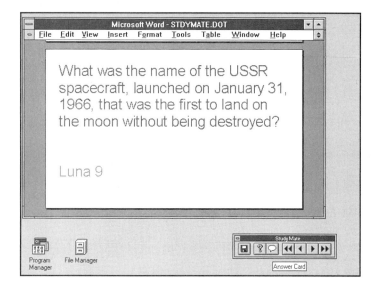

Testing Study Mate

If you haven't done so already, be sure to save your work by using **File|Save**. Next, test all the buttons to make sure they work properly. If they don't, you've got some debugging to do. Verify your code against the listings in the book if you run into any problems.

After your work is running correctly, you need to clear the template of any questions and save it empty. In the next session, you will create a set of flash cards in another document.

1. Switch to the document window if you are not there already.

2. Press the Home key to jump to the top.

3. Holding the Ctrl and Shift keys down, press the End key to jump to the end of the document to select all text.

4. Press the Delete key.

   Your document should now be cleared of all questions and answers that you entered for testing purposes.

   Before you save it a final time, you can enter a template description in Word's Summary Info dialog box. This description helps explain to the uninitiated what your template is all about.

5. Select the **File**|Summary **I**nfo command.

6. In the Title field, enter the following description for the template (as shown in Figure 2.52):

```
Use Study Mate to create a set of flash cards for reviewing study
questions or for playing a trivia game.
```

FIGURE 2.52.

Giving the template a description.

7. Close the Summary Info dialog box.

8. Select **File**|**C**lose to save your changes and close the template. Save the template as STDYMATE.DOT.

NOTE

It's always a good idea to make backup copies of your work. Use File Manager to copy the STDYMATE.DOT template, and any other templates that you create in Word's TEMPLATE directory, to some other directory, or better yet, to a floppy disk.

You might want to back up your copy of the NORMAL.DOT template also, because that has macros and toolbars that you've added, such as the Find Star Marker and Word Count utilities.

Creating Study Mate Documents

Now create your first set of flash cards as a document based on the STDYMATE.DOT template.

1. Select **File**|**N**ew to create a new document.

2. In the New dialog box, select the Stdymate template from the list of templates (as shown in Figure 2.53) and press OK.

FIGURE 2.53.

Creating a flash card document with the Study Mate template.

3. Start entering question-and-answer cards as described earlier in this chapter.

To view the Study Mate toolbar, you must turn it on using the **View|Toolbars** command. You will probably want to resize the word window and get rid of the scrollbars, toolbars, and ruler, if they are on.

You could modify the AutoOpen macro so that it does this automatically when opening a document based on the Study Mate template.

Study Mate Challenge

To make Study Mate a more effective study tool, try modifying the program so that it repeats only the questions that you get wrong.

You could add two buttons to the Study Mate toolbar. One tells Study Mate you answered correctly, and the other indicates you were incorrect. When using Study Mate, you would press either button when reviewing the answer card to see whether your reply was right or wrong.

Another enhancement would be to turn Study Mate into a testing tool that doesn't let you see the answers, and keeps score of your results. You would have to create buttons on the toolbar so that the test taker could select from a set of possible answers—perhaps labeled A, B, C, and D.

To make these changes, you will have to store values in the STDYMATE.INI file and read them back in as needed.

Summary

 In this chapter, you put Word to work and accomplished the following:

- Used Word's macro recorder to create a useful Find Star Marker utility
- Assigned a macro to a shortcut key
- Created a toolbar from which to execute your Word customizations
- Modified a recorded macro and created the Word Count utility
- Tried out the Word Basic help file as a resource for Word Basic programmers
- Learned what Word templates are, and how to store macros in them
- Created a macro library and learned how to call the procedures in it from other macros
- Learned how to create and read .INI files
- Created the Study Mate application

In the next chapter, you will cover some of the new features in Basic that never existed in old BASIC. You will examine how Excel, Access, and Visual Basic use objects. Word Basic doesn't have this capability at the moment, but it will soon.

 TRY THIS! ANSWERS

2.1. To add or modify macro assignments to the toolbar, menu, or keyboard, select the **Tools|Customize** command. In the **Categories** list of the Customize dialog box, select Macros to list the available macros. Select the macro to assign, and then make the key or menu assignment.

Use the tabs to change from toolbar, menu, and key assignments in the Customize dialog box.

2.2. The . Find should be .Find (no space).

CHAPTER 3

How Basic Interacts with the Outside World

In the last chapter, you flexed your Basic muscles a bit and accomplished a few things that I'll bet the typical Word user doesn't know are possible. To do those things, you used just a few capabilities from Word's huge library of program statements and functions.

That's the old way of doing things. There is a new and better way for a programmable desktop application to share its capabilities with the Basic programming language. That way is by using *objects.*

Word is behind Excel, Access, and Visual Basic at this time in the sense that its programmable interface is still based on a procedural model rather than an object model. In the procedural model, your program is written as a series of actions in the form of statements, functions, and subroutines.

Think about it. Your world doesn't solely consist of actions. When you grab, you grab something. When you pick up, you pick up something. You could also think of yourself as an object doing these things.

The new way of programming with objects lets you focus on the things you work with in association with what you can do with them—no more digging through an alphabetical listing of 500 or more statements and functions, trying to find the one you need. In Basic, an *object* is a software component that provides three standard ways for a Basic program to interact with it: events, methods, and properties. When you need to work with an object, you look it up first, and then you see from its events, methods, and properties what you can do to affect it (or, in the case of events, what you can do to react to it).

If the programmable interface to Word was object based, then in Word you might find objects that represent a font, a selection, a document, and so on. (For OLE automation purposes, Word has a single object, Word Basic, which is used to gain access to Word's procedural model of programmability.)

In this chapter, you're going to ditch Word temporarily so you can explore how objects are used in the newer Basics that are a part of Access, Excel, and Visual Basic. (It's likely that a future version of Word will become object-based and use Visual Basic for Applications (VBA) for its programmable engine, like Excel.)

In the process of exploring objects, you will create a username and password login facility in Microsoft Access that you can add to your own database projects. Later, in Chapter 10, "Visual Basic and Access: Secret Diary," you will create a variation of the login form in Visual Basic.

The key to Access programming is to get familiar with the objects in its environment, such as controls on forms and tables in a database. What all of the objects are and how they are used isn't something you can know completely overnight, but it's easy enough for you to catch on quickly.

At the end of the chapter, you'll briefly visit the touchy subject of naming conventions. I'll describe the variable-naming methodology used in the code in this book and explain why that methodology is used.

Declaring an Object in Code

Objects are the kind of things that reside in the computer environment. They include databases, tables, queries, forms, reports, text boxes, list boxes, combo boxes, check boxes, radio buttons, command buttons, and so on.

Because objects exist in the computing environment, you need some way to refer to them in your programs. So just as a variable can be declared as a number or string data type, a variable can also be declared as an object data type.

For example, the following line declares a variable of the type `Table`.

```
Dim tblLogin As Table
```

The variable, `tblLogin`, is meaningless until you associate it with an actual table in the database. You associate it with an actual table using the `OpenTable` method of the database object like this:

```
Set tblLogin = db.OpenTable("Login")
```

After the variable is assigned to the actual physical object, performing operations on the variable affects the object in the real world. For example, the following deletes a record in the table:

```
tbl.Delete
```

Events, Methods, and Properties

There are many objects in the Excel, Access, and Visual Basic programming environments. Being different entities, each object has its own set of events, methods, and properties.

Here are some definitions.

An *event* is something that happens while the program is running and for which the programming environment allows you to add your code in response. When the event occurs, your added code is executed. For example, events occur when a form is opened or when a button is clicked.

A *method* is an object's built-in procedure. When you invoke an object's method, the object does something. For example, you could use the `Find` method in a dynaset object to find a record within a table.

Properties are the data portion of an object. A property is a value that you can get, or that you can set. It represents some aspect of the current nature of the object, such as its color or size.

Creating a Password Form in Access

Before you can look at objects in detail, you need to get a project started that will demonstrate the concepts. Let's build a login form and complete an Access version of the `PasswordValidate` function that you spec'd out in Chapter 1, "Today's Basic."

First, create the database.

1. Double-click the Access icon in Program Manager.
2. Select **File|New** to create a new database.
3. In the New Database dialog box, select a directory to save your database to and enter `DIARY.MDB` as the name of the new database, as shown in Figure 3.1. Press OK.

FIGURE 3.1.

Creating the Diary database.

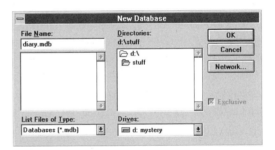

Create a Login table to store usernames and passwords.

1. In the database container window, press the **New** button to create a new table.
2. In the New Table dialog box, press the **New** Table button on the right to bypass the Table Wizard.
3. Enter the first field for the table using the following values:

Field Name:	Username
Data Type:	Text
Description:	User login name
Field Size:	10

   The Field Name, Data Type and Description are entered across the first row of the table in design view, as shown in Figure 3.2. To move the cursor to the Field Properties list at the bottom of the table design window, press F6 or click the property you want to change with the mouse.

FIGURE 3.2.

Creating a Username field.

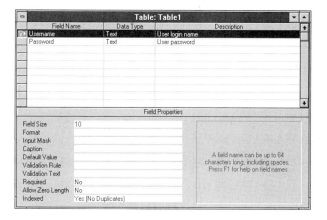

4. Enter the second field for the table:

Field Name:	Password
Data Type:	Text
Description:	User password
Field Size:	20

5. Click the square to the left of the first field name, Username, to select the row.

6. Press the toolbar button that has the key picture on it.

   A primary key will be established on the Username field, which shows a key symbol to the left of the field name, as shown in Figure 3.3. This ensures that only one record is in the table for each user name.

FIGURE 3.3

Creating a primary key on the Username field.

7. Select **File|Close** and answer **Y**es to the dialog box that asks if you want to save changes.

8. In the Save As dialog box, enter Login as the name of the table. Press OK.

In the database container, you will see the Login form has been added to the database, as shown in Figure 3.4.

FIGURE 3.4.

The Login table shows up in the Database Container.

Create a form to verify usernames and passwords against those stored in the Login table.

1. Click the Form tab on the database container.
2. Press the **N**ew button on the database container to create a new form.
3. In the New Form dialog box, press the **B**lank Form button to bypass the Form Wizard, as shown in Figure 3.5.

FIGURE 3.5.

Bypassing the Form Wizard.

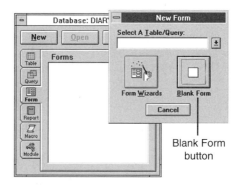

Access displays a new blank form in a form design window.

4. Drag the sides of the form so it is 2 1/2-inches wide and 1 1/2-inches tall.
5. Select the **V**iew|**P**roperties command.

    By default, Access sets the properties on a form so that it is best suited for a record editing form, allowing you to scroll through records in a table or query.

6. Select Other Properties in the combo box at the top of the Properties window. Then change the following properties (as shown in Figure 3.6):

    Pop Up: Yes
    Modal: Yes

FIGURE 3.6.

Setting a form's Other properties.

7. Select Layout Properties in the Properties window combo box and change the following properties (see Figure 3.7):

Caption:	Login
Default View:	Single Form
Scroll Bars:	Neither
Record Selectors:	No
Navigation Buttons:	No
Auto Center:	Yes
Border Style:	Dialog
Min Button:	No
Max Button:	No

FIGURE 3.7.

Setting a form's Layout properties.

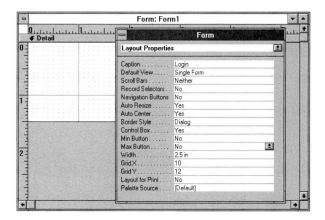

8. Close the Properties window by selecting **View|P**roperties or by pressing the Properties button on the toolbar.

Add the username and password text boxes. You can minimize the database container window to make the screen less cluttered while you work.

1. Open the Toolbox window by selecting **View|Toolbox** or by pressing the Toolbox button on the toolbar.
2. Click the Text box button on the Toolbox window.
3. Click the area of the form where you want the username text box to be placed, and drag a rectangle to draw the text box.

   Access creates a text box *and* a label.
4. Click the label to select it. Then click the label a second time to enable the text cursor within it. Enter `Username:` for the label text.
5. Click the palette button on the toolbar.
6. While you have the Palette window open, select the form and change its colors to whatever colors you desire.
7. Click the label and the text box, changing their colors and other display attributes in the Palette window as shown in Figure 3.8.

FIGURE 3.8.

Creating the Username text box.

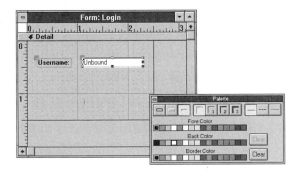

8. Add a Password text box.

   As a shortcut, you can select the Username text box and label, then press Ctrl-C and Ctrl-V to copy and paste the text box. Then you only have to change the label text for the Password label.
9. Click the label button on the toolbox and add a label for user instructions. It should say the following:

   `Enter your username and password to login to the diary.`

   Actually, if you wanted to make this more generic, you wouldn't mention in the label the name of the application being built. You could enter something like the following:

   `Enter your username and password.`

Next add OK and Cancel buttons and set the names of the controls on the form.

For the following steps, you won't be using the Access control wizards and will be creating the command button controls "manually" instead. Look for the button on the Toolbox window that has a picture of a magic wand. If the button is depressed, click it so that the button is displayed in the up position. This turns off the control wizards.

1. Click the command button on the toolbox and draw a button on the form. You can select its text like a label and change it to display OK.

2. Copy the OK button and paste another one on the form. Change the caption of the new button to say Cancel. The form should now look as shown in Figure 3.9.

FIGURE 3.9.

The Login form.

3. Open the Properties window and select Other Properties.

4. One by one, click each control on the form and enter the following names and status bar text for each:

Name	Status Bar Text
lblHint	
txtUsername	Enter your login name
txtPassword	Enter your password
cmdOK	Login
cmdCancel	Cancel login

Figure 3.10 shows the Name and Status Bar Text properties changed for the txtUsername text box.

5. Set the Default property to Yes on the cmdOK button.

This means that if you press the Enter key anytime while using the dialog box, the cmdOK button acts as if it's been clicked.

6. Set the Cancel property to Yes on the cmdCancel button.

The Cancel property is like the Default property, except that the Esc key is the key that triggers the event. Esc is usually pressed to cancel any input in a dialog box.

FIGURE 3.10.

Giving meaningful names to the controls on the Login form.

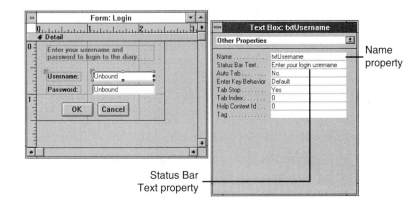

To complete the form, change the text in the password text box to white, the same color as the background of the text box. You do this so that if someone is looking over your shoulder while you enter your password, that person won't be able to read the password on the screen. He or she sees the cursor moving along but won't see the characters that are being entered.

1. Select the txtPassword control and open the Palette window. Change the Fore Color property to white, making the word Unbound disappear (as shown in Figure 3.11).

FIGURE 3.11.

Hiding the text in the txtPassword control by changing the Fore Color to white.

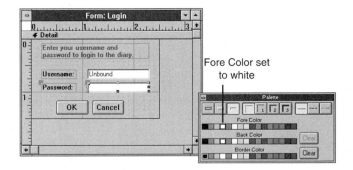

2. Select **File|Close** to save the form. Answer **Y**es to the dialog box that asks whether you want to save your changes.

3. In the Save As dialog box, enter Login as the form name and press OK.

Before you start writing the code behind the Login form, you can test it to see if it appears as it should.

1. Click the **O**pen button on the database container. The form will be displayed as shown in Figure 3.12.

FIGURE 3.12.
Testing the Login form.

2. Double-click the system bar at the top-left corner of the Login window to close it.

    Well, it looks okay. As you now know, creating such a simple little form can involve many steps.

NOTE

Most Access developers start with a copy of an existing form and make modifications to it rather than start from scratch each time. Then, for simple projects, they don't have to go through nearly as many steps as they would otherwise.

Adding a User

You need a username and password entered into the Login table.

1. Click the Table tab on the database container.
2. With the Login table selected, click the **O**pen button.
3. Enter a username in the first column and a password in the second column as shown in Figure 3.13.

    You could enter additional records for more usernames and passwords, if you like. Eventually, you would want to create a form for creating new users in the Login table, but for now this will suffice.

4. Double-click the system bar or select the **F**ile|**C**lose command to close the table.

FIGURE 3.13.

*Entering a username
and password.*

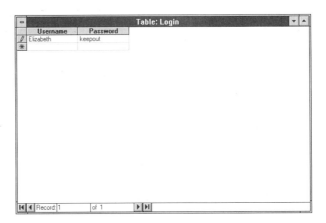

Creating a Library Module

The next step in making the Login facility work is to create a function that can validate
a username and password.

When you recognize a procedure as being one that you would find use for in other areas
of the program or in other projects, you should try to write the procedure as a library
procedure. This means that you should try to keep the procedure somewhat generic,
simple, and self-contained so that it can be used easily in other places.

The PasswordValidate function is one such procedure; it should be written as a library
procedure.

In the next few sections, follow along and create the PasswordValidate function in the
manner in which it was actually written the first time.

Create a new module by selecting the Module tab in the database container and pressing the **N**ew button.

Your module initially has in it the following line:

```
Option Compare Database    'Use database order for string comparisons
```

After creating a few hundred or so modules, I've finally gotten tired of being reminded
that the Compare Database option uses the database order for string comparisons. So I
delete the generated comment.

Enter Listing 3.1 in the declaration section of the module.

Listing 3.1. The declaration section of the Library module.

```
' Library module

  Option Compare Database
  Option Explicit

  Global Const PROGRAM = "Personal Diary"
```

The `Option Explicit` line is important. It tells Access to complain (produce an error message) if you try to use a variable in your program that you haven't declared in a `Dim` statement. You need this to catch typing mistakes that would alter the effect of your program.

If you use `Option Explicit`, it's a good idea to turn Access's syntax checking option off. You can do this by selecting the **View|O**ptions command. From the **C**ategory list, select Module Design and change the Syntax Checking option to No (see Figure 3.14).

Syntax checking set to Yes is a major nuisance as you enter the lines in your program. It reports an error any time your cursor leaves a line in the program that isn't fully syntactically correct.

Quite frequently, I need to move the cursor to another line before finishing the current line, usually to copy some text to paste into the current line that isn't completed yet. Doing so will produce the error if syntax checking is on.

So I turn the option off. You can always verify that your full program is syntactically correct by selecting the **R**un|Compile Lo**a**ded Modules command.

I've also become comfortable with my Tab Stop Width set to 2. I invented a format for entering comments in the code where the comment text is always lined up with the line of code below it. You will see this applied in all the code in this book.

FIGURE 3.14.

Setting Module environment options.

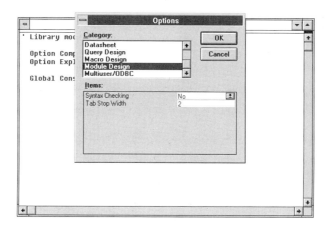

Next, enter the declaration for the `PasswordValidate` function below the text in the module's declaration section as follows (and also as shown in Figure 3.15):

```
Function PasswordValidate (strUsername As String, strPassword As String)
➡As Integer
```

FIGURE 3.15.

Entering the
PasswordValidate
declaration.

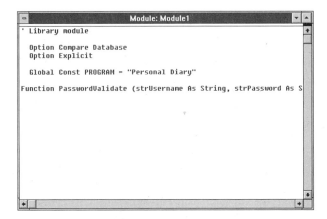

Upon moving the cursor off the line, Access moves the declaration to a section of the module specifically for this function and adds the `End Function` statement (as shown in Figure 3.16).

You can press Ctrl-Down repeatedly to cycle through all the different procedures, and the declaration section in a module. You can also select which one to view from the right combo box on the module design toolbar.

FIGURE 3.16.

A new procedure in an
Access module.

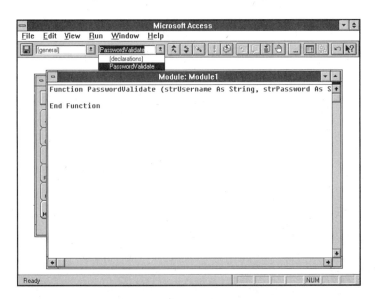

The `PasswordValidate` function is declared to receive two arguments, a username, and a password. It returns an integer that will indicate whether the password was found to be valid.

Enter the error handling code as described at the end of Chapter 1, "Today's Basic." Your procedure should now look like Listing 3.2.

Listing 3.2. Adding error handling to the `PasswordValidate` function.

```
Function PasswordValidate (strUsername As String, strPassword As String)
➥As Integer

  On Error GoTo PasswordValidateError

PasswordValidateDone:
  On Error Resume Next
  Exit Function

PasswordValidateError:
  MsgBox Error$, 48, PROGRAM
  Resume PasswordValidateDone

End Function
```

On coming into your function, you can assume that the return value is going to be False, indicating that either the username or the password is invalid. Later, as you validate that they are true, you can set the return value to True.

It's a good idea to assume a return value of False. This way, if anything goes wrong, you don't inadvertently approve a username and password that might not be valid.

Add the following comment and program line before the `On Error Goto` line:

```
' Assume failure
  PasswordValidate = False
```

Next, since you're going to have to look at the Login table, you need to declare a database variable and a table variable. Add the variable declarations to the top of your function as in Listing 3.3.

Listing 3.3. Declaring a few variables in the `PasswordValidate` function.

```
Function PasswordValidate (strUsername As String, strPassword As String)
➥As Integer

  Dim db As Database

  Dim tbl As Table
```

continues

Listing 3.3. continued

```
' Assume failure
  PasswordValidate = False

  On Error GoTo PasswordValidateError

PasswordValidateDone:
  On Error Resume Next
  Exit Function

PasswordValidateError:
  MsgBox Error$, 48, PROGRAM
  Resume PasswordValidateDone

End Function
```

The db variable will be set to the current database. The tbl variable will be assigned to an open table within the database.

Add the following lines after the line that starts with On Error Goto:

```
' Validate the username and password against the Login table
  Set db = CurrentDB()
  Set tbl = db.OpenTable("Login")
```

The first line is just a comment indicating what the next section of code is intended to do.

The Set statement is used whenever you assign an object variable to the associated object in the computer environment. Making an assignment to an object variable without the Set statement means that you are setting the value of the object being pointed to by the object variable; you are not setting the object variable itself.

That last one will be clearer as you see it in working code.

You use the CurrentDB() function provided in Access to return the database object for the currently open database and set it to the db variable. Note here that you aren't actually opening the database, as it has already been opened by the user when he or she chose **F**ile|**O**pen from the menu.

Using a Method

In the third line, you are actually using a *method* of the database object. The syntax for using a method works like this:

```
Object.Method(ArgumentList)
```

or

```
Object.Method ArgumentList
```

It's basically the same as making a function call or subroutine call, except that the name of the call is preceded by the object name and a period. Think of methods as an object's personal function and subroutine library.

When the database object's `OpenTable` method is called, a value is returned of the `Table` variable type. In your program, you set this returned value to the `tbl` variable.

```
Set tbl = db.OpenTable("Login")
```

The *blnOpened* Flag

When you are through playing, you are supposed to put the toys back in the toy box, right?

As I discussed at the end of Chapter 1, the error handling code facilitates making sure that you put away your things after you are done using them. In the above program line, you opened a table. When you open a table, you are expected at some time in your program to close it.

If you forget to close an open table, it's not the end of the world. What happens, though, is that Access can only have so many tables open at once. If you keep opening them without closing them, you eventually reach the limit where you can't open any more without first shutting down Access and starting it again.

Next, you will add some code that ensures the table is always closed before leaving the function. It's bulletproof, even when an error occurs.

Add a variable declaration for the `blnOpened` integer variable.

```
Dim blnOpened As Integer
```

The `blnOpened` variable is used as a True/False flag to indicate whether the table used in this function has been opened.

Enter a line at the end of the declarations to initialize the flag to False.

```
blnOpened = False
```

Here's a confession: the `blnOpened` variable would actually be set to False anyway when entering the function, because Basic automatically initializes its integer variables to zero. I usually initialize my variables anyway to indicate to the program reader that it matters at this point that the variable has a zero value. Otherwise, the program reader might be concerned that I've left an uninitialized variable in my program by error.

Below the line that opened the table, enter the following line to set the `blnOpened` variable to True.

```
blnOpened = True
```

To ensure the table gets closed, you add a statement after the `PasswordValidateDone` label, in a specially-designated cleanup section of the function.

Enter the following line after the `On Error Resume Next` line toward the end of the function:

```
If blnOpened Then tbl.Close
```

The function should now appear as in Listing 3.4.

Listing 3.4. `PasswordValidate` **makes sure it closes the open table.**

```
Function PasswordValidate (strUsername As String, strPassword As String)
➡As Integer

  Dim db As Database

  Dim tbl As Table
  Dim blnOpened As Integer

  blnOpened = False

' Assume failure
  PasswordValidate = False

  On Error GoTo PasswordValidateError

' Validate the username and password against the Login table
  Set db = CurrentDB()
  Set tbl = db.OpenTable("Login")
  blnOpened = True

PasswordValidateDone:
  On Error Resume Next
  If blnOpened Then tbl.Close
  Exit Function

PasswordValidateError:
  MsgBox Error$, 48, PROGRAM
  Resume PasswordValidateDone

End Function
```

There is a place in the above-described strategy where things can go wrong. It's bullet-proof, but not programmer proof. If you forget to set the `blnOpened` variable to True, the table does not get closed.

In an alternative approach, I've seen other programmers unconditionally close any possibly open object in their function's cleanup section. The `On Error Resume Next` line handles suppressing any error messages returned for attempting to close an object that was never opened.

The code would appear as in Listing 3.5.

Listing 3.5. Using `On Error Resume Next` **to allow closing all possibly open objects.**

```
Function PasswordValidate (strUsername As String, strPassword As String)
➥As Integer

  Dim db As Database

  Dim tbl As Table

' Assume failure
  PasswordValidate = False

  On Error GoTo PasswordValidateError

' Validate the username and password against the Login table
  Set db = CurrentDB()
  Set tbl = db.OpenTable("Login")

PasswordValidateDone:
  On Error Resume Next
  tbl.Close
  Exit Function

PasswordValidateError:
  MsgBox Error$, 48, PROGRAM
  Resume PasswordValidateDone

End Function
```

It feels cleaner to me to use the method described earlier, where you only close an object that has actually been opened. But this feeling is at the expense of adding an additional Boolean variable for each opened object, and adding some additional lines to the program. So you make your own decision on that one.

Setting a Property

Add this next line after the line where `blnOpened` gets set to True. It sets the Index property of the Table object.

```
  tbl.Index = "PrimaryKey"
```

The Index property indicates which of a table's indexes should be used when searching for a matching record. When you created the Login table, you made a `PrimaryKey` out of the Username field. The above line tells Access to search for records based on this key.

Setting an object's property is like setting a regular program variable. Sometimes, as in this case, you don't see an immediate result after setting a property. Properties for objects on the screen such as FontName, FontSize, Left, Top, Height, Width, ForeColor and BackColor will have an immediate affect after setting them.

Add the next line, which calls the Table object's Seek method to locate a record in the table.

```
tbl.Seek "=", strUsername
```

The Seek method works like a subroutine rather than a function. That's why there aren't any parentheses used as with the database object's OpenTable method. Like a subroutine, the Seek method doesn't return a value.

The first argument to the Seek method shows what kind of comparison operation indicates a matching record. Typically, this is passed as an equal sign (=), meaning that you are looking for an exact match.

The remaining arguments to the Seek method indicate the value to compare against the fields in the current index. If there are more fields in the index, then there are more fields passed to the Seek method. In your case, there is only one.

The way the PasswordValidate function works is that it checks if there is a record in the Login table with the same username and password as that which was passed to the function. If the username record is found, then you know they got that much right, and you compare the password field in the table to the password that was passed to the function.

Reading a Property

Enter the following lines in the program to check your search results.

```
If Not tbl.NoMatch Then
' Found the user
End If
```

The NoMatch property returns True if the search failed. You want to enter the If...Then block if you actually did find a record, so you get the opposite result in your expression by using the Not operator.

It would be nice to have a Match property. I put a comment inside the block to indicate what happened that made it possible to enter the block.

Reading a Field Value with a Table Object

The next four lines complete the function.

The code compares the value in the Password field of the current Login record against the `strPassword` variable passed to the function. If they match, then the result to the `PasswordValidate` function is set to True.

Enter the remaining four lines into the function (also shown in Figure 3.17).

```
If tbl!Password = strPassword Then
' Password checked out OK
  PasswordValidate = True
End If
```

When referencing a field value from a Table object, the exclamation point operator is used between the Table object variable and fieldname. It is valid to use a period instead, but the exclamation point tells Access that you are referencing a field in the table, not a property of the table object that might be of the same name.

Close the module window and enter `Library` as the name for the module in the Save As dialog box.

FIGURE 3.17.

Completing the `PasswordValidate` *function.*

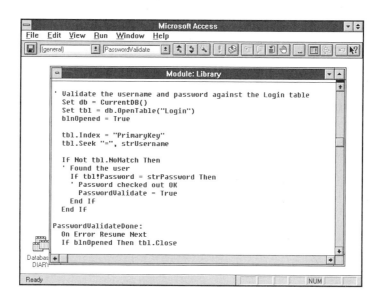

Listing 3.6 shows the completed `PasswordValidate` function.

Listing 3.6. The `PasswordValidate` function.

```
Function PasswordValidate (strUsername As String, strPassword As String)
➥As Integer

  Dim db As Database

  Dim tbl As Table
  Dim blnOpened As Integer

  blnOpened = False

' Assume failure
  PasswordValidate = False

  On Error GoTo PasswordValidateError

' Validate the username and password against the Login table
  Set db = CurrentDB()
  Set tbl = db.OpenTable("Login")
  blnOpened = True

  tbl.Index = "PrimaryKey"
  tbl.Seek "=", strUsername

  If Not tbl.NoMatch Then
  ' Found the user
    If tbl!Password = strPassword Then
    ' Password checked out OK
      PasswordValidate = True
    End If
  End If

PasswordValidateDone:
  On Error Resume Next
  If blnOpened Then tbl.Close
  Exit Function

PasswordValidateError:
  MsgBox Error$, 48, PROGRAM
  Resume PasswordValidateDone

End Function
```

I purposely showed you how that function was constructed, piece by piece in a seem-
ingly random order. This is generally the way code is produced. A program doesn't
typically get written from the top down to the bottom in one straight pass unless the
programmer has exceptional skills in planning ahead!

Testing *PasswordValidate*

You can test `PasswordValidate` from the Immediate window. For example, you could enter the following:

```
? PasswordValidate("Stephanie","itsme")
```

A 0 (False) should be printed for an invalid username and password combination. A -1 (True) should be printed if the username and password are valid. See Figure 3.18.

FIGURE 3.18.

*Testing the
PasswordValidate
function.*

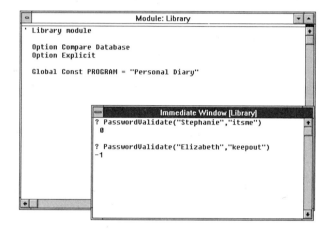

TRY THIS! QUESTION 3.1.

Add a `PasswordAssign` subroutine to the module in which you created `PasswordValidate`. The subroutine would be declared like this:

```
Sub PasswordAssign(strUsername As String, strPassword As String)
```

The `PasswordAssign` subroutine should add a username to the Login table if it isn't already there. If the username is there, then the password for that username should be changed.

You should be able to test it in the Immediate window. How would a program that uses the `PasswordAssign` function be sure that the proper user is re-assigning the password?

Create the Login Module

You know it would save you a lot of user-interface design trouble, but you can't have the users of your programs running them through the Immediate window, can you?

Nope, you're going to have to use the Login form that you created earlier in this chapter. First of all, you need some way for the form to be opened.

1. Create a new module.
2. Enter the declaration section as shown in Listing 3.7.
3. Enter the Login function as shown in Listing 3.8.
4. Close the Login module, entering Login in the Save As dialog box as the name for the module.

Listing 3.7. The declaration section for the Login module.

```
' Login module

Option Compare Database
Option Explicit

' Set to True if username/password was valid
Global gblnLoginValid As Integer
```

The gblnLoginValid variable is set by the code in the Login form to True or False, depending on whether the login was successful. You have to use a global in order for the code in the form, and the code in this module, to communicate.

Listing 3.8. The Login function.

```
Function Login () As Integer

' See if the user can enter in a valid username and password.

' Return True if login is OK.
' Return False if its an attempted break-in.

  On Error GoTo LoginError

  DoCmd OpenForm "Login", , , , , A_DIALOG

LoginDone:
  Login = gblnLoginValid
  Exit Function

LoginError:
  MsgBox Error$, 48, PROGRAM
  Resume LoginDone

End Function
```

All the `Login` function does is open the Login form and then return the value stored in `gblnLoginValid` after the Login form is closed.

Access wraps up some of its functionality in what are called macro commands. These are the commands available to you in an Access Macro object, which is intended as a less feature-rich, but easy way to program Access. To use these commands in Access Basic, the `DoCmd` statement is used before the macro command name.

The `Login` function calls the `OpenForm` macro passing Login, the name of the form to open, as the first argument, and a constant, `A_DIALOG`, as the sixth argument. The empty arguments default and are not required.

The `A_DIALOG` constant is important because it opens the form in a mode that stops execution of the current function. After the user closes the Login form, the `Login` function then proceeds to its Done section, where it checks to see what `gblnLoginValid` was assigned as.

Coding the Login Form

Now it's time to wrap all of this together and explore the remaining interface to objects you haven't used yet, *events*.

Add a module variable, `mintStrikes`, to the declarations section of the Login form module.

1. Click the Form tab on the database container, and open the Login form in **D**esign mode.
2. Select **View|Code** from the menu, or click the Code button on the toolbar.
3. Enter the declaration section for the Login form module as shown in Listing 3.9.
4. Close the module window.

Listing 3.9. The declaration for the Login form module.

```
' Login form

  Option Compare Database
  Option Explicit

' How many times user entered a bad name/password
  Dim mintStrike As Integer
```

Within the declaration section, a single variable with module scope is declared, `mintStrike`, which you can use as a counter for how many times the user tries to log in.

Next, create a `Form_Open` subroutine for the Login form using the following steps:

1. Open the Properties window and click the form to show form properties.
2. Select Event Properties in the combo box at the top of the Properties window to display a list of event names.
3. Click the text box next to the On Open event.

   A button with a down arrow will be displayed, and next to that a button with an ellipsis (…) is also displayed, as shown in Figure 3.19.

FIGURE 3.19.

Preparing to code a form's On Open event.

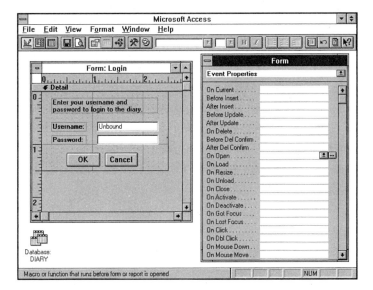

4. Click the button with the ellipsis on it.

   Access allows you to select from three builders: Expression Builder, Macro Builder, and Code Builder. See Figure 3.20.

5. In the Choose Builder dialog box, select Code Builder in the list and press OK.

Access reopens the form's module window with a subroutine declaration (sometimes called a "stub") pre-made for the form's On Open event.

FIGURE 3.20.

Selecting the Code Builder.

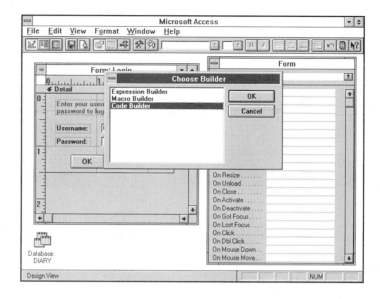

FIGURE 3.21.

Generated declaration for the Login form's On Open event.

Events Explained

The idea behind events is to allow an application like Access to provide a framework from which the Basic programmer can develop his or her application.

In older programming environments, the program ran until it needed some input from the user, then it would throw a prompt on the screen asking for a specific type of input. In those days, a run of your password program might look like this:

```
Enter your username and password.
Username:

Enter your username and password.
Username: STEPHANIE

Enter your username and password.
Username: STEPHANIE
Password:

Enter your username and password.
Username: STEPHANIE
Password: XXXXXX

Enter your username and password.
Username: STEPHANIE
Password: XXXXXX

I'm sorry, that is not a valid username and password.
```

The code in your program would have been responsible for producing everything that appears on the screen, as well as accepting and dealing with the input that is entered by the user.

The model you now program in allows the programmer to create forms just as you did with the Login form. Then you focus more on responding to the events generated by what you put on-screen.

Understanding where to place code in this kind of programming environment requires some research on the part of the programmer. Fortunately, you can quickly explore all the available events by examining what is available in the Properties window. Click the text box next to any event to move the text cursor to it, and then press F1 to get online help on the event.

A particularly helpful online help topic is the Order of Events topic (shown in Figure 3.22). From it, you can find out when the different events occur in relation to each other.

FIGURE 3.22.

Help on when events occur.

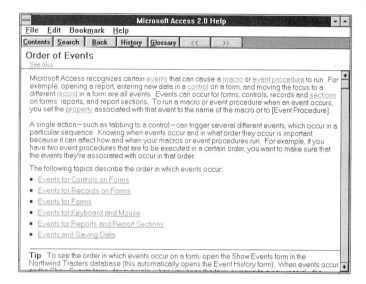

Adding Code to the On Open Event

The On Open event occurs before the form is actually displayed. You can use it to initialize two variables, gblnLoginValid and mintStrike.

Let's continue the steps where you left off.

1. Enter the code in Listing 3.10 to complete the Login form's Form_Open subroutine.
2. Close the module window.

Listing 3.10. The Form_Open **subroutine.**

```
Sub Form_Open (Cancel As Integer)

' By default, they didn't login correctly
    gblnLoginValid = False

' Zero login attempts have been tried so far
    mintStrike = 0

End Sub
```

The global variable, gblnLoginValid, is set to False to indicate a login has not been completed successfully. The module variable, mintStrike, is set to 0 to indicate that so far there have been no unsuccessful attempts at logging in.

In some events, such as the On Open event, parameters are generated in the declaration. Sometimes they are used to pass information to your code, such as the mouse position.

Other times, as with the On Open event, they can be used to pass information back to Access. The `Cancel` argument in the `Form_Open` subroutine can be set to False to tell Access to cancel displaying the form.

The *cmdOK* On Click Event

Most of what happens behind the Login form happens on the OK button's click event.

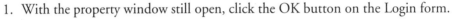

1. With the property window still open, click the OK button on the Login form.
2. Click the text box next to the On Click event to display the ellipses button, and then click the ellipses button.
3. Select Code builder.
4. Enter the `cmdOK_Click` subroutine as shown in Listing 3.11.

Listing 3.11. The `cmdOK_Click` **subroutine.**

```
Sub cmdOK_Click ()

  Dim msg As String
  Dim intIcon As Integer

  Const PROC = "cmdOK_Click"
  On Error GoTo cmdOK_ClickError

' Make sure a username and password were entered
  If CNStr(txtUsername) = "" Then
    MsgBox "Please enter a username.", 64, PROGRAM
    txtUsername.SetFocus

    GoTo cmdOK_ClickDone
  End If

  If CNStr(txtPassword) = "" Then
    MsgBox "Please enter a password.", 64, PROGRAM
    txtPassword.SetFocus

    GoTo cmdOK_ClickDone
  End If

  gblnLoginValid = PasswordValidate(CStr(txtUsername), CStr(txtPassword))

  If gblnLoginValid Then
' Successful login!
    MsgBox "Hi " & txtUsername & "!", 64, PROGRAM
    DoCmd Close
    GoTo cmdOK_ClickDone
  End If
```

```
' Count this bad attempt
  mintStrike = mintStrike + 1

' Select which message and icon to display
  Select Case mintStrike

  Case 1
    msg = "Are you supposed to be here?"
    intIcon = 32 ' Question

  Case 2
    msg = "I don't recognize you."
    intIcon = 48 ' Warning

  Case 3
    msg = "Go Away!"
    intIcon = 16 ' Stop!

  End Select

  MsgBox msg, intIcon, PROGRAM

  If mintStrike = 3 Then
  ' Three strikes and you're out!
    DoCmd Close
  Else
  ' Try again, erase the password field and set focus to it
    txtPassword = ""
    txtPassword.SetFocus
  End If

cmdOK_ClickDone:
  Exit Sub

cmdOK_ClickError:
  MsgBox Error$, 48, PROGRAM
  Resume cmdOK_ClickDone

End Sub
```

Examining *cmdOK_Click* in Detail

The first thing the cmdOK_Click subroutine does is examine the contents of the two text boxes and make sure that something was entered into them. If nothing was entered, then a message is displayed and the empty text box receives focus so the user can make an entry.

To check if a text box is empty, a CNStr function is called. You will add that function to the Library module in a moment. Its job is to ensure that the value read from the text box is read as a string so you can compare it to a string without getting an error concerning comparing different data types.

If the result of the CNStr function call is an empty string (""), then the user entered nothing in the text box or entered spaces only. See Listing 3.12.

Listing 3.12. Checking to see if a username was entered.

```
' Make sure a username and password were entered
  If CNStr(txtUsername) = "" Then
    MsgBox "Please enter a username.", 64, PROGRAM
    txtUsername.SetFocus

    GoTo cmdOK_ClickDone
  End If
```

Next, the PasswordValidate function that you wrote earlier is called. The result of the call is assigned to the gblnLoginValid global so that your Login function will know how things went.

```
gblnLoginValid = PasswordValidate(CStr(txtUsername), CStr(txtPassword))
```

The next section of code checks the gblnLoginValid value to see if the login was successful. If it is, then a friendly message is displayed, and you jump to the end of the subroutine to get out.

Listing 3.13. Say Hi if the login was successful.

```
If gblnLoginValid Then
  ' Successful login!
    MsgBox "Hi " & txtUsername & "!", 64, PROGRAM
    DoCmd Close
    GoTo cmdOK_ClickDone
  End If
```

If the login wasn't successful, then the subroutine displays one of three messages, each one progressively nastier. The subtle question icon is first, followed by the warning icon (an exclamation point), and finally the severe message icon (a stop sign).

The mintStrikes variable is used to keep track of which failed attempt you are currently on.

Listing 3.14. Choose one of three messages to display to the user who entered a bad username or password.

```
' Count this bad attempt
  mintStrike = mintStrike + 1
```

```
' Select which message and icon to display
Select Case mintStrike

  Case 1
    msg = "Are you supposed to be here?"
    intIcon = 32 ' Question

  Case 2
    msg = "I don't recognize you."
    intIcon = 48 ' Warning

  Case 3
    msg = "Go Away!"
    intIcon = 16 ' Stop!

End Select

MsgBox msg, intIcon, PROGRAM
```

The end of the subroutine checks to see if the user has failed three times. It closes the Login form if that is the case, because three times is considered excessive.

If it is on the first or second failure, then the password entered is cleared, and the password text box receives focus.

Listing 3.15. The `cmdOK_Click` subroutine decides whether or not to give the user another attempt to login.

```
If mintStrike = 3 Then
  ' Three strikes and you're out!
    DoCmd Close
  Else
  ' Try again, erase the password field and set focus to it
    txtPassword = ""
    txtPassword.SetFocus
  End If
```

The code intentionally does not clear the username field first, in case the user enters a bad username. If you enter a bad username, then the password field is still cleared, and the username field is left alone.

Giving any indication of which of the two fields is the problem would have made an easier job for the unwelcome user to hack beyond the login screen. (You need to use the built-in security features in Access to fully secure an Access database.)

The *cmdCancel* On Click Event

The Cancel button is used to close the form without receiving insults for not knowing a valid username and password.

1. Create the subroutine declaration for the cmdCancel button's On Click event as you did for the cmdOK button.
2. Enter the code in Listing 3.16 for the `cmdCancel_Click` subroutine.
3. Close the open windows, including the Login form.

Listing 3.16. The `cmdCancel_Click` subroutine.

```
Sub cmdCancel_Click ()

   DoCmd Close

End Sub
```

The *CNStr* Function

The CNStr function, which I read out loud as "sinister," is a frequently used function in my subroutine library. Every Basic coder I've worked with has some version of this function, and you'll want it in your toolkit too.

Basic has a variable type called *variant*. A variant can hold any of the basic data types which are the different types of numbers, a string, a date, or a Null.

A text box control can contain a text value or a Null. However, sometimes you really need a string, such as when you pass the value to a Basic function with a string parameter.

The CNStr function can be used to retrieve the contents of a text box and always ensure that the result is a string. It does this by converting a null value to an empty string (" ").

The CNStr function also uses the Trim$ function to remove leading, and trailing, spaces. This cleans up input, and also allows for a text box filled with spaces to be treated as empty.

Add the CNStr function as follows:

1. Open the Library module.
2. Enter the CNStr function as shown in Listing 3.17.

Listing 3.17. The sinister `CNStr` **function.**

```
Function CNStr (var As Variant) As String

' Converts a null to "".

' No error handling by intent. Let the error occur in the
' calling procedure.

  If IsNull(var) Then
    CNStr = ""
  Else
    CNStr = Trim$(CStr(var))
  End If

End Function
```

TRY THIS! QUESTION 3.2.

You're also going to need a function called `CNInt` in your library of routines, and possibly others like `CNLng` and `CNDate`. Do you know how to write the `CNInt` function?

Testing the Login Facility

Let's see if all this stuff works.

You can create an Access macro to run the `Login` function.

1. Click the Macro tab on the database container.
2. Press the **N**ew button to create a new macro.
3. In the Action column, select RunCode from the list of available actions (see Figure 3.23).
4. In the bottom half of the Macro window, enter `Login()` at the Function Name prompt (also shown in Figure 3.23).
5. Close the macro, saving it as `Macro1`.
6. Double-click the `Macro1` macro in the database container to open the Login form.

The Login form will be displayed for you to enter your name and password, as shown in Figure 3.24.

FIGURE 3.23.

Creating a macro to test the Login function.

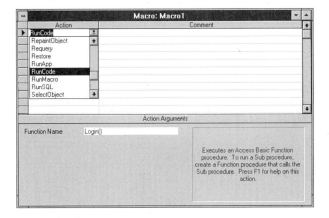

FIGURE 3.24.

Running the Login form.

Test pressing OK without entering either the username or password. Also test entering an invalid username/password combination three times. You should get the series of dialog boxes shown in Figures 3.25 through 3.27. With a valid username and password entered, you should see the message in Figure 3.28.

FIGURE 3.25.

Bad attempt number one.

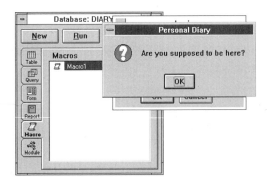

FIGURE 3.26.
*Bad attempt
number two.*

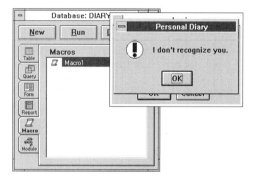

FIGURE 3.27.
*Bad attempt
number three.*

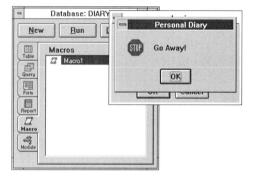

FIGURE 3.28.
Successful login!

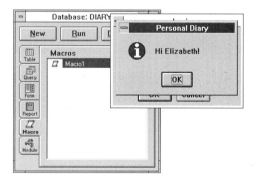

Hungarian Notation

We Basic programmers don't like to admit it, but we actually learned something useful
from the C folks. The prefixes in the variable names used throughout the code in this
book borrow from a technique called *Hungarian notation.*

This technique was introduced by Charles Simonyi, an early and legendary Microsoft programmer. I remember first seeing it in a paper of his that was passed around electronically on bulletin board systems. To be honest, I dismissed it at first because it seemed to add to the "line noise" look for which C was already famous.

The idea is that you can use one or more characters at the beginning of a variable name to signal quickly to the programmer some background information about the variable, such as its data type and how it is intended to be used.

Basic in the old days had some kind of facility for this already. Remember suffixes?

Count%	integer
Row&	a long integer
Name$	a string

These types of variable names actually still work in the current Basics, but they are about as trendy as line numbers.

What is better about Hungarian notation is that you can store more than just the data type in the variable name. For example, you can use `int` to indicate a variable is an integer, but you can also use `bln` for an integer variable, which indicates that it is intended to be used as a Boolean value and receive True or False values only.

Leszynski/Reddick Naming Convention

The prefixes used in this book for the most part match those in a proposed naming convention document authored by Stan Leszynski and Gregory Reddick. You can download a copy of this document from the MSACCESS forum on CompuServe. At the time of this writing, it's in the Modules section (library 7) as 20NAMG.DOC.

The authors of the convention spent many hours gathering input and weighing the merits of arguments to produce a set of naming prefixes they hoped the Access Basic community could adopt universally. The intent is to prescribe a common set of variable prefixes, or tags, so we all could be more apt to be capable of reading each other's programs.

In the spirit of cooperating with their effort and because I enjoy using Hungarian notation, I've used their suggested prefixes in my code. Their convention also has the distinction of being the most widely distributed convention in the Access community.

Here is a list of some of the variable prefixes used within this book.

Table 3.1. Variable prefixes used from the Leszynski/Reddick naming convention.

Data Types

int	Integer
lng	Long integer
sng	Single precision floating point number
dbl	Double precision floating point number
str	String

Forms and Controls

frm	Form
rpt	Report
ctl	Control
lbl	Label
txt	Text box
lst	List box
cbo	Combo box
cmd	Command Button
chk	Check box
grp	Option Group
opt	Option Button

Database Objects

db	Database
tbl	Table
dyn	Dynaset
snp	Snapshot
fld	Field
qry	Query

The Leszynski/Reddick naming convention also promotes using g to indicate a variable declared globally and m to indicate a variable declared within the declarations section of a module. These additional characters help indicate the scope in which a variable is used.

For example, `gstrProgramName` might be a global string storing the program name. You might have `mblnCancelled` as a module variable indicating if a Cancel button were pressed.

Variations on the Convention

The thing about any kind of programming convention is that you either love it or you hate it. You love it if it works for you and fits your style; you hate it if it doesn't, because you feel pressured by others to adopt a style that you would prefer not to use.

In this regard, other folks have also introduced their own proposed naming conventions for Basic programmers. Some programmers just ignore the issue altogether, or they explore their own naming methodologies.

By all means, use whatever works for you. Programming is a personal activity. What works for one person doesn't always work for another.

In this spirit, here are a few variations on the Leszynski/Reddick naming convention that you will see used in the code in this book. These are generally used as is, and not as prefixes for other variable names.

n	Temporary integer variable (It's easier to type than `intTemp`.)
z	Receive function call results (It's easier to type than `intReturn`.)
sz	Temporary string variable (It's easier to type than `strTemp`.)
cr	String that holds `Chr$(13)` and `Chr$(10)`, the carriage return and line feed characters
dq	String that holds `Chr$(34)`, a double quote
sq	String that holds `Chr$(39)`, a single quote
sql	String that holds SQL text (It's easier to type than `strSQL`.)
msg	String for the `MsgBox` function (It's easier to type than `strMsg`.)
bmk	String used to hold a dynaset's bookmark value

When programming in Access, I draw the line at another place, as far as using the proposed convention. I don't name actual tables, queries, forms, and so on, using prefixes. The rationale behind this is that users of my applications might see the database container.

I don't want to expose internal programming methodologies to the users of my application. The users are supposed to just have fun using the software.

I should also note that throughout this book I've used `bln` as the prefix for a Boolean integer rather than `f`, which is the prefix used in the Leszynski/Reddick proposed naming convention. I picked up `bln` from an early draft of the convention that has since been changed to use `f` (meaning "flag").

Summary

In this chapter, I covered some fundamentals on working with objects and created a login facility. You did the following:

- Discovered how Basic is moving from procedural programming toward object programming
- Learned how to declare a variable of an object type
- Defined events, methods, and properties
- Created an Access form and table
- Produced the `PasswordValidate` function step-by-step
- Learned how to open a table and read data from it
- Wrote code for form events
- Added the "sinister" `CNStr` function to your bag of tricks
- Learned about Hungarian notation and an application of it used in this book

TRY THIS! ANSWERS

3.1. Here's my version of the `PasswordAssign` function in Listing 3.18.

Listing 3.18. The `PasswordAssign` function.

```
Sub PasswordAssign (strUsername As String, strPassword As String)

    Dim db As Database

    Dim tbl As Table
    Dim blnOpened As Integer

    blnOpened = False

    On Error GoTo PasswordAssignError

    Set db = CurrentDB()
    Set tbl = db.OpenTable("Login")
    blnOpened = True

' See if the user is already in the table.
    tbl.Index = "PrimaryKey"
    tbl.Seek "=", strUsername
```

continues

Listing 3.18. continued

```
If Not tbl.NoMatch Then
' Found the user, modify their password
  tbl.Edit
Else
' New user, create a new record
  tbl.AddNew
  tbl!Username = strUsername
End If

' Write the password field and update the record
  tbl!Password = strPassword
  tbl.Update

PasswordAssignDone:
  On Error Resume Next
  If blnOpened Then tbl.Close
  Exit Sub

PasswordAssignError:
  MsgBox Error$, 48, PROGRAM
  Resume PasswordAssignDone

End Sub
```

I used the Immediate window to test assigning a new username and password (see Figure 3.29).

FIGURE 3.29.

*Testing the
PasswordAssign
subroutine.*

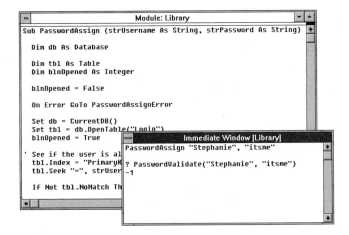

3.2. The CNInt function (shown in Listing 3.19) converts a null value into the integer zero.

Listing 3.19. The CNInt function.

```
Function CNInt (var As Variant) As Integer

' Converts a null to a zero.

' No error handling by intent. Let the error occur in the
' calling procedure.

  If IsNull(var) Then
    CNInt = 0
  Else
    CNInt = CInt(var)
  End If

End Function
```

PART II

Fun Projects

CHAPTER 4

Excel: Pretty Printer

Excel had programming before it had Basic. *The Visual Basic User's Guide for Excel* calls this former programming capability "Excel 4.0 macros."

Listing 4.1 is an example of an Excel 4.0 macro.

Listing 4.1. An Excel 4.0 macro.

```
=FORMULA("Sunday")
=SELECT("R3C2")
=FORMULA("Monday")
=SELECT("R3C3")
=FORMULA("Tuesday")
=SELECT("R3C4")
=FORMULA("Wednesday")
=SELECT("R3C5")
=FORMULA("Thursday")
=SELECT("R3C6")
=FORMULA("Friday")
=SELECT("R3C7")
=FORMULA("Saturday")
=SELECT("C1:C7")
=COLUMN.WIDTH(11.20)
=RETURN()
```

Excel 5.0 still runs macros created in the Excel 4.0 macro language. The above-mentioned user guide warns, however, that the macro language will no longer be updated to take advantage of any new features added to future versions of the product. So, if you are an Excel 4.0 macro language programmer, it's time to learn VBA.

To even the playing field, Visual Basic programmers who want to take advantage of VBA, but are unfamiliar with the Excel environment, must also learn a few things. VBA in Excel does not include the same set of application objects or programming environment that Visual Basic has. The host environment is Excel. For example, pop-up dialog boxes are created using Excel's dialog box worksheets, not a Visual Basic form object.

VBA is the Visual Basic *language* dropped into Excel, but without all that other stuff. Also note that data access objects (tables, dynasets, queries, and so on) are not presently available in Excel VBA. (In Chapter 23, "Visual Basic: S.W.A.T., Part Three—Field Reports and Time Estimates," we will use another method to make Excel read and write to an Access database.)

There is a lot you can do within Excel itself. And after all, if you develop an application within Excel, all you have to do to share it with someone else is give that person a copy of your worksheet. Unlike Visual Basic, no setup program is required here.

In this chapter you will create a worksheet-formatting utility that you will find useful again and again. In the process of building the project, you will become an expert at building Basic applications in Excel.

Introducing Pretty Printer

Often, one starts an Excel worksheet by importing data into it. If you do this enough, you might get tired of performing the same steps to make the imported data look reasonable in the worksheet and on paper after you send it to your printer.

Pretty Printer is the tool for this job. It's perhaps the quickest way to take a raw table or results from a query and make a presentable report.

The name "Pretty Printer" is borrowed from programs I downloaded from bulletin boards in my early C programming days. C programmers were always making neat utilities to clean up their source code listings and make them at least printable, if not readable too. I made this utility in the same spirit as those programmers, except that my utility works on worksheet data rather than source code listings.

If you are on any kind of electronic mail network, you can send worksheets prepared by Pretty Printer to your cohorts in e-mail land.

Excel does have an Autoformat feature that provides a variety of ways to automatically format a worksheet. The advantage that Pretty Printer has over Autoformat is that you create it; therefore, you can customize it to make it do precisely the kinds of formatting you want in your worksheets. Because this is mostly a matter of doing some macro recording, making modifications should be a cinch.

Getting Pretty Printer Test Data

To test Pretty Printer as you build it, you need a worksheet with some imported data. There are many ways to load data from external sources into Excel.

If the data is coming from Access, you can select any table or query from the Access database container and press the Excel export button on the toolbar. Excel is launched and receives the data in a new, empty workbook. You can't beat that for an easy way to transfer data between two applications.

Easier ways typically mean less flexibility, however. To get better control over what data is selected, you could initiate the data transfer from the Excel side using the provided Microsoft Query tool. This also gives you the ability to import data from other database sources, such as Btrieve, dBase, Paradox, and SQL Server.

Let's walk through the steps of using Microsoft Query to connect to a data source and pull in some data. In the following steps, I'll use Access, but remember that you could connect to other data sources also.

Establishing a Data Source

You are now going to take a whirlwind tour of Windows dialog boxes to set up a Microsoft Query data source.

1. Double-click the Excel icon from Program Manager to launch Excel with a new, empty workbook.
2. Select the **D**ata|Get External Data command.

   This brings up the Microsoft Query tool with a Select Data Source dialog box, as shown in Figure 4.1.

FIGURE 4.1.

Microsoft Query prompting for a data source.

The list of data sources are what Microsoft Query knows are available databases. If this is the first time you have used Microsoft Query, the list of data sources might be empty.

3. Press the button labeled **O**ther to define a new data source.

   The next pop-up (shown in Figure 4.2) asks you to select from one of the available ODBC data sources.

FIGURE 4.2.

The ODBC Data Sources dialog box.

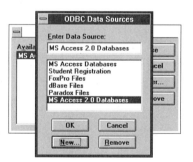

You could take a shortcut here and select Microsoft Access 2.0 Databases, and then select a default database to which you want connected. It's more convenient in the long run to define a new ODBC data source with a name that identifies which database is being used. To do this, press the **N**ew button.

The Add Data Source dialog box (shown in Figure 4.3) enables you to select from the ODBC drivers that are currently installed on your PC.

FIGURE 4.3.

The Add Data Source dialog box.

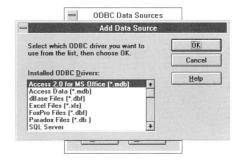

4. Select Access 2.0 for MS Office and press OK.

   The next dialog box that pops up is the ODBC Setup For Microsoft Access.

5. Press the **S**elect Database button.

   The File Open dialog box comes up to allow you to select a database.

6. Find and select the NorthWind Traders sample database that comes with Access. NWIND.MDB is in the SAMPAPPS directory off the directory in which you installed Access.

7. Enter NorthWind Traders as the Data Source Name, and enter a description if you like. (See Figure 4.4.)

FIGURE 4.4.

Selecting the NorthWind Traders database as a data source.

8. Press OK to close the dialog box.

   Back at the ODBC Data Sources dialog box, your new data source is displayed and selected in the list of available ODBC data sources, as shown in Figure 4.5.

9. Press OK to select the new data source and close the dialog box.

   This returns you to the Microsoft Query Select Data Source dialog box, which now shows the NorthWind Traders data source, as shown in Figure 4.6. The new data source shows up in this dialog box until you remove it.

FIGURE 4.5.
*The newly added
NorthWind Traders
ODBC data source.*

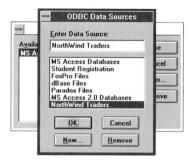

FIGURE 4.6.
*The NorthWind
Traders data source is
available to Microsoft
Query.*

Using Microsoft Query

Now you can select the data source to use in Microsoft Query and get on with selecting
your data.

1. With the NorthWind Traders data source selected, press the **U**se button.

   Microsoft Query displays a query builder similar to the QBE grid in Microsoft
   Access.

   The Add Tables dialog box appears so that you can start adding tables to your
   new query (see Figure 4.7). The tables in the NWIND.MDB database appear
   in the list of available tables.

2. Select the Products table and press the **A**dd button.

3. Now select the Suppliers table and add it as well.

   You need to include the Suppliers table in order to read and display each
   product's supplier information.

4. Press the Close button.

   Microsoft Query then displays an empty query window with the two field lists
   of your selected tables.

   A *join* indicates which records from one table are associated with a record in
   another table. For example, each product represented by a record in the
   Products table has in the Suppliers table an associated record that gives you
   information about that product's supplier.

FIGURE 4.7.

Use the Add Tables dialog box to select tables for your query.

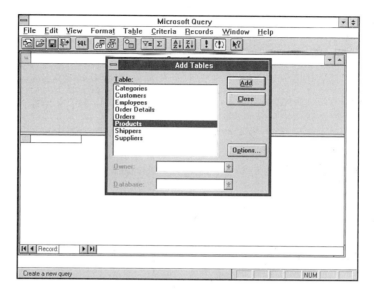

If you scroll down the field lists in both tables, you see a line connecting the SupplierID field in the Products table to the same field in the Suppliers table. A join was automatically established because the NorthWind Traders database has this and other table relationships defined within the database. See Figure 4.8.

FIGURE 4.8.

Microsoft Query automatically establishes joins between tables with defined relationships.

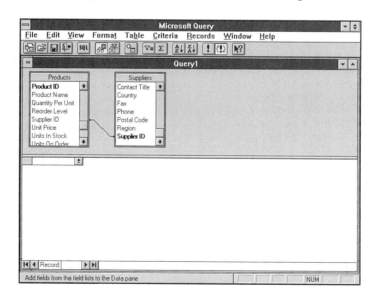

With the join established, the query produces the correct supplier data for each product. In your case, you are concerned with only the supplier's name.

5. Drag the following fields one by one into the columns of your data selection.

   From the Suppliers table, get the Company Name field. From the Products table, select and drag the Product Name, Unit Price, Quantity Per Unit, Units in Stock, and Units on Order fields.

   Note that unlike the Access QBE grid, Microsoft Query immediately displays data as you add fields to your selection.

   The final query should appear as shown in Figure 4.9.

FIGURE 4.9.

Building a query with the Microsoft Query tool.

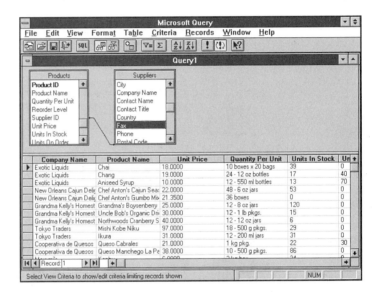

You can save your query definition so that it may be recalled in a later session with Microsoft Query.

6. Save the query as QUERY1.QRY using the **File|Save** Query command.

   Before you leave Microsoft Query, you can take a look to see what the program produces "internally" in order to produce your data selection.

7. Press the SQL button on the Microsoft Query toolbar to display a dialog box showing the generated SQL statement (as shown in Figure 4.10).

FIGURE 4.10.

Like the Access QBE grid, Microsoft Query generates SQL statements from your selections.

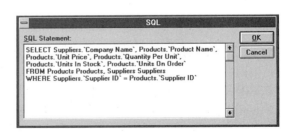

If you are like me, you are glad that you didn't have to type that SELECT statement yourself in a text editor. Be glad you have the query tool and the Access QBE grid to do this kind of work for us.

8. Press **OK** to close the SQL dialog box.

9. Select the **File|R**eturn Data to Microsoft Excel command.

Excel displays a Get External Data dialog box with a few options to choose from before the data comes in. (See Figure 4.11.)

FIGURE 4.11.

The Get External Data dialog box gives you a few useful options on how to populate the workbook.

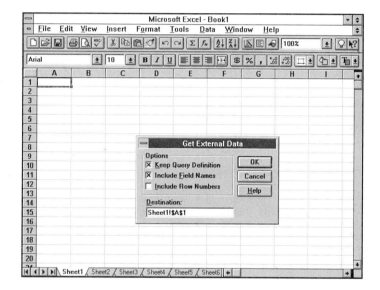

Make sure that the Include **F**ield Names option is checked, and the **D**estination for the imported data is the top left cell in the worksheet. These are the default values. The Pretty Printer utility assumes that the data was brought into the worksheet's top-left corner with field names.

Leave the **K**eep Query Definition option checked if you think you might want to refresh the workbook with a new set of data from time to time. If you are pretty sure this isn't a requirement, turn this option off to make your workbook load slightly faster. Having this option on causes the XLQUERY.XLA workbook library to be loaded each time you load your workbook.

10. Press the OK button. You now have some data in Sheet1.

You are going to clutter up the worksheet while you do some testing and macro recording. You need a saved copy so you can later reload an unmodified version of the worksheet with the data in it.

11. Use the **File|S**ave command to save your workbook as DATA.XLS.

Preliminary Results

Excel does a good job of formatting the data as it comes in. It sets the column widths correctly, and the worksheet looks neat and orderly.

If you view the worksheet in Print Preview from the **F**ile menu, you will see the result isn't exactly charming, as reports go. (See Figure 4.12.) It kind of looks like, well, a worksheet.

FIGURE 4.12.

Printing a worksheet after it is imported.

Company Name	Product Name	Unit Pr
Exotic Liquids	Chai	
Exotic Liquids	Chang	
Exotic Liquids	Aniseed Syrup	
New Orleans Cajun Delights	Chef Anton's Cajun Seasoning	
New Orleans Cajun Delights	Chef Anton's Gumbo Mix	21
Grandma Kelly's Homestead	Grandma's Boysenberry Spread	
Grandma Kelly's Homestead	Uncle Bob's Organic Dried Pears	
Grandma Kelly's Homestead	Northwoods Cranberry Sauce	
Tokyo Traders	Mishi Kobe Niku	
Tokyo Traders	Ikura	
Cooperativa de Quesos 'Las Cabras'	Queso Cabrales	
Cooperativa de Quesos 'Las Cabras'	Queso Manchego La Pastora	
Mayumi's	Konbu	
Mayumi's	Tofu	23
Mayumi's	Genen Shouyu	1
Pavlova, Ltd.	Pavlova	17
Pavlova, Ltd.	Alice Mutton	

(Window chrome: Microsoft Excel - Book1 — Next | Previous | Zoom | Print... | Setup... | Margins | Close | Help — Sheet1)

Pretty Printer Prototype

Before you start coding, it would make sense to experiment a bit and get the exact look you want for your printed worksheets—in other words, make a prototype.

Experiment with different cell formats, fonts, row spacings, print headings, and footers. Anything that is available in Excel should be available to your program. Use Print Preview to check out how each prototype would appear on a report.

Go ahead and try anything. You can always reload the untouched workbook, DATA.XLS, that you saved earlier.

The prototype I eventually came up with appears as in Figure 4.13 when in Print Preview.

FIGURE 4.13.

The Pretty Printer prototype.

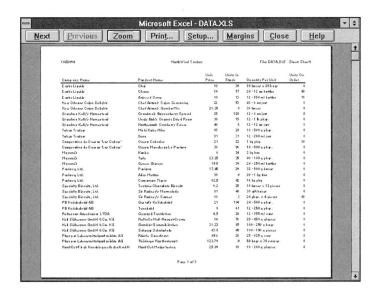

The prototype was created by applying the following changes to imported data in the worksheet:

- Change row heights of all cells from 12.75 to 15.
- Change row height of first row to 25.5.
- Bold format the first row.
- Select **W**rap Text format for the first row.
- Add a double-underline border to the first row.
- Select Fo**r**mat|**C**olumn|**A**utoFit Selection to resize all column widths.
- Insert a column between each original column with a width of 2.
- Indicate which rows to repeat at the top using **F**ile|Page Set**u**p|Sheet tab.
- Turn off gridline printing.
- Set custom headers and footers using **F**ile|Page Set**u**p|Header/Footer tab.
- Set the report to print landscape using **F**ile|Page Set**u**p|Page tab.

As you can see, there is quite a bit to do to prepare a worksheet for printing. You would want to make a utility to do this because you could have many sheets of data on which to perform the same steps on a regular basis.

Now get rid of the prototype. Save it, if you want to, under a different filename. If your prototype differs from mine, follow my example in the next section to get the hang of things, and then re-do the prototype so that you get the look that you want in your reports.

Creating Pretty Printer

1. Reload DATA.XLS so that you have a workbook in the same state as when you originally imported the data.

    You need a module worksheet to contain the Pretty Printer program.

2. Select the **I**nsert|**M**acro command.

3. From the cascading menu, select Module (as shown in Figure 4.14).

    A Module1 worksheet is inserted into your workbook.

4. Add the Option Explicit directive to the module.

FIGURE 4.14.

Creating an Excel module sheet.

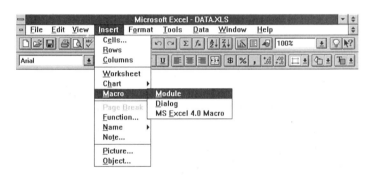

NOTE

You can tell Excel to automatically add the Option Explicit directive to each new module as it is created.

To do this, select the **T**ools|**O**ptions command. In the Module General tab, find and check the **R**equire Variable Declaration check box.

Next, add a declaration for the PrettyPrinter subroutine, and mark it to receive a macro recording.

1. A couple of lines after the Option Explicit directive, enter a new subroutine declaration in the new module worksheet.

    The declaration should look like this:

    ```
    Option Explicit
    Sub PrettyPrinter()
    End Sub
    ```

2. Place the cursor on the second line inside the subroutine declaration. This is where you want Excel to start adding code.

3. Select the **Tools**|**Record** Macro command.

4. From the cascading menu, select **M**ark Position for Recording, as shown in Figure 4.15.

FIGURE 4.15.

Telling Excel where to output recorded code.

Recorded commands are entered at the cursor.

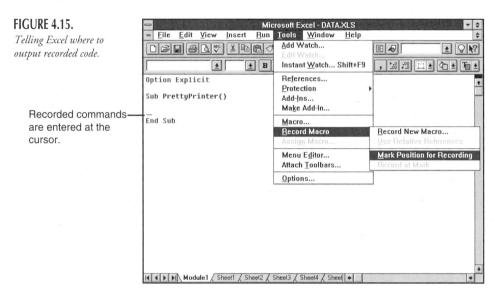

5. By pressing the Sheet1 tab, switch back to the worksheet that contains the data.

6. Turn on the formula bar if it isn't already on. Use the **View**|**F**ormula Bar command.

7. Select the **Tools**|**R**ecord Macro command again.

8. This time, select the **R**ecord at Mark command from the cascading menu, as shown in Figure 4.16.

A small toolbar window with a Stop button appears just as it did when you recorded code using Word in Chapters 1, "Today's Basic," and 2, "Word: Study Mate." Everything you do in Excel is recorded from this point on, until you press the Stop button.

You can record the whole program at once, or you can record it in one or more steps at a time. When you restart the recording after stopping it, the new code is appropriately added right where you left off. You'll record about half of the entire program at first.

FIGURE 4.16.

*Start recording an
Excel macro.*

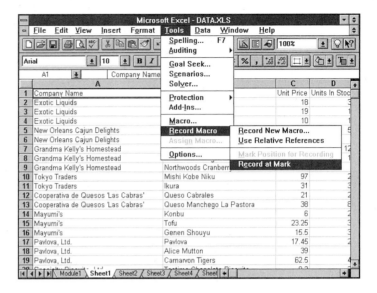

Recording Session One

1. In the workbook window, click the button at the intersection of the row and column titles.

   This selects all the cells in the worksheet.

2. Use the mouse to resize one of the rows to a height of 15.

   Because of all of the cells are selected, all of the rows will be resized.

3. Next, click the row heading button for row 1 to select all of the cells in row 1. Resize this row to a height of 25.5.

4. While row 1 is still selected, press the Bold toolbar button to change the field names to a bold font. Your worksheet should appear as shown in Figure 4.17.

5. Select the Format|Cells command.

6. In the Format Cells dialog box, click the Alignment tab and click the **W**rap Text checkbox on. (See Figure 4.18.)

7. Click the Border tab and select a **B**ottom border. Set it to a double-underline style by clicking the double underline in the Styl**e** group box. (See Figure 4.19.)

8. Press OK to close the Format Cells dialog box.

9. Press the Stop button to end the recording.

Your workbook should appear as in Figure 4.20.

FIGURE 4.17.

Recording: resizing the rows in the worksheet.

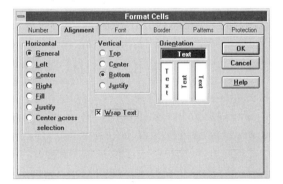

FIGURE 4.18.

Recording: setting row 1 to wrap text.

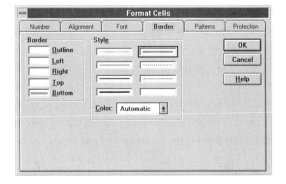

FIGURE 4.19.

Recording: placing a double-underline border below row one.

FIGURE 4.20.
Recording Session One complete.

	A	B	C	D
			Unit	Units In
1	**Company Name**	**Product Name**	**Price**	**Stock**
2	Exotic Liquids	Chai	18	3
3	Exotic Liquids	Chang	19	1
4	Exotic Liquids	Aniseed Syrup	10	1
5	New Orleans Cajun Delights	Chef Anton's Cajun Seasoning	22	5
6	New Orleans Cajun Delights	Chef Anton's Gumbo Mix	21.35	
7	Grandma Kelly's Homestead	Grandma's Boysenberry Spread	25	12
8	Grandma Kelly's Homestead	Uncle Bob's Organic Dried Pears	30	1
9	Grandma Kelly's Homestead	Northwoods Cranberry Sauce	40	
10	Tokyo Traders	Mishi Kobe Niku	97	2
11	Tokyo Traders	Ikura	31	3
12	Cooperativa de Quesos 'Las Cabras'	Queso Cabrales	21	2
13	Cooperativa de Quesos 'Las Cabras'	Queso Manchego La Pastora	38	8
14	Mayumi's	Konbu	6	2
15	Mayumi's	Tofu	23.25	3
16	Mayumi's	Genen Shouyu	15.5	

Session One Results

Now let's take a look at what was recorded.

Press the Module1 tab to view the recorded code.

The code you see on your screen should be the same as in Listing 4.2.

Listing 4.2. `PrettyPrinter` **after the first recording session.**

```
Sub PrettyPrinter()

    Cells.Select
    Selection.RowHeight = 15
    Rows("1:1").Select
    Selection.RowHeight = 25.5
    Selection.Font.Bold = True
    With Selection
        .HorizontalAlignment = xlGeneral
        .VerticalAlignment = xlBottom
        .WrapText = True
        .Orientation = xlHorizontal
    End With
    Selection.Borders(xlLeft).LineStyle = xlNone
    Selection.Borders(xlRight).LineStyle = xlNone
    Selection.Borders(xlTop).LineStyle = xlNone
    With Selection.Borders(xlBottom)
        .LineStyle = xlDouble
        .ColorIndex = xlAutomatic
    End With
    Selection.BorderAround LineStyle:=xlNone

End Sub
```

The generated code makes heavy use of Basic's new object syntax in order to control the Excel environment.

My first notion on looking at the generated code is that it could be improved a little bit to make it more readable. This is a matter of personal preference, because the code certainly will run as is. It is even more likely to run if you don't change it, because if you change it, you may introduce a programming error in your modifications.

Never one to follow my own good advice, I'm going to change it anyway.

I'll trim the code a bit by removing some lines that aren't needed. The macro recorder writes code for setting properties that you didn't modify during the recording session. This happened while you used the Format Cells dialog box.

Adding some comments to the generated code might help you remember in future edits what the function is intended to do. The macro recorder doesn't try to do this for you. That would be taking code generation a bit too far in my opinion.

You can use a single quote anywhere in a line to indicate that the following text is a comment. Excel displays a comment in green so that you can easily distinguish the comment from code that is to run.

> **NOTE**
>
> I'll tell you about my own commenting style, or lack thereof.
>
> As I become familiar with a programming environment, I tend to write a lot of comments. Later, as I find it easier to read the code, I write fewer comments because they start getting in the way.
>
> I've found that there tend to be two different camps of programmers on this: those who write a comment with every single line of code, and those who rarely write a comment at all. I have to admit that I fall in the second camp most of the time, and the code in this section is an exception.

My modified version of the recorded macro is in Listing 4.3.

Listing 4.3. Session One modified.

```
Sub PrettyPrinter()

' Select all cells
  Cells.Select

' Set the row height of all cells to 15
  Selection.RowHeight = 15
```

continues

Listing 4.3. continued

```
' Select row one
  Rows("1:1").Select

' Set the row height of row one to 25.5
  Selection.RowHeight = 25.5

' Set row one to bold
  Selection.Font.Bold = True

' Allow field names to wrap
  Selection.WrapText = True

' Set a bottom double underline border for row one
  Selection.Borders(xlBottom).LineStyle = xlDouble

End Sub
```

The Selection Property

You can reference online help if you have any questions about the code that was generated. The word *Selection* is used a lot in the code, so that's one I looked up. Put your cursor on the word and press the F1 key; you'll get a description of the word, as shown in Figure 4.21.

FIGURE 4.21.

Getting help on Selection.

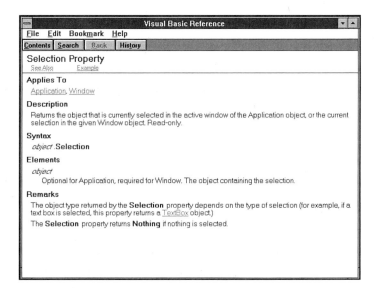

It turns out the usage of Selection is kind of tricky. The code would make you think that there is some kind of Selection object, but there isn't.

As indicated in the help topic, Selection is a property of an Application or Window object. In this particular case, the object syntax allows the Application object to be assumed, so in the generated code the object is not specified.

The Selection property returns an object of the type that is currently in selection. Yes, you heard me right; a property can sometimes return not just any run-of-the-mill data type, but can actually return an object. In your case, the returned object is the Range object.

A Range object is exactly what you think it would be—a group of cells. Most of the lines in your program involve setting properties on a Range object, where the Range object is the cells that were selected using the Select method.

You could modify the subroutine to make all this even clearer. (See Listing 4.4.)

Listing 4.4. Modifying `PrettyPrinter` **to be explicit about the selected object.**

```
Sub PrettyPrinter()

  Dim SelectedRange As Range

' Select all cells
  Set SelectedRange = Cells

' Set the row height of all cells to 15
  SelectedRange.RowHeight = 15

' Select row one
  Set SelectedRange = Rows("1:1")

' Set the row height of row one to 25.5
  SelectedRange.RowHeight = 25.5
    .
    .
    .

End Sub
```

After you understand what the Selection property returns, there really isn't a need to be this explicit. Rather than make this change, I'll leave that much of the code as it was generated.

With and *End With*

The generated code made some use of the With and End With keywords, which may be unfamiliar to Visual Basic programmers.

If you are going to set many properties of the same object within a block of code, the `With...End With` construct is a shortcut; with this construct you don't have to keep indicating which object is being set.

Code such as this

```
MyObject.Property1 = Value1
MyObject.Property2 = Value2
MyObject.Property3 = Value3
```

can be written as this:

```
With MyObject
    .Property1 = Value1
    .Property2 = Value2
    .Property3 = Value3
End With
```

You won't see a major savings in keystrokes here, but it gets better as more properties are set at the same time. There also is a slight performance gain achieved by using the `With` and `End With` keywords.

When I trimmed down the generated code, I removed the `With` and `End With` keywords because, in each case, I really needed to set only a single property.

Test the Modifications

Let's make sure the modifications didn't break anything before you move on to recording the rest of the program.

Excel enables you to save the Module1 sheet as a separate text file. You can do that and load it into the saved workbook file that contains the imported data sheet before any modifications were made to it.

1. With the Module1 worksheet in front of you, select the **File**|Save **As** command.

2. In the Save As dialog box, select a file type of Basic Code (Text).

3. Enter MODULE1.TXT as a filename and press OK. (See Figure 4.22.)

   You get a message indicating that only the active worksheet will be saved. That's all right, because that is exactly what you intended.

4. Press OK.

5. Re-open the DATA.XLS workbook you saved before you began recording. Answer Yes to the dialog box that warns you about losing your changes.

6. Create a Module1 module again by selecting the **Insert**|**Macro**|**Module** command.

7. Delete the `Option Explicit` command if it was automatically generated for you. It will be reloaded with your text file.

FIGURE 4.22.

In Excel you can save a module as a separate text file.

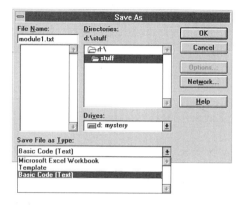

8. Select **I**nsert|**F**ile.

9. In the Insert File dialog box, select the file recently saved.

   The module loads into the worksheet starting where the text cursor is resting.

10. Click the Sheet1 tab and save the workbook now so you have a copy before running the test.

    To run the subroutine, do the following:

11. Select the **T**ools|**M**acro command.

12. Select the `PrettyPrinter` macro from the list of macros and press the **R**un button. (See Figure 4.23.)

FIGURE 4.23.

Selecting the `PrettyPrinter` macro for a test run.

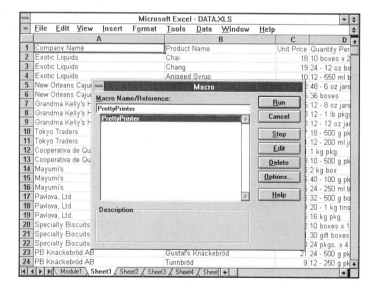

The changes to the workbook sheet will be instantaneous. If the program doesn't complete as expected, see the notes later in the chapter about debugging modules in Excel.

If you need to make a change and run the test again, re-load the saved worksheet, which has the data worksheet in the same state it was after you initially imported the data.

Do *not* save the worksheet after you run the PrettyPrinter macro. You still need a copy of the worksheet with the page unchanged to test the final version.

Recording Session Two

You can now record the second part of the Pretty Printer macro.

1. Switch back to the Module1 tab and place the cursor on the last line of the subroutine before the End Sub keywords.
2. Mark the place to receive the recorded code by selecting the **T**ools|**R**ecord Macro|**M**ark Position for Recording command.
3. Switch back to Sheet1 by pressing the Sheet1 tab.
4. Turn on the Formula bar if it is off.
5. Activate the recorder again by selecting the **T**ools|**R**ecord Macro|**R**ecord at Mark command.

The remaining steps to format the workbook sheet are these:

■ Select Format|**C**olumn|**A**utoFit Selection to resize all column widths.

■ Insert a column between each original column with a width of 2.

■ Using **F**ile|Page Set**u**p|Sheet tab, indicate which rows to repeat at the top.

■ Turn off gridline printing.

■ Set custom headers and footers using **F**ile|Page Set**u**p|Header/Footer tab.

■ Set the report to print landscape using **F**ile|Page Set**u**p|Page tab.

Record the changes to the worksheet as shown next.

1. Click the top-left corner button at the intersection of the row and column headings to select all cells in the worksheet.
2. Select the Format|**C**olumn|**A**utoFit Selection menu command.

   The columns expand or contract to the smallest possible width that allows the cell contents and the headings to display properly.

   The next step in formatting the sheet to print well is to insert a new column between each column of data. The new column is needed to add some spacing so that right-justified numbers in one column don't butt up against left-justified text in the next column.

You need to record this only for a single column because you can modify the generated program later to do the same thing for each additional column of imported data.

3. Click on cell B1.

4. Select the **I**nsert|**C**olumns command to insert a column.

5. Resize the new column so it has a width of 2. (See Figure 4.24.)

FIGURE 4.24.

Inserting a column to separate columns of data.

	A	B	C	D	E
1	**Company Name**		**Product Name**	Unit Price	tity Pe
2	Exotic Liquids		Chai	18	10 boxes x
3	Exotic Liquids		Chang	19	24 - 12 oz b
4	Exotic Liquids		Aniseed Syrup	10	12 - 550 ml
5	New Orleans Cajun Delights		Chef Anton's Cajun Seasoning	22	48 - 6 oz jar
6	New Orleans Cajun Delights		Chef Anton's Gumbo Mix	21.35	36 boxes
7	Grandma Kelly's Homestead		Grandma's Boysenberry Spread	25	12 - 8 oz jar
8	Grandma Kelly's Homestead		Uncle Bob's Organic Dried Pears	30	12 - 1 lb pkg
9	Grandma Kelly's Homestead		Northwoods Cranberry Sauce	40	12 - 12 oz ja
10	Tokyo Traders		Mishi Kobe Niku	97	18 - 500 g p
11	Tokyo Traders		Ikura	31	12 - 200 ml j
12	Cooperativa de Quesos 'Las Cabras'		Queso Cabrales	21	1 kg pkg.
13	Cooperativa de Quesos 'Las Cabras'		Queso Manchego La Pastora	38	10 - 500 g p
14	Mayumi's		Konbu	6	2 kg box
15	Mayumi's		Tofu	23.25	40 - 100 g p
16	Mayumi's		Genen Shouyu	15.5	24 - 250 ml
17	Pavlova, Ltd.		Pavlova	17.45	32 - 500 g b
18	Pavlova, Ltd.		Alice Mutton	39	20 - 1 kg tin
19	Pavlova, Ltd.		Carnarvon Tigers	62.5	16 kg pkg.

Microsoft Excel - DATA.XLS
File **E**dit **V**iew **I**nsert F**o**rmat **T**ools **D**ata **W**indow **H**elp
B1

Module1 **Sheet1** Sheet2 Sheet3 Sheet4 Sheet

The rest of your modifications to the worksheet are done in the Page Setup dialog box.

6. Open the Page Setup dialog box by selecting the **F**ile|Page Set**u**p command.

7. Click the Sheet tab.

8. Enter A1 in **R**ows to Repeat at Top text box.

9. Click the **G**ridlines checkbox so that it is unchecked (see Figure 4.25). You don't want gridlines visible in the printout.

10. Click the Header/Footer tab.

11. Press the **C**ustom Header button to enter the headings displayed at the top of a printed page.

FIGURE 4.25.

Filling in the Sheet tab.

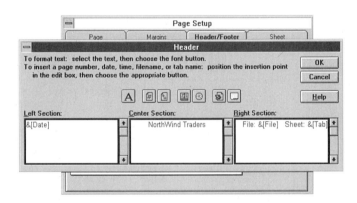

For the different sections in the page header, enter the following (and also as shown in Figure 4.26):

Left Section: `&[Date]`

Center Section: `NorthWind Traders`

Right Section: `File: &[File]    Sheet: &[Tab]`

FIGURE 4.26.

Defining the print headers.

12. Press OK to close the Headers dialog box.

13. Back in the Page Setup dialog box, click the **Cu**stom Footer button.

14. Enter the footer text.

    For the page footer, I used the center section to display the page number, and I left the other sections blank.

    Left Section: <blank>

    Center Section: `Page &[Page] of &[Pages]`

    Right Section: <blank>

15. Close the Footers dialog box.

16. Click the Page tab in the Page Setup dialog box.

17. Select **L**andscape orientation.

18. Press OK to save the page setup options.

    You are done formatting the worksheet.

19. Press the Stop button to stop the macro recorder.

Session Two Results

The macro recorder adds the code shown in Listing 4.5 to the end of your `PrettyPrinter` subroutine.

Listing 4.5. The recorded code from Session Two.

```
Cells.Select
Selection.EntireColumn.AutoFit
Range("B1").Select
Selection.EntireColumn.Insert
Columns("B:B").ColumnWidth = 2
With ActiveSheet.PageSetup
    .PrintTitleRows = "$1:$1"
    .PrintTitleColumns = ""
End With
ActiveSheet.PageSetup.PrintArea = ""
With ActiveSheet.PageSetup
    .LeftHeader = "&D"
    .CenterHeader = "NorthWind Traders"
    .RightHeader = "File: &F    Sheet: &A"
    .LeftFooter = ""
    .CenterFooter = "Page &P of &N"
    .RightFooter = ""
    .LeftMargin = Application.InchesToPoints(0.75)
    .RightMargin = Application.InchesToPoints(0.75)
    .TopMargin = Application.InchesToPoints(1)
    .BottomMargin = Application.InchesToPoints(1)
    .HeaderMargin = Application.InchesToPoints(0.5)
    .FooterMargin = Application.InchesToPoints(0.5)
    .PrintHeadings = False
    .PrintGridlines = False
    .PrintNotes = False
    .PrintQuality = 300
    .CenterHorizontally = False
    .CenterVertically = False
    .Orientation = xlLandscape
    .Draft = False
    .PaperSize = xlPaperLetter
    .FirstPageNumber = xlAutomatic
    .Order = xlDownThenOver
    .BlackAndWhite = False
    .Zoom = 100
End With
```

More Modifications

That was a lot of code for such a short little recording.

Again, because I can't seem to leave well enough alone, I modified the generated code to condense it and make it more understandable. I also added some error trapping so that a message box is displayed with an error message if anything goes sour during the run of the program.

In testing the routine, I found that a lot of screen flickering was happening. I added a command to turn off screen updates when the subroutine starts and then turn screen updates back on again when the subroutine is done.

If you turn off screen updating, be careful to make sure the routine can't exit in any way without turning it back on. This is only possible with error-handling code in place to prevent uncontrolled exits from the subroutine.

Listing 4.6 shows the second modified version.

Listing 4.6. The `PrettyPrinter` **subroutine so far.**

```
Sub PrettyPrinter()

' Trap any errors that occur
  On Error GoTo PrettyPrinterError

' Turn off screen updates until done
  Application.ScreenUpdating = False

' Select all cells
  Cells.Select

' Set the row height of all cells to 15
  Selection.RowHeight = 15

' Select row one
  Rows("1:1").Select

' Set the row height of row one to 25.5
  Selection.RowHeight = 25.5

' Set row one to bold
  Selection.Font.Bold = True

' Allow field names to wrap
  Selection.WrapText = True

' Set a bottom double underline border for row one
  Selection.Borders(xlBottom).LineStyle = xlDouble

' Select all cells
  Cells.Select
```

```
' Resize the column widths
  Selection.EntireColumn.AutoFit

' Select B1 to indicate where to insert a column
  Range("B1").Select

' Insert a column
  Selection.EntireColumn.Insert

' Set the column width on the new column to 2
  Columns("B:B").ColumnWidth = 2

' Print Page Setup options:

  With ActiveSheet.PageSetup

  ' Repeat row one at the top of each page
    .PrintTitleRows = "$1:$1"

  ' Headers
    .LeftHeader = "&D"
    .CenterHeader = "NorthWind Traders"
    .RightHeader = "File: &F    Sheet: &A"

  ' Footers
    .LeftFooter = ""
    .CenterFooter = "Page &P of &N"
    .RightFooter = ""

  ' Hide grid lines
    .PrintGridlines = False

  ' Print in landscape
    .Orientation = xlLandscape

  End With

  Application.ScreenUpdating = True

PrettyPrinterDone:
  Exit Sub

PrettyPrinterError:
  Application.ScreenUpdating = True
  MsgBox Error$(), 48, "Pretty Printer"
  Resume PrettyPrinterDone

End Sub
```

Testing the Second Round of Modifications

Let's get the modified version in your original DATA1.XLS and see how well it's going.
It is always good to catch problems early and fix them rather than waiting and debugging everything at the end.

1. Enter the modified version of the `PrettyPrinter` procedure into Module1.
2. Use the method described earlier to save the module as a text file.
3. Reload DATA1.XLS and load the new version of the `PrettyPrinter` procedure.
4. Save your workbook before testing the `PrettyPrinter` procedure with its new changes.
5. Run the macro once again and verify that it runs well with your changes so far. Figure 4.27 shows the worksheet after running the `PrettyPrinter` macro.

FIGURE 4.27.

A successful run of the `PrettyPrinter` macro.

	A	B	C	D	E
1	**Company Name**		**Product Name**	**Unit Price**	**Quantity Pe**
2	Exotic Liquids		Chai	18	10 boxes x 2
3	Exotic Liquids		Chang	19	24 - 12 oz b
4	Exotic Liquids		Aniseed Syrup	10	12 - 550 ml
5	New Orleans Cajun Delights		Chef Anton's Cajun Seasoning	22	48 - 6 oz jar
6	New Orleans Cajun Delights		Chef Anton's Gumbo Mix	21.35	36 boxes
7	Grandma Kelly's Homestead		Grandma's Boysenberry Spread	25	12 - 8 oz jar
8	Grandma Kelly's Homestead		Uncle Bob's Organic Dried Pears	30	12 - 1 lb pkg
9	Grandma Kelly's Homestead		Northwoods Cranberry Sauce	40	12 - 12 oz ja
10	Tokyo Traders		Mishi Kobe Niku	97	18 - 500 g pl
11	Tokyo Traders		Ikura	31	12 - 200 ml j
12	Cooperativa de Quesos 'Las Cabras'		Queso Cabrales	21	1 kg pkg.
13	Cooperativa de Quesos 'Las Cabras'		Queso Manchego La Pastora	38	10 - 500 g pl
14	Mayumi's		Konbu	6	2 kg box
15	Mayumi's		Tofu	23.25	40 - 100 g pl
16	Mayumi's		Genen Shouyu	15.5	24 - 250 ml l
17	Pavlova, Ltd.		Pavlova	17.45	32 - 500 g b
18	Pavlova, Ltd.		Alice Mutton	39	20 - 1 kg tin:
19	Pavlova, Ltd.		Carnarvon Tigers	62.5	16 kg pkg.

Microsoft Excel - DATA.XLS — File Edit View Insert Format Tools Data Window Help

Module1 \ **Sheet1** / Sheet2 / Sheet3 / Sheet4 / Sheet

6. Reload the worksheet if you want to run it again.

Debugging Pretty Printer

If an error occurs while you are running the program, Excel enables you to switch to the module worksheet and view the code that produced the error.

You can also step through your code to verify its correctness by setting a breakpoint and then activating the macro.

VBA in Excel is a little less capable than Visual Basic in debugging. In Visual Basic, you have the ability to modify the code when in debug mode. With VBA, you can't make any modifications to the code while it is running.

To step through the `PrettyPrinter` subroutine, perform the following steps:

1. Switch to the Module1 worksheet.
2. Move your text cursor to the first statement in the procedure.
3. Select Run|Toggle Breakpoint or press F9 to set a breakpoint at the current line.

   The line with the breakpoint is highlighted in red (see Figure 4.28).

FIGURE 4.28.

Setting a breakpoint in Excel VBA code.

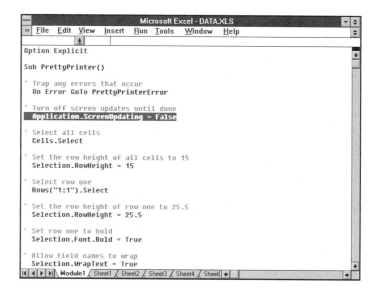

Switch back to the Sheet1 worksheet and run the macro. A debug window appears as in Figure 4.29.

FIGURE 4.29.

Execution paused at the breakpoint.

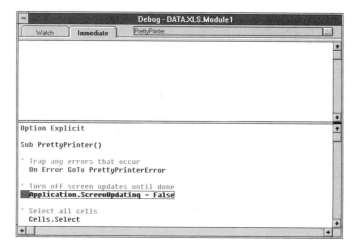

Using the Debugger to Explore

Pressing F8 steps to the next line of code. Do this repeatedly to follow execution from line to line.

You can examine the values of any variables in your code, as well as the properties of the objects used in your code or available within the spreadsheet. Select Add Watch from the Tools menu and enter the value you want to examine.

I wanted to see whether my program could know how many rows and columns of data were imported, so I dug through the help file and found the `SpecialCells` method.

The `SpecialCells` method can be used on a Range object. One of the values you can pass to `SpecialCells` is `xlLastCell`, which tells the method that you want the last used cell of the range returned. Given this cell, I can check the Row and Column properties to find where the cell is located by entering the following expressions into the Watch window:

```
Selection.SpecialCells(xlLastCell).Column
Selection.SpecialCells(xlLastCell).Row
```

To add an expression to the Watch window, do the following:

1. Select the **Tools|Add** Watch command.

2. Enter the expression to watch in the **Expression** text box, as shown in Figure 4.30.

3. Press OK.

FIGURE 4.30.

Adding an expression to the Watch window.

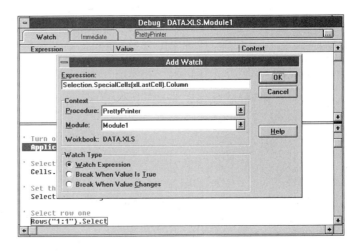

When you add the two expressions above, the Watch window indicates that the worksheet contains 6 columns and 78 rows of data. (See Figure 4.31.)

FIGURE 4.31.

Examining property values in the Watch window.

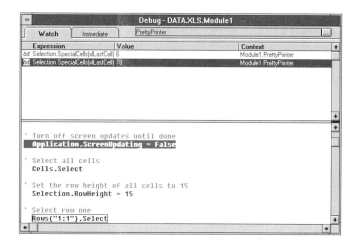

You can also view values in the Immediate window if you need to check them only once and not keep them around in the Watch window.

4. Switch to the Immediate window by clicking the Immediate tab.

5. To check how many rows are in the worksheet, you can enter the following:

```
? Selection.SpecialCells(xlLastCell).Row
78
```

The Intermediate window responds to the Print operator (?) and displays 78 for the number of rows, as shown in Figure 4.32.

FIGURE 4.32.

Examining property values in the Immediate window.

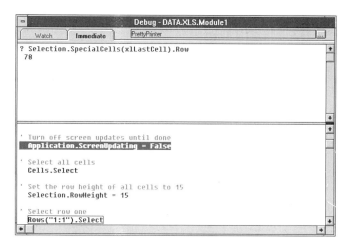

6. Press F5 to allow the program to run to the end.

Completing Pretty Printer

The final version of Pretty Printer needs to insert a column between each column of imported data. Remember, you recorded doing this for one column, but not all.

Because you don't know how many columns of imported data are coming in, you can't *hard-code* the number of columns. What you learned about the `SpecialCells` method during the debug session will help you solve this problem.

At the top of the `PrettyPrinter` subroutine you want to declare an integer variable to keep track of which column you are working on.

1. Enter the declaration for the `intColumn` variable:

    ```
    Dim intColumn As Integer
    ```

    Next, in the section of program that inserts a column in the worksheet, you need to create a loop to do as many columns as needed to insert a column between each data column.

2. Replace the code shown in Listing 4.7 with the code shown in Listing 4.8. (The final completed `PrettyPrinter` subroutine is shown in Listing 4.9.)

3. Save your workbook.

4. Run the macro again on the original worksheet of imported data. The resulting worksheet should appear as shown in Figure 4.33.

    When it runs, it seems like magic, doesn't it?

Listing 4.7. Code to replace.

```
' Select B1 to indicate where to insert a column
  Range("B1").Select

' Insert a column
  Selection.EntireColumn.Insert

' Set the column width on the new column to 2
  Columns("B:B").ColumnWidth = 2
```

Listing 4.8. Replacement code that adds each column.

```
' Start with Column B
  intColumn = 2

' Break out of the loop when past the last column
  Do While intColumn <= Selection.SpecialCells(xlLastCell).Column
```

```
' Insert a column
  Cells(1, intColumn).EntireColumn.Insert

' Set the column width on the new column to 2
  Columns(intColumn).ColumnWidth = 2

' Jump to the next column
  intColumn = intColumn + 2

Loop

' Move back to cell A1
  Cells(1, 1).Select
```

FIGURE 4.33.

Final results from the completed PrettyPrinter *subroutine.*

	A	B	C	D	E	F
					Unit Price	Quan
1	Company Name		Product Name			
2	Exotic Liquids		Chai		18	10 bo
3	Exotic Liquids		Chang		19	24 - 1
4	Exotic Liquids		Aniseed Syrup		10	12 - 5
5	New Orleans Cajun Delights		Chef Anton's Cajun Seasoning		22	48 - 6
6	New Orleans Cajun Delights		Chef Anton's Gumbo Mix		21.35	36 bo
7	Grandma Kelly's Homestead		Grandma's Boysenberry Spread		25	12 - 8
8	Grandma Kelly's Homestead		Uncle Bob's Organic Dried Pears		30	12 - 1
9	Grandma Kelly's Homestead		Northwoods Cranberry Sauce		40	12 - 1
10	Tokyo Traders		Mishi Kobe Niku		97	18 - 5
11	Tokyo Traders		Ikura		31	12 - 2
12	Cooperativa de Quesos 'Las Cabras'		Queso Cabrales		21	1 kg p
13	Cooperativa de Quesos 'Las Cabras'		Queso Manchego La Pastora		38	10 - 5
14	Mayumi's		Konbu		6	2 kg b
15	Mayumi's		Tofu		23.25	40 - 1
16	Mayumi's		Genen Shouyu		15.5	24 - 2
17	Pavlova, Ltd.		Pavlova		17.45	32 - 5
18	Pavlova, Ltd.		Alice Mutton		39	20 - 1
19	Pavlova, Ltd.		Carnarvon Tigers		62.5	16 kg

Listing 4.9. Final version of the PrettyPrinter **subroutine.**

```
Option Explicit

Sub PrettyPrinter()

  Dim intColumn As Integer

' Trap any errors that occur
  On Error GoTo PrettyPrinterError

' Turn off screen updates until done
  Application.ScreenUpdating = False

' Select all cells
  Cells.Select
```

continues

Listing 4.9. continued

```
' Set the row height of all cells to 15
  Selection.RowHeight = 15

' Select row one
  Rows("1:1").Select

' Set the row height of row one to 25.5
  Selection.RowHeight = 25.5

' Set row one to bold
  Selection.Font.Bold = True

' Allow field names to wrap
  Selection.WrapText = True

' Set a bottom double underline border for row one
  Selection.Borders(xlBottom).LineStyle = xlDouble

' Select all cells
  Cells.Select

' Resize the column widths
  Selection.EntireColumn.AutoFit

' Start with Column B
  intColumn = 2

' Break out of the loop when past the last column
  Do While intColumn <= Selection.SpecialCells(xlLastCell).Column

    ' Insert a column
      Cells(1, intColumn).EntireColumn.Insert

    ' Set the column width on the new column to 2
      Columns(intColumn).ColumnWidth = 2

    ' Jump to the next column
      intColumn = intColumn + 2

  Loop

' Move back to cell A1
  Cells(1, 1).Select

' Print Page Setup options:

  With ActiveSheet.PageSetup

    ' Repeat row one at the top of each page
      .PrintTitleRows = "$1:$1"

    ' Headers
      .LeftHeader = "&D"
      .CenterHeader = "NorthWind Traders"
      .RightHeader = "File: &F    Sheet: &A"
```

```
' Footers
  .LeftFooter = ""
  .CenterFooter = "Page &P of &N"
  .RightFooter = ""

' Hide grid lines
  .PrintGridlines = False

' Print in landscape
  .Orientation = xlLandscape

End With

Application.ScreenUpdating = True

PrettyPrinterDone:
  Exit Sub

PrettyPrinterError:
  Application.ScreenUpdating = True
  MsgBox Error$(), 48, "Pretty Printer"
  Resume PrettyPrinterDone

End Sub
```

Creating and Installing a Menu Add-In

To make Pretty Printer really useful, you need to be able to activate it from Excel while in any workbook in which you imported some data. This kind of functionality is what *menu add-ins* are all about—the ability to extend Excel by adding your own menu command.

The following instructions are going to seem a bit strange. I could say that the following is for advanced users; but to be honest, you are entering the realm of the weird here. Creating your own menu add-ins isn't the standard task you would be doing every day in Excel.

First, you need a version of the workbook that contains only Module1.

1. Delete the sheet with the imported data and all the other empty worksheets.

   To delete a worksheet, click the tab to select that sheet. Then use the Edit|Delete Sheet command.

2. Use the Insert|Macro|MS Excel 4.0 Macro command (as shown in Figure 4.34) to create a macro sheet named Macro1.

   You need this macro sheet temporarily in order to use the Insert|Name command.

FIGURE 4.34.

The data worksheets have been deleted and an Excel 4.0 macro sheet is being added.

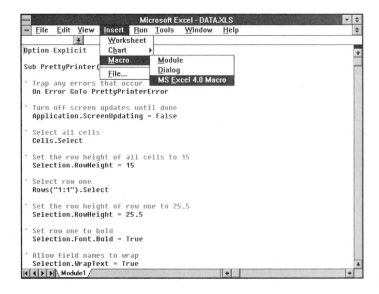

A name in Excel is an identifier for a cell, range, or expression. Names are typically used to make worksheet formulas easier to read.

What you do here is define a couple of special names that are required to make a menu add-in installable through the **T**ools|**A**dd-Ins command.

3. In the Macro1 sheet, select **I**nsert|**N**ame|**D**efine command.

Excel displays the Define Name dialog box. To define a name, enter the name to create at the Names in **W**orkbook text box and enter the definition of the name at the *Refers to:* text box. (See Figure 4.35.)

The *Refers to:* text box is difficult to use for editing a long entry. Pressing an arrow key drops the current cell coordinate into the text box rather than just moves the text cursor. This is because names in Excel typically refer to a cell address or range, but may also be used as formulas.

FIGURE 4.35.

Entering names in Excel.

Menu Add-In Special Names

Define the following three names, each of which is preceded by two underscores:

```
__Command      ={10,"Tools","Pretty Printer","PrettyPrinter",
               1,"t","Format imported data with field names on
               the first row."}
__DemandLoad =True
__ReadOnly   =True
```

The `__Command` Name installs a menu command into Excel's menu. `__Command` can be defined as a list, as in the example above, or it can be defined as a horizontal range that contains the same contents, one argument per cell.

The first argument indicates to which Excel menubar to add the command. The value for the menubar that is displayed when editing a worksheet is 10.

The second argument indicates which menu to add the command to, and the third argument is the name of the command as it appears on the menu.

The fourth argument is the name of the subroutine that gets called when your command is used. In this case, the `PrettyPrinter` subroutine is invoked upon selecting this command.

The fifth argument indicates the position in which the command should be inserted on the menu.

The sixth argument indicates which character should be used as an accelerator key. This one is a hit-or-miss thing; because you don't know what other commands were added by other menu add-ins, it's possible to use the same accelerator key as another command. **P** was already used by the Excel **Tools|P**rotection menu command, so I used **t**.

The eighth argument is the text that appears on the status line when the new menu item is selected.

The `__DemandLoad` Name is used to make your menu add-in "demand loaded." This means that only portions of the worksheet are loaded on Excel startup, and the rest is loaded only after the command is selected. You want to use this so that your add-in doesn't slow down Excel at startup; otherwise, your add-in will be too much of a nuisance to have loaded.

The `__ReadOnly` Name indicates that the final worksheet can't be modified.

Do not delete the macro sheet from the workbook. It is needed to keep the newly defined names available.

Add-In Enabled

Now that your add-in is set up to install a menu command and be demand loaded, you can focus on the actual installation itself. A menu add-in is installed through the Add-Ins dialog box from the **Tools|Add-Ins** menu command.

The Add-Ins dialog box displays the name of the add-in and a short description. (See Figure 4.36.)

FIGURE 4.36.

Pretty Printer will be installable through the Add-Ins dialog box.

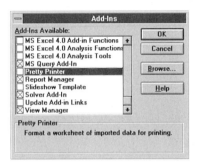

Where does this information come from? Well, this one had me stumped for a while, but I got the answer from the helpful folks monitoring the Excel forum on CompuServe. Two of the fields in the Summary Info dialog box from the **File|Summary Info** command are used.

1. Select the **File|Summary Info** command.
2. Enter Pretty Printer at the **Title** text box.
3. Enter a short description in the **Description** text box.

   Figure 4.37 shows the entries in the Summary Info dialog box.

FIGURE 4.37.

The Add-Ins dialog box uses the Title and Description fields from the Summary Info dialog box.

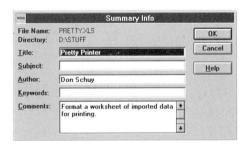

Creating the .XLA File

The final step to make your add-in installable is to create an .XLA file.

1. Save the workbook as PRETTY.XLS.

   This is going to be your backup of the code, because a workbook saved as a menu add-in (.XLA file) can no longer be edited.

2. From the **T**ools menu, select the Ma**k**e Add-In command.

3. The file to save as defaults to PRETTY.XLA (see Figure 4.38). Press OK.

4. Close the workbook.

FIGURE 4.38.
Saving the final .XLA file.

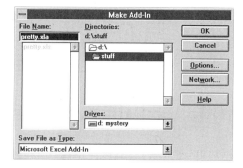

The add-in is now complete and ready to install.

User Installation

You can now install Pretty Printer in the Excel menu.

1. From the **T**ools menu select the **A**dd-Ins command.

   Pretty Printer won't show in the list of available add-ins until the Pretty Printer add-in is loaded at least once.

2. Press the **B**rowse button, and from the File Open dialog box, find and select the PRETTY.XLA file.

   Installing a menu add-in doesn't take effect until you restart Excel.

3. Exit Excel and start it up again.

   Now from the **T**ools menu you see Pretty Printer as the first command on the list, as shown in Figure 4.39.

4. Import some new data or load the DATA.XLS workbook saved earlier.

5. Select the Pretty Printer command from the Tools menu.

Because Pretty Printer is demand loaded, you will see a message on the status bar that PRETTY.XLA is loading. Next there will be a few moments while the `PrettyPrinter` subroutine executes and then the worksheet is formatted!

FIGURE 4.39.

*The added Pretty
Printer command.*

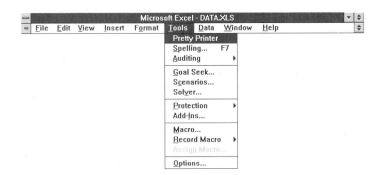

After using Pretty Printer on a worksheet, you can add formulas and make any other modifications to the worksheet before you send it to the printer for the final result.

Pretty Printer Challenge

Keep an eye out for any modifications you frequently make to worksheets, and record or program your own set of utilities to add to the Excel menu. See if you can successfully create your own installable Excel add-in.

Summary

In this chapter you not only produced a great utility, but you learned a lot about Excel in the process. Here's a list of what you did:

- Created an ODBC data source for Microsoft Query
- Created a query in Microsoft Query and imported the data into a worksheet
- Developed a prototype for Pretty Printer's expected results
- Recorded Pretty Printer code in two sessions
- Modified recorded code to make it tighter and more readable, and to give it additional functionality
- Used online help to explain what you didn't know about the recorded code
- Took a quick look at debugging Excel VBA code
- Made the Pretty Printer utility an installable menu add-in

In the next chapter, you'll create a second menu add-in for Excel called Calendar Wizard.

CHAPTER 5

Excel: Calendar Wizard

Now it's time to get to some serious coding fun. Let's apply everything you just learned in the last chapter and create a wizard in Excel.

Creating a wizard gives you an opportunity to find out what it is like to work with Excel's dialog box sheets. Pretty Printer was almost void of any user interface, and you can't expect to be able to create all your programs like that, can you?

Calendar Wizard (shown in Figure 5.1) can be used to quickly generate a printable monthly calendar as an Excel worksheet. Once the calendar is generated, important dates can be marked and reminders written in before you send the calendar to the printer for a hard copy.

FIGURE 5.1.

Calendar Wizard is a menu add-in that builds a calendar worksheet in your workbook.

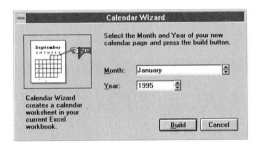

Calendar Wizard generates a single calendar page at a time. To create a calendar for a full year, you could run Calendar Wizard once for each month, and it inserts a new page into your workbook each time.

Let's start with the engine first, and do the user interface last. The engine is going to be the easy part because you can take advantage of using recorded code once again.

I'll save some repetition of what I covered in the last chapter by not detailing all the steps required to record and write the code that generates the calendar. The complete subroutine will be listed, and I'll explain the sections of interest so you understand what the code is doing.

For those of you following along closely and actually building the projects as you go, you should be able to recreate Calendar Wizard from scratch by following the details provided here and by using what you learned in Chapter 4, "Excel: Pretty Printer."

Creating a Calendar Prototype

The first step is to experiment and develop a prototype by hand so that you know what the code's target result is. The prototype I came up with is fairly basic as far as calendar pages go. See Figure 5.2 for what the calendar looks like when printed.

FIGURE 5.2.

Print preview of the calendar worksheet prototype.

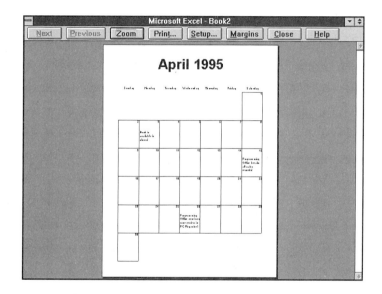

Yes, believe it or not, that *is* an Excel worksheet.

The steps to create the calendar are simple enough, but there are many. One has to resize rows, set font sizes, justify text, turn on borders, enter day titles, and enter numbers for the days. It's definitely something you wouldn't want to have to create by hand more than once.

When creating the prototype, I noticed that a calendar looks more attractive if you don't draw the squares before and after the days of the given month. This might be a special programming problem; we'll see.

Also, some months span across six rows, not just five. You run into this when you have a 30-day month that starts on a Saturday, or if you have a 31-day month that starts on a Friday or a Saturday. I sized the squares appropriately in my prototype so I could display all six rows on a printed page.

Figure 5.3 shows how the calendar looks when you view it in the worksheet.

FIGURE 5.3.

The calendar worksheet.

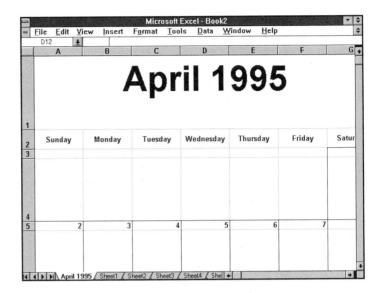

The Calendar Wizard Engine

Basically, the code to generate the calendar was written by recording each change as it was made to a worksheet. I wrote down the steps as I made my prototype and reproduced them in an empty worksheet with the macro recorder on.

I recorded only a few steps at a time, reviewing and testing the code along the way. This is the same way you created Pretty Printer in Chapter 4. Eventually I came to parts of the program that required some coding by hand.

For example, you can record entering a number for a day, setting its font to bold, and right-justifying it. But you can't record the logic to determine which day of the week a particular day falls on and how many days are in the month.

Take a brief look at Listing 5.1. It is the complete and final `CreateCalendar` subroutine. The subroutine is passed two parameters so it can generate a calendar for a specified month and year. In the next few sections, I'll explain how it all works.

Listing 5.1. The `CreateCalendar` **subroutine.**

```
Sub CreateCalendar(intMonth As Integer, intYear As Integer)

    Dim varDate As Variant
    Dim varNextMonth As Variant

    Dim intRow As Integer
    Dim intDay As Integer
```

```
   Dim intDaysInMonth As Integer
   Dim n As Integer

   On Error GoTo CreateCalendarError

' Get a date/time variable of the first day of the month
   varDate = DateValue(intMonth & "/01/" & intYear)

' Determine number of days in the month
   intMonth = intMonth + 1
   If intMonth > 12 Then
    intMonth = 1
     intYear = intYear + 1
   End If
   If intYear > 2078 Then
   ' Can't get a DateValue for 1/1/2079
     intDaysInMonth = 31
   Else
     varNextMonth = DateValue(intMonth & "/01/" & intYear)
     intDaysInMonth = varNextMonth - varDate
   End If

' Start with a new worksheet
   Sheets.Add

' Create columns for each day
   Columns("A:G").ColumnWidth = 12.29

' Create a banner displaying the month and year in big letters
   Rows("1:1").RowHeight = 100.5
   With Range("A1:G1")
     .NumberFormat = "@"
     .HorizontalAlignment = xlCenterAcrossSelection
     .VerticalAlignment = xlTop
     .WrapText = False
     .Orientation = xlHorizontal
   End With
   ActiveCell.FormulaR1C1 = Format(varDate, "mmmm yyyy")
   ActiveSheet.Name = Format(varDate, "mmmm yyyy")
   With Range("A1").Font
     .Name = "Arial"
     .FontStyle = "Bold"
     .Size = 48
   End With

' Create titles for the days of the week
   Rows("2:2").RowHeight = 26.25
   With Range("A2:G2")
     .Font.Bold = True
     .HorizontalAlignment = xlCenter
     .VerticalAlignment = xlCenter
   End With
   Range("A2").Select
   ActiveCell.FormulaR1C1 = "Sunday"
   Selection.AutoFill Destination:=Range("A2:G2"), Type:=xlFillDefault
```

continues

Listing 5.1. continued

```
' Create rows to hold day numbers and calendar notes
  For intRow = 3 To 13 Step 2
    With Range(Cells(intRow, 1), Cells(intRow, 7))
      .Font.Bold = True
      .HorizontalAlignment = xlRight
    End With
    Rows(intRow + 1).RowHeight = 85.5
    With Range(Cells(intRow + 1, 1), Cells(intRow + 1, 7))
      .HorizontalAlignment = xlLeft
      .VerticalAlignment = xlCenter
      .WrapText = True
    End With
  Next intRow

' Which day of the week is the first day of the month
  intDay = WeekDay(varDate)

' Write the day numbers and border formats for squares.
  intRow = 3
  For n = 1 To intDaysInMonth

    Cells(intRow, intDay).Select
    Selection.FormulaR1C1 = CStr(n)
    Selection.Borders(xlLeft).Weight = xlThin
    Selection.Borders(xlRight).Weight = xlThin
    Selection.Borders(xlTop).Weight = xlThin

    Cells(intRow + 1, intDay).Select
    Selection.Borders(xlLeft).Weight = xlThin
    Selection.Borders(xlRight).Weight = xlThin
    Selection.Borders(xlBottom).Weight = xlThin

    intDay = intDay + 1
    If intDay > 7 Then
      intDay = 1
      intRow = intRow + 2
    End If
  Next n

' Clear the highlighted row and move to cell A1
Cells(1, 1).Select

' Page Setup, including all defaults in the code
  With ActiveSheet.PageSetup
    .PrintArea = "$A$1:$G$14"
    .LeftHeader = ""
    .CenterHeader = ""
    .RightHeader = ""
    .LeftFooter = ""
    .CenterFooter = ""
    .RightFooter = ""
    .LeftMargin = Application.InchesToPoints(0)
    .RightMargin = Application.InchesToPoints(0)
    .TopMargin = Application.InchesToPoints(0)
```

```
      .BottomMargin = Application.InchesToPoints(0)
      .HeaderMargin = Application.InchesToPoints(0.5)
      .FooterMargin = Application.InchesToPoints(0.5)
      .PrintHeadings = False
      .PrintGridlines = False
      .PrintNotes = False
'     .PrintQuality = 300
      .CenterHorizontally = True
      .CenterVertically = True
      .Orientation = xlPortrait
      .Draft = False
      .PaperSize = xlPaperLetter
      .FirstPageNumber = xlAutomatic
      .Order = xlDownThenOver
      .BlackAndWhite = False
      .Zoom = 100
   End With

CreateCalendarDone:
   Exit Sub

CreateCalendarError:
   MsgBox Error$(), 48, "CreateCalendar"
   Resume CreateCalendarDone

End Sub
```

NOTE

Be watchful about what code the Macro Recorder produces for your programs!
In the preceding listing, the following line is commented out:

```
'     .PrintQuality = 300
```

This line was generated by the Macro Recorder when selecting page setup
options with the File|Page Setup command. As recorded, the print quality
produced is targeted for a 300 dot-per-inch laser printer. This setting would
produce an error message when you attempt to print to another type of printer.

If you comment the line out, the print quality can default to what the user
currently has set in the Page Setup dialog box.

Which Day of the Week is Day 1?

To handle dates for a calendar, you would think the program would have to be somewhat sophisticated. Really, though, it's not.

In creating Calendar Wizard, I didn't spend an iota of time researching the intricacies of how to calculate the proper placement of the days on a given month's calendar. (I did that kind of stuff before in my C days, and it's not my idea of having fun.) Instead, I let Excel's built-in date functions do the work for me.

The first problem to solve is on which day of the week to write day 1 for a given month and year. The following lines solve this problem:

```
varDate = DateValue(intMonth & "/01/" & intYear)
intDay = WeekDay(varDate)
```

The first line creates a Date variable for the first day of the month in question. It builds a date for the first day of the month as a string, and then passes it to the DateValue function which does the work of converting it into a Basic Date variable.

The next line uses the WeekDay function to determine on which day of the week the date of the Date variable would fall.

How Many Days in a Month?

The next problem to solve is how many days are in the chosen month. A Date variable stores the date using a special numbering system where the integer part of the number represents the day, and the fractional part of the number represents the time of day. You can subtract the integer part of one Date variable with the integer part of another and determine how many days apart the two values are.

Calculating the number of days in a month is easy then. Get a Date variable for the first day of next month, and subtract from it the Date variable for the first day of this month. The result is how many days are in this month.

Listing 5.2 is the portion of the program that does this.

Listing 5.2. The CreateCalendar **subroutine.**

```
' Determine number of days in the month
  intMonth = intMonth + 1
  If intMonth > 12 Then
    intMonth = 1
    intYear = intYear + 1
  End If
  If intYear > 2078 Then
  ' Can't get a DateValue for 1/1/2079
    intDaysInMonth = 31
  Else
    varNextMonth = DateValue(intMonth & "/01/" & intYear)
    intDaysInMonth = varNextMonth - varDate
  End If
```

First, the `intMonth` variable is incremented to the next month. If the month value is moving from December to January, the year is incremented and the month set back to 1, for January.

Next, the code handles a weird case that occurs only if you have chosen to create the calendar for December of 2078. I wanted Calendar Wizard to be correct and robust for any month within Excel's Date variable's range, so the code has to deal with this special case.

The last year that Excel Date variables deal with is 2078. Later you will set limits on the dialog box sheet controls to make sure that December of 2078 is the last possible month that a user is allowed to select in Calendar Wizard.

Following the code…you know coming in the subroutine that the `intYear` variable is going to be 2078 or less. If the `intYear` variable is incremented within the procedure to 2079, you know you are dealing with December of 2078 and the number of days is 31 because December always has 31 days.

That's handled right here:

```
If intYear > 2078 Then
' Can't get a DateValue for 1/1/2079
  intDaysInMonth = 31
Else
```

Finally, if you aren't dealing with the special case I've mentioned, you can get the Date variable for next month's first day and calculate the number of days in this month by subtraction, as described earlier.

```
varNextMonth = DateValue(intMonth & "/01/" & intYear)
    intDaysInMonth = varNextMonth - varDate
```

You now have all the information you need to place the day numbers on the calendar correctly. It may seem lazy to be able to produce a calendar without any concern for when a leap year falls, but if the capability is there in your development tools, use it.

Drawing the Calendar

The titles for the days of the week are entered into the calendar by using the following lines:

```
Range("A2").Select
ActiveCell.FormulaR1C1 = "Sunday"
Selection.AutoFill Destination:=Range("A2:G2"), Type:=xlFillDefault
```

The magic part is the `AutoFill` method, which uses Excel's Auto-Fill feature to write in the remaining days after Sunday. This code was created by using the Auto-Fill feature with the macro recorder turned on.

For each day in the calendar, two cells are used. The top one is shorter and is right-justified and bold to hold the day of the month number.

The bottom cell makes up the rest of the square. To display notes written on the calendar attractively, this cell is left-justified and centered vertically. My first idea was to use several rows to make up this part, but I realized it would be bothersome that way when I wrote an entry that spans multiple lines. The user would have to handle word-wrapping manually. Nix that idea!

It turns out that making the borders appear only on actual days of the month was easy. As each number for a day is entered, the borders are set to be drawn all the way around the square.

This means that adjacent borders are actually set to be drawn twice, but it didn't make any difference in the final output, and trying to "optimize" this would have been silly.

The top cell in a day has a day number written to it and is drawn by the following code:

```
Cells(intRow, intDay).Select
    Selection.FormulaR1C1 = CStr(n)
    Selection.Borders(xlLeft).Weight = xlThin
    Selection.Borders(xlRight).Weight = xlThin
    Selection.Borders(xlTop).Weight = xlThin
```

The bottom cell in a day is drawn by the following code:

```
Cells(intRow + 1, intDay).Select
    Selection.Borders(xlLeft).Weight = xlThin
    Selection.Borders(xlRight).Weight = xlThin
    Selection.Borders(xlBottom).Weight = xlThin
```

The variable, n, holds the day of the month. A separate variable, intDay, is used to hold which day you are currently on. When intDay is greater than 7, it wraps back around to 1 for Sunday again.

The loop that controls this is shown in Listing 5.3.

Listing 5.3. Looping through the days and rows on a calendar.

```
For n = 1 To intDaysInMonth

    ' Code to draw a day goes here
    .
    .
    .

    intDay = intDay + 1
    If intDay > 7 Then
      intDay = 1
      intRow = intRow + 2
    End If
  Next n
```

The program doesn't have to be concerned with which day of the week is the last day of the month. It just fills in days, starting with the day it knows is first, continues until it reaches the total days per month, and then stops.

To finish up, I recorded setting some of the options in the Page Setup dialog box. In the Margin tab, I checked the check boxes to center the page horizontally and vertically when it is printed.

On the Sheet tab, I entered the Print Area from A1 to G14. This always prints all six calendar rows so that calendars of five or six rows each print centered in the same manner. On the Sheet tab, I also turned off the option to print gridlines.

While writing and testing the function, I hard-coded the month and year, as shown in Listing 5.4.

Listing 5.4. `CreateCalendar`, **hard-coded during development.**

```
Sub CreateCalendar()

  Dim intMonth As Integer
  Dim intYear As Integer

  intMonth = 9
  intYear = 1994
  .
  .
  .
```

This way I could run and debug the subroutine by selecting it in the Macro dialog box and pressing the Run button. I created and deleted many worksheets before the program generated a complete and good-looking calendar page.

Dialog Boxes in Excel

That was the easy part. The next job is to apply Excel's dialog box sheets to create a user interface for the wizard.

Dialog boxes in Excel are like dialog boxes in Word. There just isn't a whole lot of stuff there.

If you are as spoiled as I am and you have been playing with Visual Basic and Access every day for the last couple of years, you are in for some culture shock here. For instance, controls on dialog box sheets have only one event to attach code to!

Yep, I was shocked. However, after I began to get comfortable using dialog box sheets, I began to appreciate them more. I think you will too. Their unique aspects can be kind of fun.

For one, a dialog box sheet is always available for reading or for setting its values, regardless of whether the dialog box is currently displayed. That's because a dialog box sheet is just another worksheet in the workbook. You wouldn't expect that you couldn't reference values in a cell just because it isn't on the worksheet currently on-screen, right? Well, dialog box sheets and their contents work in the same way.

I started to enjoy the simplicity of dialog box sheets. Although I couldn't control the environment as well as I could in VB or Access, I didn't have to work with all that complexity either. That can be a big help when you want to crank out something quickly.

I figure this simplicity has another benefit, in that it probably helps Excel trim its resource usage. Access has a complex and full-featured user interface model, and it's known for being a resource hog. You can't have everything without paying for it somewhere.

Dialog box sheets seem to be based on the same technology already in the product to support worksheets. A neat benefit from this is that you can place any of the controls on a regular worksheet also, because they are not restricted to dialog box sheets alone.

TRY THIS! QUESTION 5.1.

Try adding to a worksheet a button that clears a range of cells when you press it.

Creating Calendar Wizard

The best way to understand how Calendar Wizard was created is to rebuild it. Here are the steps to do it.

1. Start with an empty workbook.
2. Create a module sheet with the **Insert**|**Macro**|**Module** command.
3. Delete all the other worksheets by selecting them and using the **Edit**|**Delete** **Sheet** command.

   Select more than one sheet by holding down the Ctrl key as you click each worksheet tab. Using the **Edit**|**Delete** Sheet command then deletes all of the selected sheets in one step.

You can set an option in Excel to create less worksheets in a new workbook. Then you won't have to delete so many worksheets each time you want to get rid of the extras.

In the Options dialog box from the **T**ools|**O**ptions command, select the General tab and change the value at the **S**heets in New Workbook prompt.

4. In the module sheet, enter the `CreateCalendar` subroutine in Listing 5.1 at the beginning of the chapter and shown in Figure 5.4.

FIGURE 5.4.

Reconstructing Calendar Wizard.

```
Microsoft Excel - CALWIZ.XLS
  File  Edit  View  Insert  Run  Tools  Window  Help

Option Explicit

Sub CreateCalendar(intMonth As Integer, intYear As Integer)

    Dim varDate As Variant
    Dim varNextMonth As Variant

    Dim intRow As Integer
    Dim intDay As Integer
    Dim intDaysInMonth As Integer
    Dim n As Integer

    On Error GoTo CreateCalendarError

' Get a date/time variable of the first day of the month
    varDate = DateValue(intMonth & "/01/" & intYear)

' Determine number of days in the month
    intMonth = intMonth + 1
    If intMonth > 12 Then
      intMonth = 1
      intYear = intYear + 1
    End If
    If intYear > 2078 Then
' Can't get a DateValue for 1/1/2078
      intDaysInMonth = 31
    Else

 Dialog1  Module1
```

Creating the Calendar Wizard Dialog Box

Now let's create a dialog box sheet and build the user interface.

Select the **I**nsert|**M**acro|**D**ialog command, as shown in Figure 5.5.

Excel adds a new dialog box to the workbook. The dialog box already has OK and Cancel buttons on it. You can resize the dialog box, but repositioning it has no effect during run-time because it will always be displayed as a centered modal dialog box.

The Forms toolbar is used to select the type of control that the mouse cursor draws on the dialog box sheet. (See Figure 5.6.)

FIGURE 5.5.
Adding a Dialog box sheet.

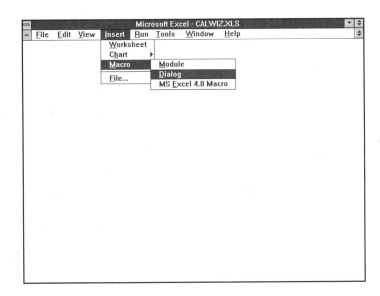

FIGURE 5.6.
Starting a new dialog box.

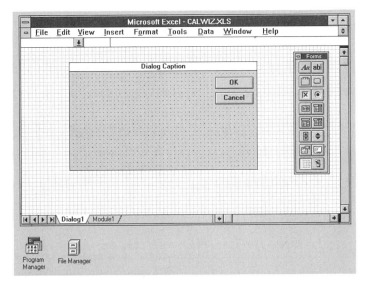

Design Considerations

Part of the idea behind wizards is to keep to the bare minimum the amount of prompting you do. Wizards aren't built to handle a variety of things in a variety of ways. That's what regular, and less easy to use, programs are for.

In your case, all you need to ask is for what month and what year they would like their calendar page generated. Then slam-dunk, you build it.

Excel dialog box sheets include a *spinner* control. That one caught my eye right away as the perfect way to allow a user to select a month and year. When the dialog box is first shown to the user, it should show the current month and year as default values. The user uses the spinners to move through months or years. When the month changes from December to January, the year should automatically increment, and automatically decrement when going backward from January to December.

Now you have your program spec. The only thing you left out is to dress up the form with a bitmap and some help text.

Adding Controls

The first control to add to the dialog box sheet is an embedded OLE object that displays the Calendar Wizard bitmap.

1. Select the **Insert|Object** command.
2. In the Object dialog box, click the Create from File tab.
3. Select a bitmap file. See Figure 5.7.

   CALWIZ.BMP is included on this book's companion CD-ROM if you want to use that; otherwise, be creative and draw your own.

FIGURE 5.7.

Inserting a bitmap on an Excel dialog box sheet.

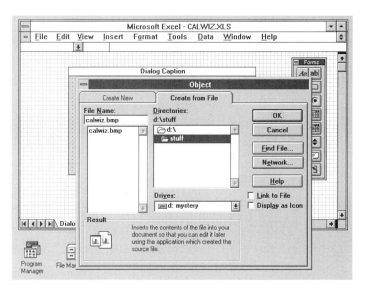

4. Position the picture on the dialog box as shown in Figure 5.8.

FIGURE 5.8.

*Positioning the
Calendar Wizard
bitmap.*

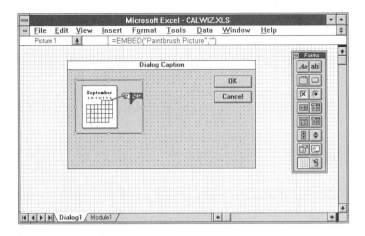

When you select a control on the dialog box, you see the name of the control on the left side of the formula bar in what's called the Name Box. The imported picture will likely be named `Picture 1`.

To rename a control, click the Name Box, enabling a text cursor in it, then erase the current name and type in the new one. I renamed the picture to `pic1`, and used Hungarian type names for each of the additional controls dropped on the form.

Next, make the following changes to the dialog sheet.

1. Click the OK button and then press the Delete key to remove it. Remove the Cancel button also. You will add your own buttons to the form later.
2. Resize the dialog box to allow for more room to drop controls.

   You may have to work with the size of the dialog box as you add controls.
3. Double-click the caption of the dialog box to make the text cursor available. Enter `Calendar Wizard` as the banner.
4. With the dialog box selected, enter `dlgCalendarWizard` in the Name Box as the name of the dialog box. (See Figure 5.9.)

Add two labels to the dialog sheet to display hint and instruction text.

1. Click the Label button on the Forms toolbox.
2. Draw a label under the picture on the dialog box, as shown in Figure 5.10.
3. Double-click the label control. Enter the following text into the label:

   `Calendar Wizard creates a calendar worksheet in your current Excel workbook.`

4. Rename the label to `lblHint`.

FIGURE 5.9.
Setting the dialog box caption and name.

Name Box

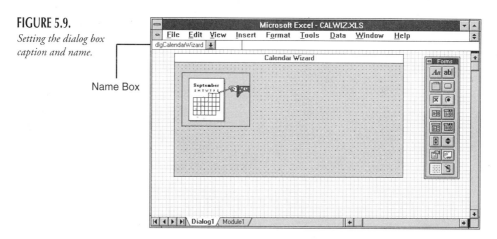

FIGURE 5.10.
Adding a label to the Calendar Wizard dialog box.

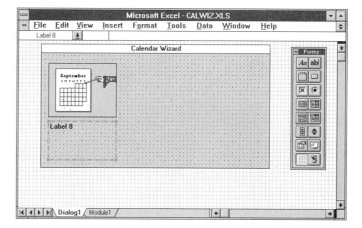

5. Add a second label, this time to the right of the bitmap and spanning across the top of the dialog box. (See Figure 5.11.)

6. Enter the following text into the new label:

   `Select the Month and Year of your new calendar page and press the build button.`

7. Name this label `lblInstructions`.

Add edit boxes and corresponding labels and spinners for entering the month and year.

1. Create two more labels named `lblMonth` and `lblYear`. They should display "Month:" and "Year:" as shown in Figure 5.12.

2. Click the Edit Box button on the Forms toolbox.

FIGURE 5.11.
Adding a second label.

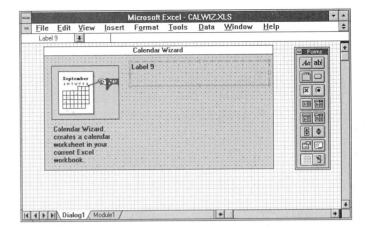

FIGURE 5.12.
*Adding Month
and Year labels.*

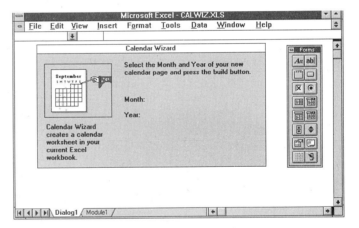

3. Draw an edit box to the right of the lblMonth label. Name the edit box
   edtMonth.

4. Create an edtYear edit box to the right of the lblYear label.

   Figure 5.13 shows the Month and Year edit boxes being added to the Calendar
   Wizard dialog.

5. Click the Spinner button on the Form toolbox.

6. Immediately to the right of the Month and Year edit boxes, add a spinner
   control for each, as shown in Figure 5.14. Label the spinner controls spnMonth
   and spnYear.

Add the remaining controls to the dialog sheet, a label and two buttons.

FIGURE 5.13.
Adding the Month and Year edit boxes.

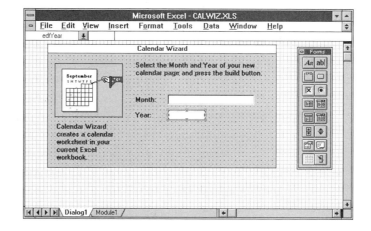

FIGURE 5.14.
Adding Spinner controls.

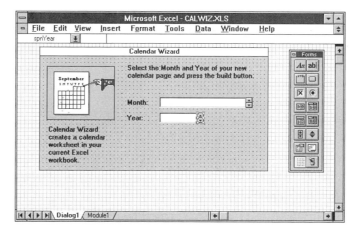

1. Add a label at the bottom of the dialog box to display a Building... message. Name this control lblBuilding.

2. Click the Create Button button on the Form toolbox.

3. Add two buttons to the dialog box.

4. Double-click the first button, and enter Build for the text displayed on the button. Rename the button to cmdBuild.

5. Enter Cancel as the displayed text for the second button. Rename this button to cmdCancel. See Figure 5.15.

Set the properties for the controls on the dialog box.

FIGURE 5.15.

*Getting all the controls
on the Calendar
Wizard dialog box.*

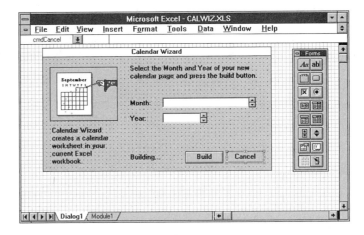

Rather than have a property sheet like Access or Visual Basic, controls in Excel get their few properties set through the Format Object dialog box.

1. Click the spinner control used with the Month edit box.

2. Select the Format|Object command as shown in Figure 5.16.

FIGURE 5.16.

*Setting properties on a
control in Excel.*

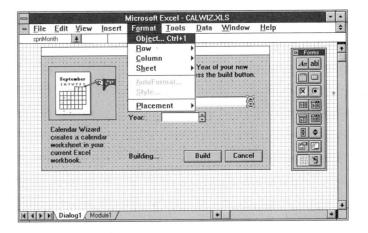

3. In the Format Object dialog box, click the Control tab and make sure the spnMonth spinner control has the following properties set as shown in Figure 5.17:

    Minimum Value: 0

    Ma**x**imum Value: 13

    Incremental Change: 1

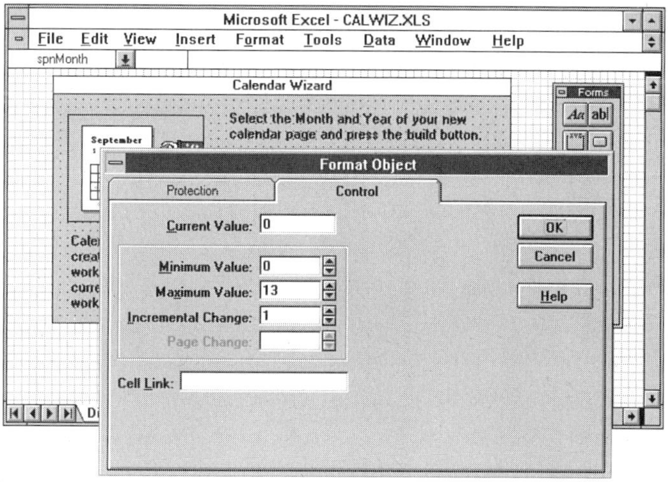

FIGURE 5.17.

Setting the spnMonth spinner to allow values from 0 to 13.

4. Set the properties for the spnYear control as follows:

   Minimum Value: 0

   Ma**x**imum Value: 180

   Incremental Change: 1

5. Click the cmdBuild button and select the Format|Object command.

6. In the Format Object dialog box, click the Control tab.

   A button in an Excel dialog box may have any of the following properties turned on:

   Default—Button is clicked by pressing the Enter key.

   Cancel—Button is clicked by pressing the Esc key.

   Di**s**miss—Dialog box is closed by clicking this button.

   H**e**lp—Button is clicked by pressing the F1 key.

7. Check the **D**efault and Di**s**miss properties (see Figure 5.18) and click OK.

8. Set the properties of the Cancel button so that the **C**ancel and Di**s**miss options are checked.

The last business you need to take care of before adding code is set the tab order of the controls on the dialog box. The tab order determines the order of controls when you press Tab to move forward and Shift-Tab to move backward through the controls on the form.

FIGURE 5.18.

Setting options for the
`cmdBuild` *button.*

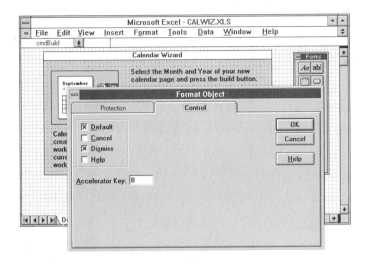

1. Select the **Tools|Tab** Order command.

   Because you took the time to create names for your controls, you can quickly identify each one in the tab order list. (See Figure 5.19.)

   When setting the tab order of controls on a dialog box, you want to think about what arrangement would be the most convenient to the person having to use the form.

FIGURE 5.19.

*Setting the tab order for
the Calendar Wizard
dialog box.*

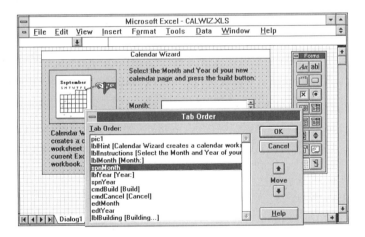

A good practice is to think of the user as someone who has absolutely no time or patience for using the software, even though you might be very proud of what you created. For this finicky, stressed, and totally impatient person, what can you do to get them in and out of the dialog box as quickly as possible?

The answer I came up with was to have the spnMonth control as the first control that can receive focus in the tab order. This allows the user to press the Up or Down keys to select a month, then press Enter to build it.

2. Set the Calendar Wizard dialog box's tab order to the following:

   pic1

   lblHint

   lblInstructions

   lblMonth

   spnMonth

   lblYear

   spnYear

   cmdBuild

   cmdCancel

   edtMonth

   edtYear

   lblBuilding

   Note that although the label and picture controls are listed in the tab order, they never receive focus. The reason for including them is so you can assign an accelerator key to them.

   For example, you can open the Format Objects dialog box and assign M as the accelerator key for the Month label. When Alt-M is pressed, the control immediately following the Month label control in the tab order receives focus.

3. Use the Format|Object command to edit the properties of the lblMonth and lblYear labels. Assign the M accelerator key to lblMonth and the Y accelerator key to lblYear.

Coding an Excel Dialog Box

Designing and putting together a dialog box is fun. Seeing it work in action for the first time is even more fun. To get there, you're going to have get into the code again.

Here's a little bit of background before you get started…

To put code behind the controls on a dialog box, you select the control on the dialog box sheet and click the Edit Code button on the toolbox. It's the button that looks like a tab control, but it's intended to represent a module sheet.

Excel creates a stub of code for you in a new module sheet. The code in Listing 5.5 was generated this way:

Listing 5.5. A generated event subroutine declaration.

```
'
'  Button1_Click Macro
'
'
Sub Button1_Click()
End Sub
```

VBA places all the code on the same edit space, one function after another. Microsoft Access and earlier versions of Visual Basic would separate the procedures from each other, each one having its own edit space. You would browse a list of procedures and select the one you wanted to work on.

VBA has preserved that same kind of interface. You can use the Object Browser as a way to navigate the code by looking at a list of modules and procedures within them, just as you do with Access and the earlier Visual Basics. It's easy. Press F2, and the Object Browser pops up as shown in Figure 5.20.

FIGURE 5.20.

Using the Excel Object Browser to navigate through your code.

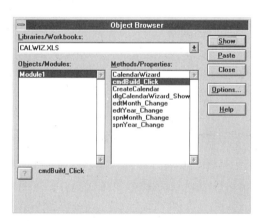

Double-click any subroutine or function, and Excel opens the module window with the cursor placed on the first line inside the declaration.

Object Browser (shown in Figure 5.21) is much better than the View Procedures window in Access 2.0. Not only do you see how your code is organized, but it also is a directory to all the information you need to use VBA and the Excel environment. Select VBA, and it lists all the constants and functions categorized by type. Select any item and press the question button; online help opens to that topic.

FIGURE 5.21.

Object Browser is a directory to Excel programming help.

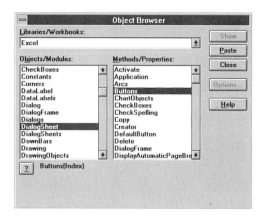

Select Excel at the **Libraries/Workbooks** prompt, and the entire object hierarchy is displayed. This is where Excel becomes a vast and rich programming environment. Virtually every feature within the product is available to the programmer here. The only problem is sorting through it all, but that is what Object Browser is for. Remember also to cheat and use the macro recorder when all else fails, if not before.

Coding the Calendar Wizard Dialog Box

To put code behind the different events on the dialog box, you need to let Excel generate the declarations for you. You will be placing code behind the following events:

- dlgCalendarWizard_Show   When the dialog box is displayed
- spnMonth_Change   When the Month spinner is changed
- edtMonth_Change   When the Month edit box is changed
- spnYear_Change   When the Year spinner is changed
- edtYear_Change   When the Year edit box is changed
- cmdBuild_Click   When the Build button is clicked

1. Click the caption of the dialog box in the dialog box sheet.

    This should select the dialog box.

2. Click the Edit Code button on the Form toolbox.

    Excel creates a new module sheet and enters a declaration for the dlgCalendarWizard_Show subroutine. (See Figure 5.22.) This subroutine is for the dialog box's Show event.

FIGURE 5.22.

Excel generates a declaration for event code.

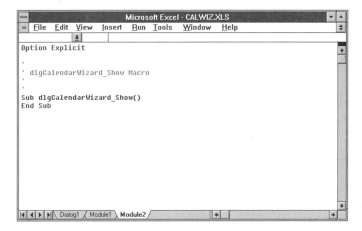

3. Click the Dialog1 tab to return to the dialog box worksheet.

4. Click the spnMonth spinner control.

5. Click the Edit Code button to generate the next subroutine declaration.

6. Repeat steps 3, 4, and 5 for each of the following controls: edtMonth edit box, spnYear spinner, edtYear edit box, and the cmdBuild button.

    The module should appear as shown in Figure 5.23.

FIGURE 5.23.

Generated declarations for six events.

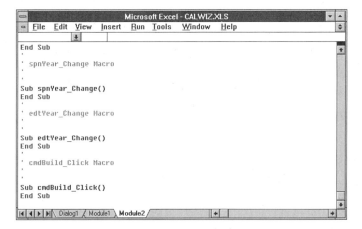

Creating the *dlgCalendarWizard_Show* Subroutine

Your job as a programmer is to fill in everything between the declaration and the closing End Sub lines. No smooth sailing here—it's coding time.

1. Add the following constant declarations after the Option Explicit line:

   ```
   Const WORKSHEET_NAME = "CALWIZ.XLS"
   ```

2. Complete the dlgCalendarWizard_Show subroutine as shown in Listing 5.6 (and also Figure 5.24).

Listing 5.6. The dlgCalendarWizard_Show **subroutine.**

```
Option Explicit

Const WORKSHEET_NAME = "CALWIZ.XLS"

'
' dlgCalendarWizard_Show Macro
'
'
Sub dlgCalendarWizard_Show()

' This subroutine gets triggered when the Calendar Wizard dialog
' is opened.

  Dim dlg As DialogSheet
  Dim spn As Spinner

  Dim varDate As Variant
  Dim intMonth As Integer
  Dim intYear As Integer

  On Error GoTo dlgCalendarWizard_ShowError

' Get the dialog
  Set dlg = Workbooks(WORKSHEET_NAME).DialogSheets("Dialog1")

' Hide the "Building..." message
  dlg.Labels("lblBuilding").Caption = ""

' Get the current month and year
  varDate = Now()
  intMonth = Month(varDate)
  intYear = Year(varDate)

' Set controls to the default values
  Set spn = dlg.Spinners("spnMonth")
  If spn.Value = 0 Then
    spn.Value = 13 - intMonth
    spnMonth_Change
  End If

  Set spn = dlg.Spinners("spnYear")
  If spn.Value = 0 Then
    spn.Value = 2079 - intYear
    spnYear_Change
  End If
```

continues

Listing 5.6. continued

```
dlgCalendarWizard_ShowDone:
  Exit Sub

dlgCalendarWizard_ShowError:
  MsgBox Error$(), 48, "dlgCalendarWizard_Show"
  Resume dlgCalendarWizard_ShowDone

End Sub
```

FIGURE 5.24.

Filling in code for the dlgCalendarWizard_Show subroutine.

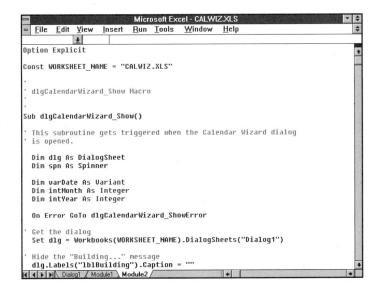

Examining the *dlgCalendarWizard_Show* Subroutine

Just before the dlgCalendarWizard_Show subroutine, you added a constant in which to store the name of the worksheet.

```
Const WORKSHEET_NAME = "CALWIZ.XLS"
```

The dlgCalendarWizard_Show subroutine, like several other subroutines you will write, starts with the following line that sets a variable pointing to the Calendar Wizard dialog box:

```
' Get the dialog
  Set dlg = Workbooks(WORKSHEET_NAME).DialogSheets("Dialog1")
```

In the preceding line, the dialog box is retrieved by first getting the object for the Calendar Wizard workbook from the workbooks collection. Within the workbook object is a DialogSheets collection from which you can retrieve the dialog box sheet by name, Dialog1.

When you create the final Calendar Wizard menu add-in, Excel saves it as CALWIZ.XLA. Before doing this you need to change the WORKSHEET_NAME constant to CALWIZ.XLA.

The next two lines hide the Building... message by erasing the caption in the lblBuilding label.

```
' Hide the "Building..." message
  dlg.Labels("lblBuilding").Caption = ""
```

Note that to reference a control on a dialog box worksheet, you use the appropriate collection. Here's a list of the collections and associated controls that you find on the Form toolbar.

Collection	Control
Buttons	Button
CheckBoxes	Check Box
DropDowns	Drop-Down
EditBoxes	Edit Box
GroupBoxes	Group Box
Labels	Label
ListBoxes	List Box
OptionButtons	Option Button
ScrollBars	Scroll Bar
Spinners	Spinner

Next in the code, the intMonth and intYear are initialized to the current month and year.

```
' Get the current month and year
  varDate = Now()
  intMonth = Month(varDate)
  intYear = Year(varDate)
```

The Show event will be triggered each time the Calendar Wizard command is selected from the Tools menu in Excel. I wanted the Month and Year values to default to the current month and year on the first time only. After that, it would be nice for them to default to the last value used so the user can click down just once to select the next month and then create the next calendar page.

The following code determines whether the default month value is used.

```
' Set controls to the default values
  Set spn = dlg.Spinners("spnMonth")
  If spn.Value = 0 Then
    spn.Value = 13 - intMonth
    spnMonth_Change
  End If
```

The spnMonth spinner is checked for a value of 0. If 0 is found, the spinner wasn't used yet, so it is set to the default.

Notice that setting the default is done by subtracting the month value from 13. This in effect reverses the month values, 1 is 12, 2 is 11, 3 is 10, and so on. I needed to do this because by default, pressing down on the spinner made the month values go down, and that felt awkward to me when using the user interface. Reversing the values makes the spinner perform as desired.

The spnMonth_Change subroutine is called to update the dialog box to display the current month. It is also the subroutine that is activated on the spnMonth's Change event, which occurs when the user clicks the up or down arrow to change the month.

The same approach is made to set the year value, except that in this case the range of values is from 1 to 2079.

```
Set spn = dlg.Spinners("spnYear")
  If spn.Value = 0 Then
    spn.Value = 2079 - intYear
    spnYear_Change
  End If
```

Creating the *spnMonth_Change* Subroutine

The next subroutine is called to update the display when the month value changes. This subroutine is triggered as a result of the spnMonth control being clicked, and it is also called by some of the other subroutines when the month text needs to be updated.

Complete the spnMonth_Change subroutine as shown in Listing 5.7.

Listing 5.7. The spnMonth_Change subroutine.

```
'
' spnMonth_Change Macro
'
'
Sub spnMonth_Change()

  Dim dlg As DialogSheet
  Dim spnMonth As Spinner
  Dim spnYear As Spinner

  Dim varDate As Variant
  Dim intMonth As Integer

  On Error GoTo spnMonth_ChangeError

  Set dlg = Workbooks(WORKSHEET_NAME).DialogSheets("Dialog1")
  Set spnMonth = dlg.Spinners("spnMonth")
```

```
    intMonth = 13 - spnMonth.Value

  If intMonth < 1 Then
    Set spnYear = dlg.Spinners("spnYear")

    spnYear.Value = spnYear.Value + 1
    spnYear_Change

    intMonth = 12
  End If

  If intMonth > 12 Then
    Set spnYear = dlg.Spinners("spnYear")

    spnYear.Value = spnYear.Value - 1
    spnYear_Change

    intMonth = 1
  End If

  spnMonth.Value = 13 - intMonth

  varDate = DateValue(CStr(intMonth) & "/01/1994")
  dlg.EditBoxes("edtMonth").Text = Format(varDate, "mmmm")
spnMonth_ChangeDone:
  Exit Sub

spnMonth_ChangeError:
  MsgBox Error$(), 48, "spnMonth_Change"
  Resume spnMonth_ChangeDone

End Sub
```

The spnMonth_Change subroutine increments the year value if going from December to January, and decrements the year if going from January to December. The spnYear_Change subroutine is called to update the Year edit box if the year changes.

The spnMonth_Change subroutine then uses the following lines to create a Date variable for the selected month, and uses the Format function to produce the month name. The month name is written to the edtMonth edit box control to be displayed.

```
varDate = DateValue(CStr(intMonth) & "/01/1994")
  dlg.EditBoxes("edtMonth").Text = Format(varDate, "mmmm")
```

The *edtMonth_Change* Subroutine

The next subroutine prohibits the user from directly typing the month into the edtMonth edit box. Any keypress into the edit box causes the Change event to occur and executes this subroutine.

The edtMonth_Change subroutine refreshes the edit box by calling the spnMonth_Change subroutine. Then it tells the user that the correct way to change the month is to use the spinner controls.

Complete the edtMonth_Change subroutine as shown in Listing 5.8.

Listing 5.8. The edtMonth_Change subroutine.

```
'
' edtMonth_Change Macro
'
'
Sub edtMonth_Change()

  Dim msg As String

' Undo the change
  spnMonth_Change

  msg = "Use the up and down arrows to change the Month value."
  MsgBox msg, 64, "Calendar Wizard"

End Sub
```

Figure 5.25 shows the edtMonth_Change subroutine being completed in the Module2 module.

FIGURE 5.25.

Completing the edtMonth_Change subroutine.

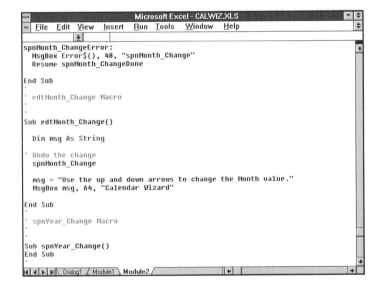

The *spnYear_Change* Subroutine

The spnYearChange subroutine is activated when the spnYear spinner control is clicked to select a different year. Only years 1900 through 2078 are valid values. The subroutine wraps the values around from 2078 to 1900 or from 1900 to 2078 if the extreme values are ever reached.

The year value is converted to text with the CStr function and written to the edtYear edit box.

Complete the spnYear_Change subroutine as shown in Listing 5.9.

Listing 5.9. The spnYear_Change subroutine.

```
'
' spnYear_Change Macro
'
'
Sub spnYear_Change()

  Dim dlg As DialogSheet
  Dim spnYear As Spinner

  Dim intYear As Integer

  On Error GoTo spnYear_ChangeError

  Set dlg = Workbooks(WORKSHEET_NAME).DialogSheets("Dialog1")
  Set spnYear = dlg.Spinners("spnYear")

  intYear = 2079 - spnYear.Value
  If intYear < 1900 Then intYear = 2078
  If intYear > 2078 Then intYear = 1900
  spnYear.Value = 2079 - intYear

  dlg.EditBoxes("edtYear").Text = CStr(intYear)

spnYear_ChangeDone:
  Exit Sub

spnYear_ChangeError:
  MsgBox Error$(), 48, "spnYear_Change"
  Resume spnYear_ChangeDone

End Sub
```

The *edtYear_Change* Subroutine

The edtYear_Change subroutine prohibits direct edits of the edtYear edit box.

Complete the edtYear_Change subroutine as shown in Listing 5.10.

Listing 5.10. The edtYear_Change **subroutine.**

```
'
' edtYear_Change Macro
'

 Sub edtYear_Change()

  Dim msg As String

' Undo the change
  spnYear_Change

  msg = "Use the up and down arrows to change the Year value."
  MsgBox msg, 64, "Calendar Wizard"

End Sub
```

The *cmdBuild_Click* Subroutine

The user builds the calendar by clicking the Build button and activating the cmdBuild_Click subroutine.

To avoid undue screen flicker, the cmdBuild_Click subroutine turns off screen updating during the duration of the CreateCalendar subroutine call. The CreateCalendar subroutine is called with the current month and year.

Whenever you turn screen updates off, you need to make sure there is no way that it will get turned back on. The cmdBuild_Click subroutine turns screen updates back on after a successful run, and also before displaying an error message in the subroutine's error handler.

Complete the cmdBuild_Click subroutine as shown in Listing 5.11.

Listing 5.11. The cmdBuild_Click **subroutine.**

```
'
' cmdBuild_Click Macro
'

 Sub cmdBuild_Click()
```

```
    Dim dlg As DialogSheet
    Dim spns As Spinners

    On Error GoTo cmdBuild_ClickError

    Set dlg = Workbooks(WORKSHEET_NAME).DialogSheets("Dialog1")

    Application.ScreenUpdating = False

    Set spns = dlg.Spinners
    CreateCalendar 13 - spns("spnMonth").Value, 2079 - spns("spnYear").Value

    Application.ScreenUpdating = True

cmdBuild_ClickDone:
    Exit Sub

cmdBuild_ClickError:
    Application.ScreenUpdating = True
    MsgBox Error$(), 48, "cmdBuild_Click"
    Resume cmdBuild_ClickDone

End Sub
```

That does it for all the event code. There is one more short procedure to enter that makes Calendar Wizard work as a menu add-in. Before you do that and create a .XLA file, let's see if this thing works!

Testing Calendar Wizard

Save the workbook.

Actually, it's very unlikely that Calendar Wizard will break Excel, but I thought it might be good to start the practice right now before you build bigger projects. As your programs get more extensive, they eventually use the features of the development environment in ways that the Microsoft's army of testers didn't and you get a resulting crash or lock up. It happens.

Another reason for saving the workbook is that you want the controls in the dialog box sheet to start as empty. In particular, the spinner controls have their Current Value property set to 0, and that indicates to the program it should default to the current month and year. If you save the workbook with these set to some other value, then that is what you will get as a default each time Calendar Wizard is loaded.

1. Save the Workbook.
2. Click the Dialog1 tab.
3. On the Forms toolbar, click the Run Dialog button.

   The Run Dialog button is the one that looks like a light switch. Calendar Wizard's dialog box should display the current month and year as shown in Figure 5.26.

FIGURE 5.26.

Testing Calendar Wizard.

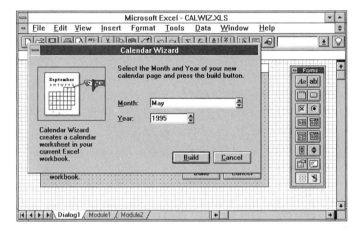

4. Use the spinner arrows to select a month and year, and then click the Build button to generate the calendar worksheet.

   After a few seconds, Excel redraws with your new calendar worksheet (as shown in Figure 5.27). Pretty neat, huh?

   What if it didn't work?

   If you got errors instead of a calendar, you'll need to check your code against the listings in the book or get familiar with the Excel debugger. You could also compare your copy against CALWIZ.XLS on this book's companion CD-ROM.

5. Close the workbook without saving it and open the version you saved before testing.

FIGURE 5.27.
A successful test run!

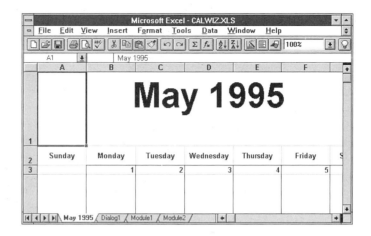

The *CalendarWizard* Subroutine

If all went well, you can now make Calendar Wizard a menu add-in.

1. Add the final subroutine, `CalendarWizard`, to Module2. See Listing 5.12.

2. Change the `WORKSHEET_NAME` constant value to `CALWIZ.XLA`.

   ```
   Const WORKSHEET_NAME = "CALWIZ.XLA"
   ```

The `CalendarWizard` subroutine opens the Calendar Wizard dialog box sheet. This function is called by selecting Calendar Wizard from the menu.

Listing 5.12. The `CalendarWizard` **subroutine.**

```
Sub CalendarWizard()

  On Error GoTo CalendarWizardError

  Workbooks(WORKSHEET_NAME).DialogSheets("Dialog1").Show

CalendarWizardDone:
  Exit Sub

CalendarWizardError:
  MsgBox Error$(), 48, "CalendarWizard"
  Resume CalendarWizardDone

End Sub
```

That completes all the code in Module2!

Make Calendar Wizard a Menu Add-In

The last step is to make a menu add-in out of your work just as you did with Pretty Printer in Chapter 4. Refer back to that chapter for more detailed instructions.

1. Create an Excel macro sheet and define the following names (as shown in Figure 5.28):

```
__Command    ={10,"Tools","Calendar Wizard","CalendarWizard",1,"C",
➥"Create a calendar worksheet."}
__DemandLoad =True
__ReadOnly   =True
```

FIGURE 5.28.

Creating the menu add-in macros.

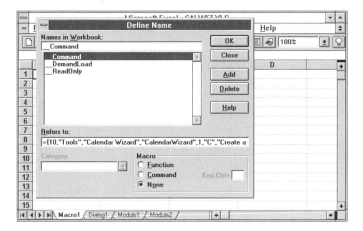

2. Select the **F**ile|Summary **I**nfo command and enter the following.

   Title: `Calendar Wizard`

   Comments: `Creates a calendar page in your workbook for the entered Month and Year.`

3. Use the **T**ools|Ma**k**e Add-In command and write the compiled version as CALWIZ.XLA. (See Figure 5.29.)

   Don't forget to keep your CALWIZ.XLS file because that is your source! You can't edit the CALWIZ.XLA file.

4. Use the **T**ools|Add-**I**ns command to bring up the Add-Ins dialog box.

5. Click the **B**rowse button in the Add-Ins dialog box then select the CALWIZ.XLA file.

6. Make sure Calendar Wizard is checked in the list of **A**dd-Ins Available and click OK.

7. Exit Excel and restart it again.

FIGURE 5.29.
*Saving the
CALWIZ.XLA file.*

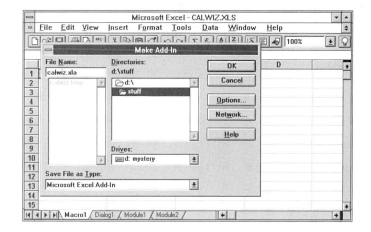

You should see a Calendar Wizard command added to the Tools menu as
shown in Figure 5.30.

FIGURE 5.30.
*Calendar Wizard is
available while using
other worksheets.*

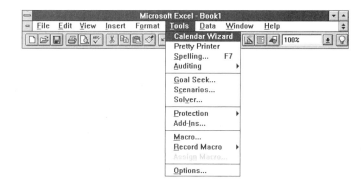

Modifying Calendar Wizard

You can improve Calendar Wizard in many ways. Here are a few ideas.

Modify Calendar Wizard so it accepts a range of months and generates a set of calendar
pages in one fell swoop.

Have Calendar Wizard generate notes for holidays and special occasions automatically.
Change the interface to prompt for which special days to be included in the calendar
currently being generated.

Finally, enable the user to select from different styles and types of calendars. Write code
that produces the different kinds of calendars.

Calendar Wizard Challenge

In creating Pretty Printer in the last chapter and Calendar Wizard in this chapter, you've learned everything you need to know to start creating your own third-party add-ins to Excel.

Can you design and create your own Excel menu add-in that is useful enough to share with your friends or even bring to market?

Summary

In this chapter you created an Excel Wizard. Here's a list of things you did along the way. You

- Created a Calendar worksheet prototype
- Created the `CalendarCreate` subroutine to generate a calendar on a worksheet
- Learned how to take advantage of Excel's date functions to solve puzzling date problems the easy way
- Learned all about Excel dialog box sheets
- Created the Calendar Wizard dialog box sheet
- Used spinner controls
- Set the tab order on a dialog box sheet
- Put code behind control events on a dialog box sheet
- Explored the Object Browser
- Used collections to reference controls on a dialog box sheet
- Made Calendar Wizard an installable menu add-in

In the next chapter I have an equally fun project in store for you. It's called "Sticky Notes."

TRY THIS! ANSWER

5.1. You can add a button to your worksheet that clears a range, without any coding. Do the following:

1. While on a worksheet page, select the **View|T**oolbars command.
2. In the Toolbars dialog box, check the Forms toolbar and press OK.
3. Click the Create Button button on the Forms toolbar.
4. Draw a button on your worksheet.

   After drawing your button, Excel displays the Assign Macro dialog box.

5. In the Assign Macro dialog box press the **R**ecord button.

6. In the Record New Macro dialog box, enter a name for the recorded macro.
   Excel displays a small window with a Stop button.

7. Select the range in your worksheet and press the Delete key.

8. Click the top left of the range to clear the range selection.

9. Press the Stop button.

CHAPTER 6

Access: Sticky Notes

You see them in nearly any workplace. Originally, they were yellow, but like most stationery products, they now come in many colors, with decorative artwork, cartoons, and cute sayings printed on them. Their functionality is incredible, and we wonder how we ever lived without them.

I'm talking, of course, about Post-it Notes™ from 3M—those little pieces of paper backed with a sticky substance that allows them to be placed somewhere and removed later without harm.

What makes Post-it Notes so useful is that they provide you a way to store information (a message, for example) beside the physical items that the information is applicable to (the telephone, for example). You are sure to get to that information when you need it, because the next time you return to the physical item, you will also return to the information.

In this chapter, I'll explain how I brought the functionality of Post-it Notes into the world of Microsoft Access. I call my implementation "Sticky Notes"; and although these notes don't use a specially formulated, patented glue, they are just as effective as their real-world counterpart.

Using Sticky Notes

You can place Sticky Notes on your application's forms while the application is running. As many as eight notes may be left on each form. When a form is closed, all associated notes disappear. Later, when the form is reopened, the notes reappear exactly where they were left before. The test form shown in Figure 6.1 has a few notes pasted on it.

FIGURE 6.1.
A test form covered
with Sticky Notes.

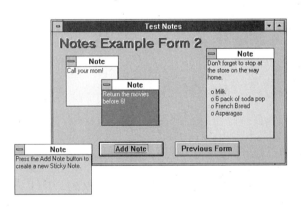

When a note is first created, it is automatically positioned in the middle of the screen. You can move it, just like any other window, by clicking the title bar and holding the mouse button down while dragging the form to its new position.

You discard a note in Sticky Notes simply by closing the note window. This is the software equivalent of picking up a note and tossing it in the trash.

You could use Sticky Notes during testing as a way to signal form design changes or bugs. You could include Sticky Notes as a feature in your final application. There are probably as many uses for Sticky Notes in Access as there are for the Post-it Notes in the world of paper documents. Whatever purposes you or your end users find for it, I guarantee that "Sticky Notes" will be a fun little project.

The Notes Table

A good way to start building any application in Access is first to define the tables. For Sticky Notes there is only one, and it is aptly called Notes.

Each record in the Notes table represents one of those yellow stickies. For each note, you need to know on which form the note was pasted, the x and y screen coordinates of the top-left corner of the note, and, of course, the actual message itself.

You will also store a number to indicate which one the note is, of the eight possible notes that may be assigned to a form. You can store a style number that will enable you to choose colors other than yellow and different sizes of "paper" for your notes.

Figure 6.2 shows the Notes table in table design view.

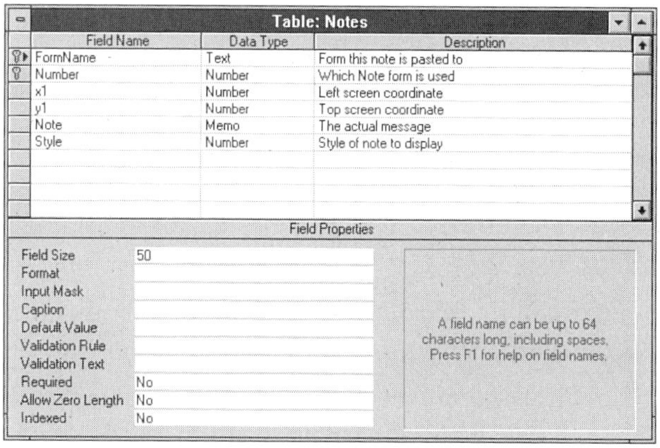

FIGURE 6.2.

Defining the Notes table.

1. Start Access and create a new, empty database.

2. Create a new Notes table with the following fields and field settings:

        Field Name: FormName
        Data Type: Text
        Description: Form this note is pasted to
        Field Size: 50

        Field Name: Number
        Data Type: Number
        Description: Which Note form is used
        Field Size: Byte

        Field Name: x1
        Data Type: Number
        Description: Left screen coordinate
        Field Size: Integer

        Field Name: y1
        Data Type: Number
        Description: Top screen coordinate
        Field Size: Integer

        Field Name: Note
        Data Type: Memo
        Description: The actual message
        Required: No
        Allow Zero Length: Yes

        Field Name: Style
        Data Type: Number
        Description: Style of note to display
        Field Size: Integer

3. While still in design view, highlight the first two rows in the table, selecting the FormName and Number fields, and press the key button on the toolbar.

    This creates a primary key using both of the selected fields. FormName and Number are used to make up the primary key, because together they uniquely identify one of the notes left by a user while running the application.

4. Close the table, saving it as Notes.

Figure 6.3 shows what the table might look like in datasheet mode after a few notes have been entered.

FIGURE 6.3.

Notes entered in the Notes table.

FormName	Number	x1	y1	Note	Style
_Form1	1	376	175	Don't forget to backup your files!	4
_Form1	2	137	216	Return the books to the library before Wednesday.	2
_Form2	1	128	175	Call your mom!	1
_Form2	2	390	162	Don't forget to stop at the store on the way home.	3
_Form2	3	194	218	Return the movies before 6!	4
_Form2	4	31	335	Press the Add Note button to create a new Sticky Note.	2
*	0	0	0		0

Record: 1   of 6

Creating the Sticky Note Forms

Next you can create the forms for the actual sticky notes.

A form must be created for each note on the screen. I chose eight as the maximum number of notes on the screen at once. Any more would probably make it difficult to see what is behind all of the notes.

You must actually create more than eight note forms, however. I've opted to allow four different styles of note forms. That means for each style you need to create eight forms, or 32 in all.

This won't be as bad as it sounds. All you need to do is create the first one and use copy-and-paste to produce the additional forms. You just have to make sure to get the first form right; otherwise, you will have to update all 32 forms or do the copy-and-paste operation again.

1. Start with a new, blank form and set the following properties:

Caption:	Note
Default View:	Single Form
Scroll Bars:	Neither
Record Selectors:	No
Navigation Buttons:	No
Pop Up:	Yes
Modal:	No
Border Style:	Thin
Min Button:	No
Max Button:	No
Width:	1 in

2. Click the detail section on the form to bring up the Properties window. Set the Height property to .75 inches. (See Figure 6.4.)

FIGURE 6.4.

Creating the Sticky Note form.

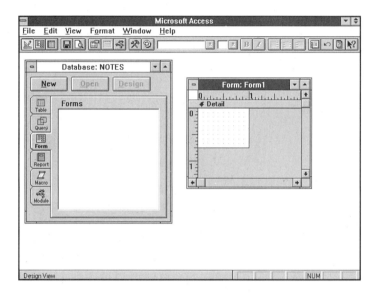

3. Add a txtNote text box control to the form, as shown in Figure 6.5.

The txtNote text box has the same height and width of the form. Its Back Color is set to standard sticky-note yellow.

The txtNote control's properties should be set as follows:

Control Name:	txtNote
Scroll Bars:	None
Left:	0 in
Top:	0 in
Width:	1 in
Height:	.75 in
Border Style:	Clear
Back Color:	65535 (Yellow)
Fore Color:	0 (Black)

To complete the form, you need to add two procedure calls to it.

4. Click the form to show the form's properties in the Properties window.

5. In the Properties window, find the On Open event. Click the button located on the right and containing the ellipsis sign (...).

FIGURE 6.5.

The txtNote control covers the entire form section.

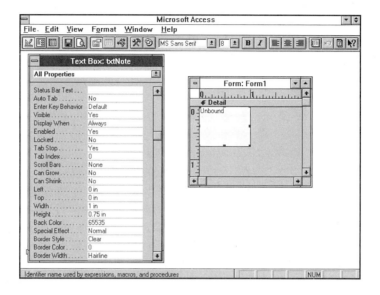

6. In the Choose Builder dialog box, select Code Builder and press OK.

7. Enter the NoteOnOpen subroutine call, as shown in Listing 6.1.

8. Find the On Close event and use the Code Builder to create a subroutine for it, as shown in Listing 6.2.

9. Close the form, saving it as Note1.

Listing 6.1. On Open event code for the Note1 form.

```
Sub Form_Open (Cancel As Integer)

   NoteOnOpen Me

End Sub
```

Listing 6.2. On Close event code for the Note1 form.

```
Sub Form_Close ()

   NoteOnClose Me

End Sub
```

Copying Forms

Next you can quickly create forms Note2 through Note8.

1. In the database container, select the Note1 form.
2. Press Ctrl-C to copy the form.
3. Press Ctrl-V to paste the copied form into the database container as a new form.
4. Enter `Note2` as the name of the new form.
5. Repeat steps 3 and 4, naming each new form Note3, Note4, and so on, until the database container shows all eight forms. See Figure 6.6.

FIGURE 6.6.

Copying forms to create a total of eight yellow Sticky Notes.

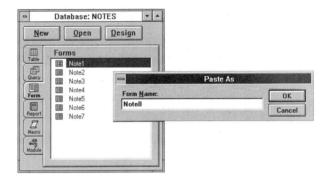

You now have the first set of eight note forms. Paste the copied form one more time as Note9 so you can use it as the basis for the next style of Sticky Note.

Being a Sticky Note Form Factory

To add a little variety to Sticky Notes, you will create three additional types of notes. Each will have a different color and a different size rectangle.

1. Open Note9 in design view.
2. Change the Width property of the text box so that it is 1.5 inches wide.

   Because the text box is larger than before, the form automatically resizes itself to accommodate the text box.
3. Change the Back Color property of the text box to 65280 (Light Green), as shown in Figure 6.7.

FIGURE 6.7.

Creating the second Sticky Note style.

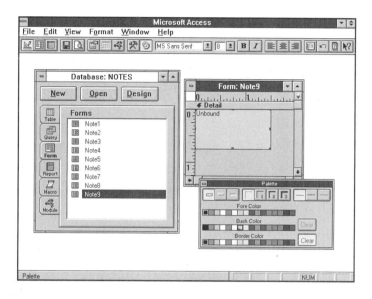

4. Close the form after saving your changes.

5. Select Note9 in the database container and copy-and-paste it as described earlier, this time creating forms Note10 through Note16.

6. Paste an additional form as Note17 to use as the basis for the third style of forms.

7. Repeat the steps above, creating a set of forms Note17 through Note24 with a third style, and forms Note25 through Note32 with a fourth style.

Style 3 should have the following txtNote properties set:

Width:	1.3021 in
Height:	1.5 in
Back Color:	16776960 (Light Blue)

Style 4 should have these settings:

Width:	·1.1042 in
Height:	.6646 in
Fore Color:	16777215 (White)
Back Color:	255 (Red)

Figure 6.8 shows forms displaying the four Sticky Note styles that we created.

FIGURE 6.8.

Four different Sticky Note styles.

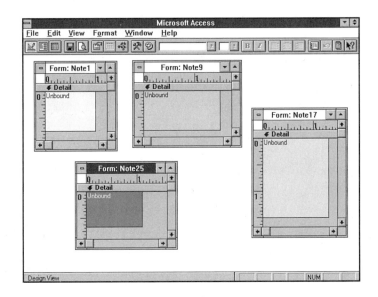

Creating the Notes Module

Now it's time to do some coding.

There are quite a few lines to type here. If you are dutifully following along and re-creating the Notes database from scratch, you might want to cheat. You can import the Notes module from the NOTES.MDB database included on the book's companion CD-ROM into your own database.

If, on the other hand, you'd rather type the code in yourself, all the procedures are listed completely here.

Nearly all the code for Sticky Notes is within the Notes Module. Putting an extensive amount of code behind the Note forms didn't make sense, because there are multiple copies of them.

In the following sections, I'll go through each procedure and explain what it does. Some of the code is fairly tricky.

1. Click the Module tab in Access.
2. Click the **N**ew button to create a new module.

   Let's save the module right now as the Notes module.
3. Select the **F**ile|**S**ave command.
4. In the Save As dialog box, enter Notes as the name of the module and press OK.

Now, as you enter each listing, be sure to save your work periodically so you don't lose much if the power goes out or something else goes wrong. It's as easy as entering Alt-F-S.

Declarations Section

At the beginning of the module is the declarations section.

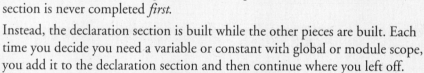

> **NOTE**
>
> It's awkward that in a programming book such as this one you typically see the declaration section listed first among the other code in the program. The truth of the matter is that, although the code is dependent on it, the declaration section is never completed *first.*
>
> Instead, the declaration section is built while the other pieces are built. Each time you decide you need a variable or constant with global or module scope, you add it to the declaration section and then continue where you left off.

Enter the declarations section, as shown in Listing 6.3.

Listing 6.3. The Notes module declarations section.

```
' Notes module

  Option Compare Database
  Option Explicit

  Const PROGRAM = "Sticky Notes"

  Const MAX_NOTES = 8
  Const NOTE_STYLES = 4

  Global Const NOTE_STYLE_CANCEL = 0
  Global Const NOTE_STYLE_YELLOW = 1
  Global Const NOTE_STYLE_GREEN = 2
  Global Const NOTE_STYLE_BLUE = 3
  Global Const NOTE_STYLE_RED = 4

  Dim mstrFormName As String

  Global gintSelectedNoteStyle As Integer

  Dim mblnClosingNotes As Integer

  Type RECT
    x1 As Integer
    y1 As Integer
```

continues

Listing 6.3. continued

```
    x2 As Integer
    y2 As Integer
End Type

Declare Function GetClientRect Lib "User" (ByVal Hwnd As Integer, r As RECT)
➥ As Integer
Declare Function GetParent Lib "User" (ByVal Hwnd As Integer) As Integer
Declare Function GetWindowRect Lib "User" (ByVal Hwnd As Integer, r As RECT)
➥ As Integer
Declare Function MoveWindow Lib "User" (ByVal Hwnd As Integer,
➥ ByVal x As Integer, ByVal y As Integer, ByVal dx As Integer,
➥ ByVal dy As Integer, ByVal blnRepaint As Integer) As Integer
```

Figure 6.9 shows the declarations section being entered in the Notes module.

FIGURE 6.9.

Creating the Notes module.

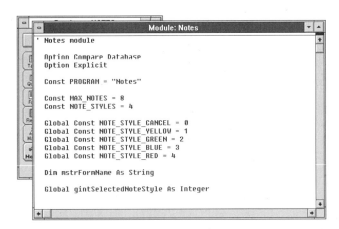

 So what is all that stuff in Listing 6.3? Here's a list of the constants being declared:

PROGRAM is used as the window caption in Msgbox calls.

MAX_NOTES defines how many notes may be displayed on a form.

NOTE_STYLES is the total number of different note styles.

NOTE_STYLE_CANCEL indicates that no style has been chosen.

NOTE_STYLE_YELLOW through NOTE_STYLE_RED indicate which style of the four Sticky Notes is being used.

Giving constants names such as NOTE_STYLE_YELLOW enhances code readability. In the section that uses the value 1 to indicate which type of Sticky Note to display, the name NOTE_STYLE_YELLOW, as opposed to simply the number 1, gives you a better idea of the meaning of the program.

A constant like MAX_NOTES enhances readability, but it has a second, more important purpose. If you decide that you want only a maximum of four notes on a form at once, you can make that change without losing any sweat. You have to change only the value that MAX_NOTES is defined as. You don't have to hunt down all the code to find where you might have left a number that is supposed to indicate the maximum number of notes on a form.

Globals and Module Variables

Next in the declaration section, some module and global variables are declared. Each of these stores a piece of information shared by two or more procedures.

Global variables have always been considered kind of a bad thing (like GoTos), but I've never been able to write a program without one (also like GoTos). The issue is that the more global information you rely on, the more likely it won't be in the state your program thought it would be.

You can minimize the likelihood of this by using a module variable, which is like a global variable although it is known only to the procedures within that module. In other words, its *scope* is limited to the code within the module.

Here are the module and global variables used in the Notes module declaration section:

```
Dim mstrFormName As String

Global gintSelectedNoteStyle As Integer

Dim mblnClosingNotes As Integer
```

The mstrFormName variable is set to indicate which form has notes displayed on it.

The gintSelectedNoteStyle variable gets set by a pop-up form that allows the user to pick which note style to use. You haven't created the form yet.

The mblnClosingNotes variable is a flag set to True to indicate that the notes are being closed because the background application form is being closed. When this flag is not set, then the note form would be closed only because the user is discarding the note.

The next part of the declaration section (shown in Listing 6.4) declares the Window's API RECT structure and some API calls. These were taken from the Windows API Utilities module in the PIM.MDB sample database that shipped with Access 1.1.

Listing 6.4. Windows API declarations in the Notes declaration section.

```
Type RECT
    x1 As Integer
    y1 As Integer
```

continues

Listing 6.4. continued

```
   x2 As Integer
   y2 As Integer
End Type

Declare Function GetClientRect Lib "User" (ByVal Hwnd As Integer, r As RECT)
➥ As Integer
Declare Function GetParent Lib "User" (ByVal Hwnd As Integer) As Integer
Declare Function GetWindowRect Lib "User" (ByVal Hwnd As Integer, r As RECT)
➥ As Integer
Declare Function MoveWindow Lib "User" (ByVal Hwnd As Integer,
➥ ByVal x As Integer, ByVal y As Integer, ByVal dx As Integer,
➥ ByVal dy As Integer, ByVal blnRepaint As Integer) As Integer
```

You will enter a CenterForm function that uses all this stuff. The CenterForm function was derived from the wu_CenterDoc function also found in the PIM.MDB database. The MoveWindow API function is also used in Sticky Notes to reposition the location of the notes to where they were the last time you viewed them.

If this API stuff freaks you out, don't worry. You won't have to become a Windows API expert to be able to build applications in Basic.

You resort to the API when you are trying to get an effect that isn't already provided within the Basic programming environment for the tool you are using. In other words, seeing API calls in the code kind of points out missing pieces in Access, Visual Basic, Excel or Word. Typically, these holes get plugged in newer versions of the products, so the need to resort to the API lessens.

In addition, when you do need to resort to the API, you aren't usually alone. Somebody has probably already treaded the same ground. My own research through the Windows Software Development Kit (SDK) help files was only in clarification of what the code in PIM.MDB was doing.

CreateNote Subroutine

The CreateNote subroutine adds a record to the Notes table and displays the new note form.

Enter the CreateNote subroutine, as shown in Listing 6.5.

Listing 6.5. The CreateNote subroutine.

```
Sub CreateNote (intStyle As Integer)

   Dim db As Database
```

```
   Dim tbl As Recordset
   Dim blnOpened As Integer

   Dim n As Integer

   blnOpened = False
   On Error GoTo CreateNoteError

   If intStyle = NOTE_STYLE_CANCEL Then
     GoTo CreateNoteDone
   End If

   If intStyle < NOTE_STYLE_CANCEL Or intStyle > NOTE_STYLES Then
     MsgBox "Invalid note style number.", 48, PROGRAM
     GoTo CreateNoteDone
   End If

   Set db = DBEngine(0)(0)

   Set tbl = db.OpenRecordset("Notes", DB_OPEN_TABLE)
   blnOpened = True

   tbl.Index = "PrimaryKey"

   For n = 1 To MAX_NOTES

     tbl.Seek "=", mstrFormName, n

     If tbl.NoMatch Then

       tbl.AddNew

       tbl!FormName = mstrFormName
       tbl!Number = n

     ' Indicate that the note should be centered
       tbl!x1 = -1
       tbl!y1 = -1

       tbl!Note = ""
       tbl!Style = intStyle

       tbl.Update

       DoCmd OpenForm "Note" & ((intStyle - 1) * MAX_NOTES + n)
       Exit For

     End If
   Next n

   If n > MAX_NOTES Then
     MsgBox "Sorry, only " & MAX_NOTES & " notes are allowed per form.", _
     ➥ 48, PROGRAM
   End If

CreateNoteDone:
   On Error Resume Next
```

continues

Listing 6.5. continued

```
If blnOpened Then tbl.Close
Exit Sub

CreateNoteError:
  MsgBox Error$, 48, PROGRAM
  Resume CreateNoteDone

End Sub
```

The first part of the subroutine verifies the `intStyle` value passed. `NOTE_STYLE_CANCEL`, or 0, can be passed to indicate that the creation of the note has been canceled. In this case, the call exits early without an error message.

If the `intStyle` value is valid, then the next step is to search the Notes table for an open slot from 1 to `MAX_NOTES` to create a note record. The search is done by looking for records by form name and note number, which is the information that makes up the primary key for the Notes table.

If a matching record is found, then you know the slot is full. If a match is not found, then it is safe to assume the searched number for the new note.

Listing 6.6. Searching for an available note number.

```
For n = 1 To MAX_NOTES

  tbl.Seek "=", mstrFormName, n

  If tbl.NoMatch Then

  ' Found a slot for a sticky note

    .
    .
    .

    Exit For

  End If
Next n
```

When a new note record is added, the fields within the record are set to default values.

Since the user has not selected a location for the note yet, the x1 and y1 coordinates are set to -1 to indicate that the note form should be centered. The Note field of the table is set to an empty string because obviously no text has been entered yet either.

The Style field is set to the value in the `intStyle` argument. With the new note record initialized, the record is saved.

Listing 6.7. Creating a new note record with default values.

```
tbl.AddNew

tbl!FormName = mstrFormName
tbl!Number = n

' Indicate that the note should be centered
tbl!x1 = -1
tbl!y1 = -1

tbl!Note = ""
tbl!Style = intStyle

tbl.Update
```

Next the note form is opened. The name of the note form that is opened is calculated using the following formula:

```
(style_number - 1) * MAX_NOTES + note_number
```

The formula works because you have the same amount of forms for each style. For example, if you choose the third style and are making the fourth note, then the formula is calculated like this:

```
(3 - 1) * 8 + 4
```

The answer is 20, which, correctly, is the fourth note form that you created in the third note style. This number is concatenated with the word "Note" to produce the actual form name.

At the end of the subroutine, an error message is displayed if the subroutine didn't successfully locate an available note number for the current form. It can tell when this occurs because the loop counter, n, would be incremented to 1 greater than the number of notes available.

NOTE

Access uses three different kinds of recordsets: Table, Dynaset and Snapshot.

A Table object is often used to take advantage of its Seek method, which utilizes the indexes of a table to provide the fastest way to locate a record in a table.

A Dynaset object is a view of the records in a database that keeps up-to-date with changes made to the records after the dynaset is opened.

A Snapshot object is a view of the records in the database that remains static, meaning that values read in from a snapshot are the same as when the snapshot was opened.

A Table object can only be set to an actual table within the database. A Dynaset or Snapshot object may be opened to a table, query, or SQL SELECT statement.

Access 2.0 introduced the Recordset object, which is a combination of all three kinds of recordsets. When you open a Recordset object you indicate whether the recordset will act as a table, dynaset, or snapshot.

NoteNumber Function

The NoteNumber function determines which note slot, from 1 to MAX_NOTES, a note form belongs to, based on the note form name. The NoteOnOpen and NoteOnClose subroutines will use this function to retrieve the appropriate note record for the current note form.

Enter the NoteNumber function, as shown in Listing 6.8.

Listing 6.8. Determining the note number from a note form name.

```
Function NoteNumber (frm As Form) As Integer

' Return a note number for the current form from 1 to MAX_NOTES

  Dim strNote As String
  Dim intNote As Integer

  On Error GoTo NoteNumberError

  strNote = frm.FormName
  intNote = CInt(Right$(strNote, Len(strNote) - 4))

  intNote = intNote Mod MAX_NOTES

  If intNote = 0 Then
    intNote = MAX_NOTES
  End If

  NoteNumber = intNote

NoteNumberDone:
  Exit Function

NoteNumberError:
  MsgBox Error$, 48, PROGRAM
  Resume NoteNumberDone

End Function
```

The `NoteNumber` function gets the form name and extracts the number from it by removing the first four characters, which are always "Note."

```
strNote = frm.FormName
intNote = CInt(Right$(strNote, Len(strNote) - 4))
```

The `Mod` function is used to extract the offset in the note form number that was added to allow for the different note styles.

```
intNote = intNote Mod MAX_NOTES
```

For example, if `MAX_NOTES` is equal to 8, and if you are dealing with note form number 23, then the remainder of 23 ÷ 8 is 7, indicating that you are using the seventh note.

However, if the `intNote` value is divisible by `MAX_NOTES`, then the `Mod` function will return 0. In this case, you know you are dealing with the last note slot.

```
If intNote = 0 Then
   intNote = MAX_NOTES
End If
```

NotesOnOpen Subroutine

The `NotesOnOpen` subroutine is called on the On Open event for each note form. The On Open event occurs just before the note is actually drawn on the screen.

You already set up the call for this subroutine, as well as the `NoteOnClose` subroutine when you created the note forms.

Enter the `NoteOnOpen` subroutine into the Notes module, as shown in Listing 6.9.

Listing 6.9. The `NoteOnOpen` **subroutine.**

```
Sub NoteOnOpen (frm As Form)

   Dim db As Database

   Dim tbl As Recordset
   Dim blnOpened As Integer

   Dim r As RECT

   Dim dx As Integer
   Dim dy As Integer

   Dim intNote As Integer
   Dim z As Integer

   blnOpened = False
   On Error GoTo NoteOnOpenError

   intNote = NoteNumber(frm)
```

continues

Listing 6.9. continued

```
Set db = DBEngine(0)(0)

Set tbl = db.OpenRecordset("Notes", DB_OPEN_TABLE)
blnOpened = True

tbl.Index = "PrimaryKey"
tbl.Seek "=", mstrFormName, intNote

If tbl.NoMatch Then
' This form was opened manually
  DoCmd Close A_FORM, frm.FormName
  GoTo NoteOnOpenDone
End If

If tbl!x1 = -1 Then

  z = CenterForm(CInt(frm.hwnd))

Else

' Find the note window position
  z = GetWindowRect(frm.hwnd, r)

  dx = r.x2 - r.x1
  dy = r.y2 - r.y1

  r.x1 = tbl!x1
  r.y1 = tbl!y1

  z = MoveWindow(frm.hwnd, r.x1, r.y1, dx, dy, True)

' Display the note
  frm!txtNote = tbl!Note

End If

NoteOnOpenDone:
  On Error Resume Next
  If blnOpened Then tbl.Close
  Exit Sub

NoteOnOpenError:
  MsgBox Error$, 48, PROGRAM
  Resume NoteOnOpenDone

End Sub
```

In the NoteOnOpen subroutine, the record for the current note is found by searching on the form name stored in mstrFormName and the calculated note number returned by the NoteNumber function.

```
tbl.Seek "=", mstrFormName, intNote
```

The `mstrFormName` module variable is the application form name is set by the `OpenNotes` subroutine, which is called when the application's form is opened.

With the record for the current note finally found, the note is displayed appropriately, depending on the information found there. If the x1 field is set to –1, then it is a note that was just added by the `CreateNote` subroutine we just looked at. New notes are centered by calling the `CenterForm` function.

```
If tbl!x1 = -1 Then

  z = CenterForm(CInt(frm.Hwnd))

Else
  .
  .
  .
```

If the note is not new, the record holds x and y coordinates used to position the note. It also contains the previously saved message, which is written to the `txtNote` text box in the note form.

To reposition the location of a note form, you can use the `MoveWindow` API call as you do in the `CenterForm` subroutine shown later.

The `MoveWindow` call takes the following arguments:

`hwnd`	Handle for a window
`intLeft`	Left coordinate
`intTop`	Top coordinate
`intWidth`	Width of window
`intHeight`	Height of window
`blnRepaint`	Repaint flag

To pass the width and height of the window, you need to first find out what they are. This is done by calling the `GetWindowRect` API call, which fills the values in the `RECT` type structure that was declared in the declarations section.

The `RECT` structure holds the window coordinates like this:

x1 –x coordinate of left border
y1 –y coordinate of the top border
x2 –x coordinate of the right border
y2 –y coordinate of the bottom border

To calculate the width of the window, you would subtract x1 from x2. Likewise, to calculate the height you would subtract y1 from y2. These values are stored in dx and dy.

```
' Find the note window position
   z = GetWindowRect(frm.Hwnd, r)

   dx = r.x2 - r.x1
   dy = r.y2 - r.y1
```

Next, the x1 and y1 values are set from the same values stored in the table and the window is moved by calling the MoveWindow function.

```
   r.x1 = tbl!x1
   r.y1 = tbl!y1

   z = MoveWindow(frm.Hwnd, r.x1, r.y1, dx, dy, True)
```

Finally, the note is retrieved from the Note field and displayed on the txtNote text box.

```
' Display the note
   frm!txtNote = tbl!Note
```

NoteOnClose Subroutine

The NoteOnClose subroutine is triggered on the OnClose event for each note form.

A note gets closed as a result of two things. Either the user throws away the note or the user closes the form that the note is attached to. In the first case, you want to delete the note record. In the second case you want to save the note record so the note can be displayed the next time the application form is opened.

Enter the NoteOnClose subroutine, as shown in Listing 6.10.

Listing 6.10. The NoteOnClose **subroutine.**

```
Sub NoteOnClose (frm As Form)

  Dim r As RECT

  Dim db As Database

  Dim tbl As Recordset
  Dim blnOpened As Integer

  Dim intNote As Integer
  Dim z As Integer

  Dim blnChange As Integer

  blnOpened = False
  On Error GoTo NoteOnCloseError

  intNote = NoteNumber(frm)

  Set db = DBEngine(0)(0)

  Set tbl = db.OpenRecordset("Notes", DB_OPEN_TABLE)
  blnOpened = True
```

```
    tbl.Index = "PrimaryKey"
    tbl.Seek "=", mstrFormName, intNote

  If tbl.NoMatch Then
    GoTo NoteOnCloseDone
  End If

  If mblnClosingNotes Then

  ' Closing the form, saving all open notes

  ' Find the note window position
    z = GetWindowRect(frm.hwnd, r)

  ' Use this flag to avoid an update if there are no changes
    blnChange = False

  ' See if there were any changes
    If tbl!x1 <> r.x1 Then
      blnChange = True
    ElseIf tbl!y1 <> r.y1 Then
      blnChange = True
    ElseIf IsNull(tbl!Note) Then
      blnChange = True
    ElseIf tbl!Note <> frm!txtNote Then
      blnChange = True
    End If

    If blnChange Then
      tbl.Edit

    ' Save the position
      tbl!x1 = r.x1
      tbl!y1 = r.y1

      ' Save the note
      tbl!Note = frm!txtNote

      tbl.Update
    End If

  Else

  ' Deleting a note
    tbl.Delete

  End If

NoteOnCloseDone:
  On Error Resume Next
  If blnOpened Then tbl.Close
  Exit Sub

NoteOnCloseError:
  MsgBox Error$, 48, PROGRAM
  Resume NoteOnCloseDone

End Sub
```

The NoteOnClose subroutine starts out like the NotesOnOpen subroutine, finding the record associated with the note form passed as an argument.

Next, the mblnClosingNotes module variable is checked to determine if the note is being deleted or if the application form is being closed.

If the note is being deleted (the user closed the note window), then the subroutine jumps to the bottom, deletes the record, and gets out, as shown in Listing 6.11.

Listing 6.11. Determining what to do with the open note.

```
If mblnClosingNotes Then

  ' Closing the form, saving all open notes
  .
  .
  .

  Else

  ' Deleting a note
    tbl.Delete

  End If
```

If the note is being closed as a result of the application form being closed, then the note needs to be saved so it can be drawn again when the form is reopened.

The GetWindowRect API function is used to fill the RECT structure with the current position of the Note window.

```
  ' Closing the form, saving all open notes

  ' Find the note window position
    z = GetWindowRect(frm.hwnd, r)
```

The save has to occur only if there has been a change to the location or substance of the message. As an optimization, the code in Listing 6.12 checks to see if updating the note record is required and skips it if not. The x1 and y1 positions, as well as the message text, are each compared against the values for the note currently on-screen.

Listing 6.12. Determining what to do with the open note.

```
  ' Use this flag to avoid an update if there are no changes
    blnChange = False

  ' See if there were any changes
    If tbl!x1 <> r.x1 Then
      blnChange = True
```

```
ElseIf tbl!y1 <> r.y1 Then
  blnChange = True
ElseIf IsNull(tbl!Note) Then
  blnChange = True
ElseIf tbl!Note <> frm!txtNote Then
  blnChange = True
End If

If blnChange Then

' A change is made, update the record
  .
  .
  .

End If
```

The excerpt in Listing 6.13 updates the notes record.

Listing 6.13. Saving the values from a note on-screen to the Notes table record.

```
tbl.Edit

' Save the position
tbl!x1 = r.x1
tbl!y1 = r.y1

' Save the note
tbl!Note = frm!txtNote

tbl.Update
```

CenterForm Function

The CenterForm function passes the hwnd property of an Access form to several Windows API calls to determine where the window should be placed for centering, and then actually centers it. The function is a simplified version of the wu_CenterDoc function from the PIM.MDB database included with Access 1.1.

Access 2.0 introduced the AutoCenter property, so you usually don't need to use this method to center a form anymore. In Sticky Notes, the windows are alternately centered or positioned by the user, so I found this function still quite useful.

Enter the CenterForm function, as shown in Listing 6.14.

Listing 6.14. The `CenterForm` function.

```
Function CenterForm (hwnd As Integer) As Integer

  Dim r As RECT
  Dim rApp As RECT

  Dim hwndApp As Integer

  Dim dx As Integer
  Dim dy As Integer
  Dim dxApp As Integer
  Dim dyApp As Integer
  Dim z As Integer

  On Error Resume Next

  z = GetWindowRect(hwnd, r)
  hwndApp = GetParent(hwnd)
  z = GetClientRect(hwndApp, rApp)

  dx = r.x2 - r.x1
  dy = r.y2 - r.y1

  dxApp = rApp.x2 - rApp.x1
  dyApp = rApp.y2 - rApp.y1

  CenterForm = MoveWindow(hwnd, (dxApp - dx) / 2, (dyApp - dy) / 2, dx, dy,
  ➥ True)

End Function
```

The `CenterForm` function uses the `GetParent` call to get a handle to the window handle for Microsoft Access. Using the coordinates for the Microsoft Access window and the Note window, it calculates the appropriate x and y coordinates to center the note in the Microsoft Access window and then centers it.

OpenNotes Subroutine

The remaining three procedures, `OpenNotes`, `CloseNote`, and `AddNote` are used to add Sticky Notes to your application.

The `OpenNotes` subroutine is called on your application form's `OnOpen` event to display any notes that were saved the last time the form was opened.

Enter the `OpenNotes` subroutine into the Notes module as shown in Listing 6.15.

Listing 6.15. The `OpenNotes` subroutine.

```
Sub OpenNotes (frm As Form)

  Dim db As Database

  Dim dyn As Recordset
  Dim blnOpened As Integer

  Dim sql As String
  Dim n As Integer

  blnOpened = False
  On Error GoTo OpenNotesError

  mstrFormName = frm.FormName

  Set db = DBEngine(0)(0)

  sql = "SELECT * FROM Notes WHERE FormName = '" & mstrFormName & "';"
  Set dyn = db.OpenRecordset(sql, DB_OPEN_DYNASET)
  blnOpened = True

  While Not dyn.EOF
    DoCmd OpenForm "Note" & (dyn!Number + (dyn!Style - 1) * MAX_NOTES)
    dyn.MoveNext
  Wend

OpenNotesDone:
  On Error Resume Next
  If blnOpened Then dyn.Close
  Exit Sub

OpenNotesError:
  MsgBox Error$, 48, PROGRAM
  Resume OpenNotesDone

End Sub
```

The `OpenNotes` subroutine is passed a form variable so it can identify the notes for this form by form name.

The following line sets the `mstrFormName` variable to the name of the form. The `CreateNote`, `NoteOnOpen`, and `NoteOnClose` subroutines all use this variable to determine to which form a note belongs.

```
mstrFormName = frm.FormName
```

The records for the notes on the current form are selected in a dynaset as shown in the following lines:

```
sql = "SELECT * FROM Notes WHERE FormName = '" & mstrFormName & "';"
Set dyn = db.OpenRecordset(sql, DB_OPEN_DYNASET)
blnOpened = True
```

Next, for each record the form number is calculated, based on the style and note number, and the form is opened.

```
While Not dyn.EOF
    DoCmd OpenForm "Note" & (dyn!Number + (dyn!Style - 1) * MAX_NOTES)
    dyn.MoveNext
  Wend
```

The actual positioning of the note and setting of its message occurs in the NoteOnOpen subroutine activated by the note form's OnOpen event.

CloseNotes Subroutine

The CloseNotes subroutine is called on an application form's OnClose event. Its job is to close any open notes.

Enter the CloseNotes subroutine as shown in Listing 6.16.

Listing 6.16. The CloseNotes subroutine.

```
Sub CloseNotes ()

  Dim n As Integer
  Dim intStyle As Integer

  On Error Resume Next

  mblnClosingNotes = True

  For intStyle = 0 To NOTE_STYLES - 1
    For n = 1 To MAX_NOTES
      DoCmd Close A_FORM, "Note" & n + MAX_NOTES * intStyle
    Next n
  Next intStyle

  mblnClosingNotes = False

End Sub
```

Rather than fuss with determining which Note forms are supposed to be open, the CloseNotes subroutine attempts to close all of them. Error handling is turned off to ignore the errors that occur when a form that isn't opened is closed.

AddNote Subroutine

The AddNote subroutine is the procedure your application calls to add a Sticky Note to the current form. It could be activated on the On Click event for an Add Note button that you add to each of your forms that use Sticky Notes.

Enter the `AddNote` subroutine, as shown in Listing 6.17.

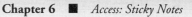

Listing 6.17. The `AddNote` subroutine.

```
Sub AddNote ()

  On Error GoTo AddNoteError

  DoCmd OpenForm "Note Style", , , , , A_DIALOG
  CreateNote gintSelectedNoteStyle

AddNoteDone:
  Exit Sub

AddNoteError:
  MsgBox Error$, 48, PROGRAM
  Resume AddNoteDone

End Sub
```

The `AddNote` subroutine opens a form named Note Style, which you will create later. The Note Style form's job is to set the `gintSelectedNoteStyle` global variable so the `AddNote` subroutine can pass the value along to the `CreateNote` subroutine.

Close the Notes module, being sure to save your changes. Fingers tired? We're done coding for a while.

Testing Sticky Notes

You won't be able to use the `AddNote` subroutine until you create the Note Style form that allows you to pick which style Note you want to create. However, you can call the `CreateNote` subroutine with a preselected Note type and see how it goes.

Let's create a test form and check it out.

1. Click the Form tab on the database container.
2. Click the **N**ew button to create a new form.
3. In the New Form dialog box, click the **B**lank Form button.

Dress up the test form any old way you like. It's just a throw-away for testing, so don't get *too* distracted.

On the one I created, I set the Back Color of the form to gray, and added a couple labels with the caption: "Notes Example Form 1".

You can get a neat 3-D effect by creating one label with its Fore Color set to White, and another with its Fore Color set to a dark color. Make sure each label has the same caption and the Back Style properties are set to Clear.

Place the dark-colored one on top of the light-colored one, slightly offset. Use the Format|Send to **B**ack command if you've got them the other way around. You will probably have to adjust the Left and Top properties through the Property window.

When you are done, continue with the following *essential* steps. First set the form's On Open event code as follows:

1. Select the **View|P**roperties command to bring up the properties window for the form.
2. Select Event Properties from the combobox at the top of the properties window.
3. Click the box next to the On Open event to activate the buttons at the right (as shown in Figure 6.10).

FIGURE 6.10.

Adding code to the test form's On Open event.

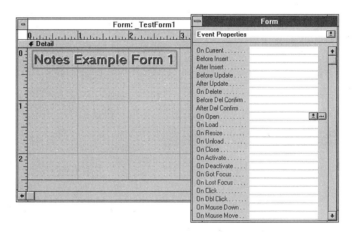

4. Click the ellipsis button. From the Choose Builder dialog box, select Code Builder.
5. Modify the Form_Open subroutine as follows (see Figure 6.11):

```
Sub Form_Open (Cancel As Integer)

  OpenNotes Me

End Sub
```

FIGURE 6.11.

Activating the OpenNotes subroutine on the test form's On Open event.

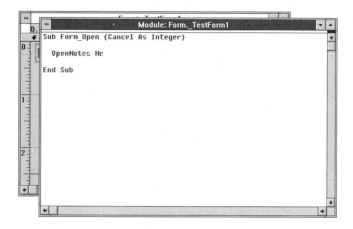

Next, enter code for the form's On Close event.

1. Close the module window.

2. Select the On Close text box in the Properties window and use Code Builder to create a subroutine for it.

3. Modify the `Form_Close` subroutine as follows:

```
Form_Close ()

    CloseNotes

End Sub
```

Next, create the Add Note button.

1. Close the module window.

2. Open the toolbox. Check to see that the toolbox Wizard button is deselected, then draw a button on the test form.

3. Set the caption of the button to say `Add Note`.

4. In the Properties window, with Other Properties displayed, rename the button to `cmdAddNote`, as shown in Figure 6.12.

5. In the Properties window, find the On Click event for the button, and use Code Builder to create a subroutine for the event.

6. Modify the `cmdAddNote_Click` subroutine as follows (see Figure 6.13):

```
cmdAddNote_Click ()

    CreateNote 1

End Sub
```

FIGURE 6.12.

Creating an Add Note button.

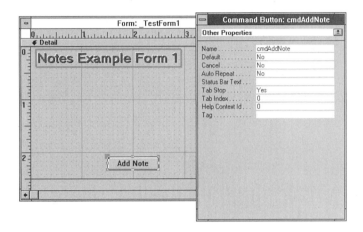

FIGURE 6.13.

Setting up a test call to the CreateNote *subroutine.*

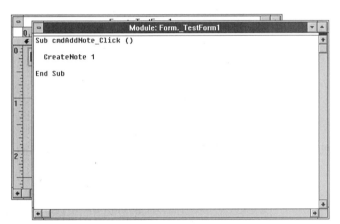

Now that the test form is completed, you are ready to try it out.

1. Close the form and save your changes.

   I saved mine as _TestForm1, using the underscore as a reminder that this is a form I'll delete eventually.

2. Select the form in the database container and open it.

3. Add eight Sticky Notes to the test form. Move each of them to a different location and enter some text into them.

4. Close the form.

5. Open the form again. Did all of the notes display correctly?

Figure 6.14 shows Sticky Notes being tested with eight notes on the screen at the same time.

FIGURE 6.14.

Testing Sticky Notes.

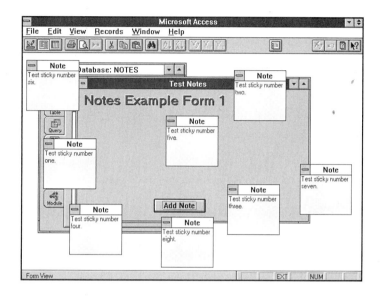

6. Try adding a ninth note. An error message should be displayed (as shown in Figure 6.15), indicating that you can add only eight notes.

FIGURE 6.15.

Testing the limits.

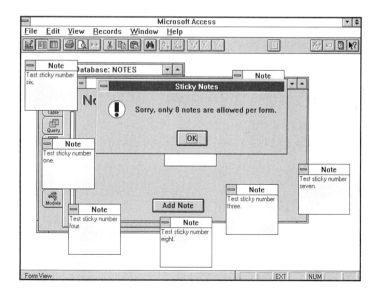

TRY THIS! QUESTION 6.1.

Create a second test form, also containing an Add Note button. (See Figure 6.1 at the beginning of the chapter.) On each form, place a button that closes the current form and opens the other. Do you know how to do this?

When you have that done, try testing Sticky Notes using both forms. As you switch from form to form, are the notes displayed properly for each form?

Remember to call the OpenNotes and CloseNotes subroutines in the second form.

Creating the Note Style Form

Now that you know that Sticky Notes basically works, you can jazz it up by allowing the user to select the style of note he or she wants.

1. Create a new form, setting the following form properties:

Caption:	Sticky Notes
Default View:	Single Form
Scroll Bars:	Neither
Record Selectors:	No
Navigation Buttons:	No
Auto Center:	Yes
Border Style:	Dialog
Min Button:	No
Max Button:	No

2. Set the Back Color of the form to gray.

3. Add a label to the top of the form that displays the following message in a bold font:

   ```
   Select which style of Sticky Note you would like to add to the current form.
   ```

4. Add four large buttons to the form. In the Properties window, name them cmdStyle1, cmdStyle2, cmdStyle3, and cmdStyle4. See Figure 6.16.

The buttons are going to be used to select from the four different note styles. Next, you need to add a bitmap of each type of Sticky Note window to the buttons.

To create the bitmaps, I ran the test form and made one of the notes appear by clicking the Add Note button. Then I captured the image of the Note window into the Windows clipboard by pressing Alt-Print Screen. Note, if you just press Print Screen, you copy the entire screen and not just the current window.

FIGURE 6.16.

Adding buttons to the Note Style form

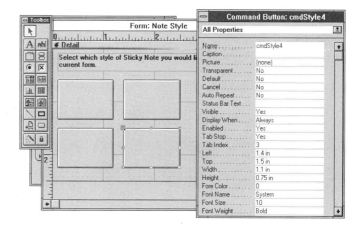

I pasted the image into Paintbrush by selecting its **Edit|P**aste command, as shown in Figure 6.17.

FIGURE 6.17.

Pasting a Sticky Note window image into Paintbrush.

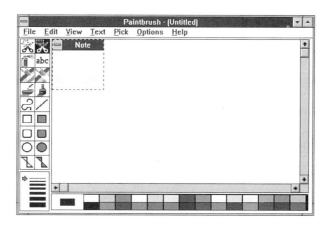

To create the final bitmap file, I selected the Paintbrush **Edit|Co**py To command while the image was still showing a dashed outline to indicate it was selected. This creates a bitmap of just the right size for the copied image.

I saved the bitmap file as NOTE1.BMP. Then I created NOTE2.BMP, NOTE3.BMP, and NOTE4.BMP by doing the same thing with the other note styles. To open one of the other notes, change the line in your test form's `cmdAddNote_Click` subroutine to pass a 2, 3, or 4 as the note style number to the `CreateNote` subroutine.

There is a shortcut, however. You can grab the bitmaps that have already been created for you from the companion CD-ROM. They are named NOTE1.BMP, NOTE2.BMP, NOTE3.BMP, and NOTE4.BMP.

Set the properties for the command buttons on the Sticky Notes form as follows:

1. Set the bitmap properties to the cmdStyle1 through cmdStyle4 buttons to the NOTE1.BMP, NOTE2.BMP, NOTE3.BMP, and NOTE4.BMP files, as shown in Figure 6.18.

FIGURE 6.18.

Adding bitmaps to the cmdStyle buttons.

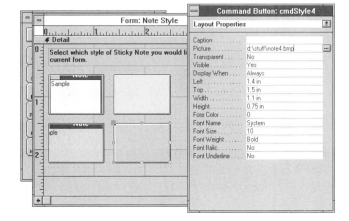

2. Resize and arrange the buttons to get a good-looking form. See Figure 6.19 for how I arranged mine.

3. Add a cmdCancel button with a Cancel caption.

FIGURE 6.19.

Layout for the Note Style form.

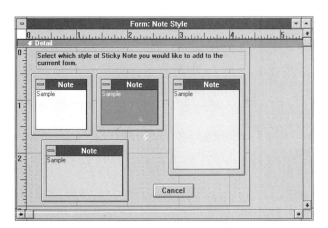

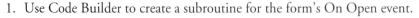

Next, you need to add some code to the form.

1. Use Code Builder to create a subroutine for the form's On Open event.

2. Modify the `Form_Open` subroutine as follows:

```
Form_Open (Cancel As Integer)

' Indicate Cancel was selected

  gintSelectedNoteStyle = NOTE_STYLE_CANCEL

End Sub
```

The `Form_Open` subroutine ensures that, by default, no style has been selected.

3. Create an On Click event subroutine for each of the cmdStyle buttons. The subroutines should match those in Listing 6.18.

4. Create a subroutine for the Cancel button's On Click event that closes the form and nothing else.

```
cmdCancel_Click ()
  DoCmd Close
End Sub
```

5. For good measure, enter the Option Explicit option into the Note Style form's declaration section:

```
' Note Style form
  Option Compare Database
  Option Explicit
```

6. Close and save the form.

Listing 6.18. The On Click event subroutines for the four cmdStyle buttons.

```
Sub cmdStyle1_Click ()

  gintSelectedNoteStyle = NOTE_STYLE_YELLOW
  DoCmd Close

End Sub

Sub cmdStyle2_Click ()

  gintSelectedNoteStyle = NOTE_STYLE_GREEN
  DoCmd Close

End Sub

Sub cmdStyle3_Click ()

  gintSelectedNoteStyle = NOTE_STYLE_BLUE
  DoCmd Close

End Sub
```

continues

Listing 6.18. continued

```
Sub cmdStyle4_Click ()

  gintSelectedNoteStyle = NOTE_STYLE_RED
  DoCmd Close

End Sub
```

That's it!

To test it, modify your test form so the Add Note button's cmdAddNote_Click subroutine calls the AddNote subroutine and not the CreateNote subroutine (see Figure 6.20). The code should look like this:

```
Sub cmdAddNote_Click ()

  AddNote

End Sub
```

FIGURE 6.20.

Calling the AddNote *subroutine.*

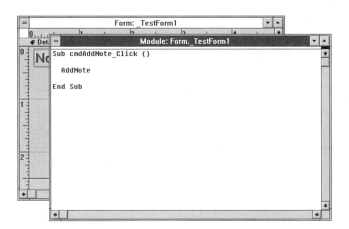

The next time you press the Add Note button, you have the option to select from the four note types, as shown in Figure 6.21.

FIGURE 6.21.

*Running the Note
Style form.*

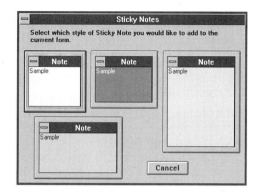

Plugging Sticky Notes into Your Access Application

To add Sticky Notes to one of your existing Access applications, do the following:

1. Import the following objects from the NOTES.MDB database into your database using the File|Import command:

   Notes table (import without the data)

   Note Style form

   Note1 through Note32 forms

   Notes module

2. Add the following subroutine calls to each form on which you wish to display notes, just as you did on the test form.

   In the `Form_Open` subroutine enter:

   ```
   OpenNotes Me
   ```

   In the `Form_Close` subroutine enter:

   ```
   CloseNotes
   ```

3. Add a button to each form to call the `AddNote` subroutine.

   In the `Button_Click` subroutine enter:

   ```
   AddNote
   ```

Enhancing Sticky Notes

You can enhance Sticky Notes by adding additional note styles.

You could add a heading at the top of each note with a label control to indicate what kind of message it is used for. The heading could be serious, like *Appointment:* or *Phone Call:*. It could be comical, as in *Your Mother called...* or *Virus Alert!*.

You could even add bitmaps to make your notes look like fancy stationery. Have fun!

Summary

I've shown you "Sticky Notes," a fun project that adds a little jazz to all of your Access projects. In this chapter, you

- Created the Notes table to store messages that you can look up by form name and note number
- Mass-produced 32 note forms
- Used some API calls, following example code from Access 1.1
- Enhanced your code's readability using constants
- Learned about global and module variable scope, and why you should be careful with globals
- Wrote a ton of code!
- Learned how to get a 3-D look for text in label controls
- Created an attractive form for selecting note styles
- Learned how to capture images for buttons
- Learned how to add Sticky Notes to other applications

TRY THIS! ANSWERS

6.1. To create a second test form, the easiest thing to do is copy the first one using Ctrl-C (copy) and Ctrl-V (paste) in the database container.

Next, add a button on each form that closes the current form and opens the next one. The subroutine behind the button's On Click event looks like this:

```
Sub cmdNextForm_Click ()

  DoCmd Close
  DoCmd OpenForm "_TestForm2"

End Sub
```

CHAPTER 7

Access: List Selection Dialog Boxes

Among the many neat user-interface breakthroughs employed in the Access wizards since Access first came out are what I call "list selection dialog boxes."

A *list selection dialog box* is a form with two lists—one representing the remaining available selections, and the other representing which items were selected. Between the two lists are four buttons labeled >, >>, <, and <<, which enable you to move items from the available list to the selected list and back again.

The Access wizards use this type of interface to enable you to choose which fields to display on a form or a report. The same technique could be used wherever a user is allowed to handpick a subset of items from a larger set, such as selecting a set of reports to send to the printer, as shown in Figure 7.1.

FIGURE 7.1.

Using the list selection technique to send reports to the printer.

In this chapter, you will create your own list selection dialog boxes that you can use in your applications. I even take this concept a step or two further than the wizards do by creating a multicolumn list selection dialog box that loads directly from an SQL Select statement.

Some of the material covered in this chapter is advanced in comparison to what I have covered in the preceding chapters, and there is a lot of code. You don't need to grasp all of it at once. The end of the chapter details the steps to use the list selection dialog boxes in your own programs. It will get you going even if some of the implementation details remain a little fuzzy at the outset.

How List Selection Dialog Boxes Work

In a list selection dialog box, the four arrow buttons do the following:

>   Move one item to the right
>>   Move all items to the right
<   Move one item to the left
<<   Move all items to the left

Another way to move an item from one list to the other is to double-click it, which pops it over to the opposite list.

Within each list on the form, an item is always selected as long as there is at least one item in the list. This marks the current position. The current position indicates which item would be moved next out of the list, or after which item a new item coming into the list would be placed. When a new item is added to the list, the new item becomes the current position, so the next item added will immediately follow it in the list.

By the nature of this design, you can't insert an item as the first item in the destination list if the list already has items in it. If you want to add a new first item, you have to delete all of the items that are currently in the list and then reinsert them after adding your new first item. Seems like kind of a bother, doesn't it? See Try This! Question 7.3 at the end of the chapter for a useful workaround to this limitation.

Creating the List Select Form

Let's get into the nitty gritties of how to create a list selection dialog box. The easiest part is creating the form. You can do this in an existing Access database project, or you can create a new database (or see LISTSLCT.MDB on the book's companion CD-ROM for a completed copy of this project).

1. Create a new form in Access with the following properties set:

Caption:	List Select
Default View:	Single Form
Scroll Bars:	Neither
Record Selectors:	No
Navigation Buttons:	No
Auto Center:	Yes
Pop Up:	Yes
Modal:	No
Border Style:	Dialog
Min Button:	No
Max Button:	No
Width:	4.7 in

2. Click the inside of the form to display the Detail0 section in the properties window. Set the Height property as follows:

Height:	1.9167 in

3. Using the Palette window, set the BackColor property of the Detail0 section to gray.

4. Drop a list box on the form with its associated label control. (See Figure 7.2.) Name the list box lstAvailable and the label control lblAvailable. Set each of the following properties:

Name:	lstAvailable
Row Source Type:	ListAvailable
Left:	0.2 in
Top:	0.3333 in
Width:	1.5097 in
Height:	1.4167 in
Special Effect:	Sunken
Font Name:	MS Sans Serif
Font Size:	8

Name:	lblAvailable
Caption:	&Available
Left:	0.2042 in
Top:	0.1667 in
Width:	1.4896 in
Height:	0.1667 in
Back Color:	12632256 (Gray)
Font Name:	MS Sans Serif
Font Size:	8
Font Weight:	Bold

FIGURE 7.2.

Creating the lstAvailable list box.

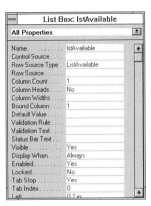

5. Select both the list box and the label and press Ctrl-C to copy them. Use Ctrl-V to paste a new list box and label on the form, as shown in Figure 7.3. Name the new list box lstSelected and the new label lblSelected. Set the following properties:

Name:	lstSelected
Row Source Type:	ListSelected
Left:	2.2 in
Top:	0.3333 in

Name:	lblSelected
Caption:	&Selected
Left:	2.2042 in
Top:	0.1667 in

FIGURE 7.3.

Adding the lstSelected list box.

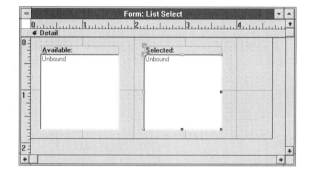

NOTE

When you created the list boxes, the Row Source Type property was set to ListAvailable for the first one and ListSelected for the second. ListAvailable and ListSelected will be Access Basic functions that are responsible for keeping the lists up to date with what should be displayed inside them.

6. Add a button to the form with the following properties:

Name:	cmdAdd
Caption:	>
Left:	1.8 in
Top:	0.5 in
Width:	0.3 in
Height:	0.1896 in
Font Name:	Small Fonts
Font Size:	6
Font Weight:	Bold

7. Copy the button and paste it on the form three times. Figure 7.4 shows the form with the four buttons added. Set the new buttons with the following properties:

Name:	cmdAddAll
Caption:	>>
Left:	1.8 in
Top:	0.7729 in

Name:	cmdRemove
Caption:	<
Left:	1.8 in
Top:	1.1667 in

Name:	cmdRemoveAll
Caption:	<<
Left:	1.8 in
Top:	1.4396 in

FIGURE 7.4.

Adding >, >>, <, and << buttons to the List Select form.

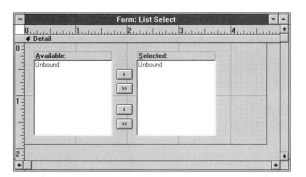

8. Create an OK button with the following properties set:

Name:	cmdOK
Caption:	OK
Default:	Yes
Left:	3.9 in
Top:	0.1667 in
Width:	0.6979 in
Height:	0.25 in
Font Name:	MS Sans Serif
Font Size:	8
Font Weight:	Bold

9. Copy the OK button and paste it. Then create a Cancel button with the following properties:

Name:	cmdCancel
Caption:	Cancel
Default:	No
Cancel:	Yes
Left:	3.9 in
Top:	0.4583 in

Figure 7.5 shows the form with the OK and Cancel buttons added.

FIGURE 7.5.

*Adding the OK and
Cancel buttons.*

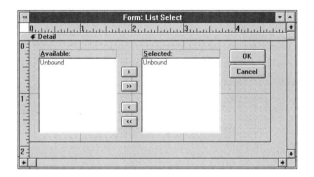

10. Select the **Edit|Tab** Order command and set the controls in the following order, as shown in Figure 7.6:

lstAvailable
cmdAdd
cmdAddAll
cmdRemove
cmdRemoveAll
lstSelected
cmdOK
cmdCancel

FIGURE 7.6.

*Adjusting the tab order
for the controls on the
List Select form.*

11. Close the form, entering List Select as the name of the form in the Save As dialog box.

Communicating Through Globals

The List Select form should be reusable so that it can be added to any application in which you want to use a list selection dialog box.

Each of these applications needs to be able to communicate with the List Select form. They need to be able to pass information to it to tell what items should be displayed and later be able to read back from it which of those items the user selected.

This communication is accomplished through the use of global variables. Globals can be read both from the program's code and the code behind the List Select form. The global variables for this purpose are declared in the List Select module, which you create next.

1. Create a new module and enter Listing 7.1 as the declaration section.

2. Close the module, saving it as List Select.

   You will be adding more to the List Select module later.

Listing 7.1. Declarations section in the List Select module.

```
' List Select module

  Option Compare Database
  Option Explicit

  Const PROGRAM = "List Select"

' Contents of the left and right lists
  Global gastrAvailable() As String
  Global gastrSelected() As String

' Width of each column in the lists
  Global gasngListWidths() As Single

' Captions on the List Select form
  Global gstrListSelectCaption As String
  Global gstrAvailableCaption As String
  Global gstrSelectedCaption As String

' Set if user cancel's List Select form
  Global gblnListSelectCancel As Integer

' Set to true to indicate its OK to open the List Select form
  Global gblnListSelectInit As Integer
```

Using your special Dick Tracy Hungarian Prefix Decoder Watch, you can learn the following information about the preceding variables from their names alone:

gastr	A global array of strings
gasng	A global array of single precision numbers
gstr	A global string
gbln	A global integer storing a Boolean value

The `gastrAvailable` and `gastrSelected` arrays contain the contents of the list boxes. Changing the contents of the list boxes involves changing these arrays and then requerying the list boxes so they can repaint with the new values in the string arrays.

The `gasngListWidths` array stores column-width settings in inches for the columns in the list boxes. The total of all values in the array should add up to 1.5 inches, which is the width of the list boxes on your form.

The next three variables can be used to change the captions displayed in the List Select form. This adds to the reusability of the form. If the strings are left blank, the captions are left as is.

gstrListSelectCaption	Caption on the form title bar
gstrAvailableCaption	Caption for the lblAvailable label
gstrSelectedCaption	Caption for the lblSelected label

The `gblnListSelectCancel` variable is a flag to indicate whether the List Select form was closed without pressing OK. You can cancel the dialog box by pressing the Cancel button or by closing it with the system bar menu.

The `gblnListSelectInit` variable is a flag used when the List Select form loads to verify that it was opened via code and not by a user opening the form from the database container. This way, when the form is opened with all of its globals properly initialized, it can display an error message and close gracefully rather than display with error messages and empty lists.

Are you confused yet? It gets worse, although it might clear up as you see all the pieces working together.

As I mentioned in the introduction to this chapter, you need to know many of these details only if you are curious about how the actual implementation works, not if you care only about using it in your own programs. That part comes later.

For the truly fearless, I'll continue explaining all the gory details as you build the project.

Coding the List Select Form

The next piece I attack is the code behind the List Select form.

1. Open the List Select form in design mode.
2. Click the Code button on the toolbar to view the List Select form module.
3. Enter the declarations section for the List Select form module as shown in Listing 7.2.

Listing 7.2. The declarations section for the List Select form.

```
' List Select form

Option Compare Database
Option Explicit

Const PROGRAM = "List Select"
Const TWIPS_PER_INCH = 1440
```

The TWIPS_PER_INCH constant is used to translate values in inches to values in twips.

> **NOTE**
>
> *Twips* are the unit of measurement used in Basic code for the placement of controls on forms and reports. As the name of the constant indicates, there are 1440 twips per inch.
>
> If twips sounds like a funny name for a unit of measurement, consider that mickeys are a unit of measurement for mouse cursor movements in Windows.

Form_Open

As is typical with Form_Open subroutines, the Form_Open subroutine for the List Select form includes several initialization steps. Here many of the global variables declared in the List Select module are used to set values on the form.

Use Code Builder to create a Form_Open subroutine on the On Open event for the form, or just type it in manually. Then fill in the Form_Open module as shown in Listing 7.3.

Listing 7.3. The Form_Open subroutine.

```
Sub Form_Open (Cancel As Integer)

  Dim strColumnWidths As String
  Dim intColumns As Integer
  Dim n As Integer

  On Error GoTo Form_OpenError

  If Not gblnListSelectInit Then
    MsgBox "Open this form with the ListSelect function.", 64, PROGRAM
    Cancel = True
    GoTo Form_OpenDone
  End If

' Default to cancel.
' The user has to press OK to accept the current selection.
  gblnListSelectCancel = True

' Set captions
  If Len(gstrListSelectCaption) > 0 Then
    Me.Caption = gstrListSelectCaption
  End If

  If Len(gstrAvailableCaption) > 0 Then
    lblAvailable.Caption = gstrAvailableCaption
  End If

  If Len(gstrSelectedCaption) > 0 Then
    lblSelected.Caption = gstrSelectedCaption
  End If

' Set the column widths
  intColumns = UBound(gasngListWidths)
  If intColumns > 0 Then
    strColumnWidths = ""
    For n = 1 To intColumns
      strColumnWidths = strColumnWidths & gasngListWidths(n) & " in;"
    Next n

    lstAvailable.ColumnCount = intColumns
    lstAvailable.ColumnWidths = strColumnWidths

    lstSelected.ColumnCount = intColumns
    lstSelected.ColumnWidths = strColumnWidths
  End If

Form_OpenDone:
  Exit Sub

Form_OpenError:
  MsgBox Error$, 48, PROGRAM
  Resume Form_OpenDone

End Sub
```

The subroutine begins by checking to see if the `gblnListSelectInit` variable has been set to True (–1). This would occur in code that initializes the global variables for the List Select form.

If the variable wasn't set, the code assumes that the other required globals weren't set either. It displays a message to indicate how to open the form properly. It then sets the Cancel argument to True, as shown in Listing 7.4, which tells Access to cancel opening the form altogether.

Listing 7.4. Checking for proper initialization.

```
If Not gblnListSelectInit Then
  MsgBox "Open this form with the ListSelect function.", 64, PROGRAM
  Cancel = True
  GoTo Form_OpenDone
End If
```

Next, the subroutine initializes the `gblnListSelectCancel` flag to True. If the form is closed in any way without this flag being set to False, the function that opened the form can safely assume that no selections were made.

```
' Default to cancel.
' The user has to press OK to accept the current selection.
  gblnListSelectCancel = True
```

The subroutine then checks to see if values were stored in the `gstrListSelectCaption`, `gstrAvailableCaption`, or `gstrSelectedCaption` global variables, as shown in Listing 7.5. The values in these globals are used to assign the form's caption and the captions of the labels above the two list boxes.

Listing 7.5. Assigning the form and label captions.

```
' Set captions
  If Len(gstrListSelectCaption) > 0 Then
    Me.Caption = gstrListSelectCaption
  End If

  If Len(gstrAvailableCaption) > 0 Then
    lblAvailable.Caption = gstrAvailableCaption
  End If

  If Len(gstrSelectedCaption) > 0 Then
    lblSelected.Caption = gstrSelectedCaption
  End If
```

The gasngListWidths global array is then read for column-width settings for the two list boxes, as shown in Listing 7.6. The size of the array indicates how many columns are used. A For...Next loop is used to retrieve the values from the array and build a string that can be used to set the Column Widths property for the list boxes. For example, if the column widths were .25, .75, and .5, the string created would be .25 in; .75 in;.5 in;.

Listing 7.6. Setting the list box column widths.

```
' Set the column widths
 intColumns = UBound(gasngListWidths)
 If intColumns > 0 Then
   strColumnWidths = ""
   For n = 1 To intColumns
     strColumnWidths = strColumnWidths & gasngListWidths(n) & " in;"
   Next n

   lstAvailable.ColumnCount = intColumns
   lstAvailable.ColumnWidths = strColumnWidths

   lstSelected.ColumnCount = intColumns
   lstSelected.ColumnWidths = strColumnWidths
 End If
```

TRY THIS! QUESTION 7.1.

Can you make the text that appears on the OK button changeable? Be sure to keep in sync with the reusable design of the List Select form and module.

List Callback Functions

Next you will create the functions that fill the lstAvailable and lstSelected list box controls. First I will give you some background information.

A list box or combo box control in Access can display values from four different kinds of sources. Each is a possible setting to the Row Source Type property.

1. Table/Query   A table, query, or SQL Select statement
2. Value List   A set of values delimited by semicolons
3. Field List   Field names for a table or query
4. The name of a specially formatted Basic function call.

You need to set the Row Source Type properties of the lstAvailable and lstSelected list boxes to the names of the appropriate Basic functions: `ListAvailable` and `ListSelected`. You can leave the Row Source property blank on each list box because it isn't required with this Row Source Type.

A list callback function is declared as shown here:

```
Function ListCallback (ctl As Control, varID As Variant, varRow As Variant,
➥ varColumn, varCode As Variant) As Variant
```

Access calls your list callback function many times while the list is being displayed. Each time Access makes a call, it is asking for a particular piece of information about the list box. It might ask how many rows are to be displayed, or the actual value for a cell on a particular row and column within the list box.

The arguments to a list callback function must be the following:

`ctl`	Points to the list box control in question
`varID`	Your identification number for the list box control
`varRow`	The current row
`varColumn`	The current column
`varCode`	Which piece of information Access needs

The first argument is Control object, and the remaining four arguments are variant data types (as shown in the declaration above).

A list callback function's return value depends on which piece of information Access is requesting, as indicated by the `varCode` argument. The possible `varCode` values follow:

0	Enables initialization, return status (0 for failure)
1	An ID for your use to identify the control
3	Number of rows
4	Number of columns
5	Column width for the column number in `varColumn`
6	Text to display for row `varRow` and column `varColumn`
9	Enables deallocation, no information returned

Now I take a look at the functions that do this work in the List Select form.

ListAvailable and *ListSelected* Functions

Enter the `ListAvailable` and `ListSelected` functions into the List Select form module, as shown in Listings 7.7 and 7.8.

Listing 7.7. The ListAvailable function.

```
Function ListAvailable (ctl As Control, varID As Variant, varRow As Variant,
➥ varColumn, varCode As Variant) As Variant

  On Error Resume Next

  Select Case varCode

  Case 0 ' Initialization
    ListAvailable = 1

  Case 1 ' Return ID
    ListAvailable = 1

  Case 3 ' Return number of rows
    ListAvailable = UBound(gastrAvailable)

  Case 4 ' Return number of columns
    ListAvailable = UBound(gasngListWidths)

  Case 5 ' Return column width
    ListAvailable = gasngListWidths(varColumn + 1) * TWIPS_PER_INCH

  Case 6 ' Return data
    ListAvailable = StrListExtract(gastrAvailable(varRow + 1), varColumn + 1)

  Case 9 ' End

  End Select

End Function
```

Listing 7.8. The ListSelected function.

```
Function ListSelected (ctl As Control, varID As Variant, varRow As Variant,
➥ varColumn, varCode As Variant) As Variant

  On Error Resume Next

  Select Case varCode

  Case 0 ' Initialization
    ListSelected = 1

  Case 1 ' Return ID
    ListSelected = 1

  Case 3 ' Return number of rows
    ListSelected = UBound(gastrSelected)

  Case 4 ' Return number of columns
    ListSelected = UBound(gasngListWidths)
```

continues

Listing 7.8. continued

```
Case 5 ' Return column width
    ListSelected = gasngListWidths(varColumn + 1) * TWIPS_PER_INCH

  Case 6 ' Return data
    ListSelected = StrListExtract(gastrSelected(varRow + 1), varColumn + 1)

  Case 9 ' End

  End Select

End Function
```

The `ListAvailable` and `ListSelected` functions are identical except that the former uses the `gastrAvailable` array and the latter uses the `gastrSelected` array. In my discussion I look at the `ListAvailable` function.

The first thing the function does is turn off error checking:

```
On Error Resume Next
```

For a list callback function, it's better this way because of the frequency with which the function is called. If an error message were displayed, it might get displayed again and again and immediately become a major nuisance.

Next, the function uses the `Select...Case` construct on the `varCode` value passed by Access:

```
Select Case varCode
```

If `varCode` is 0, the callback is being called during form loading to enable initialization. In this case, you have already allocated and filled arrays that store the contents of the list and don't have any further initialization to do.

Any non-zero value can be returned to indicate success. If you return 0, the list box does not display any data.

```
Case 0 ' Initialization
  ListAvailable = 1
```

When the `varCode` parameter is set to 1, Access is asking for an ID number for the list box. The number you return is passed in the `varID` parameter for all subsequent calls. You can use this to allow a single list callback function to be responsible for more than one list on the screen at a time.

In this case, you just return a 1 because each list has its own list callback function.

```
Case 1 ' Return ID
  ListAvailable = 1
```

A varCode value of 3 indicates that Access wants to know the total number of rows that appear in your list box. In the ListAvailable function, that is the number of items in the gastrAvailable string array.

```
Case 3 ' Return number of rows
   ListAvailable = UBound(gastrAvailable)
```

A varCode value of 4 means you need to return the number of columns in the list box. In the ListAvailable function, this is the number of column-width values in the gasngListWidths array.

```
Case 4 ' Return number of columns
   ListAvailable = UBound(gasngListWidths)
```

Access sends a varCode value of 5 when it wants to know the width of a particular column in the list box. The column in question is passed as a 0-based value (0 is the first column, 1 is the second column) in the varColumn parameter.

You are storing the column widths in a 1-based array, where each value is stored as a single precision floating-point number representing the column width in inches. To get to the appropriate value, the subroutine adds 1 to the varColumn value. Then it multiplies the value found in the array by the TWIPS_PER_INCH constant to return the measurement in twips.

```
Case 5 ' Return column width
   ListAvailable = gasngListWidths(varColumn + 1) * TWIPS_PER_INCH
```

A varCode of 6 indicates that Access wants the actual text to display in a cell within the list box. The varRow and varColumn values contain the 0-based coordinates of which cell Access is asking for:

```
Case 6 ' Return data
   ListAvailable = StrListExtract(gastrAvailable(varRow + 1), varColumn + 1)
```

The text for all columns in a particular row is stored in a single string in the gastrAvailable array. The string for the appropriate row is retrieved with the following expression:

```
gastrAvailable(varRow + 1)
```

If the list box has three columns displaying First, Middle, and Last names, a string containing values for each column would look like this:

```
"Charles¦Everett¦Schuy"
```

The entries for each column are separated by the vertical bar character (¦). The StrListExtract function is used to retrieve one of the values from the string. It is passed the actual string and a 1-based column number indicating which item to return.

The varCode variable is set to 9 when the form is being closed. Access calls the list callback function to enable it to clean up after any allocated arrays or opened tables during the initialization of the callback function. Because you are basing the list contents on global arrays that are allocated elsewhere, this is not the place to release them.

```
Case 9 ' End

End Select
```

The Move Events

Six events on the form have code behind them to move items back and forth between the lists:

cmdAdd_Click	Move one item to the right
cmdAddAll_Click	Move all items to the right
cmdRemove_Click	Move one item to the left
cmdRemoveAll_Click	Move all items to the left
lstAvailable_DblClick	Same as cmdAdd_Click
lstSelected_DblClick	Same as cmdRemove_Click

 Enter Listings 7.9, 7.10, 7.11, and 7.12 for the cmdAdd, cmdAddAll, cmdRemove and cmdRemoveAll buttons' On Click events.

Listing 7.9. The cmdAdd_Click subroutine.

```
Sub cmdAdd_Click ()

  Dim z As Integer

  z = ListTransfer(lstAvailable, gastrAvailable(), lstSelected,
  ➥ gastrSelected())

End Sub
```

Listing 7.10. The cmdAddAll_Click subroutine.

```
Sub cmdAddAll_Click ()

  Dim z As Integer

  z = ListTransferAll(lstAvailable, gastrAvailable(), lstSelected,
  ➥ gastrSelected())

End Sub
```

Listing 7.11. The `cmdRemove_Click` **subroutine.**

```
Sub cmdRemove_Click ()

  Dim z As Integer

  z = ListTransfer(lstSelected, gastrSelected(), lstAvailable,
  ➥ gastrAvailable())

End Sub
```

Listing 7.12. The `cmdRemoveAll_Click` **subroutine.**

```
Sub cmdRemoveAll_Click ()

  Dim z As Integer

  z = ListTransferAll(lstSelected, gastrSelected(), lstAvailable,
  ➥ gastrAvailable())

End Sub
```

The four subroutines listed previously economize by calling the `ListTransfer` and `ListTransferAll` functions to do the work of moving the items from one list to another. For example, the only difference between the `cmdRemove_Click` subroutine and the `cmdAdd_Click` subroutine is that the arguments to the `ListTransfer` function are switched around to move an item in the opposite direction.

Some further economizing occurs in the next two subroutines, `lstAvailable_DblClick` and `lstSelected_DblClick`. Double-clicking the lstAvailable list box has the same effect as clicking the cmdAdd button, so it makes sense that one could just call the `cmdAdd_Click` subroutine rather than reimplementing moving a list item in code.

Enter Listings 7.13 and 7.14 as the lstAvailable and lstSelected list boxes' On DblClick events.

Listing 7.13. The `lstAvailable_DblClick` **subroutine.**

```
Sub lstAvailable_DblClick (Cancel As Integer)

  cmdAdd_Click

End Sub
```

Listing 7.14. The `lstSelected_DblClick` **subroutine.**

```
Sub lstSelected_DblClick (Cancel As Integer)

  cmdRemove_Click

End Sub
```

ListTransfer

Now you get to the functions that actually do some work in moving the items back and forth between the lists.

The `ListTransfer` function moves a single item from one list to the other. This means it must remove the item from one list, shifting any following items up, then insert it into the other list, possibly shifting items in that list down to make room for it.

Enter the `ListTransfer` function into the List Select form module as shown in Listing 7.15.

Listing 7.15. The `ListTransfer` **function.**

```
Function ListTransfer (ctlSource As Control, astrSource() As String,
➥ ctlDest As Control, astrDest() As String) As Integer

' Transfer an item from one listbox to another.

' This is done by maintaining the string arrays that are the Source of the
' listboxes, and then using the Requery command to redisplay the listboxes.

  Dim strSource As String
  Dim strDest As String
  Dim strCursor As String

  Dim intSourceCount As Integer
  Dim intDestCount As Integer
  Dim n As Integer
  Dim blnFound As Integer

' Assume failure
  ListTransfer = True

  On Error Resume Next

  intSourceCount = UBound(astrSource)
  If Err <> 0 Then GoTo ListTransferDone

  intDestCount = UBound(astrDest)
  If Err <> 0 Then GoTo ListTransferDone

  On Error GoTo ListTransferError
```

```
    If intSourceCount = 0 Or IsNull(ctlSource.Column(0)) Then
      GoTo ListTransferDone
    End If

    strSource = ListString(ctlSource)

' Shift up any items that follow the deleted one
    blnFound = False
    For n = 1 To intSourceCount
      If blnFound Then
        astrSource(n - 1) = astrSource(n)
      Else
        If astrSource(n) = strSource Then
          blnFound = True
          If n < intSourceCount Then
            strCursor = astrSource(n + 1)
          ElseIf n > 1 Then
            strCursor = astrSource(n - 1)
          Else
            strCursor = ""
          End If
        End If
      End If
    Next n

' Shorten the source list
    ReDim Preserve astrSource(intSourceCount - 1) As String

' Extend the destination list
    ReDim Preserve astrDest(intDestCount + 1) As String

' Add the item to the destination list
    n = intDestCount + 1
    If intDestCount > 0 And Not IsNull(ctlDest.Column(0)) Then

      ' Add to a list based on the current position.
      strDest = ListString(ctlDest)

      For n = intDestCount To 1 Step -1
        If astrDest(n) = strDest Then
          n = n + 1
          Exit For
        End If
        astrDest(n + 1) = astrDest(n)
      Next n

      If n < 1 Then n = 1
    End If

    astrDest(n) = strSource

    ctlSource.Requery
    ctlDest.Requery

' Make the item that was added the current selection
    ctlDest = StrListExtract(strSource, 1)
```

continues

Listing 7.15. continued

```
' Set the cursor in the source list
  ctlSource = StrListExtract(strCursor, 1)

' Success
  ListTransfer = False

ListTransferDone:
  Exit Function

ListTransferError:
  MsgBox Error$, 48, PROGRAM
  Resume ListTransferDone

End Function
```

The `ListTransfer` function is passed the following arguments:

ctlSource	List box the item is coming from
astrSource	Current rows in the source list
ctlDest	List box the item is going to
astrDest	Current rows in the destination list box

The function first determines the number of items in each row by checking the length of the two string arrays passed as parameters, as shown in Listing 7.16.

Listing 7.16. Checking the length of the passed arrays.

```
On Error Resume Next

intSourceCount = UBound(astrSource)
If Err <> 0 Then GoTo ListTransferDone

intDestCount = UBound(astrDest)
If Err <> 0 Then GoTo ListTransferDone

On Error GoTo ListTransferError
```

If the source list is empty, there is no item to move, and the function exits.

```
If intSourceCount = 0 Or IsNull(ctlSource.Column(0)) Then
  GoTo ListTransferDone
End If
```

The next section of code, shown in the excerpt in Listing 7.17, can best be understood by stepping through it line by line in the debugger.

First, the ListString function is called to create a delimited string containing the contents of the current item in the list. See the section on creating the StrListExtract function toward the end of the chapter to find out about delimited strings.

Next, the subroutine loops through each item in the list. In going through the items, the function is looking for which row in the list is the currently selected item. When it is found, the blnFound flag is set to True.

The strCursor variable is set to which item—if any—should become the new current item after the present current item is removed from the list.

Listing 7.17. Updating the source list.

```
strSource = ListString(ctlSource)

' Shift up any items that follow the deleted one
blnFound = False
For n = 1 To intSourceCount
  If blnFound Then
    astrSource(n - 1) = astrSource(n)
  Else
    If astrSource(n) = strSource Then
      blnFound = True
      If n < intSourceCount Then
        strCursor = astrSource(n + 1)
      ElseIf n > 1 Then
        strCursor = astrSource(n - 1)
      Else
        strCursor = ""
      End If
    End If
  End If
Next n
```

The remaining iterations through the loop move each item up one notch in the list, overwriting the one before it. That happens in this line:

```
astrSource(n - 1) = astrSource(n)
```

If you have a list A, B, C, and D and want to remove B, the iterations would look like this:

A, B, C, D	First iteration, B not found
A, **B**, C, D	Second iteration, B is found
A, C, **C**, D	Third iteration, C copied over B
A, C, D, **D**	Fourth iteration, D copied over old C
A, C, D	List shortened

Next you need to trim up the length of the list. ReDim is called with the Preserve keyword, which resizes the string array without losing the contents of what is stored in the remaining elements after resizing it.

```
' Shorten the source list
  ReDim Preserve astrSource(intSourceCount - 1) As String
```

That was the first job, to remove the item from the source list. Now you need to add it to the next list. The first thing you must do here is lengthen the string array to provide room for an incoming item.

```
' Extend the destination list
  ReDim Preserve astrDest(intDestCount + 1) As String
```

Adding the item involves starting from the end of the list and moving backward until the appropriate slot is found to add the item, as shown in Listing 7.18. As the astrDest string array is traversed from back to front, each string in the array is moved one slot down to make room for the incoming item.

Listing 7.18. Adding an item to a list.

```
' Add the item to the destination list
  n = intDestCount + 1
  If intDestCount > 0 And Not IsNull(ctlDest.Column(0)) Then

  ' Add to a list based on the current position.
    strDest = ListString(ctlDest)

    For n = intDestCount To 1 Step -1
      If astrDest(n) = strDest Then
        n = n + 1
        Exit For
      End If
      astrDest(n + 1) = astrDest(n)
    Next n

    If n < 1 Then n = 1
  End If

  astrDest(n) = strSource
```

Suppose you are adding item B to the list E, F, G, and H. If the new item B is supposed to occupy the current F position, the iterations would look like this:

E, F, G, H, .	List extended
E, F, G, **H**, H	First iteration, H copied down
E, F, **G**, G, H	Second iteration, G copied down
E, **F**, F, G, H	Third iteration, F copied down
E, B, F, G, H	B copied into slot where F was

Next, the `Requery` method is called on the list boxes to cause them to refresh their display based on the new contents of their source arrays. This causes a chain of calls to the `ListAvailable` and `ListSelected` functions you created earlier.

```
ctlSource.Requery
ctlDest.Requery
```

The remaining step is to set the new current item in each list.

```
' Make the item that was added the current selection
ctlDest = StrListExtract(strSource, 1)

' Set the cursor in the source list
ctlSource = StrListExtract(strCursor, 1)
```

ListTransferAll

The `ListTransferAll` function has the same job as the `ListTransfer` function except that it must move all items from the source list to the destination list.

An earlier version of this function simply called the `ListTransfer` function over and over until the source list was empty. However, I rewrote it to do the work itself as an optimization to get a snappier response from it.

Enter the `ListTransferAll` function as shown in Listing 7.19.

Listing 7.19. The `ListTransferAll` function.

```
Function ListTransferAll (ctlSource As Control, astrSource() As String,
➥ ctlDest As Control, astrDest() As String) As Integer

' Transfer all of the items from one listbox to another.

  Dim strDest As String

  Dim intSourceCurrent As Integer
  Dim intDestCurrent As Integer

  Dim intSourceCount As Integer
  Dim intDestCount As Integer
  Dim n As Integer
  Dim z As Integer

' Assume failure
  ListTransferAll = True

  On Error Resume Next

  intSourceCount = UBound(astrSource)
  If Err <> 0 Then GoTo ListTransferAllDone

  intDestCount = UBound(astrDest)
  If Err <> 0 Then GoTo ListTransferAllDone
```

continues

Listing 7.19. continued

```
On Error GoTo ListTransferAllError

If intSourceCount = 0 Then GoTo ListTransferAllDone

' Extend the destination list
ReDim Preserve astrDest(intDestCount + intSourceCount) As String

intDestCurrent = intDestCount + 1

If intDestCount > 0 And Not IsNull(ctlDest) Then

  ' Add to a list based on the current position
  strDest = ListString(ctlDest)

  For intDestCurrent = intDestCount To 1 Step -1
    If astrDest(intDestCurrent) = strDest Then
      intDestCurrent = intDestCurrent + 1
      Exit For
    End If
    astrDest(intDestCurrent + intSourceCount) = astrDest(intDestCurrent)
  Next intDestCurrent

End If

For intSourceCurrent = 1 To intSourceCount

  ' Add the items to the destination list
  n = intDestCount + 1
  If intDestCount > 1 And Not IsNull(ctlDest.Column(0)) Then
    n = intDestCurrent
    intDestCurrent = intDestCurrent + 1

    If n < 1 Then n = 1
  Else
    n = intDestCurrent
    intDestCurrent = intDestCurrent + 1
  End If

  astrDest(n) = astrSource(intSourceCurrent)
  intDestCount = intDestCount + 1

Next intSourceCurrent

strDest = astrSource(intSourceCurrent - 1)

' Shorten the source list
ReDim Preserve astrSource(0) As String

lstAvailable.Requery
lstSelected.Requery

' Make the last item that was added the current selection
ctlDest = strDest

' Success
ListTransferAll = False
```

```
ListTransferAllDone:
  Exit Function

ListTransferAllError:
  MsgBox Error$, 48, PROGRAM
  Resume ListTransferAllDone

End Function
```

The ListTransferAll function works similarly to the ListTransfer function except that adjustments are made because several items are being moved at once.

For example, extending the length of the destination list is done by adding the lengths of both lists:

```
' Extend the destination list
  ReDim Preserve astrDest(intDestCount + intSourceCount) As String
```

In making room for the inserted items, items are moved down the number of slots needed for the incoming items, not just one. After the destination slots are made available, a loop inserts the source items into the destination list.

Whew! You're done with the tough ones anyway.

ListString

The next function produces a vertical bar delimited string for the current selected row in a list box.

Enter the ListString function into the List Select form module as shown in Listing 7.20.

Listing 7.20. The ListString function.

```
Function ListString (ctl As Control) As String

' Create a string delimited list from a row in the list.

  Dim sz As String
  Dim intColumns As Integer
  Dim n As Integer

  ListString = ""
  On Error GoTo ListStringError

  If IsNull(ctl) Then GoTo ListStringDone

  sz = ""
```

continues

Listing 7.20. continued

```
  intColumns = UBound(gasngListWidths) - 2

  For n = 0 To intColumns
    sz = sz & CStr(ctl.Column(n)) & "¦"
  Next n

  sz = sz & CStr(ctl.Column(n))

  ListString = sz

ListStringDone:
  Exit Function

ListStringError:
  MsgBox Error$, 48, PROGRAM
  Resume ListStringDone

End Function
```

The ListString function retrieves each value in the list box's current row using the Column property with a zero-based offset indicating which column is being retrieved.

The values are added to the sz string along with the vertical bar delimiter character, up to one before the last column. The remaining column is added without the delimiter.

Setting a Current List Item

When the List Select form first opens, neither the lstAvailable list box nor the lstSelected list box shows a selected item. You can perhaps shave a required click or two off the form for the user by selecting an item in either list whenever the lists are not empty.

Doing this isn't as easy as it would seem. You can't set the selected item in a list box just any old time while the form is loading, or Access displays an error. A good time to do this is when the On Enter event for the first control on the form is fired.

Enter the lstAvailable_Enter subroutine in Listing 7.21 for the lstAvailable list box's On Enter event.

Listing 7.21. The lstAvailable_Enter subroutine.

```
Sub lstAvailable_Enter ()

' Set a current item in each listbox

  On Error GoTo lstAvailable_EnterError

  If gblnListSelectInit Then
```

```
      gblnListSelectInit = False

   ' Select the first item if there is at least one
     If lstAvailable.ListCount > 0 Then
       lstAvailable = StrListExtract(gastrAvailable(1), 1)
     End If

   ' Select the last item if there is at least one
     If lstSelected.ListCount > 0 Then
       lstSelected = StrListExtract(gastrSelected(lstSelected.ListCount), 1)
     End If
   End If

lstAvailable_EnterDone:
   Exit Sub

lstAvailable_EnterError:
   MsgBox Error$, 48, PROGRAM
   Resume lstAvailable_EnterDone

End Sub
```

The lstAvailable_Enter function checks the gblnListSelectInit variable to determine if the form is being loaded. If this variable is set to True, it does its job of setting the current items in each list and resetting the gblnListSelectInit variable to False.

Setting the current item in each list box is done by setting the control to a value matching one of the values in its bound column.

Closing the List Select Form

To complete the List Select form module, you need code that responds to the click of the OK and Cancel buttons.

Enter Listing 7.22 and Listing 7.23 as the cmdOK and cmdCancel buttons' On Click events.

Listing 7.22. The cmdOK_Click **subroutine.**

```
Sub cmdOK_Click ()

  gblnListSelectCancel = False
  DoCmd Close

End Sub
```

Listing 7.23. The `cmdCancel_Click` subroutine.

```
Sub cmdCancel_Click ()

  DoCmd Close

End Sub
```

Both of these subroutines close the form by calling the Close macro. The `cmdOK_Click` subroutine also sets the `gblnListSelectCancel` global to False, indicating that the selections made by the user should be accepted and acted upon.

Close the List Select form and module, being sure to save your changes.

Next you will finish the List Select module started at the beginning of the chapter and create some test functions to see how all this works.

StrListExtract

This function is one of my favorites, and you will want to add it to your library of the stuff you use every day.

The `StrListExtract` function removes one item from a string of items delimited by the vertical bar character.

A delimiter character is also sometimes called a *sentinel*. A *delimiter character* is a character that separates one item of text from another. C programmers are immediately familiar with this concept because they use the Null character (a character with the ASCII value of 0) in many functions that deal with character arrays.

The term *delimiter* implies that not only does the sentinel character mark the termination of an entry, but it is also just before the point where another entry begins.

`StrListExtract` uses the vertical bar character as the delimiter character. If you called `StrListExtract` like this

```
strPhone = StrListExtract("Mimi¦555-1234¦Woodinville¦Wa",2)
```

the result stored in `strPhone` would be `555-1234`, the second item in the list.

1. Click the Module tab on the database container. Open the List Select module in design mode.
2. Enter the `StrListExtract` function as shown in Listing 7.24.

Listing 7.24. The `StrListExtract` **function.**

```
Function StrListExtract (strDelimitedList As String, intColumn As Integer)
➥ As String

' Extract a value from a delimited list of values in a string.
' The vertical bar character is used as the delimiting character.

' Example:  StrListExtract("abc¦def¦ghi",2) would return "def".

  Dim intStart As Integer
  Dim intEnd As Integer
  Dim n As Integer

  On Error GoTo StrListExtractError

' Default to nothing found
  StrListExtract = ""

  If intColumn < 1 Then GoTo StrListExtractDone

  intStart = 1
  For n = 1 To intColumn - 1
    intStart = InStr(intStart, strDelimitedList, "¦")
    If intStart = 0 Then GoTo StrListExtractDone

    intStart = intStart + 1
  Next n

  intEnd = InStr(intStart, strDelimitedList, "¦")
  If intEnd = 0 Then intEnd = Len(strDelimitedList) + 1

  StrListExtract = Mid$(strDelimitedList, intStart, intEnd - intStart)
StrListExtractDone:
  Exit Function

StrListExtractError:
  MsgBox Error$
  Resume StrListExtractDone

End Function
```

The `StrListExtract` function sets up an initial return value of an empty string. You can make a return assignment like this in a function and negate it with another return value later in the function.

An example of where this initial return value gets used is in the preceding line. If the `intColumn` value passed is negative (an invalid value), the function exits early.

```
' Default to nothing found
  StrListExtract = ""

  If intColumn < 1 Then GoTo StrListExtractDone
```

The next part of the function does the work of scanning through the string for delimiter characters to find the text to be returned. The `intStart` variable represents the starting point for each search for the next delimiter, and eventually the starting point for the text returned.

The `InStr` function can be called with two, three, or four arguments. When it is called with three arguments, the first argument represents the character offset to start the search. The second argument is the string being searched through, and the third argument is the string being searched for.

On each search, `intStart` is set to the offset for the delimiter character found. To find the next one, `intStart` is incremented by 1 so that the next search starts after the delimiter character already found:

```
intStart = 1
For n = 1 To intColumn - 1
  intStart = InStr(intStart, strDelimitedList, "¦")
  If intStart = 0 Then GoTo StrListExtractDone

  intStart = intStart + 1
Next n
```

After the loop has been iterated enough to place `intStart` on the starting character of the text to return, `InStr` is called again to find a delimiter and locate the end of the text for the current entry. If the delimiter was not found, it is safe to grab the remaining text from `intStart` on as the entry:

```
intEnd = InStr(intStart, strDelimitedList, "¦")
If intEnd = 0 Then intEnd = Len(strDelimitedList) + 1
```

The `Mid$` function is used to extract the text, using `intStart` and `intEnd` as coordinates to determine what to extract. The third argument to `Mid$` is the number of characters to extract. This is calculated by subtracting `intEnd` from `intStart`:

```
StrListExtract = Mid$(strDelimitedList, intStart, intEnd - intStart)
```

ListSelect

The `ListSelect` function is one of two functions intended for your application to call when using the List Select form. The other is `ListSelectSQL`.

Use `ListSelect` to open the List Select form.

Enter the `ListSelect` function as shown in Listing 7.25.

Listing 7.25. The `ListSelect` function.

```
Function ListSelect (astrAvailable() As String, astrSelected() As String,
➥ asngColumnWidths() As Single) As Integer

' Display a List Select dialog
'
' Returns True if user cancels or an error occurs.
'
' On success, the selected values are transfered from the
' astrAvailable array to the astrSelected array.
'

' Assume failure
  ListSelect = True

  On Error GoTo ListSelectError

  StringArrayCopy astrAvailable(), gastrAvailable()
  StringArrayCopy astrSelected(), gastrSelected()
  SingleArrayCopy asngColumnWidths(), gasngListWidths()

  gblnListSelectInit = True
  DoCmd OpenForm "List Select", , , , , A_DIALOG

  If Not gblnListSelectCancel Then
    StringArrayCopy gastrAvailable(), astrAvailable()
    StringArrayCopy gastrSelected(), astrSelected()
    SingleArrayCopy gasngListWidths(), asngColumnWidths()
  End If

  ListSelect = gblnListSelectCancel

ListSelectDone:
  Exit Function

ListSelectError:
  MsgBox Error$, 48, PROGRAM
  Resume ListSelectDone

End Function
```

The job of this function is to copy the passed arrays into the global arrays used by the List Select form, so that the results can alternately be returned depending on whether the user clicked OK or Cancel. If the user clicks OK, the results in the global arrays are copied into the passed arrays, thereby affecting the application.

The `ListSelect` function returns False (0) for success, or True (–1) to indicate an error or that the user canceled.

StringArrayCopy and *SingleArrayCopy*

The StringArrayCopy and SingleArrayCopy subroutines resize the destination array to the same size as the source array, and then copy the contents of the source array into the destination array.

Enter the StringArrayCopy and SingleArrayCopy subroutines into the List Select module as shown in Listings 7.26 and 7.27.

Listing 7.26. The StringArrayCopy **subroutine.**

```
Sub StringArrayCopy (astrSource() As String, astrDest() As String)

    Dim intLength
    Dim n As Integer

' Let error be trapped in the calling routine

    intLength = UBound(astrSource)
    ReDim astrDest(intLength) As String

    For n = 1 To intLength
        astrDest(n) = astrSource(n)
    Next n

End Sub
```

Listing 7.27. The SingleArrayCopy **subroutine.**

```
Sub SingleArrayCopy (asngSource() As Single, asngDest() As Single)

    Dim intLength
    Dim n As Integer

' Let error be trapped in the calling routine

    intLength = UBound(asngSource)
    ReDim asngDest(intLength) As Single

    For n = 1 To intLength
        asngDest(n) = asngSource(n)
    Next n

End Sub
```

ListSelectSQL

The `ListSelectSQL` function builds the `astrAvailable` and `astrSelected` arrays based on results from an SQL Select statement.

This function is helpful in preparing to call the `ListSelect` function, because your own code then doesn't have to create the delimited strings for what gets displayed in the list boxes.

Enter the `ListSelectSQL` function as shown in Listing 7.28.

Listing 7.28. The `ListSelectSQL` function.

```
Function ListSelectSQL (sql As String, astrAvailable() As String,
➡ astrSelected() As String, asngColumnWidths() As Single) As Integer

' Call this function in preparation before calling ListSelect.

' Fills the astrAvailable and astrSelected arrays with the return set
' from an SQL SELECT statement.

' The asngColumnWidths array must have the same number of columns as
' is returned by the SELECT statement.

  Dim db As Database
  Dim dyn As Recordset
  Dim blnOpened As Integer

  Dim intRecords As Integer
  Dim intFieldIndex As Integer
  Dim intColumns As Integer
  Dim n As Integer

' Assume Failure
  ListSelectSQL = True

  On Error GoTo ListSelectSQLError

  Set db = DBEngine(0)(0)

  Set dyn = db.OpenRecordset(sql, DB_OPEN_DYNASET)
  blnOpened = True

  If dyn.RecordCount = 0 Then
    MsgBox "No records selected", 48, PROGRAM
    GoTo ListSelectSQLDone
  End If

  dyn.MoveLast
  intRecords = dyn.RecordCount
  intColumns = UBound(asngColumnWidths)

  ReDim astrAvailable(intRecords) As String
  ReDim astrSelected(0) As String
```

continues

Listing 7.28. continued

```
' Copy the contents of the dynaset to an array of strings.

  dyn.MoveFirst
  For n = 1 To intRecords
    For intFieldIndex = 0 To intColumns - 2
      ' Use the vertical bar character to separate the fields from each other.
        astrAvailable(n) = astrAvailable(n) & dyn(intFieldIndex) & "¦"
    Next intFieldIndex

  ' Copy the last field, without a trailing vertical bar
    astrAvailable(n) = astrAvailable(n) & dyn(intFieldIndex)

    dyn.MoveNext
  Next n

' Success
  ListSelectSQL = False

ListSelectSQLDone:
  If blnOpened Then dyn.Close
  Exit Function

ListSelectSQLError:
  MsgBox Error$, 48, PROGRAM
  Resume ListSelectSQLDone

End Function
```

The `ListSelectSQL` function creates a dynaset based on the SQL Select statement passed.

```
Set dyn = db.OpenRecordset(sql, DB_OPEN_DYNASET)
  blnOpened = True
```

This determines how many records are in the dynaset by moving to the end and then checking the RecordCount property. The number of columns is determined by the length of the asngColumnWidths array:

```
dyn.MoveLast
intRecords = dyn.RecordCount
intColumns = UBound(asngColumnWidths)
```

The `astrAvailable` string array is resized to hold the contents of the dynaset:

```
ReDim astrAvailable(intRecords) As String
ReDim astrSelected(0) As String
```

Next, for each record in the dynaset, a delimited string is created to hold the values in each column of the current record, as shown in Listing 7.29. Each field in the record is read by using a field number starting with 0. The fields are read in the same order in which they appear in the SELECT statement.

Listing 7.29. Generating a delimited string for each record.

```
' Copy the contents of the dynaset to an array of strings.

  dyn.MoveFirst
  For n = 1 To intRecords
    For intFieldIndex = 0 To intColumns - 2
    ' Use the vertical bar character to separate the fields from each other.
      astrAvailable(n) = astrAvailable(n) & dyn(intFieldIndex) & "¦"
    Next intFieldIndex

  ' Copy the last field, without a trailing vertical bar
    astrAvailable(n) = astrAvailable(n) & dyn(intFieldIndex)

    dyn.MoveNext
  Next n
```

Close and save your changes in the List Select module.

That's it! Now you can write a few test functions and see all this in action.

Testing the List Select Form

In using the List Select form, the minimum steps you have to do are the following:

1. Initialize and fill available and selected arrays
2. Initialize and fill the column widths array
3. Call `ListSelect` to open the form
4. Extract your results from the selected array

Optionally, you can use the globals you created to set captions, and you can use the `ListSelectSQL` function to base the available list from a Select statement.

Let's start with the simplest case first.

1. Open a new module.
2. Enter the `Test1` subroutine shown in Listing 7.30.

Listing 7.30. The `Test1` subroutine.

```
Sub Test1 ()

' Test the Select List form - Test 1: Single Column

  Dim astrAvailable() As String
  Dim astrSelected() As String
  Dim asngColumnWidths() As Single
  Dim z As Integer
```

continues

Listing 7.30. continued

```
' Need to allocate these arrays to the number of items in each
' list to start with.
  ReDim astrAvailable(5) As String
  ReDim astrSelected(0) As String

' Allocate this to the number of displayed columns.
  ReDim asngColumnWidths(1) As Single

' Fill in the contents of astrAvailable and astrSelected.
' Use the vertical bar to separate values for multiple columns.
  astrAvailable(1) = "apple"
  astrAvailable(2) = "banana"
  astrAvailable(3) = "orange"
  astrAvailable(4) = "lemon"
  astrAvailable(5) = "grape"

' Fill in column width values in inches, max total is 1.5.
  asngColumnWidths(1) = 1.5

' Change the caption on the form and above the lists.
  gstrListSelectCaption = "List Select Test 1"
  gstrAvailableCaption = "&Flavors:"
  gstrSelectedCaption = "Fa&vorites:"

' Display the form.
  z = ListSelect(astrAvailable(), astrSelected(), asngColumnWidths())

  ShowResults z, astrSelected()

End Sub
```

In your test, astrAvailable is sized to 5 to include five choices that are then assigned to each element in the array. The astrSelected array is sized to 0 because the selected list starts out empty.

The asngColumnWidths array is sized to 1 because there is only one column in the list. This column is set to the full 1.5-inch width of the list boxes.

Each of the changeable captions is modified by setting the associated globals; then the ListSelect function is called to display the List Select form.

After the List Select form is closed, the test function resumes execution and calls a ShowResults subroutine to dump the contents of the astrSelected array into the Immediate window.

Enter the ShowResults subroutine shown in Listing 7.31.

Listing 7.31. The `ShowResults` **subroutine.**

```
Sub ShowResults (blnCancelled As Integer, astrSelected() As String)

' Dump test results to the Immediate window

  Dim n As Integer

  Debug.Print

  If blnCancelled Then
    Debug.Print "User cancelled"
  Else
    Debug.Print "Selected:"
    For n = 1 To UBound(astrSelected)
      Debug.Print astrSelected(n)
    Next n
  End If

  Debug.Print

End Sub
```

To test the `Test1` subroutine, do the following:

1. Select the **View|Immediate** command to open the Immediate window, as shown in Figure 7.7.

2. Enter `Test1` into the Immediate window and press Enter.

FIGURE 7.7.

Running the `Test1`
subroutine.

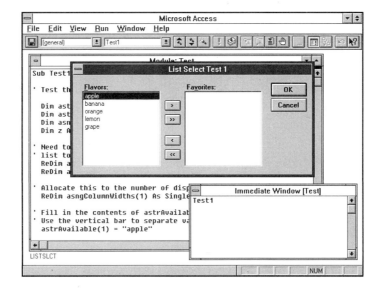

The List Select form should open, displaying the five flavor choices.

Select some or all of the flavors and press OK. The Immediate window displays which flavors have been selected, as shown in Figure 7.8.

FIGURE 7.8.

Selections are shown in the Immediate window.

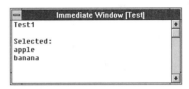

 Enter the Test2 subroutine, as shown in Listing 7.32.

Listing 7.32. The Test2 subroutine.

```
Sub Test2 ()

' Test the Select List form - Test 2: Multiple Column

  Dim astrAvailable() As String
  Dim astrSelected() As String
  Dim asngColumnWidths() As Single
  Dim z As Integer

' Need to allocate these arrays to the number of items in each
' list to start with.
  ReDim astrAvailable(5) As String
  ReDim astrSelected(2) As String

' Allocate this to the number of displayed columns.
  ReDim asngColumnWidths(3) As Single

' Fill in the contents of astrAvailable and astrSelected.
' Use the vertical bar to separate values for multiple columns.
  astrAvailable(1) = "1¦apple¦red"
  astrAvailable(2) = "2¦banana¦yellow"
  astrAvailable(3) = "3¦orange¦orange"
  astrAvailable(4) = "4¦lemon¦yellow"
  astrAvailable(5) = "5¦grape¦purple"

  astrSelected(1) = "6¦lime¦green"
  astrSelected(2) = "7¦peach¦peach"

' Fill in column width values in inches, max total is 1.5.
  asngColumnWidths(1) = .3
  asngColumnWidths(2) = .6
  asngColumnWidths(3) = .6

' Change the caption on the form and above the lists.
  gstrListSelectCaption = "List Select Test 2"
  gstrAvailableCaption = "&Flavors and Colors:"
  gstrSelectedCaption = "Fa&vorites:"
```

```
' Display the form.
  z = ListSelect(astrAvailable(), astrSelected(), asngColumnWidths())

  ShowResults z, astrSelected()

End Sub
```

This test calls the List Select form with three columns, set to column widths of .3 inches, .6 inches, and .6 inches, adding up to 1.5 inches.

Enter Test2 into the Immediate window and press Enter.

This time the List Select form displays three columns in each list box, as shown in Figure 7.9. The results dumped into the Immediate window have the vertical bar separating the column values.

FIGURE 7.9.

Test2 displays a multicolumn list.

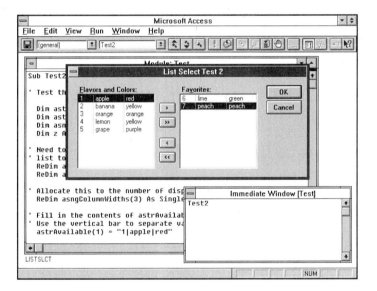

Enter the Test3 subroutine as shown in Listing 7.33.

Listing 7.33. The Test3 subroutine.

```
Sub Test3 ()

' Test the Select List form - Test 3: Using SQL to fill the lists

  Dim astrAvailable() As String
  Dim astrSelected() As String
  Dim asngColumnWidths() As Single
```

continues

Listing 7.33. continued

```
Dim sql As String

Dim z As Integer

ReDim asngColumnWidths(2) As Single

asngColumnWidths(1) = 1.2
asngColumnWidths(2) = .3

sql = "SELECT City,State FROM City ORDER BY State,City"
z = ListSelectSQL(sql, astrAvailable(), astrSelected(), asngColumnWidths())
If z Then Exit Sub

gstrListSelectCaption = "List Select Test 3"

z = ListSelect(astrAvailable(), astrSelected(), asngColumnWidths())

ShowResults z, astrSelected()

End Sub
```

Test3 uses an SQL SELECT statement as the source for the left list box. The SELECT statement returns two columns from a table named City. Because two columns are being returned, the asngColumnWidths array is sized to 2, and column width settings for two columns are entered.

To run this test, you need to create a table named City. The fields City and State must exist in the table for the SELECT statement to work.

1. Create a City table with two fields, City and State. When you save the table, Access will ask you if you want to create a primary key. Answer Yes. Switch to datasheet view and enter some records into the table (as shown in Figure 7.10).

FIGURE 7.10.

The City table.

2. Enter Test3 into the Immediate window and press Enter, as shown in Figure 7.11.

FIGURE 7.11.

The List Select form displaying data from an SQL Select statement.

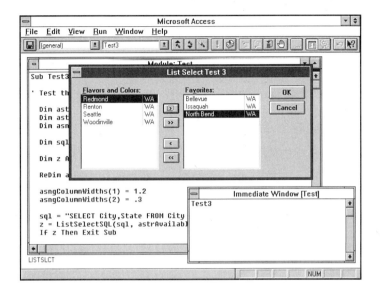

TRY THIS! QUESTION 7.2.

Can you create a `PrintReports` function that lists all the reports in your data-base, allowing you to select several reports to be sent to the printer at once?

TRY THIS! QUESTION 7.3.

Can you add up- and down-arrow buttons to the List Select form to allow you to reorder the right side list? Add the two buttons to the form and the code behind the buttons.

Summary

In this chapter you created a form to enable a user to hand-pick a subset of items from a larger set using the familiar paradigm of two lists and a set of four buttons labeled >, >>, <, and <<.

You sure dug into some code in the process. This one was a tough one. The results you get with the List Select form will make your fellow coders green with envy, though, so it was worth the trouble.

Here's that list again for those of you keeping score. In this chapter, you

- Got the full specification of how the list selection dialog box works
- Created the List Select form
- Used global variables to communicate with code behind a form
- Made the form's and its controls' captions and properties customizable through form load code
- Learned how list callback functions work as a dynamic way to fill list boxes
- Wrote code for the movement of items between two list boxes in the List Select form
- Learned about delimiter characters and created a useful StrListExtract function
- Wrote additional functions in the List Select module to simplify using the List Select form
- Wrote and ran test subroutines to check your work

In the next chapter, you take a break from the rocket science department and try your luck in Hollywood. That's right. I have a neat set of utilities for the filmmaker/screenwriter talent in all of us. Even if your cast consists of a few neighbor kids, the dog, the cat, and the hamster, you never know who might screen your masterpiece someday. This could be the beginning of a new Hollywood legend!

TRY THIS! ANSWERS

7.1. To make the caption on the OK button change, follow these steps:

1. Add a global variable to the List Select declarations section in which to pass the caption.

```
Global gstrOKButtonCaption As String
```

2. Add the following lines in the Form_Open subroutine for the List Select form, after the similar sections of code that change the form and label captions:

```
If Len(gstrOKButtonCaption) > 0 Then
  cmdOK.Caption = gstrOKButtonCaption
End If
```

3. To use the added option, set the gstrOKButtonCaption variable to the text you want to display in the OK button before calling the ListSelect function.

7.2. The function I came up with to print reports is shown in Listing 7.34.

Listing 7.34. The `PrintReports` function.

```
Function PrintReports ()

' This subroutine allows you to select reports from the current
' database and send them to the printer as a group.

  Dim astrAvailable() As String
  Dim astrSelected() As String
  Dim asngColumnWidths() As Single

  Dim sql As String

  Dim v As Variant
  Dim n As Integer
  Dim z As Integer

  ReDim asngColumnWidths(1) As Single

  asngColumnWidths(1) = 1.5

  sql = "SELECT Name FROM MSysObjects WHERE Type = -32764 ORDER BY Name"

  z = ListSelectSQL(sql, astrAvailable(), astrSelected(), asngColumnWidths())
  If z Then Exit Function

  gstrListSelectCaption = "Select Reports to Print"

  z = ListSelect(astrAvailable(), astrSelected(), asngColumnWidths())

  For n = 1 To UBound(astrSelected)
    v = SysCmd(SYSCMD_SETSTATUS, "Printing " & astrSelected(n) & "...")
    DoCmd OpenReport astrSelected(n)
  Next n

  v = SysCmd(SYSCMD_SETSTATUS, " ")

End Function
```

To get the list of reports, you need to run a SELECT statement off the MSysObjects system table, selecting each record with a Type value of –32764. This technique is commonly used, but always under the cautionary note that the MSysObjects table may change in format in a future version of Access.

Use the **View|O**ptions command and turn on the option to display hidden objects in order to see the MSysObjects table in your database.

7.3. You can add up- and down-arrow buttons to reorder the selected list, but make sure that the code behind them reorders the values in the gastrSelected array and not just the values displayed in the lstSelected list box.

Here's how I did it:

1. Add two buttons on the form, cmdUp and cmdDown, as shown in Figure 7.12.

FIGURE 7.12.

Adding the cmdUp and cmdDown buttons.

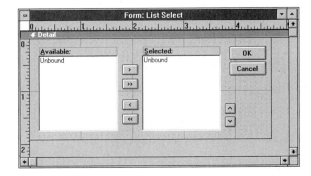

2. Enter the cmdUp_Click subroutine shown in Listing 7.35.

3. Enter the cmdDown_Click subroutine shown in Listing 7.36.

Listing 7.35. The cmdUp_Click subroutine.

```
Sub cmdUp_Click ()

  Dim sz As String

  Dim intDestCount As Integer
  Dim intCurrent As Integer

' Verify that there are items in the list and one is selected

  On Error Resume Next

  intDestCount = UBound(gastrSelected)
  If Err <> 0 Then GoTo cmdUp_ClickDone

  On Error GoTo cmdUp_ClickError

  If intDestCount < 2 Or IsNull(lstSelected.Column(0)) Then
    GoTo cmdUp_ClickDone
  End If

' Get the current item
  intCurrent = lstSelected.ListIndex + 1

' Is the item after the first?
  If intCurrent > 1 Then

    ' Swap the current item with the one above it
    sz = gastrSelected(intCurrent - 1)
```

```
    gastrSelected(intCurrent - 1) = gastrSelected(intCurrent)
    gastrSelected(intCurrent) = sz

  ' Redraw the list
    lstSelected.Requery
  End If

cmdUp_ClickDone:
  Exit Sub

cmdUp_ClickError:
  MsgBox Error$, 48, PROGRAM
  Resume cmdUp_ClickDone

End Sub
```

Listing 7.36. The cmdDown_Click subroutine.

```
Sub cmdDown_Click ()

  Dim sz As String

  Dim intDestCount As Integer
  Dim intCurrent As Integer

' Verify that there are items in the list and one is selected

  On Error Resume Next

  intDestCount = UBound(gastrSelected)
  If Err <> 0 Then GoTo cmdDown_ClickDone

  On Error GoTo cmdDown_ClickError

  If intDestCount < 2 Or IsNull(lstSelected.Column(0)) Then
    GoTo cmdDown_ClickDone
  End If

' Get the current item
  intCurrent = lstSelected.ListIndex + 1

' Is the item before the last?
  If intCurrent < intDestCount Then

    ' Swap the current item with the one after it
    sz = gastrSelected(intCurrent + 1)
    gastrSelected(intCurrent + 1) = gastrSelected(intCurrent)
    gastrSelected(intCurrent) = sz

    ' Redraw the list
    lstSelected.Requery
  End If
```

continues

Listing 7.36. continued

```
cmdDown_ClickDone:
  Exit Sub

cmdDown_ClickError:
  MsgBox Error$, 48, PROGRAM
  Resume cmdDown_ClickDone

End Sub
```

CHAPTER 8

Word: Screen Writer

Imagine yourself as the screenwriter in the following script…

<u>THE MISSING SCRIPT</u>

```
        FADE IN

        START INTERCUT SEQUENCE:

1.      INT. BRAD'S DEN - EARLY MORNING - FULL SHOT
        Brad sits in front of his computer amidst a scattering of books and papers
        that are covered with grease, crumbs, and the sugar that falls off when Brad
        eats his pastries in the morning.

2.      C.U. - A TELEPHONE RINGS

3.      BACK TO SCENE
        Brad sighs and picks up the telephone. He knows who it is.
                            BRAD
                    Yes.

4.      INT. ARLENE'S OFFICE - FULL SHOT
        Arlene's executive suite is high up a skyscraper overlooking New York.
        Through the windows behind her heavy oak desk we can see a spectacular view
        of the city.
                            ARLENE
                    Where's that damn script Brad? I TOLD YOU not to
                    take this one on unless you could pull through
                    with it. I haven't received a single e-mail from
                    you in a week!
                            BRAD (V.O. speaker phone)
                    It's in the works Arlene. I can have it to you in
                    a couple of days.

5.      C.U. - ARLENE'S HANDS TYPING FURIOUSLY ON THE KEYBOARD
                            ARLENE
                    Two days! Filming for this episode starts in two
                    days, Brad! The studio executives are up in arms
                    about this. Can I at least tell them what it's
                    about?

6.      BACK TO BRAD'S DEN - CLOSE SHOT
                            BRAD
                    Hold on a sec. Let me pull it up.

7.      BACK TO ARLENE'S OFFICE - CLOSE SHOT
        Arlene rolls her eyes in disbelief, then notices a small spider scurrying
        across her desk.

8.      C.U. SPIDER RUNNING ACROSS DESK
        Arlene's hand slams down on the spider.

9.      BACK TO ARLENE
        Arlene cringes as she looks at the underside of her hand.

10.     BACK TO BRAD'S OFFICE - BRAD'S POV OF HIS MONITOR
```

Whether or not you plan to storm Hollywood with your creations, making your very own movies can be challenging and fun. In my high school days in the late 1970s, Super 8 film was in its last days as a popular home movie format. I directed two 1/2-hour films and many shorts simply by getting together a bunch of my friends and having a go at it.

Now that the age of video has arrived, almost anyone can produce short films for about $4.00 per two-hour cassette tape, excluding, of course, the initial hefty outlay for the camera and VCR. People who don't have the video equipment themselves often can gain access to what they need through programs in local high schools and colleges.

```
        Brad's monitor shows a near empty page in Microsoft Word.

            THE Y PAPERS
            Episode 212:

        Brad clicks a button in a custom Word toolbar and examines the screen.

            hat - Washington - president - fish

  11.   C.U. BRAD
        Brad shrugs and tries again.

  12.   BACK TO BRAD'S POV

            mutant - turtles - teenage - ninja

                                    BRAD
                                (to himself)
                        Naw, there's nothing in that.

        Brad clicks the toolbar button again.

            girl - octopus - coffee - hungry

  13.   BACK TO ARLENE'S OFFICE - CLOSE SHOT
        Arlene has several different vitamin pills in her hand and is getting more
        from various bottles.

                                    ARLENE
                        I'm WAITING Brad!

                            BRAD (V.O. speaker phone)
                        It's about a girl who gets off her shift at a
                        diner in the middle of the night. She invites
                        guys she meets to her apartment, only to feed
                        them to her gigantic pet octopus.

  14.   BACK IN ARLENE'S OFFICE
        Arlene finishes typing and strikes the Enter key unusually hard to send off
        a message.

                                    ARLENE
                        OK, that'll hold off the dogs for a little while
                        anyway. Now about these deadlines...

  15.   BACK IN BRAD'S OFFICE - FULL SHOT
        Brad holds the phone away from his ear as Arlene's yelling spews out from
        it. He sets the receiver on the desk begins typing.

  16.   BRAD'S POV OF THE MONITOR

            THE Y PAPERS
            Episode 212: WOULD YOU LIKE TO FEED MY PET OCTOPUS?

        END INTERCUT SEQUENCE

                                                        FADE OUT
```

A video project has a higher degree of success if the director or filmmaker does the work of writing a script first. If you are impatient and want to jump to directing first, remember that all good directors are good writers. A good script serves as the film's master plan. If you write script keeping in mind the people and resources you will have available during filming, the work of later getting it all on film (or tape) will be much easier.

In this chapter, you will create a few useful utilities to help you grind out that script.

The programs in this chapter will help with the creative phase of generating ideas or components of the story. Then you'll experiment with Word styles to get a professional script layout on the page. The result is a swell little tool kit that you can use as the template for all of your movie script documents.

If you don't have any intentions of writing a script, you still might want to read through this chapter and pick up some tips on using Word and Word Basic. In any document creation process, you can be helped immeasurably by being able to identify what tasks can be automated, knowing how to automate them, and knowing how to use Basic to extend Word's feature set.

ACT ONE: Writer's Block

The first problem any screenwriter will have is conquering the initial writer's block that occurs when you stare at that first empty page in your script. After the story gets started, it often seems to write itself. But it has to get started!

Word Association Game

One technique that some writers use is to play a word association game. They randomly choose two or more words and then hold them up together to see if the random combination proves inspiring in any way. This is what Brad was doing in the scene at the beginning of this chapter.

To create a word association game, you'll need a document full of words to choose from. Your program will pick four words from the list and display them in a message box, as shown in Figure 8.1.

The results can be inspiring or a meaningless mess. You can run the word association game repeatedly until you find the right combination of words to get your story ideas rolling.

FIGURE 8.1.
Running the word association game.

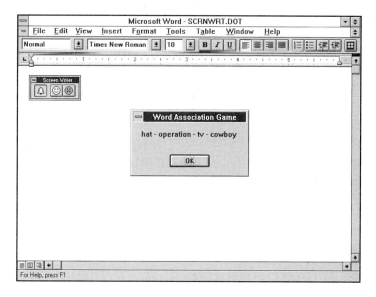

Creating the Word Association Game

The first thing you need to do is create a new Word template. This makes the utilities available for use within any document that was created based on this template.

1. In Word, select **File|New** from the menu.
2. In the New dialog box, click the **T**emplate option button, and then press OK. See Figure 8.2.

FIGURE 8.2.
Creating a new template.

Save the template right from the start and give it a name.

3. Select the **File|Save As** command.
4. In the Save As dialog box, enter `SCRNWRT.DOT` as the name of the template file (as shown in Figure 8.3).

FIGURE 8.3.

Saving
SCRNWRT.DOT.

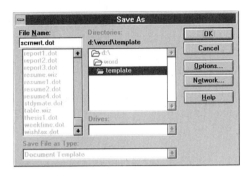

Remember that Word insists you save your templates to the TEMPLATE subdirectory in the directory in which Word was installed. When you are finished creating your template, be sure to make a backup copy in another directory in case you ever remove the Word directory entirely and re-install Word.

The next step is to create a list of words that the Word Association Game can choose from. You can do this in Word as long as you remember to save the file as a text file, not as a Word document. Notepad works well for this too, but Word's spell checker ensures that you've spelled each word correctly.

1. Select **File|New** to create a new document. Press OK in the New dialog box to accept Normal for the document template name.

2. Enter a stream of words into the document, with only one word per line. See Figure 8.4.

FIGURE 8.4.

Creating a source file
for the Word
Association Game.

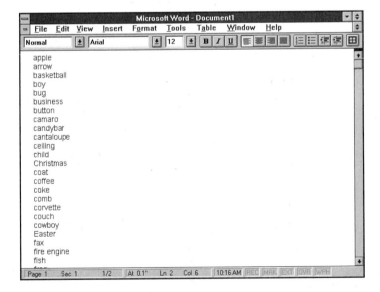

3. Select **File**|Save **A**s to save the document.

4. Enter WRDASSOC.DAT as the name of the file, and select Text Only in the Save File as **T**ype combo box as shown in Figure 8.5. Click OK.

5. Close the WRDASSOC.DAT document.

FIGURE 8.5.

Saving WRDASSOC.DAT.

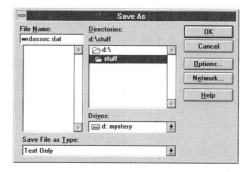

As your file gets longer, you can sort it with a DOS command to verify that you haven't entered the same word more than once. In a DOS Prompt session, enter the following:

```
rename wrdassoc.dat old.dat
type old.dat ¦ sort > wrdassoc.dat
del old.dat
```

Words entered twice will sort next to each other and will be easy to spot the next time you view the file.

Now return to the SCRNWRT.DOT template to create the WordAssociationGame macro.

1. Back in the SCRNWRT.DOT template, select the **Tools**|**M**acro command.

2. Enter WordAssociationGame as the name of the macro, and press the C**r**eate button.

3. Enter in the MAIN subroutine and the RandomWord function as shown in Listing 8.1.

4. Close the macro window by selecting the **File**|**C**lose command.

Listing 8.1. The WordAssociationGame **macro.**

```
Sub MAIN

    Dim Prog$     ' Error message window caption
    Dim File$     ' Name of data file

    Dim Text$     ' A line read in from the file
    Dim Msg$      ' Message for MsgBox
```

continues

Listing 8.1. continued

```
Dim Lines      ' Number of lines in the file

Dim n1         ' Offset for the first word
Dim n2         ' Offset for the second word
Dim n3         ' Offset for the third word
Dim n4         ' Offset for the fourth word

Dim w1$        ' First word
Dim w2$        ' Second word
Dim w3$        ' Third word
Dim w4$        ' Fourth word

Prog$ = "Word Association Game"
File$ = "WRDASSOC.DAT"

On Error Goto WordAssociationGameError

Open File$ For Input As #1

' Count how many lines are in the file
Lines = 0
While Not Eof(1)
  Line Input #1, Text$
  Lines = Lines + 1
Wend

Close #1

' Make sure there are at least 4 words in the file
If Lines < 4 Then
  Msg$ = "There must be at least 4 words in the WRDASSOC.DAT file."
  MsgBox Msg$, Prog$
  Goto WordAssociationGameDone
End If

' Select the first random word
n1 = RandomWord(Lines)

' Select the second random word
n2 = n1
While n2 = n1
  n2 = RandomWord(Lines)
Wend

' Select the third random word
n3 = n1
While n3 = n1 Or n3 = n2
  n3 = RandomWord(Lines)
Wend

' Select the fourth random word
n4 = n1
While n4 = n1 Or n4 = n2 Or n4 = n3
  n4 = RandomWord(Lines)
Wend
```

```
' Read in the chosen words

  Open File$ For Input As #1

  Lines = 0
  While Not Eof(#1)
    Line Input #1, Text$
    Lines = Lines + 1

    If Lines = n1 Then
      w1$ = Text$
    End If

    If Lines = n2 Then
      w2$ = Text$
    End If

    If Lines = n3 Then
      w3$ = Text$
    End If

    If Lines = n4 Then
      w4$ = Text$
    End If
  Wend

  MsgBox w1$ + " - " + w2$ + " - " + w3$ + " - " + w4$, Prog$

  Goto WordAssociationGameDone

WordAssociationGameError:
  If Err = 53 Then
    Error$ = "File not found: " + File$
  Else
    Error$ = "Error: " + Str$(Err)
  End If
  MsgBox Error$, Prog$

WordAssociationGameDone:
  On Error Resume Next
  Close #1

End Sub

Function RandomWord(Lines)

  RandomWord = Int(Rnd() * (Lines - 1) + 1)

End Function
```

Figure 8.6 shows the WordAssociationGame macro being entered into Word.

FIGURE 8.6.

Entering the WordAssociationGame macro.

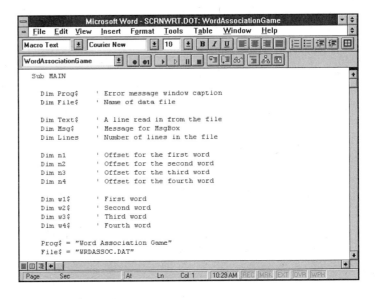

```
                Microsoft Word - SCRNWRT.DOT: WordAssociationGame

 File   Edit   View   Insert   Format   Tools   Table   Window   Help

Macro Text      Courier New        10      B  I  U

WordAssociationGame

    Sub MAIN

        Dim Prog$      ' Error message window caption
        Dim File$      ' Name of data file

        Dim Text$      ' A line read in from the file
        Dim Msg$       ' Message for MsgBox
        Dim Lines      ' Number of lines in the file

        Dim n1         ' Offset for the first word
        Dim n2         ' Offset for the second word
        Dim n3         ' Offset for the third word
        Dim n4         ' Offset for the fourth word

        Dim w1$        ' First word
        Dim w2$        ' Second word
        Dim w3$        ' Third word
        Dim w4$        ' Fourth word

        Prog$ = "Word Association Game"
        File$ = "WRDASSOC.DAT"

Page      Sec            At       Ln      Col 1      10:29 AM  REC  MRK  EXT  OVR  WPH
```

Standard Basic File I/O

The WordAssociationGame macro uses Basic file input/output (I/O) to read in the list of words stored in WRDASSOC.DAT.

These days, programming with Basic file I/O statements isn't done as frequently as it once was. That's because in most cases a better option is to store your data in tables in an Access database or other database format.

Unfortunately, the Basics in Word 6.0 and Excel 5.0 don't yet have support for programming data access objects (DAO). This means you can't program with tables, snapshots, and dynasets, as you can when using Access or Visual Basic.

Even so, there are times in Access and Visual Basic when it is still useful to read or write data in text files. These are some examples of situations where you might need to use file I/O: reading or writing data to interact with accounting software on mini or mainframe computers, writing a high-score file in a game, or writing a program's log file.

File I/O always involves the following three steps:

■ Open the file
■ Read or write to the file
■ Close the file

When we call a file *sequential,* what we really mean is that there is essentially no organization to the file other than items being stored in the same order you entered them. To read an item from a sequential file, you start from the beginning and sequentially read parts of the file until you find what you are looking for.

Opening a Sequential File

The Open statement is used to open an existing text file or create a new one. It works like this:

```
Open Filename$ For Mode As #FileNumber
```

In Basic, you identify each currently open file by the number you assigned to it as you opened it. The three modes you can open a file in are Input, Output, and Append. Opening a file for Output erases the file if it already exists, so the Append mode can be used to modify an existing file.

Here are three examples for opening WRDASSOC.DAT in the three different I/O modes.

- Open a file to read. This returns an error if the file doesn't exist.

  ```
  Open "WRDASSOC.DAT" For Input As #1
  ```

- Create a new file. If a file exists by the same name, it is deleted before creating the new one.

  ```
  Open "WRDASSOC.DAT" For Output As #1
  ```

- Open an existing file to write to. If the file doesn't exist, then a new empty file is created.

  ```
  Open "WRDASSOC.DAT" For Append As #1
  ```

Reading Data From a Sequential File

When you open a file to read data from as you do in the WordAssocationGame macro, there are several ways to read values from the file into the variables in your program. The Input and Read statements read one or more values at a time:

```
Input #FileNumber, Variable1, Variable2, ...
```

```
Read #FileNumber, Variable1, Variable2, ...
```

For example, suppose you have a text file, SHIRT.DAT that includes the lines shown in Listing 8.2.

Listing 8.2. `SHIRT.DAT.`

```
patriot, small, 25
patriot, medium, 60
patriot, large, 30
eagle, small, 60
eagle, medium, 40
eagle, large, 115
```

The `Input` statement could be used to read each value from a line in the file into a program variable like this:

```
Input #1, Style$, Size$, Amount
```

Listing 8.3 shows a test macro that reads in each line from the above SHIRT.DAT text file and displays the values one by one in a message box.

Listing 8.3. A test macro to try out the `Input` statement.

```
Sub MAIN

  Dim Style$
  Dim Size$
  Dim Amount

  Dim msg$
  Dim cr$

  cr$ = Chr$(13) + Chr$(10)

  Open "D:\STUFF\SHIRT.DAT" For Input As #1

  While Not Eof(#1)
    Input #1, Style$, Size$, Amount

    msg$ = "Style: " + Style$ + cr$ + cr$
    msg$ = msg$ + "Size: " + Size$ + cr$ + cr$
    msg$ = msg$ + "Amount: " + Str$(Amount)

    MsgBox msg$
  Wend

  Close #1

End Sub
```

Figure 8.7 shows the results after executing the test macro in Listing 8.3.

FIGURE 8.7.

Running the test macro in Listing 8.3.

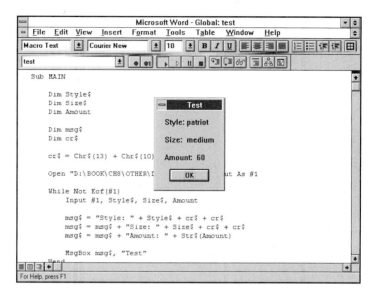

The difference between the `Read` statement and the `Input` statement is that the `Read` statement removes quotes from the first value being read. It's sort of odd that this only happens on the first variable being read into, and not on each one, but that is how it works. If your data doesn't have quotes around it in the text file, then `Read` and `Input` work identically.

Another way to read in data is by using the `Input$` function:

```
Return$ = Input$(NumberCharacters, #FileNumber)
```

The `Input$` function allows you to read a specified number of characters from the file at a time. The data read in from the file this way is done without interpretation, so commas and carriage return characters are included in the string returned. This function is useful when dealing with files that are not in the format the other input functions are familiar with.

The `Line Input` statement is used to read an entire line from a file into a string variable.

```
Line Input #FileNumber, Variable$
```

You use it in the `WordAssociationGame` macro like this:

```
Line Input #1, Text$
```

A line in a file is every character up to the carriage return, which indicates that a new line follows.

Writing Data to a Sequential File

There are only two statements for writing to a sequential file in Word Basic: `Print` and `Write`.

`Print` is really a leftover from the golden days of the BASIC programming language. In Word Basic you can print to a file, or interestingly enough, if you don't include the file number, you will print to the status bar.

The `Print` statement works like this:

```
Print #FileNumber, Expression1 Operator Expression2...
```

The expressions printed in a `Print` statement are separated by semicolons or by commas. A semicolon indicates that the following expression will be printed immediately after the preceding one. A comma indicates that the values will be separated by the tab character.

Use the `Print` statement when you need to create a file with a special format not compatible with the output produced by the `Write` statement; that is, not including comma separators between each value.

For example, suppose you need to create a SHIRT2.DAT file where the style value goes in a 12-character field, the size value is in an 8-character field, and the amount is in a 4-character field that is right justified. An individual record might look like this:

```
patriot     small    25
12345678901234567890 1234
          1          2
```

The `Write` statement creates a file with output that is easily read in later using the `Input` and `Read` statements because the output is comma delimited. The method of calling the `Write` statement is also similar to the `Input` and `Read` statements:

```
Write #FileNumber, Variable1, Variable2, ...
```

If the SHIRT.DAT file was created by a program, using the `Write` statement to write a line in the file would look like this:

```
Write #1, "patriot", "small", 25
```

Using *Seek*

The `Seek` statement allows you to change the order in which you read or write to a sequential file. The `Seek` statement works like this:

```
Seek #FileNumber, Count
```

When you use Seek, you specify the location you wish to seek by the number of characters it is from the beginning of the text file. You can get the current location by calling the Seek function:

```
Count = Seek(#FileNumber)
```

This way, you can actually close a file and later re-open it and return to the location that you were at before.

Closing a Sequential File

After reading or writing to a file, you need to close it. That's easy enough. The syntax is like this:

```
Close #FileNumber
```

TRY THIS! QUESTION 8.1.

Can you modify Listing 8.3 so that it creates a SHIRT2.DAT file with output exactly as shown in Listing 8.4?

Listing 8.4. The SHIRT2.DAT file.

```
patriot    small      25
patriot    medium     60
patriot    large      30
eagle      small      60
eagle      medium     40
eagle      large     115
```

Examining the *WordAssociationGame* Macro

Now that you know all you need to know about sequential files, let's get back to the project at hand and see how the WordAssociationGame macro works.

The WordAssociationGame macro consists of a MAIN subroutine and a RandomWord function. The RandomWord function returns a number from 1 to the number passed in the function's argument. If you pass a 10, the function returns a number from 1 to 10.

```
Function RandomWord(Lines)

  RandomWord = Int(Rnd() * (Lines - 1) + 1)

End Function
```

The RandomWord function uses the formula demonstrated in the Word Basic help file for calculating a random number. This formula is shown here:

```
Result = Int(Rnd() X (End - Start) + Start)
```

Start and End are the beginning and ending numbers in the range of integers from which you would like a number chosen. The Rnd function returns a floating point number equal to or greater than 0, but less than 1. The formula translates the result of Rnd() into an integer within the specified range.

The MAIN subroutine first declares quite a number of procedure variables, as shown in Listing 8.5.

Listing 8.5. Variable declarations in MAIN.

```
Sub MAIN

    Dim Prog$      ' Error message window caption
    Dim File$      ' Name of data file

    Dim Text$      ' A line read in from the file
    Dim Msg$       ' Message for MsgBox
    Dim Lines      ' Number of lines in the file

    Dim n1         ' Offset for the first word
    Dim n2         ' Offset for the second word
    Dim n3         ' Offset for the third word
    Dim n4         ' Offset for the fourth word

    Dim w1$        ' First word
    Dim w2$        ' Second word
    Dim w3$        ' Third word
    Dim w4$        ' Fourth word
```

The comments in the procedure do a fair job of explaining what the variables are used for. The n1, n2, n3, and n4, variables will hold the lines that contain four selected words in the WRDASSOC.DAT file. The w1$, w2$, w3$, and w4$ variables will each receive the selected words as they are read in from the file.

After the Dim statements, the Prog$ and File$ are assigned.

```
Prog$ = "Word Association Game"
File$ = "WRDASSOC.DAT"
```

The Prog$ variable is used as the message dialog caption. The File$ variable is used to identify the data file. You may need to modify this so the drive letter and path are specified for where you locate the WRDASSOC.DAT file. It should look like this:

```
File$ = "C:\WORDUTIL\WRDASSOC.DAT"
```

Or better yet, you could review how we used `GetPrivateProfileString` in Chapter 2, "Word: Study Mate," and make the data file settable through a SCRNWRT.INI file.

Next in the `MAIN` subroutine, error handling is turned on and the file is opened in Input mode and assigned to file number 1.

```
On Error Goto WordAssociationGameError

Open File$ For Input As #1
```

The subroutine then uses a loop to read in the entire contents of the file. The purpose of reading the file is to determine how many total lines, or words, are in the file.

```
' Count how many lines are in the file
  Lines = 0
  While Not Eof(1)
    Line Input #1, Text$
    Lines = Lines + 1
  Wend
```

The `Eof` function is used to check if the end of the file was reached. `Eof` returns True (-1) when the file at the specified file number has been read to the end.

Inside the `While...Wend` loop, a line is read into the `Text$` variable using the `Line Input` statement. Also, the variable `Lines` is incremented by one, indicating that there is another line in the file.

After all the lines are counted, the file is closed. The file is opened again later to read in the selected words.

```
  Close #1
```

The code that chooses four random words assumes that it can find four different words. This means that you have to be sure that there are at least four words in the file or else the program will get caught in an endless loop. The next section displays an error message and exits if fewer than four lines were read in from the file.

```
' Make sure there are at least 4 words in the file
  If Lines < 4 Then
    Msg$ = "There must be at least 4 words in the WRDASSOC.DAT file."
    MsgBox Msg$, Prog$
    Goto WordAssociationGameDone
  End If
```

Next, you begin selecting random words. Selecting a word is really a matter of selecting a line number from 1 to the number of lines that you determined are in the file.

The first word can be chosen by calling the `RandomWord` function.

```
' Select the first random word
  n1 = RandomWord(Lines)
```

Selecting the second word is also done by calling the RandomWord function, but the function must be called again if the selected word is the same as already selected for word 1.

This is done by setting word 2 equal to word 1, and then selecting word 2 repeatedly until it is not equal to word 1.

```
' Select the second random word
  n2 = n1
  While n2 = n1
    n2 = RandomWord(Lines)
  Wend
```

The third word is selected in the same manner, this time being sure that it is not the same as word 1 or word 2.

```
' Select the third random word
  n3 = n1
  While n3 = n1 Or n3 = n2
    n3 = RandomWord(Lines)
  Wend
```

And likewise for word 4, except this time being sure it is not equal to word 1, word 2, or word 3.

```
' Select the fourth random word
  n4 = n1
  While n4 = n1 Or n4 = n2 Or n4 = n3
    n4 = RandomWord(Lines)
  Wend
```

At this time, we've got the locations of the words in the file by line number, and they are stored in the n1, n2, n3, and n4 variables. Next, the program opens the file again to get the text for the selected words.

```
' Read in the chosen words

  Open File$ For Input As #1
```

A loop begins again to read the file sequentially from beginning to end. Each line is again read into the Text$ variable and the Lines variable is used to keep track of which line you are currently on.

```
  Lines = 0
  While Not Eof(#1)
    Line Input #1, Text$
    Lines = Lines + 1
```

The next few lines work like this: If the current line is equal to the line chosen for word 1, then copy Text$ into w1$.

```
  If Lines = n1 Then
    w1$ = Text$
  End If
```

If the current line is equal to the line chosen for word 2, then copy `Text$` into `w2$`, and so on for word 3 and word 4.

```
   If Lines = n2 Then
     w2$ = Text$
   End If

   If Lines = n3 Then
     w3$ = Text$
   End If

   If Lines = n4 Then
     w4$ = Text$
   End If
Wend
```

By the time the loop has executed for each line in the file, `w1$`, `w2$`, `w3$`, and `w4$` will each have the selected lines read into them.

The `MsgBox` statement is used to display the selections. The first argument to the `MsgBox` statement is created by appending each of the selected words with a dash character between them. In Word 6.0, you must use the plus (+) operator to concatenate strings rather than the ampersand (&) operator.

```
MsgBox w1$ + " - " + w2$ + " - " + w3$ + " - " + w4$, Prog$

   Goto WordAssociationGameDone
```

The next section of code is reached if an error occurs anytime during execution of the subroutine. Word Basic sets the `Err` variable to the number of the error, but doesn't have a provided `Error$` variable like the newer basics in Access, Excel, and VB.

Instead, I declared an `Error$` string variable and generated my own error message. Error number 53 is the most frequent error that would occur, meaning that the WRDASSOC.DAT file couldn't be found. For other errors, I just return the error number, which admittedly isn't a whole lot of help to the user.

```
WordAssociationGameError:
  If Err = 53 Then
    Error$ = "File not found: " + File$
  Else
    Error$ = "Error: " + Str$(Err)
  End If
  MsgBox Error$, Prog$
```

The Done section of the code closes the file opened on file number 1. The `On Error Resume Next` line is used to ignore any errors while the file is closed. This deals with the situation where you get to the Done section when the file wasn't opened in the first place.

```
WordAssociationGameDone:
  On Error Resume Next
  Close #1

End Sub
```

That's it!

Word Association Game Challenge

The more words you have in WRDASSOC.DAT, the better. Can you write a program that adds words to WRDASSOC.DAT by scanning existing documents for words?

You might attack this one in two separate programs. First, write a program that reads in a .TXT file and writes a new file with one word per line. Next, use the DOS Sort command as shown earlier to sort the words in the new file. Finally, run a second program that removes any duplicate words by again reading in one file and writing out another.

Debugging in Word

Do you think after I wrote the WordAssociationGame macro it ran successfully the first time? Well, actually I got lucky on that one and it did, but that is certainly not how it usually goes.

A good way to verify that your program works the way you expect it to is to step through it line by line in the debugger. You can watch to see that the lines execute in the order you expect them to, and you can watch the values stored in the variables in your program.

To step through the WordAssociationGame macro in the debugger, do the following:

1. Find the button on the Macro toolbar with the tooltip labeled "Step."
2. Press the Step button.

   You will see the first line in the MAIN subroutine displayed in reverse video. This is a marker indicating which line will execute on the next step.
3. Repeatedly press the Step button to watch the program execute line by line. See Figure 8.8.

   As the program executes, variables in the current procedure are set to different values. You can examine what these variables are set at.
4. Find the Show Variables button on the Macro toolbar and click it.

This displays the Macro Variables dialog box. In the dialog box is a list of each variable in your program and its current value. See Figure 8.9.

FIGURE 8.8.

Stepping through the WordAssociationGame macro.

Step button

FIGURE 8.9.

Examining variables in the Word Basic debugger.

Another technique for viewing information while the program is running is to use the Print statement in your program to write messages to the status bar. For example, after reading in a line from the WRDASSOC.DAT file, you could display it in the status bar:

```
    Line Input #1, Text$
Lines = Lines + 1

Print Text$
```

This way you can view values while your program is running, without having to stop and open the Macro Variables dialog box. If the values fly by too quickly, you could also open a file just for debugging purposes and write messages to it.

Here's another thing you can do with the debugger that is actually kind of fun to watch.

1. Close the Macro Variables dialog box if it is still open.
2. Locate and click the Trace button on the toolbar. It's the one with the white arrow.

Word executes the program in a mode that highlights each line as it executes. It's quite a dazzling little performance.

> **TRY THIS! QUESTION 8.2.**
> Write an Access or Visual Basic version of the Word Association Game. Store the words in an Access table, not in a text file.

ACT TWO: The Plot Thickens

Well, hopefully you've settled on a story idea by now and not spent all your time programming Word Basic. A good next step would be to develop some profiles for the characters in your movie. Then we'll create an experimental utility that will help us write some of the dialog for the characters.

Developing Character Profiles

To make your characters real enough that they seem to live right there on the page, you are going to need to know everything about them. Hopefully you do; after all, you created them.

However, you have to make sure that you really sat down and worked out who these people really are. Where are they from, what do they believe in, and what was their life like growing up? The more details you know about your characters, the easier it will be to write how they act and what they say.

A good way to do this is to write a profile on each character in your movie. You can start by having a set of probing questions about the character's current make-up and about their past. Generating the profile is then a matter of filling in answers to the questions.

To create the profile, you'll need a new template. The template will be used as a form for entering profile information.

You actually don't need to do any programming in this one, but I'll show you a neat technique that you can use when creating forms in Word for other purposes.

1. Select the File|New command.
2. Click the Template radio button and click OK.
3. Switch the font to Courier New. (It's neat because it looks like authentic screen-writing.)

4. Set the font size to 14 and click the Bold button on the toolbar.

5. Enter in a title at the top of the page, `Character Profile for:`.

6. Select the **View|T**oolbars command.

7. Click the Form toolbar on in the Toolbars dialog box and close it.

8. On the Forms toolbar, click the first button, the one with the "ab|" characters on it.

Word adds a text form field to the document. It displays as a gray box (see Figure 8.10). When you use this template to define your character's profile, you will only be able to enter text in the form fields. In other words, you will be able to enter answers to the prompts just as if the document was a program form and not a typical Word document.

FIGURE 8.10.

Adding a text form field to the Character Profile template.

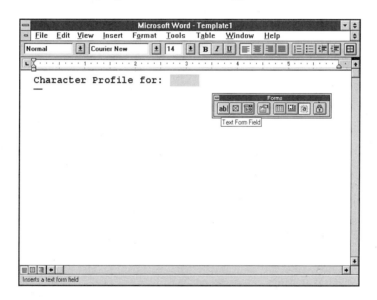

You can add text in the document to indicate the form's use.

1. Change the font size to 10. Click the Bold button to turn it off.

2. On the next line of the document, enter the following text:

   Answer the following questions about your movie character. The more detail you include, the more real your movie character will seem.

Next, you create six different sections of questions about the character to help make up the character profile: vital statistics, childhood, school years, looks and behavior, professional life, and emotions and character.

The types of questions asked here are borrowed from the suggestions in *The Screenplays—A Blend of Film Form and Content*, by Margaret Mehring, Focal Press. See Chapter 8 of *The Screenplay* for an extensive list of character-profile questions.

First, create the Vital Statistics section.

1. Skip a line, and then set the font size to 12. Turn on Bold and Underlining and enter a title for the first section of questions, `Vital Statistics`.

2. Turn off Underlining but leave Bold on. Change the font size to 10.

3. Skip another line, and then enter a series of prompts, with one per line, for the following:

   ```
   Full name:
   Sex:
   Age:
   Race:
   Height:
   Weight:
   Hair:
   Eyes:
   ```

   Don't stop at this list. You can add any other vital-statistic prompts that you feel are necessary things to know about your movie characters.

4. Position the text cursor after the colon at the end of the first prompt. Turn Bold off and enter a space.

5. Click the Text Form Field button on the Forms toolbar to add a field for the Full name prompt.

6. Repeat steps 4 and 5 to add a text form field for each prompt. Add spaces, if you like, to line up the text form fields.

Figure 8.11 shows the Vital Statistics section as it is being developed.

Next, create the Childhood section.

1. Create a title for the Childhood section as you did for the Vital Statistics section.

2. Below the title, enter a line of instructions for this section:

   ```
   Enter descriptions and moments of interest for each of the following.
   ```

3. Enter the following questions into the Childhood section:

   ```
   What country or state did the character live in as a child?:
   What was the neighborhood and house like?:
   What was the character's mother like?:
   What was the character's father like?:
   How many brothers and sisters did the character have? What were they like?:
   How did the character feel about himself?:
   ```

FIGURE 8.11.

Adding text form fields to the Vital Statistics section.

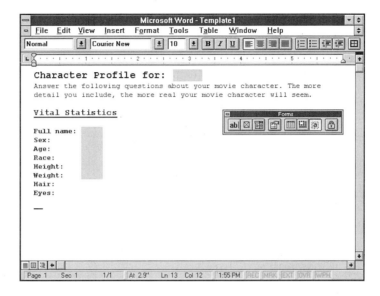

4. Add form text fields to allow answers to be entered in for each of these questions, as shown in Figure 8.12.

FIGURE 8.12.

Creating the childhood question section.

326   **Part II**   ■   *Fun Projects*

Complete the Character Profile template by entering in the remaining sections and questions:

```
School Years
Enter descriptions and moments of interest for each of the following.

Was the character popular?:
Who were the character's friends?:
How did the character relate to his teachers?:
How did the character relate to his parents?:
What accomplishments was the character the most proud of?:

Looks and Behavior
Make note of any interesting aspects about the character.

Is the character attractive?:
List any notable physical characteristics about the character.:
How does the character dress?:
How does the character talk?:
Does the character have any strange or notable habits and mannerisms?:
What are the character's hobbies and interests?:
What is the character's religion?:

Professional Life
Make note of any interesting aspects about the character at work.

How does the character earn a living?:
How does the character feel about his work?:
What are the people like that the character works with?:
Does the character take the lead, or follow others?:
What about his professional life is the character the most proud of?:
What kind of car does the character drive?:

Emotions and Character

Who does the character love, and why?:
Who does the character hate, and why?:
What makes the character laugh?:
What makes the character cry?:
What provokes rage in the character?:
Is the character enthusiastic, outwardly and risk taking?:
Is the character honest with, and sensitive, to others?:
What are the character's innermost secrets?:
```

Before you save the template, there are two quick things to do to make it function as an entry form: get rid of the gray squares, and put the document in a data entry mode. To identify the buttons mentioned in the following steps, you can use the tool-tips that are displayed when the mouse hovers above them.

1. Click the Form Field Shading button on the toolbar to make the gray boxes disappear.
2. Click the Protect Form button on the toolbar so that the button is pressed in.

Notice that Tab and Shift-Tab now can be used to cycle through the text form fields in the document. You have just created a data entry form out of a Word document!

Before closing the template, fill in the Summary Info dialog box.

1. Select the **File**|Summary **I**nfo command.

2. Enter the title of the document as `Enter a profile on a movie script character`. (See Figure 8.13.)

3. Close the Summary Info dialog box.

4. Save the template as PROFILE.DOT and close it.

FIGURE 8.13.

Entering Summary Info text for the Character Profile template.

Testing the Character Profile Template

Now you can use PROFILE.DOT as the basis for a character profile document for each character in the script.

1. From the Word menu, select **File**|**N**ew to create a new document.

2. In the New dialog box, select the Profile template as shown in Figure 8.14. Click OK.

FIGURE 8.14.

Creating a new document based on the Character Profile template.

Word displays the Character Profile template, with each field highlighted as you tab to it.

3. Enter your answers for each prompt or question. See the example in Figure 8.15.

FIGURE 8.15.

Entering a character profile.

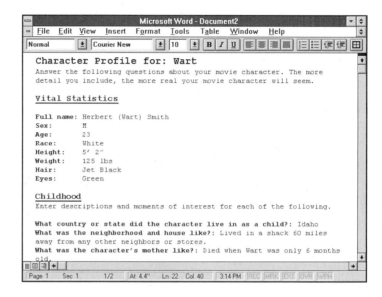

You can save and load your character profile just as you would any Word document. You can even give a copy to someone who doesn't have the PROFILE.DOT template, and that person will be able to use it.

If you add macros to the template, you must give a copy of the template itself to anyone who wants to use the macros with a document created in the template.

Adding Code to a Text Form Field

The next thing you are going to add to the Character Profile template isn't essential to its utility, but as long as we're on the subject of form fields, it's something you'll want to know about and make use of in the future.

Form fields have a limited set of events that you can attach code to, just as you can attach code to a control on a Visual Basic or Access form.

First, create a bookmark that identifies the text form field for entering the country or state the character lived in.

1. Open the PROFILE.DOT template in Word.
2. Turn on the Forms toolbar.
3. Click the Protect Form toolbar button in the Forms toolbar to turn off document protection. The button should no longer be pressed in.

4. Click the Form Field Shading button to display the gray boxes for the form fields.

5. Double-click the text form field for the first question in the Childhood section. This is the question with the following text:

```
What country or state did the character live in as a child?:
```

Word displays a Text Form Field Options dialog box. In the Field Settings **B**ookmark field, you will see the name of a bookmark for this form field, such as "Text8." You can change the name of the bookmark to be more representative of the value stored there.

6. Change the Field Settings **B**ookmark name to State (as shown in Figure 8.16), and then close the dialog box.

FIGURE 8.16.

Changing the Field Settings Bookmark on a text form field.

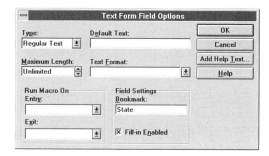

Next, create a macro that changes state abbreviations to the full state name.

1. Select the **Tools**|**M**acro command.

2. Enter `StateName` as the name of the macro to create, and press the C**r**eate button.

3. Enter the `StateName` macro as shown in Listing 8.6.

4. Close the `StateName` macro.

Listing 8.6. The `StateName` macro.

```
Sub MAIN

Dim Text$
Dim State$

State$ = "State"
Text$ = GetFormResult$(State$)

Select Case UCase$(Text$)
```

continues

Listing 8.6. continued

```
Case "CA"
    SetFormResult State$, "California"

Case "OR"
    SetFormResult State$, "Oregon"

Case "WA"
    SetFormResult State$, "Washington"

Case Else

End Select

End Sub
```

The `StateName` macro is incomplete. It checks the value stored at the text form field at the State bookmark. If the value is equal to "CA", "OR" or "WA," then it replaces the value with "California", "Oregon" or "Washington" respectively. You could modify the subroutine to translate all state codes to the full state name.

Note that the `Case Else` selection is used even though there are no statements entered for the `Case Else` condition. Word will produce an error message if there is no `Case Else` selection and the value in `Text$` doesn't match any of the `Case` values.

Next, you need to have the `StateName` macro activated at the appropriate time, which is after an entry is made in the State text form field.

1. Double-click the State text form field in the Character Profile template.
2. In the Text Form Field Options dialog box, find the Exit prompt in the group box marked Run Macro On.
3. Select the `StateName` macro in the Exit combo (see Figure 8.17), and press OK.
4. Turn Form Field Shading back off, and protect the document again.
5. Save and close the template.

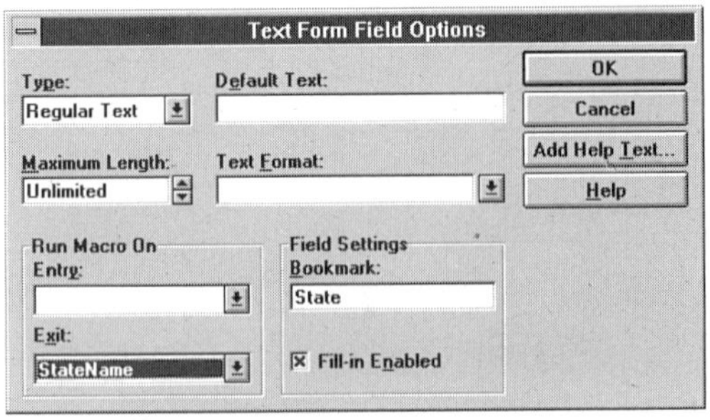

FIGURE 8.17.

Assigning the
StateName macro to
the Exit event.

Now this prompt is set up to automatically change "WA" to "Washington" as you leave the text form field. Using this technique, you can validate entries as they are entered into your Word form documents, and you can even calculate and display totals based on the values entered.

Auto Dialect

In this next program you will "abuse" one of the great new features in Word, the AutoCorrect feature. The results you get from this are only so-so, but using the program is a lot of fun.

The AutoCorrect feature enables you to tell Word that any time a particular set of characters is entered, Word should replace them with another set. This is useful in correcting very common typing mistakes. In the process of creating this book, I've had "teh" replaced with "the" about a hundred thousand or so times.

To use AutoCorrect, you normally do the following steps:

1. Select the **T**ools|**A**utoCorrect command.
2. Make sure the Replace **T**ext as You Type check box is checked.
3. Enter the text to change in the **R**eplace box.
4. Enter the replacement text in the **W**ith box.
5. Press **A**dd.

For example, I live in a city named "Woodinville," which is too darn many characters to type. To reduce the number of characters I type, I can use the AutoCorrect feature to replace "wv" with "Woodinville." (See Figure 8.18.)

FIGURE 8.18.

Manually entering an AutoCorrect entry.

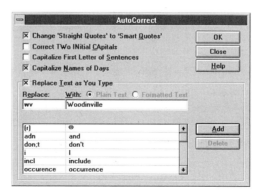

AutoCorrect is designed to be used for corrections and short-cuts. Here's where we can abuse it.

What about if you enter a bunch of AutoCorrect entries to make what you type in your document have a particular dialect or lingo? For example, "Citizens' Band talk" AutoCorrect entries might look like this:

Replace:	With:
yes	10-4 big buddy
cop	smokey
antenna	fishing pole
coffee	road tar

In experimenting with this, I got mixed results. A big problem is that the AutoCorrect feature handles only a single word in the Replace field, so you can't replace one type of phrase with another. If you were going to create a Valley Girl dialect, what word would you choose to have replaced by "Gag me with a spoon!"?

Another problem is that word replacements that make sense in one context might not in another. For example, suppose you replace the word *sick* with the phrase *so gross*. *Those people are sick* becomes *Those people are so gross*, which may work well; however, *I was sick to my stomach* becomes *I was so gross to my stomach*, which doesn't work.

You can try this now. You can load and unload a set of AutoCorrect entries all at once. This is much better than manually entering or deleting each entry at a time.

The first step is to create a source file of AutoCorrect entries. You can do this in Notepad or in Word, as long as you save the file out as a text file and not a Word document.

In the source file, each line consists of the word to be replaced, followed by a vertical bar character, followed by the replacement text. Here are a few entries from a sample file:

```
hair¦doo
mouth¦mac receptacle
eyes¦binoculars
drive¦do ninety
tv¦teevee
lunch¦french fries
dinner¦pizza
coffee¦double tall mocha grande
store¦mall
spell¦shpel
spelling¦shpelin
```

Let's give this a whirl.

1. Create a list like the one I've just shown you in Word or in Notepad. Use the vertical bar character to separate the first word with replacement words. In Figure 8.19, I used Notepad to edit my list of words.

FIGURE 8.19.

Editing DIALECT.DAT in Notepad.

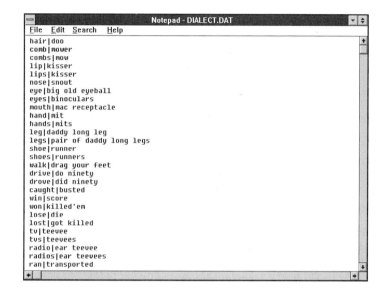

2. Save the list as DIALECT.DAT.

   If you are using Word, be sure to select Text Only in the Save File as **T**ype combo box in the Save dialog box.

3. Enter the AddDialect macro, as shown in Listing 8.7.

4. Enter the RemoveDialect macro, as shown in Listing 8.8.

Listing 8.7. The AddDialect Macro.

```
Sub MAIN

    Dim Prog$      ' Error message window caption
    Dim File$      ' Name of data file

    Dim Text$      ' A line read in from the file
    Dim Msg$       ' Message for MsgBox

    Dim w1$        ' First word or phrase
    Dim w2$        ' Second word or phrase

    Dim Bar        ' Offset for the vertical bar
    Dim Lines      ' Number of replacements added
```

continues

Listing 8.7. continued

```
Dim Added      ' Was the line added?

Prog$ = "Add Dialect"
File$ = "DIALECT.DAT"

On Error Goto AddDialectError

Open File$ For Input As #1

' Add the Auto Correct replacements
Lines = 0
While Not Eof(1)
  Line Input #1, Text$
  Added = 0

  If Len(Text$) > 3 Then
    Bar = InStr(1, Text$, "¦")
    If Bar > 0 Then
      w1$ = Left$(Text$, Bar - 1)
      w2$ = Right$(Text$, Len(Text$) - Bar)

      If Len(w1$) > 0 And Len(w2$) > 0 Then
        On Error Resume Next
        ToolsAutoCorrect .Replace = w1$, .With = w2$, .Add

        If Err = 0 Then
          Added = - 1
        End If
        Err = 0
        On Error Goto AddDialectError
      End If
    End If
  End If

  Lines = Lines + 1
  If Added = 0 Then
    Msg$ = "Line #" + Str$(Lines) + " was not added."
    Msg$ = Msg$ + Chr$(13) + Chr$(10) + Chr$(13) + Chr$(10)
    Msg$ = Msg$ + Text$

    MsgBox Msg$, Prog$
  End If
Wend

MsgBox Str$(Lines) + " AutoCorrect entries were added.", Prog$
Goto AddDialectDone

AddDialectError:
  If Err = 53 Then
    Error$ = "File not found: " + File$
  Else
    Error$ = "Error: " + Str$(Err)
  End If
  MsgBox Error$, Prog$
```

```
AddDialectDone:
  On Error Resume Next
  Close #1

End Sub
```

Listing 8.8. The RemoveDialect Macro.

```
Sub MAIN

  Dim Prog$      ' Error message window caption
  Dim File$      ' Name of data file

  Dim Text$      ' A line read in from the file
  Dim Msg$       ' Message for MsgBox

  Dim w1$        ' First word or phrase
  Dim w2$        ' Second word or phrase

  Dim Bar        ' Offset for the vertical bar
  Dim Lines      ' Number of entries deleted
  Dim Deleted    ' Was the line deleted?

  Prog$ = "Delete Dialect"
  File$ = "DIALECT.DAT"

  On Error Goto DeleteDialectError

  Open File$ For Input As #1

' Delete the Auto Correct replacements
  Lines = 0
  While Not Eof(1)
    Line Input #1, Text$
    Deleted = 0

    If Len(Text$) > 3 Then
      Bar = InStr(1, Text$, "¦")
      If Bar > 0 Then
        w1$ = Left$(Text$, Bar - 1)
        If Len(w1$) > 0 Then
          On Error Resume Next
          ToolsAutoCorrect .Replace = w1$, .Delete

          If Err = 0 Then
            Deleted = - 1
          End If
          Err = 0
          On Error Goto AddDialectError
        End If
      End If
    End If
```

continues

Listing 8.8. continued

```
   Lines = Lines + 1
   If Deleted = 0 Then
     Msg$ = "Line #" + Str$(Lines) + " was not deleted."
     Msg$ = Msg$ + Chr$(13) + Chr$(10) + Chr$(13) + Chr$(10)
     Msg$ = Msg$ + Text$

     MsgBox Msg$, Prog$
   End If
 Wend

 MsgBox Str$(Lines) + " AutoCorrect entries were deleted.", Prog$
 Goto DeleteDialectDone

DeleteDialectError:
 If Err = 53 Then
   Error$ = "File not found: " + File$
 Else
   Error$ = "Error: " + Str$(Err)
 End If
 MsgBox Error$, Prog$

DeleteDialectDone:
 On Error Resume Next
 Close #1

End Sub
```

You'll take a look at the code in a minute. First, let's create a toolbar for each of these two macros and the WordAssociationGame macro you created earlier.

1. Select the **View|T**oolbars command.
2. In the Toolbars dialog box, click the **N**ew button.
3. In the New Toolbars dialog box, enter Screen Writer as the name of the toolbar. (See Figure 8.20.)
4. Make sure that the **M**ake Toolbar Available To combo box indicates SCRNWRIT.DOT, and then press OK.

    Word displays the Customize dialog box with the **T**oolbars tab selected.
5. In the **C**ategories list, select the word Macros.
6. In the Macr**o**s list, select WordAssociationGame and drag it over to the new toolbar. (See Figure 8.21.)
7. In the Custom Button dialog box, select a picture and click the **A**ssign button, or edit your own picture for the button. (See Figure 8.22.)

FIGURE 8.20.
*Creating the Screen
Writer toolbar.*

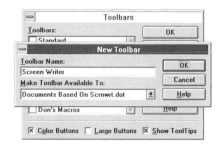

FIGURE 8.21.
*Creating a button
for the
WordAssociationGame
macro.*

Destination

Name being dragged

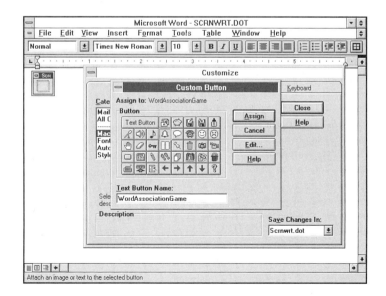

FIGURE 8.22.
*Assigning a picture
to the
WordAssociationGame
button.*

8. Add buttons for the `AddDialect` and `RemoveDialect` macros in the same manner. See Figure 8.23.

FIGURE 8.23.

Completing the Screen Writer toolbar.

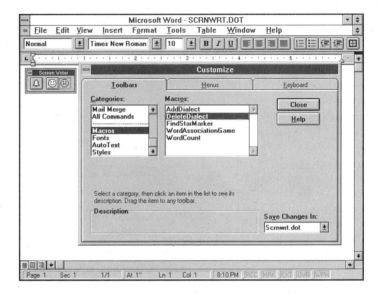

9. Close the Customize dialog box.

Testing *AddDialect* and *RemoveDialect*

You're now ready to load the AutoCorrect entries that you saved in DIALECT.DAT.

1. Click the Add Dialect button on the Screen Writer toolbar and you should get a message as shown in Figure 8.24.

2. Select the **Tools|A**utoCorrect command and verify that entries were added. See Figure 8.25.

3. You can enter a sentence or two and see how it goes.

   Here are the results I got. The first line is what I typed, and the second line is what ended up in my document:

```
My girl
My babe

My babe likes
My babe really digs

My babe really digs jazz
My babe really digs beep beep

My babe really digs beep beep music.
```

FIGURE 8.24.

Running the
AddDialect
macro.

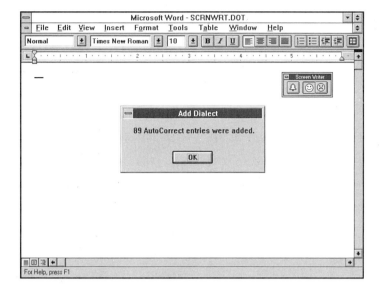

FIGURE 8.25.

A horde of new
AutoCorrect entries.

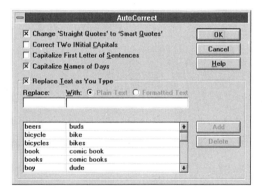

Hmmm…interesting results anyway. If you have to create any kind of serious document, you should remove the AutoCorrect entries.

4. Click the Remove Dialect button on the Screen Writer toolbar.

If all runs well, you'll get the message shown in Figure 8.26.

Let's see how all of this works.

FIGURE 8.26.

Removing the dialect.

Examining *AddDialect*

To figure out how to write the code that adds an AutoCorrect entry, I turned to the macro recorder. Using the macro recorder can instruct you on how to program things that you don't remotely care about how to do. You just want to get it done.

In this case, the recording to add an AutoCorrect entry looks like this:

```
Sub MAIN
ToolsAutoCorrect .SmartQuotes = 1, .InitialCaps = 0, .SentenceCaps = 0,
.Days = 1, .ReplaceText = 1, .Formatting = 0, .Replace = "def",
.With = "def", .Add
End Sub
```

Because the recording results are of a dialog being set, you get extra arguments that you really don't need. All you really need is this:

```
ToolsAutoCorrect .Replace = "abc",.With = "def", .Add
```

This line tells Word to add an AutoCorrect entry that replaces abc with def. Now that you know how this works, the rest is general programming stuff.

First, open the DIALECT.DAT file with read access.

```
File$ = "DIALECT.DAT"

Open File$ For Input As #1
```

Next, start a loop to read the file continually until the end is reached.

```
' Add the Auto Correct replacements
Lines = 0
While Not Eof(1)
```

Inside the loop, read each line.

```
Line Input #1, Text$
Added = 0
```

See if the line is long enough to contain an entry, which at minimum would be three characters: one character for the word to replace, a vertical bar, and one character for the word to replace with.

```
If Len(Text$) > 3 Then
```

Use the InStr function to find where the vertical bar character is located in the string.

```
Bar = InStr(1, Text$, "¦")
```

If you found a vertical bar, extract what is to the left of it and to the right.

```
If Bar > 0 Then
  w1$ = Left$(Text$, Bar - 1)
  w2$ = Right$(Text$, Len(Text$) - Bar)
```

Verify that there is text in both the left and the right strings.

```
If Len(w1$) > 0 And Len(w2$) > 0 Then
```

Turn off error handling and call the `ToolsAutoCorrect` statement to add the AutoCorrect entry. This way, if any error occurs, the rest of the file will still be loaded.

```
On Error Resume Next
ToolsAutoCorrect .Replace = w1$, .With = w2$, .Add
```

If no error occurred while adding the entry, then the `Err` system variable will be set to zero. You set a flag that the entry was added all right, and reset the `Err` variable in either case.

```
If Err = 0 Then
        Added = - 1
      End If
      Err = 0
      On Error Goto AddDialectError
    End If
  End If
End If
```

Next, if the line was not added, then an error message is displayed indicating which line has the problem, so you can find it in the source file and fix it.

```
  Lines = Lines + 1
  If Added = 0 Then
    Msg$ = "Line #" + Str$(Lines) + " was not added."
    Msg$ = Msg$ + Chr$(13) + Chr$(10) + Chr$(13) + Chr$(10)
    Msg$ = Msg$ + Text$

    MsgBox Msg$, Prog$
  End If
Wend
```

At the end of the subroutine, a message box is displayed with the number of entries successfully added.

```
  MsgBox Str$(Lines) + " AutoCorrect entries were added.", Prog$
  Goto AddDialectDone
```

Examining *RemoveDialect*

The `RemoveDialect` subroutine is nearly the same subroutine as the `AddDialect` subroutine.

The difference between the two subroutines is in how the `ToolsAutoCorrect` statement is called. To add an entry, you did this:

```
ToolsAutoCorrect .Replace = "abc",.With = "def", .Add
```

To delete the same entry, you do this:

```
ToolsAutoCorrect .Replace = "abc",.Delete
```

Each entry is still identified by the word being replaced. To know which entries to remove, you must read the AutoCorrect entry source file once again.

ACT THREE: The Printed Page

Now that you have your characters profiled and you have a dangerous tool for writing character dialog, let's look at some nonprogramming stuff and get down on the page something that has the look of an authentic movie script.

Here's the rationale. If you don't have much of a shooting plan, and if your script-writing talents are like mine (not good), you may still get some cooperation from your unpaid performers if you have a script that at least *looks* like a script!

Using Styles

America has apple pie. Word has styles.

When your document has to follow particular formatting rules, that usually means styles. A *style* is a set of formatting options saved under one name.

In defining a style, you can include the common character-formatting stuff:

- Font
- Font size
- Bold
- Underline
- Italic

You can also include in your definition of a style the following information:

- Case
- Indentation
- Line spacing
- Line justification
- Tab settings

There's more, but these are the things you will be using.

You can define different styles for the components that make up the document you are creating. Each style can be assigned to a key combination or toolbar button. As the document is being written, you can quickly switch to the style required for each type of section.

Styles For a Movie Script

The first step in creating the styles is to identify the different types of sections in your document. For a script, I've identified the following sections:

Title Script	Centered, underlined title
Headline	Left-justified directive
Numbered Headline	Left-justified directive with numbering
Description	Scene description
Character	Centered name of character
Instructions	Instructions to actor in parentheses
Spoken Dialog	Character dialog
Print	Text in shot for audience to read
Right Headline	Final right justified FADE OUT directive

You might want to review the script at the beginning of this chapter and see if you can identify each type of section.

Note that the name for each style in the preceding list has a unique character in bold. When you create the styles, you can assign a key combination of Ctrl-Shift and the bold character to turn on the style.

Creating the Styles

1. Open the SCRNWRT.DOT template if it isn't currently open.
2. Select the Format|Style command.
3. In the **L**ist combo box, select User Defined Styles.

   The list of styles then appears blank because you have not yet defined any styles. (See Figure 8.27.)
4. Click the **N**ew button.

FIGURE 8.27.
An empty style list.

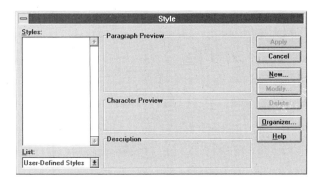

The Base Style

As you learned in Chapter 2, "Word: Study Mate," styles can be based on other styles. Also, by creating a style on which to base other styles, you eliminate the need to repeat settings in each new style you create.

The first style you create will be to simply get the font and font size correct. You'll name this style Base because it is the basis for other styles you create.

1. In the New Style dialog box, enter the following:

Name:	Base
Style **T**ype:	Paragraph
Based On:	(no style)
Style for Following Paragraph:	Base

   Figure 8.28 shows the Base style being created in the New Style dialog box.

FIGURE 8.28.

Creating the Base style.

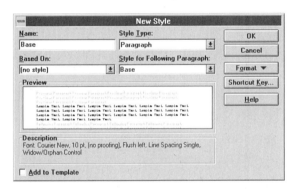

2. Click the **Fo**rmat button and click **F**ont from the drop-down menu.

3. In the Font dialog box, select a Courier New font, Regular style, with a size of 10, and click OK. See Figure 8.29.

FIGURE 8.29.

Setting the font for the Base style.

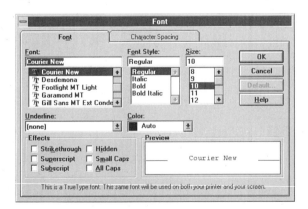

4. Click the F**o**rmat button and click **L**anguage from the drop-down menu.

5. Select English (US) or the language for which you will be using proofing tools (as shown in Figure 8.30). Click OK.

FIGURE 8.30.

Setting the Language for the Base style.

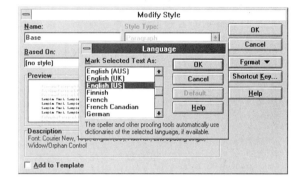

6. Click OK in the New Style dialog box.

A summary of the Base style settings are as follows:
New Style dialog box

Name:	Base
Style **T**ype:	Paragraph
Based On:	(no style)
Style for Following Paragraph:	Base

Font dialog box

Font	Courier New
F**o**nt Style	Regular
Size	10

Language dialog box

Mark Selected Text As:	English (US)

The Title Script Style—Ctrl-Shift-T

Now you can start entering styles based on your Base style. You can start with the first one you're likely to use in writing a script, the Title Script style.

1. In the Style dialog box, click the **N**ew button.

2. In the New Style dialog box, enter the following:

Name:	Title Script
Style **T**ype:	Paragraph

> **B**ased On: Base
> **S**tyle for Following Paragraph: Title Script

3. Click the F**o**rmat button and click **F**ont from the drop-down menu.

4. In the Font dialog box, set the **U**nderline combo box to Single and check the **A**ll Caps check box (see Figure 8.31). Click OK.

FIGURE 8.31.

Adding font modifica-tions to the Title Script style.

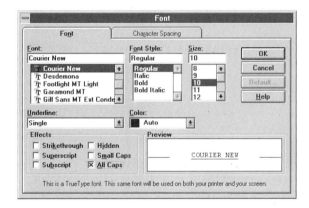

5. Click the F**o**rmat button and select **P**aragraph from the menu.

6. In the Paragraph dialog box, set the following and then click OK:

> Li**n**e Spacing: Multiple
> **A**t: 3
> Ali**g**nment: Centered

7. In the New Style dialog box, click the Shortcut Key button.

8. In the Customize dialog box, press Ctrl-Shift-T to enter that key assignment into the Press **N**ew Shortcut Key text box.

9. Click the Assign button to accept the key assignment, and then click the Close button.

10. Click OK to the New Style dialog box.

The Style dialog box now shows the Title Script style as an available style (see Figure 8.32).

You can test the new style by closing the Style dialog box, pressing Ctrl-Shift-T, and entering a script title. To continue, select F**o**rmat|**S**tyle from the menu.

FIGURE 8.32.

The Style dialog box previews the new Title Script style.

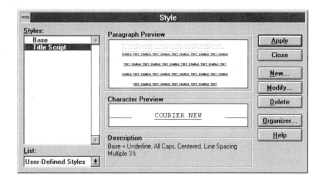

A summary of the Title Script style is as follows:

New Style dialog box
Name: Title Script
Style **T**ype: Paragraph
Based On: Base
Style for Following Paragraph: Title Script

Font dialog box
Underline: Single
All Caps: Checked

Paragraph dialog box—**I**ndents and Spacing tab
Li**n**e Spacing: Multiple
At: 3
Ali**g**nment: Centered

Shortcut Key: Ctrl-Shift-T

The Headline Style—Ctrl-Shift-H

The Headline style is used for directives like "FADE IN" at the beginning of the script. It is left-justified text in uppercase, indented by 0.4 inches.

From this point on, I'll assume you know how to get to the different dialog boxes to set the style options.

Add the Headline style with the following settings:

New Style dialog box
Name:	Headline
Style **T**ype:	Paragraph
Based On:	Base
Style for Following Paragraph:	Headline

Font dialog box
All Caps:	Checked

Paragraph dialog box—**I**ndents and Spacing tab
Left:	0.4"

Shortcut Key: Ctrl-Shift-H

The Numbered Headline Style—Ctrl-Shift-N

The Numbered Headline style is similar to the Headline style except that the left margin is all the way to the left to allow you to enter a scene or shot number.

A tab setting is added to align Numbered Headline text with text from the other styles.

1. Add the Numbered Headline style with the following settings:

   New Style dialog box
Name:	Numbered Headline
Style **T**ype:	Paragraph
Based On:	Base
Style for Following Paragraph:	Numbered Headline

   Font dialog box
All Caps:	Checked

   Shortcut Key: Ctrl-Shift-N

2. In the Tabs dialog box, enter a tab stop position of 0.4 inches and click the **S**et button (see Figure 8.33). Click OK.

FIGURE 8.33.

Setting a tab stop for the Numbered Headline style.

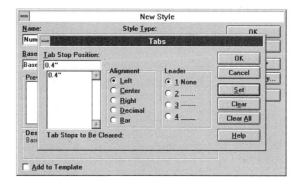

The Description Style—Ctrl-Shift-D

The Description style is used to enter brief, specific notes about the scene or characters. Description usually follows Numbered Headline text and is indented 0.4 inches to align with Headline and Numbered Headline text.

Add the Description style with the following settings:

> New Style dialog box
> **N**ame: Description
> Style **T**ype: Paragraph
> **B**ased On: Base
> **S**tyle for Following Paragraph: Description
>
> Paragraph dialog box—**I**ndents and Spacing tab
> **L**eft: 0.4"
>
> Shortcut Key: Ctrl-Shift-D

The Preview window will display the indented text, as shown in Figure 8.34.

FIGURE 8.34.

Indenting the Description style by 0.4 inches.

The Character Style—Ctrl-Shift-C

The Character style is used to center the name of the character above the scene dialog box.

Add the Character style with the following settings:

New Style dialog box
Name: Character
Style **T**ype: Paragraph
Based On: Base
Style for Following Paragraph: Character

Font dialog box
All Caps: Checked

Paragraph dialog box—**I**ndents and Spacing tab
Ali**g**nment: Centered

Shortcut Key: Ctrl-Shift-C

The Instructions Style—Ctrl-Shift-I

The Instructions style is for actor instructions that are placed above, or in the middle, of scene dialog.

The instructions are always slightly left of center and surrounded by parentheses. Instructions are off-center to make it clear to the actor that the instructions should not be read as dialog.

Add the Instruction style with the following settings:

New Style dialog box
Name: Instruction
Style **T**ype: Paragraph
Based On: Base
Style for Following Paragraph: Instruction

Paragraph dialog box— **I**ndents and Spacing tab
Left: 2"

Shortcut Key: Ctrl-Shift-I

The Spoken Dialog Style—Ctrl-Shift-S

The Spoken Dialog style is for what the actor says. This text is centered, and indented on both sides.

Add the Spoken Dialog style with the following settings:

> New Style dialog box
> **N**ame: Spoken Dialog
> Style **T**ype: Paragraph
> **B**ased On: Base
> **S**tyle for Following Paragraph: Spoken Dialog
>
> Paragraph dialog box—**I**ndents and Spacing tab
> **L**eft: 1.5"
> **R**ight: 1"
>
> Shortcut Key: Ctrl-Shift-S

Figure 8.35 shows a script written using the styles you are creating here.

FIGURE 8.35.

Writing a script with the SCRNWRT.DOT styles.

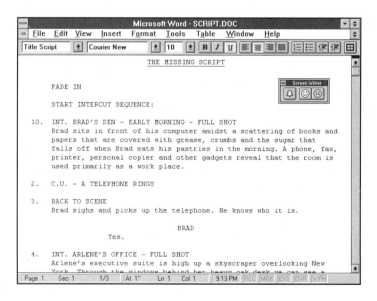

The Print Style—Ctrl-Shift-P

The Print style is used to display text that the audience would read from the screen, such as a headline in a newspaper, or typing on a computer screen.

Add the Print style with the following settings:

New Style dialog box
Name: Print
Style **T**ype: Paragraph
Based On: Base
Style for Following Paragraph: Print

Font dialog box
Underline: Single

Paragraph dialog box—**I**ndents and Spacing tab
Left: .7"
Right: .7"

Shortcut Key: Ctrl-Shift-S

The Right Headline Style—Ctrl-Shift-R

The final style is the Right Headline style. It is used to enter FADE OUT at the end of a scene.

1. Add the Right Headline style with the following settings:

    New Style dialog box
    Name: Right Headline
    Style **T**ype: Paragraph
    Based On: Base
    Style for Following Paragraph: Right Headline

    Font dialog box
    All Caps: Checked

    Paragraph dialog box—**I**ndents and Spacing tab
    Ali**g**nment: Right

    Shortcut Key: Ctrl-Shift-R

2. Make sure the document window in the template is clean of any text you entered when you tested the styles, and then save the template.

You're ready to write that cinematic masterpiece now. Create a new document based on the SCRNWRT.DOT template. All of the styles you created will be available in your new document, as well as the Screen Writer toolbar (see Figure 8.36). Don't forget to use the PROFILE.DOT template and develop some good solid character profiles.

FIGURE 8.36.

Writing with Screen Writer.

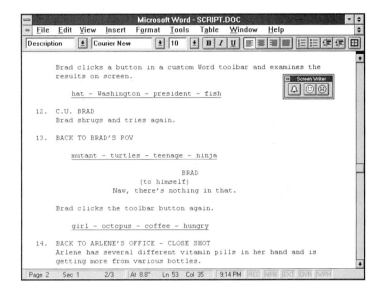

Summary

Have you started to wallpaper your study with rejection notices yet? Oh well, in this chapter you did the following:

- Created the Word Association Game
- Reviewed Basic File I/O statements and functions
- Explored debugging in Word
- Created a template to write character profiles
- Learned about Word form documents
- Wrote code for a text form field event
- Abused the AutoCorrect feature and created macros to load and unload a set of AutoCorrect entries
- Created yet another custom toolbar in Word
- Learned how to use Word styles and combined them with your programs to make a full-featured Word template

In the next chapter, it's back to Access land. This time you will build a complete application in Access. Also, you will check out a way to add some jazz to your Access forms.

TRY THIS! ANSWERS

8.1. The version I came up with is shown in Listing 8.9.

Listing 8.9. Writing SHIRT2.DAT.

```
Sub MAIN

  Dim Style$
  Dim Size$
  Dim Amount

  Open "D:\STUFF\SHIRT.DAT" For Input As #1
  Open "D:\STUFF\SHIRT2.DAT" For Output As #2

  While Not Eof(#1)
    Input #1, Style$, Size$, Amount

    Print #2, Left$(LTrim$(Style$) + "           ", 12);
    Print #2, Left$(LTrim$(Size$) + "        ", 8);
    Print #2, Right$("    " + Str$(Amount), 4)
  Wend

  Close #1
  Close #2

End Sub
```

8.2. I created a version of Word Association Game in Access Basic with the `WordAssociationGame` subroutine and the `RandomWord` functions shown in Listings 8.10 and 8.11.

Listing 8.10. The Access Basic `WordAssociationGame` subroutine.

```
Sub WordAssociationGame ()

  Dim db As Database
  Dim dyn As Dynaset

  Dim intLines As Integer

  Dim n1 As Integer
  Dim n2 As Integer
  Dim n3 As Integer
  Dim n4 As Integer

  Dim w1 As String
  Dim w2 As String
```

```
    Dim w3 As String
    Dim w4 As String

    Const PROGRAM = "Word Association Game"

    On Error GoTo WordAssociationGameError

    Set db = CurrentDB()
    Set dyn = db.CreateDynaset("Word")

    If dyn.RecordCount = 0 Then
      MsgBox "No words found"
    End If

    dyn.MoveLast
    intLines = dyn.RecordCount

  ' Select the first random word
    n1 = RandomWord(intLines)

  ' Select the second random word
    n2 = n1
    While n2 = n1
      n2 = RandomWord(intLines)
    Wend

  ' Select the third random word
    n3 = n1
    While n3 = n1 Or n3 = n2
      n3 = RandomWord(intLines)
    Wend

  ' Select the fourth random word
    n4 = n1
    While n4 = n1 Or n4 = n2 Or n4 = n3
      n4 = RandomWord(intLines)
    Wend

    dyn.MoveFirst

    intLines = 0
    Do Until dyn.EOF
      intLines = intLines + 1

      If intLines = n1 Then
        w1 = dyn!Word
      End If

      If intLines = n2 Then
        w2 = dyn!Word
      End If

      If intLines = n3 Then
        w3 = dyn!Word
      End If

      If intLines = n4 Then
        w4 = dyn!Word
```

continues

Listing 8.10. continued

```
   End If

   dyn.MoveNext
 Loop

 MsgBox w1 & " - " & w2 & " - " & w3 & " - " & w4, 0, PROGRAM

WordAssociationGameDone:
  On Error Resume Next
  dyn.Close
  Exit Sub

WordAssociationGameError:
  MsgBox Error$, 48, PROGRAM
  Resume WordAssociationGameDone

End Sub
```

Listing 8.11. The `RandomWord` function in Access Basic.

```
Function RandomWord (intLines As Integer) As Integer

  RandomWord = Int(Rnd * (intLines - 1) + 1)

End Function
```

Figure 8.37 shows the Word Association Game program being used in Access.

FIGURE 8.37.

*Running Word
Association Game
in Access.*

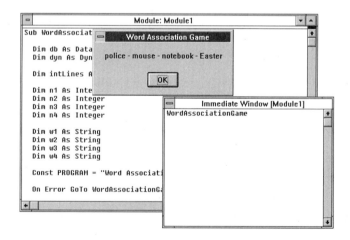

CHAPTER 9

Access: The Learning Computer

Even before computers were part of our daily life, people dreamed about computers having the same intelligence as a human. The dream is a pleasant one in some cases or a nightmare, as in movies that show intelligent machines trying to dominate the world and bring humans to extinction.

Tossing social and ethical implications aside, wouldn't it be nice if a computer could be an intelligent friend always available to remind you of what you forgot, help you with your research, or correct you when you make mistakes?

In some ways we already have this. We have daily planners to remind us of scheduled appointments and project deadlines, encyclopedias on CD-ROM complete with search engines to help us with our research, and tools like spell checkers to correct our mistakes. Even so, that's not the same as being able to have a thought-provoking "conversation" with a computer that has a lifelike intellect.

In this chapter you will create a game in Microsoft Access called The Learning Computer. No, the project is not a ground-breaking exploration in the field of artificial intelligence. The project is, however, a fun and simple experiment.

The Learning Computer demonstrates how a computer, beginning without knowing anything at all, might acquire pieces of knowledge and be able to use what it has learned.

You will also discover a method for dressing up your Access forms in an unusual way, using small, easy-to-draw bitmaps. With applications so abundant and easy to create nowadays, it's nice to be able to make your application stand out from the crowd.

A Session with the Learning Computer

Trying to guess what you are thinking about is the game the Learning Computer plays. If the computer guesses what you were thinking of, it wins; if it guesses wrong, it loses; if it gives up, it loses.

Suppose the category were "animal," and you were thinking of "cow." Your session with the Learning Computer might go like this:

Computer: Does it have four legs?
Person: Yes

Computer: Does it bark?
Person: No

Computer: Does it moo?
Person: Yes

Computer: Is it a cow?
Person: Yes

Computer: I Win!

Here's a different session when the computer loses but gets a piece of information it can use next time:

Computer: Does it have four legs?
Person: No

Computer: Is it a chicken?
Person: No

Computer: You Win! What were you thinking of?
Person: Snake

Computer: What can I ask that will identify a snake?
Person: Does it slither?

The Learning Computer Knowledge Tree

Each time the Learning Computer loses, it gets two pieces of information from the player: a new item and a question that can be asked to identify the item. The Learning Computer stores this information along with other information it has collected over different sessions with the player. The more times the computer plays, the smarter it gets.

This information must be stored in a manner that enables the computer to use it appropriately. The computer can't just randomly ask questions. It must take into account the answers to previous questions to help determine what the appropriate next question is that might lead to a correct guess.

The structure in which the information is stored can be represented in an upside-down tree, as shown in Figure 9.1.

The first question entered in a Learning Computer knowledge tree is always used as the first one in the line of questioning. Following that, the line of questioning runs down a path determined by the responses of the user.

FIGURE 9.1.

A Learning Computer knowledge tree.

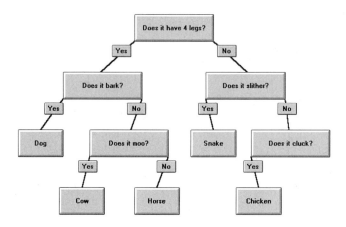

For example, the knowledge tree shown in Figure 9.1 always begins with

```
Does it have 4 legs?
```

If the player answers Yes, the left side of the tree is traversed, eliminating all the potential questions in the right side of the tree. Likewise, if the answer is No, the right side of the tree is used, eliminating the full left side of the tree.

As each question is asked and answered, another branch in the tree is eliminated until there are no more questions to ask and the computer makes a guess at what you were thinking.

Sometimes the computer doesn't have a guess and gives up. Look at the question on the bottom right of the tree, "Does it cluck?" If the player answers No to this question, the computer gives up.

The program enables you to create more than one knowledge tree. You can create one for animals and other trees on different topics, such as famous people, cartoon characters, or world capitals.

The data that makes up the knowledge tree is stored in two tables named Category and Item. Let's create these now.

1. Create a new Access database named LEARN.MDB.
2. On the database container, make sure the Table tab is selected and press the **N**ew button.
3. In the New Table dialog box, click the **N**ew Table button. (Do not select the Table **W**izards.)

4. Enter the following fields into the new table:

Field Name:	ID
Data Type:	Counter
Description:	Unique record ID

Field Name:	CategoryTitle
Data Type:	Text
Description:	Title for this category of items
Field Size:	50
Required:	Yes
Allow Zero Length:	No
Indexed:	Yes (No Duplicates)

Field Name:	FirstItemID
Data Type:	Number
Description:	Top item in the tree for this category
Field Size:	Long Integer
Default Value:	0
Required:	Yes
Indexed:	No

Next, you need to make a primary key out of the ID field.

5. Select the first row by clicking to the left of the ID field name. Click the Key toolbar button to make the ID field the primary key for the table.

6. Close the table, saving it as Category.

The Category table has three fields: ID, CategoryTitle, and FirstItemID. The ID field is a generated number that uniquely identifies each category. All records in the next table belonging to a particular category are identified by this number.

The CategoryTitle field is the name of the category as displayed in the program. The FirstItemID field indicates which question is the first question in a knowledge tree.

Now create the Item table.

1. Create another new table by pressing the **N**ew button in the database container. Skip the Table Wizard again by clicking the **N**ew Table button in the New Table dialog box.

2. Enter the following fields in the new table:

Field Name:	ID
Data Type:	Counter
Description:	Unique record ID

Field Name:	CategoryID
Data Type:	Number
Description:	Category this record belongs to
Field Size:	Long Integer
Default Value:	0
Required:	Yes
Indexed:	Yes (Duplicates OK)

Field Name:	Question
Data Type:	Text
Description:	Yes or No question
Field Size:	255
Required:	No

Field Name:	LinkYes
Data Type:	Number
Description:	Link to Yes items
Field Size:	Long Integer
Default Value:	0
Required:	Yes

Field Name:	LinkNo
Data Type:	Number
Description:	Link to No items
Field Size:	Long Integer
Default Value:	0
Required:	Yes

Field Name:	Item
Data Type:	Text
Description:	Item at end of a line of questions
Field Size:	255
Required:	No

3. Create a primary key from the ID field as you did in Step 5 for the Category table.

4. Close the table, saving it as Item.

The Item table contains the following six fields: ID, CategoryID, Question, LinkYes, LinkNo, and Item.

The ID field is a unique identifier for each record in the table. The CategoryID field holds the ID value from the Category table for the category to which an Item record belongs.

Each record in the Item table is either a question or an item. If the record is a question, the Question field contains the text for the question; otherwise, the Question field is blank. If the record represents an item, the Item field contains the name of the item.

The LinkYes and LinkNo fields can optionally store values that point to other records in the Item table. These links are the connectors that give a knowledge tree its structure.

The LinkYes and LinkNo fields are used only if the Item table record represents a question. The LinkYes field contains the ID for the next record if the user answers Yes, and the LinkNo field contains the ID for the next record if the user answers No.

Examine the contents of the Item table shown in Figure 9.2. See if you can follow the links in the table to see how it creates the tree shown in Figure 9.1.

FIGURE 9.2.

The Item table records that make up the Animals knowledge tree shown in Figure 9.1.

ID	CategoryID	Question	LinkYes	LinkNo	Item
1	1		0	0	Horse
2	1	Does it have 4 legs?	4	8	
3	1		0	0	Dog
4	1	Does it bark?	3	6	
5	1		0	0	Cow
6	1	Does it moo?	5	1	
7	1		0	0	Snake
8	1	Does it slither?	7	10	
9	1		0	0	Chicken
10	1	Does it cluck?	9	0	
(Counter)	0		0	0	

Record 1 of 10

The Learning Computer Forms

You need to create three forms for the Learning Computer game:

- Learning Computer—Select a category and begin play
- Add Category—Add a new category
- Give Up—Add an item to the knowledge tree

The rest of the interaction in the game is done with message boxes using the MsgBox function.

The first form in the Learning Computer game enables you to select a category and press a Play button to play the game. You can also add and delete categories.

When you delete a category, you delete all the information stored within that knowledge tree, so be careful.

The form is aptly named "Learning Computer." Its plain vanilla version looks like Figure 9.3.

FIGURE 9.3.

The Learning Computer form, minus enhancements.

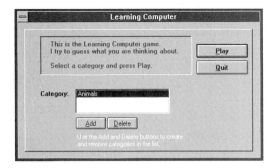

Because this is a game, I wanted to jazz up the form a bit. Also, I've always liked the idea of using small bitmaps as a method of dressing up an Access form. Using too many bitmaps in an Access application can dramatically slow down how fast your forms load, but I thought smaller bitmaps would be less of a problem.

I got a little carried away, and the resulting form is shown in Figure 9.4.

FIGURE 9.4.

The Learning Computer form, dressed up.

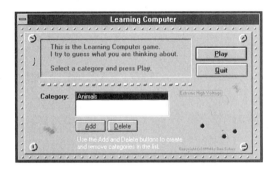

The embellishments on the form include screws, rivets, scratches, smudges, warning signs, blinking lights, and even bullet holes. I created a Form Art form to store my war chest of bitmap pictures just for this purpose. It is shown in Figure 9.5 in design mode.

FIGURE 9.5.

The Form Art collection.

At the end of the chapter I will show you some Paintbrush tips for creating your own Form Art collection.

Creating the Learning Computer Form

Here are the steps for creating the Learning Computer form from scratch:

1. In the database container, click the Form tab, then click the **N**ew button to open a new form.

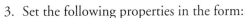

2. In the New Form dialog box, click the **B**lank Form button to build your own form from scratch rather than using the Form Wizard.

3. Set the following properties in the form:

Caption:	Learning Computer
Default View:	Single Form
Scroll Bars:	Neither
Record Selectors:	No
Navigation Buttons:	No
Auto Center:	Yes
Pop Up:	Yes
Modal:	Yes
Border Style:	Dialog
Min Button:	No
Max Button:	No
Width:	4.7181 in

4. Click inside the Detail section to view the properties for it, as shown in Figure 9.6. Set the following:

Height:	2.5785 in
Back Color:	12632256 (Light Gray)

FIGURE 9.6.

Setting the form's section properties.

Add two rectangles to the form to produce a raised panel with an indentation to display a hint text label.

1. In the Toolbox window, click the rectangle button and draw a rectangle on the form. Set the following properties in the rectangle:

Name:	boxPanel
Left:	0.141 in
Top:	0.141 in
Width:	4.4306 in
Height:	2.3021 in
Back Color:	12632256 (Light Gray)
Special Effect:	Raised

2. Draw another rectangle on the form to be an inset frame around some form instructions, as shown in Figure 9.7. Set the properties on this rectangle as listed here:

Name:	boxInset
Left:	0.4535 in
Top:	0.2813 in
Width:	2.9375 in
Height:	0.7181 in
Back Color:	12632256 (Light Gray)
Special Effect:	Sunken

FIGURE 9.7.

Creating the Learning Computer form's 3-D panels.

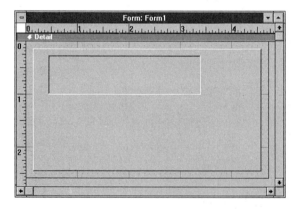

3. Place a label control inside the inset rectangle to display the following text:

```
This is the Learning Computer game.
I try to guess what you are thinking about.

Select a category and press Play.
```

4. Set the properties of the new label as follows:

Name:	lblInstructions
Left:	0.625 in
Top:	0.3438 in
Width:	2.6063 in
Height:	0.5938 in
Back Color:	12632256 (Light Gray)
Fore Color:	16711680 (Blue)
Font Weight:	Bold

Next, add a list box control to display the different knowledge tree categories.

1. Click the list box button on the Toolbox and draw a list box on the form below the inset panel.

   Access draws both a list box and a label, as shown in Figure 9.8.

FIGURE 9.8.

Adding a list box to select a knowledge tree category.

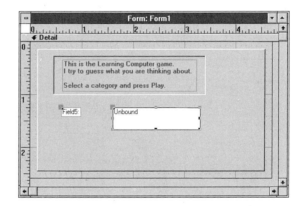

In the Properties window for the list box, the Row Source Type property is defaulted to Table/Query, which is what you want. Below that you can set the Row Source property so that it returns the ID and CategoryName fields from the Category table.

2. Click the white box where you enter the Row Source property.

   Access displays a down-arrow button and an ellipsis (...) button to the right of the white box.

3. Click the ellipsis button.

   Access opens the Query Builder window and an Add Table dialog box, as shown in Figure 9.9.

FIGURE 9.9.

Adding the Category table to a query.

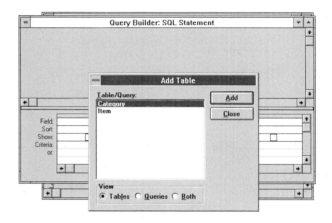

4. In the Add Table dialog box, select the Category table and click the **A**dd button. Click the **C**lose button to close the Add Table dialog box.

5. Click the ID field and drag it to the first column in the query grid.

6. Add the CategoryTitle field to the second column of the grid.

7. Change the sort order for the CategoryTitle column to Ascending, as shown in Figure 9.10.

FIGURE 9.10.

Sort the query results by category name.

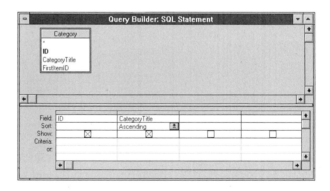

8. Close the Query Builder window, answering Yes to the message box that asks if you want to save your changes.

Access enters the following SQL SELECT statement in the Row Source property:

```
SELECT DISTINCTROW Category.ID, Category.CategoryTitle FROM Category
ORDER BY Category.CategoryTitle;
```

You can make the Category list box display the categories by name, but use the ID field in the Category table as the value for the program to identify which category is selected. This is done by hiding the first column in the list by setting its display width to 0 inches.

The Bound Column property of the list box control indicates which column in the Row Source is the value returned by the list box control. A 1 would return the first column, ID, and a 2 would return the second column, CategoryName.

Instead you can set the Bound Column to 0, which returns the current row selected in the list box. This will be helpful later when you want to tell the list box to select the first row.

Note that you can always reference values in the Row Source by using the Column property. As such, `lstCategories.Column(0)` returns ID, and `lstCategories.Column(1)` returns the CategoryName.

9. Set the remainder of the list box properties as follows:

Name:	lstCategories
Column Count:	2
Column Widths:	0 in;1.8125 in
Bound Column:	0
Tab Stop:	Yes
Tab Index:	0
Left:	1.141 in
Top:	1.2806 in
Width:	1.8125 in
Height:	0.4535 in
Special Effect:	Sunken

10. Set the properties for the list box label:

Name:	lblCategory
Caption:	Category:
Left:	0.4222 in
Top:	1.2806 in
Width:	0.625 in
Height:	0.166 in
Back Color:	12632256 (Light Gray)
Font Weight:	Bold

Figure 9.11 shows the lstCategories list box added to the form.

FIGURE 9.11.
*The completed
1stCategories list box.*

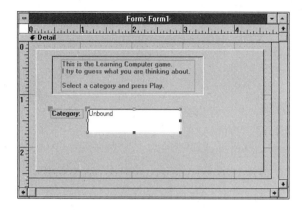

Next, you add two buttons used to maintain the available categories in the lstCategories
list box.

 Below the list box, add two buttons labeled **A**dd and **D**elete, as shown in Figure 9.12.

Name:	cmdAdd
Caption:	&Add
Tab Stop:	Yes
Tab Index:	1
Left:	1.141 in
Top:	1.8125 in
Width:	0.5729 in
Height:	0.2076 in
Font Name:	MS Sans Serif
Font Size:	8
Font Weight:	Normal
Name:	cmdDelete
Caption:	&Delete
Tab Stop:	Yes
Tab Index:	2
Left:	1.7653 in
Top:	1.8125 in
Width:	0.5729 in
Height:	0.2076 in
Font Name:	MS Sans Serif
Font Size:	8
Font Weight:	Normal

FIGURE 9.12.

Setting the cmdDelete button properties.

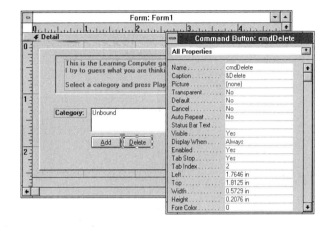

Some on-screen help text can be a big advantage when you haven't spent the time to create an online help file or a manual. Next you will add a lblHint label to explain how the **A**dd and **D**elete buttons are used.

1. Drop a label below the **A**dd and **D**elete buttons with the following caption:

   ```
   Use the Add and Delete buttons to create
   and remove categories in the list.
   ```

2. Set the properties for the new label as shown here:

Name:	lblHint
Left:	1.141 in
Top:	2.0938 in
Width:	2.125 in
Height:	0.3125 in
Back Color:	12632256 (Light Gray)
Fore Color:	16777215 (White)

Next, add **P**lay and **Q**uit buttons, as shown in Figure 9.13.

FIGURE 9.13.

The Learning Computer form.

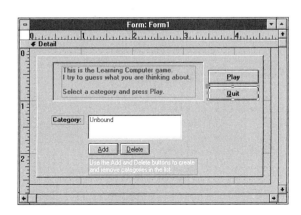

1. Add two buttons to the top right of the form with the following properties:

Name:	cmdPlay
Caption:	&Play
Default:	Yes
Tab Stop:	Yes
Tab Index:	3
Left:	3.4896 in
Top:	0.4222 in
Width:	0.9896 in
Height:	0.25 in
Font Name:	MS Sans Serif
Font Size:	8
Font Weight:	Bold

Name:	cmdQuit
Caption:	&Quit
Cancel:	Yes
Tab Stop:	Yes
Tab Index:	4
Left:	3.4896 in
Top:	0.7347 in
Width:	0.9896 in
Height:	0.25 in
Font Name:	MS Sans Serif
Font Size:	8
Font Weight:	Bold

The remaining controls to be added to the form are the Form Art bitmaps discussed at the end of the chapter.

2. Close the form, saving it as `Learning Computer`.

Before you create the remaining two forms, you can declare some globals and write the code behind the form you just created.

The Globals Module

As is typical with an application that uses multiple forms, you need to declare some global variables.

1. In the database container, click the Modules tab and click the **N**ew button to create a new module.

2. Enter the declaration section for the module, as shown in Listing 9.1.

Listing 9.1. The declaration section for the Globals module.

```
' Globals module

Option Compare Database
Option Explicit

Global Const PROGRAM = "Learning Computer"

Global gdb As Database

Global gtblCategory As Recordset
Global gtblItem As Recordset

Global gblnCategoryOpened As Integer
Global gblnItemOpened As Integer

Global gblnAnswerYes As Integer

Global cr As String
Global dq As String
```

The gdb variable is set to the current database when the Learning Computer form opens in order to open the Category and Item tables. The gdb variable is used only in the Form_Open procedure, but it must remain global for the recordset objects opened to remain valid objects.

The gtblCategory and gtblItem recordset variables are set as open table objects for the Category and Item tables. The tables remain open as long as the Learning Computer form is open. The Form_Close event has code that checks the gblnCategoryOpened and gblnItemOpened flags to see if the recordsets are open and need to be closed.

The gblnAnswerYes flag indicates whether the user answered Yes or No to the most recently asked question.

The cr and dq variables hold the carriage return characters and the double quote characters.

In this project you are going to need your sinister friend, the CNStr function. His job is to make sure that you get a string when you want a string.

Enter the CNStr function into the Globals module as shown in Listing 9.2.

Listing 9.2. The `CNStr` **function.**

```
Function CNStr (v As Variant) As String

' Convert nulls to an empty string
' Remove leading and trailing spaces

  On Error Resume Next

  If IsNull(v) Then
    CNStr = ""
  Else
    CNStr = Trim$(CStr(v))
  End If

End Function
```

Save the module with the name `Globals`.

The Learning Computer Form Module

You need to add code to the Learning Computer form for game initialization; events for the **Add**, **Delete**, **Play**, and **Quit** buttons; and the controlling game logic.

1. Open the Learning Computer form in design mode.
2. Click the Code button on the toolbar to open the Learning Computer form module.
3. Enter the declarations section as shown in Listing 9.3.

Listing 9.3. The Learning Computer form module's declaration section.

```
' Learning Computer form

  Option Compare Database
  Option Explicit
```

The *Form_Open* Subroutine

The `Form_Open` subroutine is the first code that runs when you play the Learning Computer game.

Enter the `Form_Open` subroutine into the Learning Computer form module as shown in Listing 9.4.

Listing 9.4. The Form_Open subroutine.

```
Sub Form_Open (Cancel As Integer)

  On Error GoTo Form_OpenError

' Carriage return and double quotes
  cr = Chr$(13) & Chr$(10)
  dq = Chr$(34)

  gblnCategoryOpened = False
  gblnItemOpened = False

' Note that the database object MUST be global in order for global
' recordset variables created from it to remain valid objects.

  Set gdb = CurrentDB()

' Open the Category and Item tables

  Set gtblCategory = gdb.OpenRecordset("Category", DB_OPEN_TABLE)
  gblnCategoryOpened = True

  Set gtblItem = gdb.OpenRecordset("Item", DB_OPEN_TABLE)
  gblnItemOpened = True

  gtblItem.Index = "PrimaryKey"

' Don't let the user play until a category is selected
  cmdPlay.Enabled = False
  cmdDelete.Enabled = False

Form_OpenDone:
  Exit Sub

Form_OpenError:
  MsgBox Error$, 48, PROGRAM
  Resume Form_OpenDone

End Sub
```

Form_Open first initializes two variables, cr and dq, used to construct messages in strings for the MsgBox function. The cr variable holds a carriage return character sequence, and the dq variable holds a double quote character.

```
' Carriage return and double quotes
  cr = Chr$(13) & Chr$(10)
  dq = Chr$(34)
```

Next, the gblnCategoryOpened and gblnItemOpened flags are set to False, indicating that the gtblCategory and gtblItem recordsets have not been opened yet.

```
gblnCategoryOpened = False
gblnItemOpened = False
```

The `gdb` global is set to the current database.

```
' Note that the database object MUST be global in order for global
' recordset variables created from it to remain valid objects.

  Set gdb = CurrentDB()
```

Next, in the lines shown in Listing 9.5, the `gtblCategory` and `gtblItem` recordset variables are set as the Category and Item tables are opened. The `Recordset` object, introduced in Access version 2.0, is used to open the tables instead of the `Table` object that has been in Access since 1.0.

As each table is opened, the appropriate flags `gblnCategoryOpened` and `gblnItemOpened` are set to indicate that the tables need to be closed. These flags are checked in the `Form_Close` subroutine that is activated when the form is closed.

Listing 9.5. Opening the Category and Item tables.

```
' Open the Category and Item tables

  Set gtblCategory = gdb.OpenRecordset("Category", DB_OPEN_TABLE)
  gblnCategoryOpened = True

  Set gtblItem = gdb.OpenRecordset("Item", DB_OPEN_TABLE)
  gblnItemOpened = True
```

Because the recordsets are opened as tables, you can set the Index property on either of them and use the Seek method to locate records. In this program, all seeks on the Item table are done using the PrimaryKey (the ID field). You can set that once here during initialization.

```
gtblItem.Index = "PrimaryKey"
```

The last thing that happens during initialization is the **P**lay and **D**elete buttons are disabled (grayed). They should be available only when a category is selected in the form's category list box.

```
' Don't let the user play until a category is selected
  cmdPlay.Enabled = False
  cmdDelete.Enabled = False
```

The *Form_Close* Subroutine

The `Form_Close` subroutine closes the tables opened in the `Form_Open` subroutine. This way the tables remain open and ready for use as long as the Learning Computer form is open.

Enter the `Form_Close` subroutine as shown in Listing 9.6.

Listing 9.6. The `Form_Close` subroutine.

```
Sub Form_Close ()

  On Error Resume Next

  If gblnCategoryOpened Then gtblCategory.Close
  If gblnItemOpened Then gtblItem.Close

End Sub
```

The *cmdAdd_Click* and *cmdDelete_Click* Subroutines

Next you can add code for maintaining the different knowledge tree categories.

Enter the `cmdAdd_Click` subroutine as shown in Listing 9.7.

Listing 9.7. The `cmdAdd_Click` subroutine.

```
Sub cmdAdd_Click ()

  On Error Resume Next
  DoCmd OpenForm "Add Category", , , , , A_DIALOG

End Sub
```

The `cmdAdd_Click` subroutine opens the Add Category form so the user can enter the name of the new category. The actual saving of the category occurs in the code behind that form.

Note that the form is opened with the `A_DIALOG` constant, which opens the form as a pop-up modal dialog box.

Enter the `cmdDelete_Click` subroutine as shown in Listing 9.8.

Listing 9.8. The `cmdDelete_Click` subroutine.

```
Sub cmdDelete_Click ()

  Dim lngID As Long
  Dim intRow As Integer
  Dim z As Integer
```

continues

Listing 9.8. continued

```
On Error GoTo cmdDelete_ClickError

' Which category should be deleted?
  lngID = lstCategories.Column(0)

' Which row in the listbox is being deleted?
  intRow = lstCategories

' Confirm
  z = MsgBox("Delete the " & lstCategories.Column(1) & " category?",
➥ 4 + 32 + 256, PROGRAM)
  If z <> 6 Then GoTo cmdDelete_ClickDone

' Delete
  DoCmd SetWarnings False
  DoCmd RunSQL "DELETE FROM Item WHERE CategoryID = " & lngID
  DoCmd RunSQL "DELETE FROM Category WHERE ID = " & lngID

' Refresh the list so the deleted category isn't displayed
  lstCategories.Requery

' Highlight the item after the deleted one if there is one, or the
' one before it.
  If lstCategories.ListCount > intRow Then
    lstCategories = intRow
  Else
    lstCategories = intRow - 1
  End If

' Disable the Play and Delete buttons if there are no more categories
  If lstCategories.ListCount = 0 Then
    lstCategories.SetFocus
    lstCategories_Click
  End If

cmdDelete_ClickDone:
  DoCmd SetWarnings True
  Exit Sub

cmdDelete_ClickError:
  MsgBox Error$, 48, PROGRAM
  Resume cmdDelete_ClickDone

End Sub
```

The cmdDelete_Click subroutine actually does the job of cleaning out the Item and Category tables to remove a knowledge tree. This is easier than it sounds because all the work is really just a matter of calling two SQL DELETE statements.

First, the ID number for the category is read from the first column in the lstCategories list box to determine which category has been selected to delete. Also, the current row number in the list box is saved.

```
' Which category should be deleted?
  lngID = lstCategories.Column(0)

' Which row in the listbox is being deleted?
  intRow = lstCategories
```

Before carrying out the execution, a final appeal is made to the user with a message box to see if he really wants to eliminate the category. A return value of 6 means the user clicked Yes.

```
' Confirm
  z = MsgBox("Delete the " & lstCategories.Column(1) & " category?",
➥ 4 + 32 + 256, PROGRAM)
  If z <> 6 Then GoTo cmdDelete_ClickDone
```

The records associated with this category are removed from the Item and Category tables. The SetWarnings macro is used to silence Access from displaying messages about how many records have been deleted.

```
' Delete
  DoCmd SetWarnings False
  DoCmd RunSQL "DELETE FROM Item WHERE CategoryID = " & lngID
  DoCmd RunSQL "DELETE FROM Category WHERE ID = " & lngID
```

After the records are deleted, the lstCategories list box is requeried so that the deleted category is no longer displayed.

```
' Refresh the list so the deleted category isn't displayed
  lstCategories.Requery
```

The next few lines, shown in Listing 9.9, deal with a nitpicky detail, but it's this kind of attention to details that gives your programs a professional feel.

When an item is deleted from a list box, the list box should find the next item in the list and show it as selected. If you deleted the last item in the list, the item preceding the deleted item should show as selected.

An example of where this adds real convenience is when you want to delete several items in a row. If you select the top item, you can hit the Delete button several times repeatedly to delete the selected item and those that follow it, without having to go back and forth between clicking the item in the list box and clicking the Delete button.

Is this excessively nitpicky? Yes. But if you have the time to make an application really slick, then go for it.

The code that does this uses the intRow value you saved earlier, which is set to the row you deleted. Setting the current row to this value will then be the item that followed the deleted item. If there is no item afterward, the current item is set to intRow - 1, which is the last item in the list.

Listing 9.9. Selecting the current row after a delete.

```
' Highlight the item after the deleted  one if there is one, or the
' one before it.
  If lstCategories.ListCount > intRow Then
    lstCategories = intRow
  Else
    lstCategories = intRow - 1
  End If
```

Next, the **P**lay and **D**elete buttons are disabled if there are no more items in the category list. The lstCategories_Click subroutine has code that disables the buttons, so you can call it here. Before the **D**elete button can be disabled, you have to move focus away from it to the lstCategories list box, because you can't disable a control that currently has focus without getting an error message from Access.

```
' Disable the Play and Delete buttons if there are no more categories
  If lstCategories.ListCount = 0 Then
    lstCategories.SetFocus
    lstCategories_Click
  End If
```

In the Done section of the subroutine, the SetWarnings macro is called again to turn warning messages back on.

```
cmdDelete_ClickDone:
  DoCmd SetWarnings True
  Exit Sub
```

The *lstCategories_Click* Subroutine

Each time the lstCategories list box is clicked, you need to determine whether the **P**lay and **D**elete buttons should be available.

The buttons should be disabled if there is no current selection in the list, which occurs when the list is empty. You can tell when no current item is selected because the lstCategories control returns −1. (It otherwise returns 0 or a positive number indicating which row is selected.)

Enter the lstCategories_Click subroutine as shown in Listing 9.10.

Listing 9.10. The lstCategories_Click subroutine.

```
Sub lstCategories_Click ()

' Only enable Play if a category is selected
  cmdPlay.Enabled = (lstCategories > -1)
  cmdDelete.Enabled = (lstCategories > -1)

End Sub
```

The *cmdPlay_Click* Subroutine

Now you get to the code that is actually involved with game play.

Enter the cmdPlay_Click subroutine as shown in Listing 9.11.

Listing 9.11. The cmdPlay_Click subroutine.

```
Sub cmdPlay_Click ()

  Dim msg As String
  Dim lngCategory As Long

  On Error GoTo cmdPlay_ClickError

  lngCategory = lstCategories.Column(0)

  gtblCategory.Index = "PrimaryKey"
  gtblCategory.Seek "=", lngCategory

  If gtblCategory!FirstItemID = 0 Then
  ' There are no items in this category yet.
  ' The computer loses by default.

    msg = "Hey!" & cr & cr
    msg = msg & "I don't know anything about " & dq &
    ➥ lstCategories.Column(1) & dq & "!" & cr & cr
    msg = msg & "Help me out, will ya?..."

    MsgBox msg, 48, PROGRAM

    DoCmd OpenForm "Give Up", , , , , A_DIALOG
  Else
  ' Begin play with the first item

    gtblItem.Seek "=", gtblCategory!FirstItemID

    While Play()
    Wend
  End If

cmdPlay_ClickDone:
  Exit Sub

cmdPlay_ClickError:
  MsgBox Error$, 48, PROGRAM
  Resume cmdPlay_ClickDone

End Sub
```

The cmdPlay_Click subroutine first retrieves which category is being used from the lstCategories list box.

```
  lngCategory = lstCategories.Column(0)
```

It then locates the record in the Category table for this category.

```
gtblCategory.Index = "PrimaryKey"
gtblCategory.Seek "=", lngCategory
```

The Category record contains a zero in the FirstItemID field if this is the first time playing with this category. In such a case, no data has been entered in this category, so the computer automatically loses.

```
If gtblCategory!FirstItemID = 0 Then
' There are no items in this category yet.
' The computer loses by default.
```

The program displays a message proclaiming its ignorance and asks for help.

```
msg = "Hey!" & cr & cr
msg = msg & "I don't know anything about " & dq &
➥ lstCategories.Column(1) & dq & "!" & cr & cr
msg = msg & "Help me out, will ya?..."

MsgBox msg, 48, PROGRAM
```

To collect information, the Give Up form is opened. This form gives the player the opportunity to enter the item he was thinking about and a question that leads to it.

```
DoCmd OpenForm "Give Up", , , , , A_DIALOG
```

If there is a first item, the program Seeks to that record in the Item table.

```
Else
' Begin play with the first item

gtblItem.Seek "=", gtblCategory!FirstItemID
```

With the Item table set to a Question record to start with, the program then enters a loop. Each call to the `Play` function traverses a path down the knowledge tree until the computer wins or loses.

When the game is through, `Play` returns False, and the loop ends.

```
While Play()
Wend
End If
```

Next, take a look inside the mysterious `Play` function.

The *Play* Function

For the `Play` function to work, the knowledge tree must be constructed correctly and the gtblItem recordset must be currently at a Question record.

The job of building the knowledge tree is in code behind the Give Up form, and I will look at that in a bit.

In the `cmdPlay` function, you did a Seek to the first Question record in the Items table, so at least on entering the `Play` function for the first time you know things are in a good state. It is the job of the `Play` function to make sure everything is in a good state for the next call.

Let's go ahead and enter the function before digging into any more details.

Enter the `Play` function into the Learning Computer form module, as shown in Listing 9.12.

Listing 9.12. The `Play` function.

```
Function Play () As Integer

  Dim strItem As String
  Dim lngCurrentID As Long
  Dim z As Integer
  Dim blnGiveUp As Integer

' Assume quit
  Play = False

  On Error GoTo PlayError

  blnGiveUp = False
  lngCurrentID = gtblItem!ID

' Ask a question
  z = MsgBox(gtblItem!Question, 4 + 32, PROGRAM)

  If z = 6 Then
  ' Yes
    gblnAnswerYes = True

  ' Move to the Yes link
    gtblItem.Seek "=", gtblItem!LinkYes
  Else
  ' No
    gblnAnswerYes = False

    If gtblItem!LinkNo = 0 Then
      blnGiveUp = True
    Else
    ' Move to the No link
      gtblItem.Seek "=", gtblItem!LinkNo
    End If
  End If

' Is it an item or another question?
  strItem = CNStr(gtblItem!Item)
  If Len(strItem) > 0 Then

    z = MsgBox("Is it a " & strItem & "?", 4 + 32, PROGRAM)
    If z = 6 Then
```

continues

Listing 9.12. continued

```
      MsgBox "The computer wins!", 0, PROGRAM
      GoTo PlayDone
   Else
      gtblItem.Seek "=", lngCurrentID
      blnGiveUp = True
   End If
 End If

 If blnGiveUp Then
    DoCmd OpenForm "Give Up", , , , , A_DIALOG
    GoTo PlayDone
 End If

' Continue play
 Play = True

PlayDone:
  Exit Function

PlayError:
  MsgBox Error$, 48, PROGRAM
  Resume PlayDone

End Function
```

The first thing the `Play` function does is set a return value to False. This is a precautionary measure just in case something goes wrong and the function aborts with an error.

You need to default the return value to False because the loop in the `cmdPlay_Click` subroutine would continue forever if you returned True on an error condition that occurred over and over. (Of course, in the computer world, forever is only as far away as the next Ctrl-Break, but it's better to exit clean anyway.)

```
' Assume quit
  Play = False

  On Error GoTo PlayError
```

Next, two variables are initialized. The `blnGiveUp` flag indicates that the program gives up. The `lngCurrentID` variable stores the ID of the Item record for the question you are currently on so that you can come back to it if you need to.

```
  blnGiveUp = False
  lngCurrentID = gtblItem!ID
```

The function assumes that the `gtblItem` variable is set to an Item record with a question in it. It uses the `MsgBox` function to display the question.

```
' Ask a question
z = MsgBox(gtblItem!Question, 4 + 32, PROGRAM)
```

> **NOTE**
>
> The MsgBox function's second parameter is a number indicating three things: the type of buttons displayed, the icon displayed, and the default button. To see the possible values, place your text cursor on the word MsgBox in the editor and press F1.
>
> The idea is that you add up the values for the options you want and pass that number as the value for the argument. Some people use constants like MB_YESNO, MB_ICONQUESTION, and MBDEFBUTTON2 to derive the value for the MsgBox argument.
>
> It's just about as easy to remember the numbers if you apply a little trick. That is, don't actually add up the values; just enter them like this:
>
> ```
> MsgBox strQuestion, 4 + 32 + 256, strWindowCaption
>
> 4 means display Yes and No buttons
>
> 32 means display the question icon
>
> 256 means default to the second button (No)
> ```
>
> OK, OK, OK. You can read MB_ICONQUESTION better than you can read 32. However, after about entering a million MsgBox calls, believe me, you will remember that 32 means the question icon. Besides that, the list of values is only a keystroke (F1) away.
>
> Climbing down off the soap box and back in front of the keyboard, I will get back to the Play function now.

The game player answers the question Yes or No. You check the return value of the MsgBox call to see what the player answered and what you should do next.

If the player answered Yes, you Seek to the Item record with the same ID value as stored in this record's LinkYes field. It's safe to assume that the LinkYes field always has a valid ID value because you only create Question records at the same time you create corresponding Item records.

The gblnAnswerYes global is set to True when the player answers Yes, as shown in Listing 9.13. It is set to False when they answer No. This value is needed by the code behind the Give Up form when creating records for the knowledge tree.

Listing 9.13. Dealing with a Yes answer.

```
If z = 6 Then
' Yes
  gblnAnswerYes = True

' Move to the Yes link
  gtblItem.Seek "=", gtblItem!LinkYes
```

If the player answered No, you need to check to see if there is an ID value stored in the LinkNo field, because sometimes it's empty. If it is empty, the computer loses because it doesn't have an item to guess with or any more questions. In this case the blnGiveUp flag is set to True.

If there is a value in the LinkNo field, you Seek to that record to continue, as shown in Listing 9.14.

Listing 9.14. Dealing with a No answer.

```
Else
' No
  gblnAnswerYes = False

  If gtblItem!LinkNo = 0 Then
    blnGiveUp = True
  Else
  ' Move to the No link
    gtblItem.Seek "=", gtblItem!LinkNo
  End If
End If
```

In the Item table, each record has either a Question value or an Item value. An Item value is a guess that the computer makes to see if it knows what you are thinking about.

The Play function checks the Item field for the current record. If you have Seeked to a record in the Item table that stores an Item and not a Question, you will find a value.

There is a case in the preceding code where you didn't Seek anywhere at all (when the LinkNo field doesn't have an ID value), but don't worry about that because you know you will be on a Question record in that case and the Item field will be blank.

```
' Is it an item or another question?
  strItem = CNStr(gtblItem!Item)
  If Len(strItem) > 0 Then
```

If you are on an Item record, the computer displays it as a guess using the MsgBox function.

```
    z = MsgBox("Is it a " & strItem & "?", 4 + 32, PROGRAM)
```

If the player indicates that the computer correctly deduced what the player was think-ing about, the computer displays a triumphant message and exits the function. This exit bypasses the line of code that sets the return value to True, so the play loop is termi-nated.

```
    If z = 6 Then
       MsgBox "The computer wins!", 0, PROGRAM
       GoTo PlayDone
```

If the player indicates that the computer was wrong, you Seek back to the Question record and set the blnGiveUp flag equal to True. The code behind the Give Up form expects that the current Item record is always a Question record, so that's why you had to Seek back.

```
    Else
       gtblItem.Seek "=", lngCurrentID
       blnGiveUp = True
    End If
  End If
```

Next, if the blnGiveUp flag had been set, the Give Up form is opened to make an addi-tion to the knowledge tree. This is an end-of-play condition, so you do an early exit after the Give Up dialog box is closed.

```
If blnGiveUp Then
   DoCmd OpenForm "Give Up", , , , , A_DIALOG
   GoTo PlayDone
  End If
```

Finally, if you get to the end of the function without an early exit, the play has traversed down to another Question record on the tree by following either the LinkYes field or the LinkNo field.

The current record in the Item table is a Question record, so you are ready to enter the Play function once again. The return value is set to True to indicate that play should continue.

```
' Continue play
  Play = True
```

Is all this a bit tough to follow? Try walking through the function using the knowledge tree shown at the beginning of this chapter in Figure 9.1.

Playing the game is only half the programming problem. You still have the matter of creating the records that make up the knowledge tree.

The *cmdQuit* Subroutine

To complete the code for the Learning Computer form, you need to code the **Q**uit button, which is used to close the form.

1. Enter the cmdQuit_Click subroutine as shown in Listing 9.15.
2. Close the Learning Computer form and form module, being sure to save your changes.

Listing 9.15. The cmdQuit_Click **subroutine.**

```
Sub cmdQuit_Click ()

    On Error Resume Next
    DoCmd Close

End Sub
```

Creating the Add Category Form

The Add Category form is displayed when the player clicks the **A**dd button on the Learning Computer form, as shown in Figure 9.14.

FIGURE 9.14.

Adding a new knowledge tree with the Add Category form.

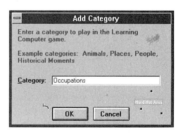

The job of this form is to create a new record in the Category table for the new category title entered by the player.

1. Create a new form with the following properties:

Caption:	Add Category
Default View:	Single Form
Scroll Bars:	Neither
Record Selectors:	No
Navigation Buttons:	No

Auto Center:	Yes
Pop Up:	Yes
Modal:	Yes
Border Style:	Dialog
Min Button:	No
Max Button:	No
Width:	3.1 in

2. Set the following properties in the form's Detail section:

Height:	1.9167 in
Back Color:	12632256 (Light Gray)

3. Add a label to the form with the following caption and properties:

Enter a category to play in the Learning
Computer game.

Example categories: Animals, Places, People,
Historical Moments

Name:	lblInstructions
Left:	0.1042 in
Top:	0.0833 in
Width:	2.8958 in
Height:	0.75 in
Back Color:	12632256 (Light Gray)
Fore Color:	16711680 (Blue)
Font Name:	MS Sans Serif
Font Size:	8
Font Weight:	Bold

4. Add a text box and label into which the Category is entered. Set the controls with the following properties:

Name:	txtCategory
Tab Stop:	Yes
Tab Index:	0
Left:	0.7979 in
Top:	1 in
Width:	2.0979 in
Height:	0.1667 in
Special Effect:	Sunken
Font Name:	MS Sans Serif
Font Size:	8
Font Weight:	Normal

Name: lblCategory
Caption: &Category:
Left: 0.1042 in
Top: 1 in
Width: 0.6979 in
Height: 0.1667 in
Font Name: MS Sans Serif
Font Size: 8
Font Weight: Bold

5. Create OK and Cancel buttons on the form with the following properties, as shown in Figure 9.15:

Name: cmdOK
Caption: OK
Default: Yes
Tab Stop: Yes
Tab Index: 1
Left: 0.8 in
Top: 1.5833 in
Width: 0.6979 in
Height: 0.25 in
Font Name: MS Sans Serif
Font Size: 8
Font Weight: Bold

Name: cmdCancel
Caption: Cancel
Cancel: Yes
Tab Stop: Yes
Tab Index: 2
Left: 1.6 in
Top: 1.5883 in
Width: 0.6979 in
Height: 0.25 in
Font Name: MS Sans Serif
Font Size: 8
Font Weight: Bold

FIGURE 9.15.

Creating the Add Category form.

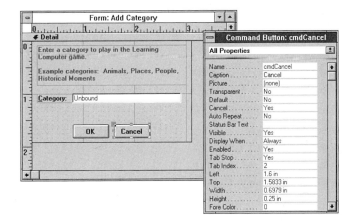

Coding the Add Category Form

Click the Code button on the toolbar and enter the declarations section as shown in Listing 9.16.

Listing 9.16. The declarations section for the Add Category form module.

```
' Add Category form

Option Compare Database
Option Explicit
```

All of the dirty work in this form occurs when the OK button is clicked. The cmdOK_Click subroutine verifies that the category name entered doesn't already exist, then it saves it as a new Category table record.

Enter the cmdOK_Click subroutine as shown in Listing 9.17.

Listing 9.17. The cmdOK_Click subroutine.

```
Sub cmdOK_Click ()

    Dim frm As Form

    Dim strCategory As String
    Dim lngID As Long
    Dim n As Integer
```

continues

Listing 9.17. continued

```
On Error GoTo cmdOK_ClickError

' Make sure they entered a category
  strCategory = CNStr(txtCategory)

  If Len(strCategory) = 0 Then
    MsgBox "Enter a category.", 48, PROGRAM
    txtCategory.SetFocus
    GoTo cmdOK_ClickDone
  End If

' See if the category already exists
  gtblCategory.Index = "CategoryTitle"
  gtblCategory.Seek "=", strCategory

  If Not gtblCategory.NoMatch Then
    MsgBox "The " & strCategory & " category already exists.", 64, PROGRAM
    GoTo cmdOK_ClickDone
  End If

' Add a category record
  gtblCategory.AddNew
  lngID = gtblCategory!ID
  gtblCategory!CategoryTitle = strCategory
  gtblCategory.Update

' Set the Category combo to the new category
  Set frm = Forms![Learning Computer]
  frm!lstCategories.Requery

  For n = 0 To frm!lstCategories.ListCount - 1
    frm!lstCategories = n
    If frm!lstCategories.Column(0) = lngID Then
      Exit For
    End If
  Next n

  frm!cmdPlay.Enabled = True
  frm!cmdDelete.Enabled = True
  frm!cmdPlay.SetFocus

  DoCmd Close

cmdOK_ClickDone:
  Exit Sub

cmdOK_ClickError:
  MsgBox Error$, 48, PROGRAM
  Resume cmdOK_ClickDone

End Sub
```

First, the subroutine verifies that the player actually entered a category name. If so, the table is searched for a matching category name to make sure the same category name isn't entered twice, as shown in Listing 9.18.

Listing 9.18. Exit early if the category title already exists.

```
' See if the category already exists
gtblCategory.Index = "CategoryTitle"
gtblCategory.Seek "=", strCategory

If Not gtblCategory.NoMatch Then
  MsgBox "The " & strCategory & " category already exists.", 64, PROGRAM
  GoTo cmdOK_ClickDone
End If
```

If the category title entered is valid, a new Category table record is created. While the record is being created, the ID counter field is saved in the lngID variable so it can be used later to set the selected item in the lstCategories list box on the Learning Computer form.

```
' Add a category record
gtblCategory.AddNew
lngID = gtblCategory!ID
gtblCategory!CategoryTitle = strCategory
gtblCategory.Update
```

A form variable is set to point to the main form, and the lstCategories list box is requeried so it displays the added category title.

```
' Set the Category combo to the new category
Set frm = Forms![Learning Computer]
frm!lstCategories.Requery
```

The items in the lstCategories list box are checked one by one to find and select the added category.

```
For n = 0 To frm!lstCategories.ListCount - 1
  frm!lstCategories = n
  If frm!lstCategories.Column(0) = lngID Then
    Exit For
  End If
Next n
```

Confident that you were able to add the category and select it as the current category, the code enables the **P**lay and **D**elete buttons. It sets focus on the **P**lay button because that is the most likely thing the player will want to do after creating a new category.

```
frm!cmdPlay.Enabled = True
frm!cmdDelete.Enabled = True
frm!cmdPlay.SetFocus
```

The subroutine ends by closing the Add Category form.

```
DoCmd Close
```

Complete the Add Category form by adding the code behind the Cancel button.

1. Enter the `cmdCancel_Click` subroutine as shown in Listing 9.19.

2. Close and save the Add Categories form.

Listing 9.19. The `cmdCancel_Click` subroutine.

```
Sub cmdCancel_Click ()

    On Error Resume Next
    DoCmd Close

End Sub
```

The Give Up Form

The final form, the Give Up form, is activated to collect new information to extend the knowledge tree.

How the information is added depends on what the current record in the Item table is and how the player answered the last question. I will get to that soon; first let's create another form.

1. Create a new form with the properties listed here:

Caption:	Learning Computer
Default View:	Single Form
Scroll Bars:	Neither
Record Selectors:	No
Navigation Buttons:	No
Auto Center:	Yes
Pop Up:	Yes
Modal:	Yes
Border Style:	Dialog
Min Button:	No
Max Button:	No
Width:	5.125 in

2. Set the following properties in the form's Detail section:

Height:	2.5625 in
Back Color:	12632256 (Light Gray)

3. Create two rectangles to produce a border effect around the form, as shown in Figure 9.16. (Note that this is primarily for the Form Art that will be added to the form.)

Name:	boxPanel
Left:	0.0313 in
Top:	0.016 in
Width:	5.0681 in
Height:	2.5417 in
Back Color:	12632256 (Light Gray)
Special Effect:	Raised

Name:	boxInset
Left:	0.2868 in
Top:	0.2.035 in
Width:	4.5521 in
Height:	2.1563 in
Back Color:	12632256 (Light Gray)
Special Effect:	Sunken

FIGURE 9.16.

Adding raised and inset rectangles on the Give Up form.

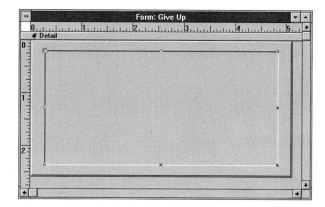

4. Create the lblMsg label with the following properties:

Name:	lblMsg
Caption:	You Win!

Left:	0.4063 in
Top:	0.2972 in
Width:	3.5313 in
Height:	0.3854 in
Back Color:	12632256 (Light Gray)
Fore Color:	16777215 (White)
Font Name:	MS Sans Serif
Font Size:	24
Font Weight:	Bold

5. Create two instruction labels with the following captions and properties, as shown in Figure 9.17:

`Enter the name of what you were thinking about.`

Name:	lblInstruction
Left:	0.391 in
Top:	0.7972 in
Width:	3.0104 in
Height:	0.1667 in
Back Color:	12632256 (Light Gray)
Fore Color:	16711680 (Blue)
Font Name:	MS Sans Serif
Font Size:	8
Font Weight:	Bold

`Enter a Yes/No question I can ask next time to identify this entry.`

Name:	lblInstructions2
Left:	0.391 in
Top:	1.3646 in
Width:	3.9896 in
Height:	0.1667 in
Back Color:	12632256 (Light Gray)
Fore Color:	16711680 (Blue)
Font Name:	MS Sans Serif
Font Size:	8
Font Weight:	Bold

FIGURE 9.17.

Placing instructions on the Give Up form.

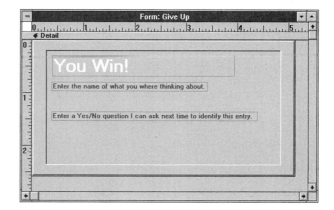

6. Drop two text boxes on the form, one for the Name of the new item and another for a Question that helps identify it. Each of the text boxes and corresponding labels uses the MS Sans Serif font size 8.

Name:	txtName
Tab Stop:	Yes
Tab Index:	0
Left:	1.091 in
Top:	1.0472 in
Width:	1.9 in
Height:	0.1667 in
Special Effect:	Sunken

Name:	lblName
Caption:	&Name
Left:	0.391 in
Top:	1.0472 in
Width:	0.5 in
Height:	0.1667 in
Back Color:	12632256 (Gray)
Font Weight:	Bold

Name:	txtQuestion
Tab Stop:	Yes
Tab Index:	1
Left:	1.091 in

Top:	1.6097 in
Width:	3.0042 in
Height:	0.6354 in
Special Effect:	Sunken
Name:	lblQuestion
Caption:	&Question
Left:	0.391 in
Top:	1.6097 in
Width:	0.5938 in
Height:	0.1667 in
Back Color:	12632256 (Gray)
Font Weight:	Bold

7. Add OK and Cancel buttons to the form.

Name:	cmdOK
Caption:	OK
Default:	Yes
Tab Stop:	Yes
Tab Index:	2
Left:	4.0472 in
Top:	0.3285 in
Width:	0.6979 in
Height:	0.25 in
Font Name:	MS Sans Serif
Font Size:	8
Font Weight:	Bold
Name:	cmdCancel
Caption:	Cancel
Cancel:	Yes
Tab Stop:	Yes
Tab Index:	3
Left:	4.0472 in
Top:	0.6618 in
Width:	0.6979 in
Height:	0.25 in
Font Name:	MS Sans Serif
Font Size:	8
Font Weight:	Bold

8. Select **File|Save** to save the form as you have completed it so far.

Figure 9.18 shows the completed Give Up form (minus artwork).

FIGURE 9.18.

Adding the functional controls to the Give Up form.

The final version of the Give Up form with some artistic embellishments is shown in Figure 9.19.

FIGURE 9.19.

The dressed-up version of the Give Up form.

Coding the Give Up Form

In case you were wondering if you would ever finish this program, you don't have too far to go. The coding here is kind of tricky, though, so wipe your eyes and try to keep it all in focus.

The job of the player at this point is to enter an item name and a question. When the question is answered Yes, that is a fair clue to the computer that points in the direction of the item entered. (You could always lie in your entries and make the computer sound like a bumbling idiot.)

Naturally, the work in the code is going to occur when the player clicks the OK button. First, add the `Option Explicit` directive in the declarations section as you always do to help catch mistyped variables.

Click the Code button on the toolbar and enter the declaration section for the Give Up form module, as shown in Listing 9.20.

Listing 9.20. The Give Up form declarations section.

```
' Give Up form

Option Compare Database
Option Explicit
```

The *cmdOK_Click* Subroutine

Enter the cmdOK_Click subroutine as shown in Listing 9.21.

Listing 9.21. The cmdOK_Click subroutine.

```
Sub cmdOK_Click ()

' Save the new entry.

  On Error GoTo cmdOK_ClickError

' Make sure a name and a question were entered

  If CNStr(txtName) = "" Then
    MsgBox "Enter a name for this entry.", 32, PROGRAM
    txtName.SetFocus
    GoTo cmdOK_ClickDone
  End If

  If CNStr(txtQuestion) = "" Then
    MsgBox "Enter a question for this entry.", 32, PROGRAM
    txtQuestion.SetFocus
    GoTo cmdOK_ClickDone
  End If

' Is this the first item for the category?
  If gtblCategory!FirstItemID = 0 Then
    AddFirstItem
  Else
    AddItem
  End If

  DoCmd Close

cmdOK_ClickDone:
  Exit Sub
```

```
cmdOK_ClickError:
  MsgBox Error$, 48, PROGRAM
  Resume cmdOK_ClickDone

End Sub
```

The `cmdOK_Click` subroutine verifies that something other than spaces has been entered in the two text boxes. Then it checks the FirstItemID field in the current Category records to see if there are any entries in this category yet.

If the FirstItemID field is 0, you are adding the first item, and the `AddFirstItem` subroutine is called, as shown in Listing 9.22. Otherwise you are adding an item to a knowledge tree already under construction.

Listing 9.22. Checking to see if this is the first item in the tree.

```
' Is this the first item for the category?
  If gtblCategory!FirstItemID = 0 Then
    AddFirstItem
  Else
    AddItem
  End If
```

Creating the Knowledge Tree

Now you get to the two subroutines that quite frankly gave me a headache: `AddFirstItem` and `AddItem`. It's not that they are difficult subroutines, it just took a while to figure out what a knowledge tree would look like, and then how to build it.

To help with the design, I used some shorthand notes via comments in the code that helped me visualize what was being created. There are four codes:

    q   A Question record
    n   A No link
    y   A Yes link
    i   An Item record

The No links and Yes links aren't records themselves—they are values plugged into the LinkYes and LinkNo fields in a record that represents a question.

When the player answers Yes, you look at the LinkYes field to see which record to Seek to next. When the player answers No, you check the LinkNo field. You looked at the code that walks through a knowledge table earlier in the `Play` function.

In the `AddFirstItem` subroutine, the first branch in the tree is created, and it looks like this:

```
            q
         n   y
               i
```

The diagram indicates that a Question record is created. Its Yes link points to an Item record. The No link is empty.

The *AddFirstItem* Subroutine

Enter the `AddFirstItem` subroutine into the Give Up form module as shown in Listing 9.23.

Listing 9.23. The `AddFirstItem` **subroutine.**

```
Sub AddFirstItem ()

' Add the first item in the tree
'
'      q
'    n y
'        i
'
  Dim lngItemID As Long

  Dim blnTransStarted As Integer

  On Error GoTo AddFirstItemError

  BeginTrans
  blnTransStarted = True

' 1. Add the first item
  gtblItem.AddNew
  lngItemID = gtblItem!ID
  gtblItem!CategoryID = gtblCategory!ID
  gtblItem!Item = txtName
  gtblItem.Update

' 2. Add the first question
  gtblItem.AddNew
  gtblItem!CategoryID = gtblCategory!ID
  gtblItem!Question = txtQuestion
  gtblItem!LinkYes = lngItemID
  lngItemID = gtblItem!ID
  gtblItem.Update
```

```
' 3. Identify the first item record for this category
  gtblCategory.Edit
  gtblCategory!FirstItemID = lngItemID
  gtblCategory.Update

  CommitTrans
  blnTransStarted = False

AddFirstItemDone:
  On Error Resume Next
  If blnTransStarted Then Rollback
  Exit Sub

AddFirstItemError:
  MsgBox Error$, 48, PROGRAM
  Resume AddFirstItemDone

End Sub
```

The `AddFirstItem` subroutine uses transaction processing, not as an optimization but to ensure that the change to the knowledge tree is complete or isn't done at all.

First the `BeginTrans` statement is used to indicate the starting point for a transaction. I always use a flag, `blnTransStarted`, when I write code using transactions. The flag is set to True to indicate that a transaction is in progress.

```
BeginTrans
blnTransStarted = True
```

If the procedure reaches the end, and the `blnTransStarted` flag was never set back to False, I know something went wrong during the transaction. The transaction is aborted by calling the `Rollback` statement. This happens in the Done section of the procedure like this:

```
If blnTransStarted Then Rollback
```

Going back to the beginning of the subroutine, to add an item to the knowledge tree you must actually create two records in the Item table: one for the item and a second one for the question.

You add the item first. This way you can store the ID for the newly added item in the variable `lngItem` so it can be used to establish a link later.

Listing 9.24 shows the code that adds the first Item record. The CategoryID field is set so you know which knowledge tree the record belongs to, then the Item field is set.

Listing 9.24. Adding an Item record.

```
' 1. Add the first item
  gtblItem.AddNew
  lngItemID = gtblItem!ID
  gtblItem!CategoryID = gtblCategory!ID
  gtblItem!Item = txtName
  gtblItem.Update
```

Next, an additional record is created in the Item table for the Question record. In this record, the question stored in the txtQuestion text box is written to the Question field, and there is no value stored in the record's Item field.

The value in the lngItemID variable is written to the LinkYes field, as shown in Listing 9.25, thereby establishing the relationship between this record and one preceding it.

Listing 9.25. Adding the first Question record.

```
' 2. Add the first question
  gtblItem.AddNew
  gtblItem!CategoryID = gtblCategory!ID
  gtblItem!Question = txtQuestion
  gtblItem!LinkYes = lngItemID
  lngItemID = gtblItem!ID
  gtblItem.Update
```

With the Question record written, the remaining step is to update the record in the Category table for this category, so that the FirstItemID field points to the first question now in the Item table.

```
' 3. Identify the first item record for this category
  gtblCategory.Edit
  gtblCategory!FirstItemID = lngItemID
  gtblCategory.Update
```

The updates to the database don't actually happen until the CommitTrans statement is issued. Following the CommitTrans statement, you set the blnTransStarted flag to False because you are no longer in the middle of a transaction.

```
  CommitTrans
  blnTransStarted = False
```

That one wasn't too bad after all. The next subroutine, AddItem, has to deal with a few more situations.

Adding New Branches to the Knowledge Tree

The various scenarios that the AddItem subroutine deals with are drawn in several diagrams in the comments at the start of the procedure, as shown in Figure 9.20.

FIGURE 9.20.

Letter diagrams in the
AddItem *subroutine*
were helpful in writing
the procedure.

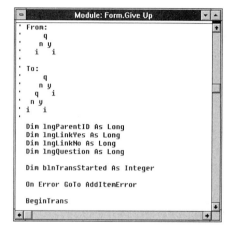

Let's take a look at each scenario:

SCENARIO ONE: The computer is on a Question record. It asks the question and the player answers Yes. The computer checks the LinkYes field and locates an Item record. The computer asks Is this the item?, and the player answers No.

At the start of the scenario, the tree looks like this:

```
        q
     n     y
             i
```

A new question is added where the old item was.

```
        q
     n     y
              q
           n     y
```

A new item is added to the Yes link for the new question:

```
        q
    n   y
          q
      n   y
            i
```

The old item is added to the No link for the new question, pushing it down a level in the tree from where it used to be.

```
        q
    n   y
          q
      n   y
    i       i
```

SCENARIO TWO: Once again, the computer is on a Question record. It asks the question, and this time the player answers No. The computer checks the No link and finds it empty, so the computer gives up without a guess.

This one is easy. Just add the new question and item as a No link.

At the start of this scenario, the tree looks like this:

```
        q
    n   y
          i
```

A new question is added to the No link:

```
          q
      n   y
    q       i
  n   y
```

The new item is added to the Yes link of the new question:

```
          q
      n   y
    q       i
  n   y
        i
```

SCENARIO THREE: The computer asks the question for the current Question record. The player answers No. The computer looks at the No link and this time finds an item. The computer guesses the item, but the player answers No.

This scenario works much like the first one. The Item record at the No link is replaced with a Question record.

This scenario begins with an item at the No link:

```
        q
     n     y
    i       i
```

A question is placed where the item is at the No link:

```
        q
     n     y
    q       i
   n   y
```

The new Item record is placed at the new Question record's Yes link:

```
        q
     n     y
    q       i
   n   y
        i
```

The old item is placed at the new Question record's No link:

```
        q
     n     y
    q       i
   n   y
  i     i
```

The *AddItem* Subroutine

Enter the AddItem subroutine into the Give Up form module as shown in Listing 9.26.

Listing 9.26. The `AddItem` subroutine.

```
Sub AddItem ()

' Scenarios:
'
' We asked a question, user answered yes.
' We asked is it the current item, user said no.
'
' From:
'       q
'     n y
'         i
'
' To:
'       q
'     n y
'         q
'       n y
'     i   i
'
' We asked a question, user answered no.
'
' From:
'       q
'     n y
'         i
'
' To:
'       q
'     n y
'     q   i
'   n y
'       i
'
' OR
'
' From:
'       q
'     n y
'     i   i
'
' To:
'       q
'     n y
'     q   i
'   n y
' i   i
'

    Dim lngParentID As Long
    Dim lngLinkYes As Long
    Dim lngLinkNo As Long
    Dim lngQuestion As Long

    Dim blnTransStarted As Integer

    On Error GoTo AddItemError
```

```
   BeginTrans
   blnTransStarted = True

   lngParentID = gtblItem!ID
   If gblnAnswerYes Then
     lngLinkNo = gtblItem!LinkYes
   Else
     lngLinkNo = gtblItem!LinkNo
   End If

' 1. Add a Yes link
   gtblItem.AddNew
   lngLinkYes = gtblItem!ID
   gtblItem!CategoryID = gtblCategory!ID
   gtblItem!Item = txtName
   gtblItem.Update

' 2. Add a Question
'    Connect the Yes link to the question
'    Connect the No link to the question
   gtblItem.AddNew
   lngQuestion = gtblItem!ID
   gtblItem!CategoryID = gtblCategory!ID
   gtblItem!Question = txtQuestion
   gtblItem!LinkYes = lngLinkYes
   gtblItem!LinkNo = lngLinkNo
   gtblItem.Update

' 3. Connect the Question
   gtblItem.Seek "=", lngParentID
   gtblItem.Edit
   If gblnAnswerYes Then
     gtblItem!LinkYes = lngQuestion
   Else
     gtblItem!LinkNo = lngQuestion
   End If
   gtblItem.Update

   CommitTrans
   blnTransStarted = False

AddItemDone:
   On Error Resume Next
   If blnTransStarted Then Rollback
   Exit Sub

AddItemError:
   MsgBox Error$, 48, PROGRAM
   Resume AddItemDone

End Sub
```

For all that it took to describe what the AddItem subroutine does, it's a pretty short procedure.

Transaction processing is used again to ensure that only a complete modification to the knowledge tree is made.

```
BeginTrans
blnTransStarted = True
```

Next, the current Item table record ID is saved so the record can be returned to later.

```
lngParentID = gtblItem!ID
```

Depending on whether the player answered Yes or No to the question in the current Item record, the new question's No link points to either the current question's Yes link or its No link, as shown in Listing 9.27.

Listing 9.27. Getting the new question's No link.

```
If gblnAnswerYes Then
  lngLinkNo = gtblItem!LinkYes
Else
  lngLinkNo = gtblItem!LinkNo
End If
```

Next, an Item record is created, as shown in Listing 9.28. The new question's Yes link points to this record.

Listing 9.28. Adding a new Item record.

```
' 1. Add a Yes link
gtblItem.AddNew
lngLinkYes = gtblItem!ID
gtblItem!CategoryID = gtblCategory!ID
gtblItem!Item = txtName
gtblItem.Update
```

The Question record is created, and its Yes and No links are established, as shown in Listing 9.29.

Listing 9.29. Adding a new Question record.

```
' 2. Add a Question
'    Connect the Yes link to the question
'    Connect the No link to the question
gtblItem.AddNew
lngQuestion = gtblItem!ID
gtblItem!CategoryID = gtblCategory!ID
gtblItem!Question = txtQuestion
```

```
gtblItem!LinkYes = lngLinkYes
gtblItem!LinkNo = lngLinkNo
gtblItem.Update
```

Next, you Seek back to the original Question record and insert the new Question record into the tree either at the Yes link or the No link, as shown in Listing 9.30.

Listing 9.30. Inserting the question into the knowledge tree.

```
' 3. Connect the Question
gtblItem.Seek "=", lngParentID
gtblItem.Edit
If gblnAnswerYes Then
  gtblItem!LinkYes = lngQuestion
Else
  gtblItem!LinkNo = lngQuestion
End If
gtblItem.Update
```

Finally, the transaction is committed.

```
CommitTrans
blnTransStarted = False
```

If I lost you there, don't feel bad. This kind of stuff takes me a few rounds to figure out, too.

The best way to understand what happens in this subroutine is to draw something similar to a football strategy diagram on a piece of paper.

Draw a box with a Q in it to represent a Question record and a circle with an I in it to represent an Item record. Draw arrows from the box to indicate Yes and No links.

Step through the procedure, modifying your drawing as each new Item record is created and links are established. See if the final drawing represents the same thing shown in the letter diagrams you viewed earlier.

The *cmdCancel_Click* Subroutine

The last procedure to enter in the application is the cmdCancel_Click subroutine.

1. Enter the cmdCancel_Click subroutine as shown in Listing 9.31.
2. Close the Give Up form, being sure to save your changes.

Listing 9.31. The `cmdCancel_Click` **subroutine.**

```
Sub cmdCancel_Click ()

  On Error Resume Next
  DoCmd Close

End Sub
```

Let's look at what you just created.

Playing the Game

To start the game, select the Learning Computer form in the database container and click the **O**pen button. You see the form for the Learning Computer game as shown in Figure 9.21.

FIGURE 9.21.

The Learning Computer game starts without any categories.

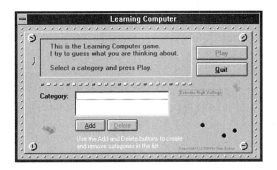

You need to add a category first, so click the **A**dd button. The Add Category dialog box, shown in Figure 9.22, appears.

FIGURE 9.22.

Adding the Transportation category.

Click the **P**lay button to start a new knowledge tree with the new category. Because the Learning Computer doesn't know anything yet about the category, it immediately gives up with the message shown in Figure 9.23.

FIGURE 9.23.

The Learning Computer whines when it has an empty knowledge table.

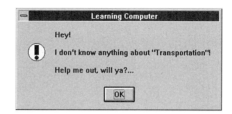

Click OK, and the Learning Computer displays the Give Up form, shown in Figure 9.24. Enter an item and a question that would reasonably lead to the item. Click OK, and you enter the first item into the knowledge tree.

FIGURE 9.24.

Entering an item and question into the knowledge tree.

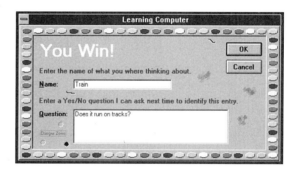

Click the **P**lay button again and the Learning Computer knows enough to ask a single question, as shown in Figure 9.25.

FIGURE 9.25.

The Learning Computer does a lot of its game play through message boxes.

If you answer Yes, the Learning Computer makes a guess at the one item it currently knows, as shown in Figure 9.26.

FIGURE 9.26.

The Learning Computer makes a guess.

If you accept the guess as the correct answer, the Learning Computer proudly exclaims that it wins. If not, you add another item into the knowledge tree and continue on from there.

Drawing Form Art

You can jazz up your Access forms as I did in my version of the Learning Computer game. Be forewarned, though: It does slow down how fast your forms load, even when you use very small bitmaps.

Here's how to do it.

Open Paintbrush to a full-screen picture. Fill the background color with what you expect to use on your Access form (typically gray).

Start drawing little pictures to adorn your forms. Use the full screen to experiment with, because you will later clip out just the pictures you want.

If you want to give your forms a rough look, you can create scratches and smudges. To create a scratch, draw short, crooked lines in black, then add a line of white below the black line to create an indented look, as shown in Figure 9.27.

FIGURE 9.27.

Drawing a scratch in Paintbrush.

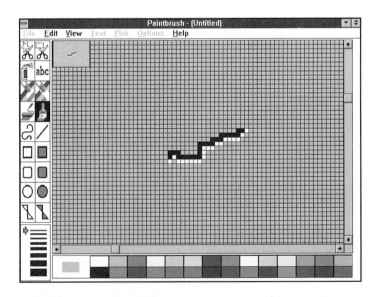

To create a smudge, use the Paintbrush spray can and spray random spots until you get a good mix that doesn't look like a set of Paintbrush spray-can dots.

Holes can be created by drawing circles or squares and then applying shading around the object to make it look indented.

To make rivets, screws, or colored lights, you change the shading so the white is to the top left of the object, giving it a raised look. A screw is a raised circle with a sunken line in the middle of it.

Use the Paintbrush **View|Zoom In** command to detail your creations, as shown in Figure 9.28.

FIGURE 9.28.

Zooming in on a smudge and a Phillips screw.

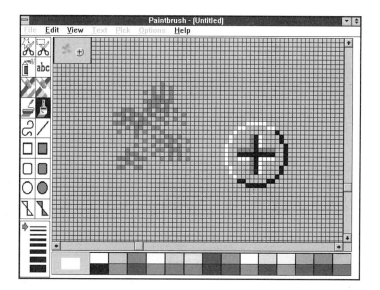

To save a drawing, click the scissors picture with the square cutout in it. Select the area you want to save by dragging a box around it, then select the **Edit|Copy To** command, as shown in Figure 9.29. When you enter a filename and save the picture, you are saving only the selected portion, not the entire Paintbrush drawing.

In Access you can create a form that becomes your Form Art gallery, as shown in Figure 9.30. To add a bitmap to the form, select the **Edit|Insert Object** command and select the bitmap file.

After the bitmaps are collected in a Form Art gallery, you can place them on other forms by copying them. Select the bitmap you want to use and press Ctrl-C to copy it. Click the form you want to paste it to and press Ctrl-V.

FIGURE 9.29.

Cutting and saving a small bitmap drawing of a Phillips screw head.

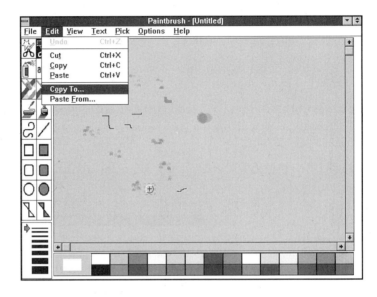

FIGURE 9.30.

Adding bitmaps to a Form Art gallery.

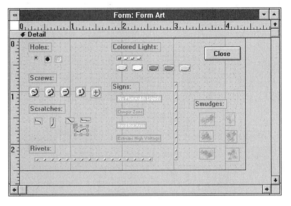

TRY THIS! QUESTION 9.1.

Now that you added some "art" to the game, do you know how to enhance the game with sound?

Write a PlayWAV subroutine that takes a WAV filename as the sound to play. Add sounds that play as the forms are displayed on screen and also as buttons are clicked.

Hint: You're going to have to look up how to use the SndPlaySound API function.

Summary

Cool! You created a unique and interesting game in Microsoft Access. This was a fairly large project to accomplish in a single chapter.

Here are all the things you did in this chapter. You

- Discovered a way to represent a tree structure in a database table
- Created the Learning Computer forms
- Used globals to keep tables conveniently open for the duration of a program run
- Created and fine-tuned the capability to add and delete knowledge tree categories
- Wrote the Learning Computer game playing engine
- Got an opinion on how to use the MsgBox function
- Used comments and shorthand codes to design knowledge tree maintenance requirements
- Wrote code that maintained the knowledge tree
- Used BeginTrans, CommitTrans, and Rollback to ensure that database updates are done in complete steps
- Experimented with Paintbrush and Form Art to jazz up your Access applications

In the next chapter you create a diary using Visual Basic and Access together as a team. You'll create your own encryption routines to hide your secrets from prying eyes.

TRY THIS! ANSWERS

9.1. To make the game play sounds, first create the Play subroutine in a new module named Sound.

1. Create a new module.
2. Enter the declarations section and PlayWAV subroutine as shown in Listings 9.32 and 9.33.
3. Enter calls to the PlayWAV subroutine in the On Open and On Click event subroutines for the forms and buttons in The Learning Computer program. You can use the WAV files found in the WINDOWS directory, or use your own, for example:

```
PlayWAV "C:\WINDOWS\TADA.WAV"
```

Listing 9.32. The Sound module declarations section.

```
' Sound module

' Includes a PlayWAV subroutine that demonstrates how to play a WAV file.

Option Compare Database
Option Explicit

Declare Function SndPlaySound Lib "MMSYSTEM.DLL" (ByVal strSoundName
➥ As String, ByVal intFlags As Integer) As Integer
```

Listing 9.33. The `PlayWAV` subroutine.

```
Sub PlayWAV (strFilename As String)

  Dim z As Integer

' These are the different flag values used in the second argument
' to the SndPlaySound function.

' Const SND_SYNC = &H0        ' Play sound before returning
  Const SND_ASYNC = &H1       ' Return immediately
  Const SND_NODEFAULT = &H2   ' Don't use default sound
' Const SND_LOOP = &H8        ' Repeat sound over and over
' Const SND_NOSTOP = &H10     ' Don't interrupt other sound

' The SndPlaySound function returns True if the sound is played,
' False if not.

  z = SndPlaySound(strFilename, SND_ASYNC + SND_NODEFAULT)

End Sub
```

CHAPTER 10

Visual Basic and Access: Secret Diary

Why would you ever need to start keeping a diary?

People like to keep some kind of remembrance of the events and personal achievements in their daily lives. However, folks today are more likely to record these events with snapshots and home videos, or by saving things like yearbooks, report cards, awards, and other collectibles than they are to actually write something down.

How many times have you found yourself in the following scenario? You dedicate yourself to organizing all of the junk buried in the closet. Soon you find a shoebox or two full of unsorted snapshots from over the years. You sit down and relive the past by digging through all those pictures, and before you know it a couple of hours have passed and the closet is in worse shape than before you started.

A photo preserves the past in a way that perhaps the most elegantly spoken words could not. However, there are some things that pictures and home videos can't capture with any accuracy. To be quite honest, the old saying "a picture is worth a thousand words" is a half-truth, if not an outright lie.

Imagine trying to convey the ideas right here on this page using pictures as the only form of communication. With pictures you can record what you and others looked like, where you have been, and what you saw. With words, you can record and preserve your thoughts.

Think of the eventful last year you just had. Wouldn't it be nice if you had taken a little time to jot a few things down here and there? Wouldn't it be interesting to see how your attitudes and feelings have changed over time?

In the age of computer communications, it is amazing how much time people spend writing notes to others through electronic mail at work or on the large national bulletin board services. People don't think anything of stomping out a few paragraphs to chat with a friend or even a stranger. But would you take the time to write even just one or two sentences a day in your own personal diary?

Why not?

Keeping a Diary Secure

Probably the main reason you don't take the time to keep a daily journal of some kind is because you are afraid that what you write will seem dumb.

What if somebody really evil got hold of it? Maybe they would embark on a devoted lifelong effort of campaigning the countryside to see how far and wide they could spread your personal embarrassment and humiliation.

Honestly, I don't think you need to worry about that kind of stuff. If anyone did read your secret diary, I'm sure they would be impressed by the thoughtful person you are and admire you simply because you had the foresight to keep a diary. Many famous people over the years kept diaries, and those diaries have become vital links to the understanding of history, even if they contain just basic notes about daily life.

If you still feel nervous about somebody intruding into the imaginative inner world of your own personal thoughts and observations, it might be reassuring to know you can keep these thoughts in a safe place.

In this chapter, you create your own password-protected Secret Diary program using Visual Basic. You also get a little help from Microsoft Access.

I can't promise you that the program will be secure enough that you could entrust it with your country's nuclear technology and diplomacy secrets. But it will be safer than those little locks on diaries you buy at the store that can be picked with a fingernail, butter knife, or paper clip.

Using Access and Visual Basic Together

To produce the Secret Diary program, you use Access and Visual Basic as a team.

When Access was introduced, many people were totally confused when deciding in which of the two—Access or Visual Basic—to develop an application.

Both products have comprehensive user-interface form objects. As of Visual Basic 3.0, both have extensive database support through Microsoft's Jet technology and data access objects. Both products are great environments for basic coding and building applications in Windows.

Here's a general definition for each product. Access is a database application development environment in the tradition of products like R:Base, dBASE, and FoxPro. Visual Basic is a general programming environment in the tradition of what BASIC, Pascal, and C programming interpreters and compilers have been.

Basically, Access is for developing database applications, and Visual Basic is for general programming projects. However, you don't have to look too far to see that the products overlap considerably as far as what you can do with them.

Which product you want to use depends on what you plan to build. You should take into account the features of both products and see which one helps get the job done fastest or produces the most desirable final product. This can be determined only on a case-by-case basis, but what I find surprising is that many times the best answer is to use them both.

In your Secret Diary program, you do just that. You use Access to set up the initial database, then use Visual Basic to build the core program, which performs just like any other quick little Windows utility. Then you can switch back to Access to use its incredible reporting capabilities to produce a quick and easy printout of the contents of your diary.

Introducing the Secret Diary

Figure 10.1 shows the Secret Diary icon in the Windows Program Manager. I have a program group titled "Usual Stuff" into which I like to copy icons for regularly used programs. (Less regularly used programs get tossed in the "Other Stuff" program group.)

FIGURE 10.1.
The Secret Diary is readily available for taking quick notes.

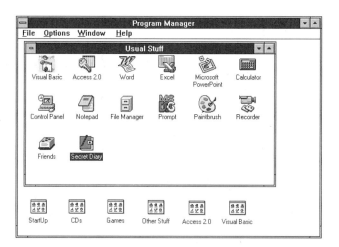

Double-click the Secret Diary icon, and the login dialog box is displayed, as shown in Figure 10.2.

FIGURE 10.2.
The Secret Diary login dialog box.

In the login dialog box, you typically enter your name and password to open the diary. However, there is a New **D**iary button to open a new diary if this is the first time you have used the program. Click this button, and the New Diary dialog box is displayed, as shown in Figure 10.3.

FIGURE 10.3.

The New Diary dialog box is used to open a new diary.

In the New Diary dialog box, you enter your name. Then you enter a password twice— once at the Password prompt and a second time at the Verify prompt. The password is hidden from view as you type it, so the Verify prompt serves as a way to ensure that the password was entered as expected.

Click OK, and the program reminds you to keep your password secure, as shown in Figure 10.4. If you forget the password, you won't be able to open your own diary. If you are careless and someone discovers your password, they will be able to open your diary.

FIGURE 10.4.

A reminder to safeguard your password.

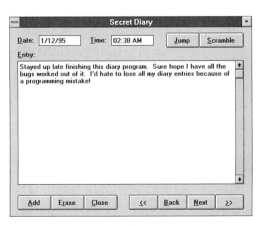

Back at the login dialog box, your name and password are automatically transferred from the New Diary dialog box so all you have to do is click OK.

If the correct password is entered, the Secret Diary window is displayed, as shown in Figure 10.5. In the window are three fields for the date, time, and diary entry. The date and time are automatically set with the current date and time. All you have to do is type the entry.

FIGURE 10.5.

Creating an entry in the Secret Diary.

To write the entry to the diary, click the **C**lose button. Your session with the program is over—it's that simple. Next time you run the program, you just enter your name and password at the login dialog box, then type in your entry and click **C**lose.

I wanted to make sure that adding an entry would be as simple as possible. If the program is convenient to use, it's more likely that diary entries will be created.

The Secret Diary Buttons

The Secret Diary window has some additional capabilities activated by the buttons on the form:

Jump	Find another entry by date
Scramble	Encrypt the display
Add	Save the current entry and start a new one
Erase	Discard the current entry
Close	Save the current entry and quit the program
<<	Move back a week
Back	Move back one entry
Next	Move forward one entry
>>	Move forward a week

The **J**ump button displays the tiny dialog box shown in Figure 10.6. You enter a date and click OK.

FIGURE 10.6.

Using the Jump To dialog box to find a diary entry by date.

If the diary finds an entry for the entered date, the entry is displayed, as shown in Figure 10.7. Having just finished the program, I entered a few fictional entries just for testing.

If there isn't an entry for the date you want to jump to, the first diary entry before that date is jumped to. If there are no entries before that date, the first entry in the diary is jumped to. I know these are mucky details, but in writing the program you have to figure out what to do for all possible situations.

The **S**cramble button is the one that's really fun. You use the **S**cramble button to quickly hide the currently displayed entry. You might use this if somebody comes up to look over your shoulder or if you want to leave the computer for a moment and don't want anyone to read your entry.

FIGURE 10.7.

Jumping to a different diary entry.

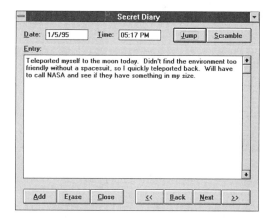

Figure 10.8 shows an entry after the **S**cramble button has been pressed.

FIGURE 10.8.

The Scramble button encrypts the currently displayed entry.

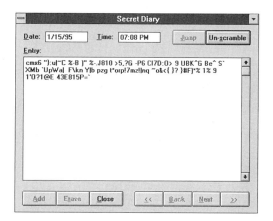

Note that clicking the **S**cramble button also disables all the other buttons except the **C**lose button. This in effect locks the program so that any unauthorized poking around can't occur.

In addition, the **S**cramble button changes to an Un-**s**cramble button. Click the Un-**s**cramble button, and the Unscramble dialog box is displayed, as shown in Figure 10.9.

FIGURE 10.9.

To unscramble an entry, you must know the login password.

Enter your password correctly, press OK, and the entry is unscrambled, as shown in Figure 10.10.

FIGURE 10.10.

A diary entry unscrambled.

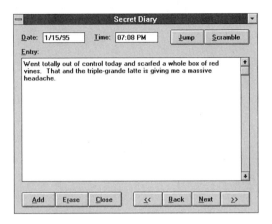

The **A**dd button is used to start a new entry. This button is needed only if you were browsing through older entries before adding the new entry. You might also use it to save the current entry and begin entering a new one.

The **E**rase button deletes the currently displayed diary entry.

The **B**ack and **N**ext buttons move back and forth through diary entries an entry at a time. The << and >> buttons jump a week back or a week forward. You can type in changes to any displayed entry, and it is saved as you move to another entry or close the diary.

I tossed around the idea that maybe a diary entry shouldn't be editable or deletable after it was entered. If it is too easy to alter past diary entries, the user would be tempted to revise or censor their historical entries from time to time. The result would probably be less interesting than the original entries.

I settled for leaving that decision up to the user. It would be frustrating not to be able to go back and correct spelling and grammatical errors. Also, if someone wants to go back and revise their diary entries, that's their business, not mine.

Creating the Diary Tables

Building the Secret Diary starts in Access. You need to create a DIARY.MDB database. In this database, you create a Login table to store user names and passwords. You also create an Entry table to store the encrypted diary entries.

First, create the Login table.

1. Create a new Access database named DIARY.MDB.

    The database should be created in a new, empty directory, where you should also store the Visual Basic project files. On my PC, I used my temporary work directory, D:\STUFF, as I have done while working on other projects in this book.

2. Create a new table without the help of the Table Wizard. In table design mode, enter the following fields, as shown in Figure 10.11:

Login table fields

Field Name:	UserID
Data Type:	Counter
Description:	Identify entries with this user

Field Name:	Username
Data Type:	Text
Description:	User login name
Field Size:	20
Required:	Yes
Allow Zero Length:	No
Indexed:	Yes (No Duplicates)

Field Name:	Password
Data Type:	Text
Description:	User password
Field Size:	20
Required:	Yes
Allow Zero Length:	No
Indexed:	No

3. Make the UserID field the primary key field by selecting it and clicking the Set Primary Key button on the toolbar.

4. Save the table as Login.

FIGURE 10.11.

Creating the Login table.

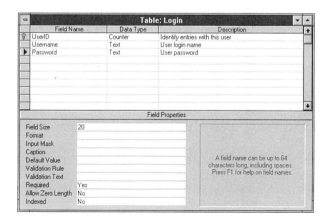

Next, create the entry table.

1. Create the Entry table with the following fields:

   Entry table fields

Field Name:	EntryID
Data Type:	Counter
Description:	Unique ID for this entry

Field Name:	UserID
Data Type:	Number
Description:	Identify user who created the entry
Field Size:	Long Integer
Default Value:	(blank)
Required:	Yes
Indexed:	No

Field Name:	Date
Data Type:	Date/Time
Description:	Date and time the entry was made
Field Size:	20
Required:	Yes
Indexed:	No

Field Name:	Entry
Data Type:	Memo
Description:	Text for this entry
Required:	No
Allow Zero Length:	Yes

FIGURE 10.12.

Creating the Entry table.

![Screenshot of the Table: Entry design view showing fields EntryID (Counter, "Unique ID for this entry"), UserID (Number, "Identify user who created the entry"), Date (Date/Time, "Date and time the entry was made"), and Entry (Memo, "Text for this entry"). Field Properties panel shows Field Size: Long Integer, Decimal Places: Auto, Required: Yes, Indexed: No, with the note "A field name can be up to 64 characters long, including spaces. Press F1 for help on field names."]

2. Make the EntryID field the primary key, as shown in Figure 10.12.

   This program always selects records from the Entry table for a user identified by the UserID field, sorted by the Date field. It makes sense, then, to create a multiple-field index on the table using the UserID and Date fields.

3. Click the Indexes button on the toolbar to open the Indexes window.

4. Enter an index name, Key1, in the line below the PrimaryKey index name.

5. In the Field Name column, select the UserID field, and set the Sort Order to Ascending.

6. In the next line, select the Date field in the Field Name column and also set it to Ascending sort order.

   The Unique property for the Key1 index should be set to No, as shown in Figure 10.13. That's because it is possible (although unlikely) that someone might want to log two diary entries under the same date and time.

FIGURE 10.13.

Creating the Key1 index in the Entry table.

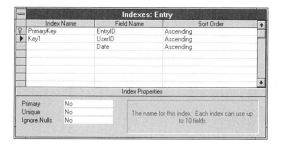

7. Close the table, saving it as Entry.

It's not required, but you can go ahead and establish relationships for the tables in the database.

1. Select the **Edit**|**R**elationships command.

2. In the Add Table dialog box, add the Login table, then the Entry table. Close the dialog box.

   Next, you establish a relationship between the two tables based on the UserID field.

3. In the Relationships window, click the UserID field in the Login table. Holding the mouse button down, drag the mouse pointer over to the UserID field in the Entry table and release the mouse button.

   Access draws a line from the UserID field in the Login table to the UserID field in the Entry table.

4. Double-click the line to bring up the Relationships dialog box.

5. In the Relationships dialog box, check the **E**nforce Referential Integrity check box, as shown in Figure 10.14. Set the relationship to One To **M**any (this is the default). Set the Cascade **D**elete Related Records option to on.

6. Close the Relationships window.

FIGURE 10.14.

Establishing a relationship between the Login and Entry tables.

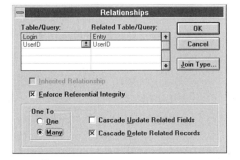

The **E**nforce Referential Integrity option ensures that no records are entered in the Entry table with an invalid UserID field value. Each entry must belong to a user.

This is a One To **M**any relationship because for a single user there are many diary entries.

The Cascade **D**elete Related Records option enables you to quickly remove all diary entries for a person by deleting his Login table record. This is probably something you won't do often except when testing the Secret Diary program.

The layout of the Relationships window is shown in Figure 10.15.

FIGURE 10.15.

The Relationships window.

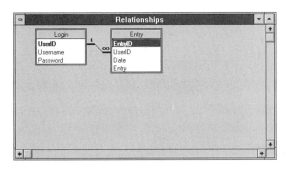

You are done with Access for now. You will be adding other objects to the database at the end of the chapter. You can close the database and Access now, or you can leave them open.

One reason you might want to leave them open is so you can view the contents of the Login and Entry tables after the Secret Diary program attempts to write to them. If you do this, be sure you don't have any of the tables open in design view while running the program, because the Secret Diary program won't be able to write records to a table that is opened this way.

> **NOTE**
>
> If you don't have a lot of RAM in your computer, you might want to close Access while working on the Visual Basic part of the program. Windows handles large demands on memory by temporarily saving memory out to its swapfile on the hard drive. This enables you to run more programs at once, but it also slows down the computer considerably because of the extra hard drive activity. I found that running Access and Visual Basic together with 8M was acceptable, but I was happier when I upgraded my PC to 16M of RAM.

Creating the Secret Diary Program

Let's start up Visual Basic.

Double-click the Visual Basic icon to start VB.

When Visual Basic first comes up on the screen, it is kind of a mess. Rather than containing the whole development environment inside a single window like Access does, VB has windows all over the place. Initially, a Menu Bar, a Toolbox, a Project Window, and the application's first form window are displayed, as shown in Figure 10.16.

FIGURE 10.16.

Starting a Visual Basic project.

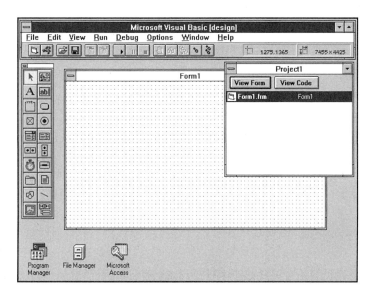

In Access, you are always building an application based on the Windows Multiple Document Interface (MDI), which means you have a parent window with child windows inside it. In Visual Basic, this is an optional capability that you will gladly discard for this kind of quick little program.

A Visual Basic project consists of one or more files listed in the Project Window. Currently the Project Window lists only one file, Form1.frm, which actually doesn't exist on disk yet because the new project hasn't been saved.

The final project contains the following files:

CHNGPWRD.FRM	Form to change your password
DIARY.FRM	Form to create and review diary entries
JUMP.FRM	Form to select a diary entry by date
LOGIN.FRM	Form to enter name and password
NEWDIARY.FRM	Form to establish name and password
PASSWORD.FRM	Form to enter password to descramble an entry
LIBRARY.BAS	Module with global variables and miscellaneous procedures

Before you write any code, you need to create each of the forms. The first form you create is the Login form, which is much like the one you created in Chapter 3, "How Basic Interacts with the Outside World," in Access.

Save the project by selecting the File|Save Project command.

Visual Basic displays the Save File As dialog box to save the project's initial form. Save it as LOGIN.FRM in the same directory where you created the DIARY.MDB database file.

Next, VB displays the Save Project As dialog box to save the project file. Enter DIARY.MAK as the name of the project file, making sure it also is saved in the same directory as before. MAK is the file extension VB uses by default for project files.

Set the properties for the form. Visual Basic has a Properties window that is similar to the one in Access.

1. Click the Form window and press F4 to display the Properties window. (You can also bring up the Properties window by selecting the Window|Properties command or by clicking the Properties button on the toolbar.)

2. Change the following properties from their default values, as shown in Figure 10.17:

Login form

BackColor:	&H00C0C0C0& (Light Gray)
BorderStyle:	3 - Fixed Double
Caption:	Secret Diary
Height:	2580
MaxButton:	False
MinButton:	False
Name:	Login
Width:	5535

FIGURE 10.17.

Setting properties for the Login form.

Setting Project and Environment Options

If you select the **O**ptions|**P**roject command, you will find that Visual Basic has by default set the project's Start Up Form option to the name of this first form, Login, as shown in Figure 10.18. This means that when the program starts, the first thing it does is display the Login form. The code that is first activated is the Login form's `Form_Load` subroutine.

FIGURE 10.18.

The Start Up Form setting determines what happens first when your program runs.

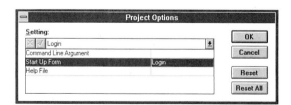

You can change this setting if your program needs to start with a different form than was first created. You can also change it so that the program doesn't load a form by default and instead runs a subroutine that you create called `Main`. You're OK here and can leave it as is.

You have some environment settings to change before you go any further.

Select the **O**ptions|**E**nvironment command.

Visual Basic displays the Environment Options dialog box. Most VB programmers have their own preferences as to what to set here. For example, you can set a color for displaying comments in your code.

The settings I used in creating the Secret Diary program are the following:

Environment Options

Tab Stop Width:	2
Require Variable Declaration:	Yes
Syntax Checking:	No
Default Save As Format:	Binary
Save Project Before Run:	No
Grid Width:	30
Grid Height:	30
Show Grid:	No
Align To Grid:	Yes

I left the color settings as they were.

The Tab Stop Width setting controls how many spaces your code is indented with each Tab key press. I use 2 primarily because other programmers I work with like their code to look this way. (Personally, I like 4 better.)

The Require Variable Declaration setting makes VB automatically insert an Option Explicit directive at the beginning of each module. That's a good idea because it helps you catch typing errors that would otherwise go unnoticed.

I turn off Syntax Checking because I often knowingly leave a line of code unfinished so that I can come back and finish it later. It's a bother to have VB tell me that the line doesn't compile correctly.

The Default Save As Format can be set to Text or Binary. When your files are saved as binary, the compiles go faster. The advantage with saving them as text is that you can look at them with any text editor.

The Save Project Before Run option can be used as a way to periodically have automatic saves in case a system error or power outage makes you lose your work. I don't like using this option because many times I make a change that I later want to abandon after seeing it run for the first time. Without this option on, I can exit VB and answer No to the forms or modules that aren't supposed to be saved.

The Grid settings are a special problem in VB. The grid concept is a neat one; it creates evenly spaced lines to which controls line up when they are dropped on the form. The dots on the form indicate where the grid lines are.

Unfortunately, the text in a Label control doesn't line up correctly with the text in a Textbox control if you use the grid with a tall grid height. With a Grid Height of 30, you can line up the text correctly, as shown in Figure 10.19.

FIGURE 10.19.

Use a fine Grid Height resolution to properly line up text in labels with text in text boxes.

I decided to set both the Height and Width of the grid to 30, then turn off the grid display by setting the Show Grid option to No.

You can set the environment options to whatever you find most comfortable. The settings remain set even when you work on other projects, so once you find what you like, you never have to set them again.

Creating the Login Form

Let's continue with the Login form.

The first control on the form is a picture box control that displays the program's icon. (This was just a way to get a little extra mileage out of a neat icon.)

The icon was drawn using an amazing Visual Basic sample program called Icon Works (shown in Figure 10.20). All of the source for the Icon Works program is included with Visual Basic in the SAMPLES\ICONWRKS directory if you are interested in digging through some code. The file for the icon is DIARY.ICO, and it is included on the book's companion CD-ROM.

1. Click the Picture box button on the Toolbox and drop a picture box control on the Login form.

    (On the back of your Visual Basic Programmer's Guide manual, you will find a picture that identifies the different buttons on the Toolbox.)

FIGURE 10.20.

*Editing the
DIARY.ICO file in
Icon Works.*

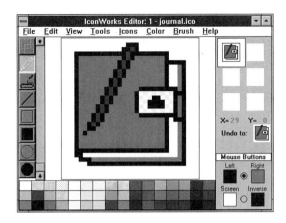

2. Set the following properties:

picDiary picture box

BackColor:	&H00C0C0C0& (Light Gray)
BorderStyle:	None
Height:	525
Left:	210
Name:	picDiary
Picture:	DIARY.ICO
TabIndex:	0
TabStop:	False
Top:	150
Width:	525

Next, you add two labels to greet the user and give a little on-screen help, as shown in Figure 10.21. Each label you create on this and following forms should have their BackColor property set to &H00C0C0C0& (Light Gray).

1. Click the Label button on the Toolbox and create a label with the following properties set:

lblHint1 label

Caption:	Hi!
ForeColor:	&H00800000& (Dark Blue)
Height:	225
Left:	870
Name:	lblHint1
TabIndex:	1
Top:	180
Width:	435

2. Create a second label with these properties:

lblHint2 label

Caption:	Enter your name and password, or press the New Diary button to create a new diary.
ForeColor:	&H00800000& (Dark Blue)
Height:	855
Left:	870
Name:	lblHint2
TabIndex:	2
Top:	390
Width:	2415

FIGURE 10.21.

Adding a picture box and on-screen help text to the Login form.

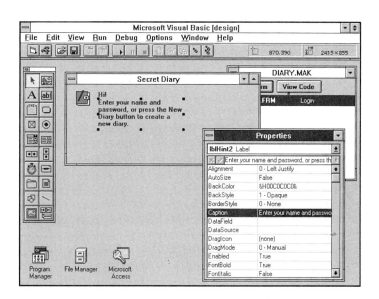

Now that you have done the pretty stuff, it's time to get the working controls on the form. First, you have two text boxes for entering the user's name and password, as shown in Figure 10.22.

Create two labels and two text boxes with the following properties:

lblName label

Caption:	&Name:
Height:	225
Left:	210
Name:	lblName

continues

lblName label

TabIndex:	3
Top:	1290
Width:	1065

txtName text box

Height:	285
Left:	1350
MaxLength:	20
Name:	txtName
TabIndex:	4
Top:	1260
Width:	1905

lblPassword label

Caption:	&Password:
Height:•	225
Left:	210
Name:	lblPassword
TabIndex:	5
Top:	1740
Width:	1065

txtPassword text box

Height:	285
Left:	1350
MaxLength:	20
Name:	txtPassword
PasswordChar:	*
TabIndex:	6
Top:	1710
Width:	1905

FIGURE 10.22.

*Adding the Name and
Password text boxes.*

The last set of controls to add to the form is a column of command buttons.

1. Add four command buttons to the form with the following properties set:

cmdOK command button

Caption:	OK
Default:	True
Height:	420
Left:	3450
Name:	cmdOK
TabIndex:	7
Top:	120
Width:	1845

cmdCancel command button

Cancel:	True
Caption:	Cancel
Height:	420
Left:	3450
Name:	cmdCancel
TabIndex:	8
Top:	600
Width:	1845

cmdNewDiary command button

Caption:	New &Diary
Height:	420
Left:	3450
Name:	cmdNewDiary
TabIndex:	9
Top:	1110
Width:	1845

cmdChangePassword command button

Caption:	&Change Password
Height:	420
Left:	3450
Name:	cmdChangePassword
TabIndex:	10
Top:	1620
Width:	1845

The completed form is shown in Figure 10.23.

2. Close the form.

> **NOTE**
>
> If you are getting tired of screen clutter, you can minimize the Project window and the Properties window while they are not being used, as shown in Figure 10.23. As icons, the windows are easier to get to than if they were fully closed.

FIGURE 10.23.

Adding command buttons to the Login form.

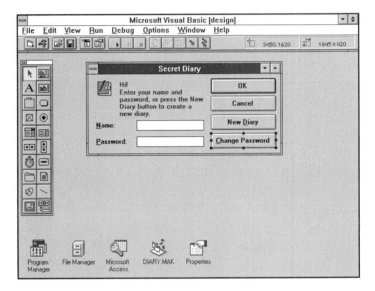

Creating the New Diary Form

The New Diary form is used initially to enter your Name and Password into the program. This creates a record in the Login table that is used to validate your password each time you open the diary.

The way the program and database are designed, it's possible to have more than one person using the same database to store their diary entries. (Each person can see only their own entries.) If you would prefer to keep separate diary files, you could instead make a copy of the final DIARY.EXE and DIARY.MDB files into separate directories for each person that has his own diary.

1. Select the File|New Form command.

2. Set the following properties on the form:

New Diary form

BackColor:	&H00C0C0C0& (Light Gray)
BorderStyle:	3 - Fixed Double
Caption:	New Diary
Height:	2325
MaxButton:	False
MinButton:	False
Name:	NewDiary
Width:	5310

3. Create a label on the form for some on-screen instructions. Set the following properties:

lblHint label

Caption:	To create a new diary, enter your name and password.
ForeColor:	&H00800000& (Dark Blue)
Height:	495
Left:	120
Name:	lblHint
TabIndex:	0
Top:	150
Width:	3555

4. Create three sets of labels and text boxes for entering the user's name, password, and verification of the password.

lblName label

Caption:	&Name:
Height:	225
Left:	150
Name:	lblName
TabIndex:	1
Top:	720
Width:	1065

txtName text box

Height:	285
Left:	1740
MaxLength:	20
Name:	txtName

continues

txtName text box

TabIndex:	2
Top:	690
Width:	1905

lblPassword label

Caption:	&Password:
Height:	225
Left:	150
Name:	lblPassword
TabIndex:	3
Top:	1110
Width:	1065

txtPassword text box

Height:	285
Left:	1740
MaxLength:	20
Name:	txtPassword
PasswordChar:	*
TabIndex:	4
Top:	1080
Width:	1905

lblVerify label

Caption:	&Verify:
Height:	225
Left:	150
Name:	lblVerify
TabIndex:	5
Top:	1500
Width:	1065

txtVerify text box

Height:	285
Left:	1740
MaxLength:	20
Name:	txtVerify
PasswordChar:	*

TabIndex:	6
Top:	1470
Width:	1905

5. Complete the form with OK and Cancel buttons, as follows:

cmdOK command button

Caption:	OK
Default:	True
Height:	405
Left:	3840
Name:	cmdOK
TabIndex:	7
Top:	150
Width:	1215

cmdCancel command button

Cancel:	True
Caption:	Cancel
Height:	405
Left:	3840
Name:	cmdCancel
TabIndex:	8
Top:	630
Width:	1215

The completed form is shown in Figure 10.24.

6. Select the **File|Save** File command to save the form, entering NEWDIARY.FRM as the filename.

FIGURE 10.24.

Creating the New Diary form.

Creating the Change Password Form

The Change Password form is another simple dialog box. This one pops up when the user clicks the **C**hange Password button in the Login dialog box.

The user must enter his name and existing password correctly or he won't be allowed to change the user password. The new password is entered twice to make sure the user didn't type it incorrectly and end up locking himself out of his own diary.

1. Create a new form with the following properties:

   ChangePassword form

BackColor:	&H00C0C0C0& (Light Gray)
BorderStyle:	3 - Fixed Double
Caption:	Change Password
Height:	2250
MaxButton:	False
MinButton:	False
Name:	ChangePassword
Width:	5325

2. Add the labels and text boxes for entering the user's name and existing password.

   lblName label

Caption:	&Name:
Height:	225
Left:	180
Name:	lblName
TabIndex:	0
Top:	180
Width:	1065

   txtName text box

Height:	285
Left:	1770
MaxLength:	20
Name:	txtName
TabIndex:	1
Top:	150
Width:	1905

   lblOldPassword label

Caption:	&Old Password:
Height:	225
Left:	180
Name:	lblOldPassword

TabIndex:	2
Top:	570
Width:	1485

txtOldPassword text box

Height:	285
Left:	1770
MaxLength:	20
Name:	txtOldPassword
PasswordChar:	*
TabIndex:	3
Top:	540
Width:	1905

3. Add the labels and text boxes for entering the new password and a verification of the new password.

lblNewPassword label

Caption:	&New Password:
Height:	225
Left:	180
Name:	lblNewPassword
TabIndex:	4
Top:	1050
Width:	1395

txtNewPassword text box

Height:	285
Left:	1770
MaxLength:	20
Name:	txtNewPassword
PasswordChar:	*
TabIndex:	5
Top:	1020
Width:	1905

lblVerify label

Caption:	&Verify:
Height:	225
Left:	180

continues

lblVerify label

Name:	lblVerify
TabIndex:	6
Top:	1440
Width:	1065

txtVerify text box

Height:	285
Left:	1770
MaxLength:	20
Name:	txtVerify
PasswordChar:	*
TabIndex:	7
Top:	1410
Width:	1905

4. Add the OK and Cancel buttons.

cmdOK command button

Caption:	OK
Default:	True
Height:	405
Left:	3870
Name:	cmdOK
TabIndex:	8
Top:	150
Width:	1215

cmdCancel command button

Cancel:	True
Caption:	Cancel
Height:	405
Left:	3870
Name:	cmdCancel
TabIndex:	9
Top:	630
Width:	1215

The Change Password form is shown in Figure 10.25.

5. Save the form with the filename CHNGPWRD.FRM.

FIGURE 10.25.
*Creating the Change
Password form.*

Creating the Secret Diary Form

You have three more forms to create. The Secret Diary form is the main form in the program, used to enter diary entries and view previous entries. You also have two tiny pop-ups to create. Let's knock out the big one first and save the easy ones for last.

1. Create a new form with the properties shown here. Set the form's Icon property to the DIARY.ICO file so when the form is minimized it displays the diary icon.

Secret Diary form

BackColor:	&H00C0C0C0& (Light Gray)
BorderStyle:	1 - Fixed Single
Caption:	Secret Diary
Height:	5535
Icon:	DIARY.ICO
MaxButton:	False
MinButton:	True
Name:	Diary
Width:	6930

2. Add two sets of labels and text boxes for entering the date and time of the entry, as shown in Figure 10.26. (Actually, the program automatically fills these in, but the user has the option to change them.)

lblDate label

Caption:	&Date:
Height:	225
Left:	210
Name:	lblDate
Top:	240
Width:	615

txtDate text box

Height:	285
Left:	810
Name:	txtDate
Top:	210
Width:	1185

lblTime label

Caption:	&Time:
Height:	225
Left:	2250
Name:	lblTime
Top:	240
Width:	615

txtTime text box

Height:	285
Left:	2850
Name:	txtTime
Top:	210
Width:	1185

I didn't list the TabIndex property settings. You will be modifying the tab order after all of the controls are on the form.

FIGURE 10.26.

Adding Date and Time fields to the Secret Diary form.

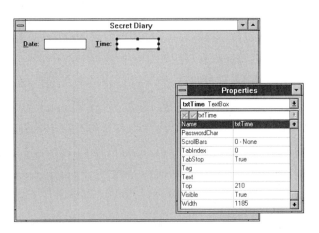

3. Add a **J**ump button for finding other entries, and a **S**cramble button for encrypting the currently displayed entry, as shown in Figure 10.27. Set the properties as listed here:

cmdJump command button

Caption:	&Jump
Height:	405
Left:	4380
Name:	cmdJump
Top:	150
Width:	945

cmdScramble command button

Caption:	&Scramble
Height:	405
Left:	5310
Name:	cmdScramble
Top:	150
Width:	1275

FIGURE 10.27.

Adding the Jump and Scramble buttons.

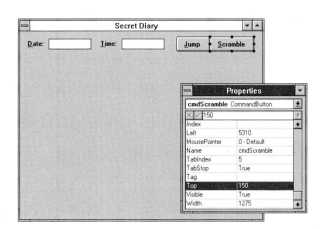

Next, you add a large, multiline text box to enter the text for a diary entry, as shown in Figure 10.28.

4. Add a label and text box with the properties shown here:

lblEntry label

Caption:	&Entry:
Height:	225
Left:	210
Name:	lblEntry
Top:	630
Width:	1065

FIGURE 10.28.

*Adding the multiple-
line Entry text box.*

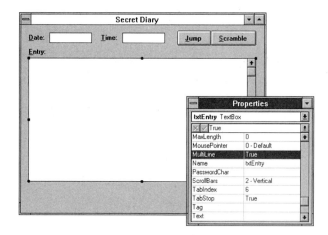

txtEntry text box

Height:	3375
Left:	210
MultiLine:	True
Name:	txtEntry
ScrollBars:	2 - Vertical
Top:	900
Width:	6375

5. Add the **A**dd, **E**rase, and **C**lose buttons with the following properties, as shown in Figure 10.29:

cmdAdd command button

Caption:	&Add
Height:	405
Left:	210
Name:	cmdAdd
Top:	4560
Width:	945

cmdErase command button

Caption:	E&rase
Height:	405
Left:	1140
Name:	cmdErase
Top:	4560
Width:	945

cmdClose command button

Caption:	&Close
Height:	405
Left:	2070
Name:	cmdClose
Top:	4560
Width:	945

FIGURE 10.29.

Adding the Add, Erase, and Close buttons.

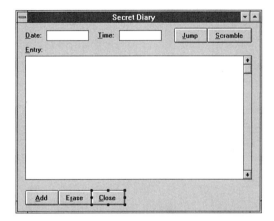

The next four command buttons are set up as a control array. Visual Basic allows you to build a set of controls like this under the same name. The controls can be distinguished from each other by the Index property. Typically, folks start at the 0 index and work up.

Why use a control array? If you have similar code that executes behind each control in the array, sometimes you can save a few lines of code with a control array. A single subroutine is written to respond to the same event for all of the controls.

For example, each of the four buttons on your form is involved with moving to another diary entry. Rather than having four On Click event subroutines, there is one. Visual Basic automatically adds an Index argument to the subroutine so that the code can distinguish which of the buttons in the array was pressed.

You will see this in more detail when you write the code behind this form.

Add the **<<**, **B**ack, **N**ext, and **>>** buttons, as shown in Figure 10.30:

cmdMove(0) command button

Caption:	&<<
Height:	405
Index:	0
Left:	3330
Name:	cmdMove
Top:	4560
Width:	825

cmdMove(1) command button

Caption:	&Back
Height:	405
Index:	1
Left:	4140
Name:	cmdMove
Top:	4560
Width:	825

cmdMove(2) command button

Caption:	&Next
Height:	405
Index:	2
Left:	4950
Name:	cmdMove
Top:	4560
Width:	825

cmdMove(3) command button

Caption:	&>>
Height:	405
Index:	3
Left:	5760
Name:	cmdMove
Top:	4560
Width:	825

FIGURE 10.30.

Adding the cmdMove control array buttons.

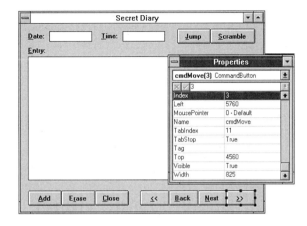

Next, you need to set the tab order of the controls on the Secret Diary form.

When the form is displayed it automatically fills in the Date and Time fields with the current date and time. The txtEntry text box should receive focus so the form is ready for the user to begin typing in an entry.

Although label controls never actually receive focus, it is important to place them properly in the tab order. When they would receive focus, they pass it along to the control immediately following them. This is important because you have used accelerator keys (the Alt key plus a letter combination) to enable direct jumps to each field.

Set the TabIndex property for each control on the form according to the following list:

TabIndex	Control
0	lblEntry Label
1	txtEntry Textbox
2	cmdAdd Command Button
3	cmdErase Command Button
4	cmdClose Command Button
5	cmdMove(0) Command Button
6	cmdMove(1) Command Button
7	cmdMove(2) Command Button
8	cmdMove(3) Command Button
9	lblDate Label
10	txtDate Textbox
11	lblTime Label
12	txtTime Textbox
13	cmdJump Command Button
14	cmdScramble Command Button

One way to set this up is to start with the lblEntry label control, set its TabIndex property to 0, then continue down the list, setting the txtEntry text box's TabIndex to 1, and so on.

A slightly easier way to do this is to start at the end of the list, at the cmdScramble command button, and work your way up, setting each TabIndex property to 0. For example, when you set the TabIndex in cmdJump to 0, the TabIndex in cmdScramble is automatically adjusted from 0 to 1.

Close the form and save it as DIARY.FRM.

The Jump and Password Forms

You have these two quick little pop-ups, then you can finally get to the code.

When the user clicks the **J**ump button, a small dialog box is displayed to enter the date of the entry to which you wish to jump.

1. Create a new form with the following properties:

   Jump form

BackColor:	&H00C0C0C0& (Light Gray)
BorderStyle:	3 - Fixed Double
Caption:	Jump To
Height:	1620
MaxButton:	False
MinButton:	False
Name:	Jump
Width:	3450

2. Add the controls listed here to the Jump To dialog box:

   lblHint label

Caption:	Enter the date of the entry to jump to.
ForeColor:	&H00800000& (Dark Blue)
Height:	495
Left:	150
Name:	lblHint
TabIndex:	0
Top:	150
Width:	2025

lblDate label

Caption:	&Date
Height:	225
Left:	150
Name:	lblDate
TabIndex:	1
Top:	810
Width:	615

txtDate text box

Height:	285
Left:	840
Name:	txtDate
TabIndex:	2
Top:	780
Width:	1185

cmdOK command button

Caption:	OK
Default:	True
Height:	405
Left:	2280
Name:	cmdOK
TabIndex:	3
Top:	90
Width:	975

cmdCancel command button

Cancel:	True
Caption:	Cancel
Height:	405
Left:	2280
Name:	cmdCancel
TabIndex:	4
Top:	570
Width:	975

After the user has clicked the **S**cramble button, it turns into an Un-**s**cramble button. The button then displays the next dialog box so the user can enter his password, verifying that it is OK for him to see the entry.

3. Create a second new form with the properties listed here:

Password form

BackColor:	&H00C0C0C0& (Light Gray)
BorderStyle:	3 - Fixed Double
Caption:	Unscramble
Height:	1605
MaxButton:	False
MinButton:	False
Name:	Password
Width:	3615

4. Add the following controls to the Password form, as shown in Figure 10.31:

lblPassword label

Caption:	&Password
Height:	225
Left:	210
Name:	lblPassword
TabIndex:	0
Top:	180
Width:	1065

txtPassword text box

Height:	285
Left:	1350
MaxLength:	20
Name:	txtPassword
PasswordChar:	*
TabIndex:	1
Top:	150
Width:	1905

cmdOK command button

Caption:	OK
Default:	True
Height:	405
Left:	720
Name:	cmdOK
TabIndex:	2
Top:	660
Width:	975

cmdCancel command button

Cancel:	True
Caption:	Cancel
Height:	405
Left:	1800
Name:	cmdCancel
TabIndex:	3
Top:	690
Width:	975

Note that while in your project the Password form is named, "Password." From a user perspective it would be thought of as the Unscramble dialog box. The user (not knowing anything about how the program was created) would identify a window or dialog box by the caption that is displayed in the title bar.

FIGURE 10.31.

Creating the Jump and Password forms.

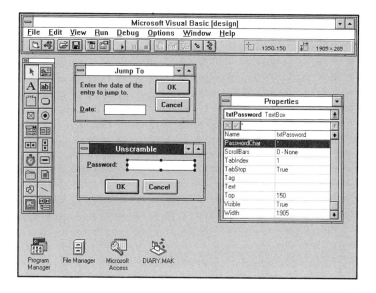

5. Close the forms. Save the Jump form as JUMP.FRM and the Password form as PASSWORD.FRM.

That puts the user-interface design work behind you. It's coding time.

Creating the Library Module

Most of the code for this application is in the form modules, but you have a little bit to take care of in a regular code module.

I called my module file LIBRARY.BAS because there are some reusable procedures in it. However, I also declare some globals in the same module that are specific to this program. You'll want to separate these into different files if you wish to use some of the procedures in other Visual Basic projects.

The LIBRARY.BAS module contains the following procedures:

(Declarations)	*Program global declarations*
CNStr	Convert a Null to an empty string
Center	Center a form
Required	Verify that a text box contains a value
CorrectEntry	Select text in a text box
Code	Encrypt a string
Decode	Decrypt an encrypted string
PasswordCreate	Create a new name and password
PasswordValidate	Verify a password entry
PasswordChange	Change a password
CountStrikes	Complain about invalid password attempts

1. Select the **File|New Module** command.
2. Fill in the declarations section as shown in Listing 10.1.

Listing 10.1. The declarations section for the LIBRARY.BAS file.

```
' Library module

Option Explicit

Global Const PROGRAM = "Secret Diary"
Global Const PASSWORD_KEY = "Babe Ruth"

Global cr As String

' Diary database
Global gdb As Database

' Table of diary entries
Global gdynEntry As Dynaset

' UserID for the person logged in.
Global glngUserID As Long

' Password for the person logged in.
Global gstrPassword As String
Global gstrUnscramblePassword As String
```

```
' How many times user entered a bad name/password
  Global gintStrike As Integer

' Date of page to jump to
  Global gvarJumpTo As Variant
```

The usage of the global variables declared in the declarations section will make more sense when you see them in action.

The PROGRAM constant is used again for the title bar in message boxes.

The PASSWORD_KEY constant is a string used in encrypting the passwords. You can make your program work differently than mine by changing this string. Don't select a string with a simple pattern such as ABC, because it tends to break down the encryption algorithm. A good mix of characters works best. "Supercalifragilisticexpialidocious" comes to mind as a good candidate if Mary Poppins doesn't mind.

```
Global Const PROGRAM = "Secret Diary"
Global Const PASSWORD_KEY = "Babe Ruth"
```

The cr variable is used to hold chr$(13) to do the job of the Enter key in a message box string:

```
Global cr As String
```

This Visual Basic program uses a database, tables, and dynasets just like Access can. You declare a database variable and a dynaset that points to the Entry table.

```
' Diary database
  Global gdb As Database

' Table of diary entries
  Global gdynEntry As Dynaset
```

The user's ID number is retrieved when they open their diary. This value is used to select their diary entries from the Entry table.

```
' UserID for the person logged in.
  Global glngUserID As Long
```

The gstrPassword variable holds the password with which the user logged in. The gstrUnscrambledPassword is set by the Password form when the user attempts to unscramble the displayed diary entry. These strings are compared to each other to determine whether the person is authorized to see the entry unscrambled.

```
' Password for the person logged in.
  Global gstrPassword As String
  Global gstrUnscramblePassword As String
```

The gintStrike variable is used to keep track of how many times in a row a bad password is entered. It's the old adage, "three strikes and you're out."

```
' How many times user entered a bad name/password
  Global gintStrike As Integer
```

The gvarJumpTo variable is used to hold the date value entered in the Jump form.

```
' Date of page to jump to
  Global gvarJumpTo As Variant
```

The *CNStr* Function

Here is my sinister friend once again. He makes sure that a string is a string is a string, and never a null.

Enter the CNStr function in the Library module as shown in Listing 10.2.

Listing 10.2. The CNStr function.

```
Function CNStr (var As Variant) As String

' Converts a null to "".

' No error handling by intent. Let the error occur in the
' calling procedure.

  If IsNull(var) Then
    CNStr = ""
  Else
    CNStr = Trim$(CStr(var))
  End If

End Function
```

The *Center* Subroutine

The Center subroutine is called in each form's Form_Load subroutine to center the form before it is displayed.

The subroutine can be called using the form module's Me variable, which is the current form object. It's done like this:

```
  Center Me
```

The form is set slightly higher than center.

Enter the Center subroutine as shown in Listing 10.3.

Listing 10.3. The `Center` **subroutine.**

```
Sub Center (frm As Form)

  On Error GoTo CenterError

  frm.Left = (Screen.Width - frm.Width) / 2
  frm.Top = ((Screen.Height - frm.Height) / 2) * .85

CenterDone:
  Exit Sub

CenterError:
  MsgBox Error$, 48, PROGRAM
  Resume CenterDone

End Sub
```

The *Required* Function

The `Required` function is called to verify that a required field has not been left blank.

If the function finds the passed control empty, it sets focus back to it and displays a message to the user that the field needs to be completed.

Enter the `Required` function as shown in Listing 10.4.

Listing 10.4. The `Required` **function.**

```
Function Required (ctl As Control, strName As String) As Integer

  On Error GoTo RequiredError

  Required = True

  If CNStr(ctl) = "" Then
    MsgBox strName & " is a required field.", 64, PROGRAM
    ctl.SetFocus
    GoTo RequiredDone
  End If

  Required = False

RequiredDone:
  Exit Function

RequiredError:
  MsgBox Error$, 48, PROGRAM
  Resume RequiredDone

End Function
```

The *CorrectEntry* Subroutine

The CorrectEntry subroutine is called to set focus back to a text box control. This subroutine is called when you are validating an entry (such as a date) and you find that the value is invalid.

The CorrectEntry subroutine selects and highlights all the text in the control so that the next keystroke can erase the entry and begin entering a corrected entry.

Enter the CorrectEntry subroutine as shown in Listing 10.5.

Listing 10.5. The CorrectEntry **subroutine.**

```
Sub CorrectEntry (ctl As Control)

  On Error GoTo CorrectEntryError

  ctl.SetFocus

  If Len(ctl.Text) > 0 Then
    ctl.SelStart = 1
    ctl.SelLength = Len(ctl.Text)
  End If

CorrectEntryDone:
  Exit Sub

CorrectEntryError:
  MsgBox Error$, 48, PROGRAM
  Resume CorrectEntryDone

End Sub
```

Roll-Your-Own Security

Now you get to the fun part—how the Secret Diary program proposes to keep your secrets secret.

In the Library module you have two functions, Code and Decode, which are responsible for encrypting and decrypting diary entries.

There is no rocket science involved here—it's a pretty simple encryption algorithm that isn't likely to hold up very well against any serious effort to crack the code. The idea is to make it just difficult enough that your average student of something other than cryptology wouldn't be able to figure it out.

If you need better security than this, you should handle it the straightforward way and use the security features provided in Access. I decided to produce this alternative because in some ways it's easier, but mostly because it's fun to have your own encryption functions.

Again, if security requirements in the project you are working on are more serious than what you are doing here, you should research and use the Access security model.

Let's look at the encryption technique used in the Secret Diary program.

The *Code* Function

The Code function takes a message string as its first argument and a key string as its second argument. The two strings are sort of blended together to produce the encrypted string. I'll look into this in detail after the listing.

Enter the Code function as shown in Listing 10.6.

Listing 10.6. The Code function.

```
Function Code (varMsg As Variant, strKey As String) As String

' Encrypt all characters from ASCII 32 to ASCII 126 in the msg string

   Dim msg As String

   Dim intLength As Integer
   Dim intKeyLength As Integer

   Dim intKeyOffset As Integer
   Dim intAsc As Integer
   Dim intKeyChar As Integer
   Dim intSkip As Integer

   Dim n As Integer

   On Error GoTo CodeError

   msg = CNStr(varMsg)

   intLength = Len(msg)
   intKeyLength = Len(strKey)
   intKeyOffset = intKeyLength

   intKeyChar = Asc(Right$(strKey, 1))

   For n = 1 To intLength
     intKeyOffset = intKeyOffset + 1
     If intKeyOffset > intKeyLength Then
       intKeyOffset = 1
     End If

     intAsc = Asc(Mid$(msg, n, 1))
```

continues

Listing 10.6. continued

```
' Only encrypt printable characters
  If intAsc > 32 And intAsc < 127 Then

    intAsc = intAsc - 32

  ' Add an offset determined by a character in the key
    intAsc = intAsc + intKeyChar

    While intAsc > 94
      intAsc = intAsc - 94
    Wend

  ' Add an offset determined by the loop counter
    intSkip = n Mod 94
    intAsc = intAsc + intSkip

    If intAsc > 94 Then
      intAsc = intAsc - 94
    End If

    Mid$(msg, n) = Chr$(intAsc + 32)
  End If

  intKeyChar = Asc(Mid$(strKey, intKeyOffset))

  Next n

  Code = msg

CodeDone:
  Exit Function

CodeError:
  MsgBox Error$, 48, PROGRAM
  Resume CodeDone

End Function
```

In finding a way to encrypt a message, you need to produce a series of steps that can produce an unreadable version of the message. Of course, you must be able to undo the steps in your decryption algorithm.

The method the Code function uses to encrypt a string is one that adds values to each character to produce a different character value. On decoding the string, the same values are subtracted to return to the original character.

The two values added to a character are as follows:

■ One of the character values from the key string

■ A counter value

The ending value must be in the range of displayable characters. As the added value becomes a number outside the range of displayable characters, it is reduced to a number within the range by allowing it to wrap around to the beginning.

Let's look at this in the code. First, the passed message is stored in the msg string variable.

```
msg = CNStr(varMsg)
```

Next, you grab the length of the message so you know how many characters to encrypt. Then you get the length of the key string and set a counter to start at the last character in the key string.

```
intLength = Len(msg)
intKeyLength = Len(strKey)
intKeyOffset = intKeyLength
```

The intKeyOffset variable cycles from 1 to the length of the key, so you can use the characters in the key one by one. The intKeyChar variable receives a numeric value that represents one of the characters in the key string.

```
intKeyChar = Asc(Right$(strKey, 1))
```

A loop starts that executes once for each character in the message.

```
For n = 1 To intLength
```

At the beginning of the loop the intKeyOffset variable is incremented to select the next character in the key string. When the offset value is greater than the number of characters in the key string, it is set back to the beginning of the string.

```
intKeyOffset = intKeyOffset + 1
If intKeyOffset > intKeyLength Then
  intKeyOffset = 1
End If
```

The intAsc variable first receives the numeric value of the original character in the message string.

```
intAsc = Asc(Mid$(msg, n, 1))
```

Not all of the characters are encrypted. This is kind of silly, but I left the nonprintable characters alone. When the **S**cramble button is pressed on the Diary form, the layout of the text in the Entry text box remains the same. It produces a neat visual effect.

```
' Only encrypt printable characters
If intAsc > 32 And intAsc < 127 Then
```

Because your character value is within the range of printable characters, you encrypt it. First, you subtract 32 from the value. This puts the character in a range from 1 to 94.

```
intAsc = intAsc - 32
```

Next, you add the key character value.

```
' Add an offset determined by a character in the key
  intAsc = intAsc + intKeyChar
```

It is possible now that the resulting value is outside the range of 1 to 94. In fact, it may be up to three times over because you haven't done any kind of verification on the character values in the key string, so they could be up to 255. (Character values range from 0 to 255.)

A loop is used to bring the value of the number down to the range of 1 to 94 chunk by chunk.

```
While intAsc > 94
   intAsc = intAsc - 94
Wend
```

Next, the loop counter is converted to a number in the range of 0 to 93 by using the modulus operator, and then adding the encrypt character value.

```
' Add an offset determined by the loop counter
  intSkip = n Mod 94
  intAsc = intAsc + intSkip
```

This creates the possibility again that the encrypted number might be out of the range of 1 to 94, so you check for that and wrap the value around if needed.

```
If intAsc > 94 Then
   intAsc = intAsc - 94
End If
```

Finally, you put the encrypted character back into the msg string variable, replacing the original character. 32 is added back to the value to place it in the range of printable character values.

```
   Mid$(msg, n) = Chr$(intAsc + 32)
End If
```

You then get the value of the next key string character in line to be used to encrypt the next character in the message string. Then the loop executes again.

```
intKeyChar = Asc(Mid$(strKey, intKeyOffset))

Next n
```

After all characters are encrypted, the resulting string is returned as a result of the function.

```
Code = msg
```

That's it. Just a series of weird but well-defined steps. You might experiment with the function and produce your own customized Code function. The tough part is making the Decode function work correctly to make sense of the encoded string. Let's take a look at what I came up with.

The *Decode* Function

The Decode function takes an encrypted string produced from the Code function as its first argument. The second argument is the same key string used by the Code function. (It has to be the same or the result will be meaningless.)

Enter the Decode function as shown in Listing 10.7.

Listing 10.7. The Decode function.

```
Function Decode (varMsg As Variant, strKey As String) As String

' Decodes a string encrypted by the Code subroutine

  Dim msg As String

  Dim intLength As Integer
  Dim intKeyLength As Integer

  Dim intKeyOffset As Integer
  Dim intAsc As Integer
  Dim intLastChar As Integer
  Dim intSkip As Integer

  Dim n As Integer

  On Error GoTo DecodeError

  msg = CNStr(varMsg)

  intLength = Len(msg)
  intKeyLength = Len(strKey)
  intKeyOffset = intKeyLength

  intLastChar = Asc(Right$(strKey, 1))

  For n = 1 To intLength
    intKeyOffset = intKeyOffset + 1
    If intKeyOffset > intKeyLength Then
      intKeyOffset = 1
    End If

    intAsc = Asc(Mid$(msg, n, 1))
    If intAsc > 32 And intAsc < 127 Then

      intAsc = intAsc - 32

    ' Subtract an offset determined by the loop counter
      intSkip = n Mod 94
      intAsc = intAsc - intSkip

      If intAsc < 1 Then
        intAsc = intAsc + 94
      End If
```

continues

Listing 10.7. continued

```
      ' Subtract an offset determined by a character in the key
        intAsc = intAsc - intLastChar

        While intAsc < 1
          intAsc = intAsc + 94
        Wend

        Mid$(msg, n) = Chr$(intAsc + 32)
      End If

      intLastChar = Asc(Mid$(strKey, intKeyOffset))

  Next n

  Decode = msg

DecodeDone:
  Exit Function

DecodeError:
  MsgBox Error$, 48, PROGRAM
  Resume DecodeDone

End Function
```

You again stuff the message into a string variable, and you again initialize the same variables.

```
msg = CNStr(varMsg)

intLength = Len(msg)
intKeyLength = Len(strKey)
intKeyOffset = intKeyLength

intLastChar = Asc(Right$(strKey, 1))
```

You also start a loop to go through each character just as you did before, and you cycle through the key string characters the same way.

```
For n = 1 To intLength
  intKeyOffset = intKeyOffset + 1
  If intKeyOffset > intKeyLength Then
    intKeyOffset = 1
  End If
```

You fetch the encrypted character from the message string. You can do the same check for a printable character, because all the encrypted characters fall within the same range of printable characters.

```
intAsc = Asc(Mid$(msg, n, 1))
If intAsc > 32 And intAsc < 127 Then
```

So far, everything is still the same as the Code function. You subtract 32 from the character value to put it in the range of 1 to 94.

```
intAsc = intAsc - 32
```

Oops! Now things are different. The last thing you did in the Code function was add a value determined by the loop counter. Now you calculate the value again with the modulus operator and subtract it from your current value.

```
' Subtract an offset determined by the loop counter
intSkip = n Mod 94
intAsc = intAsc - intSkip
```

Rather then potentially being above the range from 1 to 94, you now can potentially be below the range. You check for that and kick the value up to within the range if needed.

```
If intAsc < 1 Then
   intAsc = intAsc + 94
End If
```

Continuing the backward process, now subtract the key string character value from your encrypt character value.

```
' Subtract an offset determined by a character in the key
intAsc = intAsc - intLastChar
```

This is where you may be several times outside your allowable range of 1 to 94. You loop as many times as needed to get back into the accepted range.

```
While intAsc < 1
   intAsc = intAsc + 94
Wend
```

Hopefully all went well (the key was good) and you put the original character back into the message string. First, you add 32 to it to put the number within the range of printable characters again.

```
   Mid$(msg, n) = Chr$(intAsc + 32)
End If
```

At the end of the loop, the next key string character is read for the next iteration.

```
intLastChar = Asc(Mid$(strKey, intKeyOffset))

Next n
```

When the loop ends, the decoded message is returned as a result of the function.

```
Decode = msg
```

I hope it works.

(Actually, it works. Really. I ran it once or twice.)

The *PasswordCreate* Function

Now let's continue on with the procedures in the Library module.

The `PasswordCreate` function is an improved version of the `PasswordAssign` function you created in Chapter 3 when you were toying around with Access. Do you know what was wrong with the password functions back there?

The problem is that all you have to do is open the Login table and whoa... There are all the passwords as clear as day. Now that you have your own encryption function, how about if you encrypt the passwords in the Login table?

There is still a problem. Can't someone just run your `Decode` function against the encrypted passwords and get the real passwords? The answer is yes, they can. As long as they can get to the code and see what the constant `PASSWORD_KEY` has been assigned to, there is a big hole in your security.

Oh well, just don't tell anybody, OK? And don't you get devious and tell folks their data is secure when you know there is a back door to let yourself in.

Seriously, what you can do is modify the `PASSWORD_KEY` value as I suggested earlier, produce an executable, and hide your source code in a safe place so nobody finds out how to decrypt the passwords in your Login table.

Enter the `PasswordCreate` function as shown in Listing 10.8.

Listing 10.8. The `PasswordCreate` function.

```
Function PasswordCreate (strUsername As String, strPassword As String)
➥ As Integer

  Dim tbl As Table
  Dim blnOpened As Integer

  blnOpened = False

' Assume failure
  PasswordCreate = True

  On Error GoTo PasswordCreateError

  strUsername = CNStr(strUsername)
  strPassword = CNStr(strPassword)
  If strUsername = "" Or strPassword = "" Then
    GoTo PasswordCreateDone
  End If

  Set tbl = gdb.OpenTable("Login")
  blnOpened = True
```

```
' See if the user is already in the table.
  tbl.Index = "Username"
  tbl.Seek "=", strUsername

  If Not tbl.NoMatch Then
  ' Found the user
MsgBox "A password is already assigned for " & strUsername & ".", 48,
➥ PROGRAM
    GoTo PasswordCreateDone
  End If

' New user, create a new record
  tbl.AddNew
  tbl!Username = strUsername

' Write the password field and update the record
  tbl!Password = Code(strPassword, PASSWORD_KEY)
  tbl.Update

' Success
  PasswordCreate = False

PasswordCreateDone:
  On Error Resume Next
  If blnOpened Then tbl.Close
  Exit Function

PasswordCreateError:
  MsgBox Error$, 48, PROGRAM
  Resume PasswordCreateDone

End Function
```

First, the function checks that the name and password actually contain values.

```
  strUsername = CNStr(strUsername)
  strPassword = CNStr(strPassword)
  If strUsername = "" Or strPassword = "" Then
    GoTo PasswordCreateDone
  End If
```

Next, the Login table is opened. The global, gdb, is assumed to be set to the database that contains the Login table.

```
  Set tbl = gdb.OpenTable("Login")
  blnOpened = True
```

A check is performed to see if a user by the same name is already in the Login table.

```
' See if the user is already in the table.
  tbl.Index = "Username"
  tbl.Seek "=", strUsername

  If Not tbl.NoMatch Then
  ' Found the user
```

```
MsgBox "A password is already assigned for " & strUsername & ".", 48,
➡ PROGRAM
    GoTo PasswordCreateDone
  End If
```

If not, a record is created for the new user.

```
' New user, create a new record
  tbl.AddNew
  tbl!Username = strUsername
```

The password is encrypted before writing it to the Password field in the Login table.

```
' Write the password field and update the record
  tbl!Password = Code(strPassword, PASSWORD_KEY)
  tbl.Update
```

The *PasswordValidate* Function

The PasswordValidate function locates the Login record for a user. It then decodes the password in the record and compares it to the entered password.

The UserID value is returned if the password is valid. If it is not valid, 0 is returned.

Enter the PasswordValidate function as shown in Listing 10.9.

Listing 10.9. The PasswordValidate **function.**

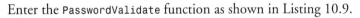

```
Function PasswordValidate (strUsername As String, strPassword As String)
➡ As Long

  Dim tbl As Table
  Dim blnOpened As Integer

  blnOpened = False

' Assume invalid
  PasswordValidate = 0

  On Error GoTo PasswordValidateError

' Validate the username and password against the Login table
  Set tbl = gdb.OpenTable("Login")
  blnOpened = True

  tbl.Index = "Username"
  tbl.Seek "=", strUsername

  If Not tbl.NoMatch Then
  ' Found the user
    If Decode(tbl!Password, PASSWORD_KEY) = strPassword Then
    ' Password checked out OK, return UserID
      PasswordValidate = tbl!UserID
    End If
  End If
```

```
PasswordValidateDone:
  On Error Resume Next
  If blnOpened Then tbl.Close
  Exit Function

PasswordValidateError:
  MsgBox Error$, 48, PROGRAM
  Resume PasswordValidateDone

End Function
```

The *PasswordChange* Function

The PasswordChange function does what you expect it would—changes a user's password. To make sure you are supposed to be doing this, it verifies the old password first.

Enter the PasswordChange function as shown in Listing 10.10.

Listing 10.10. The PasswordChange **function.**

```
Function PasswordChange (strUsername As String, strOldPassword As String,
➥ strNewPassword As String) As Integer

  Dim tbl As Table
  Dim blnOpened As Integer

  blnOpened = False

' Assume failure
  PasswordChange = True

  On Error GoTo PasswordChangeError

  Set tbl = gdb.OpenTable("Login")
  blnOpened = True

' See if the user is already in the table.
  tbl.Index = "Username"
  tbl.Seek "=", strUsername

  If tbl.NoMatch Then
  ' Couldn't find the user
    GoTo PasswordChangeDone
  End If

  If Decode(tbl!Password, PASSWORD_KEY) <> strOldPassword Then
  ' Old password is invalid
    GoTo PasswordChangeDone
  End If

' Found the user record, edit it
  tbl.Edit
```

continues

Listing 10.10. continued

```
' Write the password field and update the record
  tbl!Password = Code(strNewPassword, PASSWORD_KEY)
  tbl.Update

' Success
  PasswordChange = False

PasswordChangeDone:
  On Error Resume Next
  If blnOpened Then tbl.Close
  Exit Function

PasswordChangeError:
  MsgBox Error$, 48, PROGRAM
  Resume PasswordChangeDone

End Function
```

The *CountStrikes* Subroutine

The CountStrikes subroutine is called whenever the user enters an invalid password. The function increments the gintStrike global and displays three different messages depending on the number of incorrect password attempts.

1. Enter the CountStrikes subroutine in Listing 10.11.
2. Save the Library module as LIBRARY.BAS.

Listing 10.11. The CountStrikes subroutine.

```
Sub CountStrikes ()

  Dim msg As String
  Dim intIcon As Integer

' Count this bad attempt
  gintStrike = gintStrike + 1

' Select which message and icon to display
  Select Case gintStrike

  Case 1
    msg = "Are you supposed to be here?"
    intIcon = 32 ' Question

  Case 2
    msg = "I don't recognize you."
    intIcon = 48 ' Warning
```

```
  Case Else
    msg = "Go Away!"
    intIcon = 16 ' Stop!

  End Select

  MsgBox msg, intIcon, PROGRAM

End Sub
```

That completes the Library module. You are ready now to put code behind each of the forms you created.

Coding the Login Form

The Login form is the first form displayed in the application. It acts as an initial switch-board, because from it you can enter the New Diary form, the Change Password form, and the Secret Diary form. However, once you leave the Login form to go to the Secret Diary form, you can't come back to it without restarting the application.

1. Open the Project Window and select the Login form. Click the View Code button to open the Login form module.

2. Enter the declarations section as shown in Listing 10.12.

Listing 10.12. The Login form module's declarations section.

```
' Login form

  Option Explicit

  Dim mblnDatabaseOpened As Integer
  Dim mblnEntryOpened As Integer

' Did the user login successfully?
  Dim mblnLoginValid As Integer
```

The first two module variables, `mblnDatabaseOpened` and `mblnEntryOpened`, are set to True if the database and Entry table are opened. The Login form may have to end the program before moving on to the Secret Diary form, so these variables help indicate whether these objects need to be closed when you close down the program.

The `mblnLoginValid` variable gets set to True when the user's password is validated.

476   **Part II** ■ *Fun Projects*

The *Form_Load* Subroutine

The first code to execute in the program is in the Login form's Form_Load subroutine.

Enter the Form_Load subroutine as shown in Listing 10.13.

Listing 10.13. The Login form's Form_Load subroutine.

```
Sub Form_Load ()

  Dim strFile As String

  mblnDatabaseOpened = False
  mblnEntryOpened = False

  On Error GoTo Form_LoadError

  cr = Chr$(13)

' By default, they didn't login correctly
  mblnLoginValid = False

' Zero login attempts have been tried so far
  gintStrike = 0

' Assume the database is in the same directory as DIARY.EXE
  strFile = App.Path
  If Right$(strFile, 1) <> "\" Then
    strFile = strFile & "\"
  End If
  strFile = strFile & "DIARY.MDB"

' Open the database
  Set gdb = OpenDatabase(strFile)
  mblnDatabaseOpened = True

' Center the Login form
  Center Me

Form_LoadDone:
  Exit Sub

Form_LoadError:
  MsgBox Error$, 16, PROGRAM
  Unload Me
  Resume Form_LoadDone

End Sub
```

The cr variable is initialized to the carriage return character. The mblnLoginValid flag is initialized to False because a valid password has not been entered yet.

```
    cr = Chr$(13)

' By default, they didn't login correctly
    mblnLoginValid = False
```

The global `gintStrike` keeps track of the number of failed password attempts. You initialize it to zero (mostly out of habit, because VB already initializes integer variables to zero). The variable is global because this isn't the only form where you can enter a password.

```
' Zero login attempts have been tried so far
    gintStrike = 0
```

Next, the location of the database is determined by assuming that it is in the same directory as the program. The Path property of the Application object returns the path to the program's .EXE file. The code appends the DIARY.MDB filename to the path.

```
' Assume the database is in the same directory as DIARY.EXE
    strFile = App.Path
    If Right$(strFile, 1) <> "\" Then
      strFile = strFile & "\"
    End If
    strFile = strFile & "DIARY.MDB"
```

The database is opened and assigned to the global `gdb` database variable to be used in all of the modules.

```
' Open the database
    Set gdb = OpenDatabase(strFile)
    mblnDatabaseOpened = True
```

At the end, the `Center` subroutine you created is called to center the Login form on the screen.

```
' Center the Login form
    Center Me
```

The *cmdOK_Click* Subroutine

Behind the OK button, the code verifies that both a name and password have been entered, and then the `PasswordValidate` function is called to see if the name and password are a valid match.

Enter the `cmdOK_Click` subroutine as shown in Listing 10.14.

Listing 10.14. The Login form's `cmdOK_Click` subroutine.

```
Sub cmdOK_Click ()

  Dim sql As String

  On Error GoTo cmdOK_ClickError
```

continues

Listing 10.14. continued

```
' Make sure a name and password were entered
  If CNStr(txtName) = "" Then
    MsgBox "Please enter a name.", 64, PROGRAM
    txtName.SetFocus

    GoTo cmdOK_ClickDone
  End If

  If CNStr(txtPassword) = "" Then
    MsgBox "Please enter a password.", 64, PROGRAM
    txtPassword.SetFocus

    GoTo cmdOK_ClickDone
  End If

  glngUserID = PasswordValidate(CStr(txtName), CStr(txtPassword))
  mblnLoginValid = (glngUserID <> 0&)

  If mblnLoginValid Then
  ' Successful login!

    gintStrike = 0

    gstrPassword = txtPassword

  ' This got annoying real fast
  ' MsgBox "Hi " & txtName.Text & "!", 64, PROGRAM

sql = "SELECT * FROM Entry WHERE UserID = " & glngUserID &
➥ " ORDER BY Date"
    Set gdynEntry = gdb.CreateDynaset(sql)

    Unload Me
    GoTo cmdOK_ClickDone
  End If

  CountStrikes

  If gintStrike = 3 Then
  ' Three strikes and you're out!
    Unload Me
  Else
  ' Try again, erase the password field and set focus to it
    txtPassword = ""
    txtPassword.SetFocus
  End If

cmdOK_ClickDone:
  Exit Sub

cmdOK_ClickError:
  MsgBox Error$, 48, PROGRAM
  Resume cmdOK_ClickDone

End Sub
```

I could have used the Required function that you created in the Library module, but I decided to handle an empty name or password field without it—maybe because I wanted the message to be more polite.

Next, the PasswordValidate function is called. If the password is valid, the function returns a user ID number for the user. The mblnLoginValid flag is set to True if the login was successful.

```
glngUserID = PasswordValidate(CStr(txtName), CStr(txtPassword))
mblnLoginValid = (glngUserID <> 0&)
```

Next you branch, depending on whether the login was valid.

```
If mblnLoginValid Then
' Successful login!
```

If it was OK, the strike count is set back to zero. This way even if you have any strikes against you, you get three chances again when you enter a password later in the program.

Also, the password is saved in a global variable so you don't have to look it up in the table anymore.

```
gintStrike = 0

gstrPassword = txtPassword
```

Next is a line I commented out. As said in the comment preceding it, this was cute the first couple of times I ran the program, and it got tossed after that.

```
' This got annoying real fast
' MsgBox "Hi " & txtName.Text & "!", 64, PROGRAM
```

Using the user ID number returned by the PasswordValidate function, an SQL SELECT statement is used to open all of the diary entries for this particular user.

```
sql = "SELECT * FROM Entry WHERE UserID = " & glngUserID &
➥ " ORDER BY Date"
    Set gdynEntry = gdb.CreateDynaset(sql)
```

Then the form is closed. The Form_Unload code takes care of opening up the next form.

```
    Unload Me
    GoTo cmdOK_ClickDone
  End If
```

OK, I was lazy. Rather than using an Else block, I used a GoTo to exit the procedure early. The rest of the code in the procedure executes only if the user did not enter a password correctly.

(Actually, I code this way because I think it is easier to read. You don't have to agree with me on this.)

The `CountStrikes` subroutine is called to display an error message and increment the `gintStrikes` counter.

```
CountStrikes
```

If you find out that three consecutive bad attempts have been made, the program shuts down by unloading the Login form.

```
If gintStrike = 3 Then
' Three strikes and you're out!
   Unload Me
```

If there are one or two tries left, the password is cleared and focus returns to the Password text box.

```
Else
' Try again, erase the password field and set focus to it
   txtPassword = ""
   txtPassword.SetFocus
End If
```

The Cancel, New Diary, and Change Password Buttons

These three subroutines are pretty short.

Enter the `cmdCancel_Click`, `cmdNewDiary_Click`, and `cmdChangePassword_Click` subroutines as shown in Listings 10.15, 10.16, and 10.17.

The `cmdCancel_Click` subroutine closes the form.

Listing 10.15. The Login form's `cmdCancel_Click` subroutine.

```
Sub cmdCancel_Click ()

' Close the form
   Unload Me

End Sub
```

The `cmdNewDiary_Click` subroutine opens the New Diary form as a modal dialog box.

The code suspends execution on the Show method call until the New Diary form is closed. When the code resumes execution, it sends focus to the OK button, ready for the user to open his new diary.

Listing 10.16. The Login form's `cmdNewDiary_Click` **subroutine.**

```
Sub cmdNewDiary_Click ()

  On Error Resume Next
  NewDiary.Show 1
  cmdOK.SetFocus

End Sub
```

The `cmdChangePassword_Click` subroutine opens the Change Password form just as you opened the New Diary form.

The check on the `gintStrike` variable is added because the user must enter his existing password in the Change Password form. If he entered three consecutive bad tries, the Change Password form bails out and the Login form follows suit to end the program.

Listing 10.17. The Login form's `cmdChangePassword_Click` **subroutine.**

```
Sub cmdChangePassword_Click ()

  On Error Resume Next
  ChangePassword.Show 1
  cmdOK.SetFocus

  If gintStrike = 3 Then
    Unload Me
  End If

End Sub
```

The *Form_Unload* Subroutine

The Login form's `Form_Unload` subroutine is activated when the Login form is being closed. One of two conditions occurred that you care about: the password was entered correctly, or it wasn't.

Enter the Login form's `Form_Unload` subroutine as shown in Listing 10.18.

Listing 10.18. The Login form's `Form_Unload` **subroutine.**

```
Sub Form_Unload (Cancel As Integer)

  On Error GoTo Form_UnloadError

' Did they login correctly?
  If Not mblnLoginValid Then
```

continues

Listing 10.18. continued

```
' Close the Entry table if it was opened
  If mblnEntryOpened Then
    gdynEntry.Close
  End If

' Close the database if it was opened
  If mblnDatabaseOpened Then
    gdb.Close
  End If

' Stop the program
  End
End If

' Display the Diary form
  Diary.Show

Form_UnloadDone:
  Exit Sub

Form_UnloadError:
  MsgBox Error$, 48, PROGRAM
  Resume Form_UnloadDone

End Sub
```

The `If` block deals with the case that the password was never entered, or never entered correctly. You know this because you set `mblnLoginValid` to True only if a password is validated.

```
' Did they login correctly?
  If Not mblnLoginValid Then
```

If the Entry table was opened successfully, it is closed.

```
' Close the Entry table if it was opened
  If mblnEntryOpened Then
    gdynEntry.Close
  End If
```

Ditto on the database.

```
' Close the database if it was opened
  If mblnDatabaseOpened Then
    gdb.Close
  End If
```

Then the program terminates.

```
' Stop the program
  End
End If
```

On the other hand, if a password was entered correctly, the Diary form is loaded.

```
' Display the Diary form
  Diary.Show
```

Close the Login form module window.

I like to save my work frequently (about every five minutes). You can make sure that all of your Visual Basic work is saved by selecting the File|Save Project command. It's as easy as pressing Alt-F and Alt-V.

Testing the Login Form

You can actually run the program right now, even though it isn't complete. Press F5, and the Login form is displayed.

You can test the New Diary and Change Password forms by clicking the buttons. The pop-up forms won't center correctly because you haven't added any code to them yet.

You can also practice entering a name and password. Because there aren't any entries in the Login table yet, you get the program's responses to entering an invalid password.

Just as for the Login form in Chapter 3, the response is at first friendly, as shown in Figure 10.32. Then mildly rude, as shown in Figure 10.33. And finally obnoxious, as shown in Figure 10.34.

FIGURE 10.32.

First password failure.

FIGURE 10.33.

Second password failure.

FIGURE 10.34.

Third password failure.

The program shuts down after displaying the Stop sign message.

Coding the New Diary Form

Creating a new diary is accomplished by entering a record in the Login table for the user. This happens in the code behind the New Diary form.

1. Open the module window for the New Diary form.
2. Enter the `Form_Load` subroutine as shown in Listing 10.19, so that the form is centered when displayed.
3. Enter the `cmdOK_Click` subroutine as shown in Listing 10.20.

Listing 10.19. The New Diary form's `Form_Load` **subroutine.**

```
Sub Form_Load ()

  Center Me

End Sub
```

Listing 10.20. The New Diary form's `cmdOK_Click` **subroutine.**

```
Sub cmdOK_Click ()

  Dim msg As String

  On Error GoTo cmdOK_ClickError

  If Required(txtName, "Name") Then GoTo cmdOK_ClickDone
  If Required(txtPassword, "Password") Then GoTo cmdOK_ClickDone
  If Required(txtVerify, "Verify") Then GoTo cmdOK_ClickDone

  If txtPassword <> txtVerify Then
    msg = "The password field does not match the verification field."
    msg = msg & cr & cr
    msg = msg & "Please re-enter the password."

    MsgBox msg, 48, PROGRAM

    txtPassword = ""
    txtVerify = ""

    txtPassword.SetFocus
    GoTo cmdOK_ClickDone
  End If

  If PasswordCreate(CStr(txtName), CStr(txtPassword)) Then
    GoTo cmdOK_ClickDone
  End If

  MsgBox "Keep your password in a safe place!", 64, PROGRAM
```

```
  Login!txtName = txtName
  Login!txtPassword = txtPassword

  Unload Me

cmdOK_ClickDone:
  Exit Sub

cmdOK_ClickError:
  MsgBox Error$, 48, PROGRAM
  Resume cmdOK_ClickDone

End Sub
```

The `cmdOK_Click` subroutine's job is to make sure that a name and password were properly entered. The actual work of writing to the Login table has already been written in the `PasswordCreate` function.

The subroutine first uses the `Required` function in the Library module as a quick way to make sure that a value has been entered in each text box.

```
  If Required(txtName, "Name") Then GoTo cmdOK_ClickDone
  If Required(txtPassword, "Password") Then GoTo cmdOK_ClickDone
  If Required(txtVerify, "Verify") Then GoTo cmdOK_ClickDone
```

Next, the function compares the text entered in the password and verify fields.

You set up the text boxes so the characters entered are echoed back as star characters (*). This prohibits anyone from reading your password off the screen, but you can't read it either.

The verification step reduces the chances that the user accidentally enters something other than what he thinks he is entering.

```
  If txtPassword <> txtVerify Then
```

If the verification fails, a message is displayed.

```
  msg = "The password field does not match the verification field."
  msg = msg & cr & cr
  msg = msg & "Please re-enter the password."

  MsgBox msg, 48, PROGRAM
```

Next, the password and verify fields are cleared so they can be re-entered.

```
  txtPassword = ""
  txtVerify = ""
```

Focus is sent to the password field, and the function does an early exit.

```
  txtPassword.SetFocus
  GoTo cmdOK_ClickDone
  End If
```

If verification succeeded, the password is created by calling the `PasswordCreate` function. You check the return value of the function call and bail out if an error occurred in creating the record.

```
If PasswordCreate(CStr(txtName), CStr(txtPassword)) Then
  GoTo cmdOK_ClickDone
End If
```

If you got this far, everything went OK. You remind the user to protect his password.

```
MsgBox "Keep your password in a safe place!", 64, PROGRAM
```

For convenience, you go ahead and fill in the Name and Password fields on the Login form. This enables the user to click OK and enter the Diary form.

```
Login!txtName = txtName
Login!txtPassword = txtPassword

Unload Me
```

The last subroutine for this form responds to the Cancel button's Click event by closing the form.

1. Enter the `cmdCancel_Click` subroutine as shown in Listing 10.21.
2. Close the form module and save your work.

Listing 10.21. The New Diary form's `cmdCancel_Click` subroutine.

```
Sub cmdCancel_Click ()

  Unload Me

End Sub
```

Testing the New Diary Form

You can test the New Diary form and verify that it enters a record in the Login table. Run the program and click the New **D**iary button. Fill in a name and a password in the password and verification fields, as shown in Figure 10.35.

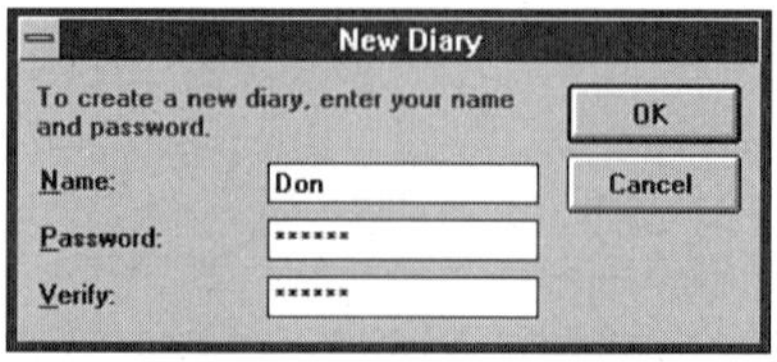

FIGURE 10.35.

Entering a name and password into the New Diary dialog box.

I misspelled the password and got the message shown in Figure 10.36.

FIGURE 10.36.
Oops!

After correctly re-entering the password and verification fields, the dialog box in Figure 10.37 is shown.

FIGURE 10.37.
A password has been assigned.

Close the program and open the database with Microsoft Access. If you open the Login table in datasheet view, you see a record like that shown in Figure 10.38.

FIGURE 10.38.
The Login table shows a new entry with the user name and encrypted password.

Can you tell what my password was?

Coding the Change Password Form

Changing the user's password should be a trivial problem, right?

There's a "gotcha" in this one. Because I decided to use the password as a key string to encrypt the diary entries, guess what happens when you change the password? I hope the entries you made in your diary the last half-year weren't really that important.

Just kidding, but if you are going to change the key, you have to change the lock too.

That's what you have to do here. To change the password, you have to decode each of the diary entries, then recode them using the new password as the key.

What a pain! I know, but did I say anywhere that this security system was perfect? Anyway, the code that does this is right here behind the Change Password form.

1. Open the Module window for the Change Password form.
2. Enter the Form_Load subroutine as shown in Listing 10.22.
3. Enter the cmdOK_Click subroutine as shown in Listing 10.23.

Listing 10.22. The Change Password form's Form_Load subroutine.

```
Sub Form_Load ()

  Center Me

End Sub
```

Listing 10.23. The Change Password form's cmdOK_Click subroutine.

```
Sub cmdOK_Click ()

  Dim msg As String
  Dim lngUserID As Long
  Dim blnLoginValid As Integer

  On Error GoTo cmdOK_ClickError

  If Required(txtName, "Name") Then GoTo cmdOK_ClickDone
  If Required(txtOldPassword, "Old Password") Then GoTo cmdOK_ClickDone
  If Required(txtNewPassword, "New Password") Then GoTo cmdOK_ClickDone
  If Required(txtVerify, "Verify") Then GoTo cmdOK_ClickDone

  If PasswordValidate(CStr(txtName), CStr(txtOldPassword)) = 0& Then
    CountStrikes

    If gintStrike = 3 Then
      Unload Me
    End If

    GoTo cmdOK_ClickDone
  End If

  gintStrike = 0

  If txtNewPassword <> txtVerify Then
    msg = "The new password field does not match the verification field."
    msg = msg & cr & cr
    msg = msg & "Please re-enter the new password."
```

```
      MsgBox msg, 48, PROGRAM

      txtNewPassword = ""
      txtVerify = ""

      txtNewPassword.SetFocus
      GoTo cmdOK_ClickDone
   End If

   If DiaryPasswordChange(CStr(txtName), CStr(txtOldPassword),
   ➥ CStr(txtNewPassword)) Then
      GoTo cmdOK_ClickDone
   End If

   MsgBox "Keep your new password in a safe place!", 64, PROGRAM

   Login!txtName = txtName
   Login!txtPassword = txtNewPassword

   Unload Me

cmdOK_ClickDone:
   Exit Sub

cmdOK_ClickError:
   MsgBox Error$, 48, PROGRAM
   Resume cmdOK_ClickDone

End Sub
```

This procedure is nearly identical to the cmdOK_Click subroutine you wrote for the New Diary form. It also borrows some code from the Login form's cmdOK_Click function to handle validating the existing password.

The new code is in the call to the DiaryPasswordChange function, used to change the Login table entry for the current user, as well as all of their Entry table records.

```
If DiaryPasswordChange(CStr(txtName), CStr(txtOldPassword),
➥ CStr(txtNewPassword)) Then
   GoTo cmdOK_ClickDone
End If
```

In the Library module you wrote a PasswordChange function. You have to create a modified version of it to handle the recoding of the diary entries.

I'm getting a little ahead of myself, because I haven't yet discussed the code that actually writes the diary entries. However, for the sake of finishing off the code behind this form, here is the DiaryPasswordChange function.

Enter the DiaryPasswordChange function as shown in Listing 10.24.

Listing 10.24. The `DiaryPasswordChange` function.

```
Function DiaryPasswordChange (strUsername As String, strOldPassword As String,
➥ strNewPassword As String) As Integer

' This is a special version of the PasswordChange function.  The entries in
' the diary is encrypted based on the password.  On changing the password,
' each of the entries must be re-encrypted.

' A transaction is used to insure that the change is made completely, or
' not at all.

  Dim tblLogin As Table
  Dim dynEntry As Dynaset

  Dim strEntry As String

  Dim blnLoginOpened As Integer
  Dim blnEntryOpened As Integer
  Dim blnTransStarted As Integer

  blnLoginOpened = False
  blnEntryOpened = False
  blnTransStarted = False

' Assume failure
  DiaryPasswordChange = True

  On Error GoTo DiaryPasswordChangeError

  Screen.MousePointer = 11

  Set tblLogin = gdb.OpenTable("Login")
  blnLoginOpened = True

' See if the user is already in the table.
  tblLogin.Index = "Username"
  tblLogin.Seek "=", strUsername

  If tblLogin.NoMatch Then
  ' Couldn't find the user
    GoTo DiaryPasswordChangeDone
  End If

  If Decode(tblLogin!Password, PASSWORD_KEY) <> strOldPassword Then
  ' Old password is invalid
    GoTo DiaryPasswordChangeDone
  End If

' Open the user's diary entries
Set dynEntry = gdb.CreateDynaset("SELECT Entry FROM Entry WHERE UserID = "
➥ & tblLogin!UserID)

' Tables are open, so the transaction can start
  BeginTrans
  blnTransStarted = True

' Decode the entries, then re-code them
  Do Until dynEntry.EOF
```

```
   strEntry = Decode(dynEntry!Entry, strOldPassword)
   dynEntry.Edit
   dynEntry!Entry = Code(strEntry, strNewPassword)
   dynEntry.Update

   dynEntry.MoveNext
 Loop

' Change the password
 tblLogin.Edit
 tblLogin!Password = Code(strNewPassword, PASSWORD_KEY)
 tblLogin.Update

 CommitTrans
 blnTransStarted = False

' Success
 DiaryPasswordChange = False

DiaryPasswordChangeDone:
 On Error Resume Next
 If blnTransStarted Then Rollback
 If blnLoginOpened Then tblLogin.Close
 If blnEntryOpened Then dynEntry.Close
 Screen.MousePointer = 0
 Exit Function

DiaryPasswordChangeError:
 MsgBox Error$, 48, PROGRAM
 Resume DiaryPasswordChangeDone

End Function
```

Depending on how prolific the diary writer is, recoding all of the entries could be a lengthy job. The first thing you do is turn on the hourglass mouse icon so the user can run to the kitchen for a candy bar.

```
Screen.MousePointer = 11
```

Next, you open the Login table and verify that a user exists with the name indicated by the strUsername argument.

```
 Set tblLogin = gdb.OpenTable("Login")
 blnLoginOpened = True

' See if the user is already in the table.
 tblLogin.Index = "Username"
 tblLogin.Seek "=", strUsername
```

If the user can't be found, you bail out of the function early.

```
 If tblLogin.NoMatch Then
 ' Couldn't find the user
   GoTo DiaryPasswordChangeDone
 End If
```

You also bail out if the second argument, strOldPassword, isn't the proper password.

```
If Decode(tblLogin!Password, PASSWORD_KEY) <> strOldPassword Then
' Old password is invalid
  GoTo DiaryPasswordChangeDone
End If
```

If everything checks out, a dynaset is created selecting the diary entries for the current user.

```
' Open the user's diary entries
Set dynEntry = gdb.CreateDynaset("SELECT Entry FROM Entry WHERE UserID = "
➥ & tblLogin!UserID)
```

Next, you use the BeginTrans statement to buffer all of the record changes in a single transaction.

This is also necessary to ensure that you either complete the entire job or you don't do it at all. If an error were to occur halfway through and you weren't using a transaction, you would be left with half of your diary unreadable.

```
' Tables are open, so the transaction can start
  BeginTrans
  blnTransStarted = True
```

A Do loop is used to run through each diary entry, as shown in Listing 10.25. The entry is first decoded using the old password, and then it is encoded with the new password and written back to the table.

Listing 10.25. Re-coding diary entries.

```
' Decode the entries, then re-code them
  Do Until dynEntry.EOF
    strEntry = Decode(dynEntry!Entry, strOldPassword)
    dynEntry.Edit
    dynEntry!Entry = Code(strEntry, strNewPassword)
    dynEntry.Update

    dynEntry.MoveNext
  Loop
```

Before you commit the transaction, you also carefully make sure that the password record is changed to remain in sync with the translated diary entries.

```
' Change the password
  tblLogin.Edit
  tblLogin!Password = Code(strNewPassword, PASSWORD_KEY)
  tblLogin.Update
```

Finally, you commit the transaction and return False to indicate that the password change and translation were successful.

```
    CommitTrans
    blnTransStarted = False

' Suooocc
    DiaryPasswordChange = False
```

To complete the module, you have the `cmdClose_Click` one-liner for closing the form without changing the password.

1. Enter the `cmdClose_Click` subroutine as shown in Listing 10.26.
2. Close the Change Password form module.

Listing 10.26. The `cmdClose_Click` subroutine.

```
Sub cmdCancel_Click ()

  Unload Me

End Sub
```

Once again, you can test your progress so far. Run the program and try out the Change Password button. Change the password, then change it back to what it was before.

Figure 10.39 shows the Change Password dialog box as a new password is being entered.

FIGURE 10.39.
Changing the password.

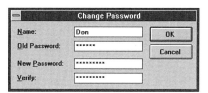

After the password is changed, the program again reminds you about keeping your password protected.

You can verify that password changes are working, but you can't verify yet that the translation of the Login table entries is working. That's because there are no entries yet. Let's correct this situation right now.

Coding the Diary Form

Now you get to the real workhorse of the diary program. The Diary form module contains the procedures listed here in the order you will look at them.

(Declarations)	*Module variable declarations*
Form_Load	Initialize the form to add a new entry
SaveEntry	Write a diary entry to the database
ShowEntry	Read and display a diary entry
cmdJump_Click	Seek a diary entry by date
cmdScramble_Click	Encrypt the view of the diary entry
cmdAdd_Click	Start a new diary entry
cmdErase_Click	Erase the current diary entry
cmdClose_Click	Close the diary form and end the program
cmdMove_Click	Move from entry to entry
txtDate_KeyPress	Miscellaneous
txtTime_KeyPress	
txtEntry_KeyPress	
txtEntry_KeyUp	
Form_Unload	Close the database

Open the Module window for the Diary form and enter the declarations section as shown in Listing 10.27.

Listing 10.27. The Diary form module's declarations section.

```
' Diary form

  Option Explicit

' Working on an entry not saved yet
  Dim mblnAddEntry As Integer

' Erasing a new entry
  Dim mblnEraseNewEntry As Integer

' The current entry is scrambled
  Dim mblnScrambled As Integer

' The current entry has been changed
  Dim mblnDirty As Integer
```

The declarations section declares four integers used as Boolean flags. Each flag represents a mode that the application can be in.

The `mblnAddEntry` flag indicates that the current entry has never been saved. The `mblnEraseNewEntry` flag is set when erasing a new entry (an entry that has never been saved before.) The `mblnScrambled` flag gets set when the **S**cramble button is clicked to encrypt the entry onscreen to keep others from reading it. The `mblnDirty` flag is set whenever a change is made to the current entry, indicating that it should be saved before going to another entry or exiting the program.

The *Form_Load* Subroutine

The `Form_Load` subroutine prepares the Diary form so that the user can begin a new diary entry.

Enter the `Form_Load` subroutine as shown in Listing 10.28.

Listing 10.28. The `Form_Load` subroutine.

```
Sub Form_Load ()

   On Error GoTo Form_LoadError

' Initially, move one beyond the last record
   If gdynEntry.RecordCount Then
      gdynEntry.MoveLast
      gdynEntry.MoveNext
   End If

' Start with a new entry
   mblnAddEntry = False
   mblnDirty = False
   cmdAdd_Click

' Center the Diary form
   Center Me

Form_LoadDone:
   Exit Sub

Form_LoadError:
   MsgBox Error$, 48, PROGRAM
   Resume Form_LoadDone

End Sub
```

The `Form_Load` subroutine first positions the `gdynEntry` dynaset's record position to the location where the next record would be added. This is the end of file position that you would usually use the EOF property to check for when traversing the entire set of records in a dynaset.

```
' Initially, move one beyond the last record
If gdynEntry.RecordCount Then
  gdynEntry.MoveLast
  gdynEntry.MoveNext
End If
```

Next, the flags are initialized and the `cmdAdd_Click` subroutine is called to prepare the form for entering a new entry.

```
mblnAddEntry = False
mblnScrambled = False
mblnDirty = False

' Start with a new entry
cmdAdd_Click
```

The `Center` subroutine is used again to center the form.

```
' Center the Diary form
Center Me
```

The *SaveEntry* Subroutine

The `SaveEntry` subroutine is called whenever you leave the current diary entry. The subroutine writes the entry to the database if any change has been made to it.

Enter the `SaveEntry` subroutine as shown in Listing 10.29.

Listing 10.29. The `SaveEntry` subroutine.

```
Sub SaveEntry ()

  Dim strEntry As String
  Dim varDate As Variant
  Dim lngEntryID As Long

  On Error GoTo SaveEntryError

  If Not mblnDirty Then
    GoTo SaveEntryDone
  End If

' Check to see if an entry was made
  strEntry = CNStr(txtEntry)
  If Len(strEntry) = 0 Then
    GoTo SaveEntryDone
  End If

' Validate the date and time

  On Error Resume Next
  varDate = CVDate(txtDate)
  If Err Then
    MsgBox "Please enter a valid date.", 48, PROGRAM
    CorrectEntry txtDate
```

```
      GoTo SaveEntryDone
   End If

   varDate = CVDate(txtTime)
   If Err Then
     MsgBox "Please enter a valid time.", 48, PROGRAM
     CorrectEntry txtTime
     GoTo SaveEntryDone
   End If

   On Error GoTo SaveEntryError

' Get the Date and Time together
   varDate = CVDate(txtDate.Text & " " & txtTime.Text)

' Save the entry
   If mblnAddEntry Then
     gdynEntry.AddNew
   Else
     gdynEntry.Edit
   End If

   gdynEntry!UserID = glngUserID
   gdynEntry!Date = varDate
   gdynEntry!Entry = Code(strEntry, gstrPassword)

' Read the counter value
   lngEntryID = gdynEntry!EntryID

   gdynEntry.Update

' Make the added entry the current record
   gdynEntry.FindFirst "EntryID = " & lngEntryID

SaveEntryDone:
   mblnAddEntry = False
   mblnDirty = False

   Exit Sub

SaveEntryError:
   MsgBox Error$, 48, PROGRAM
   Resume SaveEntryDone

End Sub
```

The SaveEntry subroutine checks the status of the mblnDirty flag to check whether the user has modified the entry in any way.

```
   If Not mblnDirty Then
     GoTo SaveEntryDone
   End If
```

Next, the code checks whether the Entry text box contains anything. For example, the user might start an entry but then erase it. When you close the Diary form, the empty entry should not be saved.

```
' Check to see if an entry was made
  strEntry = CNStr(txtEntry)
  If Len(strEntry) = 0 Then
    GoTo SaveEntryDone
  End If
```

Next, the Date and Time fields are checked to make sure they contain valid date and time expressions, as shown in Listing 10.30.

The verification is done by turning error handling off and calling the CVDate function to change the entry text to a date time value in a variant variable. The Err system variable receives a value if the call to CVDate didn't work, which means the text was a bad date or time expression.

Listing 10.30. Validating the date and time using CVDate and the Err system variable.

```
' Validate the date and time

  On Error Resume Next
  varDate = CVDate(txtDate)
  If Err Then
    MsgBox "Please enter a valid date.", 48, PROGRAM
    CorrectEntry txtDate
    GoTo SaveEntryDone
  End If

  varDate = CVDate(txtTime)
  If Err Then
    MsgBox "Please enter a valid time.", 48, PROGRAM
    CorrectEntry txtTime
    GoTo SaveEntryDone
  End If
```

With the date and time validated, error checking is turned back on. The date and time values are combined in a single variable. A date value is always an integer value.

The time value is stored as a fractional number that is the result of dividing the number 1 across the day. For example, 0.5 would be equal to 12 noon, and 0.75 would be equivalent to 6 PM.

```
  On Error GoTo SaveEntryError

' Get the Date and Time together
  varDate = CVDate(txtDate.Text & " " & txtTime.Text)
```

The mblnAddEntry flag indicates whether this is a brand-new diary entry or an existing entry is being modified.

```
' Save the entry
 If mblnAddEntry Then
   gdynEntry.AddNew
 Else
   gdynEntry.Edit
 End If
```

Finally, values are written to the fields in the record. First, the UserID field receives a value to link this record to the current user. Next, the Date field receives the date and time value. The Entry field receives the coded version of the diary entry.

```
 gdynEntry!UserID = glngUserID
 gdynEntry!Date = varDate
 gdynEntry!Entry = Code(strEntry, gstrPassword)
```

Before writing the record, you read the value assigned automatically to the EntryID counter field. You need this to locate the new record, because it won't be set as the current record automatically.

```
' Read the counter value
 lngEntryID = gdynEntry!EntryID

 gdynEntry.Update
```

After the record is written, a FindFirst call is made to locate the newly entered record.

```
' Make the added entry the current record
 gdynEntry.FindFirst "EntryID = " & lngEntryID
```

The *ShowEntry* Subroutine

The ShowEntry subroutine reads the current record from the gdynEntry dynaset and displays it as the current diary entry.

Enter the ShowEntry subroutine as shown in Listing 10.31.

Listing 10.31. The ShowEntry subroutine.

```
Sub ShowEntry ()

  On Error GoTo ShowEntryError

  txtDate = Format$(gdynEntry!Date, "Short Date")
  txtTime = Format$(gdynEntry!Date, "Medium Time")
  txtEntry = Decode(gdynEntry!Entry, gstrPassword)

  cmdScramble.Enabled = (txtEntry.Text <> "")
  cmdErase.Enabled = cmdScramble.Enabled
  mblnAddEntry = False

ShowEntryDone:
  Exit Sub
```

continues

Listing 10.31. continued

```
ShowEntryError:
  MsgBox Error$, 48, PROGRAM
  Resume ShowEntryDone

End Sub
```

The *cmdJump_Click* Subroutine

The cmdJump_Click subroutine opens the Jump form to prompt for the date of the diary entry to display. The subroutine then locates an entry in the diary on or around that date and displays it.

Enter the cmdJump_Click subroutine in Listing 10.32.

Listing 10.32. The cmdJump_Click subroutine.

```
Sub cmdJump_Click ()

  Dim lngEntryID As Long

  On Error GoTo cmdJump_ClickError

  If gdynEntry.RecordCount = 0 Then
    MsgBox "There are no entries in the diary.", 64, PROGRAM
    GoTo cmdJump_ClickDone
  End If

  Jump.Show 1

  If gvarJumpTo <> 0 Then
    SaveEntry

  ' Save the current Entry ID to see if we move anywhere
    lngEntryID = 0
    If (Not gdynEntry.BOF) And (Not gdynEntry.EOF) Then
      lngEntryID = gdynEntry!EntryID
    End If

    gdynEntry.FindLast "Date < #" & gvarJumpTo + 1 & "#"

    If gdynEntry.NoMatch Then
      gdynEntry.MoveFirst
    End If

  ' Update the form if we actually moved
    If lngEntryID <> gdynEntry!EntryID Then
      ShowEntry
    End If
  End If
```

```
cmdJump_ClickDone:
  Exit Sub

cmdJump_ClickError:
  MsgBox Error$, 48, PROGRAM
  Resume cmdJump_ClickDone

End Sub
```

The *cmdScramble_Click* Subroutine

The cmdScramble_Click subroutine takes care of the two jobs the **S**cramble button has.

First, the button scrambles the diary entry so you can't read it on-screen. Second, the button can be used to unscramble a previously scrambled entry.

Enter the cmdScramble_Click subroutine as shown in Listing 10.33.

Listing 10.33. The cmdScramble_Click **subroutine.**

```
Sub cmdScramble_Click ()

  On Error GoTo cmdScramble_ClickError

  If mblnScrambled Then
    Password.Show 1
    If gstrPassword = gstrUnscramblePassword Then
      gintStrike = 0

      txtEntry = Decode(txtEntry, gstrPassword)
      mblnScrambled = False

      cmdScramble.Caption = "&Scramble"
      txtEntry.SetFocus
    ElseIf Len(gstrUnscramblePassword) > 0 Then
      CountStrikes

      If gintStrike = 3 Then
        Unload Me
        GoTo cmdScramble_ClickDone
      End If
    End If
  Else
    SaveEntry

    txtEntry = Code(txtEntry, gstrPassword)
    mblnScrambled = True

    cmdScramble.Caption = "Un-&scramble"
  End If
```

continues

Listing 10.33. continued

```
cmdJump.Enabled = Not mblnScrambled
cmdAdd.Enabled = Not mblnScrambled
cmdErase.Enabled = Not mblnScrambled
cmdMove(0).Enabled = Not mblnScrambled
cmdMove(1).Enabled = Not mblnScrambled
cmdMove(2).Enabled = Not mblnScrambled
cmdMove(3).Enabled = Not mblnScrambled

cmdScramble_ClickDone:
  Exit Sub

cmdScramble_ClickError:
  MsgBox Error$, 48, PROGRAM
  Resume cmdScramble_ClickDone

End Sub
```

The first part of the subroutine handles a diary entry that has already been scrambled. The Password form is shown as a modal pop-up to retrieve the user's password.

```
If mblnScrambled Then
  Password.Show 1
```

If the password checks out, the entry is decoded.

```
If gstrPassword = gstrUnscramblePassword Then
  gintStrike = 0

  txtEntry = Decode(txtEntry, gstrPassword)
  mblnScrambled = False
```

Also, the Un-scramble button is changed to a **S**cramble button.

```
  cmdScramble.Caption = "&Scramble"
  txtEntry.SetFocus
```

If a password was entered and is invalid, the `CountStrikes` subroutine is called again to display the message.

```
ElseIf Len(gstrUnscramblePassword) > 0 Then
  CountStrikes
```

If three consecutive invalid passwords were entered, the Diary form is closed, terminating the program.

```
  If gintStrike = 3 Then
    Unload Me
    GoTo cmdScramble_ClickDone
  End If
End If
```

Next, you get to the code that handles encrypting the current entry. First, the `SaveEntry` subroutine is called to write the entry if it has been changed.

```
Else
   SaveEntry
```

Then the text in the Entry text box is encoded. The `mblnScrambled` flag is set to True because the program is now in that mode.

```
txtEntry = Code(txtEntry, gstrPassword)
mblnScrambled = True
```

Also, the **S**cramble button is changed to an Un-**s**cramble button.

```
cmdScramble.Caption = "Un-&scramble"
End If
```

At the end of the subroutine, all of the buttons except the **S**cramble and **C**lose buttons are disabled or enabled, depending on whether the entry is scrambled.

```
cmdJump.Enabled = Not mblnScrambled
cmdAdd.Enabled = Not mblnScrambled
cmdErase.Enabled = Not mblnScrambled
cmdMove(0).Enabled = Not mblnScrambled
cmdMove(1).Enabled = Not mblnScrambled
cmdMove(2).Enabled = Not mblnScrambled
cmdMove(3).Enabled = Not mblnScrambled
```

The *cmdAdd_Click* Subroutine

The `cmdAdd_Click` subroutine saves the current entry and begins a new one.

Enter the `cmdAdd_Click` subroutine as shown in Listing 10.34.

Listing 10.34. The `cmdAdd_Click` **subroutine.**

```
Sub cmdAdd_Click ()

   On Error GoTo cmdAdd_ClickError

   If Not mblnEraseNewEntry Then SaveEntry

   mblnAddEntry = True

   txtDate = Format$(Now, "Short Date")
   txtTime = Format$(Now, "Medium Time")
   txtEntry = ""

' Position the current record one past the last record
   If gdynEntry.RecordCount Then
      gdynEntry.MoveLast
      gdynEntry.MoveNext
   End If
```

continues

Listing 10.34. continued

```
On Error Resume Next
txtEntry.SetFocus

  cmdScramble.Enabled = False
  cmdErase.Enabled = False

cmdAdd_ClickDone:
  Exit Sub

cmdAdd_ClickError:
  MsgBox Error$, 48, PROGRAM
  Resume cmdAdd_ClickDone

End Sub
```

The `cmdAdd_Click` subroutine first calls the `SaveEntry` subroutine in case the present diary entry needs to be saved.

If the `mblnEraseNewEntry` flag is set, then the `cmdAdd_Click` subroutine is called as a result of the E**r**ase button being clicked, so in this case the `SaveEntry` subroutine is not called.

```
If Not mblnEraseNewEntry Then SaveEntry
```

The `mblnAddEntry` flag is set to True to indicate that this entry is new.

```
mblnAddEntry = True
```

The Date and Time fields are initialized with the current date and time. The Entry field is initially empty.

```
txtDate = Format$(Now, "Short Date")
txtTime = Format$(Now, "Medium Time")
txtEntry = ""
```

The current record in the Entry dynaset is set to one past the last entry.

```
' Position the current record one past the last record
  If gdynEntry.RecordCount Then
    gdynEntry.MoveLast
    gdynEntry.MoveNext
  End If
```

Next, the Entry text box receives focus so the user can start typing. The **S**cramble button is disabled because there isn't an entry to scramble yet. Likewise, the cmdErase button is disabled because there isn't an entry to erase.

```
On Error Resume Next
txtEntry.SetFocus

  cmdScramble.Enabled = False
  cmdErase.Enabled = False
```

The *cmdErase_Click* Subroutine

The cmdErase_Click subroutine erases a diary entry by deleting the associated Entry table record.

Enter the cmdErase_Click subroutine in Listing 10.35.

Listing 10.35. The cmdErase_Click subroutine.

```
Sub cmdErase_Click ()

  Dim z As Integer

  On Error GoTo cmdErase_ClickError

  z = MsgBox("Erase this diary entry?", 4 + 32 + 256, PROGRAM)
  If z Then

    If mblnAddEntry Then
    ' Abort the current entry and start a new one
      mblnEraseNewEntry = True
      cmdAdd_Click
      mblnEraseNewEntry = False
    Else
    ' Delete the current record
      If gdynEntry.RecordCount > 0 Then
        gdynEntry.Delete
      End If

      If gdynEntry.RecordCount = 0 Then
        cmdAdd_Click
      Else
      ' Try moving forward
        gdynEntry.MoveNext
        If gdynEntry.EOF Then
        ' At the end, try moving backward
          gdynEntry.MovePrevious
        End If

        If Not gdynEntry.BOF Then
        ' Found an entry, show it
          ShowEntry
        Else
        ' Deleted the last entry, start a new one
          cmdAdd_Click
        End If
      End If
    End If

  End If

cmdErase_ClickDone:
  Exit Sub
```

continues

Listing 10.35. continued

```
cmdErase_ClickError:
  MsgBox Error$, 48, PROGRAM
  Resume cmdErase_ClickDone

End Sub
```

Actually, there are few more details to erasing a diary entry than just deleting a record.

First, you need to make sure this is really what the user wants to do. Any time pressing a button can be this destructive, it's a good idea to make sure the user clicked it intentionally. (Especially because you haven't provided an Undo capability.)

```
z = MsgBox("Erase this diary entry?", 4 + 32 + 256, PROGRAM)
If z Then
```

If the user is working on an entry that hasn't been saved yet, things are easy. Just clear the entry by starting a new one.

The mblnEraseNewEntry flag is set to indicate to the cmdAdd_Click subroutine that there is no entry to be saved before initializing the form to start a new entry.

```
If mblnAddEntry Then
' Abort the current entry and start a new one
  mblnEraseNewEntry = True
  cmdAdd_Click
  mblnEraseNewEntry = False
```

If the current entry does exist in the database, it is deleted.

```
Else
' Delete the current record
  If gdynEntry.RecordCount > 0 Then
    gdynEntry.Delete
  End If
```

Then you need to determine which record to display as the current record. If there are no records, it's easy—just start a new entry.

```
If gdynEntry.RecordCount = 0 Then
  cmdAdd_Click
```

If there are records, I decided to display the record following the deleted record.

This way, for example, if you had a bad week with your girlfriend, you could start with the entry on Monday and delete each entry in the week consecutively up until Saturday night when she ditched you. She will probably be doing the same in her diary program.

```
Else
' Try moving forward
  gdynEntry.MoveNext
```

If there aren't any records after the deleted one, display the record before the deleted record instead.

```
If gdynEntry.EOF Then
' At the end, try moving backward
   gdynEntry.MovePrevious
End If
```

Finally, if a diary entry is found, it is displayed.

```
If Not gdynEntry.BOF Then
' Found an entry, show it
   ShowEntry
```

Otherwise a new diary entry is started. (I don't think you should ever get to this case, because you checked for this condition earlier.)

```
Else
' Deleted the last entry, start a new one
   cmdAdd_Click
End If
```

The *cmdClose_Click* Subroutine

I don't know about you, but I'm ready for a subroutine like this next one. The cmdClose_Click subroutine ends the program by closing the Diary form.

Enter the cmdClose_Click subroutine as shown in Listing 10.36.

Listing 10.36. The cmdClose_Click **subroutine.**

```
Sub cmdClose_Click ()

  Unload Me

End Sub
```

The *cmdMove_Click* Subroutine

That was a short break. Now back to one of the monstrosities.

The cmdMove_Click subroutine is the On Click event code for the four movement buttons: <<, **B**ack, **N**ext, and >>. An Index value is passed to the subroutine to identify which button the subroutine is being called for, with values of 0 to 3 respectively.

Enter the cmdMove_Click subroutine as shown in Listing 10.37.

Listing 10.37. The cmdMove_Click subroutine.

```
Sub cmdMove_Click (Index As Integer)

  Dim varDate As Variant
  Dim lngEntryID As Long

  On Error GoTo cmdMove_ClickError

  SaveEntry

  If gdynEntry.RecordCount = 0 Then
    cmdAdd_Click
    GoTo cmdMove_ClickDone
  End If

' Save the current Entry ID to see if we move anywhere
  lngEntryID = 0
  If (Not gdynEntry.BOF) And (Not gdynEntry.EOF) Then
    lngEntryID = gdynEntry!EntryID
  End If

  Select Case Index

  Case 0 ' Back one week
  ' Get the date value for the beginning of the current day
    If lngEntryID = 0 Then
      varDate = CVDate(Format$(Now, "Short Date"))
    Else
      varDate = CVDate(Format$(gdynEntry!Date, "Short Date"))
    End If

  ' Go back to the beginning of the day 6 days ago
    varDate = varDate - 6

  ' Search for any days before that
    gdynEntry.FindPrevious "Date < #" & varDate & "#"

  ' If not found, go to the first entry
    If gdynEntry.NoMatch Then
      gdynEntry.MoveFirst
    End If

  Case 1 ' Back one entry
    If gdynEntry.BOF Then
      gdynEntry.MoveNext
    Else
      gdynEntry.MovePrevious

      If gdynEntry.BOF Then
        gdynEntry.MoveNext
      End If
    End If

  Case 2 ' Forward one entry
    If gdynEntry.EOF Then
      gdynEntry.MovePrevious
    Else
      gdynEntry.MoveNext
```

```
      If gdynEntry.EOF Then
        gdynEntry.MovePrevious
      End If
    End If

  Case 3 ' Forward one week
  ' Get the date value for the beginning of the current day
    If lngEntryID = 0 Then
      varDate = CVDate(Format$(Now, "Short Date"))
    Else
      varDate = CVDate(Format$(gdynEntry!Date, "Short Date"))
    End If

  ' Go forward to the beginning of the day 7 days ahead
    varDate = varDate + 7

  ' Search for any days on or after that
    gdynEntry.FindNext "Date >= #" & varDate & "#"

  ' If not found, go to the last entry
    If gdynEntry.NoMatch Then
      gdynEntry.MoveLast
    End If

  End Select

' Update the form if we actually moved
  If lngEntryID <> gdynEntry!EntryID Then
    ShowEntry
  End If

cmdMove_ClickDone:
  Exit Sub

cmdMove_ClickError:
  MsgBox Error$, 48, PROGRAM
  Resume cmdMove_ClickDone

End Sub
```

Because you are leaving the current entry, you call the SaveEntry subroutine in case it needs to be saved.

```
    SaveEntry
```

Next, you might have to handle the special case when the diary still has no entries. If so, the cmdAdd_Click subroutine is called to reinitialize the form for entering the first diary entry and the subroutine exits early.

```
  If gdynEntry.RecordCount = 0 Then
    cmdAdd_Click
    GoTo cmdMove_ClickDone
  End If
```

OK, you're still here. You save the EntryID number in a variable. You can use this later to see if you moved anywhere and need to refresh the display.

```
' Save the current Entry ID to see if we move anywhere
  lngEntryID = 0
  If (Not gdynEntry.BOF) And (Not gdynEntry.EOF) Then
    lngEntryID = gdynEntry!EntryID
  End If
```

Now you select one of four code blocks to execute, depending on which button was pressed.

```
Select Case Index
```

If the << button is pressed, the code attempts to find an entry seven days before the current entry date. When moving from entry to entry by week like this, you want to take into account the number of days without concern for the actual time of day an entry is.

First, you get the date time value of the current entry without a fractional time part, as shown in Listing 10.38.

Listing 10.38. Getting the date value while ignoring the time value.

```
Case 0 ' Back one week
' Get the date value for the beginning of the current day
  If lngEntryID = 0 Then
    varDate = CVDate(Format$(Now, "Short Date"))
  Else
    varDate = CVDate(Format$(gdynEntry!Date, "Short Date"))
  End If
```

The date value is at midnight. You subtract six days from that. If you select the first entry before the resulting date and time, you will find any entries that fall within the day seven days from the date of your current entry.

```
' Go back to the beginning of the day 6 days ago
  varDate = varDate - 6

' Search for any days before that
  gdynEntry.FindPrevious "Date < #" & varDate & "#"
```

If there aren't any entries on this day, you find the latest entry before it. If there aren't any entries on or before this day, the program jumps to the first entry in the diary, because that is the closest entry to where you were headed.

```
' If not found, go to the first entry
  If gdynEntry.NoMatch Then
    gdynEntry.MoveFirst
  End If
```

Case 1 takes care of the **B**ack button, as shown in Listing 10.39. The code moves back one entry if there is an entry to move back to.

Listing 10.39. Moving back one entry.

```
Case 1 ' Back one entry
  If gdynEntry.BOF Then
    gdynEntry.MoveNext
  Else
    gdynEntry.MovePrevious

    If gdynEntry.BOF Then
      gdynEntry.MoveNext
    End If
  End If
```

The Case 2 block handles moving forward one entry, as shown in Listing 10.40.

Listing 10.40. Moving forward one entry.

```
Case 2 ' Forward one entry
  If gdynEntry.EOF Then
    gdynEntry.MovePrevious
  Else
    gdynEntry.MoveNext

    If gdynEntry.EOF Then
      gdynEntry.MovePrevious
    End If
  End If
```

The final case block works similarly to the Case 0 block, because again you are attempting to move a week of entries at a time. Case 3 is shown in Listing 10.41.

Listing 10.41. Moving forward one week.

```
Case 3 ' Forward one week
' Get the date value for the beginning of the current day
  If lngEntryID = 0 Then
    varDate = CVDate(Format$(Now, "Short Date"))
  Else
    varDate = CVDate(Format$(gdynEntry!Date, "Short Date"))
  End If

' Go forward to the beginning of the day 7 days ahead
  varDate = varDate + 7
```

continues

Listing 10.41. continued

```
' Search for any days on or after that
  gdynEntry.FindNext "Date >= #" & varDate & "#"

' If not found, go to the last entry
  If gdynEntry.NoMatch Then
    gdynEntry.MoveLast
  End If

End Select
```

At the end of the subroutine, the ShowEntry subroutine is called to display the entry to which you moved.

```
' Update the form if we actually moved
  If lngEntryID <> gdynEntry!EntryID Then
    ShowEntry
  End If
```

The Text Box KeyPress Event Code

The next three subroutines are activated each time a key is pressed in the Date, Time, or Entry text boxes.

The subroutines serve two purposes. First, if the displayed entry is scrambled, they prohibit any changes to the contents of the text boxes.

Second, when the user is allowed to edit the fields, the subroutines set the mblnDirty flag to indicate that a change has been made. An exception is made for the Ctrl-C key combination, so that you can select text with the mouse and press Ctrl-C to copy it without marking the entry as dirty.

Enter the txtDate_KeyPress, txtTime_KeyPress, and txtEntry_KeyPress subroutines as shown in Listings 10.42, 10.43, and 10.44.

Listing 10.42. The txtDate_KeyPress **subroutine.**

```
Sub txtDate_KeyPress (KeyAscii As Integer)

' Don't allow editing a scrambled entry
  If mblnScrambled Then
    KeyAscii = 0

' Ignore Ctrl C for copying
  ElseIf KeyAscii <> 3 Then
      mblnDirty = True
  End If

End Sub
```

Listing 10.43. The txtTime_KeyPress **subroutine.**

```
Sub txtTime KeyPress (KeyAscii As Integer)

' Don't allow editing a scrambled entry
  If mblnScrambled Then
    KeyAscii = 0

' Ignore Ctrl C for copying
  ElseIf KeyAscii <> 3 Then
      mblnDirty = True
  End If

End Sub
```

Listing 10.44. The txtEntry_KeyPress **subroutine.**

```
Sub txtEntry_KeyPress (KeyAscii As Integer)

' Don't allow editing a scrambled entry
  If mblnScrambled Then
    KeyAscii = 0

' Ignore Ctrl C for copying
  ElseIf KeyAscii <> 3 Then
      mblnDirty = True
  End If

End Sub
```

The *txtEntry_KeyUp* Subroutine

This next quick subroutine is used to determine whether the **S**cramble and **E**rase buttons are enabled.

The KeyUp event occurs after a key is pressed. The txtEntry_KeyUp subroutine disables the two buttons if there isn't any text to scramble or erase.

Enter the txtDate_KeyUp subroutine in Listing 10.45.

Listing 10.45. The txtDate_KeyUp **subroutine.**

```
Sub txtEntry_KeyUp (KeyCode As Integer, Shift As Integer)

  cmdScramble.Enabled = (txtEntry.Text <> "")
  cmdErase.Enabled = cmdScramble.Enabled

End Sub
```

The *Form_Unload* Subroutine

The last subroutine in the Diary form module is the Form_Unload subroutine, which is activated as the form is closed.

The subroutine calls SaveEntry in case there is an entry to be saved, then it closes the Entry table and the database.

1. Enter the Form_Unload subroutine as shown in Listing 10.46.
2. Close the Diary form module and save your work.

Listing 10.46. The Form_Unload **subroutine.**

```
Sub Form_Unload (Cancel As Integer)

  On Error Resume Next

  SaveEntry

' Close the Entry table
  gdynEntry.Close

' Close the database
  gdb.Close

End Sub
```

Time to get up and stretch. When you come back you won't have far to go.

Coding the Jump Form

There isn't much code required to make the Jump form work.

1. Open the Module window for the Jump form and enter the Form_Load subroutine as shown in Listing 10.47.
2. Enter the cmdOK_Click subroutine shown in Listing 10.48.
3. Enter the cmdCancel_Click subroutine as shown in Listing 10.49.
4. Close the Jump form module.

In the Form_Load subroutine you initialize the gvarJumpTo global variable to zero, indicating that a date has not been selected yet.

Listing 10.47. The Jump form's `Form_Load` **subroutine.**

```
Sub Form_Load ()

  gvarJumpTo = 0
  Center Me

End Sub
```

In the code behind the OK button, the entered date is verified by calling CVDate and checking the Err system variable for an error value.

If the entry is OK, it is assigned to gvarJumpTo and the form is closed.

Listing 10.48. The Jump form's `cmdOK_Click` **subroutine.**

```
Sub cmdOK_Click ()

  On Error Resume Next

  If Required(txtDate, "Date") Then GoTo cmdOK_ClickDone

  gvarJumpTo = CVDate(txtDate.Text)

  If Err = 0 Then
    Unload Me
  Else
    MsgBox txtDate.Text & " is not a valid date.", 48, PROGRAM
  End If

cmdOK_ClickDone:

End Sub
```

The cmdCancel_Click subroutine is used to close the form when the user presses Cancel without entering a date.

Listing 10.49. The `cmdCancel_Click` **subroutine.**

```
Sub cmdCancel_Click ()

  Unload Me

End Sub
```

Close the Jump form module.

Coding the Password Form

The code behind the Password form is also minimal. If the OK button is pressed, the global, gstrUnscramblePassword, receives the text entered in the Password text box.

1. Open the Module window for the Password form and enter the subroutines in Listings 10.50, 10.51, and 10.52.
2. Close the Password form module.

Listing 10.50. The Password form's Form_Load **subroutine.**

```
Sub Form_Load ()

  gstrUnscramblePassword = ""
  Center Me

End Sub
```

Listing 10.51. The Password form's cmdOK_Click **subroutine.**

```
Sub cmdOK_Click ()

  gstrUnscramblePassword = txtPassword
  Unload Me

End Sub
```

Listing 10.52. The Password form's cmdCancel_Click **subroutine.**

```
Sub cmdCancel_Click ()

  Unload Me

End Sub
```

TRY THIS! QUESTION 10.1.

A text-editing program isn't complete without some kind of keystroke recording and playback capability. A keystroke recorder will remember what you type, then retype the same entry at the press of a single key.

Fortunately, the Windows Recorder utility can be used to provide this functionality for programs that don't support this on their own (like Notepad). However, for the sake of convenience (and because it is a fun programming problem), let's create our own.

See if you can enhance the Secret Diary program so that you can use the following special key combinations to start a recording while editing a diary entry, then play it back.

Ctrl-R   Start recording keystrokes

Ctrl-S   Stop recording in progress

Ctrl-P   Play recorded keystrokes

Compiling the Program

With Visual Basic you can make an executable file out of the program that you can install as a program item in Program Manager.

1. Select the File|Make EXE File command.

   Visual Basic displays the Make EXE File dialog box, as shown in Figure 10.40.

2. Enter Secret Diary in the Application Title text box.

3. Select the Diary form in the Use Icon From combo box.

4. Make sure DIARY.EXE is the filename selected, and that it is in the same directory as DIARY.MDB.

5. Click OK.

FIGURE 10.40.

Creating the DIARY.EXE executable file.

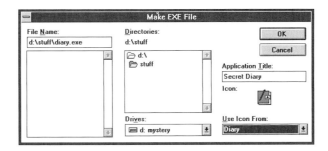

Visual Basic will hum for a little while and then you have a .EXE file.

The .EXE file created isn't exactly like a .EXE file that is created with a C compiler. The Visual Basic executable relies heavily on the VBRUN300.DLL file in the WINDOWS\SYSTEM directory.

In addition, because you have used database features, three additional .DLL files are used: MSAJT200.DLL, MSAJT112.DLL, and VBDB300.DLL. These are provided as part of the Compatibility Layer provided by Microsoft to allow Visual Basic 3.0 to work with Access 2.0. These files are also found in your WINDOWS\SYSTEM directory.

If you want to copy the Diary program to another computer after compiling it, you need to make sure the destination computer has all the files listed here.

Copy these two files you created in the same directory:

>   DIARY.EXE
>   DIARY.MDB

Copy these four files in the WINDOWS\SYSTEM directory if they aren't there already:

>   MSAJT200.DLL
>   MSAJT112.DLL
>   VBDB300.DLL
>   VBRUN300.DLL

The best way to distribute run-time .DLL files is with a full-blown setup program. Fortunately, Visual Basic includes a Setup Wizard that can be used to create distribution disks for your programs.

Creating a Secret Diary Program Item

You can create an icon in Program Manager to run the Secret Diary program.

1. Select the **File|New** command in Program Manager.
2. Select Program **I**tem in the New Program Object dialog box and click OK.
3. In the Program Item Properties dialog box, enter the following:

    Description: Secret Diary
    Command Line: D:\STUFF\DIARY.EXE
    Working Directory: D:\STUFF

    Rather than D:\STUFF, use the directory that you have DIARY.EXE and DIARY.MDB in. (Remember, DIARY.MDB must be in the same directory as DIARY.EXE.)

4. Click OK.

Diary Report

It would be nice to be able to make a printed copy of your diary entries. However, if you return to Access and open the Entry table, you find that the entries are totally un-readable, as shown in Figure 10.41.

FIGURE 10.41.

Diary entries in the Entry table are encrypted.

EntryID	UserID	Date	Entry
1	1	1/15/95 7:08:00 PM	cmx6 "):u|^C %-B]' %-J810 >5,?G -P6 CI7D:O> 9 UBK^G Be^ S^ XMb 'UpWa|. F\kn Y|b pzg t^orp|7mz||nq ~o&<{)? }#F\]'% 1% 9 1'0?1@E 43E815P='
2	1	1/12/95 2:38:00 AM	_|k;up ;& ~+.y 4'|%E"`,= 6,C= ,G/<E·B@?MH3Av ·+cP? ZQNE / L\['K_ZV vZS hkY'g qeijvc^ #wr 'l m08 ·g5n ,s\$u ,# 8++} I\[" 19 <1%8U -8TB53W 27K9IIQ·G@·A N\!SGTYUQQjS Wic'DoYo
3	1	1/5/95 5:17:00 PM	'mv"'{":yt 73}{\$·0A·2\[; /3I8 <M2+En·iO:@Y^ <A\B·PZG·Ed\KVfXSMlb·'qa Vx_Wbnfo 'gnd#wr·w·ut{mk{5w~'8·') o·%+5}##&\I·0#@\]01J<}^·.}-K\·,=<> @5LQ·LI·C=J`·.#K}·GjP·JeU·Wj·dZmq·^mr] %oic*lip|·mt·y# 5yfsR
4	1	1/20/95 4:26:00 PM	'po·~uq+·&z3{(/~}1F·5}D:'6·39·W=? FA<UZ·:5'?·L\]·=Qf·RH\[·IV\[\]Yt·9^·\[\ ukd·m\[i}: nn{o·t~k·q+)y6

Record: |◀ ◀| 1 | of 4 | ▶ ▶|

You can make a copy of your `Code` and `Decode` functions in an Access module so you can decode the entries when in Access.

Keep in mind that doing this makes it easier for someone to decode your password. With the `PASSWORD_KEY` constant value displayed in the module in the database, someone could run the `Decode` function on your Login table entry and discover your password. (Again, explore Access security features if you really need tight security on your database.)

1. Create a new module in Access.

   You will be saving the module with the name Secret Diary.

2. Enter the declarations section shown in Listing 10.53.

3. Start up Visual Basic if it isn't running already, and open the Diary project.

4. Open the LIBRARY.BAS module in Visual Basic.

5. Copy the following three procedures from Visual Basic into the Access module:

   ```
   CNStr
   Code
   Decode
   ```

6. Close Visual Basic.

7. Verify that the module in Access compiles by selecting the **R**un|Compile Loaded Modules command.

8. Save the module as `Secret Diary`.

Listing 10.53. The declarations section in the Secret Diary module in Access.

```
' Secret Diary module

Option Compare Database
Option Explicit

Global Const PROGRAM = "Secret Diary"
Global Const PASSWORD_KEY = "Babe Ruth"
```

Next, create two queries that will be used to view the decoded contents of the Entry table. Start with the User query.

1. Switch over to the Query tab in Access and open a new query.
2. In the Add Table dialog box, select the Login table.
3. In the query design window, add these fields from left to right: UserID, Password, and Username.
4. Check the Show checkbox for the first two fields and leave it blank for the Username field.
5. In the Criteria row of the Username column, enter [Enter Name].

   Your query should look like that shown in Figure 10.42.

FIGURE 10.42.

Creating the User query.

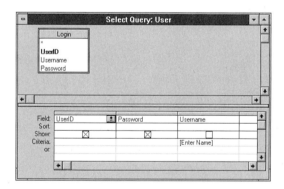

To verify you have the same thing I do, click the SQL button on the toolbar. You should see the following SELECT statement:

```
SELECT DISTINCTROW Login.UserID, Login.Password
FROM Login
WHERE ((Login.Username=[Enter Name]));
```

The query returns the UserID and Password fields from the Login table, where the Username field is equal to the [Enter Name] parameter. When you run this query, a dialog box is displayed asking for the value to use as the [Enter Name] parameter value.

Save the query and create a second query that uses the User query to display the records in the Entry table.

1. Save the query with the name User.
2. Create a second query.
3. In the Add Table dialog box, select the User query and the Entry table.
4. Create a join between the UserID field in the User query and the UserID field in the Entry table.
5. Drop the Date field from the Entry table into the first column.
6. Enter the following expression in the Field row of the second column:

```
Entry: Decode([Entry].[Entry],[Enter Password])
```

On the left side of the colon, the word indicates that this field in the query is called Entry.

On the right side of the colon is a call to the Decode function. The first argument passed is the Entry field from the Entry table. The second argument passed is another parameter like you used before. This parameter asks for a password.

The query should look like that in Figure 10.43.

FIGURE 10.43.

Creating the Decode Diary Entries query.

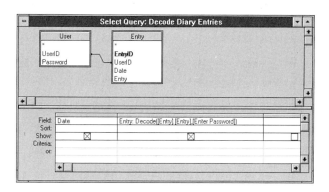

The SQL for this query follows:

```
SELECT DISTINCTROW Entry.Date, Decode([Entry].[Entry],
[Enter Password]) AS Entry
FROM User INNER JOIN Entry ON User.UserID = Entry.UserID;
```

Close the query, saving it as Decode Diary Entries.

If you open the Decode Diary Entries query, you first get prompted to enter your name, as shown in Figure 10.44.

FIGURE 10.44.

Access prompts for your name as a query parameter.

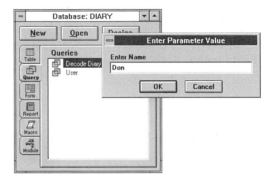

Next, you get prompted for the password, as shown in Figure 10.45. Unfortunately, your password is displayed on the screen as you enter it.

FIGURE 10.45.

The second query parameter is your password.

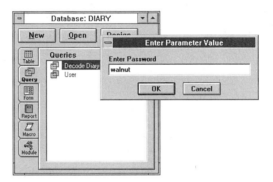

If you entered the password correctly, you see all of your decoded diary entries in datasheet view, as shown in Figure 10.46.

FIGURE 10.46.

The decoded diary entries.

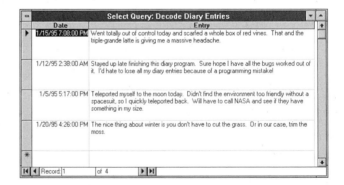

The next step would be to get the help of the Report Wizard and generate a report that you can run off of the Decode Diary Entries query. That's exactly what I did, and the results are shown in Figure 10.47.

FIGURE 10.47.

A report that uses the Decode Diary Entries query.

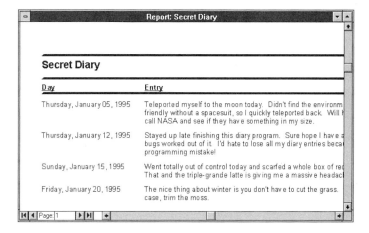

What is really neat is that when you run the report you are prompted for the name and password just as when you ran the query by itself.

Summary

In this chapter, you created a diary program using Visual Basic and Access together.

Here are some of the techniques you covered along the way. You

- Learned some general differences between Access and Visual Basic
- Created the program's tables using Access
- Looked at the environment and project options in Visual Basic
- Discovered that the Icon Works VB sample application is a good way to create icons
- Created the main form and four pop-up dialog boxes for the application
- Created a control array
- Learned a quick way to modify TabIndex settings to control tab order on a VB form
- Created a VB module with some library routines
- Used a simple algorithm to encrypt a string
- Wrote the function to decode the encrypted string

■ Modified the password functions to use encrypted passwords

■ Coded a **J**ump button to locate an entry by date

■ Coded a **S**cramble button to encrypt a diary entry on screen and lock users out of the program

■ Wrote code to add and delete diary entries

■ Wrote code to keep track of whether the diary entry is modified

■ Wrote code for the **<<**, **B**ack, **N**ext, and **>>** buttons to scan entries in the diary

■ Pasted Visual Basic code into an Access module

■ Created parameter queries as a way to enter a name and password and decode the diary entries

Chapter 11, "Excel: Time Killers, Part One," and Chapter 12, "Excel: Time Killers, Part Two," return you to Excel to create a new menu add-in with some simple but fun games.

TRY THIS! ANSWERS

10.1. This problem (adding a keystroke recording capability to the diary) took a fair amount of research and work to solve. Here's the solution I came up with, which includes a few modifications and new procedures to the Diary form module.

1. Add the module variables shown in Listing 10.54 to the Diary form module's declaration section.

2. Add the lines shown in Listing 10.55 to the end of the `txtEntry_KeyPress` subroutine. This just tells the txtEntry text box to ignore the Ctrl-P, Ctrl-R, and Ctrl-S key presses.

3. Add the `txtEntry_KeyDown` subroutine shown in Listing 10.56. This subroutine is activated on each key press. It passes the KeyDown event `KeyCode` and `Shift` arguments to the `Record` subroutine.

4. Add the `Record` subroutine shown in Listing 10.57. This subroutine translates the KeyCode and Shift values into a string that the `Sendkeys` statement can use to reproduce the key presses. The `Record` subroutine is also the procedure that controls when a recording is started, stopped, or played back.

5. Add the `Playback` subroutine shown in Listing 10.58.

Listing 10.54. Module variables for a keystroke recorder.

```
' String to receive recorded keystrokes
Dim mstrTape As String

' Recording in progress
Dim mblnRecording As Integer
```

Listing 10.55. Modification to the `txtEntry_KeyPress` subroutine.

```
' Cancel these key presses so they don't beep
  Select Case KeyAscii
  Case 16, 18, 19 ' Ctrl-P, Ctrl-R, Ctrl-S
    KeyAscii = 0
  End Select
```

Listing 10.56. The `txtEntry_KeyDown` subroutine.

```
Sub txtEntry_KeyDown (KeyCode As Integer, Shift As Integer)

  Record KeyCode, Shift

End Sub
```

Listing 10.57. The `Record` subroutine.

```
Sub Record (KeyCode As Integer, Shift As Integer)

' A keystroke recorder for Visual Basic text boxes.

' Translates the KeyCode and Shift information into a SendKeys
' playable string.

' Doesn't handle the function keys or the numeric keypad
' (but could be enhanced to do so.)

' Also doesn't do anything with the Tab key.

  Dim strKey As String
  Dim n As Integer

  Dim blnShift As Integer
  Dim blnCtrl As Integer
  Dim blnAlt As Integer

  On Error GoTo RecordError

' Are any special keys pressed?
  blnShift = ((Shift And 1) > 0)
  blnCtrl = ((Shift And 2) > 0)
  blnAlt = ((Shift And 4) > 0)

' Intercept Ctrl commands for the recorder
  If blnCtrl Then
    Select Case KeyCode

    Case 80 ' Ctrl P
      Playback
      GoTo RecordDone
```

continues

Listing 10.57. continued

```
    Case 82 ' Ctrl R
      mblnRecording = True
      mstrTape = ""
      GoTo RecordDone

    Case 83 ' Ctrl S
      mblnRecording = False
      GoTo RecordDone

    End Select
  End If

  If Not mblnRecording Then GoTo RecordDone

' Letters
  If KeyCode > 64 And KeyCode < 97 Then
    If blnShift Then
      strKey = Chr$(KeyCode)
      blnShift = False
    Else
      strKey = Chr$(KeyCode + 32)
    End If

' Numbers
  ElseIf KeyCode > 47 And KeyCode < 58 Then
    If blnShift Then
      strKey = Mid$(")!@#$%^&*(", KeyCode - 47, 1)
    Else
      strKey = Chr$(KeyCode)
    End If

  Else

  ' Other keys
    Select Case KeyCode

    Case 192 ' Apostrophe
      strKey = "`"

    Case 189 ' Minus Sign
      strKey = "-"

    Case 187 ' Equal Sign
      strKey = "="

    Case 219 ' Left Bracket
      strKey = "["

    Case 221 ' Right Bracket
      strKey = "]"

    Case 220 ' Backslash
      strKey = "\"

    Case 186 ' Semi-colon
      strKey = ";"

    Case 222 ' Single Quote
      strKey = "'"
```

```
      Case 188 ' Comma
        strKey = ","

      Case 190 ' Period
        strKey = "."

      Case 191 ' Forward Slash
        strKey = "/"

      Case 8 ' Backspace
        strKey = "{BS}"

      Case 46 ' Delete
        strKey = "{DEL}"

      Case 40 ' Down Arrow
        strKey = "{DOWN}"

      Case 35 ' End
        strKey = "{END}"

      Case 13 ' Enter
        strKey = "{ENTER}"

      Case 27 ' Escape
        strKey = "{ESC}"

      Case 36 ' Home
        strKey = "{HOME}"

      Case 45 ' Insert
        strKey = "{INSERT}"

      Case 37 ' Left Arrow
        strKey = "{LEFT}"

      Case 34 ' Page Down
        strKey = "{PGDN}"

      Case 33 ' Page Up
        strKey = "{PGUP}"

      Case 39 ' Right Arrow
        strKey = "{RIGHT}"

      Case 38 ' Up
        strKey = "{UP}"

    End Select

  ' Get Shift key version of some keys
    If blnShift Then
      If Len(strKey) = 1 Then
        n = InStr(1, "`-=[]\;',./", strKey)
        If n > 0 Then
          strKey = Mid$("~_+{}¦:" & Chr$(34) & "<>?", n, 1)
        End If
      End If
    End If

  End If
```

continues

Listing 10.57. continued

```
' Surround special characters with braces
  Select Case strKey
  Case "+", "^", "%", "~", "(", ")", "[", "]", "{", "}"
    strKey = "{" & strKey & "}"
  End Select

' Indicate if Shift, Ctrl or Alt was pressed
  If Len(strKey) > 0 Then
    If blnShift Then
      strKey = "+" & strKey
    End If
    If blnCtrl Then
      strKey = "^" & strKey
    End If
    If blnAlt > 0 Then
      strKey = "%" & strKey
    End If
  End If

' Add the key to the recording
  If Len(strKey) > 0 Then
    mstrTape = mstrTape & strKey
  End If

RecordDone:
  Exit Sub

RecordError:
  MsgBox Error$, 48, PROGRAM
  Resume RecordDone

End Sub
```

Listing 10.58. The Playback subroutine.

```
Sub Playback ()

  Dim cr As String
  Dim msg As String

  If mblnRecording Then
    cr = Chr$(13)
    msg = "Can't playback while recording." & cr & cr
    msg = msg & "Press Ctrl-S to stop recording keystrokes."
    MsgBox msg, 48, PROGRAM
  Else
    SendKeys mstrTape
  End If

End Sub
```

Excel: Time Killers, Part One

There is probably no better way to get in some real programming practice than to write a game.

Unless you are a professional game designer or author, you generally write games for the sheer fun of it. There are no anxious users with high expectations and unrealistic deadlines other than yourself.

You might find, however, that your desire for an ultra cool and fun game of your own creation can drive you to reach new programming heights that you wouldn't have achieved otherwise. In writing games, you certainly learn more about the strengths and limitations of the programming environment you are using.

If you have any reservations about game programming, I would suggest tossing them right now. By shying away from it, you not only miss the experience you gain from game programming, but you miss out on a lot of interesting technical challenges.

In the next two chapters you are going to discover that Excel is a fairly decent environment in which to program games. No, you won't be creating arcade shoot 'em ups, but you will create four interesting games.

First, you create a number-guessing game with an unexpected twist. Next, two memory games that are truly challenging. Finally, a slot machine game to which you can safely lose all your imaginary dollars. You also create a fortune cookie program, which isn't really a game but is fun because you can enter your own collection of fortunes.

The main reason for using Excel to develop the games is so that the games can be played while you are using Excel. Thanks to Excel's capability to create and install add-in extensions, you can make your games available for five-minute breaks away from your number-crunching sessions.

Let's write those games!

Components of the GAMES Workbook

The final workbook you create in this and the following chapter consists of three worksheets, six module sheets, and four dialog boxes, for a total of 13 sheets in all:

>   Options worksheet
>   Globals module

>   Number Guess dialog box
>   Number Guess module

Flash Digits dialog box
Flash Digits module

Dupe the Dupes dialog box
Dupe the Dupes module
Dupe Words worksheet

Slot Machine dialog box
Slot Machine module

Fortune Cookie module
Fortune Cookie worksheet

The regular worksheets contain game data and option settings. The dialog boxes contain the screens that the player sees. Each game has its own dialog box that pops up above the current worksheet that the player has loaded in Excel. The module sheets contain the code for each game, with some code shared in a global module.

The workbook is saved as GAMES.XLS while it is under development, but you will eventually save it in a compiled form as GAMES.XLA. The workbook has its own toolbar and menu that get installed automatically as the user adds the add-in with the **T**ools|**A**dd-**I**n command.

Creating the Workbook

This is going to be a big project. The first thing you should do is save an empty workbook as GAMES.XLS. As you do the work you can save every once in a while to minimize any work loss due to a power failure or other mishap.

1. Launch Excel from Program Manager.
2. Select **F**ile|**S**ave **A**s to save the new, empty workbook.
3. Select a directory to save the workbook in and enter GAMES.XLS as the name of the workbook. Press OK.

    Excel displays the Summary Info dialog box. The text entered here is displayed in the Add-ins dialog box when a user installs the final add-in.
4. Enter Time Killers in the **T**itle text box.
5. Enter the following into the **C**omments text box:

    Number Guess, Flash Digits, Dupe the Dupes, Slot Machine and Fortune Cookie
6. Click OK to save the dialog box as shown in Figure 11.1.

FIGURE 11.1.

Entering Summary Info for the GAMES.XLS workbook.

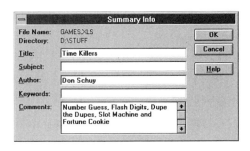

The Options Worksheet

The Options worksheet is a table you can use to tweak different game settings to get the best play out of each game. For example, you can set how many guesses the player has in the number-guessing game or you can set how often a jackpot is awarded in the slot machine game.

Clear the workbook of other worksheets and create the Options worksheet.

1. Delete all of the worksheets in the workbook except the first one. Use the **Edit|Delete Sheet** command.

   You will add each new sheet to the workbook as it is created.

2. Double-click the tab for the remaining worksheet.

   Excel displays the Rename Sheet dialog box, as shown in Figure 11.2.

3. Enter Options as the name of the worksheet and click OK.

FIGURE 11.2.

Naming the Options worksheet.

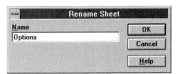

4. Resize the width of the A column to 35.00.

5. Resize the B column to a width of 10.00.

6. If the Formatting toolbar isn't being displayed, select **View|Toolbars** and check the Formatting toolbar.

7. Enter Game Options into cell A1.

8. Format cell A1 to a large font. I used Arial 16 bold.

9. Click cell A1 and drag across to cell F1 to select the cells in the top row of the worksheet.

10. Click the Center Across Columns toolbar button on the Formatting toolbar to center the title as shown in Figure 11.3.

FIGURE 11.3.

Creating a title for the Options worksheet.

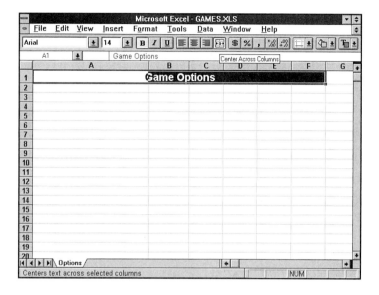

Next, enter the options for the Number Guess game.

1. In cell A3, enter the title of the first game, `Number Guess`, and click the Bold button on the Formatting toolbar.

2. In cells A4 through A7, enter the following option titles:

   ```
   Low Value

   High Value

   Maximum Tries

   Truth Percentage
   ```

3. In cells B4 through B7, enter values for each of the Number Guess game options as shown here:

   ```
   Low Value              1

   High Value           100

   Maximum Tries          6

   Truth Percentage    0.95
   ```

4. Select cell B7 (the cell containing `0.95`) and click the Percent Style button on the Formatting toolbar. Excel displays the percentage as `95%`, as shown in Figure 11.4.

FIGURE 11.4.

Entering game play options for the first game.

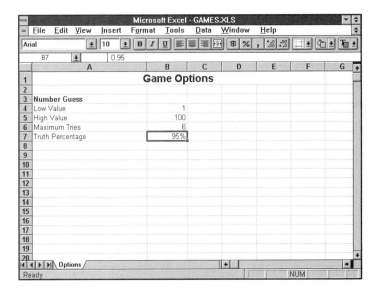

NOTE

For each game play setting in the Options worksheet, an Excel name is defined to point to the cell that contains the setting. This way the program can refer to the names and not the cells by row and column number.

In Excel VBA programming, you want to avoid using "hard-coded" row and column values in your programs wherever possible. Otherwise, when you make changes to your worksheets by adding or deleting rows or columns, you may have to look through all your code to make sure all your references to values in the worksheet point to the correct places. An Excel name automatically stays up-to-date as rows are inserted and deleted in the worksheet.

Define an Excel name for each option in the worksheet.

1. Select cell B4 by clicking it.

   On the left side of the formula bar, you should see B4 displayed in a combo box. (If the formula bar is not displayed, you can turn it on by selecting the **V**iew|**F**ormula Bar command.)

2. Click the B4 displayed in the formula bar to highlight it.

3. Enter LowValue in the formula bar combo box.

   You can verify that an Excel name was defined by selecting the **I**nsert|**N**ame|**D**efine command. This brings up the Define Name dialog box, which displays a list of all names currently defined. Selecting a name from the list displays its value in the **R**efers To text box, as shown in Figure 11.5.

The LowValue name is defined as =Options!$B$4.

FIGURE 11.5.

Examining the LowValue name setting.

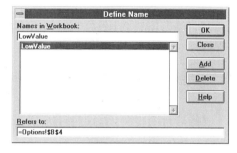

4. Create names HighValue, MaxTries, and TruthPercentage for the remaining options, using cells B5 through B7. The final list of names should appear as shown here:

LowValue   =Options!$B$4

HighValue   =Options!$B$5

MaxTries   =Options!$B$6

TruthPercentage   =Options!$B$7

You can complete the entries in the Options worksheet as you build each game.

The Number Guess Game

The Number Guess game shown in Figure 11.6 is an old and simple game, but this implementation makes it a little more interesting. In a number-guessing game, the player is supposed to guess a number from a range of numbers, typically from 1 to 10 or 1 to 100.

FIGURE 11.6.

Playing the Number Guess game.

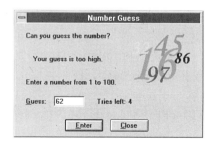

The computer's role in the game is to give clues indicating if the guess is too high or too low. A player might try to improve his odds at guessing the correct number within the allotted tries by doing a mental binary search.

First you can cut the range in half by guessing 50. If the computer indicates you are too high, you can cut the lower range of 1 to 49 in half by guessing 25. You can continue this strategy so that as you get to the last guess you have the smallest possible set of numbers to guess from.

If enough guesses are allowed, you can get the correct answer every time. It's more fun to play when you don't have as many guesses and eventually have to take a chance.

The Number Guess game you create here adds a twist by allowing the computer to lie every once in a while. You can set the percentage for which the computer tells the truth. I found that if the computer tells the truth 95 percent of the time and fibs 5 percent of the time, just about the right amount of spice is added to the game. If the computer lies any more than that, it gets pretty difficult to ever win the game.

The Number Guess Dialog Box

In creating each of the games, you create the dialog box first. The code for the games consists of functions that are activated by events in the dialog box and its controls, so it makes sense to write the code after the dialog box is created.

The Number Guess game dialog box has the following controls on it:

lblCanYou	Label, "Can you guess..."
lblEnter	Label, "Enter a number from..."
lblGuess	Label for guess edit box
edtGuess	Edit box, enter a guess
lblTriesLeft	Label, number of tries left
cmdEnter	Button, enter the value in the guess edit box
cmdClose	Button, quit
picNumbers	Paintbrush picture
lblHint	Label, display a clue

Start by creating the dialog box.

1. Create a new dialog box by selecting the **Insert|Macro|Dialog** command.

   You can keep the Options worksheet as the first sheet in the workbook by moving the new sheet.

2. Drag the tab of the dialog box to move it to the right of the Options worksheet.

3. Double-click the tab of the dialog box and rename the sheet to Number Guess.

4. Click the title bar of the dialog box frame.

   Excel displays the name of the dialog box frame in the combo box on the left side of the formula bar: `Dialog Frame 1`.

5. Change the name of the dialog box frame to dlgNumberGuess.

6. Select the text in the title bar of the dialog box and enter `Number Guess` as the title bar caption, as shown in Figure 11.7.

7. Select the **View|Toolbars** command. In the Toolbars dialog box, check the Forms toolbar so it is on, and click OK.

FIGURE 11.7.

The beginning of the Number Guess dialog box.

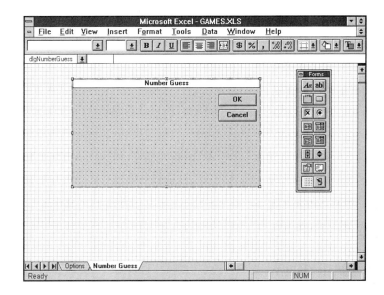

Next add controls to the dialog box.

1. Click the Label button on the Forms toolbar and draw a label in the top left area of the dialog box.

2. Enter the text `Can you guess the number?` into the new label.

3. In the formula bar, rename the label to lblCanYou.

   It isn't mandatory that you rename each of the controls as you drop them onto a dialog box. If you never reference the control in your program, it doesn't really matter what it is called. I still like to rename each of the controls so I can recognize them when I see them in the Tab Order list from the **Tools|Tab Order** command.

4. Draw another label to display messages back to the player during game play. Position the label as shown in Figure 11.8.

5. Change the name of the new label to lblHint.

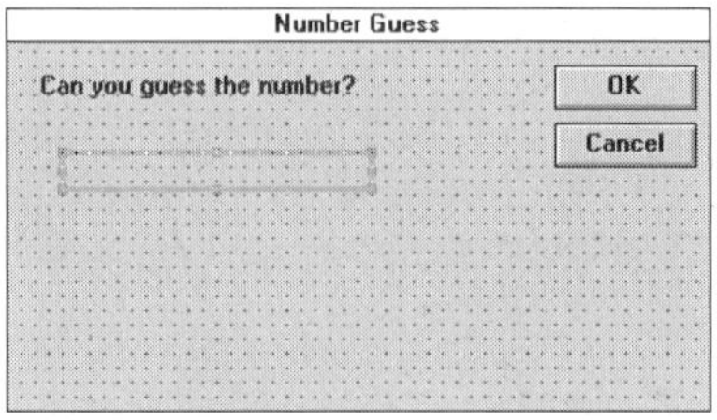

FIGURE 11.8.

*Creating an empty
label to display clues
to the player.*

6. Create a third label, lblEnter, with the text `Enter a number from 1 to 100`.

   Make the lblEnter label a little bit wider than needed so the message can be displayed completely even if the numbers are changed to larger values. The text in this label is changed by the program to reflect the values set in the Options worksheet.

7. Create a lblGuess label with the text `Guess:`.

8. Click the Edit box button on the Forms toolbar. To the right of the lblGuess label, create an edit box as shown in Figure 11.9. Change the name of the edit box to edtGuess.

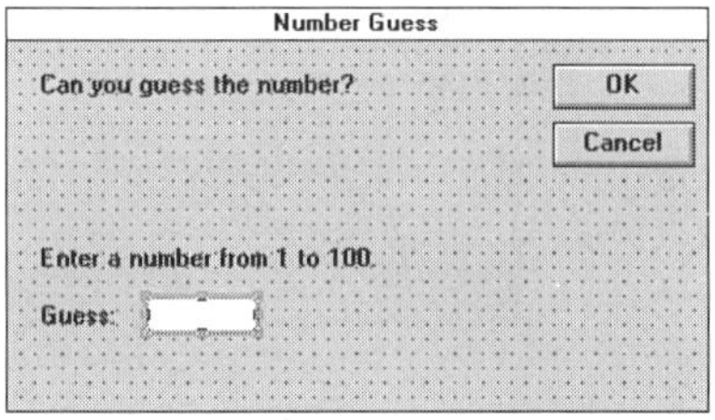

FIGURE 11.9.

*Creating the edtGuess
edit box.*

9. To the right of the edtGuess edit box, draw a label and enter `Tries left:` in the label text. Name the new label lblTriesLeft.

   Make sure the lblTriesLeft label is wide enough to display a number to the right of `Tries left:`. This label's caption is also changed while the program is running.

Resize the dialog box and utilize the OK and Cancel buttons that are already on the form.

1. Adjust the size of the form about two lines longer and two lines thinner, then move the OK and Cancel buttons to the bottom center of the form, as shown in Figure 11.10.

2. Change the caption on the OK button to Enter.

3. Rename the OK button to cmdEnter.

4. Change the caption on the Cancel button to Close.

5. Rename the Cancel button to cmdClose.

FIGURE 11.10.
Recycling the OK and Cancel buttons to make Enter and Close buttons.

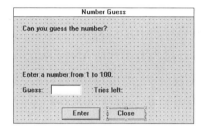

Next you can set a few properties on the controls you placed on the form.

1. Click the lblGuess control.

2. Click the Control Properties button from the Forms toolbox.

   Another way to set a control's properties is to click the control with the right mouse button. Excel displays a pop-up window that you can select the Format Object command from, as shown in Figure 11.11.

FIGURE 11.11.
Setting a control's properties.

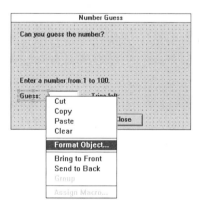

3. In the Format Object dialog box, click the Control tab, enter G in the **A**ccelerator Key text box, and click OK.

   The effect of this is that the first control that can receive focus, which is in the tab order after the lblGuess label, gets focus when the user presses the Alt-G key combination.

You need to make sure that the edtGuess edit box immediately follows the lblGuess label.

4. Select the **Tools**|**Tab** Order command.

5. Adjust the tab order so the controls are in the following order, as shown in Figure 11.12:

   lblCanYou

   lblHint

   lblEnter

   lblGuess

   edtGuess

   cmdEnter

   cmdClose

FIGURE 11.12.

Adjusting the tab order in the Number Guess dialog box.

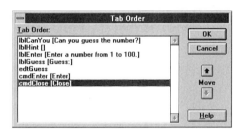

6. Select the cmdEnter button and open the Format Object dialog box.

7. The Dismiss option is checked by default. Click it so that it is not checked.

   In the Number Guess game, you want the **E**nter button to be the default button clicked when the player presses the Enter key, but you do not want that button to close the dialog box.

8. Enter E in the **A**ccelerator Key text box, as shown in Figure 11.13, and close the Format Object dialog box.

9. Open the Format Object dialog box for the cmdClose button and enter C as its accelerator key.

   You can test the dialog box even before any code is added to the program. It's a good idea to do this to check tab order and accelerator key settings to make sure the dialog box functions as expected.

10. Click the Run Dialog button on the Forms toolbox. (This is the button that looks like a light switch.)

FIGURE 11.13.

Setting properties on the cmdEnter button.

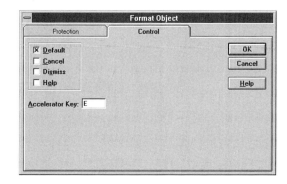

Excel will display the Number Guess dialog box as shown in Figure 11.14.

Try repeatedly entering Tab or Shift-Tab to cycle through the controls. Make sure that Alt-G takes you to the edit box, Alt-E clicks the Enter button, and Alt-C closes the dialog box.

FIGURE 11.14.

Testing the Number Guess dialog box.

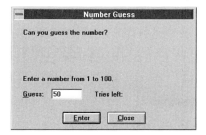

I used Paintbrush to create the bitmap for the Number Guess dialog box. First I used Paintbrush's **Text|Font** command to select the Monotype Corsiva TrueType font, as shown in Figure 11.15.

FIGURE 11.15.

Selecting fonts as artwork in Paintbrush.

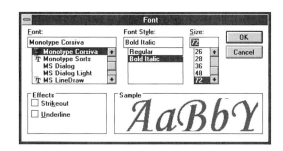

Starting with the largest font and working down, I entered different numbers onto the picture using various font sizes and colors. First I entered them separately in different areas on the picture, as shown in Figure 11.16.

FIGURE 11.16.

Creating components of the number picture.

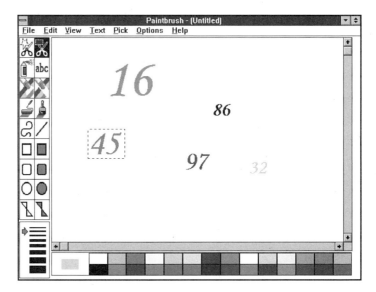

Next, I used the cut feature in Paintbrush to clip the numbers and lay them on top of each other, as shown in Figure 11.17.

FIGURE 11.17.

Overlaying the numbers in the number picture.

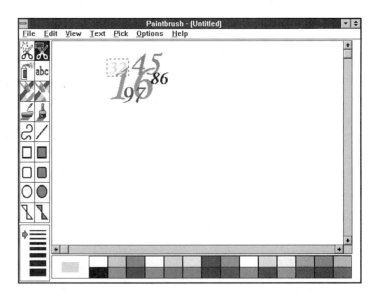

Finally, I filled in the picture with a gray background. I used the **View|Z**oom-In command to fill the smaller areas in with gray, as shown in Figure 11.18. (If I had started the Paintbrush session by setting the background color to gray, this step would have been eliminated.)

FIGURE 11.18.

Filling in the background of the number picture.

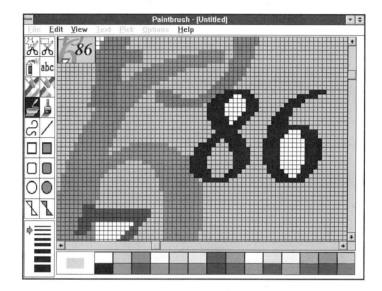

To save the bitmap, I cut a square just large enough to contain the design and used the **E**dit|**Co**py To command to save only the cut portion as a small bitmap.

The resulting bitmap is included on the book's companion CD-ROM as NUM.BMP.

1. To add the NUM.BMP picture to the dialog box, select the **I**nsert|**O**bject command.
2. In the Object dialog box, click the Create from File tab.
3. Select the NUM.BMP file created in Paintbrush and click OK.
4. Position the picture in the upper-right corner of the dialog box, as shown in Figure 11.19.

FIGURE 11.19.

Adding a picture to the Number Guess dialog box.

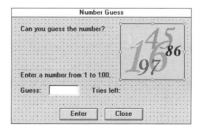

Excel defaults to displaying a thin black border around the picture.

5. Bring up the Format Object dialog box for the picture.

6. Click the Patterns tab and select **N**one for a border type. Close the Format Object dialog box.

7. Rename the picture control to picNumbers.

That completes the Number Guess dialog box except for hooking it up to the subroutines, which you haven't created yet. It's coding time!

The Globals Module

I created a Globals module as a place for global constants, variables, and subroutines that are to be shared among other modules. Most of the code in the project is specific to a particular game, and that code is organized in a set of modules—one module per game.

Within the Globals module are the following:

```
WORKBOOK_NAME constant
OpenDialog subroutine
CNStr function
```

1. Click the Number Guess tab if that sheet isn't already the current sheet.

2. Select the **I**nsert|**M**acro|**M**odule command.

   Excel creates a Module1 module between the Options worksheet and the Number Guess dialog box.

3. Rename the Module1 module as Globals.

4. Enter the declarations at the top of the Globals module as shown in Listing 11.1.

Listing 11.1. The declaration section for the Globals module.

```
' Globals

Option Explicit

Global Const WORKBOOK_NAME = "GAMES.XLS"
Const PROGRAM = "Excel Time Killers"
```

The WORKBOOK_NAME constant contains the name of the Time Killers workbook file. When the workbook is converted to a menu add-in, the constant value has to be changed from GAMES.XLS to GAMES.XLA.

The PROGRAM constant is declared so you can use the function template described in Chapter 1, "Today's Basic," for error handling in these procedures.

Following the declarations, enter the OpenDialog subroutine shown in Listing 11.2.

Listing 11.2. The OpenDialog subroutine.

```
Sub OpenDialog(strDialogName As String)

  On Error GoTo OpenDialogError

' Open the dialog'
  Workbooks(WORKBOOK_NAME).DialogSheets(strDialogName).Show

OpenDialogDone:
  Exit Sub

OpenDialogError:
  MsgBox Error$(), 48, PROGRAM
  Resume OpenDialogDone

End Sub
```

The OpenDialog subroutine is used in the entry point subroutines for each of the games that have dialog boxes.

In the following line

```
  Workbooks(WORKBOOK_NAME).DialogSheets(strDialogName).Show
```

the subroutine locates a dialog box in the games workbook and calls the Show method to display the dialog box. The rest of the subroutine is error handling.

Enter the CNStr function at the end of the Globals module as shown in Listing 11.3.

Listing 11.3. The CNStr function.

```
Function CNStr(v As Variant) As String

' Convert a null to an empty string

  If IsNull(v) Then
    CNStr = ""
  Else
    CNStr = Trim$(CStr(v))
  End If

End Function
```

As described in previous chapters, the CNStr function is used to ensure that a string is returned from a Variant type variable.

The Number Guess Module

Now you get to complete the first game by writing the code for it.

As it worked out, each of the game modules has a similar structure. They each have the following components:

- Declarations for game option variables
- Declarations for game status variables
- An entry point subroutine
- Program initialization in the dialog box's Show event
- Game round initialization in an Init subroutine
- Game play code in one button's Click event
- Other miscellaneous procedures

See if you can see this pattern develop as you look through the code.

1. Create a new module sheet. Rename it as Number Guess Module and place it after the Number Guess dialog box.
2. Enter the declarations as shown in Listing 11.4.

Listing 11.4. Declarations in the Number Guess module.

```
' Number Guess

Option Explicit

Const PROGRAM = "Number Guess"

Dim mdlg As DialogSheet

Dim mintLow As Integer
Dim mintHigh As Integer
Dim mintMaxTries As Integer
Dim msngTruthPercent As Single

Dim mintPick As Integer
Dim mintTries As Integer
Dim mintLies As Integer

Dim msg As String
Dim cr As String
```

The `mdlg` variable is set to the game's dialog box in the initialization of the program.

```
Dim mdlg As DialogSheet
```

The next four variables are set to hold the four game options stored in the Options worksheet.

```
Dim mintLow As Integer
Dim mintHigh As Integer
Dim mintMaxTries As Integer
Dim msngTruthPercent As Single
```

The next three variables change with each round of play. The `mintPick` variable holds the randomly selected number that the player is trying to guess. The `mintTries` variable holds how many tries are left for the player to guess the correct number or lose. The `mintLies` variable counts how many times the computer lies to the player. This is used at the end of the game so the computer can confess to the player about how bad it has been.

```
Dim mintPick As Integer
Dim mintTries As Integer
Dim mintLies As Integer
```

The `msg` variable is used to hold message strings as they are built before calling the `MsgBox` statement or function. The `cr` variable holds `Chr$(13)` and `Chr$(10)`, used to display a carriage return in a message box.

```
Dim msg As String
Dim cr As String
```

Enter the `NumberGuess` subroutine as shown in Listing 11.5.

Listing 11.5. The `NumberGuess` subroutine.

```
Sub NumberGuess()

  OpenDialog "Number Guess"

End Sub
```

The `NumberGuess` routine is the subroutine that starts the game. All it does is display the Number Guess dialog box. As the dialog box is opened, the next subroutine, `dlgNumberGuess_Show`, is executed, and that is where the game really begins.

The *dlgNumberGuess_Show* Subroutine

The `dlgNumberGuess_Show` subroutine is attached to the Number Guess dialog box's Show event. The Show event causes the subroutine to be executed while the dialog box is loading but before it is actually displayed.

Enter the `dlgNumberGuess_Show` subroutine in Listing 11.6 into the Number Guess module.

Listing 11.6. The `dlgNumberGuess_Show` subroutine.

```
Sub dlgNumberGuess_Show()

  Dim wsOptions As Worksheet

  On Error GoTo dlgNumberGuess_ShowError

  cr = Chr$(13) & Chr$(10)

' Get the option worksheet
  Set wsOptions = Workbooks(WORKBOOK_NAME).Worksheets("Options")

' Get the dialog
  Set mdlg = Workbooks(WORKBOOK_NAME).DialogSheets("Number Guess")

' Read the values in the Options worksheet
  mintLow = wsOptions.Range("LowValue").Value
  mintHigh = wsOptions.Range("HighValue").Value
  mintMaxTries = wsOptions.Range("MaxTries").Value
  msngTruthPercent = wsOptions.Range("TruthPercentage").Value

' Update the lblEnter label with the start and ending values
mdlg.Labels("lblEnter").Caption = "Enter a number from " & mintLow & " to "
➥ & mintHigh & "."

  InitNumberGuess

dlgNumberGuess_ShowDone:
  Exit Sub

dlgNumberGuess_ShowError:
  msg = Error$()
  If Err = 13 Then
    msg = msg & cr & cr & "Check the values in the Options worksheet."
  End If
  MsgBox msg, 48, PROGRAM
  On Error Resume Next
  mdlg.Hide
  Resume dlgNumberGuess_ShowDone

End Sub
```

The `dlgNumberGuess_Show` subroutine's main job is to initialize the module variables to prepare for a few rounds of the game. To read values from the Options worksheet, a `wsOptions` worksheet variable is assigned.

```
' Get the option worksheet
  Set wsOptions = Workbooks(WORKBOOK_NAME).Worksheets("Options")
```

Next the module variables are assigned. First, `mdlg` is set to the Number Guess dialog box. This is used to read and set the values in the controls on the dialog box.

```
' Get the dialog
  Set mdlg = Workbooks(WORKBOOK_NAME).DialogSheets("Number Guess")
```

Following that, the four play options from the Options sheet are read in.

The `Range` method is used with the Excel names you defined as you created the Options worksheet. In each case the `Range` method returns the cell that the Excel name represents. You then use the Value property on the cell to fetch the option value stored in the worksheet.

```
' Read the values in the Options worksheet
  mintLow = wsOptions.Range("LowValue").Value
  mintHigh = wsOptions.Range("HighValue").Value
  mintMaxTries = wsOptions.Range("MaxTries").Value
  msngTruthPercent = wsOptions.Range("TruthPercentage").Value
```

Pretty strange, huh? It's a great technique because it avoids referencing the values in the worksheet by row and column number.

Next the subroutine changes the lblEnter label caption to reflect the low and high values read in from the Options worksheet.

As you discovered in Chapter 5, "Excel: Calendar Wizard," while coding Calendar Wizard, to reference a control in a dialog box you must go through the appropriate collection. For labels there is the Labels collection, for buttons there is the Buttons collection, and so on.

```
' Update the lblEnter label with the start and ending values
mdlg.Labels("lblEnter").Caption = "Enter a number from " & mintLow & " to "
➥ & mintHigh & "."
```

The `Randomize` statement is used to seed the random number generator. What's all that about? Later on you're going to use the `Rnd` function to produce random numbers. Without calling the `Randomize` statement, the same sequence of random numbers is produced each time the program runs.

To truly make the game different each time you play it, the `Randomize` statement is used to seed the random number generator with a value derived from the system clock.

```
Randomize
```

After all program-related initialization is completed, the `dlgNumberGuess_Show` subroutine calls the `InitNumberGuess` subroutine for game initialization.

The `InitNumberGuess` subroutine is called repeatedly for each start of a new game, but the `dlgNumberGuess_Show` subroutine gets called again only if the dialog box is closed and then opened again.

```
InitNumberGuess
```

The error handling for the `dlgNumberGuess_Show` subroutine handles Error 13 in a special way. Error 13 is a type mismatch error; it would likely occur because one of the values from the Options worksheet was text rather than a number.

To better inform the game player about what is going on, I append an additional message to display in the error message box.

```
dlgNumberGuess_ShowError:
  msg = Error$()
  If Err = 13 Then
    msg = msg & cr & cr & "Check the values in the Options worksheet."
  End If
  MsgBox msg, 48, PROGRAM
```

Any error that occurs during program initialization would mean that the game isn't in a good state to begin play. Because of this, the error-handling code calls the `Hide` method to close the dialog box:

```
  On Error Resume Next
  mdlg.Hide
  Resume dlgNumberGuess_ShowDone
```

The *InitNumberGuess* Subroutine

As I mentioned earlier, the `InitNumberGuess` subroutine is called at the beginning of each new game. Its job is to reset any game-playing variables so the game can start off with a clean slate.

Enter the `InitNumberGuess` subroutine as shown in Listing 11.7.

Listing 11.7. The `InitNumberGuess` subroutine.

```
Sub InitNumberGuess()

' Reinitialize the game

' Hide the hint label
  mdlg.Labels("lblHint").Caption = ""

' Pick a random number from within the range
  mintPick = Int((mintHigh - mintLow + 1) * Rnd + mintLow)

' Start with zero tries used up
  mintTries = 0

' Zero out lies counter
  mintLies = 0

  ClearGuess

End Sub
```

The lblHint label is the label that displays the message `Your guess is too low` or `Your guess is too high`. At the beginning of the game any message displayed should be erased.

```
' Hide the hint label
  mdlg.Labels("lblHint").Caption = ""
```

Next, the game writer's favorite function, `Rnd`, is called to select a random number. `Rnd` returns a value from 0 up to but not including 1. The formula uses the value returned from `Rnd` to produce a number in the range from `mintLow` to `mintHigh`.

```
' Pick a random number from within the range
  mintPick = Int((mintHigh - mintLow + 1) * Rnd + mintLow)
```

The `mintTries` variable is set to 0 to indicate that no tries have been used up yet.

```
' Start with zero tries used up
  mintTries = 0
```

Also, a `mintLies` variable is set to 0. This variable tracks how many times the computer has lied.

```
' Zero out lies counter
  mintLies = 0
```

To finish up initialization, the `ClearGuess` subroutine is called to erase any entries left from a previous game.

```
ClearGuess
```

The *cmdEnter_Click* Subroutine

The next subroutine, `cmdEnter_Click`, is the game's engine. The player enters a guess by clicking the **Enter** button. (This also occurs by just pressing the Enter key, because the **Enter** button is the default button.) The `cmdEnter_Click` subroutine handles the computer's response to the entry.

Enter the `cmdEnter_Click` subroutine into the Number Guess module as shown in Listing 11.8.

Listing 11.8. The `cmdEnter_Click` subroutine.

```
Sub cmdEnter_Click()

  Dim strGuess As String
  Dim intGuess As Integer
  Dim blnTooLow As Integer

  On Error GoTo cmdEnter_ClickError
```

continues

Listing 11.8. continued

```
' Read the entered value as a string
  strGuess = CNStr(mdlg.EditBoxes("edtGuess").Text)
  If strGuess = "" Then GoTo cmdEnter_ClickDone

' See if the player entered a number
  On Error Resume Next
  intGuess = CInt(strGuess)
  If Err = 13 Then
MsgBox "Enter a number from " & mintLow & " to " & mintHigh & ".", 64,
➥ PROGRAM
    ClearGuess
    GoTo cmdEnter_ClickDone
  End If

  On Error GoTo cmdEnter_ClickError

' Player used up a try
  mintTries = mintTries + 1

' See if the player is right
  If intGuess = mintPick Then
    msg = "You're right!" & cr
    msg = msg & "The number was " & mintPick & "."
    msg = msg & cr & cr & "You win in " & mintTries & " tries."
    MsgBox msg, 0, PROGRAM

    InitNumberGuess
    GoTo cmdEnter_ClickDone
  End If

' See if the number of tries are used up
  If mintTries = mintMaxTries Then
    msg = "Sorry, but you don't have any tries left." & cr & cr
    msg = msg & "The correct number was " & mintPick & "."

  ' Confess if the computer lied
    If mintLies > 0 Then
      msg = msg & cr & cr & "I confess. I lied to you " & mintLies
      If mintLies > 1 Then
        msg = msg & " times."
      Else
        msg = msg & " time."
      End If
    End If

    MsgBox msg, 0, PROGRAM

    InitNumberGuess
    GoTo cmdEnter_ClickDone
  End If

' Is the guess too low or too high?
  If intGuess < mintPick Then
    blnTooLow = True
  End If
```

```
' Determine if the computer should tell the truth
  If Rnd >= msngTruthPercent Then
  ' Tell a lie. Reverse the too low flag
    blnTooLow = Not blnTooLow
    mintLies = mintLies + 1
  End If

' Display a hint
  If blnTooLow Then
    mdlg.Labels("lblHint").Caption = "Your guess is too low."
  Else
    mdlg.Labels("lblHint").Caption = "Your guess is too high."
  End If

  ClearGuess

cmdEnter_ClickDone:
  Exit Sub

cmdEnter_ClickError:
  MsgBox Error$(), 48, PROGRAM
  Resume cmdEnter_ClickDone

End Sub
```

The `cmdEnter_Click` subroutine first fetches the player's guess from the edtGuess edit box. The value is read as a string. If the string is empty, the player's click is ignored by jumping to the end of the subroutine.

```
' Read the entered value as a string
  strGuess = CNStr(mdlg.EditBoxes("edtGuess").Text)
  If strGuess = "" Then GoTo cmdEnter_ClickDone
```

If something was entered into the edit box, the program continues and attempts to convert it into an integer.

The `On Error Resume Next` statement is used so that the subroutine can handle a type mismatch error on its own. If a type mismatch occurs, the text entered was not a valid integer expression, and the player is told to enter a number, as shown in Listing 11.9.

Listing 11.9. Testing for a number.

```
' See if the player entered a number
  On Error Resume Next
  intGuess = CInt(strGuess)
  If Err = 13 Then
MsgBox "Enter a number from " & mintLow & " to " & mintHigh & ".", 64,
➥ PROGRAM
    ClearGuess
    GoTo cmdEnter_ClickDone
  End If

  On Error GoTo cmdEnter_ClickError
```

If the code continues to execute, a valid number was entered. The subroutine increments the mintTries counter because another guess was used up.

```
' Player used up a try
  mintTries = mintTries + 1
```

The next section of code checks to see if the player guessed correctly. If the player did, congratulations are displayed and the `InitNumberGuess` subroutine is called to perform initialization for the next game, as shown in Listing 11.10.

Listing 11.10. Game play ends if the correct number was selected.

```
' See if the player is right
  If intGuess = mintPick Then
    msg = "You're right!" & cr
    msg = msg & "The number was " & mintPick & "."
    msg = msg & cr & cr & "You win in " & mintTries & " tries."
    MsgBox msg, 0, PROGRAM

    InitNumberGuess
    GoTo cmdEnter_ClickDone
  End If
```

Continuing on, if you got this far, the player selected the wrong number. The next thing to test for is whether all tries have been used up.

```
' See if the number of tries are used up
  If mintTries = mintMaxTries Then
    msg = "Sorry, but you don't have any tries left." & cr & cr
    msg = msg & "The correct number was " & mintPick & "."
```

When the player loses, the program checks to see if the computer had ever failed to be truthful in its clues to the player. If so, the message string being built is appended to indicate how many times the computer lied, as shown in Listing 11.11.

Listing 11.11. The program confesses to the player.

```
' Confess if the computer lied
  If mintLies > 0 Then
    msg = msg & cr & cr & "I confess. I lied to you " & mintLies
    If mintLies > 1 Then
      msg = msg & " times."
    Else
      msg = msg & " time."
    End If
  End If
```

The message is displayed, and the game is initialized for the next round.

```
  MsgBox msg, 0, PROGRAM

  InitNumberGuess
  GoTo cmdEnter_ClickDone
End If
```

If the subroutine continues, the player's guess was wrong but there are still tries left.

The next part of the subroutine sets a flag indicating if the guess was too low or too high. The flag, blnTooLow, is True if the guess was too low or False if the guess was too high.

```
' Is the guess too low or too high?
  If intGuess < mintPick Then
    blnTooLow = True
  End If
```

The next section of code is where the program determines whether the computer should tell the truth or try to lead the player astray.

The Rnd function is called, and its return value is compared to the msngTruthPercent variable, which is also in the range of 0 to 1. If the Rnd value is greater than msngTruthPercent, a lie is set up to occur by reversing the value of the blnTooLow flag.

Also the mintLies counter is updated, as shown in Listing 11.12, so the program can later confess about its lie.

Listing 11.12. How the cmdEnter_Click subroutine determines whether to be truthful or to lie.

```
' Determine if the computer should tell the truth
  If Rnd >= msngTruthPercent Then
  ' Tell a lie. Reverse the too low flag
    blnTooLow = Not blnTooLow
    mintLies = mintLies + 1
  End If
```

Next, based on the value in the blnTooLow flag, the subroutine displays a hint indicating the guess is too low or too high, as shown in Listing 11.13.

Listing 11.13. Displaying a hint or lie.

```
' Display a hint
  If blnTooLow Then
    mdlg.Labels("lblHint").Caption = "Your guess is too low."
  Else
    mdlg.Labels("lblHint").Caption = "Your guess is too high."
  End If
```

At the end of the subroutine, the edit box is cleared so it is ready for the next guess.

```
ClearGuess
```

The *ClearGuess* Subroutine

The final procedure in the Number Guess module is the `ClearGuess` subroutine.

Enter the `ClearGuess` subroutine as shown in Listing 11.14.

Listing 11.14. The `ClearGuess` subroutine.

```
Sub ClearGuess()

' Display number of tries left
mdlg.Labels("lblTriesLeft").Caption = "Tries left: " & mintMaxTries -
➡ mintTries

  mdlg.EditBoxes("edtGuess").Text = ""
  mdlg.Focus = "edtGuess"

End Sub
```

The `ClearGuess` subroutine updates the message that indicates how many tries the player has left, then it clears the edtGuess edit box and sets focus to it so the player is ready to enter the next guess.

Plugging in the Number Guess Code

For the code that was just written to do anything, it needs to be attached to events that occur when the Number Guess dialog box is being used.

Only two events are used in the entire program: the dlgNumberGuess dialog box's Show event and the cmdEnter button's Click event.

1. Click the Number Guess dialog box tab.
2. Use the right mouse button to click the title bar on the Number Guess dialog box frame.

   Excel displays up a pop-up menu.
3. Select the Assign Macro command from the menu, as shown in Figure 11.20.
4. In the Assign Macro dialog box, select the `dlgNumberGuess_Show` subroutine and click OK, as shown in Figure 11.21.
5. Click the right mouse button on the **E**nter button on the Number Guess dialog box.

6. Again, select the Assign Macro command to bring up the Assign Macro dialog box.

7. This time, select the `cmdEnter_Click` subroutine and click OK.

That's it! You're ready to try out the game.

FIGURE 11.20.

Using the right mouse button menu to assign a macro to the dialog box's Show event.

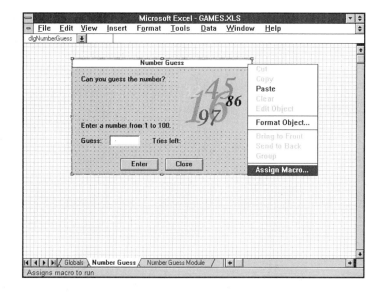

FIGURE 11.21.

Selecting the `dlgNumberGuess_Show` *subroutine.*

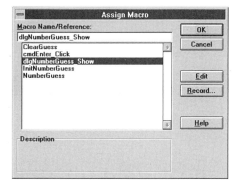

Testing the Number Guess Game

At the end of the next chapter you will create both a game menu and a toolbar to activate your games. For testing purposes, you can use the Debug window to start up the game.

1. Switch back to the Number Guess module sheet.
2. Select the **View|D**ebug Window command to display the Debug window.
3. In the Immediate window, enter `NumberGuess` (as shown in Figure 11.22).
4. Press the Enter key to execute the `NumberGuess` subroutine.

   You can also execute the `NumberGuess` subroutine by selecting it with the **T**ools|**M**acro command. However, the first time you run a program there is bound to be an error or two here or there, so it makes sense to start right out with the debugger on the first run.

FIGURE 11.22.

Use the Immediate window to test run the Number Guess game.

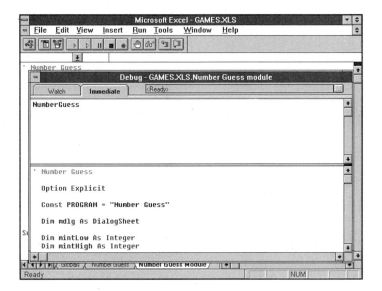

Playing the Number Guess Game

The Number Guess game is designed to play several rounds of play very quickly. At the start of the game, the edit box has focus, so you can enter your first guess. Because the **E**nter button is the default button, you can play without the mouse. Enter the guess and press the Enter key.

On each round, you are told if your guess is correct, too low, or too high. When you guess incorrectly, the edit box is cleared and receives focus so you can immediately enter your next guess. When you enter the correct guess you'll see a message like that shown in Figure 11.23.

Go ahead and give it a whirl. The game is quite fun even with its simplicity, especially given that the computer occasionally lies. You can experiment with the values on the Options worksheet to see how it affects the game play.

FIGURE 11.23.
Winning a round in the Number Guess game.

The Flash Digits Game

The second game you create is also a number game. This game tests how many digits you can remember when you see them flashed to you one digit at a time.

Sound easy? It gets difficult to play fairly quickly unless you have an extremely sharp memory. The game steadily increases the number of digits you have to remember as you play.

The Flash Digits game is shown in Figure 11.24.

FIGURE 11.24.
Playing the Flash Digits game.

Here's how it works. The game first displays a **S**tart button. You press Enter or click the **S**tart button, and the first digit is displayed.

The game displays the first digit, and the **S**tart button changes to a **N**ext button. You press Enter (or click the **N**ext button) enough times to view each digit. When the digits are all displayed, the digit window becomes blank and the **N**ext button changes to an **E**nter button.

Next you enter the number (if you can remember it) and press the Enter key. If you are right, the computer congratulates you. If you are wrong, the computer displays the correct answer so you can see where you messed up.

Let's build the game!

Adding the Flash Digits Options

The Flash Digits game has two options to customize game play: the starting number of digits you have to remember and the number of rounds of play before this number is incremented.

With the first option, you can make the game start off easy or difficult. With the second option, you control how quickly the game advances from easy to difficult.

1. Click the Options tab to display the game options worksheet.

2. In cell A9, enter `Flash Digits` and click the Bold button on the toolbar.

3. In cells A10 through A11, enter the two option titles

   ```
   Starting Number of Digits
   Number of Plays to Add a Digit
   ```

4. In cells B10 through B11, enter the option values

   ```
   Starting Number of Digits        5
   Number of Plays to Add a Digit   3
   ```

5. Click cell B10 to select it.

6. Click the combo box in the formula bar where it displays `B10`. Enter `StartDigits` as the name for this cell.

7. Click B11 and enter `PlaysToAddDigit` as the name for the B11 cell.

   The modified Options worksheet is shown in Figure 11.25.

FIGURE 11.25.

Adding game play options for the Flash Digits game.

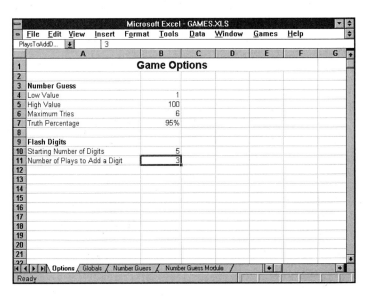

Creating the Flash Digits Dialog Box

Next you need to create the Flash Digits dialog box.

1. Select the **Insert|Macro|D**ialog command to create a new dialog box.
2. Drag the new dialog box to the last tab so that it follows the Number Guess Module.
3. Double-click the tab in the dialog box and rename the dialog box to Flash Digits.
4. Select the dialog box's title bar text and change it to Flash Digits, as shown in Figure 11.26.
5. With the dialog box frame still selected, change the dialog box frame name in the formula combo box to dlgFlashDigits.

FIGURE 11.26.

The beginning of the
Flash Digits dialog box.

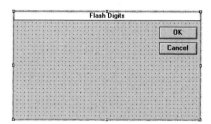

NOTE

In creating the Flash Digits dialog box, I wanted to display the number in a large window. Naturally, you would think that you could just use a label or edit box and change the font size. Believe it or not, edit boxes in Excel are restricted to a particular font and font size.

Fortunately, Excel has another type of text display called a text box. A text box in Excel isn't the same full-featured text box that you have in Access and Visual Basic for data entry. An Excel edit box is more like that. An Excel text box is used only for displaying text. It has a remarkable set of options for the appearance of the text and text box.

To use an Excel text box, you need to turn on the Drawing toolbar.

Add a text box control to the Flash Digits dialog box.

1. Use the **View|T**oolbars command to turn on both the Forms toolbar and the Drawing toolbar.

2. In the Drawing toolbar, locate the text box button. It's the one that looks like a document.

3. Click the text box button and draw a text box on the top left of the dialog box to display a large single character, as shown in Figure 11.27.

FIGURE 11.27.

Drawing the digits text box.

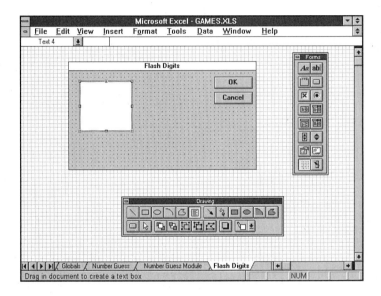

4. Close the Drawing toolbar.

5. In the formula bar, rename the text box to txtFlash.

Next, bring up the Format Object dialog box to change how the txtFlash text box is displayed.

1. Click the text box with the right mouse button to display the pop-up menu, and select the Format Object command.

   In the Patterns tab of the Format Object dialog box, you can give the text box a border and change its fill color. You can even give it rounded corners.

2. Click the Patterns tab if it isn't already the tab displayed.

3. In the Border option group, click the Custom radio button and choose a border for the text box.

   I chose a thick dotted bar for the **S**tyle, dark green for the **C**olor, and the thickest **W**eight line possible, as shown in Figure 11.28.

4. Click the Shadow and Round Corners check boxes if that is how you want your text box to display.

5. In the Fill option group, select a color for the background of the text box. I chose yellow.

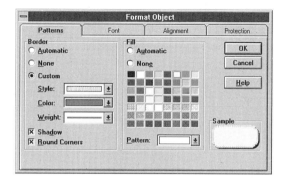

FIGURE 11.28.
Setting Pattern options on the txtFlash text box.

6. Click the Font tab in the Format Object dialog box.
7. Select the Arial font, regular weight, size 48 in black, as shown in Figure 11.29.

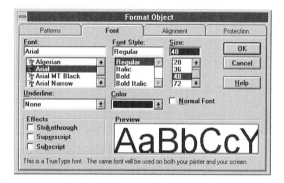

FIGURE 11.29.
Selecting a large font for the txtFlash text box.

8. Click the Alignment tab and set the Horizontal alignment to **C**enter. Leave the Vertical alignment at **T**op.
9. Click OK to close the Format Object dialog box.

Modify the existing OK and Cancel as the buttons for game play.

1. Move the OK and Cancel buttons to the lower right of the dialog box, as shown in Figure 11.30.

2. Change the caption in the OK button to read Start, but change the name of the button to cmdFlash (not cmdStart).

   The text on the cmdFlash button changes through different stages of the game play. It never says Flash, but for some reason that's what I called it. You want to use the same name because the program references the button as cmdFlash.

3. Change the caption in the Cancel button to Close and name the button cmdClose.

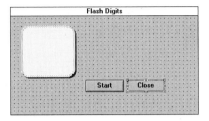

4. Click the cmdFlash button to select it, then click the Control Properties button on the Forms toolbar.

5. In the Format Object dialog box, click the Dismiss check box so that it is turned off.

   You don't want the cmdFlash button to close the dialog box when it is pressed. You can also set the **A**ccelerator Key value to s, although it isn't really required because the program updates this and the button's caption.

6. Close the Format Object dialog box.

7. Open the Format Object dialog box for the cmdClose button and set the **A**ccelerator Key to c.

8. Make sure both the **C**ancel and Dismiss options are checked, as shown in Figure 11.31, and click OK to close the Format Object dialog box.

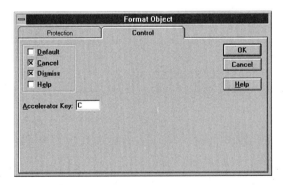

Resize the dialog box and add the following label controls.

1. Bring in the right side of the dialog box a little to shorten its width, and increase the height to give it room for a bitmap underneath the Start and Close buttons.

Don't worry about the exact height and width—you can resize it as necessary later.

2. Draw two labels at the top right of the form, one to display `Wins:` and another to display `Losses:`, as shown in Figure 11.32. Allow extra space in the labels so that the score can be displayed.

3. Change the names of the labels to lblWins and lblLosses.

FIGURE 11.32.

Adding the Wins and Losses labels.

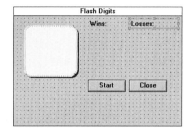

4. Draw a label to the right of the txtFlash text box. The caption for the label should read `Enter the Digits:`. Name the label lblDigits.

5. Below the lblDigits label, add an edit box named edtDigits. Make the edit box wide enough to enter fairly long numbers, as shown in Figure 11.33.

FIGURE 11.33.

Adding the edtDigits edit box.

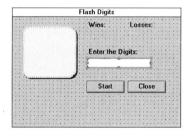

The last control to add to the form is a bitmap. I pushed my artistic abilities in Paintbrush as far as I could and created the bitmap shown in Figure 11.34.

FIGURE 11.34.

Touching up the Flash Digits dialog box with a bitmap.

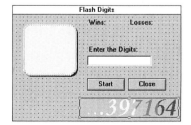

The numbers are blue on the right and gradually fade to lighter colors as you move left and then eventually vanish. It's supposed to represent the digits fading away from your memory or something like that.

1. Select the **Insert|Object** menu command to add a bitmap to the dialog box.
2. Click the Create from File tab and select a bitmap to use as a decoration on the Flash Digits dialog box.

   The DIGIT.BMP file on the companion CD-ROM is the bitmap I used here.
3. Bring up the Format Object dialog box for the inserted bitmap and change the border setting to **N**one. Close the Format Object dialog box.
4. Change the name of the bitmap to picDigits.

That's the end of this session of dialog box composing. Next you will write the code for this second game and then return to this dialog box long enough to hook the code to the dialog box events, as you did in the first game.

Coding Flash Digits

The Flash Digits module follows the same structure that was used in the Number Guess module.

1. Select the **Insert|Macro|Module** command to create a new module sheet, and drag it over to the end of the sheets in the workbook.
2. Name the new module sheet Flash Digits Module.

   First you have a declaration section that declares variables that hold the two settings in your Options worksheet and more variables for game play status.
3. Enter the declarations section of the Flash Digits module as shown in Listing 11.15.

Listing 11.15. The Flash Digits module declaration section.

```
' Flash Digits

Option Explicit

Const PROGRAM = "Flash Digits"

Dim mdlg As DialogSheet

Dim mintDigits As Integer
Dim mintPlaysToAddDigit As Integer

Dim mstrPick As String
```

```
Dim mintCurrent As Integer
Dim mintRound As Integer

Dim mintWins As Integer
Dim mintLosses As Integer

Dim msg As String
Dim cr As String
```

First, the `mdlg` variable gets set to the dialog box just as it did in the Number Guess program. It's used to reference the controls on the dialog box.

```
Dim mdlg As DialogSheet
```

The `mintDigits` and `mintPlaysToAddDigit` variables hold the two values in the Options worksheet. The `mintDigits` variable doesn't maintain a static value, however. It is the variable that keeps track of how many digits are used in a number for each play, which creeps up over time.

```
Dim mintDigits As Integer
Dim mintPlaysToAddDigit As Integer
```

The `mstrPick` string holds the randomly generated number that the user must guess to win a round.

```
Dim mstrPick As String
```

The `mintCurrent` variable keeps track of which digit is currently displayed as the player clicks through the series of digits. The `mintRound` variable keeps track of how many rounds of the game were played. This is used along with the `mintPlaysToAddDigit` variable to determine if the `mintDigits` value needs to be incremented for the next round.

```
Dim mintCurrent As Integer
Dim mintRound As Integer
```

The `mintWins` and `mintLosses` variables keep track of the score. The remaining `msg` and `cr` variables are used as they were in the Number Guess game program.

```
Dim mintWins As Integer
Dim mintLosses As Integer

Dim msg As String
Dim cr As String
```

Immediately after the declarations section is the subroutine that serves as the game entry point. It kicks off the game by opening the Flash Digits dialog box.

Enter the `FlashDigits` subroutine as shown in Listing 11.16.

Listing 11.16. The `FlashDigits` **subroutine.**

```
Sub FlashDigits()

  OpenDialog "Flash Digits"

End Sub
```

The *dlgFlashDigits_Show* Subroutine

The `dlgFlashDigits_Show` subroutine is activated when the Flash Digits dialog box is displayed. The subroutine reads in the game options from the Options worksheet and initializes program variables.

Enter the `dlgFlashDigits_Show` subroutine into the Flash Digits module as shown in Listing 11.17.

Listing 11.17. The `dlgFlashDigits_Show` **subroutine.**

```
Sub dlgFlashDigits_Show()

  Dim wsOptions As Worksheet

  On Error GoTo dlgFlashDigits_ShowError

  cr = Chr$(13) & Chr$(10)

' Get the option worksheet
  Set wsOptions = Workbooks(WORKBOOK_NAME).Worksheets("Options")

' Get the dialog
  Set mdlg = Workbooks(WORKBOOK_NAME).DialogSheets("Flash Digits")

' Read the values in the Options worksheet
  mintDigits = wsOptions.Range("StartDigits").Value
  mintPlaysToAddDigit = wsOptions.Range("PlaysToAddDigit").Value

' Init game variables
  mintRound = 0
  mintWins = 0
  mintLosses = 0

' Clear flash window
  mdlg.Text boxes("txtFlash").Caption = ""

  Randomize
  InitFlashDigits

dlgFlashDigits_ShowDone:
  Exit Sub
```

```
dlgFlashDigits_ShowError:
  MsgBox Error$(), 48, PROGRAM
  Resume dlgFlashDigits_ShowDone

End Sub
```

First, the subroutine sets the `wsOptions` and `mdlg` variables to point to the Options worksheet and the Flash Digits dialog box. Next it reads in the two game play options from the Options worksheet.

```
' Read the values in the Options worksheet
  mintDigits = wsOptions.Range("StartDigits").Value
  mintPlaysToAddDigit = wsOptions.Range("PlaysToAddDigit").Value
```

Because no rounds of the game have been played yet, the `mintRound` variable is set to zero. Also, the `mintWins` and `mintLosses` score-counting variables are set to zero.

```
' Init game variables
  mintRound = 0
  mintWins = 0
  mintLosses = 0
```

Just in case the `txtFlash` text box was saved with anything in it, the subroutine clears it here.

```
' Clear flash window
  mdlg.TextBoxes("txtFlash").Caption = ""
```

Next, the `Randomize` statement is called to seed the random number generator to ensure that a unique set of numbers is generated for each Flash Digits session.

Finally, the `InitFlashDigits` subroutine is called to initialize a single round of the game.

```
Randomize
InitFlashDigits
```

The *InitFlashDigits* Subroutine

This next subroutine is called at the start of each game. It has several assorted functions, including constructing the number used in this round of play and updating the scoreboard.

Enter the `InitFlashDigits` subroutine as shown in Listing 11.18.

Listing 11.18. The `InitFlashDigits` **subroutine.**

```
Sub InitFlashDigits()

' Reinitialize a round of the game

  Dim n As Integer
```

continues

Listing 11.18. continued

```
On Error GoTo InitFlashDigitsError

' Increment the length of the flash number every few rounds
  mintRound = mintRound + 1
  If mintRound > mintPlaysToAddDigit Then
    mintRound = 1
    mintDigits = mintDigits + 1
  End If

' Build the flash number
  mstrPick = ""
  For n = 1 To mintDigits
    mstrPick = mstrPick & Chr$(Int(10 * Rnd) + 48)
  Next n

' Debug.Print mstrPick

' Add a space as the last character
  mstrPick = mstrPick & " "

' Make a Start button
  mdlg.Buttons("cmdFlash").Caption = "Start"
  mdlg.Buttons("cmdFlash").Accelerator = "S"

' Update the scoreboard
  mdlg.Labels("lblWins").Caption = "Wins: " & mintWins
  mdlg.Labels("lblLosses").Caption = "Losses: " & mintLosses

  ClearEntry

' Set focus to the Button
  mdlg.Focus = "cmdFlash"

' No digits displayed yet
  mintCurrent = 0

InitFlashDigitsDone:
  Exit Sub

InitFlashDigitsError:
  MsgBox Error$(), 48, PROGRAM
  Resume InitFlashDigitsDone

End Sub
```

The `InitFlashDigits` subroutine first adds 1 to the `mintRound` counter to keep track of how many games have been played. If the count is greater than the value stored in `mintPlaysToAddDigit`, `mintDigits` is increased by 1 to make the flash digit number one digit longer.

When this happens, `mintRound` is set back to 1 to start the count of rounds all over again, as shown in Listing 11.19.

Listing 11.19. Determining whether to add a digit in this round of play.

```
' Increment the length of the flash number every few rounds
  mintRound = mintRound + 1
  If mintRound > mintPlaysToAddDigit Then
    mintRound = 1
    mintDigits = mintDigits + 1
  End If
```

Next the subroutine builds the number that is displayed one digit at a time to the game player.

It's easier to build and store the number as a string because you can be sure to generate a number with the appropriate number of digits. You also don't have to worry about numeric overflow with the integer or long integer variable types.

Another advantage of using a string is that retrieving each of the digits one by one can be done with the Mid$ function.

Using the Rnd function, a number between 48 and 57 is generated and then passed as an argument to the Chr$ function, which translates the number into a 0–9 digit character. Each digit is appended to the end of the string stored in the mstrPick string variable, as shown in Listing 11.20.

Listing 11.20. Building the flash digit number.

```
' Build the flash number
  mstrPick - ""
  For n = 1 To mintDigits
    mstrPick = mstrPick & Chr$(Int(10 * Rnd) + 48)
  Next n
```

While I was writing the function, I wanted to see what numbers were being generated. The next line, which is currently commented out, prints the generated number to the Immediate panel of the Debug window. You can remove the single quote to reactivate the line if you are stepping through the code in the debugger.

```
' Debug.Print mstrPick
```

After generating the digits, a space is added to the end of the mstrPick string. This space is the last character that gets written to the txtDigits text box, indicating that the number sequence has all been displayed.

```
' Add a space as the last character
  mstrPick = mstrPick & " "
```

The round of play begins by pressing the Start button. The next two lines change the caption and accelerator key for the multipurpose cmdFlash button so that it can be the Start button.

```
' Make a Start button
  mdlg.Buttons("cmdFlash").Caption = "Start"
  mdlg.Buttons("cmdFlash").Accelerator = "S"
```

Next the scoreboard is updated by writing the current win and loss counts to the lblWins and lblLosses labels.

```
' Update the scoreboard
  mdlg.Labels("lblWins").Caption = "Wins: " & mintWins
  mdlg.Labels("lblLosses").Caption = "Losses: " & mintLosses
```

The ClearEntry subroutine is called, which erases any text currently in the edtDigits edit box.

```
ClearEntry
```

Because the likely next step for the player to perform is to click the **S**tart button, the next line sets focus to it so the player can press either the Enter key or the spacebar to click it.

Admittedly, these are nitpicky details, but nitpicky details make a program fun and easy to use.

```
' Set focus to the Button
  mdlg.Focus = "cmdFlash"
```

Finally, the last part of game play initialization is to set the mintCurrent counter to zero. This variable keeps track of which digit in the flash digit number is currently displayed.

```
' No digits displayed yet
  mintCurrent = 0
```

TRY THIS! QUESTION 11.1.
Can you modify the InitFlashDigits subroutine so that capital letters are displayed instead of digits? What would you do to make this a game option?

The *cmdFlash_Click* Subroutine

The cmdFlash_Click subroutine is the game play engine.

The action performed in this subroutine depends on the current state of the game. The click could be to start the game, to read the next digit, or to enter the player's guess at what the number was.

Enter the cmdFlash_Click subroutine as shown in Listing 11.21.

Listing 11.21. The `cmdFlash_Click` subroutine.

```
Sub cmdFlash_Click()

  Dim strEntry As String

  On Error GoTo cmdFlash_ClickError

' Is this the first click?
  If mintCurrent = 0 Then
  ' Change the Start button to a Next button
    mdlg.Buttons("cmdFlash").Caption = "Next"
    mdlg.Buttons("cmdFlash").Accelerator = "N"

' Is this after the last digit?
  ElseIf mintCurrent = mintDigits Then
  ' Change the Next button to an Enter button
    mdlg.Buttons("cmdFlash").Caption = "Enter"
    mdlg.Buttons("cmdFlash").Accelerator = "E"

  ' Set focus to the Editbox
    mdlg.Focus = "edtDigits"

' Is this the entry?
  ElseIf mintCurrent = mintDigits + 1 Then
    strEntry = mdlg.EditBoxes("edtDigits").Text

    If Trim$(strEntry) = Trim$(mstrPick) Then
      MsgBox "You're right!", 0, PROGRAM
      mintWins = mintWins + 1

    Else
      MsgBox "Sorry! The answer was " & Trim$(mstrPick) & ".", 0, PROGRAM
      mintLosses = mintLosses + 1

    End If

    InitFlashDigits
    GoTo cmdFlash_ClickDone

  End If

' Display a digit
  mintCurrent = mintCurrent + 1
  mdlg.Text boxes("txtFlash").Text = Mid$(mstrPick, mintCurrent, 1)

' Don't let the player enter anything yet
  ClearEntry

cmdFlash_ClickDone:
  Exit Sub

cmdFlash_ClickError:
  MsgBox Error$(), 48, PROGRAM
  Resume cmdFlash_ClickDone

End Sub
```

At the beginning of the `cmdFlash_Click` subroutine, if the `mintCurrent` variable is set to zero, the player has clicked the **Start** button to begin a new round. The `cmdFlash_Click` subroutine changes the cmdFlash button to a **Next** button, as shown in Listing 11.22.

Listing 11.22. Changing the Start button to a Next button.

```
' Is this the first click?
  If mintCurrent = 0 Then
  ' Change the Start button to a Next button
    mdlg.Buttons("cmdFlash").Caption = "Next"
    mdlg.Buttons("cmdFlash").Accelerator = "N"
```

The player continually clicks the **Next** button to display the different digits one at a time.

If the present Click event is on the last digit, it's time for the **Next** button to change to the **Enter** button, as shown in Listing 11.23. The edtDigits text box receives focus so the player can make an entry as to which number just flashed by.

Listing 11.23. Changing the Next button to an Enter button.

```
' Is this after the last digit?
  ElseIf mintCurrent = mintDigits Then
  ' Change the Next button to an Enter button
    mdlg.Buttons("cmdFlash").Caption = "Enter"
    mdlg.Buttons("cmdFlash").Accelerator = "E"

' Set focus to the Editbox
  mdlg.Focus = "edtDigits"
```

When the `mintCurrent` variable is set to the number of digits plus 1, you know that this Click event is when the player clicked the **Enter** button to enter his or her guess.

The `strEntry` string variable receives the contents of the edtDigits edit box.

```
' Is this the entry?
  ElseIf mintCurrent = mintDigits + 1 Then
    strEntry = mdlg.EditBoxes("edtDigits").Text
```

The `strEntry` variable is compared to the `mstrPick` variable to see if the player entered the correct number. The `Trim$` function is used in both cases to remove any leading and trailing space characters before making the comparison.

If the player is correct, the program acknowledges it in a message box message, then increments the win count.

```
If Trim$(strEntry) = Trim$(mstrPick) Then
  MsgBox "You're right!", 0, PROGRAM
  mintWins = mintWins + 1
```

If the player is wrong, the correct number is displayed and the loss count is incremented.

```
Else
  MsgBox "Sorry! The answer was " & Trim$(mstrPick) & ".", 0, PROGRAM
  mintLosses = mintLosses + 1

End If
```

After displaying the results of whether the player was right or wrong, the `InitFlashDigits` subroutine is called to start a new game.

A `GoTo` statement is used to bail out of the subroutine because the rest of the code involves what happens during the middle of the game.

```
  InitFlashDigits
  GoTo cmdFlash_ClickDone

End If
```

If you are still in the subroutine at this point, the next thing to do is display the next digit in the txtFlash text box.

The `mintCurrent` variable is the offset into the `mstrPick` string where you can fetch the next character. It is incremented and then used in the `Mid$` function to extract the character.

Note that if you are already displaying the last digit, the lines here extract the extra space you left at the end of the `mstrPick` string, effectively clearing the txtFlash text box.

```
' Display a digit
  mintCurrent = mintCurrent + 1
  mdlg.TextBoxes("txtFlash").Text = Mid$(mstrPick, mintCurrent, 1)
```

Finally, the `ClearEntry` subroutine is called to erase any entries the user might have made while displaying the digits with the **N**ext button.

```
' Don't let the player enter anything yet
  ClearEntry
```

This subroutine might be a little hard to follow because it deals with three different game-playing states. You might want to mentally step through it as if you were playing the game, or better yet just set a breakpoint on the first line in the subroutine and step through it in the debugger after the program is finished.

The *ClearEntry* Subroutine

The final subroutine, `ClearEntry`, is a one-liner that clears the edtDigits edit box.

Enter the `ClearEntry` subroutine at the end of the Flash Digits module, as shown in Listing 11.24.

Listing 11.24. The `ClearEntry` subroutine.

```
Sub ClearEntry()

  mdlg.EditBoxes("edtDigits").Text = ""

End Sub
```

Whew! You've survived yet another coding session.

Hooking in the Flash Digits Code

To finish the Flash Digits game, you need to attach the `dlgFlashDigits_Show` and `cmdFlash_Click` subroutines to the appropriate Show and Click events.

1. Click the Flash Digits tab at the bottom of the workbook to display the Flash Digits dialog box.
2. Click the title bar of the dialog box with the right mouse button, then select the Assign Macro command from the pop-up menu.
3. In the Assign Macro dialog box, select the `dlgFlashDigits_Show` subroutine and click OK, as shown in Figure 11.35.

FIGURE 11.35.

Assigning the `dlgFlashDigits_Show` subroutine to the dialog box's Show event.

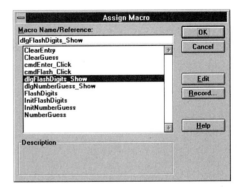

4. Click the edtDigits edit box with the right mouse button and again select the Assign Macro command from the pop-up menu.
5. Select the `cmdFlash_Click` subroutine in the Assign Macro dialog box and click OK.

Testing the Flash Digits Game

You can run the Flash Digits program from the debugger as you did earlier with the Number Guess game. If you are feeling confident that you won't need the debugger, you can go ahead and execute it from the **Tools|M**acro command.

1. Select the **Tools|M**acro command.
2. In the Macro dialog box, select the FlashDigits macro and click the **R**un button.

   The program should run without displaying any errors, although it is often easy enough to correct the problem if something does go wrong. A very common error that occurs produces a message like that shown in Figure 11.36.

FIGURE 11.36.
Oops!

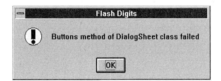

The error in this case, `Buttons method of DialogSheet class failed`, indicates that where I used the `Buttons` method to locate a button on the dialog box, a button by the name indicated could not be found. For example, the following line produces this error if there is no button named cmdFlash.

```
mdlg.Buttons("cmdFlash").Caption = "Start"
```

The solution in this case is to go to the dialog box and make sure the button is named correctly.

Playing the Flash Digits Game

If the code runs okay, game play should work like the following description.

When the Flash Digits dialog box appears, you can click the **S**tart button or press **E**nter to start the game.

The Flash Digits game displays the first number. Press Enter repeatedly until you have seen each number and the digit text box is blank again. Enter the number and press the Enter key again and the program tells you if you were right or wrong.

With the current settings in the Options worksheet, the game starts with five-digit numbers. The fourth number will be six digits, and every third number after that increases a digit, making the game tougher to play.

Summary

In this chapter you created the first two games of the Time Killers add-in workbook.

Here are some of the things you accomplished along the way:

- Got a structured overview of the GAMES.WKS workbook
- Created an Options worksheet in which to store program options
- Learned how to use Excel names to avoid hard-coded cell references
- Designed the Number Guess and Flash Digits games
- Built the dialog boxes for both games
- Wrote the Globals module
- Developed a structure for writing code for simple games
- Used the Rnd function and Randomize statement
- Used the text box drawing object to display text in a large font
- Wrote code that updated text and control properties on a dialog box
- Completed the code for two games

The next chapter continues the game writing adventure with two more games and the Fortune Cookie program.

TRY THIS! ANSWERS

11.1. To change the game so it displays characters instead of digits, you need to change the code that generates the mstrPick string.

The ASCII number value for the uppercase letter A is 65. You can find out the number for any character by entering a line like the following in the Debug window:

```
? Asc("A")
```

Because there are 26 characters in the alphabet, the range of random values includes 26 values rather than 10 as before. The change you need to make is shown in Listing 11.25.

Listing 11.25. Building a string of random characters.

```
' Build the flash characters
  mstrPick = ""
  For n = 1 To mintDigits
    mstrPick = mstrPick & Chr$(Int(26 * Rnd) + 65)
  Next n
```

To make this a game play option, you would use a Boolean variable to switch from building the string one way or the other, as shown in Listing 11.26.

Listing 11.26. Coding an option to produce digit or character sequences.

```
' Build the flash string from digits or characters
  mstrPick = ""
  For n = 1 To mintDigits
    If blnPlayDigits Then
      mstrPick = mstrPick & Chr$(Int(10 * Rnd) + 48)
    Else
      mstrPick = mstrPick & Chr$(Int(26 * Rnd) + 65)
    End If
Next n
```

You would need to set the `blnPlayDigits` variable based on either a new value in the Options worksheet or a check box added to the Flash Digits dialog box. The latter option would enable the player to switch between the two different options between rounds of the game.

CHAPTER 12

Excel: Time Killers, Part Two

In Chapter 11, "Excel: Time Killers, Part One," you completed two of the games in the GAMES.XLS workbook, Number Guess and Flash Digits. In this chapter you add two more games, Dupe the Dupes and Slot Machine, and also make the Fortune Cookie program.

After you are done programming, you create a menu and toolbar for the games and produce a final GAMES.XLA compiled add-in that you can install through Excel's **T**ools|**A**dd-**I**ns command.

As you develop the programs and final add-in workbook in this chapter, try to think about how the techniques you've used here might enhance some of your regular Excel projects. You will probably have a better idea of how the Excel dialog boxes work and how a program can be structured in Excel.

But don't let that keep you from having fun playing the games, too!

Dupe the Dupes

The next game you create caught me by surprise after I built it and ran it for the first time. The idea sounds simple enough, but it is surprisingly fun to play.

Dupe the Dupes (see Figure 12.1) is a game that displays a list of words, one by one; just like how Flash Digits displays digits one after the other. However, in this game you don't memorize the words to repeat them. Instead, you try to catch the word that shows up twice.

Sound easy? Well it's not! How many words that you saw do you think you can remember? Especially after you continue to additional rounds of the game. Sometimes you know you saw a word, but did you see it in this round or a previous one?

FIGURE 12.1.

Playing Dupe the
Dupes.

Dupe the Dupes
parachute
Next   **Dupe**   **Close**
Wins: 0   Losses: 1

In playing the game, you click a **N**ext button repeatedly to display each new word. If you find a duplicate word, you are instead supposed to click a button marked **D**upe to gain a win.

What adds suspense to the game is that any incorrect click on the **D**upe button is a loss, as well as a click on the **N**ext button if the current word is a duplicate. The game often abruptly catches you off guard as you click, click, click away on the **N**ext button and fail to notice the duplicate.

Have I got you interested? Let's do it!

Adding a Dupe the Dupes Game Option

The Dupe the Dupes game has a single game play option that determines, on average, how soon a duplicate word shows up. You can use this setting to make the game easier or harder to play.

The first thing you need to do in creating the game is add this option to the Options worksheet in your GAMES.XLS workbook.

1. Launch Excel and load the GAMES.XLS workbook created in Chapter 11.
2. Click the Options worksheet tab to display the Options worksheet.
3. In cell A13, enter Dupe the Dupes and click the Bold button on the Formatting toolbar.
4. In cell A14 enter Average Words Before Duplicate.
5. Click cell B14 and enter a value of 10.
6. Turn on the Formula bar with the **V**iew|**F**ormula Bar command if it isn't displayed.
7. With cell B14 still highlighted, enter AverageWordsBeforeDuplicate in the combo box at the left of the formula bar to create an Excel name pointing to B14.

   Figure 12.2 shows the Average Words Before Duplicate option added to the Options worksheet.

584   **Part II** ■ *Fun Projects*

FIGURE**FIGURE 12.2.**

Adding a game play option for the Dupe the Dupes game.

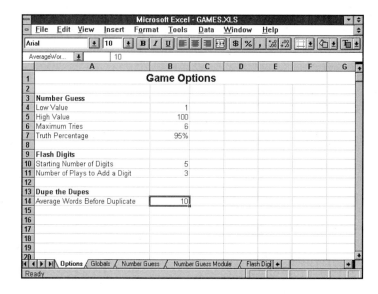

The Dupe the Dupes Dialog Box

Next, you need to create the dialog box sheet for the game.

1. Use the **Insert|Macro|Dialog** command to create a new dialog box sheet.
2. Double-click the dialog box sheet tab and rename the dialog box sheet Dupe the Dupes.
3. Drag the sheet tab all the way to the right to make it the last sheet in the workbook.
4. Change the dialog box sheet caption to Dupe the Dupes.
5. Select the dialog box sheet frame by clicking the title bar, and then enter a new name for the dialog box in the combo box in the formula bar. Change the name to dlgDupe.

For this game, you are going to need three buttons: a **S**tart/**N**ext button, a **D**upe button, and a Cancel button.

1. Click the Cancel button to select it.
2. Press Ctrl-C to copy the button.
3. Press Ctrl-V to paste a new copy of the Cancel button.

    The new button is pasted directly on top of the original Cancel button, so you might think that a new one wasn't created. Click the new button and drag it down and you have two Cancel buttons (as shown in Figure 12.3).

FIGURE 12.3.

Copying the Cancel button to make a third button.

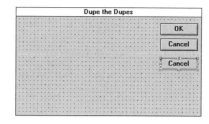

4. Drag the three buttons down the form about two-thirds of the way, aligning them horizontally as shown in Figure 12.4.

5. Change the captions of the buttons to Start, Dupe, and Close.

FIGURE 12.4.

Layout of the buttons on the Dupe the Dupes dialog box sheet.

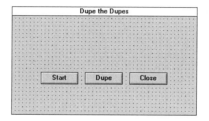

6. Using the combo box on the Formula Bar, select and change the names of the buttons to cmdNext (for the one labeled Start), cmdDupe, and cmdClose.

7. Use the right mouse button to click the cmdNext button and select Format Object from the pop-up menu.

8. Turn off the Dismiss option and enter S as the accelerator key. (See Figure 12.5.) Click OK to close the Format Object dialog box.

FIGURE 12.5.

Setting properties on the cmdNext button.

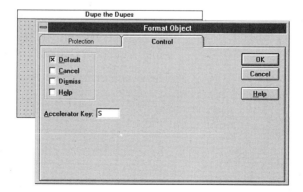

9. Open the Format Object dialog box for the cmdDupe button.

10. Turn off the **C**ancel and Di**s**miss options if they are on, and then enter a D as the accelerator key and click OK.

11. Open the Format Object dialog box for the cmdCancel button.

12. Turn on the **C**ancel and Di**s**miss options and enter a C as the accelerator key. Click OK.

Create a text box control as you did with the Flash Digits game in the last chapter. The text box should be wide enough to display any of the words used in the game.

1. Select the **View|T**oolbars command and in the Toolbars dialog box turn on the Drawing toolbar.

2. Click the text box button on the Drawing toolbar and draw a text box across the top of the dialog box, as shown in Figure 12.6.

3. Rename the text box to txtDisplay.

FIGURE 12.6.

Creating the txtDisplay text box.

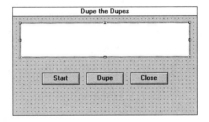

4. Click the right mouse button on the text box and select the Format Object command from the pop-up window.

5. In the Format Object dialog box, click the Patterns tab if it isn't already displayed, then select a Style, Color, and Weight for the border of the text box.

   I chose the style pattern at the bottom of the available selections, the color blue, and the thickest weight line available. (See Figure 12.7.)

6. Check the Sha**d**ow and **R**ound Corners check boxes to see if they are turned on.

7. In the Fill group box, select a color for the text box background. I chose light green.

8. Click the Font tab.

9. Select the Arial font, Bold, size 28.

10. Click the Alignment tab.

11. Select Horizontal **C**enter alignment and Vertical **C**enter alignment.

FIGURE 12.7.

Setting properties on the Patterns tab of the Format Object dialog box.

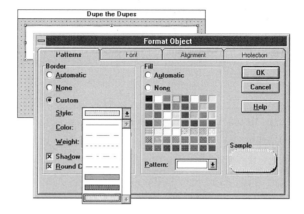

12. Click OK to accept all the changes in the Format Object dialog box.

Add two labels to record the score of the game.

1. Click the label button on the Forms toolbar and draw two labels on the bottom right portion of the dialog box sheet.

2. Enter Wins: into the first label and change the name of the label to lblWins.

3. Enter Losses: into the second label and change the name of it to lblLosses. Figure 12.8 shows the lblLosses label being created.

4. Close the Forms and Drawing toolbars.

FIGURE 12.8.

Adding lblWins and lblLosses to the Dupe the Dupes dialog box sheet.

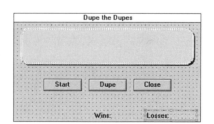

Hey, you knocked that one out fairly quickly! But before you get to write the code you need to create some data so the program has a list of words to display.

Creating the Dupe Words Worksheet

In Excel, you can store a table of supporting data for your program by just creating a worksheet and entering one record per row on the worksheet. If your data consists of several fields for each entry, then each field is in a separate worksheet column.

The data for the Dupe the Dupes is a list of words from which it can choose for display in random order. The words are entered by filling in column A on a new worksheet.

1. Use the **Insert**|**Worksheet** command to create a new worksheet.
2. Double-click the tab on the new worksheet and rename it to Dupe Words.

   If you are keeping your worksheets in the same order as mine as you develop the project, drag the worksheet tab to the right again to make it the last worksheet in the workbook.

3. Resize the width of column A to 25.00.
4. Enter a list of at least 100 words in column A (see Figure 12.9).

FIGURE 12.9.

Adding words to the Dupe Words worksheet.

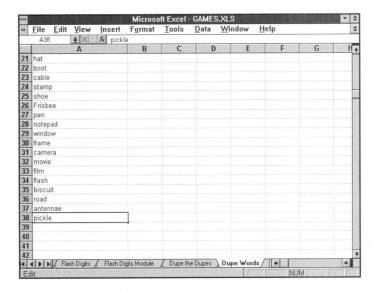

Enter as many words as you like. The more words you have, the more variety in the game.

You can use the spell checker in Excel to correct any spelling mistakes or typos you might have made while entering the words. To bring up the Excel spell checker, select the **Tools**|**S**pelling command.

Figure 12.10 shows the Excel Spelling dialog box suggesting the correct spelling for the word *satellite*.

Be careful not to enter the same word twice in the list. If there are any duplicate words, the game will appear to function incorrectly.

FIGURE 12.10.

Correcting misspellings with Excel's spell checker.

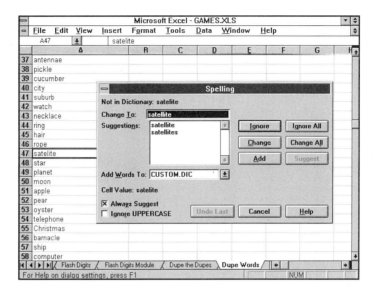

For example, the user may spot the duplicate word and hit the Dupe button expecting to win the round. Because the program is displaying words from two different rows, it wouldn't recognize the duplicate and claim that the player lost!

Next, create an Excel name for the column of words. The program will use the name in order to identify how many words are in the list.

1. Click the column head "A" to select all of column A.
2. While the column of words is selected, enter DupeWords in the combo box on the Formula Bar to create an Excel name that represents the range of cells. See Figure 12.11.

The way that the DupeWords name is defined, you can add additional words to the end of the list and the game will automatically use them.

TRY THIS! QUESTION 12.1.

Can you write a subroutine that scans the words in the Dupe Words worksheet and reports any duplicate words that are found?

FIGURE 12.11.
*Creating the
DupeWords name.*

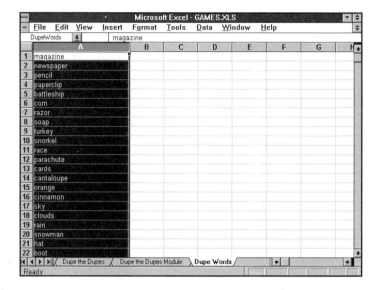

Coding the Dupe the Dupes Module

All right. You have your screen and your data. You're ready now to write the code.

1. With the Dupe Words worksheet displayed, select the **Insert|Macro|Module** command to create a new module sheet.

2. Rename the module sheet to Dupe the Dupes Module.

3. Enter the declarations, as shown in Listing 12.1.

Listing 12.1. Declarations for the Dupe the Dupes module.

```
' Dupe the Dupes

  Option Explicit

  Const PROGRAM = "Dupe the Dupes"

  Dim mdlg As DialogSheet
  Dim mwsDupeWords As Worksheet    ' Where the list of words is

  Dim mrngWords As Range           ' Range that contains word list

  Dim mintDupeAverage As Integer   ' Show a dupe on or before this number

  Dim mintWords As Integer         ' Number of words in the word list
  Dim mintCurrent As Integer       ' Current word to display
  Dim mintOffsets() As Integer     ' Which words to display
Dim mintDupe As Integer          ' Words before and including the first
➡ duplicate
```

```
Dim mintBetween As Integer      ' Number of words between the duplicates
Dim mintWordsInList As Integer  ' Total displayed words this round

Dim mintWins As Integer
Dim mintLosses As Integer

Dim msg As String
Dim cr As String
Dim dq As String
```

The variables in the declarations section store a variety of game-play information. I found it helpful in this case to write comments alongside some of the declarations to help me keep track of which variable was used for what.

The `mdlg` worksheet variable is set to the dialog box sheet. The `mwsDupeWords` worksheet variable is set to the DupeWords worksheet where the words are stored.

```
Dim mdlg As DialogSheet
Dim mwsDupeWords As Worksheet    ' Where the list of words is
```

The `mrngWords` variable is set to the range defined by the DupeWords name in the DupeWords worksheet. It is used to fetch the words within that range.

```
Dim mrngWords As Range           ' Range that contains word list
```

The `mintDupeAverage` variable is set on program startup to the value entered in the Options worksheet showing how many words, on average, should go by before the duplicate word appears in the list of words.

```
Dim mintDupeAverage As Integer   ' Show a dupe on or before this number
```

The `mintWords` variable is set to the number of words in the range the DupeWords name points to. This is one minus the number of rows in the range because the last row with the instructions is not counted.

```
Dim mintWords As Integer         ' Number of words in the word list
```

The `mintCurrent` variable counts how many words have been displayed to the user.

The `mintOffsets` array contains a set of row numbers for which words to display as the game is played. The words to display in the game are chosen ahead of time by filling in this array.

```
Dim mintCurrent As Integer       ' Current word to display
Dim mintOffsets() As Integer     ' Which words to display
```

The `mintDupe` variable contains the number of words that go by until the first occurrence of the dupe word is shown.

You don't want to always use the first word as the word to display as a duplicate, because then the game play would only be a matter of locating that first word again in the list. Instead, the player doesn't know which word is the one that is repeated.

```
Dim mintDupe As Integer          ' Words before and including the first
➥ duplicate
```

The `mintBetween` variable holds how many words are displayed between the first and second occurrence of the dupe word.

The `mintWordsInList` variable holds the total number of words displayed in a round, which is `mintDupe` plus `mintBetween` (plus one for the second occurrence of the dupe word).

```
Dim mintBetween As Integer     ' Number of words between the duplicates
Dim mintWordsInList As Integer ' Total displayed words this round
```

The `mintWins` and `mintLosses` variables keep score.

```
Dim mintWins As Integer
Dim mintLosses As Integer
```

The `msg` variable is used in constructing message box message strings. The `cr` variable holds the line feed characters and the `dq` variable holds the double quote character.

```
Dim msg As String
Dim cr As String
Dim dq As String
```

That's a lot of variables there. If the usage of any of them is unclear, they become a little clearer as you look through the code where they are used.

Next, you need to create the short entry routine for the game.

Enter the `DupeTheDupes` subroutine as shown in Listing 12.2.

Listing 12.2. The `DupeTheDupes` subroutine.

```
Sub DupeTheDupes()

  OpenDialog "Dupe the Dupes"

End Sub
```

The `DupeTheDupes` subroutine starts the game by opening the game's dialog box sheet with the `OpenDialog` subroutine that you created in the last chapter.

The *dlgDupeTheDupes_Show* Subroutine

Like your other game programs, the program initialization occurs in the dialog box sheet's Show event.

Enter the `dlgDupeTheDupes_Show` subroutine in the Dupe the Dupes module, as shown in Listing 12.3.

Listing 12.3. The `dlgDupeTheDupes_Show` subroutine.

```
Sub dlgDupeTheDupes_Show()

  Dim wsOptions As Worksheet
  Dim rng As Range

  On Error GoTo dlgDupeTheDupes_ShowError

  cr = Chr$(13) & Chr$(10)
  dq = Chr$(34)

' Get the option worksheet
  Set wsOptions = Workbooks(WORKBOOK_NAME).Worksheets("Options")
  Set mwsDupeWords = Workbooks(WORKBOOK_NAME).Worksheets("Dupe Words")

' Get the dialog
  Set mdlg = Workbooks(WORKBOOK_NAME).DialogSheets("Dupe the Dupes")

' Read the values in the Options worksheet
  mintDupeAverage = wsOptions.Range("AverageWordsBeforeDuplicate").Value * 2

' Determine the number of words in the word list
  Set mrngWords = mwsDupeWords.Range("DupeWords")
  Set rng = mrngWords.SpecialCells(xlLastCell)
  mintWords = rng.Row

  If mintDupeAverage > mintWords Then
    mintDupeAverage = mintWords
  End If

  mintWins = 0
  mintLosses = 0

  Randomize
  InitDupeTheDupes

dlgDupeTheDupes_ShowDone:
  Exit Sub

dlgDupeTheDupes_ShowError:
  MsgBox Error$(), 48, PROGRAM
  Resume dlgDupeTheDupes_ShowDone

End Sub
```

The `dlgDupeTheDupes` subroutine initializes a few variables and then calls the `InitDupeTheDupes` module to actually initialize a game round.

First, the handy `cr` and `dq` variables are set.

```
cr = Chr$(13) & Chr$(10)
dq = Chr$(34)
```

Next, the `wsOptions` variable and the `mwsDupeWords` module variable are set to the appropriate worksheets.

```
' Get the option worksheet
  Set wsOptions = Workbooks(WORKBOOK_NAME).Worksheets("Options")
  Set mwsDupeWords = Workbooks(WORKBOOK_NAME).Worksheets("Dupe Words")
```

Also, the `mdlg` variable is set to the Dupe the Dupes dialog box sheet.

```
' Get the dialog
  Set mdlg = Workbooks(WORKBOOK_NAME).DialogSheets("Dupe the Dupes")
```

Next, the `mintDupeAverage` variable is set to the value in the Options worksheet. The value is multiplied by two and used in the program as the high value for the range from which to pick the value for the number of words before the duplicate.

So technically, the variable doesn't actually store the average and is misnamed.

```
' Read the values in the Options worksheet
  mintDupeAverage = wsOptions.Range("AverageWordsBeforeDuplicate").Value * 2
```

The `mrngWords` variable is set to the range defined by the DupeWords name. Then to determine how many rows are in the range, a `rng` range variable is set to the last cell within the `mrngWords` range by calling the `SpecialCells` method.

The `SpecialCells` method can be used to return different ranges of cells, such as all the cells that have text in them, or all the cells that have errors. There are various constants you can pass to indicate what type of cell(s) you want to return.

To investigate further, place the cursor on the word SpecialCells and press F1 to view the online help description.

```
' Determine the number of words in the word list
  Set mrngWords = mwsDupeWords.Range("DupeWords")
  Set rng = mrngWords.SpecialCells(xlLastCell)
```

Once you have the last cell in the range, you can determine the number of rows in the range by checking the Row property of this cell.

```
mintWords = rng.Row
```

To avoid problems, you make sure that the number of words you intend to show before a duplicate appears is no greater than the number of words in the Dupe Words worksheet. You do some more bulletproofing in the next subroutine to make sure the program doesn't go astray for this odd situation.

```
If mintDupeAverage > mintWords Then
  mintDupeAverage = mintWords
End If
```

Next, the game score counters are initialized.

```
mintWins = 0
mintLosses = 0
```

Also, the `Randomize` statement is called to seed the random number generator with a unique value. Finally, the `InitDupeTheDupes` subroutine is called, which is the function called to initialize each round of game play.

```
Randomize
InitDupeTheDupes
```

The *InitDupeTheDupes* Subroutine

The `InitDupeTheDupes` subroutine has a little bit more work to do than your other game's initialization functions did.

The subroutine must pre-select which words to display during the entire round, including which word is the duplicate and when it shows up the first and second time.

Enter the `InitDupeTheDupes` subroutine as shown in Listing 12.4.

Listing 12.4. The `InitDupeTheDupes` subroutine.

```
Sub InitDupeTheDupes()

' Build a list of offsets that indicates which words are displayed as the
' round is played.

  Dim intList() As Integer

  Dim intWordsLeft As Integer
  Dim intSelected As Integer

  Dim i As Integer
  Dim n As Integer

  On Error GoTo InitDupeTheDupesError

' Calculate the number of words until the duplicate
  mintDupe = Int(Rnd * (mintDupeAverage / 2)) + 1

' Calculate the number of words to go by before the duplicate
  mintBetween = Int(Rnd * mintDupeAverage) + 1

' Make sure there are enough different words in the list for what is to
' be displayed.
  If mintDupe + mintBetween > mintWords Then
    Do
      If mintDupe > 0 Then
```

continues

Listing 12.4. continued

```
        mintDupe = mintDupe - 1
        If mintDupe + mintBetween = mintWords Then Exit Do
    End If

    If mintBetween > 0 Then
      mintBetween = mintBetween - 1
      If mintDupe + mintBetween = mintWords Then Exit Do
    End If
  Loop
End If

' Start with the list of words in the original order
ReDim intList(mintWords) As Integer
For n = 1 To mintWords
  intList(n) = n
Next n

' How many words are to be displayed in total?
mintWordsInList = mintDupe + mintBetween

' Allocate a list of word offsets
ReDim mintOffsets(mintWordsInList) As Integer

' Randomly pull out the words to get a list of words in random order
intWordsLeft = mintWords
For n = 1 To mintWordsInList
  intSelected = Int(Rnd * intWordsLeft) + 1

  ' Write the selected word to the play list
  mintOffsets(n) = intList(intSelected)

  ' Overwrite the selected word from the available list by sliding any
  ' following words up a notch
  For i = intSelected To mintWords - 1
    intList(i) = intList(i + 1)
  Next i

  ' The available list is one shorter now
  intWordsLeft = intWordsLeft - 1
Next n

' Clear the word display
mintCurrent = 0
mdlg.TextBoxes("txtDisplay").Text = ""

' Make a Start button
mdlg.Buttons("cmdNext").Caption = "Start"
mdlg.Buttons("cmdNext").Accelerator = "S"

' Update the scoreboard
mdlg.Labels("lblWins").Caption = "Wins: " & mintWins
mdlg.Labels("lblLosses").Caption = "Losses: " & mintLosses
```

```
InitDupeTheDupesDone:
  Exit Sub

InitDupeTheDupesError:
  MsgBox Error$(), 48, PROGRAM
  Resume InitDupeTheDupesDone

End Sub
```

During the game, you want the first appearance of the duplicate word to be as random as when it appears the second time.

The first line selects a random number between 1 and the number entered into the Options worksheet for the average number of words between duplicates. This means that the average number of words that go by before the dupe word first appears is half the average number of words between the first and second time.

```
' Calculate the number of words until the duplicate
  mintDupe = Int(Rnd * (mintDupeAverage / 2)) + 1
```

Next you calculate the second random value, which is the number of words between the first occurrence of the dupe word and the second occurrence.

```
' Calculate the number of words to go by before the duplicate
  mintBetween = Int(Rnd * mintDupeAverage) + 1
```

The next section of code (repeated in Listing 12.5) makes sure that the number of words up to and between the dupe word doesn't exceed the number of unique words in the Dupe Word list.

This section is actually kind of sloppily written because it uses a loop to decrement the count for each list one by one instead of figuring out how to make the adjustments with a mathematical formula. However, it's an odd situation that there wouldn't be enough words, so the section doesn't really merit any time spent for optimization.

The code evenly decrements the word count for both the number of words before the first dupe word, and the number of words between the first and second occurrence of the dupe word.

Listing 12.5. Making sure there are enough unique words.

```
' Make sure there are enough different words in the list for what is to
' be displayed.
  If mintDupe + mintBetween > mintWords Then
    Do
      If mintDupe > 0 Then
        mintDupe = mintDupe - 1
        If mintDupe + mintBetween = mintWords Then Exit Do
      End If
```

continues

Listing 12.5. continued

```
        If mintBetween > 0 Then
          mintBetween = mintBetween - 1
          If mintDupe + mintBetween = mintWords Then Exit Do
        End If
    Loop
  End If
```

Next, you prepare to build the list of randomly chosen words. This is a fun programming problem. Given a list of words, how do you randomly choose a set of them, making sure not to select any duplicates?

Here's how I solved it.

First, an array is dimensioned and filled in numeric order with a number for each word in the Dupe Words list.

The first element in the `intList` array stores a 1, indicating row 1 on the Dupe Words worksheet. The second element stores 2 for the second row, and so on.

```
' Start with the list of words in the original order
  ReDim intList(mintWords) As Integer
  For n = 1 To mintWords
    intList(n) = n
  Next n
```

You now calculate the total number of words that appear in the game and allocate the `mintOffsets` array that holds some of the values from the `intList` array which are randomly chosen and in random order.

```
' How many words are to be displayed in total?
  mintWordsInList = mintDupe + mintBetween

' Allocate a list of word offsets
  ReDim mintOffsets(mintWordsInList) As Integer
```

The `intWordsLeft` variable is set to how the number of words you can choose from in the list. This value decreases as words are chosen.

Next, a `For...Next` loop starts to loop as many times as words need to be selected.

```
' Randomly pull out the words to get a list of words in random order
  intWordsLeft = mintWords
  For n = 1 To mintWordsInList
```

The `intSelected` variable gets set to a random offset into the `intList` array.

```
intSelected = Int(Rnd * intWordsLeft) + 1
```

The selected word's row is stored in the `mintOffsets` array. The row is the value in the `intList` array at the offset indicated by the `intSelected` variable.

```
' Write the selected word to the play list
  mintOffsets(n) = intList(intSelected)
```

When a word is chosen, it must be removed from the available list of words so that it isn't chosen again. This is done by moving all the words after the chosen word up one notch.

```
' Overwrite the selected word from the available list by sliding any
' following words up a notch
  For i = intSelected To mintWords - 1
    intList(i) = intList(i + 1)
  Next i
```

With the hole filled, the list is now one word shorter, so the `intWordsLeft` variable is decreased by one.

This loop continues so that the list of available words shrinks while the list of selected words is filled, until all the words have been chosen.

```
' The available list is one shorter now
  intWordsLeft = intWordsLeft - 1
Next n
```

With the words chosen (as represented by the `mintOffsets` array), the game initialization continues.

The `mintCurrent` variable is set to zero, indicating that no word has been displayed yet. Also, the `txtDisplay` text box is cleared.

```
' Clear the word display
  mintCurrent = 0
  mdlg.TextBoxes("txtDisplay").Text = ""
```

The caption and accelerator of the `cmdNext` button are set to make it a **S**tart button.

```
' Make a Start button
  mdlg.Buttons("cmdNext").Caption = "Start"
  mdlg.Buttons("cmdNext").Accelerator = "S"
```

And finally, the current score is displayed by writing to the captions of the `lblWins` and `lblLosses` labels.

```
' Update the scoreboard
  mdlg.Labels("lblWins").Caption = "Wins: " & mintWins
  mdlg.Labels("lblLosses").Caption = "Losses: " & mintLosses
```

You've done all the setup. Now let's take a look at the game playing engine.

The *cmdNext_Click* Subroutine

This one is actually very easy. It's easy because you did all the work up front in the initialization code.

Not all the game play logic is in this one subroutine though, because you also have to program the **D**upe button.

Enter the `cmdNext_Click` subroutine in the Dupe the Dupes module, as shown in Listing 12.6.

Listing 12.6. The `cmdNext_Click` **subroutine.**

```
Sub cmdNext_Click()

  Dim strWord As String

  On Error GoTo cmdNext_ClickError

' Is this the start of the game?
  If mintCurrent = 0 Then
  ' Change Start button to the Next button
    mdlg.Buttons("cmdNext").Caption = "Next"
    mdlg.Buttons("cmdNext").Accelerator = "N"
  End If

  mintCurrent = mintCurrent + 1

' Is this past the duplicate?
  If mintCurrent > mintWordsInList + 1 Then

    ' Player loss
    strWord = mdlg.TextBoxes("txtDisplay").Text
    MsgBox dq & strWord & dq & " is a duplicate!", 48, PROGRAM
    mintLosses = mintLosses + 1

    InitDupeTheDupes

' Is this the duplicate?
  ElseIf mintCurrent = mintWordsInList + 1 Then

    ' Display the duplicate
    mdlg.TextBoxes("txtDisplay").Text = GetWord(mintDupe)
  ' Debug.Print GetWord(mintDupe)

  Else

    ' Display the current word
    mdlg.TextBoxes("txtDisplay").Text = GetWord(mintCurrent)
  ' Debug.Print GetWord(mintCurrent)

  End If

cmdNext_ClickDone:
  Exit Sub
```

```
cmdNext_ClickError:
  MsgBox Error$(), 48, PROGRAM
  Resume cmdNext_ClickDone

End Sub
```

The cmdNext_Click subroutine deals with different states of the game just as the cmdFlash_Click subroutine had to in the Flash Digits game. The state of the game is determined by the value in the mintCurrent variable.

First, the section of the subroutine shown in Listing 12.7 checks if mintCurrent is set to zero. If it is, then this is the click that starts the game. The **S**tart button is changed into a **N**ext button by changing its caption and accelerator key character.

Listing 12.7. The first click in a game.

```
' Is this the start of the game?
  If mintCurrent = 0 Then
  ' Change Start button to the Next button
    mdlg.Buttons("cmdNext").Caption = "Next"
    mdlg.Buttons("cmdNext").Accelerator = "N"
  End If
```

Next, the mintCurrent variable is incremented to count another click.

```
mintCurrent = mintCurrent + 1
```

At this point, if the mintCurrent variable is greater than the number of words in the word list plus one, then the player was on the second occurrence of the dupe word and passed it by clicking the **N**ext button.

```
' Is this past the duplicate?
  If mintCurrent > mintWordsInList + 1 Then
```

When the player loses this way, a message box is displayed with the bad news that the current word was a dupe. The score is updated and then InitDupeTheDupes is called again to re-initialize for another game. This is shown in Listing 12.8.

Listing 12.8. Code for when the player loses.

```
' Player loss
    strWord = mdlg.TextBoxes("txtDisplay").Text
    MsgBox dq & strWord & dq & " is a duplicate!", 48, PROGRAM
    mintLosses = mintLosses + 1

    InitDupeTheDupes
```

Given that you didn't enter the code described previously, if `mintCurrent` is equal to the number of words in the list plus one, then it's time to display the second occurrence of the duplicate.

```
' Is this the duplicate?
  ElseIf mintCurrent = mintWordsInList + 1 Then
```

The duplicate word is fetched by calling a `GetWord` function that you haven't written yet. The `mintDupe` variable holds the turn in which the dupe word came up the first time.

I left a `Debug.Print` statement in the code, although it is commented out. I used `Debug.Print` during development to gather a list of which words were being displayed in the Immediate window so I could verify that duplicate words were only showing up when they should.

```
' Display the duplicate
  mdlg.TextBoxes("txtDisplay").Text = GetWord(mintDupe)
' Debug.Print GetWord(mintDupe)
```

The remaining game state (shown in Listing 12.9) is when another word needs to be displayed in the `txtDisplay` text box.

Listing 12.9. Displaying the next word to continue the game.

```
Else

' Display the current word
  mdlg.TextBoxes("txtDisplay").Text = GetWord(mintCurrent)
' Debug.Print GetWord(mintCurrent)

End If
```

The *GetWord* Function

Here's that `GetWord` function you saw used in the `cmdNext_Click` subroutine.

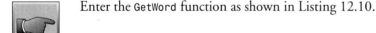Enter the `GetWord` function as shown in Listing 12.10.

Listing 12.10. The `GetWord` function.

```
Function GetWord(intRow As Integer) As String

' Retrieve a word from the word list by current order

  GetWord = mrngWords.Cells(mintOffsets(intRow))

End Function
```

The GetWord function takes a number for the current word displayed in the game. It translates that into the row number where the word can be found in the Dupe Words worksheet.

The word is retrieved by calling the Cells method on the mrngWords range with a row number.

The *cmdDupe_Click* Subroutine

There has to be a place in this program for the player to win the game. It's in here.

If the player clicks the **D**upe button at the right time, then he or she wins. Clicking at the wrong time, however, is a loss.

Enter the cmdDupe_Click subroutine as shown in Listing 12.11.

Listing 12.11. The cmdDupe_Click subroutine.

```
Sub cmdDupe_Click()

  Dim strWord As String

  On Error GoTo cmdDupe_ClickError

' Has a game started yet?
  If mintCurrent = 0 Then
    MsgBox "Click the Start button to begin a game.", 64, PROGRAM
    GoTo cmdDupe_ClickDone
  End If

  strWord = mdlg.TextBoxes("txtDisplay").Text

' Is this the duplicate?
  If mintCurrent = mintWordsInList + 1 Then
MsgBox "You are right!" & cr & cr & dq & strWord & dq &
➥ " is a duplicate.", 0, PROGRAM
    mintWins = mintWins + 1
  Else
    MsgBox "Sorry, " & dq & strWord & dq & " is not a duplicate.", 0, PROGRAM
    mintLosses = mintLosses + 1
  End If

  InitDupeTheDupes

cmdDupe_ClickDone:
  Exit Sub

cmdDupe_ClickError:
  MsgBox Error$(), 48, PROGRAM
  Resume cmdDupe_ClickDone

End Sub
```

The `cmdDupe_Click` subroutine first checks to see if the player is new to the game and clicked the **D**upe button before ever clicking the **S**tart button. If so, then the subroutine bails out with a message.

```
' Has a game started yet?
  If mintCurrent = 0 Then
    MsgBox "Click the Start button to begin a game.", 64, PROGRAM
    GoTo cmdDupe_ClickDone
  End If
```

Following this point, the game has ended either with a win or a loss. The current word is read from the `txtDisplay` text box.

```
    strWord = mdlg.TextBoxes("txtDisplay").Text
```

The program knows if the player is on the duplicate word because that will always be one past the number of words selected to be displayed.

In the code shown in Listing 12.12, the player is congratulated or told the disappointing news. In either case, the dupe word is displayed for clarification in the message box.

Listing 12.12. Displaying the game results.

```
' Is this the duplicate?
  If mintCurrent = mintWordsInList + 1 Then
MsgBox "You are right!" & cr & cr & dq & strWord & dq &
➥ " is a duplicate.", 0, PROGRAM
    mintWins = mintWins + 1
  Else
    MsgBox "Sorry, " & dq & strWord & dq & " is not a duplicate.", 0, PROGRAM
    mintLosses = mintLosses + 1
  End If
```

The game is then initialized for a new round.

```
    InitDupeTheDupes
```

You're just screaming through the code here aren't you? All you have to do is attach the macro code to the dialog box and it's ready to go.

Attaching Code to the Dupe the Dupes Dialog Box

This time around you have three different events for which you wrote code: the dialog box's Show event and two buttons' Click events.

1. Click the Dupe the Dupes tab to display the dialog box.
2. Use the right mouse button to click the dialog box's title bar, then select the Assign Macro command to bring up the Assign macro dialog box.

3. Select the `dlgDupeTheDupes_Show` subroutine from the list of subroutines and click OK. See Figure 12.12.

FIGURE 12.12.

Assigning the dlgDupeTheDupes_Show subroutine to the Show event.

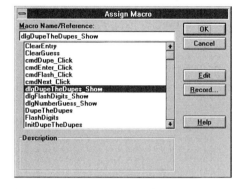

4. Click the right mouse button on the `cmdNext` button and select the Assign Macro command again.
5. Assign the `cmdNext_Click` subroutine to the click event and close the dialog box.
6. Assign the `cmdDupe_Click` subroutine to the `cmdDupe` button's click event in the same way.

Testing Dupe the Dupes

To play the game, you can run the `DupeTheDupes` macro either through the Debug window or with the **Tools|M**acro command. At the end of this chapter you create a menu and a toolbar that make launching the games much more convenient.

1. Click the Dupe the Dupes module tab.
2. Select the **View|D**ebug Window command.
3. Enter `DupeTheDupes` in the Immediate pane of the Debug window and press Enter.

Playing Dupe the Dupes

The Dupe the Dupes dialog box displays with focus set to the **S**tart button. Press Enter to start the game.

The **S**tart button changes into a **N**ext button. Click the **N**ext button after each word appears, giving yourself enough time to take in each of the words so you can recognize the duplicate when it comes.

If you see a word that you believe has already been shown once before, then click the **D**upe button. If you are correct, then your win score goes up, but if you are wrong, then your loss count is incremented.

Figure 12.13 shows the game being played to test the program.

FIGURE 12.13.

Playing the Dupe the Dupes game.

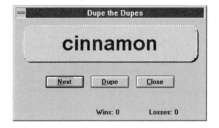

The Slot Machine Game

The Slot Machine game (shown in Figure 12.14) is a dialog box with dial windows in it. It has two buttons: **P**lay and **C**ash-In.

FIGURE 12.14.

The Slot Machine Game uses the Wingdings font to display different pictures in the dial windows.

You start with $100. Each play costs you two dollars. Click the **P**lay button to spin the dials. If the right combination comes up, then you can win up to $1000.

The amounts and odds of winning are configurable. In other words, you can "rig" the game if you like. I set the options so that the game hopefully plays somewhat realistically. The player tends to lose money at the game rather than win. I think that's pretty much how all gambling goes.

One of the challenges at playing the game is determining when to quit if you seem to be on a winning streak. Even if you get a couple of hundred dollars ahead, in no time at all you can lose it all again. Do you keep playing to take the winnings even higher?

Adding the Slot Machine Game Play Options

The Slot Machine game has more options than the other games you created. Each option plays a factor in how much the slot machine awards winnings to the player.

1. Enter `Slot Machine` into cell A16 as an Options worksheet section title. Click the Bold button to set the text to bold.

2. In cells A17 through A26, enter the following option titles:

   Low Payoff
   Chance for Low Payoff
   Medium Payoff
   Chance for Medium Payoff
   High Payoff
   Chance for High Payoff
   Jackpot
   Chance for Jackpot
   Start With
   Cost Per Pull

3. In cells B17 through B26, enter values for each of the options as shown in the table below:

Low Payoff	$5.00
Chance for Low Payoff	20.00%
Medium Payoff	$20.00
Chance for Medium Payoff	2.00%
High Payoff	$100.00
Chance for High Payoff	0.20%
Jackpot	$1,000.00
Chance for Jackpot	0.01%
Start With	$100.00
Cost Per Pull	$2.00

Cells B17, B19, B21, B23, B25, and B26 are formatted to display currency values. Cells B18, B20, B22, and B24 are formatted to display values in percentages.

You can turn on the formats by clicking in each cell, and then the dollar sign or percent sign buttons on the Format toolbar.

The actual values entered in the Percent formatted cells are:

   B18-0.2
   B20-0.02
   B24-0.002
   B26-0.0001

Figure 12.15 shows the Option worksheet as the Slot Machine game options are being added.

FIGURE 12.15.

Entering in the option values for the Slot Machine game.

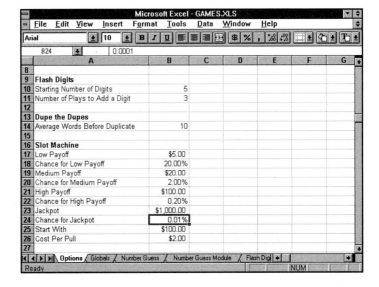

You now need to create an Excel name for each option to allow the Slot Machine program to read the values in.

1. Click cell B17 to select it.
2. Enter LowPayoff into the combo box on the formula bar.
3. Enter in names for cells B17 through B26 to finish defining the list of names listed below:

LowPayoff	=Options!$B$17
LowPayoffChance	=Options!$B$18
MediumPayoff	=Options!$B$19
MediumPayoffChance	=Options!$B$20
HighPayoff	=Options!$B$21
HighPayoffChance	=Options!$B$22
Jackpot	=Options!$B$23
JackpotChance	=Options!$B$24
StartWith	=Options!$B$25
CostPerPull	=Options!$B$26

You can verify that each of the names was entered correctly by using the **Insert|Name|Define** command to bring up the Define Name dialog box. In the dialog box you see a list of all the names defined in the workbook so far (see Figure 12.16).

FIGURE 12.16.

*Examining which
names are in the
workbook with the
Define Name dialog
box.*

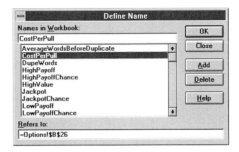

Creating the Slot Machine Dialog Box

You now create your fourth, and last, dialog box sheet for this workbook. The Slot
Machine dialog box uses three text boxes as the dial windows and a couple of buttons to
control game play.

1. Select the **Insert|Macro|D**ialog command to create a new dialog box sheet.
2. Drag the new sheet to the far right to make it the last tab in the workbook.
3. Double-click the tab and rename the dialog box sheet Slot Machine.
4. Select the caption text in the dialog box title bar and enter Slot Machine.
5. Select the dialog box, then enter dlgSlotMachine as the name of the dialog box
   frame into the combo box on the Formula Bar.

Next, add a text box as one of the three slot machine windows.

1. Turn on the Drawing toolbar.
2. Click the text box button on the drawing toolbar and draw a single rectangular
   text box, as shown in Figure 12.17.

FIGURE 12.17.

*Creating a text box for
a Slot Machine dial
window.*

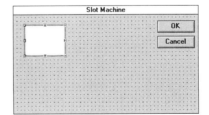

3. Click the right mouse button on the text box and select the Format Object
   command from the pop-up menu that is displayed.
4. In the Patterns tab of the Format Object dialog box, select a **S**tyle, **C**olor, and
   Weight for the border of the text box. I chose the third style from the bottom,
   blue, and the second thickest weight.

5. Click the Shadow check box so it is checked.

6. Select a background color from the colors in the Fill group box. Again, I selected blue. (See Figure 12.18.)

FIGURE 12.18.

Setting the appearance of a Slot Machine dial window.

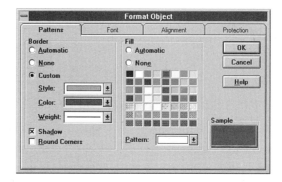

7. Click the Font tab of the Format Objects dialog box.

   This is where you're going to get some neat graphics for the different items that display in the Slot Machine dial windows.

8. Scroll down to the bottom of available fonts and select the "Wingdings" font, as shown in Figure 12.19.

9. Set the font to a regular font style, size 28.

FIGURE 12.19.

Selecting the Wingdings font for graphic characters.

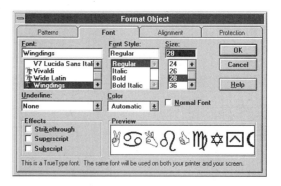

10. Click the Alignment tab.

11. Set both the horizontal and vertical text alignment to Center.

12. Click OK to close the Format Object dialog box.

To save some time, copy and paste the new text box to produce the remaining two slot machine windows.

1. Click the text box and press Ctrl-C to copy it.
2. Press Ctrl-V to paste a copy of the text box, and then drag it to the right of the first one.
3. Press Ctrl-V a second time to paste a third text box.
4. Select each text box individually and enter a name for each in the combo box in the Formula Bar. Name them from left to right, txtDial1, txtDial2, and txtDial3 (see Figure 12.20).

The names for the controls are important because the program uses them to assign values to the text box captions.

FIGURE 12.20.

Creating the Slot Machine dial windows.

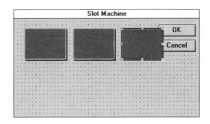

Make **P**lay and **C**ash-In buttons out of the OK and Cancel buttons.

1. Make the dialog box slightly taller by selecting the frame and dragging the bottom of it down.
2. Move the OK and Cancel buttons down near the bottom of the dialog box and bring in the right side so the dialog box isn't as wide. The layout should look like that shown in Figure 12.21.

FIGURE 12.21.

The layout of the Slot Machine dialog box.

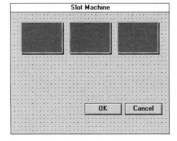

3. Change the captions of the buttons from OK and Cancel to Play and Cash-In.
4. Using the Formula Bar again, change the name of the **P**lay button to cmdPlay.
5. Change the name of the **C**ash-In button to cmdCashIn.
6. Bring up the Format Object dialog box for the cmdPlay button.

7. Turn off the Dismiss option and enter P for the **A**ccelerator Key. Close the dialog box.

8. Bring up the Format Object dialog box for the cmdCashIn button and set the **A**ccelerator Key to C. Leave the Dismiss option checked for this button and close the dialog box.

Next you create a text box to display messages to the player when they win some money.

1. Turn on the Drawing toolbar again if you turned it off.

2. Draw a wide text box in the middle of the dialog box as shown in Figure 12.22.

FIGURE 12.22.

Creating the txtMessage text box.

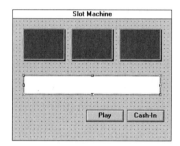

3. Click the text box using the right mouse button and select the Format Object command.

4. In the Format Object dialog box, set the Border to **N**one and the Fill color to Non**e**.

5. Click the Font tab and select the Arial font, Bold, size 14.

6. Click the Alignment tab and set the Horizontal and Vertical text alignment options to Center. Close the Format Object dialog box.

   Because the text box has no background color or border, when you click off it, it disappears from view. Click on the same area again and you see the text box selected, as shown in Figure 12.23.

7. Rename the new text box to txtMessage.

FIGURE 12.23.

The txtMessage text box has no background color or border.

Create two labels to display the game score.

1. Click the Label button on the Forms toolbar and draw a label to the left and slightly lower than the buttons.

2. Enter Cash: into the label caption and rename the label control to lblCash.

3. Draw another label below the buttons with the caption $2.00 per play. Name the label lblCostPerPull (see Figure 12.24).

Both of these labels have their text updated by the program, but in development it's nice to enter something in the caption as a reminder of what the labels are used for.

FIGURE 12.24.

The completed Slot Machine dialog box.

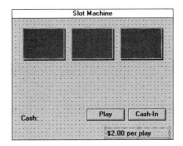

You're done here until you again have some subroutines to attach to a dialog box.

The Slot Machine Module

The Slot Machine program is kind of deceptive in nature.

Rather than first randomly choosing which symbols to display in the dial windows and *then* seeing if the player gets a reward, the game actually determines first if it is going to make an award, and afterward picks symbols that represent the reward, or lack of reward.

The symbols shown in the dial windows are a subset of the characters in the Wingdings font. I chose the ones that seemed appropriate for the game. Special combinations of the characters are chosen to represent the different cash awards as either double or triple matches.

1. Create a new Module sheet and drag it to the end of the workbook after the other sheets.

2. Rename the module sheet to Slot Machine Module.

3. Enter the declarations section as shown in Listing 12.13.

Listing 12.13. The declarations in the Slot Machine module.

```
' Slot Machine

Option Explicit

Const PROGRAM = "Slot Machine"

Dim mdlg As DialogSheet

Dim msngLowPayoff As Single
Dim msngMediumPayoff As Single
Dim msngHighPayoff As Single
Dim msngJackpot As Single

Dim msngLowPayoffChance As Single
Dim msngMediumPayoffChance As Single
Dim msngHighPayoffChance As Single
Dim msngJackpotChance As Single

Dim msngStartWith As Single
Dim msngCostPerPull As Single

Dim msngCash As Single

Dim msg As String
Dim cr As String
```

The `mdlg` variable is again used to point to the game's dialog box sheet as you did in the other game programs.

```
Dim mdlg As DialogSheet
```

Many of the variables declared are going to be set to the corresponding values in the Options worksheet. The first four store the cash awards for four different prizes.

```
Dim msngLowPayoff As Single
Dim msngMediumPayoff As Single
Dim msngHighPayoff As Single
Dim msngJackpot As Single
```

The next four hold values indicating what the chances are for the different rewards to be awarded.

```
Dim msngLowPayoffChance As Single
Dim msngMediumPayoffChance As Single
Dim msngHighPayoffChance As Single
Dim msngJackpotChance As Single
```

The `msngStartWith` and `msngCostPerPull` variables are set to the remaining two game play options, indicating how much money the player starts with and how much it costs for each round of play.

```
Dim msngStartWith As Single
Dim msngCostPerPull As Single
```

The `msngCash` variable holds how much money the player has throughout the game.

```
Dim msngCash As Single
```

The `msg` and `cr` variables are used again for creating `MsgBox` messages.

```
Dim msg As String
Dim cr As String
```

Following the declarations, the Slot Machine module declares two more module variables after a comment section that explains their use.

Enter the remainder of the declaration section as shown in Listing 12.14.

Listing 12.14. Declarations for using the Wingding characters.

```
' J - smiley face
' L - sad face
' M -bomb
' N -skull
' O -flag
' Q -airplane
' R -sun
' T -snowflake
'
' w -diamond
'
' 6 - hourglass
'
' ! - pencil
' # - scissors
' $ - glasses
' % - bell
'
' : - computer
' ' - candle
' - - mailbox
' > - tape

  Const mstrSymbols = "JLMNOQRTw6!#$%:'->"
  Dim mintSymbolsLength As Integer
```

Not that it would be any improvement, but the module editor doesn't display Wingding characters.

The comments in Listing 12.14 indicate what symbols appear for the different characters used in the program as dial window characters.

The constant, `mstrSymbols`, is declared as a string containing each of the characters used. Another variable, `mintSymbolsLength`, gets initialized to the number of characters in `mstrSymbols`.

```
Const mstrSymbols = "JLMNOQRTw6!#$%:'->"
Dim mintSymbolsLength As Integer
```

The Slot Machine program has an entry point function like the other games. This subroutine starts the game by displaying the Slot Machine dialog box.

Enter the `SlotMachine` subroutine as shown in Listing 12.15.

Listing 12.15. The `SlotMachine` subroutine.

```
Sub SlotMachine()

  OpenDialog "Slot Machine"

End Sub
```

The *dlgSlotMachine_Show* Subroutine

The Slot Machine program differs in some ways from the structure of the programs in the other games. There are more supporting subroutines and all of the game initialization occurs when the dialog box opens.

The `dlgSlotMachine_Show` subroutine reads in the game play options stored in the Options worksheet and initializes other game play variables that persist through each round of play.

In the Slot Machine game, a round of play is each click of the Play button.

Enter the `dlgSlotMachine_Show` subroutine as shown in Listing 12.16.

Listing 12.16. The `dlgSlotMachine_Show` subroutine.

```
Sub dlgSlotMachine_Show()

  Dim wsOptions As Worksheet

  On Error GoTo dlgSlotMachine_ShowError

  cr = Chr$(13) & Chr$(10)

' Get the option worksheet
  Set wsOptions = Workbooks(WORKBOOK_NAME).Worksheets("Options")

' Get the dialog
  Set mdlg = Workbooks(WORKBOOK_NAME).DialogSheets("Slot Machine")
```

```
' Read the values in the Options worksheet
  msngLowPayoff = wsOptions.Range("LowPayoff").Value
  msngMediumPayoff = wsOptions.Range("MediumPayoff").Value
  msngHighPayoff = wsOptions.Range("HighPayoff").Value
  msngJackpot = wsOptions.Range("Jackpot").Value

  msngLowPayoffChance = wsOptions.Range("LowPayoffChance").Value
  msngMediumPayoffChance = wsOptions.Range("MediumPayoffChance").Value
  msngHighPayoffChance = wsOptions.Range("HighPayoffChance").Value
  msngJackpotChance = wsOptions.Range("JackpotChance").Value

  msngStartWith = wsOptions.Range("StartWith").Value
  msngCostPerPull = wsOptions.Range("CostPerPull").Value

' Convert the percentages to a range of values
  msngMediumPayoffChance = msngMediumPayoffChance + msngLowPayoffChance
  msngHighPayoffChance = msngHighPayoffChance + msngMediumPayoffChance
  msngJackpotChance = msngJackpotChance + msngHighPayoffChance

' How much money does the play start with?
  msngCash = msngStartWith

' How much it costs to play
  msg = Format$(msngCostPerPull, "Currency") & " per play"
  mdlg.Labels("lblCostPerPull").Caption = msg

  mintSymbolsLength = Len(mstrSymbols)

  Randomize

  SymbolsNoPayoff
  Message ""
  UpdateCash

dlgSlotMachine_ShowDone:
  Exit Sub

dlgSlotMachine_ShowError:
  MsgBox Error$(), 48, PROGRAM
  Resume dlgSlotMachine_ShowDone

End Sub
```

The subroutine first starts with what by now is getting pretty routine; the initialization of several variables. First the `cr` variable is set.

```
cr = Chr$(13) & Chr$(10)
```

Next, the `wsOptions` worksheet variable is set so you can read the values in the Options worksheet.

```
' Get the option worksheet
  Set wsOptions = Workbooks(WORKBOOK_NAME).Worksheets("Options")
```

The `mdlg` dialog box sheet variable is set so you have access to the controls on the Slot Machine dialog box.

```
' Get the dialog
  Set mdlg = Workbooks(WORKBOOK_NAME).DialogSheets("Slot Machine")
```

The game prize dollar values are now read in.

```
' Read the values in the Options worksheet
  msngLowPayoff = wsOptions.Range("LowPayoff").Value
  msngMediumPayoff = wsOptions.Range("MediumPayoff").Value
  msngHighPayoff = wsOptions.Range("HighPayoff").Value
  msngJackpot = wsOptions.Range("Jackpot").Value
```

Then the chance values are read in. These numbers are floating point values in the range from 0 to 1, which is just perfect because the `Rnd` function speaks that kind of language, too.

```
msngLowPayoffChance = wsOptions.Range("LowPayoffChance").Value
msngMediumPayoffChance = wsOptions.Range("MediumPayoffChance").Value
msngHighPayoffChance = wsOptions.Range("HighPayoffChance").Value
msngJackpotChance = wsOptions.Range("JackpotChance").Value
```

Next, the remaining two options are read in.

```
msngStartWith = wsOptions.Range("StartWith").Value
msngCostPerPull = wsOptions.Range("CostPerPull").Value
```

The subroutine now modifies the values in the payoff chance variables to spread them across a range from 0 to 1.

```
' Convert the percentages to a range of values
  msngMediumPayoffChance = msngMediumPayoffChance + msngLowPayoffChance
  msngHighPayoffChance = msngHighPayoffChance + msngMediumPayoffChance
  msngJackpotChance = msngJackpotChance + msngHighPayoffChance
```

This is done so that the result of a call to the `Rnd` function falls within one of these ranges or in the remaining range that represents no payoff.

Figure 12.25 illustrates this. The bar represents a range of values from 0.0 to 1.0. The $5 block is the range from 0 to `msngLowPayoffChance`. The $20 block is the range from `msngLowPayoffChance` to `msngMediumPayoff` chance.

This goes on up to a range for the jackpot, which has the highest award in this case and the smallest chance to win. Following the range for the jackpot are the remaining values between `msngJackpotChance` and 1.0. This area represents no win.

The starting amount of cash is set next.

```
' How much money does the play start with?
  msngCash = msngStartWith
```

FIGURE 12.25.
How Slot Machine determines a win.

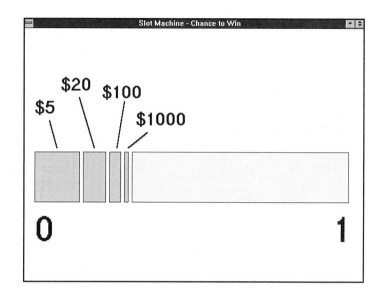

The label that displays how much it costs per play is updated with the value read from the Options worksheet.

```
' How much it costs to play
  msg = Format$(msngCostPerPull, "Currency") & " per play"
  mdlg.Labels("lblCostPerPull").Caption = msg
```

The `mintSymbolsLength` variable is set to the number of characters in the `mstrSymbols` constant. I could have made `mintSymbolsLength` a constant also, but this way you're sure to have it set to the correct number.

```
mintSymbolsLength = Len(mstrSymbols)
```

The `Randomize` statement is then called to ensure a unique game.

```
Randomize
```

Next, a few subroutines that you haven't written yet are called. The `SymbolsNoPayoff` subroutine displays appropriate symbols for a round with no reward. I wanted the game to start with some symbols displayed rather than empty dial windows.

Next, a `Message` subroutine is called to clear the txtMessage text box. Finally, the `UpdateCash` subroutine is called to update the dialog box with how much money the player has.

```
SymbolsNoPayoff
Message ""
UpdateCash
```

The *Message* Subroutine

This next one is a one-liner. Sometimes it's useful to create subroutines like this just to add some readability to the code.

The Message subroutine displays a message in the txtMessage text box. It's used in the program to indicate that the player won some money on the current round.

Enter the Message subroutine shown in Listing 12.17.

Listing 12.17. The Message **subroutine.**

```
Sub Message(strText As String)

  mdlg.TextBoxes("txtMessage").Caption = strText

End Sub
```

The *UpdateCash* Subroutine

This one is also a one-liner.

The subroutine writes to the caption of the lblCash label how much money the player has left. The Format$ function is used to create the expression in currency format.

Enter the UpdateCash subroutine as shown in Listing 12.18.

Listing 12.18. The UpdateCash **subroutine.**

```
Sub UpdateCash()

' Update the lblCash label with the current amount
  mdlg.Labels("lblCash").Caption = "Cash: " & Format$(msngCash, "Currency")

End Sub
```

The *cmdPlay_Click* Subroutine

Too bad every subroutine can't have only one line in it. This next subroutine is the game play engine. The game player, turned into an addicted gambler, repeatedly clicks the **P**lay button, which calls this subroutine each time to determine if a win occurred or another $2 was pocketed by the machine.

Enter the cmdPlay_Click subroutine into the Slot Machine module as shown in Listing 12.19.

Listing 12.19. The `cmdPlay_Click` subroutine.

```
Sub cmdPlay_Click()

  Dim sngPull As Single
  Dim sngPayoff As Single

  On Error GoTo cmdPlay_ClickError

' See if the player has enough cash to play a round
  If msngCash < msngCostPerPull Then
    msg = "You must deposit " & Format$(msngCostPerPull, "Currency")
    msg = msg & " in the machine to play."
    MsgBox msg, 64, PROGRAM
    GoTo cmdPlay_ClickDone
  End If

' Get a random "Pull" value
  sngPull = Rnd

  sngPayoff = 0#

' Did the player win a low value?
  If sngPull < msngLowPayoffChance Then
    sngPayoff = msngLowPayoff
    SymbolsLowPayoff
  ElseIf sngPull < msngMediumPayoffChance Then
    sngPayoff = msngMediumPayoff
    SymbolsMediumPayoff
  ElseIf sngPull < msngHighPayoffChance Then
    sngPayoff = msngHighPayoff
    SymbolsHighPayoff
  ElseIf sngPull < msngJackpotChance Then
    sngPayoff = msngJackpot
    SymbolsJackpot
' Beep
  Else
    SymbolsNoPayoff
  End If

  msngCash = msngCash - msngCostPerPull

  If sngPayoff > 0 Then
    Message "You won " & Format$(sngPayoff, "Currency")
    msngCash = msngCash + sngPayoff
  Else
    Message ""
  End If

  UpdateCash

cmdPlay_ClickDone:
  Exit Sub

cmdPlay_ClickError:
  MsgBox Error$(), 48, PROGRAM
  Resume cmdPlay_ClickDone

End Sub
```

First the `cmdPlay_Click` subroutine verifies that the player has enough money to play. If there isn't enough left, then a silly message asking the player to deposit some money is displayed to kind of add insult to injury since the player has lost all his or her money. (See Listing 12.20.)

This is kind of a fun way to allow the game to indicate a lost game. To play again, the player has to close the dialog box, and then restart the game from the toolbar button or menu command that you create shortly.

Listing 12.20. You can't play if you don't have any money.

```
' See if the player has enough cash to play a round
  If msngCash < msngCostPerPull Then
    msg = "You must deposit " & Format$(msngCostPerPull, "Currency")
    msg = msg & " in the machine to play."
    MsgBox msg, 64, PROGRAM
    GoTo cmdPlay_ClickDone
  End If
```

Next, the subroutine generates a random value from 0 to 1 and assigns it to the `sngPull` variable.

```
' Get a random "Pull" value
  sngPull = Rnd
```

The `sngPayoff` variable is initialized to zero. If a payoff is determined, then the variable is reassigned a value, otherwise it remains zero, which indicates no payoff.

```
  sngPayoff = 0#
```

The next part of the subroutine checks for whether or not a payoff should be made.

First, if the pull value is in the range of a low payoff, then the `sngPayoff` variable is assigned the low payoff value and a `SymbolsLowPayoff` subroutine is called to draw symbols in the dial windows indicating a low payoff.

Again, the logic of drawing the symbols last seems kind of backward. But the game player really doesn't know the difference. The player's perception of the game is that if he or she rolls the correct symbols, then he or she wins a payoff.

```
' Did the player win a low value?
  If sngPull < msngLowPayoffChance Then
    sngPayoff = msngLowPayoff
    SymbolsLowPayoff
```

If the pull value isn't in the low range, then the program checks to see if it is in the medium range,

```
ElseIf sngPull < msngMediumPayoffChance Then
  sngPayoff = msngMediumPayoff
  SymbolsMediumPayoff
```

the high range,

```
ElseIf sngPull < msngHighPayoffChance Then
  sngPayoff = msngHighPayoff
  SymbolsHighPayoff
```

or a jackpot!

```
ElseIf sngPull < msngJackpotChance Then
  sngPayoff = msngJackpot
  SymbolsJackpot
  Beep
```

Finally, if there wasn't a payoff, then the `SymbolsNoPayoff` subroutine is called to display nonwinning symbols.

```
Else
  SymbolsNoPayoff
End If
```

The cost of a round of play is deducted from the player's cash.

```
msngCash = msngCash - msngCostPerPull
```

If a win occurred, then a message is displayed to alert the player, and their cash is increased by the payoff amount.

If there was no payoff, then the message text box is cleared just in case a message is hanging around from the last round.

```
If sngPayoff > 0 Then
  Message "You won " & Format$(sngPayoff, "Currency")
  msngCash = msngCash + sngPayoff
Else
  Message ""
End If
```

At the end of the subroutine, the `UpdateCash` subroutine is called to display the amount of money the player has left.

```
  UpdateCash
```

Hmmm…just talking about this is making me anxious to play.

The *SymbolsLowPayoff* Subroutine

The next set of subroutines involves getting the proper symbols displayed to represent the payoff or lack of payoff that occurred in the `cmdPlay_Click` subroutine.

The `SymbolsLowPayoff` subroutine is called when there is a low payoff. It chooses one of the characters from the first three-fourths of the characters in the `mstrSymbols` string to be displayed twice as a match. (I arbitrarily decided that two matching characters from this set of characters would represent a low payoff.)

Enter the `SymbolsLowPayoff` subroutine shown in Listing 12.21.

Listing 12.21. The `SymbolsLowPayoff` **subroutine.**

```
Sub SymbolsLowPayoff()

' Match two of the first 3/4 of the symbols

    Dim intChar1 As Integer
    Dim intChar2 As Integer
    Dim intLength As Integer

    intLength = Int(mintSymbolsLength * 0.75)

    intChar1 = Int(Rnd * intLength) + 1
    Do
        intChar2 = Int(Rnd * mintSymbolsLength) + 1
    Loop While intChar2 = intChar1

    Match2Symbols intChar1, intChar2

End Sub
```

The subroutine first determines the range of characters it has to choose from by multiplying the number of characters in the `mstrSymbols` string by 0.75 and then rounding the result to an integer.

```
intLength = Int(mintSymbolsLength * 0.75)
```

Next, `intChar1` holds an offset for the character that is displayed twice. The `intChar1` value is calculated using a formula to select a random value from 1 to `intLength`.

```
intChar1 = Int(Rnd * intLength) + 1
```

An additional character needs to be selected. It is chosen from the entire range, but a loop is used to ensure that it is not the same character as the one chosen to be displayed as a match.

```
Do
    intChar2 = Int(Rnd * mintSymbolsLength) + 1
Loop While intChar2 = intChar1
```

Next, the Match2Symbols subroutine is called, which displays the matching characters in two of the dial windows, and in the remaining window the odd character is displayed.

```
Match2Symbols intChar1, intChar2
```

The *SymbolsMediumPayoff* Subroutine

For the player, the medium payoff is supposed to be related to getting a match from a particular set of symbols.

For the program, this means selecting the matching character from the last 1/4 of the characters in the mstrSymbols string.

Enter the SymbolsMediumPayoff subroutine as shown in Listing 12.22.

Listing 12.22. The SymbolsMediumPayoff **subroutine.**

```
Sub SymbolsMediumPayoff()

' Match two of the last 1/4 of the symbols

  Dim intChar1 As Integer
  Dim intChar2 As Integer
  Dim intOffset As Integer
  Dim intLength As Integer

  intOffset = Int(mintSymbolsLength * 0.75)
  intLength = mintSymbolsLength - intOffset

  intChar1 = Int(Rnd * intLength) + 1 + intOffset
  Do
    intChar2 = Int(Rnd * mintSymbolsLength) + 1
  Loop While intChar2 = intChar1

  Match2Symbols intChar1, intChar2

End Sub
```

The subroutine calculates an offset into the mstrSymbols string so that only the final 1/4 of the characters are used. The number of characters from after the offset to the end of the string are calculated and stored in the intLength variable.

```
intOffset = Int(mintSymbolsLength * 0.75)
intLength = mintSymbolsLength - intOffset
```

Next, the offset for the first character is calculated from among the final 1/4 characters.

```
intChar1 = Int(Rnd * intLength) + 1 + intOffset
```

The second character is then chosen inside a loop again to make sure that the selected character offset doesn't match the first character offset.

```
Do
  intChar2 = Int(Rnd * mintSymbolsLength) + 1
Loop While intChar2 = intChar1
```

At the end of the subroutine, the `Match2Symbols` subroutine is called to display the selected character symbols.

```
Match2Symbols intChar1, intChar2
```

The *HighSymbolsPayoff* Subroutine

The `SymbolsHighPayoff` subroutine is simpler than the two previous subroutines. In a high payoff, all dials display the same symbol, so only one character needs to be selected.

I decided to have any of the characters except the last one indicate a high payoff. The last character is used to indicate a jackpot.

Enter the `SymbolsHighPayoff` subroutine as shown in Listing 12.23.

Listing 12.23. The `SymbolsHighPayoff` **subroutine.**

```
Sub SymbolsHighPayoff()

' Match three of any except the last symbol

  Dim intChar1 As Integer

  intChar1 = Int(Rnd * (mintSymbolsLength - 1)) + 1
  Match3Symbols intChar1

End Sub
```

The `SymbolsHighPayoff` subroutine calculates the character offset and then calls the `Match3Symbols` subroutine to display the chosen symbol in the slot machine dial windows.

The *SymbolsJackpot* Subroutine

The `SymbolsJackpot` subroutine displays the last character in the `mstrSymbols` string in the three dial windows.

Enter the `SymbolsJackpot` subroutine as shown in Listing 12.24.

Listing 12.24. The `SymbolsJackpot` **subroutine.**

```
Sub SymbolsJackpot()

' Match three of the last symbol

  Match3Symbols mintSymbolsLength

End Sub
```

The *SymbolsNoPayoff* Subroutine

The next subroutine, `SymbolsNoPayoff`, has to choose three random symbols to display in the slot machine dial windows, where each is different from the other two.

Enter the `SymbolsNoPayoff` subroutine into the Slot Machine module as shown in Listing 12.25.

Listing 12.25. The `SymbolsNoPayoff` **subroutine.**

```
Sub SymbolsNoPayoff()

' Randomly pick 3 symbols

  Dim strDisplay As String

  Dim intChar1 As Integer
  Dim intChar2 As Integer
  Dim intChar3 As Integer
  Dim n As Integer

' Pick three different characters
  intChar1 = Int(Rnd * mintSymbolsLength) + 1
  Do
    intChar2 = Int(Rnd * mintSymbolsLength) + 1
  Loop While intChar2 = intChar1
  Do
    intChar3 = Int(Rnd * mintSymbolsLength) + 1
  Loop While intChar3 = intChar1 Or intChar3 = intChar2

  strDisplay = Mid$(mstrSymbols, intChar1, 1)
  strDisplay = strDisplay & Mid$(mstrSymbols, intChar2, 1)
  strDisplay = strDisplay & Mid$(mstrSymbols, intChar3, 1)

  DisplaySymbols strDisplay

End Sub
```

The `SymbolsNoPayoff` subroutine picks each of the symbols from the full set of characters in the `mstrSymbols` string. As the second character is chosen, the subroutine makes sure that the second selected character doesn't match the first one.

```
' Pick three different characters
  intChar1 = Int(Rnd * mintSymbolsLength) + 1
  Do
     intChar2 = Int(Rnd * mintSymbolsLength) + 1
  Loop While intChar2 = intChar1
```

Then the third character is chosen with the subroutine making sure that the third selected character doesn't match either the first or the second one.

```
Do
   intChar3 = Int(Rnd * mintSymbolsLength) + 1
Loop While intChar3 = intChar1 Or intChar3 = intChar2
```

The selected characters are extracted from the `mstrSymbols` string and concatenated to create a short three-character string, `strDisplay`.

```
strDisplay = Mid$(mstrSymbols, intChar1, 1)
strDisplay = strDisplay & Mid$(mstrSymbols, intChar2, 1)
strDisplay = strDisplay & Mid$(mstrSymbols, intChar3, 1)
```

The `strDisplay` string is passed to the `DisplaySymbols` subroutine to finally display the characters on-screen.

```
DisplaySymbols strDisplay
```

The *Match2Symbols* Subroutine

In earlier subroutines, you called the `Match2Symbols` subroutine to display the first selected character as two matching symbols, and a second character as the odd, nonmatching symbol that robs the player of the high payoff or jackpot.

Enter the `Match2Symbols` subroutine as shown in Listing 12.26.

Listing 12.26. The `Match2Symbols` subroutine.

```
Sub Match2Symbols(intChar1 As Integer, intChar2 As Integer)

  Dim strDisplay As String

  Dim intOddSlot As Integer
  Dim n As Integer

  intOddSlot = Int(Rnd * 3) + 1

  strDisplay = ""
  For n = 1 To 3
```

```
      If n = intOddSlot Then
        strDisplay = strDisplay + Mid$(mstrSymbols, intChar2, 1)
      Else
        strDisplay = strDisplay + Mid$(mstrSymbols, intChar1, 1)
      End If
    Next n

    DisplaySymbols strDisplay

End Sub
```

The `Match2Symbols` subroutine first selects which of the three dial windows is the odd one.

```
intOddSlot = Int(Rnd * 3) + 1
```

Next, the subroutine creates the same kind of three-character string as you did in the last subroutine. The code loops three times.

```
strDisplay = ""
For n = 1 To 3
```

Within the loop, if you are on the odd slot the second character selected is appended to the `strDisplay` string, otherwise the first character selected is used.

```
If n = intOddSlot Then
   strDisplay = strDisplay + Mid$(mstrSymbols, intChar2, 1)
Else
     strDisplay = strDisplay + Mid$(mstrSymbols, intChar1, 1)
  End If
Next n
```

When the loop is finished, the `strDisplay` string is created with any one of the three characters being the odd non-matching character.

The `DisplaySymbols` subroutine is called to actually update the text boxes that make up the slot machine dial windows.

```
DisplaySymbols strDisplay
```

The *Match3Symbols* Subroutine

For a three-way match, the job of creating the string to pass to the `DisplaySymbols` subroutine is much easier. You just have to repeat the same character three times in a string.

The `Match3Symbols` subroutine does this using the `String$` function, whose second argument indicates how many times to repeat the string passed as the first argument.

Enter the `Match3Symbols` subroutine as shown in Listing 12.27.

Listing 12.27. The `Match3Symbols` **subroutine.**

```
Sub Match3Symbols(intChar1 As Integer)

  DisplaySymbols String$(3, Mid$(mstrSymbols, intChar1, 1))

End Sub
```

Don't worry, you're nearly finished. Only two more subroutines to go and the Slot Machine game is coded.

The *DisplaySymbols* Subroutine

Here's the subroutine that actually updates the text boxes that represent the slot machine dial windows.

Enter the `DisplaySymbols` subroutine as shown in Listing 12.28.

Listing 12.28. The `DisplaySymbols` **subroutine.**

```
Sub DisplaySymbols(strDisplay As String)

  Dim n As Integer

  For n = 1 To 3
    mdlg.TextBoxes("txtDial" & n).Text = Mid$(strDisplay, n, 1)
  Next n

End Sub
```

The `DisplaySymbols` subroutine uses a neat trick in that it generates the name of the control to which the text is being written.

The first text box, txtDial1, gets its caption written to the first character in the `strDisplay` string. Then txtDial2 receives the second character, and finally txtDial3 receives the last character.

You don't have to do anything to "convert" the characters to their graphic symbols. When you placed the text boxes on the dialog box, you set their font to display in the Wingdings font.

The *cmdCashIn_Click* Subroutine

The final subroutine in the Slot Machine module is the subroutine that is activated when the **Cash-In** button is clicked. This subroutine ends the game by displaying the player's earnings or losses, and then closing the Slot Machine dialog box.

Enter the cmdCashIn_Click subroutine as shown in Listing 12.29.

Listing 12.29. The cmdCashIn_Click **subroutine.**

```
Sub cmdCashIn_Click()

  Dim sngNet As Single

  sngNet = msngCash - msngStartWith

  If sngNet < 0 Then
    msg = "You lost " & Format$(-sngNet, "Currency")
    msg = msg & cr & cr & "Better luck next time."
  ElseIf sngNet = 0 Then
    msg = "You broke even."
  Else
    msg = "You won " & Format$(sngNet, "Currency")
    msg = msg & cr & cr & "Come back again!"
  End If

  MsgBox msg, 0, PROGRAM

End Sub
```

The cmdCashIn_Click subroutine calculates the player's earnings by subtracting the current cash amount from the amount that the player started with.

```
sngNet = msngCash - msngStartWith
```

If the net earnings are actually net losings, then the msg variable is set so that the user is nicely scolded.

```
If sngNet < 0 Then
  msg = "You lost " & Format$(-sngNet, "Currency")
  msg = msg & cr & cr & "Better luck next time."
```

If the player quit with as much as he or she started with, then the program indicates that the player broke even.

```
ElseIf sngNet = 0 Then
  msg = "You broke even."
```

Otherwise, if the player actually won, then he or she is informed of the earnings.

```
Else
  msg = "You won " & Format$(sngNet, "Currency")
  msg = msg & cr & cr & "Come back again!"
End If
```

After the msg string is filled, it is displayed by calling the MsgBox statement.

```
MsgBox msg, 0, PROGRAM
```

Plug In the Slot Machine

You now need to attach the `dlgSlotMachine_Show`, `cmdPlay_Click` and `cmdCashIn_Click` subroutines into the dialog box.

1. Click the Slot Machine tab to display the Slot Machine dialog box sheet.
2. Click the title bar of the `dlgSlotMachine` dialog box frame using the right mouse button and select Assign Macro from the pop-up menu as shown in Figure 12.26.

FIGURE 12.26.

Assigning a macro to the `dlgSlotMachine` *dialog box's Show event.*

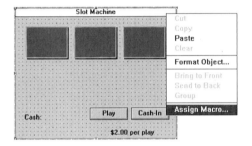

Excel displays the Assign Macro dialog box with your growing list of subroutines.

3. In the Assign Macro dialog box, select the `dlgSlotMachine_Show` subroutine (as shown in Figure 12.27) and click OK.

FIGURE 12.27.

Selecting the `dlgSlotMachine_Show` *subroutine.*

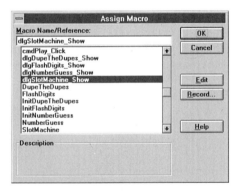

4. Assign the `cmdPlay_Click` subroutine to the cmdPlay button.
5. Assign the `cmdCashIn_Click` subroutine to the cmdCashIn button.

You just built your fourth and final game. You still have a short little Fortune Cookie program coming up, but first let's see how this one runs.

Testing the Slot Machine Game

You'd better start this one first from the Debug window, just in case it's a real disaster.

1. Click the Slot Machine Module tab.

2. Select the **View**|**D**ebug Window command to bring up the debugger.

3. Enter the name of the entry routine, `SlotMachine`, in the Immediate pane and press Enter. See Figure 12.28.

FIGURE 12.28.

Running the Slot Machine game from the Debug window.

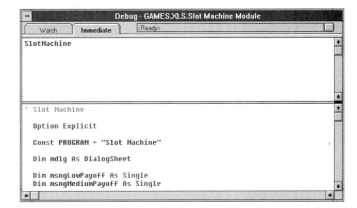

Oops! On my screen the program appeared as shown in Figure 12.29. Looks like I forgot something. The symbols in the slot machine dial windows are appearing black, which doesn't display well on a blue background.

FIGURE 12.29.

Your Slot Machine game has a minor flaw.

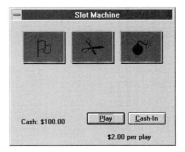

Well, it's easy enough to fix. Close the dialog box and the Debug window. Go back to the Slot Machine dialog box and open the Format Object dialog box for each of the text boxes. In the Font tab, change the **C**olor setting to white.

OK, try it again. This time my screen appeared as shown in Figure 12.30. That's much better!

FIGURE 12.30.
*The fixed Slot Machine
program.*

Click the **P**lay button.

If you win, Slot Machine displays a message indicating how much money you won. (See Figure 12.31.)

FIGURE 12.31.
*Winning some money
in Slot Machine.*

Note that you are still charged for the play even if you won.

The Fortune Cookie Program

Let's finish up your little game pack with the trivial, but always fun, Fortune Cookie program.

The Fortune Cookie program selects a fortune from a set of fortunes stored in the GAMES.XLS workbook, and then displays it in a message box.

1. Switch back over to the Options worksheet.

2. Enter Fortune Cookie into cell A28 and click the Bold button on the Formatting toolbar.

3. Enter Last Fortune for the option title into A29.

   The Last Fortune option isn't actually an option. Instead, you use it as a temporary place to store a value that the program uses and modifies each time it runs.

The idea is to prohibit the program from displaying the same fortune twice in a row.

Don't you hate it when you open two fortune cookies at the dinner table and they have the same fortune in it? It's bad luck for sure.

4. Enter an initial value of 1 into cell B29.

5. In the Formula Bar, enter `LastFortune` as the Excel name for cell B29. See Figure 12.32.

FIGURE 12.32.

The Last Fortune value is really a variable rather than a game play option.

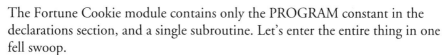

First you create the Fortune Cookie module, then a worksheet that stores the different fortunes in it.

1. Select the **I**nsert|**M**acro|**M**odule command to create a new module.

2. Rename the module sheet to Fortune Cookie Module, and drag it all the way to the end of the workbook so it is the last sheet.

   The Fortune Cookie module contains only the PROGRAM constant in the declarations section, and a single subroutine. Let's enter the entire thing in one fell swoop.

3. Enter the Fortune Cookie module as shown in Listing 12.30.

Listing 12.30. The Fortune Cookie module.

```
' Fortune Cookie

Option Explicit
```

continues

Listing 12.30. continued

```
Const PROGRAM = "Fortune Cookie"

Sub FortuneCookie()

  Dim wsFortunes As Worksheet
  Dim wsOptions As Worksheet

  Dim rng As Range

  Dim intRow As Integer
  Dim intTotalRows As Integer
  Dim intLastFortune As Integer

  On Error GoTo FortuneCookieError

  Set wsFortunes = Workbooks(WORKBOOK_NAME).Worksheets("Fortune Cookies")
  Set wsOptions = Workbooks(WORKBOOK_NAME).Worksheets("Options")

' See which fortune was displayed last
  intLastFortune = wsOptions.Range("LastFortune").Value

' Determine the number of messages in the fortune list
  Set rng = wsFortunes.Range("Fortunes")
  Set rng = rng.SpecialCells(xlLastCell)
  intTotalRows = rng.Row

  Randomize

' Select a random fortune not equal to the last one
  Do
    intRow = Int((intTotalRows * Rnd) + 1)
  Loop While intRow = intLastFortune

' Save the selected value as the last fortune
  wsOptions.Range("LastFortune").Value = intRow

' Display the fortune
  MsgBox wsFortunes.Cells(intRow, 1), 0, PROGRAM

FortuneCookieDone:
  Exit Sub

FortuneCookieError:
  MsgBox Error$(), 48, PROGRAM
  Resume FortuneCookieDone

End Sub
```

There isn't a dialog box in this program, but there are two worksheets that are referenced. The wsFortunes variable is set to the Fortune Cookies worksheet that holds the fortunes. The wsOptions variable is set to the Options worksheet.

```
Set wsFortunes = Workbooks(WORKBOOK_NAME).Worksheets("Fortune Cookies")
Set wsOptions = Workbooks(WORKBOOK_NAME).Worksheets("Options")
```

The last fortune value is read into the `intLastFortune` variable from the Options worksheet.

```
' See which fortune was displayed last
  intLastFortune = wsOptions.Range("LastFortune").Value
```

Next, a Range variable is set to the range defined by the "Fortunes" Excel name in the Fortune Cookies worksheet.

The `SpecialCells` method is used to fetch the last cell in the range and determine the number of rows in the range.

```
' Determine the number of messages in the fortune list
  Set rng = wsFortunes.Range("Fortunes")
  Set rng = rng.SpecialCells(xlLastCell)
  intTotalRows = rng.Row
```

The `Randomize` statement is called to seed the random number generator.

```
Randomize
```

A random row number is selected within a loop that executes again if the number selected is the same value as the row number read from the LastFortune Excel name.

```
' Select a random fortune not equal to the last one
  Do
     intRow = Int((intTotalRows * Rnd) + 1)
  Loop While intRow = intLastFortune
```

Once a number is selected, it is written to the cell location to which the LastFortune name points. This way the program avoids selecting this row on the next run.

```
' Save the selected value as the last fortune
  wsOptions.Range("LastFortune").Value = intRow
```

Finally, the fortune text is read from the Fortune Cookie worksheet using the `Cells` method with a specified row and column.

```
' Display the fortune
  MsgBox wsFortunes.Cells(intRow, 1), 0, PROGRAM
```

You now need to create a list of fortunes for the Fortune Cookie program to select from.

1. Select the **Insert|Worksheet** command to add a new worksheet to the workbook.
2. Rename the workbook to `Fortune Cookies`.
3. Widen column A in the workbook to about the width of the screen.
4. Enter as many fortunes as you can quickly think of, with one fortune per cell down column A.
5. Click the column A heading to select the entire column.
6. Enter `Fortunes` as a name for the range into the Formula Bar. See Figure 12.33.

FIGURE 12.33.

Creating a worksheet to store fortunes, and defining the Fortunes name.

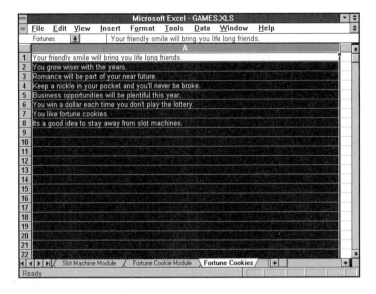

That's it! To try out the program, Select the **Tools|M**acro command and select and run the FortuneCookie macro. A fortune message should appear, as shown in Figure 12.34.

FIGURE 12.34.

Getting some advice from the Fortune Cookie program.

You can add fortunes to the Fortune Cookies worksheet by entering additional messages in the cells in column A. I made up just a few to get you started.

Creating the Games Menu

It's time to put a close to this project, but first you should create a menu and toolbar, then write the worksheet out as an Add-In workbook so the games can be played while working on other workbooks.

First you can create the menu.

1. Click on any of the module sheet tabs to make the **Tools|**Menu E**d**itor command available.

2. Make sure you have Worksheet selected in the Menu **B**ars combo box.

3. In the **M**enus list box, click on the &Help menu entry.

The ampersand character in front of each entry indicates which key is the accelerator key to select that command from the menu.

4. Click the **I**nsert button to add a new drop-down menu in the Worksheet menu.

5. Enter &Games into the **C**aption. See Figure 12.35.

FIGURE 12.35.

Adding a Games drop-down menu to the Worksheet menu bar.

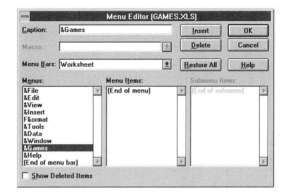

The Menu Editor dialog box displays one entry in the Menu **I**tems list box; the "(End of menu)" marker.

6. Click the "(End of menu)" marker, and then click the **I**nsert button.

7. Enter &Number Guess as the **C**aption for the first menu item.

8. In the **M**acro combo box, select the NumberGuess macro as shown in Figure 12.36.

9. Enter in the remaining menu items for each of the programs as shown in the following list:

&Number Guess	NumberGuess
&Flash Digits	FlashDigits
&Dupe the Dupes	DupeTheDupes
&Slot Machine	SlotMachine
Fortune &Cookie	FortuneCookie

Figure 12.37 shows the completed menu defined in the Menu Editor dialog box.

10. Click OK to close the Menu Editor.

To try out the menu, click to one of the worksheets in your workbook to display the Worksheets menu. You find a Games command on the menu bar just before the Help menu. See Figure 12.38.

Make sure that each program starts up correctly when calling it from the menu.

FIGURE 12.36.

Creating the first menu item in the Games menu.

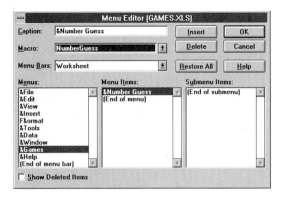

FIGURE 12.37.

Completing the Games menu.

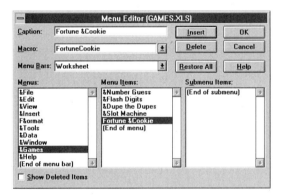

FIGURE 12.38.

Trying out the Games menu.

Creating the Time Killers Toolbar

You can up the ante on this and even make your own toolbar to activate the different games.

There are some unique things you need to know about how Excel uses Toolbars.

First, Excel has two places in which to store a toolbar. Generally, when you add toolbars or modify existing ones, you are affecting a file called EXCEL5.XLB in your Windows directory.

By default, when you create a new toolbar it is not saved in your worksheet. You must specifically make this happen.

When you create a toolbar in a workbook for distribution, the users of the workbook get their own copy of the toolbar copied automatically into their EXCEL5.XLB file when they first open the workbook.

Once they have a copy of the toolbar, they can modify it without affecting the original toolbar stored in the workbook. In fact, they can delete the toolbar from their EXCEL5.XLB file and reload the original one if they really messed it up.

This is all a lot easier than it sounds. Just follow these steps.

1. Select the **View**|**Toolbars** command.

   Excel displays the Toolbars dialog box. Before you can press the **N**ew button (it's grayed out), you need to enter a new and unique toolbar name.

2. Enter Time Killers as the Tool**b**ar Name (as shown in Figure 12.39), and then click the **N**ew button.

FIGURE 12.39.

Adding a new toolbar.

Excel displays a Customize dialog box that is similar to the one you used in Word in Chapters 2, "Word: Study Mate," and 8, "Word: Screen Writer."

Clicking the different categories displays different toolbar buttons. Add a button from the Custom set of toolbar buttons (or draw your own).

1. Select Custom from the bottom of the **C**ategories list box.
2. Select a button with a picture or grab the empty gray one if you want to start with a blank sheet in drawing your own.
3. Drag the button over to the new toolbar and drop it in as shown in Figure 12.40.

FIGURE 12.40.

Adding a button to the Time Killers toolbar.

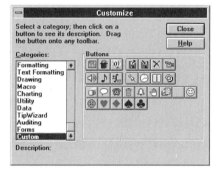

Excel displays the Assign Macro dialog box.

4. Select the `NumberGuess` subroutine from the list box (see Figure 12.41) and click OK.

FIGURE 12.41.

Assigning the `NumberGuess` *subroutine to the first toolbar button.*

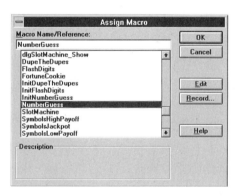

5. Add a total of five buttons to the toolbar, one for each of the following macros:

   `NumberGuess`

   `FlashDigits`

   `DupeTheDupes`

   `SlotMachine`

   `FortuneCookie`

You can bring up the Customize dialog box at any time to work on an existing toolbar by clicking with the right mouse button on the toolbar. See Figure 12.42.

FIGURE 12.42.

Bringing up the Customize dialog box to edit the Time Killers toolbar.

With the Customize dialog box open, you can edit the button image or re-assign a button to another macro by clicking with the right mouse button on the toolbar button. The popup menu shown in Figure 12.43 will appear.

FIGURE 12.43.

Preparing to edit a toolbar button image.

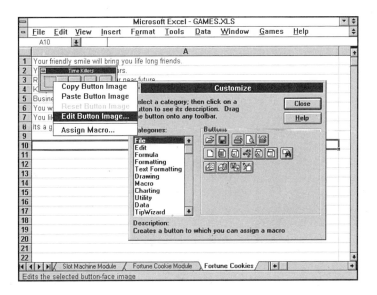

I drew my own toolbar button pictures for the Time Killer game buttons, as shown in Figure 12.44.

When you are satisfied with how the toolbar looks, you should actually store it in the GAMES.XLS workbook. When you first create it, it is written to the EXCEL5.XLB file instead.

1. Position the toolbar where you think it should appear when a user first installs it.

2. Select one of the module sheets to make the **Tools|Attach Toolbars** command available.

3. Select the **Tools**|Attach **T**oolbars command.

   Excel displays the Attach Toolbars dialog box. Listed on the left side are the custom toolbars that are currently in your EXCEL5.XLB file. Listed on the right side are any custom toolbars attached to the current workbook.

4. Select the Time Killers toolbar from the left list and click the **C**opy button. The Time Killers toolbar appears in the right list, as shown in Figure 12.45. Click OK to close the dialog box.

FIGURE 12.44.

Creating your own toolbar pictures with the Button Editor dialog box.

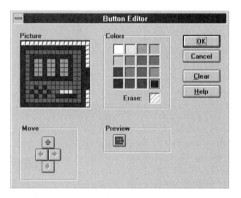

FIGURE 12.45.

Attaching a custom toolbar to the current workbook.

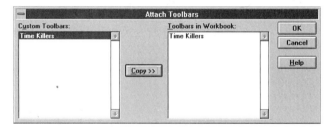

To delete a toolbar from a workbook, you open the Attach Toolbars dialog box, select the toolbar from the right list, and click the **D**elete button.

To delete a toolbar from the EXCEL5.XLB file, you select the **V**iew|**T**oolbars command and select and delete the toolbar from the Toolbars dialog box.

Creating the GAMES.XLA Menu Add-In

You can create a menu add-in out of the GAMES.XLS workbook.

First you must define the __DemandLoad name as you did when creating the .XLA files for Pretty Printer and Calendar Wizard in Chapters 4, "Excel: Pretty Printer," and 5, "Excel: Calendar Wizard."

This makes the add-in workbook load *on demand*, which means it only loads when you select one of its menu or toolbar items. This keeps the add-in from slowing down how fast Excel loads on startup.

1. Click the tab for the Options worksheet.
2. Select the **I**nsert|**N**ame|**D**efine command.
3. Enter __DemandLoad (two underscores precede the name), in the Names in **W**orkbook combo box.
4. Enter =True in the **R**efers To text box, as shown in Figure 12.46.
5. Click the **A**dd button, then click OK to close the dialog box.

FIGURE 12.46.
Defining the
DemandLoad *Excel*
Name.

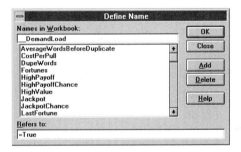

6. Save the GAMES.XLS workbook.

NOTE

You should be sure you keep a copy of the GAMES.XLS workbook, because the GAMES.XLA file is not editable. To make any changes, you need to load the GAMES.XLS workbook and then create a new GAMES.XLA file from it.

Now create the GAMES.XLA file.

1. Click the Globals module sheet tab in the workbook to display the Globals module sheet.

   You need to change the constant that stores the name of the workbook, because the workbook file is different than what you developed the programs with.

2. Look for the line that defines the WORKBOOK_NAME constant and change the definition from "GAMES.XLS" to "GAMES.XLA."

   ```
   Global Const WORKBOOK_NAME = "GAMES.XLA"
   ```

3. Select the **T**ools|Ma**k**e Add-In command.

The Make Add-In dialog box is displayed, defaulting to saving the workbook as
GAMES.XLA. See Figure 12.47.

4. Click OK.

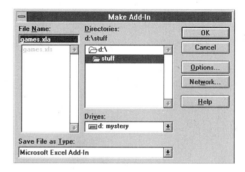

Testing the Time Killers Menu Add-In

Let's see if this works as expected. You should be able to load the workbook as a menu
add-in while any other workbook is loaded and be able to activate the games.

1. Close the GAMES.XLS workbook.

    If the only change you made to the GAMES.XLS workbook is changing the
    constant WORKBOOK_NAME to GAMES.XLA, then you can answer No to saving the
    workbook.

2. Select the **File|New** command to start with an empty workbook.

3. Select the **View|Toolbars** command.

4. Select the Time Killers toolbar displayed in the list of available toolbars and
    click the **D**elete button.

    This deletes the copy of the toolbar from your EXCEL5.XLB file.

5. Select the **Tools|Add-Ins** command.

    Excel doesn't know anything about your add-in until it is installed at least once.

6. In the Add-Ins dialog box, click the **B**rowse button.

7. In the Browse dialog box, locate the GAMES.XLA file and click OK.

    The Add-Ins dialog box now displays the Time Killers menu add-in among the
    other add-ins. It even displays the file summary information to indicate what
    the workbook library does. See Figure 12.48.

8. Click OK and Excel loads the GAMES.XLA file because it needs to copy the
    toolbar.

Excel displays the Games menu and the Time Killers toolbar. Before you test anything, get out of Excel and start all over in an empty workbook.

9. Exit Excel.

10. Launch Excel from Program Manager.

FIGURE 12.48.

Time Killers as an installable add-in library.

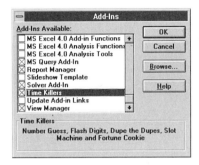

When Excel starts up, it displays the Games menu command and the Time Killers toolbar.

Click one of the buttons on the Time Killers toolbar and you see the status bar display a message, Opening GAMES.XLA. The workbook isn't loaded until you actually run one of the games!

Figure 12.49 shows the Number Guess game running in a new empty workbook.

FIGURE 12.49.

Running Excel with the Time Killers Add-In installed.

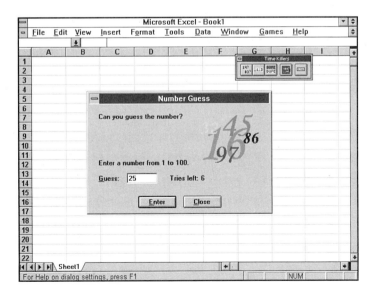

Time Killers Challenge

Take the ball and run with it.

Try creating some games of your own. You could add them to the GAMES.XLA workbook or create your own menu add-in from scratch.

Summary

In this chapter you completed your games library workbook and made it an installable add-in. Here are a few of the things you learned along the way:

- Designed and created the Dupe the Dupes game
- Solved how Dupe the Dupes selects unique words
- Stored a set of game data in a worksheet
- Designed and created a Slot Machine game
- Used Wingding fonts to display graphic characters
- Solved how Slot Machine displays winning dial combinations
- Created a Fortune Cookie program
- Created a custom menu
- Created a custom toolbar
- Made the GAMES.XLA menu add-in

In the next two chapters, you create an advanced Address Book application in Access that includes generating SQL SELECT statements by code using Query-By-Form techniques.

TRY THIS! ANSWERS

12.1. The trick to writing a subroutine that can report any duplicate words found in the Dupe Words worksheet is to have it sort the list of words first. Just as it is easier to spot duplicates from a sorted list by looking, it's also easier to spot duplicates this way in code.

(Often the best approach to solving a programming problem is to think of how you would do the same task manually.)

Listing 12.31 contains the subroutine, FindDupes. You must first click the Dupe Words worksheet tab to display the Dupe Words worksheet before you execute it. To execute the macro, select the **Tools**|**M**acro command and run it from the Macro dialog box.

Listing 12.31. The FindDupes subroutine.

```
Sub FindDupes()

    Dim wsDupeWords As Worksheet

    Dim rngWords As Range
    Dim rng As Range

    Dim strWord1 As String
    Dim strWord2 As String

    Dim intWords As Integer
    Dim n As Integer

' Get the Dupe Words worksheet
    Set wsDupeWords = Workbooks(WORKBOOK_NAME).Worksheets("Dupe Words")

' Select all of the words in column A
    wsDupeWords.Columns("A:A").Select

' Sort column A
    Selection.Sort Key1:=Range("A1"), Order1:=xlAscending, _
        Header:=xlGuess, OrderCustom:=1, MatchCase:=False, _
        Orientation:=xlTopToBottom

' Determine the number of words in the word list
    Set rngWords = wsDupeWords.Range("DupeWords")
    Set rng = rngWords.SpecialCells(xlLastCell)
    intWords = rng.Row

' Traverse the list looking for duplicates. Compare each word with the
' word following it. You'll find the match there because the words are
' sorted.
    strWord1 = rngWords.Cells(1)
    For n = 2 To intWords
        strWord2 = rngWords.Cells(n)

        If strWord1 = strWord2 Then
            MsgBox strWord1 & " is a duplicate.", 48, PROGRAM
        End If

        strWord1 = strWord2
    Next n
End Sub
```

CHAPTER 13

Access: Address Book, Part One

A Query By Form application enables the end user to perform a variety of searches in their data without having to do the work of defining and saving their own query database objects.

In the example application that you build in this and the following chapter, you apply the Query By Form methodology to an address book application.

The user of the program can search for matching records in many different ways, such as all last names beginning with an S, all persons in the state of New York, or even every person with a (206) area code.

Setting all this up isn't going to be accomplished without some work—a lot of work.

You are going to have to create some tables, queries, and forms. You will also write a bit of code. To up the ante even higher, I recklessly abandon the Access data bound forms and data bound controls when creating the entry form for the address book.

The results of all this effort demonstrate that sometimes it's worth doing things the hard way, so that your users get to do things the easy way.

It's true that you could create a very simple address book application by using the Access wizards and avoid having to do any programming at all.

Avoid programming? Why?

By knowing how to hand-code your Access applications, you will be able to reach a higher degree of sophistication and utility in your applications than you could otherwise. If you have the time, by all means get into the code.

In this chapter you create the tables and the Address Entry form to populate the tables with some data. In the next chapter you create the Address Search form and the queries that support it.

Let's take a sneak peek at what the final application will look like before you get started.

Introducing the Address Search Form

The Address Search form, shown in Figure 13.1, has two main sections. The top half of the form with all the combo boxes is not for data entry. The fields there are for entering search criteria to indicate what type of address book records should be displayed.

The bottom half of the form contains a list box that displays the matching records for the criteria entered.

Most of the fields in the search criteria section allow wildcard entries. For example, you could enter K* in the Last Name text box.

FIGURE 13.1.

The Address Search form enables you to perform many different kinds of searches.

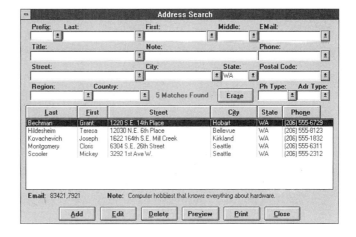

The result of this search would produce all entries with last names beginning with a K, as shown in Figure 13.2.

FIGURE 13.2.

Running a search to return all names beginning with K.

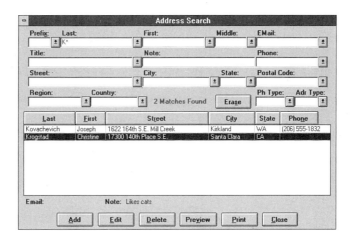

You can search for words embedded in other text. For example, each address book entry has a Note field that you can enter any miscellaneous notes in. Suppose you enter the words Member of Chess Club in this field for all members of your local chess club. You could find these entries by entering *chess* in the Note text box.

NOTE

Note that the capitalization of the words in your search entry does not have to be the same as the text being searched for to produce a matching record.

Most of the fields in the criteria section are combo boxes. From these you can view a list of all the exact matches for that field. Figure 13.3 shows the City combo box being used to select Seattle from the list of cities represented in the Address Book data.

As you add address book entries, the lists in these combo boxes reflect all the available choices in the address book data.

FIGURE 13.3.

Selecting all address book entries for people living in Seattle.

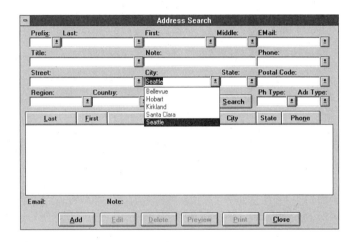

Click the **S**earch button to perform a search. The Search Pending message changes to display a total count of how many matching records were found and the **S**earch button changes to an Era**s**e button. See Figure 13.4.

When you change any of the criteria in the top half of the form, the list of results is cleared and the Search Pending message is displayed again. The Erase button is used to quickly clear the form including all entered search criteria.

FIGURE 13.4.

Results of a search display the total number of Address Book entries found for Seattle.

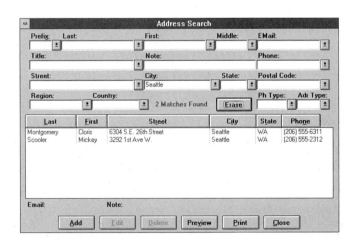

The buttons above the results list act as column headings, but they have additional functionality. When you click one of the buttons, the list is sorted primarily by that column. Each of the sorts can have subsorts defined. For example, if you sort by Last name, then First name is a subsort, so that all the Smith entries are sorted among themselves by first name.

Clicking on each record in the results list updates the two fields below the list to display the Email address and Note field entries for the selected record.

At the bottom of the form are buttons to **A**dd, **E**dit, and **D**elete address book entries. There are also Pre**v**iew and **P**rint buttons to run a report on the entries in the results list.

To select all address book entries, you can click the **S**earch button without entering any criteria. Then you can click the **P**rint button to create a report of all the records in the database.

The buttons at the bottom of the form are grayed out whenever it is not appropriate to use them. For example, when the list is clear you don't want to print a report because the report will be empty. Likewise, you can use the **E**dit and **D**elete buttons only when an item in the results list is selected.

Introducing the Address Entry Form

The second form in the Address Book application is used to add new address book entries or edit existing ones. This form, shown in Figure 13.5, is displayed after clicking the **A**dd or **E**dit button on the Address Search form.

The Address Entry form has three distinct sections that are indicated by the color of the label text for each field.

FIGURE 13.5.
The Address Entry form.

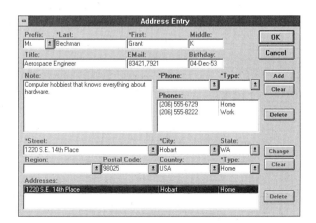

The top left section (in red) includes the Prefix, Last, First, Middle, Title, EMail, Birthday, and Note fields. This section is used to collect data for an address book entry where there is only one value per field.

The section at the middle right of the form (in blue) is used to enter phone numbers. You can enter as many phone numbers for a person in the address book as required— or none at all. Each phone number is assigned a phone number type, indicating if the number is for Home, Work, Mobile, or Fax, so that searches can be done by phone number type.

To add a phone number, you would enter the Phone and Type, and then click the Add button. The entered values move to the Phones list, indicating that the number has been entered.

The bottom section of the form (in purple) is for entering addresses. Just as with phone numbers, one person may have more than one address where you might need to contact them.

The Address Entry form doesn't impose any limit on the number of phone numbers or addresses a person may have. This is possible because phone numbers and addresses are stored in separate tables.

That's enough of the feature list for now. Let's dig into how the application was created.

Components of the Address Book Database

There are quite a few objects in the database container for this project. Actually, full-scale Access applications are known to have hundreds of objects within them, so you certainly haven't reached any limitations here.

Following is a list of all the objects in the database container, with a brief description of each:

Tables:

Address	Addresses for each person
Address Type	Valid address type codes
Enter Address	Staging area for editing addresses
Enter Phone	Staging area for editing phone numbers
Person	A person
Phone	Phone numbers for each person
Phone Type	Valid phone number type codes
Prefix	List name prefixes to choose from
State	List states to choose from

Queries:

Address Book Report	Query generated by code
Address List	Select persons by entered criteria
Addresses By City	Sort selected persons by city
Addresses By FirstName	Sort selected persons by FirstName
Addresses By LastName	Sort selected persons by LastName
Addresses By Phone	Sort selected persons by Phone
Addresses By State	Sort selected persons by State
Addresses By Street	Sort selected persons by Street

Forms:

| Address Entry | Enter new address book entries |
| Address Search | Search for persons in address book |

Reports:

| Address Book | Print selected persons |

Macros:

| AutoExec | Open the Address Search form |

Modules:

| Globals | Global declarations and procedures |

The Address Book Tables

The tables in my Address Book application are shown in Figure 13.6. This figure is the view you get in Access when using the **Edit|Relationships** command to establish relationships between the different tables.

FIGURE 13.6.

The Address Book Tables.

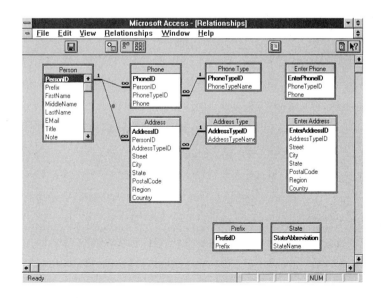

In setting relationships between different tables, you describe to Access how records in one table are related to records in another table.

In the Address Book database, the Person table has a one-to-many relationship with the Phone table (and also the Address table). The Address and Phone table records are connected by the PersonID field.

For each person in the address book, there is a single record in the Person table with its very own unique PersonID value. A single person can have several telephone numbers, such as home, work, fax, and pager. There is a record for each phone number in the Phone table. All the phone number records for a particular person have his or her PersonID.

That's where the *one-to-many* term comes from. One record in the Person table to many records in the Phone table.

In database terminology, the PersonID field in the Person table is called a *primary key*, whereas in the Phone table it is called a *foreign key*.

You can see in Figure 13.6 that relationships are also established between the Phone Type and Phone tables, and the Address Type and Address tables.

The PhoneTypeID field is a numeric code indicating a particular type of phone. The Phone Type table has two columns, one with the numeric codes and the other with the text meaning of the codes, as shown in Figure 13.7. This table is a *lookup table*.

FIGURE 13.7.

The records in the Phone Type table.

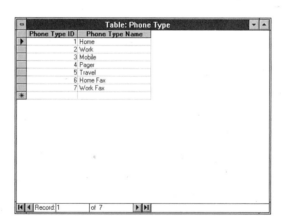

The Phone Type table has a one-to-many relationship with the Phone table because for each type of phone there may be several phone number records in the Phone table of that type. In a query, the Phone Type table is generally joined in to translate the numeric code back to the text.

The Prefix and State tables are also lookup tables that list possible values in the Prefix field of the Person table and the State field in the Address table.

For these tables I didn't establish relationships because I wanted to allow the user to enter values that are not currently in the tables, and also because the values stored in the Person and Address tables are displayable values. The tables exist only to be helpful for data entry so that a set of values is available to choose from.

The Enter Phone and Enter Address tables are temporary tables used by the program as a place to momentarily hold data during data entry. You will see how these get used as you walk through the code behind the Address Entry form.

Creating the Address Book Tables

Let's get started creating the Address Book database from scratch so you can see how it is all put together.

1. In Access, select the **File|New** command to create a new database.
2. In the New Database dialog box, enter ADDRESS.MDB for the name of the database and click OK.

Next you need to create nine new tables, starting with the Person table, which holds a record for each person in the address book.

1. With the Table tab selected in the database container, click **New**.
2. In the New Table dialog box, click the **N**ew Table button rather than using the Table Wizard.
3. Enter the following field names and data types into the Table Design window, as shown in Figure 13.8:

Field Name	Data Type
PersonID	Counter
Prefix	Text
FirstName	Text
MiddleName	Text
LastName	Text
Email	Text
Title	Text
Note	Memo
Birthday	Date/Time

4. Make the PersonID field a Primary Key by selecting it and clicking the Set Primary Key button on the toolbar. (The button with a key picture.)

FIGURE 13.8.

The Person table.

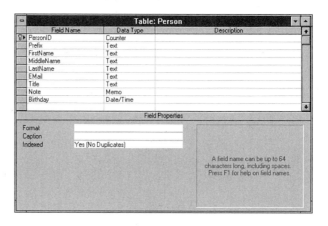

5. Set the following properties for each field as shown here. Leave the other field properties as defaulted by Access. (The data types are listed again just for reference.)

Field Name:	Prefix
Data Type:	Text
Field Size:	20

Field Name:	FirstName
Data Type:	Text
Field Size:	50
Caption:	First Name
Required:	Yes

Field Name:	MiddleName
Data Type:	Text
Field Size:	30
Caption:	Middle Name

Field Name:	LastName
Data Type:	Text
Field Size:	50
Caption:	Last Name
Required:	Yes

Field Name:	Email
Data Type:	Text
Field Size:	50

Field Name: Title
Data Type: Text
Field Size: 30

Next you add a multiple field index to the Person table. You will frequently retrieve records from this table sorted first by LastName, then by FirstName, so it makes sense to create an index for this purpose.

1. Click the Indexes button on the toolbar (the button with the lightning bolt).
2. Enter `FullName` in the Index Name column.
3. Select LastName in the Field Name column and leave the Sort Order column as Ascending.
4. On the next row, leave the Index Name column blank and select FirstName in the Field Name column. Again leave the Sort Order as the default.

   Your FullName index should be set up as shown in Figure 13.9.

FIGURE 13.9.

Creating the FullName index.

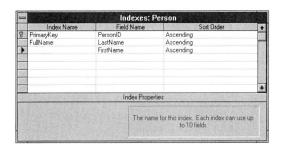

5. Close the Indexes window.
6. Close the table. In the Save As dialog box, enter `Person` as the name of the table.

The next table is the Address table, which holds a record for each address saved for a person. The PersonID field is used within this table as a foreign key, identifying which person an address table record belongs to.

With this design, there is the potential for redundant data in the Address table. This happens when there is more than one person living or working at a given address. The problem with redundant data is that if you have to change it, you have to change it in many places rather than just one.

An alternative approach would have been to keep the PersonID field out of the Address table and create an intermediate table with records holding PersonID and AddressID fields to associate persons with addresses. This would have created a many-to-many relationship between the Person and Address tables, because a person may have several addresses and an address may have several persons.

I chose the one-to-many relationship for simplicity, but also because a work address sometimes includes information such as a department number or box number that makes each employee address unique. I also felt that addresses tend to be stable enough that having to update multiple records (such as when a family or a company moves to a new address) would be a rare event. In such a case, an update query could be used to change fields that are truly identical across many records.

1. Create the Address table with the fields listed here, as shown in Figure 13.10:

Field Name	Data Type
AddressID	Counter
PersonID	Number
AddressTypeID	Number
Street	Text
City	Text
State	Text
PostalCode	Text
Region	Text
Country	Text

FIGURE 13.10.

Creating the Address table.

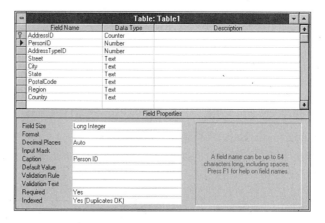

2. Make the AddressID field a primary key.

   As an optimization, the AddressID field is indexed so that searching for Address records for a particular person is quick.

3. Set the following properties for each field listed here:

Field Name:	PersonID
Data Type:	Number
Field Size:	Long Integer
Caption:	Person ID
Required:	Yes
Indexed:	Yes (Duplicates OK)

Field Name:	AddressTypeID
Data Type:	Number
Field Size:	Integer
Caption:	Address Type ID
Required:	Yes

Field Name:	Street
Data Type:	Text
Field Size:	255

Field Name:	City
Data Type:	Text
Field Size:	50

Field Name:	State
Data Type:	Text
Field Size:	20

Field Name:	PostalCode
Data Type:	Text
Field Size:	20
Caption:	Postal Code

Field Name:	Region
Data Type:	Text
Field Size:	50

Field Name:	Country
Data Type:	Text
Field Size:	50

4. Close the table and enter Address as the name to save the table as.

The Enter Address table is a temporary table used during data entry. On the Address Entry form, a list box displays each of the addresses for the person whose data is currently being added or edited. The source for this list is the Enter Address table.

The address records are copied into the Enter Address table for the edit session. The user can add, edit, or delete addresses from this list. If the user presses OK on the Address Enter form, the old address records are deleted from the Address table, and the new records are copied in.

If the user presses the Cancel button, the current Address records remain unchanged and the records in the Address Enter table are discarded without copying them into the Address table.

All but one of the fields in the Address Enter table are the same as the Address table. You can copy these fields to make creating the table go quickly.

1. Click the **N**ew button on the database container to start a new table.

2. Enter the EnterAddressID counter field as shown here:

Field Name	Data Type
EnterAddressID	Counter

3. Set the Caption property of the EnterAddressID field to Enter Address ID.

4. Make the EnterAddressID field the primary key, as shown in Figure 13.11, by selecting it and clicking the Set Primary Key button on the toolbar.

FIGURE 13.11.

A primary key is created for the Enter Address table.

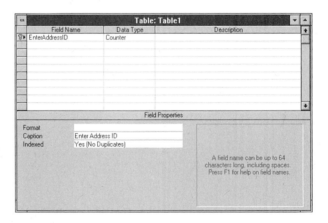

5. In the database container window, select the Address table and open it in design view by clicking the **D**esign button.

6. Select all the fields from AddressTypeID to Country, as shown in Figure 13.12. Press Ctrl-C to copy the fields into the clipboard buffer.

   To select fields for copying, you click the box to the left of the field name and drag across all the rows you want to copy.

FIGURE 13.12.

Copying fields from the Address table.

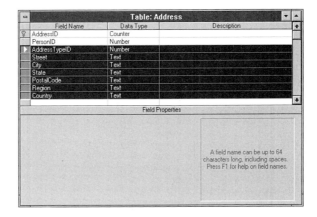

7. Close the Address table and return to the new Table window.

8. Click the first empty Field Name box below the EnterAddressID name and press Ctrl-V to paste in the copied fields, as shown in Figure 13.13.

FIGURE 13.13.

Pasting fields into the Enter Address table.

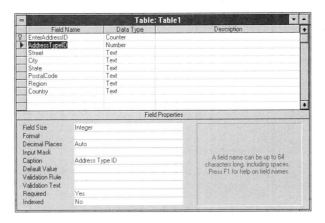

9. Close the table, saving it as Enter Address.

The next table, Address Type, is a lookup table listing the different types that an address would be classified as.

1. Create a new table with the fields shown here:

Field Name	Data Type
AddressTypeID	Number
AddressTypeName	Text

2. Set the following properties for the two fields in the Address Type table:

Field Name:	AddressTypeID
Data Type:	Number
Field Size:	Integer
Caption:	Address Type ID

Field Name:	AddressTypeName
Data Type:	Text
Field Size:	10
Caption:	Address Type Name
Required:	Yes

You can fill in the entries for this table now.

3. Click the Datasheet View button on the toolbar.

As shown in Figure 13.14, Access indicates that the table must be saved and asks if it should be saved now.

FIGURE 13.14.

A table must be saved before you can enter any records.

4. Click OK and enter Address Type as the name of the table in the Save As dialog box and click OK again.

5. In datasheet view, enter the following records into the Address Type table, as shown in Figure 13.15:

Address Type ID	Address Type Name
1	Home
2	Work
3	Travel

FIGURE 13.15.
Filling in the Address Type table.

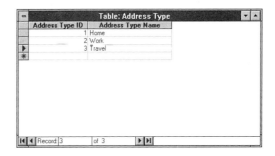

If there are additional address types that you would like to track in your database, go ahead and add them.

6. Close the Address Type table.

In Figure 13.16, the database container is now showing that you have four tables: Address, Address Type, Enter Address, and Person.

FIGURE 13.16.
You have created four tables so far.

Next you will create the Phone table and its related tables, Enter Phone and Phone Type, which are used in the same way as the Enter Address and Address Type tables.

1. Create a new table with the fields listed here:

Field Name	Data Type
PhoneID	Counter
PersonID	Number
PhoneTypeID	Number
Phone	Text

2. Make the PhoneID field the primary key.

3. Set the following properties for each field:

Field Name:	PersonID
Data Type:	Number
Field Size:	Long Integer
Caption:	Person ID
Required:	Yes
Indexed:	Yes (Duplicates OK)

Field Name:	PhoneTypeID
Data Type:	Number
Field Size:	Integer
Caption:	Phone Type ID
Required:	Yes

Field Name:	Phone
Data Type:	Text
Field Size:	30

4. Close the table, entering Phone as the name to save the table as.

In creating the Enter Phone table, you can take a shortcut and copy the PhoneTypeID and Phone fields from the Phone table just as you copied fields from the Address table to the Enter Address table.

1. Create a new table with the fields listed here:

Field Name	Data Type
EnterPhoneID	Counter
PhoneTypeID	Number
Phone	Text

2. Make the EnterPhoneID field the primary key.

3. Set the properties for the following fields. If you copied the fields from the Phone table, they are already set.

Field Name:	PhoneTypeID
Data Type:	Number
Field Size:	Integer
Caption:	Phone Type ID
Required:	Yes

Field Name:	Phone
Data Type:	Text
Field Size:	30

4. Save the table as Enter Phone.

The Phone Type table is a lookup table that stores the types that a phone number may be classified as.

1. Create a new table with the PhoneTypeID and PhoneTypeName fields shown here:

Field Name	Data Type
PhoneTypeID	Number
PhoneTypeName	Text

2. Make the PhoneTypeID field the primary key.

3. Set the field properties as follows:

Field Name:	PhoneTypeID
Data Type:	Number
Field Size:	Integer
Caption:	Phone Type ID

Field Name:	PhoneTypeName
Data Type:	Text
Field Size:	10
Caption:	Phone Type Name
Required:	Yes

4. Click the Datasheet View button on the toolbar to enter the records in the table. You are prompted to save the table; save it as Phone Type.

5. Enter the following records in the Phone Type table, as shown in Figure 13.17:

Phone Type ID	Phone Type Name
1	Home
2	Work
3	Mobile
4	Pager
5	Travel
6	Home Fax
7	Work Fax

Add any phone types that I forgot and then close the table.

You have created seven tables and have only two more left—the Prefix and State tables. These two tables are also lookup tables that provide a set of values to choose for the Prefix and State fields on the Address Entry form.

FIGURE 13.17.

*The contents of the
Phone Type table.*

Let's create the Prefix table first.

1. Create the Prefix table with the following fields:

Field Name	*Data Type*
PrefixID	Number
Prefix	Text

2. Make the PrefixID field the primary key.

3. Set the field properties as shown here:

Field Name:	PrefixID
Data Type:	Number
Field Size:	Integer
Caption:	Prefix ID

Field Name:	Prefix
Data Type:	Text
Field Size:	10
Required:	Yes

4. Save the table as Prefix and open it in datasheet view to enter the following records:

Prefix ID	*Prefix*
1	Mr.
2	Mrs.
3	Ms.
4	Dr.

   The Prefix names appear in the combo box by PrefixID order. During data entry, the user has the option to enter a prefix that doesn't exist in the table, but you want to make sure that you have included any that are used frequently.

5. Close the table.

6. Create the State table with the following fields:

Field Name	Data Type
StateAbbreviation	Text
State	Text

7. Make the StateAbbreviation field the primary key by selecting it and clicking the Set Primary Key toolbar button.

8. Set the field properties for the StateAbbreviation and State fields:

   Field Name: StateAbbreviation
   Data Type: Text
   Field Size: 2
   Caption: State Abbreviation

   Field Name: State
   Data Type: Text
   Field Size: 50
   Required: Yes

9. Save the table with the name State and enter some or all of the states as shown in Table 13.1. (The table also includes the District of Columbia.)

Table 13.1. State abbreviations.

State Abbreviation	State
AL	Alabama
AK	Alaska
AZ	Arizona
AR	Arkansas
CA	California
CO	Colorado
CT	Connecticut
DE	Delaware
DC	District of Columbia
FL	Florida
GA	Georgia
HI	Hawaii

continues

Table 13.1. continued

State Abbreviation	State
ID	Idaho
IL	Illinois
IN	Indiana
IA	Iowa
KS	Kansas
KY	Kentucky
LA	Louisiana
ME	Maine
MD	Maryland
MA	Massachusetts
MI	Michigan
MN	Minnesota
MS	Mississippi
MO	Missouri
MT	Montana
NE	Nebraska
NV	Nevada
NH	New Hampshire
NJ	New Jersey
NM	New Mexico
NY	New York
NC	North Carolina
ND	North Dakota
OH	Ohio
OK	Oklahoma
OR	Oregon
PA	Pennsylvania
RI	Rhode Island
SC	South Carolina
SD	South Dakota
TN	Tennessee

State Abbreviation	State
TX	Texas
UT	Utah
VT	Vermont
VA	Virginia
WA	Washington
WV	West Virginia
WI	Wisconsin
WY	Wyoming

Setting Table Relationships

Your next task is to set the relationships between the different tables in the database. You will be creating the Relationships view shown earlier in the chapter in Figure 13.6.

1. From the menu, select the **Edit|R**elationships command.

   Access displays an empty Relationships window, and the Add Table dialog box shown in Figure 13.18 pops up above it so you can start adding tables.

2. One by one, select each table and add it by clicking the **A**dd button.

FIGURE 13.18.

Adding all the tables to the Relationships window.

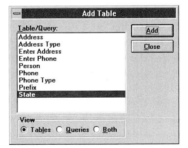

3. Close the Add Table dialog box.
4. Click the Maximize button on the Relationships window to give yourself some space to work with.
5. Rearrange the layout of the tables as shown in Figure 13.19.

Where practical, I like to resize each of the individual table windows so they can display all the fields within the table.

FIGURE 13.19.

Layout of the Address Book tables in the Relationships window.

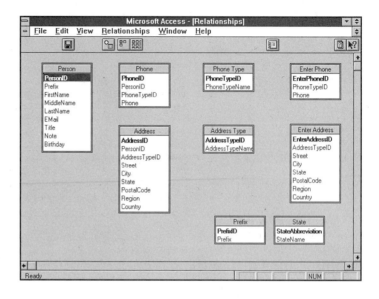

The placement of the tables doesn't affect how the database performs in any way. Only when you start creating relationships do you actually affect the database. This is what you will do next.

1. Click the PersonID field in the Person table. Holding down the mouse button, drag over to the PersonID field in the Phone table, and release the mouse button.

   Access displays the Relationships dialog box with a two-column list box indicating that the PersonID field in the Person table is joined with the PersonID field in the Phone table, as shown in Figure 13.20.

FIGURE 13.20.

Setting relationship options for a join between the Person and Phone tables.

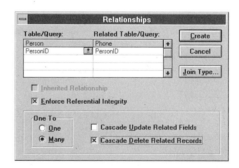

2. Click the **E**nforce Referential Integrity check box so that it is checked.

By turning this option on, you are telling Access that any record in the Phone table must have a value in its PersonID field that matches a value in the PersonID field of the

Person table. In other words, each record in the Phone table must belong to a record in the Person table.

A record in the Phone table that didn't have record in the Person table would be called an *orphan record.* The term is most likely derived from the terms used to describe the relationships between the two tables. The Person table is called a *parent table* and the Phone table is called a *child table.* (Also, the records within the tables are referred to as *parent records* and *child records.*)

By enforcing referential integrity, you are making the existence of orphan records illegal. Access produces an error message if you try to delete a parent record for which there are still child records in existence.

You can set a few additional options that affect how the database uses the Phone and Person tables.

1. Click the Cascade **D**elete Related Records check box so that it is also checked.

   Now that you have turned this option on, Access automatically deletes the child records for you when you delete a parent record that has child records, rather than producing an error.

2. Click the **J**oin Type button.

   Access displays the Join Properties dialog box.

   When you run queries that return fields from both tables, by default Access returns only records in the Person table for which there is at least one record in the Phone table.

3. Select option 2, as shown in Figure 13.21.

   Selecting option 2 enables you to create a query that produces records in the Person table even if there isn't a corresponding record in the Phone table. You want this because you don't expect every person in your address book to have a phone number.

4. Click OK in the Join Properties dialog box and click the **C**reate button in the Relationships dialog box.

FIGURE 13.21.

Defining the join type for the relationship between the Person and Phone tables.

In the Relationships window you see that Access has drawn a line from the Person table to the Phone table indicating a one-to-many relationship between the two tables. This is shown in Figure 13.22.

FIGURE 13.22.

A one-to-many relationship is established between the Person and Phone tables.

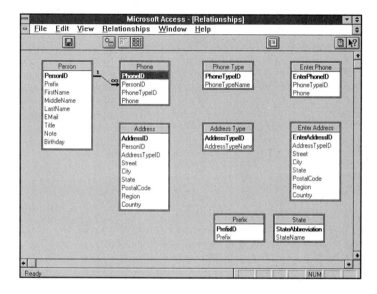

You need to set up the same type of relationship between the Person and Address tables.

1. Click the PersonID field in the Person table and drag and release the mouse button on the PersonID field in the Address table.
2. Check **E**nforce Referential Integrity and Cascade **D**elete Related Records in the Relationships dialog box.
3. Click the **J**oin Type button to bring up the Join Properties dialog box.
4. Select option 2 again. Close both dialog boxes by clicking the OK button and then the **C**reate button.

Now you have made the Address table a child table to the Person table, as shown in Figure 13.23. The 1 in the diagram indicates that one record in this table can have many records (indicated by the infinity symbol) in the child table.

You have two more relationships to define.

The Phone table has a PhoneTypeID field that represents a record in the Phone Type lookup table. The next relationship you define ensures that the PhoneTypeID value always points to an existing record in the lookup table.

For example, the Phone Type table has seven possible values for Phone Type ID: 1 through 7. It would be illegal to enter an 8 in the PhoneTypeID field of the Phone table.

FIGURE 13.23.

Adding a second relationship, this time between the Person and Address tables.

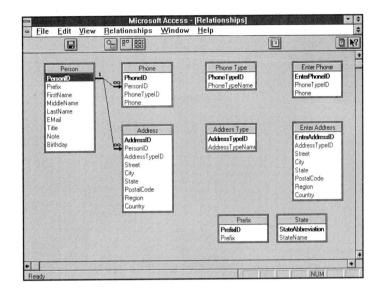

A value of 8 is meaningless because there is no corresponding record in the Phone Type table to identify what the code means.

The relationship also ensures that records in the Phone Type lookup table aren't deleted if there are still PhoneTypeID fields in the Phone table that use that record's phone type code.

1. Click the PhoneTypeID field in the PhoneType table and move left, dragging the cursor over to the PhoneTypeID field in the Phone table.

2. In the Relationships dialog box, click the **E**nforce Referential Integrity check box to turn it on.

   Do not check the Cascade **D**elete Related Records option. You don't want the deletion of a record in the Phone Type table to cause records in the Phone table to be deleted. Instead, you would prefer in this case to see an error message indicating that you shouldn't be deleting this record at this time.

   Also, you don't need to change the Join Type for this relationship, because you expect that for every PhoneTypeID value in the Phone table there is a matching PhoneTypeID value in the Phone Type table.

3. Click the **C**reate button to create the relationship.

   The next relationship works the same way as the earlier one, but it is for the Address Type and Address tables.

4. Click the AddressTypeID field in the Address Type table and drag it to the same field in the Address table.

5. Check the **E**nforce Referential Integrity option in the Relationships dialog box, and then click the **C**reate button.

Figure 13.24 shows the completed Relationships window.

FIGURE 13.24.

The Relationships window after you have defined all the relationships.

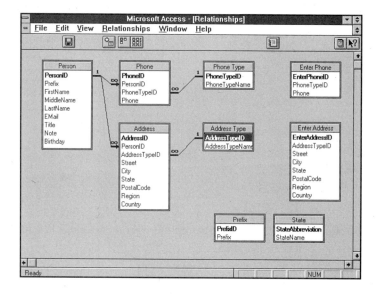

The Enter Phone, Enter Address, Prefix, and State tables have been added to the relationships diagram only to illustrate all of the tables contained in the database.

You can capture the screen and paste it into Paintbrush as a way to print the relationships diagram. Press the Print Screen button to copy the screen to the Windows clipboard.

Run Paintbrush and maximize its window. Even with the window maximized, you still need more space to be able to paste an entire screen image into the Paintbrush window. To do this, first select the **O**ptions|**I**mage Attributes command and make sure the Width and Height fields are set large enough to accommodate a large image. You can click the **D**efault button to set the image size automatically. Close the dialog box and select the Paintbrush **V**iew|Zoom **O**ut command.

Select **E**dit|**P**aste from the menu or press Ctrl-V to paste in the image. Paintbrush displays the image as a bunch of criss-crossed diagonal lines. Click anywhere off the image, and it appears in its zoomed-out form as shown in Figure 13.25.

Now select the **V**iew|Zoom **I**n command to get the normal view of the screen capture, as shown in Figure 13.26. From there the **F**ile menu is available, so you can select the **F**ile|**P**rint command to send the image to your printer.

FIGURE 13.25.

Using the View\Zoom Out command in Paintbrush to paste in a full screen shot.

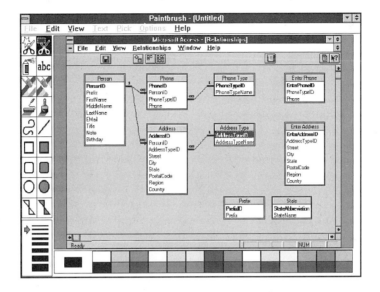

FIGURE 13.26.

Holding a Relationships screen image in Paintbrush.

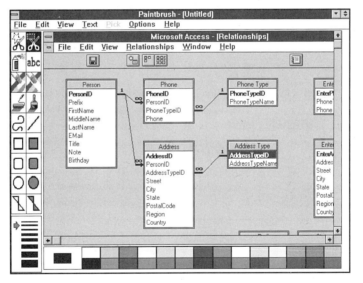

Access offers a File|Print Definition command that produces an Access report showing the defined relationships. It's not nearly as pretty as the graphical view, but it's another way to produce a report on the design of your database tables.

That's all you have to do as far as creating tables and establishing their relationships. Let's get started next on the Address Entry form so you can enter something into the tables.

Creating the Address Entry Form

In making an address book entry, you are likely to update three tables: Person, Phone, and Address.

Although it would be great to have the flexibility of using three tables to store an address book entry, it would be terrible to have to open three separate forms to make an address book entry. Instead, I combined it all inside one form.

The typical way to do this in Access is by using subforms on a main form. Why didn't I use them?

The reason is because Access-bound forms support a general-purpose record editing user interface that might not be the exact kind of user interface I want the program to have.

An example in the Address Entry form is how the phone numbers and addresses are entered. With a main form/subform relationship, the main form would have to physically write the Person record before a phone number could be entered, because the Phone record is a child record of the Person record.

What if I want my user to be able to make their field entries in any order?

Another problem to deal with is how to implement the Cancel button. If records are already written by a bound form, the code behind the Cancel button would have to reverse any changes already made to the database while the form was open. What if the user was editing rather than adding new records? You would then have to deal with the Cancel situation by restoring the edited records to their prior condition before the form was opened.

These problems can be worked around, but not without some study and full understanding of the Access event model. I find it easier to use bound forms when they really fit the task, but also avoid them when they don't. Use a bound form like a record editing form and not something else. For example, it would be better to have a Close button rather than a Cancel button if you are using a bound form.

If you work with unbound forms, the Access form event model becomes drastically simplified. You narrow yourself down to working with simple events like On Open and On Close for forms and On Click for buttons. However, you then have to provide all the record editing functionality through your own code, and that can mean a lot more coding.

After taking a look at how the Address Entry form is created, you might want to do some experimentation on your own and see if you would have implemented the form the same way (through code) or by using bound forms and subforms.

With all that said, let's take a look now at this implementation. First you need to build the form, then you write some code in a Globals module and in the code behind the form.

1. Close the Relationships window if it is still open.
2. Click the Form tab on the database container and click the **N**ew button to start a new form.
3. Click the **B**lank Form button in the New Form dialog box without selecting a table in the combo box above it.

   This is a going to be a large form, so it's easier to work on the form while it is maximized.
4. Click the Maximize button in the form design window.
5. Click on the outside of the form's detail section to select the form object (or click the little white square at the intersection of the form's horizontal and vertical rulers), and then click the Properties button on the toolbar.

   Access displays the Properties window for the new form.
6. Make sure that "All Properties" is selected in the combo box at the top of the Properties window.

   For the form and control property settings I list only those that differ from their default values, except where listing the default values helps make it clear how the control is being used.
7. Change the following form properties, as shown in Figure 13.27:

Caption:	Address Entry
Default View:	Single Form
Shortcut Menu:	No
Scroll Bars:	Neither
Record Selectors:	No
Navigation Buttons:	No
Auto Center:	Yes
Border Style:	Dialog
Min Button:	No
Max Button:	No
Width:	5.5 in

Creating the Person Record Controls

While dropping controls on the form, you might also find it useful from time to time to change the Grid X and Grid Y values to higher values to allow for a finer resolution in the placement of the controls on the form.

FIGURE 13.27.

*Setting the form
properties on the
Address Entry form.*

Form	
All Properties	
Record Source . . .	
Caption	Address Entry
Default View	Single Form
Views Allowed . . .	Both
Default Editing . . .	Allow Edits
Allow Editing	Available
Allow Updating . . .	Default Tables
Record Locks	No Locks
Allow Filters	Yes
Shortcut Menu . . .	No
Menu Bar	
Scroll Bars	Neither
Record Selectors . .	No
Navigation Buttons	No
Auto Resize	Yes
Auto Center	Yes
Pop Up	No
Modal	No

In the following instructions I give you the Left, Top, Height, and Width property settings for placement of the controls on the form.

Entering these properties through the Properties window wasn't how the form was originally constructed, but it might be the easiest method for reconstructing it if you are dutifully following these step-by-step instructions.

1. Click on the detail section (the inside of the form currently displayed as white).

   The Properties window now displays the properties for the detail section, named by default as Detail0.

2. Set the Height and Back Color properties for the detail section, as shown in Figure 13.28:

Height:	3.5826 in
Back Color:	12632256 (Light Gray)

   It's easier to use the Palette window to change the Back Color property to light gray. Click the Palette button on the toolbar and select the light gray box in the line that represents the Back Color setting.

3. Close the Palette window and click the Toolbox toolbar button to display the toolbox.

4. Click the Combo box button and click the detail section to drop a combo box and label on the form, as shown in Figure 13.29. This combo box is used to prefix a name with a title such as Mr. or Mrs.

5. Click the label of the combo box to display the properties of the label. Set the label properties as listed here:

Name:	lblPrefix
Caption:	Prefix:
Left:	0.1042 in

Top:	0.0826 in
Width:	0.5 in
Height:	1.667 in
Back Color:	12632256 (Light Gray)
Fore Color:	128 (Red)
Font Weight:	Bold

FIGURE 13.28.

Changing the Height and Back Color of the Detail section.

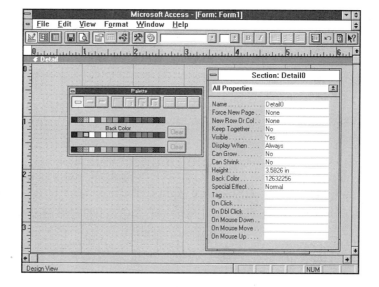

FIGURE 13.29.

Creating the first control on the form.

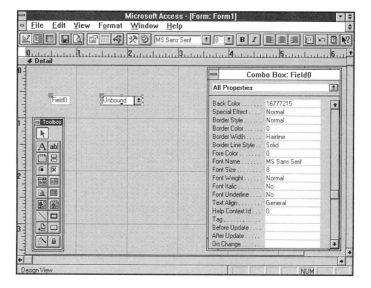

Because you have several labels to create of this type, you should use the Format|Change Default command so you have minimal settings to make on the following label controls.

As you create each new control type, you use this command again to set defaults on each type of control used on the form.

6. Select the Format|Change Default command.

The default values you just set are used by Access only when creating controls for the current form. If you wish to use modified defaults for all new forms and controls, you need to indicate which form is used as the template.

This is done from the Options dialog box from the View|Options command. Among the categories of options listed are Form and Report Design. Within the Form and Report Design options are Form Template and Report Template.

TRY THIS! QUESTION 13.1.

Create a template for a modal pop-up form. Write a function that toggles between using your template and the Normal template. Assign a keystroke to run your function so you can quickly switch between the two.

Let's continue to create the controls on the Address Entry form.

1. Click the combo box control and set the properties for it as shown here:

Name:	cboPrefix
Row Source Type:	Table/Query
Row Source:	Prefix
Column Count:	2
Column Widths:	0 in;0.6 in
Bound Column:	2
Tab Index:	0
Left:	0.1 in
Top:	0.25 in
Width:	0.6 in
Height:	0.1771 in
Special Effect:	Sunken

The Row Source for the combo box is set to display the fields in the prefix table. However, the first column is hidden by setting its display width to 0 inches. Both the bound column and the displayed column are the second column.

By default, the combo box's Limit To List property is set to No. As long as the bound column is the first column displayed in the drop-down list, the Limit To List property is used. This enables the user to enter a different prefix than those available in the list.

2. With the combo box still selected, select the Format|Change Default command as shown in Figure 13.30.

FIGURE 13.30.

Saving default settings for combo boxes based on the cboPrefix combo box.

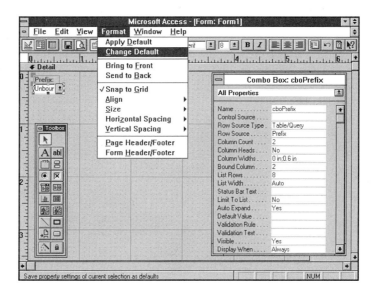

3. Click the Textbox button on the toolbox, and then click the detail section on the form to drop a label and text box on the form for entering a last name.

The label for the text box assumes some of the properties of the label control you created earlier. You haven't set default properties for a text box control yet, so it is drawn with the normal defaults.

4. Click the text box label to select it, and set the following properties:

Name:	lblLast
Caption:	*Last:
Left:	0.7146 in
Top:	0.0826 in
Width:	0.5 in
Height:	1.667 in

5. Click the text box and set the following properties:

Name:	txtLast
Tab Index:	1

continues

Left:	0.7201 in
Top:	0.25 in
Width:	1.3875 in
Height:	0.1771 in
Special Effect:	Sunken

6. Select the Format|Change Default command to save the default values for a text box.

7. Drop a second text box on the form for entering a first name.

   This time Access creates a text box that is closer to the desired object (as shown in Figure 13.31).

FIGURE 13.31.

Creating a text box from saved defaults.

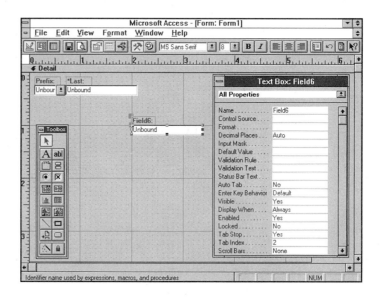

8. Set the following properties for the new label:

Name:	lblFirst
Caption:	*First:
Left:	2.125 in
Top:	0.0826 in
Width:	0.5 in
Height:	1.667 in

9. Set the properties for the new text box:

Name:	txtFirst
Tab Index:	2
Left:	2.1201 in

Top:	0.25 in
Width:	1.1792 in
Height:	0.1771 in

10. Add a text box to the form for entering a middle name or initial. Set the properties for the new label and text box as listed here:

Name:	lblMiddle
Caption:	Middle:
Left:	3.3229 in
Top:	0.0826 in
Width:	0.5 in
Height:	1.667 in

Name:	txtMiddle
Tab Index:	3
Left:	3.3201 in
Top:	0.25 in
Width:	0.6792 in
Height:	0.1771 in

That completes the first row on the form. Now is probably a good time to save the form so you don't lose too much work if disaster strikes. Don't forget to save your work every once in a while as you complete the rest of the form.

1. Select the **File|S**ave command.

2. Enter Address Entry in the Save As dialog box and click OK, as shown in Figure 13.32.

FIGURE 13.32.
*Saving your work
so far.*

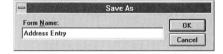

Next, add the second row of controls.

1. At the beginning of a second row, create a lblTitle label and txtTitle text box with the following properties:

Name:	lblTitle
Caption:	Title:
Left:	0.1028 in
Top:	0.4576 in
Width:	0.5 in
Height:	1.667 in

continues

Name:	txtTitle
Tab Index:	4
Left:	0.1 in
Top:	0.625 in
Width:	2.0021 in
Height:	0.1771 in

2. Create the lblEMail label and txtEMail text box with the following properties:

Name:	lblEMail
Caption:	Email:
Left:	2.125 in
Top:	0.4576 in
Width:	0.5 in
Height:	1.667 in

Name:	txtEMail
Tab Index:	5
Left:	2.1201 in
Top:	0.625 in
Width:	1.1792 in
Height:	0.1771 in

The txtBirthday control has its Format property set to display a date in the Medium Date format, which displays like 01-May-95. You can actually enter the date in other formats (such as 5/1/95) and the text box accepts it but redisplays it in the chosen format.

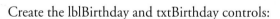

Create the lblBirthday and txtBirthday controls:

Name:	lblBirthday
Caption:	Birthday:
Left:	3.3229 in
Top:	0.4576 in
Width:	0.5833 in
Height:	1.667 in

Name:	txtBirthday
Format:	Medium Date
Tab Index:	6
Left:	3.3201 in
Top:	0.625 in
Width:	0.6792 in
Height:	0.1771 in

The text boxes on the Address Entry form are carefully placed on the form so that with the sunken effect, a small vertical bar appears to separate the text boxes, as shown in Figure 13.33.

As the controls were originally placed on the form, this effect was created by dropping each text box on the form adjacent to the text box before and after it, and then shortening the length of each text box just enough to produce the separator bar.

FIGURE 13.33.

Completing a second line of prompts on the Address Entry form.

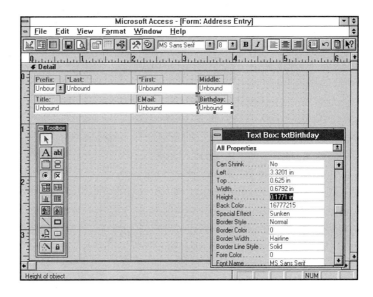

Next you create a large multiline text box for entering any type of notes about a person into the address book entry.

Add another label and text box to the form with the following properties set:

Name:	lblNote
Caption:	Note:
Left:	0.1042 in
Top:	0.8542 in
Width:	0.4583 in
Height:	1.667 in

Name:	txtNote
Enter Key Behavior:	New Line in Field
Tab Index:	7
Scroll Bars:	Vertical
Left:	0.1 in

continues

Top:	1.0208 in
Width:	2.5021 in
Height:	0.9792 in

You can test the form during development to see how it is coming along, as shown in Figure 13.34. Click the Form View button on the toolbar to switch to form view, and try entering data in the fields. The Prefix combo box should list the available name prefixes.

FIGURE 13.34.

Testing the feel of the form so far.

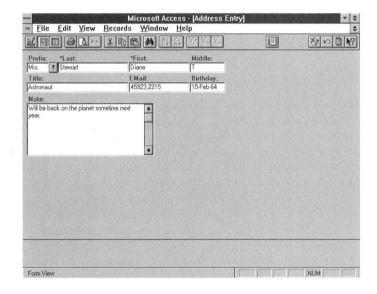

Click the Design View toolbar button to return to editing the form.

This completes the section of the form for values entered into the Person table. Next you change label colors from red to dark blue for entering records into the Phone table.

Creating the Phone Record Controls

First you add a combo box on the form to allow the user to enter a phone number.

1. Click the Combo box button on the toolbar and click the form to drop a label and combo box on the form.

2. Set the new label properties as shown here:

Name:	lblPhone
Caption:	*Phone:
Left:	2.7 in
Top:	0.8542 in

Width:	0.6 in
Height:	1.667 in
Fore Color:	8388608 (Dark Blue)

3. With the label still selected, save the new Fore Color property in the label control default by selecting the Format|Change Default command.

4. Select the new combo box and set the following properties:

Name:	cboPhone
Row Source Type:	Table/Query
Auto Expand:	No
Tab Index:	8
Left:	2.7 in
Top:	1.0208 in
Width:	1.1938 in
Height:	0.1771 in

The reason a combo box is used for the Phone field is that when you use the address book you might often find yourself making entries for different people who have the same phone number, especially when entering employees from smaller companies.

The combo box displays all the phone numbers entered into the database so far by doing a summary query on the Phone table. The next step is to create the source for this combo box.

1. In the Properties window, click the box for the Row Source property.

   Access displays two buttons, one with a down arrow to list tables and queries, and another with an ellipsis (three dots).

2. Click the ellipsis button.

   Access displays the Query Builder window (also known as the QBE grid) and the Add Table dialog box, shown in Figure 13.35.

3. Select the Phone table and click the **A**dd button. Click the **C**lose button to close the Add Table dialog box.

4. Drag the Phone field from the Phone table down to the first column in the grid.

5. Click the Totals button on the toolbar to change the query to a summary query.

6. In the Sort row of the grid, select Ascending sort order for the Phone field, as shown in Figure 13.36.

7. Close the Query Builder window, answering Yes to the dialog box that asks if you want to update the property.

FIGURE 13.35.

*Adding a table to the
query for the cboPhone
combo box's Row
Source property.*

FIGURE 13.36.

*The completed query
for the cboPhone combo
box's Row Source
property.*

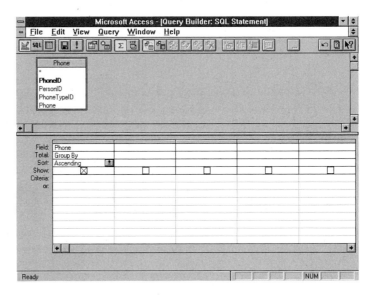

Access enters the following SQL SELECT statement into the Row Source property:

```
SELECT DISTINCTROW Phone.Phone FROM Phone GROUP BY Phone.Phone
ORDER BY Phone.Phone;
```

The next control enables the user to classify an entered phone number by one of the
phone types listed in the Phone Type table.

Drop another label and combo box on the form and set the following properties:

Name:	lblPhoneType
Caption:	*Type:
Left:	3.9201 in
Top:	0.8542 in
Width:	0.5 in
Height:	1.667 in

Name:	cboPhoneType
Row Source Type:	Table/Query
Row Source:	Phone Type
Column Count:	2
Column Widths:	0 in;0.7875 in
Bound Column:	1
Limit To List:	Yes
Auto Expand:	Yes
Tab Index:	9
Left:	3.9201 in
Top:	1.0208 in
Width:	0.7875 in
Height:	0.1771 in

The cboPhoneType control displays the PhoneTypeName field from the second column of the Phone Type table but actually returns the PhoneTypeID field, which is the numeric code for the phone type. This works because the first column has its width set to 0 inches but is set to be the bound column.

Because you already have the Phone Type table filled with data, you can test this control by switching the form to Form View mode, as shown in Figure 13.37.

The next two controls are command buttons to add the current phone entry into the list of phone numbers or clear the current phone entry. You use the Format|Change Default command again after setting the properties for the first button.

FIGURE 13.37.

Testing the cboPhoneType combo box.

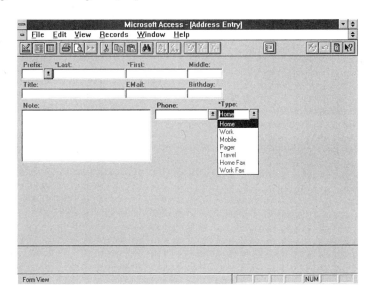

1. Click the Command Button button on the toolbox, and then click the form to add a button to the form.

2. Set the following properties on the command button control:

Name:	cmdAddPhone
Caption:	Add
Tab Index:	10
Left:	4.8 in
Top:	0.8326 in
Width:	0.6 in
Height:	0.2097 in
Fore Color:	8388608 (Dark Blue)
Font Name:	Small Fonts
Font Size:	7
Font Weight:	Bold

3. With the button still selected, select the Format|Change Default command.

In placing the next button on the form, if you simply click the form rather than drawing the button, the height and width properties are inherited from the saved defaults. This way you don't have to resize the button afterwards.

4. Drop another command button on the form, as shown in Figure 13.38, and set the following properties for it:

Name:	cmdClearPhone
Caption:	Clear
Tab Index:	11
Left:	4.8 in
Top:	1.0833 in
Width:	0.6 in
Height:	0.2097 in

The next control is a list box that you use to display the current phone numbers for the person in this address book entry. The control uses a query to read phone number records temporarily stored in the Enter Phone table for editing.

1. Click the List box button on the toolbox and click the form to drop a list box on the form.

2. Set the properties of the new label and list box as shown here:

Name:	lblPhones
Caption:	Phones:
Left:	2.7042 in
Top:	1.2292 in

Width:	0.6 in
Height:	1.667 in
Name:	lstPhones
Row Source Type:	Table/Query
Column Count:	4
Column Widths:	0 in;1.2 in;0.7875 in;0 in
Bound Column:	1
Tab Index:	12
Left:	2.7 in
Top:	1.3958 in
Width:	1.9979 in
Height:	0.6042 in
Special Effect:	Sunken

FIGURE 13.38.

Adding Add and Clear Buttons to the Address Entry form.

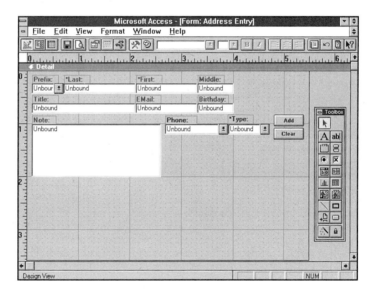

The Row Source for the list is a query returning four columns: EnterPhoneID, Phone, PhoneTypeName, and PhoneTypeID. The second and third columns are displayed, and the first and fourth columns are available to be referenced by the program.

3. Select the Row Source property text box and click the ellipsis button to enter the Query Builder window.

4. In the Add Table dialog box, add the Enter Phone and Phone Type tables, as shown in Figure 13.39. Close the Add Table dialog box.

Because of your established relationships between the tables, Access draws a line connecting the PhoneTypeID field in the Enter Phone table to the same field in the Phone Type table.

5. Drag the EnterPhoneID field from the Enter Phone table to the first column, as shown in Figure 13.40.

6. Add the Phone field from the Enter Phone table to the second column.

7. Add the PhoneTypeName field from the Phone Type table as the third column.

8. Add the PhoneTypeID field from the Enter Phone table as the fourth column.

9. Close the Query Builder window.

FIGURE 13.39.

Adding tables to the Row Source query for the lstPhones list box.

FIGURE 13.40.

The final query for the lstPhones list box Row Source property.

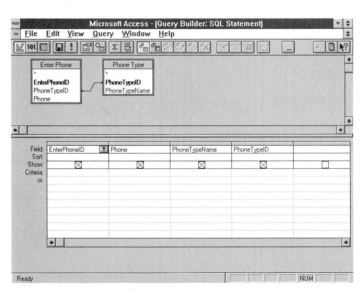

Access enters the following SQL SELECT statement into the lstPhones control's Row Source property:

```
SELECT DISTINCTROW
[Enter Phone].EnterPhoneID, [Enter Phone].Phone,
[Phone Type].PhoneTypeName, [Enter Phone].PhoneTypeID
FROM [Enter Phone]
INNER JOIN [Phone Type] ON [Enter Phone].PhoneTypeID =
➥ [PhoneType].PhoneTypeID;
```

To complete the section of the form for entering phone numbers, you need to add one more command button. The Clear button erases the text in the cboPhone and cboPhoneType combo boxes, but it doesn't actually delete a phone record. The next button is used to delete the phone number record currently selected in the lstPhones list box.

Drop a third button on the form with the following properties set:

Name:	cmdDeletePhone
Caption:	Delete
Tab Index:	13
Left:	4.8 in
Top:	1.5625 in
Width:	0.6 in
Height:	0.2097 in

You might want to save what you have so far—especially if you hear any rain and thunder outside.

Creating the Address Record Controls

Now is a good time to munch a granola bar and M&Ms for energy or pour some more coffee, because you are about to attack seven combo boxes in a row.

The bottom half of the form works just like the phone section you just completed, except there are many more fields to take care of. This section is for entering data that gets written to the Address table.

1. Drop a new combo box on the form (see Figure 13.41). Set the combo box's label to the following properties:

Name:	lblStreet
Caption:	*Street:
Left:	0.1 in
Top:	2.0826 in
Width:	0.6 in
Height:	1.667 in
Fore Color:	8388736 (Purple)

Because you changed colors, you want to save this default so it is applied to the following controls.

2. Select the Format|**C**hange Default command.

3. Set the properties for the new combo box as listed here:

Name:	cboStreet
Row Source Type:	Table/Query
Column Count:	1
Bound Column:	1
Limit To List:	No
Auto Expand:	No
Tab Index:	14
Left:	0.1 in
Top:	2.25 in
Width:	2.6 in
Height:	0.1771 in

FIGURE 13.41.

Adding the cboStreet combo box in the bottom section of the form.

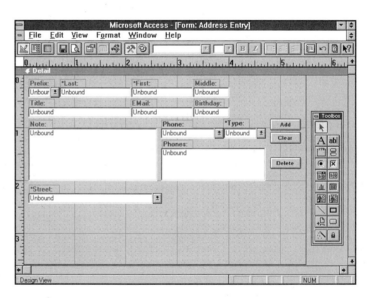

The Street, City, Region, Postal Code, and Country combo boxes all work like the Phone combo box in that they use a summary query to return a sorted list of all the entries made in these fields previously.

The idea behind this is to eliminate the need to type in the same address multiple times when you have several people living or working at the same location.

You might think that the form would take a long time to load with all these queries. Not so! Access executes each query only if the drop-down list is actually used to select an entry for the field. In many cases, the user knows that he or she has a unique entry and just types it in. Even if the list is used, only the query for the list being used is actually executed.

1. Click the ellipsis button for the cboStreet combo box's Row Source property.
2. In the Add Table dialog box, add the Address table. Close the dialog box.
3. Drag the Street field to the first column. Set the sorting of the field to Ascending order.
4. Click the Totals button on the toolbar.
5. Enter `Not Is Null` in the Criteria row, as shown in Figure 13.42. This ensures that the drop-down list doesn't contain an empty row.

FIGURE 13.42.

The Row Source query for the cboStreet combo box.

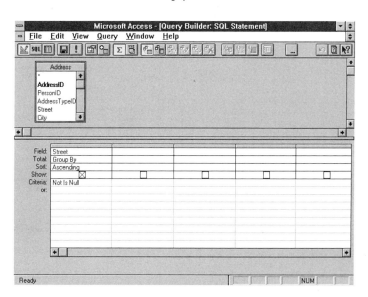

6. Close the Query Builder window.

The SQL `SELECT` statement that is entered in the cboState Row Source property looks like this:

```
SELECT DISTINCTROW Address.Street
FROM Address
GROUP BY Address.Street
HAVING ((Not Address.Street Is Null))
ORDER BY Address.Street;
```

Remember the query steps, 1 through 6. You are going to have to create the same kind of query for each of the following fields: City, Region, Postal Code, and Country.

Rather than explain these same steps over and over, I will refer you to here. Use the appropriate field for the combo box being created, rather than the Street field.

1. Add the City label and combo box with the following properties:

Name:	lblCity
Caption:	*City:
Left:	2.7201 in
Top:	2.0826 in
Width:	0.5097 in
Height:	1.667 in

Name:	cboCity
Row Source Type:	Table/Query
Column Count:	1
Bound Column:	1
Limit To List:	No
Auto Expand:	No
Tab Index:	15
Left:	2.7201 in
Top:	2.25 in
Width:	1.1729 in
Height:	0.1771 in

2. Use the Query Builder to set the Row Source property of the cboCity combo box to an SQL SELECT statement that returns each unique city in the Address table. (See the query steps 1 through 6 and Figure 13.43.)

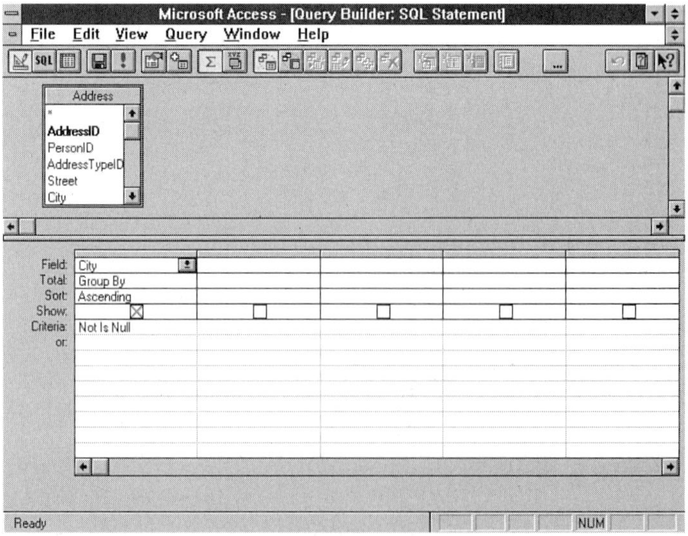

FIGURE 13.43.

The Row Source query for the cboCity combo box.

The State combo box works differently than the other combo boxes. Rather than reading its available selections from the Address table, a separate State table was created listing state abbreviations and full names.

1. Add the State label and combo box:

Name:	lblState
Caption:	State:
Left:	3.9201 in
Top:	2.0826 in
Width:	0.5 in
Height:	1.667 in

Name:	cboState
Row Source Type:	Table/Query
Column Count:	2
Column Widths:	0.25 in;1.25 in
Bound Column:	1
List Width:	1.5 in
Limit To List:	No
Auto Expand:	Yes
Tab Index:	16
Left:	3.9201 in
Top:	2.25 in
Width:	0.7771 in
Height:	0.1771 in

2. Open the Query Builder for the Row Source property of the cboState combo box.
3. Add the State table to the query and close the Add Table dialog box.
4. Place the StateAbbreviation field in the first column of the query and the StateName field in the second column.
5. Set the sort order of the StateName field to Ascending order.

The query should look like Figure 13.44.

The SELECT statement created by the Query Builder is the following:

```
SELECT DISTINCTROW State.StateAbbreviation, State.StateName
FROM State ORDER BY State.StateName;
```

The Address Entry form now has the first line of controls for the Address section. You can switch the form to Form View and verify that the cboState combo box correctly lists the states from the State table, as shown in Figure 13.45.

FIGURE 13.44.

The Row Source query for the cboState combo box.

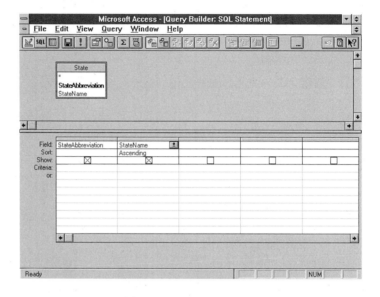

FIGURE 13.45.

Testing the cboState combo box.

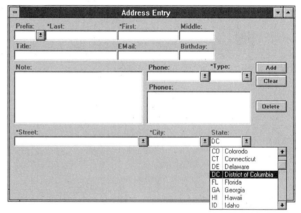

Add the next line of controls.

1. At the start of the next line of controls, add a Region label and combo box with the following properties:

Name:	lblRegion
Caption:	Region:
Left:	0.1042 in
Top:	2.4375 in
Width:	0.6 in
Height:	1.667 in

Name:	cboRegion
Row Source Type:	Table/Query
Column Count:	1
Bound Column:	1
Limit To List:	No
Auto Expand:	No
Tab Index:	17
Left:	0.1 in
Top:	2.6042 in
Width:	1.5056 in
Height:	0.1771 in

The Region field is added for addresses from countries outside the United States that use Region in addition to or in place of a State field.

2. Use the Query Builder to create a Row Source setting for the cboRegion combo box just as you did for the cboStreet and cboCity combo boxes. (See query steps 1 through 6.)

The query should return each unique Region entered in the Address table, and its SQL statement looks like this:

```
SELECT DISTINCTROW Address.Region
FROM Address
GROUP BY Address.Region
HAVING ((Not Address.Region Is Null))
ORDER BY Address.Region;
```

3. Add a Postal Code label and combo box:

Name:	lblPostalCode
Caption:	Postal Code:
Left:	1.6201 in
Top:	2.4375 in
Width:	0.8958 in
Height:	1.667 in

Name:	cboPostalCode
Row Source Type:	Table/Query
Column Count:	1
Bound Column:	1
Limit To List:	No
Auto Expand:	No
Tab Index:	18
Left:	1.6201 in

continues

Top:	2.6042 in
Width:	1.0792 in
Height:	0.1771 in

4. Follow query steps 1 through 6 once again to create a Row Source for the cboPostalCode combo box, this time for the PostalCode field. The resulting SQL SELECT statement should look like this:

```
SELECT DISTINCTROW Address.PostalCode
FROM Address
GROUP BY Address.PostalCode
HAVING ((Not Address.PostalCode Is Null))
ORDER BY Address.PostalCode;
```

5. Create a Country label and combo box:

Name:	lblCountry
Caption:	Country:
Left:	2.7201 in
Top:	2.4375 in
Width:	0.8958 in
Height:	1.667 in

Name:	cboCountry
Row Source Type:	Table/Query
Column Count:	1
Bound Column:	1
Limit To List:	No
Auto Expand:	Yes
Tab Index:	19
Left:	2.7201 in
Top:	2.6042 in
Width:	1.1729 in
Height:	0.1771 in

6. Use the Query Builder to create the Row Source property for the cboCountry combo box as you did for the other controls. (Follow query steps 1 through 6 again.) The resulting SQL SELECT statement should look like this:

```
SELECT DISTINCTROW Address.Country
FROM Address
GROUP BY Address.Country
HAVING ((Not Address.Country Is Null))
ORDER BY Address.Country;
```

The last combo box is for selecting the type of address being entered. The available selections are drawn from those you entered in the Address Type table.

7. Drop a combo box and label on the form and set the following properties:

Name:	lblAddressType
Caption:	*Type:
Left:	3.9201 in
Top:	2.4375 in
Width:	0.5 in
Height:	1.667 in

Name:	cboAddressType
Row Source Type:	Table/Query
Row Source:	Address Type
Column Count:	2
Column Widths:	0 in;0.7771 in
Bound Column:	1
Limit To List:	Yes
Auto Expand:	Yes
Tab Index:	20
Left:	3.9201 in
Top:	2.6042 in
Width:	0.7771 in
Height:	0.1771 in

This is a good breaking point to save your work once again. Figure 13.46 shows what you have so far.

FIGURE 13.46.

Completing the second row of controls on the Address section of the Address Entry form.

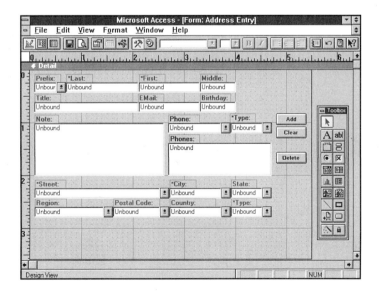

Next you create Add and Clear buttons just as you did for the Phone section of the form. You have to save the default once again after creating the first button because of the color change.

1. Drop a command button on the form and set the following properties:

Caption:	Add
Tab Index:	21
Left:	4.8 in
Top:	2.25 in
Width:	0.6 in
Height:	0.2097 in
Fore Color:	8388736 (Purple)
Font Name:	Small Fonts
Font Size:	7
Font Weight:	Bold

2. With the button still selected, select the Format|Change Default command from the menu.

3. Drop a second button with these properties:

Name:	cmdClearAddress
Caption:	Clear
Tab Index:	22
Left:	4.8 in
Top:	2.5 in
Width:	0.6 in
Height:	0.2097 in

The next control is the list box that displays the addresses that have already been entered. The data comes from the Enter Address table, which temporarily stores the address records for the address book entry being edited.

You can't have the list box display every address field, because there are too many of them. Instead, I have it displaying the required fields: Street, City, and Address Type. I lined these up in the list box with the combo boxes used earlier for entering these fields.

Click the List box button on the toolbar and drop a label and list box on the form, as shown in Figure 13.47. Set the following properties:

Name:	lblAddresses
Caption:	Addresses:
Left:	0.1042 in
Top:	2.8326 in

Width:	0.8 in
Height:	1.667 in

Name:	lstAddresses
Row Source Type:	Table/Query
Column Count:	9
Column Widths:	0 in;2.6098 in;1.182 in;0.6 in;0 in;0 in;0 in;0 in;0 in
Bound Column:	1
Tab Index:	23
Left:	0.1 in
Top:	3 in
Width:	4.6021 in
Height:	0.4597 in
Special Effect:	Sunken

FIGURE 13.47.

Adding the lstAddresses list box.

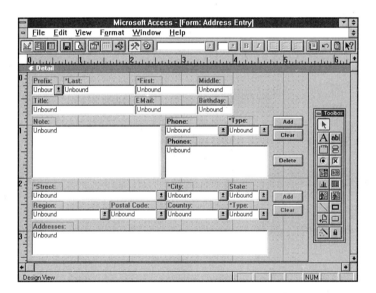

Even though only three of the fields are displayed, the Row Source for the list box must still return each of the fields for an address. This is so the program can read the address fields from the list box into the combo boxes above it when a user wants to edit an existing entry.

Many of the fields returned by the Row Source query are hidden from view by setting their display width to 0 inches.

1. Click the ellipsis button for the lstAddresses list box to bring up the Query Builder.

2. With the Add Table dialog box, add the Enter Address and Address Type tables to the Query Builder window. Close the Add Table dialog box.

3. Drag the EnterAddressID field down from the Enter Address table to the first column.

4. Place the Street and City fields from the Enter Address table in the second and third columns.

5. Place the AddressTypeName field from the Address Type table in the fourth column.

6. Place the AddressTypeID field from the Enter Address table in the fifth column.

   So far, your query should look like Figure 13.48.

FIGURE 13.48.

The first five columns of the Row Source query for the lstAddresses list box.

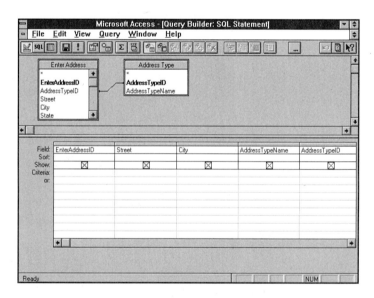

7. Click the horizontal scroll bar to show more available columns to the right.

8. Place the State, PostalCode, Region, and Country fields from the Enter Address table into the sixth, seventh, eighth, and ninth columns of the query, as shown in Figure 13.49.

9. Close the Query Builder window.

   The SQL SELECT statement generated by the Query Builder and entered into the Row Source property is the following:

```
SELECT DISTINCTROW
[Enter Address].EnterAddressID, [Enter Address].Street,
[Enter Address].City, [Address Type].AddressTypeName,
[Enter Address].AddressTypeID, [Enter Address].State,
[Enter Address].PostalCode, [Enter Address].Region,
[Enter Address].Country
FROM [Enter Address]
INNER JOIN [Address Type] ON [Enter Address].AddressTypeID =
➥ [Address Type].AddressTypeID;
```

FIGURE 13.49.

Adding the remaining four columns to the lstAddresses Row Source query.

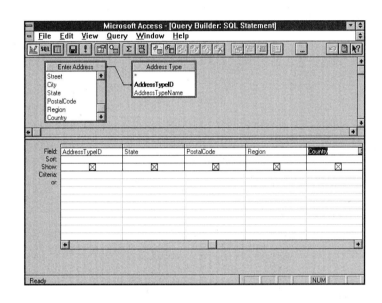

To complete the Address section of the form you need to add a Delete, OK, and Cancel button.

1. Add the Delete button to the form with the following properties:

Name:	cmdDeleteAddress
Caption:	Delete
Tab Index:	24
Left:	4.8 in
Top:	3.1042 in
Width:	0.6 in
Height:	0.2097 in

2. Create an OK button with the following properties:

Name:	cmdOK
Caption:	OK
Default:	Yes
Tab Index:	25

continues

Left:	4.7 in
Top:	0.0826 in
Width:	0.7 in
Height:	0.25 in
Font Name:	MS Sans Serif
Font Size:	8
Font Weight:	Bold

3. Select the Format|**Change** Default command so the next button can inherit the same settings. (Or copy the OK button and paste it on the form to create a Cancel button.)

4. Create a Cancel button with the following property settings:

Name:	cmdCancel
Caption:	Cancel
Cancel:	Yes
Tab Index:	26
Left:	4.7 in
Top:	0.375 in
Width:	0.7 in
Height:	0.25 in

5. Close the form, saving your work.

Wow! After all that work, the Form Wizard option isn't sounding bad at all, is it?

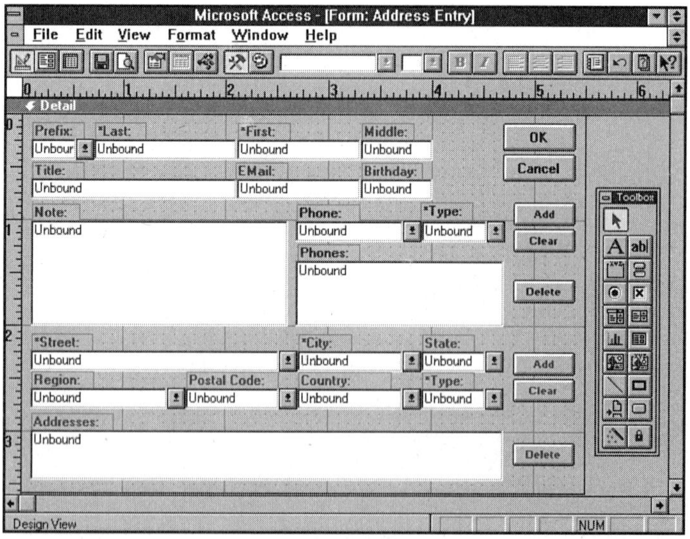

FIGURE 13.50.

The completed Address Entry form (minus code).

Let's get to the code that drives this puppy. First you have some supporting routines and declarations to enter in a Globals module.

The Globals Module

The Globals module contains the following procedures to support the Address Entry and Address Search form modules:

Declarations	
CenterForm	Center a form
CNStr	Convert a null to an empty string
CNull	Convert an empty string to a null
DumpFields	Debug print a table's field names
RequiredField	Verify a required field has been entered

1. Click the Module tab on the database container, and then click the **N**ew button to open a new module.

2. Enter the declarations section shown in Listing 13.1.

Listing 13.1. The declarations section for the Globals module.

```
' Globals module

Option Compare Database
Option Explicit

Global Const PROGRAM = "Address Book"

Global gblnAddressEditMode As Integer     ' Open Entry form in edit mode?

Type RECT
   x1 As Integer
   y1 As Integer
   x2 As Integer
   y2 As Integer
End Type

Declare Function GetClientRect Lib "User" (ByVal hwnd As Integer, r As RECT)
➥ As Integer
   Declare Function GetParent Lib "User" (ByVal hwnd As Integer) As Integer
   Declare Function GetWindowRect Lib "User" (ByVal hwnd As Integer, r As RECT)
   ➥ As Integer
Declare Function MoveWindow Lib "User" (ByVal hwnd As Integer,
➥ ByVal x As Integer, ByVal y As Integer, ByVal dx As Integer,
➥ ByVal dy As Integer, ByVal blnRepaint As Integer) As Integer
```

Some of this code you might recognize. I borrowed the Windows API declarations and the following `CenterForm` function from the Sticky Notes project in Chapter 6, "Access: Sticky Notes," which in turn borrowed the code from sample databases that came with Access Version 1.1.

(The thought occurs to me that this application would be a great place to add Sticky Notes. I'll leave that one up to you.)

Outside of the API declarations and the `PROGRAM` global constant, the only other thing in the declarations section is a `gblnAddressEditMode` flag.

This flag is set to True by the Address Search form to indicate that the Address Entry form is being opened in a special mode to edit the currently selected address book entry.

The Address Entry form is designed to be opened by itself without the Address Search form, but only for adding new entries. (Something you desperately need to do because your database is empty.)

Enter the `CenterForm` function shown in Listing 13.2.

Listing 13.2. The `CenterForm` function.

```
Function CenterForm (hwnd As Integer) As Integer

  Dim r As RECT
  Dim rApp As RECT

  Dim hwndApp As Integer

  Dim dx As Integer
  Dim dy As Integer
  Dim dxApp As Integer
  Dim dyApp As Integer
  Dim z As Integer

  On Error Resume Next

  z = GetWindowRect(hwnd, r)
  hwndApp = GetParent(hwnd)
  z = GetClientRect(hwndApp, rApp)

  dx = r.x2 - r.x1
  dy = r.y2 - r.y1

  dxApp = rApp.x2 - rApp.x1
  dyApp = rApp.y2 - rApp.y1

CenterForm = MoveWindow(hwnd, (dxApp - dx) / 2, (dyApp - dy) / 2, dx, dy,
➥ True)

End Function
```

You need the `CenterForm` function because of a nitpicky problem I ran into with the AutoCenter form property. The `Form Open` code turns off the current toolbar to make room for the form to display without being too crowded inside the Access window in standard VGA.

After shutting off the toolbar, I couldn't get the form to take into account that the toolbar is gone when it auto-centered itself. The auto-centering was still being done as if the toolbar were displayed.

I called the `CenterForm` function in the form's On Open event and it fixed the problem. I consider this a hack and would prefer to stay out of the Windows API in my Basic programming if I can, but sometimes you gotta do what you gotta do.

See the Sticky Notes project in Chapter 6 for an explanation of how the `CenterForm` function works. The next function should also be very familiar by now.

Enter the `CNStr` function as shown in Listing 13.3.

Listing 13.3. The sinister `CNStr` function, again.

```
Function CNStr (v As Variant) As String

  If IsNull(v) Then
    CNStr = ""
  Else
    CNStr = Trim$(CStr(v))
  End If

End Function
```

I'm not sure, but I think I have needed the `CNStr` function in every Access application I've ever worked on. Its job again is to make sure you get a string when you want a string. Some functions don't take kindly to being passed a Null when they really, really, really want a string.

The next function, `CNull`, does the reverse of `CNStr`. It converts empty strings to Nulls.

Enter the `CNull` function as shown in Listing 13.4.

Listing 13.4. The `CNull` function.

```
Function CNull (var As Variant) As Variant

' Convert empty strings to Null

  If CNStr(var) = "" Then
    CNull = Null
```

continues

Listing 13.4. continued

```
  Else
    CNull = var
  End If

End Function
```

The CNull function is used when writing values from controls on a form to a record in a table. If the control contains an empty string rather than a Null, I would prefer to write the Null as an indicator that the field is empty.

The *DumpFields* Subroutine

The next procedure, the DumpFields subroutine, is used for development purposes only. When you write code that reads fields in from a record to a form or the other way around, it's handy to have a list of the field names that you can paste in your code.

The DumpFields subroutine writes each of the field names for a table to the Immediate window, ready for you to start copying and pasting away.

Enter the DumpFields subroutine as shown in Listing 13.5. (This one is optional because the program doesn't actually use it.)

Listing 13.5. The DumpFields **subroutine.**

```
Sub DumpFields (strTable As String)

  Dim db As Database
  Dim tbl As Recordset
  Dim n As Integer

  Set db = DBEngine.Workspaces(0).Databases(0)
  Set tbl = db.OpenRecordset(strTable, DB_OPEN_TABLE)

  For n = 0 To tbl.Fields.Count - 1
    Debug.Print tbl.Fields(n).Name
  Next n

  tbl.Close

End Sub
```

The DumpFields subroutine opens the table in question as a Recordset object. A Recordset object has a Fields collection with a Field object for each field in the table.

A collection is a set of objects. You can reference an object in a collection by name or number. The Count property indicates how many objects are in a collection.

The loop in the subroutine cycles through each of the `Field` objects of the Fields collection and prints the value of the Name property to the Immediate window.

```
For n = 0 To tbl.Fields.Count - 1
   Debug.Print tbl.Fields(n).Name
Next n
```

To run the `DumpFields` subroutine, open a module and select the **View|Immediate Window** command to open the Immediate window. Inside the Immediate window enter the following:

```
DumpFields "Address"
```

The `DumpFields` subroutine prints the names of the fields in the Address table, as shown in Figure 13.51.

FIGURE 13.51.

Running the DumpFields utility.

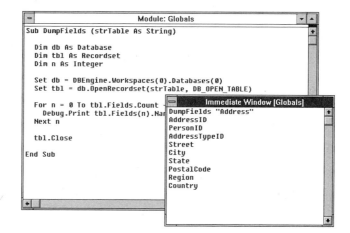

The *RequiredField* Function

The `RequiredField` function is called before writing the values from a form to a record in a table. It is called for each field on the form that must be completed. An error message is displayed if the required entry is empty.

Enter the `RequiredField` function as shown in Listing 13.6.

Listing 13.6. The `RequiredField` function.

```
Function RequiredField (strName As String, ctl As Control) As Integer

' Verify that a value was entered in the specified control

   Dim strValue As String
   Dim blnResult As Integer
```

continues

Listing 13.6. continued

```
' Default to failure
  RequiredField = True

  On Error GoTo RequiredFieldError

  strValue = CNStr(ctl)
  blnResult = (Len(strValue) = 0)

  If blnResult Then
    MsgBox strName & " is a required field", 48, PROGRAM
    ctl.SetFocus
  End If

  RequiredField = blnResult

RequiredFieldDone:
  Exit Function

RequiredFieldError:
  MsgBox Error$, 48, PROGRAM
  Resume RequiredFieldDone

End Function
```

The `RequiredField` function returns True to indicate failure, meaning that the required field was left blank. By default this is the return value, so the function returns success only if it runs in completion.

```
' Default to failure
  RequiredField = True

  On Error GoTo RequiredFieldError
```

The control is checked for a value by passing its contents to the `CNStr` function. The `CNStr` function returns an empty string if the control contains a Null, an empty string, or a string with nothing but spaces in it. Each of these cases is not considered a valid entry.

```
  strValue = CNStr(ctl)
```

If the length of the string returned by `CNStr` is 0, `blnResult` is set to True to indicate failure.

```
blnResult = (Len(strValue) = 0)
```

If a failure occurs, a message is displayed indicating that the control is required. The name of the control is passed into the function as the first argument so that a name like First Name can be displayed rather than something like txtFirstName, which isn't user friendly.

For maximum convenience, the function sets the focus to the control that is missing an entry so the user can quickly enter it and get on with his or her business.

```
If blnResult Then
  MsgBox strName & " is a required field", 48, PROGRAM
  ctl.SetFocus
End If
```

At the end of the function, the `blnResult` value is returned, which contains True for the failure condition or False for the success condition.

```
RequiredField = blnResult
```

The return value might seem backward to you, but it allows you to call the function in your subroutines like this:

```
If RequiredField("Street", cboStreet) Then GoTo cmdAddAddress_ClickDone
```

Within a single line, a control is checked and the subroutine bails out if the required entry is not found. Because of situations like this one, I often find it more helpful to return True as an error value rather than False.

Close the new module, entering `Globals` as the name to save it as.

Next you write the code behind the Address Entry form.

The Address Entry Form Module

Within the Address Entry form module are the following subroutines, which I have outlined in three categories: General, Phone Entry, and Address Entry.

General

Declarations
Form_Open
LoadAddress
cmdOK_Click
cmdCancel_Click
Form_Close

Phone Entry

cmdAddPhone_Click
cmdClearPhone_Click
cmdDeletePhone_Click
lstPhones_Click

continues

Address Entry

```
cmdAddAddress_Click
cmdClearAddress_Click
cmdDeleteAddress_Click
lstAddresses_Click
cboState_LostFocus
```

The Phone Entry and Address Entry subroutines are strictly involved with entering phone numbers and addresses. The General subroutines do everything else. Let's tackle them in the order listed previously.

1. Click the Form tab on the Access database container to get to the Address Entry form.
2. Select the Address Entry form and click the Code button on the toolbar to open the form's module.
3. Enter the declarations section as shown in Listing 13.7.

Listing 13.7. The Address Entry form module's declarations section.

```
' Address Entry form

Option Compare Database
Option Explicit

Dim mdb As Database
Dim mwsp As WorkSpace

Dim mblnOKPressed As Integer
```

Within the declarations section three variables are declared with module scope.

The `mdb` and `mwsp` variables get set to the current database and workspace. A *workspace* is a user session that may comprise multiple open databases.

You declare the workspace object variable in order to use the `BeginTrans`, `CommitTrans`, and `Rollback` methods to ensure that when you write an address book entry it gets written completely or no modification is made at all.

Actually, you don't have to declare either of these object variables globally, but it saves you from having to reassign them each time you want to use them.

The `mblnOKPressed` variable is a flag that gets set if the user presses the OK button. This is needed in the On Close event code to determine whether a change has been made that should be reflected on the Address Search form.

The *Form_Open* Subroutine

Use Code Builder to create the declaration for the Form_Open subroutine or create it by just typing it into the form module.

FIGURE 13.52.

Selecting the On Open property in the Properties window.

Complete the Form_Open subroutine as shown in Listing 13.8.

Listing 13.8. The Form_Open **subroutine.**

```
Sub Form_Open (Cancel As Integer)

  Dim lngPersonID As Long
  Dim z As Integer

  On Error GoTo Form_OpenError

' Hide the system toolbars
  Application.SetOption "Built-In Toolbars Available", False
  DoEvents

' Hide the database container or the Address Search form
  DoCmd DoMenuItem A_FormBar, 4, 3, A_Menu_Ver20

  Set mwsp = DBEngine.Workspaces(0)
  Set mdb = mwsp.Databases(0)

  If EmptyTable("Enter Phone") Then GoTo Form_OpenDone
  If EmptyTable("Enter Address") Then GoTo Form_OpenDone

  lstPhones.Requery
  lstAddresses.Requery

  If gblnAddressEditMode Then
    lngPersonID = Forms![Address Search]!lstAddresses
    Cancel = LoadAddress(lngPersonID)
  End If

  z = CenterForm(CInt(Me.Hwnd))

  mblnOKPressed = False
```

continues

Listing 13.8. continued

```
Form_OpenDone:
  Exit Sub

Form_OpenError:
  MsgBox Error$, 48, PROGRAM
  Cancel = True
  Resume Form_OpenDone

End Sub
```

The `Form_Open` subroutine initializes the Address Entry form for an editing session.

First, to keep the display simple, the Access toolbars are turned off by calling the `SetOption` method.

With the `SetOption` method, Access allows your program to easily change any of the options shown in the Options dialog box displayed with the **View|O**ptions command.

```
' Hide the system toolbars
  Application.SetOption "Built-In Toolbars Available", False
  DoEvents
```

Next the `DoMenuItem` macro is called to hide the current window, which is either the database container or the Address Search form. Either way, you want the form to be the only window open, for a clean display.

```
' Hide the database container or the Address Search form
  DoCmd DoMenuItem A_FormBar, 4, 3, A_Menu_Ver20
```

The `mwsp` variable is initialized to the current workspace and the `mdb` variable is initialized to the current database.

```
  Set mwsp = DBEngine.Workspaces(0)
  Set mdb = mwsp.Databases(0)
```

Next you call an `EmptyTable` function that deletes all the records in a given table. I chose to write my own function for this rather than using the `RunSQL` macro, in order to avoid displaying the blue progress bar at the bottom of the Access window. For such a short amount of execution time, the blue bar was just an annoying flicker rather than the helpful status indicator it normally is.

```
  If EmptyTable("Enter Phone") Then GoTo Form_OpenDone
  If EmptyTable("Enter Address") Then GoTo Form_OpenDone
```

By the time the `Form_Open` event occurs, the lstPhones and lstAddresses list boxes have already read in pointers to the records that I have just deleted.

To avoid displaying #Deleted messages, the lists need to be requeried so they are aware of the deleted records.

(In coding, miscellaneous stuff like this just happens. You figure out what you need to do to get the results you want and patch your code accordingly.)

```
lstPhones.Requery
lstAddresses.Requery
```

If the Address Entry form is being loaded by the Address Search form, the gblnAddressEditMode flag is set to True.

In such a case, the selected entry is read from the lstAddresses list box, and then the LoadAddress function is called to fill the Address Entry form with the data for this entry.

The result of the LoadAddress call is assigned to the Form_Open subroutine's Cancel argument, which if set to True aborts the opening of the Address Entry form. You don't want the form to continue loading if an error occurred while reading in the data to be edited.

```
If gblnAddressEditMode Then
    lngPersonID = Forms![Address Search]!lstAddresses
    Cancel = LoadAddress(lngPersonID)
End If
```

At the end of the subroutine, the form is centered and the mblnOKPressed variable is defaulted to False, indicating that the OK button hasn't been pressed yet.

```
z = CenterForm(CInt(Me.Hwnd))
mblnOKPressed = False
```

The *LoadAddress* Subroutine

The LoadAddress subroutine is called to fill the Address Entry form with an existing address book entry to edit.

Enter the LoadAddress subroutine as shown in Listing 13.9.

Listing 13.9. The LoadAddress subroutine.

```
Function LoadAddress (lngPersonID As Long) As Integer

    Dim frm As Form

    Dim tbl As Recordset

    Dim blnOpened As Integer

    Dim sql As String
    Dim n As Integer

    blnOpened = False
```

continues

Listing 13.9. continued

```
On Error GoTo LoadAddressError

Set tbl = mdb.OpenRecordset("Person", DB_OPEN_TABLE)
blnOpened = True

tbl.Index = "PrimaryKey"
tbl.Seek "=", lngPersonID

cboPrefix = tbl!Prefix
txtLast = tbl!LastName
txtFirst = tbl!FirstName
txtMiddle = tbl!MiddleName
txtTitle = tbl!Title
txtEMail = tbl!EMail
txtBirthday = tbl!Birthday
txtNote = tbl!Note

sql = "INSERT INTO [Enter Phone] "
sql = sql & "( PhoneTypeID, Phone ) "
sql = sql & "SELECT DISTINCTROW PhoneTypeID, Phone "
sql = sql & "FROM Phone WHERE PersonID = " & lngPersonID

DoCmd RunSQL sql

sql = "INSERT INTO [Enter Address] "
sql = sql & "( AddressTypeID, Street, City, State, PostalCode, "
sql = sql & "Region, Country ) "
sql = sql & "SELECT DISTINCTROW "
sql = sql & "AddressTypeID, Street, City, State, PostalCode, "
sql = sql & "Region, Country "
sql = sql & "FROM Address WHERE PersonID = " & lngPersonID

DoCmd RunSQL sql

lstPhones.Requery
lstAddresses.Requery

LoadAddressDone:
    On Error Resume Next
    If blnOpened Then tbl.Close
    Exit Function

LoadAddressError:
    MsgBox Error$, 48, PROGRAM
    Resume LoadAddressDone

End Function
```

On the outset, the LoadAddress subroutine knows only the PersonID value for the address entry that is to be loaded. It first opens the Person table to seek to the record identified by this ID number and gather the information stored there.

```
Set tbl = mdb.OpenRecordset("Person", DB_OPEN_TABLE)
blnOpened = True

tbl.Index = "PrimaryKey"
tbl.Seek "=", lngPersonID
```

Next the subroutine makes a brave assumption that it actually found the record. (Because this isn't a multiuser application and you had to read this record once to get the PersonID value, it's a safe assumption.)

The subroutine reads the field values and stores them in the controls on the form in the fields you created with red label text. (See Listing 13.10.)

Listing 13.10. Reading the Prefix table fields.

```
cboPrefix = tbl!Prefix
txtLast = tbl!LastName
txtFirst = tbl!FirstName
txtMiddle = tbl!MiddleName
txtTitle = tbl!Title
txtEMail = tbl!EMail
txtBirthday = tbl!Birthday
txtNote = tbl!Note
```

The code shown in Listing 13.10 is exactly the kind of code where the DumpFields subroutine comes in handy. To get a start at entering the lines, you can run the subroutine against the Person table like this:

```
DumpFields "Person"
```

After the field names are printed in the Immediate window, you can copy and paste them as a group into the module window and begin creating the lines shown in Figure 13.53.

Next the LoadAddress subroutine fills in the lstPhones list box, which has its Row Source property set to show records in the Enter Phone table.

The Enter Phone table is used as a temporary staging area for phone number edits. If the user clicks OK after the edit session, any phone numbers added, deleted, or changed in this table are applied to the Phone table also.

To start the edit session, the Phone table records for the selected person are copied into the Enter Phone table by using an SQL INSERT INTO statement.

The INSERT INTO statement takes the results of a SELECT statement and writes them to another table's fields.

FIGURE 13.53.

*Editing the
LoadAddress
subroutine.*

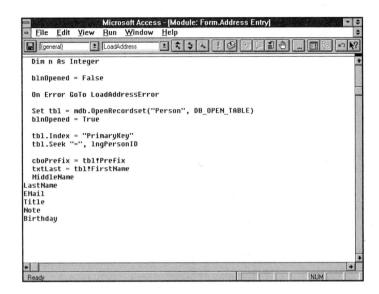

The LoadAddress subroutine builds the SQL statement in a string variable, appropriately named sql, and then executes it by calling the RunSQL statement, as shown in Listing 13.11.

Listing 13.11. Filling the temporary Enter Phone table records.

```
sql = "INSERT INTO [Enter Phone] "
sql = sql & "( PhoneTypeID, Phone ) "
sql = sql & "SELECT DISTINCTROW PhoneTypeID, Phone "
sql = sql & "FROM Phone WHERE PersonID = " & lngPersonID

DoCmd RunSQL sql
```

Likewise, the Enter Address table is updated with the Address table records for the selected person, as shown in Listing 13.12.

Listing 13.12. Filling the Enter Address table.

```
sql = "INSERT INTO [Enter Address] "
sql = sql & "( AddressTypeID, Street, City, State, PostalCode, "
sql = sql & "Region, Country ) "
sql = sql & "SELECT DISTINCTROW "
sql = sql & "AddressTypeID, Street, City, State, PostalCode, "
sql = sql & "Region, Country "
sql = sql & "FROM Address WHERE PersonID = " & lngPersonID

DoCmd RunSQL sql
```

To display the Phone and Address data, the lstPhones and lstAddresses list boxes are requeried.

```
lstPhones.Requery
lstAddresses.Requery
```

The *cmdOK_Click* Subroutine

The cmdOK_Click subroutine saves the current edits back to the Person, Phone, and Address tables. It is one of the longer procedures you have written so far.

The subroutine uses the BeginTrans and CommitTrans methods to be sure that either the entire write transaction is completed or none of it is completed. If an error occurs, it's better to abort the whole process rather than leave it half done. The subroutine uses the Rollback method to allow a kind of undo, so that all transactions since the last BeginTrans method can be undone.

Enter the cmdOK_Click subroutine as shown in Listing 13.13.

Listing 13.13. The cmdOK_Click subroutine.

```
Sub cmdOK_Click ()

    Dim frm As Form

    Dim tbl As Recordset
    Dim dynPhone As Recordset
    Dim dynAddress As Recordset
    Dim tblEnterPhone As Recordset
    Dim tblEnterAddress As Recordset

    Dim blnOpened As Integer
    Dim blnPhoneOpened As Integer
    Dim blnAddressOpened As Integer
    Dim blnEnterPhoneOpened As Integer
    Dim blnEnterAddressOpened As Integer
    Dim blnTransStarted As Integer

    Dim sql As String
    Dim lngPersonID As Long
    Dim n As Integer

    blnOpened = False
    blnPhoneOpened = False
    blnAddressOpened = False
    blnEnterPhoneOpened = False
    blnEnterAddressOpened = False
    blnTransStarted = False

    On Error GoTo cmdOK_ClickError
```

continues

Listing 13.13. continued

```
If RequiredField("Last", txtLast) Then GoTo cmdOK_ClickDone
If RequiredField("First", txtFirst) Then GoTo cmdOK_ClickDone

Set tbl = mdb.OpenRecordset("Person", DB_OPEN_TABLE)
blnOpened = True

sql = "SELECT * FROM Phone WHERE PersonID = " & lngPersonID
Set dynPhone = mdb.OpenRecordset(sql, DB_OPEN_DYNASET)
blnPhoneOpened = True

sql = "SELECT * FROM Address WHERE PersonID = " & lngPersonID
Set dynAddress = mdb.OpenRecordset(sql, DB_OPEN_DYNASET)
blnAddressOpened = True

Set tblEnterPhone = mdb.OpenRecordset("Enter Phone", DB_OPEN_TABLE)
blnEnterPhoneOpened = True

Set tblEnterAddress = mdb.OpenRecordset("Enter Address", DB_OPEN_TABLE)
blnEnterAddressOpened = True

mwsp.BeginTrans
blnTransStarted = True

If gblnAddressEditMode Then
  Set frm = Forms![Address Search]

  tbl.Index = "PrimaryKey"
  tbl.Seek "=", frm!lstAddresses
  tbl.Edit
Else
  tbl.AddNew
End If

lngPersonID = tbl!PersonID

tbl!Prefix = cboPrefix
tbl!FirstName = txtFirst
tbl!MiddleName = txtMiddle
tbl!LastName = txtLast
tbl!EMail = txtEMail
tbl!Birthday = txtBirthday
tbl!Title = txtTitle
tbl!Note = txtNote

tbl.Update

' Delete the old phone and address records.
' You can't use RunSQL with a DELETE statement inside a transaction.
  Do Until dynPhone.EOF
    dynPhone.Delete
    dynPhone.MoveNext
  Loop
```

```
   Do Until dynAddress.EOF
     dynAddress.Delete
     dynAddress.MoveNext
   Loop

   Do Until tblEnterPhone.EOF
     dynPhone.AddNew

     dynPhone!PersonID = lngPersonID
     dynPhone!PhoneTypeID = tblEnterPhone!PhoneTypeID
     dynPhone!Phone = tblEnterPhone!Phone

     dynPhone.Update
     tblEnterPhone.MoveNext
   Loop

   Do Until tblEnterAddress.EOF
     dynAddress.AddNew

     dynAddress!PersonID = lngPersonID
     dynAddress!AddressTypeID = tblEnterAddress!AddressTypeID
     dynAddress!Street = tblEnterAddress!Street
     dynAddress!City = tblEnterAddress!City
     dynAddress!State = tblEnterAddress!State
     dynAddress!PostalCode = tblEnterAddress!PostalCode
     dynAddress!Region = tblEnterAddress!Region
     dynAddress!Country = tblEnterAddress!Country

     dynAddress.Update
     tblEnterAddress.MoveNext
   Loop

   mwsp.CommitTrans
   blnTransStarted = False

   mblnOKPressed = True
   DoCmd Close

cmdOK_ClickDone:
   On Error Resume Next
   If blnTransStarted Then mwsp.Rollback
   If blnOpened Then tbl.Close
   If blnPhoneOpened Then dynPhone.Close
   If blnAddressOpened Then dynAddress.Close
   If blnEnterPhoneOpened Then tblEnterPhone.Close
   If blnEnterAddressOpened Then tblEnterAddress.Close
   DoCmd SetWarnings True
   Exit Sub

cmdOK_ClickError:
   MsgBox Error$, 48, PROGRAM
   Resume cmdOK_ClickDone

End Sub
```

The `RequiredField` function is called to verify that first and last names were entered.

```
If RequiredField("Last", txtLast) Then GoTo cmdOK_ClickDone
If RequiredField("First", txtFirst) Then GoTo cmdOK_ClickDone
```

The Person table is opened.

```
Set tbl = mdb.OpenRecordset("Person", DB_OPEN_TABLE)
blnOpened = True
```

Next you create two dynasets that select all the current Phone and Address records for this address book entry, as shown in Listing 13.14. You will be deleting each of these records and then adding records for what is currently in the Enter Phone and Enter Address tables.

Listing 13.14. Selecting existing Phone and Address records.

```
sql = "SELECT * FROM Phone WHERE PersonID = " & lngPersonID
Set dynPhone = mdb.OpenRecordset(sql, DB_OPEN_DYNASET)
blnPhoneOpened = True

sql = "SELECT * FROM Address WHERE PersonID = " & lngPersonID
Set dynAddress = mdb.OpenRecordset(sql, DB_OPEN_DYNASET)
blnAddressOpened = True
```

The Enter Phone and Enter Address tables are opened as `Recordset` objects in table mode.

```
Set tblEnterPhone = mdb.OpenRecordset("Enter Phone", DB_OPEN_TABLE)
blnEnterPhoneOpened = True

Set tblEnterAddress = mdb.OpenRecordset("Enter Address", DB_OPEN_TABLE)
blnEnterAddressOpened = True
```

With all the tables opened, you can now call the `BeginTrans` method to start a transaction.

A *transaction* is a series of record changes performed in a batch. In the program, each record change is coded as if it is happening individually. However, during execution the Jet engine actually buffers these changes in memory and applies them together when the `CommitTrans` method is called.

This enables you to program as if the updates are happening individually, but you have the security of knowing that the entire set of updates occurs only if all of them can occur without error. The last thing you want is to have your program stop at midpoint and not know how much of the data was actually changed.

Whenever I use `BeginTrans`, I like to set a `blnTransStarted` flag to indicate that a transaction has been started. The flag gets cleared after the `CommitTrans` method is called to actually perform the transaction.

In the cleanup code at the bottom of the function, I call the `Rollback` function if the `blnTransStarted` flag was never cleared, meaning that the function did not execute up to the point where the full transaction could be applied.

```
mwsp.BeginTrans
blnTransStarted = True
```

Next the subroutine checks to see if you are editing an existing address book entry or creating a new one, as shown in Listing 13.15. If you are doing an edit, the existing record is Seeked to; otherwise, a new table is created.

The Seek for an existing record is based on the PersonID field value, which is returned from the bound column on the Address Search form's lstAddresses list box.

Listing 13.15. Either an existing Person table record is edited or a new record is created.

```
If gblnAddressEditMode Then
  Set frm = Forms![Address Search]

  tbl.Index = "PrimaryKey"
  tbl.Seek "=", frm!lstAddresses
  tbl.Edit
Else
  tbl.AddNew
End If
```

The next line reads the PersonID field value into a variable. If this is a new record, the value has already been assigned to the field by Access, because it is a counter field.

```
lngPersonID = tbl!PersonID
```

The next section of code reads the values in the form's controls into the fields in the Person table record, as shown in Listing 13.16. It then calls the Update method to write the record.

Listing 13.16. Writing the Person table record.

```
tbl!Prefix = cboPrefix
tbl!FirstName = txtFirst
tbl!MiddleName = txtMiddle
tbl!LastName = txtLast
tbl!EMail = txtEMail
tbl!Birthday = txtBirthday
tbl!Title = txtTitle
tbl!Note = txtNote

tbl.Update
```

The next part of the subroutine contains a little bit of lazy coding, and I invite you to improve on it. The code updates the Phone and Address tables.

Rather than searching for existing records and updating them, the code deletes all of the existing records and writes new records. The drawback of this approach is that it makes the Access MDB file grow in size when it doesn't need to.

Space for deleted records isn't retrieved until you compact the database with the **File**|**Compact** Database command.

Another potential drawback with this approach is that you couldn't make child tables off the Phone and Address tables, because these records regularly get re-created with new PhoneID and AddressID numbers. For now though, it works.

First the Phone and Address table records for this address book entry are deleted, as shown in Listing 13.17.

Listing 13.17. Deleting the old Phone and Address table records.

```
' Delete the old phone and address records.
' You can't use RunSQL with a DELETE statement inside a transaction.
  Do Until dynPhone.EOF
    dynPhone.Delete
    dynPhone.MoveNext
  Loop

  Do Until dynAddress.EOF
    dynAddress.Delete
    dynAddress.MoveNext
  Loop
```

Next, the Enter Phone table records are copied into the Phone table, as shown in Listing 13.18.

Listing 13.18. Copying the Enter Phone records.

```
  Do Until tblEnterPhone.EOF
    dynPhone.AddNew

    dynPhone!PersonID = lngPersonID
    dynPhone!PhoneTypeID = tblEnterPhone!PhoneTypeID
    dynPhone!Phone = tblEnterPhone!Phone

    dynPhone.Update
    tblEnterPhone.MoveNext
  Loop
```

Finally, the Enter Address table records are copied into the Address table.

```
Do Until tblEnterAddress.EOF
  dynAddress.AddNew

  dynAddress!PersonID = lngPersonID
  dynAddress!AddressTypeID = tblEnterAddress!AddressTypeID
  dynAddress!Street = tblEnterAddress!Street
  dynAddress!City = tblEnterAddress!City
  dynAddress!State = tblEnterAddress!State
  dynAddress!PostalCode = tblEnterAddress!PostalCode
  dynAddress!Region = tblEnterAddress!Region
  dynAddress!Country = tblEnterAddress!Country

  dynAddress.Update
  tblEnterAddress.MoveNext
Loop
```

With all the record changes automatically stored in a temporary buffer, the CommitTrans method is called to kick it off. This is where you hear some disk activity from your hard drive.

If the transaction completes without jumping down to the error section, the blnTransStarted flag is set to False, because you are no longer in the middle of a transaction.

```
mwsp.CommitTrans
blnTransStarted = False
```

At the end of the subroutine, a flag is set to indicate that the form was closed as a result of the user clicking OK. Then the form is actually closed by calling the Close macro.

```
mblnOKPressed = True
DoCmd Close
```

The *cmdCancel_Click* Subroutine

Another way the form gets closed is when the user clicks the Cancel button.

Enter the cmdCancel_Click() subroutine as shown in Listing 13.19.

Listing 13.19. The cmdCancel_Click **subroutine.**

```
Sub cmdCancel_Click ()

  DoCmd Close

End Sub
```

The *Form_Close* Subroutine

The Form_Close event interacts with the Address Search form. You have to trust me on this one until the next chapter, when that form is actually created.

Enter the Form_Close subroutine as shown in Listing 13.20.

Listing 13.20. The Form_Close **subroutine.**

```
Sub Form_Close ()

  Dim frm As Form

  On Error Resume Next

  Set frm = Forms![Address Search]

  If Err = 0 Then
  ' The Address Search form is available

    frm.SetFocus

  ' Requery the form and update matches found
    If mblnOKPressed Then
      SendKeys "{F9}"
      DoEvents
frm!lblMatchesFound.Caption = frm!lstAddresses.ListCount &
➡ " Matches Found"
    End If
  Else
  ' Redisplay the system toolbars
    Application.SetOption "Built-In Toolbars Available", True

  ' Show the database container
    SendKeys "{F11}"
  End If

End Sub
```

This one is a bit of a hack. First the On Error Resume Next statement is called to turn off error handling. The subroutine tries to set a form variable to the Address Search form.

```
On Error Resume Next

Set frm = Forms![Address Search]
```

The Address Search form is available only if it is actually open. (It can't just be in the database container.) When your Address Search form opens the Address Entry form, it calls a menu command to hide itself. This way it is available to be redisplayed once again with all the data presently loaded still there.

The environment variable, Err, is still set even if error handling is turned off. Err is equal to 0 if no error occurred; otherwise, it is set to one of many values that indicate the type of error that did occur.

```
If Err = 0 Then
```

If no error occurred, the Address Search form is open and in hiding. It is brought back from hiding by calling the SetFocus method.

```
' The Address Search form is available

  frm.SetFocus
```

Next, if the user clicked OK to close the Address Entry form, a change has been made to an address book entry.

The F9 key is pressed (through SendKeys) to requery the Address Search form's lstAddresses list box. That's the list box that displays the resulting matches from a search.

The label that indicates how many matches have been found is also updated, as shown in Listing 13.21, because the contents of the lstAddresses list box may change.

Listing 13.21. Updating the Address Search form.

```
' Requery the form and update matches found
  If mblnOKPressed Then
    SendKeys "{F9}"
    DoEvents
frm!lblMatchesFound.Caption = frm!lstAddresses.ListCount &
➡ " Matches Found"
  End If
```

Next you deal with the simpler case where the Address Entry form is opened on its own. In this case, the Err variable contains a non-zero value to indicate that the Address Search form could not be found.

When this form opened, it hid the database container and the built-in toolbars. In Listing 13.22 both are redisplayed to return the Access environment back to normal.

Listing 13.22. Redisplay the toolbars and database container.

```
Else
' Redisplay the system toolbars
  Application.SetOption "Built-In Toolbars Available", True

' Show the database container
  SendKeys "{F11}"
End If
```

Editing Phone Numbers

You completed the heavy stuff first. Next you get to the series of subroutines that allows adding, editing, and deleting of phone numbers by using the temporary records in the Enter Phone table. Then you do the same for addresses.

The *lstPhones_Click* Subroutine

The lstPhones_Click subroutine gets executed when the user clicks on a line in the lstPhones list box. It transfers the contents of a row in the list box to the Phone and Phone Type fields for editing.

Enter the lstPhones_Click subroutine as shown in Listing 13.23.

Listing 13.23. The lstPhones_Click **subroutine.**

```
Sub lstPhones_Click ()

  On Error GoTo lstPhones_ClickError

  If lstPhones.ListIndex = -1 Then GoTo lstPhones_ClickDone

  cboPhone = lstPhones.Column(1)
  cboPhoneType = lstPhones.Column(3)

  cmdAddPhone.Caption = "Change"

lstPhones_ClickDone:
  Exit Sub

lstPhones_ClickError:
  MsgBox Error$, 48, PROGRAM
  Resume lstPhones_ClickDone

End Sub
```

First, the lstPhones_Click subroutine checks to see if a line in the list is selected. The ListIndex property is set to −1 if there is no currently selected line. The subroutine exits early in this case.

```
    If lstPhones.ListIndex = -1 Then GoTo lstPhones_ClickDone
```

Next, the subroutine copies the phone number text from the second column of the text box to the cboPhone combo box, and it copies the numeric phone number type value from the fourth column to the cboPhoneType combo box.

The cboPhoneType combo box is set up to display the text for the selected phone type number.

```
cboPhone = lstPhones.Column(1)
cboPhoneType = lstPhones.Column(3)
```

The last thing that occurs here is that the caption of the Add button is changed to Change. The form is now in a mode to edit an existing phone number entry, rather than add a new one.

```
cmdAddPhone.Caption = "Change"
```

The *cmdClearPhone_Click* Subroutine

Once you are in an edit mode, there has to be a way out without committing the change. The cmdClearPhone_Click subroutine undoes what was just accomplished by the lstPhones_Click subroutine.

Enter the cmdClearPhone_Click subroutine as shown in Listing 13.24.

Listing 13.24. The cmdClearPhone_Click **subroutine.**

```
Sub cmdClearPhone_Click ()

  On Error GoTo cmdClearPhone_ClickError

  cboPhone = Null
  cboPhoneType = Null

  lstPhones = Null

  cmdAddPhone.Caption = "Add"

  cboPhone.SetFocus

cmdClearPhone_ClickDone:
  Exit Sub

cmdClearPhone_ClickError:
  MsgBox Error$, 48, PROGRAM
  Resume cmdClearPhone_ClickDone

End Sub
```

The subroutine clears the Phone and Phone Type fields. It also clears the currently selected phone number in the lstPhones list box. The list should show a selected item only if that item is being edited.

```
cboPhone = Null
  cboPhoneType = Null

  lstPhones = Null
```

Because you are no longer in phone edit mode, the cmdAddPhone button's caption is changed from Change back to Add.

```
cmdAddPhone.Caption = "Add"
```

The last statement sets focus to the cboPhone combo box, ready for the user to enter a new phone number.

```
cboPhone.SetFocus
```

The *cmdAddPhone_Click* Subroutine

Now you get to the serious business of actually adding an entry.

Again, you write the entry to the Enter Phone table, not the Phone table. This way you can add as many phone numbers as you want and still cancel the whole shebang with the Address Entry form's Cancel button.

Enter the cmdAddPhone_Click subroutine as shown in Listing 13.25.

Listing 13.25. The cmdAddPhone_Click **subroutine.**

```
Sub cmdAddPhone_Click ()

  Dim tbl As Recordset
  Dim blnOpened As Integer

  blnOpened = False

  On Error GoTo cmdAddPhone_ClickError

  If RequiredField("Phone", cboPhone) Then GoTo cmdAddPhone_ClickDone
  If RequiredField("Type", cboPhoneType) Then GoTo cmdAddPhone_ClickDone

  Set tbl = mdb.OpenRecordset("Enter Phone", DB_OPEN_TABLE)
  blnOpened = True

  If cmdAddPhone.Caption = "Change" Then
    tbl.Index = "PrimaryKey"
    tbl.Seek "=", lstPhones
    tbl.Edit
  Else
    tbl.AddNew
  End If

  tbl!PhoneTypeID = cboPhoneType
  tbl!Phone = cboPhone

  tbl.Update

  lstPhones.Requery

  cmdClearPhone_Click

cmdAddPhone_ClickDone:
  On Error Resume Next
```

```
    If blnOpened Then tbl.Close
    Exit Sub

cmdAddPhone_ClickError:
    MsgBox Error$, 48, PROGRAM
    Resume cmdAddPhone_ClickDone

End Sub
```

First, the `cmdAddPhone_Click` subroutine checks to see if the required fields have been entered. In this case, it is both fields.

```
    If RequiredField("Phone", cboPhone) Then GoTo cmdAddPhone_ClickDone
    If RequiredField("Type", cboPhoneType) Then GoTo cmdAddPhone_ClickDone
```

Next, the Enter Phone table is opened.

```
    Set tbl = mdb.OpenRecordset("Enter Phone", DB_OPEN_TABLE)
    blnOpened = True
```

Then the code checks the caption of the cmdAddPhone button to see if you are in add or edit mode.

If you are in edit mode, the code Seeks to the existing Enter Phone record and opens it for editing, as shown in Listing 13.26. If not, a new record is added.

Listing 13.26. Edit or Add a new record to the Enter Phone table.

```
    If cmdAddPhone.Caption = "Change" Then
        tbl.Index = "PrimaryKey"
        tbl.Seek "=", lstPhones
        tbl.Edit
    Else
        tbl.AddNew
    End If
```

Next, the phone type and phone number are written to the table.

```
    tbl!PhoneTypeID = cboPhoneType
    tbl!Phone = cboPhone

    tbl.Update
```

The subroutine finishes by refreshing the lstPhones list box so it displays the new entry. It also calls the `cmdClearPhone_Click` subroutine you looked at earlier to prepare for adding the next phone number.

```
    lstPhones.Requery

    cmdClearPhone_Click
```

The *cmdDeletePhone_Click* Subroutine

The Delete button erases a phone number from the list of phone numbers displayed in the lstPhones list box.

This actually deletes the record from the Enter Phone table. If the user clicks the OK button, the phone number is also removed permanently from the Phone table.

Enter the cmdDeletePhone_Click subroutine as shown in Listing 13.27.

Listing 13.27. The cmdDeletePhone_Click **subroutine.**

```
Sub cmdDeletePhone_Click ()

  Dim tbl As Recordset
  Dim blnOpened As Integer

  On Error GoTo cmdDeletePhone_ClickError

  If lstPhones.ListCount = 0 Then GoTo cmdDeletePhone_ClickDone

  Set tbl = mdb.OpenRecordset("Enter Phone", DB_OPEN_TABLE)
  blnOpened = True

  tbl.Index = "PrimaryKey"
  tbl.Seek "=", lstPhones
  tbl.Delete

  lstPhones.Requery

  cmdClearPhone_Click

cmdDeletePhone_ClickDone:
  On Error Resume Next
  If blnOpened Then tbl.Close
  Exit Sub

cmdDeletePhone_ClickError:
  MsgBox Error$, 48, PROGRAM
  Resume cmdDeletePhone_ClickDone

End Sub
```

This subroutine works very much like the cmdAdd_Click subroutine, except that a delete is performed rather than an add or edit.

First, the subroutine checks whether there is a selected phone number to delete. If not, it closes the table and exits the subroutine. If so, it continues to the next instruction.

```
If lstPhones.ListCount = 0 Then GoTo cmdDeletePhone_ClickDone
```

Next, the Enter Phone table is opened.

```
Set tbl = mdb.OpenRecordset("Enter Phone", DB_OPEN_TABLE)
blnOpened = True
```

Then the selected phone number is Seeked to and deleted by calling the Delete method. The record to delete is identified by the bound column of the lstPhones list box.

```
tbl.Index = "PrimaryKey"
tbl.Seek "=", lstPhones
tbl.Delete
```

To close, the list box is requeried and the cmdClearPhone_Click subroutine is called to get ready for the next action.

```
lstPhones.Requery

cmdClearPhone_Click
```

Editing Addresses

The subroutines in this section are a repeat of what you just went through, except that the Enter Address records have more fields. I will be brief in my descriptions, because you already know how these work.

The *lstAddresses_Click* Subroutine

The lstAddresses_Click subroutine copies each of the field values for an address record into the controls on the Address Entry form for editing.

Many of the values come from hidden columns in the list box specifically put there for this purpose. This avoids having to re-open the Enter Phone table and Seek to the appropriate record to read in the values. (That wouldn't really be a bad way to do it, but this was easier.)

The subroutine sets the address section of the form in edit mode.

Enter the lstAddresses_Click subroutine as shown in Listing 13.28.

Listing 13.28. The lstAddresses_Click **subroutine.**

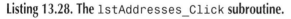

```
Sub lstAddresses_Click ()

  On Error GoTo lstAddresses_ClickError

  If lstAddresses.ListIndex = -1 Then GoTo lstAddresses_ClickDone

  cboStreet = lstAddresses.Column(1)
  cboCity = lstAddresses.Column(2)
  cboState = lstAddresses.Column(5)
  cboRegion = lstAddresses.Column(7)
  cboPostalCode = lstAddresses.Column(6)
```

continues

Listing 13.28. continued

```
cboCountry = lstAddresses.Column(8)
cboAddressType = lstAddresses.Column(4)

cmdAddAddress.Caption = "Change"

lstAddresses_ClickDone:
  Exit Sub

lstAddresses_ClickError:
  MsgBox Error$, 48, PROGRAM
  Resume lstAddresses_ClickDone

End Sub
```

The *cmdClearAddress_Click* Subroutine

The cmdClearAddress_Click subroutine clears all the fields for editing an address and returns the address section of the form to Add mode.

Enter the cmdClearAddress_Click subroutine as shown in Listing 13.29.

Listing 13.29. The cmdClearAddress_Click subroutine.

```
Sub cmdClearAddress_Click ()

  On Error GoTo cmdClearAddress_ClickError

  cboAddressType = Null
  cboStreet = Null
  cboCity = Null
  cboState = Null
  cboPostalCode = Null
  cboRegion = Null
  cboCountry = Null

  lstAddresses = Null

  cmdAddAddress.Caption = "Add"

  cboStreet.SetFocus

cmdClearAddress_ClickDone:
  Exit Sub

cmdClearAddress_ClickError:
  MsgBox Error$, 48, PROGRAM
  Resume cmdClearAddress_ClickDone

End Sub
```

The *cmdAddAddress_Click* Subroutine

The cmdAddAddress_Click subroutine writes the current address being edited to the Enter Address table.

The subroutine ensures that the Street, City, and Address Type fields have been entered.

Enter the cmdAddAddress_Click subroutine as shown in Listing 13.30.

Listing 13.30. The cmdAddAddress_Click **subroutine.**

```
Sub cmdAddAddress_Click ()

  Dim tbl As Recordset
  Dim blnOpened As Integer

  blnOpened = False

  On Error GoTo cmdAddAddress_ClickError

  If RequiredField("Street", cboStreet) Then GoTo cmdAddAddress_ClickDone
  If RequiredField("City", cboCity) Then GoTo cmdAddAddress_ClickDone
If RequiredField("Address Type", cboAddressType) Then GoTo cmdAddAddress
➥_ClickDone

  Set tbl = mdb.OpenRecordset("Enter Address", DB_OPEN_TABLE)
  blnOpened = True

  If cmdAddAddress.Caption = "Change" Then
    tbl.Index = "PrimaryKey"
    tbl.Seek "=", lstAddresses
    tbl.Edit
  Else
    tbl.AddNew
  End If

  tbl!AddressTypeID = cboAddressType
  tbl!Street = cboStreet
  tbl!City = cboCity
  tbl!State = CNull(cboState)
  tbl!PostalCode = CNull(cboPostalCode)
  tbl!Region = CNull(cboRegion)
  tbl!Country = CNull(cboCountry)

  tbl.Update

  lstAddresses.Requery

  cmdClearAddress_Click

cmdAddAddress_ClickDone:
  On Error Resume Next
  If blnOpened Then tbl.Close
  Exit Sub
```

continues

Listing 13.30. continued

```
cmdAddAddress_ClickError:
  MsgBox Error$, 48, PROGRAM
  Resume cmdAddAddress_ClickDone

End Sub
```

The *cmdDeleteAddress_Click* Subroutine

The cmdDeleteAddress_Click subroutine erases the selected address from the lstAddresses list box.

Enter the cmdDeleteAddress_Click subroutine as shown in Listing 13.31.

Listing 13.31. The cmdDeleteAddress_Click subroutine.

```
Sub cmdDeleteAddress_Click ()

    Dim tbl As Recordset
    Dim blnOpened As Integer

    On Error GoTo cmdDeleteAddress_ClickError

    If lstAddresses.ListCount = 0 Then GoTo cmdDeleteAddress_ClickDone

    Set tbl = mdb.OpenRecordset("Enter Address", DB_OPEN_TABLE)
    blnOpened = True

    tbl.Index = "PrimaryKey"
    tbl.Seek "=", lstAddresses
    tbl.Delete

    lstAddresses.Requery

    cmdClearAddress_Click

cmdDeleteAddress_ClickDone:
    On Error Resume Next
    If blnOpened Then tbl.Close
    Exit Sub

cmdDeleteAddress_ClickError:
    MsgBox Error$, 48, PROGRAM
    Resume cmdDeleteAddress_ClickDone

End Sub
```

The *cboState_LostFocus* Subroutine

The final subroutine, cboState_LostFocus, is used to make sure that entered state abbreviations display in uppercase even if they are entered in lowercase.

I added this one after countless times of forgetting to hold down the Shift key when entering a state.

1. Enter the cboState_LostFocus subroutine as show in Listing 13.32.
2. Close the form module and save your changes.

Listing 13.32. The cboState_LostFocus **subroutine.**

```
Sub cboState_LostFocus ()

  If Not IsNull(cboState) Then
    cboState = UCase$(CStr(cboState))
  End If

End Sub
```

Now it's time to put out the fire on your keyboard and give your fingers a rest. At the beginning of the next chapter you can check out the form you just created.

Summary

In this chapter you created the tables for the Address Book application and a form to populate them with data.

Here is what you also did along the way:

■ Learned what a Query By Form application is
■ Mapped out the project database objects
■ Learned about one-to-many relationships
■ Learned about primary and foreign keys
■ Examined trade-offs in the project's table design
■ Created the Address Book tables
■ Learned about referential integrity
■ Learned about parent, child, and orphan records
■ Learned about cascading deletes

■ Defined relationships for the Address Book database tables

■ Used Paintbrush to print a graphical representation of the database

■ Explored advantages of using unbound forms

■ Learned about saving form control defaults

■ Created Row Source queries with Query Builder

■ Used hidden columns in list boxes to store data

■ Used an alternative approach to subforms

■ Created the `DumpFields` subroutine to list table field names

■ Created a `RequiredField` function to test for required entries

■ Used transactions to ensure data integrity

■ Coded the Address Entry form module

You have your work set out for you in the next chapter. First you enter some data into the address book, and then you build the Address Search form and its supporting queries.

TRY THIS! ANSWERS

13.1. Writing a function to switch between form templates is a very useful development utility to have in your Access tool kit.

Here's how it's done:

1. Create your first template form. A good one to have is one with all the following properties set to make a pop-up modal dialog box:

Default View:	Single Form
Shortcut Menu:	No
Scroll Bars:	Neither
Record Selectors:	No
Navigation Buttons:	No
Auto Center:	Yes
Border Style:	Dialog
Min Button:	No
Max Button:	No
Width:	4.5 in

2. Also set the Back Color and Height properties of the detail section:

Height:	2.5 in
Back Color:	12632256 (Light Gray)

3. Save the form with the name Modal.

4. In a code module, enter the function shown in Listing 13.33.

Listing 13.33. The `ToggleFormTemplate` **function.**

```
Function ToggleFormTemplate () As Integer

  Dim strTemplate As String
  Dim blnInstall As Integer

  Const PROGRAM = "Toggle Form Template"

  On Error GoTo ToggleFormTemplateError

  strTemplate = Application.GetOption("Form Template")

  blnInstall = True

  Select Case strTemplate

  Case "Normal"
    strTemplate = "Modal"

  Case "Modal"
    strTemplate = "Normal"

  Case Else
    blnInstall = False

  End Select

  If blnInstall Then
    Application.SetOption "Form Template", strTemplate
  End If

MsgBox "The " & strTemplate & " form is installed as the Form Template.",
➥ 64, PROGRAM

ToggleFormTemplateDone:
  Exit Function

ToggleFormTemplateError:
  MsgBox Error$, 48, PROGRAM
  Resume ToggleFormTemplateDone

End Function
```

This `ToggleFormTemplate` function reads the current Form Template setting and switches it to the next template. In this version, you are switching only between the Normal template and the Modal template. You could add more.

Assign a keypress combination to run the function by creating an `AutoKeys` macro as shown in Figure 13.54.

That's it. Now press Ctrl-T to switch between the Normal and your Modal form template. A message box indicates which template is the one currently being used.

FIGURE 13.54.

An AutoKeys macro that assigns Ctrl-T to run the `ToggleFormTemplate` *function.*

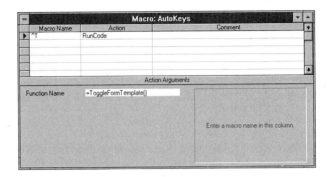

Create a new form, and it starts out with all the Modal template form settings rather than the settings that are in the Normal template.

You can also store control defaults in your form template. Add controls to your form template and use the Format|Change Default command. The control defaults are stored with your template form when you save it.

CHAPTER 14

Access: Address Book, Part Two

In this chapter you complete the Address Book application you started in Chapter 13, "Access: Address Book, Part One."

In the last chapter you set up the tables in your ADDRESS.MDB database and created the Address Entry form to start entering some data. In this chapter you get started by taking the Address Entry form for a trial run. Then you build the Address Search form.

Next you create a quick report with the Access Report Wizard to make a printed copy of your address book entries. You finish the chapter by optimizing the Address Search form with code that actually generates SQL SELECT statements based on the kind of search the user has asked the program to perform.

Get yourself ready for another long but instructive session in front of the computer.

Testing the Address Entry Form

Let's see if your Address Entry form performs as expected.

1. Select the Address Entry form in the database container and click the **O**pen button.

If the Form_Open code runs properly, you should see the form as shown in Figure 14.1.

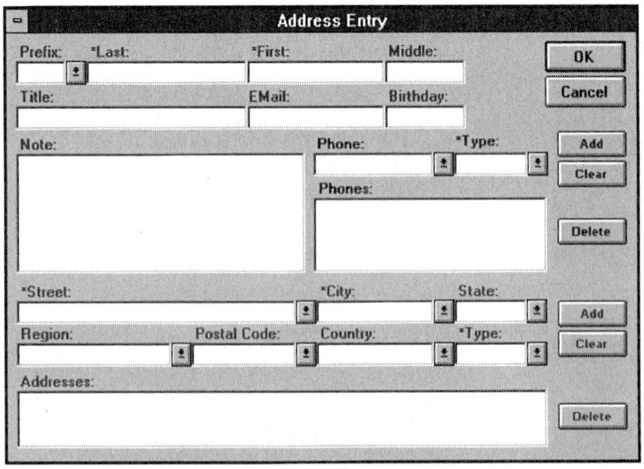

FIGURE 14.1.

Opening the Address Entry form.

If, on the other hand, you get an error message either here or in any of the following steps, it's debug time. Try to narrow down the problem to where in the code or property settings the error might be happening, then verify your code against the listings in the book.

Any experience you get debugging an application is great, but you can also cheat and look at the completed application on the book's companion CD-ROM.

I'll continue on as if everything went just peachy.

2. Fill in the red section of the form (the first two lines and the Note field) as shown in Figure 14.2.

FIGURE 14.2.

Entering Person table information into the Address Entry form.

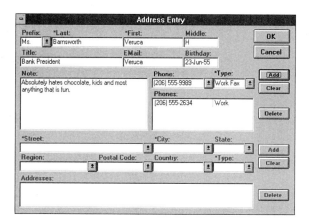

3. Enter a phone number and phone type in the blue section of the form, as shown in Figure 14.3. Click the Add button to move the new phone entry into the list of phone numbers. Repeat this for several phone numbers.

FIGURE 14.3.

Entering phone numbers into the Address Entry form.

4. Enter one or more addresses into the purple section of the form, as shown in Figure 14.4. Click the Add button to enter the new address into the address list.

FIGURE 14.4.

Entering addresses into the Address Entry form.

Address Entry
Prefix: *Last: *First: Middle: **OK**
Ms. Barnsworth Veruca H **Cancel**
Title: EMail: Birthday:
Bank President Veruca 23-Jun-55
Note: Phone: *Type: **Add**
Absolutely hates chocolate, kids and most **Clear**
anything that is fun. Phones:
(206) 555-2634 Work
(206) 555-9989 Work Fax **Delete**
(206) 555-7786 Home
*Street: *City: State:
2563 Northup Drive, #202 Belmont WA **Add**
Region: Postal Code: Country: *Type: **Clear**
98011 USA Home
Addresses:
92 S.W. Anderson Plaza Belmont Work **Delete**

5. Click OK to save your entry into the Person, Phone, and Address tables.

If the data was saved correctly, you should be able to open the Person, Phone, and Address tables in datasheet mode, as shown in Figure 14.5, and see your address book entry.

FIGURE 14.5.

Examining data entered in the Person, Phone, and Address tables.

Table: Person

PersonID	Prefix	First Name	Middle Name	Last Name
1	Ms.	Veruca	H	Barnsworth
(Counter)				

Record: 1   of 1

Table: Phone

Phone ID	Person ID	Phone Type ID	Phone
1	1	2	(206) 555-2634
2	1	7	(206) 555-9989
3	1	1	(206) 555-7786
(Counter)			

Record: 1   of 3

Table: Address

Address ID	Person ID	Address Type ID	Street	City
1	1	2	92 S.W. Anderson	Belmont
2	1	1	2563 Northup Drive	Belmont
(Counter)				

Record: 1   of 2

Note that the PersonID values in the records in the Phone and Address table appropriately match the PersonID value for the record in the Person table. This, of course, is how the Phone and Address records are linked to the Person record in the Person table.

Creating the Address Search Form

The Address Search form contains an area to enter search criteria, a Search button to perform the search, a list to display the results, and a series of buttons at the bottom of the form to perform other functions.

It's a busy form, and you have quite a bit of work to do to throw this one together.

1. Create a new form. Choose **B**lank Form from the New Form dialog box without selecting a table or query.

2. Maximize the form design window and set the following form properties:

Caption:	Address Search
Default View:	Single Form
Shortcut Menu:	No
Scroll Bars:	Neither
Record Selectors:	No
Navigation Buttons:	No
Auto Center:	Yes
Border Style:	Dialog
Min Button:	No
Max Button:	No
Width:	6.2 in

3. Click inside the detail section on the form to display the detail section's properties. Set the Height and Back Color properties as shown here:

Height:	3.8542 in
Back Color:	12632256 (Light Gray)

Note that with the height of the form you won't be able to view the entire form in design mode unless you are using a higher screen resolution than standard VGA. You have to use the form design window's vertical scroll bar to get to the bottom part of the form.

Creating Controls to Enter Search Criteria

The first control to create on the form is the cboPrefix control. This control is going to be identical to the one you created on the Address Entry form, so you can copy it from there and paste it here.

1. From the **W**indow menu, select the database container window to display it.

    Because the previous window was maximized, Access displays the database container as a maximized window.

2. Select the Address Entry form in the database container, and click **D**esign.

3. In the Address Entry form, click the cboPrefix combo box control, as shown in Figure 14.6, and press Ctrl-C to copy it into the clipboard.

FIGURE 14.6.

Copying the cboPrefix control from the Address Entry form.

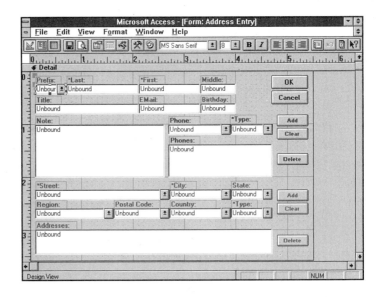

4. Switch back to the Address Search form by selecting it from the **Window** menu.

5. Press Ctrl-V to paste the control onto the form.

Access pastes the control in the top-left corner of the detail section, as shown in Figure 14.7.

FIGURE 14.7.

Pasting the cboPrefix control into the Address Search form.

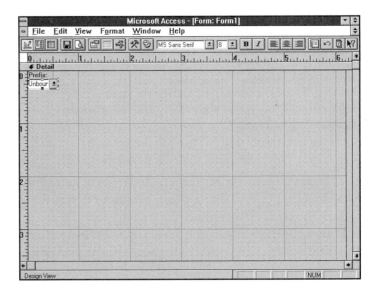

All you need to do to use this control is change the color of the label and locate it where you want it on the form. Let's also change the caption to add an accelerator key so that pressing Alt-X takes you to the top of the Address Search form.

You won't create accelerator keys for every prompt and control on the form. There aren't enough characters in the alphabet for that.

1. Set the following properties on lblPrefix control:

   Caption: Prefi&x:
   Fore Color: 0 (Black)
   Left: 0.2021 in
   Top: 0.0625 in

2. Set the following properties on the cboPrefix control:

   Left: 0.2021 in
   Top: 0.2292 in

Unfortunately, not all the controls can be copied straight from the Address Entry form. The next several controls were text boxes on the Address Entry form but are combo boxes on the Address Search form.

Each of the combo boxes contains a query that brings back all the unique values that have been entered for its corresponding field. This way a user could select a last name from a drop-down list and get all address book entries for people with that last name, and similarly for all the other fields.

First, let's save defaults based on the cboPrefix combo box.

1. Click the lblPrefix label control and select the Format|Change Default command.
2. Click the cboPrefix combo box control and select the Format|Change Default command.
3. Click the Toolbox button on the toolbar to display the Toolbox window.
4. Click the Combo box button, and then click the form to drop a combo box on the form for entering a last name.
5. Set the label and combo box properties as shown here:

   Name: blLast
   Caption: Last:
   Left: 0.825 in
   Top: 0.0625 in
   Width: 0.5 in
   Height: 0.1667 in

Name: cboLast
Tab Index: 1
Left: 0.8222 in
Top: 0.2292 in
Width: 1.5701 in
Height: 0.1771 in

Some of the properties that have already been set by default but are significant to make the cboLast control work as expected are the following:

Row Source Type: Table/Query
Column Count: 1
Bound Column: 1
Limit To List: No
Auto Expand: Yes

Next, you need to make a query that returns each of the last names entered into the Person table.

1. In the Properties window, click the ellipsis button on the Row Source property.
2. In the Add Table dialog box, select the Person table and click **A**dd. Close the Add Table dialog box.
3. Drag the LastName field to the first column in the query grid.
4. Set the Sort for the LastName field to Ascending.
5. In the Criteria row, enter Not Is Null, as shown in Figure 14.8.
6. Click the Totals button on the toolbar.
7. Close the Query Builder window.

As shown in Figure 14.9, Access enters the following SELECT statement into the Row Source property of the cboLast combo box:

```
SELECT DISTINCTROW Person.LastName
FROM Person
GROUP BY Person.LastName
HAVING ((Not Person.LastName Is Null))
ORDER BY Person.LastName;
```

The remaining combo boxes on the form have their Row Source properties set similarly to what you just did.

Rather than repeat these instructions over and over again, I'll just ask you to create a query that produces the unique values for an indicated field and table. The steps you repeat to do this are the preceding steps 1 through 7.

Good, let's shift into high gear now.

FIGURE 14.8.

Creating the Row Source query for the cboLast control.

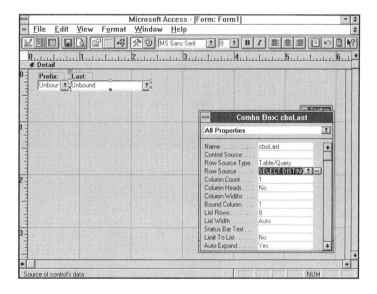

FIGURE 14.9.

Adding the cboLast combo box to the Address Search form.

1. Add the cboFirst combo box. Set the label and combo box properties as shown here:

Name:	lblFirst
Caption:	First:
Left:	2.4181 in
Top:	0.0625 in
Width:	0.5 in
Height:	0.1667 in

Name:	cboFirst
Tab Index:	2
Left:	2.4201 in
Top:	0.2292 in
Width:	1.3806 in
Height:	0.1771 in

2. As you did for the cboLast combo box, use Query Builder to set the Row Source property to a query that returns each unique FirstName field value in the Person table.

   The SQL SELECT statement generated should be the following:

```
SELECT DISTINCTROW Person.FirstName
FROM Person
GROUP BY Person.FirstName
HAVING ((Not Person.FirstName Is Null))
ORDER BY Person.FirstName;
```

3. Add the cboMiddle combo box:

Name:	lblMiddle
Caption:	Middle:
Left:	3.825 in
Top:	0.0625 in
Width:	0.5 in
Height:	0.1667 in

Name:	cboMiddle
Tab Index:	3
Left:	3.8222 in
Top:	0.2292 in
Width:	0.7875 in
Height:	0.1771 in

4. Set the Row Source property to a query that returns each unique MiddleName value in the Person table.

   The SQL SELECT statement generated should be as follows:

```
SELECT DISTINCTROW Person.MiddleName
FROM Person
GROUP BY Person.MiddleName
HAVING ((Not Person.MiddleName Is Null))
ORDER BY Person.MiddleName;
```

5. Add the cboEMail combo box:

Name:	lblEMail
Caption:	Email:
Left:	4.6271 in

Top:	0.0625 in
Width:	0.5 in
Height:	0.1667 in
Name:	cboEMail
Tab Index:	4
Left:	4.6403 in
Top:	0.2292 in
Width:	1.3806 in
Height:	0.1771 in

6. Set the Row Source property to a query that returns each unique EMail value in the Person table.

The SQL SELECT statement generated should be the following:

```
SELECT DISTINCTROW Person.EMail
FROM Person
GROUP BY Person.EMail
HAVING ((Not Person.EMail Is Null))
ORDER BY Person.EMail;
```

The first line of controls is complete, as shown in Figure 14.10.

FIGURE 14.10.

Completing the first line of controls on the Address Search form.

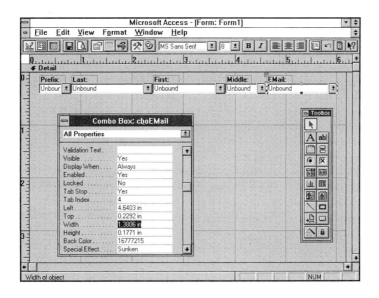

On the second line of controls you add controls for Title, Note, and Phone.

1. Add the cboTitle combo box:

Name:	lblTitle
Caption:	Title:
Left:	0.2 in
Top:	0.4375 in
Width:	0.5 in
Height:	0.1667 in

Name:	cboTitle
Tab Index:	5
Left:	0.2 in
Top:	0.6042 in
Width:	2.1938 in
Height:	0.1771 in

2. Set the Row Source property to a query that returns each unique value in the Title field of the Person table.

The following SQL SELECT statement is generated:

```
SELECT DISTINCTROW Person.Title
FROM Person
GROUP BY Person.Title
HAVING ((Not Person.Title Is Null))
ORDER BY Person.Title;
```

The next control for the Note field is a text box rather than a combo box. The typical entry in this control would be a word with wildcard characters before and after it in order to search for all notes with the given word somewhere in the text.

1. Click the Textbox button on the Toolbox window.
2. Click the form to drop a text box on it, and set the label and text box properties as follows:

Name:	lblNote
Caption:	Note:
Left:	2.4222 in
Top:	0.4375 in
Width:	0.5 in
Height:	0.1667 in

Name:	txtNote
Tab Index:	6
Left:	2.4201 in

Top:	0.6042 in
Width:	2.1792 in
Height:	0.1771 in
Special Effect:	Sunken

3. Add the cboPhone combo box and its label with the following properties:

Name:	lblPhone
Caption:	Phone:
Left:	4.6201 in
Top:	0.4375 in
Width:	0.5 in
Height:	0.1667 in

Name:	cboPhone
Tab Index:	7
Left:	4.6201 in
Top:	0.6042 in
Width:	1.4021 in
Height:	0.1771 in

The Row Source query for the cboPhone control is identical to the queries created for the earlier combo boxes except that the Phone table is used and not the Person table.

1. Use Query Builder to create a query for the cboPhone control's Row Source property. The query should return each unique phone number in the Phone table.

   The SQL SELECT statement generated should be the following:
   ```
   SELECT DISTINCTROW Phone.Phone
   FROM Phone
   GROUP BY Phone.Phone
   HAVING ((Not Phone.Phone Is Null))
   ORDER BY Phone.Phone;
   ```

2. Save your work. Select the **File|S**ave command and enter Address Search as the name of the form in the Save As dialog box.

The second row of controls is completed, as shown in Figure 14.11.

The third line of controls enables you to search by Street, City, State, or Postal Code. The Row Source queries for these controls' return values from the Address table.

FIGURE 14.11.

Completing the second row of controls on the Address Search form.

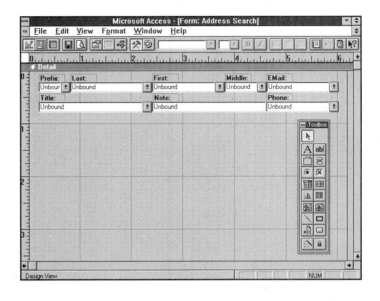

1. Add the cboStreet combo box:

Name:	lblStreet
Caption:	Street:
Left:	0.2 in
Top:	0.8125 in
Width:	0.5 in
Height:	0.1667 in

Name:	cboStreet
Tab Index:	8
Left:	0.2 in
Top:	0.9792 in
Width:	2.1938 in
Height:	0.1771 in

2. Set the Row Source property to a query that returns each unique value in the Street field of the Address table.

   The following SQL SELECT statement is generated:

```
SELECT DISTINCTROW Address.Street
FROM Address
GROUP BY Address.Street
HAVING ((Not Address.Street Is Null))
ORDER BY Address.Street;
```

3. Add the cboCity combo box and its label:

Name:	lblCity
Caption:	City:
Left:	2.4222 in
Top:	0.8125 in
Width:	0.5 in
Height:	0.1667 in

Name:	cboCity
Tab Index:	9
Left:	2.4201 in
Top:	0.9792 in
Width:	1.475 in
Height:	0.1771 in

4. Set the Row Source property to a query that returns each unique City value from the Address table.

The SQL SELECT statement generated should be as follows:

```
SELECT DISTINCTROW Address.City
FROM Address
GROUP BY Address.City
HAVING ((Not Address.City Is Null))
ORDER BY Address.City;
```

The State combo box reads its available selections from the State lookup table. You already created a combo box like this in the last chapter, so you can copy that in here.

1. Select the Address Entry from the **W**indow menu.
2. Click the cboState combo box and press Ctrl-C to copy it.
3. Switch back to the Address Search form by selecting it from the **W**indow menu.
4. Press Ctrl-V to paste the copied combo box and label into the Address Search form's Detail section.
5. Modify the properties of the lblState and cboState controls as shown here:

Name:	lblState
Left:	3.9146 in
Top:	0.8125 in
Width:	0.5 in
Height:	0.1667 in
Fore Color:	0

Name:	cboState
Tab Index:	10
Left:	3.9201 in
Top:	0.9792 in
Width:	0.6826 in
Height:	0.1771 in

6. Add the cboPostalCode combo box:

Name:	lblPostalCode
Caption:	Postal Code:
Left:	4.6271 in
Top:	0.8125 in
Width:	1 in
Height:	0.1667 in

Name:	cboPostalCode
Tab Index:	11
Left:	4.6222 in
Top:	0.9792 in
Width:	1.4021 in
Height:	0.1771 in

7. Set the Row Source property to a query that selects each unique PostalCode value from the Address table.

The SQL SELECT statement generated should be the following:

```
SELECT DISTINCTROW Address.PostalCode
FROM Address
GROUP BY Address.PostalCode
HAVING ((Not Address.PostalCode Is Null))
ORDER BY Address.PostalCode;
```

The third row of controls is completed, as shown in Figure 14.12.

Among the final row of search criteria controls is the cmdSearch button. Clicking the Search button performs the search for address book entries that match the entered criteria.

First, you have two more combo boxes to create.

1. Add the cboRegion combo box and label with the following properties:

Name:	lblRegion
Caption:	Region:
Left:	0.2 in
Top:	1.1875 in

Width:	0.6 in
Height:	0.1667 in

Name:	cboRegion
Tab Index:	12
Left:	0.2 in
Top:	1.3542 in
Width:	1.1799 in
Height:	0.1771 in

FIGURE 14.12.

The third row of controls is added to the Address Search form.

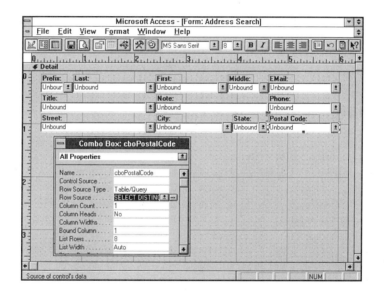

2. Set the Row Source property to a query that returns each unique Region value from the Address table.

   The SQL SELECT statement generated should look like the following:

```
SELECT DISTINCTROW Address.Region
FROM Address
GROUP BY Address.Region
HAVING ((Not Address.Region Is Null))
ORDER BY Address.Region;
```

3. Add the Country combo box:

Name:	lblCountry
Caption:	Country:
Left:	1.4 in
Top:	1.1875 in
Width:	0.7 in
Height:	0.1667 in

Name:	cboCountry
Tab Index:	13
Left:	1.4007 in
Top:	1.3542 in
Width:	1.1 in
Height:	0.1771 in

4. Set the Row Source property to a query that returns the unique Country value from the Address table.

The following SQL SELECT statement should be generated:

```
SELECT DISTINCTROW Address.Country
FROM Address
GROUP BY Address.Country
HAVING ((Not Address.Country Is Null))
ORDER BY Address.Country;
```

Creating Search State Labels

Next you create three labels that indicate the three different states the program can be in. Address Book alternately displays the different labels by setting their Visible properties.

What state each of the labels represents is clear from the text displayed in them:

■ Search Pending

■ Searching...

■ XX Matches Found

Search Pending means that the search criteria has been changed. The Search button must be clicked in order to perform the next search to bring back results that meet the entered criteria.

In a search pending state, the results list is cleared as an additional indicator that the criteria has changed. The last thing you want to do is allow the user to get confused in thinking that old search results meet the currently entered criteria.

The Searching... message is displayed briefly while a search is being performed. At least, you hope that the message is displayed briefly. At the end of the chapter you will optimize your initial implementation to make searches go as quickly as possible.

The XX Matches Found message indicates how many matching records were returned. The caption in this label is updated in code with the actual count of matches found.

1. Click the Label button on the toolbox and draw a label on the form. Enter XX Matches Found as the text in the label, and then set the following properties:

Name:	lblMatchesFound
Caption:	XX Matches Found
Left:	2.5007 in
Top:	1.3542 in
Width:	1.3097 in
Height:	0.1667 in
Fore Color:	128 (Red)
Text Align:	Center

2. Press Ctrl-C to copy the lblMatchesFound label, and then press Ctrl-V twice to paste two copies of it on the form, as shown in Figure 14.13.

FIGURE 14.13.

Pasting two copies of the lblMatchesFound label.

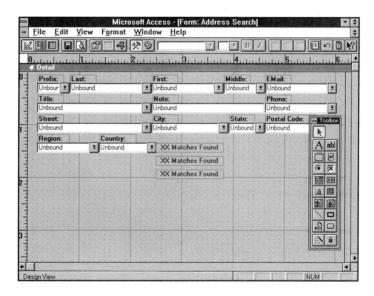

3. Set the properties of the first copy of the lblMatchesFound label as shown here to create the lblSearching label.

Name:	lblSearching
Caption:	Searching...
Left:	2.5007 in
Top:	1.3542 in

4. Set the properties of the second copy of the lblMatchesFound label as shown here to create the lblSearchPending label as shown in Figure 14.14.

Name:	lblSearchPending
Caption:	Search Pending
Left:	2.5007 in
Top:	1.3542 in

FIGURE 14.14.

The three labels are stacked on top of each other.

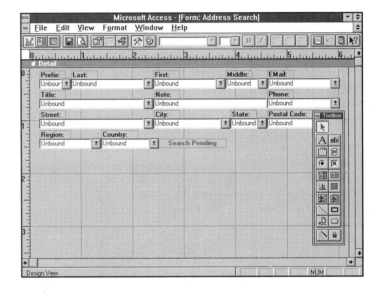

Creating the Search Button

Next you create the cmdSearch button.

1. Click the Command Button button on the toolbox and drop a button on the form with the following properties set:

Name:	cmdSearch
Caption:	&Search
Tab Index:	14
Left:	3.8326 in
Top:	1.3125 in
Width:	0.7021 in
Height:	0.25 in
Font Name:	MS Sans Serif
Font Size:	8

   At the bottom of the form you will create several buttons, so you should save the button control defaults now.

2. With the cmdSearch button selected, select the Format|Change Default command.

You have two final combo boxes to create to complete this row of controls. Fortunately, the cboPhoneType and cboAddressType combo boxes can both be copied from the Address Entry form you created in the last chapter.

1. Select the Address Entry form from the **W**indow menu.
2. Click the cboPhoneType combo box to select it. As shown in Figure 14.15, the cboPhoneType combo box is the first combo box on the form with a label that shows a *Type: caption.
3. While holding down the Shift key, click the cboAddressType combo box. This is the second combo box with a label showing a *Type: caption.
4. With both combo boxes selected, press Ctrl-C to copy them into the Windows clipboard.

FIGURE 14.15.

Selecting and copying the cboPhoneType and cboAddressType combo boxes from the Address Entry form.

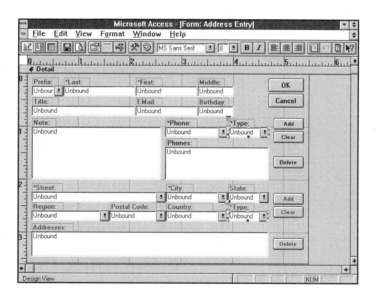

5. Return to the Address Search form by selecting it from the **W**indow menu.
6. Press Ctrl-V to paste the two controls on the form.
7. Modify the properties of the lblPhoneType label and cboPhoneType combo box as follows:

Name:	lblPhoneType
Caption:	Ph Type:
Left:	4.625 in
Top:	1.1875 in
Width:	0.7 in
Height:	0.1667 in
Fore Color:	0

Name: cboPhoneType
Tab Index: 15
Left: 4.6222 in
Top: 1.3542 in
Width: 0.7556 in
Height: 0.1771 in

8. Modify the properties of the lblAddressType label and cboAddressType combo box as shown here:

Name: lblAddressType
Caption: Adr Type:
Left: 5.3958 in
Top: 1.1875 in
Width: 0.7 in
Height: 0.1667 in
Fore Color: 0

Name: cboAddressType
Tab Index: 16
Left: 5.3993 in
Top: 1.3542 in
Width: 0.6208 in
Height: 0.1771 in

The fourth row of controls is completed, as shown in Figure 14.16.

FIGURE 14.16.

Completing the fourth row of controls on the Address Search form.

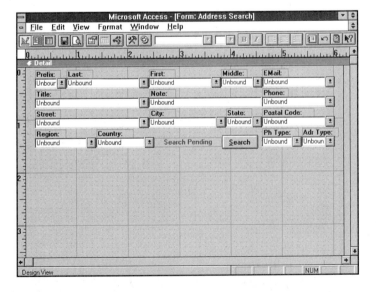

9. Select the **File|S**ave command to save your work so far.

You can test the work in progress by clicking the Form View button on the toolbar. Each of the combo boxes you created should display at least one value if something was entered in that field while testing the Address Entry form.

The Prefix, State, Phone Type, and Address Type combo boxes should display the same lists they did in the Address Entry form. The list for the Phone Type combo box is shown in Figure 14.17.

FIGURE 14.17.

Testing your half-finished Address Search form.

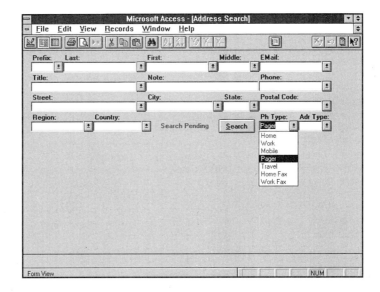

Click the Design View button to return the form to design view.

Creating Controls to Display Search Results

Your next project is to enter a row of command buttons used as headings for the results list box, then create the list box itself.

Clicking a heading button changes the sort order of the list so that the field in that column is the primary sort. Additionally, subsorts may be defined.

For example, if the cmdSortState button is pressed, the list is sorted by state names first and by city names second.

Drop six buttons on the form with the following properties, as shown in Figure 14.18:

Name:	cmdSortLast
Caption:	&Last
Tab Index:	17
Left:	0.1 in
Top:	1.625 in
Width:	1.0042 in
Height:	0.25 in

Name:	cmdSortFirst
Caption:	&First
Tab Index:	18
Left:	1.1 in
Top:	1.625 in
Width:	0.5979 in
Height:	0.25 in

Name:	cmdSortStreet
Caption:	St&reet
Tab Index:	19
Left:	1.7 in
Top:	1.625 in
Width:	1.9938 in
Height:	0.25 in

Name:	cmdSortCity
Caption:	C&ity
Tab Index:	20
Left:	3.7 in
Top:	1.625 in
Width:	0.9 in
Height:	0.25 in

Name:	cmdSortState
Caption:	S&tate
Tab Index:	21
Left:	4.6 in
Top:	1.625 in
Width:	0.5 in
Height:	0.25 in

Name:	cmdSortPhone
Caption:	Pho&ne
Tab Index:	22
Left:	5.1 in
Top:	1.625 in
Width:	0.75 in
Height:	0.25 in

FIGURE 14.18.

Adding the sort buttons.

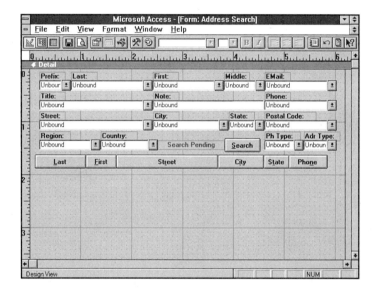

Next, you add the lstAddresses list box. I sometimes refer to this control as the results list, because that is a good description of its contents.

The Row Source for the lstAddresses list box gets changed by the program when you change sort order with the buttons above the list box. However, each query returns the same set of 10 fields: PersonID, LastName, FirstName, MiddleName, Street, City, State, Phone, EMail, and Note.

The column widths on the lstAddresses list box are set so that four of the fields are hidden from view: PersonID, MiddleName, EMail, and Note. The other six fields are displayed with column widths that match the widths of the buttons you just created.

1. Click the Listbox button on the toolbox and drop a list box on the Address Search form.

   Access automatically drops a label control with the list box. You don't need it.

2. Select the new label and delete it by pressing the Delete key.

3. Set the new list box with the following properties (as shown in Figure 14.19):

Name:	lstAddresses
Row Source Type:	Table/Query
Column Count:	10
Column Widths:	0 in;1 in;0.5903 in;0 in;2 in;0.9 in;0.5 in;7.5 in;0 in;0 in
Bound Column:	1
Tab Index:	23
Left:	0.1 in
Top:	1.875 in
Width:	5.9917 in
Height:	1.3333 in

FIGURE 14.19.

Adding the lstAddresses list box to display search results.

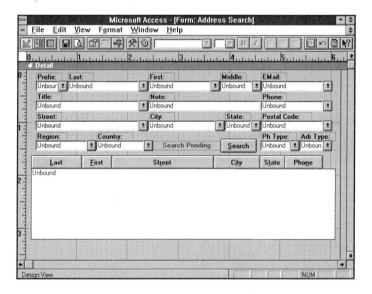

There is only so much room to display fields horizontally across a list box. To get around this limitation and display more information about the selected address book entries, some noneditable text boxes are created following the lstAddresses list box.

As the user clicks on each line in the list box, the text boxes below display additional information about the selected entry. I decided to display the EMail and Note fields this way.

Drop two text box controls on the form, as shown in Figure 14.20. Set the following properties on the new labels and text boxes:

Name: lblDisplayEmail
Caption: Email:
Left: 0.1 in
Top: 3.25 in
Width: 0.4576 in
Height: 0.1667 in
Text Align: Right

Name: txtDisplayEMail
Enabled: No
Locked: Yes
Tab Stop: No
Tab Index: 24
Left: 0.5542 in
Top: 3.25 in
Width: 1.0181 in
Height: 0.1667 in
Back Color: 12632256 (Light Gray)
Border Style: Clear

Name: lblDisplayNote
Caption: Note:
Left: 1.625 in
Top: 3.25 in
Width: 0.4479 in
Height: 0.1667 in
Text Align: Right

Name: txtDisplayNote
Enabled: No
Locked: Yes
Tab Stop: No
Tab Index: 25
Left: 2.0729 in
Top: 3.25 in
Width: 4.0292 in
Height: 0.1667 in
Back Color: 12632256 (Light Gray)
Border Style: Clear

FIGURE 14.20.

Adding two noneditable text boxes to display the Email and Note fields.

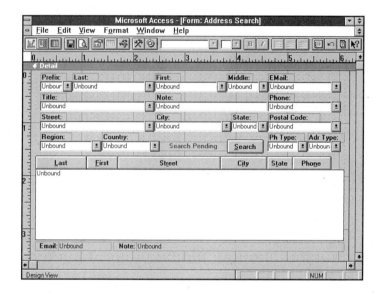

Creating the Command Buttons

At the bottom of the form is a row of buttons:

- ■ **A**dd—Add a new address book entry
- ■ **E**dit—Edit the selected address book entry
- ■ **D**elete—Delete the selected address book entry
- ■ Pre**v**iew—Print Preview a report on the listed entries
- ■ **P**rint—Print a report on the listed entries
- ■ **C**lose—Quit the program

The **A**dd and **E**dit buttons display the Address Entry form.

1. Drop six buttons on the form with the following properties, as shown in Figure 14.21:

Name:	cmdAdd
Caption:	&Add
Tab Index:	26
Left:	0.75 in
Top:	3.5417 in
Width:	0.7021 in
Height:	0.25 in

Name:	cmdEdit
Caption:	&Edit
Tab Index:	27
Left:	1.55 in
Top:	3.5417 in
Width:	0.7021 in
Height:	0.25 in

Name:	cmdDelete
Caption:	&Delete
Tab Index:	28
Left:	2.35 in
Top:	3.5417 in
Width:	0.7021 in
Height:	0.25 in

Name:	cmdPreview
Caption:	Pre&view
Tab Index:	29
Left:	0.75 in
Top:	3.15 in
Width:	0.7021 in
Height:	0.25 in

Name:	cmdPrint
Caption:	&Print
Tab Index:	30
Left:	3.95 in
Top:	3.5417 in
Width:	0.7021 in
Height:	0.25 in

Name:	cmdClose
Caption:	&Close
Tab Index:	31
Left:	4.75 in
Top:	3.5417 in
Width:	0.7021 in
Height:	0.25 in

2. Select the **File|Save** command to save your work.

FIGURE 14.21.

*Adding command
buttons to the bottom
of the form.*

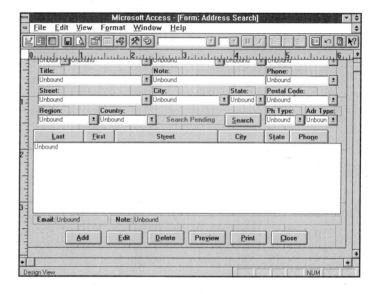

Creating a Hidden Form Header

You are almost finished with the form design window.

Before you close the form, you need to create a hidden check box control that is used by the program to signal to the lstAddresses Row Source queries that the results list should be cleared.

You will see how this gets used when you create the queries and the code behind the form. For now just trust me on this one.

One way to hide controls on a form is to place them in a Form Header or Form Footer, then make the entire section invisible by setting its Visible property to No.

1. Select the **Format|Form Header/Footer** command.

    You don't need the Form Footer section, so you can hide it even from design view by setting its height to 0 inches.

2. Drag the bottom of the Form Footer section up so that it can't be seen, or set its Height property to 0 inches in the Properties window.

3. Set the Visible property of the Form Header section to No.

4. Drop a check box control in the Form Header. Set the following properties for the new label and check box, as shown in Figure 14.22:

Name: lblClearList
Caption: chkClearList

Name: chkClearList
Default Value: True

The label of the check box is set to the name of the check box control. This is done as a quick reminder for the programmer about what the control is used for.

FIGURE 14.22.

Adding a hidden check box.

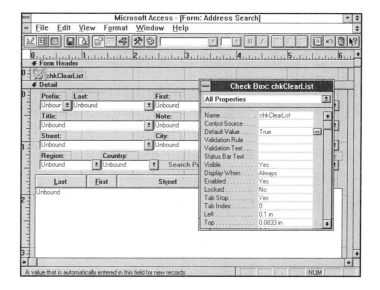

5. Close the form, being sure to save your changes.

It's nice to have the form design work done for that monstrous form. Before you code it, you need to create queries that are used to fill the lstAddresses list box with the results of each search.

Creating the Address Book Queries

I'm going to show you two ways to make Access search for address book entries that match the criteria entered into the Address Search form.

The method I'll show you now uses queries to do all the work. With large sets of data, the methodology you use here won't perform nearly as quickly as your final implementation at the end of the chapter, but you might find this method easy and quick enough for your application.

The first query, Address List, is complex. It must handle the criteria entered in each of the fields on your Address Search form and produce the correct set of matching records. Additionally, it needs to properly handle the case when fields are left blank.

The rules of the game are that if no criteria is entered for a field, you consider anything a match as far as that field is concerned. If you search without entering any criteria, all records are returned.

1. Click the Queries tab in the database container.

2. Click the **N**ew button to create a new query. At the New Query dialog box, select **N**ew Query rather than using the Query Wizards.

3. In the Add Table dialog box, shown in Figure 14.23, add three tables: Person, Phone, and Address. Click the **C**lose button to close the Add Table dialog box.

FIGURE 14.23.

Adding tables to the Address List query.

Because relationships between the tables have already been defined, Access draws the appropriate joins between the tables in the query design window.

Your query is going to be a summary query. You want it to return only the first address and phone number for a person in the address book. Otherwise you get multiple lines in the results list for the same person.

4. Click the Totals button on the toolbar.

Access adds a row below the Field row labeled Total:. This row is for entering the type of summary to be performed on each field.

5. Drag the PersonID field from the Person table to the first column.

By default, Access chooses Group By in the Total row.

6. Drag the LastName, FirstName, and MiddleName name fields from the Person table to Columns 2, 3, and 4.

7. Change the Total from Group By to First in Columns 2, 3, and 4.

If you run the query now (which you can do by clicking the Run toolbar button), you will see that Access changes the names of Columns 2, 3, and 4 by adding FirstOf to the beginning of each field name, as shown in Figure 14.24.

FIGURE 14.24.

Access adds FirstOf to the beginning of field names in a summary query.

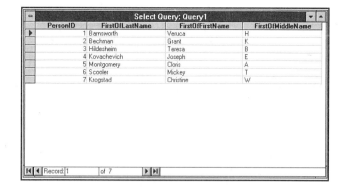

You don't have to accept those default names; you can change the names of your query's output columns.

1. In the first row of the query grid, make the following changes, as shown in Figure 14.25:

   Change `LastName` to `LastName: LastName`

   Change `FirstName` to `FirstName: FirstName`

   Change `MiddleName` to `MiddleName: MiddleName`

   The output name is at the left of the colon. You are changing the output names to be the same as the source field names.

FIGURE 14.25.

Change the output names of Columns 2, 3, and 4.

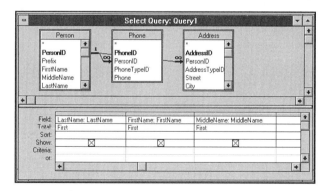

2. Drag the Street, City, and State fields from the Address table into Columns 5, 6, and 7 of the query grid.

3. In the row marked `Total:`, select First as the type of summary to perform on Columns 5, 6, and 7.

4. Change the field names as you did before:

   Change `Street` to `Street: Street`

Change `City` to `City: City`
Change `State` to `State: State`

5. Drag the Phone field from the Phone table to Column 8.

6. Drag the fields EMail and Note from the Person table to Columns 9 and 10.

7. Select First for the type of summary for Columns 8, 9, and 10.

8. Change the field names of the three new columns, as shown in Figure 14.26:

Change `Phone` to `Phone: Phone`
Change `EMail` to `EMail: Email`
Change `Note` to `Note: Note`

FIGURE 14.26.

Columns 7 through 10 of the Address List query.

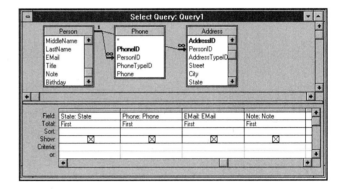

That's all the output columns the query has (10 in all). The remaining columns are used to apply criteria entered on the form so that only the appropriate records are returned.

The next column checks the value in the chkClearList check box that you placed in the form header. The criteria for this column is False. If the check box is set to True, then the criteria is not met in all cases. The end result is that no records are returned from the query.

Enter the following into Column 11 of the query:

Field: `[Forms]![Address Search]![chkClearList]`
Total: `Where`
Show: (checkbox cleared)
Criteria: `False`

The `[Forms]![Address Search]![chkClearList]` expression can be read from left to right like this:

"From the Forms collection, select the Address Search form. From the Address Search form, return the value from the chkClearList check box."

Access adds Expr1: to the beginning of the Field expression. With the Show check box cleared to indicate that this is not an output column, the Expr1: is automatically removed when you save and reload the query.

The next column's expression checks to see if there is criteria entered into the cboPrefix combo box. If the combo box is empty, the expression returns True, indicating that as far as this field is concerned the record is a match.

If the combo box contains a value, the Like operator is used to compare the value in the combo box with the value in the Prefix field in the table. The Like operator is used to allow wildcard matches.

Here's what the expression looks like in pseudocode:

> *If the control is empty*
> *Return True*
> *Else*
> *If the control matches the field*
> > *Return True*
> *Else*
> > *Return False*
> *End If*
> *End If*

In this column and all the following columns like it, you set the Criteria row value to True. This indicates that your Field expression must return True for Access to treat this record as a match.

The expression you enter into the query grid isn't quite as legible as the pseudocode.

1. Enter the following expression in the Field row of Column 12 in the Address List query.

```
IIf(IsNull([Forms]![Address
Search].[cboPrefix]),True,[Person].[Prefix] Like [Forms]![Address
Search].[cboPrefix])
```

To make entering the expression much easier, press Shift-F2 to bring up the Zoom window. This gives you a multiline edit box to enter a complex or lengthy expression in, as shown in Figure 14.27.

FIGURE 14.27.

Using the Zoom window to enter a complex expression for the Field row of Column 12.

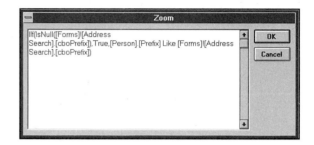

2. Set the remainder of Column 12 as follows:

   Total: Where
   Show: (checkbox cleared)
   Criteria: True

   All the remaining columns have these same three settings and differ only in the Field expression.

3. Enter Columns 13 through 27 with the following Field expressions and the Total, Show, and Criteria settings as shown in Step 2.

Column 13:

```
IIf(IsNull([Forms]![Address Search]![cboLast]),True,[Person]![LastName] Like
➡ [Forms]![Address Search]![cboLast])
```

Column 14:

```
IIf(IsNull([Forms]![Address Search]![cboFirst]),True,[Person]![FirstName] Like
➡ [Forms]![Address Search]![cboFirst])
```

Column 15:

```
IIf(IsNull([Forms]![Address Search]![cboMiddle]),True,[Person]![MiddleName]
➡ Like [Forms]![Address Search]![cboMiddle])
```

Column 16:

```
IIf(IsNull([Forms]![Address Search]![cboEMail]),True,[Person]![EMail] Like
➡ [Forms]![Address Search]![cboEMail])
```

Column 17:

```
IIf(IsNull([Forms]![Address Search]![cboTitle]),True,[Person]![Title] Like
➡ [Forms]![Address Search]![cboTitle])
```

Column 18:

```
IIf(IsNull([Forms]![Address Search]![txtNote]),True,[Person]![Note] Like
➡ [Forms]![Address Search]![txtNote])
```

Column 19:

```
IIf(IsNull([Forms]![Address Search]![cboPhone]),True,[Phone]![Phone] Like
➥ [Forms]![Address Search]![cboPhone])
```

Column 20:

```
IIf(IsNull([Forms]![Address Search]![cboStreet]),True,[Address]![Street]
➥ Like [Forms]![Address Search]![cboStreet])
```

Column 21:

```
IIf(IsNull([Forms]![Address Search]![cboCity]),True,[Address]![City] Like
➥ [Forms]![Address Search]![cboCity])
```

Column 22:

```
IIf(IsNull([Forms]![Address Search]![cboState]),True,[Address]![State] Like
➥ [Forms]![Address Search]![cboState])
```

Column 23:

```
IIf(IsNull([Forms]![Address Search]![cboPostalCode]),True,
➥[Address]![PostalCode] Like [Forms]![Address Search]![cboPostalCode])
```

Column 24:

```
IIf(IsNull([Forms]![Address Search]![cboRegion]),True,
➥[Address]![Region] Like [Forms]![Address Search]![cboRegion])
```

Column 25:

```
IIf(IsNull([Forms]![Address Search]![cboCountry]),True,
➥[Address]![Country] Like [Forms]![Address Search]![cboCountry])
```

Column 26:

```
IIf(IsNull([Forms]![Address Search]![cboPhoneType]),True,
➥[Phone]![PhoneTypeID]=[Forms]![Address Search]![cboPhoneType])
```

Column 27:

```
IIf(IsNull([Forms]![Address Search]![cboAddressType]),True,
➥[Address]![AddressTypeID]=[Forms]![Address Search]![cboAddressType])
```

That's a lot going on in a single query. In fact, you have to use the Edit|Insert Column command to make enough columns in your query grid for all the columns.

However, each expression is basically the same as Column 12 except for the last two columns. In Columns 26 and 27 you do a numeric comparison because the values returned by the combo boxes and the table fields are both numeric. In these two cases it doesn't make sense to use the Like operator.

All the expressions use the IIf function to first check for a Null in the control on the form. If the control is empty (contains a Null value), the IIf function call returns True. Otherwise the comparison is done against the criteria found in the control and the value within the corresponding field in the table. This is the logic expressed earlier in the pseudocode version.

Figure 14.28 shows the last few columns of the Address List query in the query design window.

FIGURE 14.28.

Entering the last columns into the Address List query.

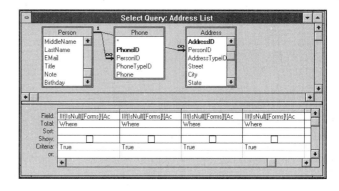

Want to see something really scary?

Maximize the query window and click the SQL View toolbar button. Access displays the SQL SELECT statement as shown in Figure 14.29.

FIGURE 14.29.

The SQL SELECT statement for the Address List query.

It's really not that bad. If you cut out the text and reformat it in Notepad, you will see a pattern emerge, and the query becomes readable. Listing 14.1 displays the SQL view of the query with reformatting.

Listing 14.1. The SQL SELECT statement behind the Address List query.

```
SELECT DISTINCTROW

Person.PersonID,
First(Person.LastName) AS LastName,
First(Person.FirstName) AS FirstName,
First(Person.MiddleName) AS MiddleName,
First(Address.Street) AS Street,
First(Address.City) AS City,
First(Address.State) AS State,
First(Phone.Phone) AS Phone,
First(Person.EMail) AS EMail,
First(Person.Note) AS [Note]

FROM (Person
LEFT JOIN Phone ON Person.PersonID = Phone.PersonID)
LEFT JOIN Address ON Person.PersonID = Address.PersonID

WHERE (
([Forms]![Address Search].[chkClearList]=False) AND

((IIf(IsNull([Forms]![Address Search].[cboPrefix]),True,
  [Person].[Prefix] Like [Forms]![Address Search].[cboPrefix]))=True) AND

((IIf(IsNull([Forms]![Address Search]![cboLast]),True,
  [Person]![LastName] Like [Forms]![Address Search]![cboLast]))=True) AND

((IIf(IsNull([Forms]![Address Search]![cboFirst]),True,
  [Person]![FirstName] Like [Forms]![Address Search]![cboFirst]))=True) AND

((IIf(IsNull([Forms]![Address Search]![cboMiddle]),True,
  [Person]![MiddleName] Like [Forms]![Address Search]![cboMiddle]))=True) AND

((IIf(IsNull([Forms]![Address Search]![cboEMail]),True,
  [Person]![EMail] Like [Forms]![Address Search]![cboEMail]))=True) AND

((IIf(IsNull([Forms]![Address Search]![cboTitle]),True,
  [Person]![Title] Like [Forms]![Address Search]![cboTitle]))=True) AND

((IIf(IsNull([Forms]![Address Search]![txtNote]),True,
  [Person]![Note] Like [Forms]![Address Search]![txtNote]))=True) AND

((IIf(IsNull([Forms]![Address Search]![cboPhone]),True,
  [Phone]![Phone] Like [Forms]![Address Search]![cboPhone]))=True) AND

((IIf(IsNull([Forms]![Address Search]![cboStreet]),True,
  [Address]![Street] Like [Forms]![Address Search]![cboStreet]))=True) AND

((IIf(IsNull([Forms]![Address Search]![cboCity]),True,
  [Address]![City] Like [Forms]![Address Search]![cboCity]))=True) AND

((IIf(IsNull([Forms]![Address Search]![cboState]),True,
  [Address]![State] Like [Forms]![Address Search]![cboState]))=True) AND

((IIf(IsNull([Forms]![Address Search]![cboPostalCode]),True,
[Address]![PostalCode] Like [Forms]![Address Search]![cboPostalCode]))
➥=True) AND
```

continues

Listing 14.1. continued

```
((IIf(IsNull([Forms]![Address Search]![cboRegion]),True,
  [Address]![Region] Like [Forms]![Address Search]![cboRegion]))=True) AND

((IIf(IsNull([Forms]![Address Search]![cboCountry]),True,
  [Address]![Country] Like [Forms]![Address Search]![cboCountry]))=True) AND

((IIf(IsNull([Forms]![Address Search]![cboPhoneType]),True,
  [Phone]![PhoneTypeID]=[Forms]![Address Search]![cboPhoneType]))=True) AND

((IIf(IsNull([Forms]![Address Search]![cboAddressType]),True,
  [Address]![AddressTypeID]=[Forms]![Address Search]![cboAddressType]))=True))

GROUP BY Person.PersonID;
```

Next, you create six additional queries—one for each sort order button above the results list on the Address Search form. Each of these queries returns the results of the
Address List query. The new queries differ from each other only in how the resulting
records are sorted.

1. Start a new query. In the New Query dialog box, click the **N**ew Query button
   instead of using the Query Wizard.
2. In the Add Table dialog box, click the **Q**ueries option in the View group box.

   Access displays a list of queries in the Table/Query list. There is currently only
   one query in the database: Address List.
3. Select the Address List query and click **A**dd. Click **C**lose to close the Add Table
   dialog box.

   In the Query design window there is a window representing the Address List
   query. It displays a star character (*) and each field returned by the query. You
   use the star to indicate that all fields should be returned, just as in an SQL
   SELECT statement.
4. Drag the star character field down from the Address List query to the first
   column in the query grid.
5. Drag the LastName field to the second column of the grid. Turn the Show
   check box off in this column and set sorting in Ascending order.
6. Drag the FirstName field to the third column of the grid. Again, turn the Show
   check box off and set the column to sort in Ascending order.

   Your query should appear as shown in Figure 14.30.

FIGURE 14.30.

The Addresses By LastName query.

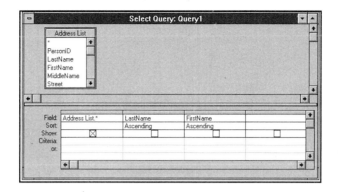

If you click the SQL View toolbar button, Access displays the SQL SELECT statement like this:

```
SELECT DISTINCTROW [Address List].*
FROM [Address List]
ORDER BY [Address List].LastName, [Address List].FirstName;
```

7. Close the query, saving it as Addresses By LastName.

8. Repeat steps 1 through 7 to create the queries listed here. Each query varies only by which fields are used to determine the sort order.

Query Name	Fields to Sort By
Addresses By FirstName	FirstName, LastName
Addresses By Street	Street
Addresses By City	City, State
Addresses By State	State, City
Addresses By Phone	Phone

The SQL SELECT statements for each of these queries are listed here:

Addresses By FirstName:

```
SELECT DISTINCTROW [Address List].*
FROM [Address List]
ORDER BY [Address List].FirstName, [Address List].LastName;
```

Addresses By Street:

```
SELECT DISTINCTROW [Address List].*
FROM [Address List]
ORDER BY [Address List].Street;
```

Addresses By City:

```
SELECT DISTINCTROW [Address List].*
FROM [Address List]
ORDER BY [Address List].City, [Address List].State;
```

Addresses By State:

```
SELECT DISTINCTROW [Address List].*
FROM [Address List]
ORDER BY [Address List].State, [Address List].City;
```

Addresses By Phone:

```
SELECT DISTINCTROW [Address List].*
FROM [Address List]
ORDER BY [Address List].Phone;
```

Coding the Address Search Form

Now it's time to enter the coding trenches once again to write the code that makes this form perform all its tricks.

Don't let the following list fool you. There actually isn't that much code in this module. Many of the subroutines are only a line or two long.

With that said, here's a map of the procedures you will be creating for the Address Search form module:

```
Declarations Section
Form_Open

SearchPending
ClearCriteria

cmdSearch_Click
MatchesFound

cmdSortLast_Click
cmdSortFirst_Click
cmdSortStreet_Click
cmdSortCity_Click
cmdSortState_Click
cmdSortPhone_Click

lstAddresses_Click

cboPrefix_AfterUpdate
cboLast_AfterUpdate
cboFirst_AfterUpdate
cboMiddle_AfterUpdate
```

```
cboEMail_AfterUpdate
cboTitle_AfterUpdate
txtNote_AfterUpdate
cboPhone_AfterUpdate
cboStreet_AfterUpdate
cboCity_AfterUpdate
cboState_AfterUpdate
cboPostalCode_AfterUpdate
cboRegion_AfterUpdate
cboCountry_AfterUpdate
cboPhoneType_AfterUpdate
cboAddressType_AfterUpdate

cboState_LostFocus

cmdAdd_Click
cmdEdit_Click
cmdDelete_Click
cmdPreview_Click
cmdPrint_Click
cmdClose_Click

GenerateRowSource
Quotes
CreateReportQuery

Form_Close
```

1. Open the Address Search form module.
2. Enter the declarations section as shown in Listing 14.2.

Listing 14.2. The Address Search form module's declarations section.

```
' Address Search form

Option Compare Database
Option Explicit

Dim mdb As Database
```

In the declarations section, you declare a database variable that gets set to the current database in the form's On Open event code.

The *Form_Open* Subroutine

As always, the Form_Open subroutine is the first subroutine that gets executed, so it handles program initialization.

Enter the Form_Open subroutine as shown in Listing 14.3.

Listing 14.3. The Form_Open **subroutine.**

```
Sub Form_Open (Cancel As Integer)

  Dim z As Integer

  On Error GoTo Form_OpenError

' Hide the system toolbars
  Application.SetOption "Built-In Toolbars Available", False
  DoEvents

' Hide the database container
  DoCmd DoMenuItem A_FormBar, 4, 3, A_Menu_Ver20

  Set mdb = DBEngine.Workspaces(0).Databases(0)

  lstAddresses.RowSource = "Addresses By LastName"
  SearchPending

  z = CenterForm(CInt(Me.Hwnd))

Form_OpenDone:
  Exit Sub

Form_OpenError:
  MsgBox Error$, 48, PROGRAM
  Cancel = True
  Resume Form_OpenDone

End Sub
```

The Form_Open subroutine starts by hiding the built-in toolbars. This gives you enough screen real estate to comfortably display the Address Search form.

A DoEvents call is required to make the toolbar disappear immediately.

```
' Hide the system toolbars
  Application.SetOption "Built-In Toolbars Available", False
  DoEvents
```

The next line calls the menu command that hides the current window, which incidentally is the database container. This is done as an additional step in cleaning up the display before your form appears.

```
' Hide the database container
  DoCmd DoMenuItem A_FormBar, 4, 3, A_Menu_Ver20
```

Next, the mdb variable is set to the current database.

```
Set mdb = DBEngine.Workspaces(0).Databases(0)
```

The lstAddresses list box has its Row Source property initialized to the query that sorts the Address List query results by LastName.

Next, a SearchPending subroutine is called to set the program in the mode where it is waiting for the user to click the Search button.

```
lstAddresses.RowSource = "Addresses By LastName"
SearchPending
```

At the end of your subroutine, the CenterForm function is called to center the form.

```
z = CenterForm(CInt(Me.Hwnd))
```

The *SearchPending* Subroutine

The SearchPending subroutine clears the results list and displays a Search Pending message.

This subroutine is called whenever an entry is made into the criteria fields, because that invalidates the currently displayed results with the displayed criteria. It is also called on program initialization in the Form_Open subroutine that you just created.

Enter the SearchPending subroutine as shown in Listing 14.4.

Listing 14.4. The SearchPending **subroutine.**

```
Sub SearchPending ()

  On Error GoTo SearchPendingError

  cmdSearch.Caption = "&Search"

  lblMatchesFound.Visible = False
  lblSearchPending.Visible = True
  chkClearList = True

' Requery combo boxes here that are dependent on other settings
' cboX.Requery

  GenerateRowSource
  lstAddresses.Requery
  lstAddresses = Null

  txtDisplayEMail = Null
  txtDisplayNote = Null
```

continues

Listing 14.4. continued

```
cmdEdit.Enabled = False
cmdDelete.Enabled = False
cmdPreview.Enabled = False
cmdPrint.Enabled = False

SearchPendingDone:
  Exit Sub

SearchPendingError:
  MsgBox Error$, 48, PROGRAM
  Resume SearchPendingDone

End Sub
```

The SearchPending subroutine first sets the caption of the cmdSearch button to Search. After a search is performed, the button caption is changed to Erase to offer an easy way to clear all entered criteria.

```
cmdSearch.Caption = "&Search"
```

Next, the Search Pending message is set to visible.

```
lblMatchesFound.Visible = False
lblSearching.Visible = False
lblSearchPending.Visible = True
```

The chkClearList check box is given a value of True. The Address List query that you created earlier returns zero records whenever this check box is set to True.

```
chkClearList = True
```

The next two lines are just notes to myself. If you were to add a combo box to the Address Search form whose contents were based on another field, this would be a good time to requery it. For example, a City combo box might be requeried to show only the city names for those cities in a selected state.

```
' Requery combo boxes here that are dependent on other settings
' cboX.Requery
```

Next, a GenerateRowSource subroutine is called. This subroutine replaces the work done by the Address List query. However, for your first version, you create an empty stub for the GenerateRowSource subroutine that does nothing.

The lstAddresses list box is requeried. With the chkClearList check box set to True, this requery has the effect of clearing the list.

The list box is assigned a Null value to erase the highlight that indicates a selected item.

```
GenerateRowSource
lstAddresses.Requery
```

```
lstAddresses = Null
```

The two text boxes below the list are also cleared because there is no currently selected item.

```
txtDisplayEMail = Null
txtDisplayNote = Null
```

At the end of the `SearchPending` subroutine, the **E**dit, **D**elete, **P**review, and **P**rint buttons are all disabled. There is no address entry selected to edit or delete, nor are any address entries in the list to print.

```
cmdEdit.Enabled = False
cmdDelete.Enabled = False
cmdPreview.Enabled = False
cmdPrint.Enabled = False
```

The *ClearCriteria* Subroutine

The `ClearCriteria` subroutine is used to erase all the values in the Address Search form's criteria fields.

Enter the `ClearCriteria` subroutine as shown in Listing 14.5.

Listing 14.5. The `ClearCriteria` subroutine.

```
Sub ClearCriteria ()

  cboPrefix = Null
  cboLast = Null
  cboFirst = Null
  cboMiddle = Null
  cboEMail = Null
  cboTitle = Null
  txtNote = Null
  cboPhone = Null
  cboStreet = Null
  cboCity = Null
  cboState = Null
  cboPostalCode = Null
  cboRegion = Null
  cboCountry = Null
  cboPhoneType = Null
  cboAddressType = Null

  SearchPending

End Sub
```

The `ClearCriteria` subroutine erases any text entered by setting each control to Null. It then calls the `SearchPending` subroutine to clear search results from the results list.

The *cmdSearch_Click* Subroutine

The cmdSearch button has two jobs. In a search pending state, the button performs a search. After a search, the button changes into an **E**rase button that can be used to quickly clear the form and start all over again.

Enter the cmdSearch_Click subroutine as shown in Listing 14.6.

Listing 14.6. The cmdSearch_Click **subroutine.**

```
Sub cmdSearch_Click ()

  On Error GoTo cmdSearch_ClickError

  If cmdSearch.Caption = "Era&se" Then
    ClearCriteria
    GoTo cmdSearch_ClickDone
  End If

  lblMatchesFound.Visible = False
  lblSearchPending.Visible = False
  lblSearching.Visible = True
  DoEvents

  chkClearList = False

  GenerateRowSource
  lstAddresses.Requery
  DoEvents

  MatchesFound
  lblSearchPending.Visible = False
  lblSearching.Visible = False
  lblMatchesFound.Visible = True

  cmdSearch.Caption = "Era&se"

  If lstAddresses.ListCount > 0 Then
    cmdPreview.Enabled = True
    cmdPrint.Enabled = True
  End If

cmdSearch_ClickDone:
  Exit Sub

cmdSearch_ClickError:
  MsgBox Error$, 48, PROGRAM
  Resume cmdSearch_ClickDone

End Sub
```

First, the subroutine checks the caption of the cmdSearch button to see what job it is supposed to be doing. If the caption is Erase, the `ClearCriteria` subroutine is called to clear the form, and the subroutine bails out.

```
If cmdSearch.Caption = "Era&se" Then
  ClearCriteria
  GoTo cmdSearch_ClickDone
End If
```

If the caption is Search, the subroutine continues.

To give some feedback to the user while the search is in progress, the `Searching...` message is displayed by setting the lblSearching label visible.

The `DoEvents` call is needed to update the form with the message before the subroutine continues.

```
lblMatchesFound.Visible = False
lblSearchPending.Visible = False
lblSearching.Visible = True
DoEvents
```

You would like to see some actual results from the Address List query this time, so the chkClearList check box is set to False.

```
chkClearList = False
```

Next, the `GenerateRowSource` subroutine is called, which again is nothing but a stub at this point because you are using the Address List query to return search results for the time being.

The actual search is kicked off when the lstAddresses list box is requeried. This activates the query assigned to the list box's Row Source property.

The `DoEvents` statement is called to pause the program until the results are returned and displayed in the lstAddresses list box.

```
GenerateRowSource
lstAddresses.Requery
DoEvents
```

Next, a `MatchesFound` subroutine is called to generate the caption for the lblMatchesFound label that indicates how many records were returned. The other labels are hidden and the lblMatchesFound label is displayed.

```
MatchesFound
lblSearchPending.Visible = False
lblSearching.Visible = False
lblMatchesFound.Visible = True
```

After a search is completed, the cmdSearch button is changed to an **E**rase button by changing its caption. As you saw at the beginning of the subroutine, changing the caption changes what the cmdSearch button does.

```
cmdSearch.Caption = "Era&se"
```

In closing, the subroutine checks the ListCount property of the lstAddresses list box to see if any matching records were found. If the list box contains any entries, the Pre**v**iew and **P**rint buttons can be enabled.

```
If lstAddresses.ListCount > 0 Then
  cmdPreview.Enabled = True
  cmdPrint.Enabled = True
End If
```

The *MatchesFound* Subroutine

The MatchesFound subroutine updates the lblMatchesFound label with the count of matching records by checking the ListCount property of the lstAddresses list box.

Enter the MatchesFound subroutine as shown in Listing 14.7.

Listing 14.7. The MatchesFound **subroutine.**

```
Sub MatchesFound ()

  lblMatchesFound.Caption = lstAddresses.ListCount & " Matches Found"

End Sub
```

The Sort Button Subroutines

The next set of subroutines changes the Row Source property on the lstAddresses list box to display the results in different orders.

The subroutines use the six different queries you created that return the results of the Address List query sorted by the LastName, FirstName, Street, City, State, or Phone fields.

Enter the subroutines shown in Listing 14.8.

Listing 14.8. The sort button On Click event subroutines.

```
Sub cmdSortLast_Click ()

  On Error GoTo cmdSortLast_ClickError
```

```
  lstAddresses.RowSource = "Addresses By LastName"
  lstAddresses.Requery

cmdSortLast_ClickDone:
  Exit Sub

cmdSortLast_ClickError:
  MsgBox Error$, 48, PROGRAM
  Resume cmdSortLast_ClickDone

End Sub

Sub cmdSortFirst_Click ()

  On Error GoTo cmdSortFirst_ClickError

  lstAddresses.RowSource = "Addresses By FirstName"
  lstAddresses.Requery

cmdSortFirst_ClickDone:
  Exit Sub

cmdSortFirst_ClickError:
  MsgBox Error$, 48, PROGRAM
  Resume cmdSortFirst_ClickDone

End Sub

Sub cmdSortStreet_Click ()

  On Error GoTo cmdSortStreet_ClickError

  lstAddresses.RowSource = "Addresses By Street"
  lstAddresses.Requery

cmdSortStreet_ClickDone:
  Exit Sub

cmdSortStreet_ClickError:
  MsgBox Error$, 48, PROGRAM
  Resume cmdSortStreet_ClickDone

End Sub

Sub cmdSortCity_Click ()

  On Error GoTo cmdSortCity_ClickError

  lstAddresses.RowSource = "Addresses By City"
  lstAddresses.Requery

cmdSortCity_ClickDone:
  Exit Sub

cmdSortCity_ClickError:
  MsgBox Error$, 48, PROGRAM
  Resume cmdSortCity_ClickDone

End Sub
```

continues

Listing 14.8. continued

```
Sub cmdSortState_Click ()

  On Error GoTo cmdSortState_ClickError

  lstAddresses.RowSource = "Addresses By State"
  lstAddresses.Requery

cmdSortState_ClickDone:
  Exit Sub

cmdSortState_ClickError:
  MsgBox Error$, 48, PROGRAM
  Resume cmdSortState_ClickDone

End Sub

Sub cmdSortPhone_Click ()

  On Error GoTo cmdSortPhone_ClickError

  lstAddresses.RowSource = "Addresses By Phone"
  lstAddresses.Requery

cmdSortPhone_ClickDone:
  Exit Sub

cmdSortPhone_ClickError:
  MsgBox Error$, 48, PROGRAM
  Resume cmdSortPhone_ClickDone

End Sub
```

The *lstAddresses_Click* Subroutine

The `lstAddresses_Click` subroutine gets called whenever an entry in the lstAddresses list box is selected.

Enter the `lstAddresses_Click` subroutine as shown in Listing 14.9.

Listing 14.9. The `lstAddresses_Click` **subroutine.**

```
Sub lstAddresses_Click ()

  On Error GoTo lstAddresses_ClickError

  If lstAddresses.ListIndex > -1 Then
    txtDisplayEMail = lstAddresses.Column(8)
    txtDisplayNote = lstAddresses.Column(9)
    cmdEdit.Enabled = True
    cmdDelete.Enabled = True
```

```
    End If

lstAddresses_ClickDone:
  Exit Sub

lstAddresses_ClickError:
  MsgBox Error$, 48, PROGRAM
  Resume lstAddresses_ClickDone

End Sub
```

The `lstAddresses_Click` subroutine verifies first that an item is selected in the list. The ListIndex property returns –1 when there is no current selection.

```
  If lstAddresses.ListIndex > -1 Then
```

With a selected item in the list, the subroutine copies two values from the hidden columns in the lstAddresses list box to the text boxes below the list box. This way the EMail name and Note for the selected address book entry are displayed.

```
    txtDisplayEMail = lstAddresses.Column(8)
    txtDisplayNote = lstAddresses.Column(9)
```

Also, the Edit and Delete buttons are enabled to act on the selected entry.

```
    cmdEdit.Enabled = True
    cmdDelete.Enabled = True
```

The After Update Event Subroutines

You have a bunch of one-liners to do now.

The After Update event occurs as focus leaves a control whose value has been changed. The Address Book program uses this event as a signal that the criteria has been changed since the last search was performed.

In each of the following subroutines, the `SearchPending` subroutine is called to clear search results and change the **Erase** button back to the **Search** button.

A subroutine is included for each control that can be used in determining which address book entries are returned.

Enter the subroutines shown in Listing 14.10.

Listing 14.10. The After Update event subroutines.

```
Sub cboPrefix_AfterUpdate ()

  SearchPending

End Sub
```

continues

Listing 14.10. continued

```
Sub cboLast_AfterUpdate ()

  SearchPending

End Sub

Sub cboFirst_AfterUpdate ()

  SearchPending

End Sub

Sub cboMiddle_AfterUpdate ()

  SearchPending

End Sub

Sub cboEMail_AfterUpdate ()

  SearchPending

End Sub

Sub cboTitle_AfterUpdate ()

  SearchPending

End Sub

Sub txtNote_AfterUpdate ()

  SearchPending

End Sub

Sub cboPhone_AfterUpdate ()

  SearchPending

End Sub

Sub cboStreet_AfterUpdate ()

  SearchPending

End Sub

Sub cboCity_AfterUpdate ()

  SearchPending

End Sub

Sub cboState_AfterUpdate ()

  SearchPending
```

```
End Sub

Sub cboPostalCode_AfterUpdate ()

  SearchPending

End Sub

Sub cboRegion_AfterUpdate ()

  SearchPending

End Sub

Sub cboCountry_AfterUpdate ()

  SearchPending

End Sub

Sub cboPhoneType_AfterUpdate ()

  SearchPending

End Sub

Sub cboAddressType_AfterUpdate ()

  SearchPending

End Sub
```

The *cboState_LostFocus* Subroutine

This next subroutine is activated on leaving the cboState combo box.

The entry in the cboState combo box should be a two-character state abbreviation. The cboState_LostFocus subroutine makes sure the entry is always displayed in uppercase characters.

Enter the cboState_LostFocus subroutine as shown in Listing 14.11.

Listing 14.11. The cboState_LostFocus **subroutine.**

```
Sub cboState_LostFocus ()

  If Not IsNull(cboState) Then
    cboState = UCase$(CStr(cboState))
  End If

End Sub
```

The Command Button On Click Event Subroutines

The next six subroutines are the code behind the On Click events for the buttons along the bottom of the form. These buttons enable you to add, edit, and delete address book entries, preview and print search results, or quit the program.

The `cmdAdd_Click` subroutine opens the Address Entry form in add mode.

Enter the `cmdAdd_Click` subroutine as shown in Listing 14.12.

Listing 14.12. The `cmdAdd_Click` **subroutine.**

```
Sub cmdAdd_Click ()

  gblnAddressEditMode = False

  On Error Resume Next
  DoCmd OpenForm "Address Entry"

End Sub
```

Before opening the Address Entry form, the `cmdAdd_Click` subroutine sets the global, `gblnAddressEditMode`, to False. This global is checked in the Address Entry form code to determine whether the form should load the entry selected in the lstAddresses list box.

In the next subroutine, `cmdEdit_Click`, the `gblnAddressEditMode` global is set to True.

Enter the `cmdEdit_Click` subroutine as shown in Listing 14.13.

Listing 14.13. The `cmdEdit_Click` **subroutine.**

```
Sub cmdEdit_Click ()

  gblnAddressEditMode = True

  On Error Resume Next
  DoCmd OpenForm "Address Entry"

End Sub
```

The `cmdDelete_Click` subroutine uses the cascading delete capability in Access to delete the Person, Phone, and Address table entries with a single record delete.

Enter the `cmdDelete_Click` subroutine as shown in Listing 14.14.

Listing 14.14. The `cmdDelete_Click` subroutine.

```
Sub cmdDelete_Click ()

  Dim tbl As Recordset
  Dim blnOpened As Integer

  Dim msg As String
  Dim z As Integer

  blnOpened = False

  On Error GoTo cmdDelete_ClickError

  msg = "Delete the address book entry for "
  msg = msg & lstAddresses.Column(2) & " "
  msg = msg & lstAddresses.Column(1) & "?"

  z = MsgBox(msg, 4 + 32 + 256, PROGRAM)
  If z <> 6 Then GoTo cmdDelete_ClickDone

  Set tbl = mdb.OpenRecordset("Person", DB_OPEN_TABLE)
  blnOpened = True

  tbl.Index = "PrimaryKey"
  tbl.Seek "=", lstAddresses
  tbl.Delete

' Requery the form
  SendKeys "{F9}"
  DoEvents
  MatchesFound

cmdDelete_ClickDone:
  On Error Resume Next
  If blnOpened Then tbl.Close
  Exit Sub

cmdDelete_ClickError:
  MsgBox Error$, 48, PROGRAM
  Resume cmdDelete_ClickDone

End Sub
```

The subroutine first constructs a message asking whether to really delete the record. The name of the person in the address book entry is constructed by reading it from the columns in the lstAddresses list box.

```
msg = "Delete the address book entry for "
msg = msg & lstAddresses.Column(2) & " "
msg = msg & lstAddresses.Column(1) & "?"
```

The constructed message is displayed with the MsgBox function. If the user doesn't respond with a Yes, the subroutine exits without deleting the record.

```
z = MsgBox(msg, 4 + 32 + 256, PROGRAM)
If z <> 6 Then GoTo cmdDelete_ClickDone
```

Next, the Person table is opened as a recordset object in table mode.

```
Set tbl = mdb.OpenRecordset("Person", DB_OPEN_TABLE)
blnOpened = True
```

The first column in the lstAddresses table contains the PersonID field value. This is the bound column, so PersonID is the value returned when directly referencing the lstAddresses list box.

The subroutine seeks to the PersonID for the selected row in the lstAddresses list box, then deletes the record.

```
tbl.Index = "PrimaryKey"
tbl.Seek "=", lstAddresses
tbl.Delete
```

When you established relationships between the Person and Phone tables and the Person and Address tables, you indicated that cascading deletes should be performed. By deleting the parent record in the Person table, the child records in the Phone and Address tables are automatically deleted.

Pretty nifty, huh?

With a record deleted, the subroutine sends the F9 character to the form so that the lstAddresses list box is requeried. DoEvents is called so the lstAddresses list box is updated before calling MatchesFound, which updates the lblMatchesFound label with the number of entries remaining in the lstAddresses list box.

```
' Requery the form
SendKeys "{F9}"
DoEvents
MatchesFound
```

The next two subroutines for the Pre**v**iew and **P**rint buttons open the Address Book report. The cmdPreview_Click subroutine hides the Address Search form before opening the report in the report preview window.

Before opening the report, each subroutine calls the CreateReportQuery subroutine. In your current version the subroutine does nothing, but in the optimized version the subroutine is responsible for generating the Row Source query for the report.

Enter the cmdPreview_Click and cmdPrint_Click subroutines as shown in Listing 14.15.

Listing 14.15. The `cmdPreview_Click` **and** `cmdPrint_Click` **subroutines.**

```
Sub cmdPreview_Click ()

  On Error Resume Next

' Hide the current window
  DoCmd DoMenuItem 0, 4, 3

  CreateReportQuery
  DoCmd OpenReport "Address Book", A_PREVIEW

End Sub

Sub cmdPrint_Click ()

  On Error Resume Next

  CreateReportQuery
  DoCmd OpenReport "Address Book", A_NORMAL

End Sub
```

The final button quits the Address Book application by closing the Address Search form.

Enter the `cmdClose_Click` subroutine as shown in Listing 14.16.

Listing 14.16. The `cmdClose_Click` **subroutine.**

```
Sub cmdClose_Click ()

  DoCmd Close

End Sub
```

Stubbing Out the SQL Generation Procedures

You will revisit the next three procedures at the end of the chapter. For now, you can declare them so they do nothing.

Enter the subroutines shown in Listing 14.17.

Listing 14.17. Temporary versions of `GenerateRowSource`, `Quotes`, **and** `CreateReportQuery`.

```
Sub GenerateRowSource ()

End Sub

Function Quotes (varMatch As Variant) As String
```

continues

Listing 14.17. continued

```
End Function

Sub CreateReportQuery ()

End Sub
```

The *Form_Close* Subroutine

To finish a working version of the Address Search form, you need to add only the
Form_Close subroutine.

Enter the Form_Close subroutine as shown in Listing 14.18.

Listing 14.18. The Form_Close **subroutine.**

```
Sub Form_Close ()

  gblnAddressEditMode = False

' Redisplay the system toolbars
  Application.SetOption "Built-In Toolbars Available", True

' Show the database container
  SendKeys "{F11}"

End Sub
```

The Form_Close subroutine first clears the gblnAddressEditMode flag. I found that if I
didn't clear the flag after a program ran, and then I opened the Address Entry form
manually, the form would get confused trying to edit a record.

Next, the subroutine turns the built-in toolbars back on and redisplays the database
container. It's always polite to return the environment back to where it was before the
program ran.

Also, while on the subject of being polite (this is strictly an opinion), never have your
program close Access when the program is finished. There is nothing more frustrating
than opening a database to check it out and then having it close your current instance
of Access.

Close the Address Search form and save your changes.

Testing the Address Search Form

In a project of this size, something is bound to go wrong. I like to turn syntax checking off while I edit code. This leaves the potential that there is a typo somewhere in the code that prohibits the program from even getting started.

To syntax-check your code, you can open all the form modules and select the **R**un|Compile Lo**a**ded Modules command. This command is there specifically to perform a test compile for folks like me who turn off syntax checking while they enter code.

If your code passed that test, the next step is to run it and see if it works. First test to see if it does the basic functions you expect it to, such as the following:

■ Add a new address book entry

■ Edit an address book entry

■ Return results when you click the **S**earch button

■ Erase results when you click the **E**rase button

■ Sort the results list by clicking sort buttons

If it passes those first tests, you are off to a good start. Enter more data into the database so you have more to work with in your tests.

Now you want to be more comprehensive and test that every piece you added to the application functions as it is expected to. This kind of testing is downright boring, but it is essential to have a really polished application when you sign off on it.

Some things you might check for are the following:

■ Does the program switch to search pending mode after changing a value in the criteria?

■ Do the search results match the criteria?

■ Does the application smoothly transition between the different forms?

■ After editing an address book entry, can you go back into it and see the changes?

■ After editing an address book entry, are the changes reflected in the results list?

■ Does the Matches Found number always match the entries in the results list?

■ Does the tab order work and make sense as you tab through controls on each form?

Keep asking questions, keep probing, and see if you can break it. Your goal in testing is to spoil your day by finding a monstrous bug or oversight that takes you hours to fix or recode. This is perhaps why programmers tend to be the worst testers.

The final test (this is somewhat tongue-in-cheek but always seems to be true) is to proudly demonstrate your program in front of someone you want to impress. If it's going to break, it will break there for sure.

Creating the Address Book Report

One test you would have expected to fail is in clicking the Preview and Print buttons, because you haven't created the report yet.

You can use the Report Wizard to create a basic report that lists the same information shown in the results list on the Address Search form. A more comprehensive report using subreports could be made to list every phone number and address for each person, but I'll let you complete that on your own.

1. Click the Reports tab on the database container.

2. Click **N**ew to create a new report.

3. In the New Report dialog box, select the Addresses By LastName query, as shown in Figure 14.31, and click the Report **W**izards button.

FIGURE 14.31.

Starting Report Wizards to create a report on the Addresses By LastName query.

4. In the Report Wizards dialog box, select the Tabular type of report and click OK, as shown in Figure 14.32.

FIGURE 14.32.

Selecting a Tabular report.

5. In the Tabular Report Wizard dialog box, shown in Figure 14.33, select the following fields to display on the report, and click **N**ext:

LastName
FirstName
MiddleName
Street
City
State
Phone

FIGURE 14.33.

Selecting which fields to display on the report.

This next step is important. You don't want the Access reporting engine sorting the fields on your report.

6. As shown in Figure 14.34, don't enter any fields to sort by in the dialog box that asks for which fields to sort by. Just click the **N**ext button.

FIGURE 14.34.

Don't select any fields to sort by.

The next dialog box asks you about the style and page orientation of your report. I chose Presentation and Portrait, as shown in Figure 14.35, but you can choose whatever you like.

7. Select a report style and page orientation. Click the **N**ext button.

FIGURE 14.35.

Choosing a report style and page orientation.

The final dialog box has several options to fill in before you click the **Finish** button.

8. Enter Address Book as the title for the report, as shown in Figure 14.36.

9. Check the box to place all fields on one page. (You will be resizing the fields anyway.)

10. Select the "Modify the report's design" option, and click the **Finish** button.

FIGURE 14.36.

At the Report Wizard finish line.

The Tabular Report Wizard generates a report like that shown in Figure 14.37.

You don't have to settle on the results that Report Wizard gave you. The first thing you can do is combine the FirstName, MiddleName, and LastName fields into one.

1. Delete the FirstName and MiddleName labels.

2. Change the text in the LastName label to Name, as shown in Figure 14.38.

3. Hold down the Shift key and click the LastName, FirstName, and MiddleName text boxes in the detail section so they are all selected.

4. Open the Properties window and set the Width and Left properties to 0.

   This hides the three text boxes from view, but they are still available to be used in expressions for other controls.

FIGURE 14.37.

Tabular Report Wizard results in report design view.

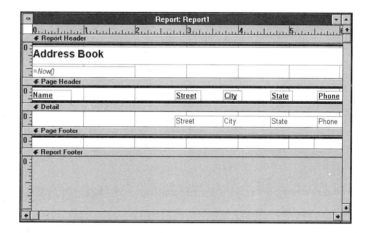

FIGURE 14.38.

The LastName, FirstName, and MiddleName text boxes have been hidden from view.

5. Click the Street text box to select it.

6. Click the detail section background, and then press Ctrl-V to paste a new copy of the Street text box.

7. Position the new text box so it is aligned with the others.

8. Enter the following formula into the text box to create a text box that displays the first, middle, and last names pieced together:

```
=[FirstName] & IIf(Not IsNull([MiddleName]),"  " & [MiddleName]) & "  "
& [LastName]
```

9. Resize and format the controls on the report so they each display the largest expected entries without losing characters.

I found that changing the font size from 10 to 8 helped ensure that fields would display completely.

FIGURE 14.39.

Arranging controls on the Address Book report.

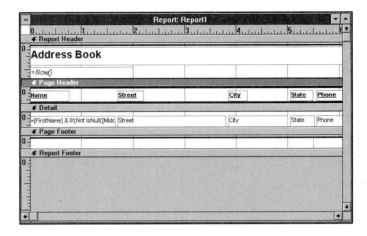

Coding the Address Book Report

1. Click the Code button on the toolbar.
2. Enter the declarations section shown in Listing 14.19.

Listing 14.19. The Address Book report module's declarations section.

```
' Address Book report

Option Compare Database
Option Explicit
```

Enter the `Report_Open` subroutine shown in Listing 14.20.

Listing 14.20. The `Report_Open` subroutine.

```
Sub Report_Open (Cancel As Integer)

  On Error GoTo Report_OpenError

  Me.RecordSource = Forms![Address Search]!lstAddresses.RowSource

Report_OpenDone:
  Exit Sub

Report_OpenError:
  If Err = 2450 Then
MsgBox "This report may only be run from the Address Search form.", 48,
➥ PROGRAM
  Else
    MsgBox Error$, 48, PROGRAM
```

```
   End If
   Cancel = True
   Resume Report_OpenDone

End Sub
```

The `Report_Open` subroutine modifies the report's Record Source property so the report runs on whatever query is currently the query used by the lstAddresses Row Source property. This way the report always prints the address book entries in the same order as they are displayed on the Address Search form.

"Aha!" you say, "That's why you didn't want the Report Wizard to define sorting in the report." That's right. Sorting in the report would override any sorting that is done beforehand in queries.

The error handling in this function traps for the error that occurs when a referenced form is not open. (I got the error number by stepping through the code, then printing Err in the Immediate window when the error occurred.)

When an error occurs, the `Cancel` argument is set to True. This tells Access not to continue with the report. I display a message to tell the user that this report can be used only from the Address Search form.

Enter the `Report_Close` subroutine as shown in Listing 14.21.

Listing 14.21. The `Report_Close` subroutine.

```
Sub Report_Close ()

  On Error GoTo Report_CloseError

' Un-hide the Address Search form.
  DoCmd OpenForm "Address Search"

Report_CloseDone:
  Exit Sub

Report_CloseError:
  MsgBox Error$, 48, PROGRAM
  Resume Report_CloseDone

End Sub
```

The `Report_Close` subroutine redisplays the Address Search form.

Close the report, saving it with the name Address Book.

Now when you click the Pre**v**iew and **P**rint buttons on the Address Book report, you can preview or print the Address Book report. A preview of the report is shown in Figure 14.40.

FIGURE 14.40.

Previewing the Address Book report.

Report: Address Book				

Address Book

01-Apr-95

Name	Street	City	State	Phone
Veruca H Barnsworth	92 S.W. Anderson Plaza	Belmont	WA	(206)
Grant K Bechman	1220 S.E. 14th Place	Hobart	WA	(206)
Teresa B Hildesheim	12030 N.E. 6th Place	Bellevue	WA	(206)
Joseph E Kovachevich	1622 164th S.E. Mill Creek	Kirkland	WA	(206)
Christine W Krogstad	17300 140th Place S.E.	Santa Clara	CA	
Cloris A Montgomery	6304 S.E. 26th Street	Seattle	WA	(206)
Mickey T Scooler	3292 1st Ave W.	Seattle	WA	(206)

Page: 1

Generating SQL in Code

The Address Book application is complete except for the promised optimization that will make it perform better with larger sets of data.

The problem with the current implementation is all those columns in the Address List query required to deal with the sixteen different fields you have allowed as criteria in a search.

Rarely, if ever, would someone use all the fields at once in entering criteria. The typical usage is to make an entry in one or two fields and then kick off the search.

This allows you to produce different sets of entries from the core set of data. In plain English, it allows you to ask different questions about your data, such as how many address book entries are from North Carolina or who are all the people in my address book whose first name starts with a W.

In your optimization you can take advantage of the real, practical usage of the application by generating an SQL SELECT statement at runtime. The generated SELECT statement's WHERE clause would have to include only criteria for which there is text entered on the form.

You can eliminate the check for a Null in each control on the form. In fact, you can even eliminate all references to the form altogether because when you build the SELECT statement you can read the values out of the controls on the form and build them right into the SELECT statement itself.

You can define a constant that allows you to programatically switch between the old search method and the new search method.

1. Open the Globals module and add the following constant to the declarations section in the Globals module, as shown in Figure 14.41:

```
Global Const GENERATE_SQL = True
```

You will modify some of the routines so they check this constant value. If GENERATE_SQL is set to True, the new method is used. If GENERATE_SQL is set to False, you go back to using the queries in the first method.

FIGURE 14.41.

A global constant is used to switch how the program works.

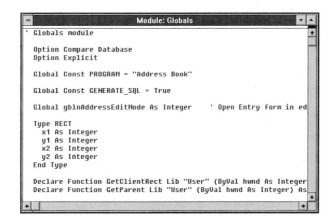

```
                        Module: Globals
' Globals module

  Option Compare Database
  Option Explicit

  Global Const PROGRAM = "Address Book"

  Global Const GENERATE_SQL = True

  Global gblnAddressEditMode As Integer      ' Open Entry form in ed

  Type RECT
    x1 As Integer
    y1 As Integer
    x2 As Integer
    y2 As Integer
  End Type

  Declare Function GetClientRect Lib "User" (ByVal hwnd As Integer
  Declare Function GetParent Lib "User" (ByVal hwnd As Integer) As
```

2. Close the Globals module.
3. Open the Address Search form module.

Each of the sort button On Click event subroutines needs to be modified.

Instead of setting the lstAddresses list box control's Row Source property to an existing query, the GenerateRowSource subroutine is called, which builds a SELECT statement and assigns that to the Row Source property.

To control what order the records are displayed in, the sort button On Click event subroutines each build a different ORDER BY clause for the SELECT statement. This is assigned to a mstrOrderBy variable declared in the form module's declaration section.

Add the mstrOrderBy string variable to the Address Search form module's declarations section as shown here:

```
Dim mstrOrderBy As String
```

Modifying the Sort Button On Click Event Subroutines

Modify the cmdSort* subroutines as shown in Listing 14.22.

Listing 14.22. The modified sort button On Click event subroutines.

```
Sub cmdSortLast_Click ()

  On Error GoTo cmdSortLast_ClickError

  If GENERATE_SQL Then
mstrOrderBy = "ORDER BY First([Person].[LastName]),
➥ First([Person].[FirstName])"
    GenerateRowSource
  Else
    lstAddresses.RowSource = "Addresses By LastName"
  End If

  lstAddresses.Requery

cmdSortLast_ClickDone:
  Exit Sub

cmdSortLast_ClickError:
  MsgBox Error$, 48, PROGRAM
  Resume cmdSortLast_ClickDone

End Sub

Sub cmdSortFirst_Click ()

  On Error GoTo cmdSortFirst_ClickError

  If GENERATE_SQL Then

    mstrOrderBy = "ORDER BY First([Person].[FirstName]),
    ➥ First([Person].[LastName])"
    GenerateRowSource
  Else
    lstAddresses.RowSource = "Addresses By FirstName"
  End If

  lstAddresses.Requery

cmdSortFirst_ClickDone:
  Exit Sub

cmdSortFirst_ClickError:
  MsgBox Error$, 48, PROGRAM
  Resume cmdSortFirst_ClickDone

End Sub

Sub cmdSortStreet_Click ()

  On Error GoTo cmdSortStreet_ClickError

  If GENERATE_SQL Then
```

```
    mstrOrderBy = "ORDER BY First([Address].[Street])"
    GenerateRowSource
  Else
    lstAddresses.RowSource = "Addresses By Street"
  End If

  lstAddresses.Requery

cmdSortStreet_ClickDone:
  Exit Sub

cmdSortStreet_ClickError:
  MsgBox Error$, 48, PROGRAM
  Resume cmdSortStreet_ClickDone

End Sub

Sub cmdSortCity_Click ()

  On Error GoTo cmdSortCity_ClickError

  If GENERATE_SQL Then

    mstrOrderBy = "ORDER BY First([Address].[City]),
    ➥ First([Address].[State])"
    GenerateRowSource
  Else
    lstAddresses.RowSource = "Addresses By City"
  End If

  lstAddresses.Requery

cmdSortCity_ClickDone:
  Exit Sub

cmdSortCity_ClickError:
  MsgBox Error$, 48, PROGRAM
  Resume cmdSortCity_ClickDone

End Sub

Sub cmdSortState_Click ()

  On Error GoTo cmdSortState_ClickError

  If GENERATE_SQL Then

    mstrOrderBy = "ORDER BY First([Address].[State]),
    ➥ First([Address].[City])"
    GenerateRowSource
  Else
    lstAddresses.RowSource = "Addresses By State"
  End If

  lstAddresses.Requery

cmdSortState_ClickDone:
  Exit Sub
```

continues

Listing 14.22. continued

```
cmdSortState_ClickError:
  MsgBox Error$, 48, PROGRAM
  Resume cmdSortState_ClickDone

End Sub

Sub cmdSortPhone_Click ()

  On Error GoTo cmdSortPhone_ClickError

  If GENERATE_SQL Then
    mstrOrderBy = "ORDER BY First([Phone].[Phone])"
    GenerateRowSource
  Else
    lstAddresses.RowSource = "Addresses By Phone"
  End If

  lstAddresses.Requery

cmdSortPhone_ClickDone:
  Exit Sub

cmdSortPhone_ClickError:
  MsgBox Error$, 48, PROGRAM
  Resume cmdSortPhone_ClickDone

End Sub
```

The *GenerateRowSource* Subroutine

Next you have the function that builds the SQL SELECT statement.

 Fill in the GenerateRowSource subroutine as shown in Listing 14.23.

Listing 14.23. The GenerateRowSource subroutine.

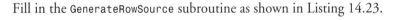

```
Sub GenerateRowSource ()

  Dim sql As String
  Dim whr As String

  Dim cr As String

  On Error GoTo GenerateRowSourceError

  If Not GENERATE_SQL Then Exit Sub

  If chkClearList = True Then
    lstAddresses.RowSource = ""
    GoTo GenerateRowSourceDone
  End If
```

```
cr = Chr$(13)

sql = "SELECT DISTINCTROW " & cr
sql = sql & "[Person].[PersonID], " & cr
sql = sql & "First([Person].[LastName]) AS LastName, " & cr
sql = sql & "First([Person].[FirstName]) AS FirstName, " & cr
sql = sql & "First([Person].[MiddleName]) AS MiddleName, " & cr
sql = sql & "First([Address].[Street]) AS Street, " & cr
sql = sql & "First([Address].[City]) AS City, " & cr
sql = sql & "First([Address].[State]) AS State, " & cr
sql = sql & "First([Phone].[Phone]) AS Phone, " & cr
sql = sql & "First([Person].[EMail]) AS EMail, " & cr
sql = sql & "First([Person].[Note]) AS [Note] " & cr

sql = sql & "FROM ([Person] " & cr
sql = sql & "LEFT JOIN [Phone] ON [Person].[PersonID] =
➥ [Phone].[PersonID]) " & cr
sql = sql & "LEFT JOIN [Address] ON [Person].[PersonID] =
➥ [Address].[PersonID] " & cr

whr = ""

If Not IsNull(cboPrefix) Then

  whr = whr & "([Person].[Prefix] Like '" & Quotes(cboPrefix) & "') AND "
  ➥ & cr
End If

If Not IsNull(cboLast) Then

  whr = whr & "([Person].[LastName] Like '" & Quotes(cboLast) & "') AND "
  ➥ & cr
End If

If Not IsNull(cboFirst) Then

  whr = whr & "([Person].[FirstName] Like '" & Quotes(cboFirst) & "') AND "
  ➥ & cr
End If

If Not IsNull(cboMiddle) Then

  whr = whr & "([Person].[MiddleName] Like '" & Quotes(cboMiddle) &
  ➥ "') AND " & cr
End If

If Not IsNull(cboEMail) Then

  whr = whr & "([Person].[EMail] Like '" & Quotes(cboEMail) & "') AND " & cr
End If

If Not IsNull(cboTitle) Then

  whr = whr & "([Person].[Title] Like '" & Quotes(cboTitle) & "') AND " & cr
End If

If Not IsNull(txtNote) Then
```

continues

Listing 14.23. continued

```
    whr = whr & "([Person].[Note] Like '" & Quotes(txtNote) & "') AND " & cr
  End If

  If Not IsNull(cboPhone) Then
    whr = whr & "([Phone].[Phone] Like '" & Quotes(cboPhone) & "') AND " & cr
  End If

  If Not IsNull(cboStreet) Then

    whr = whr & "([Address].[Street] Like '" & Quotes(cboStreet) & "') AND "
    ➥ & cr
  End If

  If Not IsNull(cboCity) Then
    whr = whr & "([Address].[City] Like '" & Quotes(cboCity) & "') AND " & cr
  End If

  If Not IsNull(cboState) Then

    whr = whr & "([Address].[State] Like '" & Quotes(cboState) & "') AND "
    ➥ & cr
  End If

  If Not IsNull(cboPostalCode) Then

    whr = whr & "([Address].[PostalCode] Like '" & Quotes(cboPostalCode)
    ➥ & "') AND " & cr
  End If

  If Not IsNull(cboRegion) Then

    whr = whr & "([Address].[Region] Like '" & Quotes(cboRegion) & "') AND "
    ➥ & cr
  End If

  If Not IsNull(cboCountry) Then

    whr = whr & "([Address].[Country] Like '" & Quotes(cboCountry)
    ➥ & "') AND " & cr
  End If

  If Not IsNull(cboPhoneType) Then

    whr = whr & "([Phone].[PhoneTypeID] = " & Quotes(cboPhoneType) &
    ➥ ") AND " & cr
  End If

  If Not IsNull(cboAddressType) Then

    whr = whr & "([Address].[AddressTypeID] = " & Quotes(cboAddressType) &
    ➥ ") AND " & cr
  End If

  If Len(whr) > 0 Then
    whr = Left$(whr, Len(whr) - 5)
    sql = sql & "WHERE (" & cr & whr & ") " & cr
```

```
   End If

   sql - sql & "GROUP BY [Person].[PersonID] "
' Default to sorting by last name
   If Len(mstrOrderBy) = 0 Then

     mstrOrderBy = "ORDER BY First([Person].[FirstName]),
     ➥ First([Person].[LastName])"
   End If

   sql = sql & cr & mstrOrderBy

   lstAddresses.RowSource = sql

' To see that SQL is generated during development, print it to
' the Immediate window
   'Debug.Print sql

GenerateRowSourceDone:
   Exit Sub

GenerateRowSourceError:
   MsgBox Error$, 48, PROGRAM
   Resume GenerateRowSourceDone

End Sub
```

The subroutine first checks the GENERATE_SQL constant and exits early if it is set so that the queries method is being used.

```
   If Not GENERATE_SQL Then Exit Sub
```

Next, the way you deal with clearing the lstAddresses list box when the chkClearList check box is set is by clearing out the Row Source property completely.

```
   If chkClearList = True Then
     lstAddresses.RowSource = ""
     GoTo GenerateRowSourceDone
   End If
```

If you are still around, an SQL statement needs to be generated to perform a search. You use carriage returns in your generated statement for two reasons. The technical reason is that Access has trouble with lines that are too long. The reason that has more significance to you is that by adding carriage returns, you can build a statement that is readable.

```
   cr = Chr$(13)
```

Next, you start piecing together a long SELECT statement.

Let me tell you how this kind of code is written. What folks generally do is start from a query that was created in Access. They change the SQL View of the query and cut the SELECT statement out and paste it into their module.

Then they use the pasted-in statement as a basis to write code like the following, which builds the full statement in a string variable. I like to use sql as the name of my string variable because it is short and clear as to what it is being used for.

In this case, I started out with the Address List query, reformatted earlier in this chapter in Notepad.

Much of the statement is generated without modification. First the selection of the fields is done, as shown in Listing 14.24.

Listing 14.24. Generating which fields are selected.

```
sql = "SELECT DISTINCTROW " & cr
sql = sql & "[Person].[PersonID], " & cr
sql = sql & "First([Person].[LastName]) AS LastName, " & cr
sql = sql & "First([Person].[FirstName]) AS FirstName, " & cr
sql = sql & "First([Person].[MiddleName]) AS MiddleName, " & cr
sql = sql & "First([Address].[Street]) AS Street, " & cr
sql = sql & "First([Address].[City]) AS City, " & cr
sql = sql & "First([Address].[State]) AS State, " & cr
sql = sql & "First([Phone].[Phone]) AS Phone, " & cr
sql = sql & "First([Person].[EMail]) AS EMail, " & cr
sql = sql & "First([Person].[Note]) AS [Note] " & cr
```

Next are the FROM clause and JOINed tables.

```
sql = sql & "FROM ([Person] " & cr

sql = sql & "LEFT JOIN [Phone] ON [Person].[PersonID] = [Phone].[PersonID])
➥ " & cr
sql = sql & "LEFT JOIN [Address] ON [Person].[PersonID] =
➥ [Address].[PersonID] " & cr
```

Next, the WHERE clause is built first in a separate string. You start with an empty WHERE clause.

```
whr = ""
```

Then a series of statement blocks check to see if a control on the Address Search form has a value in it. If the control does, the user has entered criteria that should be used to match records against for this particular field.

```
If Not IsNull(cboPrefix) Then

  whr = whr & "([Person].[Prefix] Like '" & Quotes(cboPrefix) & "') AND "
  ➥ & cr
End If
```

The preceding code generates an expression that compares the field value to the value found in the control. This expression is appended to the whr variable, which becomes a series of expressions separated by AND operators.

For example, if Mrs. is selected in the cboPrefix combo box, the following expression is added to the WHERE clause:

```
([Person].[Prefix] Like 'Mrs.') AND
```

After all the controls are checked, the subroutine checks to see if any criteria was entered. If so, the WHERE clause is added to the SELECT statement.

```
If Len(whr) > 0 Then
  whr = Left$(whr, Len(whr) - 5)
  sql = sql & "WHERE (" & cr & whr & ") " & cr
End If
```

Because this is a summary query, the GROUP BY clause is added.

```
sql = sql & "GROUP BY [Person].[PersonID] "
```

Next, the subroutine checks to see if the mstrOrderBy variable has been set. If not, it is defaulted so that sorting occurs by LastName and FirstName.

```
' Default to sorting by last name
  If Len(mstrOrderBy) = 0 Then
mstrOrderBy = "ORDER BY First([Person].[FirstName]),
➥ First([Person].[LastName])"
  End If
```

To complete the SELECT statement, the ORDER BY clause is appended. Finally, the lstAddresses list box control's Row Source property is assigned the generated SELECT statement.

```
sql = sql & cr & mstrOrderBy

lstAddresses.RowSource = sql
```

At the end of the module is a commented-out Debug.Print statement used to print the generated statement to the debug window. During development of a subroutine like this you might want to use this technique to see if your generated statement is being generated as expected.

You can even cut the printed statement out from the Immediate window (as shown in Figure 14.42) and paste it into a new query in Access to see if the generated statement is syntactically correct and produces the desired results.

```
' To see that SQL is generated during development, print it to
' the Immediate window
  'Debug.Print sql
```

FIGURE 14.42.

*Generated SQL printed
to the Immediate
window.*

```
Immediate Window [Form.Address Search]
SELECT DISTINCTROW
[Person].[PersonID],
First([Person].[LastName]) AS LastName,
First([Person].[FirstName]) AS FirstName,
First([Person].[MiddleName]) AS MiddleName,
First([Address].[Street]) AS Street,
First([Address].[City]) AS City,
First([Address].[State]) AS State,
First([Phone].[Phone]) AS Phone,
First([Person].[EMail]) AS EMail,
First([Person].[Note]) AS [Note]
FROM ([Person]
LEFT JOIN [Phone] ON [Person].[PersonID] = [Phone].[PersonID])
LEFT JOIN [Address] ON [Person].[PersonID] = [Address].[PersonID]
WHERE (
([Person].[FirstName] Like 'C*') AND
([Address].[State] Like 'WA') )
GROUP BY [Person].[PersonID]
ORDER BY First([Person].[FirstName]), First([Person].[LastName])
```

The *Quotes* Subroutine

You have a couple more changes to finish up your modification.

The Quotes function deals with a sticky situation. You are building a SELECT statement
by mixing text generated by the program and text entered by the user. There is the
potential that the user could enter something that would make your SELECT statement
syntactically invalid and an error would occur.

The Quotes function turns single quotes entered by the user into a series of two single
quotes. This tells Access that the user's single quote shouldn't terminate the string expression that your program is building.

Fill in the Quotes function as shown in Listing 14.25.

Listing 14.25. The Quotes function.

```
Function Quotes (varMatch As Variant) As String

' Change a single quote character to two consecutive single
' quote characters.

  Dim strResult As String
  Dim intOffset As Integer

  strResult = CNStr(varMatch)

  intOffset = 1
  intOffset = InStr(intOffset, strResult, "'")
```

```
  If intOffset Then
    Do While intOffset

      strResult = Left$(strResult, intOffset) & Right$(strResult,
    ➥ Len(strResult) - intOffset + 1)

      intOffset = InStr(intOffset + 2, strResult, "'")
    Loop
  End If

  Quotes = strResult

End Function
```

The *CreateReportQuery* Subroutine

The CreateReportQuery subroutine builds an actual query object out of the value in the Row Source property in the lstAddresses list box (your generated SELECT statement).

This is required because a report's RecordSource must be set to a table or query and not an SQL SELECT statement.

Enter the CreateReportQuery subroutine as shown in Listing 14.26.

Listing 14.26. The CreateReportQuery subroutine.

```
Sub CreateReportQuery ()

  Dim qdf As QueryDef

  If Not GENERATE_SQL Then GoTo CreateReportQueryDone

  On Error Resume Next
  mdb.DeleteQueryDef "Address Book Report"

  On Error GoTo CreateReportQueryError

  Set qdf = mdb.CreateQueryDef("Address Book Report", lstAddresses.RowSource)
  qdf.Close

CreateReportQueryDone:
  Exit Sub

CreateReportQueryError:
  MsgBox Error$, 48, PROGRAM
  Resume CreateReportQueryDone

End Sub
```

Close the Address Search form and save your changes.

Modifying the *Report_Close* Subroutine

Finally, you need to modify the Report_Close subroutine in the Address Book report. When you are running with the generated SQL, the report runs against the Address Book Report query.

1. Open the Address Book report module.
2. Modify the Report_Open subroutine as shown in Listing 14.27.
3. Close the report and save your changes.

Listing 14.27. The Report_Open subroutine.

```
Sub Report_Open (Cancel As Integer)

  On Error GoTo Report_OpenError

  If GENERATE_SQL Then
    Me.RecordSource = "Address Book Report"
  Else
    Me.RecordSource = Forms![Address Search]!lstAddresses.RowSource
  End If

Report_OpenDone:
  Exit Sub

Report_OpenError:
  If Err = 2450 Then

    MsgBox "This report may only be run from the Address Search form.", 48, PROGRAM
  Else
    MsgBox Error$, 48, PROGRAM
  End If
  Cancel = True
  Resume Report_OpenDone

End Sub
```

The Address Book application is a great starting point and base technology from which to develop larger applications.

Not only could you expand the Address Book into a "roll-your-own" Personal Information Manager, but you could use the Query By Form technique in many different applications. It would be especially good for cataloging applications where you want to allow the user some flexibility in how they select records from the database.

Summary

In this chapter you completed your monolithic Address Book project. But hey, this wasn't just any old Address Book, was it?

Here is a short list for those of you keeping score.

- ■ Took the Address Entry form for a test drive
- ■ Created a Query By Form user interface
- ■ Created a query to support a Query By Form interface
- ■ Used cascading deletes
- ■ Used a global constant to run different versions of a program
- ■ Built a report that runs in sync with a Query By Form
- ■ Wrote code that generated SQL SELECT statements

In the next chapter you start a project that spans four chapters to build a full-scale Access Wizard. You will learn all the techniques you need to create a truly marketable add-in product for Microsoft Access.

CHAPTER 15

Access: Picture Builder+

Access 2.0 introduced a new type of add-in extension called a *builder*. A builder is a pop-up form that helps you create a property setting or component of a larger object. Although you might use a wizard to produce an entire table, you would use a builder to complete a subtask such as adding a field to an existing table.

The builders included in Access 2.0 are

- Code Builder
- Color Builder
- Expression Builder
- Field Builder
- Macro Builder
- Menu Builder
- OBDC Connection String Builder
- Picture Builder
- Query Builder

One really neat thing about builders, wizards, and menu add-ins is the fact that they are created in Access Basic. This means that you can create your own extensions to Access for your own use or even as a marketable product.

Microsoft Access developers have been careful to put all the necessary hooks into Access to allow this. Unfortunately, the documentation for how to build your own extensions to Access is a bit skimpy. Face it, of the million or two Access users out there, how many are going to create their own builder, wizard, or menu add-in?

Well, if you are the type of person that would, the clues are there if you look deep enough. The place to start is in the actual source code for the add-ins that come with Access. Yep, you can look at them; I'll show you how. If you are fortunate enough to own the Access Developer Toolkit (ADT), you can even look at commented versions of the programs. (The library code is stripped of comments in the retail version to save disk space and memory.)

Improving Picture Builder

In this chapter, I explore how a builder is created by making one. One of the builders I particularly like in Access 2.0 is the Picture Builder, as shown in Figure 15.1. It functions as sort of a bitmap catalog when you need a picture for a command button. It offers you a selection of more than 200 pictures!

FIGURE 15.1.

The Access 2.0 Picture Builder add-in.

However, the weakness I saw in the Access 2.0 Picture Builder is that you can look at only one picture at a time. With such a large catalog of artwork, it would take much too long to browse the whole set and find just the one picture you need. This situation would only get worse as you extend the catalog by adding your own pictures to the library.

My solution to the problem was to create a slightly enhanced version of Picture Builder, so I call it "Picture Builder+." (I first wrote about my Picture Builder+ program in the December/January, 1995, premier issue of *Access/Visual Basic Advisor* from Advisor Publications, Inc. The program has since been enhanced for this book.)

Picture Builder+, shown in Figure 15.2, enables you to categorize pictures in sets of as many as 12 pictures. Each of these sets (or picture groups) is given a title. You can use the Picture Builder+ interface to quickly flip through the pictures a group at a time rather than individually.

FIGURE 15.2.

The Picture Builder+ add-in.

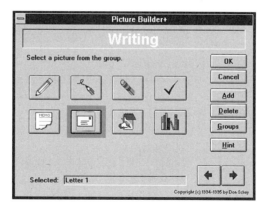

You can customize Picture Builder+ by adding your own picture groups and pictures. To add a picture, click the Add button. Use the Select Picture dialog box to select a .BMP or .ICO file, as shown in Figure 15.3.

FIGURE 15.3.

Selecting a new picture.

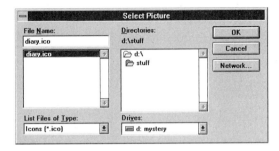

After you select the picture, a dialog box pops up so that you can enter a picture title. Then the picture and title are displayed as part of your own picture gallery, as shown in Figure 15.4.

FIGURE 15.4.

The Diary icon from Chapter 10 is added to the available pictures in Picture Builder+.

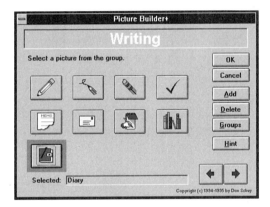

Adding and deleting pictures and picture groups can be done in Picture Builder+ by pressing the Customize button in Add-in Manager, or while you actually are using Picture Builder to select a picture for a command button. I didn't want to make folks *have* to load the Add-in Manager in order to add pictures as the original Picture Builder does.

Browsing Through the Access Library Databases

Before you can peek under the hood and see how wizards, builders, and menu add-ins work, you need to disable the automatic loading of the database libraries that occurs when Access first starts.

1. Double-click the Notepad icon in Program Manager to start Notepad.
2. Select the **File|O**pen command to open a file.

   Notepad's default is to look for a file in the directory in which you installed Windows.

3. Enter MSACC20.INI as the filename to open. This is the Access 2.0 initialization file.

4. Find the section in the .INI file that looks like Listing 15.1.

5. Modify the entries in the [Libraries] section by placing a semicolon in front of each line, as shown in Listing 15.2. Save the file with the modifications.

Listing 15.1. The [Libraries] **section of MSACC20.INI.**

```
[Libraries]
wzlib.mda=rw
wzTable.mda=rw
wzQuery.mda=rw
wzfrmrpt.mda=rw
wzbldr.mda=rw
```

Listing 15.2. Disabling the provided library databases in MSACC20.INI.

```
[Libraries]
;wzlib.mda=rw
;wzTable.mda=rw
;wzQuery.mda=rw
;wzfrmrpt.mda=rw
;wzbldr.mda=rw
```

You've just disabled all the neat wizards, builders, and menu add-ins that come with Microsoft Access. You'll want to reenable them eventually by removing the semicolons you just added to the file.

The changes you made don't take effect until you run Access the next time. If you currently have Access running, the database libraries are already loaded. Restart Access to load the libraries.

1. Close Access if you currently have it running.

2. Double-click the Access icon to start it up again.

A positive effect you will notice right away is that Access loads much faster without the libraries than it does with them. Next, open the WZBLDR.MDA file and view its contents.

1. Select the File|Open command.

   If the Open Database dialog box doesn't default to the directory you installed Access in, switch over to it.

2. Enter *.MDA in the File Name prompt and press Enter.

The Open Database dialog box displays the files with an MDA extension. In the list you see at least the following files, and possibly others if you have the Access Developer's Toolkit (ADT) or any third-party database libraries.

SYSTEM.MDA—User preferences and security information

UTILITY.MDA—Miscellaneous objects, constants, and functions

WZBLDR.MDA—Wizards and builders

WZFRMRPT.MDA—Form and report wizards

WZLIB.MDA—Library procedures and menu add-ins

WZQUERY.MDA—Query wizards

WZTABLE.MDA—Table wizards

3. Open the WZBLDR.MDA database library, as shown in Figure 15.5.

NOTE

Wait!

Before you open a library database, you may want to make a backup copy of it just in case you accidentally change the database while browsing through it. You could always reinstall Access if you modified your only copy of a library database, but it's easier to make a backup copy right now with File Manager.

FIGURE 15.5.

Opening an MDA database library.

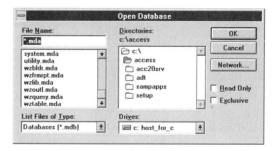

In the database container you see a variety of tables, queries, forms, and modules that are the components of the Button Wizard, Color Picker, Combo Box Wizard, Input Mask Wizard, List Box Wizard, Menu Builder, Option Group Wizard, Picture Builder, and SQL Pass Through Builder. Yep, it's all there!

Opening the database was easy. Figuring out what all that stuff does is another issue altogether. The object of the game here is dig, dig, dig. Learn from the masters. You

might not be able to understand it all, but you most definitely will pick up a few coding tricks by digging through the code you find in the modules and form modules within this database library. After all, it's written by Microsoft folks who really know their stuff.

Among the forms in this database, I found the form for the original Picture Builder and opened it in design mode as shown in Figure 15.6.

FIGURE 15.6.

Opening pb_FrmPictureBuilder in design mode.

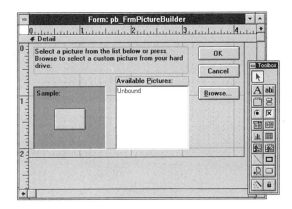

Most of the code in the database libraries resides behind the forms and not in the modules. There are a lot of tricks to be found here. For example, behind the pb_FrmPictureBuilder form, I found a function called LoadBitmapFile, as shown in Figure 15.7.

(The code displayed in the figure is from the commented source code version of WZBLDR.MDA that is included in the Access Developer's Toolkit. The retail version is the same, it just doesn't include the comments.)

FIGURE 15.7.

Snooping behind the pb_FrmPictureBuilder form.

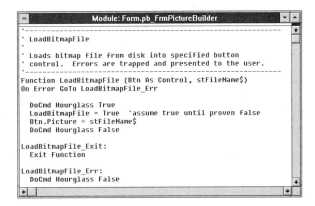

Well, that's pretty neat. As the code in the `LoadBitmapFile` function shows, all it takes to load a picture is to set with a filename a command button control's Picture property.

In the same form module you will find a `BrowseFiles_Click` subroutine demonstrating how to call the File Open common dialog box. You'll take advantage of that trick when you code Picture Builder+.

After you are done browsing, close the database. Be careful not to save any unintended changes if you accidentally made any.

Spend some time browsing the other libraries: WZFRMRPT.MDA, WZLIB.MDA, WZQUERY.MDA, and WZTABLE.MDA. It's a lot to absorb in one sitting, but you might want to get a little familiar with the contents of each library so that you know which are worthwhile to come back and explore later.

Next, undo the changes you made to the MSACC20.INI file, so your wizards will load in Access once again.

1. Reopen the MSACC20.INI file.
2. Remove the added semicolons to reenable the database libraries and then save the file.
3. Close and restart Access, and you are back to normal again.

The Picture Builder+ Database

Let's dare to walk in the footsteps of the Access gods who created all that neat stuff by proceeding to create a database library.

The Picture Builder+ database, PICBLDR.MDA, will consist of the following objects listed in the order that you will create them:

> Pic table—Picture titles and bitmaps
>
> Pic Group table—Picture group names and IDs
>
> Hint table—Hint text for two forms
>
> Option table—One-time-use startup option
>
> Picture Builder+ form—View and select pictures by group
>
> Picture Groups form—Add and delete picture groups
>
> Hint form—Pop-up to display hint text
>
> Picture Builder+ module—Entry point functions
>
> USysAddIns system table—Add-in Manager installation

You can start the project by creating the tables.

Creating the Pic Table

1. Create a new database, PICBLDR.MDB.

    Later when it's all ready, you can rename it PICBLDR.MDA.

2. Create a new table with the following fields:

Field Name	Data Type
PictureID	Counter
GroupID	Number
Position	Number
Name	Text
Picture	OLE Object

3. Set the properties for each field as follows:

Field Name	PictureID
Data Type:	Counter
Field Name:	GroupID
Data Type:	Number
Field Size:	Long Integer
Field Name:	Position
Data Type:	Number
Field Size:	Integer
Field Name:	Name
Data Type:	Text
Field Size:	50
Field Name:	Picture
Data Type:	OLE Object

4. Set the PictureID field as the primary key.

5. Click the Indexes button on the toolbar. In the Indexes window, create a second index titled Group. This index is made up of two fields, GroupID and Position, both sorted in ascending order. See Figure 15.8.

6. Save the table as Pic.

Adding Records to the Pic Table

As the starting point for your Picture Builder+ picture gallery, you can set up the table so that it is populated with some of the pictures that come with Access.

FIGURE 15.8.

*Creating the Group
index in the Pic table.*

Indexes: Pic		
Index Name	Field Name	Sort Order
PrimaryKey	PictureID	Ascending
Group	GroupID	Ascending
	Position	Ascending

Index Properties	
Primary	No
Unique	No
Ignore Nulls	No

The name for this index. Each index can use up to 10 fields.

You'll import the pictures that are stored in the bw_TblPictures table in WZLIB.MDA, a total of 45 pictures. (See the end of the chapter for a clue on how to find more pictures.)

To avoid infringing on Microsoft's copyright to their material, I've written a subroutine, ReadPictures, that extracts some of the pictures from WZLIB.MDA and places them into the Pic table so that Picture Builder+ can use them.

I can't distribute these pictures with the companion CD included in this book, but you certainly have the right to use the pictures as long as you have a licensed copy of Microsoft Access. The ReadPictures subroutine will be executed once, the first time you run Picture Builder+.

> **NOTE**
>
> Please be sure that when you use Picture Builder+, you are in compliance with copyright laws for any images you place in the Picture Builder+ database. Don't make a copy of your version of PICBLDR.MDA for others to use if it has images that you have purchased specifically for your own use.

Table 15.1 lists the records in the Pic table when it is prepared to import pictures from WZLIB.MDA.

Table 15.1. Pic table records.

PictureID	GroupID	Position	Name
1	1	2	Go to Previous
2	1	3	Go to Next
3	1	1	Go to First
4	1	4	Go to Last
5	3	11	Stop Sign

PictureID	GroupID	Position	Name
6	4	1	Pencil (yellow)
7	4	3	Eraser
8	3	1	Watch
9	3	2	Clock
10	3	3	Phone
11	5	9	Left Arrow (3D)
12	5	1	Pointing Left
13	5	5	Left Arrow (Black)
14	5	10	Right Arrow (3D)
15	5	4	Pointing Down
16	5	6	Right Arrow (Black)
17	5	12	Down Arrow (3D)
18	5	2	Pointing Right
19	5	8	Down Arrow (Black)
20	1	6	Binoculars
21	4	4	Check Mark
22	5	11	Up Arrow (3D)
23	5	3	Pointing Up
24	5	7	Up Arrow (Black)
25	4	2	Pencil (editing)
26	2	4	MS Access Table
27	2	6	MS Access Report
28	2	5	MS Access Query
29	3	5	Floppy (5.25")
30	3	6	Floppy (3.5")
31	3	9	Trash Can
32	1	5	Go to New
33	3	10	Toilet
34	4	7	Notepad (Red)
35	4	5	Memo
36	4	8	Books

continues

Table 15.1. continued

PictureID	GroupID	Position	Name
37	4	6	Letter
38	3	8	Airplane
39	3	7	Wrench
40	3	4	Handshake
41	2	3	MS Access
42	2	7	MS Access Module
43	2	2	MS Excel Document
44	2	1	MS Word Document
45	2	8	Notepad Icon

If you are following along carefully and actually re-creating this project step by step, entering all these records will be a typing exercise you might want to avoid. Instead, you can use the File|Import command to import the Pic table from the PICBLDR.MDA file included on the book's companion CD.

Alternatively, if you decide you don't want the pictures included with Access, leave the table blank. This next step is optional.

Enter (or import) into the Pic table the records listed in Table 15.1.

FIGURE 15.9.

The Pic table is ready to be loaded with pictures from WZLIB.MDA.

PictureID	GroupID	Position	Name	Picture
1	1	2	Go To Previous	
2	1	3	Go To Next	
3	1	1	Go To First	
4	1	4	Go To Last	
5	5	11	Stop Sign	
6	6	1	Pencil (yellow)	
7	6	3	Eraser	
8	5	1	Watch	
9	5	2	Clock	
10	5	3	Phone	
11	7	9	Left Arrow (3D)	
12	7	1	Pointing Left	
13	7	5	Left Arrow (Black)	
14	7	10	Right Arrow (3D)	
15	7	4	Pointing Down	
16	7	6	Right Arrow (Black)	
17	7	12	Down Arrow (3D)	
18	7	2	Pointing Right	
19	7	8	Down Arrow (Black)	
20	1	6	Binoculars	
21	6	4	Check Mark	
22	7	11	Up Arrow (3D)	

Record: 1   of 45

Creating the Pic Group Table

The Pic Group table stores the title and ID number for each picture group.

1. Create the Pic Group table with the following fields:

Field Name	Data Type
GroupID	Counter
Name	Text
SortOrder	Number

2. Set the properties for each field in the Pic Group table as follows:

Field Name	GroupID
Data Type:	Counter
Field Name:	Name
Data Type:	Text
Field Size:	50
Required:	Yes
Allow Zero Length:	No
Field Name:	SortOrder
Data Type:	Number
Field Size:	Integer
Required:	Yes
Indexed:	Yes (No Duplicates)

3. Set the GroupID field as the primary key.

Adding Records to the Pic Group Table

Picture Builder+ hasn't been bulletproofed to the point that it will work correctly if the database doesn't contain at least one picture group.

You need to enter at least one record into the Pic Group table. If you have entered the Table 15.1 records, you need to enter into the Pic Group table all the records in Table 15.2. See Figure 15.10.

Table 15.2. Pic Group table records.

GroupID	Name	Sort Order
1	Record Navigation	1
2	Microsoft Applications	2
3	Miscellaneous	3
4	Writing	4
5	Arrows	5

The Sort Order column of the Pic Group table should be numbered from 1 to the number of groups in the table. The values in this column will be swapped around as the picture groups are reordered.

The GroupID column is a counter field, so these numbers are entered automatically. There should be a matching number in this table for any GroupID value in the Pic table.

1. Enter into the Pic Group table the records shown in Table 15.2.
2. Save the table, naming it `Pic Group`.

FIGURE 15.10.

Entering records in the Pic Group table.

Creating the Hint Table

The next table is used to store some quick on-screen instructions that will be displayed in a Hint dialog box when the user presses the Hint button.

1. Create a third table with the following fields:

Field Name	Data Type
HintID	Counter
Hint	Memo

2. Set the properties for the two fields in the Hint table.

Field Name:	HintID
Data Type:	Counter

Field Name:	Hint
Data Type:	Memo
Required:	Yes
Allow Zero Length:	No

3. Enter the following text in the Hint memo field of the first record in the table. Press Ctrl-Enter twice to separate the sentences. See Figure 15.11.

```
Use the left- and right-arrow buttons to view different picture groups.
Click the Add button to add a new picture to the current picture group.
Click the Delete button to remove the currently selected picture.
Click the Groups button to add and delete picture groups.
```

4. Enter the following text as the Hint memo field of the second record in the Hint table:

```
To add a picture group,
Select the group after which you want your new group to appear.
Click the Add button.

To change a picture group name,
Select the group and click the Edit button.

To delete a picture group,
Select the group and click the Delete button.
Use the arrow keys to reorder the picture groups.
```

5. Save the table with the name Hint.

FIGURE 15.11.

Entering hint text in the Hint table.

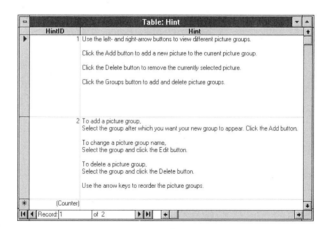

Creating the Option Table

The Option table works kind of like a Windows .INI file. The idea is to add a field to the table for each option that the program supports. The Option table never has more than one record.

An approach that I usually like better is to create a table with two fields: Name and Value. The Name field contains the name of the option, and the Value field contains the setting. With two fields, you can add settings without having to redesign the table, but you need to write a couple of subroutines for getting and setting option settings.

In Picture Builder+, I only needed a single option, so I chose the simpler approach.

1. Create the Option table with a single field:

Field Name	Data Type
ReadPictures	Yes/No

2. Open the Option table in datasheet mode.

3. Enter a Yes or No in the first record of the Option table.

   Enter a Yes in the ReadPictures field if you have prepared the Pic table to receive the pictures in WZLIB.MDA. Enter a No in the ReadPictures field if you left the table empty.

   Your program checks this option and if the setting is Yes, loads the pictures. It then sets the option to No because the pictures will never need to be loaded again.

4. Save the table, naming it Option in the Save As dialog box.

Setting Table Relationships

You have it pretty easy as far as establishing relationships between tables in the Picture Builder+ database. In this project establishing those relationships is not an optional step. You'll use the cascading delete feature to ensure that if a picture group is deleted, all its associated pictures are deleted, also.

1. Select the **Edit**|**R**elationships command.

2. In the Add Table dialog box, select and add the Pic Group and Pic tables. Close the Add Table dialog box.

3. In the Relationships window, create a join by dragging the GroupID field from the Pic Group table to the GroupID field in the Pic table.

4. In the Relationships dialog box, click the **E**nforce Referential Integrity option and the Cascade **D**elete Related Records option. Click the **C**reate button to create the join.

   The join appears between the two tables in the Relationships window as shown in Figure 15.12.

5. Close the Relationships window.

That takes care of the tables. Before you dig into the code you can create the three forms for this project.

FIGURE 15.12.

*Establishing a parent/
child relationship
between the Pic Group
and Pic tables.*

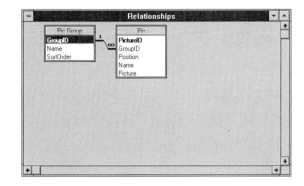

Creating the Picture Builder+ Form

Most of the action in Picture Builder+ happens in the Picture Builder+ form that you'll
create right now. With this form users can browse through all the pictures and select
the ones they want.

In this and the additional forms you create in this chapter, the font for label controls
will be set to MS Sans Serif, size 8, and Bold. Text boxes for entering or displaying values will be set to MS Sans Serif, size 8 with a Regular font weight (unless specified differently). The Back Color property of each label is set to the same color as the form,
12632256 (Light Gray).

1. Open a new form and set the following properties:

Object: **Picture Builder+ Form**

Property	Value
Caption:	Picture Builder+
Default View:	Single Form
Shortcut Menu:	No
Scroll Bars:	Neither
Record Selectors:	No
Navigation Buttons:	No
Auto Center:	Yes
Pop Up:	Yes
Modal:	Yes
Border Style:	Dialog box
Min Button:	No
Max Button:	No
Width:	4.641 in

2. Set the Height and Back Color properties for the detail section on the form.

Object: **Detail0 Section**

Property	Value
Height:	3.2708 in
Back Color:	12632256 (Light Gray)

3. Create a large text box across the top of the form to display the picture group name (see Figure 15.13).

Object: **txtName Textbox**

Property	Value
Name:	txtName
Enabled:	No
Locked:	Yes
Tab Stop:	No
Left:	0.1507 in
Top:	0.1042 in
Width:	4.3396 in
Height:	0.3542 in
Back Color:	12632256 (Light Gray)
Special Effect:	Sunken
Border Style:	Clear
Fore Color:	16777215 (White)
Font Name:	Arial
Font Size:	20
Font Weight:	Bold
Text Align:	Center

FIGURE 15.13.

Adding a text box to display the picture group name.

Text Box: txtName		
All Properties		
Back Color	12632256	
Special Effect	Sunken	
Border Style	Clear	
Border Color	0	
Border Width	Hairline	
Border Line Style	Solid	
Fore Color	16777215	
Font Name	Arial	
Font Size	20	
Font Weight	Bold	
Font Italic	No	
Font Underline	No	
Text Align	Center	
Help Context Id	0	

4. Create a label to display some quick instructions.

Object: **lblHint Label**

Property	Value
Name:	lblHint
Caption:	Select a picture from the group.
Left:	0.2035 in
Top:	0.5625 in
Width:	3.1875 in
Height:	0.2076 in

The Picture Builder+ form contains 12 buttons, each with a dark gray rectangle behind them. The rectangles are used to indicate which of the buttons is selected. All have their Visible property set to False, except the currently selected button.

You create the rectangles, as shown in Figure 15.14, before the buttons.

1. Create a rectangle control with these properties:

Object: **box1 Rectangle**

Property	Value
Name:	box1
Visible:	No
Left:	0.1951 in
Top:	0.8958 in
Width:	0.7542 in
Height:	0.6049 in
Back Color:	8421504 (Dark Gray)
Border Style:	Clear

A shortcut for creating the remaining 11 rectangles is to use copy and paste.

2. Select the box1 rectangle control and press Ctrl-C. (You can also select **Edit|Copy** from the menu to do the same thing.)

3. Press Ctrl-V to create the second rectangle and then position it by setting its properties as listed in the following text. Be sure to change the name of the rectangle to box2. Repeat the step to create box3 through box12, as shown in Figure 15.15.

FIGURE 15.14.

Creating the first rectangle.

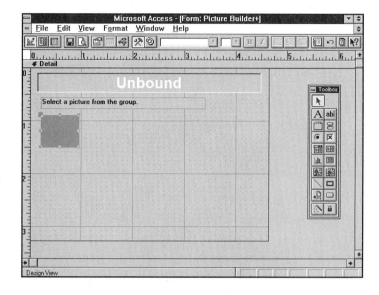

FIGURE 15.15.

Completing the box1 through box12 rectangle controls.

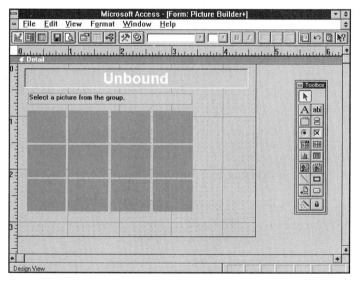

Object: **box2 Rectangle**

Property	Value
Name:	box2
Left:	1.0146 in
Top:	0.8958 in

Object: **box3 Rectangle**

Property	Value
Name:	box3
Left:	1.8285 in
Top:	0.8958 in

Object: **box4 Rectangle**

Property	Value
Name:	box4
Left:	2.65 in
Top:	0.8958 in

Object: **box5 Rectangle**

Property	Value
Name:	box5
Left:	0.1951 in
Top:	1.5417 in

Object: **box6 Rectangle**

Property	Value
Name:	box6
Left:	1.0146 in
Top:	1.5417 in

Object: **box7 Rectangle**

Property	Value
Name:	box7
Left:	1.8285 in
Top:	1.5417 in

Object: **box8 Rectangle**

Property	Value
Name:	box8
Left:	2.65 in
Top:	1.5417 in

Object: **box9 Rectangle**

Property	Value
Name:	box9
Left:	0.1951 in
Top:	2.1875 in

Object: **box10 Rectangle**

Property	Value
Name:	box10
Left:	1.0146 in
Top:	2.1875 in

Object: **box11 Rectangle**

Property	Value
Name:	box11
Left:	1.8285 in
Top:	2.1875 in

Object: **box12 Rectangle**

Property	Value
Name:	box12
Left:	2.65 in
Top:	2.1875 in

4. Add a command button to the form and then position it over the first rectangle. Set the properties for the button as listed here:

Object: **pic1 Command Button**

Property	Value
Name:	pic1
Caption:	(blank)
Enabled:	Yes
Tab Stop:	Yes
Left:	0.2785 in
Top:	0.9792 in
Width:	0.6 in
Height:	0.45 in

5. Copy the pic1 command button and paste 11 additional buttons named pic2 through pic12, as shown in Figure 15.16. Position the new buttons as follows:

Object: **pic2 Command Button**

Property	*Value*
Name:	pic2
Left:	1.091 in
Top:	0.9792 in

Object: **pic3 Command Button**

Property	*Value*
Name:	pic3
Left:	1.9035 in
Top:	0.9792 in

Object: **pic4 Command Button**

Property	*Value*
Name:	pic4
Left:	2.7306 in
Top:	0.9792 in

Object: **pic5 Command Button**

Property	*Value*
Name:	pic5
Left:	0.2785 in
Top:	1.625 in

Object: **pic6 Command Button**

Property	*Value*
Name:	pic6
Left:	1.091 in
Top:	1.625 in

Object: **pic7 Command Button**

Property	*Value*
Name:	pic7
Left:	1.9035 in
Top:	1.625 in

Object: **pic8 Command Button**

Property	Value
Name:	pic8
Left:	2.7306 in
Top:	1.625 in

Object: **pic9 Command Button**

Property	Value
Name:	pic9
Left:	0.2785 in
Top:	2.2708 in

Object: **pic10 Command Button**

Property	Value
Name:	pic10
Left:	1.091 in
Top:	2.2708 in

Object: **pic11 Command Button**

Property	Value
Name:	pic11
Left:	1.9035 in
Top:	2.2708 in

Object: **pic12 Command Button**

Property	Value
Name:	pic12
Left:	2.7306 in
Top:	2.2708 in

Next, a label and text box are added below the buttons to display the title of the selected picture.

1. Add a label and text box with the following properties:

Object: **lblSelected Label**

Property	Value
Name:	lblSelected
Caption:	Selected:

Left:	0.2806 in
Top:	2.875 in
Width:	0.625 in
Height:	0.1667 in

Object: **txtSelected Textbox**

Property	*Value*
Name:	txtSelected
Enabled:	No
Locked:	Yes
Tab Stop:	No
Left:	0.9646 in
Top:	2.875 in
Width:	2.3597 in
Height:	0.1667 in
Back Color:	12632256 (Light Gray)
Special Effect:	Sunken
Font Weight:	Bold

FIGURE 15.16.

*Adding the pic1
through pic12
command buttons.*

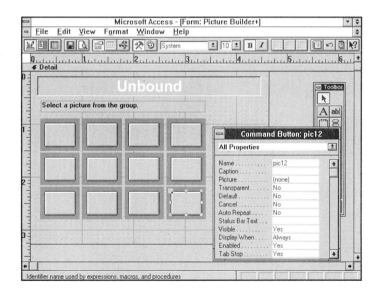

2. Add the following command buttons (see Figure 15.17). The font selected for
   the buttons is MS Sans Serif, size 8, and Bold.

Object: **cmdOK Command Button**

Property	*Value*
Name:	cmdOK
Caption:	OK
Default:	Yes
Left:	3.8125 in
Top:	0.5625 in
Width:	0.7125 in
Height:	0.25 in

Object: **cmdCancel Command Button**

Property	*Value*
Name:	cmdCancel
Caption:	Cancel
Cancel:	Yes
Left:	3.8125 in
Top:	0.8542 in
Width:	0.7125 in
Height:	0.25 in

Object: **cmdAdd Command Button**

Property	*Value*
Name:	cmdAdd
Caption:	&Add
Left:	3.8125 in
Top:	1.2083 in
Width:	0.7125 in
Height:	0.25 in

Object: **cmdDelete Command Button**

Property	*Value*
Name:	cmdDelete
Caption:	&Delete
Left:	3.8125 in
Top:	1.5 in
Width:	0.7125 in
Height:	0.25 in

Object: **cmdGroups Command Button**

Property	Value
Name:	cmdGroups
Caption:	&Groups
Left:	3.8125 in
Top:	1.7917 in
Width:	0.7125 in
Height:	0.25 in

Object: **cmdHint Command Button**

Property	Value
Name:	cmdHint
Caption:	&Hint
Left:	3.8125 in
Top:	2.1458 in
Width:	0.7125 in
Height:	0.25 in

FIGURE 15.17.

Adding command buttons to the Picture Builder+ form.

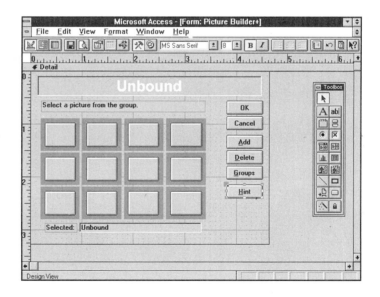

You can use a couple of pictures from the original Picture Builder to create the next two buttons. You need left- and right-arrow buttons to browse through the different picture groups.

1. Add two buttons with the following properties:

Object: **cmdPrevious Command Button**

Property	Value
Name:	cmdPrevious
Caption:	(blank)
Left:	3.5472 in
Top:	2.6646 in
Width:	0.4625 in
Height:	0.3792 in

Object: **cmdNext Command Button**

Property	Value
Name:	cmdNext
Caption:	(blank)
Left:	4.0306 in
Top:	2.6646 in
Width:	0.4625 in
Height:	0.3792 in

2. Set the picture property of each of the two buttons just created by clicking the ellipsis (…) button in the Property window. This will invoke the original Picture Builder as shown in Figure 15.18.

Select the picture titled "Left Arrow (Blue)" for the cmdPrevious button and "Right Arrow (Blue)" for the cmdNext button.

Adding the pictures this way automatically resizes the button. You have to go back and reset the Width and Height properties to preserve their settings as they were before the pictures were added.

FIGURE 15.18.

Using the Access Picture Builder to find pictures for the cmdPrevious and cmdNext buttons.

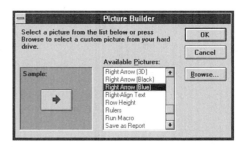

The last control on the form is a label that displays a copyright message in fine print, like you see in used car commercials.

Add a label with the following properties:

Object: lblCopyright Label

Property	Value
Name:	lblCopyright
Caption:	Copyright (c) 1994-1995 by Don Schuy
Left:	3.0826 in
Top:	3.1042 in
Width:	1.5097 in
Height:	0.125 in
Font Name:	Small Fonts
Font Size:	6
Font Weight:	Normal

Before closing and saving the form, check the tab order of the controls.

1. Select the **Edit|Tab** Order command.

2. In the Tab Order dialog box, arrange the controls in the order shown here:

cmdOK
cmdCancel
cmdAdd
cmdDelete
cmdGroups
cmdHint
cmdPrevious
cmdNext
txtName
pic1
pic2
pic3
pic4
pic5
pic6
pic7
pic8
pic9
pic10
pic11
pic12
txtSelected

The cmdOK command button is set purposely as the first control in the tab order so that it will receive focus when the form opens.

3. Close the Tab Order dialog box and then close the form. Save the form with the name `Picture Builder+`.

Figure 15.19 shows the tab order being edited in the Tab Order dialog box.

FIGURE 15.19.

Setting the tab order on the Picture Builder+ form.

The Picture Builder+ Global Variables

Before you write the code behind the Picture Builder+ form you need to declare a few global variables in a module.

The database you're creating will be loaded as a library database. Any global variables, functions, or subroutines must be named so that the names won't conflict with names in the user's database code. This is typically handled by using a prefix that identifies the variables or procedures with a particular program.

For Picture Builder+, I chose the prefix "pbp."

1. Create a new module.
2. Enter the declarations section as shown in Listing 15.3.
3. Close the module and save it with the name `Picture Builder+`.

Listing 15.3. The declarations section of the Picture Builder+ module.

```
' Picture Builder+

Option Compare Database
Option Explicit

Global Const pbp_PROGRAM = "Picture Builder+"
```

```
Global pbp_Control As Control
Global pbp_blnControlSet As Integer

Global pbp_lngCurrentGroupID As Long
Global pbp_lngHintID As Long
```

When Picture Builder+ is invoked while you are working on a form, a command button control's Picture property is modified. The pbp_Control variable is set to match the command button control with the modified property. The flag, pbp_blnControlSet, is set to True to indicate when pbp_Control is properly set.

The lngCurrentGroupID variable indicates which picture group is currently being displayed.

The lngHintID variable is set to indicate which hint should be displayed in the Hint dialog box.

With the globals declared you can enter the procedures in the Picture Builder+ form module. The Picture Builder+ module is discussed again toward the end of the chapter.

Coding the Picture Builder+ Form

There is quite a bit going on behind the Picture Builder+ form to make everything work. Here's a list of the procedures in the order that you'll look at them:

(declarations)—Declare module variables

Form_Open—Open the Pic Group and Pic tables
Form_Close—Close opened tables

ReadPictures—Load initial picture data
UpdatePics—Display the picture group pictures
SelectPic—Highlight the selected picture
cmdOK_Click—Accept the selected picture and close
cmdCancel_Click—Close the form

cmdAdd_Click—Add a new picture by filename
GetFilename—Use common dialog box to get a filename
cmdDelete_Click—Delete the selected picture

cmdGroups_Click—Display the Picture Groups dialog box

cmdHint_Click—Display the Hint dialog box

cmdPrevious_Click—Move to the previous picture group

cmdNext_Click—Move to the next picture group

The Declarations Section

Open the Picture Builder+ form module and fill in the declarations section.

1. Select the Picture Builder+ form in the database container.
2. Click the Code button on the toolbar to open the form with the module window open.
3. Enter the declarations section as shown in Listing 15.4.

Listing 15.4. The declarations section for the Picture Builder+ form module.

```
' Picture Builder+ form module

Option Compare Database
Option Explicit

Const PROGRAM = "Picture Builder+"
Const DISPLAYED_PICS = 12

Dim mdb As Database

Dim mdynPicGroup As Recordset
Dim mblnPicGroupOpened As Integer

Dim mtblPic As Recordset
Dim mblnPicOpened As Integer

Dim mintLastSelectedPic As Integer
```

The DISPLAYED_PICS constant is used to define how many pictures are on the Picture Builder+ form. A constant is used so that you can add more buttons to the form later and quickly change the program to use the added buttons.

The mdynPicGroup and mtblPic recordset variables are declared as module variables, so these recordsets need only be opened once for the duration that the form is open. The mdb variable is the database variable that the mdynPicGroup and mtblPic variables are opened with.

The mintLastSelectedPic variable is kept up-to-date with the number for the currently selected picture. The variable will always hold a value of 0 to DISPLAYED_PICS. Zero indicates that no picture has been selected.

The *Form_Open* Subroutine

The Form_Open subroutine initializes the module variables in the declaration section.

Enter the Form_Open subroutine as shown in Listing 15.5.

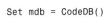

Listing 15.5. The Form_Open **subroutine.**

```
Sub Form_Open (Cancel As Integer)

  Dim sql As String

  mblnPicOpened = False
  On Error GoTo Form_OpenError

  Set mdb = CodeDB()

' Load WZBLDR.MDA pictures.  Remove this call when using your own set of
' pictures.
  ReadPictures mdb

  sql = "SELECT GroupID, Name FROM [Pic Group] ORDER BY SortOrder;"
  Set mdynPicGroup = mdb.OpenRecordset(sql, DB_OPEN_DYNASET)

  Set mtblPic = mdb.OpenRecordset("Pic", DB_OPEN_TABLE)
  mblnPicOpened = True

  mtblPic.Index = "Group"

  mintLastSelectedPic = 1
  UpdatePics 1

' If loading for customization only
  If Not pbp_blnControlSet Then
    lblHint.Caption = "Add pictures and groups to the picture library."
  End If

Form_OpenDone:
  Exit Sub

Form_OpenError:
  MsgBox Error$, 48, PROGRAM
  Cancel = True
  Resume Form_OpenDone

End Sub
```

First, the CodeDB() function is used to open the database, ensuring that the database variable points to the same database in which the code is running.

```
Set mdb = CodeDB()
```

Next, the ReadPictures subroutine is called to load initially some of the pictures from the original Picture Builder into the Pic table. This call will have no effect after the job has been done the first time the form opens.

```
' Load WZBLDR.MDA pictures.  Remove this call when using your own set of
' pictures.
  ReadPictures mdb
```

A SELECT statement is used to open the data in the Pic Group table so that the records may be retrieved in ascending order by the value in the SortOrder field.

```
sql = "SELECT GroupID, Name FROM [Pic Group] ORDER BY SortOrder;"
Set mdynPicGroup = mdb.OpenRecordset(sql, DB_OPEN_DYNASET)
```

The Pic table is opened as a Recordset object in table mode. The Index property is set to the Group index you created on the GroupID and Position fields.

```
Set mtblPic = mdb.OpenRecordset("Pic", DB_OPEN_TABLE)
mblnPicOpened = True

mtblPic.Index = "Group"
```

Next, the first picture is set as the current selected picture and then the UpdatePics subroutine is called to load the pictures on the form.

```
mintLastSelectedPic = 1
UpdatePics 1
```

The end of the subroutine checks a global, pbp_blnControlSet. This variable is set to True when Picture Builder+ is loaded so that a Picture property on a control actually can be set. The form also can be loaded simply to add or delete pictures and picture groups to or from the database.

```
' If loading for customization only
  If Not pbp_blnControlSet Then
    lblHint.Caption = "Add pictures and groups to the picture library."
  End If
```

The *Form_Close* Subroutine

The Form_Close subroutine closes the tables opened by the Form_Open subroutine.

Enter the Form_Close subroutine as shown in Listing 15.6.

Listing 15.6. The Form_Close **subroutine.**

```
Sub Form_Close ()

  On Error GoTo Form_CloseError

  If mblnPicGroupOpened Then
    mblnPicGroupOpened = False
    mdynPicGroup.Close
  End If
```

```
   If mblnPicOpened Then
     mblnPicOpened = False
     mtblPic.Close
   End If

Form_CloseDone:
   Exit Sub

Form_CloseError:
   MsgBox Error$, 48, PROGRAM
   Resume Form_CloseDone

End Sub
```

The *ReadPictures* Subroutine

The `ReadPictures` subroutine opens the WZLIB.MDA database that ships with Microsoft Access and copies the picture data from the bw_TblPictures table into your database's Pic table.

Enter the `ReadPictures` subroutine as shown in Listing 15.7.

Listing 15.7. The `ReadPictures` **subroutine.**

```
Sub ReadPictures (db As Database)

' Load pictures from the WZLIB.MDA library into the Pic table as sample data.

' This is done the first time Picture Builder+ is used to allow usage of the
' pictures provided with Access without distributing them improperly.

' Note: This subroutine assumes that the user has not already added their own
' custom pictures using the customize feature of Microsoft's Picture Builder.
' If pictures have been added, then the pictures and titles will be out of
' synchronization in Pic table.

   Dim dbWzBldr As Database
   Dim tbl As Recordset
   Dim dynSource As Recordset
   Dim dynDest As Recordset

   Dim strAccessDir As String
   Dim sql As String

   Dim blnOpened As Integer
   Dim blnDBOpened As Integer
   Dim blnSourceOpened As Integer
   Dim blnDestOpened As Integer
   Dim blnTransStarted As Integer

   Const strWizTable = "bw_TblPictures"
```

continues

Listing 15.7. continued

```
   blnOpened = False
   blnDBOpened = False
   blnSourceOpened = False
   blnDestOpened = False
   blnTransStarted = False
   On Error GoTo ReadPicturesError

   Set tbl = db.OpenRecordset("Option", DB_OPEN_TABLE)
   blnOpened = True

   If Not tbl!ReadPictures Then GoTo ReadPicturesDone

 ' Pictures have not been loaded yet

 ' Find where WZBLDR.MDA is
   strAccessDir = SysCmd(SYSCMD_ACCESSDIR)

 ' Open the WZBLDR.MDA database read-only
   Set dbWzBldr = OpenDatabase(strAccessDir & "WZBLDR.MDA", False, True)
   blnDBOpened = True

 ' Load 45 useful pictures from the bw_TblPictures table
   sql = "SELECT PictureData FROM bw_TblPictures WHERE (TBBitmapID Is Null)
   ➥ ORDER BY PictureName;"
   Set dynSource = dbWzBldr.OpenRecordset(sql, DB_OPEN_DYNASET)
   blnSourceOpened = True

   sql = "SELECT Picture FROM Pic ORDER BY Name;"
   Set dynDest = db.OpenRecordset(sql, DB_OPEN_DYNASET)
   blnDestOpened = True

 ' Copy the pictures to the Pic table
   BeginTrans
   blnTransStarted = True

   Do Until dynSource.EOF Or dynDest.EOF
     dynDest.Edit
     dynDest!Picture = dynSource!PictureData
     dynDest.Update

     dynSource.MoveNext
     dynDest.MoveNext
   Loop

   tbl.Edit
   tbl!ReadPictures = False
   tbl.Update

   CommitTrans
   blnTransStarted = False

ReadPicturesDone:
   On Error Resume Next
   If blnTransStarted Then Rollback
   If blnOpened Then tbl.Close
   If blnSourceOpened Then dynSource.Close
```

```
    If blnDestOpened Then dynDest.Close
    If blnDBOpened Then dbWzBldr.Close

    DoCmd SetWarnings True
    Exit Sub

ReadPicturesError:
    MsgBox Error$, 48, PROGRAM
    Resume ReadPicturesDone

End Sub
```

In the `ReadPictures` subroutine, the name of the table from which to import the pictures is stored in the constant `strWizTable`.

```
    Const strWizTable = "bw_TblPictures"
```

The subroutine begins by opening the Option table to see whether the pictures have already been copied. If the `ReadPictures` option is set to No, the subroutine does an early exit.

```
    Set tbl = db.OpenRecordset("Option", DB_OPEN_TABLE)
    blnOpened = True

    If Not tbl!ReadPictures Then GoTo ReadPicturesDone
```

Next, the subroutine uses the `SysCmd` function with a predefined constant `SYSCMD_ACCESSDIR` to find out from which directory Access is being run. This directory is where you would expect to find the WZBLDR.MDA library.

```
' Pictures have not been loaded yet

' Find where WZBLDR.MDA is
    strAccessDir = SysCmd(SYSCMD_ACCESSDIR)
```

The WZBLDR.MDA library is opened and assigned to the `dbWzBldr` database variable.

```
' Open the WZBLDR.MDA database read-only
    Set dbWzBldr = OpenDatabase(strAccessDir & "WZBLDR.MDA", False, True)
    blnDBOpened = True
```

The pictures you want to load are in the bw_TblPictures table. Some of the records in this table actually contain picture data, whereas other records contain an identifier that points to a specific toolbar bitmap.

Using a `SELECT` statement, the code opens a dynaset that selects only the records that contain the actual picture.

```
' Load 45 useful pictures from the bw_TblPictures table
sql = "SELECT PictureData FROM bw_TblPictures WHERE (TBBitmapID Is Null)
➡ ORDER BY PictureName;"
    Set dynSource = dbWzBldr.OpenRecordset(sql, DB_OPEN_DYNASET)
    blnSourceOpened = True
```

Next, a dynaset is opened to select the records you entered into the Pic table. There is a record for each picture you're going to extract from the bw_TblPictures table.

```
sql = "SELECT Picture FROM Pic ORDER BY Name;"
Set dynDest = db.OpenRecordset(sql, DB_OPEN_DYNASET)
blnDestOpened = True
```

The copy is done inside of a single transaction. That way it either is completely done, or won't be done at all. (The transaction also helps to speed up the program.)

```
' Copy the pictures to the Pic table
BeginTrans
blnTransStarted = True
```

In the following loop, the PictureData field from each bw_TblPictures record is copied into the Picture field of the Pic table.

```
Do Until dynSource.EOF Or dynDest.EOF
   dynDest.Edit
   dynDest!Picture = dynSource!PictureData
   dynDest.Update
```

Each of the dynasets is bumped along to the next record and the loop continues.

```
   dynSource.MoveNext
   dynDest.MoveNext
Loop
```

Once all the records have been successfully copied, the `ReadPictures` option is set to False and saved.

```
tbl.Edit
tbl!ReadPictures = False
tbl.Update
```

Finally, the transaction is committed.

```
CommitTrans
blnTransStarted = False
```

Figure 15.20 shows the Pic table in datasheet view after the `ReadPictures` subroutine is used to load pictures.

The *UpdatePics* Subroutine

The `UpdatePics` subroutine reads the pictures for the current picture group into the pic1 through pic12 command buttons on the Picture Builder+ form.

 Enter the `UpdatePics` subroutine as shown in Listing 15.8.

FIGURE 15.20.

The Pic table with picture data loaded.

PictureID	GroupID	Position	Name	Picture
1	1	2	Go To Previous	Long binary data
2	1	3	Go To Next	Long binary data
3	1	1	Go To First	Long binary data
4	1	4	Go To Last	Long binary data
5	3	11	Stop Sign	Long binary data
6	4	1	Pencil (yellow)	Long binary data
7	4	3	Eraser	Long binary data
8	3	1	Watch	Long binary data
9	3	2	Clock	Long binary data
10	3	3	Phone	Long binary data
11	5	9	Left Arrow (3D)	Long binary data
12	5	1	Pointing Left	Long binary data
13	5	5	Left Arrow (Black)	Long binary data
14	5	10	Right Arrow (3D)	Long binary data
15	5	4	Pointing Down	Long binary data
16	5	6	Right Arrow (Black)	Long binary data
17	5	12	Down Arrow (3D)	Long binary data
18	5	2	Pointing Right	Long binary data
19	5	8	Down Arrow (Black)	Long binary data
20	1	6	Binoculars	Long binary data
21	4	4	Check Mark	Long binary data
22	5	11	Up Arrow (3D)	Long binary data

Record: 1 of 45

Listing 15.8. The `UpdatePics` subroutine.

```
Sub UpdatePics (intPosition As Integer)

  Dim ctl As Control

  Dim lngGroupID As Long
  Dim n As Integer

  On Error GoTo UpdatePicsError

  lngGroupID = mdynPicGroup!GroupID
  txtName = mdynPicGroup!Name

  For n = 1 To DISPLAYED_PICS
    mtblPic.Seek "=", lngGroupID, n

    Set ctl = Me("Pic" & n)

    If mtblPic.NoMatch Then
      ctl.Picture = Null
      ctl.Visible = False
    Else
      ctl.PictureData = mtblPic!Picture
      ctl.Visible = True
    End If
  Next n

  SelectPic intPosition

UpdatePicsDone:
  Exit Sub

UpdatePicsError:
  MsgBox Error$, 48, PROGRAM
  Resume UpdatePicsDone

End Sub
```

The UpdatePics subroutine first reads the Group ID number and group name from the mdynPicGroup dynaset, which has its current record set to the picture group about to be displayed.

```
lngGroupID = mdynPicGroup!GroupID
txtName = mdynPicGroup!Name
```

Next, a loop is performed for each Pic command button on the form. The subroutine issues a Seek on the mtblPic table to see whether it can find a record for the current group and picture number.

```
For n = 1 To DISPLAYED_PICS
   mtblPic.Seek "=", lngGroupID, n
```

The next line in the program sets the ctl control type variable to one of the Pic command buttons by name.

```
Set ctl = Me("Pic" & n)
```

If a picture wasn't found in the tblPic table, the picture for this command button is cleared, and the button is hidden from view.

```
If mtblPic.NoMatch Then
   ctl.Picture = Null
   ctl.Visible = False
```

Otherwise, the command button's PictureData property is set to the data found in the table. This effectively draws the bitmap on the button's surface.

```
Else
   ctl.PictureData = mtblPic!Picture
   ctl.Visible = True
End If
Next n
```

The SelectPic subroutine is called to highlight the currently selected picture, which is passed as an argument to the UpdatePics subroutine.

```
SelectPic intPosition
```

The *SelectPic* Subroutine

The SelectPic subroutine first clears the highlight around the previously selected picture and then highlights the picture indicated by the intPosition argument.

Enter the SelectPic subroutine as shown in Listing 15.9.

Listing 15.9. The SelectPic subroutine.

```
Sub SelectPic (intPosition As Integer)

' Hilite the indicated button, if it contains a picture
```

```
   On Error GoTo SelectPicError

' Clear the previous selection
   If mintLastSelectedPic > 0 Then
     Me("Box" & mintLastSelectedPic).Visible = False
   End If

   If intPosition > 0 Then

   ' Display title of the selected picture
     mtblPic.Seek "=", mdynPicGroup!GroupID, intPosition

     If mtblPic.NoMatch Then
       intPosition = 0
     End If
   End If

   If intPosition > 0 Then
     txtSelected = mtblPic!Name

   ' Hilite the selected button
     Me("Box" & intPosition).Visible = True
   Else
     txtSelected = ""
   End If

   mintLastSelectedPic = intPosition

SelectPicDone:
   Exit Sub

SelectPicError:
   MsgBox Error$, 48, PROGRAM
   Resume SelectPicDone

End Sub
```

The previously selected picture is identified by the value in the `mintLastSelectedPic` variable. The rectangle behind this picture is set to invisible.

```
' Clear the previous selection
   If mintLastSelectedPic > 0 Then
     Me("Box" & mintLastSelectedPic).Visible = False
   End If
```

Next, the `SelectPic` subroutine tries to find a picture for the current picture group and the specified position.

```
   If intPosition > 0 Then

   ' Display title of the selected picture
     mtblPic.Seek "=", mdynPicGroup!GroupID, intPosition
```

If a record isn't found, you don't have a current picture.

```
   If mtblPic.NoMatch Then
     intPosition = 0
   End If
End If
```

The title of the selected picture is displayed. Also, the highlight behind the newly selected picture is set to visible.

```
If intPosition > 0 Then
   txtSelected = mtblPic!Name

' Hilite the selected button
   Me("Box" & intPosition).Visible = True
```

If there isn't a currently selected picture, the txtSelected text box is cleared.

```
Else
   txtSelected = ""
End If
```

After displaying which picture is selected, the mintLastSelectedPic variable is updated with the number of the currently selected picture.

```
mintLastSelectedPic = intPosition
```

The *cmdOK_Click* Subroutine

The cmdOK_Click subroutine is activated when users select the pictures they want and click OK to close the Picture Builder+ dialog box.

Enter the cmdOK_Click subroutine shown in Listing 15.10.

Listing 15.10. The cmdOK_Click **subroutine.**

```
Sub cmdOK_Click ()

   Dim ctl As Control

   On Error GoTo cmdOK_ClickError

' Transfer the picture to the destination button
   If pbp_blnControlSet And (mintLastSelectedPic > 0) Then
     Set ctl = Me("Pic" & mintLastSelectedPic)
     pbp_Control.PictureData = ctl.PictureData
   End If

' Close the form
   cmdCancel_Click

cmdOK_ClickDone:
   Exit Sub
```

```
cmdOK_ClickError:
  MsgBox Error$, 48, PROGRAM
  Resume cmdOK_ClickDone

End Sub
```

The `cmdOK_Click` subroutine checks to see whether the `pbp_blnControlSet` global flag has been set. The flag is set when Picture Builder+ is activated from the Properties window while setting the Picture property of a form on a control. Also, the `mintLastSelectedPic` variable is checked to see whether the user has actually selected one of the pictures.

If both conditions are true, the subroutine continues to transfer the picture to the control on the user's form.

The `ctl` variable is set to the Pic command button with the selected picture. The `pbp_Control` variable points to the control on the user's form. The picture is transferred by assigning the PictureData property of this control to the PictureData property setting of the Pic button that has the picture.

```
' Transfer the picture to the destination button
  If pbp_blnControlSet And (mintLastSelectedPic > 0) Then
    Set ctl = Me("Pic" & mintLastSelectedPic)
    pbp_Control.PictureData = ctl.PictureData
  End If
```

Next, the form is closed by calling the subroutine that responds when the Cancel button is pressed.

```
' Close the form
  cmdCancel_Click
```

The *cmdCancel_Click* Subroutine

The `cmdCancel_Click` subroutine is a one-liner that closes the form.

Enter the `cmdCancel_Click` subroutine.

Listing 15.11. The `cmdCancel_Click` subroutine.

```
Sub cmdCancel_Click ()

  On Error Resume Next
  DoCmd Close A_FORM, "Picture Builder+"

End Sub
```

The *cmdAdd_Click* Subroutine

The next subroutine enables users to customize Picture Builder+ by adding their own pictures to the collection of pictures stored in the Pic table.

Enter the cmdAdd_Click subroutine as shown in Listing 15.12.

Listing 15.12. The cmdAdd_Click **subroutine.**

```
Sub cmdAdd_Click ()

  Dim ctl As Control
  Dim strFilename As String
  Dim strName As String
  Dim intPosition As Integer

  On Error GoTo cmdAdd_ClickError

' Find the next available picture in this group

  For intPosition = 1 To DISPLAYED_PICS
    Set ctl = Me("Pic" & intPosition)
    If ctl.Visible = False Then
      Exit For
    End If
  Next intPosition

  If intPosition > DISPLAYED_PICS Then
    MsgBox "This picture group is full.", 48, PROGRAM
    GoTo cmdAdd_ClickDone
  End If

strFilename = GetFilename("Select Picture", "Bitmaps (*.bmp)¦*.bmp¦Icons
➥ (*.ico)¦*.ico")
  If strFilename = "" Then
    GoTo cmdAdd_ClickDone
  End If

' Load the picture in the next available button

  On Error Resume Next
  ctl.Picture = strFilename

  If Err <> 0 Then
    MsgBox "Unable to load " & strFilename & ".", 48, PROGRAM
    GoTo cmdAdd_ClickDone
  End If

  On Error GoTo cmdAdd_ClickError

' Display the button
  ctl.Visible = True
  DoEvents

' Prompt for a button title
strName = Trim$(InputBox$("Enter a title for the added picture.",
➥ "Picture Title"))
```

```
  If strName = "" Then
    strName = "Untitled"
  End If

' Save the picture to the Pic table
  mtblPic.AddNew
  mtblPic!GroupID = mdynPicGroup!GroupID
  mtblPic!Position = intPosition
  mtblPic!Name = strName
  mtblPic!Picture = ctl.PictureData
  mtblPic.Update

' Select the new picture
  ctl.SetFocus
  SelectPic intPosition

cmdAdd_ClickDone:
  Exit Sub

cmdAdd_ClickError:
  MsgBox Error$, 48, PROGRAM
  Resume cmdAdd_ClickDone

End Sub
```

When a picture group is displayed, the program shows the pic1 through pic12 command buttons as needed to display all the pictures in the group. The first thing the cmdAdd_Click subroutine does is check to see whether there are any available buttons to make visible and write a picture to.

```
' Find the next available picture in this group

  For intPosition = 1 To DISPLAYED_PICS
    Set ctl = Me("Pic" & intPosition)
    If ctl.Visible = False Then
      Exit For
    End If
  Next intPosition
```

The loop terminates as soon as an available command button is found or if all the buttons are being used. If all buttons are used, the intPosition variable is set to 1 greater than DISPLAYED_PICS. The code checks for this and displays a message if there are no available buttons in the picture group.

```
  If intPosition > DISPLAYED_PICS Then
    MsgBox "This picture group is full.", 48, PROGRAM
    GoTo cmdAdd_ClickDone
  End If
```

Next, you use a GetFilename function (written next) to display a dialog box that is used to select a bitmap or icon file. GetFilename returns an empty string if the user selects the Cancel button, in which case your subroutine bails out early.

```
strFilename = GetFilename("Select Picture", "Bitmaps (*.bmp)¦*.bmp¦Icons
➡ (*.ico)¦*.ico")
  If strFilename = "" Then
    GoTo cmdAdd_ClickDone
  End If
```

In the loop you used previously, you assigned the ctl variable to each pic command button as you checked each to see whether it was available. The ctl variable is left pointing at the command button that is ready to receive a picture.

The picture is transferred from the file to the command button simply by assigning the Picture property to the name of the picture file. Before the program does this, it turns automatic error handling off so that it can deal with the error that occurs when the filename is not a valid bitmap or icon file.

```
' Load the picture in the next available button

  On Error Resume Next
  ctl.Picture = strFilename
```

The Err system variable is checked to see whether an error occurred while Picture property was being set. If an error occurred, a message is displayed and the subroutine exits.

```
  If Err <> 0 Then
    MsgBox "Unable to load " & strFilename & ".", 48, PROGRAM
    GoTo cmdAdd_ClickDone
  End If
```

If all went well, error handling is turned back on and the subroutine continues. The code makes the button visible and calls the DoEvents statement to update the screen immediately.

```
  On Error GoTo cmdAdd_ClickError

' Display the button
  ctl.Visible = True
  DoEvents
```

Next, you use the InputBox$ function as a quick and dirty way to prompt for the new picture's title, as shown in Figure 15.21. Rather than insisting that the user enter something, use "Untitled" as the title for the picture if the InputBox$ call comes back with an empty string.

```
' Prompt for a button title
strName = Trim$(InputBox$("Enter a title for the added picture.",
➡ "Picture Title"))
  If strName = "" Then
    strName = "Untitled"
  End If
```

Now that the picture and title are collected, you can create a new entry in the Pic table for the added picture. The picture group it belongs to is saved as well as the position from 1 to DISPLAYED_PICS that the picture appears in. The name of the picture and the actual picture are stored, and then the new record is saved to the table by calling the `Update` method.

```
' Save the picture to the Pic table
  mtblPic.AddNew
  mtblPic!GroupID = mdynPicGroup!GroupID
  mtblPic!Position = intPosition
  mtblPic!Name = strName
  mtblPic!Picture = ctl.PictureData
  mtblPic.Update
```

FIGURE 15.21.

The InputBox$ function displays a generic dialog box to prompt for a text value.

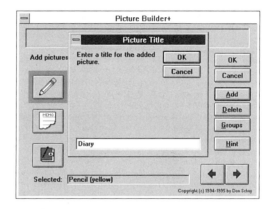

In many cases, users would enter a new picture into their collection as they were using it for the first time. For convenience the subroutine makes the new picture the currently selected one.

```
' Select the new picture
  ctl.SetFocus
  SelectPic intPosition
```

The *GetFilename* Function

Remember that you found a sample of how to use the Windows File Open dialog box inside the WZBLDR.MDA library database. This next function, `GetFilename`, is a direct result of the exploring you did.

The `GetFilename` function can be used anytime you want to allow the user to select a file. The tricky part is constructing the second argument, `strFilter`, which is used to fill in the List Files of **T**ype combo box (as shown in Figure 15.22).

The `strFilter` argument is a *delimited string* using the vertical bar character (¦) as a delimiter. (A delimited string is one where a special character is used to separate different components in the text.)

The strFilter argument is structured like this:

```
display_text | file_selector | display_text | file_selector...
```

A pair of display text and file selector entries is expected for each line in the List Files of Type combo box. In the cmdAdd_Click subroutine, you call GetFilename like this:

```
strFilename = GetFilename("Select Picture", "Bitmaps (*.bmp)|*.bmp|Icons
➡ (*.ico)|*.ico")
```

FIGURE 15.22.

The second argument to the GetFilename *function fills in the List Files of Type combo box.*

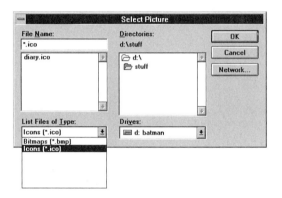

Enter the GetFilename subroutine as shown in Listing 15.13.

Listing 15.13. The GetFilename **function.**

```
Function GetFilename (strTitle As String, strFilter As String) As String

    Dim ofn As WLIB_GETFILENAMEINFO

    On Error GoTo GetFilenameError

' See the SDK docs or help files for all possible flags and their meanings.
    Const OFN_HIDEREADONLY = &H4
    Const OFN_PATHMUSTEXIST = &H800
    Const OFN_FILEMUSTEXIST = &H1000

    GetFilename = ""

    ofn.hwndOwner = Me.hwnd

' Filter: "Text (*.txt)|*.txt|All (*.*)|*.*"
    ofn.szFilter = strFilter

    ofn.nFilterIndex = 1
    ofn.szTITLE = strTitle

    ofn.Flags = OFN_HIDEREADONLY Or OFN_PATHMUSTEXIST Or OFN_FILEMUSTEXIST

' Second argument indicates if this is a file open or a file save dialog
    If Not wlib_GetFileName(ofn, True) Then
```

```
    GetFilename = Left$(ofn.szFile, InStr(1, ofn.szFile, " ") - 1)
  End If

GetFilenameDone:
  Exit Function

GetFilenameError:
  MsgBox Error$, 48, PROGRAM
  Resume GetFilenameDone

End Function
```

C language programmers familiar with the Windows API will find some familiar ground here. For the reader who doesn't have this background, I'll try to clear this up as best as I can.

At the top of the function, the ofn variable is declared as a WLIB_GETFILENAMEINFO type.

```
    Dim ofn As WLIB_GETFILENAMEINFO
```

The WLIB_GETFILENAMEINFO type is declared in WZLIB.MDA, a library database that comes with Access and always is installed unless the user removes or comments out the following line in the [Libraries] section of their MSACC20.INI FILE:

```
wzlib.mda=rw
```

If you look inside the WZLIB.MDA library you'll find the declaration for WLIB_GETFILENAMEINFO in the wlib_Util module as shown in Listing 15.14.

Listing 15.14. The WLIB_GETFILENAMEINFO declaration found in WZLIB.MDA.

```
Type WLIB_GETFILENAMEINFO
    hwndOwner As Integer
    szFilter As String * 255
    szCustomFilter As String * 255
    nFilterIndex As Long
    szFile As String * 255
    szFileTitle As String * 255
    szInitialDir As String * 255
    szTITLE As String * 255
    Flags As Long
    nFileOffset As Integer
    nFileExtension As Integer
    szDefExt As String * 255
End Type
```

In the GetFilename function, you'll be setting some of the members of the variable of type WLIB_GETFILENAMEINFO and then passing that to the wlib_GetFileName function to display the File Open common dialog box.

First, you declare some constants that will be used to derive the Flags member value.

```
' See the SDK docs or help files for all possible flags and their meanings.
  Const OFN_HIDEREADONLY = &H4
  Const OFN_PATHMUSTEXIST = &H800
  Const OFN_FILEMUSTEXIST = &H1000
```

The Flags member is used to indicate various options within a single argument by turn-ing on or off bits within a long integer number. You derive the actual Flag number value by adding the OFN constant values together.

The full list of options can be found in the SDK help text (or printed documentation) under the topic of the OPENFILENAME structure. Note that the SDK help text is included with Visual Basic and with the Access Developer's Toolkit.

I'll list the most useful options to know along with how to declare them:

The OFN_CREATEPROMPT option checks to see whether the file already exists and if not displays a dialog box to ask the user whether the file should be created.

```
  Const OFN_CREATEPROMPT = &H2000
```

The OFN_FILEMUSTEXIST option indicates that the user may only select an existing file. If they enter a filename that can't be found, the File Open dialog box displays a `Cannot find this file.` message as shown in Figure 15.23.

```
  Const OFN_FILEMUSTEXIST = &H1000
```

FIGURE 15.23.

Using the
OFN_FILEMUSTEXIST
flag to insist that the
user selects an existing
file.

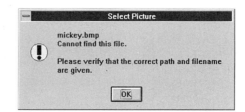

The OFN_HIDEREADONLY option is used to remove an optional Read Only check box that can appear on the File Open dialog box. The user would check this box to indicate to the application that any changes to the opened file should not be saved.

```
  Const OFN_HIDEREADONLY = &H4
```

The OFN_OVERWRITEPROMPT option is used with the Save As dialog box to prompt the user with a message box asking whether it is OK to overwrite the existing file.

```
  Const OFN_OVERWRITEPROMPT = &H2
```

The OFN_PATHMUSTEXIST option is used to insist that the entered file specification does not specify a drive or directory that doesn't exist. A message is displayed if the user enters an invalid path.

```
Const OFN_PATHMUSTEXIST = &H800
```

The OFN_READONLY option can be set to check initially the Read Only check box.

```
Const OFN_READONLY = &H1
```

You can test for the status of the Read Only check box when the user clicks the OK button in the File Open dialog box after the call to wlib_GetFileName, like this:

```
blnReadOnly = ((ofn.Flags AND &H1) = 1)
```

The blnReadOnly variable receives a True or False value, indicating whether the file was opened for read only.

Getting back to the GetFilename code you can see how all this works. First, the return value is set initially as an empty string, which indicates no filename has been selected.

```
GetFilename = ""
```

Then you start initializing the members of the ofn WLIB_GETFILENAMEINFO type variable. The hwndOwner member must be set to the current window's window handle (or hwnd property). The program's window is the parent window of the File Open dialog box.

```
ofn.hwndOwner = Me.hwnd
```

Next, the szFilter member is set to the strFilter argument. The Hungarian variable tags for the WLIB_GETFILENAMEINFO structure are faithful to their C language counterparts, so they differ from the tags used in the code in this book. The "sz" prefix is used to indicate a string and "n" is used to indicate an integer.

```
' Filter: "Text (*.txt)¦*.txt¦All (*.*)¦*.*"
ofn.szFilter = strFilter
```

The nFilterIndex member indicates which of the filters is selected by default when the dialog box opens. The value is 1-based, so a 1 (rather than a 0) indicates the first filter is used.

The szTITLE member receives the text to display in the title bar of the dialog box.

```
ofn.nFilterIndex = 1
ofn.szTITLE = strTitle
```

Next, set the Flags member value. The Or operator is used to add the different flag values into one value.

```
ofn.Flags = OFN_HIDEREADONLY Or OFN_PATHMUSTEXIST Or OFN_FILEMUSTEXIST
```

The `wlib_GetFileName` function is called with the `ofn` type variable and a True or False value indicating whether the File Open or the Save As dialog box is used. A value of True indicates the File Open dialog box is being used.

The resulting filename is found in the `szFile` member after the call. If the `wlib_GetFileName` call returns 0, all went well and there is a filename to return. It is extracted from the `szFile` member by grabbing all of the characters up to the first space character.

```
' Second argument indicates if this is a file open or a file save dialog
  If Not wlib_GetFileName(ofn, True) Then
    GetFilename = Left$(ofn.szFile, InStr(1, ofn.szFile, " ") - 1)
  End If
```

TRY THIS! QUESTION 15.1.

Can you write a `SaveFilename` function that displays the Save As common dialog box? Make it prompt users whether it is OK to overwrite files when they select an existing filename.

The *cmdDelete_Click* Subroutine

The `cmdDelete_Click` subroutine removes the currently selected picture from the Picture Builder+ form and from the Pic table in the database. A complication that the subroutine has to deal with is reordering the position numbers for the remaining records in the Pic table.

Enter the `cmdDelete_Click` subroutine as shown in Listing 15.15.

Listing 15.15. The `cmdDelete_Click` subroutine.

```
Sub cmdDelete_Click ()

  Dim intPosition As Integer
  Dim z As Integer
  Dim blnTransStarted As Integer

  blnTransStarted = False

  On Error GoTo cmdDelete_ClickError

  If mintLastSelectedPic = 0 Then
    GoTo cmdDelete_ClickDone
  End If
```

```
z = MsgBox("Delete the " & txtSelected & " picture?", 4 + 32 + 256,
➥ PROGRAM)
  If z <> 6 Then GoTo cmdDelete_ClickDone

  BeginTrans
  blnTransStarted = True

  mtblPic.Seek "=", mdynPicGroup!GroupID, mintLastSelectedPic
  If mtblPic.NoMatch Then
    GoTo cmdDelete_ClickDone
  End If

  mtblPic.Delete

  For intPosition = mintLastSelectedPic + 1 To DISPLAYED_PICS
    mtblPic.Seek "=", mdynPicGroup!GroupID, intPosition
    If mtblPic.NoMatch Then
      Exit For
    Else
      mtblPic.Edit
      mtblPic!Position = intPosition - 1
      mtblPic.Update
    End If
  Next intPosition

  CommitTrans
  blnTransStarted = False

' Reload pictures and try to hilite the pic after the deleted one
  intPosition = mintLastSelectedPic
  UpdatePics intPosition

' If that didn't work, hilite the one before it
  If mintLastSelectedPic = 0 Then
    SelectPic intPosition - 1
  End If

cmdDelete_ClickDone:
  On Error Resume Next
  If blnTransStarted Then Rollback
  Exit Sub

cmdDelete_ClickError:
  MsgBox Error$, 48, PROGRAM
  Resume cmdDelete_ClickDone

End Sub
```

The subroutine first checks to see whether a picture has been selected before the Delete button was pressed. If not, the subroutine exits.

```
If mintLastSelectedPic = 0 Then
  GoTo cmdDelete_ClickDone
End If
```

Another check is to ask the user whether he or she really wants to delete the picture. A Yes/No message is displayed, with the default answer being No.

```
z = MsgBox("Delete the " & txtSelected & " picture?", 4 + 32 + 256,
➥ PROGRAM)
  If z <> 6 Then GoTo cmdDelete_ClickDone
```

If the subroutine passes the checks, a transaction is started to make sure that your changes to the database are done completely.

```
  BeginTrans
  blnTransStarted = True
```

First, Seek to the record in the Pic table for the selected picture. If the record is found, the `Delete` method is called to remove it.

```
  mtblPic.Seek "=", mdynPicGroup!GroupID, mintLastSelectedPic
  If mtblPic.NoMatch Then
    GoTo cmdDelete_ClickDone
  End If

  mtblPic.Delete
```

Next, a loop is used to check for any pictures in the same picture group that follows the deleted one.

```
  For intPosition = mintLastSelectedPic + 1 To DISPLAYED_PICS
```

Inside the loop, if a record isn't found for the current position value, you know there are no more records to modify and the loop terminates.

```
  mtblPic.Seek "=", mdynPicGroup!GroupID, intPosition
  If mtblPic.NoMatch Then
    Exit For
```

If a record was found, the position value is decremented to move the picture up one notch to fill in for the deleted one. The loop continues until all the pictures after the deleted one have been moved up by one position.

```
  Else
    mtblPic.Edit
    mtblPic!Position = intPosition - 1
    mtblPic.Update
  End If
Next intPosition
```

The `CommitTrans` statement is used to apply the record changes you made to the database.

```
  CommitTrans
  blnTransStarted = False
```

Next, update the Picture Builder+ form by calling `UpdatePics` to reload the pictures from the database. The code tries to make the picture following the deleted one the new current picture.

```
' Reload pictures and try to hilite the pic after the deleted one
  intPosition = mintLastSelectedPic
  UpdatePics intPosition
```

In the case that you deleted the last picture in the picture group, the preceding logic isn't going to work because there is no following picture. The code then attempts to move the selected picture back by one. This will work if there are remaining pictures in the picture group; otherwise, there are no pictures to make the currently selected picture.

```
' If that didn't work, hilite the one before it
  If mintLastSelectedPic = 0 Then
    SelectPic intPosition - 1
  End If
```

The *cmdGroups_Click* Subroutine

Clicking the **G**roups button displays the Picture Groups form used to add or delete picture groups.

After the Picture Groups form is closed, the cmdGroups_Click subroutine reopens the mdynPicGroup dynaset to be current with the changes made. The Picture Builder+ form is updated to display the last selected picture group in the Picture Groups form. Because of this, the user can use the Picture Groups form as a quick way to locate and jump to another picture group.

Enter the cmdGroups_Click subroutine as shown in Listing 15.16.

Listing 15.16. The cmdGroups_Click **subroutine.**

```
Sub cmdGroups_Click ()

  Dim sql As String
  Dim lngGroupID As Long

  On Error GoTo cmdGroups_ClickError

  lngGroupID = mdynPicGroup!GroupID
  pbp_lngCurrentGroupID = lngGroupID
  DoCmd OpenForm "Picture Groups", A_NORMAL, , , , A_DIALOG

  mdynPicGroup.Close
  mblnPicGroupOpened = False

  sql = "SELECT GroupID, Name FROM [Pic Group] ORDER BY SortOrder;"
  Set mdynPicGroup = mdb.OpenRecordset(sql, DB_OPEN_DYNASET)
  mblnPicGroupOpened = True

  mdynPicGroup.FindFirst "GroupID = " & pbp_lngCurrentGroupID
  UpdatePics 1
```

continues

Listing 15.16. continued

```
cmdGroups_ClickDone:
  Exit Sub

cmdGroups_ClickError:
  MsgBox Error$, 48, PROGRAM
  Resume cmdGroups_ClickDone

End Sub
```

The *cmdHint_Click* Subroutine

The `cmdHint_Click` subroutine first sets the `pbp_lngHintID` number to 1 to indicate which Hint table record should be used as the hint. Then the Hint form is opened.

Enter the `cmdHint_Click` subroutine as shown in Listing 15.17.

Listing 15.17. The `cmdHint_Click` **subroutine.**

```
Sub cmdHint_Click ()

  On Error Resume Next
  pbp_lngHintID = 1
  DoCmd OpenForm "Hint"

End Sub
```

The *cmdPrevious_Click* Subroutine

The `cmdPrevious_Click` subroutine is called when the left-arrow button is pressed on the Picture Builder+ form.

The subroutine moves the current record pointer in the `mdynPicGroup` dynaset back by one record. If this hits the beginning of file marker (`BOF`), the record is moved back to where it was and no change occurs. If there is a picture group record, the `UpdatePics` subroutine is called to update the Picture Builder+ form with the now-current picture group.

Enter the `cmdPrevious_Click` subroutine as shown in Listing 15.18.

Listing 15.18. The `cmdPrevious_Click` **subroutine.**

```
Sub cmdPrevious_Click ()

  On Error GoTo cmdPrevious_ClickError

  mdynPicGroup.MovePrevious
  If mdynPicGroup.BOF Then
    mdynPicGroup.MoveNext
  Else
    UpdatePics 1
  End If

cmdPrevious_ClickDone:
  Exit Sub

cmdPrevious_ClickError:
  MsgBox Error$, 48, PROGRAM
  Resume cmdPrevious_ClickDone

End Sub
```

The *cmdNext_Click* Subroutine

The `cmdNext_Click` subroutine works similarly to the `cmdPrevious_Click` subroutine. The difference is, of course, that you're moving through the picture groups in a forward direction.

The subroutine checks for the end of file marker (`EOF`) to make sure that you have moved to another picture group rather than beyond the last one.

Enter the `cmdNext_Click` subroutine, as shown in Listing 15.19.

Listing 15.19. The `cmdNext_Click` **subroutine.**

```
Sub cmdNext_Click ()

  On Error GoTo cmdNext_ClickError

  mdynPicGroup.MoveNext
  If mdynPicGroup.EOF Then
    mdynPicGroup.MovePrevious
  Else
    UpdatePics 1
  End If

cmdNext_ClickDone:
  Exit Sub
```

continues

Listing 15.19. continued

```
cmdNext_ClickError:
  MsgBox Error$, 48, PROGRAM
  Resume cmdNext_ClickDone

End Sub
```

Close the Picture Builder+ module and form.

That completes the main portion of the program. It will actually run when the Picture Builder+ form is loaded. The first time you open the Picture Builder+ form, the ReadPictures subroutine loads picture data into the Pic table (unless you chose to leave that option out).

As shown in Figure 15.24, you can move from picture group to picture group with the arrow buttons, as well as add and delete pictures within a picture group.

FIGURE 15.24.

Testing the incomplete Picture Builder+ program.

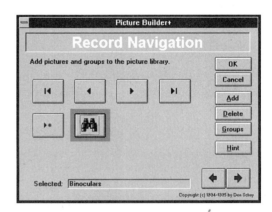

Next, create the Picture Groups form to manage adding and deleting picture groups.

Creating the Picture Groups Form

The Picture Groups form is a pop-up menu that comes up above the Picture Builder+ form. It displays a list of picture groups from which you can add or delete, or you can change the name of an existing group.

Next to the list of picture group names are up-arrow and down-arrow buttons with which the user can reorder the picture groups.

The font for all the controls is MS Sans Serif with a size of 8. The label control and buttons are set to a Bold font weight.

1. Open a new form in design mode and set the following properties:

Object: **Picture Groups Form**

Property	Value
Caption:	Picture Groups
Default View:	Single Form
Shortcut Menu:	No
Scroll Bars:	Neither
Record Selectors:	No
Navigation Buttons:	No
Auto Center:	Yes
Pop Up:	Yes
Modal:	Yes
Border Style:	Dialog box
Min Button:	No
Max Button:	No
Width:	3.1 in

2. Set the following detail section properties:

Object: **Detail0 Section**

Property	Value
Height:	2.3326 in
Back Color:	12632256 (Light Gray)

3. Add a list box and corresponding label with the following properties to the form, as shown in Figure 15.25:

Object: **lblPictureGroups Label**

Property	Value
Name:	lblPictureGroups
Caption:	Picture &Groups:
Left:	0.1 in
Top:	0.0826 in
Width:	1.0 in
Height:	0.1667 in
Back Color:	12632256 (Light Gray)
Font Weight:	Bold

Object: **lstPictureGroups Listbox**

Property	Value
Name:	lstPictureGroups
Row Source Type:	Table/Query
Column Count:	2
Column Widths:	0 in;2.1042 in
Bound Column:	1
Tab Index:	0
Left:	0.1042 in
Top:	0.25 in
Width:	2.1042 in
Height:	1.9576 in
Special Effect:	Sunken

FIGURE 15.25.

Adding the lstPictureGroups list box.

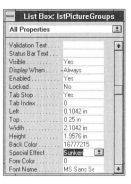

Next, you need to use the Query Builder to set the Row Source property of the lstPictureGroups list box.

1. Find the Row Source property in the property window. Click the ellipsis (…) button.

2. In the Add Table dialog box, select the Pic Group table and click the **Add** button. Close the Add Table dialog box.

3. Drag each of the fields into the columns in the query grid.

    You can do this in one step by double-clicking the Pic Group title in the table on the query window. This highlights all three fields in the table. Click the highlighted fields, drag them down to the query columns, and drop them in.

    The fields should appear in the query columns with GroupID in the first column, Name in the second column, and SortOrder in the third column.

4. Uncheck the Show check box in the SortOrder column.

5. Set the SortOrder column to Ascending sort order.

   The query should appear as shown in Figure 15.26.

6. Close the Query Builder window.

FIGURE 15.26.

Creating the Row Source query for the lstPictureGroups list box.

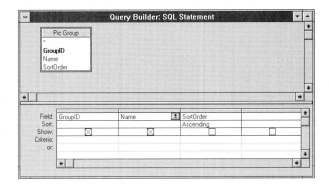

The SQL SELECT statement assigned to the Row Source property of the lstPictureGroups list box is as follows:

```
SELECT DISTINCTROW [Pic Group].GroupID, [Pic Group].Name
FROM [Pic Group]
ORDER BY [Pic Group].SortOrder;
```

Set the column width property in the list box so that the first column will be hidden, yet is the bound column. This way the user can select the picture group by name, but the program can identify the group by GroupID number.

Create two small buttons, cmdUp and cmdDown, at the bottom right of the list box.

The cmdUp command button should have a picture of an up arrow and the cmdDown command button should have a picture of a down arrow. See Figure 15.27. The files UP.BMP and DOWN.BMP on the book's companion CD can be used for this (and you could add them to your picture collection when you are done).

Object: **cmdUp Command Button**

Property	Value
Name:	cmdUp
Caption:	(Blank)
Picture:	UP.BMP
Tab Index:	1
Left:	2.3 in

continues

Property	*Value*
Top:	1.7917 in
Width:	0.2097 in
Height:	0.2097 in

Object: **cmdDown Command Button**

Property	*Value*
Name:	cmdDown
Caption:	(Blank)
Picture:	DOWN.BMP
Tab Index:	2
Left:	2.3 in
Top:	1.9986 in
Width:	0.2097 in
Height:	0.2097 in

FIGURE 15.27.

Adding the cmdUp and cmdDown arrow buttons.

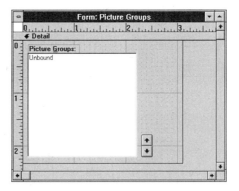

Create a set of five command buttons down the right side of the form, as shown in Figure 15.28. Make the captions **A**dd, **E**dit, **D**elete, **C**lose, and **H**int. Set the properties to match the following list:

Object: **cmdAdd Command Button**

Property	*Value*
Name:	cmdAdd
Caption:	&Add
Tab Index:	3
Left:	2.4021 in
Top:	0.125 in
Width:	0.6 in
Height:	0.25 in

Object: **cmdEdit Command Button**

Property	Value
Name:	cmdEdit
Caption:	&Edit
Tab Index:	4
Left:	2.4021 in
Top:	0.4146 in
Width:	0.6 in
Height:	0.25 in

Object: **cmdDelete Command Button**

Property	Value
Name:	cmdDelete
Caption:	&Delete
Tab Index:	5
Left:	2.4021 in
Top:	0.7076 in
Width:	0.6 in
Height:	0.25 in

Object: **cmdClose Command Button**

Property	Value
Name:	cmdClose
Caption:	&Close
Tab Index:	6
Left:	2.4021 in
Top:	1.0417 in
Width:	0.6 in
Height:	0.25 in

Object: **cmdHint Command Button**

Property	Value
Name:	cmdHint
Caption:	&Hint
Tab Index:	7
Left:	2.4021 in
Top:	1.3326 in
Width:	0.6 in
Height:	0.25 in

FIGURE 15.28.

Completing the Picture Groups form.

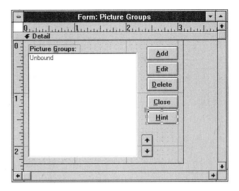

Close the form, saving it as `Picture Groups`.

Coding the Picture Groups Form

Your next task is to write the code for maintaining picture groups. This is the part of the program that really adds to the usability of Picture Builder+, because users can organize their pictures any way they like.

The Picture Groups form module contains subroutines for the `Form_Open` and `Form_Unload` events, as well as the click events for each of the buttons on the form.

1. Select the Picture Groups form in the database container and press the Code button on the toolbar to open the Picture Groups form module.
2. Enter the declarations section as shown in Listing 15.20.

Listing 15.20. The declarations section in the Picture Groups form module.

```
' Picture Groups form

Option Compare Database
Option Explicit

Const PROGRAM = "Picture Groups"
```

The *Form_Open* and *Form_Unload* Subroutines

Outside of the error handling code, the `Form_Open` and `Form_Unload` subroutines are one-liners. The two subroutines use the `pbp_lngCurrentGroupID` global to communicate between the Picture Builder+ form and the Picture Groups form what is the currently selected picture group.

The Form_Open subroutine assigns the value in pbp_lngCurrentGroupID to the lstPictureGroups list box so that the picture group displayed on the Picture Builder+ form becomes the selected picture group in the list box.

Enter the Form_Open subroutine as shown in Listing 15.21.

Listing 15.21. The Form_Open subroutine.

```
Sub Form_Open (Cancel As Integer)

  On Error GoTo Form_OpenError

  lstPictureGroups = pbp_lngCurrentGroupID

Form_OpenDone:
  Exit Sub

Form_OpenError:
  MsgBox Error$, 48, PROGRAM
  Resume Form_OpenDone

End Sub
```

The Form_Unload subroutine transfers the GroupID value in the lstPictureGroups list box back to the pbp_lngCurrentGroupID global. This way if the user has selected a different group from the list, the Picture Builder+ form can synchronize to it.

The end result is that the Picture Groups dialog box can be used as a way to quickly jump from one group to the next without having to arrow through each of the picture groups.

Enter the Form_Unload subroutine as shown in Listing 15.22.

Listing 15.22. The Form_Unload subroutine.

```
Sub Form_Unload (Cancel As Integer)

  On Error GoTo Form_UnloadError

  pbp_lngCurrentGroupID = lstPictureGroups

Form_UnloadDone:
  Exit Sub

Form_UnloadError:
  MsgBox Error$, 48, PROGRAM
  Resume Form_UnloadDone

End Sub
```

The *cmdAdd_Click* Subroutine

The cmdAdd_Click subroutine adds a picture group immediately after the selected group in the lstPictureGroups list box.

Enter the cmdAdd_Click subroutine as shown in Listing 15.23.

Listing 15.23. The cmdAdd_Click subroutine.

```
Sub cmdAdd_Click ()

    Dim db As Database
    Dim dyn As Recordset

    Dim strName As String
    Dim lngGroupID As Long
    Dim intPosition As Integer

    Dim blnTransStarted As Integer
    Dim blnOpened As Integer

    blnTransStarted = False
    blnOpened = False

    On Error GoTo cmdAdd_ClickError

strName = Trim$(InputBox$("Enter the name of the new picture group.",
➥ "Name"))
    If Len(strName) = 0 Then GoTo cmdAdd_ClickDone

    Set db = CodeDB()
    Set dyn = db.CreateRecordset("SELECT * FROM [Pic Group] ORDER BY
    ➥ SortOrder;", DB_OPEN_DYNASET)
    blnOpened = True

    If IsNull(lstPictureGroups) Then
        intPosition = lstPictureGroups.ListCount
    Else
        intPosition = lstPictureGroups.ListIndex + 1
    End If

    BeginTrans
    blnTransStarted = True

    If dyn.RecordCount Then
        dyn.MoveLast

        Do While dyn!SortOrder > intPosition
            dyn.Edit
            dyn!SortOrder = dyn!SortOrder + 1
            dyn.Update

            dyn.MovePrevious
            If dyn.BOF Then
                Exit Do
```

```
      End If
    Loop
  End If

  dyn.AddNew
  dyn!Name = strName
  dyn!SortOrder = intPosition + 1

  lngGroupID = dyn!GroupID
  dyn.Update

  CommitTrans
  blnTransStarted = False

  lstPictureGroups.Requery
  lstPictureGroups = lngGroupID

cmdAdd_ClickDone:
  On Error Resume Next
  If blnOpened Then dyn.Close
  If blnTransStarted Then Rollback
  Exit Sub

cmdAdd_ClickError:
  MsgBox Error$, 48, PROGRAM
  Resume cmdAdd_ClickDone

End Sub
```

The `InputBox$` function is used to prompt for the name of the added picture group.

```
strName = Trim$(InputBox$("Enter the name of the new picture group.",
➥ "Name"))
If Len(strName) = 0 Then GoTo cmdAdd_ClickDone
```

To insert a new record into the Pic Group table and maintain the SortOrder field values, a dynaset is opened with a `SELECT` statement to select all of the records ordered by the SortOrder field value.

```
Set db = CodeDB()
  Set dyn = db.OpenRecordset("SELECT * FROM [Pic Group] ORDER BY SortOrder;",
  ➥ DB_OPEN_DYNASET)
  blnOpened = True
```

Next, the position of the currently selected picture group is read from the lstPictureGroups list box (defaulting to the last group if there is no selected group).

```
If IsNull(lstPictureGroups) Then
  intPosition = lstPictureGroups.ListCount
Else
  intPosition = lstPictureGroups.ListIndex + 1
End If
```

Once again, because your code is going to update multiple records, you use transaction processing to ensure that the change either occurs entirely or doesn't occur at all.

```
BeginTrans
blnTransStarted = True
```

The SortOrder field must be adjusted for each of the picture groups that will appear after the new picture group. You will move to the end of the dynaset and work your way back.

```
If dyn.RecordCount Then
   dyn.MoveLast
```

Each of the picture groups after the currently selected picture group has its SortOrder value incremented by one. This creates a space for the new picture group after the current group.

```
Do While dyn!SortOrder > intPosition
   dyn.Edit
   dyn!SortOrder = dyn!SortOrder + 1
   dyn.Update
```

The loop continues by moving backward through the dynaset. The code checks for the beginning of file marker (BOF); however, this marker should never be reached if your SortOrder field values have been properly maintained by the program.

```
   dyn.MovePrevious
   If dyn.BOF Then
      Exit Do
   End If
   Loop
End If
```

After the loop has executed, you should have an available slot for the new picture group. A record is added and the name of the group and sort order position is saved.

```
dyn.AddNew
dyn!Name = strName
dyn!SortOrder = intPosition + 1
```

Before writing the record, the new GroupID value is read into a long integer variable. The GroupID field is a counter field and should be read at this time (right before the update) to let the program know the automatically generated counter value.

```
lngGroupID = dyn!GroupID
dyn.Update
```

With all the record changes completed, CommitTrans is called to apply the entire transaction to the database.

```
CommitTrans
blnTransStarted = False
```

The lstPictureGroups list box is updated by calling the Requery method to reflect the changes in the database. The new picture group is set as the selected group by assigning lstPictureGroups control to the GroupID value that was read earlier.

```
lstPictureGroups.Requery
lstPictureGroups = lngGroupID
```

The *cmdEdit_Click* Subroutine

The cmdEdit_Click subroutine enables the user to change the name of a picture group.

Enter the cmdEdit_Click subroutine as shown in Listing 15.24.

Listing 15.24. The cmdEdit_Click **subroutine.**

```
Sub cmdEdit_Click ()

  Dim db As Database
  Dim tbl As Recordset

  Dim strName As String
  Dim lngGroupID As Long

  Dim blnOpened As Integer

  blnOpened = False

  On Error GoTo cmdEdit_ClickError

  If IsNull(lstPictureGroups) Then GoTo cmdEdit_ClickDone
  lngGroupID = CLng(lstPictureGroups)

  strName = lstPictureGroups.Column(1)
strName = Trim$(InputBox$("Enter the new name for the picture group.",
➥ "Name", strName))
  If Len(strName) = 0 Then GoTo cmdEdit_ClickDone

  Set db = CodeDB()
  Set tbl = db.OpenRecordset("Pic Group", DB_OPEN_TABLE)
  blnOpened = True

  tbl.Index = "PrimaryKey"

  tbl.Seek "=", lngGroupID
  If tbl.NoMatch Then GoTo cmdEdit_ClickDone

  tbl.Edit
  tbl!Name = strName
  tbl.Update

  lstPictureGroups.Requery
  lstPictureGroups = lngGroupID

cmdEdit_ClickDone:
  On Error Resume Next
  If blnOpened Then tbl.Close
  Exit Sub
```

continues

Listing 15.24. continued

```
cmdEdit_ClickError:
  MsgBox Error$, 48, PROGRAM
  Resume cmdEdit_ClickDone

End Sub
```

The subroutine first reads the GroupID and picture group name right from the lstPictureGroups list box.

```
lngGroupID = CLng(lstPictureGroups)

strName = lstPictureGroups.Column(1)
```

The InputBox$ function is used to enable the user to edit the picture group name. The existing name is passed as the third argument so it will appear in the InputBox edit field.

```
strName = Trim$(InputBox$("Enter the new name for the picture group.",
➡ "Name", strName))
  If Len(strName) = 0 Then GoTo cmdEdit_ClickDone
```

Next, the Pic Group table is opened as a recordset in table mode.

```
Set db = CodeDB()
Set tbl = db.OpenRecordset("Pic Group", DB_OPEN_TABLE)
blnOpened = True
```

Then the code Seeks to the record for the current picture group.

```
tbl.Index = "PrimaryKey"

tbl.Seek "=", lngGroupID
If tbl.NoMatch Then GoTo cmdEdit_ClickDone
```

The record is modified with the new picture group name.

```
tbl.Edit
tbl!Name = strName
tbl.Update
```

And finally, the list box is requeried to display the change.

```
lstPictureGroups.Requery
lstPictureGroups = lngGroupID
```

The *cmdDelete_Click* Subroutine

Deleting a picture group is similar to adding one. The code must maintain the SortOrder field values in the Pic Group table. Picture groups that follow the deleted picture group have their SortOrder field value decremented by one to fill in the vacant spot left by the deleted record.

Enter the `cmdDelete_Click` subroutine as shown in Listing 15.25.

Listing 15.25. The `cmdDelete_Click` subroutine.

```
Sub cmdDelete_Click ()

  Dim db As Database
  Dim dyn As Recordset

  Dim strName As String
  Dim msg As String
  Dim cr As String

  Dim lngGroupID As Long
  Dim z As Integer

  Dim blnTransStarted As Integer
  Dim blnOpened As Integer

  blnTransStarted = False
  blnOpened = False

  On Error GoTo cmdDelete_ClickError

  If IsNull(lstPictureGroups) Then GoTo cmdDelete_ClickDone

  strName = lstPictureGroups.Column(1)
  cr = Chr$(13)

  If lstPictureGroups.ListCount = 1 Then
    msg = "Can't delete the " & strName & " picture group." & cr & cr
    msg = msg & "You must always have at least one picture group."
    MsgBox msg, 48, PROGRAM
    GoTo cmdDelete_ClickDone
  End If

msg = "Deleting a picture group also deletes any pictures in the group."
➡ & cr & cr
  msg = msg & "Are you sure you want to delete the " & strName &
  ➡ " picture group?"
  z = MsgBox(msg, 4 + 32 + 256, PROGRAM)
  If z <> 6 Then GoTo cmdDelete_ClickDone

  Set db = CodeDB()
  Set dyn = db.OpenRecordset("SELECT * FROM [Pic Group] ORDER BY SortOrder;",
  ➡ DB_OPEN_DYNASET)
  blnOpened = True

  BeginTrans
  blnTransStarted = True

  dyn.FindFirst "GroupID = " & lstPictureGroups

  dyn.Delete
  dyn.MoveNext
```

continues

Listing 15.25. continued

```
If dyn.EOF Then
   dyn.MovePrevious
   lngGroupID = dyn!GroupID
Else
   lngGroupID = dyn!GroupID

   ' Adjust sort order for groups following the deleted one
   Do Until dyn.EOF
      dyn.Edit
      dyn!SortOrder = dyn!SortOrder - 1
      dyn.Update

      dyn.MoveNext
   Loop
End If

CommitTrans
blnTransStarted = False

lstPictureGroups.Requery
lstPictureGroups = lngGroupID

cmdDelete_ClickDone:
   On Error Resume Next
   If blnOpened Then dyn.Close
   If blnTransStarted Then Rollback
   Exit Sub

cmdDelete_ClickError:
   MsgBox Error$, 48, PROGRAM
   Resume cmdDelete_ClickDone

End Sub
```

The `cmdDelete_Click` subroutine first fetches the name of the selected picture group from the lstPictureGroups list box. It also initializes the `cr` variable to use in creating messages with carriage returns in them.

```
strName = lstPictureGroups.Column(1)
cr = Chr$(13)
```

This next part is a cheesy solution to a problem that I didn't completely deal with. Rather than writing and testing the code so that it could handle a situation where the user deletes all of the picture groups, I just put the check below to prohibit them from doing that.

This is reasonable in the sense that you don't typically expect Picture Builder+ to be used while it is empty. (What good is it then?) But there is the possibility that someone might want to delete all the provided pictures and start their own collection. The user can do this now, but he or she has to add at least one picture group before he or she can delete the final provided picture group.

No excuses; this is a shortcut and could be better implemented.

```
If lstPictureGroups.ListCount = 1 Then
  msg = "Can't delete the " & strName & " picture group." & cr & cr
  msg = msg & "You must always have at least one picture group."
  MsgBox msg, 48, PROGRAM
  GoTo cmdDelete_ClickDone
End If
```

OK, if you're allowing users to delete the picture group, pop up a message first to be sure this is the destructive kind of behavior they are really in the mood for.

```
msg = "Deleting a picture group also deletes any pictures in the group."
➡ & cr & cr
  msg = msg & "Are you sure you want to delete the " & strName &
➡ " picture group?"
  z = MsgBox(msg, 4 + 32 + 256, PROGRAM)
  If z <> 6 Then GoTo cmdDelete_ClickDone
```

If you're continuing, open a dynaset with the Pic Group table records as you did in the `cmdAdd_Click` subroutine and start a transaction.

```
Set db = CodeDB()
Set dyn = db.OpenRecordset("SELECT * FROM [Pic Group] ORDER BY SortOrder;",
➡ DB_OPEN_DYNASET)
blnOpened = True

BeginTrans
blnTransStarted = True
```

Next, find the selected picture group record and delete it. Because you took the time to establish a relationship between the Pic Group table and the Pic table with the cascading delete option, all the related pictures are wiped out from the Pic table also.

The MoveNext method is called to move to the record after the deleted one.

```
dyn.FindFirst "GroupID = " & lstPictureGroups

dyn.Delete
dyn.MoveNext
```

If you've reached the end of the file, the MovePrevious method can be called to move to the record before the deleted one. The GroupID value is read so that the list box can be set to make this the current picture group:

```
If dyn.EOF Then
  dyn.MovePrevious
  lngGroupID = dyn!GroupID
```

If there are one or more records beyond the deleted picture group record, the following picture group will be established as the current picture group:

```
Else
  lngGroupID = dyn!GroupID
```

Using a loop, the following records are edited so that their SortOrder values can be decremented by one:

```
' Adjust sort order for groups following the deleted one
    Do Until dyn.EOF
      dyn.Edit
      dyn!SortOrder = dyn!SortOrder - 1
      dyn.Update

      dyn.MoveNext
    Loop
  End If
```

At the end of the subroutine, the transaction is committed and the list box is updated.

```
CommitTrans
blnTransStarted = False

lstPictureGroups.Requery
lstPictureGroups = lngGroupID
```

The *cmdUp_Click* and *cmdDown_Click* Subroutines

The cmdUp_Click and cmdDown_Click subroutines are activated when the user clicks the up- and down-arrow buttons on the form.

These two subroutines modify the SortOrder field values of the Pic Group table's records to reflect the change caused by moving a picture group up or down one notch in the sort order.

Enter the cmdUp_Click subroutine as shown in Listing 15.26.

Listing 15.26. The cmdUp_Click **subroutine.**

```
Sub cmdUp_Click ()

' Move the selected group up by one

  Dim db As Database
  Dim dyn As Recordset

  Dim lngGroupID As Long
  Dim intIndex As Integer

  Dim blnOpened As Integer
  Dim blnTransStarted As Integer

  blnOpened = False
  blnTransStarted = False

  On Error GoTo cmdUp_ClickError

  If IsNull(lstPictureGroups) Then GoTo cmdUp_ClickDone

  Set db = CodeDB()
Set dyn = db.OpenRecordset("SELECT GroupID, SortOrder FROM [Pic Group]
➨ ORDER BY SortOrder;", DB_OPEN_DYNASET)
```

```
    blnOpened = True

    lngGroupID = lstPictureGroups

    BeginTrans
    blnTransStarted = True

    dyn.FindFirst "GroupID = " & lngGroupID
    If dyn.NoMatch Then GoTo cmdUp_ClickDone

    intIndex = dyn!SortOrder
    If intIndex = 1 Then GoTo cmdUp_ClickDone

    dyn.Edit
    dyn!SortOrder = -1
    dyn.Update

    dyn.MovePrevious
    dyn.Edit
    dyn!SortOrder = intIndex
    dyn.Update

    dyn.FindFirst "SortOrder = -1"
    dyn.Edit
    dyn!SortOrder = intIndex - 1
    dyn.Update

    CommitTrans
    blnTransStarted = False

    lstPictureGroups.Requery
    lstPictureGroups = lngGroupID

cmdUp_ClickDone:
    On Error Resume Next
    If blnTransStarted Then Rollback
    If blnOpened Then dyn.Close
    Exit Sub

cmdUp_ClickError:
    MsgBox Error$, 48, PROGRAM
    Resume cmdUp_ClickDone

End Sub
```

Enter the `cmdDown_Click` subroutine as shown in Listing 15.27.

Listing 15.27. The `cmdDown_Click` subroutine.

```
Sub cmdDown_Click ()

' Move the selected group down by one
```

continues

Listing 15.27. continued

```
    Dim db As Database
    Dim dyn As Recordset
    Dim lngGroupID As Long
    Dim intIndex As Integer

    Dim blnOpened As Integer
    Dim blnTransStarted As Integer

    blnOpened = False
    blnTransStarted = False

    On Error GoTo cmdDown_ClickError

    If IsNull(lstPictureGroups) Then GoTo cmdDown_ClickDone

    Set db = CodeDB()
Set dyn = db.OpenRecordset("SELECT GroupID, SortOrder FROM [Pic Group]
➥ ORDER BY SortOrder;", DB_OPEN_DYNASET)
    blnOpened = True

    lngGroupID = lstPictureGroups

    BeginTrans
    blnTransStarted = True

    dyn.FindFirst "GroupID = " & lngGroupID
    If dyn.NoMatch Then GoTo cmdDown_ClickDone

    intIndex = dyn!SortOrder
    If intIndex = lstPictureGroups.ListCount Then GoTo cmdDown_ClickDone

    dyn.Edit
    dyn!SortOrder = -1
    dyn.Update

    dyn.MoveNext
    dyn.Edit
    dyn!SortOrder = intIndex
    dyn.Update

    dyn.FindFirst "SortOrder = -1"
    dyn.Edit
    dyn!SortOrder = intIndex + 1
    dyn.Update

    CommitTrans
    blnTransStarted = False

    lstPictureGroups.Requery
    lstPictureGroups = lngGroupID

cmdDown_ClickDone:
    On Error Resume Next
```

```
  If blnTransStarted Then Rollback
  If blnOpened Then dyn.Close
  Exit Sub

cmdDown_ClickError:
  MsgBox Error$, 48, PROGRAM
  Resume cmdDown_ClickDone

End Sub
```

The *cmdHint_Click* Subroutine

The cmdHint_Click subroutine opens the Hint form after setting the hint to display as hint number 2.

Enter the cmdHint_Click subroutine as shown in Listing 15.28.

Listing 15.28. The cmdHint_Click **subroutine.**

```
Sub cmdHint_Click ()

  On Error Resume Next
  pbp_lngHintID = 2
  DoCmd OpenForm "Hint"

End Sub
```

The *cmdClose_Click* Subroutine

The last subroutine closes the form.

1. Enter the cmdClose_Click subroutine.
2. Close the Picture Groups form.

Listing 15.29. The cmdClose_Click **subroutine.**

```
Sub cmdClose_Click ()

  DoCmd Close

End Sub
```

Creating and Coding the Hint Form

I've saved the easiest form for the end. The Hint form is modeled after the pop-up hint dialog box in the Access wizards.

Using hint forms is a quick and dirty method to implement some kind of online help without writing a Windows help file, as shown in Figure 15.29. (In Chapter 20, "Access: Survey Wizard, Part Five—Shrink-wrap and Ship It," I tackle the help compiler details so that you can produce your own help file.)

FIGURE 15.29.

*The Hint form
displaying a hint for the
Picture Group form.*

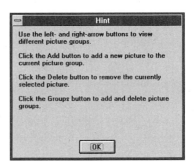

Earlier you created a Hint table to store the hint text in. This makes the Hint form a component that could be moved easily to other Access projects. The only requirement is that your project have its own global variable to identify which hint to display from the Hint table.

1. Create a new form with the typical property settings for a pop-up dialog box:

Object: **Hint Form**

Property	Value
Caption:	Hint
Default View:	Single Form
Shortcut Menu:	No
Scroll Bars:	Neither
Record Selectors:	No
Navigation Buttons:	No
Auto Center:	Yes
Pop Up:	Yes
Modal:	Yes
Border Style:	Dialog box
Min Button:	No
Max Button:	No
Width:	3.3 in

2. Set the detail section properties:

Object: **Detail0 Section**

Property	Value
Height:	2.5 in
Back Color:	12632256 (Light Gray)

Next, a label is added that covers most of the form and is used to display hint text. The label has its caption set to the string, (text added by code), as shown in Figure 15.30, which serves as a reminder when you view the form in design mode.

1. Create the lblHint label with the following properties:

Object: **lblHint Label**

Property	Value
Name:	lblHint
Caption:	(text added by code)
Left:	0.1 in
Top:	0.0826 in
Width:	3.1 in
Height:	2 in
Back Color:	12632256 (Light Gray)
Border Style:	Clear
Font Name:	MS Sans Serif
Font Size:	8
Font Weight:	Bold

2. Add an OK button to the form.

Object: **cmdOK Command Button**

Property	Value
Name:	cmdOK
Caption:	OK
Default:	Yes
Left:	1.3 in
Top:	2.1646 in
Width:	0.7042 in
Height:	0.25 in
Font Name:	MS Sans Serif
Font Size:	8
Font Weight:	Bold

FIGURE 15.30.

Creating the Hint form.

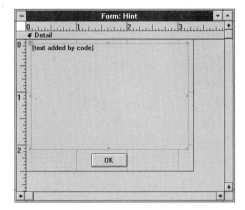

3. Click the Code button on the toolbar to open the form module.
4. Enter the declarations section as shown in Listing 15.30.

Listing 15.30. The declarations section for the Hint form module.

```
' Hint form

Option Compare Database
Option Explicit

Const PROGRAM = "Hint"
```

The Hint form's Form_Open subroutine opens the Hint table and reads the hint text into the caption of the lblHint label control. The pbp_lngHintID global variable identifies the hint to load. The pbp_lngHintID is set before opening the Hint form.

Enter the Form_Open subroutine as shown in Listing 15.31.

Listing 15.31. The Form_Open **subroutine.**

```
Sub Form_Open (Cancel As Integer)

  Dim db As Database
  Dim tbl As Recordset
  Dim blnOpened As Integer

  blnOpened = False

  On Error GoTo Form_OpenError

  Set db = CodeDB()
  Set tbl = db.OpenRecordset("Hint", DB_OPEN_TABLE)
  blnOpened = True
```

```
    tbl.Index = "PrimaryKey"

    tbl.Seek "=", pbp_lngHintID

    If tbl.NoMatch Then
      MsgBox "Invalid HintID", 48, PROGRAM
      Cancel = True
    Else
      lblHint.Caption = tbl!Hint
    End If

Form_OpenDone:
    On Error Resume Next
    If blnOpened Then tbl.Close
    Exit Sub

Form_OpenError:
    MsgBox Error$, 48, PROGRAM
    Cancel = True
    Resume Form_OpenDone

End Sub
```

1. Enter the `cmdOK_Click` subroutine as shown in Listing 15.32.
2. Close and save the Hint form.

Listing 15.32. The `cmdOK_Click` subroutine.

```
Sub cmdOK_Click ()

  DoCmd Close

End Sub
```

You have completed the forms for the Picture Builder+ program, including all the code behind them. The only thing left to complete the database library now are the details that make the program usable as a Property Builder.

Coding the Entry Point Functions

Picture Builder+ will be activated in the same way that the current Access Picture Builder is—when the user presses the ellipsis button on the Picture property in the Properties window.

Hey, wait a minute! Which builder is going to be activated when I press the ellipsis button: Picture Builder or Picture Builder+?

If there is only one builder available, pressing the ellipsis button goes directly to it. If more than one builder is available for the same property setting, Access displays the Choose Builder dialog box as shown in Figure 15.31.

FIGURE 15.31.

You can choose Picture Builder or Picture Builder+ from the Choose Builder dialog box.

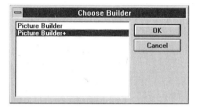

To plug Picture Builder into the Access user interface, you first need to create an entry function that Access can call. This entry point function must be declared with three string arguments; otherwise, an "invalid number of arguments" type error will occur when Access tries to call your entry point function. Even if your function doesn't use the argument values, you must declare the required arguments.

The required arguments are

strObjectName—Name of the database object being modified
strControlName—Name of the control being modified
strValue—Current value in the property setting

The strControlName argument will contain a value only if the property being modified is a control property. (You might be creating a property builder for a Form or Report property.)

An entry point function generally returns the property setting back to Access as the function's return value. However, for Picture Builder+ you're actually setting the control's PictureData property and not the Picture property. (This occurs in the Picture Builder+ form module's cmdOK_Click subroutine.)

All this will become clearer when you see the actual entry point function. You write the function in the Picture Builder+ module, which so far has a few global variable declarations in it and nothing else.

1. Open the Picture Builder+ module.
2. Enter the pbp_Entry function as shown in Listing 15.33.

Listing 15.33. The pbp_Entry **function.**

```
Function pbp_Entry (strObjectName As String, strControlName As String,
➥ strValue As String)

  On Error GoTo pbp_EntryError
```

```
Select Case Application.CurrentObjectType

Case A_FORM
  Set pbp_Control = Forms(strObjectName)(strControlName)

Case A_REPORT
  Set pbp_Control = Reports(strObjectName)(strControlName)

Case Else
  GoTo pbp_EntryDone

End Select

pbp_blnControlSet = True
DoCmd OpenForm pbp_PROGRAM, , , , , A_DIALOG

pbp_EntryDone:
  Exit Function

pbp_EntryError:
  MsgBox Error$, 48, pbp_PROGRAM
  Resume pbp_EntryDone

End Function
```

The pbp_Entry function is declared with the appropriate string arguments for a builder entry point function.

```
Function pbp_Entry (strObjectName As String, strControlName As String,
➥ strValue As String)
```

Inside the function, the CurrentObjectType property of the Application object is used to determine if a form object or report object is currently being edited.

```
  Select Case Application.CurrentObjectType
```

If it is a form, the control is located by first finding the form from the Forms collection and then by looking into the form objects default collection for the control. The first and second arguments to the pbp_Entry function point to which form and control are being modified.

```
Case A_FORM
    Set pbp_Control = Forms(strObjectName)(strControlName)
```

If the current object is a report object, the same type of statement is used to find the report first and then find the control within the report.

The global variable pbp_Control receives the control that is being modified in either case.

```
Case A_REPORT
    Set pbp_Control = Reports(strObjectName)(strControlName)
```

In the unlikely case the current object is not a form or report, the function exits.

```
 Case Else
   GoTo pbp_EntryDone

 End Select
```

The global flag, pbp_blnControlSet, is set to True to indicate that the pbp_Control variable now points to a control. The Picture Builder+ form module code checks this flag before attempting to modify the PictureData property setting in the control pointed to by the pbp_Control variable.

```
 pbp_blnControlSet = True
```

With your two global variables properly initialized, the Picture Builder+ form is opened.

```
 DoCmd OpenForm pbp_PROGRAM, , , , , A_DIALOG
```

There is an additional entry point function that you can write. In the Add-in Manager window the user can click a Customize button to customize the selected add-in. For Picture Builder+, you can use this as another way to allow the user to open the builder for the purpose of adding and deleting pictures and picture groups.

A customized entry point function takes no arguments and has no return value. The pbp_Customize function sets the pbp_blnControlSet variable to False because there is no control being edited to return a picture to. It then opens the Picture Builder+ form.

1. Enter the pbp_Customize function as shown in Listing 15.34.
2. Close the Picture Builder+ module.

Listing 15.34. The pbp_Customize **function.**

```
Function pbp_Customize ()

  On Error GoTo pbp_CustomizeError

  pbp_blnControlSet = False
  DoCmd OpenForm pbp_PROGRAM, , , , , A_DIALOG

pbp_CustomizeDone:
  Exit Function

pbp_CustomizeError:
  MsgBox Error$, 48, pbp_PROGRAM
  Resume pbp_CustomizeDone

End Function
```

Automating Picture Builder+ Installation

To make Picture Builder+ load as a database library and then be useable while working on another database project, you need to make some modifications to the MSACC20.INI file.

You can make these changes manually, but there is a trick in Access that can automate this process and make installing Picture Builder+ a no-brainer for anyone who wants to use it. First, look at what the manual changes would be so that you know what the automated method is accomplishing.

Don't make these changes to your MSACC20.INI file. Instead, use the following as a reference to verify that the automated method actually makes the proper entries.

You already took a look at the [Libraries] section of MSACC20.INI while you went snooping through the library databases that come with Access 2.0. If you renamed the PIDBLDR.MDB database to PICBLDR.MDA, you can load the database as a library with the following [Libraries] section entry:

```
[Libraries]
picbldr.mda=rw
```

That gets your library loaded on startup. Next you need to register to Access that your entry point function pbp_Entry exists as a builder for the Picture property.

This is done in the [Property Wizards] section of MSACC20.INI. If you look at the section, among the entries you will find an entry for the original Picture Builder:

```
[Property Wizards]
MSPictureBuilder=Picture, Picture Builder, PP_ENTRY,rw
```

On the left side of the equal sign is a unique Customization Name. On the right side of the equal sign are four entries separated by commas. The four entries and their settings are

> Property Name—Picture
> Display Name—Picture Builder
> Entry Point function—PP_ENTRY
> Read/Write mode—rw

The line to install pbp_Entry as a Picture property builder is shown here:

```
PictureBuilderPlus=Picture, Picture Builder+, pbp_Entry,rw
```

This line uses the Customization Name, PictureBuilderPlus, and includes the four settings shown below:

> Property Name—Picture
> Display Name—Picture Builder+
> Entry Point function—pbp_Entry
> Read/Write mode—rw

There isn't a way to register a customization function for the Add-in Manager through the MSACC20.INI file. To do that you have to complete the next step of automating this installation process.

Rather than make your users poke around the MSACC20.INI file, you can have them install Picture Builder+ as an add-in by using the Add-in Manager, as shown in Figure 15.32. The Add-in Manager is itself an add-in, so it is activated from the File|Add-ins cascading menu.

FIGURE 15.32.

Activating the Add-in Manager.

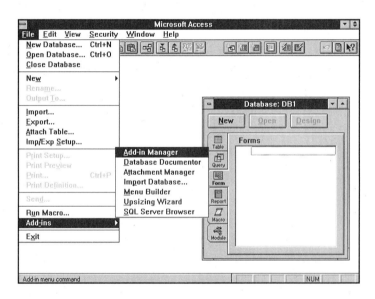

In the Add-in Manager window, the Access user should see the Picture Builder+ library listed among the installable add-ins, as shown in Figure 15.33. Users install by selecting the library and pressing the Install button. An "x" is placed by each library installed.

If the add-in you want to install is in a directory other than the Access directory, you can press the **A**dd New… button to bring up the File Open dialog box so that a user can locate the .MDA file to install. The Add-in Manager will copy this file into the Access directory so that from then on that file will be listed as an available library.

FIGURE 15.33.

Installing Picture Builder+ through the Add-in Manager.

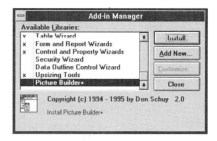

Note that within the Add-in Manager window several things about each add-in are displayed. This includes the full name of the add-in (not just the filename), an icon, a place to display the company name or person that created the add-in, a version number, and a brief message about what the current selection does.

Where does this information come from?

It comes from a hidden table that each of the database libraries contains. The table is named USysAddIns. Let's create one for the Picture Builder+ database.

1. Select the **View|O**ptions command.

2. Under the General category, change the Show System Objects option to Yes as shown in Figure 15.34. Close the Options dialog box.

FIGURE 15.34.

The Show System Objects command tells Access to display some internally maintained tables in the database container.

In the database container you will find listed several tables with names starting with the MSys prefix. You won't find a USysAddIns table, but you can import it from one of the library databases that comes with Access.

3. Select the **File|I**mport command.

4. In the Import dialog box, select Microsoft Access as the **D**ata Source and click OK.

5. In the Select Microsoft Access Database dialog box, enter `*.mda` in the File **N**ame text box to list database libraries. Select the directory you installed Access

in and choose WZBLDR.MDA from the list of library database files, as shown in Figure 15.35. Click OK.

FIGURE 15.35.

Selecting the WZBLDR.MDA database library to import the USysAddIns table.

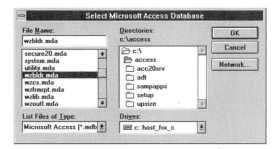

6. In the Import Objects dialog box, select Tables as the object type to import. Then find the USysAddIns table at the bottom of the list of tables, as shown in Figure 15.36. Select it and import the table by clicking the Import button. Close the Import Object dialog box.

FIGURE 15.36.

Importing the USysAddIns table.

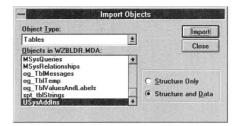

In the database container you now see the USysAddIns table.

7. Open the USysAddIns table in datasheet mode, as shown in Figure 15.37.

FIGURE 15.37.

Examining the entries of the USysAddIns table from the WZBLDR.MDA database.

PropertyName	Val1	Val2	
AddInVersion	2.0		
CompanyName	Microsoft		
Description	Manage Microsoft Access Control and Property Wizards		
DisplayName	Control and Property Wizards		
Logo			
FunctionToCallOnCustomize	Customize Input Mask	IM_Customize()	
FunctionToCallOnCustomize	Customize Command Button	bw_CustomizePictures()	
IniFileEntry	Libraries	wzbldr.mda	rw
IniFileEntry	Property Wizards	MSMenuBarBuilder	Men
IniFileEntry	Property Wizards	MSInputMaskWizard	Inpu
IniFileEntry	Control Wizards	MSCommandButtonWizard	Com
IniFileEntry	Control Wizards	MSListBoxWizard	ListB
IniFileEntry	Control Wizards	MSComboBoxWizard	Com
IniFileEntry	Property Wizards	MSForeColorBuilder	Fore
IniFileEntry	Property Wizards	MSBackColorBuilder	Back
IniFileEntry	Property Wizards	MSBorderColorBuilder	Bord
IniFileEntry	Property Wizards	MSPictureBuilder	Pictu
IniFileEntry	Menu Add-Ins	&Menu Builder	=Cus
IniFileEntry	Property Wizards	MSODBCConnectStrBuilder	ODB
IniFileEntry	Control Wizards	MSOptionGroupWizard	Optic

Record: 1   of 20

In the table you will find a bunch of entries used to install control wizards, property wizards, and property builders.

The PropertyName field is used to indicate what type of information each record is about. The Val1 through Val9 fields vary in content depending on the record type, though I found that Val4 through Val8 weren't currently being used for anything.

Table 15.3 shows a list of the different types of entries you can make in the PropertyName field, along with the associated entries that are valid in the remaining fields for each type of record.

Table 15.3. Different types of USysAddIns records.

Field	*Purpose*
AddInVersion	
Val1:	Version Number for the library
CompanyName	
Val1:	Company name and copyright notice
Description	
Val1:	Description of what is being installed
DisplayName	
Val1:	Name to appear in Available Libraries list
FunctionToCallOnCustomize	
Val1:	Name to appear in customizations list
Val2:	Entry call to customization program
IniFileEntry	
Val1:	Section name
Val2:	Option name
Val3:	Option value
Logo	
Val9:	Picture

To create your own USysAddIns table, you need to delete all the records in the imported table and add your own records to it.

1. Delete all the records in the USysAddIns table.
2. Add the records in the USysAddIns table as listed in Table 15.4.

Table 15.4. The USysAddIns records in PICBLDR.MDA.

PropertyName:	AddInVersion
Val1:	2.0

PropertyName:	CompanyName
Val1:	Copyright (c) 1994 - 1995 by Don Schuy

PropertyName:	Description
Val1:	Install Picture Builder+

PropertyName:	DisplayName
Val1:	Picture Builder+

PropertyName:	IniFileEntry
Val1:	Libraries
Val2:	picbldr.mda
Val3:	rw

PropertyName:	IniFileEntry
Val1:	Property Wizards
Val2:	PictureBuilderPlus
Val3:	Picture, Picture Builder+, pbp_Entry,rw

PropertyName:	Logo
Val9:	(Picture)

PropertyName:	FunctionToCallOnCustomize
Val1:	Customize Picture Builder+
Val2:	pbp_Customize()

Figure 15.38 shows the USysAddIns table open in datasheet view.

The first four entries in the table define the text displayed in the Add-in Manager window. The first IniFileEntry line creates an entry in the [Libraries] section of the

MSACC20.INI file that loads the PICBLDR.MDA library with read/write access on startup. The next line creates an entry in the [Property Wizards] section to register the pbp_Entry function as a Picture property builder.

FIGURE 15.38.

Filling in the USysAddIns table records.

PropertyName	Val1	Val2	Val
AddInVersion	2.0		
CompanyName	Copyright (c) 1994 - 1995 by Don Schuy		
Description	Install Picture Builder+		
DisplayName	Picture Builder+		
IniFileEntry	Libraries	picbldr.mda	rw
IniFileEntry	Property Wizards	PictureBuilderPlus	Picture, Picture Builder+,
Logo			
FunctionToCallOnCustomize	Customize Picture Builder+	pbp_Customize()	

The next record contains a bitmap in the Val9 field that is to be displayed at the lower-left corner of the Add-in Manager window. To insert a picture in this field, you would do the following:

Create a 16-color picture in Paintbrush 800 pixels wide and 600 pixels tall. Select the entire picture and copy it into the clipboard with Paintbrush's **E**dit|**C**opy command. Switch back to Access and use **E**dit|Paste **S**pecial to copy the picture into the Val9 field. In the Paste Special dialog box select "Picture" as the format to paste the picture data in.

The last record indicates to the Add-in Manager code that a customize function is available. The Add-in Manager will evaluate the expression, "pbp_Customize()", which executes the pbp_Customize function.

1. Close the table.
2. Turn the Show System Objects option off.

You're pretty much done now. Rather than just renaming the PICBLDR.MDB database to PICBLDR.MDA, I like to run the **F**ile|**C**ompact Database command to create the final library database.

1. Close the PICBLDR.MDA database.
2. Select the **F**ile|**C**ompact Database command.
3. Select the PICBLDR.MDB file as the database to compact.
4. Enter PICBLDR.MDA as the database to compact into.
5. Copy the PICBLDR.MDA file into the directory that you installed Access 2.0 into.
6. Open a database and then use the Add-in Manager to install Picture Builder+.

That's it! But software is never really done. Here are a couple ideas you might want to pursue to improve Picture Builder+: Add the capability of rearranging pictures in a picture group.

One way to do so would be to add four small arrow buttons that move the selected picture up, down, left, or right. When a picture is moved, it swaps places with the picture in the location that it is moving to.

The original Picture Builder uses the large versions of the Access toolbar button pictures. If you dig around in WZLIB.MDA you can find how the pictures are retrieved.

Can you extract these pictures and make them part of the Picture Builder+ picture library?

Summary

In this chapter you created a full-fledged, stripes-on-its-shoulder Access third-party add-in. You improved the Picture Builder provided with Access by creating one that you can use to look at more than one picture at a time.

Here's a full list of your accomplishments. You

- Learned what a builder is
- Temporarily disabled the libraries from MSACC20.INI
- Poked around the Access wizard libraries to find secrets
- Set up Picture Builder+ tables to use some of the provided pictures in WZBLDR.MDA
- Created the Picture Builder+ forms
- Created a Hint form and table you can use in other projects
- Learned how to transfer pictures from one control to another and from a file to a control
- Used the `InputBox$` function
- Wrote a `GetFilename` function to use the File Open common dialog box
- Wrote code to add and delete pictures in a picture group
- Wrote code to add, edit, and delete picture groups
- Wrote entry-point functions to activate Picture Builder+
- Created the hidden USysAddIns table so that Add-in Manager can install Picture Builder+

TRY THIS! ANSWERS

15.1. Here's the `SaveFilename` function I came up with, which is a slight modification of the `GetFilename` function you created in the chapter.

To make both of the functions more generic, you might want to pass a form variable as an argument. As coded, the functions use the `Me` variable and only work when in a form module.

```
Function SaveFilename (strTitle As String, strFilter As String) As String

  Dim ofn As WLIB_GETFILENAMEINFO

  On Error GoTo SaveFilenameError

' See the SDK docs or help files for all possible flags and their meanings.
  Const OFN_OVERWRITEPROMPT = &H2
  Const OFN_HIDEREADONLY = &H4
  Const OFN_PATHMUSTEXIST = &H800

  SaveFilename = ""

  ofn.hwndOwner = Me.hwnd

' Filter: "Text (*.txt)¦*.txt¦All (*.*)¦*.*"
  ofn.szFilter = strFilter

  ofn.nFilterIndex = 1
  ofn.szTITLE = strTitle

  ofn.Flags = OFN_OVERWRITEPROMPT Or OFN_HIDEREADONLY Or OFN_PATHMUSTEXIST

' Second argument indicates if this is a file open or a file save dialog
  If Not wlib_GetFilename(ofn, False) Then
    SaveFilename = Left$(ofn.szFile, InStr(1, ofn.szFile, " ") - 1)
  End If

SaveFilenameDone:
  Exit Function

SaveFilenameError:
  MsgBox Error$, 48, PROGRAM
  Resume SaveFilenameDone

End Function
```

PART III

Advanced Projects

CHAPTER 16

Access: Survey Wizard, Part One— Design and Interface

In the next five chapters, you will create a full-scale Access wizard from start to finish. You will not only cover the techniques to build a marketable Access add-in product, but you will actually complete one in the process!

You are going to build a Survey Wizard. The Survey Wizard can be used to generate a form, two different reports, three tables and a query; all used for the specific need of performing a survey. You will make your Survey Wizard have the same look and feel as the wizards that come with Microsoft Access.

At this stage in the game, I'll assume that you have average to expert skills in using Access. To be able to follow the instructions to build Survey Wizard, you will already have to have some experience in creating forms, be able to navigate your way through Access, and have some familiarity with Access Basic. If you've completed any of the earlier Access projects in this book, you should have no problem.

I'm also going to dispense with the numbered step-by-step instructions in this part of the book. This allows us to pick up the pace somewhat and cover more ground. You will still find each of the required property settings and all of the essential details required to follow along and reproduce the program from scratch.

If you choose to just read along rather than re-create Survey Wizard on your own, a copy of the final application is included on the companion CD-ROM. Either way, you are bound to pick up a trick or two about Access that you didn't know before.

The initial Survey Wizard screen is shown in Figure 16.1.

FIGURE 16.1.

*Survey Wizard uses
Next and Back buttons
to move from screen to
screen.*

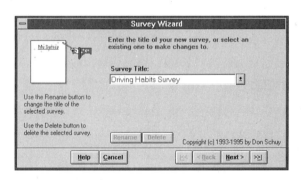

In this first chapter you deal with the fun stuff, the initial design of your application and generating the main form for it. You also will create two tables that the Survey Wizard uses to save the user's work to and you will do a little bit of coding to get started.

In Chapter 17, "Access: Survey Wizard, Part Two—Coding and Interface," you live up to your fancy design and write the code behind the Survey Wizard form. This chapter is all coding. The end result is a user interface that is easy to use and bulletproof.

In Chapters 18, "Access: Survey Wizard, Part Three—Generating Objects," and 19, "Access: Survey Wizard, Part Four—'Pretty Good Charts'," you design the objects that your wizard must produce, and implement the code that builds the objects. The build code lives behind a second form that you also create in Chapter 18.

Chapter 19 contains a bonus in that there is a set of reusable graph routines for Access reports that you can use in any Access project. In Chapter 20, "Access: Survey Wizard, Part Five—Shrink-wrap and Ship It," you polish off Survey Wizard by creating online help for it, and by making it a fully installable menu add-in.

Before you start building things, let's go over the concepts and design behind Survey Wizard.

Survey Wizard Objects

The user of Survey Wizard is a person that is creating his or her own questionnaire. The user enters what questions will be asked, and what possible answers the respondent to the questionnaire is allowed.

In this and the following chapters, I use the word *questionnaire* to mean the thing that you use to collect survey data. I use the word *survey* to mean the act or process of using a questionnaire.

If it's confusing that I'm talking about questionnaires all the time when the application is called Survey Wizard, well, just think how awkward a name like "Questionnaire Wizard" would be!

After defining the questionnaire, the Survey Wizard user has the option to create some or all of the following objects:

- Entry Report
- Questions Table
- Entry Form
- Responses Table
- Results Query
- Results Table
- Results Report

An *Entry Report* is a paper version of the questionnaire. This may be duplicated and distributed as one way to collect survey data.

The *Questions Table* contains records defining each question in the questionnaire. The Entry Report uses the Questions Table as its source data, so it's mandatory that you create this table when creating the report.

All the following objects and the Questions Table are mandatory to generate the on-line survey system with a reporting capability.

An *Entry Form* is an Access form version of the questionnaire. It would be used to collect survey data if you could somehow manage to get folks in front of your computer to take the survey. It may be more feasible to use this form in a file server network environment where many computers would have access to your survey database.

If either of those aren't viable options, the form also could be used to key into the database the data collected via the paper questionnaires.

The *Responses Table* receives the data entered into the Entry Form and is a source of data for the Results Report.

The *Results Query* is a make table query that summarizes data in the Responses Table and produces the Results Table. The *Results Table* is the data source for the Results Report.

The *Results Report* redisplays each question alongside a graph that indicates responses to the question. Use this report after your survey data is collected in order to view the trends indicated by the survey data.

Components of a Questionnaire

For Survey Wizard to be "wizard-like," you should create a user interface that is as easy as possible to use. This will be a challenge because there is quite a bit of information to enter in order to define a questionnaire.

A questionnaire is made up of questions and a means to answer the questions. Other than prompting for which questions to ask, you must also prompt for how the questions may be answered.

I decided to allow the following question/answer types:

■ A *Yes/No* question simply allows a Yes or No answer.

■ A *Write-In* question allows any written response as the answer.

■ A *Multiple-Choice* question must have selections to choose from. For simplification, I decided to limit the number of possible responses to six for each question (A through F).

- The *Range* question type is used to allow the user to reply to a question by selecting one number from a set of numbers.
- A *Percent* question type works similarly except that the numbers are shown as percentages.

The defaults for a Range question would be choices from 1 to 10, which would be typical for questions that ask to rate something on a scale of numbers. The default answer values for a Percent-type question would be 0%, 25%, 50%, 75%, and 100%.

That's everything you will be asking the Survey Wizard user for. It's not too complicated, but it is a lot of stuff to enter into a wizard form and still make it seem like a wizard. To keep a simple form design, I decided to allow the user to focus on a single question/answer definition at a time.

The Survey Wizard User Interface

As is typical for wizard programs, the Survey Wizard user interface is implemented as a multiple-page form.

Several of the pages are used to define a single question and its answering options. After defining the first question, the first of these pages is returned to in order to repeat the process and define the next question.

The flowchart in Figure 16.2 demonstrates how the Survey Wizard's multiple-page form is used to define a questionnaire.

Page 2 of the multiple-page form is used to enter a question. Then the user continues through Pages 3 and 4 to define the answering options. After the answering options are defined, the user returns to Page 2 to enter the next question.

This interface loop continues, allowing the user to enter all the questions to be included in the questionnaire. The final page is displayed when the user hits the Next button on Page 2 without entering another question. In this last page, the user starts the build of the database objects.

The code behind the user interface collects the user responses and stores them in an array of structures in memory. This array and some of the values set on the Survey Wizard forms are going to be the input to the program that actually generates the database objects.

Well, that's enough design and theory for most of us. You all know that you learn better by getting your hands dirty, so let's get to it.

FIGURE 16.2.

A map of the Survey Wizard user interface.

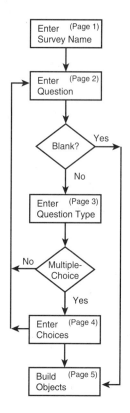

Create the Development Database

You can start by creating an empty database, SURVEY.MDB.

Eventually, when you are all done you split your development database into two library databases: SRVYBLD.MDA and SRVYRUN.MDA. As a convention, the .MDA filename extension is used for library databases, where a library database is one that can be loaded automatically each time you start Access.

For now, stick with a single database with the .MDB extension. It's easier to develop a program while it's not loaded as a library. It's also more convenient to use the .MDB extension because the Access File Open dialog box defaults to looking for .MDB files.

Create the Survey Wizard Form

Next you start creating the form that is 95 percent of the Survey Wizard interface. It is a multiple-page form that you eventually save with the name `Survey Wizard`.

Each page within your multiple-page form is going to be 2 1/4-inches high. With five pages on the form, the total height will be 11 1/4 inches. That is just over halfway to the limit of the height of a form that is 22 inches.

> ### NOTE
>
>
>
> By the way, I think I know why 22 inches was selected as the maximum height and width of an Access form. Objects placed on a form in Access are sometimes located using a coordinate system of *twips*. Because there are 1440 twips per inch, you could multiply 1440 times 22 and get a value of 31680.
>
> The interesting thing to note is that an integer in Access BASIC has a range of values from -32768 to 32767. If a form were wider or higher than 22 inches, you wouldn't be able to locate controls using integer values.
>
> Some people would argue that 22 inches is plenty, but when using this technique of multiple-page forms, the form size is kind of restrictive, especially if you wanted your multiple page form to be taller than 2 1/4 inches. You would quickly run out of pages. It's my hope that this 22-inch limit will go away in some future version of Access.

If you haven't already done so, create a new empty form and set its detail section height to 11 1/4 inches. Using the toolbox Page Break control, place four page breaks on the detail section at 2 1/4-inch intervals down the form. This would place them at 2 1/4 inches, 4 1/2 inches, 6 3/4 inches and 9 inches. Make the form 5 1/4-inches wide and give the detail section a light gray background.

Figure 16.3 shows the fourth Page Break control being added to the Survey Wizard form.

FIGURE 16.3.

Placing the fourth page break control at the 9-inch mark.

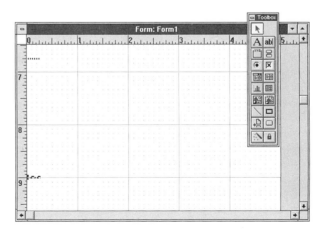

Next, enable the Form Header and Form Footer sections by selecting the Format|Form Header/Footer command. You won't need to use the Form Header section. The Form Footer section is used to display VCR buttons that the user clicks to move between the different pages in the Detail section. (You will be adding the VCR buttons to the form later.)

Following are the properties to set on the form, including the properties for the Header, Detail, and Footer sections.

In this and the following tables of property settings, I'll list mainly the properties that must be changed from their default values. You'll also find some of the properties listed with their default values unchanged because these are settings that are significant to making things work and probably shouldn't be changed.

Survey Wizard Form

A multiple-page form that is the majority of the Survey Wizard user interface.

Object: **Survey Wizard Form**

Property	Value
Caption	Survey Wizard
Default View	Single Form
Views Allowed	Form
Shortcut Menu	No
Scrollbars	Neither
Record Selectors	No
Navigation Buttons	No
Border Style	Dialog
Width	5.25 in
Grid X	64
Grid Y	64

Object: **FormHeader1 Section**

Property	Value
Visible	No
Height	0.0 in

Object: **Detail0 Section**

Property	Value
Height	11.25 in
Back Color	12632256 (Light Gray)

Object: **FormFooter2 Section**

Property	Value
Height	0.3799 in
Back Color	12632256 (Light Gray)

As we already discussed, the following page break controls should be placed in the Detail section of the form:

PageBreak0	Top: 2.25 in
PageBreak1	Top: 4.5 in
PageBreak2	Top: 6.75 in
PageBreak3	Top: 9.0 in

Creating the VCR Buttons

You now create a series of buttons in the footer section at the bottom of the form. These buttons allow the user to navigate through the different pages of the detail section when he is defining his questionnaire.

For the text on each of the buttons, I used the Arial font set to Bold with a font size of 8.

Object: **cmdCancel Command Button**
Exit the Survey Wizard without generating any objects.

Property	Value
Caption	&Cancel
Cancel	Yes
Enabled	Yes
Left	1.6 in
Top	0.05 in
Width	0.5597 in
Height	0.25 in

Figure 16.4 shows the Cancel button being added to the form.

FIGURE 16.4.

Creating the Cancel button.

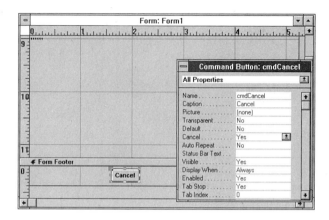

Object: **cmdFirst Command Button**

Move to the first page of the multiple-page entry sequence.

Property	Value
Caption	|&<<
Enabled	No
Left	3.1 in
Top	0.05 in
Width	0.3299 in
Height	0.25 in

Object: **cmdBack Command Button**

Move to the previous page of the multiple-page entry sequence.

Property	Value
Caption	< &Back
Enabled	No
Left	3.4201 in
Top	0.05 in
Width	0.5597 in
Height	0.25 in

Object: **cmdNext Command Button**

Move to the next page of the multiple-page entry sequence.

Property	Value
Caption	&Next >
Enabled	Yes

Left	3.9799 in
Top	0.05 in
Width	0.5597 in
Height	0.25 in

Object: **cmdLast Command Button**

Move to the last page of the multiple-page entry sequence.

Property	Value
Caption	>&>|
Enabled	Yes
Left	4.5403 in
Top	0.05 in
Width	0.3299 in
Height	0.25 in

Figure 16.5 shows the form after all the VCR buttons have been added.

FIGURE 16.5.

Completing the VCR buttons.

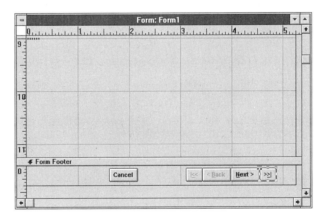

Use the **Edit|Tab** Order command to change the tab order of the buttons in the form footer. The tab order should be set so that tabbing through the buttons works circularly from left to right. However, make the cmdNext button the first button to have focus. See Figure 16.6.

cmdNext
cmdLast
cmdCancel
cmdFirst
cmdBack

FIGURE 16.6.

Setting the tab order of the VCR buttons.

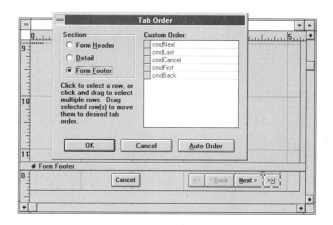

Creating Page 1

Return to the Detail section where the majority of your work is to be done. Drop the controls that make up the first page of your Survey Wizard form.

The first page has a combo box to enter the title of the survey as it appears on the top of the questionnaire. This is a required entry, so the Survey Wizard interface insists that you enter a survey title before you are allowed to continue to any other pages.

The definition of your questionnaire gets saved into tables in the Survey Wizard database, so later you can use the combo box to select it and work on your questionnaire again. It's easier than re-keying in 24 questions because you wanted to add the 25th one to your survey.

Also on the first page are Rename and Delete buttons so that you can rename or delete the title of a saved survey.

There are two labels on this and all the pages on the Survey Wizard form that display user instructions.

The label with the blue text on the top right of the page is used to indicate brief instructions about what task is being accomplished on this page. The label on the left bottom part of the form is for additional hints on how to use the form.

To polish it off, I created a picture using Windows Paintbrush (see Figure 16.7). I truly max'ed the potential of my artistic abilities and created a wizard's hand holding a magic wand.

In this picture, and in the pictures on the following pages, the sparkles and yellow glow indicate what new thing is currently being added to the questionnaire. In this case, the title is being created.

FIGURE 16.7.

Drawing the bitmap for Page 1.

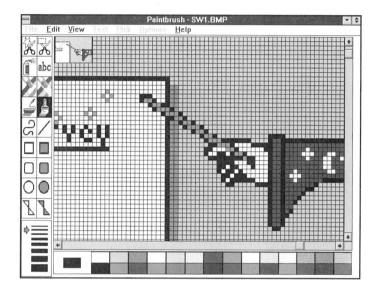

If you are creating Survey Wizard on your own, you can either draw your own picture or find it on the companion CD-ROM included with the book. The files for the bitmaps on each page of the Survey Wizard form are SW1.BMP through SW5.BMP.

In Paintbrush, I had my picture size set to 1.33-inches wide and 1.03-inches high. I drew the picture and saved the bitmap as a standard .BMP file.

Next, in Access I dropped an Unbound Object Frame control on the form. In the Insert Object dialog box I clicked the Create from **F**ile option, then pressed the **B**rowse button to locate my saved bitmap as shown in Figure 16.8.

Access did the rest and correctly sized the object frame for the size of my bitmap. See Figure 16.9.

One trick that helps remove screen flicker while your form is being displayed is to change the Back Color property of the Unbound Object Frame to the same Back Color of your form. Otherwise you see a momentary flash of white where the picture is drawn because the control is drawn empty before the picture comes in.

FIGURE 16.8.

Using the Insert Object dialog box to load a picture from a file.

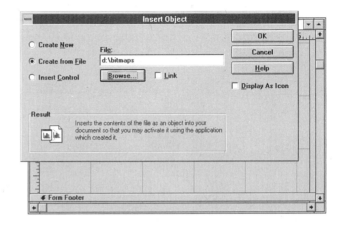

FIGURE 16.9.

Adding a bitmap to the Survey Wizard form.

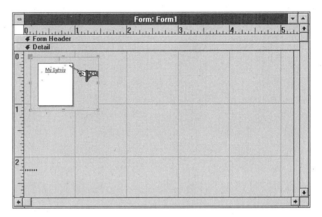

On the Survey Wizard form, the text for all the label controls is set to MS Sans Serif font, font size 8, and bold. The labels should either have their Back Color setting to the same as the form, or you can get the same effect by setting their Back Style property to Clear. I set the text for command buttons to Arial font, font size 8, and bold.

Following are the property settings for the controls on the first page of the Survey Wizard form:

Object: **bmp1 Unbound Object Frame**
Picture of the wizard materializing a questionnaire title.

Property	Value
Tab Stop	No
Left	0.1403 in

Top	0.1097 in
Back Color	12632256 (Light Gray)
Border Style	Clear

Object: **lblHint1 Label**

Hints about using the Rename and Delete buttons.

Property	Value
Caption	Use the Rename button to change the title of the selected survey. Use the Delete button to delete the selected survey.
Left	0.1097 in
Top	1.2035 in
Width	1.4896 in
Height	0.9576 in
Fore Color	0 (Black)
Font Weight	Normal

Object: **lblInstructions1 Label**

Blue instructions for Page 1.

Property	Value
Caption	Enter the title of your new survey, or select an existing one on which to make changes.
Left	1.75 in
Top	0.125 in
Width	3.25 in
Height	0.4403 in
Fore Color	12632256 (Dark Blue)
Font Weight	Bold

Object: **lblSurveyTitle Label**

Child label of the cboSurveyTitle combo box.

Property	Value
Caption	Survey Title:
Left	1.8021 in
Top	0.6771 in
Width	0.875 in
Height	0.1715 in

Object: **cboSurveyTitle Combo box**
Enter a new title or select an existing survey.

Property	Value
Row Source Type	Table/Query
Row Source	SELECT ID,Title FROM Survey ORDER BY Title;
Column Count	2
Column Widths	0 in;2.6299 in
Bound Column	2
List Rows	4
Limit To List	No
Auto Expand	Yes
Left	1.8097 in
Top	0.8646 in
Width	2.6299 in
Height	0.1903 in
Special Effect	Sunken
Font Name	MS Sans Serif
Font Size	10
Font Weight	Normal

Object: **cmdRenameSurvey Command Button**
Rename the title of the survey.

Property	Value
Caption	Rename
Enabled	No
Tab Stop	No
Left	1.8201 in
Top	1.9583 in
Width	0.6 in
Height	0.2 in
Font Name	Arial
Font Size	8
Font Weight	Bold

Object: **cmdDeleteSurvey Command Button**
Delete the selected survey.

Property	Value
Caption	Delete
Enabled	No
Tab Stop	No
Left	2.4403 in
Top	1.9583 in
Width	0.6 in
Height	0.2 in
Font Name	Arial
Font Size	8
Font Weight	Bold

Object: **lblCopyright Label**
Author's copyright message.

Property	Value
Caption	Copyright (c) 1993-1995 by Don Schuy
Left	3.2035 in
Top	2.0625 in
Width	1.9583 in
Height	0.1667 in
Fore Color	0 (Black)
Font Weight	Normal

The finished page should look like the one shown in Figure 16.10.

FIGURE 16.10.

Adding the controls for Page 1.

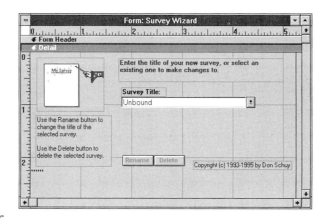

Creating Page 2

The second page of your form is where text for each question is entered.

This is by far the most complicated of the pages on the form. The page supports a feature that allows you to quickly scan through all the questions entered without having to visit the other pages on this form. Inserting and deleting questions can also be done on this page.

The controls on the second page are positioned to match the locations of the controls on Page 1. This is done so there isn't a noticeable shifting effect to where it looks like controls are moving. Instead, the controls appear to stay in the same place, but have their contents changed. Controls on the following pages are aligned to produce a smooth transition when moving from page to page throughout the form.

In the bitmap for Page 2, the wizard's magic wand moves from the title of the questionnaire over to where questions are being magically created. This bitmap is SW2.BMP on the companion CD-ROM. (See Figure 16.11.)

FIGURE 16.11.

The wizard's magic wand adds questions to the questionnaire.

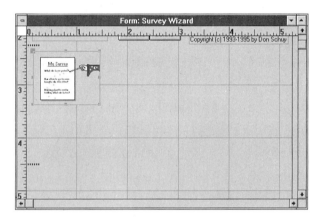

There are actually three blue instructional text box controls for Page 2. This is done because I wanted to display a different message depending on whether the user is on the first question, a middle question, or on one that may be the last question. These controls are named lblInstructions2First, lblInstructions2Next, and lblInstructions2Last.

The lblInstructions2First control is placed on the form first and has its Visible property set to Yes. The other two labels, lblInstructions2Next and lblInstructions2Last, have the same properties as lblInstructions2First except that they have their Visible property set to No.

Figure 16.12 shows the three labels before they are stacked on one another.

FIGURE 16.12.
Three labels are stacked on each other, and alternately made visible.

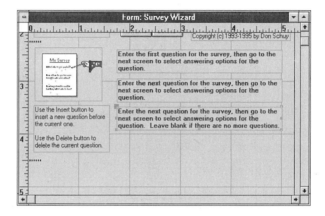

Likewise, there are two labels for the txtQuestion text box. lblFirstQuestion is the one that is actually bound to the txtQuestion text box. This label is always set to visible, but becomes obscured when the lblNextQuestion label has its visible property set to Yes.

> **NOTE**
>
> It is also possible to alternate messages by using a single label control and changing its Caption property in the program.

In the middle of the page is the txtQuestion text box. It is made large enough to make even a lengthy question visible without scrolling.

To the right of the txtQuestion control are a label and text box that display which question the user is currently working on. These two controls are duplicated on Pages 3 and 4, so while the user is working on the different parts of a question/answer definition, he or she is reminded of which question is being worked on.

Below the txtQuestion control are buttons for inserting and deleting questions, and for moving forward and backward through the set of questions.

The Insert button is used to create a new question before the current question. The Delete button does what you would expect it to and deletes the current question.

The <<, <, >, and >> buttons are used as shortcuts in order to move through the list of defined questions without having to move from Page 2 and view each question's answering options.

Here are the property settings for the controls on the second page:

Object: **bmp2 Unbound Object Frame**
Picture of the wizard creating questions.

Property	Value
Tab Stop	No
Left	0.1403 in
Top	2.3597 in
Back Color	12632256 (Light Gray)
Border Style	Clear

Object: **lblHint2 Label**
Hints on using the Insert and Delete buttons.

Property	Value
Caption	Use the Insert button to insert a new question before the current one. Use the Delete button to delete the current question.
Left	0.1097 in
Top	3.4535 in
Width	1.4896 in
Height	0.9576 in
Fore Color	0 (Black)
Font Weight	Normal

Object: **lblInstructions2First Label**
Blue instructions for Page 2 when on the first question.

Property	Value
Caption	Enter the first question for the survey, then go to the next screen to select answering options for the question.
Left	1.75 in
Top	2.375 in
Width	3.25 in
Height	0.4403 in
Fore Color	12632256 (Dark Blue)
Font Weight	Bold

Object: **lblInstructions2Next Label**
Blue instructions for Page 2 when not on the first or last question.

Property	Value
Caption	Enter the next question for the survey, then go to the next screen to select answering options for the question.
Visible	No

Other properties are the same as lblInstructions2First.

Object: **lblInstructions2Last Label**
Blue instructions for Page 2 when on a potential last question.

Property	Value
Caption	Enter the next question for the survey, then go to the next screen to select answering options for the question. Leave blank if there are no more questions.
Visible	No

Other properties are the same as lblInstructions2First.

Object: **lblFirstQuestion Label**
Child label of the txtQuestion text box. Indicates the user is entering the first question.

Property	Value
Caption	First Question:
Left	1.7903 in
Top	2.9403 in
Width	1.1771 in
Height	0.1667 in
Fore Color	0 (Black)

Object: **lblNextQuestion Label**
Indicates the user is entering question text.

Property	Value
Caption	Next Question:

Other properties are the same as lblFirstQuestion.

Object: **txtQuestion Text Box**
Receives the question text.

Property	Value
Left	1.8 in
Top	3.1201 in
Width	2.625 in
Height	1.0417 in
Special Effect	Sunken
Font Name	MS Sans Serif
Font Size	10

Object: **lblQuestion2 Label**
Label for the txtCurrentQuestion2 control.

Property	Value
Caption	Question:
Left	4.5597 in
Top	3.3903 in
Width	0.5208 in
Height	0.1667 in
Fore Color	16777215 (White)

Object: **txtCurrentQuestion2 Text Box**
Indicates which question is currently being edited.

Property	Value
Control Source	=CurrentQuestion()
Enabled	No
Locked	Yes
Tab Stop	No
Left	4.5701 in
Top	3.5903 in
Width	0.5 in
Height	0.1667 in
Fore Color	16777215 (White)

The font for the buttons on the form is Arial, bold, size 8.

Object: **cmdInsertQuestion Command Button**
Insert a question before the current one.

Property	Value
Caption	Insert
Left	1.8201 in
Top	4.2097 in
Width	0.6 in
Height	0.2 in

Object: **cmdDeleteQuestion Command Button**
Delete the current question.

Property	Value
Caption	Delete
Left	2.4403 in
Top	4.2097 in
Width	0.6 in
Height	0.2 in

Object: **cmdFirstQuestion Command Button**
Go to the first question.

Property	Value
Caption	l<<
Left	3.2806 in
Top	4.2097 in
Width	0.2701 in
Height	0.2 in

Object: **cmdBackQuestion Command Button**
Go to the previous question.

Property	Value
Caption	<
Left	3.55 in
Top	4.2097 in
Width	0.2701 in
Height	0.2 in

Object: **cmdNextQuestion Command Button**
Go to the next question.

Property	Value
Caption	>
Left	3.825 in
Top	4.2097 in
Width	0.2701 in
Height	0.2 in

Object: **cmdLastQuestion Command Button**
Go to the last question.

Property	Value
Caption	>>|
Left	4.0903 in
Top	4.2097 in
Width	0.2701 in
Height	0.2 in

When it's all done, the second page should look something like the one shown in Figure 16.13.

FIGURE 16.13.

The controls on the second page of the Survey Wizard form.

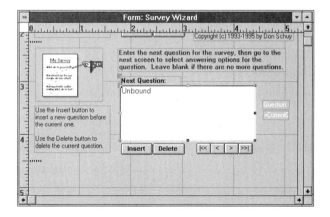

Creating Page 3

In the third page, the user defines how a question is answered by selecting one of five response types.

In the bitmap for Page 3 (SW3.BMP), the wizard's magic wand is busy filling in the answering sections of the questionnaire. See Figure 16.14.

FIGURE 16.14.

Adding a bitmap to page three.

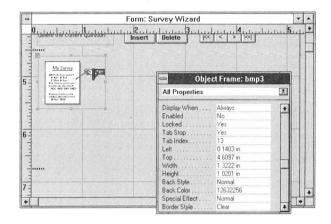

An optResponseType option group control is used to return which response type has been selected. Within this option group are five option buttons; rbtYesNo, rbtMultipleChoice, rbtWriteIn, rbtRange, and rbtPercent. They return values of 1 to 5, respectively.

When either the rbtRange or rbtPercent buttons are selected, three hidden text box controls reappear on the form in order to enter To, From, and Step values. These values define the set of numbers that are displayed as possible responses to the question.

Following are the property settings for the controls on Page 3 of the Survey Wizard form:

Object: **bmp3 Unbound Object Frame**
Picture of the wizard creating answer sections.

Property	*Value*
Tab Stop	No
Left	0.1403 in
Top	4.6097 in
Back Color	12632256 (Light Gray)
Border Style	Clear

Object: **lblHint3 Label**
Hint about using the Back button.

Property	*Value*
Caption	If you need to review which question you are working on, press the &Back button.
Left	0.1097 in

continues

Property	Value
Top	5.7035 in
Width	1.4896 in
Height	0.9576 in
Fore Color	0 (Black)
Font Weight	Normal

Object: **lblInstructions3 Label**

Blue instructions for Page 3.

Property	Value
Caption	Enter the type of response that is allowed for the current question. If Multiple-Choice is selected, the next screen lets you enter the available choices.
Left	1.75 in
Top	4.625 in
Width	3.25 in
Height	0.4403 in
Fore Color	12632256 (Dark Blue)
Font Weight	Bold

Object: **lblResponseType Label**

Child label of the optResponseType option group.

Property	Value
Caption	Response Type:
Left	1.8493 in
Top	5.1875 in
Width	0.9792 in
Height	0.1667 in

Object: **optResponseType Option Group**

Select the type of response allowed for a question.

Property	Value
Default Value	1
Left	1.7972 in
Top	5.2708 in
Width	2.625 in
Height	0.9951 in
Special Effect	Sunken

The following radio buttons have their Width and Height properties set to 0.1806 inches and 0.1375 inches, respectively. They also have their Special Effect property set as Sunken.

Object: **rbtYesNo Option Button**
Select a Yes/No response type.

Property	*Value*
Option Value	1
Left	1.9646 in
Top	5.5 in

Object: **lblYesNo Label**
Child label of the rbtYesNo option button.

Property	*Value*
Caption	Yes/No
Left	2.1715 in
Top	5.4646 in
Width	0.5097 in
Height	0.1667 in

Object: **rbtMultipleChoice Option Button**
Select a Multiple Choice response type.

Property	*Value*
Option Value	2
Left	1.9646 in
Top	5.75 in

Object: **lblMultipleChoice Label**
Child label of the rbtMultipleChoice option button.

Property	*Value*
Caption	Multiple Choice
Left	2.1715 in
Top	5.7146 in
Width	0.9646 in
Height	0.1667 in

Object: **rbtWriteIn Option Button**
Select a Write-In response type.

Property	Value
Option Value	3
Left	1.9646 in
Top	6 in

Object: **lblWriteIn Label**
Child label of the rbtWriteIn option button.

Property	Value
Caption	Write In
Left	2.1715 in
Top	5.9646 in
Width	0.5306 in
Height	0.1667 in

Object: **rbtRange Option Button**
Select a Range response type.

Property	Value
Option Value	4
Left	3.3597 in
Top	5.5 in

Object: **lblRange Label**
Child label of the rbtRange option button.

Property	Value
Caption	Range
Left	3.5625 in
Top	5.4646 in
Width	0.4479 in
Height	0.1667 in

Object: **rbtPercent Option Button**
Select a Percent response type.

Property	Value
Option Value	5
Left	3.3597 in
Top	5.75 in

Object: **lblPercent Label**
Child label of the rbtPercent option button.

Property	Value
Caption	Percent
Left	3.5625 in
Top	5.7278 in
Width	0.5208 in
Height	0.1667 in

Figure 16.15 shows the added Response Type group box and radio buttons.

FIGURE 16.15.

Page three contains an option group to select the question response type.

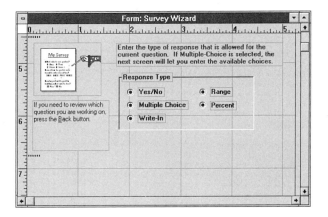

The next three text boxes are hidden from view and become visible when a Range or Percent response type is selected.

Each of the three text boxes use the MS Sans Serif font, Normal weight, and font size 8.

Object: **txtFrom Text Box**
Enter beginning value of a range of numbers.

Property	Value
Visible	No
Left	2.2347 in
Top	6.375 in
Width	0.35 in
Height	0.1701 in
Special Effect	Sunken
Text Align	Right

Object: **lblFrom Label**
Child label of the txtFrom text box.

Property	Value
Caption:	From:
Left:	1.8076 in
Top:	6.375 in
Width:	0.3847 in
Height:	0.1667 in

Object: **txtTo Text Box**
Enter ending value of a range of numbers.

Property	Value
Visible:	No
Left:	3.091 in
Top:	6.375 in
Width:	0.35 in
Height:	0.1701 in
Special Effect:	Sunken
Text Align:	Right

Object: **lblTo Label**
Child label of the txtTo text box.

Property	Value
Caption:	To:
Left:	2.7847 in
Top:	6.375 in
Width:	0.2597 in
Height:	0.1667 in

Object: **txtStep Text Box**
Enter value to increment by in creating a range of numbers.

Property	Value
Visible:	No
Left:	4.0597 in
Top:	6.375 in
Width:	0.35 in
Height:	0.1701 in

Special Effect: Sunken
Text Align: Right

Object: **lblStep Label**
Child label of the txtStep text box.

Property	Value
Caption:	Step:
Left:	3.641 in
Top:	6.375 in
Width:	0.375 in
Height:	0.1667 in

Like the second page, the third page contains a text box that indicates the position of the current question being edited.

Object: **lblQuestion3 Label**
Label for the txtCurrentQuestion3 control.

Property	Value
Caption:	Question:
Left:	4.5597 in
Top:	5.6403 in
Width:	0.5208 in
Height:	0.1667 in
Fore Color:	16777215 (White)

Object: **txtCurrentQuestion3 Text Box**
Indicates which question is currently being edited.

Property	Value
Control Source:	=CurrentQuestion( )
Enabled:	No
Locked:	Yes
Tab Stop:	No
Left:	4.5701 in
Top:	5.8403 in
Width:	0.5 in
Height:	0.1667 in
Fore Color:	16777215 (White)

The completed Page 3 is shown in Figure 16.16.

FIGURE 16.16.

Adding the Page 3 controls to the Survey Wizard form.

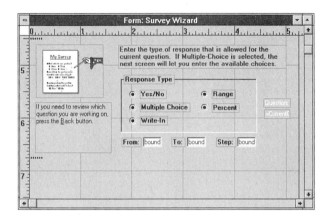

Creating Page 4

The fourth page of the Survey Wizard form is used only when Multiple Choice is selected as the question response type.

The bitmap for Page 4 is a close-up of the multiple-choice answering part of a questionnaire. This time I set the Border Style property to Normal to display a border around the picture. The bitmap file used is SW4.BMP on the companion CD-ROM. (See Figure 16.17.)

FIGURE 16.17.

Adding a bitmap for page four.

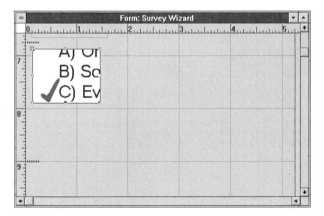

On Page 4 are six text boxes labeled A to F in which entries are made defining the possible responses to a multiple-choice question.

Here are some more controls.

Object: **bmp4 Unbound Object Frame**
Picture of a multiple-choice question being answered.

Property	Value
Tab Stop:	No
Left:	0.1403 in
Top:	6.8799 in
Back Color:	12632256 (Light Gray)
Border Style:	Normal

Object: **lblHint4 Label**
Another hint about using the Back button.

Property	Value
Caption:	If you need to review which question you are working on, press the &Back button twice.
Left:	0.1097 in
Top:	7.9535 in
Width:	1.4896 in
Height:	0.9576 in
Fore Color:	0 (Black)
Font Weight:	Normal

Object: **lblInstructions4 Label**
Blue instructions for Page 4.

Property	Value
Caption:	Enter up to six multiple-choice answers to the current question.
Left:	1.75 in
Top:	6.875 in
Width:	3.25 in
Height:	0.4403 in
Fore Color:	12632256 (Dark Blue)
Font Weight:	Bold

In the next two, you do six controls at once. First are the label controls: lblA, lblB, lblC, lblD, lblE, and lblF. Next are the text boxes: txtA, txtB, txtC, txtD, txtE, and txtF.

Objects: **lblA to lblF**
Six labels for the txtA to txtF controls.

Property	Value
Caption:	A), B), C), D), E), F)
Left:	1.8125 in
Top:	7.4535 in, 7.7097 in, 7.9597 in, 8.2097 in, 8.4549 in, 8.7097 in
Width:	0.1875 in
Height:	0.1667 in

Objects: **txtA to txtF**
Six text boxes holding possible multiple-choice answers.

Property	Value
Left:	2.0521 in
Top:	7.4535 in, 7.7097 in, 7.9597 in 8.2097 in, 8.4597 in, 8.7097 in
Width:	2.3 in
Height:	0.1667 in
Special Effect:	Sunken

Here again are controls to indicate the current question being worked on.

Object: **lblQuestion4 Label**
Label for the txtCurrentQuestion4 control.

Property	Value
Caption:	Question:
Left:	4.5597 in
Top:	7.8903 in
Width:	0.5208 in
Height:	0.1667 in
Fore Color:	16777215 (White)

Object: **txtCurrentQuestion4 Text Box**
Indicates which question is currently being edited.

Property	Value
Control Source:	=CurrentQuestion()
Enabled:	No
Locked:	Yes

Tab Stop:	No
Left:	4.5701 in
Top:	8.0903 in
Width:	0.5 in
Height:	0.1667 in
Fore Color:	16777215 (White)

The completed Page 4 is shown in Figure 16.18.

FIGURE 16.18.

Adding controls to page 4 of the Survey Wizard form.

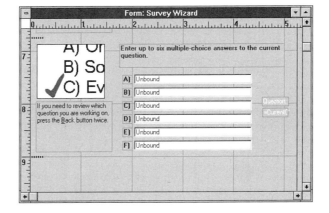

Missing Accelerator Keys

Have you noticed yet that the detail section of your form doesn't use any accelerator keys?

Accelerator keys are the underlined letters on control labels. If you press the Alt key in combination with the letter, you immediately jump to that control. (In the case of buttons, pressing the accelerator key actually activates the control.)

You do have accelerators being used within the footer section for your Cancel, <<, Back, Next, and >> buttons.

You can't use accelerator keys in the detail section of the form because as far as accelerator keys are concerned, your multiple-page form is just like any other form. If you are on page 1 and press the key combination to activate an accelerator on Page 3, then your form is going to jump to Page 3, scrolling perhaps just enough to make the selected control visible.

The design of your interface requires that you be able to control when the form moves from one page to another. It also requires that you control moving from one page to another at the right intervals so that half of one page isn't displayed alongside the other half of another page.

Don't feel bad that you couldn't get accelerator keys to work everywhere in Survey Wizard. If you take a look, you'll find that the wizards that come with Access don't use accelerator keys either because of the same reasons.

Creating Page 5

The final page of your Survey Wizard interface is used to kick off the database objects' build.

Five check boxes are used to indicate which objects to build or rebuild. By default, the Survey Entry Report and Questions Table are built. These are both required to generate the handout questionnaire.

The remaining three check boxes are used to generate objects for the online survey system. A large button labeled "Build" is used to kick off the build.

The bitmap for the final page is a picture of an Access database object assembly line. Wizard wand sparkles are fed into a machine from one side, on the other side a set of database objects are carried away via a conveyor belt. (See Figure 16.19.)

FIGURE 16.19.

Adding a bitmap to Page 5.

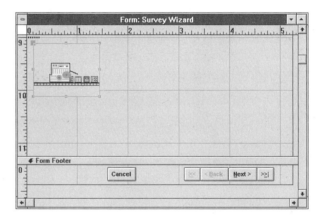

Here are the controls for Page 5:

Object: **bmp5 Unbound Object Frame**
Picture of an Access database object assembly line.

Property	Value
Tab Stop:	No
Left:	0.1403 in
Top:	9.1097 in

Back Color:	12632256 (Light Gray)
Border Style:	Clear

Object: **lblHint5 Label**
Hints about which objects to generate.

Property	Value
Caption:	Create the Entry Report and Questions Table to create a paper questionnaire. Create all the objects if you are going to collect survey data in a database.
Left:	0.1097 in
Top:	10.2035 in
Width:	1.4896 in
Height:	0.9576 in
Fore Color:	0 (Black)
Font Weight:	Normal

Object: **lblInstructions5 Label**
Blue instructions for Page 5.

Property	Value
Caption:	You are finished designing your survey! Select which database objects to make and press the Build button to create them.
Left:	1.75 in
Top:	9.125 in
Width:	3.25 in
Height:	0.4403 in
Fore Color:	12632256 (Dark Blue)
Font Weight:	Bold

Next are five check boxes and their corresponding labels. Each of the check boxes is set with Width and Height property values of 0.2292 in and 0.1347 in.

Object: **lblEntryReport Label**
Child label of the chkEntryReport check box.

Property	Value
Caption:	Entry Report
Left:	2.4806 in

continues

Property	Value
Top:	9.7646 in
Width:	0.8021 in
Height:	0.1667 in

Object: **chkEntryReport CheckBox**

Set option to create the Entry Report.

Property	Value
Default Value:	1
Left:	2.2646 in
Top:	9.8042 in
Special Effect:	Sunken

Object: **lblQuestionsTable Label**

Child label of the chkQuestionsTable check box.

Property	Value
Caption:	Entry Form
Left:	2.4806 in
Top:	10.0472 in
Width:	1.0208 in
Height:	0.1667 in

Object: **chkQuestionsTable CheckBox**

Set option to create the Questions Table.

Property	Value
Default Value:	1
Left:	2.2646 in
Top:	10.0785 in
Special Effect:	Sunken

Object: **lblEntryForm Label**

Child label of the chkEntryForm check box.

Property	Value
Caption:	Entry Form
Left:	2.4806 in
Top:	10.3375 in

Width:	0.6875 in
Height:	0.1667 in

Object: **chkEntryForm CheckBox**
Set option to create the Entry Form.

Property	Value
Default Value:	0
Left:	2.2646 in
Top:	10.3597 in
Special Effect:	Sunken

Object: **lblResponsesTable Label**
Child label of the chkResponsesTable check box.

Property	Value
Caption:	Responses Table
Left:	2.4806 in
Top:	10.6097 in
Width:	1.0826 in
Height:	0.1667 in

Object: **chkResponsesTable CheckBox**
Set option to create the Responses Table.

Property	Value
Default Value:	0
Left:	2.2646 in
Top:	10.641 in
Special Effect:	Sunken

Object: **lblResultsReport Label**
Child label of the chkResultsReport check box.

Property	Value
Caption:	Results Query, Table and Report
Left:	2.4806 in
Top:	10.8958 in
Width:	2 in
Height:	0.1667 in

Object: **chkResultsReport CheckBox**

Set option to create the Results Report and other objects.

Property	Value
Default Value:	0
Left:	2.2646 in
Top:	10.9222 in
Special Effect:	Sunken

Figure 16.20 shows Page 5 after the check boxes have been added.

FIGURE 16.20.

Adding check boxes to select which database objects are created.

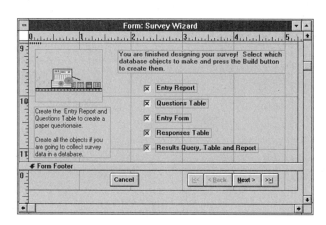

A second bitmap is added to Page 5 to help identify the objects that are generated. The bmpObjects bitmap rests to the left of the check boxes, so that a report picture is next to the chkEntryReport check box, a table picture is next to the chkQuestionsTable check box, and so on.

The last check box generates three objects: a make table query, a table, and a report. The picture to the left of this check box includes all three objects.

The bitmap used is OBJECTS.BMP, which is included on the companion CD-ROM. See Figure 16.21.

Object: **bmpObjects Unbound Object Frame**

Picture of the generated objects for each check box on Page 5.

Property	Value
Tab Stop:	No
Left:	0.1403 in
Top:	9.1097 in

Back Color:	12632256 (Light Gray)
Border Style:	Clear

FIGURE 16.21.

Adding the bmpObjects control.

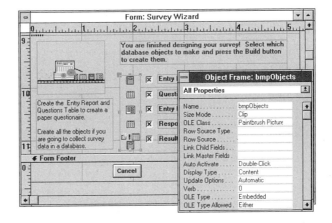

The Build button displays a magnified picture of wizard wand sparkles. The bitmap for this is SPARKLES.BMP.

Object: **cmdBuild Command Button**
Button to start build of the selected objects.

Property	Value
Picture:	(bitmap) SPARKLES.BMP
Left:	4.3597 in
Top:	10.0785 in
Width:	0.45 in
Height:	0.45 in

Object: **lblBuild Label**
Label to identify the Build button.

Property	Value
Caption:	Build
Left:	4.4056 in
Top:	10.5646 in
Width:	0.3542 in
Height:	0.1667 in

The completed fifth (and final) page is shown in Figure 16.22.

FIGURE 16.22.

Completing Page 5.

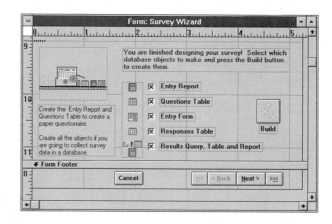

Tab Sentries

OK, you are *almost* done with your form. The last thing you need to do is add some hidden controls that are needed to make moving back and forth through the different pages work correctly.

Use of hidden controls is a well-known way to redefine the movement from control to control that occurs when the Tab key or Shift-Tab key combination is pressed.

The problem you need to work around is keeping focus from moving from one page of the form to the next, except when you want it to. This can be done by creating some strategically placed command buttons. The buttons, called *tab sentries*, have their On Current event code calling a function that redirects which control gets focus.

Command buttons are used because they can be completely hidden by setting their Transparent property. Each of these buttons should have their Height and Width properties set to 0 inches, and should have the Transparent property set to Yes.

However, initially you will want to create the buttons with a Height and Width that makes them easy to access for editing, and controls that aren't transparent. Once you have coded the form and have a fully functional interface, you can then proceed with hiding the controls.

Figure 16.23 shows the Survey Wizard form with visible tab sentry buttons.

For each of the following buttons, set the Width to 0.5 inches and the Height to 0.15 inches. Set Transparent to No.

FIGURE 16.23.

Command Buttons are added as Tab Sentries, and will be made invisible after testing.

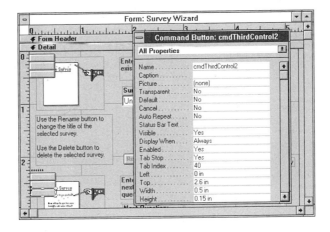

Object: cmdFirstControl1 Command Button
Send focus to first control on Page 1.

Property	Value
Left:	0.0 in
Top:	0.05 in

Object: cmdSecondControl1 Command Button
Send focus to last control on Page 1.

Property	Value
Left:	0.0 in
Top:	0.2 in

Object: cmdThirdControl1 Command Button
Send focus to first control on Page 1.

Property	Value
Left:	0.0 in
Top:	0.35 in

Object: cmdFirstControl2 Command Button
Send focus to first control on Page 2.

Property	Value
Left:	0.0 in
Top:	2.3 in

Object: **cmdSecondControl2 Command Button**
Send focus to last control on Page 2.

Property	Value
Left:	0.0 in
Top:	2.45 in

Object: **cmdThirdControl2 Command Button**
Send focus to first control on Page 2.

Property	Value
Left:	0.0 in
Top:	2.6 in

Object: **cmdFirstControl3 Command Button**
Send focus to first control on Page 3.

Property	Value
Left:	0.0 in
Top:	4.55 in

Object: **cmdSecondControl3 Command Button**
Send focus to last control on Page 3.

Property	Value
Left:	0.0 in
Top:	4.7 in

Object: **cmdThirdControl3 Command Button**
Send focus to first control on Page 3.

Property	Value
Left:	0.0 in
Top:	4.85 in

Object: **cmdFirstControl4 Command Button**
Send focus to first control on Page 4.

Property	Value
Left:	0.0 in
Top:	6.8 in

Object: **cmdSecondControl4 Command Button**
Send focus to last control on Page 4.

Property	Value
Left:	0.0 in
Top:	6.95 in

Object: **cmdThirdControl4 Command Button**
Send focus to first control on Page 4.

Property	Value
Left:	0.0 in
Top:	7.1 in

Object: **cmdFirstControl5 Command Button**
Send focus to first control on Page 5.

Property	Value
Left:	0.0 in
Top:	9.05 in

Object: **cmdSecondControl5 Command Button**
Send focus to last control on Page 5.

Property	Value
Left:	0.0 in
Top:	9.2 in

Object: **cmdThirdControl5 Command Button**
Send focus to first control on Page 5.

Property	Value
Left:	0.0 in
Top:	9.35 in

With the hidden buttons created, the tab order of the detail section should now be set as shown in Table 16.1.

Table 16.1. Tab order of the controls on the Survey Wizard form Detail section.

Tab Order	Control
1)	cmdFirstControl1
2)	cmdSecondControl1
3)	bmp1

continues

Table 16.1. continued

Tab Order	Control
4)	cboSurveyTitle
5)	cmdRenameSurvey
6)	cmdDeleteSurvey
7)	cmdThirdControl1
8)	cmdFirstControl2
9)	cmdSecondControl2
10)	bmp2
11)	txtQuestion
12)	cmdInsertQuestion
13)	cmdDeleteQuestion
14)	cmdFirstQuestion
15)	cmdBackQuestion
16)	cmdNextQuestion
17)	cmdLastQuestion
18)	txtCurrentQuestion2
19)	cmdThirdControl2
20)	cmdFirstControl3
21)	cmdSecondControl3
22)	bmp3
23)	optResponseType
24)	txtFrom
25)	txtTo
26)	txtStep
27)	txtCurrentQuestion3
28)	cmdThirdControl3
29)	cmdFirstControl4
30)	cmdSecondControl4
31)	bmp4
32)	txtA
33)	txtB

Tab Order	Control
34)	txtC
35)	txtD
36)	txtE
37)	txtF
38)	txtCurrentQuestion4
39)	cmdThirdControl4
40)	cmdFirstControl5
41)	cmdSecondControl5
42)	bmp5
43)	chkEntryReport
44)	chkQuestionsTable
45)	chkEntryForm
46)	chkResponsesTable
47)	chkResultsReport
48)	bmpObjects
49)	cmdBuild
50)	cmdThirdControl5

Figure 16.24 shows the tab order being set on the Survey Wizard form.

FIGURE 16.24.

Setting tab order for the Survey Wizard form's Detail section.

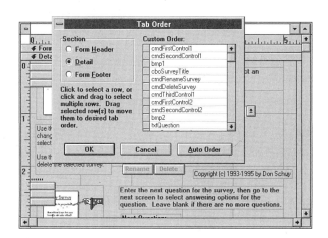

Before you start coding this monster, you need to create a couple of tables.

Creating the Survey Wizard Tables

Survey Wizard will use two tables to save a questionnaire definition to the database so that it can later be retrieved and used again.

The Survey table contains a record for each saved questionnaire. The Survey Question table contains a record for each question in a questionnaire.

Stored within the Survey table record is the title of the survey as it is entered on Page 1 of the Survey Wizard form, and the check box options for which objects were marked to be generated the last time the questionnaire was being used.

Also in the table is a BaseName field used in determining the names of the generated objects when they are built.

Object: **Survey Table**

Title and build options for a questionnaire.

Field Name	Data Type
ID	Counter
Title	Text
BaseName	Text
BuildEntryReport	Yes/No
BuildEntryForm	Yes/No
BuildResultsReport	Yes/No
BuildQuestionsTable	Yes/No
BuildResponsesTable	Yes/No

The ID field is set as the table's PrimaryKey. Following are the properties set for each field in the table. (Only the Title field differs from the defaults.)

Field Name:	ID
Data Type:	Counter
Field Name:	Title
Data Type:	Text
Field Size:	50
Required:	Yes
Indexed:	Yes (Duplicates OK)
Field Name:	BaseName
Data Type:	Text
Field Size:	50

Field Name: BuildEntryReport
Data Type: Yes/No

Field Name: BuildEntryForm
Data Type: Yes/No

Field Name: BuildResultsReport
Data Type: Yes/No

Field Name: BuildQuestionsTable
Data Type: Yes/No

Field Name: BuildResponsesTable
Data Type: Yes/No

The Survey table is shown in design mode in Figure 16.25.

FIGURE 16.25.

Designing the Survey table.

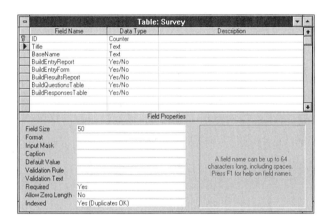

The Survey Question table stores the text for each question in a questionnaire and how a question may be answered.

The SurveyID field indicates to which questionnaire the question belongs. The ID field is a counter field, giving a unique number to each question record. The PrimaryKey is made up of both the SurveyID field and the ID field.

The Question field is a memo field to allow the question to be of any length.

A Type field indicates which of the five response types are used for the question: Yes/No, Multiple-Choice, Write-In, Range, or Percent. This value in this field is always a number from 1 to 5.

The ChoiceA through ChoiceF fields store the multiple-choice selections for a Multiple-Choice response type question.

The RangeFrom, RangeTo, and RangeStep fields hold the From, To, and Step values for a Range response type question. Likewise, there are PercentFrom, PercentTo, and PercentStep fields for a Percent response type question.

Object: **Survey Question Table**

Text and response type information for a question in a questionnaire.

Field Name	Data Type
SurveyID	Number
ID	Counter
Question	Memo
Type	Number
ChoiceA	Text
ChoiceB	Text
ChoiceC	Text
ChoiceD	Text
ChoiceE	Text
ChoiceF	Text
RangeFrom	Number
RangeTo	Number
RangeStep	Number
PercentFrom	Number
PercentTo	Number
PercentStep	Number

Together, the SurveyID and ID fields make up the PrimaryKey. This is done by selecting both rows and clicking the Primary Key button. Figure 16.26 shows the index created by doing this.

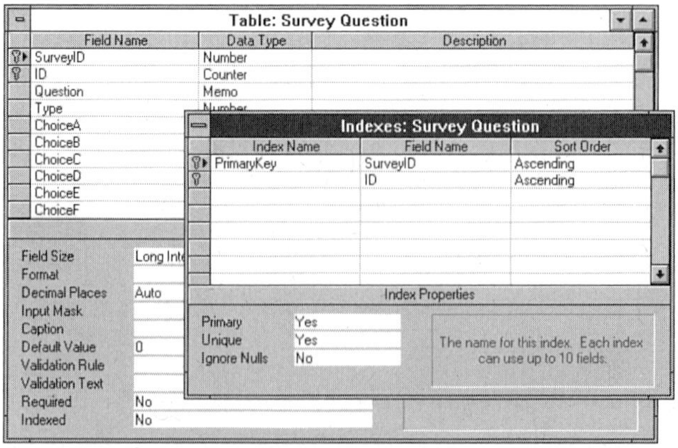

FIGURE 16.26.

The Survey Question table has a multiple-field PrimaryKey.

The following are the properties set for each field in the Survey Question table:

Field Name:	SurveyID
Data Type:	Number
Field Size:	Long Integer

Field Name:	ID
Data Type:	Counter

Field Name:	Question
Data Type:	Memo
Required:	Yes

Field Name:	Type
Data Type:	Number
Field Size:	Integer
Required:	Yes

Field Name:	ChoiceA
Data Type:	Text
Field Size:	50

Field Name:	ChoiceB
Data Type:	Text
Field Size:	50

Field Name:	ChoiceC
Data Type:	Text
Field Size:	50

Field Name:	ChoiceD
Data Type:	Text
Field Size:	50

Field Name:	ChoiceE
Data Type:	Text
Field Size:	50

Field Name:	ChoiceF
Data Type:	Text
Field Size:	50

Field Name:	RangeFrom
Data Type:	Number
Field Size:	Long Integer

Field Name:	RangeTo
Data Type:	Number
Field Size:	Long Integer

Field Name:	RangeStep
Data Type:	Number
Field Size:	Long Integer

Field Name:	PercentFrom
Data Type:	Number
Field Size:	Integer

Field Name:	PercentTo
Data Type:	Number
Field Size:	Integer

Field Name:	PercentStep
Data Type:	Number
Field Size:	Integer

Some Notes About the Code

The interface part of the Survey Wizard uses the following modules:

Error	Display error messages
Form	A few helpful one-liners
Survey Wizard Constants	Declare Survey Wizard constants
Survey Wizard Entry Point	Entry point function and globals

However, the majority of the code is in the Survey Wizard form module. This is intentional because the code doesn't take up any memory this way until the form is used. (You will write the Survey Wizard form module in the following chapter.)

I've prefixed all of the callable procedures with the character z. There are a couple reasons for it:

The first reason is to easily distinguish the callable routines from the ones that are private to the given module.

When selecting a procedure to work on, all the functions declared with a prefix of z sort to the bottom, and the module's private routines are listed first. Everyone has his or her own set of programming organizational strategies, and this one worked for me.

The second reason is that the prefix is used in hopes that it will avoid one of my function names being the same as someone else's function name.

Since Survey Wizard is to be loaded as a library, it has to have routine names that don't conflict with the names of routines in the user's current loaded database or in any other library databases. It's a common strategy in programming with Access to name your functions using a special set of prefix characters to try to make your function names unique from another programmer's.

I really would be doing better by prefixing the function names with something more lengthy than a single character, say "zdes," which is the z followed by my initials. However, for now I'll stick with just z because that makes the code easier to read.

Enough talk. It's time to dig into some code. It's probably not a good show of confidence, but I'll start right off with the module responsible for displaying error messages.

The Error Module

The error handling in Survey Wizard is done slightly different than the other programs in the book. A `strProcedure` variable is used so that the name of the procedure in which an error occurred will be displayed along with the error message.

Displaying the procedure name where the error occurred is helpful for the developer of the program because he or she knows right away which procedure needs to be fixed. This is really useful on larger scale projects.

On the other hand, the procedure name isn't much help at all to the end user of the program and may just cause confusion. Consider the following hypothetical error messages:

1) `File not found.`

2) `Error occurred in the Form_Open procedure:`
   `File not found.`

Because this was a larger project, I decided to go ahead and add the procedure name information into the error message. However, my true intention is that `zDisplayError` never gets called, but that will depend on how well I did my programming. Listing 16.1 contains the declaration section and Listing 16.2 contains the `zDisplayError` function.

Listing 16.1. The declaration section for the Error module.

```
' Error - Display error messages

Option Compare Database
Option Explicit
```

Listing 16.2. The `zDisplayError` **function.**

```
Sub zDisplayError (strProcedure As String, strError As String,
➥ strProgramName As String)

Dim msg As String
  Dim cr As String

  cr = Chr$(13) & Chr$(10)

  msg = "Error occurred in the " & strProcedure & " procedure:" & cr & cr
  MsgBox msg & strError, 48, strProgramName

End Sub
```

Don't you wish all modules in this book were so short? This next one is about the same size.

The Form Module

The Form module contains a few one-liners I found useful to have around and the `CenterForm` function you used in the Address Book application.

You need the `CenterForm` function because with the Entry Form you will run into a second case where the Access AutoCenter property setting doesn't center the form correctly for us. In this module, you rename it to `zCenterForm`.

The declaration section for the Form module is shown in Listing 16.3. It contains the necessary Windows API declarations that are used in the `zCenterForm` function.

Listing 16.3. The Form module's declaration section.

```
' Form

  Option Compare Database
  Option Explicit

  Type RECT
    x1 As Integer
    y1 As Integer
    x2 As Integer
    y2 As Integer
  End Type

  Declare Function GetClientRect Lib "User" (ByVal hwnd As Integer, r As RECT)
➥ As Integer
  Declare Function GetParent Lib "User" (ByVal hwnd As Integer) As Integer
  Declare Function GetWindowRect Lib "User" (ByVal hwnd As Integer, r As RECT)
```

```
➥ As Integer
Declare Function MoveWindow Lib "User" (ByVal hwnd As Integer,
➥ ByVal x As Integer, ByVal y As Integer, ByVal dx As Integer,
➥ ByVal dy As Integer, ByVal blnRepaint As Integer) As Integer
```

The zCenterForm function is shown in Listing 16.4.

Listing 16.4. The zCenterForm function.

```
Function zCenterForm (hwnd As Integer) As Integer

  Dim r As RECT
  Dim rApp As RECT

  Dim hwndApp As Integer

  Dim dx As Integer
  Dim dy As Integer
  Dim dxApp As Integer
  Dim dyApp As Integer
  Dim z As Integer

  On Error Resume Next

  z = GetWindowRect(hwnd, r)
  hwndApp = GetParent(hwnd)
  z = GetClientRect(hwndApp, rApp)

  dx = r.x2 - r.x1
  dy = r.y2 - r.y1

  dxApp = rApp.x2 - rApp.x1
  dyApp = rApp.y2 - rApp.y1

  zCenterForm = MoveWindow(hwnd, (dxApp - dx) / 2, (dyApp - dy) / 2, dx, dy,
  ➥ True)

End Function
```

The zCloseForm subroutine shown in Listing 16.5 is a shorthand way to close a form, ignoring any errors that occur in the process.

Listing 16.5. The zCloseForm subroutine.

```
Sub zCloseForm (frm As Form)

  On Error Resume Next
  DoCmd Close A_Form, frm.FormName

End Sub
```

The following two subroutines, zDisablePaint and zEnablePaint, are nice alternatives to using the Echo action (DoCmd Echo False and DoCmd Echo True) to suspend screen redraws. The Echo action affects all of the windows in Access. These functions allow you to temporarily suspend updates on a single form.

Where these functions have an advantage over the Echo action is when you want to re-enable screen redraws. As Echo is turned back on, the entire screen gets redrawn, including the toolbar, database container, and any other visible Access components. This sometimes causes more flicker than you were trying to avoid in the first place. Re-enabling paints on a form only causes that particular form to be redrawn.

The zDisablePaint and zEnablePaint subroutines are shown in Listings 16.6 and 16.7.

Listing 16.6. The zDisablePaint **subroutine.**

```
Sub zDisablePaint (frm As Form)

  frm.Painting = False

End Sub
```

Listing 16.7. The zEnablePaint **subroutine.**

```
Sub zEnablePaint (frm As Form)

  If frm.Painting = False Then frm.Painting = True

End Sub
```

The zTwips function (shown in Listing 16.8) converts a screen measurement in inches to a value in twips. *Twips* is the unit of measurement used to locate controls on a form from Access Basic code.

By having the zTwips function around, you can still think of placing the controls on a form in units of inches.

Listing 16.8. The zTwips **function.**

```
Function zTwips (dblInches As Double) As Integer

  zTwips = CInt(dblInches * 1440)

End Function
```

Next, you move away from creating generic stuff to code that is specific to Survey Wizard itself.

The Survey Wizard Constants Module

The Survey Wizard Constants module doesn't contain all of the constants used by the program. In fact, it only contains a small fraction of them.

The constant variables declared in this module are those that are shared among code in different modules; hence they must be declared globally.

In this module there is only a declaration section, which is shown in Listing 16.9.

Listing 16.9. Survey Wizard global constants are declared in the Survey Wizard Constants module.

```
' Survey Wizard Constants

  Option Compare Database
  Option Explicit

  Global Const zSWQuestionTypeYesNo = 1
  Global Const zSWQuestionTypeMultipleChoice = 2
  Global Const zSWQuestionTypeWriteIn = 3
  Global Const zSWQuestionTypeRange = 4
  Global Const zSWQuestionTypePercent = 5

  Global Const zSWMaximumPoints = 10
```

The constants declared include a number value to identify each question response type, and the maximum number of selection values available in a range or percent type of question.

The Survey Wizard Entry Point Module

The Survey Wizard Entry Point module contains all the global variables used by Survey Wizard as a questionnaire is defined and its objects are generated.

These globals are required so that the Survey Wizard user interface code can be separated from the code that builds the database objects. The globals hold a definition of the questionnaire in variables in memory, and become the glue between these two main pieces of the program.

Within this module, the zSW_Question user-defined data type is declared to hold all the information required to define a question within a questionnaire. Everything that the user might enter into the Survey Wizard user interface about a question is stored here. You will recognize the fields as the same ones you created in the Survey Question table.

The global, zSWaQuestion, is an array of the zSW_Question type. This array will contain all of the question definitions for a questionnaire.

The declaration section is shown in Listing 16.10.

Listing 16.10. The Survey Wizard Entry Point declarations section.

```
' Survey Wizard Entry Point
' Globals and entry point function.

' This module defines and declares the globals and zSW_Question
' structure that holds the definition of a questionnaire in memory.

' All global variables are prefixed with "zSW" in order to minimize
' naming conflicts with variable and function names in other libraries.

  Option Compare Database
  Option Explicit

  Global zSWfrm As Form

  Type zSW_Question
    strQuestion As String
    intType As Integer
    strA As String
    strB As String
    strC As String
    strD As String
    strE As String
    strF As String
    lngRangeFrom As Long
    lngRangeTo As Long
    lngRangeStep As Long
    intPercentFrom As Long
    intPercentTo As Long
    intPercentStep As Long
  End Type

  Global zSWaQuestion() As zSW_Question
  Global zSWintTotalQuestions As Integer
  Global zSWstrSurveyTitle As String

  Global zSWstrBaseName As String
  Global zSWstrEntryReport As String
  Global zSWstrEntryForm As String
  Global zSWstrResultsReport As String
  Global zSWstrResultsQuery As String
  Global zSWstrResultsTable As String
  Global zSWstrResponsesTable As String
  Global zSWstrQuestionsTable As String
```

Also in this module is the actual call that starts the Survey Wizard program. It's a one-liner that simply opens the Survey Wizard form, and is appropriately called, SurveyWizard.

Listing 16.11. The SurveyWizard **function opens the Survey Wizard form.**

```
Function SurveyWizard ()

  On Error Resume Next
  DoCmd OpenForm "Survey Wizard", A_Normal, , , A_Edit, A_Dialog

End Function
```

Summary

In this chapter you launched the Survey Wizard project and built some of the initial components, the most significant being the Survey Wizard form.

This is what you covered along the way. You

- Scoped out the objects that Survey Wizard must generate
- Designed the questionnaire and five response types
- Designed how the Survey Wizard multiple-page form allows the user to define a questionnaire
- Created the Survey Wizard form
- Learned why there is a 22-inch height and width limit on a form section
- Learned why wizards don't have accelerator keys on each control
- Created Tab Sentries to control the Tab sequence of controls on a form
- Created the Survey Wizard tables
- Got a start on the coding for the Survey Wizard user interface

So far the coding has been pretty light, but difficult to see where any of it comes together. In the next chapter you get to the real workhorse behind the user interface—the code behind the Survey Wizard form.

CHAPTER 17

Access: Survey Wizard, Part Two—Coding and Interface

In the last chapter you created an awesome form for your program. It's pretty much useless, however, until you add the magic that makes it all work. The magic is, of course, code. Lots of it!

In this chapter you write the code behind the Survey Wizard form. You also create a small pop-up form for changing survey titles.

The Survey Wizard Form Module

Most of the code you develop in this chapter is in the form module for the Survey Wizard form.

You'll need a table of contents to help make sense of where you are going. The following is a list of each of the procedures in the code behind the Survey Wizard form.

Usual Stuff
(declarations)
Warning
CNStr
CSNull
LibDLookup
TableExists
Quotes

Tab Sentries
cmdFirstControl1_Enter
cmdSecondControl1_Enter
cmdThirdControl1_Enter
cmdFirstControl2_Enter
cmdSecondControl2_Enter
cmdThirdControl2_Enter
cmdFirstControl3_Enter
cmdSecondControl3_Enter
cmdThirdControl3_Enter
cmdFirstControl4_Enter
cmdSecondControl4_Enter
cmdThirdControl4_Enter
cmdFirstControl5_Enter
cmdSecondControl5_Enter
cmdThirdControl5_Enter

Adding and Deleting Questions
AddNextQuestion
IsEmptyQuestion
DeleteEmptyQuestion

Page Two
txtQuestion_AfterUpdate
CurrentQuestion
cmdInsertQuestion_Click
cmdDeleteQuestion_Click
cmdFirstQuestion_Click
cmdBackQuestion_Click
cmdNextQuestion_Click
cmdLastQuestion_Click
UpdateQuestion
UpdateType
DeleteQuestion

Page Three
optResponseType_AfterUpdate
txtFrom_AfterUpdate
txtTo_AfterUpdate
txtStep_AfterUpdate
RangeAfterUpdate
ValidatePoints

Initialization
Form_Open

VCR Buttons
VCRButtons
VCRPage
VCRGotoControl
cmdHelp_Click
cmdCancel_Click
cmdFirst_Click
cmdBack_Click
cmdNext_Click
cmdLast_Click

Page One
cboSurveyTitle_AfterUpdate
cmdDeleteSurvey_Click
cmdRenameSurvey_Click
NoTitle
DeleteEmptyQuestion

Page Four
txtA_AfterUpdate
txtB_AfterUpdate
txtC_AfterUpdate
txtD_AfterUpdate
txtE_AfterUpdate
txtF_AfterUpdate
ChoiceAfterUpdate

Page Five
chkEntryForm_AfterUpdate
chkQuestionsTable_AfterUpdate
chkEntryReport_AfterUpdate
chkResponsesTable_AfterUpdate
chkResultsReport_AfterUpdate
CheckMandatoryObjects
cmdBuild_Click

Load and Save
ReadQuestions
Write Questions
Form_Unload

Don't let that long list scare you away. Many of the subroutines are one-liners. You do have some coding to do, but it's not an insurmountable task.

Usual Stuff

The first set of procedures you look at I've classified as "Usual Stuff." They are miscellaneous in nature and might be candidates for your stashed-away set of favorite procedures.

The Declarations Section

In the declarations section, I declare a few variables that are global within the module.

The mintCurrentQuestion variable stores which question you are currently editing. Next, mintCurrentQuestionType holds the type of answer that may be entered into the current question.

The `mintCurrentPage` variable indicates which page the user is currently looking at in the multiple-page form, and `mintLastPage` is a constant that defines how many pages are in the multiple-page form.

The declarations section is shown in Listing 17.1

Listing 17.1. The declarations section for the Survey Wizard form module.

```
' Survey Wizard form

Option Compare Database
Option Explicit

Const mstrProgramName = "Survey Wizard"

Dim mintCurrentQuestion As Integer
Dim mintCurrentQuestionType As Integer

Dim mintCurrentPage As Integer
Const mintLastPage = 5
```

The *Warning* Subroutine

Many of the modules in Survey Wizard contain a `Warning` subroutine as shown in Listing 17.2.

This subroutine calls the `zDisplayError` subroutine, passing a `mstrProgramName` constant as the third argument. The `mstrProgramName` constant is declared differently for each module to indicate which module the error occurred in.

Listing 17.2. The `Warning` subroutine.

```
Private Sub Warning (strProcedure As String, msg As String)

  zDisplayError strProcedure, msg, mstrProgramName

End Sub
```

The *CNStr* Function

As you've seen in earlier chapters, the `CNStr` function is a replacement for the `CStr` function in Access. The `CNStr` function converts a variant to a string, but also handles a null value without returning an error. It also treats a string that has nothing but spaces in it as an empty string. See Listing 17.3.

Listing 17.3. The CNStr **function.**

```
Function CNStr (v As Variant) As String

  If IsNull(v) Then
    CNStr = ""
  Else
    CNStr = Trim$(CStr(v))
  End If

End Function
```

The *CSNull* Function

The CSNull function (shown in Listing 17.4) does the opposite of what CNStr does. It converts empty strings to Null variant variables. If the string argument is nonblank, then the function returns the same string as a variant variable.

Listing 17.4. The CSNull **function.**

```
Function CSNull (sz As String) As Variant

' Convert an empty string to a null.

  If sz = "" Then
    CSNull = Null
  Else
    CSNull = CVar(sz)
  End If

End Function
```

The *LibDLookup* Function

The LibDLookup function (see Listing 17.5) is a replacement for the DLookup function. You need this to be able to do a DLookup on a table in a library database.

When your code is running inside a library database, a DLookup call would operate on tables only in the user's currently opened database. The replacement LibDLookup call in Listing 17.5 takes a database as its first argument, indicating which database the table exists in.

Listing 17.5. The `LibDLookup` **function.**

```
Function LibDLookup (db As Database, strFieldName As String,
➥ strTable As String, strCriteria As String) As Variant

' A library database version of DLookup

  Dim dyn As Recordset
  Dim blnOpened As Integer

  blnOpened = False

' Default to no match
  LibDLookup = Null

  On Error GoTo LibDLookupError

  Set dyn = db.OpenRecordset(strTable, DB_OPEN_DYNASET)
  blnOpened = True

  dyn.FindFirst strCriteria
  If Not dyn.NoMatch Then
    LibDLookup = dyn(strFieldName)
  End If

LibDLookupDone:
  On Error Resume Next
  If blnOpened Then dyn.Close
  Exit Function

LibDLookupError:
  Warning "LibDLookup", Error$
  Resume LibDLookupDone

End Function
```

The *TableExists* Function

The next function, `TableExists`, checks to see if a table of a certain name already exists in the database. `TableExists` is typically used before creating a table, to check to see if an old one by the same name needs to be deleted first.

The `TableExists` function works by attempting to reference the `TableDef` object for the specified table name. If the object exists, then `Err` is set to a non-zero value.

The `TableExists` function is shown in Listing 17.6.

Listing 17.6. The `TableExists` **function.**

```
Function TableExists (strTableName As String) As Integer

  Dim db As Database
```

```
Dim sz As String

On Error Resume Next

Set db = DBEngine(0)(0)

sz = db.TableDefs(strTableName).Name
TableExists = (Err = 0)

End Function
```

The *Quotes* Function

The Quotes function is used when you are piecing together an SQL statement or WHERE clause. Often you want to set criteria based on user input.

The Quotes function gets around the messy syntax problem that occurs when you are building a quoted string in code like this

```
whr = "Title = " & chr$(34) & strInput & chr$(34)
```

and the user's input has a double quote character also.

The result is your generated SQL is syntactically incorrect. There is a workaround. Inside a quoted string you use two double quotes to indicate a double quote character.

The Quotes function (shown in Listing 17.7) is called to translate every occurrence of a double quote character into two double quote characters.

Listing 17.7. The Quotes function.

```
Function Quotes (strArg As String) As String

' Convert a double quote character within the string to
' two double quote characters.

  Dim sz As String
  Dim dq As String
  Dim n As Integer

' Copy the string so we don't change the original
  sz = strArg

' Double quote character
  dq = Chr$(34)

  n = InStr(1, sz, dq)
  While n
    sz = Left$(sz, n) & dq & Right$(sz, Len(sz) - n)
    n = InStr(n + 2, sz, dq)
```

continues

Listing 17.7. continued

```
  Wend

  Quotes = sz

End Function
```

Tab Sentries

The next set of subroutines is the code behind the tab sentry command buttons you created on the Survey Wizard form.

The tab sentries ensure that as the user repeatedly presses the Tab or Shift-Tab keys, the focus remains on controls displayed within the current page.

There are three tab sentry command buttons per page, and you adjusted the tab order of the controls so that on each page you find the following type of arrangement:

```
cmdFirstControl
cmdSecondControl
txtOne
txtTwo
cmdThirdControl
```

The cmdFirstControl, cmdSecondControl, and cmdThirdControl are the tab sentries. The txtOne and txtTwo controls are controls displayed on the form. There can be as many controls between cmdSecondControl and cmdThirdControl as needed for the purpose of the entry being made on the page.

On entering the page, cmdFirstControl command button receives focus first. The On Enter event code for this control would send focus to the first displayed control, the txtOne text box.

As the user tabs forward, the txtTwo text box receives focus, then the cmdThirdControl command button receives focus. The On Enter event code for cmdThirdControl sends focus to the txtOne text box, giving the effect of focus wrapping from txtTwo to txtOne.

If the user is on txtOne and presses Shift-Tab to move backward, the cmdSecondControl command button receives focus. This control redirects focus back to txtTwo, so that you would wrap backward through the controls by pressing Shift-Tab repeatedly.

The VCRGotoControl subroutine is called by each of the tab sentry On Enter event subroutines to do the work of setting focus on the appropriate control.

In some cases, the control to jump to differs from time to time as not all of the controls are always enabled. For example, the Delete button on Page 1 is only enabled if a survey is selected.

Listings 17.8 through 17.12 show the On Enter event code for each of the tab sentries on the Survey Wizard form.

Listing 17.8. The tab sentry subroutines for Page 1.

```
Sub cmdFirstControl1_Enter ()

  VCRGotoControl "cboSurveyTitle", 1

End Sub

Sub cmdSecondControl1_Enter ()

' Jumps to the last control that is currently enabled.

  If cmdDeleteSurvey.Enabled Then
    VCRGotoControl "cmdDeleteSurvey", 1
  Else
    VCRGotoControl "cboSurveyTitle", 1
  End If

End Sub

Sub cmdThirdControl1_Enter ()

  VCRGotoControl "cboSurveyTitle", 1

End Sub
```

Listing 17.9. The tab sentry subroutines for Page 2.

```
Sub cmdFirstControl2_Enter ()

  VCRGotoControl "txtQuestion", 2

End Sub

Sub cmdSecondControl2_Enter ()

  If cmdLastQuestion.Enabled Then
    VCRGotoControl "cmdLastQuestion", 2
  ElseIf cmdBackQuestion.Enabled Then
    VCRGotoControl "cmdBackQuestion", 2
  Else
    VCRGotoControl "cmdDeleteQuestion", 2
  End If
```

continues

Listing 17.9. continued

```
End Sub

Sub cmdThirdControl2_Enter ()

  VCRGotoControl "txtQuestion", 2

End Sub
```

Listing 17.10. The tab sentry subroutines for Page 3.

```
Sub cmdFirstControl3_Enter ()

  VCRGotoControl "optResponseType", 3

End Sub

Sub cmdSecondControl3_Enter ()

  If txtStep.Visible Then
    VCRGotoControl "txtStep", 3
  Else
    VCRGotoControl "optResponseType", 3
  End If

End Sub

Sub cmdThirdControl3_Enter ()

  VCRGotoControl "optResponseType", 3

End Sub
```

Listing 17.11. The tab sentry subroutines for Page 4.

```
Sub cmdFirstControl4_Enter ()

  VCRGotoControl "txtA", 4

End Sub

Sub cmdSecondControl4_Enter ()

  VCRGotoControl "txtF", 4

End Sub
```

```
Sub cmdThirdControl4_Enter ()

  VCRGotoControl "txtA", 4

End Sub
```

___

Listing 17.12. The tab sentry subroutines for Page 5.

```
Sub cmdFirstControl5_Enter ()

  VCRGotoControl "chkEntryReport", 5

End Sub

Sub cmdSecondControl5_Enter ()

  VCRGotoControl "cmdBuild", 5

End Sub

Sub cmdThirdControl5_Enter ()

  VCRGotoControl "chkEntryReport", 5

End Sub
```

___

Initialization

The Form_Open subroutine in Listing 17.13 initializes a few module and global variables.

Listing 17.13. The Form_Open subroutine.

```
Sub Form_Open (Cancel As Integer)

  mintCurrentPage = 1

  mintCurrentQuestion = 0

  zSWintTotalQuestions = 0

  zSWstrBaseName = ""

' Save the form to a global so it can be easily referenced in other modules
  Set zSWfrm = Me

End Sub
```

VCR Buttons

The next set of subroutines activate the <<, **B**ack, **N**ext, and >> buttons at the bottom of the form to allow page movement through the Survey Wizard form. I like to call these the "VCR buttons" because of the similarities between these and the buttons on a VCR tape deck.

The *VCRButtons* Subroutine

The VCRButtons subroutine sets which of the VCR buttons are enabled. The << and **B**ack buttons are disabled when the current page is the first page because you can't go back any further. Likewise, the **N**ext and >> buttons are disabled when you are already at the last page.

The VCRButtons subroutine is shown in Listing 17.14.

Listing 17.14. The VCRButtons **subroutine.**

```
Sub VCRButtons (intPage As Integer)

  On Error Resume Next

  Me!cmdFirst.Enabled = (intPage > 1)
  Me!cmdBack.Enabled = (intPage > 1)
  Me!cmdNext.Enabled = (intPage < mintLastPage)
  Me!cmdLast.Enabled = (intPage < mintLastPage)

End Sub
```

The *VCRPage* Subroutine

The VCRPage subroutine is called to move from one page to the next on the Survey Wizard form. The GotoPage macro action is the line that actually does the moving.

The mintCurrentPage variable gets set to the page being jumped to. Also, the VCRButtons subroutine is called to update the Enabled properties of the VCR buttons for the new current page.

The VCRPage subroutine is shown in Listing 17.15.

Listing 17.15. The VCRPage **subroutine.**

```
Sub VCRPage (intPage As Integer)

  On Error GoTo VCRPageError

  mintCurrentPage = intPage
  DoCmd GoToPage intPage

  VCRButtons intPage

VCRPageDone:
  Exit Sub

VCRPageError:
  Warning "VCRPage", Error$
  Resume VCRPageDone

End Sub
```

The *VCRGotoControl* Subroutine

The VCRGotoControl subroutine sets the specified control so that it has focus and changes the current page setting. The primary use of this routine is by the tab sentry On Enter event code.

The VCRGotoControl subroutine is shown in Listing 17.16.

Listing 17.16. The VCRGotoControl **subroutine.**

```
Sub VCRGotoControl (strControlName As String, intPage As Integer)

  On Error GoTo VCRGotoControlError

  Me(strControlName).SetFocus

  If intPage <> mintCurrentPage Then
    mintCurrentPage = intPage
    VCRButtons intPage
  End If

VCRGotoControlDone:
  Exit Sub

VCRGotoControlError:
  Warning "VCRGotoControl", Error$
  Resume VCRGotoControlDone

End Sub
```

The *cmdHelp_Click* Subroutine

The next six subroutines are for the VCR button On Click events. There are six buttons in the footer of the Survey Wizard form: cmdHelp, cmdCancel, cmdFirst, cmdBack, cmdNext, and cmdLast.

The cmdHelp_Click subroutine (shown in Listing 17.17) can be left blank for now. You finish this one in Chapter 20, "Access: Survey Wizard, Part Five—Shrink-wrap and Ship It," when you add online help to Survey Wizard.

Listing 17.17. The cmdHelp_Click **subroutine is left blank for now.**

```
Sub cmdHelp_Click ()

End Sub
```

The *cmdCancel_Click* Subroutine

The cmdCancel_Click subroutine (shown in Listing 17.18) closes the Survey Wizard form.

Listing 17.18. The cmdCancel_Click **subroutine.**

```
Sub cmdCancel_Click ()

  On Error Resume Next
  DoCmd Close

End Sub
```

The *cmdFirst_Click* Subroutine

The cmdFirst_Click subroutine jumps back to the first page of the Survey Wizard form. The cmdFirst_Click subroutine is shown in Listing 17.19.

Listing 17.19. The cmdFirst_Click **subroutine.**

```
Sub cmdFirst_Click ()

' Moves to the starting page in defining a questionnaire. If the last
' question is empty, it is deleted.

  If mintCurrentPage = 3 Then
```

```
    If Not ValidatePoints() Then Exit Sub
  End If

  DeleteEmptyQuestion True
  If zSWintTotalQuestions Then mintCurrentQuestion = 1

  mintCurrentPage = 1
  VCRPage mintCurrentPage

End Sub
```

The *cmdBack_Click* Subroutine

The cmdBack_Click subroutine handles moving through the pages of the Survey Wizard form in the reverse order that they were traversed when the questions were defined.

There are a few complications the cmdBack_Click subroutine must deal with. The subroutine uses a Select..Case statement block to execute different code depending on which page you are moving back from. Moving back from Page 2 is the most complicated movement.

Remember from the flowchart in Figure 16.2 at the beginning of the last chapter, in moving forward through the pages in the Survey Wizard form you cycle through pages 2, 3, and 4 as each question in the questionnaire is defined. Page 4 is visited only if the selected response type in Page 3 was multiple-choice, in which case the available answers are entered.

As you move back from Page 2 to a previous question, you need to determine if the previous question is multiple choice or not, and then move to Page 4 or Page 3. If there is no previous question then you should move back to Page 1.

We also must deal with the complication of whether or not the current question is empty. If the user hasn't entered any question text, then this question should be discarded.

In moving back from Page 3, the ValidatePoints subroutine is called to validate the From, To, and Step values for Range or Percent type questions. The cmdBack_Click subroutine exits without performing the move if validation failed.

Moving back from Page 4 is easy, just move back the previous page without complications.

In moving back from Page 5 you don't move to Page 3 or 4 as you might expect. Remember that the way to move forward to Page 5 is from Page 2 without entering any question text. Moving back from Page 5 should put you on an empty Page 2 screen ready to enter the next question.

The cmdBack_Click subroutine is shown in Listing 17.20.

Listing 17.20. The cmdBack_Click **subroutine.**

```
Sub cmdBack_Click ()

  Dim blnDeleteCurrent As Integer
  Dim blnAddQuestion As Integer
  Dim intLastQuestion As Integer
  Dim n As Integer

  On Error GoTo cmdBack_ClickError

  Select Case mintCurrentPage

  Case 2
  ' Go to the end page of the last question definition (page 3
  ' or page 4), or if on the first question then go to page 1.

    n = zSWintTotalQuestions
    intLastQuestion = mintCurrentQuestion

    DeleteEmptyQuestion True

    If n <> zSWintTotalQuestions Then
      intLastQuestion = intLastQuestion + 1
    End If

    If intLastQuestion = 1 Then
      mintCurrentPage = 1
    Else
      If n = zSWintTotalQuestions Then
        mintCurrentQuestion = mintCurrentQuestion - 1
      End If

      UpdateQuestion False

      If mintCurrentQuestionType = zSWQuestionTypeMultipleChoice Then
        mintCurrentPage = 4
        txtCurrentQuestion4.Requery
      Else
        mintCurrentPage = 3
        txtCurrentQuestion3.Requery
      End If
    End If

  Case 3
    If Not ValidatePoints() Then GoTo cmdBack_ClickDone
    mintCurrentPage = 2

  Case 4
    mintCurrentPage = 3

  Case 5
  ' Don't add a question if the first one is still empty
```

```
      blnAddQuestion = True
      If zSWintTotalQuestions = 1 Then
        If IsEmptyQuestion() Then
          blnAddQuestion = False
        End If
      End If

    ' Add the empty question record back and go to it
      If blnAddQuestion Then AddNextQuestion
      mintCurrentPage = 2

    End Select

    zDisablePaint zSWfrm
    If mintCurrentPage = 2 Then UpdateQuestion True
    VCRPage mintCurrentPage
    zEnablePaint zSWfrm

cmdBack_ClickDone:
  Exit Sub

cmdBack_ClickError:
  Warning "cmdBack_Click", Error$
  Resume cmdBack_ClickDone

End Sub
```

The *cmdNext_Click* Subroutine

Now that you've dealt with going backward, the cmdNext_Click subroutine takes care of moving forward through the Survey Wizard form pages.

This subroutine deals with several special cases.

To move forward from Page 1, there must be an entry or selection in the cboSurveyTitle combo box. The NoTitle function is called to check for this.

If there is a title entered and no questions have been entered yet, then the AddNextQuestion subroutine is called to allocate the initial question in the questionnaire.

If you are leaving Page 2, you check to see if a question is being entered. If so, you go to Page 3 to define how the question may be answered. If not, then you go to Page 5 to do the build.

In leaving Page 3, you need to check to see if the question is a multiple-choice question or not. If so, then you go to Page 4 to enter the multiple-choice answers. Otherwise, you proceed to Page 2 to define the next question. Leaving Page 4 also takes you back to Page 2 to enter another question.

The cmdNext_Click subroutine is shown in Listing 17.21.

Listing 17.21. The cmdNext_Click subroutine.

```
Sub cmdNext_Click ()

  Dim n As Integer

  On Error GoTo cmdNext_ClickError

  Select Case mintCurrentPage

  Case 1
  ' From page 1, verify that a Survey Title has been entered
  ' and then goto page 2. Create a question record to edit if
  ' none already exist.

    If NoTitle() Then
      mintCurrentPage = 1
      GoTo cmdNext_ClickDone
    Else
      mintCurrentPage = 2
      If mintCurrentQuestion = 0 Then AddNextQuestion
    End If

  Case 2
  ' Leaving page 2, if the current question is not being used
  ' then it is time to go to page 5 and build the objects.
  ' Otherwise, we are editing a question and go to page 3 to
  ' enter the answer type.

    n = zSWintTotalQuestions
    DeleteEmptyQuestion True

    mintCurrentPage = 3
    If n <> zSWintTotalQuestions Then mintCurrentPage = 5

  ' If no questions are filled out, go to the last page.
    If zSWintTotalQuestions = 1 Then
      If IsEmptyQuestion() Then
        mintCurrentPage = 5
      End If
    End If

  Case 3
    If Not ValidatePoints() Then GoTo cmdNext_ClickDone

  ' If the question type is multiple-choice, go to page 4 to
  ' define the answers to select from. Otherwise, go to page
  ' 2 to enter a new question or edit an existing one.

    If mintCurrentQuestionType = zSWQuestionTypeMultipleChoice Then
      mintCurrentPage = 4
    Else
      mintCurrentPage = 2
      If mintCurrentQuestion = zSWintTotalQuestions Then
```

```
      AddNextQuestion
    Else
      mintCurrentQuestion = mintCurrentQuestion + 1
    End If
  End If

Case 4
' Go to page 2 to enter a new question or edit an existing
' one.

  mintCurrentPage = 2
  If mintCurrentQuestion = zSWintTotalQuestions Then
    AddNextQuestion
  Else
    mintCurrentQuestion = mintCurrentQuestion + 1
  End If

End Select

zDisablePaint zSWfrm
If mintCurrentPage = 2 Then UpdateQuestion True
VCRPage mintCurrentPage
zEnablePaint zSWfrm

cmdNext_ClickDone:
  Exit Sub

cmdNext_ClickError:
  Warning "cmdNext_Click", Error$
  Resume cmdNext_ClickDone

End Sub
```

The *cmdLast_Click* Subroutine

The cmdLast_Click subroutine (shown in Listing 17.22) jumps directly to Page 5 of
the Survey Wizard form to perform a build.

Listing 17.22. The cmdLast_Click subroutine.

```
Sub cmdLast_Click ()

' Moves to the final page in defining a survey. If the last
' question is empty, it is deleted.

  If mintCurrentPage = 1 Then
    If NoTitle() Then Exit Sub
  End If

  If mintCurrentPage = 3 Then
    If Not ValidatePoints() Then Exit Sub
  End If
```

continues

Listing 17.22. continued

```
DeleteEmptyQuestion True
mintCurrentQuestion = zSWintTotalQuestions

mintCurrentPage = 5
VCRPage mintCurrentPage

End Sub
```

Page 1

The next four routines are associated with Page 1 events. Page 1 of the Survey Wizard form is shown in Figure 17.1.

On Page 1 the user enters a new survey title or selects an existing questionnaire definition. The user can also rename or delete an existing questionnaire.

FIGURE 17.1.
Survey Wizard Page 1.

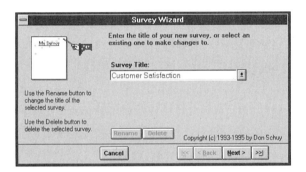

The *cboSurveyTitle_AfterUpdate* Subroutine

The cboSurveyTitle_AfterUpdate subroutine is activated after the user enters a new survey title into the cboSurveyTitle combo box or selects an existing one.

The subroutine first saves any changes made to the currently loaded questionnaire by calling the WriteQuestions function.

If the title is new, then the subroutine re-initializes a couple of variables and empties the zSWaQuestion array used to hold question definitions in memory.

If the title is a previously saved questionnaire definition, then it is loaded by calling the ReadQuestions function.

The Rename and Delete buttons are enabled if a previously saved questionnaire was selected.

The cboSurveyTitle_AfterUpdate subroutine is shown in Listing 17.23.

Listing 17.23. The cboSurveyTitle_AfterUpdate subroutine.

```
Sub cboSurveyTitle_AfterUpdate ()

  Dim dbCode As Database

  Dim v As Variant
  Dim z As Integer
  Dim bEnabled As Integer

  On Error GoTo cboSurveyTitle_AfterUpdateError

' If another survey is open, write any changes that have been made to it
  If zSWintTotalQuestions > 0 Then
    z = WriteQuestions()
  End If

' Clear the question/answer data from memory
  zSWintTotalQuestions = 0
  mintCurrentQuestion = 0
  ReDim zSWaQuestion(zSWintTotalQuestions) As zSW_Question

' Get the new survey title
  zSWstrSurveyTitle = CNStr(Me!cboSurveyTitle)
  Me!cboSurveyTitle = zSWstrSurveyTitle

' If the new title is an existing survey, load the question/answer data
  If zSWstrSurveyTitle <> "" Then
    Set dbCode = CodeDB()
v = LibDLookup(dbCode, "ID", "Survey", "Title = '" &
➥ Quotes(zSWstrSurveyTitle) & "'")

    If Not IsNull(v) Then
      z = ReadQuestions()
    End If

    bEnabled = True
  Else
    bEnabled = False
  End If

  Me!cmdRenameSurvey.Enabled = bEnabled
  Me!cmdDeleteSurvey.Enabled = bEnabled

  Me!cboSurveyTitle.Requery

cboSurveyTitle_AfterUpdateDone:
  Exit Sub

cboSurveyTitle_AfterUpdateError:
  Warning "cboSurveyTitle_AfterUpdate", Error$
  Resume cboSurveyTitle_AfterUpdateDone

End Sub
```

The *cmdDeleteSurvey_Click* Subroutine

The cmdDeleteSurvey_Click subroutine deletes the currently selected questionnaire definition from the Survey Wizard database.

The user is prompted first to be sure they really want to perform the delete. If so, then a record is deleted from the Survey table and each associated question's records are deleted from the Survey Question table.

This subroutine was originally written in Access 1.1 in an earlier version of Survey Wizard. With Access 2.0, you could use cascading deletes to make the Survey Question table records be deleted automatically when you delete the Survey table record.

The cmdDeleteSurvey_Click subroutine is shown in Listing 17.24.

Listing 17.24. The cmdDeleteSurvey_Click **subroutine.**

```
Sub cmdDeleteSurvey_Click ()

  Dim dbCode As Database

  Dim dynSurvey As Recordset
  Dim dynQuestions As Recordset

  Dim varID As Variant

  Dim blnSurveyOpened As Integer
  Dim blnQuestionsOpened As Integer
  Dim blnTransStarted As Integer

  Dim z As Integer

  blnSurveyOpened = False
  blnQuestionsOpened = False
  blnTransStarted = False

  On Error GoTo cmdDeleteSurvey_ClickError

  z = MsgBox("Delete the " & zSWstrSurveyTitle & " Survey?", 4 + 32 + 256,
  ➥ mstrProgramName)
  If z <> 6 Then GoTo cmdDeleteSurvey_ClickDone

  Set dbCode = CodeDB()

  varID = LibDLookup(dbCode, "ID", "Survey", "Title = '" &
  ➥ Quotes(zSWstrSurveyTitle) & "'")

  Me!cboSurveyTitle.SetFocus
  Me!cboSurveyTitle = Null

  If IsNull(varID) Then GoTo cmdDeleteSurvey_ClickDone
```

```
    Set dynSurvey = dbCode.OpenRecordset(
    ➡"SELECT ID FROM [Survey] WHERE ID = " & varID & ";", DB_OPEN_DYNASET)
    blnSurveyOpened = True

    Set dynQuestions = dbCode.OpenRecordset(
    ➡"SELECT ID FROM [Survey Question] WHERE SurveyID = " & varID & ";",
    ➡ DB_OPEN_DYNASET)
blnQuestionsOpened = True

    BeginTrans
    blnTransStarted = True

    Do Until dynQuestions.EOF
      dynQuestions.Delete
      dynQuestions.MoveNext
    Loop

    dynSurvey.Delete

    CommitTrans
    blnTransStarted = False

' Set number of questions to zero in order to avoid saving them again
' in cboSurveyTitle_AfterUpdate.

    zSWintTotalQuestions = 0
    cboSurveyTitle_AfterUpdate

cmdDeleteSurvey_ClickDone:
  On Error Resume Next
  If blnTransStarted Then Rollback
  If blnSurveyOpened Then dynQuestions.Close
  If blnQuestionsOpened Then dynSurvey.Close
  Exit Sub

cmdDeleteSurvey_ClickError:
  Warning "cmdDeleteSurvey_Click", Error$
  Resume cmdDeleteSurvey_ClickDone

End Sub
```

The *cmdRenameSurvey_Click* Subroutine

The Rename button is used to change the title of a saved questionnaire.

You can't simply retype the name of the questionnaire in the cboSurveyTitle combo box because Survey Wizard thinks that you are creating a new survey.

The rename button opens a small pop-up form, "Survey Wizard Rename," that you create at the end of this chapter.

The cmdRenameSurvey_Click subroutine is shown in Listing 17.25.

Listing 17.25. The `cmdRenameSurvey_Click` **subroutine.**

```
Sub cmdRenameSurvey_Click ()

  DoCmd OpenForm "Survey Wizard Rename", , , , , A_Dialog

End Sub
```

The *NoTitle* Function

The `NoTitle` function is called to see if moving beyond the first page should be allowed. A True return value indicates that no title has been entered, so it is not OK to continue.

The function checks to see if a questionnaire title has been entered into the `cboSurveyTitle` combo box. If the combo box is empty, a message is displayed and the function returns True.

The `NoTitle` function is shown in Listing 17.26.

Listing 17.26. The `NoTitle` **function.**

```
Function NoTitle () As Integer

' Default to no title found
  NoTitle = True

  On Error GoTo NoTitleError

  zSWstrSurveyTitle = CNStr(Me!cboSurveyTitle)

  If zSWstrSurveyTitle = "" Then

    MsgBox "You must enter a survey title before continuing.", 48,
    ➥ mstrProgramName
    Me!cboSurveyTitle.SetFocus
  Else
    NoTitle = False
  End If

NoTitleDone:
  Exit Function

NoTitleError:
  Warning "NoTitle", Error$
  Resume NoTitleDone

End Function
```

Adding and Deleting Questions

The next three procedures take care of adding and deleting questions to and from the zSWaQuestion array, which holds the information on each question for the questionnaire currently in memory.

The *AddNextQuestion* Subroutine

The AddNextQuestion subroutine resizes the zSWaQuestion array and initializes the newly created question with default values.

Typically, the new question is added to the end of the array; however, the subroutine can also insert a new question in front of existing questions. It does this by resizing the array, and then moving questions down a notch to make room for the inserted question.

The AddNextQuestion subroutine is shown in Listing 17.27.

Listing 17.27. The AddNextQuestion **subroutine.**

```
Sub AddNextQuestion ()

' Insert a new question record in the appropriate place within the
' zSWaQuestion array.

  Dim q As zSW_Question
  Dim n As Integer

  On Error GoTo AddNextQuestionError

  mintCurrentQuestion = mintCurrentQuestion + 1
  zSWintTotalQuestions = zSWintTotalQuestions + 1

  ReDim Preserve zSWaQuestion(zSWintTotalQuestions) As zSW_Question

' If there are other questions after the one inserted, then we need to
' move them up the array
  n = zSWintTotalQuestions
  While n > mintCurrentQuestion
    zSWaQuestion(n) = zSWaQuestion(n - 1)
    n = n - 1
  Wend

' Initialize the values for this question record
  q.strQuestion = ""
  q.intType = zSWQuestionTypeYesNo
  q.strA = ""
  q.strB = ""
  q.strC = ""
  q.strD = ""
```

continues

Listing 17.27. continued

```
  q.strE = ""
  q.strF = ""
  q.lngRangeFrom = 1
  q.lngRangeTo = 10
  q.lngRangeStep = 1
  q.intPercentFrom = 0
  q.intPercentTo = 100
  q.intPercentStep = 25

' Place the local copy into the array
  zSWaQuestion(mintCurrentQuestion) = q

AddNextQuestionDone:
  Exit Sub

AddNextQuestionError:
  Warning "AddNextQuestion", Error$
  Resume AddNextQuestionDone

End Sub
```

The *IsEmptyQuestion* Function

The IsEmptyQuestion function (shown in Listing 17.28) returns True if the txtQuestion text box on Page 2 is empty.

Listing 17.28. The IsEmptyQuestion function.

```
Function IsEmptyQuestion () As Integer

  IsEmptyQuestion = (CNStr(Me!txtQuestion) = "")

End Function
```

The *DeleteEmptyQuestion* Subroutine

Each time the user completes a question definition and clicks the Next button, the Survey Wizard form displays Page 2 ready to accept another question.

By this time, a question has already been added to the zSWaQuestion array. If the user leaves Page 2 without entering a question, the added element to the zSWaQuestion array needs to be deleted.

The DeleteEmptyQuestion subroutine first verifies that this is the exact state that the program is in, and if so, the subroutine deletes the empty question from the zSWaQuestion array by calling the DeleteQuestion subroutine.

The `DeleteEmptyQuestion` subroutine is shown in Listing 17.29.

Listing 17.29. The `DeleteEmptyQuestion` subroutine.

```
Sub DeleteEmptyQuestion (blnUpdatePage As Integer)

' Called when leaving a page. If the page being left is page 2,
' and no question is entered, then we want to delete the empty
' question record.

  Dim z As Integer

  If mintCurrentPage = 2 Then
    If mintCurrentQuestion <> 1 Then
      If mintCurrentQuestion = zSWintTotalQuestions Then

        If IsEmptyQuestion() Then
          z = DeleteQuestion(True, blnUpdatePage)
        End If

      End If
    End If
  End If

End Sub
```

Page 2

The second page of the Survey Wizard form is where new questions are added to the questionnaire. See Figure 17.2.

The page is multipurposed, however, and also allows the user to quickly browse the questions in the questionnaire, insert a new question anywhere in the list of questions, and delete a question.

FIGURE 17.2.
*Survey Wizard
Page 2.*

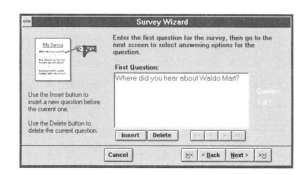

The *txtQuestion_AfterUpdate* Subroutine

Outside of the error handling, the txtQuestion_AfterUpdate subroutine (shown in Listing 17.30) is a one-liner. It saves changes made to the question text into memory.

The subroutine copies the text in the txtQuestion text box into the strQuestion member of the entry in the zSWaQuestion array that represents the current question.

Listing 17.30. The txtQuestion_AfterUpdate **subroutine.**

```
Sub txtQuestion_AfterUpdate ()

' Save any changes made to the question text

  On Error GoTo txtQuestion_AfterUpdateError

    zSWaQuestion(mintCurrentQuestion).strQuestion = CNStr(Me!txtQuestion)

txtQuestion_AfterUpdateDone:
  Exit Sub

txtQuestion_AfterUpdateError:
  Warning "txtQuestion_AfterUpdate", Error$
  Resume txtQuestion_AfterUpdateDone

End Sub
```

The *CurrentQuestion* Function

The CurrentQuestion function is called as the ControlSource for the txtCurrentQuestion2, txtCurrentQuestion3, and txtCurrentQuestion4 text boxes.

The function builds a string such as "2 of 5" to indicate which question is currently being edited of how many questions that are in the questionnaire.

Listing 17.31. The CurrentQuestion **function.**

```
Function CurrentQuestion () As String

' Let the user know which question they are working on

  CurrentQuestion = mintCurrentQuestion & " of " & zSWintTotalQuestions

End Function
```

```
    Me!cmdLastQuestion.Enabled = (mintCurrentQuestion <>
    ➥ zSWintTotalQuestions)
  End If

UpdateQuestionDone:
  Exit Sub

UpdateQuestionError:
  Warning "UpdateQuestion", Error$
  Resume UpdateQuestionDone

End Sub
```

The *UpdateType* Subroutine

The UpdateType subroutine updates the controls on Pages 3 and 4 so that they display the values stored in the zSWrQuestion array for the current question being edited.

If the question/answer type is range or percent, the txtFrom, txtTo and txtStep text boxes are made visible to display those settings.

The UpdateType subroutine is shown in Listing 17.39.

Listing 17.39. The UpdateType subroutine.

```
Sub UpdateType ()

' Updates the Survey Wizard form so that answering options for a question
' are displayed for the current question being edited.

  Dim q As zSW_Question

  Dim ctl As Control

  On Error GoTo UpdateTypeError

  q = zSWaQuestion(mintCurrentQuestion)

  Me!optResponseType = mintCurrentQuestionType

  Select Case mintCurrentQuestionType

  Case zSWQuestionTypeYesNo, zSWQuestionTypeMultipleChoice,
  ➥ zSWQuestionTypeWriteIn

    Me!txtFrom.Visible = False
    Me!txtTo.Visible = False
    Me!txtStep.Visible = False

    If mintCurrentQuestionType = zSWQuestionTypeMultipleChoice Then
      Me!txtA = q.strA
      Me!txtB = q.strB
```

continues

Listing 17.39. continued

```
        Me!txtC = q.strC
        Me!txtD = q.strD
        Me!txtE = q.strE
        Me!txtF = q.strF
      End If

    Case zSWQuestionTypeRange, zSWQuestionTypePercent

      Me!txtFrom.Visible = True
      Me!txtTo.Visible = True
      Me!txtStep.Visible = True

      If mintCurrentQuestionType = zSWQuestionTypeRange Then
        Me!txtFrom = q.lngRangeFrom
        Me!txtTo = q.lngRangeTo
        Me!txtStep = q.lngRangeStep
      Else
        Me!txtFrom = q.intPercentFrom
        Me!txtTo = q.intPercentTo
        Me!txtStep = q.intPercentStep
      End If

  End Select

UpdateTypeDone:
  Exit Sub

UpdateTypeError:
  Warning "UpdateType", Error$
  Resume UpdateTypeDone

End Sub
```

The *DeleteQuestion* Function

The DeleteQuestion function deletes the currently displayed question.

Any questions after the current one are shifted down the zSWaQuestion array before the array is reallocated one element shorter than it was before.

Because you are automatically creating question records whenever Page 2 is displayed, an empty record is added if you just deleted the last record.

The DeleteQuestion function is shown in Listing 17.40.

Listing 17.40. The DeleteQuestion **function.**

```
Function DeleteQuestion (blnExitPage As Integer, blnUpdatePage As Integer)
➥ As Integer

' Delete the current question

  Dim n As Integer

  On Error GoTo DeleteQuestionError

' If there are other questions after the one deleted, then we need to
' move them down the array.
  n = mintCurrentQuestion
  While n < zSWintTotalQuestions
    zSWaQuestion(n) = zSWaQuestion(n + 1)
    n = n + 1
  Wend

' Resize the array
  zSWintTotalQuestions = zSWintTotalQuestions - 1
  ReDim Preserve zSWaQuestion(zSWintTotalQuestions) As zSW_Question

' If we are deleting the last question and are not leaving the 2nd page,
' then if we deleted the last question we want to add an empty one.
  If mintCurrentQuestion > zSWintTotalQuestions Then
    mintCurrentQuestion = mintCurrentQuestion - 1
    If Not blnExitPage Then
      AddNextQuestion
    End If
  End If

  If blnUpdatePage Then UpdateQuestion (Not blnExitPage)

DeleteQuestionDone:
  Exit Function

DeleteQuestionError:
  Warning "DeleteQuestion", Error$
  Resume DeleteQuestionDone

End Function
```

Page 3

On Page 3 the user selects how the current question is answered (see Figure 17.3). If the question is a Range or Percent type, the txtFrom, txtTo, and txtStep text boxes are displayed so the user may set the range of numbers that are on the questionnaire as available selections.

FIGURE 17.3.
Survey Wizard Page 3.

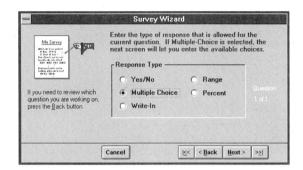

The *optResponseType_AfterUpdate* Subroutine

The `optResponseType_AfterUpdate` subroutine is called when the user selects whether a question is a yes/no, multiple-choice, write-in, range, or percent type of question.

The selection is recorded both in a module variable `mintCurrentQuestionType`, and in the `intType` member for the current question in the `zSWaQuestion` array.

Next the `UpdateType` subroutine is called to update the form with the current settings for that response type. Note that if you switch from one response type to another and then back again, you don't lose settings you originally entered for the first response type.

The `optResponseType_AfterUpdate` subroutine is shown in Listing 17.41.

Listing 17.41. The `optResponseType_AfterUpdate` **subroutine.**

```
Sub optResponseType_AfterUpdate ()

  On Error GoTo optResponseType_AfterUpdateError

  mintCurrentQuestionType = Me!optResponseType
  zSWaQuestion(mintCurrentQuestion).intType = mintCurrentQuestionType

  UpdateType

optResponseType_AfterUpdateDone:
  Exit Sub

optResponseType_AfterUpdateError:
  Warning "optResponseType_AfterUpdate", Error$
  Resume optResponseType_AfterUpdateDone

End Sub
```

The *Range AfterUpdate* Subroutines

The `txtFrom_AfterUpdate`, `txtTo_AfterUpdate`, and `txtStep_AfterUpdate` subroutines each call the `RangeAfterUpdate` subroutine to record any changes that are entered.

The `RangeAfterUpdate` subroutine checks to see if the question is a range or percent response type and saves three fields accordingly.

The `txtFrom_AfterUpdate`, `txtTo_AfterUpdate`, `txtStep_AfterUpdate` and `RangeAfterUpdate` subroutines are shown in Listing 17.42.

Listing 17.42. The `Range AfterUpdate` **subroutines.**

```
Sub txtFrom_AfterUpdate ()

  RangeAfterUpdate

End Sub

Sub txtStep_AfterUpdate ()

  RangeAfterUpdate

End Sub

Sub txtTo_AfterUpdate ()

  RangeAfterUpdate

End Sub

Sub RangeAfterUpdate ()

' Save any changes made to the From, To and Step fields

  On Error GoTo RangeAfterUpdateError

  If mintCurrentQuestionType = zSWQuestionTypeRange Then
    zSWaQuestion(mintCurrentQuestion).lngRangeFrom = Me!txtFrom
    zSWaQuestion(mintCurrentQuestion).lngRangeTo = Me!txtTo
    zSWaQuestion(mintCurrentQuestion).lngRangeStep = Me!txtStep
  Else
    zSWaQuestion(mintCurrentQuestion).intPercentFrom = Me!txtFrom
    zSWaQuestion(mintCurrentQuestion).intPercentTo = Me!txtTo
    zSWaQuestion(mintCurrentQuestion).intPercentStep = Me!txtStep
  End If

RangeAfterUpdateDone:
  Exit Sub

RangeAfterUpdateError:
  Warning "RangeAfterUpdate", Error$
  Resume RangeAfterUpdateDone

End Sub
```

The *ValidatePoints* Function

The next procedure, `ValidatePoints`, will be completed in Chapter 18. `ValidatePoints` will be used to verify that the entered From, To, and Step values are acceptable. The function returns True, indicating that the entries are OK.

A stub for the `ValidatePoints` function is shown in Listing 17.43.

Listing 17.43. A temporary `ValidatePoints` **subroutine.**

```
Function ValidatePoints()

  ValidatePoints = True

End Function
```

Page 4

Page 4 is only entered if the current question response type is multiple-choice. Here, up to six choices may be entered for the current question.

The saving of the entries on this page is lumped together into a `ChoiceAfterUpdate` subroutine, just as you lumped together the changes to `txtFrom`, `txtTo`, and `txtStep` into the `RangeAfterUpdate` subroutine. This was done mostly so you would not need to repeat the error handling code.

Page 4 of the Survey Wizard form is shown in Figure 17.4.

FIGURE 17.4.

Survey Wizard Page 4.

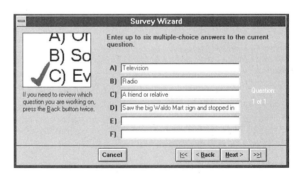

The *Choice AfterUpdate* Subroutines

The `ChoiceAfterUpdate` subroutine is called by the `txtA` through `txtF` text box `AfterUpdate` event code. A character is passed to identify which text box was changed.

The txtA_AfterUpdate, txtB_AfterUpdate, txtC_AfterUpdate, txtD_AfterUpdate, txtE_AfterUpdate, txtF_AfterUpdate, and ChoiceAfterUpdate subroutines are shown in Listing 17.44.

Listing 17.44. The Choice AfterUpdate **subroutines.**

```
Sub txtA_AfterUpdate ()

  ChoiceAfterUpdate "A"

End Sub

Sub txtB_AfterUpdate ()

  ChoiceAfterUpdate "B"

End Sub

Sub txtC_AfterUpdate ()

  ChoiceAfterUpdate "C"

End Sub

Sub txtD_AfterUpdate ()

  ChoiceAfterUpdate "D"

End Sub

Sub txtE_AfterUpdate ()

  ChoiceAfterUpdate "E"

End Sub

Sub txtF_AfterUpdate ()

  ChoiceAfterUpdate "F"

End Sub

Sub ChoiceAfterUpdate (strChoice As String)

' Store a multiple-choice answer

  On Error GoTo ChoiceAfterUpdateError

  Select Case strChoice

  Case "A"
    zSWaQuestion(mintCurrentQuestion).strA = CNStr(Me!txtA)

  Case "B"
    zSWaQuestion(mintCurrentQuestion).strB = CNStr(Me!txtB)
```

continues

Listing 17.44. continued

```
Case "C"
  zSWaQuestion(mintCurrentQuestion).strC = CNStr(Me!txtC)

Case "D"
  zSWaQuestion(mintCurrentQuestion).strD = CNStr(Me!txtD)

Case "E"
  zSWaQuestion(mintCurrentQuestion).strE = CNStr(Me!txtE)

Case "F"
  zSWaQuestion(mintCurrentQuestion).strF = CNStr(Me!txtF)

End Select

ChoiceAfterUpdateDone:
  Exit Sub

ChoiceAfterUpdateError:
  Warning "ChoiceAfterUpdate", Error$
  Resume ChoiceAfterUpdateDone

End Sub
```

Page 5

In the final page, the user selects which objects to generate and clicks the big Build button.

The effect is somewhat anticlimactic because rather than immediately generating objects, Survey Wizard displays a second form to prompt for the name as which to save the objects. Only after the user clicks OK on this next form are the objects actually generated.

Along with the code behind the Build button, there is code for the fifth page to help the user select which objects to generate.

Page 5 of the Survey Wizard form is shown in Figure 17.5.

FIGURE 17.5.
Survey Wizard Page 5.

The *Mandatory Object* Subroutines

The CheckMandatoryObjects subroutine is called when any of values in the build object check boxes are changed.

A message is displayed if the users attempt to uncheck the Questions Table or Responses Table and they are also generating a form or report that uses it.

You are allowed to skip generating the table if one already exists. You might want to correct the wording in an existing question in the survey for example. Adding or deleting questions, however, most certainly causes problems. The program doesn't currently check for this situation.

The chkEntryForm_AfterUpdate, chkQuestionsTable_AfterUpdate, chkEntryReport_AfterUpdate, chkResponsesTable_AfterUpdate, chkResultsReport_AfterUpdate, and CheckMandatoryObjects subroutines are shown in Listing 17.45.

Listing 17.45. The Mandatory Object **subroutines.**

```
Sub chkEntryForm_AfterUpdate ()

  CheckMandatoryObjects ""

End Sub

Sub chkQuestionsTable_AfterUpdate ()

  CheckMandatoryObjects "Questions"

End Sub

Sub chkEntryReport_AfterUpdate ()

  CheckMandatoryObjects ""

End Sub

Sub chkResponsesTable_AfterUpdate ()

  CheckMandatoryObjects "Responses"

End Sub

Sub chkResultsReport_AfterUpdate ()

  CheckMandatoryObjects ""

End Sub

Sub CheckMandatoryObjects (szTableControl As String)

' Some objects are mandatory when other objects are being created.
```

continues

Listing 17.45. continued

```
' For example, the Questions Table must be created if the Entry Report
' is created since this table is the record source for the report.

' This function checks the mandatory objects to be generated when they
' are needed and don't already exist.

  Dim blnQuestionsTableNeeded As Integer
  Dim blnResponsesTableNeeded As Integer

  On Error GoTo CheckMandatoryObjectsError

  blnQuestionsTableNeeded = False
  blnResponsesTableNeeded = False

  If Me!chkEntryReport = True Then
    blnQuestionsTableNeeded = True
  End If

  If Me!chkEntryForm = True Or Me!chkResultsReport = True Then
    blnQuestionsTableNeeded = True
    blnResponsesTableNeeded = True
  End If

  If blnQuestionsTableNeeded And Me!chkQuestionsTable = False Then
    If Not TableExists(zSWstrQuestionsTable) Then
      If szTableControl = "Questions" Then
        MsgBox "The Questions Table object must be generated in order to
        ➥ create the Entry Report, Entry Form or Results Report object.",
        ➥ 64, mstrProgramName

End If
      Me!chkQuestionsTable = True
    End If
  End If

  If blnResponsesTableNeeded And Me!chkResponsesTable = False Then
    If Not TableExists(zSWstrResponsesTable) Then
      If szTableControl = "Responses" Then

        MsgBox "The Responses Table object must be generated in order to
        ➥ create the Entry Form or Results Report object.", 64,
        ➥ mstrProgramName
      End If
      Me!chkResponsesTable = True
    End If
  End If

CheckMandatoryObjectsDone:
  Exit Sub

CheckMandatoryObjectsError:
  Warning "CheckMandatoryObjects", Error$
  Resume CheckMandatoryObjectsDone

End Sub
```

The *cmdBuild_Click* Subroutine

The cmdBuild_Click subroutine verifies that the user selected at least one object to build and has entered at least one question. Then the subroutine opens the Survey Wizard Save As form to prompt for a name to save objects as and to build the objects.

The cmdBuildClick subroutine is shown in Listing 17.46.

Listing 17.46. The cmbBuild_Click **subroutine.**

```
Sub cmdBuild_Click ()

  Dim blnObjectSelected As Integer
  Dim z As Integer

  On Error GoTo cmdBuild_ClickError

' Make sure that an object was selected
  blnObjectSelected = False
  If Me!chkEntryReport Then blnObjectSelected = True
  If Me!chkEntryForm Then blnObjectSelected = True
  If Me!chkResultsReport Then blnObjectSelected = True
  If Me!chkQuestionsTable Then blnObjectSelected = True
  If Me!chkResponsesTable Then blnObjectSelected = True

  If Not blnObjectSelected Then

    MsgBox "You must select at least one object to generate.", 64,
    ➥ mstrProgramName
    GoTo cmdBuild_ClickDone
  End If

' Make sure at least one question was entered
  If zSWintTotalQuestions = 1 Then
    If Len(zSWaQuestion(1).strQuestion) = 0 Then
      MsgBox "You must enter at least one question before generating any
      ➥ survey objects.", 64, mstrProgramName
GoTo cmdBuild_ClickDone
    End If
  End If

' The build code requires that the records are saved
  z = WriteQuestions()

  DoCmd OpenForm "Survey Wizard Save As", A_Normal, , , A_Edit, A_Dialog

cmdBuild_ClickDone:
  Exit Sub

cmdBuild_ClickError:
  Warning "cmdBuild_Click", Error$
  Resume cmdBuild_ClickDone

End Sub
```

Load and Save

To complete the code behind the Survey Wizard form are the functions that read in a saved questionnaire and write out new questionnaires or edit to existing ones.

The *ReadQuestions* Function

The ReadQuestions function first reads in values from the Survey table record for the selected questionnaire, and then reads each of the questions from the Survey Questions table.

The zSWaQuestion array is resized to the number of questions in the questionnaire. Each element in the array is a zSW_Question structure containing the same fields as are stored within the Survey Questions table.

The ReadQuestions function is shown in Listing 17.47.

Listing 17.47. The ReadQuestions function.

```
Function ReadQuestions () As Integer

  Dim q As zSW_Question

  Dim db As Database

  Dim dyn As Recordset
  Dim blnOpened As Integer

  Dim sql As String
  Dim vID As Variant

  blnOpened = False
  On Error GoTo ReadQuestionsError

  Set db = CodeDB()

' The ID value is on the form as a hidden column in the Survey Title
' combobox.
  vID = Me!cboSurveyTitle.Column(0)
  If IsNull(vID) Then GoTo ReadQuestionsDone

  Set dyn = db.OpenRecordset("Survey", DB_OPEN_DYNASET)
  blnOpened = True

  dyn.FindFirst "ID = " & vID
  If dyn.NoMatch Then GoTo ReadQuestionsDone

  zSWstrBaseName = CNStr(dyn!BaseName)
  Me!chkEntryReport = dyn!BuildEntryReport
  Me!chkEntryForm = dyn!BuildEntryForm
  Me!chkResultsReport = dyn!BuildResultsReport
  Me!chkQuestionsTable = dyn!BuildQuestionsTable
  Me!chkResponsesTable = dyn!BuildResponsesTable
```

```
    dyn.Close
    blnOpened = False

    sql = "SELECT * FROM [Survey Question] WHERE SurveyID = " & CLng(vID) & ";"
    Set dyn = db.CreateDynaset(sql)
    blnOpened = True

    If dyn.RecordCount Then
      dyn.MoveLast
      zSWintTotalQuestions = dyn.RecordCount
      dyn.MoveFirst

      ReDim zSWaQuestion(zSWintTotalQuestions) As zSW_Question

      Do Until dyn.EOF
        q.strQuestion = CNStr(dyn!question)
        q.intType = dyn!Type
        q.strA = CNStr(dyn!ChoiceA)
        q.strB = CNStr(dyn!ChoiceB)
        q.strC = CNStr(dyn!ChoiceC)
        q.strD = CNStr(dyn!ChoiceD)
        q.strE = CNStr(dyn!ChoiceE)
        q.strF = CNStr(dyn!ChoiceF)
        q.lngRangeFrom = dyn!RangeFrom
        q.lngRangeTo = dyn!RangeTo
        q.lngRangeStep = dyn!RangeStep
        q.intPercentFrom = dyn!PercentFrom
        q.intPercentTo = dyn!PercentTo
        q.intPercentStep = dyn!PercentStep

        zSWaQuestion(dyn!ID) = q
        dyn.MoveNext
      Loop

      mintCurrentQuestion = 1
    End If

ReadQuestionsDone:
    On Error Resume Next
    If blnOpened Then dyn.Close
    Exit Function

ReadQuestionsError:
    Warning "ReadQuestions", Error$
    Resume ReadQuestionsDone

End Function
```

The *WriteQuestions* Function

The WriteQuestions function is the opposite of the ReadQuestions function—data is being transferred, but in the opposite direction.

The function writes the Survey table record and Survey Question table records for the questionnaire definition currently loaded. The write is done inside a transaction for both speed and data integrity.

The WriteQuestions function is shown in Listing 17.48.

Listing 17.48. The WriteQuestions **function.**

```
Function WriteQuestions () As Integer

  Dim q As zSW_Question

  Dim db As Database

  Dim dynSurvey As Recordset
  Dim dynQuestions As Recordset

  Dim strTitle As String
  Dim strCriteria As String

  Dim lID As Long

  Dim intQuestion As Integer
  Dim z As Integer

  Dim blnSurveyOpened As Integer
  Dim blnQuestionsOpened As Integer
  Dim blnTransStarted As Integer

  blnSurveyOpened = False
  blnQuestionsOpened = False
  blnTransStarted = False

  On Error GoTo WriteQuestionsError

  If zSWstrSurveyTitle = "" Then GoTo WriteQuestionsDone

  DeleteEmptyQuestion False

' If no questions were entered, then don't save it.
  If zSWintTotalQuestions = 0 Then
    GoTo WriteQuestionsDone
  End If
  If zSWintTotalQuestions = 1 And zSWaQuestion(1).strQuestion = "" Then
    GoTo WriteQuestionsDone
  End If

  WriteQuestions = True

  Set db = CodeDB()

  Set dynSurvey = db.OpenRecordset("Survey", DB_OPEN_DYNASET)
  blnSurveyOpened = True

  Set dynQuestions = db.OpenRecordset("Survey Question", DB_OPEN_DYNASET)
```

```
blnQuestionsOpened = True

BeginTrans
blnTransStarted = True

strTitle = zSWstrSurveyTitle

strCriteria = "Title = " & Chr$(34) & Quotes(strTitle) & Chr$(34)
dynSurvey.FindFirst strCriteria

If Not dynSurvey.NoMatch Then
' Delete the old settings

  dynQuestions.FindFirst "SurveyID = " & dynSurvey!ID
  Do Until dynQuestions.NoMatch
    dynQuestions.Delete
    dynQuestions.FindNext "SurveyID = " & dynSurvey!ID
  Loop

  dynSurvey.Edit
Else
  dynSurvey.AddNew
  dynSurvey!Title = strTitle
End If

lID = dynSurvey!ID

dynSurvey!BaseName = CSNull(zSWstrBaseName)
dynSurvey!BuildEntryReport = Me!chkEntryReport
dynSurvey!BuildEntryForm = Me!chkEntryForm
dynSurvey!BuildResultsReport = Me!chkResultsReport
dynSurvey!BuildQuestionsTable = Me!chkQuestionsTable
dynSurvey!BuildResponsesTable = Me!chkResponsesTable
dynSurvey.Update

For intQuestion = 1 To zSWintTotalQuestions
  q = zSWaQuestion(intQuestion)

  dynQuestions.AddNew
  dynQuestions!SurveyID = lID
  dynQuestions!ID = intQuestion
  dynQuestions!question = q.strQuestion
  dynQuestions!Type = q.intType
  dynQuestions!ChoiceA = CSNull(q.strA)
  dynQuestions!ChoiceB = CSNull(q.strB)
  dynQuestions!ChoiceC = CSNull(q.strC)
  dynQuestions!ChoiceD = CSNull(q.strD)
  dynQuestions!ChoiceE = CSNull(q.strE)
  dynQuestions!ChoiceF = CSNull(q.strF)
  dynQuestions!RangeFrom = q.lngRangeFrom
  dynQuestions!RangeTo = q.lngRangeTo
  dynQuestions!RangeStep = q.lngRangeStep
  dynQuestions!PercentFrom = q.intPercentFrom
  dynQuestions!PercentTo = q.intPercentTo
  dynQuestions!PercentStep = q.intPercentStep
  dynQuestions.Update
Next intQuestion
```

continues

Listing 17.48. continued

```
  CommitTrans
  blnTransStarted = False

' Return success
  WriteQuestions = False

WriteQuestionsDone:
  On Error Resume Next
  If blnTransStarted Then Rollback
  If blnSurveyOpened Then dynSurvey.Close
  If blnQuestionsOpened Then dynQuestions.Close
  Exit Function

WriteQuestionsError:
  Warning "WriteQuestions", Error$
  Resume WriteQuestionsDone

End Function
```

The *Form_Unload* Subroutine

The final subroutine, `Form_Unload`, saves the current questionnaire that is loaded before the Survey Wizard form closes.

The `Form_Unload` subroutine is shown in Listing 17.49.

Listing 17.49. The `Form_Unload` subroutine.

```
Sub Form_Unload (Cancel As Integer)

  Dim z As Integer

  z = WriteQuestions()

End Sub
```

That's all the code behind the Survey Wizard form.

Testing the Survey Wizard Form

You should now be able to define a questionnaire, and it is automatically saved when you close the Survey Wizard form. Open the form again, and you can select your questionnaire from the Survey Title combo box.

If all is running smoothly and you can move from page to page without any problems, resize the tab sentry buttons so they have their Width and Height properties set to 0 inches. This hides them from view. It is still possible to select the tab sentry controls on the form after the tab sentry buttons have been sized like this, but you may have to hunt for a while.

The Delete button on the first page functions correctly, as do all the buttons on the second page. The From, To, and Step text boxes appear if you select a Range or Percent response type on the third page.

The Rename and Build buttons produce an error (see Figure 17.6) because the forms that they open haven't been created yet. You create the Survey Wizard Rename form next.

FIGURE 17.6.
Oops! The Build button doesn't work yet!

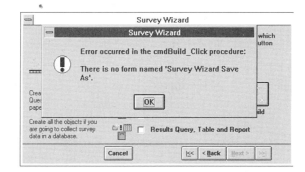

Creating the Survey Wizard Rename Form

The Survey Wizard Rename form is used to change the displayed title of the questionnaire. This title is also used to identify a saved questionnaire definition.

The form has the following properties set:

Survey Wizard Rename Form
Pop-up form to rename a survey title.

Object: **Survey Wizard Rename Form**

Property	Value
Caption:	Survey Wizard Rename
Default View:	Single Form
Views Allowed:	Form
Shortcut Menu:	No
Scrollbars:	Neither
Record Selectors:	No
Navigation Buttons:	No

Property	Value
Auto Center:	Yes
Pop Up:	Yes
Modal:	Yes
Border Style:	Dialog box
Min Button:	No
Max Button:	No
Width:	4 in

Object: **Detail0 Section**

Property	Value
Height:	1 in
Back Color:	12632256 (Light Gray)

The form has a single text box and an OK and Cancel button.

Object: **lblNewSurveyTitle Label**

Child label to the txtNewSurveyTitle text box.

Property	Value
Caption:	New Survey Title:
Left:	0.1347 in
Top:	0.1875 in
Width:	1.2 in
Height:	0.1667 in

Object: **txtNewSurveyTitle Text Box**

Enter the new title of the questionnaire.

Property	Value
Tab Index:	0
Left:	1.375 in
Top:	0.1771 in
Width:	2.5 in
Height:	0.1903 in
Special Effect:	Sunken
Font Name:	MS Sans Serif
Font Size:	10
Font Weight:	Normal

Object: **cmdOK Command Button**

Accept the entry as the changed title.

Property	Value
Caption:	OK
Default:	Yes
Tab Index:	1
Left:	1.25 in
Top:	0.625 in
Width:	0.7 in
Height:	0.25 in
Font Name:	MS Sans Serif
Font Size:	8
Font Weight:	Bold

Object: **cmdCancel Command Button**

Cancel changing the questionnaire title.

Property	Value
Caption:	Cancel
Cancel:	Yes
Tab Index:	2
Left:	2.0625 in
Top:	0.625 in
Width:	0.7 in
Height:	0.25 in
Font Name:	MS Sans Serif
Font Size:	8
Font Weight:	Bold

Figure 17.7 shows the completed Survey Wizard Rename form.

FIGURE 17.7.

*Creating the Survey
Wizard Rename form.*

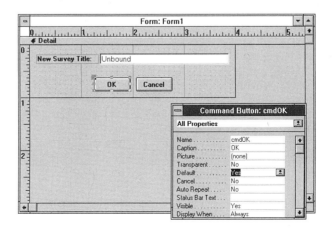

Coding the Survey Wizard Rename Form

The Survey Wizard Rename form accepts an entry for a new questionnaire title and writes it to the Survey table and back to the Survey Wizard form.

In addition to the procedures you look at here, the form module for the Survey Wizard Rename form contains its own copy of the following three procedures that are also found in the Survey Wizard form's module:

- CNStr
- Quotes
- Warning

Wasteful? The reason these were duplicated here was to avoid having to place them in modules. Given that the final application will be loaded as a library database, it's better to have code behind forms than in modules. This way, the code for a form is loaded into memory only when the form is actually used.

I admit the routines are small, so the penalty for having them loaded all the time is probably negligible. You might try this technique if you have a particularly large subroutine that needs to be in a library to support more than one form.

Don't tell anyone you heard it from me, though, OK? In general, duplicating code is a bad practice; you will likely change one version of the copy somewhere and forget to update the other copies.

The Declarations Section

Because this module is essentially part of the user interface, I decided to go with the same module name for reporting errors, Survey Wizard.

The mblnOKPressed variable gets set if the OK button on the Survey Wizard Rename form is pressed. As the form closes, the Unload event code will check the mblnOKPressed variable to determine if the title change should be used or discarded.

The declarations section is shown in Listing 17.50.

Listing 17.50. The declarations section for the Survey Wizard Rename form module.

```
' Survey Wizard Rename Form

  Option Compare Database
  Option Explicit

  Const mstrProgramName = "Survey Wizard"

  Dim mblnOKPressed As Integer
```

The *Form_Load* Subroutine

As the form opens, the Form_Load subroutine (shown in Listing 17.51) copies the title from the cboSurveyTitle on the Survey Wizard form into the text box on this form.

Listing 17.51. The Form_Load **subroutine.**

```
Sub Form_Load ()

' Copy the title from the Survey Wizard form
  txtNewSurveyTitle = CNStr(zSWfrm!cboSurveyTitle)

' Assume user cancelled
  mblnOKPressed = False

End Sub
```

The OK and Cancel Buttons

The OK and Cancel buttons both close the form. The mblnOKPressed flag is set if OK is pressed. The cmdOK_Click and cmdCancel_Click subroutines are shown in Listing 17.52.

Listing 17.52. The cmdOK_Click **and** cmdCancel_Click **subroutines.**

```
Sub cmdOK_Click ()

  mblnOKPressed = True
  zCloseForm Me

End Sub

Sub cmdCancel_Click ()

  zCloseForm Me

End Sub
```

The *Form_Unload* Subroutine

The Form_Unload subroutine (shown in Listing 17.53) validates the new questionnaire title to make sure that it isn't used on another saved questionnaire. It then locates the record for the currently loaded questionnaire and saves the changed title.

The changed title is also written to the Survey Title combo box on the Survey Wizard form and to the zSWstrSurveyTitle global variable.

Listing 17.53. The `Form_Unload` **subroutine.**

```
Sub Form_Unload (Cancel As Integer)

  Dim db As Database

  Dim dyn As Recordset
  Dim blnOpened As Integer

  Dim strNewTitle As String

  blnOpened = False

  On Error GoTo Form_UnloadError

  If mblnOKPressed Then
    strNewTitle = CNStr(txtNewSurveyTitle)

  ' Is there an entry and has it changed?
    If Len(strNewTitle) And strNewTitle <> zSWstrSurveyTitle Then

      Set db = CodeDB()
      Set dyn = db.OpenRecordset("SELECT * FROM Survey", DB_OPEN_RECORDSET)
      blnOpened = True

    ' Verify a questionnaire by this title doesn't already exist
      If dyn.RecordCount Then
        dyn.FindFirst "Title = '" & Quotes(strNewTitle) & "'"

        If Not dyn.NoMatch Then

          MsgBox "A survey by the name of " & strNewTitle &
          ➥ " already exists.", 48, mstrProgramName
          Cancel = True
          GoTo Form_UnloadDone
        End If

        dyn.FindFirst "Title = '" & Quotes(zSWstrSurveyTitle) & "'"

        If Not dyn.NoMatch Then
          dyn.Edit
          dyn!Title = strNewTitle
          dyn.Update
        End If
      End If

      zSWfrm!cboSurveyTitle = strNewTitle
      zSWstrSurveyTitle = strNewTitle
    End If
  End If

Form_UnloadDone:
  On Error Resume Next
  If blnOpened Then dyn.Close
  Exit Sub
```

```
Form_UnloadError:
  Warning "Form_Unload", Error$
  Resume Form_UnloadDone

End Sub
```

OK! Now if you press the Rename button on the Survey Wizard form, you should get something besides an error. In the next chapter you will work on that Build button.

Create an *AutoExec* Macro

To open the Survey Wizard form with those neat, thick dialog box borders, create a macro that runs the SurveyWizard function. You coded the SurveyWizard function as the entry point routine for the program.

Save the macro as AutoExec if you want it to run when you open the database. You can suspend the AutoExec macro from running if you need to by holding the Shift key down as you open the database.

Figure 17.8 shows the AutoExec macro being created in the Macro window.

FIGURE 17.8.

Creating the AutoExec *macro.*

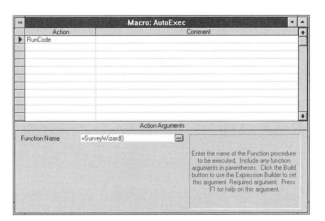

Take the form for a full test drive and define a questionnaire with many questions in it. Try the Insert, Delete, and arrow buttons on Page 2.

Summary

In this chapter, you dug deep into the coding trenches and completed the part of your Survey Wizard user interface that allows a user to define their questionnaire.

In this chapter, you coded and coded, but you also

- Outlined the contents of the Survey Wizard form module
- Used an error handling method that displays procedure names
- Wrote a replacement for DLookup that works in a code library
- Wrote a TableExists function to check to see if a table is in the current database
- Coded the tab sentries for the Survey Wizard form
- Coded the <<, **B**ack, **N**ext, and >> VCR buttons for a multiple-page form
- Coded the controls on the Survey Wizard form to define questions and response types in a questionnaire
- Wrote code to load and save a questionnaire definition into memory and then back out to tables
- Created a pop-up form to rename a questionnaire
- Created an AutoExec macro

In the next two chapters, you focus on the code that generates the database objects that Survey Wizard creates for a simple handout survey or for a full online survey system.

CHAPTER 18

Access: Survey Wizard, Part Three—Generating Objects

Did you feel a little abused in the last chapter? Sorry about that, but I did warn you there was going to be *a lot* of code. In any Access project, the user interface coding is easily half or more of the total coding that needs to be done to complete the project. And this is a sizable project.

The primary reason for having all this user interface coding is that computer users have grown more finicky over the years. We've raised our expectations of what is acceptable as a program's user interface.

This isn't a bad thing. It means that the resulting programs are immensely more useable, and as such can be used by more people—and not just folks like us, who have time to storm through a thick book like this one in order to become more familiar with their computers.

You don't *have* to write code to be able to develop applications in Access. There are Table Wizards, Form Wizards, Query Wizards, Report Wizards—wizards galore! But there is no Wizard Wizard. This is a job for us natural-born coders born with an unquenchable thirst for programming tricks and trivia and an uncanny algorithmic solving prowess for tackling the toughest of programming problems. More power to you for staying the course this far. It ought to be easy sailing from here by comparison.

Now where's that bottle of aspirin? My head hurts!

The Plan

In the last chapter, you finished the form that allows Survey Wizard users to enter which questions they want to appear in their questionnaire and how the respondent to the questionnaire may answer them.

In this chapter, you will code part of the Survey Wizard back-end engine that generates forms, reports, queries, and tables.

This code will build the Entry Report, Questions Table, Entry Form, and Responses Table. These are the first four check box build options on Page 5 of the Survey Wizard form. (See Figure 18.1.) I'll show you the design work that occurred up front before these procedures were written.

Of special interest is the Entry Form. Your code will actually produce a multiple-page form with VCR buttons, where each page on the form is for answering a single survey question.

There's quite a bit of work in this chapter, too. But keep your head up; when you finish this chapter, you will have the tools to start collecting survey data. I will save the Results Query, Results Table, and Results Report (all selected with the fifth check box) until the next chapter.

Before you begin building objects, though, you have an additional form to create.

FIGURE 18.1.
Generating the first four survey objects.

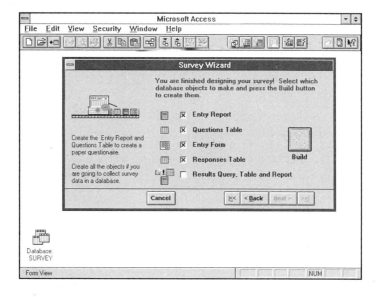

The Survey Wizard Save As Form

When you press the Build button on Page 5 of the Survey Wizard, the Survey Wizard Save As form pops up, as shown in Figure 18.2.

FIGURE 18.2.
The Survey Wizard Save As form.

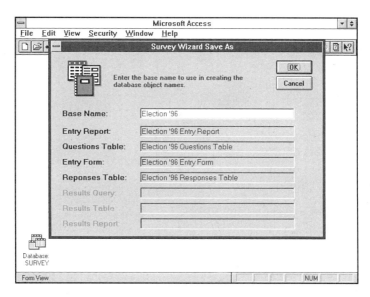

The Survey Wizard Save As form prompts for a "base name" to be used in generating the names of all the objects Survey will create. For example, the Entry Form object name will be what you entered as a base name with the text "Entry Form" added to the end of it.

Once the user enters a base name, he may press the Enter key or the Tab key in order to move to the OK button. As focus leaves the Base Name text box, some code activates to generate and display the names of the different objects that Survey Wizard will produce.

The OK button here (not our previous form's Build button) is the button that actually kicks off the build of the database objects. The Cancel button is for changing your mind, which you might want to do if you discover that you forgot to check one of the database objects that you want to generate.

If you leave and come back to the Survey Wizard Save As form, the Base Name defaults to what it was the last time so you don't have to re-enter it.

All right. Let's see how fast we can crank out this form and get beyond this user interface stuff. The Survey Wizard Save As form has the following properties set:

Survey Wizard Save As Form

Object: **Survey Wizard Save As Form**
Generates names for the Survey Wizard database objects.

Property	Value
Caption:	Survey Wizard Save As
Default View:	Single Form
Views Allowed:	Form
Shortcut Menu:	No
Scrollbars:	Neither
Record Selectors:	No
Navigation Buttons:	No
Auto Center:	Yes
Pop Up:	Yes
Modal:	Yes
Border Style:	Dialog
Min Button:	No
Max Button:	No
Width:	5.3 in

Object: **Detail0 Section**

Property	Value
Height:	3.5 in
Back Color:	12632256 (Light Gray)

The first text box on the form is the only one that is enabled to accept an entry. The remaining seven text boxes are used to display the generated names. To indicate that these fields are not editable, the Back Color property is set to Light Gray.

The labels for the bottom seven text boxes are black or grayed out, indicating whether or not the corresponding object is to be generated. This is done at run time by setting the Fore Color property in the code.

To complete the form, OK and Cancel buttons are added, along with some user instructions and a bitmap to dress it up. The following lists how each of the controls on the form are created.

The text boxes on the form use the MS Sans Serif font and have a font size of 10. They are also set to display as Sunken with a Width of 2.3 inches and a Height of 0.1903 inches.

Taking all that in, here are the remaining properties for the text boxes:

Object: **txtBaseName Text Box**
Receives the base name used to prefix the names of the generated database objects.

Property	Value
Enabled:	Yes
Tab Index:	0
Left:	.75 in
Top:	1.0826 in

Object: **txtEntryReport Text Box**
Displays the name of the Entry Report.

Property	Value
Enabled:	No
Locked:	Yes
Tab Index:	1
Left:	1.75 in
Top:	1.4146 in
Back Color	12632256 (Light Gray)

Object: **txtQuestionsTable Text Box**
Displays the name of the Questions Table.

Property	Value
Enabled:	No
Locked:	Yes
Tab Index:	2
Left:	1.75 in
Top:	1.7076 in
Back Color	12632256 (Light Gray)

Object: **txtEntryForm Text Box**
Displays the name of the Entry Form.

Property	Value
Enabled:	No
Locked:	Yes
Tab Index:	3
Left:	1.75 in
Top:	2 in
Back Color	12632256 (Light Gray)

Object: **txtResponses Table Text Box**
Displays the name of the Responses Table.

Property	Value
Enabled:	No
Locked:	Yes
Tab Index:	4
Left:	1.75 in
Top:	2.2917 in
Back Color	12632256 (Light Gray)

Object: **txtResultsQuery Text Box**
Displays the name of the Results Query.

Property	Value
Enabled:	No
Locked:	Yes
Tab Index:	5
Left:	1.75 in
Top:	2.5826 in
Back Color	12632256 (Light Gray)

Object: **txtResultsTable Text Box**
Displays the name of the Results Table.

Property	Value
Enabled:	No
Locked:	Yes
Tab Index:	6
Left:	1.75 in
Top:	2.875 in
Back Color	12632256 (Light Gray)

Object: **txtResultsReport Text Box**
Displays the name of the Results Report.

Property	Value
Enabled:	No
Locked:	Yes
Tab Index:	7
Left:	1.75 in
Top:	3.1646 in
Back Color	12632256 (Light Gray)

The properties for the corresponding text box label follow. Like the text boxes, the labels use the MS Sans Serif font with a font size of 10, but they also have their Font Weight property set to Bold.

The labels have their Back Color property set to 12632256 (Light Gray), the same as the form's detail section Back Color. The Width for the labels is 1.5 inches, and the Height is 0.1799.

Object: **lblBaseName Label**
Child label of the txtBaseName text box.

Property	Value
Caption:	Base Name:
Left:	0.2076 in
Top:	1.0826 in

Object: **lblEntryReport Label**
Child label of the txtEntryReport text box.

Property	Value
Caption:	Base Name:
Left:	0.2076 in
Top:	1.4146 in

Object: **lblQuestionsTable Label**
Child label of the txtQuestionsTable text box.

Property	Value
Caption:	Questions Table:
Left:	0.2076 in
Top:	1.7076 in

Object: **lblEntryForm Label**
Child label of the txtEntryForm text box.

Property	Value
Caption:	Entry Form:
Left:	0.2076 in
Top:	2 in

Object: **lblResponsesTable Label**
Child label of the txtResponsesTable text box.

Property	Value
Caption:	Responses Table:
Left:	0.2076 in
Top:	2.2917 in

Object: **lblResultsQuery Label**
Child label of the txtResultsQuery text box.

Property	Value
Caption:	Results Query:
Left:	0.2076 in
Top:	2.5826 in

Object: **lblResultsTable Label**
Child label of the txtResultsTable text box.

Property	Value
Caption:	Results Table:
Left:	0.2076 in
Top:	2.875 in

Object: **lblResultsReport Label**
Child label of the txtResultsReport text box.

Property	Value
Caption:	Results Report:
Left:	0.2076 in
Top:	3.1646 in

Figure 18.3 shows the Survey Wizard Save As form after the text boxes have been added to it.

FIGURE 18.3.

Adding text boxes to the Survey Wizard Save As form.

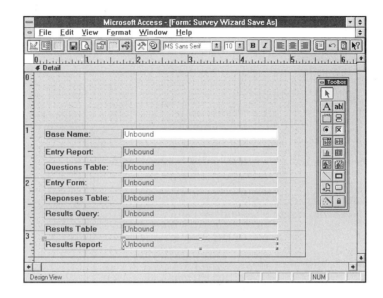

Here are the property settings for the form's OK and Cancel buttons:

Object: **cmdOK Command Button**
Accepts the object names and begins building the objects.

Property	Value
Caption:	OK
Default:	No
Cancel:	No
Tab Index:	8
Left:	4.4 in
Top:	0.1646 in
Width:	0.7 in
Height:	0.25 in
Font Name:	MS Sans Serif
Font Size:	8
Font Weight:	Bold

Object: **cmdCancel Command Button**
Closes the form, returning to the Survey Wizard form without doing a build.

Property	Value
Caption:	Cancel
Default:	No
Cancel:	Yes
Tab Index:	9
Left:	4.4 in
Top:	0.4701 in
Width:	0.7 in
Height:	0.25 in
Font Name:	MS Sans Serif
Font Size:	8
Font Weight:	Bold

A wizard form isn't complete without some user instructions and, of course, a bitmap.

Object: **lblInstructions**
Some quick, on-screen user instructions.

Property	Value
Caption:	Enter the base name to use in creating the database object names.
Left:	1.2 in
Top:	0.4146 in
Width:	2.8021 in
Height:	0.3326 in

The bitmap, shown in Figure 18.4, is a composite of enlarged pictures of table, form, and report objects to help indicate what is being created. This bitmap, SAVEAS.BMP, is included on the companion CD-ROM.

Object: **bmpSaveAs Unbound Object Frame**
Picture of generated objects.

Property	Value
Picture:	SAVEAS.BMP
Tab Stop:	No
Left:	0.3 in
Top:	0.1646 in
Back Color:	12632256 (Light Gray)
Border Style:	Clear

The completed form is shown in Figure 18.5.

FIGURE 18.4.

Touching up the SAVEAS.BMP picture in Paintbrush.

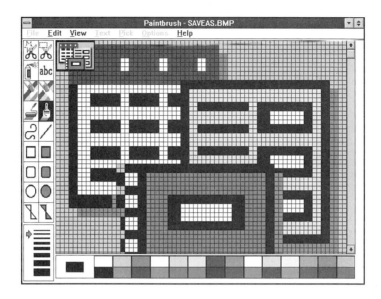

FIGURE 18.5.

Creating the Survey Wizard Save As form.

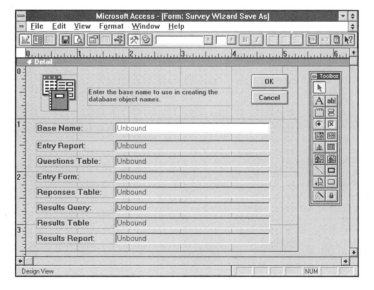

Coding the Save As Form

Following are the declaration section and procedures that are in the code module of the Survey Wizard's Save As form.

The Declarations Section

You will add to the declaration section as you go along. To start with, the declarations section has the usual minimal stuff plus a few constants declared for setting color properties, as shown in Listing 18.1.

Listing 18.1. A start on the declaration section for the Survey Wizard Save As form module.

```
' Survey Wizard Save As form

Option Compare Database
Option Explicit

Const mstrProgramName = "Survey Wizard"

Const Black = 0
Const Gray = 12632256
Const DarkGray = 8421504
Const White = 16777215
Const Blue = 8388608
```

Other Usual Stuff

The following subroutines have been shamefully copied into the module, just as you did for the Survey Wizard Rename form:

■ CNStr

■ LibDLookup

■ Quotes

■ Warning

Because we've already looked at these, I won't relist the code here. The procedures can be copied from the Survey Wizard form module and pasted into the Survey Wizard Save As form module.

User Interface Coding

The next five procedures complete the user interface portion of coding behind the Survey Wizard Save As form.

The *Form_Open* Subroutine

The Form_Open subroutine executes as the Survey Wizard Save As form opens but before the form is drawn on the screen.

The subroutine calls the `SetLabelColor` subroutine to set the colors of the labels for the text boxes that receive the generated names.

The global `zSWstrBaseName` is checked to see if the user has already selected a base name for this survey. If so, the previous base name is displayed and the object names are generated so that they will appear as last used.

The `Form_Open` subroutine is shown in Listing 18.2.

Listing 18.2. The `Form_Open` **subroutine.**

```
Sub Form_Open (Cancel As Integer)

  On Error GoTo Form_OpenError

' Display
  SetLabelColor zSWfrm!chkEntryReport, Me!lblEntryReport
  SetLabelColor zSWfrm!chkQuestionsTable, Me!lblQuestionsTable
  SetLabelColor zSWfrm!chkEntryForm, Me!lblEntryForm
  SetLabelColor zSWfrm!chkResponsesTable, Me!lblResponsesTable
  SetLabelColor zSWfrm!chkResultsReport, Me!lblResultsReport
  SetLabelColor zSWfrm!chkResultsReport, Me!lblResultsTable
  SetLabelColor zSWfrm!chkResultsReport, Me!lblResultsQuery

  If Len(zSWstrBaseName) Then
    txtBaseName.SetFocus
    Me!txtBaseName = zSWstrBaseName
    GenerateNames
  End If

Form_OpenDone:
  Exit Sub

Form_OpenError:
  Warning "Form_Open", Error$
  Resume Form_OpenDone

End Sub
```

The *SetLabelColor* Subroutine

The `SetLabelColor` subroutine is used by the `Form_Open` subroutine to indicate which objects have been selected on the Survey Wizard form to be generated.

The subroutine is passed two arguments. The first argument is one of the five check boxes from page 5 of the Survey Wizard form. The second argument is one of the labels on the Survey Wizard Save As form.

If the check box is set, the label's Fore Color property is set to Black to indicate that the object is going to be generated. The label's Fore Color property is set to Dark Gray to indicate that the object is not being generated. See Listing 18.3.

Listing 18.3. The `SetLabelColor` **subroutine.**

```
Sub SetLabelColor (chk As Control, lbl As Control)

  If chk Then
    lbl.ForeColor = Black
  Else
    lbl.ForeColor = DarkGray
  End If

End Sub
```

The *txtBaseName_AfterUpdate* Subroutine

This subroutine is activated on the txtBaseName text box's After Update event, which occurs when the contents of the text box have changed and focus leaves the text box.

The subroutine calls the GenerateNames subroutine to display the names of the database objects.

You want to be able to see the generated names before the dialog closes, so I purposely kept the Default property of the cmdOK button set to No. After the user enters a base name, he presses either the Tab key or the Enter key. The names are displayed, and focus moves to the OK button. If the user is satisfied with the names, he can press Enter to start the build. See Listing 18.4.

Listing 18.4. The `txtBaseName_AfterUpdate` **subroutine.**

```
Sub txtBaseName_AfterUpdate ()

  GenerateNames

End Sub
```

The *GenerateNames* Subroutine

The GenerateNames subroutine, shown in Listing 18.5, updates the names in the gray text boxes on the Survey Wizard Save As form.

If the entry for a base name is clear, the names are erased. If a base name is entered, the base names are displayed for those objects that have been selected to be generated on the Survey Wizard form.

Listing 18.5. The `GenerateNames` subroutine.

```
Sub GenerateNames ()

  Dim blnClear As Integer

  On Error GoTo GenerateNamesError

' Trim spaces from the entered name
  zSWstrBaseName = CNStr(Me!txtBaseName)
  Me!txtBaseName = zSWstrBaseName

  blnClear = (zSWstrBaseName = "")

  If blnClear Then
  ' Clear the names

    Me!txtEntryReport = Null
    Me!txtQuestionsTable = Null
    Me!txtEntryForm = Null
    Me!txtResponsesTable = Null
    Me!txtResultsReport = Null
    Me!txtResultsTable = Null
    Me!txtResultsQuery = Null
  Else
  ' Generate the names

    If zSWfrm!chkEntryReport Then
      Me!txtEntryReport = zSWstrBaseName & " Entry Report"
    End If

    If zSWfrm!chkQuestionsTable Then
      Me!txtQuestionsTable = zSWstrBaseName & " Questions Table"
    End If

    If zSWfrm!chkEntryForm Then
      Me!txtEntryForm = zSWstrBaseName & " Entry Form"
    End If

    If zSWfrm!chkResponsesTable Then
      Me!txtResponsesTable = zSWstrBaseName & " Responses Table"
    End If

    If zSWfrm!chkResultsReport Then
      Me!txtResultsReport = zSWstrBaseName & " Results Report"
      Me!txtResultsTable = zSWstrBaseName & " Results Table"
      Me!txtResultsQuery = zSWstrBaseName & " Results Query"
    End If
  End If

GenerateNamesDone:
  Exit Sub

GenerateNamesError:
  Warning "GenerateNames", Error$
  Resume GenerateNamesDone

End Sub
```

The *cmdOK_Click* Subroutine

The cmdOK_Click function manages the build of the database objects.

First, the subroutine checks that a base name was entered. If not, it complains, sets focus back to the base name text box, and exits.

If a base name is found, the subroutine continues. It saves the names of the database objects to globals so that they can be referenced by the build functions.

Next, the Survey Wizard Save As form is closed and the hourglass is turned on to indicate that the program is busy building the objects.

The subroutine checks the status of each check box on the Survey Wizard form and calls the appropriate build function for each check box that is checked. Each of the build functions returns False for success or True if an error occurred. The cmdOK_Click subroutine checks each return value and aborts the build if an error occurred.

If all goes well, a message box indicates that the build has completed and the Survey Wizard form is closed. See Listing 18.6.

Listing 18.6. The cmdOK_Click **subroutine.**

```
Sub cmdOK_Click ()

  Dim blnError As Integer
  Dim z As Integer

' Assume failure
  blnError = True

  On Error GoTo cmdOK_ClickError

' Verify a base name was entered
  If Len(zSWstrBaseName) = 0 Then
    MsgBox "You must enter a base name for the database objects.", 48,
    ➥mstrProgramName
    txtBaseName.SetFocus
    GoTo cmdOK_ClickDone
  End If

' Save the generated names in globals
  zSWstrEntryReport = CNStr(Me!txtEntryReport)
  zSWstrEntryForm = CNStr(Me!txtEntryForm)
  zSWstrResultsReport = CNStr(Me!txtResultsReport)
  zSWstrResultsTable = CNStr(Me!txtResultsTable)
  zSWstrResultsQuery = CNStr(Me!txtResultsQuery)
  zSWstrResponsesTable = zSWstrBaseName & " Responses Table"
  zSWstrQuestionsTable = zSWstrBaseName & " Questions Table"
```

```
' Close the Save As form
  zCloseForm Me
  DoEvents

' Begin building objects
  DoCmd Hourglass True

' Tables must be created first because other objects reference them
  If zSWfrm!chkQuestionsTable Then
    z = BuildQuestionsTable()
    If z Then GoTo cmdOK_ClickDone
  End If

  If zSWfrm!chkResponsesTable Then
    z = BuildResponsesTable()
    If z Then GoTo cmdOK_ClickDone
  End If

  If zSWfrm!chkEntryReport Then
    z = BuildEntryReport()
    If z Then GoTo cmdOK_ClickDone
  End If

  If zSWfrm!chkEntryForm Then
    z = BuildEntryForm()
    If z Then GoTo cmdOK_ClickDone
  End If

  If zSWfrm!chkResultsReport Then
    z = BuildResultsReport()
    If z Then GoTo cmdOK_ClickDone
  End If

' Success if we got here
  blnError = False

cmdOK_ClickDone:
  DoCmd Hourglass False
  If blnError Then
    MsgBox "Build failed.", 48, mstrProgramName
  Else
    MsgBox "Build completed successfully!", 64, mstrProgramName
    DoCmd Close A_Form, "Survey Wizard"
  End If
  Exit Sub

cmdOK_ClickError:
  Warning "cmdOK_Click", Error$
  Resume cmdOK_ClickDone

End Sub
```

Temporary Stubs for the Build Functions

As you write code, you usually like to keep a program compilable and runnable as you go along. That way, you can do a syntax check with the **R**un|Compile Loaded Modules command or do a test run of the program to see if it performs as expected so far.

We introduced several function calls in the cmdOK_Click subroutine that you haven't written yet. If you try to compile the program now, Access will return the error message Reference to undefined Function or array.

Entering temporary stubs for the build functions as shown in Listing 18.7 will get the program back into a compilable state again. Each function returns False to indicate a successful run.

Listing 18.7. Temporary stubs for the build functions.

```
Function BuildEntryForm () As Integer

  BuildEntryForm = False

End Function

Function BuildEntryReport () As Integer

  BuildEntryReport = False

End Function

Function BuildQuestionsTable () As Integer

  BuildQuestionsTable = False

End Function

Function BuildResponsesTable () As Integer

  BuildResponsesTable = False

End Function

Function BuildResultsReport () As Integer

  BuildResultsReport = False

End Function
```

The *cmdCancel_Click* Subroutine

Clicking the Cancel button closes the form without performing the build, as shown in Listing 18.8.

Listing 18.8. The `cmdCancel_Click` **subroutine.**

```
Sub cmdCancel Click ()

  zCloseForm Me

End Sub
```

Let's Take an Inventory

To see how all of this is coming together, let's take a look at what objects we've already created and what is left to do.

Here's what's in the database container at this point:

Survey Table
Stores the title and build options.

Survey Question Table
Stores the questions and answering options.

Survey Wizard Form
Inputs questionnaire definition.

Survey Wizard Rename Form
Changes title of the questionnaire.

Survey Wizard Save As Form
Inputs base name and build objects.

AutoExec Macro
Opens the Survey Wizard form.

Error Module
Displays error messages.

Form Module
A few form handling procedures.

Survey Wizard Constants Module
Global constants.

Survey Wizard Entry Point Module
Global variables and program entry point function.

To this you will be adding the following objects to support the Build side of the project:

Pretty Good Charts Module (next chapter)
Run-time code for displaying charts on reports.

Survey Wizard Report Run-time Module
Run-time code for generated reports.

VCR2 Module
Improved version of our VCR button code for generated forms.

You will also be writing a significant amount of code behind the Survey Wizard Save As form, which is the code that generates all of the objects.

At the end of this chapter, Survey Wizard will produce the following objects into the user's database:

Entry Report
Hand-out questionnaire.

Questions Table
Stores questions and answering options for a single survey.

Entry Form
Online questionnaire.

Responses Table
Receives data entered into the Entry Form.

Including the procedures that you have already written, all of the procedures in the code behind the Survey Wizard Save As form are listed in Table 18.1 in the order that you will be looking at them.

Table 18.1. Directory of procedures behind the Survey Wizard Save As form.

Usual Stuff

(declarations)

CNStr

LibDLookup

Quotes

Warning

User Interface

Form_Open

SetLabelColor

txtBaseName_AfterUpdate

GenerateNames

cmdOK_Click

cmdCancel_Click

Building Tables

BuildQuestionsTable

BuildResponsesTable

Building the Entry Report

BuildEntryReport

ERMultipleReport

ERMultipleChoice

ERSetFont

CreateHiddenControl

Building the Entry Form

BuildEntryForm

EFOptionButton

EFCommandButton

Building the Results Query

BuildReportsQuery

Building the Results Report

BuildResultsReport

RRMultipleChoice

RRSetFont

We've also got some *run-time* code to write. These are subroutines and functions that execute while our generated reports and forms are being used.

Procedures you will be looking at in this and the following chapter are listed in Tables 18.2 and 18.3. In this chapter, you cover everything except the procedures related to the Results Report.

Table 18.2. Directory of procedures in the Survey Wizard Report Run-time module.

Usual Stuff

(declarations)

Warning

Entry Report

zSWEntryReportDetailOnFormat

zSWEntryReportDetail2OnFormat

ShowYesNo

ShowMultipleChoice

zSWMultipleChoice

ShowWriteIn

ShowRangePercent

zSWValidatePoints

Results Report

zSWResultsReportOnOpen

zSWResultsReportDetailOnFormat

zSWResultsReportDetailOnPrint

The procedures listed in Table 18.3 are used by the multipage Entry Form to control movement from page to page.

Table 18.3. Directory of procedures in the VCR2 Run-time module.

Usual Stuff

(declarations)

Warning

VCR

zVCR2OnOpen

zVCR2Buttons

zVCR2Page

zVCR2GotoControl

zVCR2First

```
zVCR2Back
zVCR2Next
zVCR2Last
zVCR2OK
zVCR2Cancel
zVCR2BoundOnClose
```

OK, I think we have everything straight now. I didn't list the procedures in the Graph module because that entire module will be tackled in the next chapter.

Let's now look into how tables are created from code.

Building Tables

In the days of Access 1.1, having your program create a table involved jumping through a few hoops, ringing a few bells, and keeping a few spinning plates from hitting the floor while standing on your head.

If the fields in your table could be derived from fields in a pre-existing table, you could use a make table query (which is an SQL SELECT INTO statement). That's exactly what I did for my first version of Survey Wizard.

Another method was to use SendKeys statements to drive the user interface to create the tables just like you would create them manually. This worked most of the time but was a real mess when it didn't.

Thank goodness Access 2.0 introduced *Data Access Objects* (DAO), the objects, collections, properties, methods, and so on that give you programming capability over the definition of tables in your database.

In Survey Wizard, our program needs to create two tables by using DAO. The Questions Table is a copy of all of the fields in the Survey Question table, excluding the SurveyID field. This table contains the question definition records for the survey and is used as a source of information for the Entry Report and the Results Report.

The second table you generate, the Responses Table, differs in content, depending on how many and what kinds of questions are in the questionnaire definition. This table receives the data entered into the Entry Form when people enter their responses to the questionnaire online.

The *BuildQuestionsTable* Function

The BuildQuestionsTable function generates a table like that shown in Figure 18.6.

FIGURE 18.6.

*Examining a generated
Questions Table in
table design mode.*

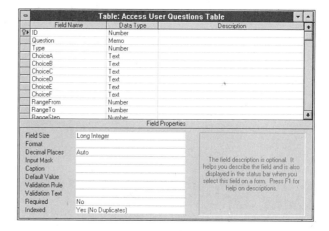

The BuildQuestionsTable function is shown in Listing 18.9. We'll take a look at this
one in detail.

Listing 18.9. The BuildQuestionsTable **function.**

```
Function BuildQuestionsTable () As Integer

   Dim dbUser As Database
   Dim dbCode As Database

   Dim tbd As TableDef
   Dim fld As Field
   Dim idx As Index

   Dim dynSource As Recordset
   Dim dynDest As Recordset

   Dim blnSourceOpened As Integer
   Dim blnDestOpened As Integer

   Dim lngID As Long
   Dim n As Integer

' Assume failure
   BuildQuestionsTable = True

   blnSourceOpened = False
   blnDestOpened = False

' Delete the table if it already exists in the database
   On Error Resume Next
   DoCmd DeleteObject A_Table, zSWstrQuestionsTable
```

```
  On Error GoTo BuildQuestionsTableError

' Open the user's database and the library database
  Set dbUser = DBEngine(0)(0)
  Set dbCode = CodeDB()

' Define the table
  Set tbd = dbUser.CreateTableDef(zSWstrQuestionsTable)

' Add the fields to the table definition
  Set fld = tbd.CreateField("ID", DB_LONG)
  tbd.Fields.Append fld

  Set fld = tbd.CreateField("Question", DB_MEMO)
  tbd.Fields.Append fld

  Set fld = tbd.CreateField("Type", DB_INTEGER)
  tbd.Fields.Append fld

  For n = 65 To 70
    Set fld = tbd.CreateField("Choice" & Chr$(n), DB_TEXT)
    fld.Size = 50
    tbd.Fields.Append fld
  Next n

  Set fld = tbd.CreateField("RangeFrom", DB_LONG)
  tbd.Fields.Append fld

  Set fld = tbd.CreateField("RangeTo", DB_LONG)
  tbd.Fields.Append fld

  Set fld = tbd.CreateField("RangeStep", DB_LONG)
  tbd.Fields.Append fld

  Set fld = tbd.CreateField("PercentFrom", DB_INTEGER)
  tbd.Fields.Append fld

  Set fld = tbd.CreateField("PercentTo", DB_INTEGER)
  tbd.Fields.Append fld

  Set fld = tbd.CreateField("PercentStep", DB_INTEGER)
  tbd.Fields.Append fld

' Add the table to the database
  dbUser.TableDefs.Append tbd

' Create the primary key index
  Set idx = tbd.CreateIndex("PrimaryKey")
  idx.Primary = True
  idx.Unique = True

' Add the ID field to the index
  Set fld = idx.CreateField("ID", DB_LONG)
  idx.Fields.Append fld

  tbd.Indexes.Append idx

' Copy question information from the Survey Question table
```

continues

Listing 18.9. continued

```
lngID = LibDLookup(dbCode, "ID", "Survey", "Title = '" &
➥ Quotes(zSWstrSurveyTitle) & "'")

Set dynSource = dbCode.OpenRecordset(
➥ "SELECT * FROM [Survey Question] WHERE SurveyID = " & lngID,
➥ DB_OPEN_DYNASET)
blnSourceOpened = True

Set dynDest = dbUser.OpenRecordset(zSWstrQuestionsTable, DB_OPEN_DYNASET)
blnDestOpened = True

Do Until dynSource.EOF

  dynDest.AddNew
  dynDest!ID = dynSource!ID
  dynDest!Question = dynSource!Question
  dynDest!Type = dynSource!Type
  dynDest!ChoiceA = dynSource!ChoiceA
  dynDest!ChoiceB = dynSource!ChoiceB
  dynDest!ChoiceC = dynSource!ChoiceC
  dynDest!ChoiceD = dynSource!ChoiceD
  dynDest!ChoiceE = dynSource!ChoiceE
  dynDest!ChoiceF = dynSource!ChoiceF
  dynDest!RangeFrom = dynSource!RangeFrom
  dynDest!RangeTo = dynSource!RangeTo
  dynDest!RangeStep = dynSource!RangeStep
  dynDest!PercentFrom = dynSource!PercentFrom
  dynDest!PercentTo = dynSource!PercentTo
  dynDest!PercentStep = dynSource!PercentStep
  dynDest.Update

  dynSource.MoveNext
Loop

' Success
  BuildQuestionsTable = False

BuildQuestionsTableDone:
  On Error Resume Next
  If blnSourceOpened Then dynSource.Close
  If blnDestOpened Then dynDest.Close
  Exit Function

BuildQuestionsTableError:
  Warning "BuildQuestionsTable", Error$
  Resume BuildQuestionsTableDone

End Function
```

The BuildQuestionsTable function first turns error handling off and attempts to delete
a table that has the same name as that being generated. If the table exists from a previous run, it is deleted. If this is the first time and the table doesn't exist, no harm is done;
you just ignore the error.

```
' Delete the table if it already exists in the database
  On Error Resume Next
  DoCmd DeleteObject A Table, zSWstrQuestionsTable
  On Error GoTo BuildQuestionsTableError
```

Next, a `TableDef` object is created. This object holds a table definition, for which there doesn't have to currently be an existing table yet.

```
' Define the table
  Set tbd = dbUser.CreateTableDef(zSWstrQuestionsTable)
```

You build the table definition by creating fields and appending them to the table definition object, as shown in Listing 18.10.

Listing 18.10. Creating field objects and appending them to the table definition object.

```
' Add the fields to the table definition
  Set fld = tbd.CreateField("ID", DB_LONG)
  tbd.Fields.Append fld

  Set fld = tbd.CreateField("Question", DB_MEMO)
  tbd.Fields.Append fld
```

After all of the fields are appended to the table definition, the table definition is appended to the `TableDefs` collection to create the actual table in the database.

```
' Add the table to the database
  dbUser.TableDefs.Append tbd
```

Next, a `PrimaryKey` index is appended to the table definition, as shown in Listing 18.11. This has the effect of creating the index in the physical table also.

Listing 18.11. Creating a `PrimaryKey` in the generated table.

```
' Create the primary key index
  Set idx = tbd.CreateIndex("PrimaryKey")
  idx.Primary = True
  idx.Unique = True

' Add the ID field to the index
  Set fld = idx.CreateField("ID", DB_LONG)
  idx.Fields.Append fld

  tbd.Indexes.Append idx
```

After the table is created, the `BuildQuestionsTable` function selects the Survey Question table records for the current questionnaire and copies their contents into the new table in the user's database, as shown in Figure 18.7.

FIGURE 18.7.

Question definition records are copied into the generated Question Table.

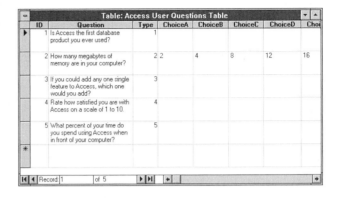

The *BuildResponsesTable* Function

The `BuildResponsesTable` function produces a table like that shown in Figure 18.8.

FIGURE 18.8.

The generated Responses Table.

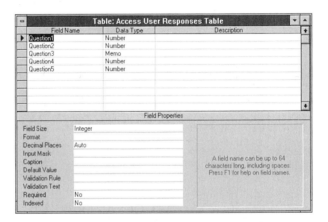

The fields in the table are simply named Question1, Question2, Question3, and so on. There is a single field for each question. The field data types vary, depending on the response type of the question:

Response Type	Field Type	Field Size
Yes/No	Number	Integer
Multiple-Choice	Number	Byte
Write-In	Memo	
Range	Number	Long integer
Percent	Number	Integer

A record is entered into the Questions Table for each time a person responds to the set of questions in the questionnaire. The data in this table is summarized when the

Results Report is executed to report on the trends that show up in the survey results. See Listing 18.12.

Listing 18.12. The `BuildResponsesTable` function.

```
Function BuildResponsesTable () As Integer

  Dim db As Database

  Dim tbd As TableDef
  Dim fld As Field

  Dim q As zSW_Question

  Dim strFieldName As String
  Dim n As Integer

' Assume failure
  BuildResponsesTable = True

  On Error GoTo BuildResponsesTableError

' Delete the table if it already exists in the database
  On Error Resume Next
  DoCmd DeleteObject A_Table, zSWstrResponsesTable
  On Error GoTo BuildResponsesTableError

  Set db = DBEngine(0)(0)

  Set tbd = db.CreateTableDef(zSWstrResponsesTable)

' Add a field to the table for each question in the survey

  For n = 1 To zSWintTotalQuestions

    strFieldName = "Question" & n
    q = zSWaQuestion(n)

    Select Case q.intType

    Case zSWQuestionTypeYesNo
      Set fld = tbd.CreateField(strFieldName, DB_INTEGER)
      tbd.Fields.Append fld

    Case zSWQuestionTypeMultipleChoice
      Set fld = tbd.CreateField(strFieldName, DB_BYTE)
      tbd.Fields.Append fld

    Case zSWQuestionTypeWriteIn
      Set fld = tbd.CreateField(strFieldName, DB_MEMO)
      tbd.Fields.Append fld

    Case zSWQuestionTypeRange
      Set fld = tbd.CreateField(strFieldName, DB_LONG)
      tbd.Fields.Append fld
```

continues

Listing 18.12. continued

```
  Case zSWQuestionTypePercent
    Set fld = tbd.CreateField(strFieldName, DB_INTEGER)
    tbd.Fields.Append fld

  End Select
Next n

db.TableDefs.Append tbd

' Success
BuildResponsesTable = False

BuildResponsesTableDone:
  Exit Function

BuildResponsesTableError:
  Warning "BuildResponsesTable", Error$
  Resume BuildResponsesTableDone

End Function
```

Designing the Survey Entry Report

Let's now look at how the Survey Entry Report is created.

The simplest way to write the code that generates a database object is to create the first database object manually and then use that as a prototype for what the code must generate. This prototype object becomes the specification that the program must live up to.

I intentionally kept my prototype object simple. I didn't add different "looks" to the report (for example, Standard, Chiseled, Shadowed, Boxed, or Embossed as in Microsoft's Wizards), nor did I add any other fancy options.

I think it would be easy enough to add options like this to Survey Wizard, but for the time being I wanted to keep it simple and get it done. Adding the different looks might be a good exercise if you have a lot of time to kill. If you do this, please send me mail. I'd love to see it.

In the Entry Report, I need to display five different types of questions and provide a helpful way for the respondent to answer them. The biggest difficulty is that I don't have any idea how long a question will be or how much space must be provided to fill in the answer.

A more sophisticated approach than the one I chose would be to have the wizard take into account the amount of text for the question and answering options and adjust to them accordingly.

Again, I opted for simplicity and decided that all questions would be displayed in the same defined amount of space. This means that if the text is really short, the area allocated for it would look a bit empty. If the text is too long, it will get truncated. In taking this approach, you have to find the right balance in which the result is visually appealing, enough space is allocated for most needs, and not too much paper is wasted.

After experimenting with the prototype for awhile, I decided to go with a shadowed box look, because that separated the questions from each other nicely and made the whole questionnaire easy to read. The first object in the prototype is a title in the report header. With the prototype report object in design mode, the title appears as shown in Figure 18.9.

FIGURE 18.9.

Creating a report heading in the Entry Report prototype.

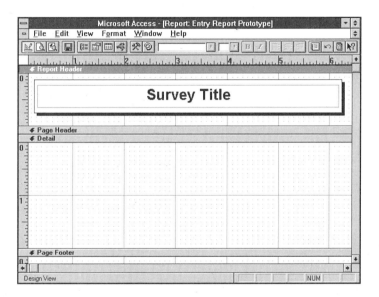

The shadowed box was constructed using two rectangles. One was set with a Back Color as black, to be used as the shadow. The shadow is placed behind the white rectangle, offset to the right and down enough so that only a little bit of it shows through as the shadow.

A label was then placed within the rectangle to display the title of the questionnaire. The label was set nearly as wide as the rectangle in hopes that it could accommodate the largest title possible. Then the Text Align property was set to center the text.

Next, in the prototype I added how Yes/No questions will be displayed within the detail section of the report. The rectangle is created again, as just described.

For the five question types, I came up with two different sizes of rectangles in the prototype. The Yes/No, Range, and Percent question types use a smaller size. The Multiple-Choice and Write-In question types use a larger size. The first thing each one has in it is a label to display the question. The size of this label remains the same for all question types.

For the Yes/No question type, I created two labels to display "Yes" and "No" and centered them inside the rectangle. (See Figure 18.10.) The idea is that the respondent would circle either one or the other when selecting an answer.

FIGURE 18.10.

Displaying Yes/No questions in the Entry Report prototype.

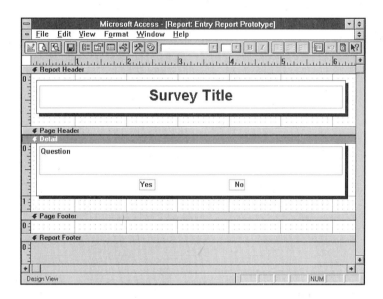

For the Multiple-Choice question type, I modified the prototype report as shown in Figure 18.11.

FIGURE 18.11

Displaying Multiple-Choice questions in the Entry Report prototype.

This time I used the larger of the two rectangles in order to allow for multiple-choice responses. I created six labels with enough space that hopefully the entire text of each multiple-choice selection would be displayed. The intent is that these labels will be created as needed, depending on whether the corresponding letter was used.

The next question type is the Write-In question (see Figure 18.12). For this, I used the large rectangle and created three lines in the answer part of the rectangle to indicate to respondents that they can fill in their answers there.

FIGURE 18.12.

Prototyping a Write-In question for the Entry Report.

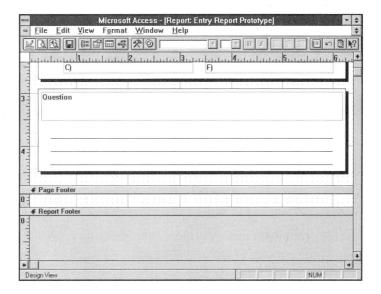

Again, the hope is that I found about the right amount of space for a response to most questions without it looking too silly when a question requires only a one-word answer.

The final two question types, Range and Percent, are basically identical. The only difference is that for percent values, a percent sign is placed at the end of the number.

There are 10 labels to place numbers in as selections for a Range or Percent question. If less than 10 selections are available, the middle labels are used first, moving outward to as many labels as are needed.

Figure 18.13 shows the prototype for Range and Percent questions.

FIGURE 18.13.

Displaying the Range and Percent type questions in the Entry Report prototype.

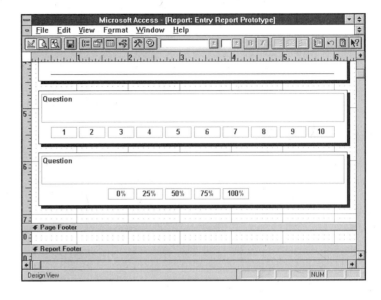

Twenty-Two Inches Is Not Enough

So now that you know what the components of the Survey Entry Report are supposed to contain, building it should be straightforward, right?

Well, in programming projects there's almost always a "gotcha" in there somewhere to make life interesting. In this case, the gotcha is that 22-inch Height and Width limitation on the size of a section of a report or form in Access.

I can't just simply start dropping each question, one after another, onto the report in the detail section. At the most, I could fit only about 20 questions on the survey before I would be out of vertical space.

I suppose there is one ugly hack that I could use to get around this limitation. I could artificially create a bunch of sort groups in the report so that I could use additional headers and footers for placing questions on them. This would work as long as I ensured that each header and footer got printed only once. With 10 sort group headers, 10 sort group footers, the report header and footer, and the detail, a total of 506 inches could be used. *Not!*

There is a saner approach. Since I've spent the time to make all of my questions appear in a certain consistent way in the report, the only difference between each question is the actual text that gets displayed.

If I can make a detail line in my report that can print any of the five question types, I can run the report off of the question data as stored in one or more tables.

Well, that's the solution I went with. And that's at least one of the reasons why you needed to create the Questions Table.

Do You Need a Wizard?

The funny thing is, if the Entry Report can produce different results based on the survey data stored within the Questions Table, do you really need a wizard at all?

To be truthful, not really. You could have just manually created one Entry Report. When the report is run, the user could be prompted to decide which of their saved questionnaires' data should be used to produce the report.

There are still a couple of good reasons to have a wizard generate this particular report. First, the Record Source property of the generated report will be preset so that the user doesn't need to be prompted for which questionnaire he is printing. Second, the Survey Wizard will reside in a library database with the goal of creating the objects in the user's database. You don't want to have to ask the user to import objects into his database.

Still, you might consider that using code to generate this first report is more of an exercise rather than a requirement for our application's needs. There will be better justification for building the Entry Form from a wizard.

How the Entry Report Works

Let's take a look at the actual generated object and get a better idea of how it works. Then you will look at the code that creates it.

The Entry Report is bound to the Questions Table that is also generated by the Survey Wizard.

The tricky part in our Entry Report object is that it needs to alternate between displaying the shorter or the larger box, depending on what question type is to be displayed.

This is done by creating a sort group on the ID field—a field that changes for each record. A sort group header is created in the report for this field so that you can use it to display one of the question types in it.

Now here's the trick: The header and the detail section are then alternately turned on and off while the report is running.

The code that does this will be in the Survey Wizard Report Run-time module. This module is code that gets executed while the generated reports run.

Figure 18.14 shows a generated report's Report Header and ID Header sections when the report is in design mode. The ID Header contains the larger of the two boxes, and it displays either three lines for a Write-In question type or six text boxes for a Multiple-Choice question type.

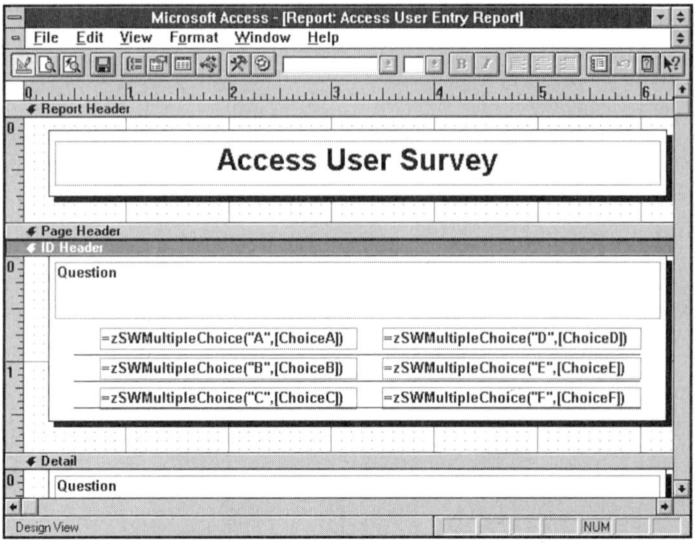

FIGURE 18.14.

The top half of the generated Entry Report in design mode.

Microsoft Access - [Report: Access User Entry Report]

File   Edit   View   Format   Window   Help

Access User Survey

♦ Report Header
♦ Page Header
♦ ID Header

Question

=zSWMultipleChoice("A",[ChoiceA])   =zSWMultipleChoice("D",[ChoiceD])
=zSWMultipleChoice("B",[ChoiceB])   =zSWMultipleChoice("E",[ChoiceE])
=zSWMultipleChoice("C",[ChoiceC])   =zSWMultipleChoice("F",[ChoiceF])

♦ Detail

Question

Design View   NUM

Figure 18.15 shows the report's Detail section and Page Footer section. The Detail section contains the smaller of the two question boxes. It has enough space to display 10 text boxes for Range or Percent type questions. Below two of these text boxes are the labels that display "Yes" and "No" for a Yes/No type question. In the Page Footer section, a page number is displayed with a dash before and after it by using the expression

```
"- " & Page & " -"
```

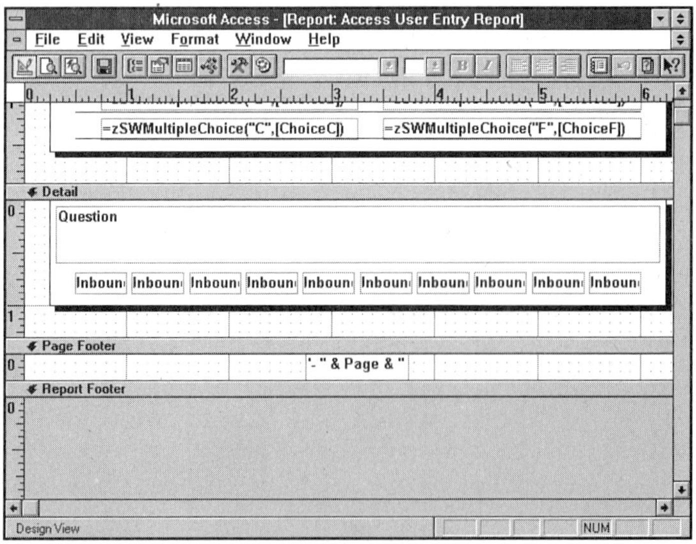

FIGURE 18.15.

The bottom half of the generated Entry Report.

Microsoft Access - [Report: Access User Entry Report]

File   Edit   View   Format   Window   Help

=zSWMultipleChoice("C",[ChoiceC])   =zSWMultipleChoice("F",[ChoiceF])

♦ Detail

Question

Inboun| Inboun| Inboun| Inboun| Inboun| Inboun| Inboun| Inboun| Inboun| Inboun|

♦ Page Footer

"- " & Page & "

♦ Report Footer

Design View   NUM

Here's an Access trivia question for you: Where does the Page value come from in an expression that displays the page count on a report?

Give up?

Page is a property for the report object. Amazingly enough, it can be referenced just by using Page in an expression without prefixing it with something, as in `Report.Page` or `Reports![MyReport].Page`.

OK, no more trivia questions. I promise.

Functions for Wizards

To write code that generates a report object and control on the report, you need to use a special set of functions.

These were missing from the Access 1.*x* documentation unless you purchased the expensive run-time license (now called the Access Developer's Toolkit, or ADT). Fortunately, the function documentation is included with the online help in Access 2.0.

The following lists and describes the function declarations. I've used Hungarian notation to indicate the argument types and a vertical bar to show where optional arguments begin. Refer to the documentation for more complete details about each of these functions.

> `CodeDB()`
> Returns the database object for the code library.
>
> `CreateControl( strFormName, intControlType, ¦ intSectionNumber,`
> `strParent, strFieldName, intLeft, intTop, intWidth, intHeight )`
> Creates a control on a form.
>
> `CreateForm( strDatabase, ¦ strFormTemplate )`
> Creates a new form database object.
>
> `CreateGroupLevel( strReportName, strGroupLevelExpression,`
> `blnShowHeader, blnShowHeader )`
> Creates a group level on a report.
>
> `CreateReport( strDatabase, ¦ strReportTemplate )`
> Creates a new report database object.
>
> `CreateReportControl( strReportName, intControlType,`
> `intSectionNumber, ¦ strParent, strFieldName )`
> Creates a control on a report.
>
> `DeleteControl( strFormName, strControlName )`
> Delete a control from a form.
>
> `DeleteReportControl( strReportName, strControlName )`
> Delete a control from a report.

If you're going to be doing a lot with Wizards, be sure to also check out the Section property in online help.

That's about as much lifting from the manuals as I can stomach for now and still feel good about myself. Let's get to the code.

The Entry Report Declarations

A lengthy list of constant declarations needs to be added to the declarations section of the Survey Wizard's Save As form module.

Many constants are declared mainly to make the code easier to read. Constants prefixed with "ER" are measurements or settings based on the Survey Entry Report prototype.

Having these values declared as constants has the additional advantage that they can be easily changed to modify the output of the report without your having to dig through the code to find where a change should be made.

The usage of each value should be clear from the names of the constants. If not, examining the code that uses them will probably help.

Listing 18.13 shows the constants added to the declaration section.

Listing 18.13. Constants declared for generating the Entry Report.

```
Const TwipsPerInch = 1440
Const Detail = 0
Const Header = 1
Const Footer = 2
Const PageHeader = 3
Const PageFooter = 4
Const Detail2 = 5    ' A sort group header in the Entry Report

Const ControlTypeLabel = 100
Const ControlTypeRectangle = 101
Const ControlTypeLine = 102
Const ControlTypeCommandButton = 104
Const ControlTypeOptionButton = 105
Const ControlTypeCheckBox = 106
Const ControlTypeOptionGroup = 107
Const ControlTypeTextbox = 109
Const ControlTypeComboBox = 111
Const ControlTypePageBreak = 118

Const Raised = 1
Const Dialog = 3

Const FontWeightNormal = 400
Const FontWeightBold = 700
```

```
Const TextAlignLeft = 1
Const TextAlignCenter = 2
Const TextAlignRight = 3

Const BackStyleClear = 0

' Entry Report constants
' Measurements (in inches) taken from the prototype Survey Entry Report

Const ERFontName = "Arial"
Const ERTitleBarFontSize = 20
Const ERFontSize = 10

Const ERSectionWidth = 6.5
Const ERReportHeaderHeight = 1#
Const ERPageFooterHeight = .25

Const ERBarLeft = .25
Const ERBarWidth = 6#
Const ERShadowOffset = .05
Const ERQuestionLabelLeft = .31
Const ERQuestionLabelWidth = 5.88
Const ERQuestionLabelTopOffset = .06
Const ERQuestionLabelHeight = .53

Const ERTitleBarTop = .125
Const ERTitleBarHeight = .63
Const ERTitleLabelTop = .23
Const ERTitleLabelHeight = .42

Const ERSmallBarHeight = 1#
Const ERLargeBarHeight = 1.56
Const ERSpaceBetweenQuestions = .25

Const ERResponseLabelTopOffset1 = .69
Const ERResponseLabelTopOffset2 = .97
Const ERResponseLabelTopOffset3 = 1.25
Const ERResponseLabelHeight = .2

Const ERYesNoWidth = .3
Const ERYesLeft = 2.25
Const ERNoLeft = 4#

Const ERMultipleChoiceLeft1 = .75
Const ERMultipleChoiceLeft2 = 3.5
Const ERMultipleChoiceWidth = 2.5

Const ERWriteInLineLeft = .5
Const ERWriteInLineWidth = 5.5
Const ERWriteInLineTopOffset1 = .94
Const ERWriteInLineSpace = .25
Const ERWriteInLineBorderWidth = 1 ' 1 point

Const ERFirstPointLeft = .5
Const ERLastPointLeft = 5.5
Const ERPointWidth = .5

Const ERPageCountLeft = 2.75
Const ERPageCountWidth = 1#
```

The *BuildEntryReport* Function

This function does most of the work. We'll take a detailed look at it following
Listing 18.14.

Listing 18.14. The `BuildEntryReport` **function.**

```
Function BuildEntryReport () As Integer

  Dim rpt As Report
  Dim ctl As Control

  Dim strReportName As String
  Dim strCaption As String

  Dim dblPointStepWidth As Double
  Dim dblPointLeft As Double

  Dim v As Variant
  Dim n As Integer
  Dim blnReportOpened As Integer

' Assume failure
  BuildEntryReport = True

  blnReportOpened = False

  On Error GoTo BuildEntryReportError

' Create the report object, defaulting to the current database and the
' current report template.
  Set rpt = CreateReport("", "")
  blnReportOpened = True

' Turn on the report header and footer through the Access 2.0 menu
' 7 = Report Design menu, 3 = Format, 10 = Report Header/Footer
  DoCmd DoMenuItem 7, 3, 10, , A_MENU_VER20

  strReportName = rpt.FormName

' Set the page dimensions
  rpt.Width = zTwips(ERSectionWidth)
  rpt.section(Header).Height = zTwips(ERReportHeaderHeight)
  rpt.section(PageHeader).Height = 0
  rpt.section(PageFooter).Height = zTwips(ERPageFooterHeight)
  rpt.section(Footer).Height = 0

' Create a group header that always tries to print. This gives us an
' alternative detail section, where at run-time we cancel one or the other.
  v = CreateGroupLevel(strReportName, "ID", True, False)

' Set report properties
  rpt.RecordSource = zSWstrQuestionsTable
  rpt.section(Detail).OnFormat = "=zSWEntryReportDetailOnFormat(Report)"
  rpt.section(Detail2).OnFormat = "=zSWEntryReportDetail2OnFormat(Report)"
```

```
' Report Header controls

' Title bar shadow

  Set ctl = CreateReportControl(strReportName, ControlTypeRectangle, Header,
➥ "", "", zTwips(ERBarLeft + ERShadowOffset), zTwips(ERTitleBarTop +
➥ ERShadowOffset), zTwips(ERBarWidth), zTwips(ERTitleBarHeight))
  ctl.ControlName = "shpTitleBarShadow"
  ctl.BackColor = Black

' Title bar
  Set ctl = CreateReportControl(strReportName, ControlTypeRectangle, Header,
➥ "", "", zTwips(ERBarLeft), zTwips(ERTitleBarTop), zTwips(ERBarWidth),
➥ zTwips(ERTitleBarHeight))
  ctl.ControlName = "shpTitleBar"
  ctl.BackColor = White

' Title bar text
  Set ctl = CreateReportControl(strReportName, ControlTypeLabel, Header, "",
➥ "", zTwips(ERQuestionLabelLeft), zTwips(ERTitleLabelTop), 0, 0)
  ctl.ControlName = "lblTitleBarCaption"
  strCaption = zSWfrm!cboSurveyTitle
  If Right$(strCaption, 6) <> "Survey" Then
    strCaption = strCaption & " Survey"
  End If
  ctl.Caption = strCaption
  ctl.TextAlign = TextAlignCenter
  ERSetFont ctl
  ctl.FontSize = ERTitleBarFontSize
  ctl.Height = zTwips(ERTitleLabelHeight)
  ctl.Width = zTwips(ERQuestionLabelWidth)

' Detail Section controls

  For n = 1 To 2
  ' Question bar shadow
    Set ctl = CreateReportControl(strReportName, ControlTypeRectangle,
➥ IIf(n = 1, Detail, Detail2), "", "", zTwips(ERBarLeft +
➥ ERShadowOffset), Detail, Detail2), "", "", zTwips(ERBarLeft +
➥ ERShadowOffset), zTwips(ERShadowOffset), zTwips(ERBarWidth),
➥ zTwips(IIf(n = 1, ERSmallBarHeight, ERLargeBarHeight)))
    ctl.ControlName = "shpBarShadow" & n
    ctl.BackColor = Black

  ' Question bar
    Set ctl = CreateReportControl(strReportName, ControlTypeRectangle,
➥ IIf(n = 1, Detail, Detail2), "", "", zTwips(ERBarLeft), 0,
➥ zTwips(ERBarWidth), zTwips(IIf(n = 1, ERSmallBarHeight,
➥ ERLargeBarHeight)))
    ctl.ControlName = "shpBar" & n
    ctl.BackColor = White

  ' Question text box
    Set ctl = CreateReportControl(strReportName, ControlTypeTextbox,
➥ IIf(n = 1, Detail, Detail2), "", "", zTwips(ERQuestionLabelLeft),
➥ zTwips(ERQuestionLabelTopOffset), zTwips(ERQuestionLabelWidth),
➥ zTwips(ERQuestionLabelHeight))
```

continues

Listing 18.14. continued

```
    ctl.ControlName = "txtQuestion" & n
    ctl.ControlSource = "Question"
    ctl.TextAlign = TextAlignLeft
    ERSetFont ctl
Next n

' Create some controls that are not displayed but that will be used
' by the run-time code to retrieve values.
CreateHiddenControl strReportName, "Type"
CreateHiddenControl strReportName, "RangeFrom"
CreateHiddenControl strReportName, "RangeTo"
CreateHiddenControl strReportName, "RangeStep"
CreateHiddenControl strReportName, "PercentFrom"
CreateHiddenControl strReportName, "PercentTo"
CreateHiddenControl strReportName, "PercentStep"

' Controls for the different answer types

' Yes
Set ctl = CreateReportControl(strReportName, ControlTypeLabel, Detail, "",
➥ "", zTwips(ERYesLeft), zTwips(ERResponseLabelTopOffset1), 0, 0)
ctl.ControlName = "lblYes"
ctl.Caption = "Yes"
ctl.TextAlign = TextAlignLeft
ERSetFont ctl
ctl.Height = zTwips(ERResponseLabelHeight)
ctl.Width = zTwips(ERYesNoWidth)

' No
Set ctl = CreateReportControl(strReportName, ControlTypeLabel, Detail, "",
➥ "", zTwips(ERNoLeft), zTwips(ERResponseLabelTopOffset1), 0, 0)
ctl.ControlName = "lblNo"
ctl.Caption = "No"
ctl.TextAlign = TextAlignRight
ERSetFont ctl
ctl.Height = zTwips(ERResponseLabelHeight)
ctl.Width = zTwips(ERYesNoWidth)

' Number line for range or percents
dblPointStepWidth = (ERLastPointLeft - ERFirstPointLeft) /
➥ (CDbl(zSWMaximumPoints) - 1#)
dblPointLeft = ERFirstPointLeft
For n = 1 To zSWMaximumPoints
' A point on the number line
    Set ctl = CreateReportControl(strReportName, ControlTypeTextbox, Detail,
    ➥ "", "", zTwips(dblPointLeft), zTwips(ERResponseLabelTopOffset1),
    ➥ zTwips(ERPointWidth), zTwips(ERResponseLabelHeight))
    ctl.ControlName = "txtPoint" & n
    ctl.TextAlign = TextAlignCenter
    ERSetFont ctl

    dblPointLeft = dblPointLeft + dblPointStepWidth
Next n
```

```
' Multiple choice selections
  ERMultipleChoice strReportName, "A", ERMultipleChoiceLeft1,
  ➥ ERResponseLabelTopOffset1
  ERMultipleChoice strReportName, "B", ERMultipleChoiceLeft1,
  ➥ ERResponseLabelTopOffset2
  ERMultipleChoice strReportName, "C", ERMultipleChoiceLeft1,
  ➥ ERResponseLabelTopOffset3
  ERMultipleChoice strReportName, "D", ERMultipleChoiceLeft2,
  ➥ ERResponseLabelTopOffset1
  ERMultipleChoice strReportName, "E", ERMultipleChoiceLeft2,
  ➥ ERResponseLabelTopOffset2
  ERMultipleChoice strReportName, "F", ERMultipleChoiceLeft2,
  ➥ ERResponseLabelTopOffset3

' Three lines for write-in answers
  For n = 1 To 3
    Set ctl = CreateReportControl(strReportName, ControlTypeLine, Detail2,
    ➥ "", "", zTwips(ERWriteInLineLeft), zTwips(ERWriteInLineTopOffset1 +
    ➥ ERWriteInLineSpace * (n - 1)), zTwips(ERWriteInLineWidth), 0)
    ctl.ControlName = "line" & n
    ctl.BorderWidth = ERWriteInLineBorderWidth
  Next n

' Add space between questions
  rpt.section(Detail).Height = rpt.section(Detail).Height +
  ➥ zTwips(ERSpaceBetweenQuestions)
  rpt.section(Detail2).Height = rpt.section(Detail2).Height +
  ➥ zTwips(ERSpaceBetweenQuestions)

' Page count
  Set ctl = CreateReportControl(strReportName, ControlTypeTextbox, PageFooter,
  ➥ "", "", zTwips(ERPageCountLeft), 0, zTwips(ERPageCountWidth),
  ➥ zTwips(ERPageFooterHeight))
  ctl.ControlName = "txtPageCount"
  ctl.ControlSource = "=" & Chr$(34) & "- " & Chr$(34) & " & Page & " &
  ➥ Chr$(34) & " -" & Chr$(34)
  ctl.TextAlign = TextAlignCenter
  ERSetFont ctl

  BuildEntryReport = False

BuildEntryReportDone:
  On Error Resume Next
  If blnReportOpened Then
    DoCmd SetWarnings False
    SendKeys zSWstrEntryReport & "~"
    DoCmd Close A_Report, rpt.FormName
    DoCmd SetWarnings True
  End If
  Exit Function

BuildEntryReportError:
  Warning "BuildEntryReport", Error$
  Resume BuildEntryReportDone

End Function
```

First, the `CreateReport` function is called and the result is assigned to a report variable. A very nice feature of this function is that the new report is opened up minimized as an icon. People don't have to see the guts of the report object as it is being generated by your program.

```
' Create the report object, defaulting to the current database and the
' current report template.
  Set rpt = CreateReport("", "")
  blnReportOpened = True
```

Next, the report header and footer are turned on by calling a menu command that toggles them on and off.

```
' Turn on the report header and footer through the Access 2.0 menu
' 7 = Report Design menu, 3 = Format, 10 = Report Header/Footer
  DoCmd DoMenuItem 7, 3, 10, , A_MENU_VER20
```

The report name (whatever Access defaulted it to) is saved into the `strReportName` variable. You need this because some of the functions take a report name as an argument.

```
  strReportName = rpt.FormName
```

Next, the width of the report is set, along with the height of the report sections (see Listing 18.15). The `zTwips` function is called in each case to translate values from inches to twips.

Listing 18.15. Setting the width of the report and the height of the report sections.

```
' Set the page dimensions
  rpt.Width = zTwips(ERSectionWidth)
  rpt.section(Header).Height = zTwips(ERReportHeaderHeight)
  rpt.section(PageHeader).Height = 0
  rpt.section(PageFooter).Height = zTwips(ERPageFooterHeight)
  rpt.section(Footer).Height = 0
```

As the comment within the code indicates, you create a section here that will be used as an alternative to the detail section. A section is created, sorted by the ID field. The ID field changes for each record, ensuring that the section always tries to print with each detail line. A header is created, but a footer is not.

```
' Create a group header that always tries to print. This gives us an
' alternative detail section, where at run-time we cancel one or the other.
  v = CreateGroupLevel(strReportName, "ID", True, False)
```

Next, the Record Source property is set to the generated Questions Table. Also, the On Format events are set to call functions in the report run-time code that will decide if each of these sections should print or if they should cancel for the current record.

Remember, you need this because, depending on which question type is being printed, either the small or large question box is printed. Additionally, these functions will handle turning on or off some of the controls on the report by setting their visible property.

The constants Detail and Detail2 are used to identify the Detail section and the ID Group Level Header section.

```
' Set report properties
  rpt.RecordSource = zSWstrQuestionsTable
  rpt.section(Detail).OnFormat = "=zSWEntryReportDetailOnFormat(Report)"
  rpt.section(Detail2).OnFormat = "=zSWEntryReportDetail2OnFormat(Report)"
```

The first three controls created display the title of the survey in the report header. See Listing 18.16.

Listing 18.16. Dropping controls in the Report Header section.

```
' Report Header controls

' Title bar shadow
Set ctl = CreateReportControl(strReportName, ControlTypeRectangle, Header,
➥ "", "", zTwips(ERBarLeft + ERShadowOffset), zTwips(ERTitleBarTop +
➥ ERShadowOffset), zTwips(ERBarWidth), zTwips(ERTitleBarHeight))
  ctl.ControlName = "shpTitleBarShadow"
  ctl.BackColor = Black

' Title bar
  Set ctl = CreateReportControl(strReportName, ControlTypeRectangle, Header,
➥ "", "", zTwips(ERBarLeft), zTwips(ERTitleBarTop), zTwips(ERBarWidth),
➥ zTwips(ERTitleBarHeight))
  ctl.ControlName = "shpTitleBar"
  ctl.BackColor = White

' Title bar text
  Set ctl = CreateReportControl(strReportName, ControlTypeLabel, Header, "",
➥ "", zTwips(ERQuestionLabelLeft), zTwips(ERTitleLabelTop), 0, 0)
  ctl.ControlName = "lblTitleBarCaption"
  strCaption = zSWfrm!cboSurveyTitle
  If Right$(strCaption, 6) <> "Survey" Then
    strCaption = strCaption & " Survey"
  End If
  ctl.Caption = strCaption
  ctl.TextAlign = TextAlignCenter
  ERSetFont ctl
  ctl.FontSize = ERTitleBarFontSize
  ctl.Height = zTwips(ERTitleLabelHeight)
  ctl.Width = zTwips(ERQuestionLabelWidth)
```

Next, the subroutine creates the two question boxes in the Detail and Group Level Header sections of the report. This is done inside a loop so that the code doesn't have to be repeated.

A call to the IIf() function is used to return the section number for the Detail section or the Group Level section. See Listing 18.17.

Listing 18.17. Creating the Question boxes in the Detail section and Group Level Header section.

```
' Detail Section controls

  For n = 1 To 2
  ' Question bar shadow
    Set ctl = CreateReportControl(strReportName, ControlTypeRectangle,
    ➥ IIf(n = 1, Detail, Detail2), "", "", zTwips(ERBarLeft +
    ➥ ERShadowOffset), Detail, Detail2), "", "", zTwips(ERBarLeft +
    ➥ ERShadowOffset), zTwips(ERShadowOffset), zTwips(ERBarWidth),
    ➥ zTwips(IIf(n = 1, ERSmallBarHeight, ERLargeBarHeight)))
    ctl.ControlName = "shpBarShadow" & n
    ctl.BackColor = Black

  ' Question bar
    Set ctl = CreateReportControl(strReportName, ControlTypeRectangle,
    ➥ IIf(n = 1, Detail, Detail2), "", "", zTwips(ERBarLeft), 0,
    ➥ zTwips(ERBarWidth), zTwips(IIf(n = 1, ERSmallBarHeight,
    ➥ ERLargeBarHeight)))
    ctl.ControlName = "shpBar" & n
    ctl.BackColor = White

  ' Question text box
    Set ctl = CreateReportControl(strReportName, ControlTypeTextbox,
    ➥ IIf(n = 1, Detail, Detail2), "", "", zTwips(ERQuestionLabelLeft),
    ➥ zTwips(ERQuestionLabelTopOffset), zTwips(ERQuestionLabelWidth),
    ➥ zTwips(ERQuestionLabelHeight))
    ctl.ControlName = "txtQuestion" & n
    ctl.ControlSource = "Question"
    ctl.TextAlign = TextAlignLeft
    ERSetFont ctl
  Next n
```

Next, some controls are created on the report so that the run-time code can reference field values in the record source of the report. It isn't good enough that these fields exist in the record source; they must actually be on the report so that the code can reference their values.

Since you don't want to actually display the controls, they are created by calling a CreateHiddenControl subroutine, shown in Listing 18.18.

Listing 18.18. Creating hidden controls.

```
' Create some controls that are not displayed, but that will be used
' by the run-time code to retrieve values.
  CreateHiddenControl strReportName, "Type"
  CreateHiddenControl strReportName, "RangeFrom"
```

```
CreateHiddenControl strReportName, "RangeTo"
CreateHiddenControl strReportName, "RangeStep"
CreateHiddenControl strReportName, "PercentFrom"
CreateHiddenControl strReportName, "PercentTo"
CreateHiddenControl strReportName, "PercentStep"
```

The next two controls are Yes and No labels for Yes/No type questions. See Listing 18.19.

Listing 18.19. Creating Yes and No labels.

```
' Yes
  Set ctl = CreateReportControl(strReportName, ControlTypeLabel, Detail, "",
  ➥ "", zTwips(ERYesLeft), zTwips(ERResponseLabelTopOffset1), 0, 0)
  ctl.ControlName = "lblYes"
  ctl.Caption = "Yes"
  ctl.TextAlign = TextAlignLeft
  ERSetFont ctl
  ctl.Height = zTwips(ERResponseLabelHeight)
  ctl.Width = zTwips(ERYesNoWidth)

' No
  Set ctl = CreateReportControl(strReportName, ControlTypeLabel, Detail, "",
  ➥ "", zTwips(ERNoLeft), zTwips(ERResponseLabelTopOffset1), 0, 0)
  ctl.ControlName = "lblNo"
  ctl.Caption = "No"
  ctl.TextAlign = TextAlignRight
  ERSetFont ctl
  ctl.Height = zTwips(ERResponseLabelHeight)
  ctl.Width = zTwips(ERYesNoWidth)
```

A loop is entered to generate 10 text box controls that display Range and Percent values for Range or Percent type questions. See Listing 18.20.

Listing 18.20. Creating the Range and Percent text boxes.

```
' Number line for range or percents
  dblPointStepWidth = (ERLastPointLeft - ERFirstPointLeft) /
  ➥ (CDbl(zSWMaximumPoints) - 1#)
  dblPointLeft = ERFirstPointLeft
  For n = 1 To zSWMaximumPoints
  ' A point on the number line
    Set ctl = CreateReportControl(strReportName, ControlTypeTextbox, Detail,
    ➥ "", "", zTwips(dblPointLeft), zTwips(ERResponseLabelTopOffset1),
    ➥ zTwips(ERPointWidth), zTwips(ERResponseLabelHeight))
    ctl.ControlName = "txtPoint" & n
    ctl.TextAlign = TextAlignCenter
    ERSetFont ctl

    dblPointLeft = dblPointLeft + dblPointStepWidth
  Next n
```

Within the larger of the two question boxes, six text boxes are created to show the multiple-choice answer selections. To save typing, I created a subroutine, ERMultipleChoice, to do the work. The letter that is being created is passed as an argument, along with the Left and Top coordinates for where the label goes. (See Listing 18.21.)

Listing 18.21. Creating the Multiple-Choice text boxes.

```
' Multiple choice selections
  ERMultipleChoice strReportName, "A", ERMultipleChoiceLeft1,
  ➥ ERResponseLabelTopOffset1
  ERMultipleChoice strReportName, "B", ERMultipleChoiceLeft1,
  ➥ ERResponseLabelTopOffset2
  ERMultipleChoice strReportName, "C", ERMultipleChoiceLeft1,
  ➥ ERResponseLabelTopOffset3
  ERMultipleChoice strReportName, "D", ERMultipleChoiceLeft2,
  ➥ ERResponseLabelTopOffset1
  ERMultipleChoice strReportName, "E", ERMultipleChoiceLeft2,
  ➥ ERResponseLabelTopOffset2
  ERMultipleChoice strReportName, "F", ERMultipleChoiceLeft2,
  ➥ ERResponseLabelTopOffset3
```

For Write-In questions, three line controls are created to help indicate where the response should be entered. (See Listing 18.22.)

Listing 18.22. Creating line controls.

```
' Three lines for write-in answers
  For n = 1 To 3
    Set ctl = CreateReportControl(strReportName, ControlTypeLine, Detail2,
    ➥ "", "", zTwips(ERWriteInLineLeft), zTwips(ERWriteInLineTopOffset1 +
    ➥ ERWriteInLineSpace * (n - 1)), zTwips(ERWriteInLineWidth), 0)
    ctl.ControlName = "line" & n
    ctl.BorderWidth = ERWriteInLineBorderWidth
  Next n
```

The height of the Detail section and ID Group Level Header section are each adjusted to leave some vertical spacing between questions as they appear on the report.

```
' Add space between questions
  rpt.section(Detail).Height = rpt.section(Detail).Height +
  ➥ zTwips(ERSpaceBetweenQuestions)
  rpt.section(Detail2).Height = rpt.section(Detail2).Height +
  ➥ zTwips(ERSpaceBetweenQuestions)
```

To finish up, a text box to display the page number is created in the Page Footer section. The Control Source of the text box is set to a formula that displays the page number with dashes around it. (See Listing 18.23.)

Listing 18.23. Creating the page count text box.

```
' Page count
  Set ctl = CreateReportControl(strReportName, ControlTypeTextbox, PageFooter,
  ➡ "", "", zTwips(ERPageCountLeft), 0, zTwips(ERPageCountWidth),
  ➡ zTwips(ERPageFooterHeight))
  ctl.ControlName = "txtPageCount"
  ctl.ControlSource = "=" & Chr$(34) & "- " & Chr$(34) & " & Page & " &
  ➡ Chr$(34) & " -" & Chr$(34)
  ctl.TextAlign = TextAlignCenter
  ERSetFont ctl
```

We're done!

In the Done section of the subroutine, you save the report by closing it. A modal dialog box pops up, asking for the object name to save.

SendKeys is used to push out the keystrokes that type in the report name and presses the Enter key. Because of how SendKeys works with pop-up dialog boxes and such, the SendKeys call is actually done before the line that closes the report object and activates the pop-up.

```
If blnReportOpened Then
   DoCmd SetWarnings False
   SendKeys zSWstrEntryReport & "~"
   DoCmd Close A_Report, rpt.FormName
   DoCmd SetWarnings True
End If
```

After this, the supporting subroutines are listed: ERMultipleChoice, ERSetFont, and CreateHiddenControl. These were each devised primarily to avoid having to repeat similar lines of code over and over again.

The *ERMultipleChoice* Subroutine

The ERMultipleChoice subroutine, shown in Listing 18.24, is called six times to create each of the text boxes that displays a possible multiple-choice answer.

The Control Source property of each text box is set to call a report run-time library function you will write later. The zSWMultipleChoice function returns a string displaying the selection letter and the text for the selection.

Listing 18.24. The `ERMultipleChoice` **subroutine.**

```
Sub ERMultipleChoice (szReport As String, szLetter As String,
➥ dblLeft As Double, dblTop As Double)

  Dim ctl As Control

  On Error GoTo ERMultipleChoiceError

  Set ctl = CreateReportControl(szReport, ControlTypeTextbox, Detail2, "", "",
  ➥ zTwips(dblLeft), zTwips(dblTop), zTwips(ERMultipleChoiceWidth),
  ➥ zTwips(ERResponseLabelHeight))
  ctl.ControlName = "txt" & szLetter
  ctl.ControlSource = "=zSWMultipleChoice(" & Chr$(34) & szLetter & Chr$(34) &
  ➥ ",[Choice" & szLetter & "])"
  ctl.TextAlign = TextAlignLeft
  ERSetFont ctl
  ctl.Visible = False

ERMultipleChoiceDone:
  Exit Sub

ERMultipleChoiceError:
  Warning "ERMultipleChoice", Error$
  Resume ERMultipleChoiceDone

End Sub
```

The *ERSetFont* Subroutine

The `ERSetFont` subroutine, shown in Listing 18.25, sets three of the control properties for the passed control.

Listing 18.25. The `ERSetFont` **subroutine.**

```
Sub ERSetFont (ctl As Control)

  On Error Resume Next
  ctl.FontName = ERFontName
  ctl.FontSize = ERFontSize
  ctl.FontWeight = FontWeightBold

End Sub
```

The *CreateHiddenControl* Subroutine

The `CreateHiddenControl` subroutine, shown in Listing 18.26, creates a text box in the top-left corner of the detail section. Its Height and Width properties are set to 0 inches.

This is a trick to make a field in the report's Record Source available in code, because otherwise the Access reporting engine just optimizes it away. The field can be referenced in code like this:

```
rpt![MyField]
```

You use the hidden controls in the report run-time code.

Listing 18.26. The `CreateHiddenControl` **subroutine.**

```
Sub CreateHiddenControl (strReportName As String, strField As String)

  Dim ctl As Control

  On Error GoTo CreateHiddenControlError

  Set ctl = CreateReportControl(strReportName, ControlTypeTextbox, Detail, "",
➥ "", 0, 0, 0, 0)
  ctl.ControlName = "txt" & strField
  ctl.ControlSource = strField

CreateHiddenControlDone:
  Exit Sub

CreateHiddenControlError:
  Warning "CreateHiddenControl", Error$
  Resume CreateHiddenControlDone

End Sub
```

You have everything you need to generate an Entry Report.

Let's take a break from the Survey Wizard Save As form module and create the Survey Wizard Report Run-time module so that you can actually run the report after it's generated.

Writing the Entry Report Run-Time Code

The report run-time code is contained in the Survey Wizard Report Run-time module. In this chapter, you will write the code that supports the Entry Report. In the next chapter you will add to this module the code to support the Results Report.

The code in this module must be loaded whenever a user opens an Entry Report generated by Survey Wizard. By using run-time code, you can make our wizard generate database objects that have more flexibility than otherwise possible with standard Access report objects.

The declarations section for this module is shown in Listing 18.27.

Listing 18.27. The declarations section for the Survey Wizard Report Run-time module.

```
' Survey Wizard Report Run-Time

  Option Compare Database
  Option Explicit

  Const mstrProgramName = "Survey Wizard Report Run-Time"
```

The module also has its own copy of the Warning subroutine, shown in Listing 18.28.

Listing 18.28. The Warning subroutine.

```
Private Sub Warning (strProcedure As String, msg As String)

  zDisplayError strProcedure, msg, mstrProgramName

End Sub
```

The *zSWEntryReportDetailOnFormat* Function

The zSWEntryReportDetailOnFormat function, shown in Listing 18.29, gets activated on the On Format event for the Detail section of the report. This section displays the shorter rectangle for Yes/No, Range, and Percent type questions.

The subroutine checks the value of the Type field for the current Question Table record in the report. This field indicates which response type is used for the current question and is also one of the hidden controls you added to the report when you generated it.

The Detail section is canceled if the question type is a Multiple-Choice or Write-In question, because those types of questions are handled by the ID Group Level Header report section.

For a Yes/No question type, two labels displaying "Yes" and "No" are made visible.

For a Range or Percent type question, the From, To, and Step values are retrieved and verified. If the number of points to display is 10 or less, the function then turns on however many text boxes it needs and writes the values along the range to them.

Listing 18.29. The `zSWEntryReportDetailOnFormat` **function.**

```
Function zSWEntryReportDetailOnFormat (rpt As Report) As Integer

  Dim intType As Integer

  On Error GoTo zSWEntryReportDetailOnFormatError

  If IsNull(rpt![Type]) Then
    DoCmd CancelEvent
    GoTo zSWEntryReportDetailOnFormatDone
  End If

  intType = CInt(rpt![Type])

  Select Case intType

  Case zSWQuestionTypeMultipleChoice, zSWQuestionTypeWriteIn
    DoCmd CancelEvent
    GoTo zSWEntryReportDetailOnFormatDone

  End Select

  ShowYesNo rpt, intType, False
  ShowRangePercent rpt, intType, False
  ShowMultipleChoice rpt, intType, False

zSWEntryReportDetailOnFormatDone:
  Exit Function

zSWEntryReportDetailOnFormatError:
  Warning "zSWEntryReportDetailOnFormat", Error$
  Resume zSWEntryReportDetailOnFormatDone

End Function
```

The *zSWEntryReportDetail2OnFormat* Function

The `zSWEntryReportDetail2OnFormat` function, shown in Listing 18.30, is called on the On Format event for the ID group header.

This function works similarly to the `zSWEntryReportDetailOnFormat` function. The first thing this function does is look at the Type control on the report to determine which question type the current question is.

The ID header is used to display Multiple-Choice and Write-In type questions only, so if the type is Yes/No, Range, or Percent, printing of the section is canceled and the function is exited.

If the question type is Multiple-Choice or Write-In, the function continues. For a Multiple-Choice type question, the `txtA` through `txtF` text box controls are set visible as needed. For a Write-In question, the three line controls are set visible.

Listing 18.30. The `zSWEntryReportDetail2OnFormat` **function.**

```
Function zSWEntryReportDetail2OnFormat (rpt As Report)

  Dim intType As Integer

  On Error GoTo zSWEntryReportDetail2OnFormatError

  If IsNull(rpt![Type]) Then
    DoCmd CancelEvent
    GoTo zSWEntryReportDetail2OnFormatDone
  End If

  intType = CInt(rpt![Type])

  Select Case intType

  Case zSWQuestionTypeYesNo, zSWQuestionTypeRange, zSWQuestionTypePercent
    DoCmd CancelEvent
    GoTo zSWEntryReportDetail2OnFormatDone

  End Select

  ShowMultipleChoice rpt, intType, False
  ShowWriteIn rpt, intType, False

zSWEntryReportDetail2OnFormatDone:
  Exit Function

zSWEntryReportDetail2OnFormatError:
  Warning "zSWEntryReportDetail2OnFormat", Error$
  Resume zSWEntryReportDetail2OnFormatDone

End Function
```

The *ShowYesNo* Subroutine

The `ShowYesNo` subroutine, shown in Listing 18.31, determines if the Yes and No labels should be displayed on the report by checking the response type of the current question record. The visible property for the label controls is set to True to make them visible or False to hide them.

The subroutine's last argument, `blnResultsReport`, is set to True if called from the Results Report run-time code. You will be adding to this and other procedures in the next chapter to handle the Results Report.

Listing 18.31. The `ShowYesNo` subroutine.

```
Private Sub ShowYesNo (rpt As Report, intType As Integer, blnResultsReport As
➥ Integer)

  Dim blnVisible As Integer
```

```
    On Error GoTo ShowYesNoError

    blnVisible = (intType = zSWQuestionTypeYesNo)

    If blnResultsReport Then
    ' Results Report

    Else
    ' Entry Report

      rpt!lblYes.Visible = blnVisible
      rpt!lblNo.Visible = blnVisible
    End If

ShowYesNoDone:
  Exit Sub

ShowYesNoError:
  Warning "ShowYesNo", Error$
  Resume ShowYesNoDone

End Sub
```

The *ShowMultipleChoice* Subroutine

The ShowMultipleChoice subroutine, shown in Listing 18.32, sets the Visible property
of the txtA through txtF controls to True or False, depending on whether the current
question is a Multiple-Choice response type.

Listing 18.32. The ShowMultipleChoice **subroutine.**

```
Private Sub ShowMultipleChoice (rpt As Report, intType As Integer,
➥ blnResultsReport As Integer)

  Dim n As Integer

  Dim blnVisible As Integer

  On Error GoTo ShowMultipleChoiceError

  blnVisible = (intType = zSWQuestionTypeMultipleChoice)

  If blnResultsReport Then
  ' Results Report

  Else
  ' Entry Report

    For n = 65 To 70
      rpt("txt" & Chr$(n)).Visible = blnVisible
    Next n
  End If
```

continues

Listing 18.32. continued

```
ShowMultipleChoiceDone:
  Exit Sub

ShowMultipleChoiceError:
  Warning "ShowMultipleChoice", Error$
  Resume ShowMultipleChoiceDone

End Sub
```

The *zSWMultipleChoice* Function

The zSWMultipleChoice function, shown in Listing 18.33, is the function assigned to the Control Source of the txtA through txtF text boxes on the Entry Report.

If a non-null value is passed to its second argument, this function returns a string with the value prefixed by the letter (A to F) of the selection.

For example, if A and 1945 are passed as arguments, this function returns A) 1945.

Listing 18.33. The zSWMultipleChoice **function.**

```
Function zSWMultipleChoice (szLetter As String, v As Variant)

  Dim strChoice As String

  On Error Resume Next

  zSWMultipleChoice = ""

  If Not IsNull(v) Then
    strChoice = Trim$(CStr(v))
    If Len(strChoice) > 0 Then
      zSWMultipleChoice = szLetter & ") " & strChoice
    End If
  End If

End Function
```

The *ShowWriteIn* Subroutine

The ShowWriteIn subroutine, shown in Listing 18.34, sets the Visible property of the three line controls displayed only for Write-In question types.

Listing 18.34. The ShowWriteIn **subroutine.**

```
Private Sub ShowWriteIn (rpt As Report, intType As Integer,
➥ blnResultsReport As Integer)

  Dim n As Integer

  Dim blnVisible As Integer

  On Error GoTo ShowWriteInError

  blnVisible = (intType = zSWQuestionTypeWriteIn)

  If blnResultsReport Then
  ' Results Report

  Else
  ' Entry Report

    For n = 1 To 3
      rpt("Line" & n).Visible = blnVisible
    Next n
  End If

ShowWriteInDone:
  Exit Sub

ShowWriteInError:
  Warning "ShowWriteIn", Error$
  Resume ShowWriteInDone

End Sub
```

The *ShowRangePercent* Subroutine

The same subroutine is used to show both Range and Percent numbers because the same set of controls is used for both. Let's look at this one in detail after Listing 18.35.

Listing 18.35. The ShowRangePercent **subroutine.**

```
Private Sub ShowRangePercent (rpt As Report, intType As Integer,
➥ blnResultsReport As Integer)

  Dim ctl As Control

  Dim lngFrom As Long
  Dim lngTo As Long
  Dim lngStep As Long
  Dim l As Long

  Dim intSkip As Integer
  Dim n As Integer
```

continues

Listing 18.35. continued

```
Dim blnVisible As Integer

On Error GoTo ShowRangePercentError

blnVisible = ((intType = zSWQuestionTypeRange) Or (intType =
➥ zSWQuestionTypePercent))

For n = 1 To zSWMaximumPoints
  rpt("txtPoint" & n).Visible = False
Next n

If blnVisible Then
  If intType = zSWQuestionTypeRange Then
    lngFrom = CLng(rpt![RangeFrom])
    lngTo = CLng(rpt![RangeTo])
    lngStep = CLng(rpt![RangeStep])
  Else
    lngFrom = CLng(rpt![PercentFrom])
    lngTo = CLng(rpt![PercentTo])
    lngStep = CLng(rpt![PercentStep])
  End If

  If zSWValidatePoints(lngFrom, lngTo, lngStep) Then
    n = 1
    intSkip = (zSWMaximumPoints - CInt((lngTo - lngFrom + lngStep) /
    ➥ lngStep)) / 2

    For l = lngFrom To lngTo Step lngStep

      If blnResultsReport Then
      ' Results Report

      Else
      ' Entry Report

        Set ctl = rpt("txtPoint" & n + intSkip)
      End If

      If intType = zSWQuestionTypePercent Then
        ctl = CStr(l) & "%"
      Else
        ctl = CStr(l)
      End If

      ctl.Visible = True

      n = n + 1
    Next l

  End If
End If

ShowRangePercentDone:
  Exit Sub
```

```
ShowRangePercentError:
  Warning "ShowRangePercent", Error$
  Resume ShowRangePercentDone

End Sub
```

The `ShowRangePercent` subroutine first turns off each of the text boxes used to display Range or Percent values. If the question is a Range or Percent type, it will later selectively turn these back on for as many text boxes as are required to display the values in the range.

```
blnVisible = ((intType = zSWQuestionTypeRange) Or (intType =
➡ zSWQuestionTypePercent))

For n = 1 To zSWMaximumPoints
  rpt("txtPoint" & n).Visible = False
Next n
```

Next, the From, To, and Step values are retrieved, and the `zSWValidatePoints` function is called to make sure that the selected range will produce no more than 10 different numbers. (See Listing 18.36.)

Listing 18.36. Reading the From, To, and Step values from hidden controls and validating them.

```
If blnVisible Then
  If intType = zSWQuestionTypeRange Then
    lngFrom = CLng(rpt![RangeFrom])
    lngTo = CLng(rpt![RangeTo])
    lngStep = CLng(rpt![RangeStep])
  Else
    lngFrom = CLng(rpt![PercentFrom])
    lngTo = CLng(rpt![PercentTo])
    lngStep = CLng(rpt![PercentStep])
  End If

  If zSWValidatePoints(lngFrom, lngTo, lngStep) Then
```

Next, the Skip value is determined. This indicates how many text box controls to the left are skipped in order to center the set of numbers on the page.

```
n = 1
intSkip = (zSWMaximumPoints - CInt((lngTo - lngFrom + lngStep) /
➡ lngStep)) / 2
```

The subroutine then loops through the set of numbers, selecting one of the txtPoint text box controls for each number, as shown in Listing 18.37.

Listing 18.37. Selecting a control to write a number to.

```
For l = lngFrom To lngTo Step lngStep

  If blnResultsReport Then
  ' Results Report

  Else
  ' Entry Report

    Set ctl = rpt("txtPoint" & n + intSkip)
  End If
```

The number is written to the selected text box as a string. If the question response type is Percent, the percentage sign is appended to the string.

The text box is set to be visible, and the loop continues. See Listing 18.38.

Listing 18.38. Writing a Percent or Range number to a text box on the Entry Report.

```
  If intType = zSWQuestionTypePercent Then
    ctl = CStr(l) & "%"
  Else
    ctl = CStr(l)
  End If

  ctl.Visible = True

  n = n + 1
Next l
```

The *zSWValidatePoints* Function

The zSWValidatePoints function (shown in Listing 18.39) ensures that the From, To, and Step values produce no more then 10 numbers in a set.

Listing 18.39. Writing a Percent or Range number to a text box on the Entry Report.

```
Function zSWValidatePoints (lngFrom As Long, lngTo As Long, lngStep As Long)
➥ As Integer

' Verify that the From, To, and Step values make sense

  Dim lngPoints As Long

' Return False to indicate bad values
  zSWValidatePoints = False
```

```
' Does step make any progress?
  If lngStep = 0 Then Exit Function

' Does step move in the right direction?
  If lngTo - lngFrom > 0 Then
    If lngStep < 0 Then Exit Function
  Else
    If lngStep > 0 Then Exit Function
  End If

' Do we reach the To value within the maximum number of steps?
  lngPoints = (lngTo - lngFrom + lngStep) / lngStep
  If lngPoints > zSWMaximumPoints Then Exit Function

' Return all is OK
  zSWValidatePoints = True

End Function
```

Validation During Data Entry

It would be best to not only validate the From, To, and Step values when they are used at run time, but also as the user enters them into the Survey Wizard form.

Now that we have a zSWValidatePoints function, return to the Survey Wizard form module and complete the ValidatePoints function as shown in Listing 18.40.

Listing 18.40. The completed ValidatePoints function in the Survey Wizard form module.

```
Function ValidatePoints ()

' If the question type is range or percent, verify the From, To and Step
' values.

  ValidatePoints = True

  If mintCurrentQuestionType = zSWQuestionTypeRange Or mintCurrentQuestionType
  ➥ = zSWQuestionTypePercent Then
    If Not zSWValidatePoints(CLng(txtFrom), CLng(txtTo), CLng(txtStep)) Then
      MsgBox "The From, To and Step values must produce number sequence
      ➥ consisting of no more than 10 numbers.", 48, mstrProgramName
      txtFrom.SetFocus
      ValidatePoints = False
    End If
  End If

End Function
```

Running the Entry Report

Cool! We're set to see Survey Wizard do its first bit of magic. And its about time, huh?

Enter a series of questions, making sure to try at least one of each response type. When you get to page 5, check the Entry Report and Questions Table. You can check the Responses Table also if you like. The Responses Table will be generated, but you don't need it at this point.

Figure 18.16 shows Page 5 of the Survey Wizard form with the Entry Report, Questions Table, and Responses Table checked.

FIGURE 18.16.

Test building the Entry Report and tables.

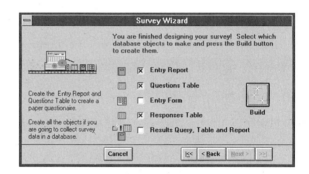

Click the Build button to bring up the Survey Wizard Save As form. Enter a base name and click OK. Hopefully, you will get the message shown in Figure 18.17.

FIGURE 18.17.

A successful build.

Click OK in the message box and the Survey Wizard form automatically closes. Find the generated report in the database container and open it. The one I created is shown in Figure 18.18.

All right, we're just warming up. This next one is going to be awesome!

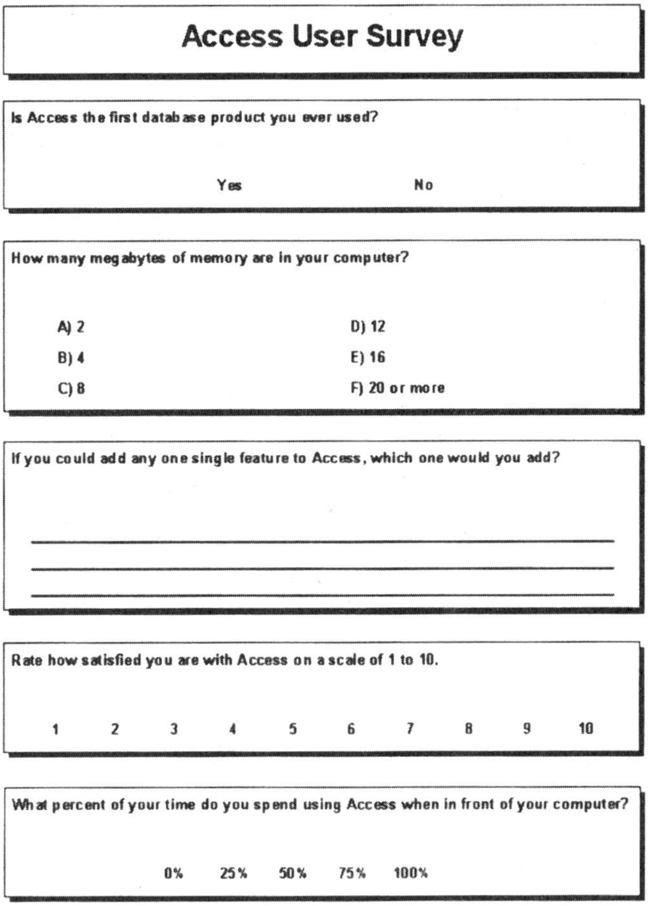

FIGURE 18.18.
Printing an Access User questionnaire.

Access User Survey

Is Access the first database product you ever used?

Yes   No

How many megabytes of memory are in your computer?

A) 2   D) 12

B) 4   E) 16

C) 8   F) 20 or more

If you could add any one single feature to Access, which one would you add?

_____

_____

_____

Rate how satisfied you are with Access on a scale of 1 to 10.

1   2   3   4   5   6   7   8   9   10

What percent of your time do you spend using Access when in front of your computer?

0%   25%   50%   75%   100%

Designing the Entry Form

I saved the fun one in this chapter for last. The next object to be created is the Entry Form.

In designing the Entry Form, I was faced with the same dilemma I had to deal with in the Entry Report—the fact that the size of each section within a form is only so big (22 inches by 22 inches).

Potentially, many controls would have to be dropped on the form if the user created a very long questionnaire. It would be difficult to fit them all in this space without crowding things.

One possible solution would be to take the same approach that you did in the Entry Report: the same controls would be reused to display the different question and answering options. Some run-time code would be involved, probably to set certain controls as visible or not, depending on the question type. Even though this strategy would have been perfectly reasonable, it's not the approach I took.

Instead, I found that if I created a multiple-page form that moved horizontally as well as vertically to get to different pages, I might have a reasonable number of pages to satisfy most survey needs.

I chose to make the detail section for each page on my prototype 2 inches high and 4.4 inches wide. This allowed me to go 11 rows down and 5 columns across for a total of 55 different pages.

With one question displayed per page, this would allow up to 55 questions per questionnaire. The actual maximum number of questions turned out to be 53 because I decided to use the first and last pages for user instructions.

The familiar <<, **B**ack, **N**ext, and >> buttons are used to move through the different pages.

I wrote a new version of the VCR procedures that would handle moving both horizontally and vertically to display the larger set of pages. These procedures are in a VCR2 module. They are designed to be generic enough so that you can use them in other projects where you might also need multiple-page forms.

Figure 18.19 shows a rough sketch of what the generated form would look like in design mode, given that the questionnaire being created had 39 questions. Within the detail section are columns of 11 pages. You could have up to five columns, but since only 39 questions are being used in the survey, you need only four. On the left side of the form, between each row, is a page break control, indicated by a black line.

As indicated by the order of the pages in the diagram, movement from page to page moves down a column and then starts at the top of the next column when the first column is used up.

In the form footer are multiple sets of VCR buttons, one set per column of pages. This is needed because when you scroll the detail section of the form to the right, all other sections scroll also.

FIGURE 18.19.

The layout of a VCR2 multiple-page form

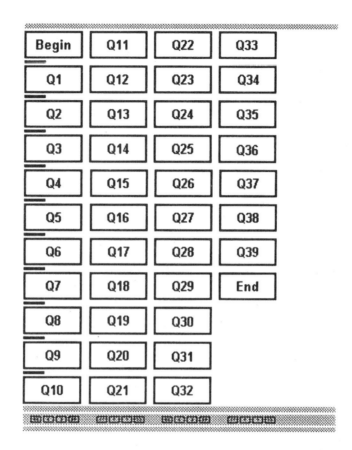

As much as possible (without spending a lot of time on it), I tried to position and size the buttons so that you can't tell any difference when the form moves from one column to the next. The buttons still have some noticeable changes in position or length when moving pages causes a move to different columns of pages.

Next you need to know what is being created on each page; this includes the beginning page of instructions, a page for each question type, and an ending instructions page. I experimented with this by manually creating a prototype before I did any coding, but the figures I've included here are from running an actual generated form and not my prototype.

On the first page, two labels are used to display the title of the questionnaire and some user instructions (see Figure 18.20).

FIGURE 18.20.

Page One of the
generated Entry Form.

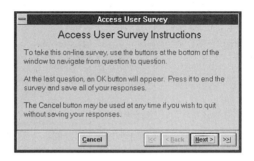

In each of the five question type pages, a label at the top of the page displays up to four lines of text for the question.

A Yes/No question type is answered by selecting one of two radio buttons within a hidden option group (see Figure 18.21). The option group is the actual control that is bound to the field receiving the answer to this question. By default, this field is Null, so neither Yes nor No is selected. Selecting Yes writes a –1 to the bound field; selecting No writes a 0.

FIGURE 18.21.

A Yes/No question on
the Entry Form.

For responding to a multiple-choice question, a hidden option group is created with up to six answers showing as option buttons. The field bound to the option group will receive a value from 1 to 6 when one of the selections is made. (See Figure 18.22.)

FIGURE 18.22.

A Multiple-Choice
question on the Entry
Form.

A Write-In question type is easily supported with a text box control, as shown in Figure 18.23.

FIGURE 18.23.

A Write-In question on the Entry Form.

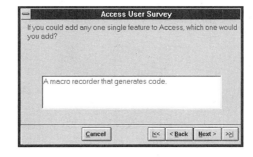

An option button solution is again used for the Range and Percent question types. (See Figure 18.24.)

FIGURE 18.24.

A Range question on the Entry Form.

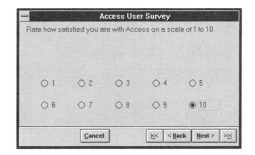

The Percent question type differs from a Range question only in that percent signs are displayed. (See Figure 18.25.)

FIGURE 18.25.

A Percent question on the Entry Form.

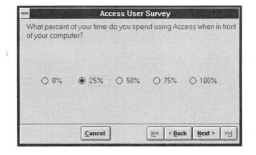

The final page redisplays the questionnaire title and some closing instructions to remind users how to save or cancel their entries. (See Figure 18.26.)

FIGURE 18.26.
The final page of the generated Entry Form.

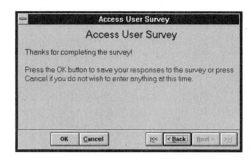

Have I gotcha hooked? You need to code the massive function that builds this puppy, and then the VCR2 run-time code.

The Entry Form Declarations

Back to the Survey Wizard Save As form. The code shown in Listing 18.41 needs to be added to the declarations section.

Listing 18.41. Survey Wizard Save As form module declarations for the Entry Form.

```
' Entry Form Constants

  Const EFFontName = "MS Sans Serif"
  Const EFFontSize = 10
  Const EFButtonFontName = "Arial"
  Const EFButtonFontSize = 8

  Const EFMaximumDetailHeight = 22#

  Const EFSectionWidth = 4.4      ' Allows 5 columns of pages
  Const EFDetailHeight = 2#       ' Allows 11 rows of pages
  Const EFHeaderHeight = 0#
  Const EFFooterHeight = .38

  Const EFButtonWidth = .56
  Const EFShortButtonWidth = .33
  Const EFButtonHeight = .25
  Const EFButtonTop = .05

  Const EFOKButtonLeft = .64
  Const EFCancelButtonLeft = 1.2
  Const EFFirstButtonLeft = 2.48
  Const EFBackButtonLeft = 2.81
  Const EFNextButtonLeft = 3.37
  Const EFLastButtonLeft = 3.93

  Const EFBannerTop = .06
  Const EFBannerHeight = .3
  Const EFBannerFontSize = 14
```

```
Const EFInstructionsLeft = .13
Const EFInstructionsTop = .44
Const EFInstructionsHeight = 1.44
Const EFInstructionsWidth = 4.16

Const EFQuestionLeft = .13
Const EFQuestionTop = .06
Const EFQuestionHeight = .69
Const EFQuestionWidth = 4.17
Const EFQuestionFontSize = 10

Const EFOptionGroupLeft = .13
Const EFOptionGroupTop = .94
Const EFOptionGroupWidth = 4.17
Const EFOptionGroupHeight = 1.05

Const EFAnswerOptionButtonLeft1 = .38
Const EFAnswerOptionButtonLeft2 = 2.41

Const EFAnswerOptionButtonTop1 = .84
Const EFAnswerOptionButtonTop2 = 1.24
Const EFAnswerOptionButtonTop3 = 1.64

Const EFAnswerLabelLeft1 = .56
Const EFAnswerLabelLeft2 = 2.59

Const EFAnswerLabelTop1 = .81
Const EFAnswerLabelTop2 = 1.21
Const EFAnswerLabelTop3 = 1.61

Const EFAnswerLabelWidth = 1.6
Const EFAnswerLabelHeight = .34

Const EFWriteInLeft = .44
Const EFWriteInTop = 1.08
Const EFWriteInHeight = .62
Const EFWriteInWidth = 3.48

Const EFRangeOptionButtonLeft = .44
Const EFRangeLabelLeft = .62
Const EFRangeSpacing = .72

Const EFRangeOptionButtonTop1 = 1.11
Const EFRangeOptionButtonTop2 = 1.53
Const EFRangeLabelTop1 = 1.08
Const EFRangeLabelTop2 = 1.5
Const EFRangeLabelHeight = .2
Const EFRangeLabelWidth = .42

Dim mintEFHorizontalPages As Integer
Dim mintEFVerticalPages As Integer
Dim mintEFPages As Integer
```

The *BuildEntryForm* Function

The lengthy BuildEntryForm function, shown in Listing 18.42, builds the Entry Form.

Following the listing, I'll take the time to detail what is happening in the function. This will help you if you're interested in customizing the function or want to build your own multi-page form wizard. If you aren't interested in all of the gory details, you can skip it.

Listing 18.42. The BuildEntryForm **function.**

```
Function BuildEntryForm () As Integer

  Dim q As zSW_Question

  Dim frm As Form
  Dim blnFormOpened As Integer

  Dim ctl As Control

  Dim strTitle As String
  Dim strFormName As String
  Dim strControl As String
  Dim sz As String
  Dim cr As String

  Dim lngFrom As Long
  Dim lngTo As Long
  Dim lngStep As Long
  Dim l As Long

  Dim dblOptionButtonTop As Double
  Dim dblOptionButtonLeft As Double
  Dim dblLabelTop As Double
  Dim dblLabelLeft As Double

  Dim intVerticalPage As Integer      ' 0-based
  Dim intHorizontalPage As Integer    ' 1-based

  Dim intTopOffset As Integer
  Dim intLeftOffset As Integer
  Dim intQuestion As Integer
  Dim n As Integer

  Dim blnCreateButtons As Integer

' Assume failure
  BuildEntryForm = True

  blnFormOpened = False

  On Error GoTo BuildEntryFormError

  cr = Chr$(13) & Chr$(10)

' Create the form object, defaulting to the current database and the
' current form template.
```

```
    Set frm = CreateForm("", "")
    blnFormOpened = True

    strFormName = frm.FormName

' Add the word "Survey" to the title if it isn't already there
    strTitle = Trim$(zSWfrm!cboSurveyTitle)
    If InStr(1, strTitle, "Survey") = 0 Then
      strTitle = strTitle & " Survey"
    End If

' Turn on the form header and footer
' 3 = Form Design menu, 3 = Format, 10 = Form Header/Footer
    DoCmd DoMenuItem 3, 3, 10, , A_MENU_VER20

' Number of pages is number of questions plus one for the instruction page
    mintEFPages = zSWintTotalQuestions + 2
    If mintEFPages > 55 Then
      MsgBox "53 is the maximum number of questions available on a survey entry
      ➥ form. Any extra questions will not be used.", 48, mstrProgramName
      mintEFPages = 55
    End If

' Determine number of horizontal and vertical pages

    mintEFVerticalPages = CInt(EFMaximumDetailHeight / EFDetailHeight)
    If mintEFVerticalPages > mintEFPages Then
        mintEFVerticalPages = mintEFPages
    End If

    mintEFHorizontalPages = mintEFPages / mintEFVerticalPages
    If mintEFPages Mod mintEFVerticalPages Then
        mintEFHorizontalPages = mintEFHorizontalPages + 1
    End If

' Set page dimensions
    frm.Section(Header).Height = zTwips(EFHeaderHeight)
    frm.Section(Footer).Height = zTwips(EFFooterHeight)
    frm.Section(Detail).Height = zTwips(EFDetailHeight) * mintEFVerticalPages
    frm.Width = zTwips(EFSectionWidth) * mintEFHorizontalPages

' Set form properties
    frm.RecordSource = zSWstrResponsesTable
    frm.Caption = strTitle
    frm.OnOpen = "=zVCR2OnOpen(Form," & mintEFPages & "," &
    ➥ zTwips(EFDetailHeight) & "," & zTwips(EFSectionWidth) & ")"
    frm.OnClose = "=zVCR2BoundOnClose(Form)"
    frm.DefaultView = 0 ' Single form
    frm.ScrollBars = 0 ' None
    frm.PopUp = True
    frm.Modal = True
    frm.RecordSelectors = False
    frm.NavigationButtons = False
    frm.BorderStyle = Dialog

' These properties make it so the form may enter only new records
    frm.AllowEditing = -1    ' Available
    frm.DefaultEditing = 1   ' Data Entry
```

continues

Listing 18.42. continued

```
' Page Header
  frm.Section(Header).Visible = False

' Detail section
  frm.Section(Detail).BackColor = Gray

' Page Footer
  frm.Section(Footer).BackColor = Gray
  frm.Section(Footer).SpecialEffect = Raised

' Create the instructions page

' Banner
  Set ctl = CreateControl(strFormName, ControlTypeLabel, Detail, "", "", 0,
  ➥ zTwips(EFBannerTop))
  ctl.ControlName = "lblBanner"
  ctl.FontName = EFFontName
  ctl.FontSize = EFBannerFontSize
  ctl.ForeColor = Blue
  ctl.BackStyle = BackStyleClear
  ctl.TextAlign = TextAlignCenter

  ctl.Caption = strTitle & " Instructions"

  ctl.Height = zTwips(EFBannerHeight)
  ctl.Width = zTwips(EFSectionWidth)

' Instructions
  Set ctl = CreateControl(strFormName, ControlTypeLabel, Detail, "", "",
  ➥ zTwips(EFInstructionsLeft), zTwips(EFInstructionsTop))
  ctl.ControlName = "lblInstructions"
  ctl.FontName = EFFontName
  ctl.FontSize = EFFontSize
  ctl.ForeColor = Black
  ctl.BackStyle = BackStyleClear
  ctl.TextAlign = TextAlignLeft
  ctl.Height = zTwips(EFInstructionsHeight)
  ctl.Width = zTwips(EFInstructionsWidth)

  sz = "To take this on-line survey, use the buttons at the bottom of the
  ➥ window to navigate from question to question." & cr & cr
  sz = sz & "At the last question, an OK button will appear. Press it to end
  ➥ the survey and save all of your responses." & cr & cr
  sz = sz & "The Cancel button may be used at any time if you wish to quit
  ➥ without saving your responses."
  ctl.Caption = sz

' Need a control to get focus

' First hidden control
  Set ctl = CreateControl(strFormName, ControlTypeCommandButton, Detail, "",
  ➥ "", intLeftOffset, intTopOffset + zTwips(.1), 0, 0)
  ctl.ControlName = "cmdFirstControl1"
  ctl.Transparent = True
  ctl.OnEnter = "=zVCR2GotoControl(" & Chr$(34) & "cmdWait" & Chr$(34) & ",1)"
```

```
' Control to receive focus
  Set ctl = CreateControl(strFormName, ControlTypeCommandButton, Detail, "",
➥ "", intLeftOffset, intTopOffset + zTwips(.2), 0, 0)
  ctl.ControlName = "cmdWait"
  ctl.Transparent = True

' Last hidden control
  Set ctl = CreateControl(strFormName, ControlTypeCommandButton, Detail, "",
➥ "", intLeftOffset, intTopOffset + zTwips(.3), 0, 0)
  ctl.ControlName = "cmdLastControl1"
  ctl.Transparent = True
  ctl.OnEnter = "=zVCR2GotoControl(" & Chr$(34) & "cmdWait" & Chr$(34) & ",1)"

  intVerticalPage = 1
  intHorizontalPage = 1
  blnCreateButtons = True

' Create a page for each question

  For intQuestion = 1 To zSWintTotalQuestions + 1

    intTopOffset = zTwips(EFDetailHeight) * intVerticalPage
    intLeftOffset = zTwips(EFSectionWidth) * (intHorizontalPage - 1)

    If intVerticalPage = 0 Then
      blnCreateButtons = True
    End If

    If blnCreateButtons Then
      blnCreateButtons = False

    ' Create the VCR control buttons

    ' OK
      Set ctl = CreateControl(strFormName, ControlTypeCommandButton, Footer,
➥ "", "", zTwips(EFOKButtonLeft) + intLeftOffset, zTwips(EFButtonTop),
➥ zTwips(EFButtonWidth), zTwips(EFButtonHeight))
      EFCommandButton ctl, "cmdOK" & intHorizontalPage, "OK", "=zVCR2OK()"
      ctl.Default = True
      ctl.Visible = False

    ' Cancel
      Set ctl = CreateControl(strFormName, ControlTypeCommandButton, Footer,
➥ "", "", zTwips(EFCancelButtonLeft) + intLeftOffset,
➥ zTwips(EFButtonTop), zTwips(EFButtonWidth), zTwips(EFButtonHeight))
      EFCommandButton ctl, "cmdCancel" & intHorizontalPage, "&Cancel",
➥ "=zVCR2Cancel()"
      ctl.Cancel = True

    ' First
      Set ctl = CreateControl(strFormName, ControlTypeCommandButton, Footer,
➥ "", "", zTwips(EFFirstButtonLeft) + intLeftOffset,
➥ zTwips(EFButtonTop), zTwips(EFShortButtonWidth),
➥ zTwips(EFButtonHeight))
      EFCommandButton ctl, "cmdFirst" & intHorizontalPage, "¦&<<",
➥ "=zVCR2First()"
```

continues

Listing 18.42. continued

```
' Back
  Set ctl = CreateControl(strFormName, ControlTypeCommandButton, Footer,
  ➡ "", "", zTwips(EFBackButtonLeft) + intLeftOffset,
  ➡ zTwips(EFButtonTop), zTwips(EFButtonWidth), zTwips(EFButtonHeight))
  EFCommandButton ctl, "cmdBack" & intHorizontalPage, "< &Back",
  ➡ "=zVCR2Back()"

' Next
  Set ctl = CreateControl(strFormName, ControlTypeCommandButton, Footer,
  ➡ "", "", zTwips(EFNextButtonLeft) + intLeftOffset,
  ➡ zTwips(EFButtonTop), zTwips(EFButtonWidth), zTwips(EFButtonHeight))
  EFCommandButton ctl, "cmdNext" & intHorizontalPage, "&Next >",
  ➡ "=zVCR2Next()"

' Last
  Set ctl = CreateControl(strFormName, ControlTypeCommandButton, Footer,
  ➡ "", "", zTwips(EFLastButtonLeft) + intLeftOffset,
  ➡ zTwips(EFButtonTop), zTwips(EFShortButtonWidth),
  ➡ zTwips(EFButtonHeight))
  EFCommandButton ctl, "cmdLast" & intHorizontalPage, ">&>¦",
  ➡ "=zVCR2Last()"
End If

' Page Break
If intHorizontalPage = 1 Then
  If intVerticalPage < mintEFVerticalPages Then
    Set ctl = CreateControl(strFormName, ControlTypePageBreak, Detail, "",
    ➡ "", 0, intVerticalPage * zTwips(EFDetailHeight))
    ctl.ControlName = "pgb" & intVerticalPage
  End If
End If

If intQuestion <= zSWintTotalQuestions Then

  q = zSWaQuestion(intQuestion)

  Select Case q.intType

  Case zSWQuestionTypeWriteIn
    strControl = "txtQuestion" & intQuestion

  Case Else
    strControl = "optQuestion" & intQuestion

  End Select

' First hidden control
  Set ctl = CreateControl(strFormName, ControlTypeCommandButton, Detail,
  ➡ "", "", intLeftOffset, intTopOffset + zTwips(.1), 0, 0)
  ctl.ControlName = "cmdFirstControl" & intQuestion + 1
  ctl.Transparent = True
  ctl.OnEnter = "=zVCR2GotoControl(" & Chr$(34) & strControl & Chr$(34) &
  ➡ "," & intQuestion + 1 & ")"

' Question
  Set ctl = CreateControl(strFormName, ControlTypeLabel, Detail, "", "",
  ➡ intLeftOffset + zTwips(EFQuestionLeft), intTopOffset +
  ➡ zTwips(EFQuestionTop))
```

```
    ctl.ControlName = "lblQuestion" & intQuestion
    ctl.FontName = EFFontName
    ctl.FontSize = EFQuestionFontSize
    ctl.ForeColor = Blue
    ctl.BackStyle = BackStyleClear
    ctl.TextAlign = TextAlignLeft
    ctl.Height = zTwips(EFQuestionHeight)
    ctl.Width = zTwips(EFQuestionWidth)
    ctl.Caption = q.strQuestion

' Answer Type

    If q.intType <> zSWQuestionTypeWriteIn Then
    ' Option group
      Set ctl = CreateControl(strFormName, ControlTypeOptionGroup, Detail,
      ➥ "", "", intLeftOffset + zTwips(EFOptionGroupLeft), intTopOffset +
      ➥ zTwips(EFOptionGroupTop), zTwips(EFOptionGroupWidth),
      ➥ zTwips(EFOptionGroupHeight))
      ctl.ControlName = "optQuestion" & intQuestion
      ctl.ControlSource = "Question" & intQuestion
      ctl.BorderStyle = 0 ' Clear
    End If

    Select Case q.intType

    Case zSWQuestionTypeYesNo
      EFOptionButton strFormName, intQuestion, "Yes", -1, "Yes",
      ➥ intLeftOffset, intTopOffset, EFRangeOptionButtonLeft +
      ➥ EFRangeSpacing, EFRangeOptionButtonTop1, EFRangeLabelLeft +
      ➥ EFRangeSpacing, EFRangeLabelTop1, q.intType
      EFOptionButton strFormName, intQuestion, "No", 0, "No", intLeftOffset,
      ➥ intTopOffset, EFRangeOptionButtonLeft + EFRangeSpacing * 3#,
      ➥ EFRangeOptionButtonTop1, EFRangeLabelLeft + EFRangeSpacing * 3,
      ➥ EFRangeLabelTop1, q.intType

    Case zSWQuestionTypeMultipleChoice
      EFOptionButton strFormName, intQuestion, "A", 1, q.strA,
      ➥ intLeftOffset, intTopOffset, EFAnswerOptionButtonLeft1,
      ➥ EFAnswerOptionButtonTop1, EFAnswerLabelLeft1, EFAnswerLabelTop1,
      ➥ q.intType
      EFOptionButton strFormName, intQuestion, "B", 2, q.strB,
      ➥ intLeftOffset, intTopOffset, EFAnswerOptionButtonLeft1,
      ➥ EFAnswerOptionButtonTop2, EFAnswerLabelLeft1, EFAnswerLabelTop2,
      ➥ q.intType
      EFOptionButton strFormName, intQuestion, "C", 3, q.strC,
      ➥ intLeftOffset, intTopOffset, EFAnswerOptionButtonLeft1,
      ➥ EFAnswerOptionButtonTop3, EFAnswerLabelLeft1, EFAnswerLabelTop3,
      ➥ q.intType
      EFOptionButton strFormName, intQuestion, "D", 4, q.strD,
      ➥ intLeftOffset, intTopOffset, EFAnswerOptionButtonLeft2,
      ➥ EFAnswerOptionButtonTop1, EFAnswerLabelLeft2, EFAnswerLabelTop1,
      ➥ q.intType
      EFOptionButton strFormName, intQuestion, "E", 5, q.strE,
      ➥ intLeftOffset, intTopOffset, EFAnswerOptionButtonLeft2,
      ➥ EFAnswerOptionButtonTop2, EFAnswerLabelLeft2, EFAnswerLabelTop2,
      ➥ q.intType
      EFOptionButton strFormName, intQuestion, "F", 6, q.strF,
```

continues

Listing 18.42. continued

```
    ➥ intLeftOffset, intTopOffset, EFAnswerOptionButtonLeft2,
    ➥ EFAnswerOptionButtonTop3, EFAnswerLabelLeft2, EFAnswerLabelTop3,
    ➥ q.intType

  Case zSWQuestionTypeWriteIn
    Set ctl = CreateControl(strFormName, ControlTypeTextbox, Detail, "",
    ➥ "", intLeftOffset + zTwips(EFWriteInLeft), intTopOffset +
    ➥ zTwips(EFWriteInTop), zTwips(EFWriteInWidth),
    ➥ zTwips(EFWriteInHeight))
    ctl.ControlName = "txtQuestion" & intQuestion
    ctl.ControlSource = "Question" & intQuestion
    ctl.FontName = EFFontName
    ctl.FontSize = EFFontSize
    ctl.SpecialEffect = 2 ' Sunken

  Case zSWQuestionTypeRange, zSWQuestionTypePercent

    If q.intType = zSWQuestionTypeRange Then
      lngFrom = q.lngRangeFrom
      lngTo = q.lngRangeTo
      lngStep = q.lngRangeStep
    Else
      lngFrom = CLng(q.intPercentFrom)
      lngTo = CLng(q.intPercentTo)
      lngStep = CLng(q.intPercentStep)
    End If

    If zSWValidatePoints(lngFrom, lngTo, lngStep) Then
      n = 1
      dblOptionButtonTop = EFRangeOptionButtonTop1
      dblLabelTop = EFRangeLabelTop1
      dblOptionButtonLeft = EFRangeOptionButtonLeft
      dblLabelLeft = EFRangeLabelLeft

      For l = lngFrom To lngTo Step lngStep
        EFOptionButton strFormName, intQuestion, CStr(l), l, Cstr(l),
        ➥ intLeftOffset, intTopOffset, dblOptionButtonLeft, dblOptionButtonTop,
        ➥ dblLabelLeft, dblLabelTop, q.intType
        n = n + 1
        If n = 6 Then
          dblOptionButtonTop = EFRangeOptionButtonTop2
          dblLabelTop = EFRangeLabelTop2
          dblOptionButtonLeft = EFRangeOptionButtonLeft
          dblLabelLeft = EFRangeLabelLeft
        Else
          dblOptionButtonLeft = dblOptionButtonLeft + EFRangeSpacing
          dblLabelLeft = dblLabelLeft + EFRangeSpacing
        End If
      Next l
    End If

  End Select

' Second hidden control
  Set ctl = CreateControl(strFormName, ControlTypeCommandButton, Detail,
  ➥ "", "", intLeftOffset, intTopOffset + zTwips(.2), 0, 0)
```

```
      ctl.ControlName = "cmdLastControl" & intQuestion + 1
      ctl.Transparent = True
      ctl.OnEnter = "=zVCR2GotoControl(" & Chr$(34) & strControl & Chr$(34) &
  ➥ "," & intQuestion + 1 & ")"

      intVerticalPage = intVerticalPage + 1
      If intVerticalPage = mintEFVerticalPages Then
        intHorizontalPage = intHorizontalPage + 1
        intVerticalPage = 0
      End If
    End If
  End If

Next intQuestion

' Thank you screen banner
Set ctl = CreateControl(strFormName, ControlTypeLabel, Detail, "", "",
➥ intLeftOffset, intTopOffset + zTwips(EFBannerTop))
ctl.ControlName = "lblBanner2"
ctl.FontName = EFFontName
ctl.FontSize = EFBannerFontSize
ctl.ForeColor = Blue
ctl.BackStyle = BackStyleClear
ctl.TextAlign = TextAlignCenter
ctl.Caption = strTitle

ctl.Height = zTwips(EFBannerHeight)
ctl.Width = zTwips(EFSectionWidth)

' Thank you screen instructions
Set ctl = CreateControl(strFormName, ControlTypeLabel, Detail, "", "",
➥ intLeftOffset + zTwips(EFInstructionsLeft), intTopOffset +
➥ zTwips(EFInstructionsTop))
ctl.ControlName = "lblThankYou"
ctl.FontName = EFFontName
ctl.FontSize = EFFontSize
ctl.ForeColor = Black
ctl.BackStyle = BackStyleClear
ctl.TextAlign = TextAlignLeft
ctl.Height = zTwips(EFInstructionsHeight)
ctl.Width = zTwips(EFInstructionsWidth)
sz = "Thanks for completing the survey!" & cr & cr
sz = sz & "Press the OK button to save your responses to the survey "
sz = sz & "or press Cancel if you do not wish to enter anything at this
➥ time." & cr & cr
ctl.Caption = sz

' Thank you screen first hidden control
Set ctl = CreateControl(strFormName, ControlTypeCommandButton, Detail, "",
➥ "", intLeftOffset, intTopOffset + zTwips(.1), 0, 0)
ctl.ControlName = "cmdFirstControl" & zSWintTotalQuestions + 2
ctl.Transparent = True
ctl.OnEnter = "=zVCR2GotoControl(" & Chr$(34) & "cmdWait2" & Chr$(34) & ","
➥ & zSWintTotalQuestions + 2 & ")"

' Control to receive focus
Set ctl = CreateControl(strFormName, ControlTypeCommandButton, Detail, "",
➥ "", intLeftOffset, intTopOffset + zTwips(.2), 0, 0)
ctl.ControlName = "cmdWait2"
```

continues

Listing 18.42. continued

```
ctl.Transparent = True

' Thank you screen last hidden control
    Set ctl = CreateControl(strFormName, ControlTypeCommandButton, Detail, "",
    ➥ "", intLeftOffset, intTopOffset + zTwips(.3), 0, 0)
    ctl.ControlName = "cmdLastControl" & zSWintTotalQuestions + 2
    ctl.Transparent = True
    ctl.OnEnter = "=zVCR2GotoControl(" & Chr$(34) & "cmdWait2" & Chr$(34) & ","
    ➥ & zSWintTotalQuestions + 2 & ")"

' Success
    BuildEntryForm = False

BuildEntryFormDone:
  On Error Resume Next
  If blnFormOpened Then
    DoCmd SetWarnings False
    SendKeys zSWstrEntryForm & "~"
    DoCmd Close A_Form, frm.Name
    DoCmd SetWarnings True
  End If
  Exit Function

BuildEntryFormError:
  Warning "BuildEntryForm", Error$
  Resume BuildEntryFormDone

End Function
```

The form is initially created by calling the `CreateForm` function, as shown in Listing 18.43.

Listing 18.43. Creating the Entry Form.

```
  Set frm = CreateForm("", "")
  blnFormOpened = True

  strFormName = frm.FormName

' Add the word "Survey" to the title if it isn't already there
  strTitle = Trim$(zSWfrm!cboSurveyTitle)
  If InStr(1, strTitle, "Survey") = 0 Then
    strTitle = strTitle & " Survey"
  End If
```

The Form Header and Footer are turned on so that you have a footer section to drop VCR buttons into.

```
' Turn on the form header and footer
' 3 = Form Design menu, 3 = Format, 10 = Form Header/Footer
  DoCmd DoMenuItem 3, 3, 10, , A_MENU_VER20
```

Next, the number of pages is calculated (see Listing 18.44). The user is told if any questions will have to be dropped because of the 53-page limit.

Listing 18.44. Calculate the number of pages in the multiple-page form.

```
' Number of pages is number of questions plus one for the instruction page
  mintEFPages = zSWintTotalQuestions + 2
  If mintEFPages > 55 Then
    MsgBox "53 is the maximum number of questions available on a survey entry
    ➥ form. Any extra questions will not be used.", 48, mstrProgramName
    mintEFPages = 55
  End If
```

The function calculates how many pages down the form will go. This is needed to determine the height of the Detail section.

```
' Determine number of horizontal and vertical pages

  mintEFVerticalPages = CInt(EFMaximumDetailHeight / EFDetailHeight)
  If mintEFVerticalPages > mintEFPages Then
      mintEFVerticalPages = mintEFPages
  End If
```

The number of page columns is calculated in order to know how wide to make the form.

```
  mintEFHorizontalPages = mintEFPages / mintEFVerticalPages
  If mintEFPages Mod mintEFVerticalPages Then
      mintEFHorizontalPages = mintEFHorizontalPages + 1
  End If
```

The form's section Height and Width properties are set using the measurements just taken.

```
' Set page dimensions
  frm.Section(Header).Height = zTwips(EFHeaderHeight)
  frm.Section(Footer).Height = zTwips(EFFooterHeight)
  frm.Section(Detail).Height = zTwips(EFDetailHeight) * mintEFVerticalPages
  frm.Width = zTwips(EFSectionWidth) * mintEFHorizontalPages
```

Many of the form's properties are set, including the Record Source and On Open and On Close events (see Listing 18.45).

Listing 18.45. Setting the form properties.

```
' Set form properties
  frm.RecordSource = zSWstrResponsesTable
  frm.Caption = strTitle
  frm.OnOpen = "=zVCR2OnOpen(Form," & mintEFPages & "," &
    ➡ zTwips(EFDetailHeight) & "," & zTwips(EFSectionWidth) & ")"
  frm.OnClose = "=zVCR2BoundOnClose(Form)"
  frm.DefaultView = 0 ' Single form
  frm.ScrollBars = 0 ' None
  frm.PopUp = True
  frm.Modal = True
  frm.RecordSelectors = False
  frm.NavigationButtons = False
  frm.BorderStyle = Dialog

' These properties make it so the form may enter only new records
  frm.AllowEditing = -1   ' Available
  frm.DefaultEditing = 1   ' Data Entry

' Page Header
  frm.Section(Header).Visible = False

' Detail section
  frm.Section(Detail).BackColor = Gray

' Page Footer
  frm.Section(Footer).BackColor = Gray
  frm.Section(Footer).SpecialEffect = Raised
```

Next, banner and instruction labels are created on the first page of the form. A message is constructed, then set to display in the instructions label by setting its Caption property. See Listing 18.46.

Listing 18.46. Creating controls on the first page.

```
' Create the instructions page

' Banner
  Set ctl = CreateControl(strFormName, ControlTypeLabel, Detail, "", "", 0,
    ➡ zTwips(EFBannerTop))
  ctl.ControlName = "lblBanner"
  ctl.FontName = EFFontName
  ctl.FontSize = EFBannerFontSize
  ctl.ForeColor = Blue
  ctl.BackStyle = BackStyleClear
  ctl.TextAlign = TextAlignCenter

  ctl.Caption = strTitle & " Instructions"

  ctl.Height = zTwips(EFBannerHeight)
  ctl.Width = zTwips(EFSectionWidth)
```

```
' Instructions
 Set ctl = CreateControl(strFormName, ControlTypeLabel, Detail, "", "",
➡ zTwips(EFInstructionsLeft), zTwips(EFInstructionsTop))
 ctl.ControlName = "lblInstructions"
 ctl.FontName = EFFontName
 ctl.FontSize = EFFontSize
 ctl.ForeColor = Black
 ctl.BackStyle = BackStyleClear
 ctl.TextAlign = TextAlignLeft
 ctl.Height = zTwips(EFInstructionsHeight)
 ctl.Width = zTwips(EFInstructionsWidth)

 sz = "To take this on-line survey, use the buttons at the bottom of the
➡ window to navigate from question to question." & cr & cr
 sz = sz & "At the last question, an OK button will appear. Press it to end
➡ the survey and save all of your responses." & cr & cr
 sz = sz & "The Cancel button may be used at any time if you wish to quit
➡ without saving your responses."
 ctl.Caption = sz
```

Just as our Survey Wizard form needed to have tab sentries, so does the generated Entry Form. These controls are command buttons that are hidden by setting their height and width to zero and having their transparent property set to True.

On the first page, you also need to generate a control that can receive focus, because the two labels can't. A hidden cmdWait command button is created for this purpose. (See Listing 18.47.)

Listing 18.47. Creating tab sentries and a cmdWait command button.

```
' Need a control to get focus

' First hidden control
 Set ctl = CreateControl(strFormName, ControlTypeCommandButton, Detail, "",
➡ "", intLeftOffset, intTopOffset + zTwips(.1), 0, 0)
 ctl.ControlName = "cmdFirstControl1"
 ctl.Transparent = True
 ctl.OnEnter = "=zVCR2GotoControl(" & Chr$(34) & "cmdWait" & Chr$(34) & ",1)"

' Control to receive focus
 Set ctl = CreateControl(strFormName, ControlTypeCommandButton, Detail, "",
➡ "", intLeftOffset, intTopOffset + zTwips(.2), 0, 0)
 ctl.ControlName = "cmdWait"
 ctl.Transparent = True

' Last hidden control
 Set ctl = CreateControl(strFormName, ControlTypeCommandButton, Detail, "",
➡ "", intLeftOffset, intTopOffset + zTwips(.3), 0, 0)
 ctl.ControlName = "cmdLastControl1"
 ctl.Transparent = True
 ctl.OnEnter = "=zVCR2GotoControl(" & Chr$(34) & "cmdWait" & Chr$(34) & ",1)"
```

With the first page completed and ready to hold user instructions, the program now enters a loop that creates a page for each question.

The `intVerticalPage` and `intHorizontal` page variables keep track of which page you're working on. The `blnCreateButtons` variable is a flag that when True indicates to code that follows it that it's time to create VCR buttons for a column of pages. (See Listing 18.48.)

Listing 18.48. Entering loop to generate each page.

```
intVerticalPage = 1
intHorizontalPage = 1
blnCreateButtons = True

' Create a page for each question

For intQuestion = 1 To zSWintTotalQuestions + 1
```

The `intTopOffset` and `intLeftOffset` variables hold the coordinates in twips of the top-left position of the page being created.

```
intTopOffset = zTwips(EFDetailHeight) * intVerticalPage
intLeftOffset = zTwips(EFSectionWidth) * (intHorizontalPage - 1)
```

If this is the first question within a column of pages, the VCR buttons need to be created for the column.

To save some repetitive typing, the properties for each button are set by calling the `EFCommandButton` subroutine. Its fourth argument is the code to activate for the button's On Click event. (See Listing 18.49.)

Listing 18.49. Creating the VCR command buttons.

```
If intVerticalPage = 0 Then
  blnCreateButtons = True
End If

If blnCreateButtons Then
  blnCreateButtons = False

' Create the VCR control buttons

' OK
  Set ctl = CreateControl(strFormName, ControlTypeCommandButton, Footer,
➥ "", "", zTwips(EFOKButtonLeft) + intLeftOffset, zTwips(EFButtonTop),
➥ zTwips(EFButtonWidth), zTwips(EFButtonHeight))
  EFCommandButton ctl, "cmdOK" & intHorizontalPage, "OK", "=zVCR2OK()"
  ctl.Default = True
  ctl.Visible = False
```

```
' Cancel
  Set ctl = CreateControl(strFormName, ControlTypeCommandButton, Footer,
  ➥ "", "", zTwips(EFCancelButtonLeft) + intLeftOffset,
  ➥ zTwips(EFButtonTop), zTwips(EFButtonWidth), zTwips(EFButtonHeight))
  EFCommandButton ctl, "cmdCancel" & intHorizontalPage, "&Cancel",
  ➥ "=zVCR2Cancel()"
  ctl.Cancel = True

' First
  Set ctl = CreateControl(strFormName, ControlTypeCommandButton, Footer,
  ➥ "", "", zTwips(EFFirstButtonLeft) + intLeftOffset,
  ➥ zTwips(EFButtonTop), zTwips(EFShortButtonWidth),
  ➥ zTwips(EFButtonHeight))
  EFCommandButton ctl, "cmdFirst" & intHorizontalPage, "¦&<<",
  ➥ "=zVCR2First()"

' Back
  Set ctl = CreateControl(strFormName, ControlTypeCommandButton, Footer,
  ➥ "", "", zTwips(EFBackButtonLeft) + intLeftOffset,
  ➥ zTwips(EFButtonTop), zTwips(EFButtonWidth), zTwips(EFButtonHeight))
  EFCommandButton ctl, "cmdBack" & intHorizontalPage, "< &Back",
  ➥ "=zVCR2Back()"

' Next
  Set ctl = CreateControl(strFormName, ControlTypeCommandButton, Footer,
  ➥ "", "", zTwips(EFNextButtonLeft) + intLeftOffset,
  ➥ zTwips(EFButtonTop), zTwips(EFButtonWidth), zTwips(EFButtonHeight))
  EFCommandButton ctl, "cmdNext" & intHorizontalPage, "&Next >",
  ➥ "=zVCR2Next()"

' Last
  Set ctl = CreateControl(strFormName, ControlTypeCommandButton, Footer,
  ➥ "", "", zTwips(EFLastButtonLeft) + intLeftOffset,
  ➥ zTwips(EFButtonTop), zTwips(EFShortButtonWidth),
  ➥ zTwips(EFButtonHeight))
  EFCommandButton ctl, "cmdLast" & intHorizontalPage, ">&>¦",
  ➥ "=zVCR2Last()"
End If
```

A page break control is created for each page that falls on the first column (except the last page). (See Listing 18.50.)

Listing 18.50. Creating a page break control.

```
' Page Break
  If intHorizontalPage = 1 Then
    If intVerticalPage < mintEFVerticalPages Then
      Set ctl = CreateControl(strFormName, ControlTypePageBreak, Detail, "",
      ➥ "", 0, intVerticalPage * zTwips(EFDetailHeight))
      ctl.ControlName = "pgb" & intVerticalPage
    End If
  End If
```

Next, the function determines the name of the control that is to receive focus when entering this page. (See Listing 18.51.)

Listing 18.51. Getting the name of the first control to receive focus on the page.

```
q = zSWaQuestion(intQuestion)

Select Case q.intType

Case zSWQuestionTypeWriteIn
  strControl = "txtQuestion" & intQuestion

Case Else
  strControl = "optQuestion" & intQuestion

End Select
```

The first hidden control is generated for the page, and then the label that displays text for this question. (See Listing 18.52.)

Listing 18.52. Creating a tab sentry and question label.

```
' First hidden control
  Set ctl = CreateControl(strFormName, ControlTypeCommandButton, Detail,
  ➥ "", "", intLeftOffset, intTopOffset + zTwips(.1), 0, 0)
  ctl.ControlName = "cmdFirstControl" & intQuestion + 1
  ctl.Transparent = True
  ctl.OnEnter = "=zVCR2GotoControl(" & Chr$(34) & strControl & Chr$(34) &
  ➥ "," & intQuestion + 1 & ")"

' Question
  Set ctl = CreateControl(strFormName, ControlTypeLabel, Detail, "", "",
  ➥ intLeftOffset + zTwips(EFQuestionLeft), intTopOffset +
  ➥ zTwips(EFQuestionTop))
  ctl.ControlName = "lblQuestion" & intQuestion
  ctl.FontName = EFFontName
  ctl.FontSize = EFQuestionFontSize
  ctl.ForeColor = Blue
  ctl.BackStyle = BackStyleClear
  ctl.TextAlign = TextAlignLeft
  ctl.Height = zTwips(EFQuestionHeight)
  ctl.Width = zTwips(EFQuestionWidth)
  ctl.Caption = q.strQuestion
```

If you aren't currently doing a Write-In type question, you need to create an option group to contain the option buttons you will be creating next. (See Listing 18.53.)

Listing 18.53. Creating a bound option group for a question.

```
' Answer Type

If q.intType <> zSWQuestionTypeWriteIn Then
' Option group
  Set ctl = CreateControl(strFormName, ControlTypeOptionGroup, Detail,
  ➡ "", "", intLeftOffset + zTwips(EFOptionGroupLeft), intTopOffset +
  ➡ zTwips(EFOptionGroupTop), zTwips(EFOptionGroupWidth),
  ➡ zTwips(EFOptionGroupHeight))
  ctl.ControlName = "optQuestion" & intQuestion
  ctl.ControlSource = "Question" & intQuestion
  ctl.BorderStyle = 0 ' Clear
End If
```

Next, the function creates the controls that users will use to select or write in their answers. For option buttons, the `EFOptionButton` subroutine is called.

Two option buttons are created for a Yes/No question. (See Listing 18.54.)

Listing 18.54. Creating a Yes/No question.

```
Select Case q.intType

Case zSWQuestionTypeYesNo
  EFOptionButton strFormName, intQuestion, "Yes", -1, "Yes",
  ➡ intLeftOffset, intTopOffset, EFRangeOptionButtonLeft +
  ➡ EFRangeSpacing, EFRangeOptionButtonTop1, EFRangeLabelLeft +
  ➡ EFRangeSpacing, EFRangeLabelTop1, q.intType
  EFOptionButton strFormName, intQuestion, "No", 0, "No", intLeftOffset,
  ➡ intTopOffset, EFRangeOptionButtonLeft + EFRangeSpacing * 3#,
  ➡ EFRangeOptionButtonTop1, EFRangeLabelLeft + EFRangeSpacing * 3,
  ➡ EFRangeLabelTop1, q.intType
```

Option buttons are created for each of the Multiple-Choice selections. (See Listing 18.55.)

Listing 18.55. Creating a Multiple-Choice question.

```
Case zSWQuestionTypeMultipleChoice
  EFOptionButton strFormName, intQuestion, "A", 1, q.strA,
  ➡ intLeftOffset, intTopOffset, EFAnswerOptionButtonLeft1,
  ➡ EFAnswerOptionButtonTop1, EFAnswerLabelLeft1, EFAnswerLabelTop1,
  ➡ q.intType
  EFOptionButton strFormName, intQuestion, "B", 2, q.strB,
  ➡ intLeftOffset, intTopOffset, EFAnswerOptionButtonLeft1,
  ➡ EFAnswerOptionButtonTop2, EFAnswerLabelLeft1, EFAnswerLabelTop2,
  ➡ q.intType
  EFOptionButton strFormName, intQuestion, "C", 3, q.strC,
```

continues

Listing 18.55. continued

```
 ➥ intLeftOffset, intTopOffset, EFAnswerOptionButtonLeft1,
 ➥ EFAnswerOptionButtonTop3, EFAnswerLabelLeft1, EFAnswerLabelTop3,
 ➥ q.intType
EFOptionButton strFormName, intQuestion, "D", 4, q.strD,
 ➥ intLeftOffset, intTopOffset, EFAnswerOptionButtonLeft2,
 ➥ EFAnswerOptionButtonTop1, EFAnswerLabelLeft2, EFAnswerLabelTop1,
 ➥ q.intType
EFOptionButton strFormName, intQuestion, "E", 5, q.strE,
 ➥ intLeftOffset, intTopOffset, EFAnswerOptionButtonLeft2,
 ➥ EFAnswerOptionButtonTop2, EFAnswerLabelLeft2, EFAnswerLabelTop2,
 ➥ q.intType
EFOptionButton strFormName, intQuestion, "F", 6, q.strF,
 ➥ intLeftOffset, intTopOffset, EFAnswerOptionButtonLeft2,
 ➥ EFAnswerOptionButtonTop3, EFAnswerLabelLeft2, EFAnswerLabelTop3,
 ➥ q.intType
```

A text box is created for entering in a Write-In answer. (See Listing 18.56.)

Listing 18.56. Creating a Write-In question.

```
Case zSWQuestionTypeWriteIn
  Set ctl = CreateControl(strFormName, ControlTypeTextbox, Detail, "",
  ➥ "", intLeftOffset + zTwips(EFWriteInLeft), intTopOffset +
  ➥ zTwips(EFWriteInTop), zTwips(EFWriteInWidth),
  ➥ zTwips(EFWriteInHeight))
  ctl.ControlName = "txtQuestion" & intQuestion
  ctl.ControlSource = "Question" & intQuestion
  ctl.FontName = EFFontName
  ctl.FontSize = EFFontSize
  ctl.SpecialEffect = 2 ' Sunken
```

Option buttons are created for selections to a Range or Percent question. (See Listing 18.57.)

Listing 18.57. Creating Range and Percent questions.

```
Case zSWQuestionTypeRange, zSWQuestionTypePercent

If q.intType = zSWQuestionTypeRange Then
  lngFrom = q.lngRangeFrom
  lngTo = q.lngRangeTo
  lngStep = q.lngRangeStep
Else
  lngFrom = CLng(q.intPercentFrom)
  lngTo = CLng(q.intPercentTo)
  lngStep = CLng(q.intPercentStep)
End If
```

```
    If zSWValidatePoints(lngFrom, lngTo, lngStep) Then
      n = 1
      dblOptionButtonTop = EFRangeOptionButtonTop1
      dblLabelTop = EFRangeLabelTop1
      dblOptionButtonLeft = EFRangeOptionButtonLeft
      dblLabelLeft = EFRangeLabelLeft

      For l = lngFrom To lngTo Step lngStep
        EFOptionButton strFormName, intQuestion, CStr(l), l, Cstr(l),
        ➡ intLeftOffset, intTopOffset, dblOptionButtonLeft, dblOptionButtonTop,
        ➡ dblLabelLeft, dblLabelTop, q.intType
        n = n + 1
        If n = 6 Then
          dblOptionButtonTop = EFRangeOptionButtonTop2
          dblLabelTop = EFRangeLabelTop2
          dblOptionButtonLeft = EFRangeOptionButtonLeft
          dblLabelLeft = EFRangeLabelLeft
        Else
          dblOptionButtonLeft = dblOptionButtonLeft + EFRangeSpacing
          dblLabelLeft = dblLabelLeft + EFRangeSpacing
        End If
      Next l
    End If

  End Select
```

A second tab sentry is created as the last control on the current page. This sentry sends focus to the option group or the text box if the current page is a Write-In question. (See Listing 18.58.)

Listing 18.58. Creating the second hidden control.

```
' Second hidden control
Set ctl = CreateControl(strFormName, ControlTypeCommandButton, Detail,
➡ "", "", intLeftOffset, intTopOffset + zTwips(.2), 0, 0)
ctl.ControlName = "cmdLastControl" & intQuestion + 1
ctl.Transparent = True
ctl.OnEnter = "=zVCR2GotoControl(" & Chr$(34) & strControl & Chr$(34) &
➡ "," & intQuestion + 1 & ")"
```

At the end of the loop for creating pages, the subroutine increments the vertical page counter. If you run out of pages in the current column, the vertical page counter is reset to 0 and the horizontal page counter is incremented to move to the next column of pages. (See Listing 18.59.)

Listing 18.59. Keeping track of the current page.

```
      intVerticalPage = intVerticalPage + 1
      If intVerticalPage = mintEFVerticalPages Then
        intHorizontalPage = intHorizontalPage + 1
        intVerticalPage = 0
      End If
    End If

  Next intQuestion
```

After all the pages that display questions are finished, the final page is created with some closing instructions on how to save the user responses. First, two labels are created to hold the survey title and the instructions.(See Listing 18.60.)

Listing 18.60. Creating controls on the last page.

```
' Thank you screen banner
  Set ctl = CreateControl(strFormName, ControlTypeLabel, Detail, "", "",
  ➥ intLeftOffset, intTopOffset + zTwips(EFBannerTop))
  ctl.ControlName = "lblBanner2"
  ctl.FontName = EFFontName
  ctl.FontSize = EFBannerFontSize
  ctl.ForeColor = Blue
  ctl.BackStyle = BackStyleClear
  ctl.TextAlign = TextAlignCenter
  ctl.Caption = strTitle

  ctl.Height = zTwips(EFBannerHeight)
  ctl.Width = zTwips(EFSectionWidth)

' Thank you screen instructions
  Set ctl = CreateControl(strFormName, ControlTypeLabel, Detail, "", "",
  ➥ intLeftOffset + zTwips(EFInstructionsLeft), intTopOffset +
  ➥ zTwips(EFInstructionsTop))
  ctl.ControlName = "lblThankYou"
  ctl.FontName = EFFontName
  ctl.FontSize = EFFontSize
  ctl.ForeColor = Black
  ctl.BackStyle = BackStyleClear
  ctl.TextAlign = TextAlignLeft
  ctl.Height = zTwips(EFInstructionsHeight)
  ctl.Width = zTwips(EFInstructionsWidth)
  sz = "Thanks for completing the survey!" & cr & cr
  sz = sz & "Press the OK button to save your responses to the survey "
  sz = sz & "or press Cancel if you do not wish to enter anything at this
  ➥ time." & cr & cr
  ctl.Caption = sz
```

Then, just like in the first page, you need to create our two hidden controls and an additional one to receive focus since you don't have any other controls that can receive focus on the last page. (See Listing 18.61.)

Listing 18.61. Creating tab sentries and `cmdWait2` on the last page.

```
' Thank you screen first hidden control
  Set ctl = CreateControl(strFormName, ControlTypeCommandButton, Detail, "",
  ➡ "", intLeftOffset, intTopOffset + zTwips(.1), 0, 0)
  ctl.ControlName = "cmdFirstControl" & zSWintTotalQuestions + 2
  ctl.Transparent = True
  ctl.OnEnter = "=zVCR2GotoControl(" & Chr$(34) & "cmdWait2" & Chr$(34) & ","
  ➡ & zSWintTotalQuestions + 2 & ")"

' Control to receive focus
  Set ctl = CreateControl(strFormName, ControlTypeCommandButton, Detail, "",
  ➡ "", intLeftOffset, intTopOffset + zTwips(.2), 0, 0)
  ctl.ControlName = "cmdWait2"
  ctl.Transparent = True

' Thank you screen last hidden control
  Set ctl = CreateControl(strFormName, ControlTypeCommandButton, Detail, "",
  ➡ "", intLeftOffset, intTopOffset + zTwips(.3), 0, 0)
  ctl.ControlName = "cmdLastControl" & zSWintTotalQuestions + 2
  ctl.Transparent = True
  ctl.OnEnter = "=zVCR2GotoControl(" & Chr$(34) & "cmdWait2" & Chr$(34) & ","
  ➡ & zSWintTotalQuestions + 2 & ")"
```

Yowee! Did you follow all of that?

The *EFOptionButton* Subroutine

The `EFOptionButton` subroutine (shown in Listing 18.62) is used in the `BuildEntryForm` function to create an option button.

Listing 18.62. The `EFOptionButton` subroutine.

```
Sub EFOptionButton (strFormName As String, intQuestion As Integer,
➡ strLetter As String, lngOptionValue As Long, strOptionText As String,
➡ intLeftOffset As Integer, intTopOffset As Integer,
➡ dblAnswerOptionButtonLeft As Double,
➡ dblAnswerOptionButtonTop As Double,
➡ dblAnswerLabelLeft As Double,
➡ dblAnswerLabelTop As Double, intType As Integer)

  Dim ctl As Control

  Dim strCaption As String

  On Error GoTo EFOptionButtonError

  If Len(strOptionText) Then
  ' Button
    Set ctl = CreateControl(strFormName, ControlTypeOptionButton, Detail,
    ➡ "optQuestion" & intQuestion, "", intLeftOffset +
    ➡ zTwips(dblAnswerOptionButtonLeft), intTopOffset +
```

continues

Listing 18.62. continued

```
    ➥ zTwips(dblAnswerOptionButtonTop))
    ctl.ControlName = "rbt" & strLetter & intQuestion
    ctl.OptionValue = lngOptionValue

  ' Label
    Set ctl = CreateControl(strFormName, ControlTypeLabel, Detail, "rbt" &
    ➥ strLetter & intQuestion, "", intLeftOffset +
    ➥ zTwips(dblAnswerLabelLeft), intTopOffset + zTwips(dblAnswerLabelTop))
    ctl.ControlName = "lbl" & strLetter & "_" & intQuestion

    Select Case intType

    Case zSWQuestionTypeMultipleChoice
      strCaption = strLetter & ") " & strOptionText

    Case zSWQuestionTypePercent
      strCaption = strOptionText & "%"

    Case Else
      strCaption = strOptionText

    End Select

    Select Case intType

    Case zSWQuestionTypeYesNo, zSWQuestionTypeRange, zSWQuestionTypePercent
      ctl.Height = zTwips(EFRangeLabelHeight)
      ctl.Width = zTwips(EFRangeLabelWidth)

    Case Else
      ctl.Height = zTwips(EFAnswerLabelHeight)
      ctl.Width = zTwips(EFAnswerLabelWidth)

    End Select

    ctl.FontName = EFFontName
    ctl.FontSize = EFFontSize
    ctl.Caption = strCaption
    ctl.BackColor = Gray
    ctl.ForeColor = Black
  End If

EFOptionButtonDone:
  Exit Sub

EFOptionButtonError:
  Warning "EFOptionButton", Error$
  Resume EFOptionButtonDone

End Sub
```

The *EFCommandButton* Subroutine

The EFCommandButton subroutine is called in the BuildEntryForm subroutine to create and set properties for a command button. See Listing 18.63.

Listing 18.63. The EFCommandButton **subroutine.**

```
Sub EFCommandButton (ctl As Control, strControlName As String,
➥ strCaption As String, strOnPush As String)

  On Error GoTo EFCommandButtonError

  ctl.FontName = EFButtonFontName
  ctl.FontSize = EFButtonFontSize
  ctl.FontWeight = FontWeightBold
  ctl.ControlName = strControlName
  ctl.Caption = strCaption
  ctl.OnPush = strOnPush

EFCommandButtonDone:
  Exit Sub

EFCommandButtonError:
  Warning "EFCommandButton", Error$
  Resume EFCommandButtonDone

End Sub
```

This completes the Entry Form build code. Figure 18.27 shows a generated form in design mode.

FIGURE 18.27.

A multiple-page form created by Survey Wizard.

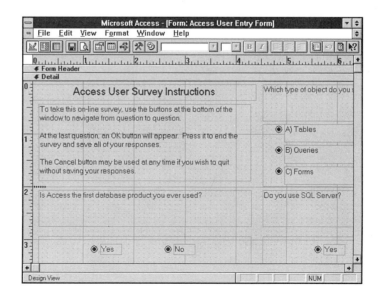

The next section lists the run-time code required to use the generated form.

The VCR2 Module

The VCR2 module is a modification of an earlier VCR module that was eventually incorporated into the Survey Wizard form module. In other words, the old VCR module got tossed in the bit bucket.

The improved VCR2 module will handle our cool new multiple-page forms that take advantage of the maximum width of the form object in order to squeeze out more page real estate. I discussed this neat discovery while designing Survey Wizard's Entry Form.

An advantage of having VCR2 in a module is that you could potentially use it with other non-Survey Wizard forms created by a program or manually. You will have to make sure you build your form appropriately. Review how the `BuildEntryForm` function generates the Entry Form if you wish to do this.

The VCR2 module declares several module-level variables to keep track of the status of the displayed form. (See Listing 18.64.)

Listing 18.64. The VCR2 declarations section.

```
' VCR2 module

  Option Compare Database
  Option Explicit

  Const mstrProgramName = "VCR2 Dialog Control"
  Const TwipsPerInch = 1440

  Dim mfrm As Form

  Dim mintCurrentPage As Integer
  Dim mintLastPage As Integer
  Dim mintHorizontalPage As Integer

  Dim mintPageHeight As Integer
  Dim mintPageWidth As Integer
  Dim mintPagesPerColumn As Integer
  Dim mintColumns As Integer

  Dim mblnVCR2OK  As Integer
  Dim mblnVCR2Cancel  As Integer
  Dim mblnNext As Integer
```

The VCR2 module also has its own copy of the `Warning` subroutine. (See Listing 18.65.)

Listing 18.65. The `Warning` **subroutine.**

```
Private Sub Warning (strProcedure As String, msg As String)

  zDisplayError strProcedure, msg, mstrProgramName

End Sub
```

The *zVCR2OnOpen* Function

The `zVCR2OnOpen` function, shown in Listing 18.66, gets activated on the form's On Open event while the form is opening.

The subroutine initializes the variables within the declaration section, sizes the form and centers it, and then initializes the VCR buttons as to whether they are visible or enabled.

You use the `zCenterForm` function from the Form module here to center the form because setting the AutoCenter property doesn't center the form correctly.

This is just a guess, but the centering done through AutoCenter most likely occurs before our use of the MoveSize macro action has any effect, so the AutoCenter centering is based on the actual width of the form, even if it is many columns of pages wide.

Listing 18.66. The `zVCR2OnOpen` **function.**

```
Function zVCR2OnOpen (frmArg As Form, intPages As Integer,
➥ intPageHeightArg As Integer, intPageWidthArg As Integer) As Integer

  Dim sz As String
  Dim v As Variant
  Dim n As Integer
  Dim z As Integer

  On Error GoTo zVCR2OnOpenError

  mintLastPage = intPages
  mintCurrentPage = 1

  mintPageHeight = intPageHeightArg
  mintPageWidth = intPageWidthArg

  mintPagesPerColumn = (22 * TwipsPerInch) / mintPageHeight
  mintColumns = (intPages - 1) / mintPagesPerColumn + 1

  DoCmd MoveSize , , mintPageWidth + 16  ' Add 16 for border width

' Use the API to center the form, because AutoCenter will center based on
' the actual width of the form, not just what is displayed.
```

continues

Listing 18.66. continued

```
z = zCenterForm(CInt(frmArg.Hwnd))

Set mfrm = frmArg

On Error Resume Next

If mintLastPage = 1 Then
  mfrm!cmdFirst1.Visible = False
  mfrm!cmdBack1.Visible = False
  mfrm!cmdNext1.Visible = False
  mfrm!cmdLast1.Visible = False
Else
  mintHorizontalPage = 1
  zVCR2Buttons 1
End If

mblnVCR2OK = False
mblnVCR2Cancel = False

zVCR2OnOpenDone:
  Exit Function

zVCR2OnOpenError:
  Warning "zVCR2OnOpen", Error$
  Resume zVCR2OnOpenDone

End Function
```

The *zVCR2Buttons* Subroutine

The zVCR2Buttons subroutine, shown in Listing 18.67, enables/disables the VCR buttons as needed.

If you're on the first page, it doesn't make sense to be able to use the << or **B**ack buttons. If you're on the last page, it doesn't make sense to be able to use the **N**ext and >> buttons.

Listing 18.67. The zVCR2Buttons **subroutine.**

```
Private Sub zVCR2Buttons (intPage As Integer)

  Dim ctl As Control
  Dim n As Integer

  On Error Resume Next

' Move the focus to a control that is enabled

  If intPage = 1 Then
    mblnNext = True
```

```
  ElseIf intPage = mintLastPage Then
    mblnNext = False
  End If

  If mblnNext Then
    Set ctl = mfrm("cmdNext" & mintHorizontalPage)
  Else
    Set ctl = mfrm("cmdBack" & mintHorizontalPage)
  End If

  ctl.Enabled = True
  ctl.SetFocus

  For n = 1 To mintColumns
    If n = mintHorizontalPage Then
      mfrm("cmdOK" & n).Visible = (intPage = mintLastPage)
      mfrm("cmdCancel" & n).Enabled = True
      mfrm("cmdFirst" & n).Enabled = (intPage > 1)
      mfrm("cmdBack" & n).Enabled = (intPage > 1)
      mfrm("cmdNext" & n).Enabled = (intPage < mintLastPage)
      mfrm("cmdLast" & n).Enabled = (intPage < mintLastPage)
    Else
      mfrm("cmdOK" & n).Visible = False
      mfrm("cmdCancel" & n).Enabled = False
      mfrm("cmdFirst" & n).Enabled = False
      mfrm("cmdBack" & n).Enabled = False
      mfrm("cmdNext" & n).Enabled = False
      mfrm("cmdLast" & n).Enabled = False
    End If
  Next n

End Sub
```

The *zVCR2Page* Subroutine

The zVCR2Page function uses the GoToPage macro action to switch pages.

In calling GoToPage, the vertical page coordinate is passed along with an offset in twips to set the horizontal page coordinate. After changing pages, the subroutine calls zVCR2Buttons to update the VCR buttons for the current page. (See Listing 18.68.)

Listing 18.68. The zVCR2Page subroutine.

```
Sub zVCR2Page (intPage As Integer)

  Dim intVerticalPage As Integer

  On Error GoTo zVCR2PageError

  mintHorizontalPage = Int((intPage - 1) / mintPagesPerColumn) + 1
```

continues

Listing 18.68. continued

```
intVerticalPage = intPage Mod mintPagesPerColumn
If intVerticalPage = 0 Then
  intVerticalPage = mintPagesPerColumn
End If

mintCurrentPage = intPage
DoCmd GoToPage intVerticalPage, (mintHorizontalPage - 1) * mintPageWidth, 0

  zVCR2Buttons intPage

zVCR2PageDone:
  Exit Sub

zVCR2PageError:
  Warning "zVCR2Page", Error$
  Resume zVCR2PageDone

End Sub
```

The *zVCR2GotoControl* Function

The zVCR2GotoControl function, shown in Listing 18.69, is used to set focus to a specific control, changing the current page if necessary.

The function's main usage is from the On Enter events of the hidden tab sentry controls, so focus does not leave the current page; instead, it loops around the controls within it.

Listing 18.69. The zVCR2GotoControl **function.**

```
Function zVCR2GotoControl (strControlName As String, intPage As Integer)
➡ As Integer

  On Error GoTo zVCR2GotoControlError

  mfrm(strControlName).SetFocus

  If intPage <> mintCurrentPage Then
    mintCurrentPage = intPage
    zVCR2Buttons intPage
  End If

zVCR2GotoControlDone:
  Exit Function

zVCR2GotoControlError:
  Warning "zVCR2GotoControl", Error$
  Resume zVCR2GotoControlDone

End Function
```

The VCR Button On Click Event Functions

The next four functions are activated on the On Click events for the <<, **B**ack, **N**ext, and >> buttons in the form footer. Each of these functions uses the zVCR2Page subroutine to move to the desired page.(See Listing 18.70.)

Listing 18.70. The zVCR2First **function.**

```
Function zVCR2First () As Integer

  zVCR2Page 1

End Function

Function zVCR2Back () As Integer

  mblnNext = False

  If mintCurrentPage > 1 Then
    zVCR2Page mintCurrentPage - 1
  End If

End Function

Function zVCR2Next () As Integer

  mblnNext = True

  If mintCurrentPage < mintLastPage Then
    zVCR2Page mintCurrentPage + 1
  End If

End Function

Function zVCR2Last () As Integer

  zVCR2Page mintLastPage

End Function
```

The OK and Cancel Buttons

The next two functions get activated by the OK and Cancel buttons' On Click events. These functions each set their own flag to indicate how the form was closed, and then they close the form.

The blnVCROK and blnVCRCancel flags are checked in the zVCR2BoundOnClose function when the form closes. (See Listing 18.71.)

Listing 18.71. The `zVCR2OK` and `zVCR2Cancel` **functions.**

```
Function zVCR2OK ()

  On Error Resume Next

  mblnVCR2OK = True
  DoCmd Close A_Form, mfrm.FormName

End Function

Function zVCR2Cancel () As Integer

  On Error Resume Next

  mblnVCR2Cancel = True
  DoCmd Close A_Form, mfrm.FormName

End Function
```

The *zVCR2BoundOnClose* Function

The name of the last function, `zVCR2BoundOnClose`, indicates that it is used on a bound form. There would be another version of this function if the form wasn't bound to a record source.

On our form, if the user clicks OK, the record edited should be saved. If Cancel is pressed, the record shouldn't be saved. If the user double-clicks the top-left system box, none of the flags will be set, so the program asks whether or not to save the record. (See Listing 18.72.)

Listing 18.72. The `zVCR2BoundOnClose` **function.**

```
Function zVCR2BoundOnClose (frm As Form)

  Dim dyn As Recordset
  Dim z As Integer
  Dim blnCancel As Integer

  On Error GoTo zVCR2BoundOnCloseError

  blnCancel = False

  If mblnVCR2Cancel Then
    blnCancel = True

  ElseIf Not mblnVCR2OK Then
    z = MsgBox("Do you want to save your responses?", 32 + 3, mstrProgramName)

    If z = 7 Then
```

```
        blnCancel = True

    ElseIf z = 2 Then
    ' Cancel closing the form
      DoCmd CancelEvent
    End If
  End If

  If blnCancel Then
  ' Delete the current record being edited

    On Error Resume Next
    Set dyn = frm.RecordsetClone
    dyn.Bookmark = frm.Bookmark
    dyn.Delete
  End If

zVCR2BoundOnCloseDone:
  Exit Function

zVCR2BoundOnCloseError:
  Warning "zVCR2BoundOnClose", Error$
  Resume zVCR2BoundOnCloseDone

End Function
```

With the run-time code completed, our generated survey Entry Forms are ready to go.
You will take the Entry Form for a test spin at the beginning of the next chapter.

Summary

You have four of the five objects generated now.

Using the Entry Report and Questions Table, you can print a hand-out questionnaire
to start collecting survey data.

Using the Entry Form and Responses Table, you can set up your database on a file server
and have participants on your network open the database and enter their answers right
into the database.

Here's a list of your accidents, accomplishments, and adventures for this chapter. You

- ■ Designed and created the Survey Wizard Save As form
- ■ Completed the Survey Wizard user interface coding
- ■ Used temporary stub functions to keep our program compilable and runnable
  during development
- ■ Outlined the objects we've created so far and what's left to do

- Outlined the procedures behind the Survey Wizard Save As form and two run-time modules
- Wrote code to generate the Questions Table and Responses Table
- Developed a prototype for the Entry Report
- Learned how to create shadowed boxes in a report
- Found a work-around for the 22-inch report section size limitation
- Learned a trick to create an alternative report detail section
- Reviewed the Create and Delete functions for Wizard programming
- Went hog-wild with constants to make our code readable and modifiable
- Wrote the code to generate the Entry Report
- Created hidden controls on a report to make Record Source fields available to our code
- Wrote run-time code that modifies sections in the Entry Report while the report is printing
- Designed a multi-page Entry Form to beat the 22-inch section limitation again
- Can you believe it? Wrote code that generates a VCR button multiple-page form
- Wrote reusable run-time code for our multiple-page Entry Form

Stay tuned! In the next chapter you will build the Results Report and a terrific set of graph routines that you can use in any of your database projects

CHAPTER 19

Access: Survey Wizard, Part Four— "Pretty Good Charts"

The main headline for this chapter is stolen from a programmer I used to work with, and I hope he doesn't mind. He had this idea of selling his own programs under a company name of Pretty Good Software.

The lighthearted concept was to avoid any kind of hype and oversell. He felt basically good about his programs and knew that his targeted users would think they were pretty darn good, too.

Programs like this don't strive to do everything and may even have a few quirks here or there, but they also are a simple and direct approach to a specific task.

In this chapter, I'll implement my own charting capability for Access report objects. I call these Pretty Good Charts, as shown in Figure 19.1. They are an alternative to using Microsoft Graph, which I found pretty darn amazing but a little too sophisticated for my current needs.

FIGURE 19.1.

Using Pretty Good Charts to create a bar graph.

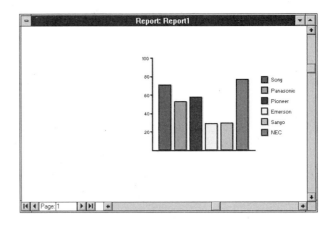

Another reason I shy away from Microsoft Graph is because the first version of Survey Wizard was created in Access 1.1. It was easy to use Microsoft Graph in your reports, but making a wizard that used Microsoft Graph was a challenge.

Things changed for the better in Version 2.0 of Access. The new version of Microsoft Graph included in this version uses OLE automation so that it can be driven by other programs. However, now that I've got my own amazingly fast chart routines (without the overhead of having to load a second application), I think I'll stick with them.

Reviewing Your Progress

In the last three chapters you developed the Survey Wizard user interface and wrote the code that generates the objects behind four of the five check boxes on the final build screen.

As was promised, in this chapter you will create the Results Report and its supporting objects. You will also create the Pretty Good Charts module.

The job of the Results Report is to display summarized data collected in an online survey so that the report's reader can quickly identify the general response to each question. To accomplish this, you will also need to generate a make table query that produces the total values for the report.

Additionally, you will take a run through a generated Entry Form so that you will have some test data to run the report on.

What Is a Wizard, Really?

Before you get started… I've run into folks that had completely different ideas of what a wizard is. It might be helpful if I explain my own definition. I can't claim to be an authority on the topic, but from some careful examination and pondering about what Microsoft is doing with wizards, I believe the following is a correct definition.

Wizards are an additional software layer above a full-featured software product. A full-featured product offers extreme flexibility, but makes it more difficult for novice users (and sometimes even advanced users) to figure out what combination of steps are needed to create a complete document in some commonly desired way. I'm using the word *document* here generically to mean anything that application software creates.

Wizards have evolved from the template concept. For example, in previous days when you wanted to create a business letter, you loaded templates into your word processor. As a starting point, you found a template you liked and then made it your own by entering your information into it.

Wizards are more advanced than templates because they have code behind them that runs. When the wizard runs, it prompts the user for the minimum information needed to generate the desired object. Predefined defaults are used to fill in the multitude of options the user wasn't prompted for.

This combination of code and defaults takes the template concept further because the object you start with is nearly done, as opposed to just the basic skeleton being done as with a template.

To keep the end result from being too rigidly predefined, the Access form and report wizards offer the user a selection of styles for their generated object.

A *style* is a set of options applied all at once. This holds true to the concept of asking the user only the minimum questions needed in order to generate a useable "document." In a sense, the process is kind of like selecting one template from a set of templates.

The real power in wizards is that once the object is generated, you don't have to stop. You can then use the full-featured program to customize the object in more ways than the wizard offered options for. In essence, with a wizard you get a simple-to-use user interface, but you are not hindered by it. (This statement is underlaid with the assumption that the generated object is easy to understand and modify. Unfortunately, that is not always true.)

Wizards are characterized also by their style of user interface. Rather than having large complex forms with many fields, wizards free the screen from clutter by prompting for only a few things at a time.

VCR-style buttons are used to move between these screens. Each screen typically displays user instructions to indicate which task is being accomplished at that screen.

Some people deny that wizards are extremely powerful tools because the simple interface makes them seem like a toy. As far as I'm concerned, those people can stare at all the overcrowded screens they want if it makes them feel sophisticated; but it's not for me.

Does Survey Wizard fit the wizard model? Well, as I discussed in the last chapter, it doesn't fit perfectly. The objects generated by Survey Wizard don't allow much room for modification after executing the wizard to generate them. Maybe Survey Wizard fits more into the category of an Application Builder?

One thing Survey Wizard definitely will be is a full-fledged, stripes-on-its-shoulder, Access menu add-in. You will take care of that in the next chapter when you move Survey Wizard into two installable library databases.

Performing an Online Survey

Let's define a questionnaire. Following are some questions to enter, or you can define your own. You can use the Entry Form to fill in some dummy data and use it in testing the Results Report, or if there are some family members and friends around, you might have them take the survey.

First, enter the title of the survey as shown in Figure 19.2.

Next, cycle through Pages 2 through 4 as needed to enter the questions.

1. **Do you obey all traffic laws?** (Yes/No)
2. **How much above or below the speed limit do you typically drive?** (Multiple-Choice)
   A) 10 miles below
   B) 5 miles below

C) Right on the speed limit

D) 5 miles above

E) 10 miles above

F) As fast as I can

3. **Do you always come to a complete stop at a stop sign?** (Yes/No)

4. **Normally, how far do you follow behind the car in front of you on the freeway?** (Multiple-Choice)

A) As far as possible

B) I apply the two-second rule

C) A couple of car lengths

D) One car length

E) A couple of feet

F) A couple of inches

Figure 19.3 shows question 4 being added to the questionnaire. Figure 19.4 shows the multiple-choice answers being entered for question 4.

FIGURE 19.2.

Creating a Driving Habits questionnaire.

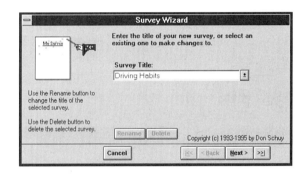

FIGURE 19.3.

Entering a multiple-choice question into page two.

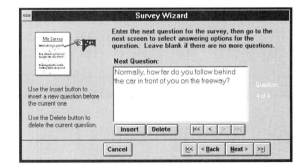

FIGURE 19.4.

Entering the multiple-choice selections into page four.

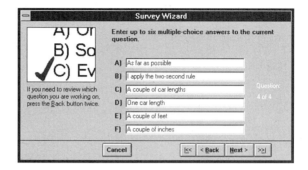

5. **Who drives better?** (Multiple-Choice)

   A) Men
   B) Women
   C) Sex makes no difference

6. **What sex are you?** (Multiple-Choice)

   A) Male
   B) Female

7. **When you are in the car, what percent of the time do you do the driving?**
   (0%, 20%, 40%, 60%, 80%, 100%)

   Set the percentages by entering From, To, and Step values of 0, 100, and 20, respectively. See Figure 19.5.

FIGURE 19.5.

Defining the percent values on page three.

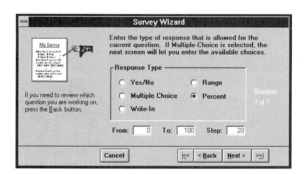

8. **Do you consider yourself a better and safer driver than typical drivers?**
   (Yes/No)

9. **How do you rate your own driving safety skills?** (Range: 1, 2, 3, 4, 5, 6, 7, 8, 9, 10 [1 is worst, 10 is best])

10. **How many accidents have you been involved in within the last five years?** (Multiple-Choice)

   A) My record is clean
   B) One, not my fault
   C) One, my fault
   D) Two
   E) Three or more

11. **If buying automobile insurance wasn't mandatory, would you buy it anyway?** (Yes/No)

12. **How old are you?** (Multiple-Choice)

   A) Under 20
   B) 21 to 25
   C) 26 to 30
   D) 31 to 40
   E) Over 40

13. **Do you or have you ever ridden a motorcycle regularly?** (Yes/No)

14. **Do you support the helmet law? (Motorcycle riders have to use a helmet.)** (Yes/No)

I found it helpful to identify each question with a number, and I typed in the number along with each question. Later you might want to modify Survey Wizard so that it automatically numbers questions for you.

On Page 5, check the Entry Form check box. This automatically checks the Responses Table check box, also. Press the Build button, as shown in Figure 19.6, to open the Survey Wizard Save As dialog box.

FIGURE 19.6.

Selecting Build options for the Driving Habits survey.

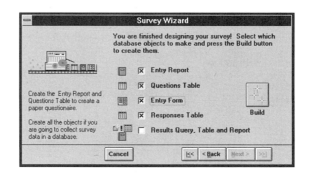

In the Survey Wizard Save As form, enter a base name. I entered `Driving`, as shown in Figure 19.7. Then click OK to build the objects.

FIGURE 19.7.

*Entering a base name
for the Driving Habits
survey.*

Survey Wizard Save As		
Enter the base name to use in creating the database object names.		OK / Cancel
Base Name:	Driving	
Entry Report:	Driving Entry Report	
Questions Table:	Driving Questions Table	
Entry Form:	Driving Entry Form	
Reponses Table:	Driving Responses Table	
Results Query:		
Results Table:		
Results Report:		

To create the printed handout version of the questionnaire, select the generated report object named "Driving Entry Report" in the database container and use the **F**ile | **P**rint command from the menu. The previously-listed questions produce an attractive three-page questionnaire.

However, for the sake of collecting data in the database, you need to use the generated Entry Form. If you want other people to open the database and use your form, you can make an AutoExec macro automatically open the form and then close Access after the form is closed.

Hey, wait a minute! Didn't Chapter 14, "Access: Address Book, Part Two," say "Never have your program close Access when it's done." OK, it did. Just remember that making your program close Access is rude. If you are sure that the only reason your user will be using Access is to run the program in your database, maybe it's OK. You could also make your macro just close the current database.

Following are the commands to enter in an AutoExec macro to minimize the database container, open the Entry Form, and then exit Access.

AutoExec Macro

Action:	Minimize
Action:	OpenForm
Form Name:	Driving Entry Form
View:	Form
Data Mode:	Add
Window Mode:	Dialog
Action:	DoMenuItem
Menu Bar:	Form

Menu Name:	File
Command:	Exit

Be careful to make sure that the Data Mode setting in the OpenForm action is set to Add (as shown in Figure 19.8). This ensures that each time the form is opened, it edits a new Responses Table record rather than an existing one.

FIGURE 19.8.

Creating an AutoExec macro to open the online Driving Habits survey.

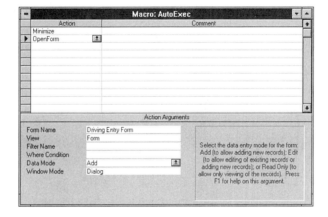

To make the macro close the database only rather than exit Access, change the last command to the following:

Modified AutoExec Macro

Action:	DoMenuItem
Menu Bar:	Form
Menu Name:	File
Command:	Close

NOTE

You can always bypass an AutoExec macro and open a database normally by holding down the shift key when you open an Access database.

Note that most Access users know about this, and can bypass the AutoExec macro also if they want to.

Next, you can make a Program Manager program item for the database. Hold down the Ctrl key as you click the Access icon and drag it to an empty spot in the Program Manager window just as if you were moving it. Release the mouse button, and Program Manager makes a copy of the item.

Next, select the new item and press Alt-Enter. This brings up the Program Item Properties dialog box. Change the description and command-line settings:

Description:

`Driving Habits Survey`

Command Line:

`C:\ACCESS\MSACCESS.EXE D:\STUFF\SURVEY.MDB`

Your command-line setting will differ depending on where MSACCESS.EXE and SURVEY.MDB are located on your system.

You also can change the picture by clicking the Change **I**con button and then selecting an Access icon in the Change Icon dialog box or clicking **B**rowse to find other icon choices, as shown in Figure 19.9.

FIGURE 19.9.

Selecting a picture for the Program Manager icon that opens the SURVEY.MDB database.

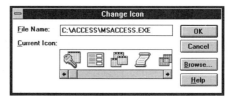

When you are done, you can double-click the new Program Manager program item to run Access and bring up the survey form, as shown in Figure 19.10.

FIGURE 19.10.

Using a Program Manager program item to load a survey form.

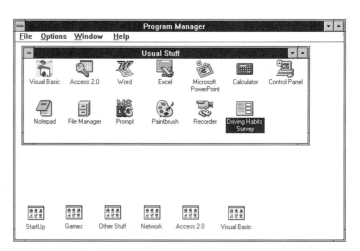

The first page of the form displays the user instructions, as shown in Figure 19.11.

FIGURE 19.11.

Page one of the Entry Form.

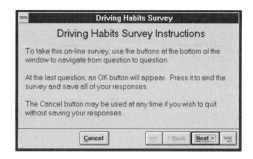

Click **N**ext and the first question is displayed. Answer each question, clicking **N**ext each time to move through the questionnaire. Figure 19.12 shows a multiple-choice question. Figure 19.13 shows a percent-type question.

FIGURE 19.12.

Answering a multiple-choice question in the survey entry form.

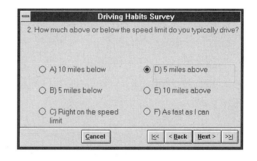

FIGURE 19.13.

Answering a percent-type question.

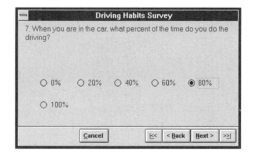

After answering all the questions, click OK on the last page to save your responses, as shown in Figure 19.14. Clicking OK creates a single record in the Responses Table.

If you opted to close Access in your AutoExec macro, the program closes after you click OK or Cancel on the Entry Form.

Go ahead and have several people take the survey, or if you can't do that right now, fake the survey by making several entries yourself. Take the survey at least three times with varying responses to produce a good set of test data.

FIGURE 19.14.
Clicking OK on the last page saves answers to a record in the Responses Table.

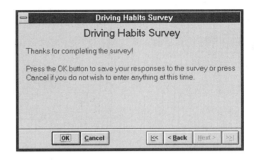

Calculating Results Report Totals

Now take a look at how the generated Results Report gets its data.

As noted before, the Entry Form results are written to the generated Responses Table. Each record within this table represents the answers entered by one person taking the survey.

The table is pretty much unintelligible on its own. As shown in Figure 19.15, other than the ID field, the field names are simply Question1 through QuestionN for the number of questions in the survey.

FIGURE 19.15.
The fields in a generated Responses Table.

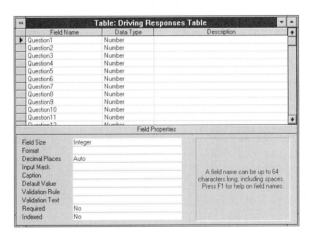

The data type of each field depends on what type of question the field represents. For a yes/no question, an integer number field is used to receive either –1 for True or 0 for False. A byte-sized number field is used for multiple-choice questions. This field receives a value from 1 to 6 corresponding to the position of the chosen selection.

A long integer is used for a range question because the questionnaire designer may have use for range values that extend below –32767 or above 32767, the minimum and maximum values an integer can represent.

An integer was used for the percent-type question because these values must be between 0 and 100.

The only question type that isn't numeric is the write-in question. A memo field is used for the write-in question type to allow lengthy responses. Because it contains text that can be virtually anything, the write-in type question can't be meaningfully summarized in the Results Report.

The data in the Responses Table must be tabulated before a meaningful report can be created. This is the job of the Results Query. The Results Report Query returns a record for each question in the survey. This record includes a count of how many times each possible answer to a question was used.

For example, if the question was a yes/no type, the Results Report Query record has a count of how many times Yes was chosen and how many times No was chosen. You might think that it took a highly skilled master query to do this tabulation, but in fact the implementation I came up with is kind of crude.

Figure 19.16 shows what part of the query looks like in design mode.

FIGURE 19.16.

The Results Query in the query design grid.

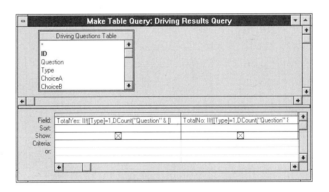

Many of the fields returned by the query are calculated. The TotalYes field uses DCount() to count how many times Yes was the response. Here's the entire expression:

```
TotalYes: IIf([Type]=1,DCount("Question" & [ID],"[Driving Responses Table]",
➡"Question" & [ID] & " = -1"),Null)
```

The expression checks the Type field to see whether the question type is 1 (yes/no). If it is, the DCount() function counts all the records for which the current question contains a –1 (to indicate Yes).

There are similar expressions to get the total counts for TotalNo, TotalA through TotalF for multiple-choice questions, and Total1 through Total10 for range or percent questions.

You might expect that relying on a query with DCount() used all over the place can be awfully slow, and in fact that was the case. On my initial tests it took up to two minutes for the report to display some results.

Two minutes! Yuk!

I'm sure the query could have been defined better to serve as the Record Source for a report, but I used a simple trick to radically speed things up. I changed the query to a Make Table query and then changed the report to run off the generated table rather than the query. That's where the Results Table comes in.

I modified the report so that it prompts for whether or not the survey results need to be "recalculated" each time the report opens. This is done via a function that executes on the On Open event for the report.

This effectively gives the user the option to regenerate the Results Table that the Results Report is bound to each time the report is previewed or printed. I liked this method because if I based the report off a query, all the calculations would have to be redone each time the report was run. With this method I needed only to redo the calculations when I knew that my survey data had been updated.

The end result is that even when the recalculation is done, the report opens in a few seconds rather than a few minutes. I can't tell you what's going on inside the Access report engine, but I've found that general reports always run faster from tables than they do from queries.

Designing the Results Report

Well, that's how the report gets its data. Now what does the actual report look like?

The Results Report is similar to the Entry Report you created in Chapter 18, "Access: Survey Wizard, Part Three—Generating Objects." After tossing around a lot of ideas, I decided I wanted the Results Report to display the questions and possible answers, not just the results. This way one could look at the report and see what was being asked as well as what was being answered.

Figure 19.17 shows the Results Report in report design mode.

It's not pretty, is it?

That mess within the detail section is a lot of stacked label and text box controls. Code that runs behind the report's On Print event turns on the appropriate controls, depending on which question type is currently being printed. This process works exactly as does the Entry Report.

FIGURE 19.17.

The generated Results Report.

```
┌─────────────────────────────────────────────────────────────┐
│ ═        Microsoft Access - [Report: Driving Results Report]  ▼│▲│
│ ▫ File  Edit  View  Format  Window  Help                     │▲│
│ ┌────────────────────────────────────────────────────────────│
│ │0. . . . .|. .1. . . .|. . .2. . . .|. . .3. . . .|. . .4. . . .|. . .5. . . .|. . .0. .│
│ ◀ Report Header                                               │
│                                                               │
│    ┌──────────────────────────────────────────────────────┐  │
│    │            Driving Habits Survey                      │  │
│    └──────────────────────────────────────────────────────┘  │
│                                                               │
│ ◀ Page Header                                                 │
│ ◀ Detail                                                      │
│    ┌──────────────────────────────────────────────────┐      │
│    │ Question                                          │      │
│    │                                                   │      │
│    └──────────────────────────────────────────────────┘      │
│    =zSWMultipleChoice("A",[ =zSWM   Write-In Question.        │
│    =zSWMultipleChoice("B",[  =zSWMultipleChoice("E",[(        │
│    =zSWMultipleChoice("C",[  =zSWMultipleChoice("F",[(        │
│                                                               │
│ ◀ Page Footer                                                 │
│                                    =". " & Page & "-          │
│                                         "                     │
│ Design View                                         NUM       │
└───────────────────────────────────────────────────────────────┘
```

One difference is that in this report there are two controls for each possible printed answer value. One control displays normal text and the other displays bold text.

The run-time code evaluates which answer was selected the most and highlights it by displaying the bold text version. In case of ties, more than one answer may be highlighted.

In each report I leave a small space to display a graph. It's not good enough to indicate which answer was selected the most because the reader of the survey needs to know how decisively respondents chose one option over another.

I used a chart prototype before actually digging into the coding. I created a bar chart by dropping rectangle and label objects onto a 6 1/2- by 4-inch section on a report. My prototype is shown in Figure 19.18.

Using the measurements off the prototype, I wrote the code that would draw a chart. I knew that I wouldn't always want my charts to display as large as 6 1/2- by 4-inches, so I introduced scaling into the chart function.

The resulting function draws a bar chart and is called in the report run-time code like this:

```
z = pgcReportBarChart(rpt, ChartTop, ChartLeft, ChartHeight, ChartWidth,
➥ intValues, maintData(), mastrLegend(), malngColors())
```

FIGURE 19.18.

Prototyping a bar chart with rectangle and label objects.

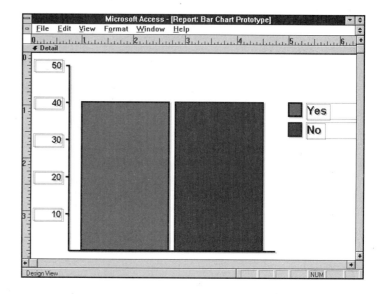

The arguments to the pgcReportBarChart function are as follows:

rpt	The report object
ChartTop	Location of the top of the chart in inches
ChartLeft	Location of the left side of the chart in inches
ChartHeight	Height of the chart in inches
ChartWidth	Width of the chart in inches
intValues	Number of values and resulting number of bars
aintData()	Array of integer values
astrLegend()	Array of legend titles
alngColors()	Array of color values for fill colors

Get ready to look at some code now.

The Pretty Good Charts Module

The Pretty Good Charts module draws three types of charts: bar charts, line charts, and pie charts.

After you look over the code in the module, I'll show you how to use the chart subroutines in your own project. The module is pretty close, but not quite self-contained. If you want to use it in a separate project, be sure to grab the Error and Form modules, too, because the zDisplayError subroutine and the zTwips function are used.

The Pretty Good Charts Declarations Section

The declaration section (shown in Listing 19.1) declares a few constants affecting the layout and look of the charts, and also a few module variables.

Listing 19.1. The declarations section for the Pretty Good Charts module.

```
' Chart module
' Draw simple bar, line and pie charts on a report

 Option Compare Database
 Option Explicit

 Const mstrProgramName = "Pretty Good Chart"

 Const XShadowOffset = .03
 Const YShadowOffset = .03

 Const XAxisLeft = .75
 Const YAxisTop = .25

 Const Black = 0
 Const Gray = 12632256
 Const Red = 255

 Dim mdblChartTop As Double
 Dim mdblChartLeft As Double
 Dim mdblChartHeightRatio As Double
 Dim mdblChartWidthRatio As Double
 Dim mdblXAxisRight As Double
 Dim mdblYAxisBottom As Double
```

The *Warning* Subroutine

Yep, you've seen this one a few times now. Like the other modules, the Pretty Good Charts module has the Warning subroutine defined (see Listing 19.2).

Listing 19.2. The Warning **subroutine.**

```
Private Sub Warning (strProcedure As String, msg As String)

  zDisplayError strProcedure, msg, mstrProgramName

End Sub
```

The *X* and *Y* Scaling Functions

To produce charts of any size, the X and Y functions (shown in Listing 19.3) allow the program to express coordinates in the scale of the prototype.

The X function scales an X coordinate of a value between 0 and 6 1/2-inches to fit within the size and location of the chart. It also converts this value to Twips by calling the zTwips function.

Likewise, the Y function scales and adjusts a Y coordinate that would range from a value of 0 to 4 inches.

Listing 19.3. The X **and** Y **functions.**

```
Private Function X (dblX As Double) As Integer

  X = zTwips(dblX * mdblChartWidthRatio + mdblChartLeft)

End Function

Private Function Y (dblY As Double) As Integer

  Y = zTwips(dblY * mdblChartHeightRatio + mdblChartTop)

End Function
```

The *DrawLine* Subroutine

The DrawLine subroutine (see Listing 19.4) uses the report object's Line method to draw a black line. The function is passed coordinates based on the prototype, so it converts them by using the X and Y functions.

Listing 19.4. The DrawLine **subroutine.**

```
Private Sub DrawLine (rpt As Report, dblX1 As Double, dblY1 As Double,
➥ dblX2 As Double, dblY2 As Double)

  rpt.Line (X(dblX1), Y(dblY1))-(X(dblX2), Y(dblY2)), Black

End Sub
```

DrawShadowLine

The DrawShadowLine subroutine (shown in Listing 19.5) works like the DrawLine function except that it draws the line shifted slightly to the right and down. It also always draws a gray line.

The DrawShadowLine subroutine is always called before the DrawLine function in order to draw a line's shadow and to produce a 3-D-like appearance.

Listing 19.5. The DrawShadowLine **subroutine.**

```
Private Sub DrawShadowLine (rpt As Report, dblX1 As Double, dblY1 As Double,
➥ dblX2 As Double, dblY2 As Double)

  rpt.Line (X(dblX1 + XShadowOffset), Y(dblY1 + YShadowOffset))-
  ➥(X(dblX2 + XShadowOffset), Y(dblY2 + YShadowOffset)), Gray

End Sub
```

The *DrawAxis* Subroutine

The DrawAxis subroutine draws the bar and line charts' X and Y axis. See Listing 19.6.

Listing 19.6. The DrawAxis **subroutine.**

```
Private Sub DrawAxis (rpt As Report)

' Draw the y axis
  DrawLine rpt, XAxisLeft, YAxisTop, XAxisLeft, mdblYAxisBottom

' Draw the x axis
  DrawLine rpt, XAxisLeft, mdblYAxisBottom, mdblXAxisRight, mdblYAxisBottom

End Sub
```

The *DrawBox* Subroutine

The DrawBox subroutine (shown in Listing 19.7) is passed a fill color and draws a filled box with a gray shadow and black outline.

Listing 19.7. The `DrawBox` **subroutine.**

```
Private Sub DrawBox (rpt As Report, dblX1 As Double, dblY1 As Double,
➥ dblX2 As Double, dblY2 As Double, lngColor As Long)

  rpt.Line (X(dblX1 + XShadowOffset), Y(dblY1 + YShadowOffset))-
  ➥(X(dblX2 + XShadowOffset), Y(dblY2 + YShadowOffset)), Gray, BF
  rpt.Line (X(dblX1), Y(dblY1))-(X(dblX2), Y(dblY2)), lngColor, BF
  rpt.Line (X(dblX1), Y(dblY1))-(X(dblX2), Y(dblY2)), Black, B

End Sub
```

The *ScaleGraph* Subroutine

The `ScaleGraph` subroutine is used to determine what values should be displayed as tick-mark values on a bar or line chart. The results are passed back in the `intHigh` and `intStep` variables.

The `intHigh` variable receives the largest value. The `intStep` variable receives the first value, which is also the value to step by to reach the `intHigh` value in five tick marks.

The `ScaleGraph` subroutine is shown in Listing 19.8.

Listing 19.8. The `ScaleGraph` **subroutine.**

```
Private Sub ScaleGraph (aintData() As Integer, intValues As Integer,
➥ intHigh As Integer, intStep As Integer)

' Determine how to scale the graph by checking the range of values used.

  Dim n As Integer

  On Error GoTo ScaleGraphError

  intHigh = 0
  For n = 1 To intValues
    If aintData(n) > intHigh Then
      intHigh = aintData(n)
    End If
  Next n

  If intHigh < 5 Then
    intHigh = 5
  ElseIf intHigh < 10 Then intHigh = 10
  ElseIf intHigh < 25 Then intHigh = 25
  ElseIf intHigh < 50 Then intHigh = 50
  ElseIf intHigh < 75 Then intHigh = 75
  ElseIf intHigh < 100 Then intHigh = 100
  ElseIf intHigh < 250 Then intHigh = 250
  ElseIf intHigh < 500 Then intHigh = 500
  ElseIf intHigh < 750 Then intHigh = 750
```

```
     ElseIf intHigh < 1000 Then intHigh = 1000
     ElseIf intHigh < 2500 Then intHigh = 2500
     ElseIf intHigh < 5000 Then intHigh = 5000
     ElseIf intHigh < 7500 Then intHigh = 7500
     ElseIf intHigh < 10000 Then intHigh = 10000
     Else intHigh = 25000
     End If

     intStep = intHigh / 5

ScaleGraphDone:
   Exit Sub

ScaleGraphError:
   Warning "ScaleGraph", Error$
   Resume ScaleGraphDone

End Sub
```

The *YPoint* Function

The YPoint function is used to translate in inches a data value into a Y coordinate. See Listing 19.9.

Listing 19.9. The YPoint function.

```
Private Function YPoint (intData As Integer, intHigh As Integer) As Double

' Determine the height of a bar on a bar chart or the Y coordinate of a
' point on a line chart.

   Dim dbl As Double

   dbl = CDbl(intData)
   If dbl > CDbl(intHigh) Then
     dbl = CDbl(intHigh)
   End If

   YPoint = dbl / CDbl(intHigh) * (mdblYAxisBottom - YAxisTop)

End Function
```

The *DrawTickMarks* Subroutine

The DrawTickMarks subroutine (shown in Listing 19.10) draws the ticks along the Y axis of a bar or line chart and prints the numbers that each tick mark represents.

Listing 19.10. The DrawTickMarks subroutine.

```
Private Sub DrawTickMarks (rpt As Report, intStep As Integer)

' Draw the report border, axis shadow and tick marks

    Dim dblY As Double

    Dim intTick As Integer
    Dim intFillZeros As Integer

    Dim i As Integer
    Dim n As Integer

    On Error GoTo DrawTickMarksError

' How wide the lines will be
    rpt.DrawWidth = 12 * mdblChartHeightRatio

    rpt.FontSize = 12 * mdblChartHeightRatio
    rpt.FontName = "Arial"

' Draw a border around the chart
    ' rpt.Line (X(0#), Y(0#))-(X(6.5), Y(4#)), Black, B

' Draw the y axis shadow
    DrawShadowLine rpt, XAxisLeft, YAxisTop, XAxisLeft, mdblYAxisBottom

' Draw the x axis shadow
    DrawShadowLine rpt, XAxisLeft, mdblYAxisBottom, mdblXAxisRight,
    ➥ mdblYAxisBottom

' Draw the tick marks and step values
    For n = 1 To 5
        dblY = mdblYAxisBottom - YPoint(n, 5)

        rpt.CurrentX = X(.05)
        rpt.CurrentY = Y(dblY) - rpt.TextHeight(CStr(intTick)) / 2

        intTick = intStep * n

        ' Print blank zeros as needed to right justify the number
        intFillZeros = 6 - Len(CStr(intTick))

        rpt.ForeColor = RGB(255, 255, 255) ' White
        For i = 1 To intFillZeros
            rpt.Print "0";
        Next i

        rpt.ForeColor = Black
        rpt.Print CStr(intTick)

        DrawShadowLine rpt, XAxisLeft - .06, dblY, XAxisLeft, dblY
        DrawLine rpt, XAxisLeft - .06, dblY, XAxisLeft, dblY
    Next n

DrawTickMarksDone:
    Exit Sub
```

```
DrawTickMarksError:
  Warning "DrawTickMarks", Error$
  Resume DrawTickMarksDone

End Sub
```

The *pgcReportBarChart* Function

Now that all the supporting functions are in place, `pgcReportBarChart` is the function that actually creates a bar chart.

Figure 19.19 shows a sample of the output created by this function.

FIGURE 19.19.

A bar chart created by the `pgcReportBarChart` *function.*

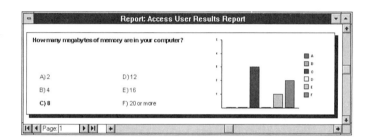

The first thing the `pgcReportBarChart` function does is assign some constant values and module globals that determine scaling as well as the chart's layout.

Note how the 6 1/2- and 4-inch values are used with the width and height to determine the ratio that is needed to translate the report's prototype measurements to the size of the chart being generated.

The function is surprisingly short for what is being created. Within a loop, each legend title and box is drawn and each bar on the chart is drawn. The height of the bar is determined by using the `YPoint` function.

The `pgcReportBarChart` subroutine is shown in Listing 19.11.

Listing 19.11. The `pgcReportBarChart` **function.**

```
Function pgcReportBarChart (rpt As Report, dblTop As Double,
➡ dblLeft As Double, dblHeight As Double, dblWidth As Double,
➡ intValues As Integer, aintData() As Integer, astrLegend() As String,
➡ alngColors() As Long) As Integer

' This function implements a "do-it-yourself" bar chart on a report by
' using the Line method to draw it. Coordinates passed are in inches.
```

continues

Listing 19.11. continued

```
' Arguments:

' rpt                   - Currently running report
' dblTop, dblLeft       - Coordinates where to draw the chart
' dblHeight, dblWidth   - Size of the chart
' intValues             - Number of values in data set
' aintData()            - One value for each bar
' astrLegend()          - Legend titles for each bar
' alngColors()          - Color for each bar

' The arrays should have the values stored in indexes 1 to intValues.
' The values in aintData() must be zero or positive.

    Dim dbl As Double
    Dim dblBarWidth As Double
    Dim dblBarHeight As Double
    Dim dblLegendTop As Double

    Dim intHigh As Integer
    Dim intStep As Integer
    Dim n As Integer

    On Error GoTo pgcReportBarChartError

    Const SpaceBetweenBars = .125
    Const SpaceBetweenLegendTitles = .4

    mdblChartTop = dblTop
    mdblChartLeft = dblLeft
    mdblChartHeightRatio = dblHeight / 4#
    mdblChartWidthRatio = dblWidth / 6.5
    mdblXAxisRight = 4.75
    mdblYAxisBottom = 3.75

    ScaleGraph aintData(), intValues, intHigh, intStep

    DrawTickMarks rpt, intStep

' Calculate the width of a bar
    dblBarWidth = (3.5 - SpaceBetweenBars * (intValues - 1)) / intValues

    dbl = 1#
    dblLegendTop = .95
    rpt.FontSize = 14 * mdblChartHeightRatio
    For n = 1 To intValues
    ' Draw the legend box and title

        DrawBox rpt, 5#, dblLegendTop, 5.25, dblLegendTop + YAxisTop, _
        ➥ alngColors(n)

        rpt.CurrentX = X(5.35)
        rpt.CurrentY = Y(dblLegendTop + .016)
        rpt.Print astrLegend(n)
```

```
' Draw the bar

    dblBarHeight = YPoint(aintData(n), intHigh)

    DrawBox rpt, dbl, mdblYAxisBottom - dblBarHeight, dbl + dblBarWidth,
    ➥ mdblYAxisBottom, alngColors(n)

    dbl = dbl + dblBarWidth + SpaceBetweenBars
    dblLegendTop = dblLegendTop + SpaceBetweenLegendTitles
  Next n

  DrawAxis rpt

pgcReportBarChartDone:
  Exit Function

pgcReportBarChartError:
  Warning "pgcReportBarChart", Error$
  Resume pgcReportBarChartDone

End Function
```

The *pgcReportLineChart* Function

Having a single chart type in Pretty Good Charts simply won't do. In addition to a bar chart, there are two more functions, one to create a line chart and another to create a pie chart.

Figure 19.20 shows a line chart.

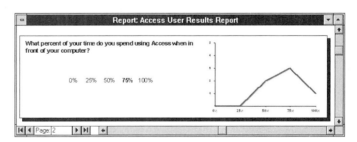

The line chart function does nearly the same thing as the bar chart function except that instead of drawing boxes, it draws lines from the previous (X,Y) coordinates to the current ones.

The pgcReportLineChart function is shown in Listing 19.12.

Listing 19.12. The pgcReportLineChart **function.**

```
Function pgcReportLineChart (rpt As Report, dblTop As Double,
➡ dblLeft As Double, dblHeight As Double, dblWidth As Double,
➡ intValues As Integer, aintData() As Integer, astrLegend() As String,
➡ alngColors() As Long) As Integer

' This function draws a line chart. See the pgcReportBarChart function for
' details on the arguments passed.

    Dim dblBottomOffset As Double
    Dim dblX1 As Double
    Dim dblX2 As Double
    Dim dblY1 As Double
    Dim dblY2 As Double
    Dim dblSpaceBetweenPoints As Double

    Dim intHigh As Integer
    Dim intStep As Integer
    Dim intTextWidth As Integer
    Dim n As Integer

    On Error GoTo pgcReportLineChartError

    Const SpaceBetweenLegendTitles = .4

    mdblChartTop = dblTop
    mdblChartLeft = dblLeft
    mdblChartHeightRatio = dblHeight / 4#
    mdblChartWidthRatio = dblWidth / 6.5
    mdblXAxisRight = 6#
    mdblYAxisBottom = 3.5

    ScaleGraph aintData(), intValues, intHigh, intStep

    DrawTickMarks rpt, intStep

    dblSpaceBetweenPoints = (mdblXAxisRight - XAxisLeft) / (CDbl(intValues) -
➡ 1#)
    dblBottomOffset = mdblYAxisBottom - .01

    rpt.FontSize = 14 * mdblChartHeightRatio
    For n = 1 To intValues

      dblX2 = XAxisLeft + dblSpaceBetweenPoints * (CDbl(n) - 1#)

    ' Write a tick line and legend value to a point on the X axis

      rpt.DrawWidth = 12 * mdblChartHeightRatio
      DrawShadowLine rpt, dblX2, mdblYAxisBottom, dblX2, mdblYAxisBottom + .06
      DrawLine rpt, dblX2, mdblYAxisBottom, dblX2, mdblYAxisBottom + .06

      intTextWidth = rpt.TextWidth(astrLegend(n))
      rpt.CurrentX = X(dblX2) - intTextWidth / 2
      rpt.CurrentY = Y(mdblYAxisBottom + .1)
      rpt.Print astrLegend(n)
```

```
    ' Draw the line connecting this dot with a previous dot

    If n > 1 Then

       dblX1 = dblX2 - dblSpaceBetweenPoints

       dblY1 = dblBottomOffset - YPoint(aintData(n - 1), intHigh)
       dblY2 = dblBottomOffset - YPoint(aintData(n), intHigh)

       rpt.DrawWidth = 18 * mdblChartHeightRatio

       DrawShadowLine rpt, dblX1, dblY1, dblX2, dblY2
       rpt.Line (X(dblX1), Y(dblY1))-(X(dblX2), Y(dblY2)), Red

    End If

  Next n

  rpt.DrawWidth = 12 * mdblChartHeightRatio
  DrawAxis rpt

pgcReportLineChartDone:
  Exit Function

pgcReportLineChartError:
  Warning "pgcReportLineChart", Error$
  Resume pgcReportLineChartDone

End Function
```

The *pgcReportPieChart* Function

The pie chart function gave me the most trouble.

The documentation for the Circle method is incorrect in that it indicates setting the report's Back Style property if you need to fill in a circle or pie slice. A report doesn't have a Back Style property!

I was truly stumped, so I raised the issue on the MSACCESS forum on CompuServe and at the local Access user group. Several people came running to my rescue, and I thank them heartily.

Their answer was that the Fill Color property, which must be set to 0, is the correct property to set. With this valuable piece of Access trivia, you can produce a pie chart, as shown in Figure 19.21.

The pie chart function calculates start and end values for the different slices in the pie.

I wanted the function to draw the slices starting from the top and circling clockwise. Because the Circle method draws counterclockwise, I just reversed the order in which the data was used, starting with the last value in the data set.

FIGURE 19.21.

A pie chart created by the pgcReportPieChart *function.*

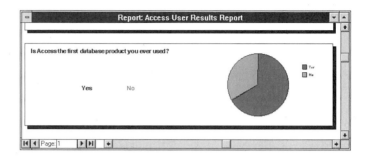

The pgcReportPicChart function is shown in Listing 19.13.

Listing 19.13. The pgcReportPieChart function.

```
Function pgcReportPieChart (rpt As Report, dblTop As Double,
➥ dblLeft As Double, dblHeight As Double, dblWidth As Double,
➥ intValues As Integer, aintData() As Integer, astrLegend() As String,
➥ alngColors() As Long) As Integer

' This function draws a pie chart. See the pgcReportBarChart function for
' details on the arguments passed.

    Dim intTotal As Integer
    Dim intHorzCenter As Integer
    Dim intVertCenter As Integer
    Dim intHorzCenter2 As Integer
    Dim intVertCenter2 As Integer
    Dim intRadius As Integer
    Dim dblLegendTop As Double
    Dim sngStart As Single
    Dim sngEnd As Single
    Dim sngStep As Single
    Dim n As Integer

    On Error GoTo pgcReportPieChartError

    Const SpaceBetweenLegendTitles = .4

    mdblChartTop = dblTop
    mdblChartLeft = dblLeft
    mdblChartHeightRatio = dblHeight / 4#
    mdblChartWidthRatio = dblWidth / 6.5

    dblLegendTop = .95

' How wide the lines will be
    rpt.DrawWidth = 12 * mdblChartHeightRatio

    rpt.FontSize = 14 * mdblChartHeightRatio
    rpt.FontName = "Arial"

    For n = 1 To intValues
    ' Draw the legend box and title
```

```
    DrawBox rpt, 5#, dblLegendTop, 5.25, dblLegendTop + YAxisTop,
    ➡ alngColors(n)

    rpt.CurrentX = X(5.35)
    rpt.CurrentY = Y(dblLegendTop + .016)
    rpt.Print astrLegend(n)

    dblLegendTop = dblLegendTop + SpaceBetweenLegendTitles
  Next n

  intHorzCenter = X(2.75)
  intVertCenter = Y(2#)
  intHorzCenter2 = X(2.75 + XShadowOffset)
  intVertCenter2 = Y(2# + YShadowOffset)
  intRadius = Y(1.5)

  intTotal = 0
  For n = 1 To intValues
    intTotal = intTotal + aintData(n)
  Next n

' Access documentation incorrectly indicates that you need to set the
' BackStyle property to make the pie slice fill with a color.
' Actually, they meant the FillStyle property as a Report object doesn't
' even have a BackStyle property!

  rpt.FillStyle = 0

' Draw the shadow for the whole pie
  rpt.FillColor = Gray
  rpt.Circle (intHorzCenter2, intVertCenter2), intRadius, Gray

' Draw the pie slices
  sngStart = 1.570795
  For n = intValues To 1 Step -1
    sngStep = CSng(aintData(n)) * 3.14159 * 2# / CSng(intTotal)
    sngEnd = sngStart + sngStep

    If sngEnd > 3.14159 * 2# Then
      sngEnd = sngEnd - 3.14159 * 2#
    End If

    rpt.FillColor = alngColors(n)
    rpt.Circle (intHorzCenter, intVertCenter), intRadius, Black, -sngStart,
    ➡ -sngEnd

    sngStart = sngEnd
  Next n

pgcReportPieChartDone:
  Exit Function

pgcReportPieChartError:
  Warning "pgcReportPieChart", Error$
  Resume pgcReportPieChartDone

End Function
```

Testing Pretty Good Charts

To test the chart functions, create an empty report with its Detail section set to 4 inches high and the report Width set to 6 inches. Then set the Detail section's On Print property, as shown in Figure 19.22, to call the `TestChart` function like this:

```
=TestChart([Report])
```

FIGURE 19.22.

Setting the On Print event for the Detail section.

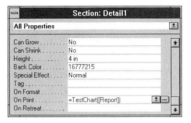

At the end of the test function are three lines that call the chart drawing functions. Two of the lines are commented out so that one of the charts is drawn. You can switch between charts by changing which of the three lines are commented out.

The `TestChart` function is shown in Listing 19.14.

Listing 19.14. The `TestChart` function.

```
Function TestChart (rpt As Report) As Integer

    ReDim aintData(6) As Integer
    ReDim astrLegend(6) As String
    ReDim alngColors(6) As Long

    Const ChartTop = 0#
    Const ChartLeft = 0#
    Const ChartHeight = 4#
    Const ChartWidth = 6.5

    Dim z As Integer

    On Error GoTo TestChartError

    aintData(1) = Rnd * 100
    aintData(2) = Rnd * 100
    aintData(3) = Rnd * 100
    aintData(4) = Rnd * 100
    aintData(5) = Rnd * 100
    aintData(6) = Rnd * 100

    astrLegend(1) = "Sony"
    astrLegend(2) = "Panasonic"
    astrLegend(3) = "Pioneer"
```

```
astrLegend(4) = "Emerson"
astrLegend(5) = "Sanyo"
astrLegend(6) = "NEC"

alngColors(1) = RGB(255, 0, 0)
alngColors(2) = RGB(0, 255, 0)
alngColors(3) = RGB(0, 0, 255)
alngColors(4) = RGB(255, 255, 0)
alngColors(5) = RGB(0, 255, 255)
alngColors(6) = RGB(255, 0, 255)

' Remove the comment for the type of chart you want to graph

  z = pgcReportBarChart(rpt, ChartTop, ChartLeft, ChartHeight, ChartWidth, 6,
➥ aintData(), astrLegend(), alngColors())
' z = pgcReportLineChart(rpt, ChartTop, ChartLeft, ChartHeight, ChartWidth, 6,
➥ aintData(), astrLegend(), alngColors())
' z = pgcReportPieChart(rpt, ChartTop, ChartLeft, ChartHeight, ChartWidth, 6,
➥ aintData(), astrLegend(), alngColors())

TestChartDone:
  Exit Function

TestChartError:
  MsgBox Error$, 48, "TestChart"
  Resume TestChartDone

End Function
```

Figures 19.23, 19.24, and 19.25 show line, pie, and bar charts that were drawn by calling the TestChart function as previously described.

FIGURE 19.23.

Testing the line chart.

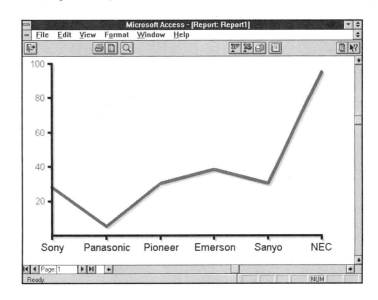

Part III ■ *Advanced Projects*

Testing the pie chart.

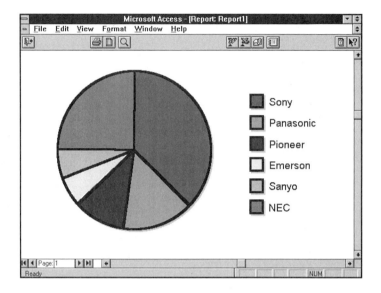

FIGURE 19.25.

Testing the bar chart.

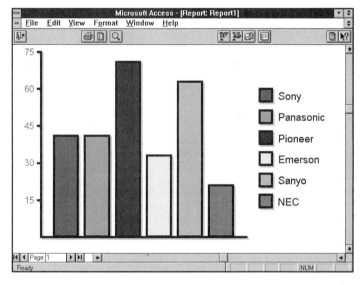

Note that the three Pretty Good Chart functions for drawing charts—
pgcReportBarChart, pgcReportLineChart, and pgcReportPieChart—take the same arguments, so they are easily interchangeable. You could use them in a program where the type of chart is selected at run time.

The *BuildResultsQuery* Function

Next, move back to the Survey Wizard Save As form module and look at the code that generates the two objects: the Results Query and the Results Report. The third object, Results Table, is generated as a result of executing the Results Query.

The best way to understand the BuildResultsQuery function (shown in Listing 19.15) would be to look at one of the queries it produces. Not the SQL, mind you; I mean the QBE (Query By Example) design window.

Note that this function was "reverse engineered" by creating a query by hand and then writing the code that produced the same SQL statement. The function is ugly, but it works!

Listing 19.15. The BuildResultsQuery **function.**

```
Function BuildResultsQuery () As Integer

  Dim db As Database
  Dim qry As QueryDef

  Dim sql As String
  Dim q As String

  Dim strLetter As String

  Dim n As Integer

' Assume failure
  BuildResultsQuery = True

  On Error GoTo BuildResultsQueryError

' Build an obscene SQL statement in a string variable for use in creating
' the Results Query

  q = Chr$(34)

  sql = "SELECT DISTINCTROW [" & zSWstrQuestionsTable & "].*, "
  sql = sql & "DCount(" & q & "Question" & q & " " & [ID]," & q & "[" &
➥ zSWstrResponsesTable & "]" & q & ") AS TotalResponses, "
  sql = sql & "IIf([Type]=1,DCount(" & q & "Question" & q & " " & [ID]," & q &
➥ "[" & zSWstrResponsesTable & "]" & q & "," & q & "Question" & q &
➥ " " & [ID] & " " & q & " = -1" & q & "),Null) AS TotalYes, "
  sql = sql & "IIf([Type]=1,DCount(" & q & "Question" & q & " " & [ID]," & q &
➥ "[" & zSWstrResponsesTable & "]" & q & "," & q & "Question" & q &
➥ " " & [ID] & " " & q & " = 0" & q & "),Null) AS TotalNo, "

  For n = 0 To 5
    strLetter = Chr$(65 + n)
```

continues

Listing 19.15. continued

```
    sql = sql & "IIf([Type]=2 And Not IsNull([Choice" & strLetter & "]),
    ➥DCount(" & q & "Question" & q & " & [ID]," & q & "[" &
    ➥ zSWstrResponsesTable & "]" & q & "," & q & "Question" & q & " & [ID]
    ➥ & " & q & " = " & n + 1 & q & "),Null) AS Total" & strLetter & ", "
    Next n

  sql = sql & "IIf([Type]=4 Or [Type]=5,IIf([Type]=4,[RangeFrom],
  ➥[PercentFrom]),Null) AS [From], "
  sql = sql & "IIf([Type]=4 Or [Type]=5,IIf([Type]=4,[RangeTo],[PercentTo])
  ➥,Null) AS To, "
  sql = sql & "IIf([Type]=4 Or [Type]=5,IIf([Type]=4,[RangeStep],
  ➥[PercentStep]),Null) AS Step, "
  sql = sql & "IIf(IsNull([From]),Null,([To]-[From])/[Step]+1) AS StepCount, "

  sql = sql & "IIf(IsNull([Step]),Null,DCount(" & q & "Question" & q & " & 
  ➥ [ID]," & q & "[" & zSWstrResponsesTable & "]" & q & "," & q &
  ➥ "Question" & q & " & [ID] & " & q & " = " & q & " & [From]))
  ➥ AS Total1, "

  For n = 1 To 9
    sql = sql & "IIf(IsNull([Step]),Null,IIf([StepCount]<" & n & ",Null,
    ➥DCount(" & q & "Question" & q & " & [ID]," & q & "[" &
    ➥ zSWstrResponsesTable & "]" & q & "," & q & "Question" & q & " & [ID]
    ➥ & " & q & " = " & q & " & [From]+[Step]*" & n & "))) AS Total" & n +
    ➥ 1
    If n < 9 Then sql = sql & ", "
  Next n

  sql = sql & " INTO [" & zSWstrResultsTable & "]"
  sql = sql & " FROM [" & zSWstrQuestionsTable & "] WITH OWNERACCESS OPTION;"

  Set db = DBEngine(0)(0)

' Delete the query if it already exists
  On Error Resume Next
  db.DeleteQueryDef zSWstrResultsQuery
  On Error GoTo BuildResultsQueryError
*
' Create the query
  Set qry = db.CreateQueryDef(zSWstrResultsQuery, sql)
  qry.Close

' Success
  BuildResultsQuery = False

BuildResultsQueryDone:
  Exit Function

BuildResultsQueryError:
  Warning "BuildResultsQuery", Error$
  Resume BuildResultsQueryDone

End Function
```

Building the Results Report

Next, you need to return to the Survey Wizard Save As form module's declaration section and add the constants that define the layout of the Results Report. (See Listing 19.16.)

Listing 19.16. The Results Report constants for the Survey Wizard Save As form module.

```
' Results Report constants

  Const RRFontName = "Arial"
  Const RRTitleBarFontSize = 20
  Const RRFontSize = 8

  Const RRSectionWidth = 6.5
  Const RRReportHeaderHeight = 1#
  Const RRDetailSectionHeight = 1.83
  Const RRPageFooterHeight = .25

  Const RRBarLeft = .25
  Const RRBarWidth = 6#
  Const RRShadowOffset = .05
  Const RRQuestionLabelLeft = .36
  Const RRQuestionLabelWidth = 3.5
  Const RRQuestionLabelTopOffset = .06
  Const RRQuestionLabelHeight = .53

  Const RRTitleBarTop = .125
  Const RRTitleBarHeight = .63
  Const RRTitleLabelTop = .23
  Const RRTitleLabelLeft = .31
  Const RRTitleLabelHeight = .42

  Const RRResponseLabelTopOffset1 = .75
  Const RRResponseLabelTopOffset2 = 1#
  Const RRResponseLabelTopOffset3 = 1.25
  Const RRResponseLabelHeight = .17

  Const RRYesNoWidth = .25
  Const RRYesLeft = 1.35
  Const RRNoLeft = 2.15

  Const RRMultipleChoiceLeft1 = .5
  Const RRMultipleChoiceLeft2 = 2.1
  Const RRMultipleChoiceWidth = 1.5

  Const RRWriteInLeft = 2.5
  Const RRWriteInWidth = 1.5

  Const RRFirstPointLeft = .45
  Const RRLastPointLeft = 3.6
  Const RRPointWidth = .3

  Const RRPageCountLeft = 2.75
  Const RRPageCountWidth = 1#
```

The *BuildResultsReport* Function

The BuildResultsReport function is similar in many ways to the BuildEntryReport function.

The function looks complicated, but writing it was mainly a matter of describing via code the existing prototype report. Create the object, set its properties, create the object, set its properties, and so on. You get the picture.

Reviewing how you created the Entry Report will help clear things up.

Within the function, the BuildResultsQuery function is called to produce the make table query. Then the make table query is executed to produce an empty copy of the table to which this report is bound.

The BuildResultsReport function is shown in Listing 19.17.

Listing 19.17. The BuildResultsReport **function.**

```
Function BuildResultsReport () As Integer

' The report generated is always the same other than the setting of the
' Record Source property. However, the report is still generated via code
' so that it may be dropped in the user's current database by the wizard.

    Dim rpt As Report
    Dim ctl As Control

    Dim strReportName As String
    Dim strCaption As String

    Dim dblPointStepWidth As Double
    Dim dblPointLeft As Double

    Dim n As Integer
    Dim z As Integer

    Dim blnReportOpened As Integer

    blnReportOpened = False
    On Error GoTo BuildResultsReportError

    z = BuildResultsQuery()
    If z Then GoTo BuildResultsReportDone

    Set rpt = CreateReport("", "")
    blnReportOpened = True

' Turn on the report header and footer through the Access 2.0 menu
' 7 = Report Design menu, 3 = Format, 10 = Report Header/Footer
    DoCmd DoMenuItem 7, 3, 10, , A_MENU_VER20

    strReportName = rpt.FormName
```

```
' Set the page dimensions
  rpt.Width = zTwips(RRSectionWidth)
  rpt.Section(Header).Height = zTwips(RRReportHeaderHeight)
  rpt.Section(PageHeader).Height = 0
  rpt.Section(PageFooter).Height = zTwips(RRPageFooterHeight)
  rpt.Section(Detail).Height = zTwips(RRDetailSectionHeight)
  rpt.Section(Footer).Height = 0

' Execute the make table query to create the record source for this report
  DoCmd SetWarnings False
  DoCmd OpenQuery zSWstrResultsQuery
  DoCmd SetWarnings True

' Set report properties
  rpt.RecordSource = zSWstrResultsTable
  rpt.OnOpen = "=zSWResultsReportOnOpen(Report," & Chr$(34) &
➥ zSWstrResultsQuery & Chr$(34) & ")"
  rpt.Section(Detail).OnFormat = "=zSWResultsReportDetailOnFormat(Report)"
  rpt.Section(Detail).OnPrint = "=zSWResultsReportDetailOnPrint(Report)"

' Report Header controls

' Title bar shadow
  Set ctl = CreateReportControl(strReportName, ControlTypeRectangle, Header,
➥ "", "", zTwips(RRBarLeft + RRShadowOffset), zTwips(RRTitleBarTop +
➥ RRShadowOffset), zTwips(RRBarWidth), zTwips(RRTitleBarHeight))
  ctl.ControlName = "shpTitleBarShadow"
  ctl.BackColor = Black

' Title bar
  Set ctl = CreateReportControl(strReportName, ControlTypeRectangle, Header,
➥ "", "", zTwips(RRBarLeft), zTwips(RRTitleBarTop),
➥ zTwips(RRBarWidth), zTwips(RRTitleBarHeight))
  ctl.ControlName = "shpTitleBar"
  ctl.BackColor = White

' Title bar text
  Set ctl = CreateReportControl(strReportName, ControlTypeLabel, Header, "",
➥ "", zTwips(RRTitleLabelLeft), zTwips(RRTitleLabelTop), 0, 0)
  ctl.ControlName = "lblTitleBarCaption"
  strCaption = zSWfrm!cboSurveyTitle
  If Right$(strCaption, 6) <> "Survey" Then
    strCaption = strCaption & " Survey"
  End If
  ctl.Caption = strCaption
  ctl.TextAlign = TextAlignCenter
  RRSetFont ctl, FontWeightBold
  ctl.FontSize = RRTitleBarFontSize
  ctl.Height = zTwips(RRTitleLabelHeight)
  ctl.Width = zTwips(ERQuestionLabelWidth)

' Detail Section controls

' Question textbox
  Set ctl = CreateReportControl(strReportName, ControlTypeTextbox, Detail, "",
➥ "", zTwips(RRQuestionLabelLeft), zTwips(RRQuestionLabelTopOffset),
➥ zTwips(RRQuestionLabelWidth), zTwips(RRQuestionLabelHeight))
```

continues

Listing 19.17. continued

```
ctl.ControlName = "txtQuestion" & n
ctl.ControlSource = "Question"
ctl.TextAlign = TextAlignLeft
RRSetFont ctl, FontWeightBold

' Create some controls that are not displayed, but will be used to retrieve
' values by the run-time code.
CreateHiddenControl strReportName, "Type"
CreateHiddenControl strReportName, "RangeFrom"
CreateHiddenControl strReportName, "RangeTo"
CreateHiddenControl strReportName, "RangeStep"
CreateHiddenControl strReportName, "PercentFrom"
CreateHiddenControl strReportName, "PercentTo"
CreateHiddenControl strReportName, "PercentStep"
CreateHiddenControl strReportName, "From"
CreateHiddenControl strReportName, "To"
CreateHiddenControl strReportName, "Step"
CreateHiddenControl strReportName, "TotalNo"
CreateHiddenControl strReportName, "TotalYes"
For n = 1 To 10
  CreateHiddenControl strReportName, "Total" & n
Next n
For n = 1 To 6
  CreateHiddenControl strReportName, "Total" & Chr$(64 + n)
Next n

' Controls for the different answer types

' Create an additional one for each, set to Bold so that can be turned on
' to indicate a value selected the most.

' Yes
Set ctl = CreateReportControl(strReportName, ControlTypeLabel, Detail, "",
➥ "", zTwips(RRYesLeft), zTwips(RRResponseLabelTopOffset1), 0, 0)
ctl.ControlName = "lblYes"
ctl.Caption = "Yes"
ctl.TextAlign = TextAlignLeft
RRSetFont ctl, FontWeightNormal
ctl.Height = zTwips(RRResponseLabelHeight)
ctl.Width = zTwips(RRYesNoWidth)

' Yes Bold
Set ctl = CreateReportControl(strReportName, ControlTypeLabel, Detail, "",
➥ "", zTwips(RRYesLeft), zTwips(RRResponseLabelTopOffset1), 0, 0)
ctl.ControlName = "lblYesBold"
ctl.Caption = "Yes"
ctl.TextAlign = TextAlignLeft
RRSetFont ctl, FontWeightBold
ctl.Height = zTwips(RRResponseLabelHeight)
ctl.Width = zTwips(RRYesNoWidth)
ctl.Visible = False

' No
Set ctl = CreateReportControl(strReportName, ControlTypeLabel, Detail, "",
➥ "", zTwips(RRNoLeft), zTwips(RRResponseLabelTopOffset1), 0, 0)
ctl.ControlName = "lblNo"
```

```
  ctl.Caption = "No"
  ctl.TextAlign = TextAlignRight
  RRSetFont ctl, FontWeightNormal
  ctl.Height = zTwips(RRResponseLabelHeight)
  ctl.Width = zTwips(RRYesNoWidth)

' No Bold
  Set ctl = CreateReportControl(strReportName, ControlTypeLabel, Detail, "",
➥ "", zTwips(RRNoLeft), zTwips(RRResponseLabelTopOffset1), 0, 0)
  ctl.ControlName = "lblNoBold"
  ctl.Caption = "No"
  ctl.TextAlign = TextAlignRight
  RRSetFont ctl, FontWeightBold
  ctl.Height = zTwips(RRResponseLabelHeight)
  ctl.Width = zTwips(RRYesNoWidth)
  ctl.Visible = False

' Number line for range or percents
  dblPointStepWidth = (RRLastPointLeft - RRFirstPointLeft) /
➥ (CDbl(zSWMaximumPoints) - 1#)
  dblPointLeft = RRFirstPointLeft
  For n = 1 To zSWMaximumPoints
  ' A point on the number line
    Set ctl = CreateReportControl(strReportName, ControlTypeTextbox, Detail,
➥ "", "", zTwips(dblPointLeft), zTwips(RRResponseLabelTopOffset1),
➥ zTwips(RRPointWidth), zTwips(RRResponseLabelHeight))
    ctl.ControlName = "txtPoint" & n
    ctl.TextAlign = TextAlignCenter
    RRSetFont ctl, FontWeightNormal

  ' Bold version
    Set ctl = CreateReportControl(strReportName, ControlTypeTextbox, Detail,
➥ "", "", zTwips(dblPointLeft), zTwips(RRResponseLabelTopOffset1),
➥ zTwips(RRPointWidth), zTwips(RRResponseLabelHeight))
    ctl.ControlName = "txtPoint" & n & "Bold"
    ctl.TextAlign = TextAlignCenter
    RRSetFont ctl, FontWeightBold
    ctl.Visible = False

    dblPointLeft = dblPointLeft + dblPointStepWidth
  Next n

' Multiple choice selections
  RRMultipleChoice strReportName, "A", RRMultipleChoiceLeft1,
➥ RRResponseLabelTopOffset1
  RRMultipleChoice strReportName, "B", RRMultipleChoiceLeft1,
➥ RRResponseLabelTopOffset2
  RRMultipleChoice strReportName, "C", RRMultipleChoiceLeft1,
➥ RRResponseLabelTopOffset3
  RRMultipleChoice strReportName, "D", RRMultipleChoiceLeft2,
➥ RRResponseLabelTopOffset1
  RRMultipleChoice strReportName, "E", RRMultipleChoiceLeft2,
➥ RRResponseLabelTopOffset2
  RRMultipleChoice strReportName, "F", RRMultipleChoiceLeft2,
➥ RRResponseLabelTopOffset3
```

continues

Listing 19.17. continued

```
' Display a message if the question was a Write-In type
  Set ctl = CreateReportControl(strReportName, ControlTypeLabel, Detail, "",
  ➥ "", zTwips(RRWriteInLeft), zTwips(RRResponseLabelTopOffset1), 0, 0)
  ctl.ControlName = "lblWriteIn"
  ctl.Caption = "Write-In Question."
  ctl.TextAlign = TextAlignRight
  RRSetFont ctl, FontWeightBold
  ctl.Height = zTwips(RRResponseLabelHeight)
  ctl.Width = zTwips(RRWriteInWidth)
  ctl.TextAlign = 2 ' Centered

' Page count
  Set ctl = CreateReportControl(strReportName, ControlTypeTextbox, PageFooter,
  ➥ "", "", zTwips(RRPageCountLeft), 0, zTwips(RRPageCountWidth),
  ➥ zTwips(RRPageFooterHeight))
  ctl.ControlName = "txtPageCount"
  ctl.ControlSource = "=" & Chr$(34) & "- " & Chr$(34) & " & Page & " &
  ➥ Chr$(34) & " -" & Chr$(34)
  ctl.TextAlign = TextAlignCenter
  RRSetFont ctl, FontWeightBold

' Success
  BuildResultsReport = False

BuildResultsReportDone:
  On Error Resume Next
  If blnReportOpened Then
    DoCmd SetWarnings False
    SendKeys zSWstrResultsReport & "~"
    DoCmd Close A_Report, rpt.FormName
    DoCmd SetWarnings True
  End If
  Exit Function

BuildResultsReportError:
  Warning "BuildResultsReport", Error$
  Resume BuildResultsReportDone

End Function
```

Although `BuildResultsQuery` and `BuildResultsReport` get the job done, they are not pretty to look at. Don't feel bad if you didn't feel a rush of appreciation for them.

The next two subroutines are called by the `BuildResultsReport` function.

The *RRMultipleChoice* Subroutine

The `RRMultipleChoice` subroutine creates two text boxes to display a multiple-choice selection on the Results Report. The first one is in the Normal Font Weight and the second one is in Bold. See Listing 19.18.

Listing 19.18. The RRMultipleChoice **subroutine.**

```
Sub RRMultipleChoice (strReportName As String, strLetter As String,
➡ dblLeft As Double, dblTop As Double)

  Dim ctl As Control

  On Error GoTo RRMultipleChoiceError

  Set ctl = CreateReportControl(strReportName, ControlTypeTextbox, Detail, "",
  ➡ "", zTwips(dblLeft), zTwips(dblTop), zTwips(RRMultipleChoiceWidth),
  ➡ zTwips(RRResponseLabelHeight))
  ctl.ControlName = "txt" & strLetter
  ctl.ControlSource = "=zSWMultipleChoice(" & Chr$(34) & strLetter & Chr$(34)
  ➡ & ",[Choice" & strLetter & "])"
  ctl.TextAlign = TextAlignLeft
  RRSetFont ctl, FontWeightNormal
  ctl.Visible = False

  Set ctl = CreateReportControl(strReportName, ControlTypeTextbox, Detail, "",
  ➡ "", zTwips(dblLeft), zTwips(dblTop), zTwips(RRMultipleChoiceWidth),
  ➡ zTwips(RRResponseLabelHeight))
  ctl.ControlName = "txt" & strLetter & "Bold"
  ctl.ControlSource = "=zSWMultipleChoice(" & Chr$(34) & strLetter & Chr$(34)
  ➡ & ",[Choice" & strLetter & "])"
  ctl.TextAlign = TextAlignLeft
  RRSetFont ctl, FontWeightBold
  ctl.Visible = False

RRMultipleChoiceDone:
  Exit Sub

RRMultipleChoiceError:
  Warning "RRMultipleChoice", Error$
  Resume RRMultipleChoiceDone

End Sub
```

The *RRSetFont* Subroutine

The RRSetFont subroutine is used to set three control properties in one call. See Listing 19.19.

Listing 19.19. The RRSetFont **subroutine.**

```
Sub RRSetFont (ctl As Control, intFontWeight As Integer)

  On Error Resume Next
  ctl.FontName = RRFontName
  ctl.FontSize = RRFontSize
  ctl.FontWeight = intFontWeight

End Sub
```

That completes the changes to the Survey Wizard Save As form module. The remaining codes are changes and additions to the report run-time code.

The Survey Wizard Report Run-Time Module

You need to add code to the Survey Wizard Report Run-Time module to support the new report. I'll list the full procedures, but keep in mind that you already did much of this coding when you created run-time code for the Entry Report.

The first change is to add some variables and constants to the declarations section. The three arrays are used to hold data passed to the chart functions. See Listing 19.20.

Listing 19.20. The Survey Wizard Report Run-Time module declaration section.

```
' Survey Wizard Report Run-Time

  Option Compare Database
  Option Explicit

  Const mstrProgramName = "Survey Wizard Report Run-Time"

  Dim maintData(10) As Integer
  Dim mastrLegend(10) As String
  Dim malngColors(10) As Long

  Const TwipsPerInch = 1440
  Const Black = 0
```

The *ShowYesNo* Subroutine

The ShowYesNo subroutine is modified to display or hide the Yes and No labels on a results report. See Listing 19.21.

If the results are being displayed, either the Yes or No Bold label is displayed to indicate which one was chosen the most often. There may also be a tie, in which case the Bold versions of both are displayed.

Listing 19.21. The ShowYesNo **subroutine.**

```
Private Sub ShowYesNo (rpt As Report, intType As Integer, blnResultsReport
➥ As Integer)

  Dim blnVisible As Integer

  On Error GoTo ShowYesNoError
```

```
    blnVisible = (intType = zSWQuestionTypeYesNo)

  If blnResultsReport Then
  ' Results Report

    rpt!lblYes.Visible = False
    rpt!lblNo.Visible = False
    rpt!lblYesBold.Visible = False
    rpt!lblNoBold.Visible = False

    If blnVisible Then
      If rpt![TotalYes] >= rpt![TotalNo] Then
        rpt!lblYesBold.Visible = True
      Else
        rpt!lblYes.Visible = True
      End If

      If rpt![TotalNo] >= rpt![TotalYes] Then
        rpt!lblNoBold.Visible = True
      Else
        rpt!lblNo.Visible = True
      End If
    End If
  Else
  ' Entry Report

    rpt!lblYes.Visible = blnVisible
    rpt!lblNo.Visible = blnVisible
  End If

ShowYesNoDone:
  Exit Sub

ShowYesNoError:
  Warning "ShowYesNo", Error$
  Resume ShowYesNoDone

End Sub
```

The *ShowMultipleChoice* Subroutine

Ditto the preceding, except this time the multiple choice text boxes are turned on or off. If they are made visible, the selection that was chosen the most is highlighted by turning the Bold version of that text box on. See Listing 19.22.

Listing 19.22. The ShowMultipleChoice **subroutine.**

```
Private Sub ShowMultipleChoice (rpt As Report, intType As Integer,
➡ blnResultsReport As Integer)

  Dim ctl As Control
```

continues

Listing 19.22. continued

```
Dim intCount As Integer
Dim intLargest As Integer

Dim n As Integer

Dim blnVisible As Integer

On Error GoTo ShowMultipleChoiceError

blnVisible = (intType = zSWQuestionTypeMultipleChoice)

If blnResultsReport Then
' Results Report

  For n = 65 To 70
    rpt("txt" & Chr$(n)).Visible = False
    rpt("txt" & Chr$(n) & "Bold").Visible = False
  Next n

  If blnVisible Then

  ' Find the largest value
    intLargest = 0
    For n = 65 To 70
      Set ctl = rpt("Total" & Chr$(n))

      If Not IsNull(ctl) Then
        intCount = ctl
        If intCount > intLargest Then
          intLargest = intCount
        End If
      End If
    Next n

  ' Bold the ones that match the largest value
    For n = 65 To 70
      Set ctl = rpt("Total" & Chr$(n))
      If Not IsNull(ctl) Then
        intCount = ctl
        If intCount = intLargest Then
          rpt("txt" & Chr$(n) & "Bold").Visible = True
        Else
          rpt("txt" & Chr$(n)).Visible = True
        End If
      End If
    Next n
  End If
Else
' Entry Report

  For n = 65 To 70
    rpt("txt" & Chr$(n)).Visible = blnVisible
  Next n
End If

ShowMultipleChoiceDone:
  Exit Sub
```

```
ShowMultipleChoiceError:
  Warning "ShowMultipleChoice", Error$
  Resume ShowMultipleChoiceDone

End Sub
```

The *ShowWriteIn* Subroutine

Only one line has been added to the ShowWriteIn subroutine (see Listing 19.23).

If the current question is a write-in question, the report simply displays a label that says Write-In Question. That's because the report can't really do anything with write-in results because they can't be summarized.

A report for write-in questions hasn't been supplied. You might want to create a separate report that lists all the responses individually.

Listing 19.23. The ShowWriteIn **subroutine.**

```
Private Sub ShowWriteIn (rpt As Report, intType As Integer,
➥ blnResultsReport As Integer)

  Dim n As Integer

  Dim blnVisible As Integer

  On Error GoTo ShowWriteInError

  blnVisible = (intType = zSWQuestionTypeWriteIn)

  If blnResultsReport Then
  ' Results Report

    rpt!lblWriteIn.Visible = blnVisible
  Else
  ' Entry Report

    For n = 1 To 3
      rpt("Line" & n).Visible = blnVisible
    Next n
  End If

ShowWriteInDone:
  Exit Sub

ShowWriteInError:
  Warning "ShowWriteIn", Error$
  Resume ShowWriteInDone

End Sub
```

The *ShowRangePercent* Subroutine

The ShowRangePercent subroutine turns on text boxes to display the range or percent values if the question is a range- or percent-type question.

Again, the one or more values that have been selected the most often are highlighted by turning on the Bold versions of the text boxes.

The ShowRangePercent subroutine is shown in Listing 19.24.

Listing 19.24. The ShowRangePercent **subroutine.**

```
Private Sub ShowRangePercent (rpt As Report, intType As Integer,
➥ blnResultsReport As Integer)

  Dim ctl As Control

  Dim lngFrom As Long
  Dim lngTo As Long
  Dim lngStep As Long
  Dim l As Long

  Dim intCount As Integer
  Dim intLargest As Integer
  Dim intSkip As Integer
  Dim n As Integer

  Dim blnVisible As Integer

  On Error GoTo ShowRangePercentError

  blnVisible = ((intType = zSWQuestionTypeRange) Or (intType =
➥ zSWQuestionTypePercent))

  For n = 1 To zSWMaximumPoints
    rpt("txtPoint" & n).Visible = False
    If blnResultsReport Then
      rpt("txtPoint" & n & "Bold").Visible = False
    End If
  Next n

  If blnResultsReport Then
    If blnVisible Then

    ' Find the largest value
      intLargest = 0
      For n = 1 To zSWMaximumPoints
        Set ctl = rpt("Total" & n)
        If IsNull(ctl) Then
          Exit For
        Else
          intCount = ctl
          If intCount > intLargest Then
            intLargest = intCount
          End If
        End If
```

```
      Next n
    End If
  End If

  If blnVisible Then
    If intType = zSWQuestionTypeRange Then
      lngFrom = CLng(rpt![RangeFrom])
      lngTo = CLng(rpt![RangeTo])
      lngStep = CLng(rpt![RangeStep])
    Else
      lngFrom = CLng(rpt![PercentFrom])
      lngTo = CLng(rpt![PercentTo])
      lngStep = CLng(rpt![PercentStep])
    End If

    If zSWValidatePoints(lngFrom, lngTo, lngStep) Then
      n = 1
      intSkip = (zSWMaximumPoints - CInt((lngTo - lngFrom + lngStep) /
      ➥ lngStep)) / 2

      For l = lngFrom To lngTo Step lngStep

        If blnResultsReport Then
        ' Results Report

          If rpt("Total" & n) = intLargest Then
            Set ctl = rpt("txtPoint" & n + intSkip & "Bold")
          Else
            Set ctl = rpt("txtPoint" & n + intSkip)
          End If
        Else
        ' Entry Report

          Set ctl = rpt("txtPoint" & n + intSkip)
        End If

        If intType = zSWQuestionTypePercent Then
          ctl = CStr(l) & "%"
        Else
          ctl = CStr(l)
        End If

        ctl.Visible = True

        n = n + 1
      Next l

    End If
  End If

ShowRangePercentDone:
  Exit Sub

ShowRangePercentError:
  Warning "ShowRangePercent", Error$
  Resume ShowRangePercentDone

End Sub
```

The *zSWResultsReportOnOpen* Function

The On Open event code for the Results Report initializes the color values used in the charts.

The function then displays a message box asking whether to recalculate the survey totals. If the user selects Yes, the Results Query is executed to generate a new Results Table.

The zSWResultsReportOnOpen subroutine is shown in Listing 19.25.

Listing 19.25. The zSWResultsReportOnOpen **subroutine.**

```
Function zSWResultsReportOnOpen (rpt As Report, strMakeTableQuery As String)
➥ As Integer

  Dim z As Integer

  On Error GoTo zSWResultsReportOnOpenError

  malngColors(1) = RGB(255, 0, 0)
  malngColors(2) = RGB(0, 255, 0)
  malngColors(3) = RGB(0, 0, 255)
  malngColors(4) = RGB(255, 255, 0)
  malngColors(5) = RGB(0, 255, 255)
  malngColors(6) = RGB(255, 0, 255)
  malngColors(7) = RGB(127, 0, 0)
  malngColors(8) = RGB(0, 127, 0)
  malngColors(9) = RGB(0, 0, 127)
  malngColors(10) = RGB(127, 127, 0)

' Prompt for whether or not the results should be recalculated
  z = MsgBox("Recalculate survey results?", 4 + 32, mstrProgramName)

' Run the make table query to generate new survey results
  If z = 6 Then ' Yes
    DoCmd SetWarnings False
    DoCmd OpenQuery strMakeTableQuery
    DoCmd SetWarnings True
  End If

zSWResultsReportOnOpenDone:
  Exit Function

zSWResultsReportOnOpenError:
  Warning Error$, "zSWResultsReportOnOpen"
  Resume zSWResultsReportOnOpenDone

End Function
```

The *zSWResultsReportDetailOnFormat* Function

The `zSWResultsReportDetailOnFormat` function was required to prevent errors from occurring when the Detail section tried to print with no current record. In such cases, this function cancels printing the section. (See Listing 19.26.)

Listing 19.26. The `zSWResultsReportDetailOnFormat` **subroutine.**

```
Function zSWResultsReportDetailOnFormat (rpt As Report) As Integer

  Dim intType As Integer

  On Error GoTo zSWResultsReportDetailOnFormatError

  If IsNull(rpt![Type]) Then
    DoCmd CancelEvent
    GoTo zSWResultsReportDetailOnFormatDone
  End If

zSWResultsReportDetailOnFormatDone:
  Exit Function

zSWResultsReportDetailOnFormatError:
  Warning "zSWResultsReportDetailOnFormat", Error$
  Resume zSWResultsReportDetailOnFormatDone

End Function
```

The *zSWResultsReportDetailOnPrint* Function

The final function, `zSWResultsReportDetailOnPrint`, is executed on the report Detail section's On Print event.

The `ShowYesNo`, `ShowRangePercent`, `ShowMultipleChoice`, and `ShowWriteIn` subroutines are called to turn on the appropriate controls for the current record's question type.

Next, depending on the question type, the chart arrays are filled with data and legend text.

Here's an interesting one: Rather than use rectangle controls to create the shadowed box, the subroutine draws the boxes instead. This is done because the functions that draw a chart can draw only on the report background. You will need to be aware of this limitation when using the chart functions.

Finally, depending on the question type, the appropriate chart function is called. Having interchangeable chart functions is a big advantage here.

I chose to use bar charts for multiple-choice questions, line charts for range or percent questions, and pie charts for yes/no questions.

The zSWResultsReportDetailOnPrint subroutine is shown in Listing 19.27.

Listing 19.27. The zSWResultsReportDetailOnPrint **subroutine.**

```
Function zSWResultsReportDetailOnPrint (rpt As Report) As Integer

  Dim strLetter As String

  Dim intType As Integer
  Dim intValues As Integer
  Dim n As Integer
  Dim z As Integer

  Const ChartTop = .04
  Const ChartLeft = 3.75
  Const ChartHeight = 1.48
  Const ChartWidth = 2.46

  On Error GoTo zSWResultsReportDetailOnPrintError

  intType = CInt(rpt![Type])

' Show the appropriate response text

  ShowYesNo rpt, intType, True
  ShowRangePercent rpt, intType, True
  ShowMultipleChoice rpt, intType, True
  ShowWriteIn rpt, intType, True

' Set the chart data

  Select Case intType

  Case zSWQuestionTypeYesNo
    intValues = 2
    maintData(1) = rpt![TotalYes]
    maintData(2) = rpt![TotalNo]
    mastrLegend(1) = "Yes"
    mastrLegend(2) = "No"

  Case zSWQuestionTypeMultipleChoice
    intValues = 0
    For n = 1 To 6
      strLetter = Chr$(64 + n)
      If Not IsNull(rpt("Choice" & strLetter)) Then
        intValues = intValues + 1
        maintData(intValues) = rpt("Total" & strLetter)
        mastrLegend(intValues) = strLetter
      End If
    Next n

  Case zSWQuestionTypeRange, zSWQuestionTypePercent
    intValues = 0
    For n = rpt![From] To rpt![To] Step rpt![Step]
      intValues = intValues + 1
```

```
      maintData(intValues) = rpt("Total" & intValues)
      mastrLegend(intValues) = Str$(n)
      If intType = zSWQuestionTypePercent Then
        mastrLegend(intValues) = mastrLegend(intValues) & "%"
      End If
    Next n

  End Select

' Draw a box
  rpt.DrawWidth = 1
  rpt.Line (.25 * TwipsPerInch, 0# * TwipsPerInch)-(6.25 * TwipsPerInch,
  ➡ 1.56 * TwipsPerInch), Black, B

' Draw a shadow for the box
  rpt.Line (.3 * TwipsPerInch, 1.56 * TwipsPerInch)-(6.31 * TwipsPerInch,
  ➡ 1.62 * TwipsPerInch), Black, BF
  rpt.Line (6.25 * TwipsPerInch, .05 * TwipsPerInch)-(6.31 * TwipsPerInch,
  ➡ 1.62 * TwipsPerInch), Black, BF

' Draw the chart

  Select Case intType

  Case zSWQuestionTypeYesNo
    z = pgcReportPieChart(rpt, ChartTop, ChartLeft, ChartHeight, ChartWidth,
    ➡ intValues, maintData(), mastrLegend(), malngColors())

  Case zSWQuestionTypeMultipleChoice
    z = pgcReportBarChart(rpt, ChartTop, ChartLeft, ChartHeight, ChartWidth,
    ➡ intValues, maintData(), mastrLegend(), malngColors())

  Case zSWQuestionTypeRange, zSWQuestionTypePercent
    z = pgcReportLineChart(rpt, ChartTop, ChartLeft, ChartHeight, ChartWidth,
    ➡ intValues, maintData(), mastrLegend(), malngColors())

  End Select

zSWResultsReportDetailOnPrintDone:
  Exit Function

zSWResultsReportDetailOnPrintError:
  Warning "zSWResultsReportDetailOnPrint", Error$
  Resume zSWResultsReportDetailOnPrintDone

End Function
```

Running the Results Report

The Survey Wizard is fully functional now!

Open the Results Report and you get the message box shown in Figure 19.26.

FIGURE 19.26.

Being prompted to recalculate the survey totals.

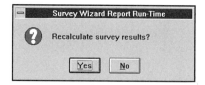

Answer Yes if you haven't calculated totals since you last ran the report.

Figures 19.27 through 19.30 show the printed Results Report of the Driving Habits survey.

FIGURE 19.27.

Driving Habits Survey results, Page 1.

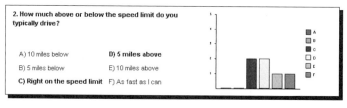

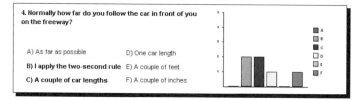

FIGURE 19.28.

Driving Habits Survey results, Page 2.

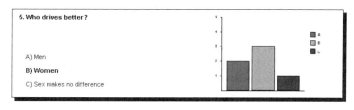

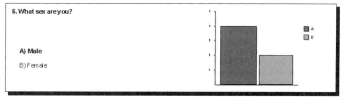

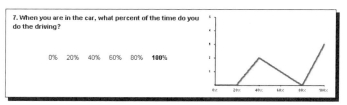

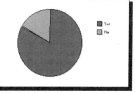

FIGURE 19.29.
Driving Habits Survey results, Page 3.

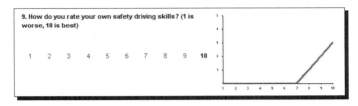

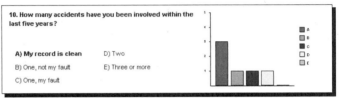

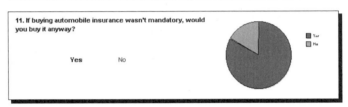

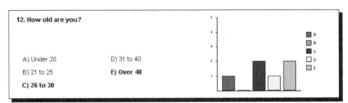

FIGURE 19.30.

Driving Habits Survey results, Page 4.

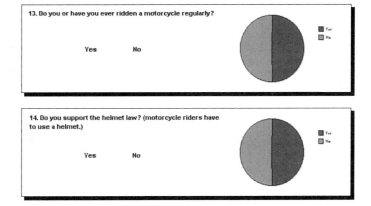

Summary

Hey, you did it! You have a fully functional online survey system with reporting capability.

Here are some of the highlights that occurred throughout this chapter. You

- Figured out what a wizard *really* is
- Created a questionnaire
- Activated the questionnaire Entry Form from a Program Manager icon
- Entered some test data on which to report
- Designed the Results Query and Results Report
- Prototyped the Bar Chart
- Coded functions to draw bar, line, and pie charts
- Applied scaling to make charts of any size
- Wrote a text function to prove that chart routines work anywhere
- Wrote code to generate the Results Query and Results Report
- Wrote the run-time code for the Results Report

In the next chapter you take a break from coding and get Survey Wizard ready to ship. You'll split it into two installable library databases, and then you'll create online help to document it.

Cool!

CHAPTER 20

Access: Survey Wizard, Part Five— Shrink-wrap and Ship It

This chapter focuses on making Survey Wizard a "shippable" product.

The first task at hand is to transform the SURVEY.MDB database into a pair of library databases. You will test how to call Survey Wizard from the Access menu to create objects in a new empty database.

Then you'll blow the dust off of the Windows Help Compiler and discover all of the gory details that go into how the Survey Wizard help file is created. You finish up by making Survey Wizard an installable menu add-in, just as you did with the Picture Builder+ database in Chapter 15, "Access: Picture Builder+" (see Figure 20.1).

FIGURE 20.1.

Survey Wizard is installable through the Access Add-in Manager.

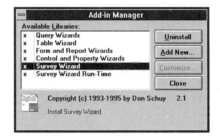

First, let's address a few notes on the makeup of an application designed to run as a library database.

The Importance of Using Code Behind Forms

With Version 2.0, Access went Visual Basic in style by allowing the placement of *code behind forms* (CBF).

This is a welcome change. CBF enables developers to build larger applications because only portions of the application need to be loaded at a time. Module code is loaded as soon as the application starts and remains in memory for the duration of the run. Code behind a form affects your computer's available resources only when the form is loaded and used.

You may need to experiment with CBF to see if it truly benefits the application you are working on. A drawback with CBF is that forms can load somewhat slower than they did before.

To counter this slow speed, you may want to pre-load some of the more frequently used forms in your application as hidden forms. When the pre-loaded form is needed, you just set its Visible property to True and the user gets instant feedback. However, be aware that code behind the pre-loaded forms is loaded at all times just as if it were in a module.

If you are building an extension to Access in the form of a builder, wizard, or menu add-in, then CBF is an essential ingredient to your project.

Access add-ins are implemented as database libraries that are loaded at startup. This procedure makes your add-in available to affect a user's open database. If you have done any poking around in your MSACC20.INI file, you have probably seen the following section that indicates which libraries are being loaded:

```
[Libraries]
wzlib.mda=rw
wzQuery.mda=rw
wzbldr.mda=rw
wzTable.mda=rw
wzfrmrpt.mda=rw
picbldr.mda=rw
```

Suppose that you made the next killer add-in for Access 2.0 and a few thousand excited users installed it on their machine. If you didn't do things right, your database library could wind up using a good chunk of precious memory resources on all those machines! Not only that, your application could significantly slow down how fast Access loads on all those computers, too.

By using CBF, you minimize the impact your database library has on a computer running Access. The module in a typical add-in declares a few global constants and a few variables if necessary; then a minimally sized function called an *entry point* opens up the first form.

Back in Chapter 16, "Access: Survey Wizard, Part One—Design and Interface," you created the SurveyWizard function in the Survey Wizard Entry Point module. For a recap, it's shown again here in Listing 20.1.

Listing 20.1. The SurveyWizard entry point function.

```
Function SurveyWizard ()

  On Error Resume Next
  DoCmd OpenForm "Survey Wizard", A_Normal, , , A_Edit, A_Dialog

End Function
```

Avoiding Name Conflicts

Another benefit in using CBF is that you don't need to worry about name conflicts with declarations in other database libraries. All the constants, variables, and procedures in a form module are limited in scope to that module only.

For code that remains in a code module, you still need to be careful to place a prefix before each function or other name declaration that will hopefully ensure it remains unique. For the Survey Wizard libraries, you should be OK as long as some other programmer isn't going wild with z, zSW and pgc prefixes.

Writing Code for Libraries

My first version of Survey Wizard didn't run correctly as a library database, so I had to make some adjustments here and there. We have coded Survey Wizard the correct way this time, but just in case you want to develop your own menu add-in, I will list some of the issues I ran into.

To open objects in the library database you need to use the CodeDB() function to return the database object, rather than the Access 1.1 CurrentDB() function or the Databases(0) element of the Databases collection. CodeDB() returns the database that the library code is running from. CurrentDB() and the Databases(0) element return the user's open database, which they've opened with the **File**|**O**pen menu command.

NOTE

The shorthand way you've been using to set a database variable to the current database is

```
Set db = DBEngine(0)(0)
```

The DBEngine object represents the Microsoft Jet database engine. The default collection for the DBEngine object is the Workspaces collection. The first (0) represents the first Workspace object in the Workspaces collection.

A Workspace object is a session from login to logout with the Jet database engine. The default collection for a Workspace is the Databases collection. The second (0) represents the first database in the Workspaces collection.

The following line also sets a db Database variable to the current database:

```
Set db = DBEngine.Workspaces(0).Databases(0)
```

You cannot use the RunSQL macro action to affect tables in your library database. Instead, you need to write code to accomplish the same thing with Recordsets.

The DLookup function has the same problem as RunSQL when intended for use on tables within the library database. DLookup tries to find the table you specify among the tables in the open database. The work-around is the LibDLookup function you created in Chapter 17, "Access: Survey Wizard, Part Two—Coding and Interface."

Let's make those libraries.

Creating the Libraries

Rather than a single library database, you are going to create two: SRVYBLD.MDA and SRVYRUN.MDA.

The SRVYBLD.MDA library contains the pieces you need for Survey Wizard to generate forms and reports in a person's current database.

The SRVYRUN.MDA library contains run-time code that must be loaded to run those generated forms and reports. In addition, SRVYRUN.MDA must be loaded whenever you have SRVYBLD.MDA loaded because procedures and variables in SRVYRUN.MDA are referenced in SRVYBLD.MDA.

The following table lists objects in each library:

SRVYRUN.MDA *Survey Wizard Run-Time Library*	*SRVYBLD.MDA* *Survey Wizard Build Library*
Error module	Survey table
Form module	Survey Question table
Pretty Good Charts module	Survey Wizard form
Survey Wizard Constants module	Survey Wizard Rename form
Survey Wizard Report Run-Time module	Survey Wizard Save As form
VCR2 module	Survey Wizard Entry Point module

SRVYRUN.MDA

To create a library database, follow these steps:

1. Choose the **F**ile|**N**ew command just like you would to create any other database.
2. In the New Database dialog box, type a filename with the .MDA filename extension rather then the .MDB extension. In our case, type SRVYRUN.MDA and click OK (see Figure 20.2).
3. Choose the **F**ile|**I**mport command to import the objects from your development .MDB database into the library.
4. In the Import dialog box, select Microsoft Access as the **D**ata Source.

FIGURE 20.2.

*Creating the
SRVYRUN.MDA file.*

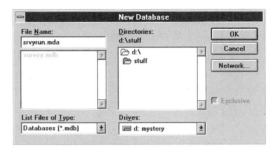

5. In the Select Microsoft Access Database dialog box, select SURVEY.MDB. Access reads the list of objects from the SURVEY.MDB database and displays them in the Import Objects dialog box.

6. Select Modules as the Object **T**ype to import (see Figure 20.3).

FIGURE 20.3.

*Importing modules into
SRVYRUN.MDA.*

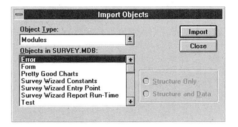

7. One by one, import these six modules into the database:

   Error module
   Form module
   Pretty Good Charts module
   Survey Wizard Constants module
   Survey Wizard Report Run-Time module
   VCR2 module

8. When you are done, you can click the Module tab on the database container and see the imported modules (see Figure 20.4).

A good test to perform before you close the database is to make sure that all the code still compiles without errors.

In splitting objects out of the former database, the possibility exists that code in one of the imported modules references a global declared in a module you forgot to import. Or worse yet, you may not have organized the code in a manner that enables you to easily split it apart.

FIGURE 20.4.
*Contents of the
SRVYRUN.MDA
library.*

To do this sanity check, open one of the modules and choose the **R**un|Compile Lo**a**ded
Modules command. Assuming all went well, you can close the database.

Your first library database is done!

SRVYBLD.MDA

You create the next library exactly the same way except you import the objects from the
second list, which contains two tables, three forms, and a single module:

> Survey table
> Survey Question table
> Survey Wizard form
> Survey Wizard Rename form
> Survey Wizard Save As form
> Survey Wizard Entry Point module

You can select the **S**tructure Only option when importing the tables if you don't want
to copy the questionnaires you created while testing the development library database
(see Figure 20.5). The **S**tructure Only option imports the tables without the data.

FIGURE 20.5.
*Importing the Survey
Wizard tables.*

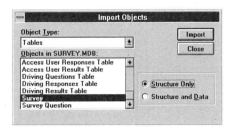

After importing the objects, you should do the compile sanity check just as you did with the first library. In this database you have code behind forms, so you first need to open the form modules for each of the three forms. The **R**un|Compile Lo**a**ded Modules command doesn't compile code behind forms unless the code window is open.

On trying the compile I got the error shown in Figure 20.6.

FIGURE 20.6.

Oops! The code in SRVYBLD.MDA doesn't compile!

The error is expected. My compile died on a line using the zSWQuestionTypeYesNo constant that is declared in the Survey Wizard Constants module in the SRVYRUN.MDA. Actually, SRVYBLD.MDA needs *a lot* of things in the SRVYRUN.MDA library.

You can resolve this problem by installing SRVYRUN.MDA as a library database. Close down Access and open the MSACC20.INI file in your WINDOWS directory (typically C:\WINDOWS). In the [Libraries] section, add the following line:

```
d:\stuff\srvyrun.mda=r
```

Rather than d:\stuff, you want to use the appropriate file specification for wherever your copy of SRVYRUN.MDA is (see Figure 20.7).

The =r indicates that the library should open in read-only mode. Opening this library in read-only is okay because you are only running code from it and not making any updates to it.

FIGURE 20.7.

You install the SRVYRUN.MDA database library by modifying MSACC20.INI.

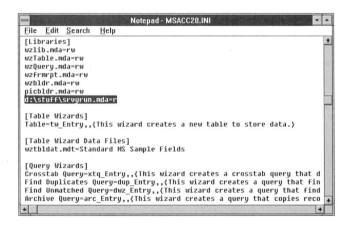

Now open the SRVYBLD.MDA library again and try the sanity check compile. No errors? Great!

Testing the Library

OK, the big moment is here. It's one thing to test the wizard in its own database, but will it all function correctly outside of the open database?

Jump back to the MSACC20.INI file and add a line to install the SRVYBLD.MDA library in read/write mode. The full [Libraries] section should look something like Listing 20.2.

Listing 20.2. The [Libraries] **section of the MSACC20.INI file.**

```
[Libraries]
wzlib.mda=rw
wzTable.mda=rw
wzQuery.mda=rw
wzfrmrpt.mda=rw
wzbldr.mda=rw
picbldr.mda=rw
d:\stuff\srvyrun.mda=r
d:\stuff\srvybld.mda=rw
```

You can also use the MSACC20.INI file to add a command to the Access menu that will start up Survey Wizard. In the [Menu Add-Ins] section, add the following line:

```
&Survey Wizard==SurveyWizard()
```

Notice that you use two equal signs, not just one.

Next, add the following line to the [Options] section to enable debugging of library databases:

```
DebugLibraries=1
```

The preceding option modifies your View Procedures window, creating an additional combo box that enables you to select which database you want to view code from (see Figure 20.8).

FIGURE 20.8.

The View Procedures
window can give you
access to modules in
other libraries.

NOTE

The DebugLibraries option enables you to work with your code after it's installed as a library. This option is nice but it has some drawbacks. Each time you compile your code, Access needs to compile all the library code, too, including the wizard libraries that ship with Access. This process slows down compilation a bit.

A worse problem is that if you do any global name changes with the **Edit|Replace** command while coding, you can accidentally change code in the wizard libraries. Just be sure to turn the DebugLibraries option back off before you forget about it.

With the aforementioned MSACC20.INI file changes saved, restart Access. Remember, for the changes to take effect, you must close Access and load it again.

Open a new database. The new **S**urvey Wizard command is available from the **F**ile|**A**dd-ins cascading menu, along with the menu add-ins that come with Access out of the box (see Figure 20.9).

Choose the **S**urvey Wizard command from the menu to open the form, as shown in Figure 20.10.

Did the Survey Wizard form come up? If it did things are looking really good. Enter some questions to define a questionnaire, and then select all of the build options and generate the objects.

I hope your screen reads like mine…(see Figure 20.11).

FIGURE 20.9.

*Adding the
Survey Wizard
command to the
Access menu.*

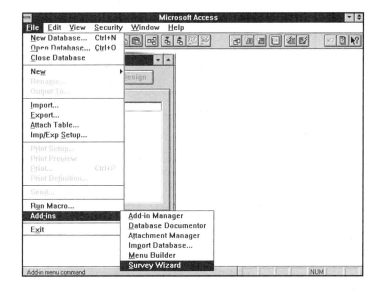

FIGURE 20.10.

*Survey Wizard is
activated in a test
database.*

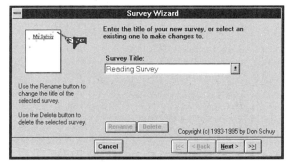

FIGURE 20.11.

A successful build!

The final test is to see if all the generated objects work. Run the Entry Report, Entry
Form, and then finally the Results Report. Figure 20.12 shows the results I got.

FIGURE 20.12.

Ship It!

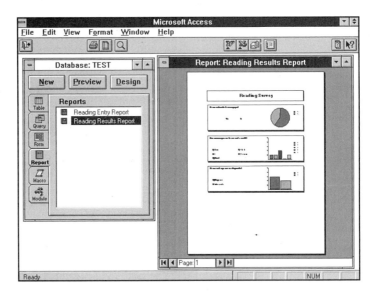

Now you have the data being collected via the generated multi-page form and you have reports on the collected data with your own charting capability. All this is created inside a new empty database!

But aren't you forgetting something—like the documentation?

The Help File Project

You have some more work to do. It's time to put Access in the background for awhile and crank up Word.

If you have been polishing up your writing skills, you have an advantage over your fellow programmers who only know the techie stuff. However, if you feel your writing skills are kind of weak then look at it this way: creating a help file can be an opportunity to get in some needed writing practice.

Writing help files is truly for a person of many skills. This task involves organizing, writing, drawing, using special codes, compiling, and testing. The operating environment is Windows and command line DOS, and the applications you use are Word, Paintbrush, Access, File Manager, WINHELP.EXE, the Help Compiler, and your favorite simple editor, such as Notepad or the DOS editor. The source files you use involve an .RTF format Word document, bitmaps, and .MAP and .PRJ project files that include preprocessor directives similar to C language.

Sounds like a big mess, doesn't it?

The folks at Microsoft probably have gotten their fair share of flak over the years for how help file creation works, but it's really not that hard. Creating help files is a lot like programming. Your source looks just different enough from the final result that it's kind of a thrill each time you compile a file and check out the results.

This section demonstrates the process of building a help file step-by-step and helps you put all the various pieces of help file construction into perspective. Just follow the instructions on setting up the Survey Wizard's help source files and you will have the basis to start your own help file project.

Gathering the Pieces

Make sure you have a copy of the Help Compiler that is up to date with the version of Word you are using. The version that came with my copy of Visual Basic 3.0 was stamped Version 3.10.504 and didn't run against Word 6.0 .RTF files. (An .RTF file is a Word document saved as a rich text format file.)

The Help Compiler version that came with the Access Developer Toolkit was stamped with a slightly higher version number, 3.10.505, and it worked fine with Word 6.0 .RTF files. If you type HC31 at the DOS prompt you should get a message indicating which version of the Help Compiler you have:

```
C:\>hc31
Microsoft (R) Help Compiler Version 3.10.505
Copyright (c) Microsoft Corp 1990 - 1992. All rights reserved.

Syntax: HC [<Help project filename.hpj>]
```

The Help Compiler is basically two files: HC31.EXE is the compiler and HC31.ERR contains the compiler's error messages. (You might also find versions of these files as HC.EXE and HC.ERR.) Additional files included are a compiler for producing multiple resolution bitmap files and a hot-spot editor, but you don't need those files for this task.

You have two strategies for dealing with all the technical details of creating help files. You can compose your help text and not worry about how it compiles until all the text is written, or you can maintain a compilable help file as you write it.

The former strategy may help you focus more on content and less on technical details while you are writing. You will eventually need to make the technical pass through the document and other files to turn your work into a compilable help file.

You may find the second approach more efficient because at any time the help file is compilable and viewable. Whenever you write a help file for someone else, the person wants to be able to see the work in progress. Handing someone a help file is easier than walking the person through your Word document and explaining all the funny codes.

The first thing to do when creating a help file is to set up the minimum pieces. After the file is compiled and viewable, you can begin a cycle of adding text to it, compiling it, and then viewing it. Repeat this cycle until all the text is written and you're satisfied with the results.

Create a directory where you can do your help file work. In this example the directory is C:\SWHELP. Within this directory you will create the following files:

SURVEY.HPJ	Help project file
SURVEY.MAP	Map of topic ID numbers
SURVEY.RTF	Help source document
BITMAPS.LST	List of bitmap files
GO.BAT	DOS batch file

Kicking Off a Compile with GO.BAT

First, create the GO.BAT file using Notepad or the DOS editor. This file is a one-line command file that saves a few keystrokes each time you launch the Help Compiler.

Type the following line in GO.BAT:

```
hc31 survey.hpj
```

Typing GO at the DOS prompt runs the Help Compiler against the SURVEY.HPJ help project file, which you now must create.

The SURVEY.HPJ Help Project File

The .HPJ file is a plain vanilla ASCII text file created in Notepad or the DOS editor just as you created GO.BAT. The file should contain the lines shown in listing 20.3.

Listing 20.3. The SURVEY.HPJ help project file.

```
[OPTIONS]
ROOT = C:\SWHELP
BMROOT = C:\SWHELP\BITMAPS
TITLE = Survey Wizard
CONTENTS = HelpContents
ERRORLOG = C:\SWHELP\SURVEY.ERR
REPORT = ON
WARNING = 3
COMPRESS = OFF

[FILES]
SURVEY.RTF
SURVEY2.RTF

[BITMAPS]
#include <BITMAPS.LST>
```

```
[MAP]
#include <SURVEY.MAP>

[CONFIG]
BrowseButtons()
```

Doesn't a help project file look kinda like the offspring you would get if you bred a Windows .INI file with a C-language, source-code header file?

Yeah, I thought so, too.

The good news is that you can use the preceding example with minor modifications in all your help file projects. Change the `C:\SWHELP` directory references and the `SURVEY` references to the appropriate directory and name for your help project. Then change the `TITLE` text and you are set to go.

Let's take a look at the different sections in the help project file.

The `[OPTIONS]` section is for exactly that: options. The following list briefly indicates what each of the settings are. Refer to the Help Compiler Guide for the complete details.

ROOT	Where the help source files are located
BMROOT	Where the help bitmap files are located
TITLE	Text to appear on the WinHelp program's title bar
CONTENTS	Name of default topic first displayed
ERRORLOG	File to receive help compiler screen output
REPORT	Indicates if error messages should be reported
WARNING	Indicates level of errors to report (3 means all)
COMPRESS	Level of compression

You may want to change the `COMPRESS` option to `MEDIUM` or `HIGH` to try out the two levels of compression. This step may potentially make your help file smaller. My help project file has no compression to allow for the fastest possible load time of the help file.

The `[FILES]` section indicates which .RTF source files are being compiled. Typically folks just throw all topics in one document, but you can break up a help project across multiple files for better organization.

```
[FILES]
SURVEY.RTF
SURVEY2.RTF
```

You could put help text for pop-up topics in a second file, SURVEY2.RTF. These topics are short word definitions that don't branch off to any other help topics. In a sense, this second document would be a glossary for your help file.

The [BITMAPS] section should contain a list of all .BMP files to be included in the resulting help file. Any bitmap referenced in the help file needs to be listed in the [BITMAPS] section. For ease of use in maintaining this list, you may want to use the #include directive to point to another file, BITMAPS.LST, that contains the actual list:

```
[BITMAPS]
#include <BITMAPS.LST>
```

The [MAP] section should contain a series of #define directives that tie a help topic name to a help topic ID number. You may want to again use the #include directive to maintain this list in a separate text file, SURVEY.MAP:

```
[MAP]
#include <SURVEY.MAP>
```

The Windows help file system has a limited programmable capability using Help File Macros. You can use these macros to add buttons and menus to the WinHelp interface, launch other Windows programs, or even register DLL functions and execute them.

Any macros within the [CONFIG] section of the help project file are automatically executed on loading of the help file. The [CONFIG] section in SURVEY.HPJ calls the BrowseButtons() macro because this macro is required for WinHelp to make the << and >> buttons available:

```
[CONFIG]
BrowseButtons()
```

The SURVEY.MAP File

The next step is to create the SURVEY.MAP text file. Within the help source document, each topic is referenced by name. Within a C, Visual Basic, or Access application, each topic is identified by a number that was assigned in a help project's [MAP] section.

The [MAP] section links these two systems together by using the #define directive to associate a name with a number. In Help Compiler lingo these terms are known as *context strings* and *context IDs*.

To start, your SURVEY.MAP file will list a single topic, the HelpContents topic as shown here:

```
#define HelpContents 1
```

Later, as you decide to make topics available directly without going through the Help Contents page, you can add new entries.

Creating Help File Bitmaps

Now you can create some bitmaps and get that part of the help project file going, too.

Create a directory off the C:\SWHELP directory called BITMAPS. You set up BMROOT in your help project file to indicate where you want to store bitmaps.

Next, use your hidden artistic skills and draw an icon or logo-type picture to use alongside the title with each help topic.

An example is shown in Figure 20.13.

FIGURE 20.13.
Creating LOGO.BMP.

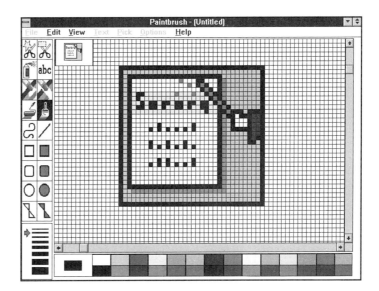

You can skip the logo if you like, but one graphic that is helpful to have in nearly any help file is a bullet graphic.

A bullet is usually a dot placed before an item in a bulleted list. In Paintbrush, you can create a simple bullet by setting the image size to five pixels wide and seven pixels high. Zoom into the picture and fill the pixels as shown in Figure 20.14.

In Survey Wizard's help file I wanted to be a little more creative, so my BULLET.BMP looks like a hand pointing a finger to each bulleted item. I also created a bitmap to indicate a section of steps to perform, and a bitmap to indicate a See Also section. These bitmaps are shown in Figures 20.15, 20.16, and 20.17.

FIGURE 20.14.
*A typical
BULLET.BMP
close up.*

FIGURE 20.15.
BULLET.BMP.

FIGURE 20.16.
123.BMP.

1..
2..
3..

FIGURE 20.17.
EYES.BMP.

Naturally, you will be adding more bitmaps as you write the help file. With all the bitmaps in the C:\SWHELP\BITMAPS directory, generating the BITMAPS.LST file is easy. In a DOS prompt window, set your default directory to the C:\SWHELP directory. Next, enter the following DOS command:

```
dir /b bitmaps\*.*> bitmaps.lst
```

The text file, BITMAPS.LST, is created with the following contents:

```
LOGO.BMP
BULLET.BMP
123.BMP
EYES.BMP
```

The Help File Source Document

Next, you can create the initial .RTF files in Word and try compiling a short help file.

A help file is built from units called topics. Although you certainly can deviate from the rules, the Help Compiler Guide recommends that a help topic contain roughly one or two screens of text per topic.

A help source document contains one topic after another separated by page breaks. The first few characters in a topic are special footnote characters that the help compiler uses to identify the help topic and features used by the help text author. In addition, specially formatted text within the body of the help topic indicates jumps to other help topics.

If you get the feeling that editing a document like this is going to take some getting used to, you're right. I was apprehensive about creating help files at first. However, if you keep to it, eventually all the special formatting and footnotes will become second nature and people will marvel at the ease with which you can crank out help files. So let's charge on and get past this first one.

In Word, select a font to use in your document from the fonts that come with Windows 3.1. Then your text will appear the same on other machines as you originally compose it. A good choice may be Arial, with a font size of 10.

> **NOTE**
>
> There are many freeware, shareware, and commercially available products to help you with your help file authoring. These products vary in sophistication and features, but all strive to make the help file creation process easier and more productive so that you can focus more on the content of your help file rather than the technical details behind creating it.

Writing the Help Topic

The following steps describe how to insert a few footnotes as the first characters in your topic:

1. Choose **I**nsert|Foot**n**ote from the menu.
2. In the Footnote and Endnote dialog box, select the **C**ustom Mark radio button and type # as the custom mark (see Figure 20.18).

FIGURE 20.18.

Creating a custom footnote.

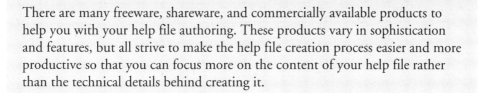

3. Close the dialog box, and the Footnote window opens with the cursor next to your footnote character.
4. In the Footnote window, type a unique help topic name as a single word much like a variable name where no spaces are allowed. For the first topic, type `HelpContents`.
5. Next, click the document window and choose **I**nsert|Foot**n**ote again. This time type a custom mark using the dollar sign character, $.

   The dollar sign footnote indicates the topic name as it would be displayed in the help text Search dialog box's list of topics. The text is also displayed if you choose the History button in WinHelp to list the topics you have already viewed.

6. Type `Help Contents` as the footnote text.

7. Insert a third footnote using an uppercase K as the custom mark. This type of footnote supports the WinHelp Search dialog box. Use the footnote to indicate which search keywords should list this topic among the help topics they point to. Make sure to type a semicolon after each keyword.

8. For this topic type `contents;` as the footnote text.

9. Insert one final footnote character, this time using the plus sign (+) as the custom mark. This footnote indicates where a topic fits within a topic browse sequence. A *topic browse sequence* is a chain of related topics in which you may use the << and >> buttons to move from topic to topic in sequential order.

    The contents of this footnote should contain the name of the browse sequence, a colon, and a number to indicate where this topic shows up in the sequence compared to other topics. You may want to leave a gap between numbers in the sequence so you can insert additional topics later without having to renumber all the browse sequence numbers.

    If you plan on using a single sequence for the entire help file, you may choose to call your sequence *browse*, which also helps you remember the meaning of the footnote.

10. Type `browse:0010` for the plus custom mark footnote text.

    The footnotes for our first help topic are shown in Figure 20.19.

FIGURE 20.19.

Custom footnotes for a help topic.

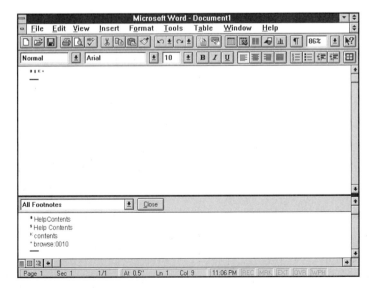

Adding a Bitmap

So far this help topic contains only some funny footnote characters and an empty page. You can start by adding the logo bitmap and a title at the top of the help topic.

To put a bitmap in the text, type an open brace and bmc, followed by the name of the bitmap, and then the closing brace, like this:

`{bmc logo.bmp}`

Make sure that any bitmaps you reference in your text are also listed in the BITMAPS.LST file you created earlier. If you add any new bitmaps, just place the bitmap file in the BITMAPS directory and re-run the DOS trick described earlier to regenerate BITMAPS.LST.

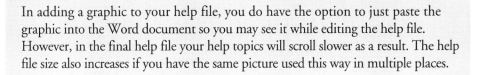

NOTE

In adding a graphic to your help file, you do have the option to just paste the graphic into the Word document so you may see it while editing the help file. However, in the final help file your help topics will scroll slower as a result. The help file size also increases if you have the same picture used this way in multiple places.

Creating a Non-Scrollable Title Region

Following the graphic, type the title of the help topic, Survey Wizard Help Contents. Select this text and set it to bold with a font size of 18. After the title, change the font back to normal, font size 10, and press Enter to start a new line.

The document should appear as shown in Figure 20.20.

You can make your title a non-scrollable region. Select the text in the title from {bmc logo.bmp} through Contents. Choose the Format|Paragraph command. Click the Text Flow tab and check Keep with Next (see Figure 20.21). That's it. The text you now enter will scroll under the title you just created.

A Help Contents page is typically a directory to the major topics in the help file. You may want to start with one or two lines about what the program does. For Survey Wizard I used this text:

> "Survey Wizard is a Microsoft Access Menu Add-in. With Survey Wizard you can generate a paper questionnaire or generate a complete on-line survey system for use within your current database project."

Next, you want to list the main topics, which brings us to the final and most important help file trick: how to set up the topic jumps.

FIGURE 20.20.

A title for the Help Contents topic.

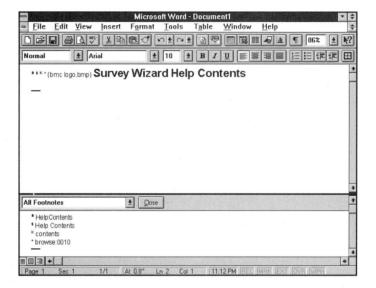

FIGURE 20.21.

Creating a non-scrollable region.

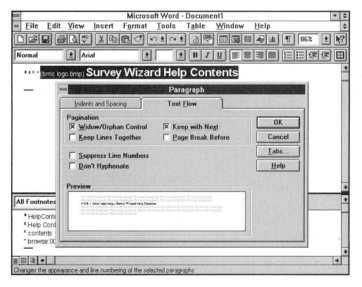

Creating Topic Jumps

A topic jump is text highlighted in green and underlined. When you click the text, the help file either displays a pop-up window containing additional text, or the main window changes to display the topic you're jumping to.

You implement topic jumps by formatting text one way to indicate what is to be highlighted in green on the screen. Then you follow the specially formatted text with hidden text that identifies the topic to jump to when the user clicks on the highlighted text.

For your first jump, you can create a pop-up window that defines a menu add-in by following these steps:

1. Select Menu Add-in from the paragraph under the topic title.

2. Choose the Format|Font command. The Font dialog box has a combo box for underline styles. Select a single underline. (If you have the Formatting toolbar displayed, you can also use the Underline button to accomplish the same thing.)

   The single underline indicates that this topic jump will be a pop-up help topic.

3. Immediately following the underlined text, type the name of the topic you're jumping to. This name should be the same value you typed somewhere in the help document (or related help document) as a pound sign (#) footnote. For this topic type MenuAddIn. Remember that the help topic ID names do not have spaces in them.

4. Now you need to format the help topic ID as hidden text. Highlight the text, MenuAddIn, and choose Format|Font again. In the Font dialog box click the Hidden check box (see Figure 20.22). This option makes the text disappear.

FIGURE 20.22.

Formatting text as hidden.

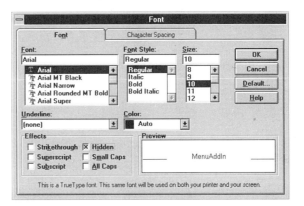

5. You need to be able to see the text to edit it. From the **T**ools menu choose **O**ptions to bring up the Options dialog box. Click the View tab and you see a group of check boxes under the group title Nonprinting Characters.

6. Clicking the **Hi**dden Text check box makes hidden text display with a dashed underline (see Figure 20.23). You also may want to check the Paragraph **M**arks check box, which is explained in the next set of steps.

FIGURE 20.23.

Telling Word to display hidden text.

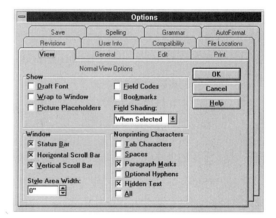

On closing the Options dialog box you see the MenuAddIn topic jump displayed with a dashed underline (see Figure 20.24).

FIGURE 20.24.

The MenuAddIn topic jump is visible.

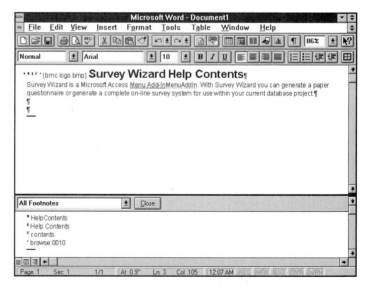

Next you can create several topic jumps that actually switch to a different help file page. These steps are exactly the same as the preceding instructions except you use a double underline rather than a single underline.

Even though you are working on a contents page, you shouldn't list too many topic jumps one right after another because it's difficult to quickly scan the list and locate the topic you need.

Instead, the topics are organized among the following categories: Installation, Defining a Survey, Building the Objects, and Using the Generated Survey. Each of these main topics is set to bold with a font size of 12 (see Figure 20.25). The topics below the main categories are indented a couple of spaces.

FIGURE 20.25.

Grouping topic jumps by category.

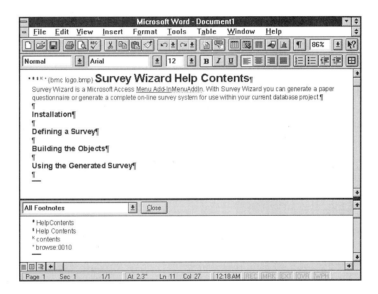

Underneath the category of Installation are two topics: Installing Survey Wizard and Copyright Notice (see Figure 20.26).

Format the topics this way:

1. Format Installing Survey Wizard as double underlined using the Format|Font command.

2. Immediately after the word Wizard, type `InstallingSurveyWizard` as the help topic ID, formatted as hidden.

   Don't repeat the formatting steps for each new jump topic. Instead, copy the line for the first topic and paste it as lines for the new topics. Then edit both the underlined text and the hidden text to change it to the appropriate value for each topic. This method goes faster than entering the text each time unformatted and reapplying the formats each time.

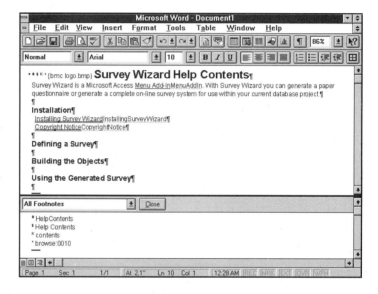

NOTE

The reason you turned on the display of paragraph marks is to avoid a problem that causes warning-level error messages to show up when compiling the help file.

When the paragraph mark is not displayed, you can accidentally include the paragraph mark as part of the text being formatted as hidden. With the paragraph mark displayed, you can see the dashed underline extend underneath it and correct the problem if necessary.

3. To complete the first help topic, insert a page break to indicate the end of the help topic page. The final help document will be a series of topics, each ending with a page break. To insert a page break, choose **I**nsert|**B**reak and make sure that **P**age Break is selected for the type of break.

The completed Help Contents topic page is shown in Figure 20.27.

FIGURE 20.27.

The completed Help Contents topic page.

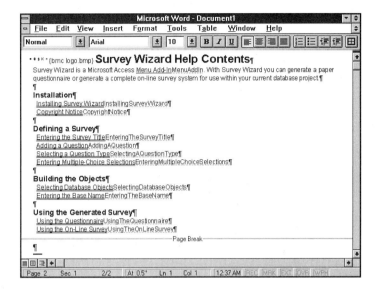

Being a Help Topic Factory

You are probably thinking that you just went through an awful lot of work to create a single help topic. However, the next topic is going to be less painful because much of the work is already done for you. The following steps show you how to create your next topic:

1. Move your cursor to the top left of the screen edit window, before the first footnote you entered.

2. Holding down the Shift key, press the down arrow repeatedly until you have selected the entire help topic including the page break.

3. Copy all the selected text into the clipboard buffer.

4. Move your cursor underneath the page break and paste the copied text.

   Use this copied page as the basis for your next help topic. You can delete most of the text, but keep the full title section.

   If you look in the footnote window you find that the four footnotes you created also copied. To set up the footnotes for this second topic all you need to do is change the values of the copied footnotes to what they should be for this new topic.

5. To create the Installing Survey Wizard topic, use the following values for the footnotes:

```
# InstallingSurveyWizard
$ Installing Survey Wizard
K installation;setup;Add-in Manager;
+ Browse:0020
```

6. Next change the topic title from Survey Wizard Help Contents to Installing Survey Wizard.

7. Following the title, type the body of text for the topic.

8. At the end of the topic, add a See Also: section to list jumps to related topics. You can cut jumps from the first topic and paste them as-is if the jump goes to the same topic. Or you can paste the text from another jump and replace the displayed text and hidden jump text with the help topic to jump to. The main thing you are saving here is having to reapply all the special formatting.

Word has another quick way to copy formats: the Format Painter. This method is described in the following steps:

1. Select at least one character from a word with formats applied to it.

2. Click the paintbrush button on the standard toolbar. The mouse cursor changes shape to a paintbrush alongside the familiar I-beam.

3. Select the characters to format by clicking and dragging the mouse over the text to format. When you release the mouse button, the selected text inherits the same formats as the characters originally selected.

You may want to add a System Requirements topic to describe the minimum hardware and software requirements that a program needs to run efficiently. In the case of an Access application, your users need the base requirements to run Access, plus more if your application is larger than usual. This topic is a good place to use a bullet bitmap when displaying the listed requirements.

Figure 20.28 shows the System Requirements topic during editing.

FIGURE 20.28.

Creating the System Requirements help topic.

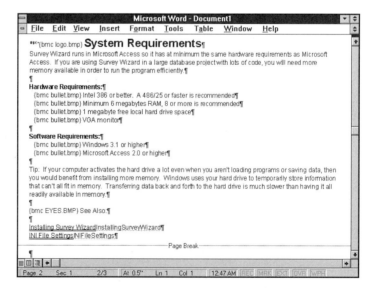

Creating SURVEY2.RTF

In your help project file you listed a second .RTF file, SURVEY2.RTF. Each topic in this file contains text for a pop-up window. This document is easier to create because the pound sign (#) footnote to identify each topic is the only help file coding technique required.

Figure 20.29 shows the SURVEY2.RTF document with two topics defined: MenuAddIn and Objects.

FIGURE 20.29.

Creating SURVEY2.RTF.

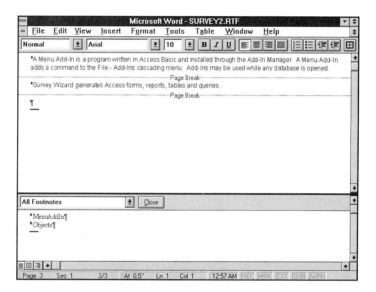

Compiling the Help Project

You have enough material now that you should try a test compile and see how the help file is looking.

Save the two documents as .RTF files. In the Save As dialog box, you must select Rich Text Format in the Save File as **T**ype combo box (see Figure 20.30). Save the main help document as SURVEY.RTF and the second document as SURVEY2.RTF.

You also need to close the document windows. Word keeps a lock on the files if you don't close them.

Next, in your DOS prompt session, set default to the SWHELP directory and run the Help Compiler using the batch file you created earlier:

```
C:
CD \SWHELP
GO
```

FIGURE 20.30.

Saving the help file document as a Rich Text Format file.

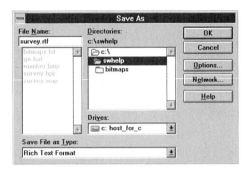

If all goes well, you may get a few WARNING 4113 messages about unresolved jumps and nothing else. The unresolved jumps are expected because you haven't created some of the topics to which you already set up jumps. The final version of the help documents shouldn't produce this message during the compile, but for now this message is OK.

In your DOS session you can review the errors with the DOS editor by entering this line:

```
edit survey.err
```

The log file displays something like the screen shown in Figure 20.31.

FIGURE 20.31.

Viewing the Help Compiler output in SURVEY.ERR.

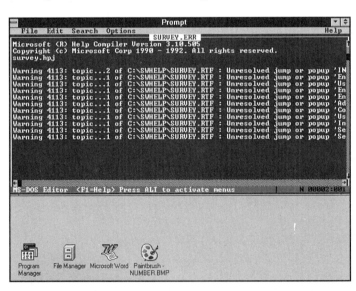

Note that you can use Alt-Enter to switch between running your DOS session full screen or running it in a window. With your DOS session in a window, you can view the errors as you fix them in the Word document.

Use Alt-Tab as a quick way to switch between applications, including your DOS session. If using DOS so much is making you feel less than civilized, you can always use Windows Notepad to view the error log file rather than the DOS editor.

Testing the Help File

Now you can take a look at what you generated.

In File Manager, locate the newly created SURVEY.HLP file and double-click it to open it. This action invokes WinHelp and displays the Help Contents page (see Figure 20.32).

FIGURE 20.32.
Viewing the Help Contents page.

You should see the words Menu Add-in highlighted in green with a dashed underline. Clicking the highlighted text should display the definition of a Menu Add-in in a pop-up window as shown in Figure 20.33.

You didn't create a topic jump to go directly to the System Requirements page from the Help Contents page, but you can get there through the **S**earch button in WinHelp. Click the **S**earch button, then in the Search dialog box select installation, setup, or system requirements. Then click the **S**how Topics button.

The System Requirements topic is displayed in the list box at the bottom of the Search dialog box as shown in Figure 20.34.

FIGURE 20.33.

Viewing pop-up help.

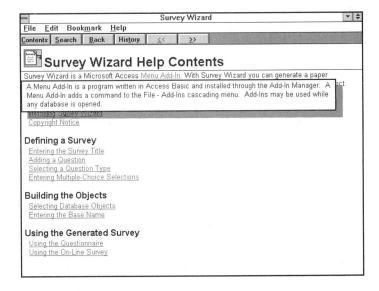

FIGURE 20.34.

Using the Search dialog box to get to the System Requirements topic.

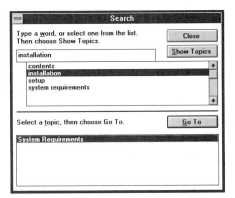

Click the **G**o To button, and the Systems Requirements help topic appears as shown in Figure 20.35.

You also can test the browse sequence buttons as a way to flip back and forth between the two topics. This feature is not that impressive yet with only two topics, however.

FIGURE 20.35.

Viewing the System Requirements help topic.

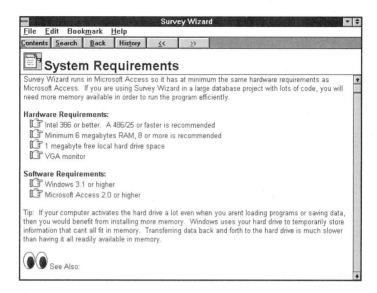

Creating a Help File Outline

At this point, you may want to save the files as a starting point for your own help project. You can rename the files and update the project files appropriately, then change the titles and content within the .RTF files to describe your own application.

One method of mapping out what needs to be done in a help file is copying a topic page that has the footnotes, title, and a See Also section, then pasting the page in for each topic you think you need in the file.

Use this method to build an outline. Change all the titles and footnote values and fill in the See Also section with jumps to the appropriate topics.

Compile the help file and review it in WinHelp to see that you have all the topics organized appropriately and that you present all the information the user needs.

Then, to finish the help file, you go back to each empty topic and fill in the content, having all the technical work of creating the help file already done. You may start with this method but end up adding some additional topics along the way.

More Tips for the Help File Author

Use periodic compiles to test your work in progress. These tests save you from having to go back and make major changes later. If you keep File Manager and the DOS session open then you can quickly Alt-Tab to DOS, type GO to compile, Alt-Tab to File Manager, and double-click the .HLP file to view it.

Before writing any help files you may want to look at the various help files on your computer to get an idea of what authors are doing with them. Among certain types of programs you may find a common structure of help file (at least across the Microsoft applications).

For example, all the Windows' utilities have a simple structure that differs considerably from the help files created for Word, Excel, and Access. Viewing existing help files may help you formulate an idea of what is needed and expected in the content and structure of the help file.

How extensive you think your help file documentation should be is ultimately up to you, but be considerate of your help file readers. Nobody likes to read long, drawn-out help files any more than they like reading thick software manuals, but not finding enough help is also frustrating. My strategy in creating a help file for Survey Wizard was to be comprehensive enough to make sure folks could use the program, but short enough that folks would also take the time to read it.

As a personal favor to me, *please* do not fill your help file with sentences like this:

"Enter your last name at the Last Name prompt."

Your help file readers aren't looking for what's inherently obvious. They are looking for an overview of what the program does or maybe some details about a not-so-obvious feature of the program. Maybe readers need to know how one part of the program fits in with the other parts of the program.

Whatever you do, don't shortchange your help file readers by doing a sloppy job. If you take pride in how your software works then take that pride and apply it to your help file also. Take care to do a spell check and try to remember everything you learned in school about writing clearly and directly.

Test the help file thoroughly. All the topics should display cleanly and be easy to read. Play the role of the targeted readers and try to determine if they are getting the answers they need.

Using Screen Shots

Writing a help file can be tough. You may have difficulty expressing in words what exactly is happening on-screen.

A good way to convey information is to use pictures. A useful feature in Windows is its ability to take a snapshot at any time of what is on-screen. All you need to do is press the Print Scrn button, and a copy of the screen image is placed in the Windows clipboard. You can also use Alt-Print Scrn to capture only the image of a modal dialog box, without the background windows.

Use the Paintbrush program to work with the captured image. If you have a full-screen image in the clipboard, you want to choose the **View|Zoom O**ut command before pasting the image. With Paintbrush, you can select a part of the image and use the **Edit|Co**py To command to write a portion of the picture out as a separate bitmap file.

In Survey Wizard's help file, I wanted to quickly relate parts of the image to the text. I created a set of boxed numbers in a bitmap that I could copy and paste on the images for my help file. The bitmap of numbers is shown in Figure 20.36.

FIGURE 20.36.

Copying a number box out of NUMBER.BMP.

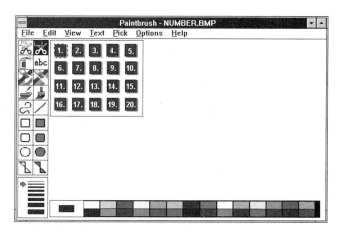

The numbers are pasted onto a screen shot as shown in Figure 20.37.

The completed SURVEY.HLP help file is included on this book's companion CD-ROM, along with the source files used to create it. The CD-ROM also includes a variety of additional topics and bitmaps that hopefully do the proper job of documenting the application.

FIGURE 20.37.

Pasting number boxes into a help file screen shot.

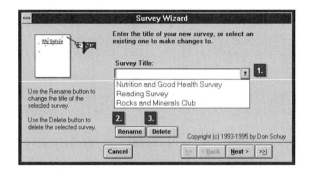

Plugging Help into SRVYBLD.MDA

The final step in implementing a help file is to plug it into the application. The simplest case is to always jump to the Help Contents page. If your application is a quick utility with only one or two screens, that option may be the best.

A good approach may be to have a topic on each screen or window in the program. When users summon help they get a topic that gives them an overview of what is being accomplished at the current screen with a list of topic jumps to more detailed information.

To link Survey Wizard to the help file you need to open the SRVYBLD.MDA database and modify the forms. First you need to temporarily disable SRVYBLD.MDA as a library database so you can open it normally. Comment out the line in MSACC20.INI that loads the library, as shown in Figure 20.38.

FIGURE 20.38.

Commenting out the SRVYBLD.MDA line in MSACC20.INI.

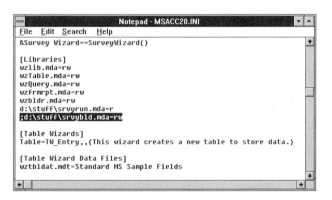

Next, open the SRVYBLD.MDA database.

Each form has a Help File property and a Help Context ID property that you can set via the properties window as shown in Figure 20.39.

FIGURE 20.39.

Setting the Help File and Help Context ID properties.

Access enables you to also assign separate help context ID numbers to each control on a form. The help file in the form's Help File property is assumed. Figure 20.40 shows the Help Context ID property being set for a command button control.

FIGURE 20.40.

Setting the Help File ID for a control on a form.

For Survey Wizard, I wanted to be able to jump to a different help topic for each page in Survey Wizard's multiple-page form. So I set all the controls on a page to the help topic for that page. The Survey Wizard Rename and Survey Wizard Save As forms each also have their own topic. If focus is on any of the buttons in the form footer, then the contents page is the initial help topic viewed.

Listing 20.4 shows the final SURVEY.MAP file, which makes eight of the help topics available from the Access forms.

Listing 20.4. The SURVEY.MAP file.

```
#define HelpContents 1
#define EnteringTheSurveyTitle 100
#define AddingAQuestion 110
#define SelectingAQuestionType 120
#define EnteringMultipleChoiceSelections 130
#define SelectingDatabaseObjects 140
#define EnteringTheBaseName 200
#define RenamingASurvey 300
```

Table 20.1 summarizes which Help File and Help Context ID property settings are set on the forms and controls in Survey Wizard.

Table 20.1. SRVYBLD.MDA Help File and Help Context ID settings.

Property	Setting
Survey Wizard Form	
Help File:	SURVEY.HLP
Help Context ID:	1
Controls on page 1	
Help Context ID:	100
Controls on page 2	
Help Context ID:	110
Controls on page 3	
Help Context ID:	120
Controls on page 4	
Help Context ID:	130
Controls on page 5	
Help Context ID:	140
VCR Buttons in form footer	
Help Context ID:	1
Survey Wizard Save As Form	
Help File:	SURVEY.HLP
Help Context ID:	200

Property	Setting
Survey Wizard Rename Form	
Help File:	SURVEY.HLP
Help Context ID:	300

Creating a Help Button

This section describes how to add a Help button to the form footer of the Survey Wizard form. The Help button serves as an on-screen hint that on-line help is available.

The properties for the cmdHelp button are shown in this list:

Object: **cmdHelp Command Button**
Startup WinHelp with help for the current page.

Property	Value
Caption:	&Help
Enabled:	Yes
Left:	1.0472 in
Top:	0.05 in
Width:	0.5597 in
Height:	0.25 in
Font Name:	Arial
Font Size:	8
Font Weight:	Bold

You can place the cmdHelp button in the tab order just before the Cancel button.

You can make the Help button context-sensitive and bring up help for the currently displayed page by calling Windows Help directly from the code. First, in the declarations section of the Survey Wizard form, add the declaration for the WinHelp API function as shown in Listing 20.5.

Listing 20.5. The declaration for the WinHelp function.

```
Declare Function WinHelp Lib "User" (ByVal hwnd As Integer,
➡ ByVal lpHelpFile As String, ByVal wCommand As Integer,
➡ dwData As Any) As Integer
```

Next, complete the cmdHelp_Click subroutine as shown in Listing 20.6.

Listing 20.6. The cmdHelp_Click **subroutine.**

```
Sub cmdHelp_Click ()

' Activate Windows Help with a context number for the current page.

    Dim dwData As Long
    Dim z As Integer

    On Error Resume Next

' What help context number
    dwData = 100 + (mintCurrentPage - 1) *10

    z = WinHelp(Me.hWnd, "SURVEY.HLP", 1, ByVal dwData)

End Sub
```

You now have everything you need to get the help file created and going.

Be sure you install the help file in a place where it can be found, or Windows Help will show up with an empty blue screen and an error message. You can place SURVEY.HLP either in the user's Access directory, where the library files will eventually go, or in the user's WINDOWS directory.

Add-In Manager Enabled

Now that you have the help file, what about installation?

You can make the Survey Wizard database libraries Add-in Manager installable just as you did with the Picture Builder+ database library you created in Chapter 15.

Choose the **View|O**ptions command and set Show System Objects to Yes. With SRVYBLD.MDA open, use the **File|I**mport command to import the USysAddins table from WZLIB.MDA in your Access directory.

Open the table in datasheet mode and change the contents of the records as listed in Table 20.2.

Table 20.2. The contents of the USysAddIns table in SRVYBLD.MDA.

Field	*Value*
PropertyName:	AddInVersion
Val1:	2.1
PropertyName:	CompanyName
Val1:	Copyright (c) 1993-1995 by Don Schuy
PropertyName:	Description
Val1:	Install Survey Wizard
PropertyName:	DisplayName
Val1:	Survey Wizard
PropertyName:	IniFileEntry
Val1:	Libraries
Val2:	srvybld.mda
Val3:	rw
PropertyName:	IniFileEntry
Val1:	Menu Add-ins
Val2:	&Survey Wizard
Val3:	=SurveyWizard()
PropertyName:	Logo
Val9:	Picture

The complete table is shown in Figure 20.41 (with the unused columns Val4 through Val8 not showing).

FIGURE 20.41.

Creating a USysAddIns
table for the
SRVYBLD.MDA
database library.

	Table: USysAddIns			
PropertyName	**Val1**	**Val2**	**Val3**	**Val9**
AddInVersion	2.1			
CompanyName	Copyright (c) 1993-1995 by Don Schuy			
Description	Install Survey Wizard			
DisplayName	Survey Wizard			
IniFileEntry	Libraries	srvybld.mda	rw	
IniFileEntry	Menu Add-Ins	&Survey Wizard	=SurveyWizard()	
Logo				Picture

Record: 1   of 7

You also must create a USysAddIns table for the SRVYRUN.MDA database library.

Remember that you need to modify MSACC20.INI so the SRVYRUN.MDA database isn't loaded before you open the database to make the modification. At this point, remove all your modifications to the MSACC20.INI file. Then you can see how successfully the libraries install with the Add-in Manager. Be sure to also remove the DebugLibraries line.

The records for the USysAddIns table for SRVYRUN.MDA are listed in Table 20.3.

Table 20.3. The contents of the USysAddIns table in SRVYRUN.MDA.

Field	*Value*
PropertyName:	AddInVersion
Val1:	2.1
PropertyName:	CompanyName
Val1:	Copyright (c) 1993-1995 by Don Schuy
PropertyName:	Description
Val1:	Install Survey Wizard Run-Time
PropertyName:	DisplayName
Val1:	Survey Wizard Run-Time
PropertyName:	IniFileEntry
Val1:	Libraries

Field	Value
Val2:	srvyrun.mda
Val3:	r
PropertyName:	Logo
Val9:	Picture

You may want to paste in a different picture for each library. See Chapter 15 for details on how to create and paste a logo picture into the USysAddIns table.

Installing Survey Wizard

Survey Wizard is finally complete. To use it, just copy the following three files into your Access directory:

> SRVYBLD.MDA
> SRVYRUN.MDA
> SURVEY.HLP

Restart Access and use the Add-in Manager to install the two libraries (see Figure 20.42). If the libraries don't initially show up in the Add-ins list, use the **A**dd New button and locate the library files.

FIGURE 20.42.

*Installing the completed
Survey Wizard
database libraries.*

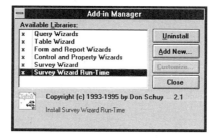

Summary

In this chapter, you completed the final touch-ups required to make Survey Wizard a real product!

Here's what you discovered along the way:

- The importance of using code behind forms in database libraries
- Tips on writing code for libraries
- Creating a run-time code library for supporting custom database objects
- Creating the Survey Wizard build library for generating objects
- Adding a custom command to the Menu Add-ins menu to start Survey Wizard
- Creating the project files for compiling a Windows help file
- Inserting a bitmap and non-scrollable region in a help file
- Adding topics to the help file source document and setting up jumps to other topics
- Using Copy and Paste to remove some of the help file creation drudgery
- Compiling and testing the help file
- Tips on authoring help files
- Connecting the help file to Access forms using help context ID numbers
- Creating a help button that uses the `WinHelp` API call to activate on-line help
- Creating the USysAddIns tables for our library databases

You have completed your first advanced project. In the next chapter you start your second advanced project, the S.W.A.T. issues tracking database, and you build a terrific database maintenance menu for all your Access databases.

CHAPTER 21

Access: S.W.A.T., Part One—Table Design and Database Maintenance

Many of the projects you have created in this book are of a size that can be developed over one or two weekends of playing around in your spare time. Some are even small enough to do in a few hours in the evening.

Larger projects like Survey Wizard are developed over a longer period of time and may require some means to track your progress. (I developed Survey Wizard in off-hours over a period of several months.) Keeping track of the elements of a large project is challenging.

If you are working on projects of this size or larger, one of the most useful tools you can create is undoubtedly an *issues database.*

In this chapter, you take a look at exactly why you might need an issue-tracking system. Of course, that means you are going to build one. You will create the tables for it in this chapter and leave the rest for the remaining chapters.

Also in this chapter, you build a run-time maintainable menu that can open forms and reports, execute queries and macros, and even execute Basic language expressions to run your code. The resulting menu and issues-tracking system are two valuable components that you can add to any database project.

Some Definitions

What are issues? Well for the purposes here, an *issue* is a reason that justifies that additional work be done on a project.

Issues fall within the following three categories:

> *Bug*—A program defect. The program does not function as it was intentionally written to perform.
>
> *Change*—A modification on how the program accomplishes one of its original features. Changes usually increase efficiency or ease of use.
>
> *Enhancement*—A modification to the program that adds a new capability.

Bugs Do Exist

Uh oh,…I went and said the *B* word.

Some people take the position that bugs should not and do not ever exist (except when there is something incredibly wrong). That's an overreaction, because bugs *do* exist.

I don't mind saying the *B* word. Some people like to hide behind other words that somehow fog the reality that bugs exist. They call bugs anomalies, problems, aberrations, or unexpected behaviors. How about UAE or GPF? Well, the list goes on.

They're all bugs to me. Bugs do exist in software. Bugs are in my software and they are in software created by large corporations too. And unless you are truly perfect, bugs will exist in your programs, also.

Only by recognizing imperfection can one strive for perfection. If you recognize that bugs exist (even in your own programs), you are more apt to hunt them down and kill them.

Programming is starting to sound like a violent activity, isn't it? Well, it isn't exactly.

There may be a time when you spend an entire weekend tracking down an ever-elusive problem that is corrupting files or doing some other kind of nasty thing. The bug has all of your coworkers totally perplexed. You finally find it, tweak one or two lines of code, and all of a sudden you are the hero programmer that saved the program, saved the company, and saved everyone's jobs. Invigorated, you bask in glory over your bug-squashing prowess.

Too bad, but it's not usually that dramatic. In truth, bug hunting is kind of humiliating. When you hunt for a bug, eventually you or someone else finds the problem and it's in *your* code. It's always a dumb mistake too. (Did you ever hear of a smart mistake?)

Bugs aren't little creatures that get into your programs. They are programming mistakes. You make them! However humiliating it is, it's unrealistic to assume that there are no mistakes in the software you create. I'm quite certain that there is a bug or two (or three...or four...) in the software developed in this book, even though my goal was to make sure there wasn't one.

With that admission, another thing I want to say before you send me back the CD with an angry letter, is that quite often bugs are harmless. You've all heard stories of software glitches (there's another word for bug) that cost a company millions of dollars. Those are rare.

Most bugs at most are a minor annoyance requiring some kind of work-around so you can still get the results you want from the software. Bugs do make your programs look cheap though, so get rid of them as best as you can!

Changes and Enhancements

One thing that a bug certainly is *not* is a change or enhancement request. Don't think that bugs exist in your programs when folks are actually talking about features that they want the software to do; features that weren't part of the original intent of the program.

You might go so far as to say that change and enhancement requests are bugs in the program's specification, but that's not really being fair, is it?

Too much left-brain thinking for me…let's switch gears. Consider the following statement:

Good software never dies, it just gets rewritten.

The more useful your programs are, the more likely that they need changes made to them. Sounds kind of backward doesn't it? Well, it's true.

A useful program is used more heavily. Hence, more requests come in to add this or change that to make it even more useful.

Just like you have to recognize that there may be bugs in your programs, you also have to recognize that you may need to make changes to the programs in order to keep up with your user's demands. If you don't update the program and keep pace with the users, they will eventually find some other way to accomplish what they want, and your software may not be a part of it.

Tracking Issues

Rather than ignore that issues (bugs, changes, and enhancements) exist, you want to celebrate the fact that they are there.

Collect them. Collect them as if they were cherished collectibles like Action Comics Issue Number 1.

Only by gathering up the issues can you have any idea of how well the program accomplishes its job and what can be done to make it better. Long-lasting programs evolve through a cycle of being heavily used and abused along with periods of new development.

Issues are collected in an issues-tracking system. This can be in many forms, such as a simple list of things to do in the next version, a collection of notes from talking to users, or a new program specification. However, if your project is anything but small, you'll find that you can control the issues better if you use a database for your issues-tracking system.

Here's one way to look at it. If you are at the point where you start assigning version numbers to your program, you are definitely in need of a *real* issues-tracking system.

Where Can I Buy an Issues-Tracking System?

In my software development experience, I've found that a good issues-tracking system is one of the developer's most useful tools. However, you don't see many of them available as marketable products.

What gives?

The reason for this is because this is a high-level piece of software that must address an organization's specific working environment and needs. As such, you may have to modify the issues-tracking system you build in this book considerably to make it work for you, particularly in the area of the type of information being recorded along each issue.

Introducing S.W.A.T.

All right, what does the S.W.A.T. acronym stand for?

Well, I haven't thought of anything that fits. The name comes from the Special Weapons And Tactics (S.W.A.T.) police unit that was popularized in a television show by the same name in the 1970s. I liked both the play on words where you would "swat a bug" in addition to the idea of S.W.A.T. as a high precision force.

OK, it's corny, but the best name, *Raid,* is already taken. (Raid is the name of a program used internally by Microsoft to track development issues.)

The main form in S.W.A.T. is shown in Figure 21.1.

FIGURE 21.1.

Entering an issue in the S.W.A.T. Issue form.

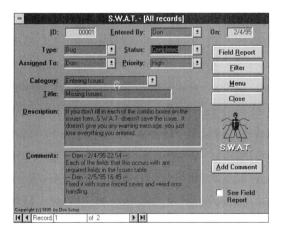

The Goals of S.W.A.T.

S.W.A.T. is intended to work as an issues-tracking system for a single-person project or for a group project of up to five people. To make S.W.A.T. effective, I've focused on the following areas:

- ■ Accessibility
- ■ Ease-of-use

■ Applicability

■ Information value

Let me explain what I mean by these terms. You'll find that they tend to overlap each other in some ways.

Accessibility involves how easily you can get to the program. Probably the best example of an accessible program is the Windows Notepad utility. No matter how many other mega-apps you have open in Windows, you usually will have no difficulty launching the Notepad utility to jot down a few notes and save them in a text file. It's easy, fast, and right there when you need it.

I've tried to make S.W.A.T. accessible in two ways. First, I kept the program simple. S.W.A.T. is an Access database, so there is the overhead of having to load Access. However, the number of forms in S.W.A.T. is minimal, so for an Access application it loads quickly.

I've also provided a Field Report feature so that issues can be recorded off-site in a Word template. Having this template prevents you from having to install and load the S.W.A.T. application simply to record an issue. Each user does not have to secure access to the database.

Ease-of-use is important in S.W.A.T. for more than just the usual reasons. In order for S.W.A.T. to be effective, it has to be the simplest and easiest way for people to communicate with each other about the project.

An issues-tracking system breaks down when people side-step it out of convenience. If the data-entry form is complicated or difficult to use and the user is in a hurry, the user may resort to passing the information to the developer through some other means: e-mail, a note on paper, or a brief telephone conversation.

If data entry is difficult, the developer may also find it easier to just go ahead and make the program change without ever entering it into the issues tracking system.

The result of all this side-stepping is that there is no record that the issue ever existed or was ever fixed. The problem is compounded when it turns out that the developer's change didn't completely address the issue or the issue was misinterpreted.

Applicability involves whether the information being kept in the issues-tracking system actually helps the people that use it. This issue goes along with the question of ease of use. You shouldn't have to fill in a screen full of 20 fields to enter an issue if you really need only five of the fields.

In designing a system, some people by habit gather every possible field they can think of for the program. This is bad for two reasons.

First, users are shocked to find out how much work they must do to complete the entry form. This leads again to side-stepping the program. Second, users have to sort through the clutter of additional unneeded information in order to find the information that they need.

In S.W.A.T., I attempted to minimize the types of data to the bare essentials. As you modify S.W.A.T. for your own needs, you can add fields that your organization needs.

The last term, *informational value*, covers how effective S.W.A.T. is in giving you information about the status and active issues in the development project. This works with the concept of applicability; it is useless to derive statistics on data you really don't need.

The primary information that S.W.A.T. must provide is what issues need to be worked on by any one individual. To find this information, I've added a filtering capability. For example, you can create a filter that returns all of the bugs assigned only to you (see Figure 21.2).

FIGURE 21.2.

Use the Filter form in S.W.A.T. to return only issues assigned to you.

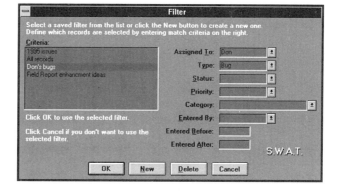

Some of the additional questions you might want S.W.A.T. to help you answer include:

- How stable is the software?
- How capable are you at responding to the issues?
- When do you believe a reliable version of the software can be completed?
- What things should you be focusing on for the next version?
- How well are the folks on your team performing?

None of these questions can be answered simply by looking at the raw data in an issues-tracking system. You'll have to interpret the data carefully to get the entire picture. You can export the S.W.A.T. data into Excel and see if, by looking at the data combined with your experience and intuition, you can determine how things are going.

Ownership and Accountability

This next aspect about an issues-tracking system sounds a little bit negative at first, but it doesn't have to be that way.

One of the most useful features of an issues-tracking system is its capability to assign an issue to an individual. Without an issues-tracking system, you undoubtedly find yourself in the situation where you thought someone else was taking care of an issue.

This can be good and bad. It's good in the sense that you know who to go to if an issue is not resolved. It's good also because people can quickly locate which items they need to fix.

It's bad in the sense that folks sometimes use the information in an issues-tracking system as a way to measure productivity among the different people working on a project. These results may be skewed.

For example, you find that George is fixing roughly half of the issues that Joan is. It makes Joan appear to be top-notch. On the other hand, you might think that George tends to produce code that is less error-prone, hence the reason for fewer issues on his code. Now which of the programmers appears to be doing a better job?

To find the real answers about how the project is going, you may have to look deeper than the issues-tracking system. A dry spell in collecting issues might indicate that a program has become stable, or it may instead be the result of a decline in the amount of usage or testing an application receives. Which one is it?

If you are careful in how you interpret the results of the issues-tracking system, you will be better informed about how your software project is really progressing.

A second useful aspect about assigning an issue to an individual is that it helps to move the issues to resolutions. Suppose Sam enters a change request. Candice is assigned to do the work, but on looking at it, she doesn't fully comprehend the issue. Rather than try to track down Sam, Candice leaves a comment in the issue and assigns it back to him. The next time Sam is in S.W.A.T., he finds the issue assigned to him and realizes he left out some important information when reporting the issue. He responds with the additional information and then assigns it back to Candice, who can now make the change.

All this happened without Sam or Candice having to interrupt each other. Yet the issue is still resolved quickly because both Sam and Candice like to keep a minimal number of open issues on their plates. (This is equivalent to the traditional in-basket that folks have on their desks.)

The Components of S.W.A.T.

In S.W.A.T., you use each of the Office applications covered in this book: Word, Excel, and Access.

The database and main program are in Access. Word is used for gathering information in Field Reports. The program uses OLE Automation to enable the S.W.A.T. program to call up Word to view or print a Field Report. Excel extracts some of the data collected in the SWAT.MDB database for analysis.

In the remainder of this chapter, you create the tables in the SWAT.MDB database and whip up some quick forms with the Form Wizard to populate some lookup tables. You also build the Menu form that I mentioned at the opening of the chapter.

In Chapter 22, "Visual Basic: S.W.A.T., Part Two—Creating the S.W.A.T. Forms," you create and code the main forms in the SWAT.MDB database. In Chapter 23, "Visual Basic: S.W.A.T., Part Three—Field Reports and Time Estimates," you create the Field Report template and make S.W.A.T. control Word with OLE Automation. You also create an Access report to make a quick printout of the issues on which you are working. You finish Chapter 23 by using Excel to analyze the collected data in your issues database.

Designing the S.W.A.T. Tables

The schema for the S.W.A.T. database is shown in Figure 21.3.

FIGURE 21.3.

Using the Relationships window to view the tables in the S.W.A.T. database.

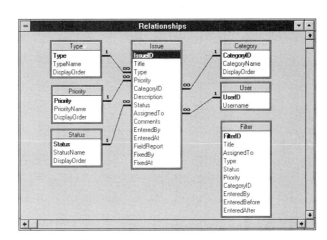

The design recognizes the following objects: User, Issue, Category, and Filter.

A *user* is a person who uses the program. A user receives a generated ID number. This number is used in the AssignedTo, EnteredBy, and FixedBy fields to identify the user for each of these concerns.

An *issue* is all of the information regarding a development issue (bug, change, or enhancement).

A *category* is how issues may be classified to different parts of the project. For example, you might have categories such as User Interface and Reporting. The Category and User tables are lookup tables, but they differ from the other lookup tables because their contents vary depending on the project.

The *Filter table* contains many of the fields in the Issue table. When a filter is applied, only the records from the Issue table that contain matching values are returned.

The remaining tables are lookup tables that remain the same: Type, Priority, and Status. (A *lookup table* identifies a numeric code with its textual meaning.)

The *Type table* stores codes that indicate whether an issue is a bug, change, or enhancement. The *Priority table* stores codes for High, Medium, and Low priorities. The *Status table* stores codes that identify the working status of an issue: In Progress, On Hold, Completed, Dropped, and Closed.

Missing from the schema is a way to track different products. The idea is that you have a separate S.W.A.T. database for each project.

You don't need to start a new database to work on a new version of the same project. Any issues left open are still in effect on the new version of the software. However, it might make sense to add a Version field and corresponding lookup table so that you can identify the version of the program for which an issue is targeted to be completed.

Creating the S.W.A.T. Tables

I'm talking too much. Let's start building. (SWAT.MDB and other associated files are on the book's companion CD, in case you want to read along.)

Start Access and create a new database, SWAT.MDB. Add the following tables: User, Category, Type, Priority, Status, Issue, and Filter, as shown next.

The User table contains two fields, UserID and Username.

You can store user-specific information in this table. For example, you can create a LastFilterID field that stores the last filter used. The next time the user uses S.W.A.T., the filtering can be set automatically.

Object: **User Table**
Stores user names and corresponding UserID numbers.

Field Name	Data Type
UserID	Counter
Username	Text

Set the UserID field as the User table's primary key. Set the properties for the fields in the User table as shown here:

Field Name	UserID
Data Type	Counter
Description	User ID number

Field Name	Username
Description	User name
Data Type	Text
Field Size	30
Required	Yes
Allow Zero Length	No
Indexed	Yes (No Duplicates)

Adding records to the User table is automatic when each new user logs in to S.W.A.T.

The next four tables contain a DisplayOrder field. This field indicates in what order the records should display when appearing in a drop-down list of a combo box.

Create the Category table.

Object: **Category Table**
Defines how issues may be classified among different areas of the project.

Field Name	Data Type
CategoryID	Counter
CategoryName	Text
DisplayOrder	Number

The CategoryID field is set as the primary key.

Field Name	CategoryID
Data Type	Counter
Description	Category ID

Field Name	CategoryName
Data Type	Text

continues

Description	Category name
Field Size	30
Required	Yes
Allow Zero Length	No
Indexed	No

Field Name	DisplayOrder
Data Type	Number
Description	Display order
Field Size	Integer
Required	Yes
Indexed	Yes (No Duplicates)

You will use the Form Wizard to make a quick form for filling in entries in this table later in this chapter.

Create the Type table.

Object: Type Table
Contains codes for the different issue types.

Field Name	Data Type
Type	Number
TypeName	Text
DisplayOrder	Number

Set the Type field as the primary key and set the field properties as shown here:

Field Name	Type
Data Type	Number
Field Size	Integer
Description	Type code

Field Name	TypeName
Data Type	Text
Description	Type name
Field Size	20
Required	Yes
Allow Zero Length	No
Indexed	No

Field Name	DisplayOrder
Data Type	Number
Description	Display order

Field Size	Integer
Required	Yes
Indexed	Yes (No Duplicates)

Switch to datasheet view and enter the following records into the Type table.

Type	TypeName	DisplayOrder
1	Bug	1
2	Change	2
3	Enhancement	3

Create the Priority table.

Object: **Priority Table**

Contains codes for the different issue priorities.

Field Name	Data Type
Priority	Number
PriorityName	Text
DisplayOrder	Number

Set the Priority field as the primary key.

Field Name	Priority
Data Type	Number
Field Size	Integer
Description	Priority code
Field Name	PriorityName
Data Type	Text
Description	Priority name
Field Size	20
Required	Yes
Allow Zero Length	No
Indexed	No
Field Name	DisplayOrder
Data Type	Number
Description	Display order
Field Size	Integer
Required	Yes
Indexed	Yes (No Duplicates)

In datasheet view enter the following records into the Priority table. Figure 21.4 shows the priority values.

Priority	Priority Name	Display Order
1	High	1
2	Medium	2
3	Low	3

FIGURE 21.4.

Entering the priority values in the Priority table.

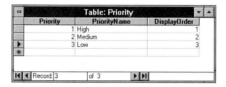

Create the Status table.

Object: **Status Table**

Contains codes for the work states.

Field Name	Data Type
Status	Number
StatusName	Text
DisplayOrder	Number

Set the Status field as the primary key.

Field Name	Status
Data Type	Number
Field Size	Integer
Description	Status code
Field Name	StatusName
Data Type	Text
Description	Status name
Field Size	20
Required	Yes
Allow Zero Length	No
Indexed	No
Field Name	DisplayOrder
Data Type	Number
Description	Display order
Field Size	Integer
Required	Yes
Indexed	Yes (No Duplicates)

In datasheet view, enter the following records into the Status table.

Status	Status Name	Display Order
1	In Progress	1
2	On Hold	2
3	Completed	3
4	Dropped	4
5	Closed	5

That does it for the lookup tables. Next, you need to create the Issue table.

Object: **Issue Table**
Stores all collected information about an issue with the project.

Field Name	Data Type
IssueID	Counter
Title	Text
Type	Number
Priority	Number
CategoryID	Number
Description	Memo
Status	Number
AssignedTo	Number
Comments	Memo
EnteredBy	Number
EnteredAt	Date/Time
FieldReport	Text
FixedBy	Number
FixedAt	Date/Time

Set the IssueID field as the primary key. Set the properties for the different fields as shown here:

Field Name	IssueID
Data Type	Counter
Description	Issue ID
Field Name	Title
Data Type	Text
Description	40 character title for the issue
Field Size	40
Required	Yes

continues

Allow Zero Length	No
Indexed	No
Field Name	Type
Data Type	Number
Description	Is this a bug, change, or enhancement?
Field Size	Integer
Validation Rule	>0 And <4
Required	Yes
Indexed	No
Field Name	Priority
Data Type	Number
Description	How does the issue rate in urgency compared to other issues?
Field Size	Integer
Validation Rule	>0 And <4
Required	Yes
Indexed	No
Field Name	CategoryID
Data Type	Number
Description	Under which part of the product does this issue fall?
Field Size	Long Integer
Required	Yes
Indexed	No
Field Name	Description
Data Type	Memo
Description	Full description of the problem, including steps to reproduce it, if applicable.
Required	Yes
Allow Zero Length	No
Field Name	Status
Data Type	Number
Description	Where does this issue currently stand?
Field Size	Integer
Validation Rule	>0 And <6
Required	Yes
Indexed	No

Field Name	AssignedTo
Data Type	Number
Description	Who is currently working on this issue?
Field Size	Long Integer
Required	Yes
Indexed	No

Field Name	Comments
Data Type	Memo
Description	Comments entered while resolving the issue.
Required	No
Allow Zero Length	Yes

Field Name	EnteredBy
Data Type	Number
Description	Who originally entered the issue?
Field Size	Long Integer
Required	Yes
Indexed	No

Field Name	EnteredAt
Data Type	Date/Time
Description	When was the issue originated?
Default Value	Now( )
Required	Yes
Indexed	No

Field Name	FieldReport
Data Type	Text
Description	Path for the field report Word document.
Field Size	255
Required	No
Allow Zero Length	Yes
Indexed	No

Field Name	FixedBy
Data Type	Number
Description	Who resolved the problem?
Field Size	Long Integer
Required	No
Indexed	No

continues

Field Name	FixedAt
Data Type	Date/Time
Description	When was the issue closed?
Required	No
Indexed	No

Figure 21.5 shows the Issues table in design view.

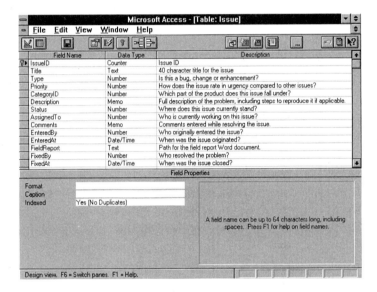

The final table to create is the Filter table. Many of the fields in the Filter table match those in the Issue table. You can copy them in directly, but if you do so, be sure to check the property settings. Required entries in the Issue table are not required in a Filter table record, and no validation rules are set.

Object: **Filter Table**

Stores criteria to match against when filtering Issue records in the Issue form.

Field Name	Data Type
FilterID	Counter
Owner	Number
Title	Text
AssignedTo	Number
Type	Number
Status	Number
Priority	Number

CategoryID	Number
EnteredBy	Number
EnteredBefore	Date/Time
EnteredAfter	Date/Time

Set the FilterID field as the primary key.

Field Name	FilterID
Data Type	Counter
Description	Filter ID

Field Name	Owner
Data Type	Number
Description	Who does this filter belong to?
Field Size	Long Integer
Required	Yes
Indexed	No

Field Name	Title
Data Type	Text
Description	Title of this filter
Field Size	60
Required	Yes
Allow Zero Length	No
Indexed	No

Field Name	AssignedTo
Data Type	Number
Description	Who is currently working on this issue?
Field Size	Long Integer
Required	No
Indexed	No

Field Name	Type
Data Type	Number
Description	Is this a bug, change, or enhancement?
Field Size	Integer
Required	No
Indexed	No

Field Name	Status
Data Type	Number
Description	Where does this issue currently stand?

continues

Field Size	Integer
Required	No
Indexed	No

Field Name	Priority
Data Type	Number
Description	How does the issue rate in urgency compared to other issues?
Field Size	Integer
Required	No
Indexed	No

Field Name	CategoryID
Data Type	Number
Description	Under which part of the product does this issue fall?
Field Size	Long Integer
Required	No
Indexed	No

Field Name	EnteredBy
Data Type	Number
Description	Who originally entered the issue?
Field Size	Long Integer
Required	No
Indexed	No

Field Name	EnteredBefore
Data Type	Date/Time
Description	When was the issue originated?
Required	No
Indexed	No

Field Name	EnteredAfter
Data Type	Date/Time
Description	When was the issue originated?
Required	No
Indexed	No

Creating Lookup Table Maintenance Forms

It's easy enough to open up table in datasheet view and fill in some records just as you did with the Priority, Status, and Type tables. However, for lookup tables that you expect to edit more often than usual, you can create a form to do the job.

To be quite honest, you aren't gaining a whole lot here other than aesthetics. However there isn't much effort you need to put into it. Use the Form Wizard to create the forms and then perform minor tweaks on them to get the look you want.

Click the Form tab in the database container and click the **N**ew button to start a form. Select Category as the table on which to base the form and click the Form **W**izards button. See Figure 21.6.

FIGURE 21.6.

Use the Form Wizard to create forms for maintaining records in lookup tables.

In the Form Wizards dialog box, select the Tabular Form Wizard, as shown in Figure 21.7. This wizard generates a continuous form that displays several of the lookup values at once.

FIGURE 21.7.

Selecting the Tabular Form Wizard.

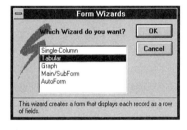

In the first screen of the Tabular Form Wizard, select CategoryName and SortOrder as the fields to display on the form. See Figure 21.8.

FIGURE 21.8.

Selecting which fields to display on the Category form.

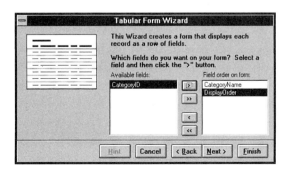

In the next wizard screen, select Embossed as the form style. This style creates sunken text boxes on the form, as shown in Figure 21.9.

FIGURE 21.9.

Choose the Embossed form style.

In the final screen, select the option to Modify the form's design and click the Finish button. See Figure 21.10.

FIGURE 21.10.

The final screen in the Tabular Form Wizard.

The generated form, shown in Figure 21.11, is pretty close to what you want.

FIGURE 21.11.

The Catalog form generated by the Tabular Form Wizard.

I made the following changes to clean it up and get the look I wanted:

■ Added a space in the column labels so that CategoryName reads as Category Name and DisplayOrder reads as Display Order.

■ Widened the DisplayOrder text box so that it more closely matches the column label.

■ Widened the form to leave space between the last field and the right side of the form.

■ Behind the large white Category label is a label with the same text in gray. It is offset to the right and below just enough to produce a shadow effect. I changed the Fore Color of this to Black.

■ Set the Back Color of the form sections and labels to dark gray.

■ Set the Back Color of the text boxes to Teal.

■ Set the Auto Center property of the form to Yes.

You can modify the Catalog form so that each time it opens, it displays the records by order of the SortOrder field, as shown in Figure 21.12. Change the Record Source property on the form to the following:

```
SELECT * FROM Category ORDER BY DisplayOrder;
```

FIGURE 21.12.

Modifying the Catalog form.

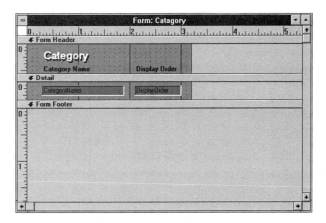

My final form is shown in Figure 21.13. I chose the dark colors to fit the S.W.A.T. theme of bug squishing.

You can create forms for the other lookup tables in the same manner. I found that it is easier to copy the Catalog form and use it as a basis for creating the next one than it is to start the Form Wizard again and develop the form from scratch.

FIGURE 21.13.
*Entering categories with
the Catalog form.*

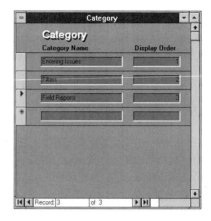

I created additional forms for the Priority, Status, Type, and User tables, with each form
by the same name of the table.

A Database Maintenance Menu

Now, I will get lost on a major tangent outside of the objective of completing S.W.A.T.
It will be worth it though; I promise. You will return to the subject of the issues-tracking system at the beginning of the next chapter.

A useful utility in any Access database project is a menu that can open the various lookup
table forms, preview and print reports, execute action queries, or run a procedure you
wrote in Access Basic for a special operation.

You might say, "Well, the database container can do that." However, the database container shows all of your development forms, queries, and so on, alongside the objects
that you want users of the application to use.

A menu form guides the users to the components of the application they need and can
even provide help text to indicate what each component of the application is for.

The impulse way to create a menu is to drop some buttons on a form and then write the
code behind each of the buttons to perform the desired operation. Pretty soon, you run
out of space for all the buttons and either create a menu that calls menus, or you do
something like you do here.

Introducing…the S.W.A.T. Database Maintenance Menu (see Figure 21.14).

In the S.W.A.T. menu is a list box that lists the different forms. As you click each selection from the list, the text in the light gray box below the list shows a descriptive note
about the form.

FIGURE 21.14.
S.W.A.T. has its own database maintenance menu.

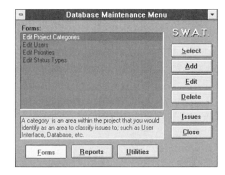

Below the description box are three toggle buttons that allow you to switch from Forms to Reports or Utilities. Suppose you write a program that empties the Issues and Filter tables in the S.W.A.T. database. You can add a Utility menu item, as shown in Figure 21.15.

FIGURE 21.15.
The S.W.A.T. menu can execute programs you've written in Access Basic.

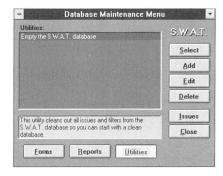

When you select the Reports button, a check box appears at the bottom-right corner of the menu so you can choose whether to preview a report on-screen or send it to the printer (see Figure 21.16).

FIGURE 21.16.
The S.W.A.T. menu lets you preview reports as well as print them.

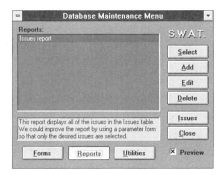

A menu like this is driven off of a table, of course. I've seen menus like this in many applications, but something I've added that you don't usually see is the capability to add, edit, and delete commands from the menu while the menu is open. This way, folks don't have to figure out the structure of your menu table to add a form to the menu; they simply click the Add button.

When you click the Add button, the Add Menu Item dialog box appears, as shown in Figure 21.17.

FIGURE 21.17.

The Add Menu Item pop-up form.

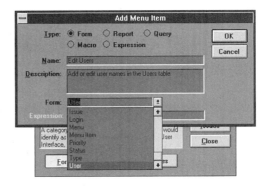

There are five types of menu items that you can add to the menu. The last three—Query, Macro, and Expressions—are clumped together in the Utilities category.

In the Add Menu Item form, you enter the name and description of the menu item. The name is the text that appears in the list of menu items. The description is the text that appears in the gray box below the list when an item is selected.

If the menu item is a Form, you can use the combo box below the description text box to select from the forms currently in the database (as was shown in Figure 21.17). If you change the menu item type to Report, Query, or Macro, the label for this combo box changes appropriately and all of the database's reports, queries, or macros are displayed in the list.

If you select an Expression menu item type, the database object combo box is disabled and the Expression text box below it is used instead. In this text box, you can enter any expression that properly evaluates when passed to the Access Basic `Eval()` function. If you wrote a function named `ClearDatabase`, for example, you enter the following in this text box to execute it:

```
ClearDatabase()
```

Not only can you call your own functions, but you can call any Access functions as well. As a silly example, suppose you create a menu item that displays a message with the `MsgBox` function. The entry can be like the following:

FIGURE 21.19.
*Adding the lstMenu
list box.*

Object: **lblDescription Label**
Display notes about the currently selected menu item.

Property	Value
Name	lstDescription
Caption	<Filled by code>
Left	0.1 in
Top	1.8333 in
Width	2.7917 in
Height	0.4271 in
Back Color	12632256 (Light Gray)
Special Effect	Sunken

The next control on the form is an option group that returns an appropriate value, depending on which of three toggle buttons is currently pressed.

Object: **grpMenu Option Group**
Option group containing the Forms, Reports, and Utilities toggle buttons.

Property	Value
Name	grpMenu
Default Value	1
Tab Index	1
Left	0.1 in
Top	2.2917 in
Width	2.8 in
Height	0.4146 in
Back Style	Clear
Border Style	Clear

Figure 21.20 shows the grpMenu option group.

FIGURE 21.20.

Adding the grpMenu option group (before setting the border to Clear).

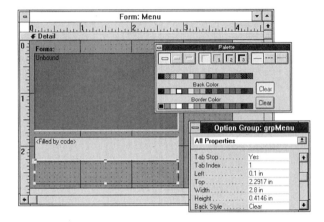

Inside the option group, add the following toggle buttons. The Option Value property for each button indicates which value the grpMenu control returns when the button is pressed.

Object: **tglForms Toggle Button**
Pressed to display menu items that open forms.

Property	Value
Name	tglForms
Caption	&Forms
Option Value	1
Left	0.2 in
Top	2.375 in
Width	0.8021 in
Height	0.25 in

Object: **tglReports Toggle Button**
Pressed to display menu items that open reports.

Property	Value
Name	tglReports
Caption	&Reports
Option Value	2
Left	1.1 in
Top	2.375 in

Width	0.8021 in
Height	0.25 in

Object: **tglUtilities Toggle Button**

Pressed to display menu items that run action queries, run macros, or evaluate expressions.

Property	Value
Name	tglUtilities
Caption	&Utilities
Option Value	3
Left	2 in
Top	2.375 in
Width	0.8021 in
Height	0.25 in

Figure 21.21 shows the three toggle buttons.

FIGURE 21.21.

The three toggle buttons are placed in the now invisible grpMenu option group.

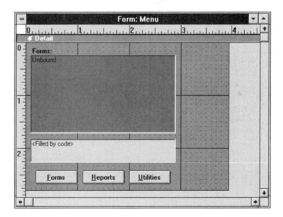

Next, add the following six command buttons down the right side of the form.

Object: **cmdSelect Command Button**

Activate the selected menu item.

Property	Value
Name	cmdSelect
Caption	&Select
Tab Index	2
Left	3.05 in

continues

Property	Value
Top	0.4576 in
Width	0.8021 in
Height	0.25 in

Object: **cmdAdd Command Button**

Display the Add Menu Item dialog box.

Property	Value
Name	cmdAdd
Caption	&Add
Tab Index	3
Left	3.05 in
Top	0.75 in
Width	0.8021 in
Height	0.25 in

Object: **cmdEdit Command Button**

Display the Edit Menu Item dialog box.

Property	Value
Name	cmdEdit
Caption	&Edit
Tab Index	4
Left	3.05 in
Top	1.0417 in
Width	0.8021 in
Height	0.25 in

Object: **cmdDelete Command Button**

Delete the selected menu item.

Property	Value
Name	cmdDelete
Caption	&Delete
Tab Index	5
Left	3.05 in
Top	1.3326 in
Width	0.8021 in
Height	0.25 in

Object: **cmdIssues Command Button**
Close the Menu form and open the Issue form.

Property	Value
Name	cmdIssues
Caption	&Issues
Tab Index	6
Left	3.05 in
Top	1.7076 in
Width	0.8021 in
Height	0.25 in

Object: **cmdClose Command Button**
Close the Menu form and display the database container.

Property	Value
Name	cmdClose
Caption	&Close
Tab Index	7
Left	3.05 in
Top	2 in
Width	0.8021 in
Height	0.25 in

Figure 21.22 shows the Menu form's command buttons.

FIGURE 21.22.

Adding the Menu form's command buttons.

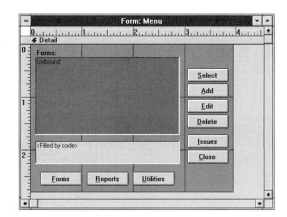

Add a check box to indicate whether reports should be viewed on-screen or sent to the printer.

Object: **chkPreview Check Box**
Indicates whether reports are previewed rather than printed.

Property	Value
Name	chkPreview
Default Value	1
Tab Index	8
Left	3.1 in
Top	2.4146 in
Width	0.1806 in
Height	0.1458 in
Special Effect	Sunken

Object: **lblPreview Label**
Label for the chkPreview check box.

Property	Value
Name	lblPreview
Caption	&Preview
Left	3.2806 in
Top	2.4146 in
Width	0.6042 in
Height	0.1667 in

Finally, for window dressing, add a couple of labels to the form to display the name of the program with a shadowed effect.

Object: **lblSwat1 Label**
Shadow for the S.W.A.T. program title.

Property	Value
Name	lblSwat1
Caption	S.W.A.T.
Left	3.0597 in
Top	0.1431 in
Width	0.7917 in
Height	0.2396 in

Fore Color	0 (Black)
Font Name	MS Sans Serif
Font Size	12
Font Weight	Bold

Object: **lblSwat2 Label**
The foreground S.W.A.T. program title.

Property	Value
Name	lblSwat2
Caption	S.W.A.T.
Left	3.05 in
Top	0.125 in
Width	0.7917 in
Height	0.2396 in
Fore Color	16777215 (White)
Font Name	MS Sans Serif
Font Size	12
Font Weight	Bold

Figure 21.23 shows the completed Menu form.

FIGURE 21.23.
The completed Menu form.

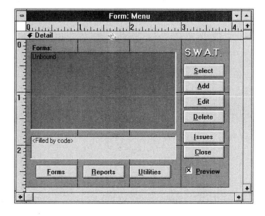

The Globals Module

Before you dig into the code behind the Menu form, you need to declare a few globals and add a couple of your familiar procedures to the project.

Open a new module and add the declarations, as shown in Listing 21.1.

Listing 21.1. The declarations section in the Globals module.

```
' S.W.A.T. globals

  Option Compare Database
  Option Explicit

  Global Const PROGRAM = "S.W.A.T."

' Globals for the database maintenance menu
  Global gintObjectType As Integer
  Global glngAddedItem As Integer
  Global glngEditItem As Integer

  Global gblnEditItemCancel As Integer
```

Each of the variables declared in the declarations section is used in communication between the Menu form and the Menu Item form, which adds and edits menu items. You'll
see how they are used as you go through the code.

Enter the CNLng and CNStr functions, as shown in Listings 21.2 and 21.3.

Listing 21.2. The CNLng function.

```
Function CNLng (v As Variant) As Long

  If IsNull(v) Then
    CNLng = 0
  Else
    CNLng = CLng(v)
  End If

End Function
```

Listing 21.3. The CNStr function.

```
Function CNStr (v As Variant) As String

  If IsNull(v) Then
    CNStr = ""
  Else
    CNStr = Trim$(CStr(v))
  End If

End Function
```

Another function that you can borrow from previous projects is the RequiredField function (see Listing 21.4). Use this function to verify that an entry was made in a text box or other control.

Listing 21.4. The RequiredField function.

```
Function RequiredField (strName As String, ctl As Control) As Integer

' Verify that a value was entered in the specified control

  Dim strValue As String
  Dim blnResult As Integer

' Default to failure
  RequiredField = True

  On Error GoTo RequiredFieldError

  strValue = CNStr(ctl)
  blnResult = (Len(strValue) = 0)

  If blnResult Then
    MsgBox strName & " is a required field", 48, PROGRAM
    ctl.SetFocus
  End If

  RequiredField = blnResult

RequiredFieldDone:
  Exit Function

RequiredFieldError:
  MsgBox Error$, 48, PROGRAM
  Resume RequiredFieldDone

End Function
```

In the next chapter, you add some additional declarations and procedures to the Globals module, but this is all you need to complete right now.

Coding the Menu Form

Next, you need to add the code behind the Menu form. Some of the code interacts with forms that you haven't created. In actual development, some of the code for the forms in this project was developed simultaneously, of course.

The Declarations Section

The declarations section of the Menu form module declares three variables to keep track of which menu item is currently selected in each of the three menu item groups (see Listing 21.5). As the user switches back and forth between the groups, the program can reselect the menu item that was selected the last time you viewed the same group.

Listing 21.5. The declarations section for the Menu form module.

```
' Menu form module

  Option Compare Database
  Option Explicit

  Dim mlngSelectedForm
  Dim mlngSelectedReport
  Dim mlngSelectedUtility

  Dim mblnLoadingIssues
```

The *Form_Load* Subroutine

The Form_Load subroutine hides the database container to get a clean display (see Listing 21.6). It then calls the grpMenu_Click subroutine to do the same kind of initialization that occurs when switching between the different types of menus.

Listing 21.6. The Form_Load **subroutine.**

```
Sub Form_Load ()

' Hide the database container
  DoCmd DoMenuItem 0, 4, 3, A_MENU_VER20

  grpMenu_Click

End Sub
```

The *grpMenu_Click* Subroutine

The grpMenu_Click subroutine is shown in Listing 21.7. Take a look at this one in detail.

Listing 21.7. The grpMenu_Click **subroutine.**

```
Sub grpMenu_Click ()

  Dim sql As String

  On Error GoTo grpMenu_ClickError

  sql = "SELECT * FROM [Menu Item] WHERE Type = " & grpMenu
```

```
    lstMenu.RowSource = sql
    lstMenu.Requery

  chkPreview.Visible = (grpMenu = 2)

  Select Case CInt(grpMenu)
  Case 1
    lstMenu = mlngSelectedForm
    lblMenu.Caption = "Forms:"
  Case 2
    lstMenu = mlngSelectedReport
    lblMenu.Caption = "Reports:"
  Case 3
    lstMenu = mlngSelectedUtility
    lblMenu.Caption = "Utilities:"
  End Select

  If lstMenu.ListIndex < 0 Then
    lstMenu.SetFocus
    DoEvents
    SendKeys "{Down}"
  End If

  lstMenu_Click

grpMenu_ClickDone:
  Exit Sub

grpMenu_ClickError:
  MsgBox Error$, 48, PROGRAM
  Resume grpMenu_ClickDone

End Sub
```

The grpMenu_Click event occurs when one of the toggle buttons is clicked. The grpMenu option group control returns the Option Value property setting for the button that was clicked.

The grpMenu_Click subroutine constructs a SELECT statement that returns each of the menu items for the type of menu items displayed. The lstMenu list box has its Row Source property set to the statement and then is requeried to display the new selection.

```
  sql = "SELECT * FROM [Menu Item] WHERE Type = " & grpMenu
  lstMenu.RowSource = sql
  lstMenu.Requery
```

Next, the Preview check box is visible only if the report menu items appear.

```
  chkPreview.Visible = (grpMenu = 2)
```

Next, the current item in the list and the caption above the list are set, depending on which items are displayed. The module level variables return the selection to the same item that was selected when last viewing the same list.

```
Select Case CInt(grpMenu)
Case 1
  lstMenu = mlngSelectedForm
  lblMenu.Caption = "Forms:"
Case 2
  lstMenu = mlngSelectedReport
  lblMenu.Caption = "Reports:"
Case 3
  lstMenu = mlngSelectedUtility
  lblMenu.Caption = "Utilities:"
End Select
```

In case no item is selected in the list, the next few lines set focus to the list box and press the down-arrow key to select the first item in the list (if there is one).

```
If lstMenu.ListIndex < 0 Then
  lstMenu.SetFocus
  DoEvents
  SendKeys "{Down}"
End If
```

The `lstMenu_Click` subroutine is called to perform further initialization that occurs each time an item is selected in the list.

```
lstMenu_Click
```

The *lstMenu_Click* Subroutine

The `lstMenu_Click` subroutine updates the `lblDescription` label with the text corresponding to the selected menu item (see Listing 21.8).

Although the lstMenu list box displays only a single field, it actually contains all of the fields in a Menu Item table record. The description is loaded into the fourth column of the list box.

The subroutine also updates the module level variables that store the items that were last selected in a list.

Listing 21.8. The `lstMenu_Click` subroutine.

```
Sub lstMenu_Click ()

  On Error GoTo lstMenu_ClickError

  lblDescription.Caption = lstMenu.Column(3)

' Save current selection so when the menu is returned, you can restore it.

  Select Case CInt(grpMenu)
  Case 1
    mlngSelectedForm = lstMenu
  Case 2
    mlngSelectedReport = lstMenu
```

```
Case 3
  mlngSelectedUtility = lstMenu
End Select

lstMenu_ClickDone:
  Exit Sub

lstMenu_ClickError:
  MsgBox Error$, 48, PROGRAM
  Resume lstMenu_ClickDone

End Sub
```

The *cmdSelect_Click* Subroutine

Within any form, there always seems to be one procedure where all the action occurs. Usually, it's a cmdOK_Click subroutine. In this form, the action happens right here.

The cmdSelect_Click subroutine performs the menu selection, the action depending on the type of menu item selected (see Listing 21.9).

Listing 21.9. The cmdSelect_Click **subroutine.**

```
Sub cmdSelect_Click ()

  Dim db As Database
  Dim qrydef As QueryDef
  Dim blnOpened As Integer

  Dim v As Variant

  blnOpened = False

  On Error GoTo cmdSelect_ClickError

  If lstMenu.ListIndex = -1 Then
    MsgBox "You must select an entry from the menu first.", 64, PROGRAM
    GoTo cmdSelect_ClickDone
  End If

  Select Case CInt(grpMenu)

  Case 1 ' Form
    DoCmd OpenForm lstMenu.Column(5)

  Case 2 ' Report
    If chkPreview = 1 Then
      DoCmd OpenReport lstMenu.Column(5), A_Preview
    Else
      DoCmd OpenReport lstMenu.Column(5)
    End If
```

continues

Listing 21.9. continued

```
Case 3
  Select Case CInt(lstMenu.Column(4))
  Case 1 ' Query
    Set db = DBEngine(0)(0)
    Set qrydef = db.OpenQueryDef(lstMenu.Column(5))
    blnOpened = True

    qrydef.Execute

  Case 2 ' Macro
    DoCmd RunMacro lstMenu.Column(5)

  Case 3 ' Expression
    v = Eval(lstMenu.Column(5))
    If Not IsNull(v) Then
      If CStr(v) <> "" Then
        MsgBox "Return value = " & v, 0, PROGRAM
      End If
    End If

  End Select

End Select

cmdSelect_ClickDone:
  On Error Resume Next
  If blnOpened Then qrydef.Close
  Exit Sub

cmdSelect_ClickError:
  MsgBox Error$, 48, PROGRAM
  Resume cmdSelect_ClickDone

End Sub
```

After checking that a menu item has been selected and bailing out if not, the cmdSelect_Click subroutine checks the grpMenu control to determine whether the menu item is a form, report, or utility.

```
Select Case CInt(grpMenu)
```

If the item is a form, cool; just open it and you are done.

The name of the object is stored in the sixth column of the lstMenu list box (the column property is zero based). This column holds the Argument field from the Menu Item table.

```
Case 1 ' Form
  DoCmd OpenForm lstMenu.Column(5)
```

A report is only slightly more complicated. Before opening the report (which normally prints it), you check the Preview check box. If the check box is checked, A_Preview is passed to open the report in preview mode.

```
Case 2 ' Report
  If chkPreview = 1 Then
    DoCmd OpenReport lstMenu.Column(5), A_Preview
  Else
    DoCmd OpenReport lstMenu.Column(5)
  End If
```

If the menu item is a Utility, another Select Case statement is used based on the UtilityType value stored in the fifth column of the lstMenu list box.

```
Case 3
  Select Case CInt(lstMenu.Column(4))
```

If the menu item is a query, the query definition opens as a QueryDef object and executes. You'll get a reasonable error message if the query you selected is a SELECT query rather than an action query.

```
Case 1 ' Query
  Set db = DBEngine(0)(0)
  Set qrydef = db.OpenQueryDef(lstMenu.Column(5))
  blnOpened = True

  qrydef.Execute
```

If the item is a macro, it is executed with the RunMacro action.

```
Case 2 ' Macro
  DoCmd RunMacro lstMenu.Column(5)
```

Finally, the really fun one occurs here. If the menu item is an expression, it is passed into the Eval() function in order to execute it.

The Eval() function returns the value derived from the expression (if there is one). I decided to ignore Null and zero return values, but display all others.

```
Case 3 ' Expression
  v = Eval(lstMenu.Column(5))
  If Not IsNull(v) Then
    If CStr(v) <> "" Then
      MsgBox "Return value = " & v, 0, PROGRAM
    End If
  End If
```

The *cmdAdd_Click* Subroutine

The cmdAdd_Click subroutine opens the Menu Item form, which really does the work of adding a new menu item (see Listing 21.10). Then the subroutine handles messy details to update the Menu form in case a new item was added to the menu.

Listing 21.10. The `cmdAdd_Click` subroutine.

```
Sub cmdAdd_Click ()

  On Error GoTo cmdAdd_ClickError

  glngEditItem = 0

  gintObjectType = grpMenu
  DoCmd OpenForm "Menu Item", , , , , A_Dialog

  If Not gblnEditItemCancel Then
    If glngAddedItem > 0 Then
      grpMenu_Click
      lstMenu = glngAddedItem
      lstMenu_Click
    End If
  End If

cmdAdd_ClickDone:
  Exit Sub

cmdAdd_ClickError:
  MsgBox Error$, 48, PROGRAM
  Resume cmdAdd_ClickDone

End Sub
```

In communicating with the Menu Item form, the `glngEditItem` variable is set to 0 to indicate that, rather than editing an item, you are creating a new one.

```
glngEditItem = 0
```

Next, the `ginObjectType` variable is set with the current menu item type. The Menu Item form uses this so that it defaults to creating the same type of item currently listed on the Menu form.

```
gintObjectType = grpMenu
```

Then, the form is opened as a dialog box, so the code is suspended until the form is closed.

```
DoCmd OpenForm "Menu Item", , , , , A_Dialog
```

Next, the code checks the state of two variables to determine whether a new item was added.

```
If Not gblnEditItemCancel Then
  If glngAddedItem > 0 Then
```

If the item was added, the following lines refresh the lstMenu list box, select the added item, and refresh the description text for the selected menu item.

```
       grpMenu_Click
       lstMenu = glngAddedItem
       lstMenu_Click
     End If
  End If
```

The *cmdEdit_Click* Subroutine

The `cmdEdit_Click` subroutine works much like the subroutine you just looked at (see Listing 21.11).

In this case, you set the `glngEditItem` variable with the `ItemID` value for the Menu Item table record being edited. The Menu Item form switches into edit mode when it finds that the global has been set.

Listing 21.11. The `cmdEdit_Click` subroutine.

```
Sub cmdEdit_Click ()

  On Error GoTo cmdEdit_ClickError

  If lstMenu.ListIndex = -1 Then GoTo cmdEdit_ClickDone

  glngEditItem = lstMenu

  gintObjectType = grpMenu
  DoCmd OpenForm "Menu Item", , , , , A_Dialog

  If Not gblnEditItemCancel Then
    grpMenu_Click
    lstMenu = glngEditItem
    lstMenu_Click
  End If

  glngEditItem = 0

cmdEdit_ClickDone:
  Exit Sub

cmdEdit_ClickError:
  MsgBox Error$, 48, PROGRAM
  Resume cmdEdit_ClickDone

End Sub
```

The *cmdDelete_Click* Subroutine

The `cmdDelete_Click` subroutine deletes a menu item (see Listing 21.12). (I know this is obvious, but for some reason I still felt compelled to state it.)

Listing 21.12. The cmdDelete_Click **subroutine.**

```
Sub cmdDelete_Click ()

  Dim db As Database
  Dim dyn As Recordset
  Dim blnOpened As Integer

  Dim msg As String
  Dim dq As String
  Dim z As Integer

  blnOpened = False

  On Error GoTo cmdDelete_ClickError

  If lstMenu.ListIndex = -1 Then GoTo cmdDelete_ClickDone

  dq = Chr$(34)
  msg = "Delete the " & dq & lstMenu.Column(2) & dq & " menu item?"
  z = MsgBox(msg, 4 + 32 + 256, PROGRAM)
  If z <> 6 Then GoTo cmdDelete_ClickDone

  Set db = DBEngine(0)(0)
  Set dyn = db.OpenRecordset(lstMenu.RowSource, DB_OPEN_DYNASET)
  blnOpened = True

  dyn.FindFirst "ItemID = " & lstMenu
  If dyn.NoMatch Then GoTo cmdDelete_ClickDone

  dyn.Delete
  lstMenu.Requery

  dyn.MoveNext
  If dyn.EOF Then
    dyn.MovePrevious
  End If

  If Not dyn.BOF Then
    lstMenu = dyn!ItemID
  End If
  lstMenu_Click

cmdDelete_ClickDone:
  On Error Resume Next
  If blnOpened Then dyn.Close
  Exit Sub

cmdDelete_ClickError:
  MsgBox Error$, 48, PROGRAM
  Resume cmdDelete_ClickDone

End Sub
```

The subroutine first checks to make sure that an item was selected.

```
If lstMenu.ListIndex = -1 Then GoTo cmdDelete_ClickDone
```

> **NOTE**
>
> Here's a tip. Always check the `ListIndex` for a value of –1 if you want to determine whether an item in the list is selected. I originally tried to accomplish this with the `IsNull` function, figuring that if a list box didn't have anything selected in it, it returns a Null value.
>
> Not so (or at least some of the times not so). A list box control can contain a value, possibly from a prior selection, while it doesn't show a selected value. Weird, huh?

Before deleting anything, the code performs its usual message box thing to make absolutely sure the user is in a destructive mood.

```
dq = Chr$(34)
msg = "Delete the " & dq & lstMenu.Column(2) & dq & " menu item?"
z = MsgBox(msg, 4 + 32 + 256, PROGRAM)
If z <> 6 Then GoTo cmdDelete_ClickDone
```

Next, open a recordset based on the `SELECT` statement stored in the `lstMenu` RowSource property. That's pretty tricky isn't it?

The idea is to produce a recordset with the same contents and same order as the list box. Not only do you need the recordset to delete the selected menu item, but you need it to help you determine which logical record should be current in the menu list box.

```
Set db = DBEngine(0)(0)
  Set dyn = db.OpenRecordset(lstMenu.RowSource, DB_OPEN_DYNASET)
  blnOpened = True
```

Next, the code does a silly check to make sure that what you are deleting actually exists.

```
dyn.FindFirst "ItemID = " & lstMenu
If dyn.NoMatch Then GoTo cmdDelete_ClickDone
```

Then, the record is deleted. The `Requery` method updates the menu list with the deleted menu item removed.

```
dyn.Delete
lstMenu.Requery
```

Next, you need to determine which item in the menu list to show as selected because you deleted the one that was selected. The rule I use in situations like this is to select the item after the deleted item. If there isn't an item after the deleted item, you select the item that was before the deleted item.

The code first tries to move the dynaset to an item after the deleted item. If the EOF property is set, you moved beyond the last record (indicating that you just deleted the last record). In that case, the `MovePrevious` method is called to move back.

This moves past the marker for the deleted record also (maybe because at this point it no longer exists).

```
dyn.MoveNext
If dyn.EOF Then
  dyn.MovePrevious
End If
```

Checking first to determine that you didn't move back to the BOF marker, the menu list sets the current record in the recordset. The only time you find yourself with the BOF property set is when you delete the only remaining record.

```
If Not dyn.BOF Then
  lstMenu = dyn!ItemID
End If
```

The `lstMenu_Click` subroutine updates the description label for the selected menu item.

```
lstMenu_Click
```

The *cmdIssues_Click* Subroutine

Whew! After that last one, you can use a short procedure. Here it is.

The `cmdIssues_Click` subroutine sets a flag indicating that the Issues form is open, and then it closes the Menu form and opens the Issues form (see Listing 21.13).

The flag is used in the `Form_Unload` subroutine to determine whether to display the database container.

Listing 21.13. The `cmdIssues_Click` subroutine.

```
Sub cmdIssues_Click ()

  On Error GoTo cmdIssues_ClickError

  mblnLoadingIssues = True
  DoCmd Close
  DoCmd OpenForm "Issue"

cmdIssues_ClickDone:
  Exit Sub

cmdIssues_ClickError:
  MsgBox Error$, 48, PROGRAM
  Resume cmdIssues_ClickDone

End Sub
```

The *cmdClose_Click* and *Form_Unload* Subroutines

The cmdClose_Click subroutine closes the form, of course (see Listing 21.14).

Listing 21.14. The cmdClose_Click subroutine.

```
Sub cmdClose_Click ()

  DoCmd Close

End Sub
```

As the form goes away, the Form_Unload subroutine checks the mblnLoadingIssues flag to determine whether the Issues form is being loaded (see Listing 21.15). If not, the database container is visible again.

Listing 21.15. The Form_Unload subroutine.

```
Sub Form_Unload (Cancel As Integer)

  If Not mblnLoadingIssues Then
  ' Show the database container
    SendKeys "{F11}"
  End If

  mblnLoadingIssues = False

End Sub
```

Creating the Menu Item Form

Dying to see all of this work? Let's crank out the Menu Item form. After that, there isn't too much code you have to put behind it before you are in business.

Start a new form with the following properties:

Menu Item Form
Add or edit records in the Menu Item table.
Object: **Menu Item Form**

Property	Value
Caption	Add Menu Item
Default View	Single Form

continues

Property	Value
Shortcut Menu	No
Scrollbars	Neither
Record Selectors	No
Navigation Buttons	No
Auto Center	Yes
Pop Up	Yes
Modal	Yes
Border Style	Dialog
Min Button	No
Max Button	No
Width	4.65 in

Object: **Detail0 Section**

Property	Value
Height	1.9146 in
Back Color	8421504 (Dark Gray)

Next, you need an option group to drop option buttons in for selecting which type of menu item to create.

Object: **grpType Option Group**

Option group containing five option buttons; one for each menu item type.

Property	Value
Name	grpType
Tab Index	0
Left	0.9826 in
Top	0.0826 in
Width	2.6979 in
Height	0.4174 in
Back Style	Clear
Border Style	Clear

Object: **lblType Label**

Label for the grpType option group.

Property	Value
Name	lblType
Caption	&Type

Left	0.0938 in
Top	0.125 in
Width	0.7917 in
Height	0.1667 in

Next, add the five option buttons and corresponding labels for the Form, Report, Query, Macro, and Expression menu item types.

Object: **optForm Option Button**

Select the Form menu item type.

Property	Value
Name	optForm
Option Value	1
Left	0.9847 in
Top	0.125 in
Width	0.1806 in
Height	0.1375 in

Object: **lblForm Label**

Label for the optForm option button.

Property	Value
Name	lblForm
Caption	Form
Left	1.1646 in
Top	0.125 in
Width	0.4167 in
Height	0.1667 in

Object: **optReport Option Button**

Select the Report menu item type.

Property	Value
Name	optReport
Option Value	2
Left	1.6854 in
Top	0.125 in
Width	0.1806 in
Height	0.1375 in

Object: **lblReport Label**
Label for the optReport option button.

Property	Value
Name	lblReport
Caption	Report
Left	1.8646 in
Top	0.125 in
Width	0.5 in
Height	0.1667 in

Object: **optQuery Option Button**
Select the Query menu item type.

Property	Value
Name	optQuery
Option Value	3
Left	2.4847 in
Top	0.125 in
Width	0.1806 in
Height	0.1375 in

Object: **lblQuery Label**
Label for the optQuery option button.

Property	Value
Name	lblQuery
Caption	Query
Left	2.6646 in
Top	0.125 in
Width	0.5 in
Height	0.1667 in

Object: **optMacro Option Button**
Select the Macro menu item type.

Property	Value
Name	optMacro
Option Value	4
Left	0.9847 in

Top	0.3326 in
Width	0.1806 in
Height	0.1375 in

Object: **lblMacro Label**

Label for the optMacro option button.

Property	Value
Name	lblMacro
Caption	Macro
Left	1.1646 in
Top	0.3326 in
Width	0.5 in
Height	0.1667 in

Object: **optExpression Option Button**

Select the Expression menu item type.

Property	Value
Name	optExpression
Option Value	5
Left	1.6847 in
Top	0.3326 in
Width	0.1806 in
Height	0.1375 in

Object: **lblExpression Label**

Label for the optExpression option button.

Property	Value
Name	lblExpression
Caption	Expression
Left	1.8646 in
Top	0.3326 in
Width	0.7396 in
Height	0.1667 in

Figure 21.24 shows an option group and option buttons on the Menu Item form.

Next, you need to add the text boxes to enter the menu item name and description.

FIGURE 21.24.

Adding an option group and option buttons to the Menu Item form.

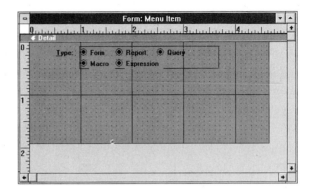

The text boxes and combo box on the form have their Back Color properties set to 8421376 (Teal) and are Sunken. The Text Align property is set to Right for the corresponding labels for these controls.

Object: **txtName Text Box**
Enter the menu item name.

Property	Value
Name	txtName
Tab Index	1
Left	0.9792 in
Top	0.625 in
Width	2.6979 in
Height	0.1667 in

Object: **lblName Label**
Label for the txtName text box.

Property	Value
Name	lblName
Caption	&Name:
Left	0.0938 in
Top	0.625 in
Width	0.7917 in
Height	0.1667 in

Object: **txtDescription Text Box**
Enter a description of the menu item displayed when the item is selected.

Property	Value
Name	txtDescription
Tab Index	2
Left	0.9792 in
Top	0.875 in
Width	2.6979 in
Height	0.4618 in

Object: **lblDescription Label**
Label for the txtDescription text box.

Property	Value
Name	lblDescription
Caption	&Description:
Left	0.05 in
Top	0.875 in
Width	0.8438 in
Height	0.1667 in

Figure 21.25 shows the Name and Description text boxes.

FIGURE 21.25.

Adding the Name and Description text boxes.

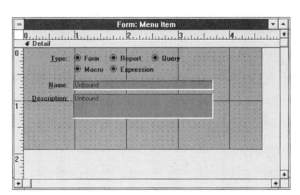

Next, you need to add a combo box to select a form, report, or other object. The Row Source property for the combo box is set by code.

Object: **cboObject Combo Box**

Select a database object.

Property	Value
Name	cboObject
Row Source Type	Table/Query
Row Source	(blank)
Column Count	1
Limit To List	Yes
Enabled	No
Tab Index	3
Left	0.9917 in
Top	1.4146 in
Width	1.8542 in
Height	0.1667 in

Object: **lblObject Label**

Label for the cboObject combo box.

Property	Value
Name	lblObject
Caption	&Form:
Left	0.1 in
Top	1.4146 in
Width	0.7917 in
Height	0.1667 in

Add a text box to receive expressions when adding an expression menu item.

Object: **txtExpression Text Box**

Enter an expression to evaluate when the menu item is selected.

Property	Value
Name	txtExpression
Tab Index	4
Left	0.9847 in
Top	1.6667 in
Width	2.6979 in
Height	0.1667 in

Object: **lblExpression Label**
Label for the txtExpression text box.

Property	Value
Name	lblExpression
Caption	&Expression:
Left	0.1021 in
Top	1.6667 in
Width	0.8333 in
Height	0.1667 in

Add the OK and Cancel buttons.

Object: **cmdOK Command Button**
Accept the new or changed menu item.

Property	Value
Name	cmdOK
Caption	OK
Default	Yes
Tab Index	5
Left	3.8347 in
Top	0.125 in
Width	0.6979 in
Height	0.25 in

Object: **cmdCancel Command Button**
Close the form without accepting the change.

Property	Value
Name	cmdCancel
Caption	Cancel
Cancel	Yes
Tab Index	6
Left	3.8347 in
Top	0.4167 in
Width	0.6979 in
Height	0.25 in

Figure 21.26 shows the completed Menu Item form.

FIGURE 21.26.

*The completed Menu
Item form.*

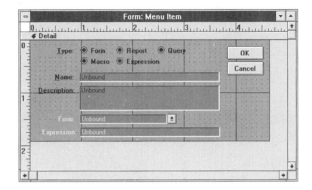

Coding the Menu Item Form

There are no module-level variables declared in the Menu Item form module's declaration section (see Listing 21.16).

Listing 21.16. The Menu Item form's declaration section.

```
' Menu Add form module

  Option Compare Database
  Option Explicit
```

The *Form_Load* Subroutine

If the form is opened in edit mode, the Form_Load subroutine loads the controls on the form with the Menu Item field values for the record being edited (see Listing 21.17).

Listing 21.17. The Form_Load subroutine.

```
Sub Form_Load ()

  Dim db As Database
  Dim tbl As Recordset
  Dim blnOpened As Integer

  blnOpened = False

  On Error GoTo Form_LoadError

  glngAddedItem = 0
  gblnEditItemCancel = True
```

```
    If gintObjectType = 0 Then
      gintObjectType = 1
    End If

    grpType = gintObjectType
    grpType_Click

    If glngEditItem > 0 Then
      Set db = DBEngine(0)(0)
      Set tbl = db.OpenRecordset("Menu Item", DB_OPEN_TABLE)

      tbl.Index = "PrimaryKey"

      tbl.Seek "=", glngEditItem

      If Not tbl.NoMatch Then

        Me.Caption = "Edit Menu Item"

        txtName = tbl!Name
        txtDescription = tbl!Description

        gintObjectType = tbl!Type

        If gintObjectType = 3 Then
          gintObjectType = gintObjectType + tbl!UtilityType - 1
        End If
        grpType = gintObjectType
        grpType_Click

        If gintObjectType = 5 Then ' Expression
          txtExpression = tbl!Argument
        Else
        ' Ignore the error if the object was deleted
          On Error Resume Next
          cboObject = tbl!Argument
        End If

      End If
    End If

Form_LoadDone:
  On Error Resume Next
  If blnOpened Then tbl.Close
  Exit Sub

Form_LoadError:
  MsgBox Error$, 48, PROGRAM
  Resume Form_LoadDone

End Sub
```

The Form_Load subroutine initializes glngAddedItem to 0, indicating that at this time no menu item has been added.

The `gblnEditItemCancel` flag is set to indicate that an edited menu item has not been saved.

```
glngAddedItem = 0
gblnEditItemCancel = True
```

The `gintObjectType` variable is initialized to 1 for Forms if there isn't a default menu item type set.

```
If gintObjectType = 0 Then
  gintObjectType = 1
End If
```

Next, the appropriate option button is set and the `grpType_Click` subroutine is called to respond to the setting.

```
grpType = gintObjectType
grpType_Click
```

The `glngEditItem` variable is checked to determine whether the form was called to edit an existing menu item.

```
If glngEditItem > 0 Then
```

If so, the Menu Item table is opened and the program finds the appropriate record in order to perform the edit.

```
Set db = DBEngine(0)(0)
Set tbl = db.OpenRecordset("Menu Item", DB_OPEN_TABLE)

tbl.Index = "PrimaryKey"

tbl.Seek "=", glngEditItem
```

If the record is found, the form goes into edit mode. First, the caption of the title bar indicates that an edit, rather than an add, is in progress.

```
If Not tbl.NoMatch Then

  Me.Caption = "Edit Menu Item"
```

Next, the name and description are loaded.

```
txtName = tbl!Name
txtDescription = tbl!Description
```

The type code is read from the record (returning a 1 to 3 value for form, report, or utility).

```
gintObjectType = tbl!Type
```

If the type is a utility, the `UtilityType` field is also read to derive the actual menu item type.

```
If gintObjectType = 3 Then
  gintObjectType = gintObjectType + tbl!UtilityType - 1
End If
```

Setting the grpType option group control to the value turns on the appropriate option button.

```
grpType = gintObjectType
grpType_Click
```

Finally, either the expression text box or the object combo box is loaded, depending again on which menu item type is being edited.

```
If gintObjectType = 5 Then ' Expression
  txtExpression = tbl!Argument
Else
' Ignore the error if the object was deleted
  On Error Resume Next
  cboObject = tbl!Argument
End If
```

The *grpType_Click* Subroutine

The grpType_Click subroutine updates the Menu Item form for whichever menu item type is selected (see Listing 21.18).

If the menu item type is an expression, the cboObject combo box is disabled and the expression text box is enabled. Otherwise, the subroutine uses the system table, MSysObjects, to load the cboObject combo with the names of the database objects that may be selected.

Listing 21.18. The grpType_Click subroutine.

```
Sub grpType_Click ()

  Dim sql As String

  On Error GoTo grpType_ClickError

  If IsNull(grpType) Then GoTo grpType_ClickDone
  gintObjectType = CInt(grpType)

  cboObject = Null
  txtExpression = Null

  cboObject.Enabled = (gintObjectType <> 5)
  txtExpression.Enabled = (gintObjectType = 5)

  sql = ""

' Object types used in MSysObjects
'
' Form = -32768
' Report = -32764
' Query = 5
' Macro = -32766
```

continues

Listing 21.18. continued

```
Select Case gintObjectType

Case 1 ' Form
  sql = "SELECT Name FROM MSysObjects WHERE Type = -32768"
  lblObject.Caption = "Form:"

Case 2 ' Report
  sql = "SELECT Name FROM MSysObjects WHERE Type = -32764"
  lblObject.Caption = "Report:"

Case 3 ' Query
  sql = "SELECT Name FROM MSysObjects WHERE Type = 5"
  lblObject.Caption = "Query:"

Case 4 ' Macro
  sql = "SELECT Name FROM MSysObjects WHERE Type = -32766"
  lblObject.Caption = "Macro:"

Case 5 ' Expression
  lblObject.Caption = "Form:"

End Select

If Len(sql) > 0 Then
  cboObject.RowSource = sql
  cboObject.Requery
End If

grpType_ClickDone:
  Exit Sub

grpType_ClickError:
  MsgBox Error$, 48, PROGRAM
  Resume grpType_ClickDone

End Sub
```

The *cmdOK_Click* Subroutine

The cmdOK_Click subroutine either adds a new menu item record or it updates an existing one with the changes entered by the user (see Listing 21.19).

Listing 21.19. The cmdOK_Click **subroutine.**

```
Sub cmdOK_Click ()

  Dim db As Database
  Dim tbl As Recordset
  Dim blnOpened As Integer

  Dim strName As String
```

```
    blnOpened = False

    On Error GoTo cmdOK_ClickError

' Check that everything was entered

    If RequiredField("Name", txtName) Then GoTo cmdOK_ClickDone
    If RequiredField("Description", txtDescription) Then GoTo cmdOK_ClickDone
    If cboObject.Enabled Then
      strName = Choose(gintObjectType, "Form", "Report", "Query", "Macro")
      If RequiredField(strName, cboObject) Then GoTo cmdOK_ClickDone
    Else
      If RequiredField("Expression", txtExpression) Then GoTo cmdOK_ClickDone
    End If

' Write the new menu item to the Menu Item table

    Set db = DBEngine(0)(0)
    Set tbl = db.OpenRecordset("Menu Item", DB_OPEN_TABLE)

    If glngEditItem > 0 Then
      tbl.Index = "PrimaryKey"
      tbl.Seek "=", glngEditItem

      If tbl.NoMatch Then
        tbl.AddNew
      Else
        tbl.Edit
      End If
    Else
      tbl.AddNew
    End If

    tbl!Name = txtName
    tbl!Description = txtDescription

    If gintObjectType < 3 Then
    ' Form or Report
      tbl!Type = gintObjectType
    Else
    ' Utility (Query, Macro or Expression)
      tbl!Type = 3
      tbl!UtilityType = gintObjectType - 2
    End If

    If gintObjectType = 5 Then ' Expression
      tbl!Argument = txtExpression
    Else
      tbl!Argument = cboObject
    End If

    glngAddedItem = tbl!ItemID
    tbl.Update

    gblnEditItemCancel = False
    DoCmd Close
```

continues

Listing 21.19. continued

```
cmdOK_ClickDone:
  On Error Resume Next
  If blnOpened Then tbl.Close
  Exit Sub

cmdOK_ClickError:
  MsgBox Error$, 48, PROGRAM
  Resume cmdOK_ClickDone

End Sub
```

The cmdOK_Click subroutine first uses the RequiredField function to verify that each of the required entries has been made. If the entries have been made, the subroutine opens the Menu Item table as a recordset object in table mode in order to make the change.

```
' Write the new menu item to the Menu Item table

  Set db = DBEngine(0)(0)
  Set tbl = db.OpenRecordset("Menu Item", DB_OPEN_TABLE)
```

If the glngEditItem global has been set (by code in the Menu form), the subroutine attempts to find the record and edit it. Otherwise, a new record is added to the table.

```
  If glngEditItem > 0 Then
    tbl.Index = "PrimaryKey"
    tbl.Seek "=", glngEditItem

    If tbl.NoMatch Then
      tbl.AddNew
    Else
      tbl.Edit
    End If
  Else
    tbl.AddNew
  End If
```

The name and description text are saved.

```
  tbl!Name = txtName
  tbl!Description = txtDescription
```

Then, the Type and UtilityType fields are saved.

```
If gintObjectType < 3 Then
' Form or Report
  tbl!Type = gintObjectType
Else
' Utility (Query, Macro or Expression)
  tbl!Type = 3
  tbl!UtilityType = gintObjectType - 2
End If
```

The Argument field is read from the cboObject combo box or the txtExpression text box, depending again on the menu item type.

```
If gintObjectType = 5 Then ' Expression
  tbl!Argument = txtExpression
Else
  tbl!Argument = cboObject
End If
```

The glngAddedItem variable is set to indicate to the Menu form which item should be displayed as current in the menu list.

```
glngAddedItem = tbl!ItemID
tbl.Update
```

The gblnEditItemCancel flag is set to False, indicating to the Menu form that a change has been made. The Menu Item table is updated with the new record and the form is closed.

```
gblnEditItemCancel = False
DoCmd Close
```

The other way to close the form is the Cancel button. The cmdCancel_Click subroutine leaves the gblnEditItemCancel flag set to True so the Menu form knows that no change has been made (see Listing 21.20).

Listing 21.20. The cmdCancel_Click subroutine.

```
Sub cmdCancel_Click ()

  DoCmd Close

End Sub
```

That completes the Menu and Menu Item forms. You should now be able to add the lookup table forms to the menu and experiment with the other types of menu items.

Summary

In this chapter, you devoted some time to figuring out why the heck you need an issues-tracking system and what some of the design considerations are in making one.

You got a start at building one by creating the tables in the S.W.A.T. database. Then you got lost on a major but fruitful tangent and created a run-time modifiable menu for all of your database-maintenance needs.

Oh yeah, here's that list again. In this chapter, you

- Defined the difference between a bug, change, or enhancement.
- Defined four guiding principles: accessibility, ease-of-use, applicability, and informational value. These principles are used in designing a software solution.
- Looked at the pluses and minuses behind ownership and accountability.
- Developed the schema for the issues-tracking system.
- Used the Form Wizard to generate a quick form for editing lookup table values.
- Created a run-time modifiable database maintenance menu.

OK, no more getting lost on tangents. In the next chapter, you get down to serious business and create your S.W.A.T. forms. Of course, you also write the code that runs behind them.

CHAPTER 22

Visual Basic: S.W.A.T., Part Two— Creating the S.W.A.T. Forms

In the last chapter, you were side-tracked a bit, but it was a nice bit of side-tracking because you created a pretty decent database maintenance menu. Think of it as a bonus app. Yeah, that's it.

Well, there will be no side-tracking or tangents in this chapter; I promise. You have some work to do. You need to create the primary forms that make up the S.W.A.T. issue-tracking system.

The Objects in the S.W.A.T. Database

Take a look at what you have created and what you hope to have in the database container by the end of the chapter. This is what is in the database right now:

Category Table
What categories issues can be classified by

Filter Table
Saved settings used to select subsets of the Issue records

Issue Table
Data about each issue tracked in the database

Menu Item Table
Items displayed in the database maintenance menu

Priority Table
Priority levels that may be assigned to an issue

Status Table
Current work states that an issue can be in

Type Table
Different types of issues (bug, change, or enhancement)

User Table
Names and IDs of the users

Category Form
Created by Tabular Form Wizard to edit categories in the Category table

Menu Form
Database maintenance menu used to open lookup table forms and miscellaneous other functions

Menu Item Form
Add menu items to the Menu form

You also may have created forms for editing and viewing records in the Priority, Status, Type, and User tables just as you did for the Category table (by using the Tabular Form Wizard).

You will add the following objects to the database in this chapter. They are listed in the order in which you create them:

Login Form
Identify the user or create a new user record

AutoExec Macro
Activate the Login form

Issue Form
The application's main form, used to enter and edit issue records

Filter Form
Save criteria that produces a subset of records in the Issue form

In Access, using bound forms as opposed to unbound forms is the norm. If the tool is there, use it, right? However, as I mentioned in an earlier chapter, quite often I don't use bound forms in my Access applications because the user-interface requirements don't fit the model of a standard record-editing form. In the S.W.A.T. database, the Issue form does fit the requirements, but the Filter form does not.

Creating the Login Form

The Login form in S.W.A.T. identifies the user for a few reasons. The first reason is that saved filters store the user so that, upon browsing the list of filters, you have to choose only from your own filters.

Other uses for user IDs deal with editing an Issue record. When you add a comment, S.W.A.T. can automatically enter text that identifies the comment with your name. And when you mark an issue as completed, S.W.A.T. automatically writes your user ID to a field, indicating who completed the issue.

Also, when you attempt to close an issue, S.W.A.T. verifies your user ID against the one recorded as creating the issue. The person that creates the issue is the only person authorized to close the issue. This is primarily to give the person a chance to review the program, fix or change, and comment on the resolution.

I didn't implement security in S.W.A.T., so there is no password field on the Login form. If you feel you need security in your issues-tracking system to prohibit one person from logging in as another, you have to add those modifications to the program.

Create a new form with the usual set of properties for a pop-up form; however, leave the Modal property set to No.

Login Form
Identify the user or create a new user record.

Object: **Login Form**

Property	Value
Caption	Login
Default View	Single Form
Shortcut Menu	No
Scrollbars	Neither
Record Selectors	No
Navigation Buttons	No
Auto Center	Yes
Pop Up	Yes
Modal	No
Border Style	Dialog
Min Button	No
Max Button	No
Width	3 in

Object: **Detail0 Section**

Property	Value
Height	1.1646 in
Back Color	8421504 (Dark Gray)

Add a combo box to the form to enter the username of the person logging in. The combo box has the Limit To List property set to False in order to allow the user to enter a name that isn't already in the list. Figure 22.1 shows the cboUsername combo box.

Object: **cboUsername Combo Box**
Enter the name of the user.

Property	Value
Name	cboUsername
Row Source Type	Table/Query
Column Count	1
Column Widths	1 in
Bound Column	1
Status Bar Text	Select your name from the list

Limit To List	No
Auto Expand	Yes
Tab Index	0
Left	0.8938 in
Top	0.8326 in
Width	0.9896 in
Height	1.6666 in
Back Color	8421376 (Teal)
Special Effect	Sunken

Object: lblUsername Label

Label for the cboUsername combo box.

Property	Value
Name	lblUsername
Caption	Username:
Left	0.1 in
Top	0.0833 in
Width	0.6875 in
Height	0.1667 in

FIGURE 22.1.

Creating the cboUsername combo box.

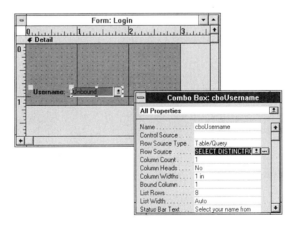

The Row Source property for the cboUsername combo box should be set to a query that returns the Username field from the User table in sorted order. The criteria in the query are set to filter out the username, "Unassigned," which is a special User table record you will create.

Figure 22.2 shows the query constructed in the Query Builder.

FIGURE 22.2.

Creating a query to set the Row Source property in the cboUsername combo box.

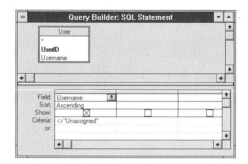

The SELECT statement derived from this query is shown here:

```
SELECT DISTINCTROW User.Username
FROM User
WHERE ((User.Username<>"Unassigned"))
ORDER BY User.Username;
```

Next, add the Issues, Menu, and Cancel buttons.

Object: **cmdIssues Command Button**
Open the S.W.A.T. Issue form for working with issues.

Property	Value
Name	cmdIssues
Caption	&Issues
Default	Yes
Tab Index	1
Left	2.2 in
Top	0.0833 in
Width	0.7083 in
Height	0.25 in

Object: **cmdMenu Command Button**
Open the Menu form.

Property	Value
Name	cmdMenu
Caption	&Menu
Tab Index	2
Left	2.2 in
Top	0.375 in
Width	0.7083 in
Height	0.25 in

Object: **cmdCancel Command Button**
Cancel login and display the database container.

Property	Value
Name	cmdCancel
Caption	Cancel
Cancel	Yes
Tab Index	3
Left	2.2 in
Top	0.6667 in
Width	0.7083 in
Height	0.25 in

Two labels are added to display the program title in large characters.

Object: **lblSwat1 Label**
Shadow for the S.W.A.T. program title.

Property	Value
Name	lblSwat1
Caption	S.W.A.T.
Left	0.225 in
Top	0.1104 in
Width	1.5 in
Height	0.4167 in
Fore Color	0 (Black)
Font Name	MS Sans Serif
Font Size	24
Font Weight	Bold

Object: **lblSwat2 Label**
The foreground S.W.A.T. program title.

Property	Value
Name	lblSwat2
Caption	S.W.A.T.
Left	0.2 in
Top	0.0833 in
Width	1.5 in
Height	0.4167 in
Fore Color	16777215 (White)

Property	Value
Font Name	MS Sans Serif
Font Size	24
Font Weight	Bold

The completed form is shown in Figure 22.3.

FIGURE 22.3.

The completed Login form.

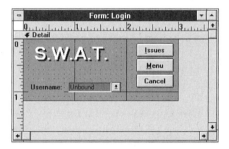

Coding the Login Form

When users log into S.W.A.T., their user IDs and names are stored in two global variables, glngUserId and gstrUsername; the rest of the program can use this information.

You need to add these two globals as well as two others that you use later: glngFilterID and gblnFilterChanged. The declarations section of the Globals module should be modified as shown in Listing 22.1.

Listing 22.1. The declaration section in the Globals module.

```
' S.W.A.T. globals

  Option Compare Database
  Option Explicit

  Global Const PROGRAM = "S.W.A.T."

  Global gstrUsername As String
  Global glngUserID As Long

  Global glngFilterID As Long
  Global gblnFilterChanged As Integer

' Globals for the database maintenance menu
  Global gintObjectType As Integer
  Global glngAddedItem As Integer
  Global glngEditItem As Integer

  Global gblnEditItemCancel As Integer
```

Next, open the module for the Login form and enter its declaration section, as shown in Listing 22.2.

Listing 22.2. The declaration section for the Login form module.

```
' Login form module

  Option Compare Database
  Option Explicit

  Dim mblnMenu As Integer
```

The only module variable declared is a flag that is set to True if the Menu form should be opened instead of the Issues form.

The *Form_Load* Subroutine

The Login form's `Form_Load` subroutine (see Listing 22.3) calls the menu command to hide the database container from view and initializes the global and module level variables.

Listing 22.3. The `Form_Load` **subroutine.**

```
Sub Form_Load ()

' Hide the database container
  DoCmd DoMenuItem 0, 4, 3, A_MENU_VER20

  glngUserID = 0
  glngFilterID = 0

  mblnMenu = False

End Sub
```

The *cmdIssues_Click* and *cmdMenu_Click* Subroutines

Whether the user hits the Issues button or the Menu button, the `cmdIssues_Click` subroutine handles the work of verifying the username and opening the appropriate form.

The `cmdMenu_Click` subroutine shown in Listing 22.4 sets a flag indicating that the Menu button has been clicked, and then calls the `cmdIssues_Click` subroutine.

Listing 22.4. The `cmdMenu_Click` subroutine.

```
Sub cmdMenu_Click ()

  mblnMenu = True
  cmdIssues_Click
  mblnMenu = False

End Sub
```

The `cmdIssues_Click` subroutine uses the `DLookup` function to determine whether a user exists with the entered user name (see Listing 22.5). If not, the subroutine asks the user if she or he is new, in which case the program adds a record to the User table, allowing the user to proceed.

The program then checks the `mblnMenu` flag to determine whether the Menu form or the Issue form should be opened.

Listing 22.5. The `cmdIssues_Click` subroutine.

```
Sub cmdIssues_Click ()

  Dim db As Database
  Dim tbl As Recordset
  Dim blnOpened As Integer

  Dim strUsername As String

  Dim cr As String
  Dim dq As String
  Dim msg As String
  Dim v As Variant
  Dim z As Integer

  blnOpened = False

  On Error GoTo cmdIssues_ClickError

  strUsername = CNStr(cboUsername)

  If Len(strUsername) = 0 Then
    MsgBox "Please enter your name.", 0, PROGRAM
    cboUsername.SetFocus
    GoTo cmdIssues_ClickDone
  End If

  v = DLookup("UserID", "User", "Username = '" & cboUsername & "'")
  If IsNull(v) Then

    z = MsgBox(strUsername & ", are you a new user?", 4 + 32 + 256, PROGRAM)
```

```
   If z = 6 Then

   ' Create a new user record

     Set db = DBEngine(0)(0)
     Set tbl = db.OpenRecordset("User", DB_OPEN_TABLE)
     tbl.AddNew
     tbl!Username = strUsername

     glngUserID = tbl!UserID
     tbl.Update

     MsgBox "Welcome aboard " & strUsername & "!", 0, PROGRAM

   Else

     cr = Chr$(13)
     dq = Chr$(34)

     msg = "Sorry, but I didn't find a record of a user by "
     msg = msg & "the name of " & dq & strUsername & dq & "." & cr & cr
     msg = msg & "Please re-enter your name."

     MsgBox msg, 64, PROGRAM
     cboUsername.SetFocus

     GoTo cmdIssues_ClickDone

   End If

   Else

     glngUserID = CLng(v)

   End If

   gstrUsername = strUsername
   DoCmd Close
   If mblnMenu Then
     DoCmd OpenForm "Menu"
   Else
     DoCmd OpenForm "Issue"
   End If

cmdIssues_ClickDone:
   Exit Sub

cmdIssues_ClickError:
   glngUserID = 0
   MsgBox Error$, 48, PROGRAM
   Resume cmdIssues_ClickDone

End Sub
```

The *cmdCancel_Click* and *Form_Unload* Subroutines

The cmdCancel_Click subroutine closes the form. No user will have been identified (see Listing 22.6).

Listing 22.6. The cmdCancel_Click **subroutine.**

```
Sub cmdCancel_Click ()

  DoCmd Close

End Sub
```

On the form's Unload event, the program checks the glngUserID variable to determine whether a user was successfully identified. If not, the database container appears because neither the Issue nor Menu form is open (see Listing 22.7).

Listing 22.7. The Form_Unload **subroutine.**

```
Sub Form_Unload (Cancel As Integer)

  If glngUserID = 0 Then
  ' Show the database container
    SendKeys "{F11}"
  End If

End Sub
```

Creating the *AutoExec* Macro

Next, you should create an AutoExec macro to open the Login form automatically when the database is opened.

The macro need only contain a single command, OpenForm, with the Login form selected as the Form Name argument. The macro is shown in design view in Figure 22.4.

FIGURE 22.4.

The AutoExec *macro opens the Login form when the database is initially opened.*

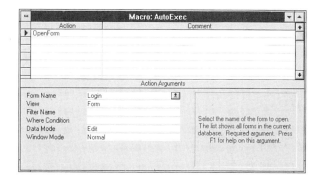

Entering User Names

You don't have the Issue form created yet, but you can log in and use the Menu form. You can open the Login form by running the AutoExec macro you just created or by opening the form from the database container.

Enter Unassigned in the Username combo box to create a record in the User table with that username (see Figure 22.5). This extra user name is used in the Assigned To prompt on the Issue form so you can identify any unassigned forms.

FIGURE 22.5.

Creating the Unassigned user name.

Click the Menu button. S.W.A.T. displays a message box asking you whether you are a new user (see Figure 22.6). Click the **Y**es button; the cmdIssue_Click subroutine writes the record, displays a welcome message to the new user, and then opens the Menu form.

FIGURE 22.6.

Answer Yes to create the Unassigned username.

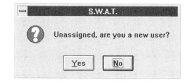

Close the Menu form and open the Login form again to create a username record for yourself. Afterwards, each time you open the Login form, your name appears in the drop-down list of the Login form.

Creating the Issue Form

The Issue form is where issues are originally created and where the programmers, testers, and other folks who work on the issues record their progress.

You may find yourself using this form frequently, so you want to make sure that it is comfortable to use. I'll be up front and acknowledge that you may have to modify this form to make it serve its purpose for you. Please do. Improving S.W.A.T. in any way to better serve your needs will not only increase the value that this tool has for you, but will also be a rewarding programming exercise.

With all that said, take a look at the version that I came up with. To re-create it, you need to open a new form and maximize the form design window. It's also helpful to remove the Ruler by selecting the **View|R**uler command to toggle it off.

The form has the Form Header and Form Footer sections turned on. Those are turned on using the **Format|Form H**eader/Footer command, which is also a toggle option. The Header section isn't actually used, so you can set the Height property to 0 inches. The Footer section is used as a place to drop some hidden controls. You can hide the entire Footer section from the user's view by setting the Footer section's Visible property to False.

The property settings for the form and different sections on the form follow:

Issue Form
The application's main form, used to enter and edit issue records.

Object: **Issue Form**

Property	Value
Record Source	Issue
Caption	S.W.A.T.
Default View	Single Form
Shortcut Menu	Yes
Scrollbars	Neither
Record Selectors	No
Navigation Buttons	Yes
Auto Center	Yes
Border Style	Dialog

Min Button	Yes
Max Button	No
Width	5 in

Object: **FormHeader1 Section**

Property	Value
Height	0 in

Object: **Detail0 Section**

Property	Value
Height	3.5938 in
Back Color	8421504 (Dark Gray)

Object: **FormFooter2 Section**

Property	Value
Height	0.7917 in
Back Color	8421504 (Dark Gray)

In standard VGA, there is just enough room to view the entire detail section while working on it. To view the footer section, you need to scroll down the design window a bit (see Figure 22.7).

FIGURE 22.7.

Creating the different sections on the Issue form.

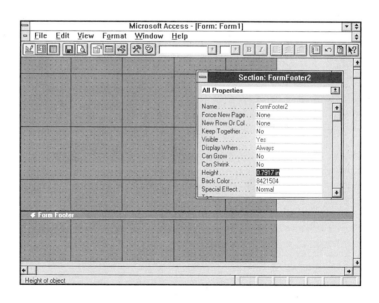

Let's start adding controls at the top of the detail section. The txtIssueID and txtEnteredAt text boxes have their Back Color property set to 12632256 (Light Gray). That's intended as a visual cue to indicate that the fields are not modifiable. However, you can set focus to the txtIssueID text box and use the Edit|Find command to locate an issue by number.

The remaining controls for editing text all use a Back Color setting of 8421376 (Teal). All of the text boxes and combo boxes have their Special Effect properties set to Sunken.

Object: **txtIssueID Text Box**
Displays the Issue ID number.

Property	Value
Name	txtIssueID
Control Source	IssueID
Format	00000
Status Bar Text	Issue ID
Enabled	Yes
Locked	No
Tab Index	0
Left	1.0083 in
Top	0.0833 in
Width	0.5938 in
Height	0.1771 in
Back Color	12632256 (Light Gray)

Object: **lblIssueID Label**
Label for the txtIssueID text box.

Property	Value
Name	lblIssueID
Caption	&ID:
Left	0 in
Top	0.0833 in
Width	0.9 in
Height	0.1667 in

Set the value cboEnteredBy combo box to default to the current user. It is probable that at times you might enter a new issue under another person's name, such as when someone phones in an issue. The users identified in this field are assigned the issue after the issue is marked as completed so that they can review the work done and close it.

The defaulting is done by calling a UserID() function that you will be adding to the Globals module.

Object: **cboEnteredBy Combo Box**

Identifies the person who created the issue.

Property	Value
Name	cboEnteredBy
Control Source	EnteredBy
Row Source Type	Table/Query
Column Count	2
Column Widths	0 in;1 in
Bound Column	1
Status Bar Text	Who originally entered the issue?
Limit To List	Yes
Auto Expand	Yes
Default Value	=UserID()
Tab Index	1
Left	2.7104 in
Top	0.0833 in
Width	0.9896 in
Height	0.1771 in
Text Align	Left

Object: **lblEnteredBy Label**

Label for the cboEnteredBy combo box.

Property	Value
Name	lblEnteredBy
Caption	&Entered By:
Left	1.7813 in
Top	0.0833 in
Width	0.8229 in
Height	0.1667 in

The Row Source property of the cboEnteredBy combo box should be set to a query that returns both the UserID and Username fields of the User table.

Before creating the query, open the User table in datasheet view and see what UserID number was generated for the Unassigned user. It will most likely be a 1 unless you entered other usernames in the table first. The query should filter out the Unassigned user, as shown in Figure 22.8.

FIGURE 22.8.

Creating a query for the cboEnteredBy Row Source property.

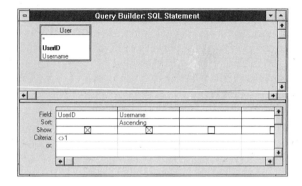

The SELECT statement generated for the Row Source property by the Query Builder is as follows:

```
SELECT DISTINCTROW User.UserID, User.Username
FROM User
WHERE ((User.UserID<>1))
ORDER BY User.Username;
```

The txtEnteredAt text box displays when the Issue table record was created. You have this field initialized on the table level by calling the Now function (see Figure 22.9).

Object: **txtEnteredAt Text Box**
Displays the date the issue was entered.

Property	Value
Name	txtEnteredAt
Control Source	EnteredAt
Format	Short Date
Status Bar Text	When was the issue originated?
Enabled	No
Locked	Yes
Tab Index	2
Left	4.1979 in
Top	0.0833 in
Width	0.5 in
Height	0.1771 in
Back Color	12632256 (Light Gray)

Object: **lblEnteredAt Label**
Label for the txtEnteredAt text box.

Property	Value
Name	lblEnteredAt
Caption	On:
Left	3.8 in
Top	0.0833 in
Width	0.2979 in
Height	0.1667 in

FIGURE 22.9.

Adding the first row of controls on the Issue form.

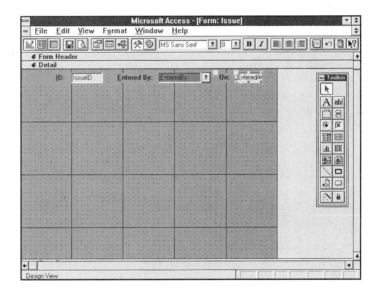

Adding the Issues Form Combo Boxes

Next, you have to add a series of combo boxes for selecting Type, Status, Assigned To, Priority, and Category values.

Object: **cboType Combo Box**

Indicate whether the issue is a bug, change, or enhancement.

Property	Value
Name	cboType
Control Source	Type
Row Source Type	Table/Query
Column Count	2
Column Widths	0 in;1 in
Bound Column	1

Property	Value
Status Bar Text	Is this a bug, change or enhancement?
Limit To List	Yes
Auto Expand	Yes
Tab Index	3
Left	1.0021 in
Top	0.4167 in
Width	1 in
Height	0.1771 in
Text Align	Left

Object: **lblType Label**
Label for the cboType combo box.

Property	Value
Name	lblType
Caption	T&ype:
Left	0 in
Top	0.4167 in
Width	0.9 in
Height	0.1667 in

The Row Source property in the cboType combo box should be set to a query that returns the Type and TypeName fields from the Type table sorted by the SortOrder field. The SortOrder field allows you to impose a specific sort order on how the values show up in the drop-down list of the combo box.

The query in the Query Builder window is shown in Figure 22.10.

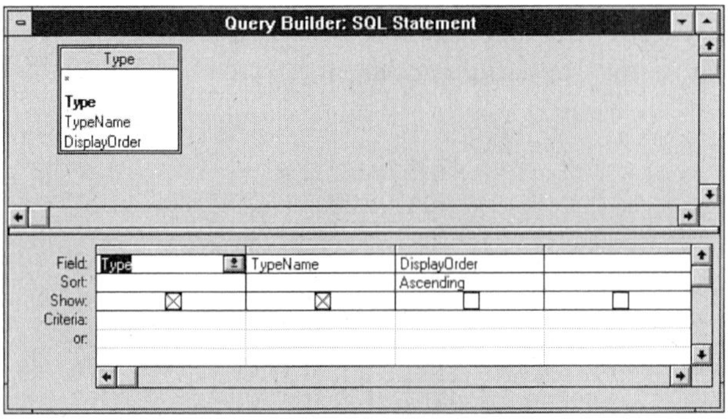

FIGURE 22.10.

The Row Source query for the cboType combo box.

The SELECT statement produced for the Row Source property follows:

```
SELECT DISTINCTROW Type.Type, Type.TypeName
ГПOM Typc
ORDER BY Type.DisplayOrder;
```

In the life of an issue, it will contain different values in the Status field. I gave the combo box a default value of 1, which is the code for the "In Progress" status value.

Object: cboStatus Combo Box

Indicates in what stage the issue is.

Property	Value
Name	cboStatus
Control Source	Status
Row Source Type	Table/Query
Column Count	2
Column Widths	0 in;1 in
Bound Column	1
Status Bar Text	Where does this issue currently stand?
Limit To List	Yes
Auto Expand	Yes
Default Value	1
Tab Index	4
Left	2.6958 in
Top	0.4167 in
Width	1 in
Height	0.1771 in
Text Align	Left

Object: lblStatus Label

Label for the cboStatus combo box.

Property	Value
Name	lblStatus
Caption	&Status:
Left	2.1042 in
Top	0.4167 in
Width	0.5 in
Height	0.1667 in

The Row Source property value for the cboStatus combo box returns the Status and StatusName fields from the Status table sorted by the SortOrder field. The SELECT statement for this follows:

```
SELECT DISTINCTROW Status.Status, Status.StatusName
FROM Status
ORDER BY Status.DisplayOrder;
```

The cboAssignedTo combo box identifies ownership of the issue. This ownership can transfer around quite a bit during the life of the issue, depending on who has worked on it and collected information on it. Eventually, the field receives the value of the creator of the issue, so that she or he can close the issue.

The default value of the combo box is set to the UserID value of the Unassigned user.

Object: **cboAssignedTo Combo Box**
Identifies the person who is working on the issue.

Property	Value
Name	cboAssignedTo
Control Source	AssignedTo
Row Source Type	Table/Query
Column Count	2
Column Widths	0 in;1 in
Bound Column	1
Status Bar Text	Who is currently working on this issue?
Limit To List	Yes
Auto Expand	Yes
Default Value	1
Tab Index	5
Left	1.0042 in
Top	0.6667 in
Width	1 in
Height	0.1771 in
Text Align	Left

Object: **lblAssignedTo Label**
Label for the cboAssignedTo combo box.

Property	Value
Name	lblAssignedTo
Caption	Assig&ned To:
Left	0 in

Top	0.6667 in
Width	0.9 in
Height	0.1667 in

The cboAssignedTo combo box returns each of the UserID and Username fields in the User table including the Unassigned user. The SELECT statement for this query follows:

```
SELECT DISTINCTROW User.UserID, User.Username
FROM User
ORDER BY User.Username;
```

The cboPriority combo box assigns a priority value to the issue of High, Medium, or Low priority (the values in the Priority table). For this combo box, I used a default value of 3, indicating Low priority.

The reasoning behind choosing Low priority is that if you assign a high priority to an item, you are in effect interrupting someone's current work schedule. By defaulting to a Low priority, you force the user to make the decision to raise the priority of an issue.

Object: **cboPriority Combo Box**
Indicates the immediacy of the issue.

Property	Value
Name	cboPriority
Control Source	Priority
Row Source Type	Table/Query
Column Count	2
Column Widths	0 in;1 in
Bound Column	1
Status Bar Text	How does the issue rate in urgency compared to other issues?
Limit To List	Yes
Auto Expand	Yes
Default Value	3
Tab Index	6
Left	2.6979 in
Top	0.6667 in
Width	1 in
Height	0.1771 in
Text Align	Left

Object: **lblPriority Label**
Label for the cboPriority combo box.

Property	Value
Name	lblPriority
Caption	&Priority:
Left	2.1042 in
Top	0.6667 in
Width	0.5 in
Height	0.1667 in

The Row Source property for the cboPriority combo box should return the Priority and PriorityName fields from the Priority table. The SELECT statement is shown here:

```
SELECT DISTINCTROW Priority.Priority, Priority.PriorityName
FROM Priority
ORDER BY Priority.DisplayOrder;
```

The final combo box is for classifying an issue by program area.

Object: **cboCategoryID Combo Box**
Classify an issue by the area of the program that it relates to.

Property	Value
Name	cboCategoryID
Control Source	CategoryID
Row Source Type	Table/Query
Column Count	2
Column Widths	0 in;1.8021 in
Bound Column	1
Status Bar Text	Which part of the product does this issue fall under?
Limit To List	Yes
Auto Expand	Yes
Tab Index	7
Left	1.0021 in
Top	1 in
Width	1.8125 in
Height	0.1771 in
Text Align	Left

Object: **lblCategory Label**
Label for the cboCategoryID combo box.

Property	Value
Name	lblCategory
Caption	Cate&gory:
Left	0 in

Top	1 in
Width	0.9 in
Height	0.1667 in

Set the Row Source property for the cboCategoryID combo box to return the CategoryID and CategoryName fields from the Category table sorted by the DisplayOrder field. The SELECT statement for this is shown here:

```
SELECT DISTINCTROW Category.CategoryID, Category.CategoryName
FROM Category
ORDER BY Category.DisplayOrder;
```

Figure 22.11 shows what is completed on the form at this point.

FIGURE 22.11.

Adding the combo boxes to the Issue form.

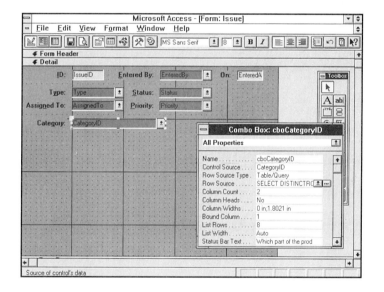

Adding the Issues Form Text Boxes

Next, you add three text boxes to the form to enter the issue Title, Description, and Comments.

Object: **txtTitle Text Box**
Enter a brief title to identify the issue.

Property	*Value*
Name	txtTitle
Control Source	Title
Status Bar Text	Enter a brief title to identify the issue (40 chars maximum)
Tab Index	8

Property	Value
Left	1.0021 in
Top	1.25 in
Width	2.1042 in
Height	0.1771 in

Object: **lblTitle Label**

Label for the txtTitle text box.

Property	Value
Name	lblTitle
Caption	&Title
Left	0 in
Top	1.25 in
Width	0.9 in
Height	0.1667 in

Object: **txtDescription Text Box**

Receives a full explanation of the issue.

Property	Value
Name	txtDescription
Control Source	Description
Status Bar Text	Full description of the problem, including steps to reproduce it if applicable.
Tab Index	9
Left	1 in
Top	1.5833 in
Width	2.6979 in
Height	0.75 in

Object: **lblDescription Label**

Label for the txtDescription text box.

Property	Value
Name	lblDescription
Caption	&Description
Left	0 in
Top	1.5833 in
Width	0.9 in
Height	0.1667 in

Object: **txtComments Text Box**
Receives notes about the progress of the issue as people work on it.

Property	Value
Name	txtComments
Control Source	Comments
Status Bar Text	Comments entered while resolving the issue.
Tab Index	10
Left	1 in
Top	2.4167 in
Width	2.6979 in
Height	1 in

Object: **lblComments Label**
Label for the txtComments text box.

Property	Value
Name	lblComments
Caption	&Comments
Left	0 in
Top	2.4167 in
Width	0.9 in
Height	0.1667 in

Figure 22.12 shows the text boxes added for Title, Description, and Comments.

FIGURE 22.12.

Adding text boxes to the Issue form for Title, Description, and Comments.

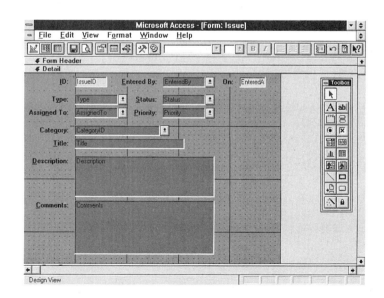

Adding the Issue Form Command Buttons

The Issue form has five visible buttons, as well as two invisible buttons that act as tab sentries.

The Add Comment button starts a new comment section in the Comment text box. The user's name and the date and time appear at the end of the text currently in the Comment text box and the cursor appears on the line after "Ready to enter the next message."

Object: cmdAddComment Command Button

Starts a new comment in the txtComment text box.

Property	Value
Name	cmdAddComment
Caption	&Add Comment
Status Bar Text	Add a comment, marked with username, date, and time.
Tab Index	11
Left	3.9 in
Top	2.5833 in
Width	1 in
Height	0.25 in

The Field Report button opens a dialog box to associate a Word document with the current issue. The Filter button displays the Filter dialog box. The Menu button closes the Issue form and opens the Menu form. The Close button closes the Issue form and redisplays the database container.

Object: **cmdFieldReport Command Button**
Open the Field Report dialog box.

Property	Value
Name	cmdFieldReport
Caption	Field &Report
Status Bar Text	View the field report for this issue
Tab Index	12
Left	3.9 in
Top	0.4167 in
Width	1 in
Height	0.25 in

Object: **cmdFilter Command Button**
Open the Filter dialog box.

Property	Value
Name	cmdFilter
Caption	&Filter
Status Bar Text	Select a subset of issue records
Tab Index	13
Left	3.9 in
Top	0.7083 in
Width	1 in
Height	0.25 in

Object: **cmdMenu Command Button**
Open the database maintenance menu.

Property	Value
Name	cmdMenu
Caption	&Menu
Status Bar Text	Display the database maintenance menu
Tab Index	14
Left	3.9 in
Top	1 in
Width	1 in
Height	0.25 in

Object: **cmdClose Command Button**
Close the Issue form.

Property	Value
Name	cmdClose
Caption	C&lose
Status Bar Text	Close the form
Tab Index	15
Left	3.9 in
Top	1.2917 in
Width	1 in
Height	0.25 in

Figure 22.13 shows the command buttons added to the Issue form.

FIGURE 22.13.

The visible command buttons are added to the Issue form.

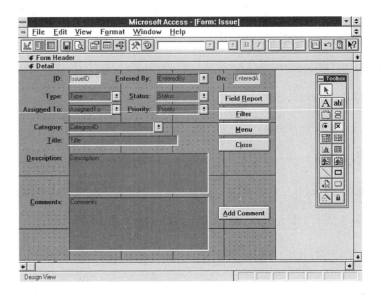

As you move from control to control on a bound form with the Tab key, eventually you get to the last control in the tab order. Press the Tab key once again and the bound form automatically moves off the current record and onto the next record. (You can also use Shift-Tab to move to the previous record from the first control in the tab order.)

I found this behavior undesirable in the Issue form. To make the form stay on the current record, I added two tab sentry command buttons to alter which control has focus before the form moves from one record to the next. (This happens in the On Got Focus event code that you add later.)

You can hide the tab sentry command buttons by setting their Height and Width properties to zero.

Object: **cmdSentry1 Command Button**
Tab sentry 1.

Property	Value
Name	cmdSentry1
Caption	(Blank)
Tab Index	16
Left	0 in
Top	0 in
Width	0 in
Height	0 in

Object: **cmdSentry2 Command Button**
Tab sentry 2.

Property	Value
Name	cmdSentry2
Caption	(Blank)
Tab Index	17
Left	0 in
Top	0 in
Width	0 in
Height	0 in

Figure 22.14 shows the Tab Sentry command buttons.

FIGURE 22.14.
The Tab Sentry command buttons before they are hidden from view.

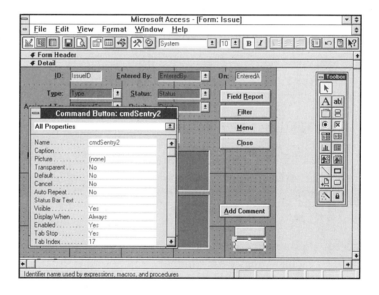

Finishing the Detail Section

Next, place a check box on the form to indicate whether a field report Word document exists with additional information about the issue. The check box is not editable; it is set when the user opens the Field Report dialog box and selects the Word document to associate it with this issue.

Object: **chkSeeFieldReport Check Box**
Indicates whether a field report exists for the current issue.

Property	Value
Name	chkSeeFieldReport
Enabled	No
Locked	Yes
Tab Index	18
Left	3.9847 in
Top	3.1417 in
Width	0.1299 in
Height	0.1299 in
Special Effect	Sunken

Object: **lblSeeFieldReport Label**

Label for the chkSeeFieldReport check box.

Property	Value
Name	lblSeeFieldReport
Caption	See Field Report
Left	4.1722 in
Top	3.125 in
Width	0.6146 in
Height	0.3021 in

The next control is an attempt to decorate the form. I must admit that this time around my hidden artistic talents didn't come out from hiding. Oh well.

The picture represents a bug being targeted in a gun-sight. The idea is to combine the S.W.A.T. themes of swatting bugs and a high-tech police force.

Object: **picBug Object Frame**

Picture of a bug targeted for elimination.

Property	Value
Name	picBug
OLE Class	Paintbrush Picture
Enabled	No
Locked	Yes
Tab Index	19
Left	4.0854 in
Top	1.6667 in
Width	0.5625 in
Height	0.5833 in

Figure 22.15 shows the bitmap being edited in the Windows Paintbrush utility.

FIGURE 22.15.

A bitmap of a bug targeted for elimination.

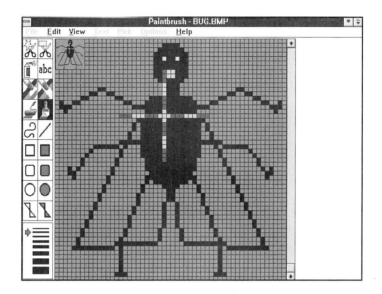

Below the bitmap are two labels that display the name of the program with the shadowed effect.

Object: **lblSwat1 Label**
Shadow for the S.W.A.T. program title.

Property	Value
Name	lblSwat1
Caption	S.W.A.T.
Left	4.0479 in
Top	2.2681 in
Width	0.6875 in
Height	0.1979 in
Fore Color	0 (Black)
Font Name	MS Sans Serif
Font Size	10
Font Weight	Bold

Object: **lblSwat2 Label**
The foreground S.W.A.T. program title.

Property	Value
Name	lblSwat2
Caption	S.W.A.T.
Left	4.0382 in
Top	2.25 in
Width	0.6875 in
Height	0.1979 in
Fore Color	16777215 (White)
Font Name	MS Sans Serif
Font Size	10
Font Weight	Bold

The completed detail section is shown in Figure 22.16.

FIGURE 22.16.

The Issue form's detail section.

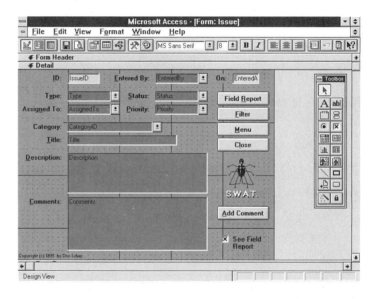

Adding Controls in the Form Footer Section

Within the footer section, add three text boxes to make it easy for the program to change the settings in the corresponding fields. The text boxes should be bound to the FieldReport, FixedBy, and FixedAt fields from the Issue table.

The appearance of these text boxes is not important because the entire section is hidden from view. However, this list shows the properties in the order you set them.

Object: **txtFieldReport Text Box**
Used to read and write to the FieldsReport field.

Property	Value
Name	txtFieldReport
Control Source	FieldReport
Left	1 in
Top	0.0417 in
Width	2 in
Height	0.1771 in

Object: **lblFieldReport Label**

Label for the txtFieldReport text box.

Property	Value
Name	lblFieldReport
Caption	Field Report
Left	0 in
Top	2.4167 in
Width	0.9 in
Height	0.1667 in

Object: **txtFixedBy Text Box**

Used to read and write to the FixedBy field.

Property	Value
Name	txtFixedBy
Control Source	FixedBy
Left	1 in
Top	0.3021 in
Width	0.6458 in
Height	0.1771 in

Object: **lblFixedBy Label**

Label for the txtFixedBy text box.

Property	Value
Name	lblFixedBy
Caption	Fixed By:
Left	0 in
Top	0.3021 in
Width	0.9 in
Height	0.1667 in

Object: **txtFixedAt Text Box**
Used to read and write to the FixedAt field.

Property	Value
Name	txtFixedAt
Control Source	FixedAt
Left	1 in
Top	0.5625 in
Width	0.6458 in
Height	0.1771 in

Object: **lblFixedAt Label**
Label for the txtFixedBy text box.

Property	Value
Name	lblFixedAt
Caption	Fixed At:
Left	0 in
Top	0.5625 in
Width	0.9 in
Height	0.1667 in

Figure 22.17 shows the text boxes in the hidden footer section.

FIGURE 22.17.

Adding bound text boxes in the hidden footer section.

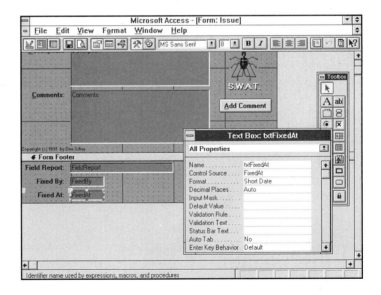

Coding the Issue Form

The majority of the code behind the Issue form deals with the filtering capability of the program. The remaining code handles some special conditions while editing an issue record, and moving to and from the other forms.

Here's a directory of the procedures in the Issue form module in the order in which you look at them.

(Declarations)	Declarations Section
`Form_Load`	Initialization
`FilterTitle`	Set the title caption of the window
`Form_Current`	Update the See Field Report check box
`UserID`	Return the current user's ID number
`cboStatus_Click`	Processing after an issue status change
`cmdAddComment_Click`	Write header for a comment
`cmdFilter_Click`	Apply a selected filter
`Where`	Add a condition to filter's `Where` clause
`RemoveFilter`	Show all records again
`cmdSentry1_GotFocus`	Tab sentry
`cmdSentry2_GotFocus`	Tab sentry
`Form_BeforeUpdate`	Validate required fields
`cmdMenu_Click`	Open the Menu form
`cmdClose_Click`	Return to the database container
`Form_Unload`	Show the database container if needed

The Declarations Section

In the declarations section, declare two flags. Set the `mblnCancelUpdate` flag when validation fails while trying to save the current Issue record.

Set the `mblnLoadingMenu` variable when closing the form to indicate whether the database container window should be redisplayed (see Listing 22.8).

Listing 22.8. The declarations section in the Issue form module.

```
' Issue form module

Option Compare Database
```

continues

Listing 22.8. continued

```
Option Explicit

Dim mblnCancelUpdate As Integer
Dim mblnLoadingMenu As Integer
```

The *Form_Load* and *FilterTitle* Subroutines

When the Issue form is first loaded there is no filtering applied. The Form_Load subroutine calls the FilterTitle subroutine to indicate on the Issue form's title bar that all records are available (see Listing 22.9).

Listing 22.9. The Form_Load **subroutine.**

```
Sub Form_Load ()

  mblnLoadingMenu = False
  FilterTitle "All records"

End Sub
```

The FilterTitle subroutine sets the caption of the title bar so that it displays the program name along with the filter being applied to the Issue form (see Listing 22.10).

Listing 22.10. The FilterTitle **subroutine.**

```
Sub FilterTitle (strFilter As String)

' Display the filter title in the form's title bar
  Me.Caption = PROGRAM & " - [" & strFilter & "]"

End Sub
```

The *Form_Current* Subroutine

The Form_Current subroutine is activated when a record becomes the currently displayed record in the Issue form (see Listing 22.11).

The subroutine determines whether a filename has been stored in the FieldReport field. If so, the subroutine checks the See Field Report check box. This check indicates to the user that a field report exists.

Listing 22.11. The `Form_Current` **subroutine.**

```
Sub Form_Current ()

  chkSeeFieldReport = (Len(CNStr(txtFieldReport)) > 0)

End Sub
```

The *UserID* Function

The `UserID` function is a one-liner that simply returns the user ID of the current user. This value is stored in the `glngUserID` global. The function is needed as a way to default the Entered By combo box to the current user (see Listing 22.12).

Listing 22.12. The `UserID` **function.**

```
Function UserID () As Long

  UserID = glngUserID

End Function
```

The *cboStatus_Click* Subroutine

The `cboStatus_Click` subroutine executes whenever the user changes the value in the cboStatus combo box (see Listing 22.13).

Listing 22.13. The `cboStatus_Click` **subroutine.**

```
Sub cboStatus_Click ()

' Give the person that switches the issue status to Completed credit for
' completing the issue. Also, when an issue is completed or dropped, it
' is assigned back to the person that originated the issue as they are
' the only one with the authority to close it.

  Dim msg As String

  On Error GoTo cboStatus_ClickError

' Is issue completed?
  If cboStatus = 3 Then
    txtFixedBy = glngUserID
    txtFixedAt = Now
  End If
```

continues

Listing 22.13. continued

```
' Is issue completed or dropped?
  If cboStatus = 3 Or cboStatus = 4 Then
    cboAssignedTo = cboEnteredBy
  End If

' Is issue being closed?
  If cboStatus = 5 Then
    If cboEnteredBy <> glngUserID Then
      msg = "An issue may only be closed by the person "
      msg = msg & "who originally entered it."
      MsgBox msg, 64, PROGRAM

      cboStatus = cboStatus.OldValue
    End If
  End If

cboStatus_ClickDone:
  Exit Sub

cboStatus_ClickError:
  MsgBox Error$, 48, PROGRAM
  Resume cboStatus_ClickDone

End Sub
```

The subroutine first determines whether the status of the issue has changed to "Completed." If it has, the FixedBy and FixedAt fields record who completed the issue. Therefore, the person who actually made the fix is the only person who can mark it as completed, otherwise the system incorrectly stores who fixed the issue.

```
' Is issue completed?
  If cboStatus = 3 Then
    txtFixedBy = glngUserID
    txtFixedAt = Now
  End If
```

Next, a check determines whether the issue is again marked as "Completed" or "Dropped." The action taken here is to automatically assign the issue to the person who originally entered it into the database, so that this person may review it to close the issue.

```
' Is issue completed or dropped?
  If cboStatus = 3 Or cboStatus = 4 Then
    cboAssignedTo = cboEnteredBy
  End If
```

If the issue is being closed, the subroutine verifies that the person closing the issue is the same as the person who created the issue. If not, the subroutine switches back to the previous status by using the `OldValue` property.

```
' Is issue being closed?
  If cboStatus = 5 Then
```

```
   If cboEnteredBy <> glngUserID Then
     msg = "An issue may only be closed by the person "
     msg = msg & "who originally entered it."
     MsgBox msg, 64, PROGRAM

     cboStatus = cboStatus.OldValue
   End If
 End If
```

The *cmdAddComment_Click* Subroutine

The cmdAddComment_Click subroutine appends text to the text already in the txtComments text box (see Listing 22.14). The added text identifies a new comment with the current user's name and the date and time of the entry.

The subroutine places the cursor automatically at the end of the entry ready for the new comment. You do this by setting the txtComments SelStart property to the length of the text in the text box.

Listing 22.14. The cmdAddComment_Click **subroutine.**

```
Sub cmdAddComment_Click ()

  Dim sz As String
  Dim cr As String

  On Error GoTo cmdAddComment_ClickError

  cr = Chr$(13) & Chr$(10)

  sz = CNStr(txtComments)

  If Len(sz) > 0 Then
    If Right$(sz, 1) <> cr Then
      sz = sz & cr
    End If
  End If

  sz = sz & "— " & gstrUsername & " - "
  sz = sz & Format$(Now, "Short Date") & " "
  sz = sz & Format$(Now, "Short Time") & " — " & cr

  txtComments = sz
  txtComments.SetFocus
  txtComments.SelStart = Len(sz)

cmdAddComment_ClickDone:
  Exit Sub

cmdAddComment_ClickError:
  MsgBox Error$, 48, PROGRAM
  Resume cmdAddComment_ClickDone

End Sub
```

The *cmdFilter_Click* Subroutine

The cmdFilter_Click subroutine opens the Filter form to allow the user to define and select a filter (see Listing 22.15). If a filter is selected, this subroutine constructs the Record Source query to select the appropriate Issue table records.

Listing 22.15. The cmdFilter_Click **subroutine.**

```
Sub cmdFilter_Click ()

  Dim db As Database

  Dim rs As Recordset

  Dim tblFilter As Recordset
  Dim blnOpened As Integer

  Dim sql As String
  Dim whr As String

  Dim lngFilterID As Long
  Dim lngIssueID As Long

  blnOpened = False

  On Error Resume Next

' Save the record
  DoCmd DoMenuItem 0, 0, 4, A_MENU_VER20

  On Error GoTo cmdFilter_ClickError

  If mblnCancelUpdate Then
    mblnCancelUpdate = False
    GoTo cmdFilter_ClickDone
  End If

  lngFilterID = glngFilterID
  DoCmd OpenForm "Filter", , , , , A_Dialog

  lngIssueID = CNLng(txtIssueID)

  If glngFilterID = 0 Then
' No filter was selected

' Was a filter being used before?
    If lngFilterID <> 0 Then
      RemoveFilter
    End If
  Else
' A filter was selected

    Set db = DBEngine(0)(0)
    Set tblFilter = db.OpenRecordset("Filter", DB_OPEN_TABLE)

    tblFilter.Index = "PrimaryKey"
```

```
    tblFilter.Seek "=", glngFilterID

' Is it different then before?
  If (lngFilterID <> glngFilterID) Or gblnFilterChanged Then

  ' Generate the new record source for the form

    If tblFilter.NoMatch Then

    ' Shouldn't ever get here
      MsgBox "Unable to load selected filter.", 48, PROGRAM
      RemoveFilter

    Else

      sql = "SELECT * FROM ISSUE "
      whr = ""

    ' The Where subroutine adds a condition to the whr variable
    ' for each of these fields when a non-zero value is found in
    ' the filter record.

      Where tblFilter, "AssignedTo", whr
      Where tblFilter, "Type", whr
      Where tblFilter, "Status", whr
      Where tblFilter, "Priority", whr
      Where tblFilter, "CategoryID", whr
      Where tblFilter, "EnteredBy", whr

      If IsDate(tblFilter!EnteredBefore) Then
        If Len(whr) > 0 Then
          whr = whr & "AND "
        End If

        whr = whr & "EnteredAt < #" & tblFilter!EnteredBefore & "# "
      End If

      If IsDate(tblFilter!EnteredAfter) Then
        If Len(whr) > 0 Then
          whr = whr & "AND "
        End If

        whr = whr & "EnteredAt > #" & tblFilter!EnteredAfter & "# "
      End If

      If Len(whr) > 0 Then
        sql = sql & "WHERE " & whr
      End If

      Me.RecordSource = sql & ";"
      Me.Requery

      FilterTitle CNStr(tblFilter!Title)
    End If
  Else

  ' Make sure the filter wasn't deleted
    If tblFilter.NoMatch Then
```

continues

Listing 22.15. continued

```
        RemoveFilter
      End If

    End If
  End If

' Resync the form to the record that was displayed before
' we changed filters.

  If lngIssueID > 0 Then
    Set rs = Me.RecordsetClone
    rs.FindFirst "IssueID = " & lngIssueID

    If Not rs.NoMatch Then
      Me.Bookmark = rs.Bookmark
    End If
  End If

cmdFilter_ClickDone:
  On Error Resume Next
  If blnOpened Then tblFilter.Close
  Exit Sub

cmdFilter_ClickError:
  MsgBox Error$, 48, PROGRAM
  Resume cmdFilter_ClickDone

End Sub
```

Before you can apply a filter (which might exclude viewing the current record), the current record is saved.

```
On Error Resume Next

' Save the record
DoCmd DoMenuItem 0, 0, 4, A_MENU_VER20
```

The subroutine turns on error-handling after the save, and then checks the module variable, `mblnCancelUpdate`, to determine whether validation failed while saving the record.

```
On Error GoTo cmdFilter_ClickError

If mblnCancelUpdate Then
  mblnCancelUpdate = False
  GoTo cmdFilter_ClickDone
End If
```

Next, the subroutine saves the currently used `FilterID` in a local variable so you can later compare it to determine whether a new filter was selected. Then, the subroutine opens the Filter form as a pop-up dialog box.

```
lngFilterID = glngFilterID
DoCmd OpenForm "Filter", , , , , A_Dialog
```

After the Filter dialog box closes, the subroutine saves the current IssueID. If you requery the form with a newly selected filter, you use this to try to return to the same record that was being edited.

```
lngIssueID = CNLng(txtIssueID)
```

The subroutine checks the glngFilterID global for a value of 0, which indicates that the user clicked the OK button on the Filter form while there was no filter selected. If there was a filter loaded, calling the RemoveFilter subroutine removes the filtering.

```
If glngFilterID = 0 Then
' No filter was selected

' Was a filter being used before?
  If lngFilterID <> 0 Then
    RemoveFilter
  End If
```

The Else clause indicates a few possibilities. The users may have clicked OK to select a new filter. They may also have clicked Cancel. In any case, if they modified the filter that they were using, the form needs to be requeried to reflect the change to the filter.

First, the Filter table opens as a table. Then, the subroutine locates the record for the selected filter.

```
Else
' A filter was selected

  Set db = DBEngine(0)(0)
  Set tblFilter = db.OpenRecordset("Filter", DB_OPEN_TABLE)

  tblFilter.Index = "PrimaryKey"
  tblFilter.Seek "=", glngFilterID
```

Next, the subroutine determines whether a different filter was picked before or whether the current filter was changed. If so, the new filter is applied by generating the Record Source property setting for the form.

```
' Is it different then before?
  If (lngFilterID <> glngFilterID) Or gblnFilterChanged Then

    ' Generate the new record source for the form
```

Just for bulletproofing, check the NoMatch property to make sure that the filter record was found.

```
    If tblFilter.NoMatch Then

    ' Shouldn't ever get here
      MsgBox "Unable to load selected filter.", 48, PROGRAM
      RemoveFilter

    Else
```

The subroutine begins generating the Record Source property setting, which is a SELECT statement that returns all fields from the Issue table. It also has a WHERE clause that is, in effect, the filter.

```
sql = "SELECT * FROM ISSUE "
whr = ""
```

The Where subroutine is passed the tblFilter table variable, which points to the record in the Filter table for the generated filter. The second argument indicates which field is to be checked for possible criteria; the whr string variable receives modifications to the WHERE clause.

```
' The Where subroutine adds a condition to the whr variable
' for each of these fields when a non-zero value is found in
' the filter record.

Where tblFilter, "AssignedTo", whr
Where tblFilter, "Type", whr
Where tblFilter, "Status", whr
Where tblFilter, "Priority", whr
Where tblFilter, "CategoryID", whr
Where tblFilter, "EnteredBy", whr
```

The program takes care of the EnteredBefore and EnteredAfter criteria values right here. The modified WHERE clause returns records in which the EnteredAt field is less than the EnteredBefore field.

```
If IsDate(tblFilter!EnteredBefore) Then
  If Len(whr) > 0 Then
    whr = whr & "AND "
  End If

  whr = whr & "EnteredAt < #" & tblFilter!EnteredBefore & "# "
End If
```

Then, the WHERE clause is modified to return only records in which the EnteredAt field is greater than the EnteredAfter value.

```
If IsDate(tblFilter!EnteredAfter) Then
  If Len(whr) > 0 Then
    whr = whr & "AND "
  End If

  whr = whr & "EnteredAt > #" & tblFilter!EnteredAfter & "# "
End If
```

If criteria were defined and you have a WHERE clause, the clause appears at the end of the SELECT statement.

```
If Len(whr) > 0 Then
  sql = sql & "WHERE " & whr
End If
```

Then, assign the SELECT statement to the Record Source property and requery the form.

```
        Me.RecordSource = sql & ";"
        Me.Requery
```

Because you applied a filter, the `FilterTitle` subroutine displays the name of the filter being used in the form's title caption.

```
        FilterTitle CNStr(tblFilter!Title)
    End If
```

The next section of code handles the case in which the users click Cancel to indicate that they don't want to change filters, but also delete the previously used filter from the list of available filters. It's a weird case, but might happen.

The subroutine deals with this situation by calling the `RemoveFilter` subroutine, which reverts to no filtering used.

```
    Else
    ' Make sure the filter wasn't deleted
        If tblFilter.NoMatch Then
            RemoveFilter
        End If

    End If
End If
```

At the end of the subroutine, the code attempts to relocate the issue that the user was working on before changing filters.

```
' Resync the form to the record that was displayed before
' we changed filters.

  If lngIssueID > 0 Then
```

Set a `recordset` variable as a clone of the form's underlying recordset. Then, use the `FindFirst` method to locate the record in the cloned `recordset`.

```
    Set rs = Me.RecordsetClone
    rs.FindFirst "IssueID = " & lngIssueID
```

If the record is found, have the form set to that record by setting its `Bookmark` property to the current `Bookmark` property for the cloned `recordset`.

```
    If Not rs.NoMatch Then
        Me.Bookmark = rs.Bookmark
    End If
  End If
```

The *Where* Subroutine

The `Where` subroutine was used in the `cmdFilter_Click` subroutine to generate the `WHERE` clause for the `SELECT` statement that is the mechanics behind an Issue form filter (see Listing 22.16).

Each call to the Where subroutine affects selection by a single field, which is indicated as the second argument by name.

Listing 22.16. The Where subroutine.

```
Sub Where (tblFilter As Recordset, strFieldName As String, whr As String)

' Add a condition to the WHERE clause of the Issue form RecordSource
' SELECT statement.

  On Error GoTo WhereError

  If CNLng(tblFilter(strFieldName)) > 0 Then
    If Len(whr) > 0 Then
      whr = whr & "AND "
    End If

    whr = whr & strFieldName & " = "
    whr = whr & tblFilter(strFieldName) & " "
  End If

WhereDone:
  Exit Sub

WhereError:
  MsgBox Error$, 48, PROGRAM
  Resume WhereDone

End Sub
```

The Where subroutine checks the current tblFilter record to determine whether criteria have been established for the passed field name.

```
  If CNLng(tblFilter(strFieldName)) > 0 Then
```

If so, the subroutine appends an expression to the WHERE clause. The subroutine appends the AND operator if criteria exist in the WHERE clause.

```
    If Len(whr) > 0 Then
      whr = whr & "AND "
    End If
```

An expression is added to compare the value in the named field for the current Issue table record against the value selected in the Filter table record.

```
    whr = whr & strFieldName & " = "
    whr = whr & tblFilter(strFieldName) & " "
  End If
```

The *RemoveFilter* Subroutine

Fortunately, the job of removing a filter is much simpler than the job of constructing one. The RemoveFilter subroutine accomplishes this job by setting the RecordSource property back to the Issue table (see Listing 22.17).

Listing 22.17. The RemoveFilter **subroutine.**

```
Sub RemoveFilter ()

  On Error GoTo RemoveFilterError

  FilterTitle "All records"
  Me.RecordSource = "Issue"
  Me.Requery

RemoveFilterDone:
  Exit Sub

RemoveFilterError:
  MsgBox Error$, 48, PROGRAM
  Resume RemoveFilterDone

End Sub
```

The Tab Sentry Subroutines

The tab sentries are activated on the tab sentry command button's On Got Focus events. The subroutines switch focus to other controls, which effectively prohibits the user from using the Tab key to move the focus past the tab sentries (see Listings 22.18 and 22.19).

Listing 22.18. The cmdSentry1_GotFocus **subroutine.**

```
Sub cmdSentry1_GotFocus ()

  txtIssueID.SetFocus

End Sub
```

Listing 22.19. The cmdSentry2_GotFocus **subroutine.**

```
Sub cmdSentry2_GotFocus ()

  cmdClose.SetFocus

End Sub
```

The *Form_BeforeUpdate* Subroutine

The Form_BeforeUpdate subroutine makes a series of calls to the RequiredField subroutine in the Globals module to verify that a value is entered in each of the required fields (see Listing 22.20).

The subroutine is activated each time Access attempts to write a record to the Issue table. To communicate how successful the write attempt was, set the mblnCancelUpdate flag if the write didn't occur.

Listing 22.20. The Form_BeforeUpdate **subroutine.**

```
Sub Form_BeforeUpdate (Cancel As Integer)

' Validate that all required fields have been entered.

  mblnCancelUpdate = True

  If RequiredField("Entered By", cboEnteredBy) Then
    Cancel = True
    Exit Sub
  End If

  If RequiredField("Type", cboType) Then
    Cancel = True
    Exit Sub
  End If

  If RequiredField("Status", cboStatus) Then
    Cancel = True
    Exit Sub
  End If

  If RequiredField("AssignedTo", cboAssignedTo) Then
    Cancel = True
    Exit Sub
  End If

  If RequiredField("Priority", cboPriority) Then
    Cancel = True
    Exit Sub
  End If

  If RequiredField("CategoryID", cboCategoryID) Then
    Cancel = True
    Exit Sub
  End If

  If RequiredField("Title", txtTitle) Then
    Cancel = True
    Exit Sub
  End If

  If RequiredField("Description", txtDescription) Then
```

```
        Cancel = True
        Exit Sub
    End If

    mblnCancelUpdate = False

End Sub
```

The *cmdMenu_Click* and *cmdClose_Click* Subroutines

The cmdMenu_Click subroutine sets a flag indicating that the Menu is being opened, and then it closes the Issue form by calling the cmdClose_Click subroutine just as if the user clicked the Close button (see Listing 22.21).

Listing 22.21. The cmdMenu_Click **subroutine.**

```
Sub cmdMenu_Click ()

    mblnLoadingMenu = True
    cmdClose_Click

End Sub
```

The cmdClose_Click subroutine first attempts to save the current Issue record before closing the form (see Listing 22.22). If the mblnCancelUpdate flag is set as a result of required fields not being entered, the close is canceled.

The subroutine checks the mblnLoadingMenu flag to see whether it was called by the cmdMenu_Click subroutine. If it was, the Menu form is opened.

Listing 22.22. The cmdClose_Click **subroutine.**

```
Sub cmdClose_Click ()

    On Error Resume Next

' Save the record
    DoCmd DoMenuItem 0, 0, 4, A_MENU_VER20

    On Error GoTo cmdClose_ClickError

' If the update was cancelled, don't close the form

    If mblnCancelUpdate Then
        mblnCancelUpdate = False
    Else
        DoCmd Close A_Form, Me.Name
```

continues

Listing 22.22. continued

```
    If mblnLoadingMenu Then
      DoCmd OpenForm "Menu"
    End If
  End If

cmdClose_ClickDone:
  Exit Sub

cmdClose_ClickError:
  MsgBox Error$, 48, PROGRAM
  Resume cmdClose_ClickDone

End Sub
```

The *Form_Unload* Subroutine

The final subroutine behind the Issue form, Form_Unload, is called because the form is closed (see Listing 22.23). The subroutine determines whether the Menu form is loaded. If not, the database container is redisplayed.

Listing 22.23. The Form_Unload **subroutine.**

```
Sub Form_Unload (Cancel As Integer)

  If Not mblnLoadingMenu Then
  ' Show the database container
    SendKeys "{F11}"
  End If

End Sub
```

That's all of the coding you need to do behind the Issue form for now. In Chapter 23, "Visual Basic: S.W.A.T., Part Three—Field Reports and Time Estimates," you add code for the Field Report button's On Click event.

At this point, you can log in and enter issues into the S.W.A.T. database, as well as switch between the Menu and Issue forms.

While entering issues, you can use all of the record-editing capabilities on the toolbar and menu. For example, you can use the **Edit**|**Un**do Current Record command after modifying a field in a record. Another useful capability is the Find button (or **Edit**|**Find** command), used for locating an issue record by issue number.

Creating the Filter Form

The Filter form contains a list on the left side of the form showing the title for each saved filter. As each filter is selected from the list, the combo boxes and text boxes on the right side of the form show the entered criteria.

As was with the other forms in this application, the controls for entering text have their Back Color set to 8421376 (Teal) and are Sunken.

The properties for the Filter form are as follows:

> **Filter Form**
> Select or define a filter.

Object: **Filter Form**

Property	Value
Caption	Filter
Default View	Single Form
Shortcut Menu	No
Scrollbars	Neither
Record Selectors	No
Navigation Buttons	No
Auto Center	Yes
Pop Up	Yes
Modal	No
Border Style	Dialog
Min Button	No
Max Button	No
Width	5.9 in

Object: **Detail0 Section**

Property	Value
Height	3.0833 in
Back Color	8421504 (Dark Gray)

The lstFilter list box holds 10 of the eleven fields found in the Filter table. The Row Source property is set to a SELECT statement in the Form Load event code. The column widths of the list box are set so that only the second column in the row source is displayed.

Object: **lstFilter List Box**
Select a filter from the saved filters.

Property	Value
Name	lstFilter
Row Source Type	Table/Query
Column Count	10
Column Widths	0 in;2.5959 in;0 in;0 in;0 in;0 in;0 in; 0 in;0 in;0 in
Bound Column	1
Status Bar Text	Select the filter to edit
Tab Index	0
Left	0.1 in
Top	0.5833 in
Width	2.5958 in
Height	1.1847 in

Object: **lblFilter Label**
Label for the lstFilter list box.

Property	Value
Name	lblFilter
Caption	&Criteria:
Left	0.1042 in
Top	0.4167 in
Width	0.5938 in
Height	0.1667 in

Figure 22.18 shows the lstFilter list box.

FIGURE 22.18.

Adding the lstFilter list box.

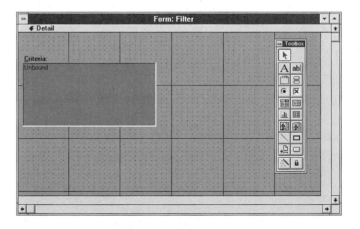

Next, add a series of six combo boxes to the form. Like the lstFilter list box, the contents of the drop-down lists in the combo boxes are set in code. Note that the Row Source Type properties on these combo boxes are set to Value List and not Table/Query.

Object: **cboAssignedTo Combo Box**

Indicate that matching issues must be assigned to this user.

Property	Value
Name	cboAssignedTo
Row Source Type	Value List
Column Count	2
Column Widths	0 in;1 in
Bound Column	1
Status Bar Text	Who is currently working on this issue?
Limit To List	Yes
Auto Expand	Yes
Tab Index	1
Left	3.9 in
Top	0.5833 in
Width	1.1042 in
Height	0.1771 in

Object: **lblAssignedTo Label**

Label for the cboAssignedTo combo box.

Property	Value
Name	lblAssignedTo
Caption	Assigned &To:
Left	2.9 in
Top	0.5833 in
Width	0.9056 in
Height	0.1667 in

Object: **cboType Combo Box**

Indicate that matching issues must be of this type.

Property	Value
Name	cboType
Row Source Type	Value List
Column Count	2
Column Widths	0 in;1 in

Property	Value
Bound Column	1
Status Bar Text	Is this a bug, change, or enhancement?
Limit To List	Yes
Auto Expand	Yes
Tab Index	2
Left	3.9 in
Top	0.8333 in
Width	1.1042 in
Height	0.1771 in

Object: **lblType Label**
Label for the cboType combo box.

Property	Value
Name	lblType
Caption	T&ype:
Left	2.9 in
Top	0.8333 in
Width	0.9056 in
Height	0.1667 in

Object: **cboStatus Combo Box**
Indicate that matching issues must be in this status box.

Property	Value
Name	cboStatus
Row Source Type	Value List
Column Count	2
Column Widths	0 in;1 in
Bound Column	1
Status Bar Text	Where does this issue currently stand?
Limit To List	Yes
Auto Expand	Yes
Tab Index	3
Left	3.9 in
Top	1.0833 in
Width	1.1042 in
Height	0.1771 in

Object: **lblStatus Label**
Label for the cboStatus combo box.

Property	Value
Name	lblStatus
Caption	&Status:
Left	2.9 in
Top	1.0833 in
Width	0.9056 in
Height	0.1667 in

Object: **cboPriority Combo Box**
Indicate that matching issues must have this priority.

Property	Value
Name	cboPriority
Row Source Type	Value List
Column Count	2
Column Widths	0 in;1 in
Bound Column	1
Status Bar Text	How does the issue rate in urgency compared to other issues?
Limit To List	Yes
Auto Expand	Yes
Tab Index	4
Left	3.9 in
Top	1.3333 in
Width	1.1042 in
Height	0.1771 in

Object: **lblPriority Label**
Label for the cboPriority combo box.

Property	Value
Name	lblPriority
Caption	&Priority:
Left	2.9 in
Top	1.3333 in
Width	0.9056 in
Height	0.1667 in

Object: **cboCategoryID Combo Box**
Indicate that matching issues must be categorized by this category.

Property	Value
Name	cboCategoryID
Row Source Type	Value List
Column Count	2
Column Widths	0 in;1.9056 in
Bound Column	1
Status Bar Text	Under which part of the product does this issue fall?
Limit To List	Yes
Auto Expand	Yes
Tab Index	5
Left	3.9 in
Top	1.5833 in
Width	1.9063 in
Height	0.1771 in

Object: **lblCategory Label**
Label for the cboCategoryID combo box.

Property	Value
Name	lblCategory
Caption	Cate&gory:
Left	2.9 in
Top	1.5833 in
Width	0.9056 in
Height	0.1667 in

Object: **cboEnteredBy Combo Box**
Indicate that matching issues were entered by this user.

Property	Value
Name	cboEnteredBy
Row Source Type	Value List
Column Count	2
Column Widths	0 in;1 in
Bound Column	1
Status Bar Text	Who originally entered the issue?
Limit To List	Yes
Auto Expand	Yes
Tab Index	6

Left	3.9 in
Top	1.8333 in
Width	1.1042 in
Height	0.1771 in

Object: **lblEnteredBy Label**

Label for the cboEnteredBy combo box.

Property	Value
Name	lblEnteredBy
Caption	&Entered By:
Left	2.9 in
Top	1.8333 in
Width	0.9056 in
Height	0.1667 in

Figure 22.19 shows the criteria combo boxes.

FIGURE 22.19.

Adding the criteria combo boxes to the Filter form.

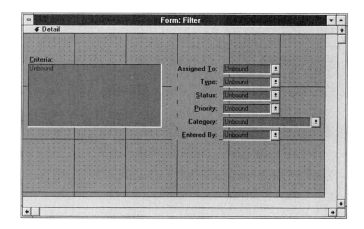

In order to filter the Issue table records by date entered, add two text boxes to the Filter form.

Object: **txtEnteredBefore Text Box**

Indicate that matching issues were entered before a specified date.

Property	Value
Name	txtEnteredBefore
Format	Short Date
Status Bar Text	When was the issue originated?
Tab Index	7

Property	Value
Left	3.9 in
Top	2.0833 in
Width	0.6042 in
Height	0.1667 in
Back Color	12632256 (Light Gray)

Object: **lblEnteredBefore Label**

Label for the txtEnteredBefore text box.

Property	Value
Name	lblEnteredBefore
Caption	Entered &Before:
Left	2.65 in
Top	2.0833 in
Width	1.1563 in
Height	0.1667 in

Object: **txtEnteredAfter Text Box**

Indicate that matching issues were entered after a specified date.

Property	Value
Name	txtEnteredAfter
Format	Short Date
Status Bar Text	When was the issue originated?
Tab Index	8
Left	3.9 in
Top	2.3333 in
Width	0.6042 in
Height	0.1667 in
Back Color	12632256 (Light Gray)

Object: **lblEnteredAfter Label**

Label for the txtEnteredAfter text box.

Property	Value
Name	lblEnteredAfter
Caption	Entered &After:
Left	2.65 in
Top	2.3333 in
Width	1.1563 in
Height	0.1667 in

Then add the OK, New, Delete, and Cancel buttons to the bottom of the form.

Object: **cmdOK Command Button**

Use the selected filter on the Issue form.

Property	Value
Name	cmdOK
Caption	OK
Default	Yes
Status Bar Text	Use the selected filter
Tab Index	9
Left	1.35 in
Top	2.75 in
Width	0.7083 in
Height	0.25 in

Object: **cmdNew Command Button**

Add a new filter to the list of filters.

Property	Value
Name	cmdNew
Caption	&New
Status Bar Text	Create a new filter
Tab Index	10
Left	2.15 in
Top	2.75 in
Width	0.7083 in
Height	0.25 in

Object: **cmdDelete Command Button**

Delete the selected filter.

Property	Value
Name	cmdDelete
Caption	&Delete
Status Bar Text	Delete the selected filter
Tab Index	11
Left	2.95 in
Top	2.75 in
Width	0.7083 in
Height	0.25 in

Object: **cmdCancel Command Button**
Close the form without changing the current filter.

Property	Value
Name	cmdCancel
Caption	Cancel
Cancel	Yes
Status Bar Text	Do not use the selected filter
Tab Index	12
Left	3.75 in
Top	2.75 in
Width	0.7083 in
Height	0.25 in

Figure 22.20 shows the Filter form command buttons.

FIGURE 22.20.

Adding the Filter form command buttons.

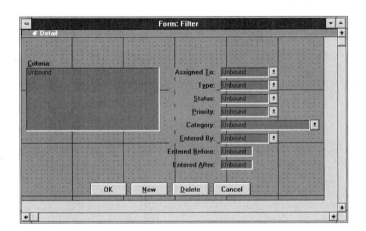

The rest is decoration. You can add a couple of labels with hints on how to use the form. Also add the lblSwat1 and lblSwat2 labels to display the program name on the form.

Object: **lblHint Label**
First of two labels to display hint text.

Property	Value
Name	lblHint
Left	0.1042 in
Top	0.0833 in
Width	5 in
Height	0.3333 in

The caption of the lblHint label should be set to the following:

```
Select a saved filter from the list or click the New button
to create a new one.
Define which records are selected by entering match criteria on the right.
```

Object: **lblHint2 Label**
Second label to display hint text.

Property	Value
Name	lblHint2
Left	0.1042 in
Top	1.8333 in
Width	2.6 in
Height	0.5521 in

The caption for the second hint label is set as follows:

```
Click OK to use the selected filter.
```
```
Click Cancel if you don't want to use the selected filter.
```

The easiest way to enter label text with carriage returns is to type it on the label control and not through the Property window. Use Ctrl-Enter to put a carriage return in the text.

Object: **lblSwat1 Label**
Shadow for the S.W.A.T. program title.

Property	Value
Name	lblSwat1
Caption	S.W.A.T.
Left	4.8097 in
Top	2.4347 in
Width	0.7917 in
Height	0.2396 in
Fore Color	0 (Black)
Font Name	MS Sans Serif
Font Size	12
Font Weight	Bold

Object: **lblSwat2 Label**
The foreground S.W.A.T. program title.

Property	Value
Name	lblSwat2
Caption	S.W.A.T.
Left	4.8 in
Top	2.4167 in
Width	0.7917 in
Height	0.2396 in
Fore Color	16777215 (White)
Font Name	MS Sans Serif
Font Size	12
Font Weight	Bold

The completed Filter form is shown in Figure 22.21.

FIGURE 22.21.

The Filter form.

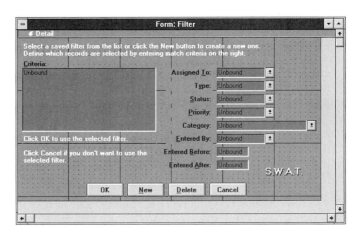

Coding the Filter Form

The Filter form's job is basically to edit records in the Filter table. However, it also allows the user to select one of the existing filters in order to apply it to the Issue form.

The way the Filter form accomplishes its jobs are less than conventional, but it gave me the user interface I wanted. Here's a list of the procedures you will be looking at:

(Declarations)	Declarations section
Form_Open	Load the drop-down lists and filter list.
SetRowSource	Generate a Value List type Row Source.
LoadRecord	Load settings from the Filter table.
lstFilter_Click	Load settings for the selected filter.

`ClearFilter`	Clear the settings on the form.
`SaveRecord`	Save the settings to the Filter table.
`cmdOK_Click`	Use the selected filter.
`cmdNew_Click`	Add a new filter.
`cmdDelete_Click`	Delete the selected filter.
`cmdCancel_Click`	Close the form without using the filter.
`Form_Close`	Clean up.

You also have a series of one-liners to react to the After Update event for many of the controls on the form:

```
cboAssignedTo_AfterUpdate
cboType_AfterUpdate
cboStatus_AfterUpdate
cboPriority_AfterUpdate
cboCategoryID_AfterUpdate
cboEnteredBy_AfterUpdate
txtEnteredBefore_AfterUpdate
txtEnteredAfter_AfterUpdate
```

The Declarations Section

The declarations section for the Filter form module is shown in Listing 22.24. Module-level variables are declared so that you can open a dynaset on the Filter table for the duration that the form is open.

Listing 22.24. The Filter form module's declaration section.

```
' Filter form module

Option Compare Database
Option Explicit

Dim mdb As Database
Dim mdyn As Recordset
Dim mblnOpened As Integer
```

The *Form_Open* Subroutine

The Form_Open subroutine uses the SetRowSource subroutine to fill the different combo boxes on the form (see Listing 22.25). It also fills the lstFilters list box and sets the mdyn recordset variable.

Listing 22.25. The Form_Open subroutine.

```
Sub Form_Open (Cancel As Integer)

  Dim sql As String

  mblnOpened = False

  On Error GoTo Form_OpenError

  Set mdb = DBEngine(0)(0)

  sql = "SELECT UserID AS ID, Username AS Name "
  sql = sql & "FROM User ORDER BY Username;"
  SetRowSource cboAssignedTo, sql

  sql = "SELECT Type AS ID, TypeName AS Name "
  sql = sql & "FROM Type ORDER BY DisplayOrder;"
  SetRowSource cboType, sql

  sql = "SELECT Status AS ID, StatusName AS Name "
  sql = sql & "FROM Status ORDER BY DisplayOrder;"
  SetRowSource cboStatus, sql

  sql = "SELECT Priority AS ID, PriorityName AS Name "
  sql = sql & "FROM Priority ORDER BY Priority.DisplayOrder;"
  SetRowSource cboPriority, sql

  sql = "SELECT CategoryID AS ID, CategoryName AS Name "
  sql = sql & "FROM Category ORDER BY Category.DisplayOrder;"
  SetRowSource cboCategoryID, sql

  sql = "SELECT UserID AS ID, Username AS Name "
  sql = sql & "FROM User "
  sql = sql & "WHERE Username <> 'Unassigned' "
  sql = sql & "ORDER BY Username;"
  SetRowSource cboEnteredBy, sql

  sql = "SELECT * FROM Filter "
  sql = sql & "WHERE Owner = " & glngUserID & " "
  sql = sql & "ORDER BY Title;"

  Set mdyn = mdb.OpenRecordset(sql, DB_OPEN_DYNASET)
  mblnOpened = True

  sql = "SELECT FilterID, Title, AssignedTo, Type, Status, Priority, "
  sql = sql & "CategoryID, EnteredBy, EnteredBefore, EnteredAfter "
  sql = sql & "FROM Filter "
  sql = sql & "WHERE Owner = " & glngUserID & " "
  sql = sql & "ORDER BY Title;"

  lstFilter.RowSource = sql

  If glngFilterID > 0 Then
    lstFilter = glngFilterID
    LoadRecord
  Else
    SendKeys "{Down}"
```

```
   End If

Form OpenDone:
  Exit Sub

Form_OpenError:
  MsgBox Error$, 48, PROGRAM
  Resume Form_OpenDone

End Sub
```

The `mdb` module level database variable is set to the current database.

```
Set mdb = DBEngine(0)(0)
```

Next, for the `SetRowSource` subroutine, create a `SELECT` statement that returns two fields: ID and Name. By renaming the output field names in the `SELECT` statement, the job of the code in `SetRowSource` is generic so that it can be a subroutine rather than code pasted over and over in this procedure.

The `SetRowSource` subroutine generates a RowSource property setting using the values it retrieves from the query produced by the `SELECT` statement.

```
sql = "SELECT UserID AS ID, Username AS Name "
sql = sql & "FROM User ORDER BY Username;"
SetRowSource cboAssignedTo, sql
```

This procedure is repeated for each of the combo boxes on the form (not listed here).

Next, set the `mdyn` variable to a `recordset`, selecting the records in the Filter table sorted by Title. Only Filter table records that belong to the current user are returned.

```
sql = "SELECT * FROM Filter "
sql = sql & "WHERE Owner = " & glngUserID & " "
sql = sql & "ORDER BY Title;"

Set mdyn = mdb.OpenRecordset(sql, DB_OPEN_DYNASET)
mblnOpened = True
```

A `SELECT` statement is generated for the lstFilter Row Source property that produces the same selection as previously shown, except that not all fields are returned.

```
sql = "SELECT FilterID, Title, AssignedTo, Type, Status, Priority, "
sql = sql & "CategoryID, EnteredBy, EnteredBefore, EnteredAfter "
sql = sql & "FROM Filter "
sql = sql & "WHERE Owner = " & glngUserID & " "
sql = sql & "ORDER BY Title;"

lstFilter.RowSource = sql
```

The end of the subroutine checks the `glngFilterID` variable to determine whether a filter is currently in use. If it is, the lstFilter list box is set to show this fact.

```
If glngFilterID > 0 Then
   lstFilter = glngFilterID
   LoadRecord
```

If not, `SendKeys` presses the Down key. This result selects the first item in the lstFilter list box because it initially has focus.

```
Else
   SendKeys "{Down}"
End If
```

The *SetRowSource* Subroutine

The idea behind using the `SetRowSource` subroutine as a way to fill in combo boxes is to create an initial blank entry in the list. Each of the combo boxes on the form is bound to column 1, which holds a numeric value, but actually displays column 2, a text value.

When a combo box is set up this way, it doesn't matter if you have the Limit To List property set to True or False; you still can select only a value from the list. This limitation prohibits users from blanking out the value in the control once they have made a selection. (Not a good situation in this case, because part of editing a filter might mean removing criteria on a field.)

Figure 22.22 shows the Priority combo box, cleared by choosing the blank entry from the list of available selections.

FIGURE 22.22.

The combo boxes on the Filter form display an empty row used to clear the combo box.

![Filter dialog box screenshot. Header reads "Select a saved filter from the list or click the New button to create a new one. Define which records are selected by entering match criteria on the right." Left panel labeled "Criteria:" shows a list with "Don's bugs". Below: "Click OK to use the selected filter." and "Click Cancel if you don't want to use the selected filter." Right side shows fields: Assigned To: Don, Type: Bug, Status:, Priority:, Category: (dropdown showing High, Medium, Low), Entered By:, Entered Before:, Entered After:, with S.W.A.T. text. Buttons at bottom: OK, New, Delete, Cancel.]

The `SetRowSource` subroutine does all this by generating a *value list,* a set of column values for the control separated by semicolons (see Listing 22.26). The values come in pairs because there are two columns in the combo box. The first column is the ID number and the second column is the name.

Listing 22.26. The `SetRowSource` subroutine.

```
Sub SetRowSource (ctl As Control, sql As String)

' Manually generate a value list for a combo box Row Source property in
' order to add a blank value to the list of available selections.

' Assumes there are two fields, ID and Name in the passed SELECT statement.

    Dim dyn As Recordset
    Dim blnOpened As Integer

    Dim sz As String

    blnOpened = False
    On Error GoTo SetRowSourceError

    Set dyn = mdb.OpenRecordset(sql, DB_OPEN_DYNASET)
    blnOpened = True

' Add the blank value first
    sz = "0;;"

' Add the values in the dynaset
    Do Until dyn.EOF
      sz = sz & dyn!ID & ";" & dyn!Name & ";"
      dyn.MoveNext
    Loop

    ctl.RowSource = sz

SetRowSourceDone:
    On Error Resume Next
    If blnOpened Then dyn.Close
    Exit Sub

SetRowSourceError:
    MsgBox Error$, 48, PROGRAM
    Resume SetRowSourceDone

End Sub
```

The `SetRowSource` subroutine opens a dynaset type `recordset` to the passed `SELECT` statement. The subroutine assumes that the `SELECT` statement produces ID and Name fields for each record.

```
Set dyn = mdb.OpenRecordset(sql, DB_OPEN_DYNASET)
blnOpened = True
```

The value list is stored in the `sz` string variable. The first entry is created immediately, which is the blank text entry with the ID of 0.

```
' Add the blank value first
    sz = "0;;"
```

The remaining entries are created by pulling the ID and Name field values from each record and appending them to the end of the sz string.

```
' Add the values in the dynaset
  Do Until dyn.EOF
    sz = sz & dyn!ID & ";" & dyn!Name & ";"
    dyn.MoveNext
  Loop
```

The Row Source property is then set to the value list.

```
ctl.RowSource = sz
```

The *LoadRecord* and *lstFilter_Click* Subroutines

The `LoadRecord` subroutine locates the Filter table record selected in the lstFilter list box (see Listing 22.27). It then loads the settings stored in the table to the controls on the right side of the Filter form.

Listing 22.27. The `LoadRecord` subroutine.

```
Sub LoadRecord ()

  On Error GoTo LoadRecordError

  If lstFilter.ListIndex = -1 Then GoTo LoadRecordDone

  mdyn.FindFirst "FilterID = " & lstFilter

  cboAssignedTo = mdyn!AssignedTo
  cboType = mdyn!Type
  cboStatus = mdyn!Status
  cboPriority = mdyn!Priority
  cboCategoryID = mdyn!CategoryID
  cboEnteredBy = mdyn!EnteredBy
  txtEnteredBefore = mdyn!EnteredBefore
  txtEnteredAfter = mdyn!EnteredAfter

LoadRecordDone:
  Exit Sub

LoadRecordError:
  MsgBox Error$, 48, PROGRAM
  Resume LoadRecordDone

End Sub
```

The `lstFilter_Click` subroutine is activated each time the user selects a different filter from the lstFilters list box (see Listing 22.28). The `LoadRecord` subroutine populates the form with the currently selected filter.

Listing 22.28. The `lstFilter_Click` **subroutine.**

```
Sub lstFilter_Click ()

  LoadRecord

End Sub
```

The *ClearFilter* Subroutine

The `ClearFilter` subroutine erases the current settings on the Filter form (see Listing 22.29).

Listing 22.29. The `ClearFilter` **subroutine.**

```
Sub ClearFilter ()

  On Error GoTo ClearFilterError

  cboAssignedTo = Null
  cboType = Null
  cboStatus = Null
  cboPriority = Null
  cboCategoryID = Null
  cboEnteredBy = Null
  txtEnteredBefore = Null
  txtEnteredAfter = Null

ClearFilterDone:
  Exit Sub

ClearFilterError:
  MsgBox Error$, 48, PROGRAM
  Resume ClearFilterDone

End Sub
```

The *SaveRecord* Subroutine

The `SaveRecord` subroutine locates the record for the currently selected filter and writes the settings on the Filter form to it (see Listing 22.30).

The `gblnFilterChanged` global flag indicates that the current Filter has been modified. (The `cmdFilter_Click` subroutine in the Issue form module used this global flag to indicate that the Issue form's Record Source property needed to be regenerated.)

Listing 22.30. The `SaveRecord` subroutine.

```
Sub SaveRecord ()

  On Error GoTo SaveRecordError

  If lstFilter.ListIndex = -1 Then GoTo SaveRecordDone

  mdyn.FindFirst "FilterID = " & lstFilter

  mdyn.Edit
  mdyn!AssignedTo = cboAssignedTo
  mdyn!Type = cboType
  mdyn!Status = cboStatus
  mdyn!Priority = cboPriority
  mdyn!CategoryID = cboCategoryID
  mdyn!EnteredBy = cboEnteredBy
  mdyn!EnteredBefore = txtEnteredBefore
  mdyn!EnteredAfter = txtEnteredAfter
  mdyn.Update

  gblnFilterChanged = True

SaveRecordDone:
  Exit Sub

SaveRecordError:
  MsgBox Error$, 48, PROGRAM
  Resume SaveRecordDone

End Sub
```

The *AfterUpdate* Subroutines

This next bit of code may seem a bit silly, but it was the easiest way to get the job done.

When manually handling the reading and writing of the Filter table records, you need to be sure that a changed filter is updated before another one is loaded. If you mess up, users may lose changes they make.

Rather than finding all occurrences where I would need to save the record and track whether the record has been dirtied, I took the easy way out. As each field on the form is modified, the `SaveRecord` subroutine is immediately called by the changed control's After Update event.

This means that the record can be saved many more times than is required (depending on how many fields the users edit). However, in practice, this was perfectly acceptable.

Listing 22.31 shows the `AfterUpdate` subroutines for eight controls on the Filter form. They each simply call the `SaveRecord` subroutine.

Listing 22.31. The After Update event code for many of the controls on the Filter form.

```
Sub cboAssignedTo_AfterUpdate ()

  SaveRecord

End Sub

Sub cboType_AfterUpdate ()

  SaveRecord

End Sub

Sub cboStatus_AfterUpdate ()

  SaveRecord

End Sub

Sub cboPriority_AfterUpdate ()

  SaveRecord

End Sub

Sub cboCategoryID_AfterUpdate ()

  SaveRecord

End Sub

Sub cboEnteredBy_AfterUpdate ()

  SaveRecord

End Sub

Sub txtEnteredBefore_AfterUpdate ()

  SaveRecord

End Sub

Sub txtEnteredAfter_AfterUpdate ()

  SaveRecord

End Sub
```

The *cmdOK_Click* Subroutine

Users click the OK button to indicate that they want to use the filter currently selected
in the lstFilter list box. Doing so closes the Filter form to return to the Issue form with
the new filter applied.

The cmdOK_Click subroutine sets the glngFilterID variable to pass back the information that a filter has been selected to the Issue form (see Listing 22.32). If there aren't any filters in the lstFilter list box, the global is set to 0 to indicate that any filter currently used should be removed.

Listing 22.32. The cmdOK_Click **subroutine.**

```
Sub cmdOK_Click ()

  If lstFilter.ListIndex = -1 Then
    glngFilterID = 0
  Else
    glngFilterID = CNLng(lstFilter)
  End If

  DoCmd Close

End Sub
```

The *cmdNew_Click* Subroutine

The cmdNew_Click subroutine creates a new record in the Filter table, and then prepares the Filter form to edit it (see Listing 22.33).

Listing 22.33. The cmdNew_Click **subroutine.**

```
Sub cmdNew_Click ()

  Dim sz As String
  Dim lngFilterID As Long

  On Error GoTo cmdNew_ClickError

  sz = InputBox$("Enter a title for your new filter.", "Title")
  sz = Trim$(Left$(sz, 60))

  If Len(sz) = 0 Then GoTo cmdNew_ClickDone

  mdyn.AddNew
  mdyn!Owner = glngUserID
  mdyn!Title = sz

  lngFilterID = mdyn!FilterID
  mdyn.Update

  lstFilter.Requery
  lstFilter = lngFilterID

  ClearFilter
```

```
   mdyn.Close
   mblnOpened = False

   Set mdyn = mdb.OpenRecordset("SELECT * FROM Filter ORDER BY Title",
   ➡ DB_OPEN_DYNASET)
mblnOpened = True

cmdNew_ClickDone:
   Exit Sub

cmdNew_ClickError:
   MsgBox Error$, 48, PROGRAM
   Resume cmdNew_ClickDone

End Sub
```

The `cmdNew_Click` subroutine first prompts the user for the name of the new filter. The `InputBox$` function is a quick way to get this prompt done. The resulting name is trimmed off to 60 characters because the Title field in the Filter table can only accept up to 60 characters.

```
   sz = InputBox$("Enter a title for your new filter.", "Title")
   sz = Trim$(Left$(sz, 60))

   If Len(sz) = 0 Then GoTo cmdNew_ClickDone
```

A record is added in the Filter table by using the `mdyn recordset` variable. The Owner field in the table is set to the UserID of the current user to identify the Filter.

```
   mdyn.AddNew
   mdyn!Owner = glngUserID
   mdyn!Title = sz
```

Before writing the record, the program reads the automatically generated FilterID (a counter field) from the table.

```
   lngFilterID = mdyn!FilterID
   mdyn.Update
```

After the record is written, the lstFilter list box is requeried to display the new record. The newly added filter is selected by setting the list box equal to the FilterID of the new record.

```
   lstFilter.Requery
   lstFilter = lngFilterID
```

Next, the `ClearFilter` subroutine erases settings left on the form from the previously selected filter.

```
   ClearFilter
```

The module level variable, mdyn, closes and reopens so that it contains an up-to-date recordset in the same sort order as the lstFilter list box.

```
mdyn.Close
mblnOpened = False

Set mdyn = mdb.OpenRecordset("SELECT * FROM Filter ORDER BY Title",
➥ DB_OPEN_DYNASET)
mblnOpened = True
```

The *cmdDelete_Click* Subroutine

The cmdDelete_Click subroutine deletes a filter, of course (see Listing 22.34). You saw logic like this in the Menu form in the previous chapter.

Listing 22.34. The cmdDelete_Click **subroutine.**

```
Sub cmdDelete_Click ()

' Delete the selected filter, then requery and resync the
' lstFilter list box.

    Dim z As Integer

    On Error GoTo cmdDelete_ClickError

    If lstFilter.ListIndex = -1 Then GoTo cmdDelete_ClickDone

z = MsgBox("Delete the " & lstFilter.Column(1) & " filter?",
➥ 4 + 32 + 256, PROGRAM)
    If z <> 6 Then GoTo cmdDelete_ClickDone

    mdyn.FindFirst "FilterID = " & lstFilter
    mdyn.Delete

    lstFilter.Requery

    mdyn.MoveNext
    If mdyn.EOF Then
        mdyn.MovePrevious
    End If

    If mdyn.BOF Then
        ClearFilter
    Else
        lstFilter = mdyn!FilterID
        LoadRecord
    End If

cmdDelete_ClickDone:
    Exit Sub

cmdDelete_ClickError:
    MsgBox Error$, 48, PROGRAM
```

```
      Resume cmdDelete_ClickDone

End Sub
```

The `cmdDelete_Click` subroutine first confirms that there is a selection to delete and that the user is certain he or she wants to do it. If both are yes, the subroutine finds and deletes the record by using the `mdyn` recordset variable.

```
  mdyn.FindFirst "FilterID = " & lstFilter
  mdyn.Delete
```

The lstFilter list box is requeried to remove the deleted record.

```
  lstFilter.Requery
```

Next, use the `mdyn` recordset to determine which filter to set as the current filter.

```
  mdyn.MoveNext
  If mdyn.EOF Then
    mdyn.MovePrevious
  End If
```

If there is no filter to make current, use the `ClearFilter` subroutine to clear the form. Otherwise, select the chose filter and load it onto the form.

```
  If mdyn.BOF Then
    ClearFilter
  Else
    lstFilter = mdyn!FilterID
    LoadRecord
  End If
```

The *cmdCancel_Click* and *Form_Close* Subroutines

The Cancel button closes the form without changing the current filter selection (see Listing 22.35).

Listing 22.35. The `cmdCancel_Click` subroutine.

```
Sub cmdCancel_Click ()

  DoCmd Close

End Sub
```

When the form closes, the `Form_Close` subroutine takes care of closing the `mdyn` recordset (see Listing 22.36).

Listing 22.36. The `Form_Close` **subroutine.**

```
Sub Form_Close ()

  On Error Resume Next
  If mblnOpened Then
    mdyn.Close
    mblnOpened = False
  End If

End Sub
```

Using S.W.A.T. to Track S.W.A.T.

You can now use S.W.A.T. to monitor issues in one of your projects. Why not use it to catalog bugs, changes, and enhancements to S.W.A.T. itself?

The list of categories I have set in S.W.A.T. to do this includes

General
Entering Issues
Filters
Field Reports
Maintenance Menu
Excel Analysis

The General category is for miscellanies that don't fit well within the other category. Field Reports and Excel Analysis are categories you will be involved with in Chapter 23.

Log issues for any enhancement ideas you might have, as well as changes you want to make to the program. And if I've left any bugs in there, be sure to log those too!

Summary

In this chapter, you learned how to build the primary forms that make S.W.A.T. a capable issues-tracking system.

Here are some issues that you tackled along the way. You

■ Created a security-relaxed Login form that allows new users into the database

■ Created a bound Issues form

■ Used tab sentries to eliminate the automatic scrolling from record to record

- Used hidden controls to update non-displayed fields on a bound form
- Wrote your own filtering capability using generated SELECT statements for the Issue form's Record Source property
- Added your own record validation code to ensure that incomplete records aren't lost when a form closes
- Created the Filter form
- Developed a work-around solution to allow clearing an entry in a combo box

In the next and final chapter of this book, you expand on the capabilities of S.W.A.T. with Access reports, Word templates, OLE Automation, and Excel.

CHAPTER 23

Visual Basic: S.W.A.T., Part Three—Field Reports and Time Estimates

Throughout this book, you have created many projects; each one used one of the major desktop applications in Microsoft Office as a full-fledged and serious program development environment. In this final chapter of programming Microsoft Office, you take a look at a couple of the ways that these products are used together.

Each of the three Office applications covered in this book fits within its traditional application categories. Access is the desktop database, Excel is the spreadsheet, and Word is the word processor. Although the functionality of Access, Excel, and Word frequently overlap, they each have distinct advantages when tackling a project that fits within the traditional realm.

A sign I remember seeing in a Shakey's pizza parlor when I was a kid read something like this:

> "Shakey's and the bank have made an agreement. Shakey's does not cash checks, and the bank does not sell pizza."

If you can push that analogy just a bit, think of Access as the pizza parlor and Word or Excel as the bank. If you are going to create a document, Access reporting often can do it, but Word is likely the better tool. Also, if you are going to create a database, Word probably isn't the best place to start. Being a spreadsheet package, Excel is the best place to do your heavy number crunching and what-if scenario modeling, but not the best place to compose a novel or store piles of data in tables.

Enhancing S.W.A.T. from All Directions

The S.W.A.T. database is certainly complete enough to use as-is at the end of Chapter 22, "Visual Basic: S.W.A.T., Part Two—Creating the S.WA.T Forms." However, in this chapter you add some accessories to S.W.A.T. that make it even more useful and capable.

First, you use Word to create a template for collecting detailed information about issues (generally bugs) reported from off-site locations. What is useful about this strategy is that the off-site users of your applications don't have to be connected in some way to the S.W.A.T. database to report issues. They still have a method to provide useful information that can improve the software.

Next, you modify S.W.A.T. in Access so that it drives Word through OLE automation. S.W.A.T. uses Word to automatically view or print the field report associated with an issue in the database.

Your journey then takes you to Excel to take a look at budgeted programming time on the issues in the S.W.A.T. database versus the actual programming time required to complete them.

The heavy spreadsheet users I've known over the years have always found a need to import data into their spreadsheets, do some calculations and manipulating, and then export the modified data back into the database.

With Excel, it is pretty clear-cut how to read some data into the worksheet, but less straightforward how to send data the other way. Along this line, you write some procedures to help with this process and develop a strategy that might also work for other applications you are working on that involve Excel and Access.

Creating the Field Report Word Template

In Chapter 8, "Word: Screen Writer," you created a Word template to enter character profiles as part of your screen writer utilities. Creating the Field Report template for S.W.A.T. is basically the same job; so you're in familiar territory there.

Launch Word and select the **File|New** command. In the New dialog box, select the **T**emplate option button and click OK. Next, turn on the Forms toolbar by selecting the **View|T**oolbars command and checking the Forms toolbar in the list of toolbars.

You are ready now to begin entering the template. You may want to create a field report for each program for which you are collecting issues, or create a single field report that generically covers them all.

In the example here, you create a field report to report issues on the S.W.A.T. program.

In designing the field report, be considerate of the person's time involved in completing the document. If the field report is too extensive, the chances that it will be used are greatly diminished.

A factor that weighs against this strategy is that you may also like to collect as much information as possible, just in case you need it to reproduce a bug. Quite often, a bug that shows up regularly on someone else's computer does not show up on the developer's computer. The field report can signal what is different between those two environments.

Figure 23.1 shows the first screen of text in the S.W.A.T. field report.

At the top of the field report template under the document title are some instructions about how the template is used.

You can certainly provide instructions in documentation you send along with the template, but why not include the instructions right in the template itself? This way you know that the users have the instructions in front of them while completing the field report.

FIGURE 23.1.

You can include user instructions in the template.

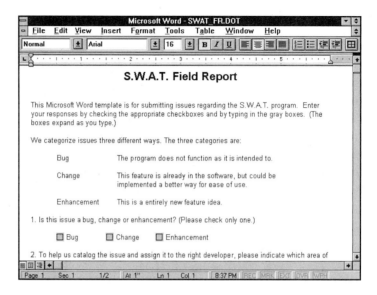

As a precursor to asking users how they classify the issue as a bug, change, or enhancement, the document defines these terms. Following the question, three check boxes are placed in the document by using the check box button on the Form toolbar.

On the Form toolbar is a button showing an *a* character with diagonal shading lines behind it. Clicking this button turns on gray shading for each of the controls dropped onto the template form. I found it useful to leave the shading on because the text boxes are invisible without it, which makes entry confusing.

Figure 23.2 shows questions 2, 3, and 4.

The second question allows the user to identify the issue to one of the categories defined in the Category table in the S.W.A.T. database.

The third question is the meat of the field report, where the user enters in a description of the issue. In other issue-tracking systems and user surveys I've seen this question broken up into several questions like the following:

What is the issue?

What steps are needed to reproduce the issue?

What benefit is gained or problems are solved by the issue?

Separating this into many questions is helpful in that it focuses the user on the different pieces of information that are needed. However, a problem is that it causes the user to have to duplicate information in order to complete the field report. Consider the following answers to the previous three questions:

What is the issue?
When I run your program it immediately crashes my computer.

What steps are needed to reproduce the issue?
Run your program.

What benefit is gained or problems are solved by the issue?
My computer will not crash. I will be able to use your program.

FIGURE 23.2.

The second screen in the S.W.A.T. Field Report template.

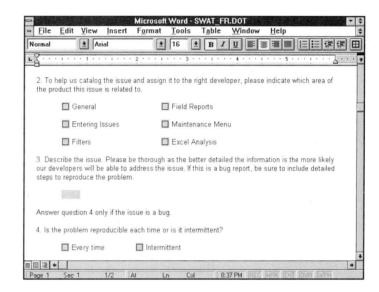

See what I mean? The second and third answers don't provide any additional information that isn't already provided in the first answer.

Question four is used specifically for bugs and asks whether the problem is intermittent or occurs each time. This is important for the programmers because knowing that the bug is intermittent helps underscore that they may have to try many different things before they can successfully reproduce it. An intermittent bug may require more extensive testing after the fix to be sure that problem has truly been addressed.

Figure 23.3 shows question five in the field report, created to help the user identify the equipment on which the software is running.

How extensive this section is depends again on your needs. An advantage with developing programs inside of a host application like Access, Excel, and Word is that hardware-related issues are, for the most part, addressed by the host.

FIGURE 23.3.

The field report has a section to collect information about the user's PC.

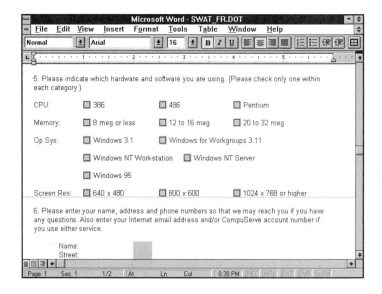

I developed an Access application once that caused Access to GPF and terminate on some machines but not others. The problem turned out to be with a bitmap that was pasted onto a form directly from Paintbrush. The video card driver on some machines had a problem displaying the bitmap.

This previous kind of issue is rare, so my hardware questions on the field report don't go as far as asking what video card and device drivers are installed on the user's PC. The main thing you want to know is how much memory is on the computer. If the issue is that the program is slow, it may be that the user's PC needs to be upgraded in order to run the programs successfully.

Figure 23.4 shows questions six and seven in the S.W.A.T. field report. This part of the field reports compiles contact information from the user, which is necessary to follow up on the issue, especially if the bug is difficult to reproduce. It's also useful if you want to be able to notify the user of the progress made on the issue. Question seven allows the users to indicate whether they are interested in being notified.

Using a field report as a way to collect information probably works best for consultants who contact their clients frequently enough to be able to collect the resulting Word documents created to report issues. In this case, question six may only need to prompt for the user's name.

The final section on the S.W.A.T. field report, shown in Figure 23.5, indicates how the user might get the information back to the developer. If the user and the developer are not connected to each other via a network or an e-mail system where they can transfer files, then the most convenient method for the user may be to fax the document to the developer. This means that the developer doesn't have the actual issue document electronically, but at least the information has been communicated.

FIGURE 23.4.

Sections in the field report for users to provide their address information.

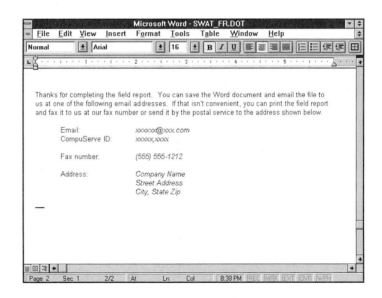

FIGURE 23.5.

The end of the field report indicates how the user can get the information back to the developer.

The field report sample created here is on the book's companion CD-ROM as SWAT_FR.DOT.

Creating the Field Report Form

Supposing that you can collect field report documents from the users of your programs, this next section shows you how to make Access automatically launch Word and display or print the field report documents.

Even if you don't have a need for this particular feature of S.W.A.T., pay close attention because the technique you use here is useful for many applications. For example, you might create a database that catalogs business forms, sales literature, specifications, or article submissions for a newsletter or magazine.

To accomplish this task, you use OLE automation. In a nutshell, *OLE automation* is where an application registers its programmable capabilities to the Windows environment so that other applications with programming languages can use these capabilities. In effect, one application can drive the other via remote control.

In the earlier days of Windows, this kind of application interaction was accomplished exclusively through DDE (*Dynamic Data Exchange*).

First step, you have a small pop-up form to create in your S.W.A.T. database. The properties for the form are shown here.

> **Field Report Form**
> View or print an issue's field report.

Object: **Field Report Form**

Property	Value
Caption	Field Report
Default View	Single Form
Shortcut Menu	No
Scrollbars	Neither
Record Selectors	No
Navigation Buttons	No
Auto Center	Yes
Pop Up	Yes
Modal	No
Border Style	Dialog
Min Button	No
Max Button	No
Width	4.2 in

Object: **Detail0 Section**

Property	Value
Height	1.25 in
Back Color	8421504 (Dark Gray)

Add a text box to the form so the user can enter a filename.

Object: **txtFieldReport Text box**

Enter the filename for the issue's field report.

Property	Value
Name	txtFieldReport
Status Bar Text	Enter the filename for the field report (or press the Browse button)
Tab Index	0
Left	1.0021 in
Top	0.5833 in
Width	2.1979 in
Height	0.1667 in
Back Color	8421376 (Teal)

Object: **lblFieldReport Label**

Label for the txtFieldReport text box.

Property	Value
Name	lblFieldReport
Caption	&Field Report:
Left	0.1 in
Top	0.5833 in
Width	0.8021 in
Height	0.1667 in

Figure 23.6 shows the Field Report form after adding the text box.

FIGURE 23.6.

Adding the txtFieldReport text box.

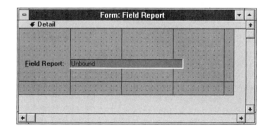

Next, add the following five buttons.

Object: **cmdBrowse Command Button**

Open a File Open dialog box to select the field report document.

Property	Value
Name	cmdBrowse
Caption	&Browse...
Status Bar Text	Select the field report document
Tab Index	1
Left	0.9 in
Top	0.9167 in
Width	0.8021 in
Height	0.25 in

Object: **cmdOpen Command Button**

Use OLE automation to open the document in Word.

Property	Value
Name	cmdOpen
Caption	&Open
Status Bar Text	Open the field report in Microsoft Word
Tab Index	2
Left	1.8 in
Top	0.9167 in
Width	0.7083 in
Height	0.25 in

Object: **cmdPrint Command Button**

Use OLE automation to print the document in Word.

Property	Value
Name	cmdPrint
Caption	&Print
Status Bar Text	Print the field report using Microsoft Word
Tab Index	3
Left	2.6 in
Top	0.9167 in
Width	0.7083 in
Height	0.25 in

Object: **cmdOK Command Button**
Close the form, accepting the change.

Property	Value
Name	cmdOK
Caption	OK
Default	Yes
Tab Index	4
Left	3.4 in
Top	0.0833 in
Width	0.7083 in
Height	0.25 in

Object: **cmdCancel Command Button**
Close the form, ignoring the change.

Property	Value
Name	cmdCancel
Caption	Cancel
Cancel	Yes
Tab Index	5
Left	3.4 in
Top	0.375 in
Width	0.7083 in
Height	0.25 in

With the command buttons added, the form appears as shown in Figure 23.7.

FIGURE 23.7.

*Adding the command
buttons.*

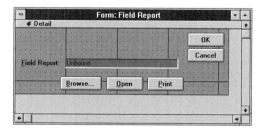

You can now add a hint label to the form with some brief user instructions.

Object: **lblHint Label**
Display hint text.

Property	Value
Name	lblHint
Caption	Click the Open button to view the Field Report in Microsoft Word. Click Print to print the document.
Left	0.1042 in
Top	0.0833 in
Width	3.0938 in
Height	0.4167 in

The completed form is shown in Figure 23.8.

FIGURE 23.8.

The Field Report form.

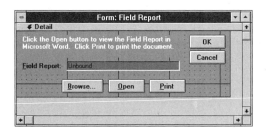

Completing the Globals Module

Before you write the code behind the Field Report form, you need to make a few additions to the Globals module.

First, add the two global variables to the Global module declaration section, as shown in Listing 23.1.

Listing 23.1. Two more global variables for the declaration section in the Globals module.

```
Global gstrFieldReport As String
Global gWord As Object
```

The `gstrFieldReport` string variable communicates back to the Issue form the name of the field report document file that has been selected. (The Issue form is where this information is updated to the database.)

The `gWord` variable is declared as an Object variable data type. The variable is your program's link to an instance of another application such as Word or Excel. An important note to observe here is that the variable *must* be declared globally or at least within the declarations section of a module that remains active.

Why? If the variable is declared locally in a procedure, like other variables in the procedure, all trace of the variable is lost once the procedure exits. This, in effect, destroys your connection to the application (and has the effect of closing it). When you invoke Word to allow the user to read a field report, you need to leave Word active after the procedure that does this terminates, otherwise the user will never get a chance to view the document.

Next, add the GetFilename function to the Globals module, as shown in Listing 23.2. This is a slightly modified version from the one used in Picture Builder+. Passed as the first argument to the function is a Form variable so the function can be called from any form. Refer to Chapter 15, "Access: Picture Builder+," for details on how this function works.

Listing 23.2. The GetFilename **function.**

```
Function GetFilename (frm As Form, strTitle As String, strFilter As String)
➡ As String

  Dim ofn As WLIB_GETFILENAMEINFO

  On Error GoTo GetFilenameError

' See the SDK docs or help files for all possible flags and meanings.
  Const OFN_HIDEREADONLY = &H4
  Const OFN_PATHMUSTEXIST = &H800
  Const OFN_FILEMUSTEXIST = &H1000

  GetFilename = ""

  ofn.hwndOwner = frm.hwnd

' Filter: "Text (*.txt)¦*.txt¦All (*.*)¦*.*"
  ofn.szFilter = strFilter

  ofn.nFilterIndex = 1
  ofn.szTITLE = strTitle

  ofn.Flags = OFN_HIDEREADONLY Or OFN_PATHMUSTEXIST Or OFN_FILEMUSTEXIST

' Second argument indicates if this is a file open or a file save dialog
  If Not wlib_GetFileName(ofn, True) Then
    GetFilename = Left$(ofn.szFile, InStr(1, ofn.szFile, " ") - 1)
  End If

GetFilenameDone:
  Exit Function

GetFilenameError:
  MsgBox Error$, 48, PROGRAM
  Resume GetFilenameDone

End Function
```

Coding the Field Report Form

Next, open the module for the Field Report form and enter the declarations section as shown in Listing 23.3.

Listing 23.3. The declaration section for the Field Report form module.

```
' Field Report form module

Option Compare Database
Option Explicit

Dim mblnLoading As Integer
```

Before the Field Report form is opened, the gstrFieldReport variable is set by code in the Issue form. This variable indicates which document filename (if any) is the field report for the current issue shown on the Issue form.

The Form_Open subroutine sets the txtFieldReport text box to display the field report filename. The Form_Open subroutine is shown in Listing 23.4.

Listing 23.4. The Form_Open **subroutine.**

```
Sub Form_Open (Cancel As Integer)

  mblnLoading = True
  txtFieldReport = gstrFieldReport

End Sub
```

Also set in the Form_Open subroutine is the mblnLoading flag, which indicates that the form is in the process of loading. This flag is used in the next subroutine, txtFieldReport_GotFocus. The Field Report text box is the first control in the tab order so its GotFocus event is guaranteed to occur after the form is displayed.

The txtFieldReport_GotFocus subroutine, shown in Listing 23.5, checks the mblnLoading flag and if it is still True, sets it to False. This way, the remaining code in the subroutine is executed only the first time the GotFocus event occurs.

Next, the subroutine checks to see whether the txtFieldReport text box contains a filename. If it does, the subroutine sets focus to the cmdOpen command button, which is likely what the user wants to do. If the txtFieldReport text box is empty, the focus remains at the text box so the user may enter the filename for the field report.

Listing 23.5. The `txtFieldReport_GotFocus` **subroutine.**

```
Sub txtFieldReport_GotFocus ()

' Default to the Open button having focus if a Field Report
' is available.

  If mblnLoading Then
    mblnLoading = False

    If Len(CNStr(txtFieldReport)) > 0 Then
      cmdOpen.SetFocus
    End If
  End If

End Sub
```

All that work to set the control that has focus when the form opens may seem like more bother than it's worth. As users, we've all gotten pretty finicky about how your applications behave. However, attention to detail is what makes an application have a professional feel to it, so you might as well do it if you know how.

The *cmdBrowse_Click* Subroutine

All that's left to write in the Field Report form module is the code that runs behind each button.

The `cmdBrowse_Click` subroutine, shown in Listing 23.6, calls the `GetFilename` function to allow the user to select a word document filename. The resulting filename is written to the txtFieldReport text box on the form.

Listing 23.6. The `cmdBrowse_Click` **subroutine.**

```
Sub cmdBrowse_Click ()

  Dim strPath As String
  Dim sz As String

  On Error GoTo cmdBrowse_ClickError

' Build the filter
  sz = "Word Documents (*.doc)|*.doc|"
  sz = sz & "Text Files (*.txt)|*.txt|"
  sz = sz & "All Files (*.*)|*.*"

' Call the open file dialog
  strPath = GetFilename(Me, "Select Word Document", sz)

  If Len(strPath) > 0 Then
```

continues

Listing 23.6. continued

```
    txtFieldReport = strPath
  End If

cmdBrowse_ClickDone:
  Exit Sub

cmdBrowse_ClickError:
  MsgBox Error$, 48, PROGRAM
  Resume cmdBrowse_ClickDone

End Sub
```

Using the *Word.Basic* Object

Before you get to the next subroutine, you need a quick primer on OLE automation with Microsoft Word.

The Word developers managed to provide full programmability to their product through a single supported object, the Basic object. Excel on the other hand has many objects (see Appendix B on the companion CD-ROM for information on programming with objects in Excel, Access, and Visual Basic).

What makes the Word.Basic object so powerful is that every Word Basic statement is available through the object as a method of the Word.Basic object.

The steps to writing OLE automation procedures to control Word follow:

1. Record a macro in Word where you perform manually what you want your program to do.
2. View the macro to see what statements were recorded.
3. Look up the statements in the Word Basic help file to find information about the statement arguments.
4. Translate the code to method calls from a Word.Basic object variable.

> **NOTE**
>
> The Word Basic help file is the WRDBASIC.HLP file in the directory in which you installed Microsoft Word. (Installing this file is optional, so you may not find it on your computer. Rerun Word Setup if you need to get this file.)
>
> To get to the Word Basic help file, you need to view the contents page of the Word help file, and then select "Programming with Microsoft Word" from the available topics. I like to create an icon in Program Manager so I can jump

> directly to the Word Basic help file. Just drag the WRDBASIC.HLP file in File
> Manager to a window in Program Manager and the icon is created.

In performing the translation, you need the Word Basic help file to determine which
order the arguments must be passed into the method from the Word.Basic object. Some
of the arguments may be required and others are optional.

Word Basic uses named arguments. When you record code in Word with the macro
recorder, the code produced uses named arguments. For example, look at the following
recording of the **File|Print** command:

```
FilePrint .AppendPrFile = 0, .Range = "0", .PrToFileName = "", .From = "",
.To = "", .Type = 0, .NumCopies = "1", .Pages = "", .Order = 0,
.PrintToFile = 0, .Collate = 1, .FileName = ""
```

In the Word Basic help file, you'll find that there is an additional argument passed to
the FilePrint statement (Background) that doesn't show up in the code produced by
the macro recorder. Figure 23.9 shows the first screen in the topic on the FilePrint
statement.

FIGURE 23.9.

*Viewing the
WRDBASIC.HLP help
topic for the
FilePrint statement.*

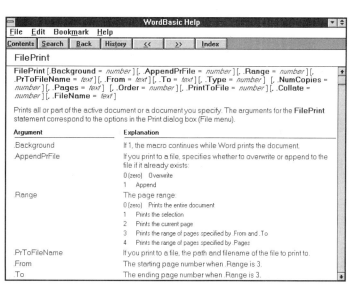

At the top of the help file topic is a syntax diagram indicating how the statement is used.
Brackets around an argument indicate that the argument is optional. As it turns out, all
of the arguments in the FilePrint statement are optional. That means that in Word
Basic you call it like this:

```
FilePrint
```

Each of the arguments defaults to whatever is documented as the default value. Through OLE automation, you make the call like this:

```
gWord.FilePrint
```

Simple, huh? OK, let's look at a call that specifies an argument. Suppose you want your code to print two copies of the current document. In Word Basic, you do it like this:

```
FilePrint .NumCopies = 2
```

It's not quite so easy with OLE automation because you don't have named arguments. What you need to do is count the arguments up to the NumCopies argument. There are Background, AppendPrFile, Range, PrToFileName, From, To, Type, and then NumCopies. NumCopies is the eighth argument. You can default all of the arguments before NumCopies by making the call like this:

```
FilePrint , , , , , , , 2
```

The *cmdOpen_Click* Subroutine

OK, now it's time to put what you just learned to good use. The cmdOpen_Click subroutine in Listing 23.7 uses OLE automation to open a field report in Word.

Listing 23.7. The cmdOpen_Click **subroutine.**

```
Sub cmdOpen_Click ()

  Dim strFilename As String
  Dim cr As String

  On Error Resume Next

' Make sure there is a document to print
  strFilename = Dir$(txtFieldReport)

  If Len(strFilename) = 0 Then
    cr = Chr$(13)
    MsgBox "File not found:" & cr & cr & txtFieldReport, 48, PROGRAM
    GoTo cmdOpen_ClickDone
  End If

' Attempt to open the document
  gWord.FileOpen txtFieldReport

' If an error occurred, it's likely because Word is not active
  If Err <> 0 Then
    On Error GoTo cmdOpen_ClickError

  ' Activate word
    Set gWord = CreateObject("Word.Basic")
```

```
     ' Try to open the document again
       gWord.FileOpen txtFieldReport
    Fnd If

    On Error GoTo cmdOpen_ClickError

   ' Maximize Word to see the document full screen
     gWord.AppMaximize "Microsoft Word", 1

   ' Close the form
     cmdOK_Click

  cmdOpen_ClickDone:
    Exit Sub

  cmdOpen_ClickError:
    MsgBox Error$, 48, PROGRAM
    Resume cmdOpen_ClickDone

  End Sub
```

The cmdOpen_Click subroutine first turns error-handling off and uses the Dir$ function to test for whether the file exists.

```
  On Error Resume Next

 ' Make sure there is a document to print
   strFilename = Dir$(txtFieldReport)
```

The Dir$ function returns an empty string if it can't find the file. The subroutine displays a message in this case and does an early exit.

```
If Len(strFilename) = 0 Then
    cr = Chr$(13)
    MsgBox "File not found:" & cr & cr & txtFieldReport, 48, PROGRAM
    GoTo cmdOpen_ClickDone
  End If
```

Next, with error-handling still off, the subroutine attempts to tell Word to open the file.

What!? But you haven't set the gWord variable to anything yet! That's right, except that it may be set from a previous run of this same subroutine. The only way to tell is to go ahead and try to use the object variable.

Even if this subroutine has already been run, you have no idea whether Word is still active because the user might have selected File|Exit and closed Word after viewing the last field report. The method used next is fool-proof because it doesn't assume at any time that the Word connection is still valid.

```
 ' Attempt to open the document
   gWord.FileOpen txtFieldReport
```

After the attempt to open a document, you were either successful or an error occurred. The subroutine checks the `Err` variable. If it's anything but 0 for success, you need to try to activate Word.

```
' If an error occurred, it's likely because Word is not active
  If Err <> 0 Then
```

Inside the `If...Then` block, error-handling is turned on. This time around, if you can't communicate to Word, let the user know with an error message.

```
    On Error GoTo cmdOpen_ClickError
```

To activate Word, the subroutine calls the `CreateObject` function with the name of the OLE automation object you want to use. This function starts up Word in addition to making the `gWord` object variable a valid OLE automation object.

```
    ' Activate word
    Set gWord = CreateObject("Word.Basic")
```

After the `gWord` object variable is set, it attempts to call `FileOpen` again.

```
    ' Try to open the document again
    gWord.FileOpen txtFieldReport
  End If
```

If execution has progressed to this part of the subroutine, you have a valid connection to Word and the document is open. Error-handling is turned on in case it is still off; the `AppMaximize` statement is called in Word to maximize the Word window.

```
    On Error GoTo cmdOpen_ClickError

' Maximize Word to see the document full screen
  gWord.AppMaximize "Microsoft Word", 1
```

The user may still have to press Alt-Tab to switch from Access over to Word. If the Word window was already maximized, the `AppMaximize` statement has no effect, so Word is left in the background. I attempted to fix this by entering a call to the `AppMinimize` statement directly before the `AppMaximize` call, but unfortunately it produced a GPF. Hey, it happens.

The *cmdPrint_Click* Subroutine

This next subroutine works similarly to `cmdOpen_Click`, of course. The only difference is in which Word commands are executed. The `cmdPrint_Click` subroutine, shown in Listing 23.8, issues a background print to print a document without having to load the document into Word.

Listing 23.8. The cmdPrint_Click subroutine.

```
3ub cmdPrint_Click ()

  Dim strFilename As String
  Dim cr As String

  On Error Resume Next

' Make sure there is a document to print
  strFilename = Dir$(txtFieldReport)

  If Len(strFilename) = 0 Then
    cr = Chr$(13)
    MsgBox "File not found:" & cr & cr & txtFieldReport, 48, PROGRAM
    GoTo cmdPrint_ClickDone
  End If

' Attempt to print the document as a background file
  gWord.FilePrint , , , , , , , , , , , , txtFieldReport

' If an error occurred, it's likely because Word is not active
  If Err <> 0 Then
    On Error GoTo cmdPrint_ClickError

  ' Activate Word
    Set gWord = CreateObject("Word.Basic")

  ' Some screen flicker is going to happen here because the user will
  ' momentarily see Word startup.

  ' In order to issue the print command we need to have a document open
    gWord.FileNew

  ' Minimize Word
    gWord.AppMinimize "Microsoft Word", 1

  ' Attempt to print the document again
    gWord.FilePrint , , , , , , , , , , , , txtFieldReport
  End If

' If we got here then let them know the document is on its way to the
' printer
  MsgBox "Document printing", 64, PROGRAM

' Close the form
  cmdOK_Click

cmdPrint_ClickDone:
  Exit Sub

cmdPrint_ClickError:
  MsgBox Error$, 48, PROGRAM
  Resume cmdPrint_ClickDone

End Sub
```

While investigating the `FilePrint` statement in the Word Basic help file, I found that it takes a `FileName` argument to print as the last argument. This argument is what saves you from having to tell Word to load the document before printing it.

`FileName` is the thirteenth argument, so twelve commas are used to skip all of the other arguments before specifying a filename. Like `cmdOpen_Click`, the `cmdPrint_Click` subroutine attempts to use the `gWord` object variable as if it has been properly set, even though it may not be.

```
' Attempt to print the document as a background file
  gWord.FilePrint , , , , , , , , , , , , txtFieldReport
```

And as before, if an error occurred, the subroutine attempts to activate Word.

```
' If an error occurred, it's likely because Word is not active
  If Err <> 0 Then
     On Error GoTo cmdPrint_ClickError

     ' Activate Word
     Set gWord = CreateObject("Word.Basic")
```

Before Word can issue the `Print` command, it needs to have a current document open. Yes, even if you are specifying a filename to print. To open a document, the `FileNew` statement is called.

As the comment in the code indicates, there is a momentary flash on the screen as Word is shown before it is minimized.

```
     ' Some screen flicker is going to happen here because the user will
     ' momentarily see Word startup.

     ' In order to issue the print command we need to have a document open
     gWord.FileNew

     ' Minimize Word
     gWord.AppMinimize "Microsoft Word", 1
```

The subroutine attempts again to print the document, now that it has a valid OLE automation object to Word.

```
     ' Attempt to print the document again
     gWord.FilePrint , , , , , , , , , , , , txtFieldReport
  End If
```

At the end of the subroutine, a message box appears indicating that the document is successfully printing.

```
' If we got here then let them know the document is on its way to the
' printer
  MsgBox "Document printing", 64, PROGRAM
```

The *cmdOK_Click* and *cmdCancel_Click* Subroutines

The cmdOK_Click and cmdCancel_Click subroutines, shown in Listings 23.9 and 23.10, both close the field report form. The cmdOK_Click subroutine assigns the gstrFieldReport global with the entry in the txtFieldReport text box.

Listing 23.9. The cmdOK_Click **subroutine.**

```
Sub cmdOK_Click ()

  On Error GoTo cmdOK_ClickError

  gstrFieldReport = CNStr(txtFieldReport)
  DoCmd Close A_Form, "Field Report"

cmdOK_ClickDone:
  Exit Sub

cmdOK_ClickError:
  MsgBox Error$, 48, PROGRAM
  Resume cmdOK_ClickDone

End Sub
```

Listing 23.10. The cmdCancel_Click **subroutine.**

```
Sub cmdCancel_Click ()

  DoCmd Close

End Sub
```

That completes the code behind the Field Report form. You have a subroutine to add to the Issue form that will open the Field Report form.

The *cmdFieldReport_Click* Subroutine

Open the Issue form module and enter the cmdFieldReport_Click event, as shown in Listing 23.11.

Listing 23.11. The cmdFieldReport_Click **subroutine.**

```
Sub cmdFieldReport_Click ()

  On Error GoTo cmdFieldReport_ClickError
```

continues

Listing 23.11. continued

```
gstrFieldReport = CNStr(txtFieldReport)
DoCmd OpenForm "Field Report", , , , , A_Dialog

If Len(gstrFieldReport) = 0 Then
' Don't dirty the record unless the Field Report name is being erased
' on purpose.
  If Len(CNStr(txtFieldReport)) > 0 Then
    txtFieldReport = ""
  End If
Else
  txtFieldReport = gstrFieldReport
End If

' Update the See Field Report check box
  Form_Current

cmdFieldReport_ClickDone:
  Exit Sub

cmdFieldReport_ClickError:
  MsgBox Error$, 48, PROGRAM
  Resume cmdFieldReport_ClickDone

End Sub
```

Remember that you created a txtFieldReport text box in the hidden footer section of the Issue form. The control is bound to the FieldReport field within the Issue table so you can write directly to the table by writing to this control.

Before opening the Field Report form, the cmdFieldReport_Click subroutine sets the gstrFieldReport global to the current field report filename. (This may very well be blank in case a field report document has not been selected.)

```
gstrFieldReport = CNStr(txtFieldReport)
DoCmd OpenForm "Field Report", , , , , A_Dialog
```

After the Field Report form is closed, the gstrFieldReport variable may contain a new setting for the FieldReport field in the Issue table.

If the global is an empty string, the code checks first that the table stores something other than a null or empty string before writing the field value. This is to avoid dirtying a new record with an empty string value.

```
If Len(gstrFieldReport) = 0 Then
' Don't dirty the record unless the Field Report name is being erased
' on purpose.
  If Len(CNStr(txtFieldReport)) > 0 Then
    txtFieldReport = ""
  End If
```

Otherwise, if there is a field report filename, it is written to the table by writing the value to the txtFieldReport text box.

```
Else
    txtFieldReport = gstrFieldReport
End If
```

The Issue form's `Form_Current` subroutine updates the check box on the form that indicates whether a field report exists. By calling that subroutine, you don't have to do the same thing here.

```
' Update the See Field Report check box
  Form_Current
```

The Importance of Time Estimates

Your next enhancement to the S.W.A.T. issue tracking system is a job for Excel. When it comes to the dynamic world of budgeting and forecasting, a spreadsheet is the natural tool.

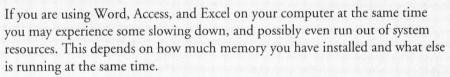

> If you are using Word, Access, and Excel on your computer at the same time you may experience some slowing down, and possibly even run out of system resources. This depends on how much memory you have installed and what else is running at the same time.
>
> If you've got 8MB on your computer or less, you certainly should avoid running all three applications at once. My computer has 16MB on it and it runs all three at the same time without any trouble.

If you are paying for programming work done by others, you need estimates to a reasonable degree of accuracy for how much time will be spent on a project. Spending time is of course spending money, so it's no comfort to you that programming time is a difficult thing to estimate. Everyone has had one of those two-hour fixes that took three days.

As a programmer, it is likely that you have to submit estimates on how long it will take you to accomplish a set of programming tasks. It's not one of your favorite jobs because you are usually held accountable to those estimates. I have a friend who would regularly take any programmer's estimate and multiply it by two and a half to get the actual amount of time it would take to finish the job. He said his system seemed to produce estimates that were more accurate.

Through experience and practice, you will be able to produce more accurate time esti-mates. Part of this experience comes from becoming familiar with what it takes to get a job done and knowing how to stay clear of programming areas that cause you delays. Another part is just plain and simple: get organized.

Developing an issues tracking system is a big step toward being organized. A tracking system allows you to accumulate the data that you need to know in order to determine how much work is involved in a project. Each issue is an objective to accomplish that takes time.

You can become better organized by going one step farther and actually assigning a time estimate with each issue in the database. This is better than trying to produce a single estimate for an entire project without looking at the issues individually. Why? Because a project is typically a moving target.

While the project (called A) is being worked on, your users are likely to decide that they need things in the project that they didn't think of beforehand (called B). Other parts of the project (A) all of a sudden lose significance. You find yourself using an estimate to create A when you are now creating a little bit of A and a lot of B.

When this occurs, it will be helpful to be able to revise your estimates quickly. If you've estimated issues individually, this is easier because you need only select those issues that are now important and produce the sum of estimates for the issues that are active.

Adding the Budget and Actual Fields

Let's add a couple fields to the Issue table for your time estimate needs. Open the S.W.A.T. database and open the Issue table in design mode. Add the following fields to the end of the table:

Field Name	Budget
Data Type	Number
Description	Time budgeted for this issue.
Field Size	Single
Default Value	0
Required	No
Indexed	No

Field Name	Actual
Data Type	Number
Description	Actual time used to fix this issue.
Field Size	Single
Default Value	0

| Required | No |
| Indexed | No |

Figure 23.10 shows the result.

FIGURE 23.10.

Adding Budget and Actual fields to the Issue table.

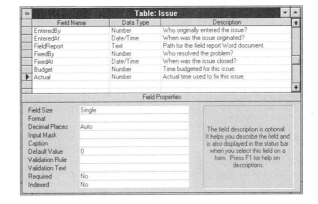

If you indeed plan to make tracking budgeted and actual times for each issue in your database a habit, you probably need to modify the Issue form to display these fields, as shown in Figure 23.11. (This change is not included in the version of SWAT.MDB on the companion CD.)

FIGURE 23.11.

Budget and Actual text boxes are added to the bottom of the Issue form.

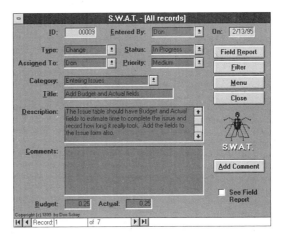

Introducing the Time Estimates Workbook

The Time Estimates workbook, SWAT.XLS, is a scratch pad for working with budgeted and actual programming time values. The Time Estimates worksheet is the main worksheet in the workbook. It contains three buttons: Import Issues, Clear, and Export Changes.

Clicking the Import Issues button reads data from the Issues table into the Time Estimates worksheet, as shown in Figure 23.12.

FIGURE 23.12.

The Time Estimates worksheet.

Issue ID	Title	Budget	Actual
9	Add Budget and Actual fields	0.25	0.25
10	Database corrupted	0.5	0
11	No reports in menu	2	0
12	Save last used filter	0.5	0
13	Need better error reporting	1	0
14	Default Type to a bug	0	0
15	S.W.A.T. logo needs work	0.5	0
	Total:	4.75	0.25

Clicking the Clear button erases the data. This button isn't required except that you might want to save the workbook without any data loaded into it. Clicking the Import Issues button performs the clear also before importing a new set of records.

Here's the first neat part. When you click the Export Changes button, the values in the Budget and Actual columns are written back to the Issue table in the S.W.A.T. database.

Now click the Options tab to show the Options worksheet. The first set of options, Files and Directories, tells the program where to find the SWAT.MDB database and the user's SYSTEM.MDA database. (You'll read about the reason for that in a little bit.)

Now for neat part number two. In the bottom half of the Options worksheet are the Filter options. This set of options contains a set of combo boxes that you can use to determine which set of Issue records is imported into the Time Estimates worksheet. See Figure 23.13.

How does it all work? Well, it uses the Excel set of SQL functions provided in the XLODBC.XLA add-in library. Using these functions, you can generate SQL SELECT statements in code and execute them to produce different sets of data in the Time Estimates worksheet.

To write back the changed records, an SQL UPDATE statement is generated and executed for each row of data in the Time Estimates worksheet.

FIGURE 23.13.
The Options worksheet.

	A	B	C	D
1	**Files and Directories**			
2	Database Directory	D:\BOOK\CH23\FILES		
3	Database	SWAT.MDB		
4	System Database	D:\ACCESS20\SYSTEM.MDA		
5				
6	**Filter**			
7	Type	Bug		
8	Status	In Progress		
9	Assigned To	Don		
10	Priority	High		
11	Category			
12				
13		General		
14		Entering Issues		
15		Filters		
16		Field Reports		
17		Maintenance Menu		
		Excel Analysis		

Time Estimates \ *Options* / *Issues module* / *MDB modi.*

You'll see how all of this works in the code, but first let's create the worksheets.

Creating the Time Estimates Worksheet

Create a new workbook in Excel. Save the workbook as SWAT.XLS.

Rename Sheet1 to "Time Estimates." Widen column B so that it can display the titles of your Issues. I set it to a width of 48.57.

Select cells A1 through E3 and change the shading to dark gray. (This is done with the Format|Cells command, setting the Cell Shading option in the Patterns tab of the Format Cells dialog box.)

Turn on the Forms toolbar and place three large buttons in the gray bar across the top of the form with the labels, "Import Issues," "Clear," and "Export Changes," as shown in Figure 23.14.

Set row 4 to a height of 19.50. Enter the following as column headings in cells A4 through D4:

A4	Issue ID
B4	Title
C4	Budget
D4	Actual

Set the font for cells A4 through D4 to Arial, size 11, Bold.

FIGURE 23.14.

Adding command buttons to the Time Estimates worksheet.

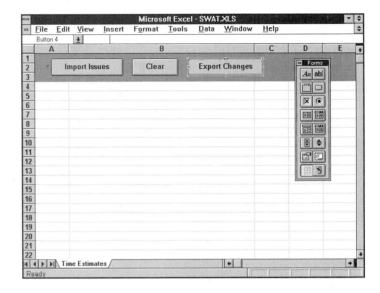

Click cell A5 to select it. On the left side of the formula bar is the name box. Enter ImportCell to create a name defined as cell A5. The ImportCell name is used as a marker in the code to indicate where to import data into. Figure 23.15 shows creating the ImportCell name.

FIGURE 23.15.

Creating the ImportCell name.

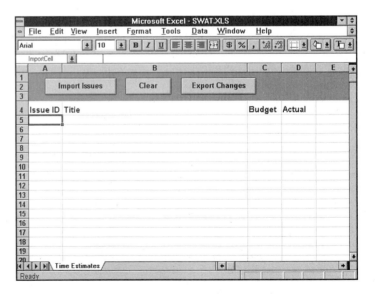

Creating the Options Worksheet

Create a second worksheet with the worksheet name, Options.

Set the width of column A to 28.00 and the width of column B to 36.00. Set the height of rows 1 and 6 to 25.50.

With the Arial font, size 14 and bold, enter `Files and Directories` into cell A1 and `Filter` into cell A6. Enter the following titles for the options stored in this worksheet:

A2	Database Directory
A3	Database
A4	System Database
A7	Type
A8	Status
A9	Assigned To
A10	Priority
A11	Category

The worksheet should look like the one shown in Figure 23.16.

FIGURE 23.16.

Creating titles in the Options worksheet.

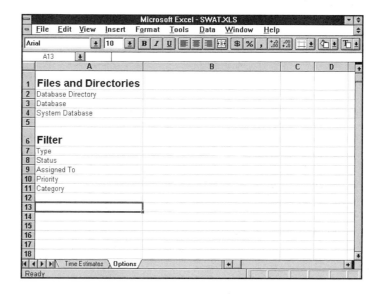

Select the following cells and enter the listed names in the name box:

B2   DatabaseDirectory
B3   Database
B4   SystemDatabase

These names are used in the code to read the entries that you type in the corresponding cells.

Fill these in now so they match the environment on your PC. In B2, enter the directory in which SWAT.MDB resides. In B3, enter SWAT.MDB (or another name if you have renamed the S.W.A.T. database). In B4, enter the full path and filename of the Access system database (this is typically C:\ACCESS\SYSTEM.MDA or C:\MSOFFICE\ACCESS\SYSTEM.MDA).

Set the height of rows 7 through 11 to 15.00. This makes each row tall enough to fit a drop-down in the row. Open the Forms toolbar, and then draw a drop-down control in cell B7. Get the drop-down sized just right so it fits in the borders of the cell perfectly.

Next, click the drop-down control with the right mouse button. A pop-up menu appears. Select Copy from the menu. You can then select each of the cells from B8 to B11 and paste in a drop-down control by clicking the right mouse button and selecting Paste, or by pressing Ctrl-V.

The form should appear as shown in Figure 23.17.

FIGURE 23.17.

Adding drop-down controls to the Options worksheet.

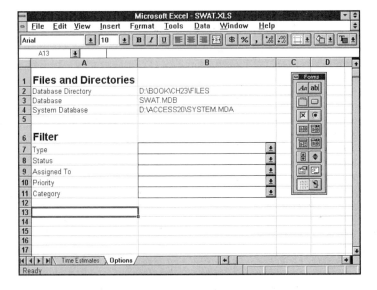

Each of the drop-down controls needs to be named so that it can be referenced in the code. I used a prefix of "cbo," which isn't exactly accurate because the controls are not combo boxes but are Excel drop-down controls. From top to bottom, select each and enter the names in the name box as shown here:

```
cboType
cboStatus
cboAssignedTo
cboPriority
cboCategory
```

Creating the Lookup Tables Worksheet

Next, you need to create the sources for the drop-down controls on the Options worksheet. Add a new worksheet to the workbook with the name *Lookup Tables.*

Store the same lookup table values that are in several of the tables in the database in this worksheet. The drawback with this design, of course, is that the worksheet will not reflect any changes made to the lookup tables in the database unless the worksheet is manually updated. I decided to go with this, but if you want to perfect the application you can write code that updates this worksheet from the database.

In cells A1 through B5 enter the following table:

Type	TypeName
0	
1	Bug
2	Change
3	Enhancement

Note that in this and the following tables, you can open the corresponding tables in Access, select all of the records, and copy them into the clipboard. Then in Excel, you can paste the values directly into the Lookup Tables worksheet and modify them as needed to produce the results you are looking for.

Next, select cells B2 through B5 and enter `TypeName` in the name box on the left side of the function bar. The name you just created will be the entries that show up in the `cboType` drop-down control starting with a blank, and then Bug, Change, and Enhancement.

In cells A7 through B13 enter the following:

Status	StatusName
0	
1	In Progress
2	On Hold
3	Completed
4	Dropped
5	Closed

Select cells B8 through B13 and enter StatusName in the name box.

In cells A15 through B19 enter the following:

Priority	PriorityName
0	
1	High
2	Medium
3	Low

Select cells B20 through B23 and enter PriorityName as a name in the name box, as shown in Figure 23.18.

FIGURE 23.18.

Creating the PriorityName name.

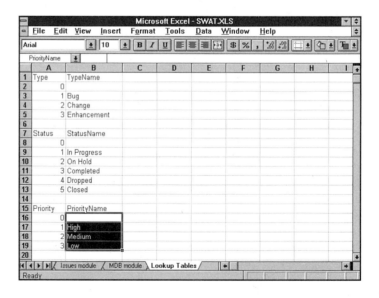

Starting at cell A21, enter the following table or create your own entries based on the categories defined in your S.W.A.T. database. The CategoryID value should be the appropriate ID number for each category as found in the Category table.

CategoryID	CategoryName
0	
6	General
1	Entering Issues
2	Filters
3	Field Reports
4	Maintenance Menu
5	Excel Analysis

Create a CategoryName name for the cells starting at B22 to the end of the table.

At the second row after the last table, create a new table for user names as shown here:

UserID	Username
0	
1	Unassigned
2	Don
3	Robin

Create a Username name for the cells in column B starting with the blank entry, as shown in Figure 23.19.

FIGURE 23.19.
Creating the Username name.

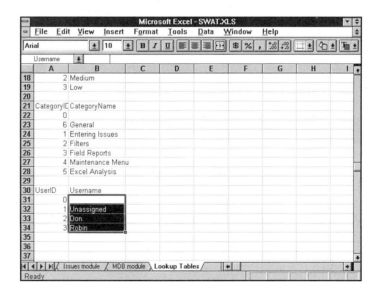

Now set the drop-down controls to display the contents of the lookup tables. Switch back to the Options worksheet. Click the right mouse button on the drop-down control for the Type option. From the pop-up menu, select Format Object, as shown in Figure 23.20.

FIGURE 23.20.

Select the Format Object command from the pop-up menu to bring up the Format Object dialog box.

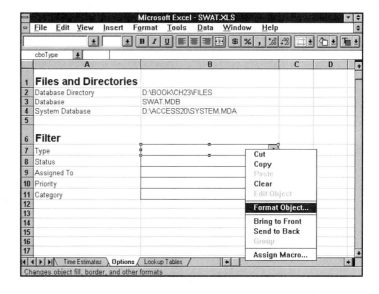

In the Format Object dialog box, click the Control tab. In the **I**nput Range text box enter TypeName, which is the name you defined for the entries in the first table on the Lookup Tables worksheet. See Figure 23.21.

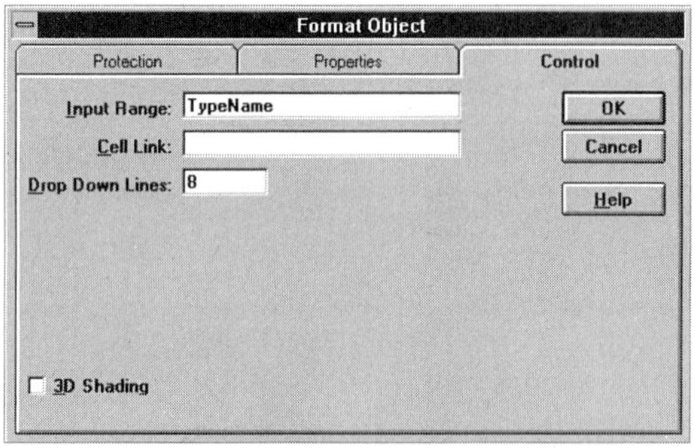

FIGURE 23.21.

Defining the Input Range for a drop-down control.

Close the Format Object dialog box. Now if you click the down arrow on the cboType drop-down control, it displays four entries: a blank line, Bug, Change, and Enhancement, as shown in Figure 23.22.

The extra blank line is used as a way to clear the value in the drop-down control. The user may want to import all Issue records that are bugs, and then later import all issues regardless of type.

FIGURE 23.22.

Selecting Type from the cboType drop-down control.

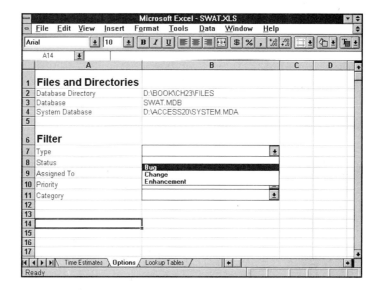

Set the input range for the remaining drop-down controls as follows:

Drop-Down	Input Range
cboStatus	StatusName
cboAssignedTo	Username
cboPriority	PriorityName
cboCategory	CategoryName

Working with the Excel SQL Functions

You have two module sheets to code. The MDB module contains four procedures that make programming interaction with an Access database easy. The Issues module utilizes the code in the MDB module for this particular application. (You may want to use the procedures in the MDB module in other Excel-to-Access projects.)

The Excel SQL functions use ODBC to gain access to various data sources including SQL Server. At present you use them to reach data in an Access database. The full set of functions is listed here:

SQLBind	Indicate where to place SELECT results
SQLClose	Close a connection to a data source
SQLError	Return detailed error messages
SQLExecQuery	Execute an SQL statement
SQLGetSchema	Retrieve information about the database

SQLOpen	Establish a connection with a data source
SQLRequest	All-in-one function to connect to a data source, execute a query, and retrieve results
SQLRetrieve	Retrieve results from a query
SQLRetrieveToFile	Retrieve results from a query to a file

NOTE

The documentation for the Excel SQL functions is in the VBA_XL.HLP help file. This is the help file displayed on selecting "Programming with Visual Basic" from the Excel help contents page. Just as you did with the WRDBASIC.HLP help file, you may want to create a Program Manager icon that loads the help file directly without having to go through the main Excel help file.

The Excel SQL functions are provided by the XLODBC.XLA add-in, which is found in the LIBRARY\MSQUERY subdirectory; a subdirectory of your main Excel directory. To use the functions, you must first establish a reference to the XLODBC.XLA file. Select the **T**ools|Re**f**erences command, and then click the **B**rowse button in the References dialog box. In the Browse dialog box, locate the XLODBC.XLA file as shown in Figure 23.23, and click OK.

FIGURE 23.23.

Establishing a reference to the XLODBC.XLA add-in library.

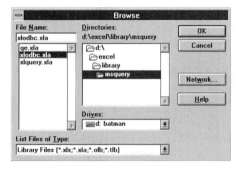

The MDB Module

The MDB module contains the following procedures:

Connect	Establish a connection with an Access database
Disconnect	Disconnect from the Access database
RunSQL	Execute an SQL statement
Retrieve	Place SELECT statement results in a worksheet

Outside of a few comments, the declarations section for the MDB module (shown in Listing 23.12) declares two globals: ghDB and gblnConnect.

The ghDB variable is set when a connection to the ODBC data source is established. This handle is then passed to other SQL functions so they know with which connection they are working. The gblnConnect flag is set when the connection is made to indicate to your program that it should disconnect when the program is done using the connection.

Listing 23.12. Declarations in the MDB module.

```
' MDB module
' Simple interface to execute SQL statements against an Access database.

' The code in this module requires that you load the XLODBC.XLA library
' included in the LIBRARY\MSQUERY directory off of the directory that
' you installed Excel into on your harddrive.

' Procedures:
'
'   Connect strDatabase, strDefaultDir, strSystemDB
'   Disconnect
'   RunSQL(sql)
'   Retreive(rng)

  Option Explicit

  Global ghDB As Integer          ' Handle for the ODBC connection
  Global gblnConnect As Integer   ' Flag set if open succeeded
```

The Connect Subroutine

The Connect subroutine builds a connect string argument to pass to the SQLOpen function in order to establish a connection with an Access database.

The contents of the connect string argument vary depending on the data source used. For an Access database, three of the pieces of information that must be provided are: database filename, directory to find the database file, and which system database file to use. Because these three vary depending on the application and whose computer you are running the program on, I've made them arguments to the Connect subroutine.

The Connect subroutine is shown in Listing 23.13.

Listing 23.13. The Connect subroutine.

```
Sub Connect(strDatabase As String, strDefaultDir As String,
➡ strSystemDB As String)
```

continues

Listing 23.13. continued

```
' Connect to an Access database as an ODBC data source

' Example call:
'   Connect "SWAT.MDB", "D:\SWAT", "C:\ACCESS\SYSTEM.MDA"

  Dim v As Variant
  Dim sz As String

  On Error GoTo ConnectError

' Build a connection string
  sz = "DSN=MS Access 2.0 Databases;"
  sz = sz & "DBQ=" & strDatabase & ";"
  sz = sz & "DefaultDir=" & strDefaultDir & ";"
  sz = sz & "FIL=MS Access;"
  sz = sz & "JetIniPath=MSACC20.INI;"
  sz = sz & "SystemDB=" & strSystemDB & ";"
  sz = sz & "UID=Admin;"

' Make the connection
  v = SQLOpen(sz, , 4)
  If IsError(v) Then
    MsgBox "Unable to connect to data source.", 48, PROGRAM
    GoTo ConnectDone
  End If

  ghDB = v
  gblnConnect = True

ConnectDone:
  Exit Sub

ConnectError:
  MsgBox Error$(), 48, PROGRAM
  Resume ConnectDone

End Sub
```

The Connect subroutine pieces together the connection string using the supplied arguments for the database filename, default directory, and system database filename.

```
' Build a connection string
  sz = "DSN=MS Access 2.0 Databases;"
  sz = sz & "DBQ=" & strDatabase & ";"
  sz = sz & "DefaultDir=" & strDefaultDir & ";"
  sz = sz & "FIL=MS Access;"
  sz = sz & "JetIniPath=MSACC20.INI;"
  sz = sz & "SystemDB=" & strSystemDB & ";"
  sz = sz & "UID=Admin;"
```

Next, the subroutine calls the SQLOpen function to establish the connection. A variant variable is returned as a result of the call. The result contains the connection ID number if the connection was successfully made, or otherwise the #N/A error value. The IsError function checks the return value for a successful connection.

```
' Make the connection
  v = SQLOpen(sz, , 4)
  If IsError(v) Then
    MsgBox "Unable to connect to data source.", 48, PROGRAM
    GoTo ConnectDone
  End If
```

If the connection is good, the ghDB variable receives the connection ID and the gblnConnect flag is set to True.

```
  ghDB = v
  gblnConnect = True
```

The *Disconnect* Subroutine

The Disconnect subroutine, shown in Listing 23.14, checks the gblnConnect flag to see whether the connection is established. If there is a connection, it then calls SQLClose to disconnect from the data source.

Listing 23.14. The Disconnect **subroutine.**

```
Sub Disconnect()

  Dim v As Variant

  On Error GoTo DisconnectError

  If gblnConnect Then
    v = SQLClose(ghDB)
    If IsError(v) Then
      MsgBox "An error occurred while disconnecting from data source.", 48,
      ➥ PROGRAM

      GoTo DisconnectDone
    End If

    gblnConnect = False
  End If

DisconnectDone:
  Exit Sub

DisconnectError:
  MsgBox Error$(), 48, PROGRAM
  Resume DisconnectDone

End Sub
```

The *RunSQL* Function

Now this one is an interesting function, mainly because of the SQLExecQuery function. The RunSQL function calls SQLExecQuery to perform an SQL statement.

What's different is in how the SQLExecQuery function must be called. The second argument is an array of strings, where each string must not exceed 127 characters or the function doesn't work. (This is probably a bug.)

OK, you can live with that, except that the help topic for SQLExecQuery doesn't have any explanation about what form the second argument is in at all. It doesn't even indicate that the argument must be an array of strings!

It happens. When you run into something like this you do have places to figure things out. First check your MSDN and TechNet CDs if you have them. While scanning the CDs, look for a code sample. If you don't find the information you need there, try the forums on CompuServe where all the gurus that have time to kill hang out, including some of the brightest folks from Microsoft Product Support Services (PSS).

Listing 23.15 shows the RunSQL function, which manages to use SQLExecQuery without a hitch.

Listing 23.15. The RunSQL function.

```
Function RunSQL(sql As String) As Integer

' Perform an SQL statement in the connected ODBC data source.

' Using the SQLExecQuery function, the SQL statement must be passed in
' lines not exceeding 127 characters in length. The entire statement is
' broken up into lines in the astrSQL string array.

    Dim astrSQL() As String
    Const MAX_LINE_LENGTH = 127

    Dim msg As String
    Dim cr As String

    Dim v As Variant
    Dim intLines As Integer
    Dim n As Integer

' Assume failure
    RunSQL = True

    On Error GoTo RunSQLError

    If Not gblnConnect Then GoTo RunSQLDone

    intLines = (Len(sql) + MAX_LINE_LENGTH) \ MAX_LINE_LENGTH
    ReDim astrSQL(1 To intLines) As String
```

```
  For n = 1 To intLines
    astrSQL(n) = Mid$(sql, (n - 1) * MAX_LINE_LENGTH + 1, MAX_LINE_LENGTH)
  Next n

  v = SQLExecQuery(ghDB, astrSQL)
  If IsError(v) Then
    cr = Chr$(13)
    msg = "An error occurred executing the following SQL statement:" & cr & cr
    msg = msg & sql
    MsgBox msg, 48, PROGRAM
    GoTo RunSQLDone
  End If

' Success
  RunSQL = False

RunSQLDone:
  Exit Function

RunSQLError:
  MsgBox Error$(), 48, PROGRAM
  Resume RunSQLDone

End Function
```

At the top of the RunSQL function, the astrSQL variable is declared as an array of strings. Also a constant, MAX_LINE_LENGTH, is defined to indicate the maximum number of characters allowed in a string within the string array.

```
Dim astrSQL() As String
Const MAX_LINE_LENGTH = 127
```

The subroutine does an early exit if the gblnConnect flag indicates that you don't have a connection to a data source.

```
If Not gblnConnect Then GoTo RunSQLDone
```

Next, the number of lines required to break up the SQL statement in lines no greater than 127 characters is calculated. The astrSQL array is allocated for the number of lines calculated.

```
intLines = (Len(sql) + MAX_LINE_LENGTH) \ MAX_LINE_LENGTH
ReDim astrSQL(1 To intLines) As String
```

In a loop, the Mid$ function is used to extract first the characters 1–127, and then 128–254, and then 255–381, and so on until the entire statement is broken up into strings of no greater length than the maximum number of characters.

```
For n = 1 To intLines
  astrSQL(n) = Mid$(sql, (n - 1) * MAX_LINE_LENGTH + 1, MAX_LINE_LENGTH)
Next n
```

The `SQLExecQuery` function is called with the connection ID number and the `astrSQL` array. The result of the call is checked using the `IsError` function.

```
v = SQLExecQuery(ghDB, astrSQL)
If IsError(v) Then
```

If an error did occur, an error message is produced that displays the SQL statement that didn't execute.

```
    cr = Chr$(13)
    msg = "An error occurred executing the following SQL statement:" & cr & cr
msg = msg & sql
    MsgBox msg, 48, PROGRAM
    GoTo RunSQLDone
  End If
```

If all went well, the return value of the `RunSQL` function is set to False to indicate success.

```
' Success
  RunSQL = False
```

Figure 23.24 shows the `RunSQL` function being entered in the MDB module.

FIGURE 23.24.

Editing the RunSQL function.

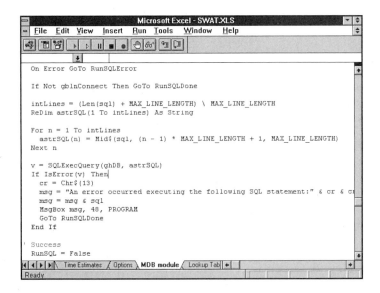

The *Retrieve* Function

Using the `RunSQL` function, you can execute SQL statements, including `SELECT` statements that return results. But where do the results go?

If you use the `SQLBind` function, you can indicate before calling `SQLExecQuery` where the results should be placed. Then the results are automatically written to the worksheet when you call `SQLExecQuery`.

The other method, as I've used here, is to call the `SQLRetrieve` function after the `SQLExecQuery` call specifying the area in the worksheet to write results to. With this method, results of the `SELECT` statement are buffered until you explicitly ask that they be transferred into the worksheet.

> **NOTE**
>
> You have no obligation to retrieve the buffered results. If you call `SQLExecQuery` a second time, any previous buffered results are discarded.

The `Retrieve` function in Listing 23.16 takes a range object as its argument to indicate where in the worksheet the data should be written to. The function doesn't do much else other than hand the argument over to the `SQLRetrieve` function along with the connection ID.

Listing 23.16. The `Retrieve` function.

```
Function Retrieve(rng As Range) As Integer

  Dim v As Variant

' Assume failure
  Retrieve = True

  On Error GoTo RetrieveError

  If Not gblnConnect Then GoTo RetrieveDone

  v = SQLRetrieve(ghDB, rng)
  If IsError(v) Then
    MsgBox "An error occurred retrieving results of a database query.", 48,
    ➡ PROGRAM

    GoTo RetrieveDone
  End If

' Success
  Retrieve = False

RetrieveDone:
  Exit Function

RetrieveError:
  MsgBox Error$(), 48, PROGRAM
  Resume RetrieveDone

End Function
```

The Issues Module

Now let's put your simplified database interface to work. Create a second module worksheet named *Issues module*. Within this module, you will create the following procedures:

`ConnectSWAT`	Connect to the S.W.A.T. database
`ImportIssues`	Import data from the Issue table
`Where`	Add criteria to the WHERE clause of the SELECT statement used to return Issue data
`LastImportedRow`	Last row in the worksheet with imported data
`Clear`	Erase imported data
`ExportIssues`	Write data back to the Issue table

Declare the PROGRAM constant in the declaration section, as shown in Listing 23.17.

Listing 23.17. Declarations in the Issues module.

```
' S.W.A.T. Issues module

' Import/Export issue data into the Time Estimates worksheet

  Global Const PROGRAM = "S.W.A.T."
```

The *ConnectSWAT* Function

The first procedure in the module is the ConnectSWAT function, shown in Listing 23.18. It reads the database directory, database filename, and system database values from the Options worksheet and calls the Connect subroutine to establish a connection to the S.W.A.T. database.

Listing 23.18. The ConnectSWAT function.

```
Function ConnectSWAT() As Integer

' Connect to the S.W.A.T. database

  Dim wsOptions As Worksheet

  Dim strDatabaseDirectory As String
  Dim strDatabase As String
  Dim strSystemDatabase As String

' Assume failure
  ConnectSWAT = True

  On Error GoTo ConnectSWATError
```

```
' Get the option worksheet
  Set wsOptions = Worksheets("Options")

' Read the values in the Options worksheet
  strDatabaseDirectory = wsOptions.Range("DatabaseDirectory").Value
  strDatabase = wsOptions.Range("Database").Value
  strSystemDatabase = wsOptions.Range("SystemDatabase").Value

' Connect to the database
  Connect strDatabase, strDatabaseDirectory, strSystemDatabase

' Return success if connected
  ConnectSWAT = (Not gblnConnect)

ConnectSWATDone:
  Exit Function

ConnectSWATError:
  MsgBox Error$(), 48, PROGRAM
  Resume ConnectSWATDone

End Function
```

The *ImportIssues* Subroutine

The ImportIssues subroutine (shown in Listing 23.19) generates a SELECT statement to return data from the Issue table in the S.W.A.T. database. The SELECT statement is generated because the WHERE clause will differ depending on what criteria have been indicated in the drop-down controls on the Options worksheet.

Listing 23.19. The ImportIssues subroutine.

```
Sub ImportIssues()

  Dim ws As Worksheet

  Dim sql As String
  Dim whr As String
  Dim sz As String

  Dim z As Integer

  On Error GoTo ImportIssuesError

' Erase the current data
  Clear

' Connect to the S.W.A.T. database
  If ConnectSWAT() Then GoTo ImportIssuesDone

' Get the Time Estimates worksheet
```

continues

Listing 23.19. continued

```
Set ws = Worksheets("Time Estimates")

' Generate a SELECT statement based on the filter values in the Options
' worksheet
sql = "SELECT IssueID, Title, Budget, Actual FROM Issue"
whr = ""

' Construct the WHERE clause for any criteria that has been set on the
' Options worksheet
If Where("cboType", "TypeName", "Type", whr) Then GoTo ImportIssuesDone
If Where("cboStatus", "StatusName", "Status", whr) Then GoTo
➥ ImportIssuesDone
If Where("cboAssignedTo", "Username", "AssignedTo", whr) Then GoTo
➥ ImportIssuesDone
If Where("cboPriority", "PriorityName", "Priority", whr) Then GoTo
➥ ImportIssuesDone
If Where("cboCategory", "CategoryName", "CategoryID", whr) Then GoTo
➥ ImportIssuesDone

If Len(whr) > 0 Then
  sql = sql & " WHERE " & whr
End If

' Execute the SELECT statement
z = RunSQL(sql & ";")
If z Then GoTo ImportIssuesDone

' Put the results in the Time Estimates worksheet
z = Retrieve(ws.Range("ImportCell"))

' Find out how many rows were imported
intLastRow = LastImportedRow()

' Enter an equation to sum the Budget and Actual columns
ws.Cells(intLastRow + 2, 2).Value = "Total:"
ws.Cells(intLastRow + 2, 3).Formula = "=SUM(C5:C" & intLastRow & ")"
ws.Cells(intLastRow + 2, 4).Formula = "=SUM(D5:D" & intLastRow & ")"

ImportIssuesDone:
  On Error Resume Next
' Disconnect from the S.W.A.T. database
  Disconnect
  Exit Sub

ImportIssuesError:
  MsgBox Error$(), 48, PROGRAM
  Resume ImportIssuesDone

End Sub
```

The ImportIssues subroutine first calls the Clear subroutine to erase any data that was imported from a previous run of the ImportIssues subroutine.

```
' Erase the current data
  Clear
```

Next, a connection to the S.W.A.T. database is established, exiting early if the connection was not accomplished.

```
' Connect to the S.W.A.T. database
  If ConnectSWAT() Then GoTo ImportIssuesDone
```

A worksheet variable is set to the Time Estimates worksheet.

```
' Get the Time Estimates worksheet
  Set ws = Worksheets("Time Estimates")
```

The SQL SELECT statement is generated next in the SQL string variable. The statement returns four fields from the Issue table.

```
' Generate a SELECT statement based on the filter values in the Options
' worksheet
  sql = "SELECT IssueID, Title, Budget, Actual FROM Issue"
  whr = ""
```

Next, a series of calls is made to the Where subroutine. Each call has the potential of appending a criteria expression to the whr string variable, such as Type = 1.

```
' Construct the WHERE clause for any criteria that has been set on the
' Options worksheet
  If Where("cboType", "TypeName", "Type", whr) Then GoTo ImportIssuesDone
  If Where("cboStatus", "StatusName", "Status", whr) Then GoTo
  ➥ ImportIssuesDone
  If Where("cboAssignedTo", "Username", "AssignedTo", whr) Then GoTo
  ➥ ImportIssuesDone
  If Where("cboPriority", "PriorityName", "Priority", whr) Then GoTo
  ➥ ImportIssuesDone
  If Where("cboCategory", "CategoryName", "CategoryID", whr) Then GoTo
  ➥ ImportIssuesDone
```

If the whr variable received any expressions, the SQL string is appended with a WHERE clause.

```
  If Len(whr) > 0 Then
    sql = sql & " WHERE " & whr
  End If
```

The generated SELECT statement is executed by calling the RunSQL function.

```
' Execute the SELECT statement
  z = RunSQL(sql & ";")
  If z Then GoTo ImportIssuesDone
```

The results of the SELECT statement are entered in the Time Estimates worksheet in the place marked by the ImportCell name.

```
' Put the results in the Time Estimates worksheet
  z = Retrieve(ws.Range("ImportCell"))
```

Next, the last row that contains data is determined by calling the `LastImportedRow` function.

```
' Find out how many rows were imported
  intLastRow = LastImportedRow()
```

Two rows that follow the last row of imported data, a `Total:` string is entered in column two along with equations in columns three and four to calculate the total budgeted and actual programming time for the imported issues.

```
' Enter an equation to sum the Budget and Actual columns
  ws.Cells(intLastRow + 2, 2).Value = "Total:"
  ws.Cells(intLastRow + 2, 3).Formula = "=SUM(C5:C" & intLastRow & ")"
  ws.Cells(intLastRow + 2, 4).Formula = "=SUM(D5:D" & intLastRow & ")"
```

In the Done section of the subroutine, the connection to the S.W.A.T. database is terminated.

```
ImportIssuesDone:
  On Error Resume Next
' Disconnect from the S.W.A.T. database
  Disconnect
  Exit Sub
```

The *Where* Function

The `Where` function (shown in Listing 23.20) adds an expression to the end of the `whr` string variable passed as its fourth argument.

Listing 23.20. The `Where` function.

```
Function Where(strDropdown As String, strRangeName As String,
➡ strField As String, whr As String) As Integer

' Append an expression to the WHERE clause for selecting Issue table records

  Dim wsLookup As Worksheet
  Dim wsOptions As Worksheet

  Dim intListIndex As Integer
  Dim intRow As Integer
  Dim intCode As Integer

' Assume failure
  Where = True

  On Error GoTo WhereError

' Get the worksheets
  Set wsLookup = Worksheets("Lookup Tables")
  Set wsOptions = Worksheets("Options")

  intListIndex = wsOptions.DrawingObjects(strDropdown).ListIndex
  If intListIndex > 1 Then
```

```
        intRow = wsLookup.Range(strRangeName).Row
        intRow = intRow + intListIndex - 1
        intCode = wsLookup.Cells(intRow, 1)

        If Len(whr) > 0 Then
          whr = whr & " AND "
        End If
        whr = whr & strField & " = " & intCode
      End If

      Where = False

  WhereDone:
    Exit Function

  WhereError:
    MsgBox Error$(), 48, PROGRAM
    Resume WhereDone

  End Function
```

The `Where` function uses the Lookup Tables worksheet to read the numeric code associated with a selection made in a drop-down list on the Options worksheet. The subroutine starts by setting worksheet variables to both of these worksheets.

```
' Get the worksheets
  Set wsLookup = Worksheets("Lookup Tables")
  Set wsOptions = Worksheets("Options")
```

The `strDropdown` argument indicates which drop-down control you need to look at in the Options worksheet. The `intListIndex` variable is assigned to the value returned by the drop-down control's `ListIndex` property.

The value will be 0 if no item was selected, 1 if the blank line was selected, or a value greater than 1 if a selection was made from the items in the list.

```
  intListIndex = wsOptions.DrawingObjects(strDropdown).ListIndex
  If intListIndex > 1 Then
```

If an item was selected, the appropriate row is calculated to find the corresponding numeric code for the selected item. The number is read from the Lookup table's worksheet into the `intCode` variable.

```
    intRow = wsLookup.Range(strRangeName).Row
    intRow = intRow + intListIndex - 1
    intCode = wsLookup.Cells(intRow, 1)
```

Before appending an expression to the `whr` string variable, it is checked to see whether it already contains an expression. If so, the `AND` operator is added to separate the two expressions and indicate that both the former and latter criteria must be met.

```
    If Len(whr) > 0 Then
      whr = whr & " AND "
    End If
```

Finally, the expression is appended to the whr string variable.

```
    whr = whr & strField & " = " & intCode
  End If
```

The *LastImportedRow* Function

The LastImportedRow function determines which row in the Time Estimates worksheet is the last row that contains imported data.

The function starts with the first row in the worksheet that potentially contains imported data; then it checks each value in column A to find a value of 0. (A blank cell returns the value of 0.) Once the 0 is found, the function can deduce that the row before it is the last imported row.

The LastImportedRow function is shown in Listing 23.21.

Listing 23.21. The LastImportedRow function.

```
Function LastImportedRow() As Integer

' Count how many rows were imported

  Dim ws As Worksheet

  Dim lngIssueID As Long
  Dim intRow As Integer

  On Error GoTo LastImportedRowError

  Set ws = Worksheets("Time Estimates")

  intRow = 5
  Do
    lngIssueID = ws.Cells(intRow, 1)
    If lngIssueID = 0 Then Exit Do

    intRow = intRow + 1
  Loop

  LastImportedRow = intRow - 1

LastImportedRowDone:
  Exit Function

LastImportedRowError:
  MsgBox Error$(), 48, PROGRAM
  Resume LastImportedRowDone

End Function
```

The *Clear* Subroutine

The Clear subroutine (shown in Listing 23.22) uses the ClearContents method to erase any data imported into the Time Estimates worksheet.

Listing 23.22. The Clear subroutine.

```
Sub Clear()

' Erase the imported rows from the Time Estimates worksheet

  Dim ws As Worksheet
  Dim rng As Range

  Dim intStartRow As Integer
  Dim intEndRow As Integer

  On Error GoTo ClearError

  Set ws = Worksheets("Time Estimates")
  intStartRow = ws.Range("ImportCell").Row
  intEndRow = ws.UsedRange.Rows.Count

  If intEndRow >= intStartRow Then
    Set rng = ws.Range(Cells(intStartRow, 1), Cells(intEndRow, 4))
    rng.ClearContents
  End If

ClearDone:
  On Error Resume Next
  Exit Sub

ClearError:
  MsgBox Error$(), 48, PROGRAM
  Resume ClearDone

End Sub
```

The *ExportIssues* Subroutine

The ExportIssues subroutine, shown in Listing 23.23, utilizes the SQL UPDATE statement to modify records in the S.W.A.T. database. The values in the Budget and Actual columns are written to the appropriate records in the Issue table.

Listing 23.23. The ExportIssues subroutine.

```
Sub ExportIssues()

' Update the Issue table in the database with the values in the Budget and
' Actual columns
```

continues

Listing 23.23. continued

```
    Dim ws As Worksheet
    Dim rng As Range

    Dim sql As String
    Dim intStartRow As Integer
    Dim intEndRow As Integer

    Dim lngIssueID As Long
    Dim sngBudget As Single
    Dim sngActual As Single

    On Error GoTo ExportIssuesError

    Set ws = Worksheets("Time Estimates")
    intStartRow = ws.Range("ImportCell").Row

' This may be larger than the actual number of rows currently in the
' Time Estimates worksheet.
    intEndRow = ws.UsedRange.Rows.Count

' Connect to the S.W.A.T. database
    If ConnectSWAT() Then GoTo ExportIssuesDone

    For intRow = intStartRow To intEndRow
      lngIssueID = ws.Cells(intRow, 1)

    ' Check to see if we moved past the last row with data
      If lngIssueID = 0 Then Exit For

      sngBudget = ws.Cells(intRow, 3)
      sngActual = ws.Cells(intRow, 4)

    ' Create an UPDATE statement for the current row
      sql = "UPDATE Issue SET "
      sql = sql & "Budget = " & sngBudget & ", "
      sql = sql & "Actual = " & sngActual & " "
      sql = sql & "WHERE IssueID = " & lngIssueID

    ' Execute the UPDATE statement
      z = RunSQL(sql & ";")
      If z Then GoTo ExportIssuesDone
    Next intRow

ExportIssuesDone:
    On Error Resume Next
' Disconnect from the S.W.A.T. database
    Disconnect
    Exit Sub

ExportIssuesError:
    MsgBox Error$(), 48, PROGRAM
    Resume ExportIssuesDone

End Sub
```

The `ExportIssues` subroutine starts by setting a worksheet variable to the Time Estimates worksheet. The `intStartRow` variable is set to the first row that receives imported data, as marked by the `ImportCell` name.

```
Set ws = Worksheets("Time Estimates")
intStartRow = ws.Range("ImportCell").Row
```

The `intEndRow` variable is set to a value that is potentially the last row of imported data. The `UsedRange` property of the worksheet object returns the area used in the worksheet. This doesn't reliably tell you which is the last row of imported data, because an import run before may have contained more rows than is currently in the worksheet.

```
' This may be larger than the actual number of rows currently in the
' Time Estimates worksheet.
intEndRow = ws.UsedRange.Rows.Count
```

Next, the subroutine connects to the S.W.A.T. database:

```
' Connect to the S.W.A.T. database
If ConnectSWAT() Then GoTo ExportIssuesDone
```

Then a loop begins to traverse the rows of imported data:

```
For intRow = intStartRow To intEndRow
```

Inside the loop, the `IssueID` field value for the associated record in the Issue table is read from the A column.

```
lngIssueID = ws.Cells(intRow, 1)
```

If the value read is 0, you've come to an empty row and the loop can terminate.

```
' Check to see if we moved past the last row with data
If lngIssueID = 0 Then Exit For
```

Next, the values in columns three and four are read into the `sngBudget` and `sngActual` variables.

```
sngBudget = ws.Cells(intRow, 3)
sngActual = ws.Cells(intRow, 4)
```

An SQL `UPDATE` statement is generated that updates the Budget and Actual fields for the record in the Issue table with the `IssueID` value read from column A.

```
' Create an UPDATE statement for the current row
sql = "UPDATE Issue SET "
sql = sql & "Budget = " & sngBudget & ", "
sql = sql & "Actual = " & sngActual & " "
sql = sql & "WHERE IssueID = " & lngIssueID
```

The `RunSQL` function is called to execute the `UPDATE` statement. Then the loop continues for each row of imported data.

```
' Execute the UPDATE statement
z = RunSQL(sql & ";")
If z Then GoTo ExportIssuesDone
Next intRow
```

Enabling the Time Estimate Worksheet Buttons

Before the command buttons on the Time Estimate worksheet will work, you need to assign the appropriate subroutines from the Issue module to them.

Switch back to the Time Estimate worksheet. Click the right mouse button on the Import Issues button. In the pop-up menu, select Assign Macro, as shown in Figure 23.25.

FIGURE 23.25.

Opening the Assign Macro dialog box.

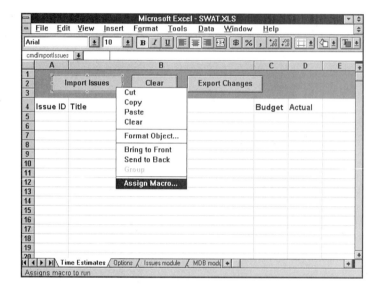

In the Assign Macro dialog box, select the ImportIssue subroutine and click OK, as shown in Figure 23.26.

FIGURE 23.26.

Assigning the ImportIssue subroutine to the Import Issue button.

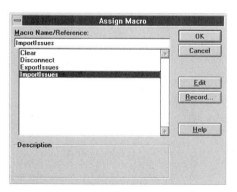

Assign the Clear subroutine to the Clear button and the ExportIssues subroutine to the Export Changes button.

Running the Time Estimates Workbook

The first time I clicked the Import Issues button, I received some odd results. Some of the imported data was in the wrong columns in the Time Estimates worksheet!

Upon investigation, I found that if the Budget and Actual fields in the Issue table contained Null values, the import performs as expected. I corrected this by running an update query in the S.W.A.T. database in Access to enter zero values in any of the fields that were Null. I reran the import in the Time Estimates worksheet and after that, everything came in fine.

By default, any new records entered into the Issue table have the Budget and Actual fields set to 0, so this problem occurred only with records entered before the Budget and Actual fields were added to the table.

Outside of that problem, the program worked as expected in my testing. The Time Estimates workbook doesn't do much in the way of showing off Excel's analytical powers, but you've accomplished the first essential step in making Excel read and write data into an Access database.

I'll leave the rest up to you. Add fields to the Issue table as needed to track the information that is of concern to you and the folks with whom you work. Then find creative ways to work with this data in Excel to find out what this data can tell you about your software projects.

Summary

In this chapter, you enhanced the S.W.A.T. issue tracking system with capabilities provided by Word and Excel.

Here's a log of your explorations along the way. You

- Created a field report template in Word
- Created the Field Report dialog box in Access
- Learned how to program the `Word.Basic` OLE automation object
- Wrote code to open and print Word documents from Access
- Added Budget and Actual fields to the Issue table
- Created the Time Estimate, Options, and Lookup Tables worksheets
- Discovered the Excel SQL functions
- Wrote a simplified interface to use the Excel SQL functions

■ Wrote code to import data into an Excel worksheet using SQL statements generated at run time

■ Wrote code to export modified data back into the Access database using the SQL UPDATE statement

From Casual Programmer to Professional Programmer

A question that programmers often hear is this:

"How does one become a professional programmer?"

Programming is a creative profession that is both rewarding and challenging. So it makes sense that a programmer is asked this question just as a filmmaker would get asked, "How does one get into movies?" or a writer is asked, "How does one get into writing?"

If you are a casual programmer wanting to make the move to professional programming, I have good news for you. You are already doing exactly what you should be doing—that's writing programs.

The important thing to do is keep the focus on acquiring skills and just keep writing programs. As you become more and more capable, you'll be able to snag that job opportunity when it pops up. When you already have the skills that employers need, it's a lot less difficult to find the type of work that you want to do. You may even change roles in your present job as your co-workers learn about the valuable skills you have already acquired.

Don't wait for someone to tell you to write a program. A writer doesn't wait for someone to tell him or her to write a novel; a writer will just do it.

Some of your early efforts may be total flops. A tendency that newer programmers have is to write about 10 times as many lines in their programs than is actually required to get the job done. Eventually your program may get so complicated that even you don't understand it anymore.

It's okay!

The largest adjustments to your programming skills will occur from the lessons you learn when things don't turn out exactly as you wish they would.

Try to keep your programming projects at an accomplishable scale. Word and Excel are wonderful programming environments for writing quick little utilities. As you move on up to larger projects, divide the work into smaller units so you can feel good about each milestone that you reach.

Read books and magazines—lots of them. If courses are available at your local college, take the time to attend them. Be sure to enhance that experience by reading as many programming books as you can get your hands on. Books are relatively cheap compared to other forms of education. Moreover, by spending time with books, you will be improving your reading comprehension skills, and that is critical to becoming a successful professional programmer.

Share your programs with others. You'll learn from the critiques they give you about your work (and that hurts sometimes). Sharing your programs is also important in that it lets people know about what you've learned to do. If you have access to online services, upload your programs so that other folks have a chance to take a look at them. You'll get some valuable tips and earn some admiration, too.

Finally, write programs that are fun to write and fun to use. To motivate yourself to dig through all this technical stuff, you're going to need to reward yourself regularly. What better way to do that than write the programs that you would like to see on your own computer.

You are definitely on your way. As soon as folks know what you can do, you'll have too many programs to write and too many books to read to keep up with it all. No matter how busy you become, you're going to like programming, I promise.

PART IV

Appendix

A   Using the Accompanying CD-ROM Software

Using the Accompanying CD-ROM Software

All of the programs developed in the chapters within this book are included on the companion CD-ROM, ready to run and examine. The CD-ROM is a read-only form of media, so you will need to copy the files to your hard drive before you can use and modify them.

The files on the disc are uncompressed and installed into a PMO directory on your hard drive by the Install program. The total disk space used after the files are installed is 8.5 megabytes.

To run the Install program, do the following:

1. Put the companion CD-ROM in your CD-ROM drive.
2. In Program Manager, select the File|Run command.
3. Enter `d:\install` in the Run dialog box and click OK. (Although this is typically drive letter D, use the appropriate drive letter for your CD-ROM drive.)

Table A.1 indicates where you can find each of the projects in the book. Generally, each program can be found in a directory named after the chapter in which the program is created. In the case of projects such as Address Book that span multiple chapters, the files are located in a directory named after the first chapter about the project.

Table A.1. Where to find the programs in the PMO directory.

Program	Directory
Good Morning	PMO\CH01
Don's Macros	PMO\CH02
Study Mate	PMO\CH02
Login Form Example	PMO\CH03
Pretty Printer	PMO\CH04
Calendar Wizard	PMO\CH05
Sticky Notes	PMO\CH06
List Selection Dialog Boxes	PMO\CH07
Screen Writer Utilities	PMO\CH08
The Learning Computer	PMO\CH09
Secret Diary	PMO\CH10
Excel Time Killers	PMO\CH11
Address Book	PMO\CH13

Program	Directory
Picture Builder+	PMO\CH15
Survey Wizard	PMO\CH16
S.W.A.T.	PMO\CH21

Note that several of the projects are Excel or Access add-in libraries. If you've installed the add-ins to use the software, you will have to uninstall the add-ins temporarily in order to open the workbook or database files to examine and modify the programs.

Following are instructions for getting started with each program. See the chapters for complete details.

Good Morning (Chapter 1)

Application: Excel
Directory: PMO\CH01
Files: SINGTO.XLS

The Good Morning program is an introductory program example written in Excel VBA. The program displays a short song that is sung to the tune of "Happy Birthday."

To run the program, load the SINGTO.XLS worksheet. Select the View|Debug Window command. In the Immediate pane of the Debug Window, enter Main and press the Enter key.

Don's Macros (Chapter 2)

Application: Word
Directory: PMO\CH02
Files: DONNRML.DOT

The DONNRML.DOT file is a template containing two Word Basic macros, FindStarMarker and WordCount.

The FindStarMarker macro searches for the next occurrence of three star characters (***) in the document, which is used to identify an unfinished section in the document.

The WordCount macro displays a dialog box into which the user enters a word. The macro then displays a count of how many times the word occurs in the document.

To use the template, copy the DONNRML.DOT file into the TEMPLATE directory. When creating a Word document, select Donnrml from the list of templates in Word's New dialog box.

The DONNRML.DOT template also contains a custom toolbar that can be used to activate the macros. To display the toolbar, select the View|Toolbars command and check the box next to Don's Macros in the Toolbars list box.

Study Mate (Chapter 2)

Application:	Word
Directory:	PMO\CH02
Files:	STDYMATE.DOT
	SPACE.DOC

The STDYMATE.DOT file is a Word template that is used to create a set of flash cards and randomly display them using Word. Study Mate is a useful program for preparing for an exam.

To use Study Mate, copy the STDYMATE.DOT file into the TEMPLATE directory in the directory in which you installed Word on your hard drive. Select File|New in Word to create a new document. In the New dialog box, select Stdymate from the list of available templates.

Study Mate works best when you do the following:

Select the View|Page Layout command so that Word displays the document in pages. The template has the page height and width set to display a page with the proportions of an index card.

Turn off any toolbars that are displayed by using the View|Toolbars command. Turn on the Study Mate toolbar, which displays the Study Mate buttons to save your document, pick a random card, show an answer card, and move through the cards in sequential order.

You might also turn off the status bar and the vertical and horizontal scroll bars. These options are set from the Options dialog box displayed when selecting the View|Options command.

Finally, resize the Word window to about the size that a single flash card is displayed at a time. Figure A.1 shows Word configured and ready to go for a round with Study Mate.

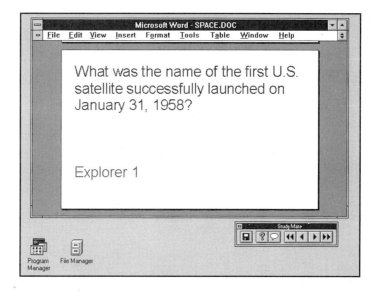

When creating a set of flash cards, the first page in your document is the first question. The second page is the answer card for the first page. Pages 3 and 4 are the question and answer for the second card, and so on.

Use Alt-Q to use a Word style for entering questions. Use Alt-A to use a Word style for entering answers. I like to include the question on the answer card.

Click the Random Card button on the Study Mate toolbar to have Study Mate randomly select a question. The SPACE.DOC file is an example set of Study Mate flash cards.

Login Form Example (Chapter 3)

Application: Access
Directory: PMO\CH03
Files: DIARY.MDB

The DIARY.MDB database contains an introductory program, which displays a Login form that prompts for a username and password. The program gives the user three attempts to enter a valid username and password.

To run the program, open the database in Access. Run the `Macro1` macro, or open the Login form using the database container. To change the usernames and passwords, open the Login table in datasheet view.

Pretty Printer (Chapter 4)

Application:	Excel
Directory:	PMO\CH04
Files:	PRETTY.XLA
	PRETTY.XLS
	DATA.XLS
	QUERY1.QRY

The Pretty Printer program is an Excel menu add-in that is used to beautify a worksheet of imported data in order to produce a quick report.

The PRETTY.XLA file is a compiled version of the workbook. Open PRETTY.XLS if you want to look at the program code.

To install Pretty Printer as a menu add-in, select the **T**ools|**A**dd-**I**ns command. In the Add-Ins dialog box, click the Browse button and locate the PRETTY.XLA file. Excel adds Pretty Printer as an available add-in within the Add-Ins Available list box in the Add-Ins dialog box. Close Excel and restart it. Now, under the Tools menu, you see an entry for Pretty Printer.

To use Pretty Printer, you first need to import some data into a worksheet. You can open the DATA.XLS worksheet, which already has some sample data, or you can import your own.

The data in DATA.XLS comes from the Access Northwind Traders example database and was derived from the query stored in QUERY1.QRY. You can load this query by using the **F**ile|**O**pen command in Microsoft Query. Microsoft Query asks you to redefine the data source. Select Microsoft Access 2.0 Databases as the ODBC data source, and select the NWIND.MDB database that is in the SAMPAPPS directory where you installed Access.

See the chapter for complete instructions on importing data into Excel using Microsoft Query.

When the data is in your worksheet, select the **T**ools|**P**retty Printer command to activate the Pretty Printer program and modify the current worksheet.

Calendar Wizard (Chapter 5)

Application: Excel
Directory: PMO\CH05
Files: CALWIZ.XLA
CALWIZ.XLS
CALWIZ.BMP

The Calendar Wizard program is an Excel menu add-in that generates a calendar month page as a new worksheet in the current workbook.

To install Calendar Wizard as a menu add-in, select the **Tools|Add-I**ns command. In the Add-Ins dialog box, click the Browse button and locate the CALWIZ.XLA file. Excel adds Calendar Wizard, preselected, as one of the available add-ins in the Add-Ins dialog box. Close the dialog box and exit Excel.

The next time you restart Excel, the Calendar Wizard command will be available from the Tools menu. Select the **Tools|**Calendar Wizard command and the Calendar Wizard dialog box is displayed as shown in Figure A.2.

FIGURE A.2.

Running Calendar Wizard.

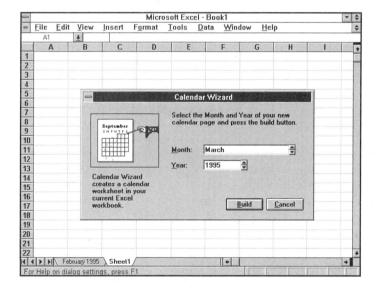

Select the month and year for your calendar page and press the Build button. Calendar Wizard generates a calendar page that you can send to the printer with the File|Print command.

The CALWIZ.XLA file is a compiled version of the program. To examine and work with the code, you need to open the CALWIZ.XLS workbook. The CALWIZ.BMP file is the bitmap used on the Calendar Wizard dialog box.

Sticky Notes (Chapter 6)

Application:	Access
Directory:	PMO\CH06
Files:	NOTES.MDB
	NOTES1.BMP
	NOTES2.BMP
	NOTES3.BMP
	NOTES4.BMP

Sticky Notes isn't an application on its own; it's a component that you can add to your own Access projects. Sticky Notes enables you to leave pop-up notes on the different forms within your Access projects.

The NOTES.MDB database contains a test form named _TestForm1. Open the form to see Sticky Notes work, as shown in Figure A.3.

FIGURE A.3.

Opening the _TestForm1 form to try out Sticky Notes.

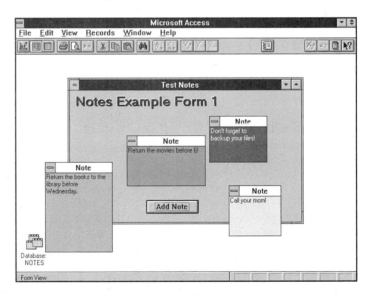

Click the Add Note button to display the Sticky Notes dialog box, which enables you to select from one of four note styles. Sticky Notes are removed by simply closing the note window while it is being displayed.

NOTE1.BMP, NOTE2.BMP, NOTE3.BMP, and NOTE4.BMP are the bitmaps used in the Sticky Notes dialog box.

See Chapter 6 for details on how to add Sticky Notes to your database projects.

List Selection Dialog Boxes (Chapter 7)

Application:	Access
Directory:	PMO\CH07
Files:	LISTSLCT.MDB
	UP.BMP
	DOWN.BMP

The LISTSLCT.MDB database contains a List Select form and a List Select module that together are used to display list selection dialog boxes in your Access projects. A list selection dialog box is one in which items from a list on the left can be selected by moving them to a list on the right.

To see the List Selection dialog box in action, open the LISTSLCT.MDB database in Access. Open the Test module and select the **View|I**mmediate Window command. There are three test procedures that show off different capabilities of the List Selection dialog box.

Test1	Show a single column list selection dialog box
Test2	Show a multiple column list selection dialog box
Test3	Load a list selection dialog box using a SELECT expression

To run either of the tests, enter the subroutine name in the Immediate Window and press Enter. The List Select dialog box is displayed, as shown in Figure A.4.

FIGURE A.4.

Testing the List Select dialog box.

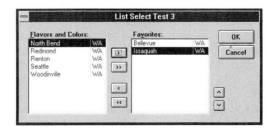

Study the example procedures and the chapter to find out how to use List Selection dialog boxes in your Access project.

Screen Writer Utilities (Chapter 8)

Application: Word
Directory: PMO\CH08
Files: SCRNWRT.DOT
                WRDASSOC.DAT
                PROFILE.DOT
                DIALECT.DAT
                SCRIPT.DOC
                WRDASSOC.MDB

The Screen Writer Utilities is a mixed collection of tools that a screen writer might use to help him or her write a movie script.

The SCRNWRT.DOT file is a Word template containing the Word Association Game and Auto Dialect programs. To use the template, copy it into the TEMPLATE directory of the directory that you installed Microsoft Word into. Then, base your new document on the Scrnwrt template.

The SCRNWRT.DOT template has its own toolbar. Select the View|Toolbars command and turn on the Screen Writer toolbar in the Toolbars dialog box.

Click the button with a picture of a bell to play the Word Association Game. The Word Association Game displays four randomly drawn words from the WRDASSOC.DAT text file (see Figure A.5). This file must be in your current working directory, or the program will display a message indicating it can't find the file.

The Auto Dialect program uses Word's AutoCorrect feature to replace a word with another word or phrase. Click the happy face button to load the AutoCorrect definitions stored in the DIALECT.DAT text file. Click the unhappy face button to unload the AutoCorrect definitions. The DIALECT.DAT file must be in the current working directory or a File not found error message will appear.

Both WRDASSOC.DAT and DIALECT.DAT are text files that you can edit in Notepad.

SCRNWRT.DOT also contains a set of Word styles that are helpful in formatting a document to look like a movie script. See the chapter for a list of which styles are defined and what they do.

FIGURE A.5.
*Using the Word
Association Game from
SCRNWRT.DOT.*

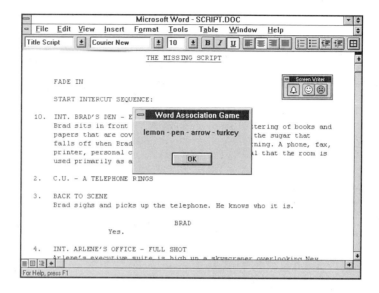

The PROFILE.DOT Word template is an example Word form used to collect information about a character in your screenplay.

The WRDASSOC.MDB file is a second version of the Word Association Game, written in Access Basic for the Try This answer 8.2. The words for the program are stored in a Word table within the database. To run the program, open the Module1 module. Open the Immediate window, type WordAssociationGame, and press Enter.

The Learning Computer (Chapter 9)

> Application: Access
> Directory: PMO\CH09
> Files: LEARN.MDB

The Learning Computer is a computer game in which the computer asks you a series of questions to try to guess what you are thinking. When the computer is wrong, it asks you to enter what the answer is, as well as a question that it can ask the next time around to point to the same conclusion. In this way the game "learns" as it plays.

To play the game, open the LEARN.MDB database in Access. An AutoExec macro is used to immediately start the program and display the dialog box shown in Figure A.6.

Select a category from the list, and click the Play button. You can add and delete categories of your own by using the Add and Delete buttons.

FIGURE A.6.

Playing the Learning Computer game.

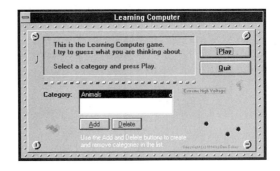

Secret Diary (Chapter 10)

Application:	Visual Basic and Access
Directory:	PMO\CH10
Files:	DIARY.EXE
	DIARY.MDB
	DIARY.MAK
	CHNGPWRD.FRM
	DIARY.FRM
	JUMP.FRM
	LOGIN.FRM
	NEWDIARY.FRM
	PASSWORD.FRM
	LIBRARY.BAS
	DIARY.ICO

The Secret Diary program is written in Visual Basic 3.0 using the Access 2.0 Compatibility Layer. To run the program, you need the following DLLs in your WINDOWS\SYSTEM directory:

    MSABC200.DLL
    MSAJT112.DLL
    MSAJT200.DLL
    VBDB300.DLL
    VBRUN300.DLL

You also need SHARE.EXE, which is typically found in your DOS directory. The JET database engine DLLs require that you have an entry in your computer's AUTOEXEC.BAT file similar to the following:

```
C:\DOS\SHARE.EXE /L:500
```

We have installed the appropriate DLL files to run this program. The install only placed the DLLs on your system if they were not there previously, or were newer than your existing versions of those files.

An icon for DIARY.EXE has been created in Program Manager within the group "Programming Microsoft Office."

Double-click the Diary icon in Program Manager to run the program. Note that the database, DIARY.MDB, must be in the same directory as the DIARY.EXE file.

The program displays a dialog box to enter your name and password. You need to create a new diary first, so click the New Diary button. In the New Diary dialog box, enter your name, password, and password again in the Verify text box.

Back at the Secret Diary dialog box, you can now click OK to open your new diary and start making entries. See Chapter 10 for additional details about using the program.

The DIARY.MAK file is the Visual Basic project file for the program. To examine the program, open this file in Visual Basic. Visual Basic loads the .FRM and .BAS files into the Project window.

The DIARY.ICO file is the icon used for the program.

Excel Time Killers (Chapters 11 and 12)

Application: Excel
Directory: PMO\CH11
Files: GAMES.XLA
GAMES.XLS
NUM.BMP
DIGIT.BMP

The Excel Time Killers is a set of simple but challenging games that you can load into Excel as an add-in. This enables you to take time out and play the games while any other workbook is loaded into Excel.

To install the add-in, select the Tools|Add-Ins command. Click the Browse button in the Add-Ins dialog box. Find the GAMES.XLA file in the Browse dialog box and click OK. In the Add-Ins dialog box, make sure that Time Killers is checked and close the dialog box.

Excel adds a Games menu to the toolbar with commands to play each of the games, as shown in Figure A.7.

FIGURE A.7.
The Time Killer games are selected from a Games menu.

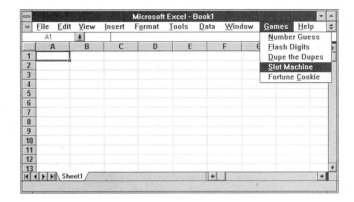

In the Number Guess game, you are given six tries to guess a number from 1 to 100. The computer tells you whether your guess is high or low; but, watch out because every once in a while, the computer lies.

In the Flash Digits game, press Enter repeatedly to see a series of digits flash by one at a time. When the digit window is clear again, enter the complete number if you can remember it. The game tracks your wins and losses. The more you play, the longer the number sequences get.

Dupe the Dupes is also a simple but challenging memory game, like Flash Digits. Press Enter repeatedly (or click the Next button), and the game displays a stream of words one at a time. At the first occurrence of a duplicate word, you are supposed to click the Dupe button. If you don't catch it, and click Next instead, you lose!

In Slot Machine, the player starts with $100. Click Play to deposit $2 into the slot machine. If you match symbols in the slot machine windows, you win and the slot machine displays your earnings. Either way, your current cash in pocket is updated in the dialog box. The trick here is to quit while you are ahead.

The Fortune Cookie command displays a dialog box with your fortune.

Each of the games are modifiable by working on the source code version of the workbook, GAMES.XLS. For example, you can tweak the loss/earning ratios in Slot Machine, or add fortunes to the Fortune Cookie program. See Chapters 11 and 12 for full details.

The NUM.BMP and DIGIT.BMP files are the bitmaps used in the Number Guess and Flash Digits games.

Address Book (Chapters 13 and 14)

Application:	Access
Directory:	PMO\CH13
Files:	ADDRESS.MDB
	TEMPLATE.MDB

The Address Book program is a sophisticated approach to storing and searching for people and address information in a computer address book.

To use the application, open the ADDRESS.MDB database in Access. An AutoExec macro starts the program right away.

The Address Search form is displayed with many combo boxes, one each for the various fields that are used in an address book entry. To perform a search, enter any criteria in the combo boxes and click the Search button.

The results list on the bottom half of the form displays any address book entries that match each of the criteria entered at the top of the form.

Use the buttons at the bottom of the form to add, edit, and delete address book entries, as well as to print a report showing all of the currently selected records.

On clicking Add or Edit, the Address Entry form is displayed. The form contains three different sections identified by color labels. The red section contains fields about the person. The blue section contains telephone number information. The magenta section contains address information. A person may have more than one phone number and more than one address. Figure A.8 shows the Address Entry form.

FIGURE A.8.

The Address Entry form.

The TEMPLATE.MDB database demonstrates switching between different form templates in Access. You can use form templates as a quick way to create a form with a common set of settings, such as on a pop-up modal form.

Open the database. Press Ctrl-T to switch from the Normal form template to a pop-up modal form template. When you create a new form, instead of seeing the Normal form you see a new form created like the Modal form in the TEMPLATE.MDB database. Press Ctrl-T again to switch back to the Normal form.

TEMPLATE.MDB uses an `AutoKeys` macro so that Ctrl-T activates the `ToggleFormTemplate` function in the Form Template module.

Picture Builder+ (Chapter 15)

Application: Access
Directory: PMO\CH15
Files: PICBLDR.MDA
               UP.BMP
               DOWN.BMP

The Picture Builder+ program is an Access Builder add-in used to set the Picture property on command buttons.

Picture Builder+ is installed using the Access Add-In Manager. Select the File|Add-Ins|Add-In Manager command. In the Add-In Manager dialog box, click the Add New button and select the PICBLDR.MDA database. Close the Add-In Manager dialog box and close Access. When you restart Access, Picture Builder+ will be available.

To run Picture Builder+, create a new form. Add a command button to the form and open the Properties window to modify the command button properties. In the Picture property, click the ellipses (...) button.

Access displays the Choose Builder dialog box. Select Picture Builder+ and click OK.

The Picture Builder+ dialog box (shown in Figure A.9) displays up to 12 icons at a time in a picture category. Click the blue left and right arrow buttons at the bottom right of the dialog box to switch between picture groups.

The UP.BMP and DOWN.BMP files are bitmaps used in creating Picture Builder+.

FIGURE A.9.
The Picture Builder+ dialog box.

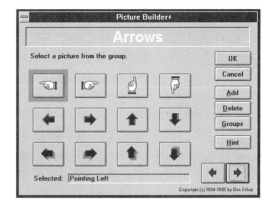

To set a picture for the button on your form, select the button and click OK. Click the Add button to add a new picture to the currently displayed picture group. Click the Groups button to add new picture groups.

Survey Wizard (Chapters 16 to 20)

Application:	Access
Directory:	PMO\CH16
Files:	SRVYBLD.MDA
	SRVYRUN.MDA
	SURVEY.HLP
	SW1.BMP
	SW2.BMP
	SW3.BMP
	SW4.BMP
	SW5.BMP
	OBJECTS.BMP
	SPARKLES.BMP
	SAVEAS.BMP
	SWHELP.EXE
	BITMAPS.EXE

Survey Wizard is an Access menu add-in that creates Access forms, reports, tables, and queries to produce a handout questionnaire and online survey system with graphic reporting capabilities. Survey Wizard includes a Windows help file, SURVEY.HLP, for complete documentation on using the program.

To install Survey Wizard, select the File|Add-Ins|Add-In Manager command. Click the Browse button in the Add-In Manager dialog box to first select the SRVYRUN.MDA file, and then the SRVYBLD.MDA file. The Add-In Manager copies the .MDA files into the directory that you installed Access 2.0 into. You need to manually copy the SURVEY.HLP file into the Access 2.0 directory using File Manager.

Close Access and restart it. Open an existing or new database. Select File|Add-Ins from the menu, and you see a Survey Wizard command has been added. Select the Survey Wizard command to start Survey Wizard.

Survey Wizard is a multiple-page form (like other Access wizards). In the first form, enter your survey title. In the following screens, add your questions to the survey as shown in Figure A.10. At any time, you can press F1 to get help on the current screen.

FIGURE A.10.

Entering a question in Survey Wizard.

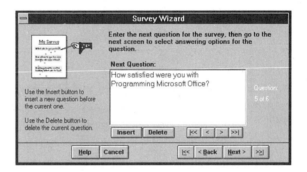

Click the Next button without entering a question and Survey Wizard brings you to the Build screen. Select the objects to build and click the Build button.

If you are only creating a handout survey report, you can select Entry Report and Questions Table. If you are creating a full online survey system, click all objects. Survey Wizard displays a Save As dialog box. Enter a name to prefix all of the generated database objects, and click OK.

After the objects are generated, you use them by opening them from the database container. See Chapters 16, 17, 18, 19, and 20 for full details about using Survey Wizard and how it was created.

The .BMP files are the bitmaps used on the Survey Wizard forms. The SWHELP.EXE file is a self-extracting archive with all of the files used in creating the SURVEY.HLP file. The BITMAPS.EXE file is a self-extracting file containing the bitmaps used in the Survey Wizard help file. See Chapter 20 for details on using the files in SWHELP.EXE and BITMAPS.EXE.

S.W.A.T. (Chapters 21 to 23)

Application: Access, Word, Excel
Directory: PMO\CH21
Files: SWAT.MDB
SWAT_FR.DOT
SWAT.XLS
BUG.BMP

S.W.A.T. is an issues tracking system developed in Access, but with some added capabilities provided by Word and Excel. An issues tracking system is one of a programmer's most useful tools. It enables programmers to ensure that they are working on the most pressing issues that meet the needs of the users of the program.

To start using S.W.A.T., open the SWAT.MDB database in Access. At the Login dialog box, enter your name as you would like to enter it each time you use S.W.A.T., and click the Menu button. (From the Login form, you can go to either the Issue form or the Database Maintenance Menu form.) The program asks whether you are a new user. Click Yes and the Database Maintenance Menu form is displayed.

In the menu, select the Categories form and click the Select button. A continuous form is displayed. Enter categories in your project to which you want to classify bugs, changes, and enhancements, such as User Interface, Database, Data Entry, and so on.

Click the Issues button to switch over to the Issue form. There, you can start entering issues into the database, classifying them by type, current working status, who the issue is assigned to, what priority it has, and which of the categories it belongs to.

Click the Filter button to define filters. A filter is criteria that affects which records are displayed on the Issue form. Click the Field Report button to associate a user-written field report document to the issue record.

Field reports are written using the SWAT_FR.DOT template, which should be copied to the TEMPLATE directory where Word was installed for each user who wants to create a field report. The template is a Word form with check boxes and text boxes that a user fills in to report an issue.

The SWAT.XLS workbook imports budget data from the Issue database, enables the user to modify the records, and then exports the data back out to the database.

To use the SWAT.XLS workbook, open it in Excel. Switch to the Options worksheet and fill in the Database Directory and System Database options. Switch back to the Time Estimates worksheet and click the Import Issues button to read data from each of the records in the Issue table of SWAT.MDB into the worksheet. You can modify the values in the Budget and Actual columns, and then click the Export Changes button to write the data back to the SWAT.MDB database.

On the Options worksheet are combo boxes in the Filter section to establish criteria for which Issue records are read into the worksheet. You need to update the Lookup Tables worksheet to make the Assigned To and Category combo boxes display the available selections.

The BUG.BMP file is the bitmap used on the Issue form in SWAT.MDB.

See Chapters 21, 22, and 23 for full details about the S.W.A.T. programs, as well as the rationale behind using an issue tracking system.

Bonus Files

You will also find on the CD-ROM a BONUS directory loaded with useful and educational public domain and shareware files collected from popular online services.

Read the notices that accompany each file, for many of the programs are shareware, requiring you to send payment to the shareware author if you continue to use the program beyond a specified trial period.

Sams Publishing and the author of this book did not create these files and warn you that all of the files shall be used at your own risk.

The shareware and freeware example applications in the BONUS directory include two contributions from Ken Getz, the world's foremost Access expert. Those contributions are CTLMPH (used to change one control type into another) and RTSIZE (used for resizing form controls at runtime). You may need to use the popular PKUNZIP shareware utility to expand these files.

Index

Add to Your Sams Library Today with the Best Books for Programming, Operating Systems, and New Technologies

The easiest way to order is to pick up the phone and call

1-800-428-5331

between 9:00 a.m. and 5:00 p.m. EST.

For faster service please have your credit card available.

ISBN	Quantity	Description of Item	Unit Cost	Total Cost
0-672-30494-5		Access 2 Unleashed (Book/Disk)	$34.95	
0-672-30453-8		Access 2 Developer's Guide, Second Edition (Book/CD-ROM)	$44.95	
0-672-30647-6		Microsoft Office Developer's Guide	$45.00	
0-672-30568-2		Teach Yourself OLE Programming in 21 Days	$39.99	
0-672-30385-X		Excel 5 Super Book	$39.95	
0-672-30338-8		Inside Windows File Formats	$29.95	
0-672-30447-3		Teach Yourself Visual Basic for Applications in 21 Days	$29.95	
0-672-30364-7		WIN32 API Desktop Reference (Book/CD-ROM)	$49.95	
0-672-30239-X		Windows Developer's Guide to Application Design	$34.95	
0-672-30685-9		Windows NT 3.5 Unleashed, Second Edition	$39.99	
0-672-30611-5		Your Windows 95 Consultant, Pre-Release Edition	$25.00	
❏ 3 ½" Disk		Shipping and Handling: See information below.		
❏ 5 ¼" Disk		TOTAL		

Shipping and Handling: $4.00 for the first book, and $1.75 for each additional book. Floppy disk: add $1.75 for shipping and handling. If you need to have it NOW, we can ship product to you in 24 hours for an additional charge of approximately $18.00, and you will receive your item overnight or in two days. Overseas shipping and handling adds $2.00 per book and $8.00 for up to three disks. Prices subject to change. Call for availability and pricing information on latest editions.

201 W. 103rd Street, Indianapolis, Indiana 46290

1-800-428-5331 — Orders   1-800-835-3202 — FAX   1-800-858-7674 — Customer Service

Book ISBN 0-672-30706-5

PLUG YOURSELF INTO...

The Macmillan Information SuperLibrary™

Free information and vast computer resources from the world's leading computer book publisher—online!

FIND THE BOOKS THAT ARE RIGHT FOR YOU!

A complete online catalog, plus sample chapters and tables of contents give you an in-depth look at *all* of our books, including hard-to-find titles. It's the best way to find the books you need!

- **STAY INFORMED** with the latest computer industry news through our online newsletter, press releases, and customized Information SuperLibrary Reports.

- **GET FAST ANSWERS** to your questions about MCP books and software.

- **VISIT** our online bookstore for the latest information and editions!

- **COMMUNICATE** with our expert authors through e-mail and conferences.

- **DOWNLOAD SOFTWARE** from the immense MCP library:
    - Source code and files from MCP books
    - The best shareware, freeware, and demos

- **DISCOVER HOT SPOTS** on other parts of the Internet.

- **WIN BOOKS** in ongoing contests and giveaways!

TO PLUG INTO MCP: → WORLD WIDE WEB: **http://www.mcp.com**

GOPHER: gopher.mcp.com

FTP: ftp.mcp.com

Install

The companion CD-ROM contains applications developed in the book, as well as a Bonus directory containing popular programs and utilities.

The Bonus directory contains programs that you may choose to copy to your hard drive. The Bonus directory files will not be included in the install program.

Software Installation Instructions

1. Insert the CD-ROM into your CD-ROM drive.
2. From File Manager or Program Manager, choose Run from the File menu.
3. Type `<drive>INSTALL` and press Enter, where `<drive>` corresponds to the drive letter of your CD-ROM drive. For example, if your CD-ROM is drive D:, type `D:INSTALL` and press Enter.
4. Follow the on-screen instructions in the installation program. Files will be installed to a directory named `\PMO` unless you choose a different directory during installation.

For a full install, you will need 12–13MB free. You may choose, however, to do a partial install.